Handbook of Orthography and Literacy

HANDBOOK OF ORTHOGRAPHY AND LITERACY

Edited by

R. Malatesha Joshi
Texas A & M University

P. G. Aaron
Indiana State University

LEA
2006

LAWRENCE ERLBAUM ASSOCIATES, PUBLISHERS
Mahwah, New Jersey   London

KH

Director, Editorial:	Lane Akers
Editorial Assistant:	Bonita D'Amil
Cover Design:	Kathryn Houghtaling Lacey
Textbook Production Manager:	Paul Smolenski
Full-Service Compositor:	TechBooks
Text and Cover Printer:	Hamilton Printing Company

This book was typeset in 10/12 pt. Times, Italic, Bold, Bold Italic.
The heads were typeset in Helvetica Bold, and Helvetica Bold Italic.

Lawrence Erlbaum Associates, Inc., Publishers
10 Industrial Avenue
Mahwah, New Jersey 07430
www.erlbaum.com

Library of Congress Cataloging-in-Publication Data

Handbook of orthography and literacy / edited by R. Malatesha Joshi,
P. G. Aaron.
  p. cm.
  Includes bibliographical references and index.
  ISBN 0-8058-4652-2 (hardback : alk. paper)—ISBN 0-8058-5467-3 (pbk. : alk. paper)
1. Language acquisition. 2. Literacy. 3. Language and languages—Orthography and spelling.
I. Joshi, R. Malatesha. II. Aaron, P. G.

  P118.H349   2005
  418—dc22   2005015076

Books published by Lawrence Erlbaum Associates are printed on
acid-free paper, and their bindings are chosen for strength and durability.

Printed in the United States of America
10 9 8 7 6 5 4 3 2 1

10/19/06

Contents

Contributors

P. G. Aaron
Dept. of Educational and School Psychology
College of Education
Indiana State University
Terre Haute, IN 47809 USA

Salim Abu-Rabia
Faculty of Education
University of Haifa
Mount Carmel
Haifa 31905, Israel

Athanasios Aidinis
Department of Psychology
Aristotle University of Thessaloniki
Thessaloniki, Greece

Nobuhiko Akamatsu
Department of English
Doshisha University
Imadegawa-Karasume
Kamigyo-ku, Kyoto 602-8580 Japan

Katie J. Alcock
Department of Psychology
Lancaster University
Fylde College
Lancaster LA1 4YF, United Kingdom

Elena Andonova
Central and East European Center for
    Cognitive Science
Department of Cognitive Science
New Bulgarian University
21 Montevideo Street
Sofia 1618, Bulgaria

Dorit Aram
The Constantiner School of Education
Tel Aviv University
Tel Aviv, 69978, Israel

Mikko Aro
Department of Psychology
University of Jyväskylä
Niilo Mäki Institute
Jyväskylä, Finland

Bahman Baluch
Department of Experimental Psychology
School of Health and Social Sciences
Middlesex University EN3 4SF
United Kingdom

Anna M. T. Bosman
Radboud University Nijmegen
Faculty of Social Sciences
Department of Special Education
PO Box 9104, 6500 HE Nijmegen
The Netherlands

Regina Boulware-Gooden
Neuhaus Education Center
Houston, Texas, USA

Peter Bryant
Department of Experimental Psychology
Oxford Brookes University
Gipsy Lane
Oxford OX3 0BP
United Kingdom

Marketa Caravolas
Dept. of Psychology
University of Liverpool
Liverpool, United Kingdom

Cláudia Cardoso-Martins
Departamento de Psicologia
Universidade Federal de Minas Gerais
Av. Antonio Carlos 6627
31270-901 — Belo Horizonte, MG, Brazil

James W. Chapman
Department of Learning and Teaching
Massey University
Private Bag 11 222
Palmerston North, New Zealand

Him Cheung
Department of Psychology
The Chinese University of Hong Kong
Shatin, PT, Hong Kong

Bonnie Wing-Yin Chow
Department of Psychology
The Chinese University of Hong Kong
Shatin, PT, Hong Kong

Valéria Csépe
Research Institute for Psychology of the
   Hungarian Academy of Sciences
   H-1068 Budapest
Szoni utca 83-85, Hungary

Chris Davis
School of Behavioural Science
Department of Psychology
The University of Melbourne
3010, Australia

Hélène Deacon
Psychology Department
Dalhousie University
Halifax, Nova Scotia
B3H 4J1, Canada

Aydin Yücesan Durgunoğlu
Department of Psychology
University of Minnesota Duluth
1207 Ordean Court
Duluth, MN 55812-3010, USA

Linnea C. Ehri
Program in Educational Psychology
CUNY Graduate School
365 Fifth Avenue
New York, NY 10016, USA

Carsten Elbro
Department of General and Applied
   Linguistics
University of Copenhagen
86 Njalsgade
DK-2300 Copenhagen S, Denmark

Michel Fayol
LAPSCO-CNRS (UMR 6024) & Université
   de Clermont-Ferrand
34, Avenue Carnot
63037 Clermont-Ferrand Cedex (France)

Xiwu Feng
La Guardia Community College, New York,
   NY, USA

Martine A. R. Gijsel
Radboud University Nijmegen
Faculty of Social Sciences
Department of Special Education
PO Box 9104, 6500 HE Nijmegen
The Netherlands

Usha Goswami
Professor of Education
University of Cambridge
Faculty of Education
Shaftesbury Road
Cambridge, CB2 2BX
United Kingdom

I. P. Gowramma (Rajni Chengappa)
All India Institute of Speech and Hearing
Mysore, Karnataka, India

Saskia de Graaff
Radboud University Nijmegen
Faculty of Social Sciences
Department of Special Education
PO Box 9104, 6500 HE Nijmegen
The Netherlands

Elena L. Grigorenko
Moscow State University, Russia and
   Center for the Psychology of Abilities
   Competencies, and Expertise (PACE)
Yale University, 340 Edwards Street
New Haven, CT 06520-8358, USA

Bente E. Hagtvet
Institute of Special Needs Education
University of Oslo
Norway
Turid Helland
Centre of Logopedics
University of Bergen
Bergen, Norway

Torleiv Høien
Dyslexia Research Foundation
Stavanger, Norway

Leena Holopainen
Department of Special Education
University of Joensuu
Joensuu, Finland

Jean-Pierre Jaffré
LEAPLE-CNRS (UMR 8606) & Université
    Paris V
7 rue Guy-Môquet
94801 Villejuif Cedex (France)

Armina Janyan
Central and East European Center for
    Cognitive Science
Department of Cognitive Science
New Bulgarian University
21 Montevideo Street
Sofia 1618, Bulgaria

Remo Job
DPSS, University of Padova and
    University of Trento
Via Venezia 8
35100 Padova, Italy

Rhona S. Johnston
Department of Psychology
University of Hull
Hull HU6 7RX
United Kingdom

R. Malatesha Joshi
MS 4232, Reading Education
College of Education and Human
    Development
Texas A & M University
College Station, TX 77843-4232, USA

Prathibha Karanth
MVS College of Speech & Hearing
Vidya Nagar
Mangalore 547 013
DK. Karnataka, India

Jeesum Kim
School of Behavioural Science
Department of Psychology
The University of Melbourne
3010, Australia

Ofra Korat
Faculty of Social Sciences
School of Education
Bar Ilan University
Ramat-Gan 52900, Israel

Karin Landerl
Department of Psychology
University of Salzburg
Hellbrunnerstrasse 34
A-5020 Salzburg, Austria

Annukka Lehtonen
Department of Psychiatry
University of Oxford
Warneford Hospital
Oxford OX3 7JX, United Kingdom

Matti Leiwo
Department of Languages
University of Jyväskylä, Finland

Iris Levin
The Constantiner School of Education
Tel Aviv University
Tel Aviv, 69978, Israel

Solveig-Alma H. Lyster
Institute of Special Needs Education
University of Oslo, Norway

Heikki Lyytinen
Department of Psychology
University of Jyväskylä
Niilo Mäki Institute
Jyväskylä, Finland

Paula Lyytinen
Department of Psychology
University of Jyväskylä, Finland

Catherine McBride-Chang
Department of Psychology
The Chinese University of Hong Kong
Shatin, PT, Hong Kong

Claudio Mulatti
DPSS, University of Padova and
    University of Trento
Via Venezia 8
35100 Padova, Italy

Giok Lian Ng
Advent Links—Southeast Asia Union
    College
Centre for Children and Family Studies
299 Thomson Road
Singapore 307652

Thomas Nicholson
School of Education
The University of Auckland
Private Bag 92019
Auckland, New Zealand

Terezinha Nunes
Oxford Brookes University
Gipsy Lane, Oxford OX3 0BP
United Kingdom

Richard K. Olson
Department of Psychology
UCB 345
University of Colorado
Boulder, CO 80309, USA

Ingrida Paunina
Latvian Language Institute of
    University of Latvia
Riga, Latvia

Francesca Peressotti
University of Padova
Via Venezia 8
35100 Padova, Italy

Jörgen Pind
Department of Psychology
University of Iceland
IS-101, Reykjavík, Iceland

Costas D. Porpodas
Division of Psychology
Dyslexia Unit
Department of Education
University of Patras
26500 Patras, Greece

Dorit Ravid
Department of Communications Disorders
The Constantiner School of Education
Tel Aviv University, Tel Aviv, 69978
Israel

Agnieszka A. Reid
41 Corrie Road
Cambridge, CB1 3QP
United Kingdom

Javier S. Sainz
Applied Psycholinguistics Unit
Department of Cognitive Processes
Universidad Complutense de Madrid
Madrid, Spain

Philip H. K. Seymour
Department of Psychology
University of Dundee
Dundee, DD1 4HN
Scotland, United Kingdom

Ieva Sprugevica
University of Latvia
Riga, LV 1050, Latvia

Haitham Taha
Faculty of Education
University of Haifa
Mount Carmel
Haifa 31905, Israel

Verena Thaler
Department of Psychology
University of Salzburg
Hellbrunnerstrasse 34
A-5020 Salzburg, Austria

Asko Tolvanen
Department of Psychology
University of Jyväskylä, Finland

Rebecca Treiman
Department of Psychology
Washington University in St. Louis
Campus Box 1125
One Brookings Drive
St. Louis, MO 63130-4899, USA

William E. Tunmer
Department of Learning and Teaching
Massey University
Private Bag 11 222
Palmerston North, New Zealand

Richard L. Venezky
Unidel Professor of Educational Studies
School of Education
University of Delaware
Newark, DE 19716
USA (Deceased 11th June 2004)

Joyce E. Watson
School of Psychology
University of St Andrews
St Andrews, KY16 9JU
Scotland, United Kingdom

Introduction to the Volume

Until about two decades ago, the study of writing systems and its relationship to literacy acquisition has been generally modeled after studies of the English language. It was also tacitly believed, if not overtly stated, that what is true of English is also true of other writing systems. During the past 20 years or so, information technology has boomed with incredible rapidity and made the mastery of literacy skills an inevitable requirement. Reading and writing have therefore become a necessity for survival, and literacy and literacy acquisition have taken the center stage in psychological, educational, and linguistic studies. Furthermore, computerization of the world has interconnected cognitive psychologists, linguists, and educators, which has enabled them to communicate with each other with ease. A combination of these events has aroused researchers with different language backgrounds from different countries to examine the connection between their writing systems and literacy acquisition. The present volume is an assemblage of such research work undertaken in different languages by experts who are researchers in the field of literacy and who are also native speakers of the language they describe in their respective chapters. This volume contains the names of 70 such researchers and scholars, and we thank them collectively for their time and effort. A close reading of this volume will show that theirs is a superb and lasting contribution to the field of literacy studies.

Most of the information presented in these chapters was delivered at the Advanced Study Institute on Orthography and Literacy in Il Ciocco, Italy, during November of 2002. The conference was sponsored and supported by the Scientific Affairs Division of the North Atlantic Treaty Organization. We are grateful for their support.

At this point, it will be helpful to introduce some of the terms that the reader will encounter in this volume.

Writing system: Written language described in terms of linguistic units; for example, morphemic writing (Chinese), syllabic writing (Japanese Kana), alphabetic–syllabic system (Kannada and Tamil), and alphabetic writing (Italian and Spanish).

Orthography: Visual representation of language as conditioned by phonological, syntactic, morphological, and semantic features of the language. Examples of orthographies are Chinese orthography and English orthography.

Script: The graphic format in which writing is represented. Examples are Roman script and Arabic script.

The writing systems described in this volume range from Finnish, which has an almost one-to-one grapheme–phoneme correspondence to that of English, which is described often as having the most inconsistent grapheme–phoneme relationship. In other words, these writing systems vary widely in their orthographic depth. The question then arises whether the nature of orthography has an effect on the ease with which children learn to read and write. If so, it is legitimate to ask whether the research findings that come from the study of the English writing system can be applied to other orthographies as well.

Studies reported in this volume make it clear that what is true of acquisition of literacy skills in English need not be true of all orthographies. These findings provide general support to the orthographic-depth hypotheses, which indicate that the degree of correspondence between orthography and the phonology of the written word is one of the many factors that has an influence on the rate at which literacy skills are acquired.

The chapters in this Volume are grouped into three parts. Part I deals with the acquisition of literacy in different writing systems. The research reported in Part II includes chapters that make direct comparisons of literacy acquisition in English and other orthographic systems. The chapters included in Part III are more pragmatic in nature in the sense that they explore literacy acquisition from developmental and instructional perspectives.

The relationship between orthography and literacy is addressed either directly or indirectly by almost every one of the 27 chapters contained in Part I of the volume. More important, these authors give brief sketches of the nature of the orthographic system they have studied. A total of 25 orthographies are described. This part of the volume serves as a handy reference source for knowing about the orthographies of languages such as Icelandic, Kannada, and Kishwahili.

The eight chapters included in Part II of the volume address this question by a direct comparison of the acquisition of reading skills by children who speak different languages. The overall conclusion that emerges from these studies is that orthographic depth does have an influence on literacy acquisition, primarily by slowing down the rate of acquisition of reading skills. However, eventually, most children who have to contend with deep orthographies such as English become normal readers, albeit slowly. Most, but not all. Even though deep orthography may exacerbate reading problems encountered by potentially weak readers of an orthography such as English, even some children who learn shallow orthographies remain poor readers, primarily because they are slow readers. Thus it appears that dyslexia is not an "orthography-limited" symptom, but also has an internal cognitive, biological, and genetic component.

The seven chapters in Part III deal with the pragmatic issues of literacy acquisition such as instructional strategies for promoting reading and spelling skills. This section ends with a look into the future of literacy research.

We thank Lane Akers and Paul Smolenski of Lawrence Erlbaum Associates and Susan Detwiler and Peggy Rote of TechBooks, as well as Emily Ocker-Dean and Mary Ghong, doctoral students at Texas A & M University, for their help at various stages of preparing the volume.

—R. M. Joshi
—P. G. Aaron

I

Literacy Acquisition in Different Writing Systems

1

Evolution of an Alphabetic Writing System: The Case of Icelandic

Jörgen Pind
University of Iceland

Iceland has a literary tradition reaching back for almost a millennium, with the earliest written Icelandic documents dating from the 11th century. During the 13th and 14th centuries numerous important literary works—sagas, poetry, histories—were produced. In the 12th century an alphabet was created for Icelandic in an important treatise, commonly termed the *First Grammatical Treatise*, written by an unknown author. The treatise elaborates on the letters needed for showing the phonemic distinctions of the language; it also shows a realization of the fact that numerous other considerations apply in writing than purely phonemic ones. The current Icelandic orthography has been gradually shaped over the past centuries, with the latest changes being introduced in 1973–1974. Establishing the current Icelandic system of writing has involved a struggle between two opposing viewpoints, one viewpoint arguing for the necessity of being true to the origins of words and the long tradition of writing, the other wanting to move the writing closer to pronunciation. The most recent changes introduced were, though, primarily motivated by educational concerns. The current Icelandic orthography is a compromise between these different viewpoints. The result is a writing system that is relatively transparent for the reader but rather difficult for the speller.

INTRODUCTION

In this chapter I give an outline of the history of the Icelandic writing system and briefly discuss some aspects of literacy in Iceland. Two factors make the Icelandic case somewhat unique. First, the Icelandic language is quite conservative and has remained relatively stable in its morphology and syntax, though the phonology has undergone considerable changes. Because of this conservatism, Icelanders can still read the literature of the earlier centuries. Second, of considerable interest is the fact that there exists an important document from the earliest period of Icelandic writing called the *First Grammatical Treatise* (FGT). In this work the author, who remains unknown, describes in great detail his considerations when applying the Latin alphabet

A man inflicted a *wound* (sar) on me; I inflicted many *wounds* (sǫr) on him. The priest *swore* (sor) the *fair* (sør) oaths only. (p. 17)

After having thus established the necessity of the nine vowel symbols in this manner, the FG also argues for the necessity of adding two more distinctions to the set of vowels, again illustrating the need for this by an analysis of minimal pairs. These are, first, the feature of nasality in which "each one of these nine letters will bring forth a new one if it is spoken in the nose (p. 17)." This the FG marks by putting a dot over the vowel letter. Add to this that "it is well known that there is another distinction in the vowels, both in those that were in the alphabet before, and in the new ones that have been added [i.e. the nasal vowels]. This is a distinction which changes the meaning, according to whether the letter is long or short (p. 17)." This distinction, the FG proposes to mark with a stroke. So this makes for an inventory of 36 vowel symbols in all! Again these distinctions are carefully documented by the use of minimal pairs of the sort shown earlier.

The analysis of the FG is highly sophisticated, as are the arguments brought forth to support it. It is clear that he has a precise understanding of the importance of distinction in the phonological system for which he uses a specific term, *grein*. His manner of establishing the necessary distinctions is of course the same as the method of substitution introduced by the structural linguists of the 20th century. A change of the vowel sound in a word will *skipta máli*, change the discourse, and thus it is also necessary to change the vowel symbol.

The FG uses a similar approach with the consonants, but details are not given of his treatment of them here (the details can be found in the excellent monographs by Benediktsson, 1972, and Haugen, 1972). The FG's treatment of the consonants are of interest because they show well his education in classical Latin grammar (as shown most clearly by Holtsmark, 1936). In classical grammar the letter was conceived of very differently from what is now customary. In his *Ars Maior*, Donatus gives the following definition of the letter: *Littera est pars minima vocis articulatae* [the letter is the minimal part of speech]. This understanding, moving between speech and writing, survived for a long time, as shown by Abercrombie (1949). The FG adheres to the classical conception according to which each letter has three attributes, its name (*nomen*; *nafn* in the FGT), its shape (*figura*; *líkneski* or *vöxtur* in the FGT), and pronunciation (*potestas*; *jartein* or *atkvæði* in the FGT). The vowels pose no particular problem in this respect for the scholastically minded FG. However, for the consonants, things are a bit more difficult. For one thing, a vowel names itself but this is not so for the consonants, explaining the long discussion in the FGT on the correct manner of naming the consonants. Consonants need an adjacent vowel to make up their name, and their pronunciation is also often difficult to ascertain because "the sound of a consonant . . . is not easy to distinguish, for it is short and closely blended or grown together with the vowel with which it is combined (p. 21)." In modern terminology we would say that consonants are coarticulated with the adjacent vowels (Liberman, Cooper, Shankweiler, & Studdert-Kennedy, 1967). However, in general, the FG finds that the Latin consonants do a passably good job of representing the consonants of Icelandic except that they do not distinguish between long and short consonants. He proposes to write the long ones with uppercase letters (e.g., N and R), the short ones with the ordinary lowercase consonant symbols. One symbol added to the Latin consonants is the letter þ (thorn). This letter is part of the Runic alphabet but was probably adopted from Anglo-Saxon by the FG, who uses it to denote both the voiced and voiceless dental fricatives. The voiced one later received its own letter, ð. Both these letters are part of the current Icelandic alphabet (see Fig. 1.1).

The manner in which the FG proceeds suggests that he is proposing a more or less phonetically correct system of spelling for Icelandic. Unfortunately, the manuscript of the FGT dates from the 14th century and bears the mark of the orthography then current (except that

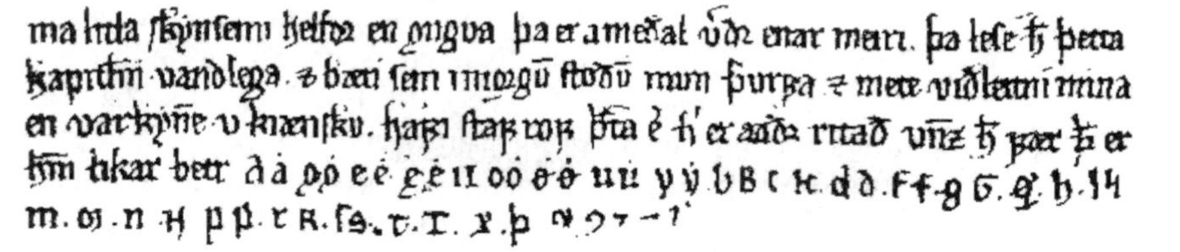

FIG. 1.1. The end of the FGT in the *Codex Wormianus* illustrating the alphabet for Icelandic as proposed in the Treatise.

in illustrating the use of minimal pairs the scribe is obviously at great pains to remain true to the original; which may, of course, not be the treatise as left by the FG). However, modern commentators (Benediktsson, 1972; Haugen, 1972; Holtsmark, 1936) have expressed doubt as to whether the system of writing proposed by the FG was to be used consistently in the spelling of every word, in effect constituting a phonetic transcription, or whether it was primarily to be employed in those cases in which there was a danger of misunderstanding arising because of homophony. The following remarks from the treatise definitely suggest that the FG is well aware that establishing an alphabet for a language does by no means solve all problems as regards the manner in which individual words should be written:

> If I were to write another discourse, which there might be good reason for and plenty of material, if only I had the wits to do it, concerning the letters that make up the nature of each word or the way in which all the letters should be combined,—then that would be an entirely different work and much larger, and so I cannot take up that subject in this one (p. 21).

These remarks suggest that the FG saw the need for a "spelling dictionary" or some similar treatise to illustrate the proper and correct writing of the language.

The alphabet established by the FG forms the core of the present Icelandic alphabet, though changes in the phonology of the language have been considerable, especially as regards the vowel system (Benediktsson, 1959). Nasalization of vowels seems to have disappeared around the time the treatise was written. In the 16th century the quantity system underwent a drastic change so that quantity is no longer free to vary but depends on context. Thus a vowel is short if followed by one or no consonants (with some exceptions); otherwise it is long (Pind, 1986, 1999). The accent mark, which used to denote length, now symbolizes differences in quality (i [ɪ] vs. í [i]), diphthongs (ó [ou] or á [au]), or even a combination of semivowel and vowel (é [je]). Current Icelandic speech has eight vowels and five diphthongs. Some vowels that were distinguished in the writing of the FG are no longer distinguished in pronunciation (e.g., e and ę; ǫ and ø; i and y).

WRITING BEFORE THE AGE OF PRINTING

The orthography of the medieval Icelandic manuscripts was not standardized, despite the efforts of the FG. According to an authority on early Icelandic writing, the FGT influenced the writings of "most scribes" in the 13th century and, to some extent, also those in the 14th century (Karlsson, 1989). The move to standardize the orthography gained momentum with the advent of printing (the first printed book, the New Testament in an Icelandic translation, dates from 1540) but did not reach its final form until the first decades of the 20th century with some changes being introduced actually as late as 1974.

With the advent of printing, reading materials became much more widely available and the need for a unified spelling became more apparent. Numerous attempts were made to provide a rational and consistent system of spelling. The need for this became widely felt toward the end of the 18th century with the advent of magazines and newspapers and especially at the beginning of the 20th century, when universal schooling was mandated by law. Shortly afterwards, in 1918, the first government regulations for spelling were published; this was supplanted by another regulation in 1929 and a third one in 1973–1974. The last changes led to intense and heated debates even in the Icelandic Parliament.

An early writer on Icelandic orthography and spelling was Jón Ólafsson (1705–1779), secretary to Árni Magnússon (1663–1730), the great collector of Icelandic manuscripts. At the beginning of his essay on spelling Ólafsson notes that spelling can be based on three principles: "1. The method of our predecessors, as found in their ancient books; 2. On the origins of word, and 3. Daily pronunciations as well as the custom of learned men" (Helgason, 1929, p. 81).

This quote nicely illustrates the opposing viewpoints on which spelling can be based, in particular whether to base spelling on the daily pronunciation or on ancient custom, reflecting the "origins of words." Over the next centuries scholars and writers, and, in the 20th century, politicians too, engaged in fierce debates over the proper way to spell Icelandic, arguing either for a spelling based on pronunciation or one based on adherence to traditional principles. It should not come as a surprise that the latter viewpoint has usually carried great weight, considering how old the Icelandic tradition of writing in fact is. Interestingly, in the last round of spelling reforms, instituted in 1973–1974, yet another viewpoint was given considerable weight, namely educational considerations.

I do not describe in detail the history of Icelandic spelling (a good overview can be found in Jónsson, 1959) but just mention the major steps in this evolutionary history. This history clearly shows that current Icelandic spelling involves a compromise among different principles.

The first major step towards a unified spelling for Icelandic was taken by the famous Danish linguist Rasmus Kristian Rask (1787–1832) who published an Icelandic reading primer in 1830, "for the children of gentlemen," as it says in the title (R. Rask, 1830). Rask had early become interested in Icelandic and wrote a scholarly treatise on the origins of the Old Icelandic language (R. Rask, 1818), which is one of the founding documents of comparative grammar in the 19th century. Earlier he had written an Icelandic grammar, and later he prepared the first major Icelandic dictionary for publication. Rask was one of the founders of the Icelandic literary society, founded in Copenhagen in 1816, which has played an important part in intellectual affairs in Iceland since. Rask also argued forcefully for spelling reforms in his native Danish (K. Rask, 2002).

Rask's reading primer had two aims. The first was to establish the use of Latin letterforms for the customary Gothic letterforms that up to that time had mostly been used for printing. The other was to establish a consistent system of spelling. These were ambitious goals for a reading primer, as indeed Rask acknowledges! As far as spelling is concerned, Rask argued for a conservative approach, wanting to base spelling on the model of earlier writing. Thus he kept the i/y distinction, wrote è for the earlier long e (now spelled é but pronounced [je]), wanted to keep the letter z for those cases in which ðs, ds, or ts were pronounced as [s]. He established the rule, since adhered to consistently in Icelandic spelling, of writing -nn at the end of disyllabic adjectives in their masculine form and -n in their feminine form; thus *iðin kona* [industrious woman] and *iðinn maður* [industrious man]. This distinction is not heard in the pronunciation but makes the spelling consistent with other cases in which the distinction is heard in the pronunciation, for example, *mikil kona* [great woman], *mikill maður* [great man].

In general, Rask wanted his spelling to be faithful to older stages of Icelandic writing and to give morphological considerations their due. However, he did not do this consistently. Thus he did not adopt the custom of distinguishing between æ and œ (both now pronounced [ai]) to show the different origins of the two vowels, but he stated that it is necessary to keep this distinction in published editions of earlier Icelandic literature.

In 1835 the first volume of the Icelandic literary magazine *Fjölnir* by a group of young radical intellectuals was published. One of the principals of the journal was Konráð Gíslason (1808–1891), later to become professor of Old Icelandic at the University of Copenhagen. In the second volume of the magazine Gíslason wrote a long essay on Icelandic spelling and argued forcefully for a phonetically based spelling. This was a radical break with earlier traditions. It involved the abolition, for example, of y from the alphabet as well as numerous other changes. One of Gíslason's arguments against the earlier system of spelling was that the advocates of etymologically based spelling were not consistent in their approach, sometimes being faithful to this approach (e.g., in the spelling of i/y, in other cases not, e.g., æ/œ).

In 1850 Halldór Kr. Friðriksson (1819–1902), who was a teacher of the Icelandic language at the Reykjavík grammar school for almost 50 years, published a book on spelling, an exhaustive treatise, in which he carefully argued for an etymologically based spelling. This may be seen as a direct response to the attempted spelling reforms of Gíslason. Friðriksson's spelling became known as the "school spelling" as it was taught at the Reykjavík grammar school for a long period. It was much more archaic than the spelling of Rask because it introduced items such as the æ/œ distinction that otherwise had not been in common use in Icelandic spelling.

Another attempt to move spelling closer to pronunciation was proposed by Björn M. Ólsen (1850–1919), who succeeded Friðriksson as teacher of Icelandic at the Reykjavík grammar school. Ólsen was an outstanding linguist and later became the first rector of the University of Iceland when it was founded in 1911. Ólsen based his arguments on the needs for spelling reforms primarily on educational considerations. He (Ólsen, 1889) cataloged the spelling errors found in essays written by students entering or graduating from the Reykjavík grammar school. Ólsen analyzed 200 essays by pupils entering and the same number of essays from those graduating from the school. In the former set of essays Ólsen counted 1,008 errors in all (based on Friðriksson's rules for spelling) but 300 errors in the essays of the graduating students (and this in spite of the fact that these were considerably longer). The major categories of errors involved i/y, s/z, and -nn/-n. Table 1.1 shows the proportion of errors as regards these categories.

From these data Ólsen drew the conclusion that the letters y and z should be abolished from the Icelandic alphabet because they posed unnecessary difficulties for the speller and did not serve a useful orthographic purpose.

Icelandic spelling was finally standardized by government decree in 1918 in response to the introduction of mandated schooling. This spelling did in fact abolish z from the spelling, but it was reintroduced in another regulation in 1929. It was finally abolished in the final reform

TABLE 1.1

Three Classes of Spelling Errors (Expressed as a Percentage of All Errors)

Type of Error	Entering Class (%)	Graduating Class (%)
i/y	20.2	27.7
s/z	7.6	22
-nn/-n	9.1	8.7

Note: From essays written by entering and graduating students at the Reykjavík grammar school near the end of the 19th century (Ólsen, 1889).

undertaken in 1973–1974. This reform met with fierce opposition, and the Icelandic Parliament passed a resolution to the effect that these reforms should be rescinded. However, the reforms had the support of all the teachers' unions in the country as well as that of the professor of modern Icelandic grammar at the university, and thus the Ministry of Education refused to comply with the wishes of the parliament.

LITERACY IN ICELAND

The extensive vernacular literature of the medieval period points to widespread literacy, or at least literacy that was not confined to the clergy, as many of the major manuscripts were made at the order of wealthy farmers. However, literacy figures are hard to come by so nothing definite can be said on this score. It is certainly an exaggeration to claim, as scholars of a romantic persuasion in earlier times did, that the whole population was literate. Evidence can be had from a much later time, from figures of literacy gathered in the 18th century, admittedly a difficult period in the history of the country. As illustrated in Fig. 1.2, from the data from the south of Iceland, literacy is growing in the period up to the middle of the century (ability to read became a prerequisite for confirmation in 1746). Interestingly, from the same data, an early indication of the effect of "print exposure" on literacy can be seen in Fig. 1.3. This figure shows that illiteracy is 100% in household with no books, falling to 0% in households owning 20 or more books!

After universal—or near universal—literacy became the norm at the beginning of the 20th century, the view became widely accepted that learning to read in Icelandic was not a difficult task, though learning to spell might be quite difficult. This view was reflected in the remark

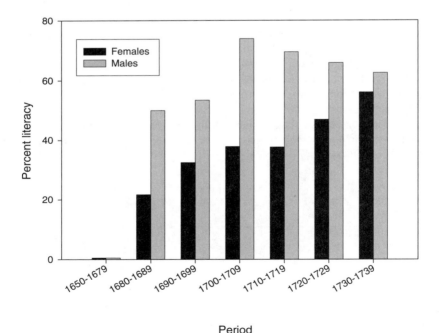

Period

FIG. 1.2. The growth of literacy in Iceland according to church registers from the south of Iceland (Guttormsson, 1989).

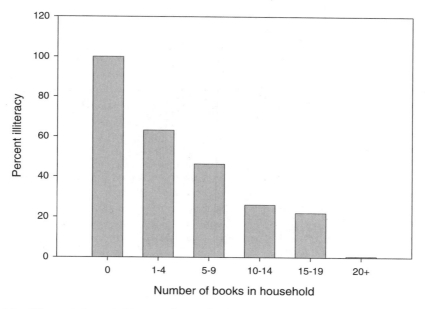

FIG. 1.3. Illiteracy in households according to church registers from the south of Iceland and the number of books in the households (Guttormsson, 1989).

made by Wayne O'Neil, currently professor of linguistics at MIT, at a conference in 1971, later published in the landmark book *Language by Ear and by Eye* (Kavanagh & Mattingly, 1972):

> In Iceland a child starts school at 7 if he has already learned to read at home; otherwise, he must wait a year (p. 329).

O'Neil had been a Fulbright scholar in Iceland and so could be expected to be knowledgeable about this. However, presumably the statement reflects more the common belief among Icelanders up until just a few years ago that learning to read is easy. In earlier times children were indeed taught to read at home, especially in the countryside, but this was definitely the exception by 1970. In any case it is clear that until quite recently reading has not been considered problematic in Iceland. Interestingly, difficulties in spelling have long been recognized, as already mentioned, and have led to heated debates over issues of spelling reform. However, currently there is much interest in reading problems and dyslexia, which has become a widely recognized problem. It is, however, difficult to estimate the occurrence of reading problems because almost no standardized diagnostic instruments are available.

Reading instruction has changed over the past century, moving from the letter/word method to a predominantly phonic approach in the first grades. A failed attempt was made to introduce a "whole-word" method by an Icelandic educator who had studied at the Teachers College at Columbia University in the earlier part of the 20th century. The phonics approach was solidified by Ísak Jónsson (1898–1963), who was probably the most influential primary school educator of the 20th century.

A phonics approach would seem well suited to the Icelandic orthography as the mapping from print to sound is, in most cases, quite regular. Icelandic children in general do not have great trouble in learning to decode print. This can be seen from a study conducted by Ingibjörg Sigurjónsdóttir as part of her master's degree in psychology at the University of Iceland in 2001. The study involved 134 children in grades 1–4 in three schools. Ingibjörg measured,

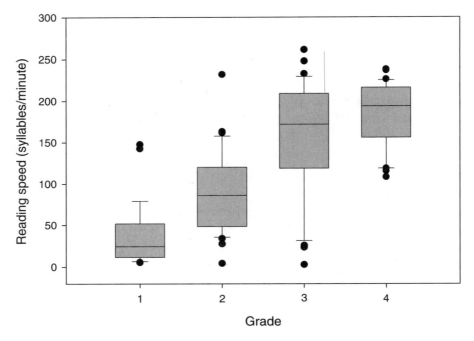

FIG. 1.4. The growth in reading speed in a sample of 134 children from the first four grades in the Icelandic primary schools. Reading rate is here measured as the number of syllables read per minute. Based on unpublished data from Ingibjörg Sigurjónsdóttir (2001).

among other things, their reading speed. Her results are shown in Fig. 1.4, which show steady progress in reading connected text aloud in the first three grades, leveling off in the fourth grade.

Further evidence on reading acquisition can be obtained from the IEA study of reading conducted in 1990–1991 (Elley, 1992). In this study Icelandic 9-year-old children were ranked 8 out of 27 countries studied and 14-year-olds were ranked 5–7 out of 31 countries.

CONCLUSIONS

In this chapter the main events in the evolution of the current Icelandic orthography have been traced. The literary tradition in Iceland extends back for almost a millennium. The adoption of the Latin alphabet for the writing of the Icelandic language was described in great detail in the so-called *First Grammatical Treatise* from the middle of the 12th century. The alphabet adopted by the First Grammarian still forms the core of the current Icelandic alphabet. Intense debates over spelling have taken place over the past two centuries, with the last spelling reforms being undertaken in 1973–1974. The current Icelandic spelling is a compromise between opposing viewpoints arguing either for an orthography that is close to the pronunciation or one that remains faithful to the long tradition of writing in the country. Educational considerations have played an important part in the last round of changes. Interestingly, even "aesthetic" viewpoints have played a part in shaping the orthography and explain the great reluctance shown by the majority of Icelanders toward abolishing the i/y distinction. This has generally been believed to alter the "look" of the writing too much to be acceptable. Abolishing the distinction between æ and œ met with general approval because, in that case, the look of the writing was unchanged. Indeed, making this distinction is a tricky matter needing considerable linguistic insight because little support is to be had from the visual shape of the words. This is very different for the linguistically comparable i/y distinction. In those cases the look of the words is believed to provide a salient cue for the correct spelling.

The current Icelandic orthography is pretty regular in the mapping from print to sound, making it relatively easy for most children to learn to decode. The mapping from sound to print is much more difficult to master, as shown by the amount of time needed to make pupils proficient spellers (Sigurðsson & Þórðarson, 1987).

REFERENCES

Abercrombie, D. (1949). What is a letter? *Lingua, II*, 54–63.

Anderson, S. R. (1985). *Phonology in the twentieth century: Theories of rules and theories of representations*. Chicago: University of Chicago Press.

Benediktsson, H. (1959). The vowel system of Icelandic: A survey of its history. *Word, XV*, 282–312.

Benediktsson, H. (1965). *Early Icelandic script as illustrated in vernacular texts from the twelfth and thirteenth centuries*. Reykjavík: The Manuscript Institute of Iceland.

Benediktsson, H. (1972). *The first grammatical treatise*. Reykjavík: Institute of Linguistics.

Elley, W. B. (1992). *How in the world do students read*? The Hague: The International Association for the Evaluation of Educational Achievement.

Guttormsson, L. (1989). Læsi [Literacy]. In F. F. Jóhannsson (Ed.), *Íslensk þjóð menning [Icelandic Culture]* (Vol. VI, pp. 117–144). Reykjavík: Þjóðsaga.

Haugen, E. (1972). *First grammatical treatise : The earliest Germanic phonology, an edition, translation [from the Old Norse] and commentary*. London: Longman.

Helgason, J. (1929). *Jón Ólafsson frá Grunnavík* (Safn Fræðafélagsins, Vol. V). Copenhagen: Hið íslenska fræðafélag.

Holtsmark, A. (1936). *En islandsk scholasticus fra det 12. århundrede* [An Icelandic scholar from the 12th century]. In Norwegian Oslo: Jacob Dybvad.

Jónsson, J. A. (1959). Ágrip af sögu íslenzkrar stafsetningar [Overview of the history of Icelandic spelling]. *Íslenzk tunga – Lingua Islandica, I*, 71–119.

Karlsson, S. (1989). Tungan [The language]. In F. F. Jóhannsson (Ed.), *Íslensk þjóð menning* [Icelandic Culture] (Vol. VI, pp. 1–54). Reykjavík: Þjóðsaga.

Kavanagh, J. F., & Mattingly, I. G. (Eds.). (1972). *Language by ear and by eye: The relationships between speech and reading*. Cambridge, MA: MIT Press.

Liberman, A. M., Cooper, F. S., Shankweiler, D. P., & Studdert-Kennedy, M. (1967). Perception of the speech code. *Psychological Review, 74*, 431–461.

Ólsen, B. M. (1889). Um stafsetning [On spelling]. *Tímarit um uppeldi og menntamál, II*, 3–24.

Pind, J. (1986). The perception of quantity in Icelandic. *Phonetica, 43*, 116–139.

Pind, J. (1999). Vowel and consonant duration as cues for quantity in Icelandic. *Journal of the Acoustical Society of America, 106*, 1045–1053.

Rask, K. (2002). *Rasmus Rask: Store tanker i et lille land* [Rasmus Rask: Great thoughts in a small country]. Copenhagen: Gads forlag.

Rask, R. (1818). *Undersøgelse om det gamle Nordiske eller Islandske Sprogs Oprindelse* [An investigation into the origins of the old Nordic or Icelandic language]. Copenhagen: Gyldendal.

Rask, R. (1830). *Lestrarkver handa heldri manna börnum* [Reading primer for the children of gentlemen]. Copenhagen: Hið íslenska bókmenntafélag.

Sigurðsson, B., & Þórðarson, S. (1987). Hvernig geta börn lært stafsetningu? [How can children learn to spell?] *Íslenskt mál og almenn málfræð i, 9*, 7–22.

Sigurjónsdóttir, I. (2001). Lestur barna í 1.–4. bekk og tengsl hans við Ravens Progressive Matrices [Children's Nading in grades 1–4 and its relation to Ravens Progressive Matrices]. Unpublished manuscript, University of Iceland.

2

Literacy Acquisition in Norwegian

Bente E. Hagtvet
University of Oslo

Turid Helland
University of Bergen

Solveig-Alma H. Lyster
University of Oslo

Norwegian belongs to the North German group of the Indo-European languages. It has developed from Old Norse with a rich morphology into a modern language with less morphological complexity. Morphemic reading, however, is still needed. Norwegian orthography is described as semi-transparent. Studies of Norwegian children show that even subjects with dyslexia break the alphabetic code rather easily. However, automaticity of decoding skills appears to be generally slow to develop in Norwegian children. This developmental picture is supported by large-scale international comparative studies in which a fair proportion of older Norwegian children (ages 14–15 years) read laboriously, and with limited comprehension. This chapter discusses the role of orthography from a developmental perspective. It argues that largely because of the fairly systematic sound–letter correspondence of Norwegian orthography, learning the sound–letter relationships associated with early reading is easy even for children at risk of developing reading problems. However, even subtle variations in phonological qualities such as word length and minor irregularities in degree of phoneme–grapheme correspondence appear to have a negative impact on reading speed and fluency and, in many cases, reading comprehension as well. How these issues interact with the individual child's linguistic and cognitive skills and with the teaching methods used in school is not clear and should be the focus of future research.

PHONOLOGICAL, MORPHOLOGICAL AND ORTHOGRAPHIC NATURE OF NORWEGIAN ORTHOGRAPHY

From Old Norse to Contemporary Norwegian

The Norwegian script, together with the Icelandic, Danish, and Swedish, form the North Germanic group of the Germanic branch of the Indo-European languages. Scripts in Old Norse date back to the period of the Vikings, about the 10th century C.E. Modern Swedish, Danish, and Norwegian languages are closely related to each other with minor variations in phonology, morphology, syntax, and semantics of the spoken languages, in addition to orthography of the written languages. These differences can be described as merely dialectical. Oral, even more so than written, communication flows relatively easily among the three languages. Danish orthography, however, is less transparent than Swedish and Norwegian orthographies. Icelandic, on the other hand, is close to the Old Norse language and cannot be immediately understood by Norwegians today.

Politically, Norway was in union first with Denmark, and then with Sweden. The languages of these two countries dominated Norwegian written language. Modern written Norwegian did not start to develop until 200 years ago. In the 19th century, two eminent dialect researchers, Knud Knudsen (1812–1895) and Ivar Aasen (1813–1896), developed their own Norwegian grammars and orthographic dictionaries. The result of their works is that today we have two standard, official orthographies: urban Norwegian (*bokmål*), which originally developed from Danish and was based on the southern and eastern dialects centred around Oslo, and rural Norwegian (*nynorsk*), which is based on dialects of the western parts of the country. Norwegian has furthermore many different dialects, which are appreciated and used officially.

With a total of about 4.7 million inhabitants and users of the Norwegian language, this diversity may look trivial from the outside. However, for years the presence of these two orthographies has caused discussion and controversy among the Norwegian population.[1] The orthographies are regularly being reformed, not only in accordance with dialectal changes, but also in accordance with the ongoing debate of the two official orthographies.[2]

Norwegian has developed from the synthetic Old Norse into a modern Norwegian with a less complicated morphology, especially when it comes to cases. A few remnants of the cases in Old Norse are seen in inflections of the pronouns and also in nouns in some dialects. Nouns, adjectives, and pronouns are inflected in singular and plural in congruence with the three grammatical genders of the language. Verbs are conjugated according to tense. Syntactically, Norwegian is quite similar to English, except for the use of "to do" in interrogative and negative sentences. Rather, interrogation is marked by inversion (verb–subject) and a tonal rise at the end of the sentence. Inversion is always seen in any sentence starting with an adverbial phrase.

The Structure of the Language: The Alphabet and the Word Classes

Roughly speaking, the Norwegian language comprises 40 phonemes[3] and 29 letters. The alphabet consists of 20 consonant phonemes: b [b], (c), d[d], f[f], g[g], h[h], j[j], k[k], l[l], m[m], n[n] p[p], (q), r[r], s[s], t[t], v[v], (w), (x), and (z). The parentheses indicate that the letters are not used in any word of Norwegian origin, but are seen in imported words. Four different graphemes make three different consonant phonemes: kj/tj[ç], skj[ʃ], and ng[ŋ], and the eastern dialects have the retroflexes rt[ʈ], rd[ɖ], rn[ɳ], and rs[ʂ]. A tendency to fail to distinguish between [ʃ] and [ç], fading out the [ç], is seen in young people's oral language. The Norwegian alphabet has nine vowels, which can be either short or long: a[a]/[ɑ]/[a:]/[ɑ:], e[ɛ]/[æ]/[e:], i [ɪ]/[i:], o[ʊ]/[u:], u[ʉ]/,[ʉ:], y[ɣ]/[y], æ[æ:], ø[œ]/[ø:], and å[ɔ][o:]. Further, there are four diphthongs: ei[æɪ], au[æʉ], øy[œ], and ai[ai] (Endresen, 1996; Moen, 1993). A recent newspaper survey reported that Norwegian parents no longer want to name their children with traditional names containing the letters 'æ', 'ø', or 'å', probably because the difficulty in making a personal computer readily accept these letters.

---

[1] Both orthographies are taught in junior and senior high school, but one of the orthographies is chosen as the main orthography for each class or school.

[2] Up until the 1960s the two orthographies were assimilated, leading to three fractions: one rural *nynorsk*, one urban *bokmål*, and one for a joint venture (*samnorsk*). Today the third, joint alternative is not debated, and the two orthographies, *nynorsk* and *bokmål* exist side by side. In this chapter only the urban *bokmål* is referred to, as it is most frequently used in mass media and in Norwegian literature. About 80% of the population use this orthography.

[3] Notated per the International Phonetic Alphabet.

The number of spellings for the 40 Norwegian phonemes is relatively high and somewhat more complex compared with the more-or-less one-to-one correspondence between for example, the Finnish phonemes and graphemes. Nevertheless, the difference between the number of phonemes and graphemes in the Norwegian script is fairly small compared with those in for example French, in which approximately 30 phonemes are represented by more than 130 graphemes. As to English, Dewey (1971) reported 561 different ways of spelling 41 English phonemes (English is often reported as having approximately 44 phonemes), showing that the English script is all by itself at the very "deep" end on a continuum from highly regular and transparent to highly irregular and deep orthography. Despite the fair simplicity and regularity of sound–letter correspondences in Norwegian, orthographic challenges are quite numerous, caused by consonant clusters.

Many Norwegian words have consonant clusters, and some combinations such as *oftest* [most often], *nifst* [scary], or *kringkasting* [broadcasting] may be especially difficult. Typically, the first syllable is stressed in Norwegian multi-syllabic words: skole ['skuːlɛ] (school); *merkelig* ['mærkɛlɪ] (strange). There are also two tonemes, often called toneme 1 and toneme 2, differentiating the meaning of some words with identical spelling or words that would otherwise have had the same pronunciation: (1'lœvɛ) [the leaf, the foliage] and (2'lœvɛ) [lion] (see Kristoffersen, 2000; Moen, 2000; Simonsen, Endresen, & Hovdhaugen, 1996, for further studies on Norwegian phonology).

Basic units of the written Norwegian language are words, which grammatically are categorised into 10 word classes: nouns, articles, pronouns, verbs, adjectives, adverbs, prepositions, conjunctions, numerals, and interjections. Norwegian nouns have three grammatical genders: masculine (*m*), feminine (*f*), and neuter (*n*). The nouns are marked by a preceding indefinite article: *en* (*m*), *ei* (*f*), and *et* (*n*) in the singular. The plural has no indefinite article, but is marked by endings according to grammatical gender. Table 2.1 shows how regular nouns are inflected in *bokmål*.

A few nouns have irregular inflections, usually shown by changes in the stem vowel (brother: *en bror–broren–brødre–brødrene*). The adjectives usually modify and precede a noun and are inflected in agreement with the noun. The definite form of the adjective demands a definite article. The inflections for *m* and *f* are identical: *en fin gutt–den fin/e gutten–fin/e gutter–de fin/e guttene*; for *n*: *et fin/t hus–det fin/e huset–fin/e hus–de fin/e husene*. Adjectives are indicated either by the inflectional endings (*-ere* in the comparative and *-est* in the superlative), or by the modifiers 'more' and 'most'.

TABLE 2.1
Nouns: Inflectional Classes in Norwegian *Bokmål*

Gender	Singular, Indefinite	Singular, Definite	Plural, Indefinite	Plural, Definite
M	En gutt (a boy)	gutt/en (the boy)	gutt/er (boys)	gutt/ene (the boys)
F	Ei jente (a girl)	jent/a (the girl)	jent/er (girls)	jent/ene (the girls)
N	Et hus (the house)	hus/et (the house)	hus (houses)	hus/a/ene (the houses)

Note. M: masculine; *F*: feminine; *N*: neuter.

TABLE 2.2
Verb Conjugation in Norwegian *Bokmål*

Conjugation	Infinitive	Present	Past	Past Participle
Regular [to dance]	å dans/e	dans/er	dans/et	har dans/et
Irregular [to ask]	å be	be/r	ba	har be/dt

Norwegian verbs are conjugated by tense, and there are both regular and irregular conjugations, as shown in Table 2.2. The subject marks grammatical person, with no effect on the verb. The modal auxiliaries are used in approximately the same way as in English. There are no grammatical progressive aspects in Norwegian. The rest of the 10 word classes are not conjugated, with an exception of the adverbs, which are indicated in the same way as adjectives.

Structure and Challenges of the Norwegian Script

Although Norwegian script is described as fairly transparent, it is not transparent to the same degree as Italian, Spanish, or Finnish (Elley, 1992). The reasons why some words are not written the way they are spoken are etymological, but to a far lesser degree than in English orthography. For instance, the first two letters of Norwegian interrogatives *hvem* [who], *hva* [what], and *hvor* [where], are pronounced as one phoneme, much like the English words 'who' and 'when'. Presumably all Norwegians have a memory of their first-grade step into literacy: the walls of the classroom covered by red and blue letters, the vowels and the consonants. In a comparatively shallow orthography, synthesising these letters into words would be easy. However, authors of Norwegian ABC textbooks will testify that pronouncing these words is not that easy for beginning readers. The pronouns '*jeg*' [ɪ], *meg* [me], *deg* (you, accusative of *du* [you]), *seg* [herself/himself, reflexive pronoun] are all pronounced with '-ei' after the onset. The conjunction *og* [and] is pronounced as if it should be spelled 'å' which is the infinitive marker in Norwegian. Two other rather tricky phonemes are [v] and [j] when they occupy the initial position in a word. As a rule, these phonemes are written as 'v' and 'j', respectively, but quite frequently they have another letter added to them. High-frequency exception words have to be learned from an early stage on.

Somewhat humorously, but with some truth to it, the double consonant is called the most expensive letter combination in the Norwegian language, as it has caused many extra training lessons at school. The problematic double consonant is not a matter of the consonant phoneme, but of the preceding vowel sound—whether it is short or long. In some languages, the long vowel sound is marked by a double vowel. In Norwegian, a long vowel sound is followed by a single consonant whereas a short vowel sound is followed by a double consonant. Some words have retained the spelling from Old Norse as manifested by 'mute letters' at the end of the words, as in *land* (/lan/, meaning land) and *sild* (/sil/, meaning herring), contrary to the expectation that there should not be a letter or that there should be a double consonant.

Vowels can also cause problems, as there is not always a phoneme-to-grapheme correspondence. This concerns above all the letter 'o', which is sometimes pronounced [ʊ], as in *bort* (/bʊʈ/, meaning away), and sometimes [ɔ], as in *godt* (/gɔt/, meaning good). Similarly, the letter 'e' is often pronounced [æ], as in *her* (/hær/, meaning here).

A couple of other features of the Norwegian orthography need to be mentioned. Many function words, as well as some short words, have a rule-breaking spelling of their own. Because these words are not semantically dense, little attention may be paid to them as they are read. The reason why many individuals with reading and writing disabilities often misspell these words may be that the combination of irregular spelling and low semantic loading makes them harder to memorise compared with content words.

Compound words are widely used in Norwegian, adding a creative element to the language in the sense that a compound word can be made up on the spot, if needed. The two (or more) words that are combined are then written as one word, as in *tog/stasjon/s/betjenten*, meaning the train station operator. An 's', a reminiscence of a genitive from Old Norse, is sometimes (but not always) seen in compound words and may be a challenge to young writers. Many compounds are high-frequency words, such as *matematikkundervisning* [teaching of mathematics], *klatrestativ* [climbing frame], and *brannslukningsapparat* [fire extinguisher]. These long words cause problems for beginning and slow readers. Another typical way of creating new words in Norwegian is by the compilation of affixes. Much-used prefixes are 'u-', 'unn-', 'inn-', 'an-', 'be-', and 'for-', and frequent suffixes are '-ning', '-ing', and '-else'. Prefixes and suffixes can be seen in the same word, for example, *inn + flyt + else* [influence] and *an + be + fal + ing* [recommendation]. Affixes in nouns do not influence the spelling of the word roots, but may change the pronunciation and thereby reduce the transparency of the written language.

Finally, the Norwegian language has many words with a rather complex phonological structure, especially for word onsets. Word onsets such as 'str-', 'skr-', 'fr-', 'tr-', and 'br-' are very common, as well as words with more than one consonant cluster. Examples are *struts* [ostrich], *skrumpe* [shrink], and *straks* [soon]. The complex phonological structure in combination with compound words may then easily produce words such as *strakstiltak* [immediate measure] consisting of the words *straks*, *til*, and *tak*, and with two consonant clusters in the first word.

In summary, a semantically simple text will have quite a few words with exceptional spelling, showing that there are many pitfalls even in a rather shallow orthography such as Norwegian. Both grammatical meta-knowledge and linguistic meta-knowledge are required for reading and writing Norwegian. Rules, exceptions to the rules, and exceptions to the exceptions pose problems to children who are learning to read and spell, particularly to those with weaknesses in language processing ability.

THE ROLE OF ORTHOGRAPHY IN LITERACY ACQUISITION AND PROBLEMS OF READING AND SPELLING IN NORWAY

The Influence of Orthography on Reading Development and Reading Disability

The research literature is not at all clear about the extent to which the orthographies of the script influence the ease with which children learn to read and spell. There appears to be general agreement, however, that significant individual differences in literacy development could be accounted for by the properties of the language (Caravolas, 1993; Goulandris, 2003; Hagtvet & Lyster, 2003; Landerl, 2003; Leong & Joshi, 1997; Wimmer & Goswami, 1994). The influence of factors such as phoneme–grapheme correspondence, the distinctiveness or stress pattern of the phonological system, and the characteristics of the morphological system on reading and spelling development, however, is still not well understood (Goulandris, 2003). How these issues interact with the linguistic–cognitive skills of the individual and with the teaching methods used in school is even more unclear. A hypothesis with much theoretical appeal assumes that the closer the number of graphemes is to the number of phonemes, the

multiple-letter graphemes representing one phoneme: *lenger* [longer/anymore]; *bort* [away]. Words and non-words with a complex or less distinct phonological structure, such as *bnof* [nonword], and *damer* [ladies], also caused problems. Poor and good readers, in other words, showed different spelling patterns only when they spelled words with a challenging orthography or phonology. To some extent their spelling performance was moreover influenced by the degree of familiarity of a word. *Jeg* (/jæi/, meaning 'ɪ') was, for example, much easier than *seg* (/sæi/, meaning 'herself/himself'), even though the degree of irregularity is the same. Thus reading experience appeared to have an impact on how well an irregular word was spelled. The correlation between word reading and spelling was found to be .77, suggesting that most good readers were good spellers and that most poor readers were also poor spellers.

Helland (2002) studied a group of 33 older Norwegian dyslexic adolescents who were 11 to 16 years old and had IQs in the average range. With the phase model of Frith used as a frame of reference, a subgroup of 23 of the 33 participants was defined as being in "the alphabetic phase" of their literacy development. Of these 23 participants, 8 had problems in comprehension and mathematics. The other subgroup of 10 participants had reached an 'unstable orthographic phase'.[6] Both groups scored below average on accuracy and speed measures when they read short regular words. Furthermore, the groups read short, regular words with equal accuracy, but the 10 participants in the unstable orthographic phase read them faster. As to reading speed of longer and irregular words, there was no group difference, but the "orthographic readers" read these words more accurately. This group also showed more advanced spelling.

Taken together, these studies offer a number of theoretically important suggestions regarding the role of orthography in literacy acquisition and reading disability. First, breaking the alphabetic code appears fairly simple even in a semi-transparent orthography such as the Norwegian. However, automatised reading is not. These findings differ from the studies of English-speaking readers, which report that poor readers have problems in manipulating the phonological structure of language even at a basic alphabetic level (Lennox & Siegel, 1994).

Second, the speed of reading is affected by variables such as word length, phonological complexity, and orthographic complexity suggesting that fluent reading presupposes rapid integration of phonological and orthographic processes. Morphological information inherent in the orthographic system is a constituent part of this integration process connecting phonology and semantics.

Third, there appears to be a developmental interdependence between accuracy and speed of reading in which 'accuracy precedes speed'.[7]

We now explore the impact of orthography on reading performance by examining how Norwegian children and youths in general score in international comparative reading studies.

INCIDENCE OF READING PROBLEMS

The Challenges of Defining Literacy and Literacy Problems

With a well-developed school system, compulsory schooling from the age of 6 years on (before 1997 from the age of 7 years), and a healthy economic condition, one would expect the incidence of reading problems in Norway to be low . Relatively speaking, this is indeed the case, but the incidence of reading problems varies with the criteria used for defining reading problems.

---

[6] There was no correlation between age/years of schooling and reading/spelling scores.

[7] This relation between accuracy and speed of reading is further empirically documented in a Danish study including 576 Danish participants 8–12 years old showing that fluency in reading was achieved at the point where 80–90% of the words of a test could be read with accuracy (Nielsen et al., 1992).

Reading skills have been defined in various ways depending on time, tradition, purpose, and so forth. Today, it is generally agreed that reading is a complex process encompassing decoding abilities and comprehension abilities. In addition to reading skills, writing skills are also used to define problems with written language. To encompass the many aspects of reading and writing, the term 'literacy skills' is often preferred.

Literacy in the Adult Population

The most recent study of reading skills and reading deficiencies in the adult population is the International Adult Literacy Survey (IALS) (2000), comprising 22 nations, in which Norway participated in the third round of data collection in 1998. The IALS is a large-scale collaboration among governments, national statistical agencies, research institutions, and the Organization for Economic Co-operation and Development (OECD).

In the IALS study 'literacy' is defined functionally as understanding and employing printed information in daily activities, at home, at work and in the community (The Final OECD Report of the International Adult Literacy Survey, 2000). Literacy is operationally defined in terms of three domains of skills: prose literacy, document literacy, and quantitative literacy. Nationally representative samples of the adult population from 16 to 65 years old participated in the study. Norway received the following rankings which were based on mean scores: Prose literacy (3), document literacy (2), and quantitative literacy (4). However, as much as 30% of the population still functioned below Level 3, that is, the level defined as critical in terms of 'functional literacy'.[8] Furthermore, Norway was among the six countries in which less than 15% of the population functioned at Literacy Level 1, indicating a severe literacy deficit in everyday life and at work. Even in Sweden, which was the nation ranked at the top on all measures, about 8% of the population functioned at Literacy Level 1. The equivalent figure for Norway was 9%.[9]

Taken together, the IALS results show that Norway has a relatively high literacy level, but that about 10% of the adult population read at a critically low level and another 20% at a marginal level.

Age was negatively correlated with literacy skills, with older cohorts tending to score lower than younger cohorts.[10] Other variables predicting adult literacy skills were home background (in particular the level of education of parents) and active use of literacy skills at work. Most studies of literacy skills of adults and older schoolchildren have not looked at orthography as an explanatory variable for differences in literacy skills.

---

[8] Five levels of literacy were identified corresponding to measured ranges of scores achieved on various tests. Level 1 'indicates persons with very poor skills, where the individual may, for example, be unable to determine the correct amount of medicine to give a child from information given on the package'. At Level 2 'respondents can deal only with simple material which is clearly laid out, and in which the tasks involved are not too complex'. Level 3 is considered a critical minimum skill level for coping with the demands of modern life and work, and Levels 4 and 5 refers to command of higher-order information processing skills (The OECD Report, 2000).

[9] The fact that the IALS describes reading problems in terms of a continuum suggests that an incidence figure for reading problem is indeed a very relative entity. In Denmark for example, which is a country with social, political, and cultural values similar to those of Norway, different comparative studies of adult literacy have come up with widely differing figures for reading problems: 45% (IALS) and 12% (Elbro, Møller, & Nielsen, 1995). There are probably good reasons for this difference in incidence figures—reasons related to differences in screening instruments and criteria used to define literacy. Elbro and collaborators (1995) also defined literacy functionally and focused on texts from daily life (newspaper articles, documents, forms at the post office, etc.). The tests are, however, quite different from those used by IALS and somewhat stricter criteria have been applied when deciding the cutoff between 'problems' and 'normality' (whereas the IALS included a rather large group of individuals, including so-called 'marginal reading problems').

[10] In the study by Elbro et al. (1995), 'incidence of reading problems' varied strongly across ages: 4% (age 18–29), 9% (age 30–44), 25% (age 45–59), 27% (age 60–67).

TABLE 2.3

Mean Student Ability Scores (With Standard Deviations) for All Domains, Arranged in Order
of Overall Achievement

Country	Rank	Grade/Age	Overall	Narrative	Expository	Documents
Finland	1	3 / 9.7	569 (70)	568 (83)	569 (81)	569 (88)
United States	2	4 / 10.0	547 (74)	553 (96)	538 (80)	550 (81)
Sweden	3	3 / 9.8	539 (94)	536 (100)	543 (112)	539 (106)
Norway	8	3 / 9.8	524 (91)	525 (102)	528 (103)	519 (101)
Denmark	26	2 / 9.8	475 (111)	463 (119)	467 (127)	496 (125)

Note. International mean score = 500.

Incidence of Reading Problems in Children

Over the past 15 years, Norway has taken part in a number of large-scale international comparative reading literacy studies of children 9 to 15 years of age. In general, the results place
Norway above the international average, but well below what one might expect on the basis
of her high composite development index (CDI).[11]

The IEA Reading Literacy Study of 1990–1991 The international association for the evaluation of education achievement (IEA) was based on representative national samples of 9- and
14-year-old pupils from 32 countries ($N = 1,500-3,000$ per country). This study was planned
and organized by The International Association for the Evaluation of Educational Achievement
with the aim of assessing "the average levels of reading literacy of representative samples of
all students in the grades where most 9- and 14-year-olds were to be found" (Elley, 1992).
Three domains of reading were used for this survey: narrative prose, expository prose, and
documents. Starting school at the age of 7 years the Norwegian children were assessed at the
end of Grade 3 (mean age 9.8 years) and at the end of Grade 8 (mean age 14.8).[12]

For several reasons, Finland, Sweden, Denmark and the United States provide interesting units for comparison. All nations except Denmark were ranked at the top for 9-year-old
children, and they render great importance to education. As previously mentioned, the orthographic systems of the languages of these countries vary in degree of transparency. The mean
student ability scores (and standard deviations) for all domains, ranked in the order of overall
achievement, are presented in Table 2.3 for the 9-year-olds and in Table 2.4 for the 14-year-olds.

Table 2.3 shows that the Norwegian pupils at 9 years of age scored above the international
mean in all the literacy domains, but somewhat below the rank the Composite Development
Index (CDI) status would predict (Elley, 1992). Furthermore, results across genres were quite
stable, but with a rather large standard variation relative to the top-ranking country, Finland,
indicating that a fair number of children read below the national mean. The lowest 5% of the
participants furthermore read extremely poorly relatively speaking. This is a most unexpected
finding, given that socioeconomically Norway is one of the most homogeneous countries in
the survey.

---

[11] (Composite Development Index is a composite based on a set of selected national indicators GNP per capita, public
expenditure per student on education, life expectancy, low birth weigth, newspapers per 100 populations, % adult
literacy).

[12] School entrance age was in 1997 reduced to six in Norway, but not in Sweden and Finland. This has of course no
impact on the IEA-results, which were obtained before the reform.

TABLE 2.4
Mean Student Ability Scores (With Standard Deviations) for All Domains, Arranged
in Order of Overall Achievement

Country	Rank	Grade/Age	Overall	Narrative	Expository	Documents
Finland	1	8/14.7	560 (65)	559 (84)	541 (71)	580 (82)
Sweden	3	8/14.8	546 (80)	556 (93)	533 (91)	550 (90)
United States	9	9/15.0	535 (85)	539 (98)	539 (107)	528 (84)
Denmark	13	8/14.8	525 (77)	517 (83)	524 (94)	532 (88)
Norway	17	8/14.8	516 (71)	515 (76)	520 (86)	512 (82)

Note. International mean score = 500.

In terms of the potential impact of orthography on the results a rather complex picture is revealed where Finland with the most transparent orthography scores the highest followed by Sweden and Norway with semi-transparent orthographies. Of the Nordic countries Denmark with the deepest orthograhy ranks the lowest. However, the USA with the deepest orthography of all the countries in the table ranks second. This indicates that while orthography appears to play a part during early reading development as suggested by the relative ranks of the Nordic countries, the causal pattern is complex, which is also argued by the authors of the study.

Table 2.4 illustrates equivalent results for the 14-year-olds and shows that Norway has had the largest negative change in ranking, both overall and for the different literacy domains of all these top-ranking countries. There may be numerous substantive explanations to this negative change in Norwegian scores (for example inefficient teaching methods or subtle impacts from orthography) as well as methodological explanations and characteristics of tests (e.g., lower sensitivity of tests at 14 years old than at 97 years old). Sampling bias may also be a possible explanation. We will get back to the causal at pattern below.

The Programme for International Student Assessment (PISA) (2001) is another large-scale comparative reading study in which Norway has participated. One of the main purposes of the project was to compare a large body of aspects associated with reading: retrieval of specific information, interpretation of written texts, and reflection and evaluation of information given in written texts. The focus, in other words, was on 'reading to learn' rather than on 'learning to read'. In this survey, 15-year-olds from 31 countries participated.

The results showed that Norwegian 15-year-olds—while still scoring marginally above average relative to the other OECD countries—ranked 13th in overall competence in reading comprehension, again after Finland and Sweden, but ahead of the United States, and also ahead of Denmark, which were ranked 15th and 16th, respectively. Compared with the IEA study, this study may be seen as an improvement in reading competence. However, the variation in reading skills was higher among the Norwegian pupils than was the case for the participants from the other Nordic countries. Also, gender differences in favour of girls had increased in all countries, but only Finland and New Zealand had larger gender differences than Norway. Further, as many as 16% of the pupils read at Level 1, in which students are capable of completing only the least complex reading tasks. In short, Norwegian schools appear to foster or 'get' a high proportion of poor readers.

In addition to reading skills, attitudes towards reading were evaluated. It turned out that Norwegian pupils manifested the least positive attitudes after Belgium and the United States, but girls were more positive than boys.

only 2 of the 10 subjects in the "orthographic phase-group". This suggests that the phonological deficit in very poor readers may be associated with a more general language problem than is the case with marginally poor readers and. This again raises the question of the universality of the manifestations of dyslexia across languages. Carefully planned comparative studies are needed to establish in more detail the complex interactive set of variables influencing literacy development in different orthographies, and in particular in relation to poor reading skills.

REFERENCES

Caravolas, M. (1993). Language-specific influences of phonology and orthography on emergent literacy. In J. Altarriba (Ed.), *Cognition and culture: A cross-cultural approach to psychology.* Amsterdam: Elsevier.

Dewey, G. (1971). *English spelling: Roadblock to reading.* New York: Teachers College Press.

Ehri, L. C. (1992). Reconceptualizing the development of sight word reading and its relationship to recoding. In P. Gough, L. C. Ehri & R. Treiman (Eds.), *Reading Acquisition* (pp. 107–143). NJ: Lawrence Erlbaum Associates.

Elbro, C., Møller, S., & Nielsen, E. M. (1995). Functional reading difficulties in Denmark. A study of adult reading of common texts. *Reading and Writing an Interdisciplinary Journal, 7,* 257–276.

Elley, W. B. (1992). *How in the world do students read? IEA study of reading literacy.* The International Association for the Evaluation of Educational Achievement. IEA Headquarters, The Hague, The Netherlands.

Endresen, R. T. (1996). Fonologi. In H. G. Simonsen, R. T. Endresen & E. Hovdhaugen (Eds.), *Språkvitenskap* (4th ed., pp. 38–75). Oslo: Universitetsforlaget AS.

Gallagher, A., Frith, U., & Snowling, M. J. (2000). Precursors of literacy-delay among children at genetic risk of dyslexia. *Journal of Child Psychology and Psychiatry, 41,* 203–213.

Goulandris, N. (2003). Introduction: Developmental dyslexia, language and orthographies. In N. Goulandris (Ed.), *Dyslexia in different languages. Cross-linguistic comparisons* (pp. 1–14). London: Whurr.

Hagtvet, B. E., Horn, E., & Lyster, S. A. H. (June, 2003). *Connections between spoken and written language: Early precursors of written language problems.* Paper presented at The Annual Meeting of the Society for the Scientific Study of Reading, Boulder, CO.

Hagtvet, B. E., & Lyster, S. (2003). The spelling errors of good and poor decoders: a developmental cross-linguistic perspective. In N. Goulandris (Ed.), *Dyslexia in different languages. Cross linguistic comparison* (pp. 181–207). London: Whurr.

Hagtvet, B. E., & Lyster, S. A. H., & Horn, E. (2004). Underlying sources of fluent reading of text: Phonemic awareness naming speed and other sub-skills. Paper presented at The Annual Meeting of the Society for the Scientific Study of Reading, Amsterdam, July 2004.

Helland, T. (2002). Single word Reading and spelling in dyslexia Vary with Neuro-cognitive functions. In T. Helland (2002), *Neuro-Cognitive Functions in Dyslexia. Variations According to Language Comprehension and Mathematics Skills.* Doctoral thesis. University of Oslo, Norway.

Henry, M. K. (1993). Morphological structure: Latin and Greek roots and affixes as upper grade code strategies. *Reading and Writing: An Interdisciplinary Journal, 5,* 227–241.

IALS (the International Adult Literacy Survey) (2000). Literacy in the Information Age: Final Report of the International Adult Literacy Survey, OECD, Paris 2000.

Jaffré, J. P. (1997). From writing to orthography: The functions and limits of the notion of system. In M. Fayol (Ed.), *Learning to spell. Research, theory, and practice across languages* (pp. 1–20). Mahwah, NJ: Lawrence Erbaum Associates.

Korkman, M., & Häkkinen-Rihu, P. (1994). A new classification of developmental language disorders (DLD). *Brain and Language, 4,* 96–116.

Kristoffersen, G. (2000). *The Phonology of Norwegian.* Oxford, UK: Oxford University Press.

Landerl, K. (2003). Dyslexia in German-speaking children. In N. Goulandris (Ed.), *Dyslexia in different languages. Cross-linguistic comparisons* (pp. 15–32). London: Whurr.

Lennox, C., & Siegel, L. S. (1994). The role of phonological and orthographic processes in learning to spell. In G. D. A. Brown & N. C. Ellis (Eds.), *Handbook of spelling. Theory, processes and intervention* (pp. 93–109). New York: Wiley.

Leong, C. K., & Joshi, R. M. (1997). Relating phonologic and orthographic processing to learning to read and spell. In C. K. Leong & R. M. Joshi (Eds.), *Cross-language studies of learning to read and spell* (pp. 1–29). Boston: Kluwer Academic Publishers.

Lyster, S. A. H. (1998). Preventing reading failure: A follow-up study. *Dyslexia, 4,* 132–144.

TABLE 2.4
Mean Student Ability Scores (With Standard Deviations) for All Domains, Arranged
in Order of Overall Achievement

Country	Rank	Grade/Age	Overall	Narrative	Expository	Documents
Finland	1	8/14.7	560 (65)	559 (84)	541 (71)	580 (82)
Sweden	3	8/14.8	546 (80)	556 (93)	533 (91)	550 (90)
United States	9	9/15.0	535 (85)	539 (98)	539 (107)	528 (84)
Denmark	13	8/14.8	525 (77)	517 (83)	524 (94)	532 (88)
Norway	17	8/14.8	516 (71)	515 (76)	520 (86)	512 (82)

Note. International mean score = 500.

In terms of the potential impact of orthography on the results a rather complex picture is revealed where Finland with the most transparent orthography scores the highest followed by Sweden and Norway with semi-transparent orthographies. Of the Nordic countries Denmark with the deepest orthograhy ranks the lowest. However, the USA with the deepest orthography of all the countries in the table ranks second. This indicates that while orthography appears to play a part during early reading development as suggested by the relative ranks of the Nordic countries, the causal pattern is complex, which is also argued by the authors of the study.

Table 2.4 illustrates equivalent results for the 14-year-olds and shows that Norway has had the largest negative change in ranking, both overall and for the different literacy domains of all these top-ranking countries. There may be numerous substantive explanations to this negative change in Norwegian scores (for example inefficient teaching methods or subtle impacts from orthography) as well as methodological explanations and characteristics of tests (e.g., lower sensitivity of tests at 14 years old than at 97 years old). Sampling bias may also be a possible explanation. We will get back to the causal at pattern below.

The Programme for International Student Assessment (PISA) (2001) is another large-scale comparative reading study in which Norway has participated. One of the main purposes of the project was to compare a large body of aspects associated with reading: retrieval of specific information, interpretation of written texts, and reflection and evaluation of information given in written texts. The focus, in other words, was on 'reading to learn' rather than on 'learning to read'. In this survey, 15-year-olds from 31 countries participated.

The results showed that Norwegian 15-year-olds—while still scoring marginally above average relative to the other OECD countries—ranked 13th in overall competence in reading comprehension, again after Finland and Sweden, but ahead of the United States, and also ahead of Denmark, which were ranked 15th and 16th, respectively. Compared with the IEA study, this study may be seen as an improvement in reading competence. However, the variation in reading skills was higher among the Norwegian pupils than was the case for the participants from the other Nordic countries. Also, gender differences in favour of girls had increased in all countries, but only Finland and New Zealand had larger gender differences than Norway. Further, as many as 16% of the pupils read at Level 1, in which students are capable of completing only the least complex reading tasks. In short, Norwegian schools appear to foster or 'get' a high proportion of poor readers.

In addition to reading skills, attitudes towards reading were evaluated. It turned out that Norwegian pupils manifested the least positive attitudes after Belgium and the United States, but girls were more positive than boys.

The most recent large-scale comparative study in which Norway participated is The Progress in Reading Literacy Study of 2003. (PIRLS, 2003), which examined the reading comprehension level of 9-year-olds. The study confirmed the previous findings, but also added a dramatic twist. Of the 17 OECD countries that participated in this study, Norway was ranked almost the lowest. These findings have caused political turmoil because this cohort of Norwegian fourth graders included children who had had one more year of schooling than children in the previous international literacy studies. (Children started school at the age of 6 years after the 1997 Reform, when school entry age was lowered by one year).

To obtain a comparative measure of low-scoring readers in each country, PIRLS identified the 25th percentile as a lower benchmark. Only 80% of the Norwegian sample had scores above this benchmark, whereas as many as 86% of the Swedish and 98% of the Dutch sample had such high scores. This is a challenging finding, as the Dutch, Swedish, and Norwegian orthographies have a similar level of transparency. The PIRLS study showed that, among the Norwegian poor readers, 63% were boys and 37% were girls, although a clear gender difference was not observed among good readers (46% boys and 54% girls).

In summary, these international studies are different in scopes and measures and also indefinite as to the impact of orthography on literacy development. Yet some results of relevance to the issues at stake in this chapter stand out with fair consistence: The incidence of poor Norwegian adolescent and adult readers is higher than one would expect on the basis of Norway's high CDI score and egalitarian school system, as are inter-individual variations and gender differences. Futhermore, judging from the IEA-results, the scores of Norwegian pupils appear to deteriorate with age (from age 9 to age 14) relative to those of pupils from other comparable nations. In the IEA-study of "reading literacy" Norway had the largest negative change in ranking from age 9 to age 14. Also, the lowest 5% of the participants at age 9 read extremely poorly. Taken together these findings suggest that relative to other countries with a comparable CDI-status, a fair amount of Norwegian children appear to face larger reading comprehension problems the older they become. Other international comparative studies corroborate this finding. In the PISA-study (2001) focusing "reading to learn" as many as 16% of the Norwegian 15-year-olds read at the lowest level of literacy, and in the IALS-study, as many as 30% of the adults read below the level defined as critical in terms of "functional literacy".

According to the authors of the international studies the variables that contributed to the observed variations in literacy skills appeared to be multiple with CDI scores and the quality of the environmental input judged the most influential ones. Orthography was granted only a minor impact, if considered at all. It is true enough that Finland, the best reading nation in the world, had the most consistent grapheme-phoneme system they argued. Yet other nations with deeper orthographies did almost as well while nations with shallow orthographies did more poorly. Rather, the high quality of teacher training, an emphasis on teaching reading strategy from an early age, and a widespread interest in reading and schooling in the Finnish culture was highlighted as more probable explanations (e.g., Elley, 1992).

While not disregarding the importance of quality teaching and well developed school systems, we would like to underscore that the international comparative studies converge with studies of reading disabled children on the two developmental key issues highlighted in the preceding passage (beginning reading appears on the whole simpler for Norwegian pupils than is continued reading, and continued reading (involving fluency and advanced comprehension) appears surprisingly difficult for a fair number of Norwegian adolescents and adults). We will argue that the semi-transparent Norwegian orthography may play a part in explaining these findings. However, with little systematic focus on the possible impact from orthography on literacy development in the international studies (and also in other studies including Norwegian samples), its explanatory potential and more precise impact as to the case of Norway has to be hypothesized mainly by implication.

SUMMARY AND CONCLUSIONS

Two strands of Norwegian studies have been investigated for the purpose of exploring the role of orthography on the development of literacy skills in Norwegian children. One strand referred to developmental studies of children with reading disabilities. The other regarded large scale international comparative studies of typical development of "reading literacy". The converging evidence states that breaking the alphabetic code in a "semi-transparent" Norwegian script (and with a reading instruction which is generally phonics oriented) is fairly easy. This regarded typically developing children as well as children with problems in learning to read and spell. We tend to see this in connection with a fairly shallow (semi-transparent) orthographic system where connections between the phonemic structure of spoken language and the orthographic structure of the script are regular enough for even the slow learner to understand and master the alphabetic code at a basic level within a reasonable amount of time. This causes almost all Norwegian children to be fairly accurate readers and spellers, in particular when reading and spelling short and orthographically simple words.

The converging evidence furthermore relates to "continued reading". Both typically developing Norwegian adolescents and adults and those who struggle with reading and spelling appear to be "set back" relative to relevant comparison groups when reading demanding texts. Also, relative to other countries with a comparable CDI-status, a large amount of Norwegian children appear to read at the lowest level of literacy, and in the IALS-study, as many as 30% of the adults read below the level defined as critical in terms of "functional literacy". Good text comprehension presupposes among other things automated and fluent decoding skills in addition to good understanding of the semantic content of words. We hypothesize that for reading disabled children event a semi-transparent orthography with moderate irregularities in phoneme-grapheme corespondence may slow down the automation of sound and letters causing reading comprehension to suffer. We see this in connection with characteristics of fluent reading where rapid integration of phonological and semantic processes is crucial and heavily dependent on variables such as word length, sound length, phonological complexity and orthographic complexity. The meaning making processes in fluent reading is therefore presumably strongly influenced by morphological information inherent in the orthographic system and also by more subtle irregularities between sound- and letter patterns. In sum therefore, even in a semi-transparent orthography like the Norwegian the orthographic system may be a barrier to fluent reading and reading comprehension via its impact on rapid and automated integration of phonology and semantics, and in particular in poor readers.

How does the observation that the Norwegian reading disabled children had problems in integrating phonology and semantics (reading speed and fluency), but not in breaking the alphabetic code, fit in with the hypothesis that a phonological weakness is crucial in most serious reading problems? In our view, the Norwegian results do not necessarily challenge the 'phonological deficit hypothesis'. Rather, they challenge the way we have perceived its manifestations and the issue of specificity of phonological difficulties, that is, whether reading disability is primarily associated with a specific phonological dysfunction, or whether it reflects a more general language problem. Many researchers, for example Ehri (1992), claim that phonological recoding underlies the storage of sight words in memory, that is, phonological recoding supports children's development of orthographic knowledge and their ability to use an orthographic strategy. If phonology is important in "orthographic reading" (and spelling), phonological weaknesses may at least partly explain why it was so difficult for the Norwegian poor readers to accelerate their speed of reading. Regarding specificity, it is interesting to note that in Helland's study of impaired reading in 11- to 16-year-olds 15 out of 23 subjects in the "alphabetic phase-group" (i.e., the children with the most serious problems including problems with accuracy) had a history of delayed language development; this was the case for only 2 of the 10 subjects in the "orthographic phase-group". This suggests that the phonological deficit in very poor readers may be associated with a more general language problem than is the case with marginally poor readers and. This again raises the question of the universality of the manifestations of dyslexia across languages. Carefully planned comparative studies are needed to establish in more detail the complex interactive set of variables influencing literacy development in different orthographies, and in particular in relation to poor reading skills.

REFERENCES

Caravolas, M. (1993). Language-specific influences of phonology and orthography on emergent literacy. In J. Altarriba (Ed.), *Cognition and culture: A cross-cultural approach to psychology.* Amsterdam: Elsevier.

Dewey, G. (1971). *English spelling: Roadblock to reading.* New York: Teachers College Press.

Ehri, L. C. (1992). Reconceptualizing the development of sight word reading and its relationship to recoding. In P. Gough, L. C. Ehri & R. Treiman (Eds.), *Reading Acquisition* (pp. 107–143). NJ: Lawrence Erlbaum Associates.

Elbro, C., Møller, S., & Nielsen, E. M. (1995). Functional reading difficulties in Denmark. A study of adult reading of common texts. *Reading and Writing an Interdisciplinary Journal, 7,* 257–276.

Elley, W. B. (1992). *How in the world do students read? IEA study of reading literacy.* The International Association for the Evaluation of Educational Achievement. IEA Headquarters, The Hague, The Netherlands.

Endresen, R. T. (1996). Fonologi. In H. G. Simonsen, R. T. Endresen & E. Hovdhaugen (Eds.), *Språkvitenskap* (4th ed., pp. 38–75). Oslo: Universitetsforlaget AS.

Gallagher, A., Frith, U., & Snowling, M. J. (2000). Precursors of literacy-delay among children at genetic risk of dyslexia. *Journal of Child Psychology and Psychiatry, 41,* 203–213.

Goulandris, N. (2003). Introduction: Developmental dyslexia, language and orthographies. In N. Goulandris (Ed.), *Dyslexia in different languages. Cross-linguistic comparisons* (pp. 1–14). London: Whurr.

Hagtvet, B. E., Horn, E., & Lyster, S. A. H. (June, 2003). *Connections between spoken and written language: Early precursors of written language problems.* Paper presented at The Annual Meeting of the Society for the Scientific Study of Reading, Boulder, CO.

Hagtvet, B. E., & Lyster, S. (2003). The spelling errors of good and poor decoders: a developmental cross-linguistic perspective. In N. Goulandris (Ed.), *Dyslexia in different languages. Cross linguistic comparison* (pp. 181–207). London: Whurr.

Hagtvet, B. E., & Lyster, S. A. H., & Horn, E. (2004). Underlying sources of fluent reading of text: Phonemic awareness naming speed and other sub-skills. Paper presented at The Annual Meeting of the Society for the Scientific Study of Reading, Amsterdam, July 2004.

Helland, T. (2002). Single word Reading and spelling in dyslexia Vary with Neuro-cognitive functions. In T. Helland (2002), *Neuro-Cognitive Functions in Dyslexia. Variations According to Language Comprehension and Mathematics Skills.* Doctoral thesis. University of Oslo, Norway.

Henry, M. K. (1993). Morphological structure: Latin and Greek roots and affixes as upper grade code strategies. *Reading and Writing: An Interdisciplinary Journal, 5,* 227–241.

IALS (the International Adult Literacy Survey) (2000). Literacy in the Information Age: Final Report of the International Adult Literacy Survey, OECD, Paris 2000.

Jaffré, J. P. (1997). From writing to orthography: The functions and limits of the notion of system. In M. Fayol (Ed.), *Learning to spell. Research, theory, and practice across languages* (pp. 1–20). Mahwah, NJ: Lawrence Erbaum Associates.

Korkman, M., & Häkkinen-Rihu, P. (1994). A new classification of developmental language disorders (DLD). *Brain and Language, 4,* 96–116.

Kristoffersen, G. (2000). *The Phonology of Norwegian.* Oxford, UK: Oxford University Press.

Landerl, K. (2003). Dyslexia in German-speaking children. In N. Goulandris (Ed.), *Dyslexia in different languages. Cross-linguistic comparisons* (pp. 15–32). London: Whurr.

Lennox, C., & Siegel, L. S. (1994). The role of phonological and orthographic processes in learning to spell. In G. D. A. Brown & N. C. Ellis (Eds.), *Handbook of spelling. Theory, processes and intervention* (pp. 93–109). New York: Wiley.

Leong, C. K., & Joshi, R. M. (1997). Relating phonologic and orthographic processing to learning to read and spell. In C. K. Leong & R. M. Joshi (Eds.), *Cross-language studies of learning to read and spell* (pp. 1–29). Boston: Kluwer Academic Publishers.

Lyster, S. A. H. (1998). Preventing reading failure: A follow-up study. *Dyslexia, 4,* 132–144.

Lyster, S. A. H. (2002). The effects of morphological versus phonological awareness training in kindergarten on reading development. *Reading and Writing: An Interdisciplinary Journal, 15*, 261–294.

Lyster, S. A. H. (2003). Morphological awareness and reading development. Evidence from a six year follow-up study. Paper Presented at Bangor Dyslexia Conference, University of Wales, Bangor, July, 2003.

Moen, I. (1993). Functional lateralization of the perception of Norwegian word tones: Evidence from a dichotic listening experiment. *Brain & Language, 44*, 400–413.

Moen, I. (2000). Fonetikk og fonologi. In M. Lind, H. Uri, I. Moen & K. M. Bjerkan (Eds.), *Ord som ikke vil. Innføring i språkpatologi*. Oslo: Novus forlag.

Nielsen, J. C., Allerup, P., Ankerdal, H., Gamby, G., Poulsen, A., & Søegård, A. (1992). *IL-prøverne. Håndbok*. [The Individual Reading Test. Handbook]. Copenhagen: Dansk psykologisk forlag.

PIRLS. (2001). *(Progress in International Reading Literacy Study)*. In I. V. S. Mullis, I. V. S. Martin, E. J. Gonzales & A. M. Kennedy (Eds.), PIRLS 2001 International Report: IEA's Study of Reading Literacy Achievement in Primary Schools. Chestnut Hill: Boston College.

PISA. (2001). (Program for International Student Assessment) Knowledge and Skills for Life. OELD, Paris, 2001.

Scarborough, H. (1989). Prediction of reading disability from familial and individual differences. *Journal of Educational Psychology, 81*, 101–108.

Scarborough, H. (1990). Very early language deficits in dyslexic children. *Child Development, 61*, 1728–1743.

Scarborough, H. (1991). Early syntactic development of dyslexic children. *Annals of Dyslexia, 41*, 207–220.

Seidenberg, M. S., & McClelland, J. L. (1989). A distributed developmental model of word recognition and naming. *Psychological Review, 96*, 523–568.

Simonsen, H. G., Endresen, R. T., & Hovdhaugen, E. (1996). *Språkvitenskap. En elementær innføring* (8th ed.). Oslo: Universitetsforlaget.

Snowling, M. (1987). *Dyslexia: A cognitive developmental perspective*. Oxford, UK: Basil Blackwell.

Snowling, M., & Nation, K. A. (1997). Language, phonology and learning to read. In C. Hulme & M. Snowling (Eds.), *Dyslexia: Biology, cognition and intervention* (pp. 153–166). London: Whurr.

Treiman, R., & Cassar, M. (1997). Spelling acquisition in English. In C. A. Perfetti, L. Rieben, & M. Fayol (Eds.), *Learning to spell* (pp. 61–80). Mahwah, NJ: Laurence Erlbaum Associates.

Vellutino, F. R. (1979). *Dyslexia: Theory and research*. Cambridge, MA: MIT Press.

Wimmer, H., & Goswami, U. (1994). The influence of orthographic consistency on reading development: word recognition in English and German children. *Cognition, 51*, 91–103.

3

Literacy Acquisition in Danish: A Deep Orthography in Cross-Linguistic Light

Carsten Elbro
University of Copenhagen

Danish and English are similar in many ways. Both are Germanic languages with deep orthographies. Both in Denmark and in the United States, reading and writing are usually taught through a variety of approaches such as phonics, whole word, and whole language. Because Danish orthography also shares some basic similarities with English, Danish children would be expected to acquire reading and writing skills in ways that are similar to those of English-speaking children. This is so in spite of the fact that Danish children do not receive formal instruction in reading until the age of 7 years. The available evidence summarized in this chapter suggests that initial reading and spelling development in Danish is indeed similar to that in English.

WHY STUDY READING IN DANISH?

Reading acquisition has been studied far more extensively in English than in any other language. This means that the standard models of reading acquisition have been developed and validated in terms of English. Little is known about how these models generalize to other alphabetic orthographies—not to mention syllabic and morphemic orthographies. Some comparisons have been made, though, between English and other, more regular, orthographies.

However, almost all of these comparisons rest on somewhat soft grounds because orthography is far from the only difference between languages. When English and French are compared, for instance, a deep orthography with many deviations from a simple one-to-one phoneme–grapheme writing system (English) is compared with a system with a much more predictable pronunciation of written words (French) (e.g., Goswami, Gombert, & Barrera, 1998). Furthermore, the two languages have rather different syllabic structures. There are also differences between the ways reading is taught in the two languages. Consequently, observed differences in reading acquisition in English and French may be difficult to interpret because they may stem from differences in orthography, language, teaching methods, and so forth. Similarly, comparisons of reading acquisition in English and German (e.g., Landerl, Wimmer, & Frith, 1997) are probably influenced not only by differences in the orthographies—German orthography is much more shallow than English orthography—but also by differences in teaching methods. German children are initially taught to read exclusively through the synthetic phonics method, whereas initial reading instruction in English uses a mixture of methods.

These differences make Danish interesting from an international perspective, because Danish is similar to English in at least three respects: Danish, like English, is a Germanic language; Danish also has a somewhat deep orthography; and initial reading in Danish is traditionally taught by means of a variety of instructional methods, such as whole-word look-and-say, contextual cues use, some phonics, and easy book reading. We can therefore expect reading acquisition in Danish to parallel that in English.

Needless to say, there are also differences between the Danish and English orthographies. For example, unlike English, Danish has only a few vowel digraphs, mainly in French loan words that have preserved their French spelling. Danish also has three extra vowel letters (æ, ø, and å). Nevertheless, these differences appear to be minor when the entire language structure is taken into consideration. The basic similarities between English and Danish therefore permit us to study the effects of orthographic structure on literacy acquisition. So far, however, only a few cross-linguistic studies have been carried out, and they are presented in this chapter.

The studies in this chapter have mostly been conducted within the framework of a reading acquisition model that assumes that literacy development follows the principle of economy: That is, the most productive and reliable grapheme–phoneme associations are learned first and complex associations are learned later. This means that standard pronunciations of the single letters are learned first because, in addition to the one-to-one association, their number is also determined by how many letters are there in the alphabet. More complex grapheme–phoneme associations are acquired progressively with these simple associations used as the base, and this progressive development occurs in *overlapping waves*. This means that the knowledge of other principles of orthography is collected from early on, but each principle is made use of in spelling over a period of time.

This general model gives rise to several expectations. First, if standard pronunciations of the single letters are learned first, then any deviation from a simple grapheme–phoneme correspondence may cause difficulties for beginning readers. Even common digraphs—in which two letters regularly represent one phoneme—can be expected to cause difficulties. Second, spelling patterns in which single letters have more than one pronunciation are expected to pose difficulties for novice readers. In a language such as English with many such patterns, the acquisition of literacy skills is likely to be a protracted affair. Third, morphemic spelling patterns are expected to be a major challenge because they are based on morphology, information that is categorically different from phonology. Fourth and finally, word-specific orthographic forms that do not conform to either phonologic or morphologic conventions are expected to be the ones that will be acquired last.

INITIAL READING DEVELOPMENT IS SLOW IN DANISH

A large-scale IEA (which stands for the International Association for the Evaluation of Educational Achievement) study of reading literacy conducted in 1922 reported that Danish 9-year-old children ranked 24th among children from 27 countries (Elley, 1992). The Danish students were on average the slowest readers among children from all participating European countries. This was found in both word decoding and in reading of narrative and expository texts. Since then, because of increased awareness about literacy education, the reading accuracy of Danish

9-year-olds has improved from below the international average to somewhat above it; but reading speed still remains relatively low (Allerup, Mejding, & Zeuner, 2001).

In Denmark, formal schooling starts when the child reaches 7 years of age. Before this, very little informal reading instruction takes place at home. Therefore, Danish children are at a position of disadvantage when compared with children of the same age in other countries where formal schooling starts when children are 6 years, or even 5 years, of age, as in Britain.

A small-scale study of initial reading development in 13 European orthographies including Danish and English (Seymour, Aro, & Erskine, 2003) indicated that Danish and English children are far behind other children by the end of the first school year. One would expect English-speaking children, because they started school much earlier, to have done better, but that did not happen. Even though Danish children knew as many letters as children from other countries and could name more than 90% of the letters by the end of the first school year, they were able to read monosyllabic nonwords with an accuracy rate of only about 60%. The corresponding figure was around 90% or higher for children who spoke other European languages. Only the English-speaking (Scottish) children read worse (40% correct) than Danish children.

By the age of 14 years, Danish youths, however, read relatively better. In the 1992 IEA study Danish youth came in at the 13th place out of 31 participating countries. This result was corroborated in the 2000 OECD PISA study (Andersen et al., 2001) in which the performance of Danish 15-year-olds came very close to the average of youths from 33 participating countries.

Together, these studies suggest that the initial phase of reading development is slow in Danish. There may be many reasons for this. The particular difficulties of the Danish orthography may be one of them; this probably is exacerbated by the relatively late school start in Denmark.

DANISH DEPTHS

Danish orthography was already old when a national norm was first established around the year 1200. From the very beginning, Danish orthography reflected several obsolete pronunciations. For example, even though Danish words like *lov* [law] had been pronounced with a final /w/ sound for generations, scribes working during the 13th century spelled such words with a final -*gh* (*logh*) in conformity with the archaic pronunciation. Similarly, the *th* sound (as in *myth*) had long since been replaced with /ð/ (as in *with*) in the final position, yet Danish scribes continued to insert -*th* in words that did not have that sound anymore. The developmental changes in the pronunciation of spoken Danish were so numerous during the early middle ages that, by about 1300, a majority of words contained segments that made the grapheme–phoneme correspondence of these words opaque (Skautrup, 1944, 257–258).

The scribes who instituted the first national spelling norm were, without doubt, learned men, who came from various parts of the country and who spoke different Danish dialects (or regional variants). Hence one possible reason for the initial orthographic conservatism may be that the scribes may have wished to select spellings that were not based on any one spoken Danish dialect as norm. Instead, the scribes appear to have chosen old-fashioned, possibly high-status, Danish as the basis for spelling.

Whatever the reason for the initial conservatism of Danish spelling may be, things have become worse since the 1200s. Written language is by nature more conservative than spoken language. Spelling reforms usually lag far behind changes in pronunciation, and spoken Danish has changed more than most Germanic languages since the 1200s. For instance, spoken Swedish has stayed much closer than Danish to its East Nordic root, which is one major reason why Swedish orthography is much more shallow than Danish orthography.

In addition, Danish has been more accepting than most languages of foreign loan words. This means that Danish has imported many orthographic complexities along with imported words. In comparison, Norwegian spelling of loan words conforms much more closely to Norwegian spelling conventions. For example, Danish *psykologi* [psychology] has a silent *p* whereas Norwegian *sykologi* does not; in the Danish word *nation* (from the Latin), the middle /ʃ/ sound is spelled with a *t* whereas the Norwegian spelling is *nasjon*, with a standard digraph *sj*; Danish *tusch* [Indian ink, from the German] uses a German spelling of the /ʃ/ sound whereas Norwegian *tusj* uses the standard *sj*; and Danish *niveau* (from the French) has the French *eau* for the /o/ sound whereas Norwegian spelling is more simple, *nivo*.

The changes in spoken language and the influx of foreign words and their spellings from other languages are two main reasons why Danish orthography deviates from a simple phoneme–grapheme structure. In addition, some orthographies, like those of English and Danish, also represent morphology to some extent. Examples of the influence of morphology on spelling are *bomb–bombardment*, *damn–damnation*, and *boys* versus *boy's*. Deep orthographies, such as those of English and Danish, differ from shallow ones because they reflect such morphological information even when it conflicts with simple grapheme–phoneme correspondences.

From a present-day perspective, however, the consequences of the three sources of orthographic irregularity are difficult to identify and isolate with precision. It may be pedagogically more productive to disregard the historical perspective and take a look at orthographies as they appear from a contemporary perspective. Four orthographic principles may be distinguished. For the sake of simplicity, they are presented in their order of acquisition in the next section. The first is the basic phonemic principle that is common to all alphabetic orthographies.

TAKING THE PLUNGE

The Alphabetic Principle 1: Standard Letter Sounds

Single, abstract letters (graphemes) represent single, abstract segments of speech (phonemes). This is the basic principle of all alphabetic orthographies—including deep ones such as those of English and Danish. This is the principle that Danish children acquire first, as we shall see.

Danish children are taught the letter names directly during the first months of Grade 1. In some cases, the introduction to the letters takes a full semester. Sometimes, but not always, letter sounds are taught along with letter names.

However, the basic alphabetic principle faces a challenge in Danish and in all other Germanic languages. There are not enough letters in the Latin alphabet to match all the phonemes. The Latin alphabet had enough letters to represent spoken Latin, but the Germanic languages that borrowed it have more sounds. The problem is particularly pressing for the Danish vowels. It can be argued that there are 12 Danish vowel phonemes that qualitatively differ from each other (Elbro, 2001). Therefore, even disregarding vowels that differ only in length, there are too few letters in the alphabet to represent all the Danish vowel phonemes. Attempts to deal with this problem have resorted to three solutions, all of which make the orthography deviate from a simple phonemic script.

First, one letter may represent more than one phoneme; for example, written *s* may represent /s/ in *press*, /z/ in *present*, /ʃ/ in *pressure*, and /ʒ/ in *pleasure*. Each Danish vowel letter regularly represents two or more different short-vowel phonemes and at least one long-vowel phoneme.

Second, special letters may be added to the Latin alphabet. Danish, like Norwegian, has three additional vowel letters, *æ* (originally *ae*), *ø* (originally *oe*), and *å* (originally *aa*).

Third, fixed letter combinations (e.g., *ng* in *ring*, and *sh* in *shoe*) can be used for representing single phonemes (/ŋ/ and /ʃ/). Such fixed letter combinations, or *complex graphemes* or *digraphs*, are very common in English; and they exist in all Germanic orthographies. The *ng* (as in *ring*) digraph is a very widespread example. Another complex grapheme in Danish is *sj* that represents /ʃ/.

Digraphs and trigraphs are complex graphemes

Digraphs such as *ng*, *sj*, and *sh* are fixed letter patterns that generally represent only one phoneme. Digraphs are interesting in the study of reading development because they have highly regular pronunciations on the one hand, but, on the other hand, they deviate from the basic alphabetic principle that each letter corresponds to a sound. Therefore, if children initially associate single letters with single (standard) sounds, complex graphemes should pose a problem for them. It should be harder for them to read words like ***shin*** with complex graphemes compared with words like ***spin*** and ***pen***, even though *spin* has more sounds than *shin*.

To my knowledge, there has been only one study that investigated the acquisition of complex graphemes in Danish. That is the study reported below. The study also examined complex grapheme acquisition in English and German. The materials used were nonwords with complex consonant graphemes (e.g., ***shig***), matched nonwords with consonant clusters instead of complex graphemes (e.g., ***spig***), and matched nonwords with the same number of sounds but fewer letters (e.g., ***deg***). These "words" are listed in the appendix. Details of the participants are shown in Table 3.1.

The results indicated that words with complex graphemes were significantly harder to read than both types of control words with and without consonant clusters (Table 3.2). The tendencies, with Grade 3 as an example, can be clearly seen in Fig. 3.1. The effect was confirmed for English and Danish in a repeated-measures analysis of variance with three word types × two languages × two grade levels and planned contrasts between the words with digraphs and the other two word types: $F(1, 109) = 85.1$, $p < .001$, and $F(1, 109) = 137.9$, $p < .001$, respectively. Grade level had a significant main effect: $F(1, 109) = 6.6$, $p < .05$. Language did not significantly interact with other factors.

A second analysis of variance looked at all three languages and Grades 3 and 4 (between subjects), but only two word types (within subjects). This analysis indicated a strong main effect of word type, $F(1, 146) = 125.8$, $p < .001$; a main effect of grade level, $F(1, 146) = 4.7$, $p < .05$; and an effect of language, $F(2, 146) = 12.6$, $p < .001$. A post hoc test (Scheffé,

TABLE 3.1
The Participants

Language	Grade Level	N	Mean Age Mean Age	SD
English	3	30	7,4	0,4
(Scottish)	4	30	8,6	0,4
German	1	13	7,5	0,6
(Austrian)	2	20	8,3	0,4
	3	20	9,1	0,4
	4	19	10,4	0,4
Danish	3	19	9,11	0,4
(proper)	4	34	10,8	0,6

TABLE 3.2

Mean Reading Accuracy of Nonwords With Complex Consonant Graphemes, Consonant
Clusters, and Simple Consonant Graphemes in Three Languages

Language	Grade Level	Consonant Graphemes		
		Digraphs	Clusters	Simple
English	3	53.7 (26.6)	73.3 (27.9)	74.3 (24.0)
	4	62.2 (20.3)	80.0 (22.5)	82.7 (18.4)
Danish	3	57.9 (23.3)	70.2 (24.9)	77.8 (24.6)
	4	70.6 (21.9)	84.3 (20.7)	87.9 (15.1)
German	1	67.3 (27.7)	—	92.3 (12.0)
	2	73.8 (19.0)	—	92.5 (18.3)
	3	80.0 (17.4)	—	93.8 (13.8)
	4	81.6 (14.0)	—	92.1 (16.8)

Note. Standard deviations are given in parentheses.

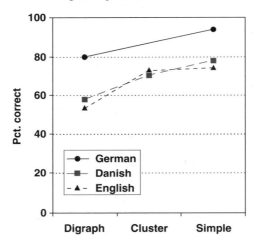

FIG. 3.1. Reading accuracy in grade 3 in three languages with words containing digraphs (e.g.,
shig) compared with consonant clusters (e.g., *spig*) and simple consonants (e.g., *deg*).

$p < .05$) indicated that the language effect was caused by significantly higher scores in German
than in both Danish and English. None of the interaction effects was significant.

The results of this study support three general hypotheses. First, it is obvious that German
children who learn to read a relatively shallow orthography by means of a synthetic phonics
approach develop basic decoding skills more rapidly than do English and Danish children.

Second, the results support the hypothesis that deviations from the basic alphabetic
principle—that each grapheme represents one phoneme—are acquired more slowly. These
letter patterns challenge beginning readers in all alphabetic orthographies regardless of the
depth of the orthography. Not only English and Danish children were affected by complex
graphemes; readers of the more regular German orthography were also affected. It should also
be noted that the complex graphemes had a disruptive effect on children's reading even though
the complex graphemes have predictable pronunciations in both Danish and German.

Third, the results are in accordance with the general idea that reading development starts with the acquisition of the basic alphabetic principle, that is, learning the phonemes associated with each letter of the alphabet.

The Alphabetic Principle 2: Letter Patterns

As spoken Danish has continued to develop, orthographic conservatism has resulted in many inconsistencies between spelling and sound. Many of these orthographic complexities are nonetheless rather predictable because the changes in pronunciation have occurred in similar sound contexts across many words. The general development means that regularities may still exist between *strings* of letters and the corresponding *strings* of sounds—even though the *individual* grapheme–phoneme relationships have become opaque. For example, consider how the standard sound of written *o* and *ou* is modified by context in English (collected from Carney, 1994):

-o- → /ɒ/ (*hot, mob*)
-ou- → /aʊ/ (*doubt, about*)
*-ou*gh → /əʊ/ (*though, dough*)
*-ou*ght → /ɔ:/ (*ought, thought*)

Note that the letter pattern *-ought* has a completely predictable pronunciation as a whole (this rime is pronounced the same way in all words) although the individual letters of the pattern have mostly nonstandard pronunciations. Another example is the so-called magic *e-* rule in English. A final *e-* changes the vowel in words like *cape* and *bite* from the short standard sounds /æ/ as in *cap* and /ɪ/ as in *bit* into tense (long) variants, /eɪ/ and /aɪ/. In other words, *a* and *i* receive *conditional* pronunciations in words with final *e*'s.

Similar situations exist in most alphabetic orthographies, even though they many not have as many in English. The regularities of letter patterns exist *above* the single-letter–sound level, but *below* the morphemic and lexical levels. Implicit knowledge of letter patterns is likely to be an important part of the internalized orthographic code (or the *cipher*). An overview of the most common letter patterns in Danish may be seen in Elbro (2001, p. 78–79). A detailed account of Danish letter-to-sound correspondences is provided in Becker-Christensen (1988).

The acquisition of regular letter patterns (such as *-ought* and *-ake*) was studied with the same groups of schoolchildren who took part in the preceding study of digraphs. The study focused on patterns in which the vowel letter receives a conditional pronunciation, because such patterns are very common in Danish. The expectation was that words with conditional vowel pronunciations would be more difficult to learn than words with standard pronunciations—indicating that conditional pronunciations are learned *later* than standard pronunciations. The materials were nonwords with vowel letters with a conditional pronunciation (e.g., *pake*) and matched nonwords in which the same vowel letters had standard pronunciations (e.g., *pask*). The English part of the study was also conducted with real words. The materials are listed in the appendix.

The results showed significant effects of letter patterns with conditional letter sounds in both languages and at each grade level (Elbro et al., 2000; Juul & Elbro, 2001) (see Fig. 3.2). A repeated-measures ANOVA with two word types × two languages × two grade levels showed a significant main effects of word type, $F(1, 109) = 81.7$, $p < .001$; grade level, $F(1, 109) = 8.7$, $p < .01$; and language, $F(1, 109) = 8.1$, $p < .01$; and a significant interaction effect of word type and language, $F(1, 109) = 8.4$, $p < .01$. The analysis thus suggests that nonwords such as *pake* were significantly harder to read than nonwords with standard sounds such as *pask* for both third and fourth graders. The same was found with English real words, even

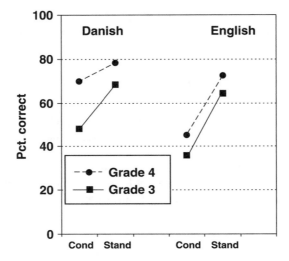

FIG. 3.2. Reading accuracy with words with conditional versus standard vowel letter sounds. Means are shown for grades 3 and 4 in Danish and English.

though the effect was significantly smaller in Danish. This difference in orthographic effect suggests that Danish children are about to master the conditional vowel grapheme–phoneme rules by Grade 4 whereas the English-speaking children have a longer way to go.

The fact that words with conditional pronunciations are relatively difficult indicates that orthographies with such conditional pronunciations are more difficult to learn than other, more regular orthographies. The parallel results for Danish and English suggest that letter patterns with conditional vowel letter pronunciations are a general problem, regardless of the language.

Vowel Length

The orthographic representation of vowel length is no problem in Latin because vowel length is not distinctive. It is, however, a potential problem in Germanic languages and in many other languages (including Finnish and Greenlandic) in which vowel length (or tenseness) is distinctive. Many languages use more than one way to represent vowel length. A simple doubling (gemination) of a letter that represents a long sound (as opposed to a short one) would seem the most straightforward way. This is the principle used by both Greenlandic and Finnish, which have very regular orthographies. Nevertheless, the acquisition of the representation of phoneme length appears to be a problem in both languages (e.g., Jacobsen, 1994). The difficulty may be similar to the one with digraphs—two letters representing one sound.

The most common way of representing short, stressed vowels in Danish is by *consonant doubling* (in polysyllabic words). It works as in English to distinguish between, for example, *bitter* with a short (lax) vowel and *biter* with a long (tense) vowel. The convention is, of course, used very frequently. Not surprisingly, it is also acquired from an early point in both reading and writing Danish (Elbro et al., 2000; Juul, 2004).

One major problem in Danish orthography is that the convention for representing vowel length is not used consistently with unstressed vowels. Although it is relatively safe to assume that double consonants are preceded by a short vowel in Danish, a single consonant is less reliably associated with a long vowel. Therefore, for unstressed vowels, word-specific knowledge is needed, and this is acquired rather slowly (Juul, 2004).

Rime Analogy Is Not a Flotation Device

The orthographic rime comprises the vowel letter and the consonants that follow it. The status of the rime in the development of decoding is controversial (e.g., Bowey, Vaughan, & Hansen, 1998). On the one hand, it is clear that many regular orthographic patterns coincide with the rimes; and it is generally the case that consonants after the vowel exert greater influence on the pronunciation of the vowel than consonants before the vowel. On the other hand, there is such a large number of different rimes that it would seem a rather uneconomic strategy to try to internalize their individual pronunciations.

A more economic strategy would be to internalize the *minimal* letter patterns that predict a conditional pronunciation. For example, in Danish it would be economic to remember the conditional pronunciation of -*u* as /ɔ/ when it is followed by an -*m* (as opposed to the standard pronunciation /u/ as in *bus* [bus]). This minimal rule would cover several rimes at once, for example, -*umf*, -*ums*, and -*umt*, in addition to the simple -*um*. Therefore, each of these rimes and their pronunciations would *not* have to be stored separately.

The presence of a digraph in the rime should *not* pose any particular problem to the reader if the rime is recognized as a whole. In such cases, the frequency of the rime as a whole would be an important predictor of how easily the word is read. On the other hand, if rimes are not recognized as wholes, their internal structure is likely to play a role. In that case, the frequency of digraphs in the rimes will be an important predictor of how easily the word is read. These two hypotheses were assessed by means of the data from the study of the impact of digraphs. A plot of the relation between digraph frequency and reading accuracy is shown in Fig. 3.3(a), and rime frequency is plotted against reading accuracy in Fig. 3.3(b). The Danish reading data are averages across Grades 3 and 4.

It is clear that the frequency of the digraphs [Fig. 3.3(a)] provided a much better fit to the reading scores than did the frequency of the rimes [Fig. 3.3(b)]. Unfortunately, the English words were not ranked differently according to digraph and rime frequencies, so a comparison

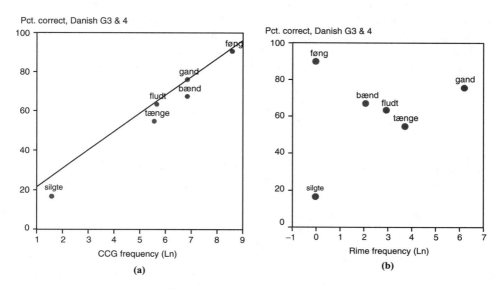

FIG. 3.3.   (a) Reading accuracy in Danish plotted against the frequency of the complex consonant graphemes (CCGs.) in the words; (b) the same reading performance but now plotted against the frequencies of the rimes that contained the CCGs.

TABLE 3.3
Danish Study of Effects of Rime (VCC) vs. Small Unit (VC) Frequency

	Rime	
VC	+ Frequent	− Frequent
+ Frequent	−ink …	−ins …
− Frequent	−uft …	−ums …

is not possible. However, the Danish results suggest that digraphs are dealt with as problem units rather than as an integral part of the whole rime.

A study by Shkoza (2000) confirmed this result. She studied the effects of planned contrasts between words with high- versus low-frequency rimes and high- versus low-frequency vowel–consonant combinations. (See Table 3.3 for an overview of the contrasts with examples of rimes). In this comparison, all the test words had conditional vowel pronunciations; but there were also some filler words with standard vowel pronunciations. The participants were Danish school children from grades 2 to 4.

The results were very clear in that only the frequency of the relevant spelling pattern (the vowel–consonant combination) influenced reading accuracy. The rime frequency of which the pattern was a part did not.

Again, these results are in line with the general idea that children adopt a principle of economy as they internalize the conventions of the orthography. Small orthographic units are more productive, and hence more economical, than large units.

Nonetheless, whole rimes may be useful entities in reading instruction. The corresponding rhymes are easily accessible and well known from poetry and language games. Therefore the regular spelling of some rimes may be useful for demonstrations of regularities above the single-letter level. It is unlikely, however, that *rhyme analogy* in general is a major strategy in reading development in Danish—even though Danish orthography has many irregularities.

BOYS WILL BE *BOY'S*

The Morphemic Principle in Spelling

Sometimes spelling reflects the morphological structure of the word rather than just the phonemic structure. The smallest meaningful unit, a morpheme, may sometimes be spelled in only one way in spite of variations in pronunciation, as is the case with the -*ed* past-tense ending that is pronounced /d/, *beamed*; /t/, *dropped*; or /ɪd/, *rested*; depending on the end of the verb root. In the case of the -*ed* ending, the morphemic principle overrules the phonemic principle and causes the orthography to increase in depth.

Learning to use the morphemic principle appears to be a long-lasting problem for Danish schoolchildren. The problems in Danish are similar to problems in English. Danish also has a number of homophones that are spelled differently. For example, verbs with roots that end in -*r* (e.g., *bor* [the root of drill]) have identically sounding infinitives and present-tense forms that are spelled differently, *at bore* [to drill] and *borer* [drills], respectively. The derived noun, *en borer* [a driller], is also a homophone. Other examples are the homophones -*ene* (plural definite noun) versus -*ende* (present participle of verb) and -*ed* (end of some noun roots) versus -*et* (past participle of verbs). These word endings can be spelled correctly only by reference to the morphological structure.

In a cross-sectional study of 142 Danish students from Grades 4, 6, 8, and 10, Juul and Elbro (2004) found that the silent *r* and similar morphologically determined letters were applied correctly in only about 50% of the items, even by children in Grade 8; by Grade 10, their accuracy was about 90%. When errors occurred, it was almost always because students provided a standard spelling of the sound pattern they heard. Hence the results of the study indicated that morphological spelling knowledge is indeed acquired over a long period of time.

SEEING *READ* IN *READY*

The Morphemic Principle in Reading

The role of morphological decomposition in decoding is a controversial issue. However, once the reader has learned to recognize the root word such as *read*, this orthographic knowledge would be helpful in reading words that contain that root (e.g., *reads, reading, reader, unreadable, readability*, etc.).

A major problem with prelexical morphological decomposition is that it cannot distinguish between real morphemes and pseudomorphemes. Before a word is recognized, it is impossible to know whether or not a particular letter string is in fact the morpheme it looks like. For example, *read* might be a root in *ready* but it is not, and *car* might be a root in *carrot* but it is not. As pointed out by Taft (1981) and others, high-frequency prefixes may facilitate decoding based on morpheme analysis; but the evidence is not very strong.

However, morphological analysis may be a used as a compensatory strategy by dyslexic readers. In one study, Elbro found that dyslexic adolescents rely more on morphological word structure than do younger typical readers with a similar level of word decoding ability (see Elbro and Arnbak, 1996). In comparison, there was a significantly smaller effect of morphology on a group of younger typical readers matched for reading level (Elbro, 1990).

WORD-SPECIFIC SPELLING–SOUND RELATIONS

When spelling patterns and the morphemic principle are taken into account, deep orthographies are not as unpredictable as they might seem at first. Nevertheless, Danish has very many words in which one or more letters have unique pronunciations. This is the case for some highly frequent words that have preserved their odd spelling precisely because they are so common, for example Danish *de* [they] pronounced with an /i/ rather than standard /ɛ/ or /e/, or any of the conditional pronunciations. Other examples are Danish *af* [of, from] with a silent *f*, *kobber* [copper] with /w/ for written *b*, and *otte* [eight] with a nonstandard, long vowel /ɔ:/ for written *o*. In addition, there are numerous words of foreign origin that have preserved their non-Danish spellings. Examples are relatively new loan words from French and English such as *mayonnaise*, *gear*, and *juice* (the unique spellings are emphasized).

In addition to these words with unique spelling-to-sound relationships, there are many inconsistent spelling patterns in Danish (as in English). For example, the -*uk* pattern is pronounced /ɔk/ in some words (e.g., *luk* [close]) and /uk/ in other words (e.g., *kluk* [cluck]). As a consequence, the reader needs lexical orthographic knowledge.

The general framework for understanding reading development put forward in this chapter would predict that such word-specific spellings are acquired late in reading development. Unfortunately, there are very few studies of reading in Danish that have tested this prediction. There is good evidence from English, however, that word-specific orthographic knowledge is indeed acquired relatively late (when word frequency is controlled). Zinna, Liberman, and Shankweiler (1986, exp. 1) studied children's reading of three types of words: words with standard letter sounds (e.g., *green*, *paint*), words with consistent spelling patterns (e.g., *beach*, *mount*), and words with inconsistent spelling patterns (e.g., *steak*, *touch*). It was very clear that children in Grades 3 and 5 made many more errors in the words with inconsistent spelling patterns than in the words with consistent patterns, whereas the words with standard letters sounds were the easiest. Not surprisingly, these differences were especially large for low-frequency words. The results suggest that word-specific letter pronunciations are indeed learned later than words with consistent letter–sound patterns.

One Danish study has compared acquisition of spelling patterns and word-specific spelling (Juul, 2003). In this study, 140 children in Grades 4 and 6 were asked to spell words with consistent standard spellings (e.g., /i/ spelled *i*), words with consistent conditional spelling (e.g., /e/ spelled *i* before /s/), and words with inconsistent spellings (e.g., /ɛ/ spelled *æ* before /s/). Both vowels and consonants were studied as the critical segments of the words. The results supported the hypothesis about the developmental sequence: Proficient spellers were at or near ceiling with both standard spellings and consistent conditional spellings, but less adept with the word-specific spellings. Poor spellers were good at standard spellings, but lagged behind in both consistent conditional spellings and word-specific spellings. Together, the results are in line with the general idea that the acquisition of orthographic knowledge starts with standard letter–sound relationships and progresses toward less common and less productive orthographic patterns.

CONCLUSIONS

Danish is a Germanic language with a comparatively deep orthography. Reading and writing are usually taught by a mixed approach in Danish schools. Hence Danish has some basic similarities with English, and Danish children would be expected to acquire reading and writing abilities in ways that are somewhat similar to those of English-speaking children—even though Danish children do not receive formal instruction in reading until the age of 7 years. The available evidence summarized in this chapter suggests that initial reading and spelling development in Danish is, indeed, similar to that of English.

Almost all comparisons between reading in English and in other languages have focused on differences that are hypothesized to be consequences of the deeper English orthography. Comparisons with Danish are particularly interesting because they make it possible to see whether the orthographic complexities that are generally presumed to be a challenge to English readers are also problems to readers in other languages. Some complexities such as digraphs exist even in shallow orthographies such as German. There is now some evidence that digraphs do seem to be a challenge across orthographies—even when there are few of them and even if the orthography is shallow. This finding has far-reaching implications. One implication is that such possibly universal complexities may reflect universal phases (or trends) in reading development: Some aspects of orthographies (the complexities) are learnd *after* the standard grapheme–phoneme correspondences are learned. Another implication is that cross-orthographic complexities provide a metric for comparisons of the relative difficulty of orthographies; in principle, it is possible to measure the complexities of orthographies.

The complexities of the Danish orthography are obviously not mastered all at once. The results from recent studies of reading and spelling acquisition in Danish conform to a general framework for the development of reading and writing: Short letter patterns are learned more quickly than patterns comprising many letters, and consistent (reliable) patterns are learned more quickly than inconsistent ones.

At least four different developmental waves can be distinguished during literacy development in Danish (and English) (cf. Siegler, 1986):

Wave 1. Learning of Single-Letter–Single-Sound Correspondences.   The dominant strategy during the initial phase of learning to read and write is to associate one sound with one letter and one letter with one sound. The preferred sound is often the one present in the letter name. This strategy results in problems with digraphs and all other forms that deviate from simple letter–sound relationships.

Wave 2. Learning of Letter–Sound Patterns With Conditional Pronunciations.   Conditional pronunciations (e.g., *mat, mate; rat; rate*) are learned at first in the smallest possible units (e.g., vowel–consonant combinations) rather than as part of bigger units (e.g., rimes).

Wave 3. Learning of Spelling Based on Morphemic Orthographic Knowledge.   These patterns are acquired relatively late. Even the spellings of some frequently occurring morphemes continue to be a challenge when they are distinguished in spelling, but not in pronunciation, such as the genitive apostrophe in English or the present tense *−r* in Danish. However, some morphographic units with invariant spelling of morphemes, such as the *−ed* verb ending, are learned earlier.

Wave 4. Learning of Word-Specific Orthographic Patterns.   This is a lifelong process. Needless to say, some high-frequency words are learned as whole patterns ("sight words") from the very beginning of reading development. Although the orthographic representations of individual morphemes (or words) may be recognized following only a few presentations, there are so many of them that their acquisition is never really complete.

APPENDIX

Materials in the Study of Digraphs

Language	Digraph	Consonant Cluster	Simple Consonant
Danish	sjål	spål	jål
	føng	føsp	føm
	gand	gasp	gan
	hvam	svam	vam
	hjælle	pjælle	jælle
	tænge	tækle	tæse
	silgte	silste	silte
	bænd	bælk	bæn
	fludt	flusk	flut
English	shig	spig	peb
	dack	besk	cag
	ladge	dand	pon
	knop	skop	mun
	wemb	famp	bip
	ling	twid	tud
	shid	spid	deg
	dotch	twonk	pon
	wrin	trin	rit
German	schore		sore
	bung		bun
	dech		def
	kosch		kos

Materials in the Study of Conditional Vowel Letter Sounds

Language	Conditional	Standard
English	pake	pask
	bline	blin
	clind	clend
	nold	nond
	peather	deacher
	wab	wak
	squas	squag
	whap	whang
	rall	bramp
	hode	hont
	dyth	yath
Danish	kotter	søtter
	fumme	jalle
	ginse	hamse
	gosse	goser*
	vunke	biffe
	tummer	siffen
	tejser	fæbes*
	molse	dæske
	gimme	mæsle

*Two Danish nonwords with long vowels gave rise to many errors. They were subsequently left out of the data analyses.

ACKNOWLEDGMENTS

Many of the studies summarized in this chapter were carried out with support from the Danish Research Council for the Humanities (contract No. 9602075). The Scottish part of the study was conducted by Philip H. K. Seymour, and data were collected by Jane Erskine. The Austrian part of the study was conducted by Karin Landerl. Data for the Danish part of the international study were collected by Louise Rønberg, Mette Nygaard Petersen, and Line Dahl Jørgensen. The author thanks all these collaborators, participants, and their teachers.

REFERENCES

Allerup, P., Mejding, J., & Zeuner, L. (2001). *Færdigheder i læsning og matematik. Udviklingstræk omkring årtusindskiftet* [Reading and math abilities. Developmental trends around the turn of the decennium]. Copenhagen: Socialforskningsinstituttet.

Andersen, A. M., Egelund, N., Jensen, T. P., Krone, M., Lindenskov, L., & Mejding, J. (2001). *Forventninger og færdigheder—danske unge i en international sammenligning* [Expectations and abilities. Danish youths in an international comparison]. Copenhagen: Socialforskningsinstituttet.

Becker-Christensen, C. (1988). *Bogstav og lyd. Dansk retskrivning og rigsmålsudtale* [Letter and sound. Danish spelling and received pronunciation]. Copenhagen: Gyldendal.

Bowey, J. A., Vaughan, L., & Hansen, J. (1998). Beginning readers' use of orthographic analogies in word reading. *Journal of Experimental Child Psychology, 68*, 108–133.

Carney, E. (1994). *A survey of English spelling*. London: Routledge.

Elbro, C. (1990). *Differences in dyslexia. A study of reading strategies and deficits in a linguistic perspective*. Copenhagen: Munksgaard.

Elbro, C. (2001). *Læsning og læseundervisning* [Reading and the teaching of reading]. Copenhagen: Gyldendal.

Elbro, C., & Arnbak, E. (1996). The role of morpheme recognition and morphological awareness in dyslexia. *Annals of Dyslexia, 46*, 209–240.

Elbro, C., Juul, H., Shkoza, B. H., Wimmer, H., Landerl, K., Seymour, P. H. K., & Wood, R. (2000, July 24–28). *Conditional letter sounds and reading development in different orthographies.* Paper presented at the International Congress of Psychology, Stockholm.

Elley, W. B. (1992). *How in the world do students read? IEA study of reading literacy.* The Hague: The International Association for the Evaluation of Educational Achievement.

Goswami, U., Gombert, J. E., & Barrera, L. F. (1998). Children's orthographic representations and linguistic transparency: Nonsense word reading in English, French and Spanish. *Applied Psycholinguistics, 19,* 19–52.

Jacobsen, B. (1994). *Grønlandsk læseundersøgelse: en ortografisk, fonologisk og morfologisk undersøgelse* [Greenlandic reading investigation: An orthographic, phonological and morphological study]. Unpublished doctoral dissertation. Copenhagen: University of Copenhagen.

Juul, H. (2003). Typer af stavefejl og typer af stavefærdighed [Types of spelling errors and types of spelling ability]. *Danske Talesprog, 4,* 59–74.

Juul, H. (2004). *Knowledge of context sensitive spellings as a component of spelling competence: Evidence from Danish. Applied Psycholinguistics* (in print).

Juul, H., & Elbro, C. (2001). Når bogstavets lyd afhænger af sammenhængen. Om tilegnelsen af videregående afkodningsfærdighed [When the letter sound depends on the context. On the acquisition of advanced decoding ability]. *Psykologisk Pædagogisk Rådgivning, 38,* 3–13.

Juul, H., & Elbro, C. (2004). The links between grammar and spelling: A cognitive hurdle in deep orthographies? *Reading and Writing: An Interdisciplinary Journal, 17* (in press).

Landerl, K., Wimmer, H., & Frith, U. (1997). The impact of orthographic consistency on dyslexia: A German–English comparison. *Cognition, 63,* 315–334.

Rittle-Johnson, B., & Siegler, R. S. (1999). Learning to spell: Variability, choice, and change in children's strategy use. *Child Development, 70,* 332–348.

Seymour, P. H., Aro, M., & Erskine, J. M. (2003). Foundation literacy acquisition in European orthographies. *British Journal of Psychology, 94,* 143–174.

Shkoza, B. H. (2000). *Rimstrategier ved afkodning—en undersøgelse af Læsere i 2. til 4. klasse.* ('Rime analogy strategiei in decoding—a study of readers in 2nd to 4th grades'). Copenhagen: University of Copenhagen (unpublished thesis).

Siegler, R. S. (1986). *Children's thinking.* Englewood Cliffs, NJ: Prentice-Hall.

Skautrup, P. (1944). Det danske sprogs historie [The history of the Danish language] (Vol 1). Copenhagen: Gyldendal.

Taft, M. (1981). Prefix stripping revisited. *Journal of Verbal Learning and Verbal Behavior, 20,* 289–297.

Zinna, D. R., Liberman, I. Y., & Shankweiler, D. (1986). Children's sensitivity to factors influencing vowel reading. *Reading Research Quarterly, 21,* 465–479.

4

Children's Language Development and Reading Acquisition in a Highly Transparent Orthography

Heikki Lyytinen and Mikko Aro
University of Jyväskylä and Niilo Mäki Institute, Jyväskylä

Leena Holopainen
University of Joensuu

Matti Leiwo, Paula Lyytinen, and Asko Tolvanen
University of Jyväskylä

In this chapter we discuss the relation between early language skills and reading acquisition in the context of the Finnish language. Roughly one third of Finnish children acquire reading skills before school entry; apparently in part because of the transparent nature of the Finnish orthography and also in part because of the availability of written material in the home and children's attendance at day-care centers. The results from the Jyväskylä Longitudinal Study of Dyslexia (JLD, Lyytinen et al., 2004) which we summarize in this article reveal that, although the process of acquiring fluent reading in Finnish can be relatively effortless, a number of children still face problems in mastering reading skill. Approximately 6% of children do not achieve accurate reading skill when 90% accuracy in reading pseudowords is used as the criterion. The reasons for such reading difficulties in Finnish children are attributed at least in part to speech processing problems which compromise language development and acquisition of reading and challenge achievements in spelling accuracy and reading fluency. Every reader of Finnish is affected by the agglutinative nature of the language which results in longer than average word length. Finally, the role of phoneme awareness in reading Finnish in comparison to less regular orthographies is examined.

FINNISH ORTHOGRAPHY FACILITATES THE ACQUISITION OF BASIC DECODING SKILLS IN MOST CHILDREN

In this section we describe the features of Finnish orthography that may have an effect on the development of early literacy skills. For a more detailed description, see Lyytinen, Aro, and Holopainen (2004).

Grapheme–Phoneme Correspondences in Finnish. In the Finnish orthography, the grapheme-phoneme (G-P) correspondences are regular and symmetrical. There are 21 Finnish phonemes: 8 vowel phonemes[1] (/i/, /y/, /u, /e, /o/, /ö/, /ä/, and /a/) and 13 consonant

---

[1] The graphemes *y*, *ö*, and *ä* mark front vowels /ü/, /œ/, and /æ/, respectively.

phonemes (/p/, /t/, /k/, /m/, /n/, /l/, /r/, /s/, /h/, /j/, /v/ and more marginal /d/ and /ŋ/). Three additional "foreign" consonant sounds (/b/, /g/, /f/) are used in recent loan words. The phoneme /ŋ/ is marked with the letter *n* when short in front of /k/ (in combination *nk*) and as a bigraph *ng* when long. Other phonemes are marked with a corresponding single-letter grapheme. Thus the number of letters with a corresponding phoneme is 23. As already mentioned, all of these G-P correspondences are regular in both directions.

Phonemic quantity is a distinctive feature in Finnish word production. All phonemes (with the exception of /d/, /h/, /j/ and /v/) can have two phonological lengths, long and short. Thus words like *tuli* (tuli) [fire], *tulli* (tul:i) [customs], and *tuuli* (tu:li) [wind] have different meanings. The long quantity is marked by the doubling of the corresponding letter. With regard to articulation, the stop consonants /p/, /t/, and /k/ are lengthened by a longer voiceless occlusion before the explosion of the sound.

Syllables in Finnish.   There are 10 types of syllables: CV, CVC, CVV, CVVC, VC, V, VV, CVCC, VVC, and VCC. The number of distinct syllables in Finnish is estimated to be slightly over 3,000. Open syllables are more frequent than closed syllables. A syllable (or a word) never begins with a consonant cluster, with the exception of some loan words such as *traktori (tractor)*. Consonant clusters can appear at the end of the syllables but not at the end of the word. The longest syllables consist of four phonemes.

In spoken Finnish, the main stress is placed on the first syllable, and the secondary stress on the third, fifth, etc., that is, on every second syllable of words (with some exceptions), and the final syllable is always unstressed. Because of this regular stress pattern, the syllable is a perceptually salient unit in the segmentation of spoken language. The basic rule for syllabification in reading is that there is a syllable boundary before every CV- combination (e.g., par.ta, kat.to, kelk.ka). Syllabification of written words closely matches the phonological syllable segments of spoken words. However, in the case of stop consonants, the syllabification does not perfectly correspond to phonological syllable segments of spoken language.

Explicit segmentation of syllables forms a central component of early reading and spelling instruction, and syllables are explicitly delineated in the reading materials of beginning readers. Because words can be quite long, working memory capacity is easily exceeded at the level of the phonemes. The standard instruction methods guide children in the use of the syllable as a substage of assembly, thus reducing the memory demands during recoding.

Words in Finnish.   Almost all Finnish words are multisyllabic. There are only approximately 50 monosyllabic words, and most of these are conjunctions and interjections. Because of highly productive compounding, a rich derivational system, and agglutinative and fusional morphology, the words tend to be relatively long. The mean length of a written word is 7.86 letters and correspondingly contains about the same number of phonemes (Pääkkönen, 1990). The agglutinative and fusional morphological system results in words that contain multiple segments of semantic information, as can be seen in the following examples:

taloissani [in my houses]

stem	plural	case	possessive
talo	+i	+ssa	+ni

or *näytettyämme* [after we have shown]

stem	derivative	past participle	case	possessive
näy	+te	+tty	+ä	+mme

Any noun can have over 2,000 orthographic forms with different combinations of case (15), plural marker, possessives (6), and a variety of clitics. This number is even higher for verbs.

When one takes into account derivation and compounding, the same stem can exist in a large number of orthographic contexts. Because the morphology is also fusional, the stem may have several different allomorphs depending on the inflection (e.g., *käsi* [hand], *käde+n*, hand+genitive, *kät+tä,* hand+partitive). On the other hand, the same stem can be used in several words, for example, *kirja* [book], *kirjoittaa* [write], *kirjain* [letter], *kirjailija* [author], and *kirjasto* [library]. These allomorphic variations and derivational affixes force readers toward careful phonemic analysis of words, but the variation also adds to the predictability in reading: The stem forms limit the range of the following suffixes, the phonemic variation of the suffixes depends on the stem, and transparent derivations form semantic networks that can benefit semantic analysis. Affixes, on the other hand, frequently occur in the language (across words) and also reinforce their acquisition in writing. Because small morphemic chunks are semantically distinct, children learn to recognize them even though their critical parts may be only one phoneme/letter in size. This may be helpful in the acquisition of spelling skills.

Finnish orthography differs in many ways from that of English. The features of the orthography that may have an effect on reading development and the nature of reading problems in general are described in more detail toward the end of this chapter. Finnish is an extremely regular and purely phonemic orthography. It stands in stark contrast to English which is one of the most irregular orthographies and relies on morphological information at the expense of phonemic information. In Finnish, the G-P correspondences are regular and symmetrical at the level of single letters (23 phonemes that map onto single letters and one phoneme that is represented by a digraph). The syllables are simple, and consonant clusters are relatively rare, whereas diphthongs and vowel combinations are relatively frequent. Because of the agglutinative nature of morphology, Finnish words are relatively long and can have different orthographic forms depending on the derivational or inflectional suffixes. An exciting feature of Finnish is the variation of phonetic duration which can vary substantially but the proportion of which within a word is in a key position for semantic distinctiveness (for details, see Lehtonen, 1970; Richardson 1998, Richardson, Leppänen, Leiwo, & Lyytinen, 2003). It is a feature of interest to reading research, as we subsequently demonstrate (for a closer review, see Lyytinen, Leppänen, Richardson, & Guttorm, 2003).

The acquisition of phonological recoding skill seems to be a major difficulty for beginning readers in irregular orthographies such as English (Seymour, Aro, & Erskine, 2003). Nonetheless, a number of Finnish children also struggle with the acquisition of literacy skills, albeit of such a transparent, alphabetic orthography. This means that even when the acquisition of phonological recoding skill is facilitated by the orthography, there are obviously other obstacles that hinder mastery of accurate reading and spelling and also fluent reading. This could mean that the language-related background of developmental reading problems is wider than is being postulated in theories that emphasize the exclusive role of phonology. On the other hand, the subsets of phonological skills of relevance to early reading skills may be more dependent on the language and orthography than has been generally thought thus far. From this perspective, knowledge from different orthographies adds to our knowledge of reading development and, it is hoped, helps toward our understanding of the true universal nature of developmental dyslexia.

ASSESSING THE LANGUAGE BASIS OF FAMILIAL RISK FOR EARLY READING FAILURE

In the Jyväskylä Longitudinal Study of Dyslexia (JLD), we began the follow-up study of children who were at familial risk for dyslexia ($N = 107$) and their controls ($N = 93$) from birth and follow them into school age. We assessed the contribution of quantity-related aspects such as difficulty in discriminating phonemic quantity in speech processing during infancy. Three types of experimental approaches were used: (a) recording brain event-related potentials (ERPs) to sounds and speech stimuli, (b) assessing categorical perception of variations of speech sound by use of behavioral head-turning techniques, and (c) assessing the ability of children to imitate minimal pairs such as *mato* (mato) [worm] and *matto* (mat:o) [rug].

In addition to concentrating on this special quantity feature, we also conducted more global and intensive assessments of early language development in the JLD. We followed language production and comprehension by using structured parental reports of vocalization and vocabulary growth during the first years. We assessed vocalization by identifying the ages at which infants reached important, established milestones (P. Lyytinen, Poikkeus, Leiwo, Ahonen, & Lyytinen, 1996). Assessment of vocabulary growth was conducted in terms of both production and comprehension of spoken items. This type of assessment was based on the use of the MacArthur Communicative Development Inventories (CDI; Fenson et al., 1994; P. Lyytinen, Poikkeus, Laakso, Eklund, & Lyytinen, 2001) and the Reynell Developmental Language Scales (RDLSs; Reynell & Huntley, 1987). The CDI covered the ages from 1 to 2.5 years; the RDLS was administered when the children were 18 and 30 months old. This test validated the parental reports (based on the CDI) of their children's receptive and expressive language (P. Lyytinen, Poikkeus, & Laakso, 1997). In addition, the development of symbolic play was followed when the children were between the ages of 14 and 18 months (P. Lyytinen, Laakso, Poikkeus, & Rita, 1999).

The parental reports of the ages at which their child's developmental milestones of vocalization and later language production and comprehension were reached revealed no significant group differences before the age of 2 years. At 2 years of age, a child's maximum sentence length was the first measure that showed a difference (P. Lyytinen et al., 2001) between the groups. In addition, early symbolic play assessed when the toddler was 14 months old revealed significant correlations to subsequent language development (P. Lyytinen, Eklund, & Lyytinen, 2003; P. Lyytinen et al., 2001).

Our findings showed that assessments carried out during infancy may give indications concerning future reading readiness. ERPs to speech sound obtained immediately after birth differentiated children with and without risk for dyslexia (Guttorm, Leppänen, Richardson, & Lyytinen, 2001) and revealed cues about critical brain processing features associated with later language development and reading. These ERP-indices predicted reliably later global language composite scores (Guttorm et al., 2005). The predictive ERPs were based on contrasts between responses to syllable sounds that differed in temporal features such as voice onset times (ba, da, ga). Responses to /ga/ especially differentiated the groups and predicted later language development. The results were linked to duration whereby the formant transitions (specifically of F2) of the synthetic consonant sounds were longest (45 ms) in /ga/. It has to be emphasized that, in Finnish, the voiced /b, d, g/ and the voiceless stops /p, t, k/ are not in phonological opposition, and hence the differences are subphonological.

The next analysis was specifically associated with duration-specific processing because the critical stimuli differed from each other in vowel duration (/ka/–/ka:/). Here, as in our later ERP-studies, an oddball paradigm was used to assess brain responses to an infrequent deviant syllable presented among repeated syllables. The difference (deviancy from repeated sounds) of interest was the increase or decrease of duration. Preliminary analyses of the data reveal that, already at birth, babies' differential responses to duration discriminate the groups. However, only results from the next age of assessment—6 months of age—have thus far been analyzed in detail to document differences related to processing vowel duration between children who were and were not at risk (Leppänen, Pihko, Eklund, & Lyytinen, 1999).

Also at the age of 6 months, babies' processing of stop consonant duration (based on a longer silence associated with the long consonant sound and reflected in the brain responses) was assessed by use of the pseudowords /ata/ and /atta/ as repeated and deviant stimuli. The results clearly differentiated the groups (Leppänen et al., 2002). The lengthening of the duration of /t/ affected the ERP–response in both hemispheres of all children. However the amplitudes were reliably higher in the left hemisphere of the children in the control group. The ERPs of the at-risk children tended to respond to the deviant sound mainly in the right hemisphere. Preliminary analyses also reveal that ERP responses to /ata-atta/ stimuli have a significant correlation with later language development in the at-risk groups.

From different experiments, the ERPs of the at-risk children tend to agree on one issue: The differential brain processing of speech stimuli between groups seems to be dominantly related to hemisphere-specific differences (for a review of the early ERP–results from the JLD, see Lyytinen et al., 2003). When compared with the left hemisphere, the right hemisphere of children who were at risk for reading failure was more active than in children who were not at risk.

The JLD children were studied in their categorization of duration on a short to long /ata-atta/ continuum with a head-turning paradigm. The infants were 6 months of age. It transpired that at-risk children had clear difficulties in perceiving durational cues indicating the change from short to long sound, just like the adults with dyslexia (see Richardson, Leppänen, Leiwo, & Lyytinen, 2003). What makes both ERP and these behavioral results especially interesting is the association of the ERPs of interest (especially the hemispheric difference) with the behavioral results from behavioral categorical perception studies at the same age. Richardson et al. (2003) showed that children require 30 ms or more of a longer silence (the cue making consonant sounds such as /t/ to be perceived as long) for perceiving the /t/ phoneme as crossing the categorical border between short and long. The association between ERPs in the oddball situation to the lengthening of the same sound and its categorical perception is especially clear among at-risk children.

The imitation experiments of the 18-month-old JLD–children (Richardson, 1998) showed that the children were able to imitate the temporal aspects of quantity distinction in a similar manner. It seems, however, that both the dyslexic adults and the at-risk children had more difficulties in the production of the durational cues of length in word-final vowel phonemes in the studied CVCV and CVCCV structures.

LANGUAGE DEVELOPMENT AND EARLY
ACQUISITION OF READING

Several early language related skills correlate to reading at the early school age (see Table 4.1.). A reliable association is seen between early receptive speech and reading. However, the most strong correlations are between letter naming and reading reaching at best a level of .5 to distributionally very well-behaved text reading measures at the end of the first grade, four years after the predictor was assessed. The table shows that also expressive speech— maximum sentence length at 2.5 years of age and inflectional skills assessed using a Berko type task tapping language skills in a little bit wider sense—have highly significant correlations.

The most thoroughly analyzed production data related to early phonological development of the JLD children come from the examination of word-production skills, especially of how accurately the children produce words in spontaneous naming behavior within a play context. Turunen (2003) analyzed words produced by the children of the JLD at the age of 2.5 years. She failed to find any significant differences between the at-risk group and the control group in their production of correct word structures in the naming of familiar objects, or in the total number

TABLE 4.1

Correlations for Early Language Measures, Reading and Spelling During the First Grade.

| Early Language Measures | Reading Measures at School | | | |
| | At the End of First Semester | | At the End of Second Semester | |
	Word Recognition	Spelling Pseudowords	Reading (a Story)	Spelling Pseudowords
1.5 years				
Symbolic play at 14 months	.14*	.22**	.12	.09
Vocabulary production	.15*	.24**	.08	.16*
2.5 years				
Maximum sentence length	.27**	.28**	.29***	.19*
Reynell receptive	.30***	.29***	.24**	.23**
3.5 years				
Inflectional morphology	.28***	.33***	.22**	.27***
Letter naming	.38***	.27***	.48***	.17*

Note. Ns from 145 (JLD children assessed at the end of the second semester) to 196 (first semester).
$*p < .05$, $**p < .005$, $***p < .001$.

of named items. The examination covered the production of four- and three-syllable word structures, heavy unstressed syllables, homorganic and heterorganic consonant sequences and diphthongs, and the phonemes /r/ and /s/. It may be that possible group differences between at-risk and control children can be observed only in linguistically more demanding tasks such as pseudoword repetition, or in more detailed phonetic analyses.[2]

There were statistically significant differences between the groups in relation to reading before they entered the school (Turunen, 2003; see Table 4.2). Approximately one third of Finnish children can read before entering school, one third have no obvious reading skills although they may know a lot of letters, and one third have some preliminary blending ability (e.g., in their readiness to spell their own first name). At the age of 2.5 years, children's speech production accuracy differed reliably among these three groups of the JLD, who were identified just before the start of formal reading instruction and labeled as non-readers, middle group, and early readers. Early readers clearly produced more target items than did middle and poor readers. The groups also differed significantly in the production of word level phonological structures such as four- and three-syllable words and heavy unstressed syllables.

No differences were found in the production of difficult heterorganic consonant clusters, with the exception of diphthongs, and phonemes /s/ and /r/. These word-level measures also significantly predicted spontaneous reading acquisition. It must be noted, however, that the correlations become markedly smaller soon after children have been exposed to reading instruction.

P. Lyytinen et al. (2001) showed that a substantially higher number of members identified as late talkers at 2 years of age among the familial risk group compared with similarly defined late talkers of the control group failed to reach the age norm in language during the next

---

[2] It must be noted, however, that apparently no more than half of the children in the group will really be affected and face reading failure. This means that the assessment should be quite reliable and the differences quite robust in order to reach statistical significance.

TABLE 4.2

Phonological Production at Age 2.5 Years of Poor, Middle, and Early Readers at the Age
of 7 Years. The Attempts to Name (Namings) and the Number of Accurate Productions
of the Labeled Feature are Listed.

Naming Categories	Skill Level of Reading			F-Value
	Poor	Middle	Early	
Number of namings (max = 38)	25.0	26.5	29.9	4.84*
Namings of four-syllable targets (max = 8)	4.1	3.9	5.5	8.95***
Correct four-syllable forms	3.2	3.3	4.8	6.70**
Namings of heterorganic targets (max = 6)	4.1	4.5	4.6	ns.
Correct sequences	2.1	2.9	2.5	ns.
Namings of heavy unstressed syllable targets (max = 12)	6.6	7.4	8.4	5.42**
Correct heavy syllable	4.3	5.6	6.5	5.21**

Note. Modified from Turunen, 2003.
$*p < .05, **p < .01, ***p < .001.$

few years of life. This means that apparently those at real risk for dyslexia are much more likely to belong to the group who will face reading failure at school. This is why a closer look of this subgroup may be warranted. In Turunen's study, children diagnosed as late talkers at 2 years of age were less advanced in their production at all phonological levels (word, syllable, phoneme, and phoneme sequence) in comparison with the other members of the JLD at-risk or control groups, but no differences were found between similarly defined late talkers selected from the at-risk and control groups. A good example of the difference between late talkers and non-late talkers independent of the main groups is the naming and production of words *pyörä* /pyœræ/ [bike] and *pöytä* /pœytæ/ [table] with front vowels in all positions of the words. The at-risk children and the control children managed to produce the front vowels well and had almost no problems with "frontness" whereas seven children diagnosed as late developers at the ages of both 2 and 5 years could not articulate the vowels of the two words and produced forms that do not obey the front-vowel harmony rule of Finnish words (Leiwo, Turunen, & Koivisto, 2002).

At 3.5 years of age, the JLD children participated in a computer-based assessment of *phonological skills* (Puolakanaho, Poikkeus, Ahonen, Tolvanen, & Lyytinen, 2003, 2004). Computer animations were used to make tasks commonly used to assess phonological skills at later ages interesting and reliable for the assessment of younger children between the ages of 3.5 and 5.5 years. Phonological awareness at different levels of units (word, syllable, and phoneme) and preliminary blending skill (continuation of phonological units) were assessed. The results revealed that a substantial proportion of children as young as 3.5 years of age were aware of the syllabic units—apparently because of the syllable-based stress pattern of spoken Finnish. The mean correct score was 7.4 out of 12. The accuracy scores reflecting phonemic level awareness were naturally lower (approximately 12% correct). Because about 10% of the JLD children knew most Finnish letters at this age and more than 20% identified a few most common letters, phonemic awareness may be associated with letter knowledge. Children tend to say the letter name when they have to identify the first sound in words. Knowing the letter names helps to produce phonemic awareness because vowel names are identical to the

TABLE 4.3

Correlations Between Reading and Nonreading Measures at the End of the First Grade.

	Reading Measures					
Nonreading Measures	Text Reading Accuracy	Pseudoword Reading Accuracy	Text Reading Speed	Pseudoword Reading Speed	Spelling Accuracy	Single-Word Reading Speed and Accuracy
Phonological skills before school	.42**	.29	.55**	.11	.41**	.40**
RAS	.32*	.42**	.51***	.33*	.39**	.42**
RAN	.42**	.31*	.37*	.19	.26**	.26
Categorical perception	.47**	.33*	.40**	.11	.51***	.33*

Note. The measure representing phonological segmentation was deduced before the children started school to reduce the influence of reading skill thereupon; other nonreading measures were carried out simultaneously with reading and spelling assessments at the end of the second semester of the first grade.
$^*p < .05$, $^{**}p < .001$, $^{***}p < .001$

long-duration phonemic sounds (represented in writing by the repeat of the vowel; e.g., the name for a is /a:/).

The groups differed reliably in all but the synthesis of phonological units in which the difference marginally failed to reach significance at 3.5 years of age. The phonological measures—and especially the repetition of pseudoword-type tasks—correlated significantly with different early reading measures until the end of the first grade.

JLD children with and without familial risk for dyslexia differ very clearly in language measures such as. Boston naming (Kaplan, Goodglass, & Weintraub, 1983), and an inflectional morphology test (P. Lyytinen et al., 2001; Lyytinen & Lyytinen, 2004) at the age of 3.5 years, and the differences increase as functions of age (H. Lyytinen et al., 2001). It is interesting to note that the groups did not differ consistently on any performance-related IQ measure taken at any age. Consistently, none of the observed language-related differences between groups was affected, even when the effect of the nonverbal IQ was controlled for (H. Lyytinen et al., 2001). The main differential source of variance between children with and without risk for dyslexia in language assessments reflects specifically their perception, discrimination, identification, and/or manipulation of speech sound of various unit sizes and is found in more global assessments of expressive or receptive language skills. It must be added that both categorical perception of speech units associated with duration and more pure auditory tasks—such as discrimination of modulated sounds (a task provided by John Stein and his colleagues)—correlate highly with emergent reading measures; but so do more global language measures such as rapid naming (RAN) and the rapid alternating stimulus test (RAS; see Table 4.3 for examples from the JLD data).

DEVELOPMENTAL PATHS OF READING-RELATED LANGUAGE SKILLS

The JLD's language assessments comprised follow-ups of receptive and expressive language, vocabulary growth, naming accuracy and speed, phonological, morphological, and

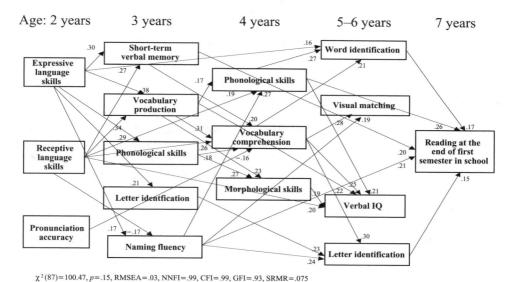

FIG. 4.1.   Predictive paths of language skills to reading at the end of the first semester in school. To ensure readability of the figure, the connections within each age level have not been drawn.

Assessment of expressive and receptive language skills is based on the RDLS (Reynell & Huntley, 1987) and the pronunciation accuracy is based on the number of correct names of pictures articulated correctly (Turunen, 2003). Memory was assessed with the digit span task modified by Gathercole and Adams (1994). Vocabulary production is based on the Boston naming test (Kaplan et al., 1983), naming fluency on the RAN (Denckla & Rudel, 1976; short version), and assessment of letter identification finger-pointing of letters whose names are pronounced to the child. Phonological assessments were conducted with computer-animated tests (see Puolakanaho et al., 2003). Vocabulary knowledge was based on the Peabody picture vocabulary test (Dunn & Dunn, 1981). Morphological skills were assessed with a Berko-type test (Lyytinen & Lyytinen, 2004), and a word-identification test that required the child to identify an orally presented word from a list of nine written words. In the visual matching task, the child had to recognize a shown form from four alternatives (the visual material contained non-letter forms, numbers, letters, and letter sets), verbal IQ was based on the Wechsler Preschool and Primary Scale of Intelligence—Revised (Wechsler, 1989). The criterion reading measure is a composite score of nationally normed timed mechanical reading tests based on the number of (a) words correctly identified and (b) number of errors detected in a list of written words.

orthographic skills at each age level. The differences between groups with and without familial risk tend to increase in language measures as functions of age and also occur after controlling for nonverbal IQ (H. Lyytinen et al., 2001). However, parental education and both environmental and biological factors tend to make a significant additional contribution in regression models that predict early reading. Depending on which kind of early reading measure is used, the total contributions of these language measures explain close to 80% of variance among the children who have completed the first semester of school. The highest percentages are reached if multiple phonological skills assessed just before the beginning of school are included in the model. The main reason is that almost all typical phonological measures (excluding nonword repetition) are so close to reading of Finnish that their correlation is at the level of the reliability (>.7) of the variables. Preliminary path analyses (see Figure 4.1) reveal expected connections from a very early age to the reading status reached at the end of the first semester of school, when the distribution of a composite score of mechanical reading skill has reached quite a normal form.

We computed the path analyses illustrated in Figure 4.1 by proceeding from the reading status and finding the highest predictive routes to identify the contribution of skills at earlier ages. Each age stage variable was added to the model, step by step, from a later to earlier age. The model was built favoring the path between successive age stages and estimated by using the maximum likelihood method. The nonsignificant predictors were eliminated one by one, and modification indices were used to identify paths crossing stages, thus favoring indirect connections. In the end, all non-significant covariances between measures from the same age were also eliminated. Before analysis, the distributions of the predictors were corrected (using Prelis 2.0) and, after this, missing values were imputed using an EM algorithm. The final data comprises 170 JLD subjects whose scores were available at the time (early spring 2003) of the execution of this analysis. In Figure 4.1, the within-age stage connections have not been drawn. All significant predictors directly connected to reading skills have been marked in the figure using standardized coefficients.

Early receptive and expressive language makes the widest and strongest relative contribution to the successful path to reading. Early expressive language skills are also directly connected to both early letter knowledge and word identification. The development of letter-identification skills forms its own path to reading. Phonological skills form a path that has multiple connections to vocabulary and in its early stage is connected to naming fluency. With the exception of the role of the early "general" language skills, the nonspecific language measures (such as verbal IQ or vocabulary) have no direct connection to reading according to this model, which explains about 40% of the variance of reading at the end of the first semester of school.

PHONEMIC AWARENESS, EARLY LETTER KNOWLEDGE, AND READING SKILLS

The most interesting phase of pre-reading development covers the time from when children first become aware of letters and phonemes to the start of formal reading instruction. This happens in the very literacy-oriented Nordic countries relatively early, although formal reading instruction begins at the age of 7 years. The value of literacy is documented by the fact that the ability to read Catechismus has historically been required before couples obtain permission to marry (Lundberg & Nilsson, 1986).

The acquisition of basic phonological recoding skills is a relatively rapid process for beginning readers in Finnish. Although no formal reading instruction takes place before school, children are typically introduced informally to letters and words during the kindergarten year preceding school entry. In a follow-up study, Holopainen, Ahonen, Tolvanen, and Lyytinen (2000) report that half of the children knew all Finnish letters when they entered school. At school entry, one fourth of the children reached 90% decoding accuracy of syllables and pseudowords. During the first semester of the first grade, the children are taught most of the letter sounds and they practice phonological assembly with familiar letters from the very beginning of reading instruction. The single letters map onto phonemes in a regular manner, as described at the beginning of this chapter. Thus, after the basic letter sounds are learned, phonemic blending skill is required for mastering basic recoding.

Aro et al. (1999) monitored the development of phonological skills and reading in a group of children whose school entry had been postponed and who were participating in a special kindergarten group. The development of the children was followed from the year preceding school entry until the end of the first semester of the first grade. The results indicated that there was considerable inter-individual variation in the emergence of phonological skills. For some children, the development was gradual whereas others showed sudden progress. Rhyme detection and phoneme identification skills seemed to be present to some degree 1 year before the children entered school. All children showed emergence of phoneme-identification and syllable-deletion skills before the acquisition of phonological recoding, although children were unable to reliably solve phoneme synthesis and phoneme deletion tasks before mastering phonological recoding. These phonemic awareness tasks require high levels of analytical skills and conscious representations of the phonological segments. The results support the notion that these phonemic skills develop as a product of reading instruction or reading acquisition. This conclusion is further supported by the fact that five out of six children gave only letter-name responses in the phoneme-identification task, both before and after learning to read. Similar findings regarding the use of letter-name responses are reported by Holopainen et al. (2000).

In their study, Holopainen, Ahonen, and Lyytinen (2001) reported that preschool phonological awareness skills differentiated those children who showed very fast reading acquisition after school entry. These same skills failed to identify children whose reading acquisition was delayed; but a preschool letter-knowledge task differentiated the children with delayed reading from children who acquired reading skill normally. This finding casts doubt on the predictive value of phonemic awareness tasks in Finnish. A number of children also performed quite poorly on phonological awareness tasks at the beginning of school despite their becoming good readers shortly after school entry. Holopainen et al. also reported that the earliest readers in their study were close to perfect in their letter knowledge a year before school entry.

Interestingly, Mann and Wimmer (2002), in their recent study, compared phonemic awareness and reading skills in groups of Austrian and American children in kindergarten, grade 1, and grade 2. The American children outperformed the Austrian children at kindergarten age in phonemic identity judgment tasks, as well as in letter knowledge and reading ability. However, by the end of first grade, the Austrian children performed at the same level as the American children on phoneme awareness tasks. The Austrian children also had perfect knowledge of letters; they also read pseudowords more accurately than did the American children. These differences do not support the notion that phonemic awareness is the result of phonological reorganization triggered by the development of spoken language skills. Instead, the authors interpret the differential development of Austrian and American children as supporting the literacy hypothesis on phoneme awareness. The inducement of phoneme awareness requires more than just experiences supporting primary language development. It seems to develop typically as a result of learning to read.

PREDICTING LATER STAGES OF READING

As yet, the JLD project cannot provide predictions of mature reading because only a few of the children have reached later grades. This is why we report here predictive correlations obtained from another Finnish study (Holopainen et al., 2001; Holopainen, Ahonen, & Lyytinen, submitted). In these studies, a reading-related development of a random sample of Finnish children was followed from preschool age to fourth grade. They reveal that the language skills that children acquire before school entry can be used to predict both success and failure of long-term reading instruction. This conclusion was reached by assessment of verbal and nonverbal skills of a random sample of 89 children who were assessed at the age of 6 years, one year before the start of formal synthetic phonics reading instruction. After two years of schooling, participants were divided into four reading groups depending on the duration of instruction required to reach 90% decoding accuracy in the reading of pseudowords. These reading groups were the precocious decoders (PDs), who read at school entry, early decoders (EDs), who reached the criterion within the first 4 months in grade 1, and ordinary decoders (ODs), who reached this criterion within 9 months. The last group, late decoders (LDs), failed to reach the criterion within the first 2 years of instruction.

The most interesting difference emerged between the ODs and the LDs. These groups were significantly different in (and the membership predictable from) pseudoword repetition accuracy and naming speed assessed before entry into school. Naming speed was also associated with slow reading speed at the end of the second grade. As described at the end of this chapter, Finnish words are long and generally consist of a large number of syllables because of multiple inflections. Consequently, slow reading seems to be a characteristic of Finnish adults with dyslexia (Leinonen et al., 2001).

The pseudoword repetition task requires several phonological processes: accurate phonological representation of the input, good phonological working memory to keep an unfamiliar representation in mind, and the ability to keep the phonological representations distinct for accurate co-articulation of the output. Pseudoword repetition covers these critical skills so well that no other phonological measure can add significantly to the discrimination between ODs and LDs. Interestingly, the phonological awareness task seems to play a significant role in discriminating only PDs and EDs from ordinary and late decoders. Phonological awareness, however, did not differentiate between the OD and the LD groups. This challenges the value of phonological awareness measures used in studies of deep orthographies such as English as predictors of later reading problems. In short, children who may achieve a relatively low phonological awareness score but who are exposed to reading instruction in a highly transparent language, in this case, Finnish, can become very accurate readers in about 6 months. The obvious reason is that reading instruction itself develops awareness of the 24 phonemes that children should master to acquire reading skill. These results indicate that assessments and interventions for children with potential problems in reading acquisition should be expanded to include a wider battery of functions (especially pseudoword repetition) to identify individuals who are in need of additional support.

The role of naming dysfluency in reading may indicate that automatization is affected by difficulties in retrieving accurate phonemic representations of words. On the other hand, the contribution of naming speed to reading significantly increased the prediction made by the phonological measures showing the independence of these two predictors. This begs the question as to whether failure to automatize can be solely a result of phonological weakness. The speed factor could alternatively affect the establishment of fluent identification of larger graphemic chunks.

The extent to which phonological awareness acquired before reading instruction contributes to reading achievement at later stages of reading is an interesting question. Phonological awareness (as determined by single-phoneme identification, phoneme deletion, syllable deletion, and phoneme-blending tasks) assessed before children's entry into school did not predict their later reading, but phonological awareness measured at the end of the first grade predicted both reading accuracy and reading fluency in the fourth grade. Because the orthographic representations available to readers can substantially help in the solving of phonological tasks, it was of interest to ascertain the correlation of phonological awareness and later reading when reading accuracy in the year before school entry and in the first grade was partialled out from their association. As expected, the effect of the phonological awareness measure taken before school entry was no longer a significant predictor of fourth-grade reading accuracy. Earlier reading accuracy was the best predictor. This was also the case in the prediction of reading fluency in the fourth grade: first-grade fluency, together with pseudoword repetition measures, was the strongest predictor in jointly explaining over 50% of the variance.

Performance in pseudoword repetition identified those children who were unable to achieve accurate reading skills during the first 3 years of synthetic phonics instruction. Difficulty with both the segmentation of words into phonemes and with the mental organization of the articulatory output may explain difficulties in both pseudoword repetition and reading acquisition. This finding shows that some basic phonological feature also affects readers of a highly regular orthography. Children learn to identify phonemes but may continue to make errors in complex word-level features such as phonemic length which is based on the relative duration of consecutive sound segments rather than on absolute duration. Studies of very young children who were at risk for dyslexia suggested that phonological representations entail word-level problems in using sub-phonemic duration cues. Inaccuracies in the categorical perception of speech based on the variation of the duration of consecutive sounds can widely affect the development of phonological segmentation and manipulation skills. Although semantic support at the word level helps children to avoid errors in the reading of familiar words, even the spelling of familiar words seems to be affected. This is shown in the analysis of spelling errors committed by children who are not good readers and adults in the JLD study (Lyytinen, Leinonen, Nikula, Aro, & Leiwo, 1995).

IMPLICATIONS OF THE FINNISH ORTHOGRAPHY FOR THE BEGINNING READER

From the perspective of phonological recoding, the simple Finnish G-P correspondence system has distinct advantages. As noted at the beginning of the chapter, the number of phonemes is relatively small and G-P conversion rules are perfectly regular. Because there are only single letter graphemes (with one exception), the written word also makes the abstract phonemic structure explicit for the reader. Consequently phonological assembly is a fairly simple serial process of putting the letter sounds together. As long as beginning readers are able to perform phonemic synthesis after mastering the basic letter-sound correspondences, they have the tools for recoding any given word or pseudoword. This stands in marked contrast to the requirements of an irregular orthography such as English, in which readers first have to be able to perform orthographic segmentation of multi-letter graphemes (*thief*→*/th/ /ie/ /f/*) and in which the knowledge of basic letter sounds is insufficient in terms of being able to use the G-P correspondences. In English, readers also have to take context into consideration and irregular words completely elude phonemic assembly. Compared with irregular orthographies, it seems plausible to conclude that the regularity of the Finnish orthography makes it relatively easy to master and thus to systematically apply phonological recoding in the early stage of reading development.

This effect of orthographic depth on the acquisition of early reading skills has been shown in a cross-linguistic comparison by Seymour et al. (2003). This conclusion is also supported by international comparison studies (Elley, 1994) and the recent PISA study[3] (OECD, 2001, OECD, 2002). These PISA studies reveal that, internationally, Finnish children are at the top in terms of their ultimate reading achievement, comprehension, and use and interpretation of written texts. Even Finnish dyslexic children are usually able to master phonological recoding and attain relatively good accuracy in their reading skills. Their problems seem to manifest in poor fluency.

The English-based models of reading acquisition typically describe separate processes of phonological recoding and direct word recognition. Because of the synthetic and agglutinative

---

[3] The Programme for International Student Assessment (PISA) is an international assessment of the skills and knowledge of 15-year olds, a project of the Organisation for Economic Co-operation and Development (OECD) and participating member countries.

nature of Finnish, the use of a direct strategy for word recognition in beginning reading would be inefficient. In sentences, the nouns and verbs are inflected; hence the ability to recognize the uninflected root does not suffice. In the case of fusional structures, even the stem has different allomorphs in different inflections, and also the suffixes may have several allomorphs. Thus, the number of possible word forms for any given item is excessive. For a beginning reader, this means that phonological recoding is the only efficient route toward word recognition. In practice, reading instruction methods in Finland are almost uniformly based on phonics approaches.

From the point of view of early literacy skills, Finnish orthography has two specific hurdles. These relate to the marking of the phonemic quantity and to the length of the words. To correctly code phonemic quantity in reading, and especially to correctly mark it in writing, children require sensitivity to the phonological and sub-phonological cues of length and syllable-segmentation. However, in the coding of double-stop consonant letters that demarcate long-quantity, phonological syllable segmentation does not necessarily help in the identification of quantity. It is also worthy of note that, at the morphographic level, there are a few irregularities in marking the phonemic quantity: After some lexical morphemes before clitics, in some compound words (e.g., *sadetakki* /sadet:ak:i/ [raincoat], and at some word boundaries in sentences, the initial consonant of the suffix or the word that follows geminates in spoken standard Finnish. However, in these cases, the long quantity is not marked in the orthography. Another problem for beginning readers relates to the length of the words. The memory demands of recoding are high because a large number of phonemes require to be assembled before pronunciation is accessed. For slow, beginning recoders, this often means that the assembly process can become disrupted. Consequently, children are usually instructed to use the syllable as a subroutine in phonological assembly. In general, syllables play a central role in reading and spelling instruction and problems in syllable segmentation or syllabification are also typically reflected in reading and spelling skills. Furthermore, it has to be emphasized that the preceding lexical context often predicts the selection of the morpheme and the stem from the selection of its allomorph.

THE ROLE OF PHONEMIC AWARENESS MAY HAVE BEEN EXAGGERATED IN EXPLAINING SUCCESS OR FAILURE IN READING

The phoneme is a very abstract speech unit to a child who has not been exposed to letters. It seems likely that, in the Finnish context, being exposed to letters creates a sufficient basis for the achievement of phonemic awareness. This is documented by the fact that a large majority of Finnish children have full mastery of all Finnish letter-names before school entry. Those who fail to name letters tend to have difficulties in following the synthetic phonic instruction—instruction which very successfully helps a similarly large majority of Finnish children to accurately decode any short word/nonword within 3–4 months of instruction. Children who, at this stage, have difficulties in the simple G-P association learning process also fail to show accurate speech perception in the most complex challenge of Finnish phonology—the interpretation and classification of duration into short and long which persists as the most usual indicator of reading difficulties in adulthood. A similarly common problem is dysfluency of reading which is affected by the agglutinative nature of Finnish, that is, long words in many contexts can only be read with accuracy through phoneme-by-phoneme decoding.

REFERENCES

Aro, M. (2005). Learning to read. In R. M. Joshi & P. G. Aaron (Eds.), *Handbook of orthography and literacy* (pp. 531–550). Hillsdale: Lawrence Erlbaum Associates.

Aro, M., & Wimmer, H. (2003). Learning to read: English in comparison to six more regular orthographies. *Applied Psycholinguistics, 26,* 619–634.

Aro, M., Aro, T., Ahonen, T., Räsänen, P., Hietala, A., & Lyytinen, H. (1999). The development of phonological abilities and their relation to reading acquisition: Case studies of six Finnish children. *Journal of Learning Disabilities, 32,* 457–463.

Denckla, M. B., & Rudel, R. G. (1976). Naming of object-drawings by dyslexic and other learning disabled children. *Brain and Language, 3,* 1–15.

Dunn, L. M., & Dunn, L. M. (1981). *Peabody Picture Vocabulary Test—Revised.* Circle Pines, MN: American Guidance Service.

Douglas, V. I., & Peters, K. G. (1979). Toward a clearer definition of the attentional deficit of hyperactive children. In G.A. Hale & M. Lewis (Eds.), *Attention and cognitive development* (pp. 173–247). New York: Plenum.

Elley, W. (1994). *The IEA study of reading literacy: Achievement and instruction in thirty-two school systems.* Oxford: Pergamon.

Fenson, L., Dale, P. S., Reznick, J. S., Bates, E., Thal, D., & Pethick, S. J. (1994). Variability in early communicative development. *Monographs of the Society for Research in Child Development, 59* (5, Serial No. 242).

Gathercole, S. E., & Adams, A.-M. (1994). Children's phonological working memory: Contributions of long-term knowledge and rehearsal. *Journal of Memory and Language, 33,* 672–688.

Guttorm, T. K., Leppänen, P. H. T., Poikkeus, A.-M., Eklund, K. M., Lyytinen, P., & Lyytinen, H. (2005). Brain event-related potentials (ERPs) measured at birth predict later language development in children with and without familial risk for dyslexia. *Cortex, 41.*

Guttorm, T. K., Leppänen, P. H. T., Richardson, U., & Lyytinen, H. (2001). Event-related potentials and consonant differentiation in newborns with familial risk for dyslexia. *Journal of Learning Disabilities, 34,* 534–544.

Holopainen, L., Ahonen, T., & Lyytinen, H. (2001). Predicting reading delay in reading achievement in a highly transparent language. *Journal of Learning Disabilities, 34,* 401–414.

Holopainen, L., Ahonen, T., & Lyytinen, H. (submitted). Development of reading and linguistic abilities: Results from a Finnish longitudinal study.

Holopainen, L., Ahonen, T., Tolvanen, A., & Lyytinen, H. (2000). Two alternative ways to model the relation between reading accuracy and phonological awareness at preschool age. *Scientific Studies of Reading, 4*(2), 77–100.

Kaplan, E., Goodglass, H., & Weintraub, S. (1983). *The Boston Naming Test* (2nd ed.). Philadelphia: Lea & Febiger.

Lehtonen, J. (1970). *Aspects of quantity in standard Finnish.* Studia Philogica Jyväskyläensia 6. University of Jyväskylä.

Leinonen, S., Müller, K., Leppänen, P. H. T., Aro, M., Ahonen, T., & Lyytinen, H. (2001). Heterogeneity in adult dyslexic readers: Relating processing skills to the speed and accuracy of oral text reading. *Reading & Writing, 14,* 265–296.

Leiwo, M., Turunen, P., & Koivisto, J. (2002). Suomen vokaaliharmonian kehitys—vaikeasti kuvattava vaikeus. *Puhe ja Kieli, 22,* 105–112.

Leppänen, P. H. T., Pihko, E., Eklund, K. M., & Lyytinen, H. (1999). Cortical responses of infants with and without a genetic risk for dyslexia: II. Group effects. *NeuroReport, 10,* 969–973.

Leppänen, P. H. T., Richardson, U., Pihko, E., Eklund, K. M., Guttorm, T. K., Aro, M., & Lyytinen, H. (2002). Brain responses to changes in speech sound durations differ between infants with and without familial risk for dyslexia. *Developmental Neuropsychology, 22,* 407–422.

Lundberg, I., & Nilsson, L.-G. (1986). What church examination records can tell us about the inheritance of reading disability? *Annals of Dyslexia, 36,* 217–236.

Lyytinen, H., Ahonen, T., Eklund, K., Guttorm, T. K., Laakso, M.-L., Leinonen, S., Leppänen, P. H. T., Lyytinen, P., Poikkeus, A.-M., Puolakanaho, A., Richardson, U., & Viholainen, H. (2001). Developmental pathways of children with and without familial risk for dyslexia during the first years of life. *Developmental Neuropsychology, 20,* 535–554.

Lyytinen, H., Aro, M., Eklund, K., Erskine, J., Guttorm, T. K., Laakso, M.-L., Leppänen, P. H. T., Lyytinen, P., Poikkeus, A.-M., Richardson, U., & Torppa, M. (2004). The development of children at familial risk for dyslexia: birth to school age. *Annals of Dyslexia, 54,* 2 184–220.

Lyytinen, H., Aro, M., & Holopainen, L. (2004). Dyslexia in highly orthographically regular Finnish. In I. Smythe, J. Everatt & R. Salter (Eds.), *The international handbook of dyslexia* (pp. 81–91). West Sussex, UK: Wiley.

Lyytinen, H., Leinonen, S., Nikula, M., Aro, M., & Leiwo, M. (1995). In search of the core features of dyslexia: Observations concerning dyslexia in the highly orthographically regular Finnish language. In V. W. Berninger

(Ed.), *The varieties of orthographic knowledge II: Relationships to phonology, reading, and writing* (pp. 177–204). Dordrecht, The Netherlands: Kluwer Academic.

Lyytinen, H., Leppänen. P. H. T., Richardson, U., & Guttorm, T. (2003). Brain functions and speech perception in infants at risk for dyslexia. In V. Csepe (Ed.), *Dyslexia: Different brain, different behavior* (pp. 113–152). Neuropsychology and Cognition Series. Dordrecht, The Netherlands: Kluwer.

Lyytinen, P., Eklund, K., & Lyytinen, H. (2003). The play and language behavior of mothers with and without dyslexia and its association to their toddlers' language development. *Journal of Learning Disabilities, 36*, 1, 74–86.

Lyytinen, P., Laakso, M.-L., Poikkeus, A.-M., & Rita, N. (1999). The development and predictive relations of play and language across the second year. *Scandinavian Journal of Psychology, 40*(3), 177–186.

Lyytinen, P., & Lyytinen, H. (2004). Growth and predictive relations of vocabulary and inflectional morphology in children with and without familial risk for dyslexia. *Applied Psycholinguistics, 25*, 397–411.

Lyytinen, P., Poikkeus, A.-M., & Laakso, M.-L. (1997). Language and symbolic play in toddlers. *International Journal of Behavioral Development, 21*, 289–302.

Lyytinen, P., Poikkeus, A.-M., Laakso, M.-L., Eklund, K., & Lyytinen, H. (2001). Language development and symbolic play in children with and without familial risk for dyslexia. *Journal of Speech, Language and Hearing Research, 44*, 873–885.

Lyytinen, P., Poikkeus, A.-M., Leiwo, M., Ahonen, T., & Lyytinen, H. (1996). Parents as informants of their child's vocal and early language development. *Early Child Development and Care, 126*, 15–25.

Mann, V., & Wimmer, H. (2002). Phoneme awareness and pathways into literacy: A comparison of German and American children. *Reading and Writing, 15*, 653–682.

OECD 2001 (2001). Knowledge and skills for life. First results from PISA 2000. Organization for Economic Cooperation and Development. Paris: OECD.

OECD 2002 (2002). Reading for change. Performance and engagement across countries. Results from PISA 2000. Paris: OECD.

Puolakanaho, A., Poikkeus, A.-M., Ahonen, T., Tolvanen, A., & Lyytinen, H. (2003). Assessment of three-and-a-half-year old children's emerging phonological awareness in a computer-animation context. *Journal of Learning Disabilities, 36*, 416–423.

Puolakanaho, A., Poikkeus, A.-M., Ahonen, T., Tolvanen, A., & Lyytinen, H. (2004). Emerging phonological awareness as a precursor of risk in children with and without familial risk for dyslexia. *Annals of Dyslexia, 54*, (2) 221–243.

Pääkkönen, M. (1990). *Grafeemit ja konteksti. Tilastotietoja suomen yleiskielen kirjaimistosta*. Helsinki: Suomalaisen Kirjallisuuden seura.

Reynell, J., K., & Huntley, M. (1987). *Reynell Developmental Language Scales manual* (2nd ed.). Windsor, UK: NFER—Nelson.

Richardson, U. (1998). *Familial dyslexia and sound duration in the quantity distinctions of Finnish infants and adults*. Studia Philologica Jyväskyläensia, 44 (diss.).

Richardson, U., Leppänen, P. H. T., Leiwo, M., & Lyytinen, H. (2003). Speech perception of infants with high familial risk for dyslexia differ at the age of 6 months. *Developmental Neuropsychology, 23*, 385–397.

Seymour, P. H. K., Aro, M., & Erskine, J. M. (2003). Foundation literacy acquisition in European orthographies. *British Journal of Psychology, 94*, 143–174.

Turunen, P. (2003). *Production of word structures. A constraint-based study of 2; 6 year old Finnish children at-risk for dyslexia and their controls*. Jyväskylä Studies in Languages, 54 (diss).

Van der Leij, A., Lyytinen, H., & Zwarts, F. (2001). The study of infant cognitive processes in dyslexia. In A. J. Fawcett (Ed.), *Dyslexia: Theory and good practice* (pp. 160–181). London: Whurr.

Wechsler, D. (1989). *Wechsler Preschool and Primary Scale of Intelligence–Revised*. San Antonio, TX: The Psychological Corporation.

5

Sources of Information Children Use in Learning to Spell: The Case of Finnish Geminates

Annukka Lehtonen
University of Oxford, U.K.

Two experiments were designed to investigate the ways in which children use orthographic, phonological, and morphological information in spelling double consonants (geminates) in Finnish. In the first experiment, children had to choose out of two pseudo-word spellings the one that looked more like a real word on the basis of orthographic or phonological information. In the second experiment, children spelled real words containing target consonant clusters in either word stems or inflections. The results showed that even children just starting school were able to use orthographic information to their advantage in spelling, whereas phonological aspects of spelling rules were acquired only later on. During the first school year also the use of morphological information began to emerge. Thus children seem to use multiple kinds of information in spelling from very early on.

INTRODUCTION

Traditionally the study of literacy development has been dominated by research concentrating on English orthography. However, languages differ in their structure and the characteristics of their orthography, and English with its deep morphophonological orthography and relatively simple morphological structure is by no means the norm. This is increasingly acknowledged in the field, as the past decade has seen a remarkable increase in the number of studies investigating literacy acquisition in languages other than English, including studies concerning bilingualism and cross-linguistic comparisons in a variety of languages. Because languages differ from each other in multiple ways, they provide different kinds of opportunities for investigating the factors affecting literacy development. Finnish is an interesting language for this kind of research for several reasons. It has an almost perfectly transparent orthography, phoneme length in addition to phoneme quality distinguishes between meanings, and the morphological structure of the language is very complex.

Characteristics of Finnish

Orthography

The most remarkable characteristic of Finnish orthography is that it is very transparent, because the relationships between graphemes and phonemes are regular and consistent. This is true for both spelling-to-sound and sound-to-spelling relationships, so that each letter denotes only one sound and each sound can be spelled with only one letter. This makes Finnish symmetrically transparent, unlike, for example, French and German, which are more transparent in their spelling-to-sound relationships than in their sound-to-spelling relationships and thus easier to read than to spell. The only exception to the one-to-one phoneme–grapheme mappings in Finnish is the nasal consonant phoneme /ŋ/, which is represented by the digraph *ng*. Finnish uses the Roman alphabet to represent its 13 consonants and 8 vowels. It is worth noting that Finnish has fewer phonemes than, for example, English, as there are only 21 phonemes compared with the 44 that are used in English. Therefore not all the letters of the Roman alphabet are used in Finnish, for example, *c* and *w* are never used to represent Finnish phonemes. Consequently Finnish gives young readers and spellers two kinds of advantages in acquiring the alphabetic principle. First, the number of different sounds that need to be distinguished and represented is smaller than in languages that are richer in phonemes. Second, the way in which phonemes are mapped onto letters is much more straightforward than in most other orthographies. A further constraining factor is the small number of legal syllable structures allowed in Finnish. Finnish allows only 14 basic syllable types, and therefore syllables provide quite stringent phonotactic constraints for Finnish words and possibly give guidelines for beginning and more advanced spellers.

Phoneme Length in Finnish

Although many languages, such as English, code only for phoneme quality, in Finnish it is also necessary to pay attention to phoneme quantity, that is, the duration of phonemes in terms of time. There is a difference between short phonemes, which are spelled with a single letter, and long phonemes, which are spelled with two identical letters. The distinction in Finnish is like the difference in duration in pronouncing the letter *a* in the English words *bat* and *bad* (Treiman, 1993), rather than the qualitative difference in pronouncing the same letter in the words *hat* and *hate*. The difference between *bat* and *bad* does not distinguish between meaning in English, but does so in Finnish. Both consonants and vowels can appear as long in Finnish. Long consonants are referred to as geminates. Examples of how the length of phonemes distinguishes between meanings are provided in Table 5.1.

TABLE 5.1
Examples of How Length Affects Meaning in Finnish

Finnish	English
T*aka*	Back
T*akka*	A fireplace
T*aakka*	A burden
T*akaa*	From behind
T*akkaa*	Of a fireplace
T*aakkaa*	Of a burden

Whereas determining phoneme quality is relatively straightforward in Finnish, defining the length of a phoneme is more complicated, as length is not an absolute concept. Rather, it depends on the total duration of the word in question and also on the other phonemes in the word (Lehtonen, 1970). However, there is no evidence as of yet that normally developing Finnish school-age children have problems distinguishing between short and long phonemes in speech, whereas they often make errors in representing long phonemes with two letters in the early phases of literacy acquisition. Problems in representation of length also provide one potential marker of reading and spelling problems in Finnish, both for children and adults (Lyytinen, Leinonen, Nikula, Aro, & Leiwo, 1995). This might be partly because the spelling of long phonemes deviates from the "one-sound, one-letter" rule that otherwise holds well in the Finnish orthography because of its transparent nature. Therefore we can say that representing phoneme length is an inconsistent aspect of this otherwise very regular orthography.

Morphology

Finnish is a very complex language with respect to morphological structure. Possession, plurals, prepositions, and some particles are all expressed by inflections added to the ends of words, so Finnish is a good example of an agglutinative language (see Table 5.2). In practice, this means that words are long and can take on a vast number of different forms. Each noun can have over 2,000 different forms and each verb as many as 10,000. The morphology is particularly complex as words often have several different stems, which are used depending on the type of inflection that is attached to the end of the word in different occasions. Table 5.3 shows an example of this.

This kind of morphological structure sets certain requirements for how it can be processed. Niemi and Laine (1995) point out that there simply is not enough time to go through all the possible forms of words if they were all represented as separate entries in the lexicon. Indeed, several studies looking at reading in Italian (Caramazza, Laudana, & Romani, 1988), which is another highly inflected and agglutinative language, and Finnish (Niemi, Laine, & Tuominen, 1994) suggest that word stems and inflections are represented separately in the lexicon of Italian and Finnish readers. This work is still at a preliminary stage, however, and we do not know how the representations develop or how they may affect spelling or be affected by spelling.

Most of the aforementioned research in Finnish has investigated case inflections. Finnish has 14 different case inflections, and they are used instead of word order to express the role of a word in a sentence. They are very frequent in the language and children acquire them relatively early. Thus, if morphological information were to influence children's literacy acquisition, case inflections would probably be involved, and this is why the focus in this study was the possible role of case inflections in spelling.

TABLE 5.2
Examples of Finnish Morphology

Finnish	Translation
Taloissammekin	In our houses as well
TALO + *I* + **SSA** + MME + KIN	House + *s* + **in** + our + as well

TABLE 5.3
Some Finnish Case Inflections Showing How the Stem
of the Word (in Boldface) Changes

Finnish	*English*
Vesi	Water
Veden	Of water
Vettä	Some water
Vetenä	As water
Vedeksi	Into water
Vedessä	In water
Vedestä	From water
Veteen	To water
Vedellä	With water

The Types of Information That Children Use in Spelling

The development of children's spelling skills is generally considered an increasingly sophisticated process of understanding how the sounds of words can be represented by letters or letter groups. The specifics of this developmental progression have been outlined in several spelling models, for example, those of Frith (1985) and Ehri (1992). The different models agree on many of the main characteristics of spelling development. Initially, children do not attempt to represent the sounds in words, but their "spellings" are letters and numbers jumbled together with no clear correspondence to the words that they are supposed to represent. Children's first attempts at representing the sound structure of words are incomplete, as they represent some of the correct sounds, but not all of them. Both letter-name knowledge and children's phonological knowledge affect the outcome of these early spelling attempts. The next step is considered to be the "phonetic" stage of spelling, in which children's spellings represent the complete sound structure of the words. However, they still fail to consider many of the conventional constraints of the orthography of the language (orthographic rules), such as legal letter position and the types of letters that can appear adjacent to each other. Children also overlook many morphologically regular spelling sequences. The ability to use orthographic and morphological information in spelling is considered to be a more sophisticated approach on the way to proficiency than the children in the semiphonetic or phonetic stage are capable of. A question that the spelling models disagree on and that has not been resolved yet is whether children use qualitatively different spelling strategies at different times. If this were the case, we would expect to find that children use different kinds of information in spelling at different points in time. In contrast, if we were to learn that children can use different types of knowledge to their advantage in spelling from early on, this would be evidence against the strict stage model approach.

One way to investigate how children's ability to use different kinds of knowledge affects their developing spelling skills is to look at how a specific aspect of spelling develops over time. The study by Cassar and Treiman (1997) of children's knowledge of the use of letter doublets offers a good example of this approach. They used an orthographic constraints test, in which children were shown non-word pairs and asked to choose the member of the pair that looked more like a real word. Cassar and Treiman (1997) compared legal and illegal doublets in final (legal) and initial (illegal) positions of the word. They also ran an experiment in which the non-words were read out loud, so that it was possible to test children's knowledge of the phonological rule associated with letter doublets, that is, that a consonant letter doublet usually follows a short vowel (Carney, 1994). The results showed that first graders chose non-words with final doublets and legal doublets more often than they chose non-words with initial or illegal doublets. Kindergartners were similarly sensitive to the legal position of doublets, whereas they were still at chance when having to choose between legal and illegal doublets. This suggests that already very young children know something about the orthographic rules that govern letter doublet use. However, it was not until sixth grade and above that children had begun to master the phonological rule of doublet spelling.

These results illustrate two important issues. First, even kindergartners can make certain judgements on the basis of orthography, although their spelling is still on the semiphonetic or phonetic level. Although these children have not been learning to spell for very long yet, they have been exposed to print in their environment and have had the opportunity to pick up information about the conventions of their orthography implicitly. Second, we can see that information of the function of spelling sequences is acquired gradually, depending on the nature of the information involved. Although kindergartners already seemed to know about the allowed position of doublets, it takes an additional year for them to work out that not all letters are allowed to double. More sophisticated aspects of spelling, like the phonological relationship between the medial doublet and the preceding vowel, are not mastered until considerably later.

Pacton, Perruchet, Fayol, and Cleeremans (2001) investigated French children's performance in the orthographic constraints test. They controlled the frequency of letter doublets by using consonants that differ in their frequency of doubling. This is possible because there are consonants (e.g., c, d, v) that are frequent as single letters, but double rarely, whereas other consonants (e.g., l, m, s) are frequent as both single and double letters. Pacton et al. (2001) also investigated children's learning of the rule about the doublet position by using doublets of letters that are never doubled. Thus children's responses should not have been biased by the number of times that they had seen these doublets in either initial or final position. The results showed that, even when the frequency of the single consonants making up the doublets was controlled, children preferred more frequent doublets and thus showed sensitivity to the frequency of doublets per se already in their first school year. This sensitivity increased from grade 2 to grade 3. Moreover, children were more likely to choose medial doublets (legal in French) than initial or final doublets (illegal in French) even when all the doublets were made up of consonants that cannot be doubled in French and children could not have responded on the basis of how often they had seen the doublets. These results corroborate those of Cassar and Treiman (1997) and suggest that children in the semiphonetic and phonetic stages of spelling development already possess some orthographic knowledge that they can bring into their spelling.

Before we draw any firm conclusions about children's concept of doublets in spelling, it is important to note that doublets have different functions in different orthographies. In English, doublets usually follow a short vowel, and in principle this should also help children to know that doublets are not allowed in the initial position of a word. In French doublets do not have a phonological function at all, so their role is exclusively orthographic. Yet another type of function appears in Finnish, in which doublets represent the length of phonemes. Italian doublets have a similar function, but the phoneme–grapheme relationships in Italian are somewhat more irregular than those of Finnish. These cross-linguistic differences offer an interesting opportunity to investigate the interaction between orthography and phonology. French children have only orthographic information to guide them in the use of doublets, which allows us to look at the development of orthographic information alone. English children have to learn quite a complex rule about doublets, involving both phonology and orthography, and indeed they begin to follow it only at the age of 12 years and above. However, already beginning spellers seem to know something about the consistent rule that specifies the legal position of doublets, that is, that doublets are not allowed in the initial position of a word.

In Finnish, however, the relationship between consonant doublets (geminates) in orthography and phonology is not consistent with respect to the geminate position within a word. A long consonant in the middle of the word is always marked by a geminate. However, if we look at the initial position of the word, there are word forms (e.g., singular second-person imperative: "*Come* here," "*Eat* this") that will make the first consonant of the following word lengthen in pronunciation. This lengthening in the initial position is not represented in spelling, however; initial geminates are never allowed in the Finnish orthography. The reason for this phenomenon is historical. These word forms used to end in a consonant, and although this is no longer marked in spelling, it is realised in pronunciation (Laaksonen & Lieko, 1998). This means that children cannot simply follow the phonological rule in spelling. Instead, they have to take into account the orthographic constraint that geminates are illegal at word beginnings.

This experiment investigated how children's knowledge of the orthographic and phonological aspects of the geminate spelling rule affects their performance in an orthographic constraints test and whether the two types of knowledge interact. Children's knowledge of the allowed position of geminates was compared, as the orthographic cue of the legal position of geminates is very straightforward in Finnish, but not explicitly taught.

If Finnish children are sensitive to orthographic constraints as English-speaking children are, they would be expected to be less likely to accept geminates in the initial than in the medial position of words. It is not obvious, however, that one would see this pattern of responding in the first-year children, as at the time of testing they had not yet been exposed to any formal literacy instruction. Therefore any knowledge they may demonstrate is more likely to be due to informal exposure to print. Additionally, the aim was to investigate children's mastery of the phonological aspect of the geminate spelling rule, that is, that geminates are used to mark long consonants in speech. First-year children were not expected to make the distinction between long and short consonants yet, as this usually emerges in spelling only some months after the start of formal literacy instruction. However, the better at spelling the children become, the more attention they should pay to the length of the phonemes that they hear.

The older children's performance is of interest, because their errors could show us whether phonological and orthographic information interact in the course of spelling development. These children have had plenty of experience of reading and spelling already. Thus they are likely to know that initial doublets are not allowed, but also that long phonemes should be represented by geminates. Therefore they actually have two types of conflicting information that might lead them to accept disproportionally many word-initial geminates. Third-year children should be less likely than second-year children to show the effect of the conflict between the types of information, as they are much more competent in spelling in general and their knowledge of the spelling system is far more extensive.

As long consonants are only pronounced at the beginning of the word if they are preceded by certain types of words, it was necessary to use a modified version of the orthographic constraints test, that is, short sentences in which the target pseudo-word was always the second word. Children in years 1–3 were tested at the beginning of the school year, when the first-year children have not received any formal instruction in reading or spelling yet. Therefore it was necessary to use a test for which the requirements for reading and spelling were minimized. This problem was solved by reading out loud each sentence and the pseudo-word in it, then asking children to circle, out of two choices, the pseudo-word spelling that looked more like a real word. This way, children did not need to know how to read that well, and, as they had to only circle one of the options, they did not have to write anything either. This ensured that data could be collected from all first-year children, regardless of the fact that their reading and spelling skills were very limited at this stage.

To investigate the development of and interaction between children's orthographic and phonological knowledge, the test had four conditions. The test sentences included words with a long/short phoneme pronounced at the beginning of some target words and a long/short phoneme in the middle of other target words. The phonemes in the initial position always had to be spelled with one letter, whereas a long phoneme in the middle of the word was spelled with a letter doublet and a short phoneme with a single letter. Thus orthography and phonology are in conflict in the condition in which a long phoneme is pronounced at the beginning of the word.

STUDY 1

Method

Participants

121 children in Years 1–3 in a primary school in Espoo, Finland, were tested. The mean ages of the children were 7 : 2 years, 8 : 2 years, and 9 : 2 years. The reason for the high mean ages is that in Finland children go to school in the autumn of the year when they turn 7 years old. The children were tested in August, 10 days after the schools had started in the new academic year, so the first-year children had not received any formal literacy training yet.

The Task and the Procedure

Children were seen as a group in a single experimental session and the task was administered to the whole class at once, so about 25 children were doing the task simultaneously.

The Task.   The orthographic constraints test consisted of 24 sentences. Each of these was three words long and contained a pseudo-word as the second word. The pseudowords varied according to two variables: the length of the target phoneme and the position of the target phoneme. In half of the words, the target phoneme was long in pronunciation, in half it was short. Half of the words had the target phoneme in the initial position of the word, whereas in half of the words the target phoneme was in the middle of the word. The most interesting condition was the one in which a long phoneme appeared in the initial position and was spelled with a single letter, as here phonology and orthography contradicted each other. There was no equivalent incongruence in the target phonemes that were in the medial position of the word. Table 5.4 illustrates the design of the task. The target phoneme is printed in bold, and there

TABLE 5.4
The design of the orthographic constraints task and examples of items

Phoneme	Position	
	Initial	*Medial*
Short	Paksu **S**oaki (**SS**oaki) painaa.	Kaunis nei**L**e (nei**LL**e) laulaa.
	Nuori **L**aire (**LL**aire) nukkuu.	Vanha rai**S**i (rai**SS**i) lepää.
Long	Heitä **K**itri (**KK**itri) ulos.	Pieni muo**SS**i (muo**S**i) nauraa.
	Kisko **P**atso (**PP**atso) irti.	Vihreä tai**LL**e (tai**L**e) herää.

Note. The target phonemes are given in boldface type. The wrong choices are in parentheses.

is only one condition for which a geminate is appropriate. Each experimental word was five phonemes long and with each item the children had a choice between a five-letter word and a six-letter spelling. The reliability of the task was .78 (Cronbach's alpha).

There were two versions of the task with the items in different randomised orders to avoid order effects. In half of the items, the correct choice was on the right-hand side of the response sheet, in half of the items it was the left-hand side word. To make sure that children were paying attention to the right words of the sentence, the two choice words were printed in capital letters and in a bigger font size (20 pt) than the other words of the sentences (14 pt).

The children were given three practice items, in which the choice was between two words that only differed from each other by one phoneme (and one letter). Geminates were not used in the practice words, as this might have given the children some guidelines about how to perform the task. However, the words had to differ from each other both orthographically and phonologically. Therefore letters that are visually confusable were used, for example, N–M, R–P, and L–T.

Procedure.   The experimenter started by introducing herself and a toy cat she had with her. Then she handed out the response sheets and children heard the following instructions: The cat had found some new words nobody had ever heard before. The problem was that now someone should decide how to spell these words, but the cat, unlike all the children, did not know anything about reading or spelling of words. Therefore he needed help and was asking the children to tell how the words should be spelled. The experimenter would help here and read out and repeat every row of words that the children had on the sheet in front of them. The children's task was "to circle one of the words written with big letters, the one that looked more like a real word."

Any questions the children had were answered, and the experiment started with the three practice items. Between these, the experimenter went round the classroom making sure every child was circling only one word at a time, not more and not less, and in general knew what to do.

Results

Children received one point every time they chose a word with a geminate in it. This was thus a measure of how likely they were to choose a geminate in the various experimental conditions, and, by looking at the condition in question, it was possible to determine whether the choice was appropriate orthographically, phonologically, or both. The means of the scores in the different conditions are presented in Fig. 5.1. It is important to note that the only time that the choice of a geminate was appropriate was in the doublet/medial condition.

The scores showed that children in Year 1 chose initial geminates less often than they choose medial geminates, irrespective of whether the phoneme that they heard was short or long. Year 2 children chose initial geminates less often than did Year 1 children, and they were also unaffected by the length of the initial phoneme they heard. Year 3 children were even less likely to choose initial geminates than were the younger children. However, Year 1 children chose medial geminates on hearing a long phoneme only slightly more often than when hearing a short phoneme, and their scores were very close to the chance level of responding, which was 3. Year 2 children chose geminates more often for long medial phonemes and therefore seemed to pay more attention to the length of medial phonemes that they heard. The Year 3 children were almost always choosing a medial geminate when they heard a long medial phoneme and a single letter when they heard a short medial phoneme.

These results were confirmed by repeated-measures analyses of variance. Therefore we can say that, although first-year children were more likely to accept geminates in the medial position than in the initial position, whether they heard a long or a short phoneme in either position did not make a significant difference to their answers. Second-year children were

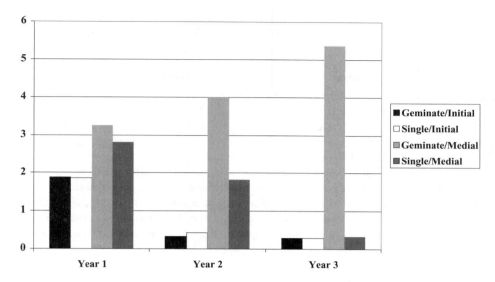

FIG. 5.1. The mean number of geminate choices in different conditions (out of six).

significantly more likely to choose geminates when they heard a long phoneme than when they heard a short one, but this was true only when the long phoneme was in the medial position. The second-year children rejected doublets in the initial position irrespective of whether they heard a long or a short phoneme. Hence there was no interaction between orthographic and phonological knowledge, in which children would have been more likely to accept initial geminates because they paid attention to the length of the phoneme involved. The third-year children were even more likely than the second-year children to choose medial doublets when they heard a long phoneme and less likely to do so when they heard a short phoneme. Also, they almost always rejected initial geminates. Consequently it appears that third-year children pay attention to the length of the phoneme and are able to represent it correctly in their spelling, as well as following the orthographic rule that word-initial geminates are illegal.

One-sample *t* tests were used to see whether children's scores were significantly different from chance. These showed that the second- and third-year children's scores were significantly different from chance in all conditions. However, the first-year children's scores in the medial conditions were not significantly different from chance, although they were in the correct direction. This further supports the suggestion that the first-year children did not pay attention to the length of the phonemes they heard. If they had taken length into account, they should have performed better than chance in the task.

Discussion

The results show us that first-year children already have some knowledge of the fact that words are not supposed to begin with a geminate. However, these young children do not pay attention to the length of phonemes yet, and therefore they are equally likely to choose a medial geminate whether they hear a long or a short phoneme. Second-year children have enough experience of reading and spelling to know that phoneme length matters, and they also know that consonant length is represented with geminates. Therefore they are significantly more likely than chance to choose medial geminates when they hear long phonemes and to choose single-letter spellings when they hear a short phoneme in the middle of the word. However, although the second-year children pay attention to length most of the time, they are far from perfect, because they choose geminates for long phonemes about two thirds of the time and a geminate for short phonemes about one third of the time. In contrast, third-year children are almost at ceiling in choosing a geminate for long word-medial phonemes and a single-letter spelling for short word-medial phonemes. Therefore we can say that, by the beginning of their third school year, children have mastered both the orthographic and phonological rules governing the use of geminates.

It is important to note that, when the length of phonemes is taken into account, second- and third-year children also follow the orthographic rule concerning initial geminates; they are significantly less likely than the first-year children to choose initial geminates. This indicates two issues. First, children's orthographic knowledge develops from the first year to the second year, and older children are overall less likely to choose initial geminates. Second-year children are not significantly different from third-year children in this skill, so it seems that this orthographic rule is mastered during the first year of schooling, although, as was pointed out earlier, school entrants already have some knowledge of it. Second, phonological information does not override orthographic information, and thus learning about the length of phonemes during the first school year does not increase children's tendency to choose initial geminates. In general, the condition under which orthographic knowledge and phonological knowledge conflict does not produce any additional problems to children in any age group.

STUDY 2

Study 1 showed us that children have access to orthographic knowledge from early on and also begin to learn about the phonological function of geminates during the first school year. This indicates that children are able to use multiple kinds of information to work out the rules governing the Finnish spelling system. Another possible source of information in spelling is morphology. Ravid and Gillis (in press) have suggested that a language that is morphologically complex predisposes children to use their morphological knowledge in spelling. They compared Hebrew (a morphologically complex language with a deep orthography) and Dutch (a morphologically simple language with a relatively transparent orthography) and found that children were using morphological information in spelling more extensively in Hebrew than in Dutch. Nunes, Bryant, and Bindman (1997) have showed that English children's morphological awareness gradually begins to affect their spelling as they develop more sophisticated spelling strategies and start to appreciate the morphological regularities of the English spelling system. Similar results have been demonstrated in Portuguese and Greek (Bryant, Nunes, & Aidinis, 1999; Rego, 1999). This work prompts us to ask whether morphological information might also be involved in Finnish children's spelling attempts in addition to the influences of orthographic and phonological information that we already saw. Because Finnish is morphologically complex, it should present numerous opportunities for the use of morphological information.

Investigation of children's geminate spelling provided a way of inspecting this question. Children were asked to do a spelling-to-dictation task that compared spelling of geminates such as *ss* and *ll* when these appear either in the word stem or in the case inflection. Other types of consonant clusters were included, too, to get a measure of children's spelling of consonants when it is necessary to consider only phoneme identity, not phoneme length. It was hypothesised that if children were able to take advantage of the morphological structure of the word, they would be likely to spell geminates and consonant clusters better when these are in case inflections than when they are in word stems. Several studies reviewed earlier suggest that speakers of highly inflected languages parse inflected words into stems and inflections (Caramazza et al., 1988; Niemi et al., 1994). If this is the case, children would be likely to find spelling of consonant sequences easier in inflections. Case inflections have low type frequency, as there are only 14 of them, whereas their token frequency is high, because they are repeatedly used both in spoken and written language. In contrast, word stems have high type frequency, as there are so many different stems, but their token frequency is low because of the low number of stems of any one type. Therefore case inflections lend themselves much better to frequency-based learning than stems do. Children were tested twice, halfway through and at the end of their first school year, to find out whether there is a developmental pattern to children's possible use of morphological information in spelling.

Method

Participants

41 children in a primary school in Espoo, Finland, were tested in December of their first school year and 4 months later in April, towards the end of their first school year. The mean age of the children at Time 1 was 7:4 years and at Time 2 7:8 years. There were 15 boys and 26 girls.

The Task and Procedure

The spelling tasks discussed here were given as part of a larger longitudinal study of children's spelling development and were administered in a single session to groups of about 10 children each.

The spelling task consisted of 24 nouns that varied according to two variables: position of phoneme cluster (word stem/case inflection) and type of phoneme cluster (geminate/mixed cluster). The design of the tasks is presented in Table 5.5. A different set of words at Times 1 and 2 had to be used as spelling development in Finnish is such a rapid process that I was concerned about possible ceiling effects at Time 2 if the same word set had been used. This time there was no conflict of different kinds of information, as in Study 1. Instead, the question was whether the morphological structure of the words would affect children's spelling performance. The reliability of the spelling task at Time 1 was .92 and at Time 2 it was .87 (Cronbach's alpha).

Results

Scoring

Children received one error point for each incorrect spelling of a cluster and each condition was scored separately. As a result, each child got four error scores. The means and standard deviations of these are presented in Tables 5.6 (Time 1) and 5.7 (Time 2).

TABLE 5.5
The Design and Some Examples of the Words in the Spelling Task

	Position	
Phoneme	Word Stem	Case Inflection
Geminate	reiSSu	kerhoSSa
	siveLLin	tunniLLa
Mixed Cluster	riSTeys	kuoroSTa
	keLTainen	hiekaLTa

TABLE 5.6
Means (and Standard Deviations) of the Children's Error Scores in the
Spelling Task at Time 1

	Geminate	Mixed Cluster
Word Stem	1.80 (2.08)	.20 (.51)
Case Inflection	1.88 (2.52)	.46 (.78)

Note. Maximum score 6 in each condition.

TABLE 5.7
Means (and Standard Deviations) of the Children's Error Scores in the
Spelling Task at Time 2

	Geminate	Mixed Cluster
Word Stem	2.56 (2.21)	.56 (.98)
Case Inflection	1.34 (1.98)	.61 (.92)

Note. Maximum score 6 in each condition.

We can see that it made no difference whether the geminates were in the word stems or inflections at Time 1. However, at Time 2, geminates produced much higher error rates in the stem condition than in the inflection condition, whereas there was no corresponding difference in the mixed-cluster condition. In general, geminates seem to cause more errors than mixed clusters whether they were in the stem or in the inflection condition. Children's most common error in geminate spelling was to leave out one letter of the geminate. Mixed clusters caused children to spell letters incorrectly and to miss out letters. These types of errors occurred both with the first and the second letter of the cluster.

Analyses

The means were inspected by a repeated-measures analysis of variance, in which the within-subjects variables were position (stem/inflection) and phoneme (geminate/mixed cluster).

Time 1.   At Time 1, there was a significant main effect of phoneme, $F(1,40) = 25.128$, $p < .001$, because children made more errors when they spelled geminates than when they spelled mixed clusters. This could be expected on the basis of earlier results and the difference is particularly dramatic at this early phase of spelling development, when many children largely ignore phoneme length instead of just making the occasional error with geminates. There was no significant main effect of position or any interactions, so it seems that children's spelling at the end of their first term at school is not facilitated by the morphological structure of the word at all.

Time 2. At Time 2, there were significant main effects of both position, $F(1,40) = 13.892$, $p = .001$, and phoneme, $F(1,40) = 20.811$, $p < .001$, and a significant interaction between these, $F(1,40) = 22.732$, $p < .001$. The interaction was inspected by paired-sample t tests with Bonferroni corrections, $\alpha = .013$. These indicated that, although geminates caused significantly more errors in stems than in case inflections, $t(40) = 5.294$, $p < .001$, it made no significant difference whether mixed clusters appeared in stems or in inflections. This suggests that the morphological structure of words influences children's spelling and supports the hypothesis about the nature of this facilitation; children are spelling geminates better in case inflections than in word stems. What is interesting is that facilitation occurs in only geminate spelling, which agrees with the idea that geminate spelling requires somewhat different processes than mixed-cluster spelling. Mixed clusters, which only require sound–letter decoding, are quite straightforward to deal with in a transparent orthography such as Finnish. Children's error rates in spelling these types of clusters are relatively low, and therefore there is not much room for improvement through other strategies. In contrast, geminate spelling requires children to pay attention to both phoneme identity and phoneme length. This is more demanding than just sound–letter decoding, and therefore additional strategies, such as cues provided by the morphological structure of the word, are more likely to aid geminate than mixed cluster spelling.

GENERAL DISCUSSION

These two experiments set out to examine how children's orthographic, phonological, and morphological knowledge affect their developing spelling skills. The particular aspect of spelling that was of interest was geminate spelling, which is interesting for two reasons. First, the phonological aspect of the geminate spelling rule in Finnish determines a relationship between phoneme length and geminates, as geminates are used to spell long phonemes. Second, the geminate spelling rule in Finnish is conditional on orthographic position, as word-initial geminates are not allowed even when a long consonant appears at the beginning of the word.

Study 1 showed that already first-year children at the beginning of the school year are less likely to accept geminates in the initial than in the medial position of the word. Therefore they demonstrate some knowledge of the orthographic rules of Finnish. However, first-year children are largely ignorant of the phonological function of geminates. Consequently they are equally likely to accept word-medial geminates and single-letter spellings whether they hear a short or a long consonant in the middle of the word.

Second-year children, on the other hand, reject word-initial geminates even more readily than do first-year children and are also able to pay attention to the length of the phoneme they hear. Because of this, they choose medial geminates predominantly when they hear a long phoneme and single-letter spellings on hearing a short phoneme. This tendency is even more pronounced in the third-year children's performance, which is close to ceiling in all conditions. The conflict of phonological and orthographic information in the word-initial geminate condition does not affect the second- or third-year children. Although they do know that long phonemes should be spelled with geminates, they do not accept initial geminates even when they hear a long phoneme in the initial position of the word.

Study 2 investigated whether children benefit from the morphological structure of the word when they spell geminates. The results showed that the morphological structure of the word makes no difference in children's performance halfway through the first school year, but 4 months later in the spring these same children were already spelling geminates significantly better in case inflections than word stems. Therefore the morphological structure of the word does facilitate spelling, although only of geminates. Mixed consonant clusters were spelled equally well whether they were in stems or inflections.

The results of Study 1 show that even children who have received no formal instruction in literacy skills can have some knowledge of what words are supposed to look like. Before entering school, children will have seen written words on many occasions and are able to notice some characteristics of words. Given the late age of school entry in Finland, children's opportunities for this type of informal learning are many. Although the first-year children still chose an initial geminate about one third of the time, the fact that they were better than expected by chance is nevertheless quite a sophisticated achievement, as the Finnish orthography does allow word-initial vowel doublets. Therefore children cannot merely reject all word-initial letter doublets. Rather, they have to have some idea of the doublets that are allowed and those that are not. As Pacton et al. (2001) pointed out, French first-year children are more likely to reject double vowels, which are not legal in French, than double consonants, which are. This agrees with the results obtained from Finnish children. One possible way for acquiring this kind of knowledge is through frequency-based learning, which has been suggested both by Pacton et al. (2001) and Cassar and Treiman (1997). However, more carefully controlled experiments would have to be conducted to test this hypothesis in Finnish children.

It is not surprising that the first-year children at the beginning of the school year in Study 1 were unaffected by phoneme length. Although this is a distinction that children of this age do not find particularly hard in spoken language, the concept of short and long phonemes seems to become explicit in reading and spelling only gradually during the first school year. This was confirmed by the results obtained from the older children. They were able to choose geminates appropriately according to whether they heard a long or a short phoneme, and this skill improved with increasing age.

An interesting finding was that, although second- and third-year children had conflicting orthographic and phonological information in the condition under which they heard a long initial phoneme, this did not affect their performance. Thus children take into account what they know about the orthographic constraints of their language when they begin to work out the phonological function of geminates. The independence of orthographic and phonological information is illustrated by the fact that, during the year when children learn to represent long phonemes with geminates, they reach near floor level in the number of chosen geminates in the initial position of the word. However, it is possible that when children start learning the phonological function of geminates, there is a time when they also accept initial geminates, phonological information overriding the orthographic rules about geminates. This phase might not have been caught in the study, as detecting it would require testing children longitudinally and probably also at shorter intervals than a whole year. Additional studies are thus required.

Therefore, during the first year of schooling, children's orthographic knowledge of geminates solidifies and they also start to appreciate the phonological function of geminates. This is also the time when, as shown by Study 2, children become sensitive to the morphological structure of words, specifically in geminate spelling. Halfway through the first school year, many children are still likely to decode words laboriously, using sound-to-letter mappings and failing to pay attention to geminates or the morphological structure of the words they are spelling. However, just a few months later we see significant facilitation of geminate spelling in case inflections. This suggests that geminate spelling requires different processing than other consonant clusters, which can be spelled more easily by use of the regular one-to-one mappings between phonemes and graphemes that Finnish provides. The spelling of geminates, on the other hand, is a more complicated process and is affected by children's ability to analyse the morphological structure of the word they are spelling.

Why do children spell geminates better in case inflections than in word stems? There are two potential explanations. One possibility is that these children, like the English children studied by Nunes et al. (1997), begin to notice the morphological function of inflections because of their developing morphological awareness skills. This would require further study that looks at whether children's performance in morphological awareness tasks would predict their ability to spell case inflections better than their spelling of stems.

It is also possible that the results are due to more implicit morphological processing, that is, the ability of speakers of highly inflected languages to parse words to stems and inflections. Additionally, as was already suggested, the high token frequency and low type frequency of case inflections make them salient learning targets, whereas stems possess the opposite frequency characteristics. Children's performance in the orthographic constraints test suggested that they are sensitive to the position of geminates in words from early on; this could in part explain their superior spelling of geminates in case inflections. The present results do not allow us to determine in more detail whether morphological parsing is involved, which would necessitate a degree of morphological knowledge, or whether children just pay attention to case inflections because they are frequent orthographic patterns.

However, independent of whether the difference between spelling geminates in stems and inflections is due to morphological awareness or to learning of orthographic spelling patterns, the phenomenon demonstrates that, as early as in the second half of their first school year, children begin to appreciate the phonological aspect of the geminate spelling rule. Moreover, children pay attention to spelling patterns in different parts of words and may possibly parse words to stems and inflections as they spell them. The finding that the difference between spelling stems and inflections emerges only for geminates, not mixed consonant clusters, suggests that it is possible for children to learn the consistent phoneme–grapheme mappings without the help provided by the morphological knowledge. Children learn these mappings before they start to appreciate the morphological structure of words. However, learning to spell geminates takes longer and improves with children's growing ability to pay attention to the morphological structure of words.

In summary, the studies we presented suggest that Finnish children can use multiple sources of information when they are learning to spell. Even before the start of formal teaching, first-year children know something about the legal position of geminates, and during their first year at school they begin to appreciate the phonological function of geminates, that is, that they represent phoneme length. During this process, children seem to be helped by the morphological structure of words, as they are more likely to spell geminates correctly in case inflections than in word stems. Consequently, the results do not support strict stage models of spelling, which postulate that children in different stages of spelling development use qualitatively different information in spelling and that, for example, orthographic information in spelling would be a sophisticated strategy that children in the semiphonetic or phonetic stage of spelling would not be able to consider. In contrast, children seem to be able to use different kinds of knowledge to their advantage in spelling from early on.

One issue that needs to be addressed is the way in which these results might be important for the study of spelling in general. As already pointed out, English is quite an exceptional orthography, thanks to its deep morphophonological structure. Despite this, most spelling models are based on English orthography. Studies of orthographies other than English are trying to extend the work done in English by answering two questions. First, they attempt to find out which processes affect spelling development independent of the structure of orthography. Second, they try to investigate how properties characteristic to particular orthographies affect the ways in which children learn to spell.

The two studies presented here contribute to the first question by showing that, just as English and French children are, young Finnish children seem to be sensitive to the legal position of letter doublets. Also, like English children, Finnish children take longer to learn the phonological than the orthographic aspect of the geminate spelling rule. With regard to the second question, the most obvious characteristics specific to Finnish is that it requires children to learn the difference between short and long phonemes in spelling. This suggests that learning about the phonological properties of words is not just about learning phoneme identity and how this is expressed in spelling, but other phonological aspects can be involved as well, depending on the language in question. Several other languages code for phoneme length; for example, in Hungarian this is done by use of accents on top of letters. Also, it is important to note that spelling development in Finnish is much more rapid than in English, and therefore children start appreciating the phonological role of geminates already during the second half of their first year at school, whereas English-speaking children learn it only in the sixth grade.

There are several ways in which we could improve the studies to investigate the conclusions even further. First, it would be important to test the children's reading and spelling levels to see how this relates to their ability to use orthographic and phonological knowledge in the orthographic constraints test. It would also be informative to do a version of the orthographic constraints test with vowel doublets as well as geminates as targets, as Finnish does allow vowel doublets in word-initial positions. This way we could find out whether children are merely using a general rule of the type "no doublets at the beginning of words allowed" or whether they are actually sensitive to the different properties of consonants and vowels. Third, we need to explore the reason for the facilitation we find in inflections as opposed to word stems. To investigate whether it is due to morphological processing, we should look at children's performance in morphological awareness tests. A way to find out if the facilitation is due to orthographic processing of the position of case inflections would be to ask children to spell words in which the case inflection is not the final inflection of the word. This way, we would gain more detailed information about the kinds of knowledge young children can use to their advantage when they are learning to spell.

ACKNOWLEDGEMENTS

I thank Peter Bryant for his comments on an earlier version of this chapter and many helpful discussions. I am also grateful to the teachers and pupils of the schools in Finland who participated in the studies presented here.

REFERENCES

Bryant, P. E., Nunes, T., & Aidinis, A. (1999). Different morphemes, same spelling problems: Cross-linguistic developmental studies. In M. Harris & G. Hatano (Eds.), *Learning to read and write: A cross-linguistic perspective* (pp. 112–133). Cambridge, UK: Cambridge University Press.

Caramazza, A., Laudana, A., & Romani, C. (1988). Lexical access and inflectional morphology. *Cognition, 28,* 297–332.

Carney, E. (1994). *A survey of English spelling.* London: Routledge.

Cassar, M., & Treiman, R. (1997). The beginnings of orthographic knowledge: Children's knowledge of double letters in words. *Journal of Educational Psychology, 89,* 631–644.

Ehri, L. (1992). Review and commentary: Stages of spelling development. In S. Templeton & D. Bear (Eds.), *Development of orthographic knowledge and the foundations of literacy: A memorial Festschrift for Edmund H. Henderson* (pp. 307–332). Hillsdale, NJ: Lawrence Erlbaum Associates.

Frith, U. (1985). Beneath the surface of developmental dyslexia. In K. Patterson, M. Coltheart and J. Marshall (Eds.), *Surface dyslexia.* Hove, UK: Lawrence Erlbaum Associates.

Laaksonen, K., & Lieko, A. (1998). *Suomen kielen äänne- ja muoto-oppi* [The phonology and structure of the Finnish language]. Helsinki: Finn Lectura.

Lehtonen, J. (1970). *Aspects of quantity in standard Finnish*. Studia Philologica Jyväskyläensia, 6. University of Jyväskylä.

Lyytinen, H., Leinonen, S., Nikula, M., Aro, M., & Leiwo, M. (1995). In search of the core features of dyslexia: Observations concerning dyslexia in the highly orthographically regular Finnish language. In V. Berninger (Ed.), *The varieties of orthographic knowledge II: Relationships to phonology, reading, and writing* (pp. 177–204). Dordrecht, the Netherlands: Kluwer Academic.

Niemi, J., & Laine, M. (1995). Suomen kielen sanojen mentaalisen käsittelyn malli [A mental model for the processing of Finnish words]. *Suomen Logopedis-foniatrinen aikakauslehti, 14,* 65–71.

Niemi, J., Laine, M., & Tuominen, J. (1994). Cognitive morphology in Finnish. Foundations of a new model. *Language and Cognitive Processes, 9,* 423–446.

Nunes, T., Bryant, P., & Bindman, M. (1997). Morphological spelling strategies: Developmental stages and processes. *Developmental Psychology, 4*: 637–649.

Pacton, S., Perruchet, P., Fayol, M., & Cleeremans, A. (2001). Implicit learning out of the lab: The case of orthographic regularities. *Journal of Experimental Psychology: General, 130,* 401–426.

Ravid, D., & Gillis, S. (in press). Teachers' perception of spelling patterns and children's spelling errors: A cross-linguistic perspective. In M. Neef, A. Neijt, & R. Sproat (Eds.), *Consistency in writing systems*. Tübingen, Germany: Niemeyer Verlag.

Rego, L. (1999). Phonological awareness, syntactic awareness and learning to read and spell in Brazilian Portuguese. In M. Harris & G. Hatano (Eds.), *Learning to read and write: A cross-linguistic perspective* (pp. 71–88). Cambridge, UK: Cambridge University Press.

Treiman, R. (1993). *Beginning to spell*. New York: Oxford University Press.

6

Orthography and Literacy in French

Jean-Pierre Jaffré
CNRS Villejuif, France
Université Blaise-Pascal CNRS, Paris

Michel Fayol
CNRS and Université Clermont-Ferrand, France
Université Blaise-Pascal CNRS, Paris

As a starting point, this chapter presents a brief description of the early history of the French writing system. Subsequently the linguistic aspects of French orthography are discussed. Studies of acquisition of literary skills by French children indicate that they may not go through a logographic stage when they learn to read but rather they latch on to the phonological principles as a starting point. Even though the French language is more regular than English as far as orthography is concerned, this statement is only partially true. French is more consistent than English when one proceeds from spelling to phonology; it is, however, less consistent when one proceeds from phonology to spelling. In addition, French morphology is more opaque when compared with that of English, which makes French difficult to master. This is so because there are many graphemes that have no phonological counterparts. One source of difficulty for poor readers is inflectional morphology rules because there is a considerable amount of difference between written and spoken forms of French. The unlikely event that any orthographic reforms would even be envisaged in France has given rise to a paradoxical situation: The French have great difficulty in learning to master their orthography, but they are extremely fond of it.

Studies of literacy have so far paid little attention to French orthography. This neglect is particularly regrettable, because the French system of orthography, although like many others is alphabetic, also is highly original in many respects.

French is a Romance language, and, as such, it has inherited a number of features from the original Latin, in the same way as Italian, Portuguese, and Rumanian have. Unlike these closely related languages, however, French started off by being a language that was spoken in the north of Europe by Germanic settlers. A few centuries later, when the system of orthography was developing, this Germanic influence had some important consequences that have left their mark right up to the present day: The Germanic period resulted in the erosion of the final letters of words that convey essential grammatical information.

Romance languages are inflectional languages in which the words generally have a lexical component combined with a grammatical one. This morphological specificity focuses in these languages on the structure of the verbs. In the imperfect indicative singular, for example, the Italian verb *partire* [to leave] has three separate forms (*partivo, partivi, partiva*) and the corresponding Portuguese and Spanish verbs (*partir*) have two (*partía, partías*); whereas in French, the corresponding verb has only one form (/partɛ/). The morphology of the nouns can be seen to have followed a similar pattern. In Spanish, for example, the singular case of nouns differs from the plural (*griego, griegos* [Greek, Greeks] (as it does in Portuguese (*grego, gregos*) and Italian (*greco, greci*), whereas in French, the singular and plural of many nouns are homophones (/grɛk/, *grec, grecs*). This homophony, which results largely from a process of morphological erosion, has led some authors to state that the French language is the least Latinate of all the Romance languages (Posner, 1996, p. 245).

THE THEORETICAL BACKGROUND

In many respects, the orthography of French nevertheless resembles many other orthographies, especially those involving the use of an alphabet. To present this particular theoretical point, we assume that, strictly speaking, all systems of writing are closely related to the corresponding spoken language. This relationship can be expressed in terms of two main principles, which we have called the *phonographic* and *semiographic* principles (Jaffré, 2003).

The phonographic principle is fundamental to the structure of writing systems. It makes it possible for correspondences to be set up between graphic units, or graphemes, and phonemes, or syllables. Phonography is in fact the key to writing systems, because it constitutes the "grammar" on which they are based. Without phonography, graphic systems would not be able to function properly. This is why the emergence of phonography, which started when the Sumerian rebus developed around 3000 B.C.E., was of such importance to the future development of writing systems. It also explains why so much attention has been paid in studies on the acquisition of reading and writing to the issue of phonological awareness. In this connection, it can be noted incidentally that some convergence occurs between morphogenesis and ontogenesis, because young children's ability to learn how to read and write depends on their becoming aware of the recurrent nature of the phonographic relationships involved (Read, 1986; Jaffré, 2000).

The semiographic principle is the name given to the set of processes used in a writing system to directly or indirectly represent the significant forms (the lexemes and morphemes) of a language. Some writing systems, especially the first ones to emerge, opted for a nonphonographic type of representation, such as that used in the initial phases in the development of the Sumerian system. This option eventually became too awkward to handle because of the large number of signs[1] of which each language is composed. Very young children attempting to copy this process by using a nonphonographic strategy of this kind quickly realize what an impossible task this is to tackle (Bousquet, Cogis, Ducard, Massonnet, & Jaffré, 1999). Although linguistic meaning is the *raison d'être* of all writing systems, it does not provide all writing systems with a proper basis for acquiring it; it can do so indirectly, however, by serving as a complement to the phonographic basis.

There have been many examples of this semiographic pattern throughout the history of writing systems, including the Sumerian and ancient Egyptian determinatives, which stand for classes of words or categories (such as gender or number). In the Egyptian hieroglyphs, for example, these signs served to differentiate between man and woman, masculine and feminine, or wood and iron. Some features of the Chinese writing system also function in a fairly

---

[1] The item *sign* should be taken here to mean "significant form," that is, approximately a *word*.

similar way. The Chinese characters are another example of a system based on twofold graphic principles because approximately 90% of these characters consist of two components. First there is a *phonetic* component, which corresponds to the syllabic structure of the language, and then there is the *radical*, which makes for better graphic legibility. The radical makes it possible to distinguish between potential homophones and thus to avoid ambiguity. As we will see, the orthography of French also involves the use of a similar process, as the semiographic principle is far from playing a minor role, although it did not contribute to the actual fundamentals of the writing system. The semiographic principle can therefore be said to be the superstructure of a system, the foundations of which is phonography (Hannas, 1997).

THE ORTHOGRAPHY OF FRENCH: SOME LINGUISTIC ASPECTS

Like most other orthographies, the French system consists of a repertory of graphemes that can serve various functions. Phonograms are graphic units that correspond to phonemes (or syllables in other writing systems). The phonograms are a necessary component of semiograms, but they are not the only component. Some of them can also play a morphological role (as does the *ai* in *(il) savait* [he knew]), which is why they have sometimes been called morphonograms. They differ, however, from real morphograms, which serve specifically morphological purposes (as in the case of the *t* in *(il) savait*). In addition, many letters are used in French for logographic purposes, in a more random way, no doubt, to distinguish between homophonic sounds (/sã/ *sang* [blood] vs. /sã/ *cent* [a hundred]).

A statistical analysis of the graphemes occurring in French (Catach, 1980) has shown that most of the letters of the alphabet play a phonographic role (e.g., *film* [film], *demain* [tomorrow], etc.). In fact, something like 85% of all the graphemes in French are phonograms. A much smaller proportion of the letters—about 4%—have grammatical and lexical functions (*grand* [tall], *les femmes* [women]. Last, there is a nonnegligible group of letters (amounting to about 13% of all the letters) that are simply etymological and historical traces devoid of any real linguistic function ("s" in *néanmoins* [nevertheless], *frais* [cold], etc.).

Phonography in French

The phonography of French is characterized by a high rate of polyvalence, as there are only about 30 phonemes corresponding to as many as 130 phonograms. It is worth noting, however, that the polyvalence is greater on the graphic production side (which corresponds to phonography in the strictest sense of the term) than on the side of reading (which corresponds to graphophony), in which relationships occur more regularly. The vocalic area is especially ambiguous. The phoneme /e/, for example, can be represented by *é* (*été* [summer], *e* (*manger* [to eat]); the phoneme /ɛ̃/, by "in" (*fin* [thin], *ain* (*main* [hand]), or *ein* (*rein* [kidney]); the phoneme /ã/ by *an* or *en* (*enfant* / [child]), and so on. The phonographic correspondences are not so consistent, although they tend to be more so in the case of consonants than in that of vowels. Some consonants (such as *p*, *b*, and *d*) are fairly regular, whereas others are more variable. This is so in the case of /ʒ/, for example, which corresponds to *j* in only 49% of the occurrences, whereas *g* and *ge* are used to serve the other distributions of this consonant. There is generally more competition in the case of the vowels. Some phonograms, such as *u*, *ou*, and *on*, are quite regular, but there are usually several phonographic options for processing a single phoneme. One has to choose, for example, between *an* (44%) and *en* (47%) to represent /ã/, among *in* (45%), *ain* (21%), or *en* (23%) to represent /ɛ̃/; and among *o* (75%), *au* (21%), and even *eau* (3%) to represent /o/. Generally speaking, the conventions pertaining to the writing of vowels in French are therefore more complex than those relating to consonants. On the whole, 68% of the vowels are regular in the phonographic sense of the term, compared with 99% of the consonants occurring in the initial position (Peereman & Content, 1999).

However, to be of any value, a quantitative approach to phonograms will have to take the frequency with which the words occur into account. The trigram *eau*, for example, is a fairly infrequent phonogram, and yet the words in which it occurs (such as *beau* [beautiful] and *eau* [water]) are quite frequent. This logographic frequency can obviously provide some solutions to the problems of polyvalence that arise. It plays an important role because it influences the users' cognitive representations (Bybee & Hopper, 2001). Despite this fact, and because orthography has to comply with the norms and is not allowed to resort to the use of variants, any graphic polyvalence encountered will require relatively complex cognitive calculations. This is what has been found to occur in French when learners are faced with ambiguities that are due to polyvalence, which they attempt to solve by means of the logographic aspects. In this case, they will tend to make use of a strategy based on the similarity between *ain* in *main* [hand] and the *in* in *matin* [morning].

The orthography of French is generally held to be particularly irregular, especially at the phonographic level. The level of irregularity of monosyllables has been said to be greater than 50%, compared with only 5% at the orthophonographic level (Ziegler, 1998, p. 85). However, one cannot deny the fact that there nevertheless exists some phonographic consistency in French. Although in this respect the orthography of French is at least apparently more complex than that of Spanish, Italian, or German, which are often said to be more transparent, it is at least more regular than that of English, in which there are as many as 1,120 graphemes corresponding to only 40 phonemes, which works out to 28 graphemes per phoneme on the average (Nyikos, 1988[2]). Appearances can sometimes be somewhat deceptive, however.

As we saw earlier, lexical frequency can sometimes help out when the phonographic complexity causes problems. However, many other difficulties arise, owing mainly to the fact that the orthography of French differs in many respects from its European counterparts. In particular, it contains a large number of nonphonographic graphemes (morphograms and logographic letters) that nevertheless play grammatical and lexical roles, respectively. Their recurrence causes many errors in children, of course, but it also does so even in experienced adult writers (Fayol, Largy, & Lemaire, 1994; Jaffré, 2002). The specificities of French orthography are therefore outlined here, focusing on what we have called the semiographic aspects (see preceding discussion).

Semiography in French

Phonograms serve to form the written signs called semiograms. The process of construction involved can result from a phonographic reanalysis that yields relatively transparent orthographies, as in the case of Spanish and Italian, for example, or in that of the Japanese *kana*. In French, many written words come under this heading, although some distributional factors also come into play. A word such as *principe* [principle] results, for example, from a more or less regular combination between a series of phonograms to which some specific additional rules have been applied: the presence of the digram *in*, the position of *c* before *i*, the ending *e*, and so forth. All French speakers who have acquired a little experience in using the orthography are obviously familiar with these characteristics.

The process of semiographic analysis involved in phonography is one of the main sources from which writing systems stem. During this process, phonograms acquire a new status

---

[2] Cited by Coulmas (2003, p. 184).

in keeping with the mixedness of orthography. The trigram *eau*, which corresponds to the phoneme /o/, is to be found in several words, in which its status is that of a phonogram (*bateau* [boat], *chapeau* [hat], *château* [castle], *seau* [bucket], etc.). From the morphological point of view, however, each of these words can be viewed differently, as belonging to a particular series (*bateau*, *batelier* [boat, boatman], *chapeau*, *chapelier* [hat, hatter], etc.), which justifies the use of the *e* in *eau* and shows how the trigram *eau* has a morphological role to play. Another similar example is that of the phonogram *ai*, which is often used to form the imperfect tense of verbs (*prenait* [took], *donnait* [gave], etc.).

Morphonograms of this kind occur in most systems of orthography. To quote just one example, the vowels and consonants of the Arabic writing system tend to have specific semiographic (lexical vs. grammatical) functions, whereas in Japanese, the *kana* syllabary is specialized rather in the notation of grammatical units.

It might be tempting to keep to this relatively mechanistic method of accounting for writing systems. In the alphabetical sphere at least, some systems are quite amenable to descriptions of this kind, although there is more to them than mechanistic accounts would suggest. In many cases, however, the presence of nonphonographic components has resulted in orthographies that are less transparent, such as those which have developed in English and French. It is almost as if the semiographic requirements created the need for some more specific components. In the alphabetic writing systems, leaving aside those of the other kind (Chinese, Japanese, etc.), the rules of some board games seem to imply that a letter has to be either a vowel or a consonant. If this were true, however, the sequences of letters forming words would by definition have a phonographic correspondence. Now there are many letters that act as graphemes without being phonograms.

In French, for example, some letters serve to make distinctions between homophones. This does not mean that all homophones are heterographs. One needs only leaf through a French dictionary to be able to see that the homophones that are homographs (*bassin* [pond], *bassin* [bowl]; *son* [his or her], *son* [sound]) are more numerous than the homophones that are heterographs (*sain* [sane], *saint* [saint]): words of the latter kind occur more frequently, however. Most alphabetical orthographies, especially in English, in which the letters of the alphabet often serve logographic purposes, follow a similar pattern. In fact, there are whole dictionaries of heterographic homophones.[3]

On the grammatical side of French orthography, however, contrary to what happens in English,[4] the morphograms predominate in the context of both verbs (*il prend* [*he takes*], *il allait* [*he went*], *donner*] [*to give*], etc.) and nouns (*chevaux* [*horses*], *routes* [*roads*], etc.). This difference has had some noteworthy effects as far as literacy is concerned. Contrary to obtaining lexical skills, which are largely acquired as a function of the subject's knowledge of the world, the acquisition of grammatical skills requires abstract thinking about the way a language works and the corresponding graphic options available. This specific metalinguistic activity seems to be more complex than the mere processing of lexical representations. In any case, it is at this very level that the largest number of problems are encountered by those attempting to master the orthography of the French language.

It should be pointed out here that morphograms in French do not follow a homogeneous pattern. There are many factors liable to either facilitate or complicate their mental processing. Some morphograms have become integrated into a distributional context, for example, as in the case of the *x* in *aux* (*chevaux* [*horses*]) or the *t* in *ait* ([il] *parlait* [(*he*) *talked*]). In the first case, the regularity of the graphic co-occurrence, ritualized by conventional schoolteaching methods

---

[3] See, for example, *English Guides, 6: Homophones*. Collins Cobuild, London: Harper Collins Publishers 1995.

[4] In English, grammatical morphonograms are the rule: The correspondences with speech are always transparent in the case of a past irregular verb (*took*) as well as that of a plural noun (*cats*).

whereby the three letters are always written together, creates a link between the morphogram x and the morphonogram *au*, resulting in a composite but highly stable unit. It looks almost as if the x took advantage of the phonographic reason for the *au*–/o/, reinforced by the consistency of the distribution of *aux* forming the plural of words ending in /o/. This convergence may at least explain why children manage to learn these particular rules at quite an early age.

It sometimes happens, however, that some graphic distributions compete with others and thus interfere with the phonographic information. Some morphonograms, such as *ai*, can be followed in French by either *s* (*je savais* [*I knew*]), *t* (*il savait* [*he knew*]), or *ent* (*ils savaient* [*they knew*]). This orthographic neighborhood, the complexity of which is naturally increased by the homophony, sets up a competition between the cues to be processed that can be quite problematic. The addition of pronouns can of course help to lessen the ambiguity, but, as we will subsequently see when we come to discuss the chains of agreement, the inconsistent morphological patterns and the redundancy they entail give rise to problems that are not at all easy to solve.

There is more still to be said, however, about the difficulties involved in learning the orthography of French. Apart from the morphonograms we have mentioned, which are complex but provide phonographic information, there is another, more autonomous kind of morphographic unit, called the morphogram. One example is the final, silent *s*. This typical mark of agreement in the number of nouns and adjectives is one of the main points on which mistakes are made not only by children but also by adults, who also tend to omit the *s*. Although it is associated at quite an early age with the idea of plurality, this morphogram also carries strong metamorphological connotations, as commonly described by learners: "You have to put an *s* on the end because there are several of them." In French, there are practically no other letters that work this way, except perhaps for the feminine ending *e* (*amie* [*girlfriend*]), *élue* [*elected*]), but in this case the morphographic function of the letter is less transparent because it also occurs at the end of some masculine nouns (*arbre* [*tree*], *centre* [*center*], *costume* [*costume*], *musée* [*museum*], etc.).

On the other hand, mastering the use of the *s* requires knowledge of the pattern of grammatical homophony, the main morphographic obstacle that has to be overcome in French. Unlike the *x* which, as we previously saw, benefits from the presence of the phonographic helper *au*–/o/, the *s* is the only graphic sign used to mark the plural of most words. The *s* alone indicates the number of *routes* [roads], *causes* [causes], and so forth. It can be backed up, of course by the redundancy resulting from the laws of graphic agreement, which lend the would-be user a helping hand: *les routes verglacées* [icy roads], *les causes perdues* [lost causes]. However, the fact of belonging to a morphosyntactical chain can work both ways. The presence of a morphonogram (*les* vs. *le* or *la*) certainly provides an indirect phonographic cue, the proximity of which helps to keep the idea of plurality in the user's working memory. On the other hand, the redundancy of the graphic marks (morphonograms and morphograms) also makes the presence of some of them less indispensable, especially when the user is writing them.

Last but not least, we come to what must be the be-all and end-all of all the morphographic difficulties arising in French. Up to this point, it has been possible to talk about the existence of links, however indirect, between morphography and phonography. Even in the most complex case of close homophony, whether it is a question of number (*le jour* vs. *les jours* [the day vs. the days]) or a question of verb endings (*je savais* vs. *il savait* [I knew vs. he knew]), it is often possible to use co-occurring morphemes (determinants or pronouns), which can be extremely helpful although they do not always provide the whole solution. In any case, we have been dealing with entities that occupy a morphosyntactical space: The pattern of distribution of the most problematic cases is complementary to that of the phonographic cues available. This is no longer what occurs with the homophony that involves the verbs ending in /e/, especially when an opposition occurs between the past participle and the infinitive. Here the modal distinction focuses on a single graphic mark (*donner* vs. *donné* [to give vs. given]) for which there are no morphosyntactic clues available. It seems likely that learning to decipher situations of this kind may involve making analogies with paradigms in which phonographically distinct forms (*prendre* vs. *pris* [to take vs. taken]) carry out similar modal functions. Here we have yet another example of how the morphography—the most independent aspect of the French writing system, that is, that which has seemingly turned its back on the phonographic origins—actually makes use of the phonography, although in this case it does so rather indirectly.

On the semiographic side, the orthography of French involves the use of a whole range of units with widely different statuses. The nature of the relationships between these units and the phonography can also serve to show what a high degree of orthographic complexity the French language involves. There are a number of conclusions to be drawn here from the psycholinguistic point of view, especially as regards the difficulty of learning the French system of orthography. From the linguistic point of view, the picture we have just drawn of the French orthography can usefully serve to show the limits of the theories suggesting that orthography is an autonomous entity. Our description of the written language tends to show that, as it is an entity that occupies a two-dimensional space because of the specific requirements that have to be satisfied, it is not just a system of notation attempting to slavishly copy the spoken language. At the same time, as Vachek (1945/1949) so aptly noted, although the degree of correspondence between the spoken and written forms of a language are bound to vary considerably from one linguistic community to another, an orthography and the corresponding written norms have nothing to gain by neglecting the link with the spoken norms. In this respect, the morphography of French provides a highly original illustration of this duality.

Semiography and History

The fact that the semiography of French is specific and complex is due to its history, which, as we mentioned at the beginning, sets it apart from all the other Romance languages. Without replacing the newly emerging French language, the Germanic tongue spoken by the Franks before the 9th century profoundly affected its phonology (Marchello-Nizia, 1999). In particular, the system of accentuation used by these communities led to a weakening of the final vowels, which was to have important effects at a later stage on the verbal paradigms (Posner, 1996, p. 45). To see what this involved, one need look at only the conjugation of the verb *partir* [*to leave*] in French and compare it with its Italian and Spanish equivalents (see table). In the latter two languages, the inflections are denoted by phonograms, and the information is so transparent that, in these two languages, there is no need to add the corresponding pronouns.

French	Italian	Spanish
je pars	parto	parto
tu pars	parti	partes
il part	parte	parte
ils partent	partono	parten
nous partons	partiamo	partimos
vous partez	partite	partís

In French, on the contrary, there obviously exists a high level of homophony among the various oral forms: In the present indicative, this verb is conjugated in fact with only four different forms: /paR/ (*pars, part*), /paRt/ (*partent*), /paRtⁿ/ (*partons*), and /paRte/ (partez). This why personal pronouns were gradually added in the 15th century to make up for the lack of information provided by the verbs, although the marks *e*, *s*, and *ent*, which are remnants of the former Latin morphology, were not removed. What is so paradoxical about this situation is the fact that we managed to play on both fronts at the same time, "having our cake and eating it too," so to speak, using a palliative linguistic strategy (adding the pronouns) while still keeping the original etymological components. One might have expected the morphology of the written system to make do with the former solution, as the spoken system has done.

The outcome might easily have been simpler if Latin had not left such strong, long-lasting imprints on French culture. During a decisive period for the development of French orthography (between the 14th and 17th centuries), the Latin clerks and the master printers both gave priority to the etymological written forms of which the morphographic material would subsequently mainly consist, to the detriment of an orthography of a more transparent kind.

It should be added at this point that the French system of orthography was one of the first in Western Europe to become standardized, as centralized decision making was already being carried out at quite an early stage in the country's history. This system thus acquired a stability that has been hard to shake ever since, despite the considerable linguistic changes that have occurred. As a result of the large-scale educational projects introduced in the 19th century, the conventional orthography was taught in the schools without any attempt being made to render it more accessible to the new users of the written language. French children all over the country simply had to learn to master a system of orthography designed by and for an elite section of the population, and to achieve this aim and overcome the problems involved, they were simply given an extremely thorough grounding in the grammatical rules of French (Chervel, 1977). This approach to orthography obviously left its mark on the minds of the users themselves. Accustomed, as they had become, to the historically marked forms, many people were reluctant to accept any changes; they actually viewed the idea of introducing changes as an insult to the language instead of realizing that an attempt was being made to provide a linguistic tool that was more in keeping with the needs of the times.

A quick look at the morphogenesis of French orthography, that is, at the way in which it has developed over the centuries, should suffice to convince us, however, that this overattachment to the conventional forms is quite unjustifiable. For those who attempt to learn or use it, the French system of orthography poses a more difficult set of problems than any other system. This is mainly because the morphology departs greatly from the Latin more than other Romance languages do and is actually less transparent. We have already mentioned how the Germanic influence led to the loss of the accentuated final vowels, thus setting the French writing system apart from that of the other Romance languages (Posner, 1996, p. 69). The process of linguistic change that subsequently occurred reduced the Latin words to their initial accentuated syllables and changed the quality of nearly all the remaining phonemes (Perret, 1998, p. 85). This explains in particular the alternating pattern shown by irregular verb forms such as *je peux* versus *nous pouvons* [I can versus we can].

This was the background against which the French system of orthography gradually developed from the period known as Middle French (12th–15th centuries) onward. During several centuries, two main conflicting tendencies could be observed. Those supporting the first, more phonological tendency wanted the writing system to resemble the spoken word as closely as possible, whereas those on the other side favored etymological, historical, morphological, and semantic solutions, attaching particular importance to the need to be able to distinguish between homophonic monosyllables. This analytical approach to the language, the effects of which have remained perceptible up to the present day, was constantly moving the orthography of French in the opposite direction from its Italian and Spanish cousins (Catach, 2001, p. 79).

This battle over orthography[5] between the Ancients and the Moderns led in fact to some important changes. The graphic forms used in the works published by the great authors of the Renaissance period look more modern to us now than those published in the 16th century. This tendency was reversed before long, however, by the upsurge of the etymological approach encouraged by the printers, who wanted to standardize the orthography. The traditional or *ancient* orthography was in fact an extraordinarily complex invention of scholars who did all they could to make the written language resemble the Latin ideal as closely as possible, based on the belief that this procedure would make the language easier to read. In the *Cahiers de Mézeray* (1673), Bossuet made the following comment, for example: "We do not read letter by letter; but the whole pattern of the word makes its impression on the eyes and on the mind, so that if this pattern suddenly changes considerably, the words lose the features which make them recognizable to the sight and the eyes are no longer satisfied."

The so-called new orthography, that of Du Bellay, Ronsard, and Marot, for example, had come to stay, at least for some time. Some of the innovations they proposed during the 16th century, such as changes in the accentuation (*pres > pré*), the abolition of components, such as diphthongs (*dangier > danger*), diacritical internal consonants and the final diacritical *z* (*libertez > libertés*), and so forth, were readily adopted. However, the old orthography won many points as well, as regards the mute final *x* (*heureux* [happy]), the mute final *z* in verbs (*vous chantez* [you sing]), the double consonants (*allumer* [to light]), and so forth.

This in any case was the situation from the 17th century onward, when the history of the French orthographic system joined forces with that of the Académie Française and its *Dictionnaire*. In 1694, the first edition was written with the traditional orthography, and this option has never been really seriously questioned ever since that time (Pellat, 2003). Some minor amendments have been introduced of course, especially in the 1740 edition, which contributed decisively to the emergence of the present-day French orthography. After a relatively active period of innovation, the academicians gradually made do with attempting to conserve the current usage, not to say lapsing into conservatism. A hesitant approach and a good helping of half-measures might well sum up the work that went into the ninth and latest edition of the *Dictionnaire*, which started to be published at the end of the 20th century.

THE ORTHOGRAPHY OF FRENCH: THE PSYCHOLINGUISTIC ASPECTS

The orthography of French belongs to the alphabetic sphere, and the underlying secret to the way it works is therefore based on the making of associations between phonemes and graphemes. As the result of specific historical conditions (such as the emergence of many homophones and the influence of a predominantly Latin culture) along with the early advent of centralized linguistic policies, the orthography that came into being was not very transparent, however. The effects of this duality (the presence of a phonographic dimension plus an important etymological dimension) are still perceptible in present-day psycholinguistic studies on the French system of orthography.

As we have seen, the orthography of French is not at all transparent. The number of letters available is much smaller than the number of phonemes to be transcribed, and this has resulted in many bigrams and even trigrams. On the other hand, many of the letters are devoid of any phonographic function and have been given a morphographic role to play. This orthography nevertheless constitutes a system that relies heavily (although not exclusively: see "The Orthography of French: Some Linguistic Aspects," in this chapter, and also Martinet, 2001) on the alphabetical principle.

---

[5] Catach (1963) coined the expression *la bataille de l'orthographe*.

The Twofold Pathway

To make comparisons with other more regular (e.g., the German, Spanish, and Portuguese) and less regular (e.g., the English) orthographic systems and how they are learned we adopted the model developed by Frith (1985) as a descriptive framework. This model involves three developmental phases, namely the logographic, phonographic and orthographic phases, depending on the main information-processing strategy used by learners. This model was inspired by neuropsychological data that show that double dissociations occur in patients with language impairments.

The first type of disorder can be illustrated an examination of the case of an English-speaking patient, P. R. (Shallice, 1981), who was able to write and spell more than 90% of the regular words (such as *potato*) and irregular words (such as *symbol*) that were dictated to him, as long as they were words with which he was familiar. His performances were very poor, however (<20%), when he was asked to transcribe pseudowords. This pattern of performance corresponds to a condition known as phonological dysgraphia, which specifically affects the processes involved in the transcoding of sequences of phonemes into sequences of graphemes.

That same year, Beauvois and Dérouesné (1981) reported the case of a French-speaking patient, R. G., who was able to produce a plausible transcription of 99% of the pseudowords dictated to him, but who had difficulty in writing words he knew. His performances varied depending on the regularity of the correspondences between the phonemes and the graphemes. He obtained a high score (>90%) on regular words such as *mur* [wall] and *chou* [cabbage], but much lower scores when the phonemes involved transcriptional ambiguities such as /o/ → *o, au, eau* and /f/ → *f, ph*. This pattern of performance corresponds to what is known as surface dysgraphia, which is a variably severe condition affecting the ability to write some words although the ability to transcribe other words in which regular correspondences between phonemes and graphemes occur in French remains intact (for example, /o/ is more frequently rendered by *o* in French than by *eau*).

The existence of these two patterns of impairment has led neuropsychologists to suggest that the processing of written alphabetical language may involve two different processes, regardless of whether they are to be read or written. On the one hand, there is the direct (or lexical) pathway, whereby the items required are obtained directly from a sort of orthographic repertory in which regular and irregular words are stored. The items taking the other, more indirect, so-called assembly pathway, undergo a process of conversion from phonemes into graphemes (or vice versa, depending on whether they are to be read or written). Each of these two pathways might require different processes when people are learning how to master the appropriate mode of written language processing.

The Logographic Phase

Frith has defined the logographic phase as being based on direct associations involving no phonological mediation between a concrete visual pattern (a logo) and a meaning. The recognition of these patterns might be based on the use of various cues. For example, the colors green and white are an indispensable part of the logo associated with *Perrier* (the French brand of mineral water). The cues can also include salient letters or groups of letters. Alphabetical information is used in a semantico–picturorial system (in which a visual pattern is associated with a meaning), which in the second place relates the picture of a word to an oral form. In the early stages of learning, at least, no rules or regularities seem to be used to shift from the written to the oral form or vice versa.

As far as learning how to read in English is concerned, the logographic phase can lead to the development of an early repertory consisting of anything from 10 to 100 words (Seymour & Elder, 1986). In French, the existence of a repertory of this kind has been questioned (Rieben

& Saada-Robert, 1997; Sprenger-Charolles & Bonnet, 1996) because French children have to learn a more regular orthographic system than do English children. In addition, because French children are exposed to teaching methods that focus heavily on the correspondences between phonemes and graphemes, they do not seem to acquire these logographic processing abilities.

The results of studies on the first stages in learning to produce written French have not provided any further proof that a logographic phase actually occurs. Ferreiro and Teberosky (1988) and Freinet (1975) have reported that children begin by separating iconic productions from those of other kinds and make negative statements about written words: for example, "That's not a drawing." A graphic object is then transformed into a series of marks that are not yet very systematic but that make it at least partly interpretable. Children then begin to look actively for qualitative variations in the nature, quantity, and positions of the letters. Last, they attempt to perform a more systematic type of coding that enables them to read and understand alphabetic writing and the underlying principles. This understanding is based on the categorization of letters and on their arrangement within words (Fijalkow & Fijalkow, 1991; Gombert & Fayol, 1992).

Some authors have also addressed the question as to how children learn to write their own first name and have shown how this process plays a specific role in the genesis of writing (Besse, de Gaulmyn & Luis, 1993). The very first logographic pattern to be mastered in childhood paves the way for producing a few other familiar words (such as *Daddy*, *Mommy*, and hello). By making a few changes in the arrangement of the letters, for example, a child can also use his or her first name as a basis for producing other words with different meanings (Jaffré, 1988, 1992).

In short, data of two kinds are now being published that cast some doubt on the likelihood that there may exist a logographic phase—in French. First, children confronted with alphabetical systems such as French, in particular, seem to acquire few, if any, processes that enable them to match up meanings directly with graphic patterns. Second, because children's writing performances necessarily reflect their use of analytical mechanisms, the results obtained are not very consistent with the logographic processing of whole words at a time. The model developed by Frith is therefore not in line with what seems to occur in French during this early learning phase.

The Alphabetical Phase

The type of processing characteristic of this phase is based on the systematic use of correspondences between phonemes and graphemes or between larger segments of words. When reading or writing consists of recomposing a word by use of intralexical components, a process of assembly takes place, which can be defined by opposition with the addressing process, which consists of directly pairing a graphemic pattern with a mental representation (Barry, 1994). A great deal of controversy is still going on as to the exact nature of the units used in this assembling process, however (see subsequent discussion).

Even in French, which is one of the most irregular orthographic systems, the regularity of the correspondences is the most crucial factor (Catach, 1980; Gak, 1976; Veronis, 1986). Letters, graphemes, and series of graphemes have to be matched up with phonemes and sequences of phonemes. For this purpose, learners have to be able to spot intralexical configurations (syllables and phonemes) within the discourse they hear and to relate them to graphemes and series of graphemes. The fact that this matching activity is so fundamental to writing explains the importance of phonological awareness (Gombert, 1990) and phonological mediation (Sprenger-Charolles, Siegel, & Bonnet, 1998).

The alphabetical phase begins when children discover that writing is a transcription of speech. Comparative studies on how the orthographies of various languages are learned have shown that the learning occurs all the earlier and all the more easily if the orthography is a transparent one. German, Spanish, Greek, Italian, and Portuguese children are all able to read familiar words as well as new words more quickly and accurately than their English and French counterparts are. On the production side, the orthography of German and Spanish children is generally quite plausible, and it is all the more likely to be acceptable and in keeping with the conventional rules as the material they are dealing with is regular.

Learners are confronted with a threefold problem. First, they have to be able to cut up the spoken word into segments that have first to be spotted. Then, they have to be able to pick out the graphemes present in the words and identify them. Last, they have to match up phonemic patterns with graphemic patterns. Depending on the orthographic system involved, the size and consistency of these patterns can vary considerably from one context to another, but contextual differences are difficult to perceive at this stage.

Studies on the setting up of correspondences between phonemes and graphemes have shown that children with a knowledge of the alphabet use the names of letters to produce the sounds corresponding to the oral language (Read, 1986). They write *LFA* for *elephant*, for example, or *GT* for *jeter* [to throw]. Children tend to give the syllable a special status. They attempt to segment sequences of sounds into syllables and to make fairly systematic associations between a syllable and a letter (Jaffré, 1992), especially when a sequence of phonemes resembles the name of a letter (/b/ in *belette* [weasel], which can be written as *blt*, or *carotte* [carrot], which is sometimes written *KRT*). By using a phonological approach to orthography and by aptly segmenting the sequences of sounds into syllables, children can learn to discover the alphabetic principles and yet they can make mistakes that are contrary to these principles (Read, 1986). It is particularly easy to proceed by syllabic segmentation in French, in which the syllables are fairly simple and clearly delimited (at least for French people).

Resorting to phonological mediation in this way has a whole series of effects. The results of a set of longitudinal studies by Sprenger-Charolles et al. (Sprenger-Charolles & Casalis, 1995; Sprenger-Charolles & Siegel, 1997; Sprenger-Charolles, Siegel & Béchennec, 1997) were not only mutually coherent, but were also consistent with the hypothesis that phonological mediation comes into play at an early stage of development and continues to be used for a long time. Children tend to read regular words more accurately and to write them more correctly than they do irregular words. When they encounter words of the latter kind, they will often regularize them (e.g., /fam/ is transcribed as *fam* instead of *femme* [woman] or *femme* is pronounced as /fæm/). One of the main conclusions to be drawn from these findings concerns the long-term impact of phonological mediation. The data obtained in these studies show that children's early performances in tests requiring phonological skills—and hence their ability to use phonological mediation—are good predictors of their subsequent performances in reading and writing irregular words. The predictive value of early phonological skills turned out to be even greater than that of children's early performances in irregular word-reading tests. Phonological mediation therefore seems to be one of the main mechanisms underlying self-learning processes (Share, 1999; Sprenger-Charolles, 1992), but the question as to how this mechanism functions still remains to be elucidated.

In short, we can say that, in French, as in the other alphabetical orthographies, the alphabetical phase begins by an attempt to find systematic correspondences between phonemes and graphemes when a children are learning to read and to write. This phase depends on children's phonological awareness and promotes the development of this awareness. It leads children to write, read, or both, by using a phonological approach, which consists of associating each grapheme systematically with each phoneme. However, whenever children have to learn systems that are as irregular as French, the learning process becomes rather long and arduous, and errors continue to be made even late in life. Even in the case of these irregular orthographies, however, the learning process is still based on the acquisition of correspondences and the processing of regularities, and the implementation of this method gradually leads to the advent of the final orthographic phase.

From the Alphabetical Phase to the Orthographic Phase

The alphabetical and orthographic phases begin to overlap when children are at a very early age, leading to the coexistence in adults of two different reading and writing processes. The second process begins as soon as the conventional reading and writing of words is no longer just a matter of forming simple, consistent associations between phonemes and graphemes. Intralexical contextual cues are identified (e.g., the *ch* is written correctly in both *écharde* [splinter] and *orchidée* [orchid]), double consonants are appropriately used (e.g., *allumer* [to light] vs. *éluder* [*to elude*]) and plural associations are rightly formed between phonemes and graphemes (e.g., /e/→ *é, er, et, ai*; /o/→ *o, au, eau*): These associations are known to be more easily predicted when one is reading (in which graphemes have to be associated with phonemes) than when one is writing (in which phonemes have to be associated with graphemes) (Ziegler, Jacobs, & Stone, 1996). The question therefore now arises as to how it becomes possible to read and write items that do not obey any regular rules of correspondence.

There are two possible answers to this question. First, the orthographic form of a given familiar word may be directly recovered from long-term memory by means of the direct pathway (e.g., *thym* [thyme], *théâtre* [theater]). Second, new items may be dealt with on the basis of the correspondences between phonemes and graphemes (e.g., /a/→ *a*). However, in a system as irregular as French, learners can use these correspondences to correctly transcribe or read only about half of all the words (Veronis, 1986). Other infralexical methods of processing are therefore no doubt available. Two of the potential candidates have been investigated so far. One possible method consists of the memorization of statistical regularities (for example, some double consonants occur only in specific situations, as in the case of the *ss* between two vowels). The other possible method is based on lexical analogies (a pseudoword such as /orkim/ will be transcribed as *orchime*, for example, by analogy with *orchidée* [orchid], or *orquime* by analogy with *arquer* [to bend]). Therefore there are four possible ways, not just two, of accounting for the reading and writing performances of learners who are already familiar with the alphabetical principles.

The complexity of the graphemes can affect the way words are written in French. The difficulties that arise here are not due to the fact that the graphemes corresponding to some phonemes (such as /u/) consist of two or three letters (as in the case of *ou*, which means or) and not just one. Alegria and Mousty (1994) have established that these context-independent digrams are learned concomitantly with the graphemic monograms. Difficulties occur when a single phoneme or grapheme corresponds to several graphemes or phonemes, respectively: /s/, for example, can be written as *s, c, ss*, or *t*. The orthographic form most frequently used by children in general is *s*, even if this solution is not appropriate in the context with which they are presented (e.g., between two vowels, for which *ss* is required). It is only by about the fifth grade that orthographic rules of this kind are mastered. Children therefore seem to start to learn how to write by using a simplified system of orthography (Alegria & Mousty, 1996).

The data available in the literature show that children at a very early age are able to notice some of the orthographic regularities that occur in French. By the end of the second grade, they are as capable as adults in rejecting pseudowords such as *llumir* or *lumirr*, in which double consonants have been placed at the beginning and end, which never happens in French. At the same time, they accept *lummir*, and even *lukkir*, in which double consonants, even of a kind they have never encountered before (as in *lukkir*), occur in the middle of the item with which they are presented (Pacton, Fayol, & Perruchet, 2002a, 2002b; Pacton, Perruchet, Fayol, & Cleeremans, 2001). These findings confirm and extend the results of previous studies that showed that children's writing systems are influenced by orthographic regularities (Treiman, 1993) at a much earlier age than what the stage-by-stage models of orthographic learning (such as that proposed by Frith, 1985) suggest. It turns out that the set of correspondences between a series of phonemes and a series of graphemes on which they base their transcriptions is much larger than the set of correspondences they have learned between a series of phonemes and series of graphemes.

Children also learn to write hitherto unknown words by transcribing some words that they already know (Goswami, Gombert, & Barrera, 1998; Martinet, 2001). A child who knows how to write *ticket*, for example, may attempt to write /bike/→ *bicket* by analogy. Here again, children have larger reference sets of correspondences available when working from graphemes to phonemes than in the opposite direction (see however Sprenger-Charolles et al., 1998). Investigations by Content (1993) shows that orthographic neighborhood is used as early as the second grade by children learning to read French. Like adults (Segui, 1991), children tend to read pseudowords aloud, comparing them with similar frequently occurring words with which they are already familiar.

To sum up, before they have learned to completely master the correspondences between phonemes and graphemes, children are able to resort to the phonology and, in parallel, to learn to recognize the correspondences between statistical features of lexical items. Their use of phonological mediation has several consequences. First, they establish systematic associations between the phonemic and the graphemic configurations occurring specifically in French (Lott, 1970). Both types of configurations have some clearly identifiable statistical patterns of occurrence: Some series of phonemes and graphemes are more likely to occur than others. Establishing correspondences between these series gives rise to the realization that other probabilistic associations may occur: There is a roughly equal overall likelihood of /ã/ being written as *an* or *en*, whereas /o/ is written as *o* more frequently than as *au* or *eau*. (Fayol, Lété, & Gabriel, 1996; Pacton & Fayol, 2003). On the other hand, these patterns of frequency in the correspondences between phonemes and graphemes vary depending on their position in the words and on their environment. The grapheme *eau*, for example, is more frequently encountered at the end than in the middle of words. Infralexical associations of this kind between series of phonemes and series of graphemes (Bonin, Peereman, & Fayol, 2001), depending on their environment, are established at a very early age. Children's ability to memorize and use them is strongly dependent on the level of reading skill they have reached (Alegria & Mousty, 1997).

In an irregular system such as French, however, it does not suffice by any means to have acquired some phonological awareness and some knowledge about the correspondences occurring between phonemes and graphemes to be able to read and write correctly. Among the other aspects that have to be taken into account is morphology. For example, /kur/ can be written as *cour* [courtyard], *court* [short], *cours* [course], and so forth. There is no difference among the pronunciations of all these words. The relationships between modes of processing and phonological and orthographic units are therefore not the only relationships that have to be set up. The practice of reading also leads to the building up of probabilistic associations of other kinds, namely between phonological, orthographic, or both, configurations and semantic modes of processing. In French, these associations often, although not always, correspond to morphological features.

Morphology

From the linguistic point of view, orthography, phonology, morphology, and semantics are all different ways in which words can be described. In an inflectional language such as French, studies on the morphology are of fundamental importance, as the morphology covers not only the syntactic mechanisms involved in the composition of sentences, but also the processes underlying the formation of words. Theoretically, for example, the formation of the word *lecteur* [reader] involves a combination between two morphemes (or two minimum units of significance): *lect-*, a radical relating to the nature of an action, and *-eur*, an affix evoking the agent performing that action.

The question as to how the morphology of a language is processed is particularly relevant in the framework of the French writing system. Rey-Debove (1984) noted that 75% of the 35,000 French words are morphologically complex and that they can therefore be analyzed in terms of their morphemic constituents. A distinction has to be made here between what occurs in inflectional morphology (e.g., conjugated verb forms, inflectional forms of nouns and adjectives, which constitute surface variants of a single word and are predictable) and in derivational morphology, in which a root is combined with at least one affix (a prefix, as in *refaire* [to redo] or a suffix, as in *laitier* [milkman]).

From the psycholinguistic point of view, the problem thus arises as to whether, how, and when morphological information contributes to the perception and production of written language. Various ideas have been expressed on this subject, which are not mutually exclusive but actually form a continuum and apply to all orthographic systems. At one end of the continuum, we have the theories according to which morphological information simply reflects covariations of the phonological, orthographic, and semantic properties of the words (Seidenberg, 1987; Seidenberg & McClelland, 1989). At the other end, we have the theories according to which morphology is thought to be a real psychological factor and the morphological information is therefore used for both perception and production. The theories of the latter kind can be divided into three subgroups. Those in the first subgroup suggest that all words, whether they are morphologically simple or complex, are perceived and represented in their entirety (this is the "full-listing" hypothesis). In this case, the morphology is therefore taken to play only a secondary role. Some theorists have put forward the opposite point of view, however, that all morphologically complex (i.e., composite) words undergo a process of prelexical decomposition (Taft & Forster, 1975). In between these two extremes, there is an intermediary school of thought according to which coexisting morphologically complex and morphologically decomposed forms are liable to be activated simultaneously and to compete with each other during word-processing operations. Generally speaking, the authors of most present-day studies on French tend to agree with the latter description.

The Role of Morphology in the Perception of Language

Three main principles have been described to date as far as the contribution of morphology to language perception is concerned.

First, it has been established that pseudo-prefixed items (such as *préfet* [prefect]) are recognized or named by subjects more slowly than are prefixed items (such as *prénom* [first name]) (Pillon, 1993). The morphological structure of words therefore affects the choice of the analytical processes mobilized in order to identify them.

Second, the effects of the frequency of occurrence of items (the time taken to recognize an item will be all the shorter as this item occurs more frequently) are visible both in the case of the lexical surface frequency (as in the case of *laitage* [dairy product], or *laiterie* [dairy]) and in that of the cumulative frequency (of either the radical base or the root, as in the case of *lait* [milk]) between all the words formed with a given root (in this case, *lait* + *laitage* + *laitier* + *laiterie*). In French, a combined effect of these two frequencies has been found to occur in the case of words with suffixes (such as *laitier* [milkman]) but not those with prefixes. The latter are subject only to a lexical frequency effect (Beauvillain, 1996; Colé, Beauvillain & Segui, 1989; Colé, Segui & Taft, 1997). At least some morphological information therefore seems to be explicitly represented in the form of separate units in adults.

Third, results obtained in priming tests designed to distinguish at least partly between the role of the morphology and that of formal aspects such as phonological or orthographic similarity have shown that the learners' responses to a target word (such as *laitier*) were faster and more accurate when these words were preceded by a priming item including the corresponding basic morpheme (such as *lait*) rather than by a nonrelated item (Grainger, Colé & Segui, 1991). A morphological priming effect was found to occur when two consecutively presented words had the same prefix (e.g., *enjeu* [stake] and *envol* [taking flight]) and not just the same orthographic component at the beginning (e.g., *engin* [machine]) (Giraudo, 1999), even when the items belonging to the same family had rather different phonological, orthographic, or both forms (e.g., *barbe* [beard] and *imberbe* [beardless]). This finding again supports the idea that, in French, the roots and prefixes are explicitly represented in the form of morphological units to be processed and that they are processed at the supralexical stage, rather than at the prelexical stage. The findings differ somewhat from this account in the case of suffixed derivational items, which may be decomposed during encoding stage of reading and the roots may be processed first.

The data published so far on the processing of morphological information in language perception have focused mainly on derivational morphology and on a small number of root words and affixes (such as *re-*, *dé-*, *in-*, *-able*, *-eur*, *-ment*). These findings show that adults' performances are compatible with a model in which morphological aspects are explicitly represented, at least as far as the roots and prefixes are concerned. The results obtained on the processing of suffixes are not so clear-cut, however. The processing of suffixes seems to mobilize both a computational component, because the words are decomposed, and a direct recovery mechanism, because the words are represented as such and can therefore be recovered directly. The few rare data available about the processing of the inflectional morphology of the number of nouns (New, 2002) are consistent with the latter conclusions.

The Role of Morphology in Language Production

Morphological processing involved in French language production has been mainly investigated in the case of the inflectional morphology (e.g., the marks of number), and less attention has been paid to derivational morphology (Pacton et al., 2002a, 2002b). The inflectional morphological rules of number in French have some quite unique characteristics: As we have seen in the discussion on linguistic aspects, there is often no phonological correspondence, at least when these rules apply to nouns, adjectives, and verbs. In the spoken language, plurality is mainly signaled by a determinant (such as *le/la* or *un/une* in the singular and *les/des* in the plural), whereas the other segments of the phrase rarely contain any audible plural signs (Dubois, 1965). This specificity poses problems not only to young learners but also to many adult users.

Inflectional morphological rules of number in written French are highly regular and productive. Apart from a few exceptions, plurals of nouns and adjectives are formed by the addition of an *s* at the end of nouns and *nt* at the end of verbs. It seems quite likely that the morphemes *s* and *nt* may be explicitly represented and that they may be combined with the roots in keeping with rules of pluralization whereby "if a noun or adjective is plural, add '*s*'"; and "if a verb is plural, add '*nt*'" (Anderson, 1983, 1995). However, some authors are of the opinion that the inflected instances may be directly recovered from memory without any calculations being necessary.

These alternative hypotheses were studied by use of tests involving agreement in number between homophonic items (about which no phonological information was available), the plural form of which varies depending on whether they are nouns or adjectives (when they take *s*) or verbs (when they take *nt*). Some of the errors made by the subjects varied depending on the characteristics of the items (e.g., depending on whether or not there was a verbal homophone corresponding to a given noun). The data obtained in this study are particularly interesting, as they show that agreements are based on the recovery of specific instances from memory rather than by the application of rules. Largy, Fayol, and Lemaire (1996) have reported that educated adults with a good working knowledge of the rules of verb agreement in number nevertheless made errors *(il les **asperge*** [he sprinkles them]). It is possible that because the nominal form *(une **asperge*** [asparagus]) corresponding to this verb *(asperger* [to sprinkle]) is more common than the verb, these adults wrote *asperges* and not *aspergent*. Errors of a similar kind have been reported by Pacton, Fayol, and Perruchet (2004) in the agreement of adjectives (wrongly written with *nt* at the end) that were less common than their verbal homophones (e.g., *fixe* [permanent]). The occurrence of errors of this kind shows that a process of recovery from memory is involved when people are dealing with inflected forms. They suggest that the rules of agreement are not sufficient to explain such morphological processing (Fayol et al., 1994).

Adults are, of course, perfectly able to use rules of agreement, but mobilizing and applying these rules are costly and time-consuming operations in cognitive terms. When educated adults have to make verbal agreements in sentences in which the verb comes before the subject (the subject nearly always comes before the verb in French) (e.g., *Sur les pentes glisse le skieur* [Down the slopes slides the skier]), making the agreement is a demanding task, as shown by the poor performances obtained by subjects in a secondary task (Hupet, Fayol, & Schelstraete, 1998). This shows that agreements of this kind are made most of the time not by the application of the rules, but probably by the recovery of the inflected form from the memory in which it is stored. In most cases, this method works quite successfully. It fails to do so only in the most extreme cases such as those in which the item that must be made to agree has a more common homophone that takes a different mark of agreement. This method is quite appropriate for written French, as it gives a high success rate at the lowest possible cost.

All in all, the data available at present about the morphological production of written French have mainly focused on the inflectional morphology of number. They show that adults have two possible ways of making agreements at their disposal. They can either use the cognitively costly rules of agreement or recover the appropriate flexed instances directly from the working memory, in which they therefore seem to be explicitly represented and stored.

Learning the Morphological Rules

In adults, the representation and use of morphological units seems to occur by means of a fairly well-stabilized system. The basic morphological units can be said to be part of the mental lexicon, and the procedures (i.e., the rules) applied to them mobilize these units during both their perception (when they are decomposed) and their production (when they are re-combined). This picture is at odds with what is generally thought to occur during learning processes. The authors of studies on learning tend to favor the idea that morphological abilities develop after children have acquired a lexical repertory and that they are able to detect any regularities occurring in a corpus and to note the structures of any correlations (Pacton et al., 2001).

The first example worth mentioning in this respect concerns the statistical regularities that occur between the gender of nouns and their endings. In French, most nouns have been given a fairly arbitrary gender *(lune* [moon] is feminine, and *soleil* [sun] is masculine). Children therefore have no "natural" categories to which they might refer when learning the gender of nouns. They seem to rely on the consistency of the associations they encounter between the gender and the phonological and orthographic forms of words. Some endings are certainly strongly associated with gender: 91.9% of all the words ending in /m/ and 93.3% ending in /ã/ are masculine, and 75.4% of all the words ending in /i/ are feminine (Surridge, 1993; Tucker, Lambert, & Rigault, 1977). The authors of several studies have established that children are able to use regularities of this kind at a very early age to determine the gender of the new nouns they encounter (Karmiloff-Smith, 1979). Adults also rely on orthographic endings to determine the gender of words (Andriamamonjy, 1997). At all ages, people therefore use quasi regularities extracted from the corpus of nouns to determine the probable gender of newly encountered nouns. However, in French, these regularities are not sufficiently systematic; there is no feminine suffix, for example, that might be used to form (and unmistakably label) all feminine words.

The second example concerns the fact that regularities can begin to look more systematic when morphological marks are systematically associated with semantic distinctions. In French, for instance, the noun *renardeau* [baby fox] is formed with the root *renard* [fox] plus the derivational morpheme *eau*, a suffix used as a diminutive. Derivational suffixes of this kind greatly constrain the transcription of phonemes. In the cases already mentioned, /o/ is written as *eau* (rather than *o* or *au*). Consequently, when individuals have noted these regularities and are faced with an unknown item ending in /o/, which they recognize as a diminutive, they will no doubt systematically write *-eau*. When individuals have noted that /o/ is a diminutive and have also learned the appropriate orthography, they will write *eau* to transcribe this phoneme; in other words, they will apply the appropriate rule.

Pacton et al. (2002a, 2002b, submitted) have explored the effects of probabilistic grapho-tactic regularities and those of morphological regularities (which can be described by a rule) as well as the possible interactions between these two kinds of regularities on the transcription of the sounds /o/ and /ɛt/ in second- to fifth-grade children. The graphotactic regularities focused on the fact that the probability of /o/ being written as *eau* and that of /ɛt/ being written as *ette* at the end of words varies depending on the consonants occurring before /o/ and /ɛt/. The morphological regularities focused on the fact that, in some morphologically complex words, /o/ is written as *eau* (rather than as *o* or *au*) and /ɛt/ is written as *ette* (rather than *aite* or *ète*) when they are used as diminutive suffixes (as in *renard-eau* [fox cub] and *vach-ette* [*heifer*]). Because similar results have been obtained on /ɛt/ and /o/, we have described only those obtained on /o/.

The results obtained in pseudoword dictation tests have shown that graphotactic constraints do have effects: *Eau* was used more frequently by the participants when it came after a consonant that is usually followed by *eau* (e.g., /vitaro/) than when it came after a consonant that is never followed by *eau* (e.g., /vitafo/). The extent of this effect was not found to vary, however, depending on the school level reached by the children. The transcription of /o/ was also found to be influenced by morphological constraints: /o/ was more frequently written as *eau* in the "diminutive" condition than in the "base" condition; and this effect increased with the level of schooling reached by the children. One of the most important findings obtained here was that the effects of the graphotactic constraints did not differ significantly depending on whether the pseudowords were dictated in the "base" or "diminutive" condition, and that they did not depend on the school level reached, even after 5 years of written language practice.

These findings are not very consistent with the idea that subjects acquire increasingly abstract rule-based knowledge about the regularities occurring in the material they encounter. They are in agreement, however, with the distributional statistical findings suggesting that an implicit learning process takes place and that a gradual tendency toward abstraction develops (Pacton et al., 2001, 2002a, 2002b), involving gradients of generalization that depend on the similarity between familiar and newly encountered forms.

Little research has been carried out so far on the role of derivational morphology in French (Colé & Fayol, 2000). Lecocq, Casalis, Leuwers, and Watteau (1996) studied a group of French-speaking children between 5 and 8 years of age who performed tasks in which they had to interpret and produce derivative or inflected forms for words (*sucre, sucrier* [sugar, sugar bowl]) involving a change in the base (*fou, folie* [mad, madness]), and pseudowords.

The authors also compared the performances of second-grade children who were good and poor readers. The results showed on the one hand that children have little ability to carry out morphological analysis before they have learned to read and that this ability continues to develop well beyond the second grade. On the other hand, the poor readers obtained lower scores than the good readers specifically in writing words involving inflectional morphological rules, whereas no such difference between the oral versus written modality was observed in the case of words involving derivational morphological rules. This difference is probably attributable to the characteristics of French, a language in which the inflectional morphology differs considerably between the written and spoken forms (Fayol, 1997; Jaffré & Fayol, 1997). A study by Colé, Royer, Hilton, Marec, and Gombert (in press) also investigated the role of word morphology in reading acquisition. The use of word morphology in reading was observed in good readers as early as the first grade and in poor readers by the second grade. Dyslexic children were found to rely more heavily on the morphology than normal readers did, probably because they were using a compensatory strategy.

Even after children have had 5 years of practice in writing, their orthographic behavior does not seem to be governed by rules when they are dealing with aspects to which rules do apply, but have never been explicitly taught. This finding suggests that these children had learned regularities that were roughly transposable to any items that were similar to those with which they were already familiar. This is not morphology in the strictest sense of the term. However, suffixes such as *eau* and *ette* are not always used as suffixes, and their use does not seem to have emerged spontaneously from what the children knew from their personal experience of writing. This result is in line with the results obtained by Lecocq et al. (1996), which show that morphological comprehension develops at a fairly late stage and continues to improve during primary school, although some early signs of its use become apparent in children at a very early age (Colé et al., in press). It is not possible on the basis of the data available to determine whether this pattern of use is common to all children and whether it includes all possible morphological combinations.

It therefore appears that the inflectional morphology of French is learned at a fairly late stage in development and that the learning process continues for a long period of time (Fayol, Thévenin, Jarousse, & Totereau, 1999; Totereau, Thévenin, & Fayol, 1997). The ability to interpret the plural ending *s*, which is specific to nouns and adjectives, is mastered earlier in life than the plural ending *nt* of verbs. These two marks begin to be produced quite late in childhood and tend to be overgeneralized (adding *s* to verbs, in particular) before stabilizing when children are about 9–10 years of age. The use of the verbal ending *nt* seems to have become automatized when children are about 10 years of age. (Fayol, Hupet, & Largy, 1999).

CONCLUSION

Recent studies on the orthography of French illustrate quite clearly what Ziegler et al. (1996) have termed "the inconsistency mystery of French." When one is working from spelling to phonology, French looks quite a consistent language, but it is highly inconsistent in the way it proceeds when one is working from phonology to spelling. In addition, although the 130 phonograms that make up this writing system provide the main basis of its semiographic structure, a whole series of specifically graphic units also intervene, the mastery of which requires a high level of metalinguistic ability. Last, the coexistence of these very different kinds of units has made for a highly complex system of orthography that constitutes a special case among all the alphabetical systems.

The orthography of English is no doubt one of those that resembles that of French most closely, but there is one important difference worth mentioning. The morphology of written

English is practically transparent, whereas that of French is remarkably opaque, which makes it even more difficult to master. The reasons for the specificities of the French exception are mostly linguistic and historical. When French was developing, it underwent several influences, especially Germanic ones, that deflected it from following the Latin archetype. At a later stage in history, an elitist cultural and political group strongly attached to the Latin culture took great pains to give the orthography of French a form that has actually changed very little since then.

The conjunction of all these processes has given rise to many psycholinguistic problems. As with all the other alphabetic orthographies, the acquisition of the French naturally involves mastering the underlying phonographic processes. The orthography of French is certainly less regular in this respect than that of Italian or Spanish, whereas it is more regular than that of English. The greatest difficulties are due, however, to the unique morphographic features of French, as there are many graphemes that have no phonographic counterparts. Schoolteachers spend a great deal of time "instilling into their pupils" the orthography of verbal homophones (*donner* vs. *donné* [to give vs. given]), and the rules of agreement in gender and number (*les jeunes femmes étaient parties depuis longtemps* [young women left since a long time]), with conspicuously unequal results. Because it still seems quite impossible to even envisage making any orthographic reforms in France, we are faced with a somewhat paradoxical situation: Although the French have great difficulty in learning to master their orthography, they are nevertheless extremely fond of it.

Comparisons with writing systems of other kinds might help to throw some useful light on this question. The more transparent alphabetical orthographies, such as the Spanish and Italian ones, can certainly serve to show the advantages of systems based on more consistent phonographic relationships. However, in view of the graphic specificities of French already mentioned, it might also be worth looking at some writing systems that have morphographic units similar to those occurring in French. The Chinese characters with their *radicals* come under this heading, as do the Japanese *kanji*.

REFERENCES

Alegria, J., & Mousty, P. (1994) On the development of lexical and non-lexical spelling procedures of French-speaking normal and disabled children. In G. D. A. Brown & N. C. Ellis (Eds.), *Handbook of spelling: Theory, process, and intervention* (pp. 211–226). Chichester, NY: Wiley.

Alegria, J., & Mousty, P. (1996). The development of spelling procedures in French-speaking, normal and learning-disabled children: Effects of frequency and lexicality. *Journal of Experimental Child Psychology, 63*, 312–338.

Alegria, J., & Mousty, P. (1997). Lexical spelling processes in reading disabled French-speaking children. In C. A. Perfetti, L. Rieben, & M. Fayol (Eds.), *Learning to spell. Research, theory, and practice across languages* (pp. 115–128). Mahwah, NJ: Lawrence Erlbaum Associates.

Anderson, J. R. (1983). *The architecture of cognition*, Cambridge, MA: Harvard University Press.

Anderson, J. R. (1995). *Learning and memory: An integrated approach*. New York: Wiley.

Andriamamonjy, P. (1997). *Le traitement du genre grammatical au cours de la lecture de mots isolés et de phrases*. Unpublished doctoral thesis, Université de Nice-Sophia Antipolis, France.

Barry, C. (1994). Spelling routes (or roots or rutes). In G. D. A. Brown & N. C. Ellis (Eds.), *Handbook of spelling: Theory, process, and intervention* (pp. 27–50). Chichester, NY: Wiley.

Beauvillain, C. (1996). The integration of morphological and whole-word form information during eye fixations on prefixed and suffixed words. *Journal of Memory and Language, 35*, 801–820.

Beauvois, M. F., & Dérouesné, J. (1981). Lexical or orthographic agraphia. *Brain, 104*, 21–49.

Besse, J.-M., de Gaulmyn, M.-M., & Luis, M.-H. (1993). Du pouvoir lire son prénom au savoir lire-écrire. In J.-P. Jaffré & J. David (Eds.), La genèse de l'écriture: systèmes et acquisitions, *Etudes de Linguistique Appliquée, 91*, 8–21.

Bonin, P., Peereman, R., & Fayol, M. (2001). Do phonological codes constraint the selection of orthographic codes in written picture naming? *Journal of Memory and Language, 45*, 688–720.

Bousquet, S., Cogis, D., Ducard, D., Massonnet, J., & Jaffré, J.-P. (1999). Acquisition de l'orthographe et mondes cognitifs, *Revue Française de Pédagogie, 126*, 23–38.

Bybee, J., & Hopper, P. (2001), Introduction to frequency and the emergence of linguistic structure. In J. Bybee & P. Hopper (Eds.), *Frequency and the emergence of linguistic structure* (pp. 1–26). Amsterdam: Benjamins.

Catach, N. (1963). Un point d'histoire de la langue: La bataille de l'orthographe aux alentours de 1900, *Le Français Moderne*, Paris: Éditions d'Artrey, *XXXI, 2,* 111–120.

Catach, N. (1980). *L'orthographe française: Traité théorique et pratique.* Paris: Nathan (new editions in 1986 and 1989).

Catach, N. (2001). *Histoire de l'orthographe française.* (posthumous ed.). Paris: Honoré Champion.

Chervel, A. (1977). *. . . et il fallut apprendre à écrire à tous les petits français; histoire de la grammaire scolaire.* Paris: Payot.

Colé, P., Beauvillain, C., & Segui, J. (1989). On the representation and processing of prefixed and suffixed derived words: a differential frequency effect. *Journal of Memory and Language, 28,* 1–13.

Colé, P., & Fayol, M. (2000). Reconnaissance des mots écrits et apprentissage de la lecture: Rôle des connaissances morphologiques. In M. Kail & M. Fayol (Eds.), *L'acquisition du langage, Vol. 2* (pp. 151–181). Paris: Presses Universitaires de France.

Colé, P., Royer, C., Hilton, H., Marec, N., & Gombert, J.-E. (in press). Morphology in reading acquisition and in dyslexia. In J.-P. Jaffré, J.-C. Pellat, & M. Fayol (Eds.), *The semiography of writing. Scripts and linguistic meanings.* Dordrecht, The Netherland: Kluwer.

Colé, P., Segui, J., & Taft, M. (1997). Words and morphemes as units of lexical access. *Journal of Memory and Language, 37,* 312–330.

Content, A. (1993). Le rôle de la médiation phonologique dans l'acquisition de la lecture. In J.-P. Jaffré, L. Sprenger-Charolles, & M. Fayol (Eds.), *Lecture–ecriture–acquisiton: Les actes de la Villette* (pp. 80–96). Paris: Nathan.

Coulmas, F. (2003). *Writing systems. An introduction to their linguistic analysis.* Cambridge, UK: Cambridge University Press.

Dubois, J. (1965). *Grammaire structurale de Français.* Paris: Larousse.

Fayol, M. (1997). *Des idées au texte.* Paris: Presses Universitaires de France.

Fayol, M., Hupet, M., & Largy, P. (1999). The acquisition of subject–verb agreement in written French. From novices to experts errors. *Reading and Writing, 11,* 153–174.

Fayol, M., Largy, P., & Lemaire, P. (1994). Cognitive overload and orthographic errors: When cognitive overload enhences subject–verb agreement errors. A study in French written language. *The Quarterly Journal of Experimental Psychology, 47A,* 437–464.

Fayol, M., Lété, B., & Gabriel, M. A. (1996). Du développement de la correspondance un phonème-plusieurs graphèmes chez les enfants de 6 à 7 ans. *Linguistique of Didactique de Langes (LIDIL), 13,* 67–85.

Fayol, M., Thévenin, M. G., Jarousse, J.-P., & Totereau, C. (1999). From learning to teaching to learning French written morphology. In T. Nunes (Ed.), *Learning to read: An integrated view from research and practice* (pp. 43–64). Dordrecht, The Netherlands: Kluwer.

Ferreiro, E., & Teberosky, A. (1988). *Literacy before schooling.* New York: Heinemann.

Fijalkow, J., & Fijalkow, É. (1991). L'écriture inventée ou cycle des apprentissages. Etude génétique. *Les Dossiers de l'Éducation, 18,* 125–167.

Freinet, C. (1975). *La méthode naturelle. L'apprentissage de la langue.* Verviers, Belgium: Marabout.

Frith, U. (1985). Beneath the surface of developmental dyslexia. In K. E. Patterson, J. C. Marshall, & M. Coltheart (Eds.). *Surface dyslexia: Cognitive and neuropsychological studies of phonological reading* (pp. 301–330). Hillsdale, NJ: Lawrence Erlbaum Associates.

Gak, V. G. (1976). *L'orthographe du français, essai de description théorique et pratique.* Paris: Société d' Etuds Linguistique et Anthropologicals de France.

Giraudo, H. (1999). *Le codage des informations morphologiques dans la perception des mots écrits.* Unpublished doctoral thesis, Université de Provence, France.

Gombert, J.-E. (1990). *Le développement métalinguistique.* Paris: Presses Universitaires de France.

Gombert, J.-E., & Fayol, M. (1992). Writing in preliterate children. *Learning and Instruction, 2,* 23–41.

Goswami, U. C., Gombert, J.-E., & Fraca de Barrera, L. (1998). Children's orthographic representations and linguistic transparency: Nonsense word reading in English, French, and Spanish. *Applied Psycholinguistics, 19,* 19–52.

Grainger, J., Colé, P., & Segui, J. (1991). Masked morphological priming in visual word recognition. *Journal of Memory and Language, 30,* 370–384.

Hannas, W. C. (1997). *Asia's orthographic dilemma.* Honolulu: University of Hawai'i Press.

Hupet, M., Fayol, M., & Schelstraete, M. A. (1998). Effects of semantic variables on the subject–verb agreement processes in writing. *British Journal of Psychology, 89,* 59–75.

Jaffré, J.-P. (1988). Lecture et écriture: Convergences métalinguistiques, *Langue Française, 80,* 20–32.

Jaffré, J.-P. (1992). Le traitement élémentaire de l'orthographe: Les procédures graphiques, *Langue Française, 95,* 27–48.

Jaffré, J.-P. (2000). Ce que nous apprennent les orthographes inventées. In C. Fabre-Cols, (Ed.), *Apprendre à lire des textes d'enfants* (pp. 50–60). Brussels: DeBoeck/Duculot.

Jaffré, J.-P. (2002). L'écriture & les nouvelles technologies. Ce que les unes nous apprennent de l'autre [on-line]. Available Office AudioVisuel de l'Université de Poitiers, http://imedias.univ-poitiers.fr/rhrt/index.htm.

Jaffré, J.-P. (2003). Orthography. In W. J. Frawley (Ed.). *The international encyclopedia of linguistics, Vol. 4* (2nd ed.). Oxford, UK: Oxford University Press.

Jaffré, J.-P., & Fayol, M. (1997). *Orthographe: des systèmes aux usages.* Paris: Flammarion.

Karmiloff-Smith, A. (1979). *A functional approach to child language.* Cambridge, UK: Cambridge University Press.

Largy, P., Fayol, M., & Lemaire, P. (1996). On confounding verb/noun inflections. A study of subject-verb agreement errors in French. *Language and Cognitive Processes, 11,* 217–255.

Lecocq, P., Casalis, S., Leuwers, C., & Watteau, N. (1996). *Apprentissage de la lecture et compréhension d'énoncés.* Lille, France: Presses Universitaires de Lille.

Lott, D. (1970). Knowledge of intraword redundancy by beginning readers. *Psychonomic Science, 19,* 343–344.

Marchello-Nizia, C. (1999). *Le Français en diachronie: Douze siècles d'évolution.* Paris: Ophrys.

Martinet, C. (2001). *Le rôle de la phonologie dans l'acquisition des connaissances lexicales orthographiques.* Unpublished doctoral thesis, Université Pierre Mendès France, Grenoble, France.

New, B. (2002). *La base lexique et l'étude expérimentale de la flexion nominale en français.* Unpublished doctoral thesis, Université René Descartes, Paris.

Nyikos, J. (1988). A linguistic perspective of illiteracy. In Sheila Empleton (Ed.), *The 14th LACUS Forum 1987* (pp. 146–163). Lake Blaff, IL. Linguistic Association of Canada and the United States.

Pacton, S., & Fayol, M. (2003). How do children use morphosyntactic information when they spell adverbs and present participle? *Scientific Studies of Reading, 7,* 273–287.

Pacton, S., Fayol, M., & Perruchet, P. (2002a). Acquérir l'orthographe du français: Apprentissages implicites et explicites. In A. Florin & J. Morais (Eds.), *La maîtrise du langage.* Rennes, France: Presses Universitaires de Rennes.

Pacton, S., Fayol, M., & Perruchet, P. (2002b). The acquisition of untaught orthographic regularities in French. In L. Verhoeven, C. Elbro, and P. Reitsma (Eds.), *Precursors of functional literacy* (pp. 121–138). Amsterdam: Benjamins.

Pacton, S., Fayol, M., & Perruchet, P. (2004). Frequency and position effects on adjective-verb homophone spelling errors. Manuscript submitted for publication.

Pacton, S., Perruchet, P., Fayol, M., & Cleeremans, A. (2001). Implicit learning out of the lab: The case of orthographic regularities. *Journal of Experimental Psychology: General, 130,* 401–426.

Peereman, R., & Content, A. (1999). LEXOP: A lexical database providing orthography–phonology statistics for French monosyllabic words. *Behavior Research Methods, Instruments, & Computers, 31,* 376–379.

Pellat, J.-C. (2003). Variation et plurisystème graphique au XVIIᵉ siècle. *Faits de Langue, 22,* 139–150.

Perret, M. (1998). *Introduction à l'histoire de la langue française.* Paris: Éditions SEDES.

Pillon, A. (1993). *La mémoire des mots.* Brussels, Belgium: Mardaga.

Posner, R. (1996). *The Romance languages.* Cambridge, UK: Cambridge University Press.

Read, C. (1986). *Children's creative spelling.* London: Routledge & Kegan Paul.

Rey-Debove, J. (1984). Le domaine de la morphologie lexicale. *Cahiers de Lexicologie, 45,* 3–19.

Rieben, L., & Saada-Robert, M. (1997). Relations between word-search strategies and word-copying strategies in children aged 5 to 6 years old. In C. A. Perfetti, L. Rieben & M. Fayol (Eds.), *Learning to spell. Research, theory, and practice across languages* (pp. 295–318). Mahwah, NJ: Lawrence Erlbaum Associates.

Segui, J. (1991). La reconnaissance visuelle de mots. In R. Kolinsky, J. Morais, & J. Segui (Eds.), *La reconnaissance des mots dans les différentes modalités sensorielles* (pp. 99–118). Paris: Presses Universitaires de France.

Seidenberg, M. S. (1987). Sublexical structures in visual word recognition: Access units or orthographic redundancy? In M. Coltheart (Ed.), *Attention and performance XII: Reading.* Hillsdale, NJ: Lawrence Erlbaum Associates.

Seidenberg, M. S., & McClelland, J. L. (1989). A distributed developmental model of word recognition and naming. *Psychological Review, 96,* 523–568.

Seymour, P. H. K., & Elder, L. (1986). Beginning reading without phonology. *Cognitive Neuropsychology, 3,* 1–36.

Shallice (1981). Phonological agraphia and the lexical route in writing. *Brain, 104,* 412–429.

Share, D. L. (1999). Phonological recoding and orthographic learning: A direct test of the self-teaching hypothesis. *Journal of Experimental Child Psychology, 72,* 95–129.

Sprenger-Charolles, L. (1992). L'évolution des mécanismes d'identification des mots. In M. Fayol, J.-E. Gombert, P. Lecocq, L. Sprenger-Charolles, & D. Zagar (Eds.), *Psychologie cognitive de la lecture* (pp. 141–193). Paris: Presses Universitaires de France.

Sprenger-Charolles, L., & Bonnet P. (1996). New doubts on the importance of the logographic stage: A longitudinal study of French children. *Current Psychology of Cognition, 15,* 173–208.

Sprenger-Charolles, L., & Casalis, S. (1995). Reading and spelling acquisition in French first graders. *Reading and Writing, 7,* 1–25.

Sprenger-Charolles, L., & Siegel, L. (1997). A longitudinal study of the effects of syllabic structure on the development of reading and spelling skills in French. *Applied Psycholinguistics, 18,* 485–505.

Sprenger-Charolles, L., Siegel, L., & Béchennec, D. (1997). Beginning reading and spelling acquisition in French: A longitudinal study. In C.A. Perfetti, L. Rieben, & M. Fayol (Eds.), *Learning to spell. Research, theory, and practice across languages* (pp. 339–360). Mahwah, NJ: Lawrence Erlbaum Associates.

Sprenger-Charolles, L., Siegel, L., & Bonnet, P. (1998). Reading and spelling acquisition in French: The role of phonological mediation and orthographic factors. *Journal of Experimental Child Psychology, 68*, 134–165.

Surridge, M. E. (1993). Gender assignment in French: The hierarchy of rules and the chronology of acquisition. *International Review of Applied Linguistics in Language Teaching, 31*, 77–95.

Taft, M., & Forster, K. I. (1975). Lexical storage and retrieval of prefixed words. *Journal of Verbal Learning and Verbal Behavior, 14*, 638–647.

Totereau, C., Thévenin, M. G., & Fayol, M. (1997). The development of the understanding of number morphology in written French. In C. Perfetti, M. Fayol, & L. Rieben (Eds.), *Learning to spell* (pp. 97–114). Hillsdale, NJ: Lawrence Erlbaum Associates.

Treiman, R. (1993). *Beginning to spell*. New York: Oxford University Press.

Tucker, G. R., Lambert, W. E., & Rigault, A. A. (1977). *The French speaker's skill with grammatical gender: An example of rule-governed behavior*. The Hague, The Netherlands: Mouton.

Vachek, J. (1945–1949). Some remarks on writing and phonetic transcription, *Acta Linguistica, 5*, 86–93.

Veronis, J. (1986). Etude quantitative sur le système graphique et phono-graphique du français. *European Bulletin of Cognitive Psychology, 6*, 501–553.

Ziegler, J. C. (1998). La perception des mots, une voie à double sens? *Annales de la Fondation Fyssen, 13*, 81–88.

Ziegler, J. C., Jacobs, A. M., & Stone, G. O. (1996). Statistical analysis of the bidirectional inconsistency of spelling and sound in French. *Behavior, Research Methods, Instruments, & Computers, 28*, 504–515.

7

The Acquisition of Literacy in Italian

Remo Job
University of Padova and University of Trento

Francesca Peressotti
University of Padova

Claudio Mulatti
University of Padova and University of Trento

People at different times and in different places have come up with different solutions to the problem of how to express graphically the sounds of language. Furthermore, languages differ greatly in the extent to which they rely on different mechanisms to encode relevant information. For example, some rely heavily on morphological devices whereas others do so to a much lesser degree. Thus reading and writing and their acquisition may be sensitive to, and affected by, different constraints brought about by the type of language in which people become literate. In this chapter, we examine some issues on this topic with respect to Italian. The chapter is organized as follows: First, some features of the language relevant for reading and writing are outlined. Next, some empirical data on the strategies Italian children use in learning to read and write are presented. Finally, some of the difficulties encountered by children in the acquisition of literacy are discussed.

SOME FEATURES OF ITALIAN

Orthography and Phonology

The mapping of orthography into phonology is quite regular in Italian, and thus, according to the distinction between deep and shallow orthographies, Italian falls into the latter class. However, the system is not totally regular as there are a few letters that have word-specific pronunciations. Also, the mapping from phonology to orthography, although quite transparent, is not totally regular as some sounds may have word-specific orthographic realizations.

In Table 7.1 the main correspondences between letters and sound for reading and writing are presented. The schema is adapted from that presented by Lepsky and Lepsky (1981), but some changes have been made to account for the pronunciation of some multiletter graphemes.

Let us first consider the mapping of print to sound. Of the 21 letter comprising the Italian alphabet, 12 have a one-to-one correspondence between a single letter and a phoneme (a, b, d, f, l, m, n, p, q, r, t, v). Of the remaining letters, h is silent and functions as a diacritic grapheme (e.g., *giro* [tour] /'dʒiro/ vs. *ghiro* [dormouse] /'giro/), five (c, g, i, u, s) are read according

TABLE 7.1
A Simplified Schema of the Relationship Between Sounds and Letters in Italian

From Sounds to Letters	From Letters to Sounds	
[i] *i*	*a*	[a]
[e] *e*	*b*	[b]
[a] *a*	*c (+ a, o, u, consonant)*	[k]
[o] *o*	*(+i, e)*	[tʃ]
[u] *u*	*ch*	[k]
[p] *p*	*ci (+ vowel)*	[tʃ]
[b] *b*	*d*	[d]
[t] *t*	*e*	[e]
[d] *d*		[ɛ]
[k] *c (+ a, o, u, consonant)*	*f*	[f]
ch (+ i, e)	*g (+ a, o, u, consonant)*	[g]
q	*(+ i, e)*	[dʒ]
	gh	[g]
[g] *g (+ a, o, u, consonant)*	*gi (+ vowel)*	[dʒ]
gh (+ i, e)	*gl (+ i)*	[ʎ]
	gli (+ vowel)	[ʎ]
[f] *f*	*gn*	[ɲ]
[v] *v*	*gni (+ vowel)*	[ɲ]
[s] *s*	*h*	
[z] *s*		
[ʃ] *sc (+ i, e)*	*i*	[i]
		[j]
sci (+ vowel)	*l*	[1]
	m	[m]
[ts] *z*	*n*	[n]
[dz] *z*	*o*	[o]
		[ɔ]
[tʃ] *c (+ i, e)*	*p*	[p]
ci (+ vowel)	*q*	[k]
	r	[r]
	s	[s]
		[z]
[dʒ] *g (+ i, e)*	*sc (+ i, e)*	[ʃ]
gi (+ vowel)	*sci (+ vowel)*	[ʃ]
	t	[t]
[m] *m*	*u*	[u]
		[w]
[n] *n*	*v*	[v]
[ɲ] *gn*	*z*	[ts]
[1] *l*		[dz]
[ʎ] *gl (+ i)*		
[r] *r*		

Note. Modified from Lepsky and Lepsky (1981).

to context-sensitive rules, and three (e, o, z) have each two possible pronunciations that are lexically based.

The letter c is pronounced as the velar /k/ when in front of the vowels a, o, and u, and in front of a consonant. When followed by either the vowels i or e it is pronounced as the palatal / tʃ/. The letter g too has a velar pronunciation /g/ when followed by the vowels a, o, and u, or by a consonant (except n) and has the palatal pronunciation /dʒ/ in front of i and e. When followed by the consonant n and by a vowel, g corresponds the phoneme /ɲ/ as in *sogno* [dream]. The cluster gl followed by the vowel i corresponds to the phoneme /ʎ/ in the following cases: At the end of a word (e.g., *figli* [sons]); at the end of a root (e.g., *maglietta* [T-shirt]), or when i is followed by another vowel (e.g., *aglio* [garlic]). It is pronounced /gli/ in words' initial position (e.g., *glicerina* [Glycerine]) or when gli is preceded by n (e.g., *anglicano* [Anglican]). In this perspective, then, the highly frequent word *gli* (both a pronoun [him] and a determiner marked for masculine gender and plural number) may be considered an exception.

When unstressed, and adjacent to a vowel, the letter i functions as the semiconsonant /j/, and the letter u functions as the semiconsonant /w/ (*cuore* [heart] /'kwɔre/). In all other the cases, i and u are pronounced /i/ and /u/, respectively.

The letter s can be pronounced as /z/ or /s/ according to the context in which it occurs (Nespor, 1993): It is /z/ before a sounding consonant and when it occurs between two non-consonant segments, but it is pronounced /s/ otherwise.

Finally, there are three letters that each have two possible pronunciations that are not predictable from the context in which they occur. When accented, e can correspond to /ɛ/, as in *finestra* [window] or to /e/, as in *teso* [stretched]; also o can be open or closed, as shown by the minimal pair *botte*: /'bɔtte [blows] and /'botte/ [barrel]. The letter z can be pronounced /ts/ as in *ozio* [idleness] or /dz/ as in *zero* [zero]. These three letters thus are those giving rise to lexically based pronunciations, that is, they require lexical knowledge for arriving at the correct phonological form. However, it should be noted that the distinction is subjected to regional variation, and within a given dialect the distinction tends to disappear for most items.

In addition to the clusters gn and gl, we should mention the trigraph sci that by itself or followed by either a, o, or u, corresponds to the phoneme /ʃ/, as in *sciame* [swarm].

The mapping from phonology to orthography is univocal for most, but not all, sound–letter pairs (see Table 7.1). In particular, the phoneme /k/ maps into c, q, and cq. In these cases then, lexical information is needed to spell the words correctly.

An accent is not marked in Italian unless the word is stressed on the last syllable, in which case the last letter is explicitly marked (e.g., *però* [but]). Thus word stress is lexically based. The majority of polysyllabic words are iambic, that is, they are accented on the penultimate syllable, even if there is a sizable group of dactylic words (Colombo, 1992) whose stress falls on the antepenultimate syllable.

The syllabic structure of words is quite "regular," in the sense that CV and CVC syllables prevail, and these may be less complex—acoustically and orthographically—than other types of syllabic structures (Näslund, Schneider, & van den Broek, 1997).

Morphology

The morphology of Italian is quite rich and productive (Scalise, 1983). Except for function words (including adverbs), the words of the major grammatical classes are morphologically complex. Nouns and adjectives are generally marked for gender—masculine and feminine—and for number—singular and plural. Most masculine nouns and adjective take the suffix –o for singular and –i for plural, as in *tavolo* [table] and *tavoli* [tables], and most feminine nouns and adjectives take the suffix –a for singular and –e for plural (e.g., *sedia, sedie* [chair, chairs]). There is also a class of nouns and adjectives that takes the suffix—e for singular and –i for

TABLE 7.2

Inflected Forms of the Regular Verb Amare (To Love)

						Tense				
Person	Present	Past Definitive	Imperfect	Future	Conditional	Subjunctive Present	Subjunctive Imperfect	Imperative	Present Participle	Past Participle
1st singular	amo	amai	amavo	amerò	amerei	ami	amassi		amando	amato (singular, masculine)
2nd singular	ami	amasti	amavi	amerai	ameresti	ami	amassi	ama		amata (singular, feminine)
3rd singular	ama	amò	amava	amerà	amerebbe	ami	amasse	ami		amati (plural, masculine)
1st plural	amiamo	amammo	amavamo	ameremo	ameremmo	amiamo	amassimo	amiamo		amate (plural, feminine)
2nd plural	amate	amaste	amavate	amerete	amereste	amiate	amaste	amate		
3rd plural	amano	amarono	amavano	ameranno	amerebbero	amino	amassero	amino		

plural—and is thus opaque with respect to the word's grammatical gender. To illustrate, *cane* [dog] and *tigre* [tiger] are masculine and feminine, respectively. Also, there are exceptions. Some masculine nouns end in –a (e.g., *sistema* [system]) and some feminine nouns end in –o (e.g., *mano* [hand]). According to Padovani and Cacciari (2003), about 71% of nouns ending in –o are masculine and about 68% of nouns ending in –a are feminine. Of the nouns ending in e about 17% are masculine and 20% are feminine, the remaining being bigender.

Usually plurals tend to preserve the phonological value of the stem (e.g., *parco* /parko/ [park], *parchi* /parki/ [parks]) but some do not (e.g., *porco* /porko/ [pork], *porci* /portʃi/ [porks]).

Italian has a quite rich system of prefixation and suffixation, the latter used, among others, for diminutives (e.g., *ragazzo* [boy]; *ragazzino* [little boy]) and pejoratives (*ragazzaccio* [bad boy]).

The verb system is also morphologically complex. For each verb there are more than 40 inflected forms, each form being marked for time, person, aspects, and, in the past participle, for gender. There are three declensions in Italian. The first groups the largest number of verbs (about 3,000). These are characterized by the stem vowel "a" (e.g., *am-a-re* [to love]) and, for the most part, are regular, there being only four irregular verbs in this group (*fare* [to make], *dare*, [to give], *andare*, [to go], and *stare* [to stay]). The second declension groups the smallest number of verbs (about 400). They are characterized by the stem vowel "e" (e.g., *ved-e-re* [to see]). This class presents the highest incidence of exceptions: According to Orsolini and Marslen Wilson (1997), 95% of these verbs are irregular. The third declension groups about 500 verbs characterized by the stem vowel "i," as in *sent-i-re* [to hear]. About 10% of these verbs are irregular.

For regular verbs, the inflected forms are derived from the verb root by the addition of suffixes (see examples in Table 7.2). For the irregular verbs, irregularities regard mostly the inflected forms of the present, the past definite, and the past participle.

LEARNING TO READ AND WRITE IN ITALIAN

Until recently, no general formal instructions on reading and writing were given to Italian children before the age of 6 years, when they started elementary school.[1] At present, instruction is provided in the last years of most kindergarten classes so that children have some alphabetical skills when enrolling in school. Furthermore, Italian children develop quite early phonemic awareness abilities (Cossu, Shankwailer, Liberman, Katz, & Tola, 1988; Cossu, 1999), so they are quite proficient in tasks requiring metaphonological skills.

The methods used to teach literacy vary greatly, and most teachers used mixed methods comprising aspects of global methods (whole words and sentences) and phonemic methods (stressing the relationship between graphemes and phonemes; see, for example, Santoro & De Lorenzo, 2000).

Reading

To analyze some of the empirical data available on the acquisition of literacy in Italian, it may be useful to set them against an explicit model of reading acquisition. Several models of the acquisition of reading and writing abilities are available (e.g., Frith, 1985; Marsh, Friedman, Welch, & Desberg, 1981; Seymour & McGregor, 1984). The models differ from each other on many aspects, but it may be accurate to characterize them as postulating three developmentally separate stages: (a) A holistic stage in which the verbal material is recognized as a

---

[1] Italian children enter elementary school when they are 6 years old. After 5 years, they enter middle school (corresponding to Grades 6–8).

FIG. 7.1.   Examples of the stimuli used by Job and Reda (1996), in the first line, a car brand logo is represented (condition C+W+). In the second line, the same logo is altered (condition C+W−). In the third line, the brand name without the graphic context is reported (condition C−W+). Finally, in the last line, the brand name is altered (condition C−W−).

perceptual pattern. Only after having recognized the word as a whole can the child produce the corresponding phonological form. (b) A stage in which an analytic strategy allows single letters to be identified and pronounced. In this case, the phonological forms obtained corresponds to the blending of the letters that have been decoded. (c) A stage in which morphological and orthographic patterns are exploited to retrieve the phonological forms of words. Frith (1985) calls these stages logographic, alphabetic, and orthographic, respectively.

Given the highly regular mapping from orthography to phonology in Italian, it may be predicted that the logographic stage does not play a role in the acquisition of reading in this language. However, the data are not consistent on this issue. Job and Reda (1996), following the research strategy used by Masonheimer, Drum, and Ehri (1984), selected 14 logos that were judged to be familiar to children attending kindergarten, and presented them either intact, or with some alterations. The four conditions thus obtained are depicted in Fig. 7.1 and can be described as follows:

Condition **C+W+**: The stimuli were the exact copies of each logo, with the correctly written item(s);

Condition **C+W−**: The written item(s) appearing in each logo was altered by an exchange of two letters in the string or by inversion of the order of the two;

Condition **C−W+**: The written item(s) appearing in each logo was presented without the graphic context;

Condition **C**−**W**−: The written item(s) appearing in each logo was presented without the graphic context and was altered by an exchange of two letters within a string or by inversion of the order of the two strings.

In addition to these stimuli, each participant was presented with the following written stimuli:

1. His or her name, correctly written or altered in two ways: by an exchange of letters in initial position and by an exchange of letters in middle positions
2. A list of words and nonwords. The 16 words varied in length and frequency, the 16 nonwords in length
3. The letters of the alphabet.

Participants were required to read aloud each stimulus. The test required two sessions for completion.

Of the 55 children taking part in the study, some were attending kindergarten and some the first year of elementary school. According to their reading performance on the list of words, children were classified into one of three classes:

1. Nonreaders (30 children, mean age: 5 years 8 months, range 5 years 4 months–6 years 9 months)
2. Prereaders (10 children, mean age: 6 years 2 months, range 5 years 6 months–6 years 8 months)
3. Readers (15 children, mean age: 6 years 4 months, range 5 years 8 months–6 years 9 months).

The results show the following pattern for the logos: In the C+W− category, nonreaders made more false-positive identification and semantic errors than did prereaders, who, in turn, made more false-positive identification and semantic errors than did readers. Conversely, prereaders, and even more so readers, made visually similar errors (50% of letters that were common between stimulus and response) to stimuli in the C−W+ and C−W− categories. In the same categories nonreaders gave unrelated responses or omissions, and this in spite of the fact that nonreaders had some knowledge about letter names. These results cannot be taken as evidence for a logographic stage because of the large number of semantic errors (see also Ehri, 1987).

However, as mentioned, each of the same sample of children was also presented with his or her printed name (e.g., Enrico) and two altered forms. In the first, the two initial letters of the name were exchanged (e.g., Nerico); in the second, two middle letters were exchanged (e.g., Enirco). Interestingly, even nonreaders could recognize their name 70% of the time when correctly written. Crucially, although they never read the letter string correctly when the name was altered, they made very few false-positive identifications: 24% when middle letters were exchanged and 6% when initial letters were exchanged. This rate of false positive is quite low and seems to support the notion of a logographic stage: Children could recognize their own names and could correctly reject the altered forms, but they could not read them aloud. Because it is unlikely that they had previously seen their name written in the specific form we presented them with, they must have based their responses on knowledge about the letters, and yet they could not use this knowledge to read slightly different sequences.

The next two stages in Frith's model are the alphabetic stage, in which the strategy children use is based on the decoding of the letters that compose a word, and the orthographic stage, in which children use linguistic units that take into account morphological as well as orthographic patterns. As already mentioned, the mapping from print to sound is quite regular in Italian, but the reader must process and use graphemes that quite often are multiletter and context sensitive. Thus it may be hypothesized that the alphabetic strategy requires that some effort be mastered even in a regular language like Italian.

According to some authors (e.g., Landerl, Wimmer, & Frith, 1997) the mastering of decoding skills in languages with consistent orthographies is best indexed by reading speed rather than by accuracy. Indeed, Stella and Cerruti Biondino (2002) have presented longitudinal data showing that for both Italian typical readers and dyslexic readers there is an increase in reading speed from second grade to eighth grade (last year of middle school in Italy). However, whereas in second grade the difference between typical readers and dyslexic children is 1.36 syllables/second, in eighth grade the difference increases to 2.51 syllables/second. This pattern is consistent with the view that, in transparent orthographies, typical readers acquire efficient decoding skills more rapidly, whereas dyslexic children lag behind in mastering and automatically activating the connections between phonological and orthographic representations.

Unfortunately, an analysis of accuracy is not reported in the study, but the nature of the errors participants make in reading may be of some help for determining how literacy is acquired even in transparent languages. Data on this issue have been reported by Tressoldi (1996), who considered accuracy as well as reading times in his cross-sectional study. A sample of 929 children from second to eighth grade were administered several tests taken from Cornoldi and Colpo (1981), to investigate text reading, and from Sartori, Job, and Tressoldi (1995), to investigate word and nonword reading and homophonic strings discrimination. The expected increase in reading rate from the second to the eighth grade varied as a function of the linguistic material: It was largest for connected text (from 2.1 to 5.3 syllables/second), intermediate for words (from 1.6 to 4.6 syllables/second), and smallest for nonwords (from 1.1 to 2.6 syllables/second). As for accuracy, the rate of errors decreased rapidly for both word and nonword stimuli, with words being less error prone than nonwords at each school level. However, the ability to discriminate nonhomographic homophones developed quite slowly. In sixth grade, errors were still about 10% in this task. The author interprets this pattern as showing that Italian readers enter the orthographic stage quite late and argues that this may be due to the regularity of the language that does not require the development of strategies based on linguistic units larger than letters or syllables.

In Tressoldi's study, errors in reading words were below 5% starting from third grade. Thus it is indeed the case that accuracy is high in learning to read Italian. Nevertheless, it would be interesting to know if the errors children make, although few, are typologically different for the different reading proficiency levels. This would be expected if the children pass through different reading stages. Sonzogni (1989) presents data that show this to be the case. Her aim was to identify whether the proposed stages of Frith's model could account for Italian children's performance in different school levels. To do so, she investigated the reading accuracy of an unselected sample of 133 children from second to fifth grades. To analyze their performances, Sonzogni applied the criteria of Snowling, Stackhouse, and Racks (1986) for classifying reading errors, but she further constrained those criteria to take into account relevant psycholinguistic variables. The results of her study are reported in Table 7.3. There are several interesting findings to note. First, the types of errors children produce in reading aloud allow classifying them, save a few cases, in one of the stages postulated by the model. Further, the strategies identified tend to covary with age, but only to some degree: A few children in second grade already make use of the orthographic strategy and some children in fifth grade still use an alphabetic strategy. Finally, reading strategy, rather than age level, accounts for correct reading performance in the sample—both quantitatively and qualitatively.

To investigate whether children pass from the use of an alphabetic strategy to the use of an orthographic strategy, Job (1994) designed a study in which children were presented with words

TABLE 7.3
Percentage of Children's Use of Different Reading Strategies From Second to
Fifth Grade (Sonzogni, 1989)

| Grade | Prealphabetic | Alphabetic | | Orthographic | Unclassified |
		First Step	Second Step		
2	18	38	41	3	—
3	11	33	33	22	—
4	6	14	49	31	2
5	14	8	16	62	7

and nonwords written either with the homogeneous case (CAT) or in case alternation (cAt). The assumption underlying the choice of these experimental conditions was that the alphabetic strategy takes single letters as the basic unit of reading whereas the orthographic strategy is based on morphological and orthographic units that may involve multiletter sequences. If this is true, then the case-alternation format should hinder the performance of children who use the orthographic strategy more than that of children who use the alphabetic strategy. From a developmental point of view, this experimental design is interesting because it predicts that case alternation would disrupt older children's performance more than it would younger children's performance.

High- and low-frequency words and nonwords were used. Words varied for length and frequency. Nonwords varied for length. Stimuli had different internal structure, but no multiletter graphemes were included.

Half of the 36 children who took part in the study attended the second grade (mean age, 7 years 4 months), and half attended the fifth-grade (mean age, 10 years 3 months).

Each child was presented with several lists of six stimuli written either homogeneously or with case alternation and was asked to read them aloud. The dependent variable was the difference between the reading time of case-alternated stimuli and the reading time of homogeneous stimuli. Such a difference, expressed as percentage of reading time increase, is reported in Table 7.4. The fact that the difference is always positive indicates that case-alternated stimuli always took longer to read than did the comparison homogenous stimuli. However, statistical analyses showed that the increase was not the same for younger and older children: The main

TABLE 7.4
Percentage of Increase in Reading Times for CaSe-AlTeRnAtEd stimuli
Compared with Homogeneous Stimuli

Grade	High-Frequency Words (%)	Low-Frequency Words (%)	Nonwords (%)
2	62	17	15
5	91	69	44

effects of age and type of stimuli, and the interaction between them, were significant. As can be seen, for both age groups, high-frequency words are the most disrupted by case alternation. However, for low-frequency words, only some of which may be part of the younger readers' visual lexicon, the two groups diverge: The disruption is similar to that for nonwords for second graders whereas it is very high (69%) for fifth graders.

This pattern is compatible with stage models of reading that postulate an earlier stage during the acquisition of reading in which the strategy employed is based on letter identity, and a later stage in which the word, the morphemic level, or both, becomes relevant. It is noteworthy that for nonwords the difference is smaller than that for low-frequency words for both age groups. So it seems that younger and older children use a similar strategy in reading nonwords, and this is not an orthographic strategy. Rather, the strategy exploits the grapheme-to-phoneme conversion route that has been established on the basis of the alphabetic strategy.

Writing

Two aspects of the acquisition of writing have been the focus of investigation by Italian researchers: decoding skills and the strategies underlying the written production of texts. Although for decoding skills there are fewer studies on the writing than on reading (for a recent review see Tressoldi, 2002), the studies on the written production of texts, an area of study that is at the interface between psychology and education, are numerous.

As for the first issue, that is, the acquisition of decoding skills, one set of data has been reported in the study by Tressoldi (1996) previously cited. The same sample of children tested for reading was also asked to write to dictation (a) words, (b) nonwords, and (c) simple sentences containing homophones. The dependent variable was accuracy. Errors to words and nonwords did not differ significantly (even though there was a trend for nonwords to give rise to more errors than words) and decreased from about 10% in second grade to 2% in fifth grade. Errors to homophones, instead, were high but decreased steadily (from 74% in second grade to 18% in fifth grade to 6% in eighth grade).

Tressoldi suggests that Italian children rely on the alphabetic strategy to write both words and nonwords up to the fifth grade, thus delaying the use of the orthographic strategy in writing. A similar conclusion, with some qualifications, has been reached by Sonzogni (1989) on the basis of the analysis of the writing performance of the sample of 133 children mentioned in the preceding subsection. She asked her participants to write to dictation both words and nonwords, and then she analyzed their accuracy. Unlike the participants who took part in Tressoldi's study, the children in her study made more errors in writing nonwords than words: In second grade, errors to words and nonwords stimuli were 9% and 18%, respectively; the corresponding figures for Grades 3, 4, and 5 were 5% versus 9%, 5% versus 10%, and 4% versus 7%, respectively. Also, by the fifth grade, 57% of the children used an orthographic strategy. However, the author points out that children tended to use the alphabetic strategy in writing longer than in reading, and always acquired the orthographic strategy in reading before using it accurately in writing.

The studies on written text production started in the late 1980s, under the influence of the cognitive approach, paradigmatically represented by the model of Hayes and Flower (1980). This model presents a view of writing as articulated in three processes: planning, translating, and revising.

A first research line has analyzed the strategies used by students in different grades (mainly, elementary and middle) and the difficulties they have to deal with when composing specific text types relevant for instruction. Studies in this area have investigated planning in expository (Boscolo, 1990, 1996) and narrative writing (Pontecorvo & Paoletti, 1991), revising in narrative and argumentative writing (Boscolo, 1991), integrating information in argumentative writing (De Bernardi & Antolini, 1996), and in text synthesis (De Bernardi & Levorato, 1991).

Studies on text composition were fostered also by the development of personal computer technology, which suggested interesting possibilities for analyzing new ways of learning and designing more effective learning environments. In particular, narrative writing was used for analysis of collaborative planning (e.g., Pontecorvo & Zucchermaglio, 1991) and revising (Zammuner, 1995). The interest in the social dimension of writing was also linked to the social constructivist approach to literacy learning, with its conceptualization of writing as a social and cultural practice (Boscolo, 1995; Pontecorvo, 1997).

One research line has investigated the ways in which students of different degrees of writing competence take into account the readers' need for understanding, as well as the ways to improve their sense of audience (Boscolo & Cisotto, 1999; Lumbelli, Paoletti, Camagni, & Frausin, 1996; Lumbelli, Paoletti, & Frausin, 1999). On the other hand, studies have been conducted from the cognitive perspective of writing, on how writing various text types (e.g., notes, outlines, personal comments) can facilitate conceptual change and improve learning in scientific and historical domains (e.g., Boscolo & Mason, 2001; Mason, 1998, 2001; Mason & Boscolo, 2000). Last, motivational aspects of writing have been investigated, that is, how a stimulating writing environment may improve students' writing abilities as well as their interest in writing and learning (Boscolo, 2002; Boscolo & Carotti, 2003).

DIFFICULTIES IN ACQUIRING LITERACY

It may be productive to distinguish two types of difficulties children may be confronted with when acquiring literacy: those pertaining to the decoding skills involved in mapping orthography to phonology and vice versa; and those pertaining to the abilities necessary to comprehend written texts. These two aspects of literacy are quite distinct, and the sources of difficulties in the acquisition process may be quite different. For this reason, we briefly discuss them in turn.

Decoding Skills

Irrespective of the degree of regularity of the mapping from orthography to phonology, dyslexic adults show a reduced activation of the left temporal lobe during reading tasks (Paulesu et al., 2001). However, in matched reading tests, the Italian participants in the study by Paulesu et al. performed better than either French or English participants. Furthermore, from a developmental point of view, the incidence of dyslexia among Italian children, as compared with that of American children, is much lower, as reported by the seminal paper by Lindgren, De Renzi, and Richman (1985) . This pattern leads to the conclusion that the orthographic irregularity of a language can modulate the degree of success in learning to read and can affect the actual manifestation of dyslexic symptoms. Nevertheless, the acquisition of reading and spelling is quite effortful even for a language with a transparent orthography, and a number of children experience difficulties in learning to read and write properly in Italian.

According to different sources, there are an estimated 2.5%–8% school-age Italian children who suffer reading and spelling difficulties at the decoding level. Stella (2001) reports that, on the bases of children's performance on standardized tests, in elementary school 3.8% pupils have difficulties in reading and 4.1% have difficulties in writing. The analogous figures for children in middle school (11 to 14 years old) are 3.6% and 4.5%, respectively. In the same survey, 1.8% of elementary school children, and 2% of middle school children showed difficulties in text comprehension.[2]

There are numerous cases of Italian developmental dyslexic people reported in the literature. Rather than review all of them, it may be sufficient to note that the most frequently reported cases present either a profile of surface dyslexia, with word reading more impaired than nonword reading (e.g., Job, Sartori, Masterson, & Coltheart, 1984; Zoccolotti et al., 1999), or a profile of phonological dyslexia, with nonword reading more impaired than word reading (Lucca, Job & Vio, 1989; Sartori & Job, 1983) or a profile of letter-by-letter reading (e.g., Job & Rapagnani, 1996).

In group studies, Zoccolotti, Judica, De Luca, and Spinelli (2002) reported abnormal eye movements for Italian dyslexic children when reading connected text, especially affecting the number and the amplitude of saccadic movements: Their participants presented with a high number of saccadic movements of small amplitude (De Luca, Borrelli, Judica, Spinelli, & Zoccolotti, 2002; De Luca, Di Pace, Judica, Spinelli, & Zoccolotti, 1999). However, unlike what is reported for English dyslexic readers (Pavlidis, 1981), the incidence of regressions for Italian dyslexic readers is no higher than that of control readers. This pattern of frequent, small-amplitude fixations has been interpreted as showing that Italian dyslexic children, the majority of whom have surfacelike dyslexia, use letters and syllables as decoding units. Furthermore, these authors (e.g., Spinelli, De Luca, Judica, & Zoccolotti, 2002) have also shown that crowding (i.e., the influence of surrounding visual elements on the recognition of a target element) negatively affected dyslexic children compared with age-matched control children in processing both words and symbols. This suggests an impairment at some prelinguistic stage of analysis. Interestingly, only a subgroup of dyslexic children, about 30% of the sample, showed this pattern of performance.

Written Text Comprehension

Some children, in spite of having normal decoding skills, may present with difficulties in comprehending what they read. As the difficulties are restricted to, or mainly present in, processing written texts as compared with oral texts, they cannot be due to intellectual (in)abilities per se (Joshi, Williams, & Wood, 1998).

In a series of studies, Cornoldi and coworkers have shown that Italian students who are poor comprehenders are less able than good readers to inhibit irrelevant information in memory tasks (Cornoldi, De Beni, Palladino, & Pazzaglia, 2002; De Beni, Palladino, Pazzaglia, & Cornoldi, 1998). Thus one source of difficulty may be working memory limitations, which prevents filtering out information not specific to the task. Furthermore, poor comprehenders are less skilled than control readers in metacognitive tasks, as indexed by their difficulty in monitoring the task they are performing, their inability to apply efficient processing strategies, and their poor perception of typological differences of texts. Thus metacognitive factors also affect negatively the reading performance of poor comprehenders (Cornoldi, De Beni, & Pazzaglia, 1996).

It is not clear at the present time what the joint causal role of working memory deficits and metacognitive inabilities may be in written text processing. From their studies, Cornoldi et al. (2002) propose the working hypothesis that metacognitive abilities directly influence comprehension, whereas working memory affects comprehension only indirectly through the effects it exerts on metacognitive abilities.

---

[2] In passing, it may be interesting to note that these figures are substantially lower than those estimated by teachers for both school levels.

CONCLUSIONS

This chapter reviewed some of the factors affecting the acquisition of literacy in Italian, focusing mainly on those related to the orthography-to-phonology interface. The reason is twofold. On the one hand, this is the area most focused on by Italian researchers investigating the acquisition and disorders of reading and writing. On the other hand, there are reasons to believe that comprehension processes beyond the decoding stage are less affected by language-specific factors. Thus, even if it may be hypothesized that there are some language-specific effects on working memory, such as word length (Italian words tend to be longer than words in English), their influence on comprehension should not be substantial.

Two aspects can be singled out from the studies on Italian just reviewed, and both point to the relevance of investigating the acquisition of literacy in Italian.

The first is that the empirical data collected allow us to provide a description of the processes involved in the acquisition of reading and writing as well as some of the difficulties children encounter in such enterprise. In turn, this may be instrumental in developing intervention programs that may be able to alleviate such difficulties. In this perspective, the studies conducted have shown that some features of the language, such as orthographic consistency, modulate the rate and mode of the acquisition of abilities involved in processing written language. In particular, the data show that reading speed is a crucial factor in the acquisition of reading and a reliable indicator of difficulties in mastering such ability. The data also show that typologically different errors provide important cues for determining the stage in the acquisition process the child is at and the specific type(s) of difficulties the child is experiencing. For writing, accuracy rather than speed was investigated, and so at present no data are available about the relationship between speed and the acquisition, disorders, or both, of writing.

The second aspect that emerges from review studies relates to the possibility of carrying on comparative studies of writing systems with different orthographic structures. These studies would contribute to a better understanding of the constraints and the mechanisms languages use to process information within and across modality. To this end, direct cross-linguistic comparisons may be especially helpful in disentangling some of the general issues pertaining to the acquisition of reading and writing.

REFERENCES

Boscolo, P. (1990). The construction of expository text. *First Language, 10*, 217–230.

Boscolo, P. (1991). Strategies of restructuring narrative and argumentative texts in elementary school children. In M. Carretero, M. Pope, R.-J. Simons, & J. I. Pozo (Eds.), *Learning and instruction: European research in an international context* (Vol. 3, pp. 293–309). Oxford, UK: Pergamon.

Boscolo, P. (1995). The cognitive approach to writing and writing instruction: A contribution to a critical appraisal. *Cahiers de Psychologie Cognitive, 14*, 343–366.

Boscolo, P. (1996). The use of information in the construction of expository text. In M. Orsolini, L. B. Resnick, C. Pontecorvo & B. Burge (Eds.), *Children's early text construction* (pp. 209–227). Mahwah, NJ: Lawrence Erlbaum Associates.

Boscolo, P. (Ed.). (2002). La scrittura nella scuola dell'obbligo [Writing in elementary and middle school]. Rome-Bari: Laterza.

Boscolo, P., & Carotti, L. (2003). Does writing contribute to improving high school students' approach to literature? *L1 – Educational Studies in Language and Literature, 3*, 197–224.

Boscolo, P., & Cisotto, L. (1999). On reading–writing relationships: How young writers construe the reader's need for inferences. In S. R. Goldman, A. C. Graesser, & P. van den Broek (Eds.), *Narrative comprehension, causality, and coherence: Essays in honor of Tom Trabasso* (pp. 161–178). Mahwah, NJ/London: Lawrence Erlbaum Associates.

Boscolo, P., & Mason, L. (2001). Writing to learn, writing to transfer. In P. Tynjälä, L. Mason, & K. Lonka (Eds.), *Writing as a learning tool: Integrating theory and practice* (pp. 83–104). Dordrecht, The Netherlands: Kluwer.

Colombo, L. (1992). Lexical stress effect and its interaction with frequency in word pronunciation. *Journal of Experimental Psychology: Human Perception and Performance, 18*, 987–1003.

Cornoldi, C., & Colpo, M. (1981). *La verifica della lettura*. Florence: Organizzazioni Speciali.

Cornoldi, C., De Beni, R., Palladino, P., & Pazzaglia, F. (2002). Lettori che non capiscono. In G. Di Stefano & R. Vianello (Eds.), *Psicologia dello sviluppo e problemi educativi*. Florence: Giunti.

Cornoldi, C., De Beni, R., & Pazzaglia, F. (1996). Profiles of reading comprehension difficulties: An analysis of single cases. In C. Cornoldi & J. Oakhill (Eds.), *Reading comprehension difficulties: Processes and intervention*. Mahwah, NJ: Lawrence Erlbaum Associates.

Cossu, G. (1999). The acquisition of Italian orthography. In M. Harris and G. Hatano (Eds.), *Learning to read and write: A cross-linguistic perspective* (pp. 10–33). Cambridge: University Press.

Cossu, G., Shankwailer, D., Liberman, I. Y., Katz, L. E., & Tola, G. (1988). Awareness of phonological segments and reading ability in Italian children. *Applied Psycholinguistics, 9*, 1–16.

De Beni, R., Palladino, P., Pazzaglia, F., & Cornoldi, C. (1998). Increases in intrusion errors and working memory deficit of poor comprehenders. *Quarterly Journal of Experimental Psychology, 51A*, 305–320.

De Bernardi, B., & Antolini, E. (1996). Structural differences in the production of written arguments. *Argumentation, 10*, 175–196.

De Bernardi, B., & Levorato, C. (1991). How writers integrate information in written text production: A developmental study. *European Journal of Psychology of Education, 6*, 143–153.

De Luca, M., Borrelli, M., Judica, A., Spinelli, D., & Zoccolotti, P. (2002). Reading words and pseudowords: An eye movement study of developmental dyslexia. *Brain and Language, 80*, 617–626.

De Luca, M., Di Pace, M., Judica, A., Spinelli, D., & Zoccolotti, P. (1999). Eye movement patterns in linguistic and non-linguistic tasks in developmental surface dyslexia. *Neuropsychologia, 37*, 1407–1420.

Ehri, L. C. (1987). Learning to read and spell words. *Journal of Reading Behavior, 19*, 5–31.

Frith, U. (1985). Beneath the surface of developmental dyslexia. In K. Patterson, J. Marshall & M. Coltheart (Eds.) *Surface dyslexia*. London: Lawrence Erlbaum Associates.

Hayes, J. R., & Flower, L. S. (1980). Identifying the organization of writing processes. In L. W. Gregg & E. R. Steinberg (Eds.), *Cognitive processes in writing*. Hillsdale, NJ: Lawrence Erlbaum Associates.

Job, R. (1994, September). Development of reading and writing in Italian. Paper presented at the NATO Advanced Study Institute on Cognitive and Linguistic Bases of Reading, Writing and Spelling. Algarve, Portugal.

Job, R., & Rapagnani, C. (1996). Analisi e riabilitazione di un caso di lettura "lettera-per-lettera" in età evolutiva. *Psichiatria dell'Infanzia e dell'Adolescenza, 63*, 713–729.

Job, R., & Reda, P. (1996). Lo stadio logografico nell'acquisizione della lettura. In P. Boscolo, F. Cristante, A. Dellantonio, & S. Soresi (Eds.), *Aspetti qualitativi e quantitativi nella ricerca psicologica* (pp. 69–79). Padua: Il Poligrafo.

Job, R., Sartori, G., Masterson, J., & Coltheart, M. (1984). Surface dyslexia in Italian. In R. N. Malatesha and H. A. Whitaker (Eds.), *Dyslexia: A global issue*. The Hague, Netherlands: Nijhoff.

Joshi, R. M., Williams, K. A., & Wood, J. R. (1998). Predicting reading comprehension from listening comprehension: Is this the answer to the IQ debate? In C. Hulme & R. M. Joshi (Eds.), *Reading and spelling*. Mahwah, NJ: Lawrence Erlbaum Associates.

Landerl, K., Wimmer, H., & Frith, U. (1997). The impact of orthographic consistency on dyslexia: A German–English comparison. *Cognition, 3*, 315–334.

Lepsky, A. L., & Lepsky, G. (1981). *La lingua italiana*. Milan: Bompiani.

Lindgren, S. D., De Renzi, E., & Richman, L. C. (1985). Cross-national comparisons of developmental dyslexia in Italy and United States. *Child Development, 56*, 1404–1417.

Lucca, A., Job, R., & Vio, C. (1989). Uno studio su soggetto singolo di idslessia evolutiva: Un contributo metodologico. *Ricerche di Psicologia, 1*, 63–93.

Lumbelli, L., Paoletti, G., Camagni, C., & Frausin, T. (1996). Can the ability to monitor local coherence in text comprehension be transferred to writing? In G. Rijlaarsdam, H. van den Bergh, & M. Couzijn (Eds.), *Effective teaching and learning of writing*. Amsterdam: Amsterdam University Press.

Lumbelli, L., Paoletti, G., & Frausin, T. (1999). Improving the ability to detect comprehension problems: From revising to writing. *Learning and Instruction, 9*, 143–166.

Marsh, G., Friedman, M. P., Welch, V., & Desberg P. (1981). A cognitive developmental theory of reading acquisition. In T. G. Waller & G. E. Mackinnon (Eds.), *Reading Research: Advances in Theory and Practice, Vol. 3*. New York: Academic Press.

Mason, L. (1998). Sharing cognition to construct scientific knowledge in school context: The role of oral and written discourse. *Instructional Science, 25*, 359–389.

Mason, L. (2001). Introducing talk and writing for conceptual change: A classroom study. *Learning and Instruction, 11*, 305–329.

Mason, L., & Boscolo, P. (2000). Writing and conceptual change. What changes? *Instructional Science, 28*, 199–226.

Masonheimer, P. E., Drum, P. A., & Ehri, L. C. (1984). Does environmental print identification leads children into word reading? *Journal of Reading Behavior, 16*, 257–271.

Näslund, J. C., Schneider, W., & van den Broek, P. (1997). Beginning reading in Germany and the U.S.A.: A comparison of phonological segmentation, decoding, lexical access and comprehension. In C. K. Leong & R. M. Joshi (Eds.), *Cross-language studies of learning to read and spell.* Dordrecht, The Netherlands: Kluwer.

Nespor, M. (1993). *Le strutture del linguaggio. Fonologia.* Bologna: il Mulino.

Orsolini, M., & Marslen Wilson, W. (1997). Universal in morphologyical representation: Evidence from Italian. *Language and Cognitive Processes, 12,* 1–47.

Padovani, R., & Cacciari, C. (2003). Il ruolo della trasparenza morfologica delle parole in Italiano. *Giornale Italiano di Psicologia, 30,* 749–771.

Paulesu, E., Démonet, J-F., Fazio, F., McCroy, E., Chanoine, V., Brunswick, N., Cappa, S. F., Cossu, G., Habib, M., Frith, C. D., & Frith, U. (2001). Dyslexia: Cultural diversity and biological unity. *Science, 291,* 2165–2167.

Pavlidis, G. T. (1981). Do eye movements hold the key to dyslexia? *Neuropsychologia, 19,* 57–64.

Pontecorvo, C. (1997). *Writing development: An interdisciplinary view.* Amsterdam/Philadelphia: Benjamins.

Pontecorvo, C., & Paoletti, G. (1991). Planning story completion in a collaborative computer task. *European Journal of Psychology of Education, 6,* 199–212.

Pontecorvo, C., & Zucc(hermaglio, C. (1991). Computer use in learning about language. *European Journal of Psychology of Education, 6,* 15–27.

Santoro, A., & De Lorenzo, R. (2000). *Vocabolaquario. Metodo grafico-fonemico per acquisire e migliorare le abilità di scrittura e lettura.* Trento: Erikson.

Sartori, G., & Job, R. (1983). Phonological impairment in Italian: Acquired and developmental dyslexia. In D. Rogers & J. A. Sloboda (Eds.), *The acqusition of symbolic skills.* New York: Plenum.

Sartori, G., Job, R., & Tressoldi, P. E. (1995). *Batteria per la valutazione della dislessia e disortografia evolutiva.* Florence: Organizzazioni Speciali.

Scalise, S. (1983). *Morfologia lessicale.* Padua: Clesp Editrice.

Seymour, P. H. K., & McGregor, C. J. (1984). Developmental dyslexia. A cognitive experimental analysis of phonological, morphememic and visual impairments. *Cognitive Neuropsychology, 1,* 43–83.

Snowling, M., Stackhouse, J., & Rack, J. (1986). Phonological dyslexia and dysgraphia. A developmental analysis. *Cognitive Neuropsychology, 3,* 309–339.

Sonzogni, G. M. (1989). Strategie di lettura e di scrittura e sviluppo cognitivo in bambini di scuola elementare. Unpublished thesis, University of Padova, Italy.

Spinelli, D., De Luca, M., Judica, A., & Zoccolotti, P. (2002). Crowding effects on word identification in developmental dyslexia. *Cortex, 38,* 179–200.

Stella, G. (2001). *In classe con un allievo con disordini dell'apprendimento.* Florence: Fabbri.

Stella, G., & Cerruti Biondino, E. (2002). La dislessia evolutiva lungo l'arco della scolarità obbligatoria. In S. Vicari & M. C. Castelli (Eds.), *I disturbi dello sviluppo.* Bologna: Il Mulino.

Tressoldi, P. E. (1996). L'evoluzione della lettura e della scrittura dalla 2$^\wedge$ elementare alla 3$^\wedge$ media. *Età Evolutiva, 53,* 43–55.

Tressoldi, P. E. (2002). I disturbi della scrittura. In S. Vicari & M. C. Castelli (Eds.), *I disturbi dello sviluppo.* Bologna: Il Mulino.

Zammuner, V. L. (1995). Individual and cooperative computer-writing and revising: Who gets the best results? *Learning and Instruction, 5,* 101–124.

Zoccolotti, P., De Luca, M., Di Pace, E., Judica, A., Orlandi, M., & Spinelli, D. (1999). Markers of developmental surface dyslexia in a language (Italian) with high grapheme–phoneme correspondence. *Applied Psycholinguistics, 20,* 191–216.

Zoccolotti, P., Judica, A., De Luca, M., & Spinelli, D. (2002). Diagnosi e riabilitazione dei disturbi di lettura in ragazzi italiani di età scolare. In S. Vicari & M. C. Castelli (Eds.), *I disturbi dello sviluppo.* Bologna: Il Mulino.

8

Reading and Spelling Acquisition and Dyslexia in German

Karin Landerl and Verena Thaler
University of Salzburg

This chapter reviews empirical findings on reading and spelling acquisition and dyslexia in German. The orthography of German is characterized by high consistency of grapheme–phoneme correspondences, and the main method of reading instruction is phonics. The reading and spelling instruction of young children acquiring German orthography are clearly phoneme based. The predictive power of early phonological awareness for later reading skills is lower for German than it is for English, probably because early differences in phonological awareness are evened out by the combination of a phonics teaching approach and experience with a phonologically transparent orthography. Even dyslexic children are able to acquire a high level of reading accuracy for both words and nonwords. Their main problem is a serious and highly persistent deficit in reading fluency. Deficits in reading fluency are closely related to deficits in rapid automatized naming that are manifest even before the onset of reading instruction. A first attempt to remediate deficits in reading fluency was of limited success, showing that such deficits do not result from missing reading practice but rather constitute a neurocognitive disorder.

SOME INFORMATION ON GERMAN ORTHOGRAPHY AND READING INSTRUCTION

The most striking difference between German and English orthography is that German is characterized by highly predictable grapheme–phoneme correspondences (GPCs), also termed high-feed-forward consistency. The only inconsistent consonant grapheme is *v*, which is sometimes pronounced /f/ as in *Vater* and sometimes /v/ as in *Vase*. Few other graphemes have context-dependent pronunciation, that is, the pronunciation changes from one to another in certain contexts. *S* is usually pronounced as /s/, but in onset clusters when followed by *p* or *t* it is pronounced /ʃ/ in most German dialects. The grapheme *h* is pronounced /h/ if it precedes a vowel (e.g., *hat*), but is silent if it follows a vowel (e.g., *mehr*). In English, consistency of GPCs for vowels is much lower. This is not the case for German, in which consistency of GPCs for vowel quality is just as high as it is for consonants. A good example is the letter *a*, which is consistently pronounced as /a/ in the German words *Hand*, *Hass*, *Ball*, and *Garten*, whereas the pronunciation is different for each of the English equivalents *hand*, *hate*, *ball*, and *garden*. Thus, with respect to GPCs, German can be categorized as a shallow orthography.

Just like English, German adheres to the principle of morpheme consistency; that is, the spelling of morphemes is preserved in different word forms (e.g., *fahren*, *Fahrer*, *Gefährt*). However, in contrast to English, it never overrides the phonological principle. Sometimes the German umlaut graphemes can help to retain both morpheme and phonological consistency. For a number of words, plural formation involves a change of the main vowel. For example, the plural of /bal/ [ball] is /bɛlə/. The spellings of the two word forms are *Ball* and *Bälle*. The grapheme *ä* corresponds consistently to the vowel phoneme /ɛ/ so that the phonological word form can be derived from the letter sequence unequivocally. At the same time, the singular and plural word forms are visually similar, thus retaining consistency at the morphemic level.

The principle of morpheme consistency is probably the main reason why German is much less consistent in the direction from phoneme to grapheme, also termed feedback consistency. Whereas in reading there is almost always only one possible translation of a grapheme into a phoneme, in spelling, one has to choose among various possible translations of a phoneme into a grapheme. This explains why German (just like English) has a considerable number of homophonic spellings, for example, *mehr–Meer* [more–sea], *viel–fiel* [a lot–fell], *Lied–Lid* [song–eyelid], *Wal–Wahl* [whale–election]. The orthographic marking of vowel length is especially inconsistent and tricky. Short vowels are marked by two following consonants—but there are a limited number of high-frequency words (mainly function words and prepositions) for which the short vowel is not orthographically marked. For long vowels, there are three different kinds of orthographic marking, doubling of the vowel (*Moos*, *Haar*), putting a "silent h" after the vowel (e.g., *Bahn*, *mehr*), or no orthographic marking at all (*baden*, *Regen*). There are no clear algorithms for the orthographic marking (e.g., *Tal*, *Zahl*, *Saal*). Thus, with respect to spelling, German is rather at the deep end of the continuum of orthographic depth.

Initial reading instruction in the German-speaking countries makes use of the consistency of German orthography by relying on a slowly advancing phonics program in the first year of school. In kindergarten, there is no reading preparation at all, that is, no letter training is provided. Before school parents will only provide information about letters if children show consistent interest. The philosophy is that learning to read and spell is the children's main task in primary school and should not start earlier. Critical features of the phonics program in first grade are the main GPCs—including all multiletter graphemes (e.g., *sch*, *ch*, *ck*, *au*, *eu*, *ei*, *ie*)—which are directly presented and immediately used for word reading. There are also modeling and training on how to read words by means of grapheme–phoneme translation and blending. This training starts with words like *Mimi* and *Mama*, for which blending is easy to demonstrate and to practice, and uses graphical devices to mark syllable boundaries. In the beginning, the blending ritual results in word preforms, which characteristically have artificially lengthened phonemes and incorrect stress assignments. However, because of the consistency of German orthography, these preforms are usually close enough to the target pronunciation. With respect to grapheme teaching, it should be noted that letter names are avoided and that the multiple-letter graphemes are introduced in the same way as the single-letter graphemes. The important aspect of this approach is that the straightforward GPCs do not have to be detected, but rather are systematically presented.

EARLY READING AND SPELLING IN GERMAN IS MAINLY PHONEME BASED

A reasonable expectation is that the combination of a phonologically transparent orthography and a systematic phonics teaching approach makes the acquisition of phoneme synthesis in word recognition and phoneme analysis in word spelling relatively easy for German children. This was indeed confirmed. Wimmer and Hummer (1990) looked at reading and spelling skills of German-speaking children after only a few months of formal reading instruction. Their study included a group of children with normal reading development as well as a group of children who experienced serious difficulties. Wimmer and Hummer found that their young participants (even those who experienced difficulties) were well able to read completely unfamiliar nonwords and most of them could also spell those nonwords. The main difference between typically progressing and delayed readers was that the typically progressing children were able to read about two thirds of the presented items under short-term presentation and performed at ceiling without time restrictions. The delayed readers, however, could work out only about half of the words and 35% of the nonwords under short-term presentation. When they were presented with the same items without time limitation, they could read about 70% of the words and 50% of the nonwords correctly. Reading errors consisted mainly of nonwords beginning with the first letter(s) of the target, indicating a faulty left-to-right decoding strategy. Most spelling errors consisted of spellings that were at least partially phonologically correct. These findings clearly indicate that German-speaking first graders have a good understanding of the phonological component of the orthography they are learning. Systematic grapheme–phoneme translation is their main reading strategy.

Treiman (1993) has argued that the spelling of consonant clusters poses a major phonological difficulty to young children because the clusters are treated as phonological units, such as syllable onset or coda of the rime, and are difficult to segment into their separate phonemes. German provides an interesting test case for this conclusion because, similar to English, German has many words with consonant clusters (e.g., *blau–blue*, *drei–three*, *Hand–hand*, *Wolf–wolf*), and one should therefore expect that German-speaking children should have similar difficulties with the spelling of consonant clusters as English children. However, after only 9 months of formal reading instruction, German first graders did not show particular problems with consonant clusters (Wimmer & Landerl, 1997). For onset clusters, only four phonemically incorrect spellings were observed among the whole sample of 68 children. For end clusters, seven misspellings occurred. The relative ease of consonant-cluster spelling in German does not mean that consonant clusters do not pose any difficulties for phonemic segmentation. It does suggest, however, that such segmentation difficulties are easily overcome by the combination of a consistent orthography and an instructional regime that induces children to early word recognition in reading by means of grapheme–phoneme decoding. This laborious procedure provides systematic segmentation training that makes the phonemic composition of consonant clusters transparent.

EARLY PREDICTION OF READING DEVELOPMENT IN GERMAN

Research on English has identified early phonological skills as a strong predictor of later reading development (for reviews see Catts, 1991; Goswami & Bryant, 1990; Pennington, 1991). Phonological skills are necessary for understanding the alphabetic principle that the segments of written language, that is, the graphemes, stand for phonemes, segments of spoken language. Does the higher orthographic consistency of German compared with that of English make a difference in the relevance of early phonological skills? Empirical evidence shows that early reading in German is more strongly based on phonological decoding than in English. This could mean that young German readers are even more dependent on a good understanding of phonological segments. However, German orthography provides a much more systematic representation of the underlying phonological structure than English does. It is plausible that experience with such a consistent representational system in combination with phonics instruction helps children with early phonological deficits to improve their phonological skills to a sufficient level to cope with the requirements of reading acquisition.

Wimmer, Landerl, Linortner, and Hummer (1991) found that children's performance on a vowel substitution task carried out at the beginning of Grade 1 was reliably correlated with reading and spelling skills 9 months later. In a follow-up study (Landerl & Wimmer, 1994), it was shown that vowel substitution assessed at children's school entry predicted reading accuracy and speed up to the end of Grade 3 and orthographic spelling skills even up to the end of Grade 4. In contrast to findings with English children (Goswami & Bryant, 1990), with German children we did not find a strong relationship of early rhyme recognition skills with reading and spelling at the end of Grade 1. Interestingly, however, early rhyme awareness did predict reading fluency (but not reading accuracy) and orthographic spelling in Grades 2 and 3. In Grade 4, early rhyme awareness was no longer predictive for any of the reading and spelling measures (Wimmer, Landerl, & Schneider, 1994).

These findings on early predictions of literacy are well in line with the observed differences in reading development in German versus English. Young German readers rely heavily on a left-to-right strategy of phonological decoding; that is, they sound out the grapheme sequence. Thus the phonological skill that is most relevant for their early reading development is phoneme awareness. The lower prediction of rhyme awareness in German compared with English readers can probably be explained by the fact that orthographic consistency is higher on the rime level than on the phoneme level in English (Treiman, Mullenix, & Bijeljac-Babic, 1995). Although rhyme awareness may be helpful in cracking the alphabetic code in English, it is not essential in German. Once children are familiar with the alphabetic code, the next requirement is to establish an orthographic lexicon. Such a lexicon is essential for two reasons: First, it allows fast and direct word recognition in reading, which is much less laborious than a systematic indirect decoding procedure; and second, an orthographic lexicon is indispensable for spelling in German. Simply translating the sound sequence into adequate graphemes is not sufficient, but the child has to memorize the orthographically correct spelling. Current theories suggest that orthographic representations are closely connected to phonological representations; that is, they are phonologically underpinned (Ehri, 1992; Perfetti, 1992). Once again the most important phonological segment for the connections between orthographic and phonological representations in German is the phoneme; however, it is probably efficient to have connections between larger orthographic and phonological segments such as onsets, rhymes, and syllables. Such larger units would speed up the reading process for words that include these segments, and they would also be helpful for spelling. Thus a stronger reliance on the orthographic lexicon in Grades 2 and 3 compared with that in Grade 1 would explain the pattern of correlations that we found for rhyme awareness in German orthography.

However, the findings on early prediction of reading and spelling that were discussed so far are of little practical relevance. Rhyme awareness in German turned out to be a less reliable predictor than it is in English but phoneme awareness was a good predictor; however, it mainly predicted the good readers and did not allow identification of those children who showed difficulties in reading acquisition later. All children who showed good performance on the vowel substitution test at the beginning of Grade 1 developed good reading skills over the following months and so did most of the children who had poor phoneme manipulation skills to start with. Very few from a large group of children who were deficient in phoneme awareness at school entry fell behind their classmates in reading during first grade.

A plausible explanation for the fact that the vowel substitution task predicted good rather than poor readers is that it taps into the most challenging level of phonological skills, that is, explicit awareness of individual phonemes. Children were asked to replace the /a/ in one- and two-syllable words with /i/, so, for example, /bal/ became /bil/ and /mama/ was /mimi/. To be able to fulfill the requirements of this task, the /a/ vowel has to be identified, segmented from the rest of the word, and replaced with /i/, and then the sounds must be blended into a coherent pronunciation again. It is likely that this complex procedure overtaxed many 6-year-olds' phonological skills.

In later studies, we made every attempt to use easier phonological tasks with which only those children who develop reading problems later on should have had difficulties. In a large-scale longitudinal study (Mayringer, Wimmer, & Landerl, 1998) we assessed alliteration and rhyme detection, plural formation, nonword repetition, articulation speed, rapid automatized naming (RAN), and letter knowledge in a sample of 560 boys at the beginning of Grade 1. However, once again the correlations of the single predictors with reading and spelling at the end of the school year were disappointingly low, and even a combined phonological predictor score showed only a limited relationship with the literacy measures. These low correlations could be partly due to the low level of difficulty of some of the tasks, causing a reduced variance because many children performed at ceiling. However, when children were classified into at-risk and no-risk groups, it turned out that only 31% of those children who developed reading skills below the 10th percentile could be identified correctly; and even if the at-risk rate were doubled and the lowest 20% on a combined predictor score were classified as at risk, sensitivity could be increased to only 52%, that is, only about half of the later poor readers could be identified. Interestingly, the best single predictor was not one of the phonological awareness measures, but RAN, that is, fast naming of a sequence of pictured objects (Denckla & Rudel, 1976).

One explanation for the weak prediction of early phonological awareness for early reading could be that the phonological requirements of the first stages of reading acquisition in the consistent German orthographic system are so low that even children with a phonological deficit can fulfill them whereas later on phonological skills do differentiate between good and poor readers. However, in a follow-up study 2 years later, when the children were at the end of Grade 3 (Wimmer, Mayringer, & Landerl, 2000), it turned out that those children who had poor phonological awareness skills (the lowest 10% on alliteration and rhyme detection at school entry) did not show any reading difficulties in Grade 3. Both reading accuracy and reading speed were well within the average range not only for word recognition, but even for nonword decoding. The phonological awareness deficit group did, however, show a spelling deficit. Although they were able to spell words phonologically, that is, they represented every phoneme in a dictated word in an adequate way, their spellings did not often conform to the orthographic conventions of German. Once again this finding is somewhat surprising because one would expect children with a deficit in phonological awareness to have problems with the phonological aspect of spelling. However, phonologically correct spelling of words and nonwords from a very early point in development even for dyslexic children was replicated in a number of our studies (Landerl & Wimmer, 2000; Wimmer, 1993, 1996) and can probably also be explained by the phonological transparency of German orthography. It is highly interesting that an early deficit in phonological awareness skills has a negative influence on the development of orthographic spelling skills. Remember that German orthography has many inconsistent phoneme–grapheme correspondences. Thus it seems that phonological awareness is relevant to understanding the relationships between spoken and written words only when these relationships are more complex whereas even children with deficits in phoneme awareness can be trained to understand and apply the basic alphabetic principle that graphemes represent phonemes.

In contrast to the children with an early phonological awareness deficit who developed poor orthographic spelling but adequate reading skills, another group identified by Wimmer et al. (2000) showed deficit in RAN. Ten percent of the first grade sample who had the slowest naming speed on an object-naming RAN task, showed deficient reading speed for both words and nonwords at the end of Grade 3. Interestingly, the group with an early RAN deficit also developed a deficit in spelling. The explanation for this finding is not completely clear. One theoretically plausible interpretation would be that slow naming speed prevents children from developing phonologically underpinned orthographic representations because they are too slow to activate the phonemic code as fast as the visual letter code processing would require. The findings of this study are discussed again in the next section on dyslexia in the context of the double-deficit theory (Wolf & Bowers, 1999).

In summary, the evidence on early prediction of reading and spelling skills shows that phonological awareness is not a very strong predictor in German and that early deficits in phonological awareness are not detrimental for reading development. The phonological transparency of the orthography as well as the intense practice in phonemic decoding provided by the widely used phonics instruction methods can be assumed to be protective factors. That deficits in phonological awareness can be overcome rather easily is also evident from the fact that early training in phonological awareness was found to be very helpful for children who were identified as having a phonological deficit (Schneider, Roth, & Ennemoser, 2000). Among a sample of at-risk children who received treatment during their last kindergarten year only 16% developed spelling problems in the following 2 years in school. Treatment was especially helpful if it combined phonological awareness training with training of letters, a finding similar to the English findings by Hatcher, Hulme, and Ellis, 1994. Among this combined group, the percentage of children who had problems later was just as low as among a group of no-risk control children.

DEVELOPMENTAL DYSLEXIA IN GERMAN: A DEFICIT IN READING FLUENCY

In the phonologically transparent German orthography, even children with serious reading difficulties acquire the process of phonological decoding skills after a short delay. It is only in the very first stages of reading acquisition that problems with this process can still occur. Wimmer (1996) describes early reading and spelling performance of a sample of 12 first graders who were later (in Grade 4) diagnosed as dyslexic. After the first 7 months in school, only two children from this group were not yet able to carry out the sounding-out procedure. Another seven were slow and error prone (between 17% and 79% correct in a nonword-reading task). Three children were able to decode both words and nonwords with a high degree of accuracy, even though their reading was very slow and laborious. Three years later, at the end of Grade 4, these dyslexic children no longer showed problems with respect to the decoding accuracy. Their main problem now was that their reading was extremely slow and laborious. Their reading speed was about 2 years below that of their chronological age.

The finding that reading accuracy is generally high and reading fluency is the main problem of dyslexia in German has been reported in a number of studies (Wimmer, 1993, 1996; Wimmer, Mayringer, & Landerl, 1998). Wimmer and Mayringer (2002), for example, report a standard word-reading rate of between 170 and 190 syllables per minute for 9-year-old German-speaking children whereas dysfluent readers managed to read only between 70 and 95 syllables per minute. Similar findings of high reading accuracy but deficient reading fluency in dyslexic children have also been reported for other consistent orthographies like Norwegian (Lundberg & Hoien, 1990), Spanish (Rodrigo & Jimenez, 1999), Dutch (Yap & van der Leij, 1993), or Italian (Zoccolotti et al., 1999). Deficits in reading fluency are not only a serious impairment but also are highly persistent: Klicpera, Gasteiger-Klicpera, and Schabmann (1993) report that a large majority of German-speaking children with a fluency deficit in Grade 2 still showed seriously delayed reading speed in Grade 8.

A DEFICIT IN PHONEME AWARENESS IS NOT THE CORE PROBLEM OF DYSLEXIA

The dominant Anglo–American view of the cognitive deficits that underlie dyslexia is that they are phonological in nature (e.g., Snowling, 2000). Because of an inborn deficit in phonological processing, dyslexic children cannot fully appreciate the often redundant correspondences between written and spoken words in alphabetic orthographies. Some theorists assume that such a phonological deficit is language inherent (e.g., Elbro, 1996; Snowling, 2000; Studdert-Kennedy & Mody, 1995) whereas others would argue that it is a reflection of a broader cognitive–neurological problem (e.g., Nicolson & Fawcett, 1990; Stein, 2001; Tallal, 1984). The general assumption is that such a phonological deficit is language independent and leads to problems in all alphabetic orthographies.

Based on findings in English, one dominant theoretical view of the phonological deficit hypothesis is that dyslexic people have difficulties in gaining access to the phonemic level of speech. According to this view, they have difficulties in segmenting the speech stream into separate phonological segments. Segmentation is assumed to be especially difficult for the smallest phonological segments that are most relevant for alphabetic skills, that is, phonemes. Shankweiler (1999), for example, came to the conclusion that "phonological awareness is largely absent in dyslexic children and adults" (p. 119). Obviously such an inability to understand the phoneme structure would be detrimental for anybody trying to acquire an alphabetic orthography that depicts phonemes.

In a study comparing dyslexia in German and English (Landerl, Wimmer, & Frith, 1997) we did indeed find a reliable deficit for both German and English participants on a spoonerism task in which children had to exchange the consonantal onsets of word pairs (e.g., *boat* and *fish* become *foat* and *bish*). The spoonerism task is a widely used phonological awareness test, and it is generally assumed that failure to perform this task is due to failure to correctly segment, manipulate, and blend the relevant subword phonological segments. Interestingly, however, a closer look at the errors that the dyslexic participants made revealed that, contrary to theoretical predictions, the children were well able to cope with the requirements on explicit phonological awareness tasks (Landerl & Wimmer, 2000). A typical error was that a child produced one correct response but failed on the second one. For example, for the items *fish* and *boat*, some children responded *bish* and *fish*, *bish* and *boat*, or simply *bish* (or *foat*). The important point is that the single correct response word *bish* indicates that both of the stimulus words were adequately segmented at the onset-rime level: The child isolated the /b/ in *b-oat* and the /ɪʃ/ in *f-ish* to come up with *bish*. It is more likely that a child producing such a response was overtaxed by the complex demands this task makes on phonological working memory and monitoring skills. When such errors that indicated intact phonological awareness were accepted as correct, dyslexic children's error rates dropped from 73% to 26% for the English and from 63% to 15% for the German sample. Furthermore, de Jong and van der Leij (2003) could get 12-year-old Dutch dyslexic adolescents, after an intensive training session, to perform the spoonerism test on the same level as that of normally developing readers. The methodological criticism toward some phonological awareness tasks like spoonerisms is that they measure not only explicit phonological awareness but other cognitive skills as well, so much so that the phonology-based interpretation of poor performance becomes tenuous.

Another task that gives a good impression of children's understanding of the sound structure of language is nonword spelling. To produce correct spelling of a nonword, the child has to segment and identify the constituent phonemes of the dictated nonwords. However, in contrast to spoonerisms, here the demands on working memory and monitoring skills are greatly reduced: the child has on paper what is already transcribed and can easily check what still has to be done. Of course, spelling is also a highly familiar and heavily practiced skill. It turned out that the very same children who showed serious problems on the spoonerism task were quite accurate in spelling one-, two-, and three-syllable nonwords. In fact, the 12-year-old German-speaking dyslexic adolescents performed at ceiling, indicating good access to the phoneme structure of the speech stream.

Thus we are left with the disconcerting finding that dyslexic readers show problems on the spoonerism task (which requires explicit segmentation only on the onset-rime level but places many additional cognitive demands on participants), but do not show marked deficits in nonword spelling (which requires full segmentation and identification on the linguistically more difficult phoneme level but places comparably little extra cognitive demands on children). In a second study, Landerl and Wimmer (2000) followed up on this discrepancy and gave 9-year-old German dyslexic children a nonword-spelling task and a phoneme segmentation task in which children were asked to name the phonemes of each item. To facilitate comparison of task performance, we used more or less the same items in both tasks. The main focus was on consonant clusters because they are difficult to segment for linguistic reasons. We did replicate the finding that German-speaking dyslexic children perform as well as typically developing children when asked to spell nonwords. Both groups, dyslexic children as well as control children, showed slightly lower performances on phoneme segmentation than on nonword spelling, which once again confirms our argument that phonological awareness tests are sometimes difficult for nonlinguistic reasons such as higher memory demand. Dyslexic children performed as accurately as control children in segmenting consonant clusters in word onset position. The only difference between the two groups became evident for clusters in the end position in which dyslexic children could still correctly segment 74% of the clusters but were outperformed by the typically developing children, who were correct on 83% of the items. Once again there is no linguistic reason that would explain why end clusters should be more difficult for dyslexic readers than onset clusters are. Memory problems are a more likely reason.

An important point about this study is that the 9-year-old German-speaking dyslexic children not only performed as well as younger reading level control children, but they were indistinguishable from normally developing children of the same age. An obvious explanation for their good performance is, of course, once again the phonological transparency of German orthography in addition to phonics instruction. Emphasizing segmenting and blending of phonemes helps dyslexic children to develop competent phoneme awareness. The relevant point is that dyslexic children can get good phoneme awareness but nevertheless show serious reading and spelling problems. By now it is also clear that even many English dyslexic readers develop phoneme awareness over time and are at ceiling on phoneme awareness tasks as adults (e.g., Griffiths & Frith, 2002; Paulesu et al., 2001), although there is also evidence suggesting that not all English dyslexic adults reach a normal level of performance (Bruck, 1992). However, in general, we have to conclude that phoneme awareness deficits can hardly be the core problem of dyslexia.

NO DEFICIT IN PHONEME AWARENESS, BUT STILL A PHONOLOGICAL DEFICIT

The evidence from group comparison studies of children with normal and deficient reading development in phonologically transparent orthographies with respect to phonological deficits is inconsistent. Sometimes the difference between dyslexic children and control children is reliable though not dramatic (Caravolas & Volin, 2001; Landerl, 2001; Wimmer, 1993; Wimmer et al., 1998), sometimes dyslexic readers' performance is just as good as those of normal readers (de Jong & van der Leij, 2003; Landerl & Wimmer, 2000). On the other hand, a cognitive task that clearly differentiates between dyslexic and normal readers is the RAN of visual stimuli

(Landerl, 2001; Wimmer et al., 1998; Yap & van der Leij, 1993). In this paradigm, participants are asked to name lists of recurring pictures of objects, colors, digits, or letters (Denckla & Rudel, 1976) and a consistent finding is that dyslexic readers perform at a slower speed than normal readers. This task plays a special role in a recent theoretical explanation of dyslexia assuming that two different deficits can underlie difficulties in reading acquisition. In this so-called double-deficit account (Wolf & Bowers, 1999), phonological deficits are assumed to cause the "classic" symptoms of dyslexia, that is, poor understanding of how print represents speech and therefore low reading accuracy, specific deficits with phonological decoding and phonological errors in spelling. The second cognitive deficit proposed by Wolf and Bowers that can cause dyslexia is a naming-speed deficit. Children with such a deficit should not have particular difficulties with the phonological aspects of an alphabet, but would develop low reading fluency and would show deficits in spelling. Children with a double deficit, that is, with deficits in both cognitive domains should show the most serious reading and spelling problems.

A plausible explanation for the findings in consistent orthographies could be that the phonological deficit subtype plays a minor role because, owing to the phonological transparency of the orthography, such deficits do not have a strong negative influence. The consistent input of orthography might help children with phonological deficits to overcome their problems. Thus, in group studies comparing dyslexic and normal readers, deficits in phonological awareness are sometimes evident and sometimes not, depending on the number of children of the phonological subtype in the sample. Naming-speed deficits, on the other hand, might explain the marked deficit in reading fluency as well as deficits in spelling that were found to be the main problem of dyslexic readers in consistent orthographies.

This was examined in two studies with German-speaking participants. In the already discussed study by Wimmer et al. (2000) children were grouped according to phonological and naming-speed deficits *before* the onset of formal reading acquisition, at the beginning of Grade 1, and their reading and spelling skills were assessed at the end of Grade 3. Consistent with expectations, it turned out that children with an early phonological deficit did not show any reading problems at the end of Grade 3, not even in nonword decoding. The only problem these children experienced was with spelling, but they did not make phonological spelling errors as the double-deficit theory would predict. Those children who had started off with a naming-speed deficit developed a marked problem with reading fluency for both words and nonwords, but not with reading accuracy. This group too showed a deficit in orthographic spelling. Interestingly, although the performance of the double-deficit group was highly comparable with that of the naming-speed deficit group, the additional phonological deficit did not aggravate the reading and spelling difficulties.

In a second analysis (Wimmer & Mayringer, 2002), children were grouped according to their reading and spelling performance at the end of Grade 3. A group of dysfluent readers showed extremely slow reading speed but good accuracy and age-adequate spelling skills. Another group was diagnosed as having a single spelling deficit. Their reading fluency was within an acceptable range for their age. The main question was whether these groups were different with respect to cognitive deficits 3 years earlier, when they entered school.

The group of dysfluent readers showed no deficits in phonological short-term memory and phonological awareness, but only in RAN. The poor spellers, on the other hand, did have poor phonological awareness and short-term memory when formal reading instruction started. The evidence with respect to rapid naming was somewhat inconsistent for this group. In Study 1 the poor spellers tended to be only slightly slower than controls with no significant difference, whereas, in a second sample, poor spellers' naming speed was just as low as that of the dysfluent readers.

These findings provide a plausible explanation for the fact that earlier group studies of German-speaking participants sometimes did and sometimes did not find evidence for a phonological deficit. The participants of our studies were almost without exception selected because of reading problems. The detailed analysis of subtypes, however, shows that phonological awareness is more strongly related with spelling than with reading. It is likely that the group difference in phonological awareness became evident only in those studies in which enough children with spelling as well as reading problems were among the participants.

Thus, as discussed earlier, phonological awareness is relevant for spelling but not so much for reading in German. A plausible reason is that phoneme–grapheme consistency is rather low in German (compared with the very high GPC in reading). To be able to produce orthographically correct spellings, the buildup of an orthographic lexicon is indispensable. In this view, phonological awareness is mainly relevant for the buildup of phonologically sustained orthographic representations. If children suffer from a phonological awareness deficit, they cannot form the close associations between graphemic and phonological representations that are needed. Such a deficit in the buildup of orthographic representations would be detrimental in English because of the inconsistency in both directions, from graphemes to phonemes and from phonemes to graphemes, both reading and spelling are dependent on the availability of orthographic representations. In German, a lack of phonologically underpinned orthographic representations is more detrimental for spelling than for reading.

Naming speed, on the other hand, is closely related to reading fluency. The theoretical explanation for this relationship has yet to be established. Bowers, Golden, Kennedy, and Young (1994) hypothesized that slow naming speed might index how slowly the letters in words are identified, with slower speeds inhibiting the quick buildup of orthographic codes for common patterns. Reading would then be slow both because grapheme–phoneme conversion is slow and because orthographic representations for direct recognition are not available. The latter problem would also cause deficits in orthographic spelling skills.

Furthermore, the cognitive basis of naming-speed deficits is not very clear. Some theorists argue that both phonological awareness deficits and rapid-naming deficits are a consequence of a more general cognitive deficit, namely a deficit in general automatization skills (Nicolson & Fawcett, 1990, 1995). Such a general deficit in automatization skills should also become evident in motoric tasks such as balancing on a beam, especially if balance has to be kept while another cognitive task (e.g., verbal semantic categorization) has to be carried out so that the balancing has to be done automatically. This theoretical account seemed highly interesting for German because it would provide a plausible explanation for the extremely slow and laborious reading of German-speaking dyslexic children. However, in two studies (Mayringer et al., 1998; Wimmer, Mayringer, & Raberger, 1999) it turned out that German children who have specific deficits in reading acquisition do not show any evidence for a more general deficit in automatization skills as measured by the balancing tasks developed by Nicolson and Fawcett (1990, 1995). The evidence rather suggests that children with attention deficit hyperactivity disorder (ADHD) are likely to have problems with the balancing task. Comorbidity between dyslexia and ADHD is well established (Willcutt & Pennington, 2000).

By now many theorists subsume naming-speed deficits as yet another indication of a phonological deficit because rapid-naming tasks require fast access to phonological representations. Snowling (2000) assumes that dyslexic children's phonological representations are of poor quality. Therefore they are not readily available to form the necessary associations with the graphemes of the spelling system. For the same reason many dyslexic children have difficulties to access the subword phonological segments they would need to perform phonological awareness tasks; and, once again for the same reason, retrieval and output of phonological word forms as required in RAN tasks take slightly but reliably longer than in phonologically competent children. However, if phonological awareness tasks and rapid-naming tasks depend on the same underlying phonological skills, how can we explain that a considerable number of children shows deficits in one but not the other kind of task and that the correlation between these two types of tasks is typically rather low?

A reconciling factor might be speed of phonological processing. A major contribution of both research on consistent orthographies and of the double-deficit approach was to introduce speed into the discussion of reading and spelling deficits. It might be very interesting to look at the speed of processing in phonological awareness tasks. Some dyslexic readers might be able to develop phonological awareness skills that are good enough to perform the standard phonological awareness tasks with high accuracy, but difficulties might still be evident from higher reaction times. Indeed, this is how phonological deficits are now sometimes assessed in dyslexic adults (Paulesu et al., 2001; Ramus et al., 2003). Therefore, instead of proposing two independent cognitive deficits, we could assume that children can be deficient along different dimensions of the same cognitive deficit, namely accuracy and speed of phonological processing. Some children with a reading disability have fast but imprecise access to phonology whereas others have slow but precise access to their phonological representations. Both groups would suffer from an inefficient phonological system. Of course, there are children who have slow and inaccurate access to phonology—the double-deficit children in Wolf and Bower's (1999) terminology. Correlations between RAN and phonological awareness tasks would then be low because speed and accuracy of access to phonological representations are not necessarily associated with each other.

Even if naming-speed and phonological awareness deficits are manifestations of the same underlying phonological problem, slow access to phonology seems to be the more serious manifestation—at least in a consistent orthography like German. Children with fast but in-accurate access to phonology (no naming-speed deficit but poor phonological awareness) can be trained on the phonological segments that are relevant for learning to read and spell an alphabetic orthography. Their main problem is to develop phonology-based orthographic representations, but the more consistent an orthography, the less important it is to have ortho-graphic representations. Wimmer et al. (2000) found that children who had a naming-speed deficit when they entered school developed poor orthographic spelling skills in addition to slow reading speeds. Wimmer and Mayringer (2002) report two studies in which they selected groups of children with poor spelling but age-adequate reading skills. In their first study these poor spellers showed normal naming speed (but low phonological awareness) whereas in Study 2 this group was deficient in naming speed as well as in phonological awareness. Therefore the more typical pattern seems to be that this group too shows poor spelling, that is, they too have a deficit in developing orthographic representations, maybe for the very same reason as the other group: Their phonological representations are not readily available to form mutlilevel associations beween phonological and graphemic segments.

READING FLUENCY: HARD TO REMEDIATE

Intervention programs for English-speaking dyslexic children mainly focus on improvement of reading accuracy. It has been demonstrated repeatedly that trainings focusing on the im-provement of phonological awareness are successful in improving dyslexic children's reading accuracy (Torgesen, Rashotte, Alexander, Alexander, & MacPhee, 2003). Such programs may be useful for German-speaking dyslexic children during the very first stages of reading ac-quisition. However, in general, German dyslexic readers are able to develop good phonemic awareness and high reading accuracy in this comparably transparent orthographic writing system. As demonstrated in this chapter, the main problem of dyslexic children in German is their low reading fluency.

One explanation of the typical dysfluency problem in consistent orthographies is that these children suffer from an impairment to form memory representations of frequently read words (Reitsma, 1983; Share, 1999). Therefore they cannot rely on fast direct visual word recogni-tion but have to rely on slow and laborious letter-by-letter phonological decoding, even for high-frequency words. Reading fluency should increase if memory representations of consonant-cluster spellings could be formed and associated with the corresponding phonological segment. Such graphophonological representations for complex onsets would prevent children from laborious decoding.

In a training study (Thaler, Ebner, Wimmer, & Landerl, 2004) we attempted to induce graphophonological memory representations for consonantal word onsets in the following way. The study focused on four different onset clusters with eight items per onset, resulting in 32 training items. The training sequence for a word such as *Fluss* [river] was like this: The word spelling appeared repeatedly on a computer screen. For the first presentation, the whole-word pronunciation was provided by the computer. Then the computer accentuated the onset cluster by visually highlighting first the whole cluster *Fl* and then the individual graphemes of the cluster. Simultaneously, the pronunciations for the whole cluster /flə/ and for the individual graphemes were provided either by the computer or by the child. Finally, the word appeared again on the screen without any highlighting, and the child had to read the whole word aloud. To measure progress over the training sessions, all 32 training words were presented again one by one at the end of each session with the instruction to read them as quickly as possible. Thus, altogether, each of the 32 training words was presented six times within each training session, five times in immediate sequence and a sixth time at the end of the session.

A sample of 20 dysfluent readers (8–11 years) received this computerized training of repeated reading of this limited set of 32 training words over a period of up to 25 days. Each day, training words were presented up to six times with special emphasis on the onset segment. Posttests were carried out 1 and 5 weeks after the last training day. A considerable increase in reading fluency was achieved for the trained words that remained stable for both posttests; however, the training did not lead to age-adequate word-recognition speed. Generalization to untrained words starting with a trained onset cluster (transfer words) was statistically reliable but very small in real terms.

Although these findings of resistance to our remedial attempts are obviously disappointing, they are important from a theoretical point of view. It has been widely assumed that cracking the alphabetic code is the main stumbling block for dyslexic children. However, the participants in our training did not have particular problems with the alphabetic code, as was evident from their high reading accuracy even before training. They were subjected to intensive practice under well-controlled conditions, but nevertheless, they were not able to reach age-adequate reading speed, even for words for which they were intensively trained. This finding shows that dysfluent reading is not "just" a delay in reading development, but a serious and persistent problem. Further evidence comes from the already mentioned longitudinal studies (Wimmer & Mayringer, 2002; Wimmer et al., 2000) demonstrating that children who show deficient reading speed in third grade already showed a cognitive deficit before the onset of reading acquisition, namely a deficit in RAN.

The disconcerting conclusion is that there is a group of poor readers, namely dysfluent readers, who were largely neglected by research. This is especially the case in phonologically transparent orthographies like German, but the same phenomenon of dysfluent reading has also been reported for English (Lovett, 1987; Wolf & Bowers, 1999). Even more disconcertingly, we do not have a good idea of how to help these children.

REFERENCES

Bowers, P. G., Golden, J., Kennedy, A., & Young, A. (1994). Limits upon orthographic knowledge due to processes indexed by naming speed. In V. W. Berninger (Ed.), *The varieties of orthographic knowledge: Theoretical and developmental issues* (pp. 173–218). Dordrecht, The Netherlands: Kluwer.

Bruck, M. (1992). Persistence of dyslexics' phonological awareness deficits. *Developmental Psychology, 28,* 874–886.

Caravolas, M., & Volin, J. (2001). Phonological spelling errors among dyslexic children learning a transparent orthography: The case of Czech. *Dyslexia, 7,* 229–242.

Catts, H. W. (1991). Phonological processing deficits and reading disability. In A. G. Kamhi & H. W. Catts (Eds.), *Reading disabilities: A developmental language perspective* (pp. 67–132). Boston: Allyn & Bacon.

de Jong, P. F., & van der Leij, A. (2003). Developmental changes in the manifestation of a phonological deficit in dyslexic children learning to read a regular orthography. *Journal of Educational Psychology, 95,* 22–40.

Denckla, M. B., & Rudel, R. G. (1976). Rapid automatized naming (RAN): Dyslexia differentiated from other learning disabilities. *Neuropsychologia, 14,* 471–479.

Ehri, L. C. (1992). Reconceptualizing the development of sight word reading and its relationship to recoding. In P. Gough, L. C. Ehri, & R. Treiman (Eds.), *Reading acquisition* (pp. 107–143), Hillsdale, NJ: Lawrence Erlbaum Associates.

Elbro, C. (1996). Early linguistic abilities and reading development: A review and a hypothesis. *Reading and Writing, 8,* 453–485.

Goswami, U., & Bryant, P. (1990). *Phonological skills and learning to read.* Hove, UK: Lawrence Erlbaum Associates.

Griffiths, S., & Frith, U. (2002). Evidence for an articulatory awareness deficit in adult dyslexics. *Dyslexia, 8,* 14–21.

Hatcher, P., Hulme, C., & Ellis, A. W. (1994). Ameliorating early reading failure by integrating the teaching of reading and phonological skills: The phonological linkage hypothesis. *Child Development, 65,* 41–57.

Klicpera, Ch., Gasteiger-Klicpera, B., & Schabmann, A. (1993). *Lesen und Schreiben—Entwicklung und Schwierigkeiten* [Reading and spelling—development and difficulties]. Bern, Switzerland: Huber.

Landerl, K. (2001). Word recognition deficits in German: More evidence from a representative sample. *Dyslexia: An International Journal of Research and Practice, 7,* 183–196.

Landerl, K., & Wimmer, H. (1994). Phonologische Bewußtheit als Prädiktor für Lese- und Schreibfertigkeiten in der Grundschule [Phonological awareness as predictor for reading and spelling in primary school]. *Zeitschrift für Pädagogische Psychologie, 8,* 153–164.

Landerl, K., & Wimmer, H. (2000). Deficits in phoneme segmentation are not the core problem of dyslexia: Evidence from German and English children. *Applied Psycholinguistics, 21,* 243–262.

Landerl, K., Wimmer, H., & Frith, U. (1997). The impact of orthographic consistency on dyslexia: A German–English comparison. *Cognition, 63,* 315–334.

Lovett, M. W. (1987). A developmental approach to reading disability: Accuracy and speed criteria of normal and deficient reading skill. *Child Development, 58,* 234–260.

Lundberg, I., & Hoien, T. (1990). Patterns of information processing skills and word recognition strategies in developmental dyslexia. *Scandinavian Journal of Educational Research, 34,* 231–240.

Mayringer, H., Wimmer, H., & Landerl, K. (1998). Die Vorhersage früher Lese- und Rechtschreibschwierigkeiten: Phonologische Schwächen als Prädiktoren [Prediction of early reading and spelling difficulties. Phonological deficits as predictors]. *Zeitschrift für Entwicklungspsychologie und Pädagogische Psychologie, 30,* 57–69.

Nicolson, R. I., & Fawcett, A. J. (1990). Automaticity: A new framework for dyslexia research? *Cognition, 30,* 159–182.

Nicolson, R. I., & Fawcett, A. J. (1995). Dyslexia is more than a phonological disability. *Dyslexia, 1,* 19–36.

Paulesu, E., Démont, J. F., Fazio, F., McCrory, E., Chanoine, V., Brunswick, N., Cappa, S. F., Habib, M., Frith, C. D., & Frith, U. (2001). Dyslexia: Cultural diversity and biological unity. *Science, 291,* 2165–2167.

Pennington, B. F. (1991). *Diagnosing learning disorders: A neuropsychological framework.* New York: Guilford.

Perfetti, C. A. (1992). The representation problem in reading acquisition. In P. B. Gough, L. C. Ehri, & R. Treiman (Eds.), *Reading acquisition* (pp. 145–174). Hillsdale, NJ: Lawrence Erlbaum Associates.

Ramus, F., Rosen, S., Dakin, S., Day, B. L., Castellote, J. M., White, S., & Frith, U. (2003). Theories of developmental dyslexia: Insights from a multiple case study of dyslexic adults. *Brain, 126,* 841–865.

Reitsma, P. (1983). Printed word learning in beginning readers. *Journal of Experimental Child Psychology, 36,* 321–339.

Rodrigro, M., & Jimenez, J. E. (1999). An analysis of the word naming errors of normal readers and reading disabled children in Spanish. *Journal of Research in Reading, 22,* 180–197.

Schneider, W., Roth, E., & Ennemoser, M. (2000). Training phonological skills and letter knowledge in children at risk for dyslexia: A comparison of three kindergarten intervention programs. *Journal of Educational Psychology, 92,* 284–295.

Shankweiler, D. (1999). Words to meanings. *Scientific Studies of Reading, 3,* 113–127.

Share, D. L. (1999). Phonological recoding and orthographic learning: A direct test of the self-teaching hypothesis. *Journal of Experimental Child Psychology, 72,* 95–129.

Snowling, M. (2000). *Dyslexia* (2nd ed.). Oxford, UK: Blackwell.

Stein, J. (2001). The sensory basis of reading problems. *Developmental Neuropsychology, 20,* 509–534.

Studdert-Kennedy, M., & Mody, M. (1995). Auditory temporal perception deficits in the reading impaired: A critical review of the evidence. *Psychonomic Bulletin & Review, 2,* 508–514.

Tallal, P. (1984). Temporal or phonetic processing deficit in dyslexia? That is the question. *Applied Psycholinguistics, 5*, 167–169.

Thaler, V., Ebner, E.-M., Wimmer, H., & Landerl, K. (2004). Training reading fluency in dysfluent readers with high reading accuracy: Word specific effects but low transfer as untrained words. *Annals of Dyslexia, 54*(1), 89–113.

Torgesen, J., Rashotte, C. A., Alexander, A., Alexander, J., & MacPhee, K. (2003). Progress towards understanding the instructional conditions for remediating reading difficulties in older children. In B. Foorman (Ed.), *Preventing and remediating reading difficulties: Bringing science to scale* (pp. 275–297). Parkton, MD: York Press.

Treiman, R. (1993). *Beginning to spell.* New York: Oxford University Press.

Treiman, R., Mullenix, J., & Bijeljac-Babic, R. (1995). The special role of rimes in the description, use, and acquisition of English orthography. *Journal of Experimental Psychology: General, 124*, 107–136.

Willcutt, E. G., & Pennington, B. F. (2000). Comorbidity of reading disability and attention-deficit/hyperactivity disorder: Differences by gender and subtype. *Journal of Learning Disabilities, 33*, 179–191.

Wimmer, H. (1993). Characteristics of developmental dylexia in a regular writing system. *Applied Psycholinguistics, 14*, 1–33.

Wimmer, H. (1996). The early manifestation of developmental dyslexia: Evidence from German children. *Reading and Writing, 8*, 171–188.

Wimmer, H., & Hummer, P. (1990). How German-speaking first graders read and spell: Doubts on the importance of the logographic stage. *Applied Psycholinguistics, 11*, 349–368.

Wimmer, H., & Landerl, K. (1997). How learning to spell German differs from learning to spell English. In C. A. Perfetti, L. Rieben, & M. Fayol (Eds.), *Research, theory, and practice across languages* (pp. 81–96). Mahwah, NJ: Lawrence Erlbaum Associates.

Wimmer, H., Landerl, K., Linortner, R., & Hummer, P. (1991). The relationship of phonemic awareness to reading acquisition: More consequence than precondition but still important. *Cognition, 40*, 219–249.

Wimmer, H., Landerl, K., & Schneider, W. (1994). The role of rhyme awareness in learning to read a regular orthography. *British Journal of Developmental Psychology, 12*, 469–484.

Wimmer, H., & Mayringer, H. (2002). Dysfluent reading in the absence of spelling difficulties: A specific disability in regular orthographies. *Journal of Educational Psychology, 94*, 272–277.

Wimmer, H., Mayringer, H., & Landerl, K. (1998). Poor reading: A deficit in skill-automatization or a phonological deficit? *Scientific Studies of Reading, 2*, 321–340.

Wimmer, H., Mayringer, H., & Landerl, K. (2000). The double-deficit hypothesis and difficulties in learning to read a regular orthography. *Journal of Educational Psychology, 92*, 668–680.

Wimmer, H., Mayringer, H., & Raberger, T. (1999). Reading and dual-task balancing: Evidence against the automatization deficit explanation of developmental dyslexia. *Journal of Learning Disabilities, 32*, 473–478.

Wolf, M., & Bowers, P. G. (1999). The double-deficit hypothesis for the developmental dyslexias. *Journal of Educational Psychology, 91*, 415–438.

Yap, R., & van der Leij, A. (1993). Word processing in dyslexics: An automatic decoding deficit? *Reading and Writing, 5*, 261–279.

Zoccolotti, P., de Luca, M., di Pace, E., Judica, A., Orlandi, M., & Spinelli, D. (1999). Markers of developmental surface dyslexia in a language (Italian) with high grapheme–phoneme correspondence. *Applied Psycholinguistics, 20*, 191–216.

9

Double Dutch: The Dutch Spelling System and Learning to Spell in Dutch

Anna M. T. Bosman, Saskia de Graaff,
and Martine A. R. Gijsel
Radboud University Nijmegen

In this chapter, a concise description of Dutch orthography and its relation to reading and spelling is presented. Dutch, a member of the West-Germanic language group, reached its modern status in the 16th century. In the beginning of the 19th century, Dutch spelling started to show uniformity. The first set of spelling rules, presented by Siegenbeek in 1804 and extended by te Winkel in 1863, still constitutes the basic principles on which Dutch orthography is based. Dutch is best characterised as a language that contains two types of words, native-Dutch words and non-native-Dutch words. The most recent, comprehensive description of Dutch orthography is presented by the Dutch linguist Nunn (1998). Here, we present her hybrid model because it appears to account for most of the spelling variations in Dutch. It is a combination of two distinct sets of phoneme–grapheme conversion rules, one for native-Dutch words and one for non-native-Dutch words, with a set of autonomous spelling rules, that apply to both native- and non-native-Dutch words. Although written Dutch is morphophonemic, this feature has different consequences for reading and spelling. That is, grapheme-to-phoneme relations appear to be more consistent than phoneme-to-grapheme relations, which renders written Dutch relatively transparent for reading but somewhat opaque for spelling. Finally, we describe how the relationship between phonemes and graphemes, as well as autonomous spelling rules, affects reading for beginning readers and spelling for both beginning and advanced spellers.

Dutch is spoken by about 20 million people and is the standard language of the Netherlands and one of the three standard languages of Belgium; the other official languages of Belgium are French and German. Dutch is also the standard language of the Netherlands Antilles, formerly known as the Dutch West Indies, and Suriname, a former colony of the Netherlands. However, daily conversations in the Antilles are mostly in Papiamentu (Creole Spanish) and in Suriname in Sranan (Creole English) or Sarnami (a language from India). Despite the name and its historical relation to Dutch, Afrikaans or South-African Dutch has been a separate language since the 19th century as a result of the interaction among Dutch, Hottentots (a native-African language), and languages such as Malay and Portuguese (van der Wal, 1992).

The goal of this chapter is to present a description of Dutch orthography with a focus on its most salient reading and spelling aspects. This paper has three main parts. It starts with an introduction of the emergence of the Dutch language and its development towards a standard spelling system, followed by a linguistic description of Dutch orthography, and ends with a discussion of some of the major spelling and reading problems encountered by beginning readers and spellers.

THE ORIGIN AND DEVELOPMENT OF THE DUTCH LANGUAGE

The Dutch language is a member of the West-Germanic language group along with German, Afrikaans, Yiddish, Flemish, Friesian, and English. These languages, together with other European (e.g., Balto-Slavic, Celtic, and Italian) and Asian language groups, originate from the prehistoric Proto-Indo-European language spoken around 5000 B.C.E., most likely between Eastern Europe and the Aral Sea in southern Russia. The first, reconstructed phase of the Germanic language group is Proto-Germanic that arose approximately 1000 B.C.E. Linguists date the origin of Old Dutch to around 700 C.E., its transition into Middle Dutch to 1100 C.E., and the emergence of Modern Dutch to the 16th century.

There is both a linguistic reason and a cultural reason for the occurrence of the transition from Old Dutch into Middle Dutch in the 12th century. The linguistic reason is that unstressed vowels turned into schwa [ə], for example, *vogal* became *vogel* [bird]. The cultural reason is the emergence of an extensive written literature. The beginning of Modern Dutch is strongly related to the fact that a standard, written language came into being and was also boosted by a number of linguistic changes that occurred during that period. Examples are changes in conjunctions and pronouns and the disappearance of suffixes (van der Sijs, 2001a; van der Wal, 1992).

Before focusing the attention on the major topic of this chapter, that is, the Dutch spelling system, we would like to take the opportunity to explain why the English word for our language is Dutch, and not for instance, Netherlandish, Hollandish, or even Netherish. After all, most English words that refer to European languages reveal a clear relationship with the name of the country: Finnish, Spanish, French, German, Portuguese, Italian, and so forth. Flemish, the variety of Dutch spoken in a major part of Belgium is also derived from the word Fleming, the name for the people in Belgium who live in Vlaanderen [Flanders].

Back to the question: Why did 'Dutch' become the English term for the language spoken in the Netherlands? During the Middle Ages, particularly in the 16th and 17th centuries, Dutch had a profound effect on the English language. Many current English words happen to be Dutch loan words. For example, the English word 'yacht' came from the Dutch word *jacht*, 'booze' from an Old Dutch word *buizen*, which means to drink. Later examples are 'aardvark,' 'wildebeast', and 'apartheid'. The most recent Dutch loan word in the English language is 'klapskate' from the Dutch *klapschaats* (see van der Sijs, 2001b, for more examples).

In the 16th century, *Dietsch* or *Duutsch* was the Dutch word for the language spoken in the Netherlands, meaning 'language of the people'. Thus, four centuries ago, the English borrowed our word *Duutsch*, and, because they never returned it, *Dutch* is still the English word for the language spoken in the present-day Netherlands. Although the English forever borrowed the old word *Duutsch*, developments in the Netherlands led to a change from *Dietsch* into *Nederduits* [Nether German]. Subsequently, as a result of the foundation of *het Koninkrijk der Nederlanden* [Kingdom of the Netherlands], the Dutch word for the language spoken in the Netherlands became *Nederlands* (N. van der Sijs, personal communication, February 12, 2002).

Although the first signs of a standard language became visible in the 16th century, it lasted until the beginning of 1800 before Dutch spelling started to show uniformity. In 1804,

Siegenbeek published his regulations that described how to deal with many spelling variations, but left other variations unexplained. In line with Siegenbeek's regulations, te Winkel (1863) wrote an explanation of Siegenbeek's spelling rules that resulted in the first official Dutch spelling list (te Winkel & de Vries, 1866). These spelling rules were officially accepted by the Dutch government in 1883. Since then, two more official spelling reforms took place. One occurred in 1954 and the most recent one in 1995.

Unlike in France, where a number of scholars are appointed in *L'Académie Française* to fight the invasion of foreign words in the French language, the Dutch were rather tolerant and freely adopted (and still do) words from languages such as Latin, Greek, French, German, and English. Thus, linguistically, the Dutch language broadly comprises two types of words: indigenous words and borrowings. Indigenous words are those words that already existed when the Germanic language group was not diversified. Borrowings enter(ed) the Dutch language from other languages. The Dutch etymologist van der Sijs (1996) distinguishes three types of borrowings: semantic borrowings, translation borrowings, and loan words. Semantic borrowings occur when extant Dutch words (both indigenous words and borrowings) receive an additional meaning derived from another language. For example, the Dutch word *administratie* [accounting], borrowed from the French, became polysemic after the introduction of the English meaning related to government, as in the *Reagan-administratie*. The indigenous Dutch word *stem* first meant voice, but received a second meaning through a semantic borrowing from French *voix*, meaning vote. Translation borrowings are foreign words translated into indigenous Dutch words. Usually, both meaning and composition of the foreign word are adopted. For example, the Dutch word *grootvader* came from the French word *grand-père* [grandfather], and the word *ezelsbrug* [mnemonic] come from the Latin words *pons asinorum*. Loan words take phonology, meaning, or both from the language of origin; examples are *imperium* from Latin, *finish* from English, and *pizza* from Italian.

Loan words are the most common borrowings in the Dutch language and are often subdivided in naturalized words, strange words, and bastard words (from te Winkel, 1865). Naturalized words are morphologically and phonologically identical to indigenous words; the borrowing *kerk* [church] is an example of a naturalized word. It strongly resembles the indigenous word *werk* [work], but is borrowed from the Greek word *kuriakon*; and similarly with respect to the word *beschuit* [Dutch rusk], which is borrowed from the French word *biscuit*; it has the appearance of an indigenous word as a result of the use of the prefix *be*.

Strange words usually retain phonology, morphology, and spelling of the source language; examples are *thriller* and *computer* from English, *grammatica* [grammar] from Latin, and *bureau* [desk] and *douche* [shower] from French. Bastard words are loan words with spelling and phonology adapted to indigenous words; examples are *fitheid* from fitness, *empirisch* from empirical, and *citroen* from the French word citron [lemon].

In sum, indigenous words and loan words constitute the two most important, etymological categories of Dutch words. Although it is tempting to conclude that a formal description of Dutch spelling should therefore be based on this etymological distinction, it is not the most useful option. There are two major reasons. One, Dutch language users are largely unaware of the origin of words. Two, the phonology and spelling of a large number of loan words are identical to indigenous words. Nunn (1998), who recently investigated Dutch orthography, proposed distinguishing between two types of words for which two different sets of spelling rules can be developed. The distinction is based on formal criteria and the result was a set of native words and a set of non-native words. Nunn preferred the terms 'native' and 'non-native' for these two types of words, as opposed to the terms 'indigenous words' and 'loan words' because the former typology is based on formal, linguistic criteria, whereas the latter is based on the origin of words.

THE DUTCH SPELLING SYSTEM

Written Dutch uses all 26 signs or letters of the Roman alphabet (i.e., a, b, c, d, e, f, g, h, i, j, k, l, m, n, o, p, q, r, s, t, u, v, w, x, y, z) with the additional digraph IJ, which has a special status. Some linguists consider it a separate letter by indicating that, when used at the beginning of a sentence, both I and J are capitalized, for example, *IJdel* [vain] and IJs [ice]. Although the Roman alphabet is by no means the only alphabetic writing system, it is the world's predominant one and is the basis of the International Phonetic Alphabet (IPA), the most common system for transcribing the sounds of a language (see Albright, 1958). Some alphabetic writing systems generally represent only consonants, for example, Hebrew and Arabic. The Roman alphabet, however, is a fully phonetic system, that is, both consonants and vowels are represented by letters or letter clusters. Alphabets with unique and unequivocal correspondences between letters and sounds are called phonemic alphabets. Spanish and Finnish are examples of the application of the Roman alphabet system that approximate this ideal. Most Roman alphabetic writing systems, however, contain a certain number of inconsistencies between letters and sounds (Coulmas, 1996).

English orthography is notorious with respect to the number of inconsistencies between sounds and letters. The sound /i/, for example, has at least six possible spellings: e as in 'here', y as in 'entry', ey as in 'key', ee as in 'deep', ea as in 'leaf', and ie as in 'chief'. Simon and Simon (1973) maintained that the word 'she' has in principle 36 possible spellings. The [ʃ] can be spelled nine different ways (ti, sh, ci, ssi, si, c, ch, t, s), and [i] in four different ways (e, ea, ee, ie). Stone, Vanhoy, and Van Orden (1997) computed the percentage of one-syllable words with inconsistent sound-to-spelling relations and found that this reached as high as 72.3%. Inconsistencies in the English language are not limited to sound-to-spelling relations; spelling-to-sound relations also contain a number of inconsistencies, albeit fewer. Pronunciation of the word 'pint', for example, is highly inconsistent regarding the pronunciation of words with identical rime; 'dint', 'hint', 'lint', 'mint', and 'tint'. The gh has different pronunciations in *through* and *tough*, as does ea in 'leaf' and 'deaf' and u in 'pull' and 'dull'. Stone et al. (1997) found 31.0% of the same corpus of one-syllable words to be spelling-to-sound inconsistent. They concluded that sound-to-spelling inconsistency is higher than spelling-to-sound inconsistency.[1] In other words, there are more possible ways to spell a word than there are possible ways to pronounce a word. It is not only in English but also in other alphabetic languages that an asymmetry between sound-to-spelling and spelling-to-sound consistency exists (see Ziegler, Stone, & Jacobs, 1996, for French; Bosman & Mekking, 2005; and van Kruysbergen, Bosman, & Stone, 1998, for Dutch). This asymmetry explains why spelling is often more difficult than reading.

In the remainder of this section, we focus on Dutch sound-to-spelling relations. Regarding the description of Dutch orthography, its phonemes serve as the starting point. Alphabetic languages strive for a consistent relationship between the phonemes of the language and a limited set of graphic signs, that is, graphemes. A grapheme is the orthographic counterpart of the phoneme. The graphemes constitute all the letters of the alphabet plus all letter combinations that represent the phonemes.

As already stated, most alphabetic languages contain a certain number of spelling-to-sound inconsistencies, and Dutch is no exception. Despite this problem, Siegenbeek (1805) made the

---

[1] Until recently, no distinction was made between sound-to-spelling and spelling-to-sound consistency. Languages were referred to as being either regular or transparent or irregular or opaque. English was always considered opaque, whereas Spanish or Dutch were considered transparent. The work of both Stone et al. (1997) and Ziegler et al. (1996) shows that we need to be precise, because consistency depends on the direction from which it is assessed and may diverge greatly within languages.

first attempt to provide a systematic description of Dutch orthography. The account presented by his successor te Winkel in 1863 coincides with that of Siegenbeek. Because te Winkel's account is more explicit, we chose to base our discussion on his principles. He took the phoneme–grapheme relations as the first basic principle for a systematic description of Dutch orthography.

Prescriptive Account of te Winkel

The first principle of te Winkel (1863) is the *Principle of Received Pronunciation* and states that, 'write by means of letter signs all the elements that can be heard in a word if it is pronounced correctly by civilized people' (p. 13). This principle is also known as the phonological principle (Cohen & Kraak, 1972) or the phonemic principle (Booij, Hamans, Verhoeven, Balk, & van Minnen, 1979). Because many of the spellings at that time were not or could not be captured by the main principle of received pronunciation, te Winkel (1865) developed additional principles. Each of these principles is illustrated by examples.

The second is the *Principle of Uniformity*; it actually contains two rules. The first is, 'always write the same word with the same letters, when pronunciation and declension or conjugation allow this'. The second part of the principle is, 'give derived words the same shape as the primary word and give component parts of compound words the same shape as their compound, as far as the pronunciation allows this' (te Winkel, 1865, p. 19). The principle of uniformity was introduced to prevent spelling changes resulting from the effect of sound rules like final devoicing. For example, a, d, on the end of a Dutch word, in contrast to a, d, at the end of an English word, is devoiced, and thus is pronounced [t]. Although the words *tand* (tɑnt) [tooth] and *klant* (klɑnt) [customer] have identical final pronunciation, they are spelled differently, because their plurals are pronounced and spelled differently, *tanden* (tɑndən) [teeth] and *klanten* (klɑntən) [customers], respectively. Maintaining similar spelling in the singular version of a plural word, in derived words from primary words, and in component parts of compound words guarantees uniformity in spelling.

The third is the *Principle of Etymology* and states that, 'the choice between letters with the same sound is decided by the derivation or the older form that was used then and could still be distinguished clearly, but has now become indistinguishable, provided that no other rules or special circumstances make this choice not advisable' (te Winkel, 1865, p. 22). The principle of etymology was introduced to respect the existing practice. It also prevented the emergence of homophones. For example, the Dutch language has two different spellings for the phoneme [ɛi], EI and IJ. The words *meiden* [girls] and *mijden* [to avoid] are pronounced identically (mɛidən). Similarly for the word pair *pauw* (pɑu) [peacock] and *touw* (tɑu) [rope], the rime of these words have identical pronunciation [ɑu], but they are spelled differently, because originally these words were pronounced differently.

The fourth is the *Principle of Analogy* and was added for cases that are not accounted for by the principle of uniformity. It states that, 'where the three above named spelling rules fall silent, one acts on analogy; words are written in the same way as other words whose spelling is known with certainty and that are apparently formed in a similar way' (te Winkel, 1865, p. 24). Proper spelling of the word *stationsstraat* [station street] requires a double S because of the analogy to *stationsweg* [station road]. The second S is the initial letter of *straat* and the first one is a morpheme that links *station* to *straat*, in a similar fashion as *station* is linked to *weg* by an S. This rule is required, because the double S is inaudible and thus cannot be derived from the first principle, the principle of received pronunciation.

The combination of the principle of uniformity and the principle of analogy is referred to as the *Morphological Principle* (Cohen & Kraak, 1972). This principle shows that Dutch spelling is morphophonemic rather than phonemic, because the one-to-one relation between phonemes and graphemes is more often valid for morphemes than for entire words. Although these principles capture a large number of the spelling variants that occur in the Dutch language, there remain a number of spelling variants not accounted for. Nunn's (1998) recent work is an attempt to fill this void.

Nunn's Hybrid Model of Dutch Orthography

The Dutch linguist Nunn (1998) argued that deviations from the one-to-one correspondence in the approach of te Winkel actually comprise three types of spelling variants, namely, apparent variants, competing variants, and conditioned variants (the competing and conditioned variants cluster into real variants). Apparent variants are adequately described by the morphological principle. These variants are called apparent because they disappear if the spelling is taken as a code for the pronunciation of morphemes rather than phonemes. Recall the example of *tand* which is spelled with a D, but pronounced with a T[tɑnt] as a result of the plural spelling *tanden*.

Competing variants are adequately described by the principle of etymology. Recall the difference in spelling, but current similarity in pronunciation between the words *pauw* and *touw*, as a result of a historical difference in pronunciation.

The conditioned variants, however, are not accounted for by te Winkel's four principles. Conditioned variants are context-specific spelling variants. The degree of regularity (in psycholinguistic terms also referred to as degree of structure) in the set of conditioned variants (these spellings are often predictable and regular) motivated Nunn (1998) to propose a hybrid model for Dutch orthography. Her hybrid model is in fact a combination of two major competing accounts. The first account, defended by the Dutch linguists Booij (1995), Cohen and Kraak (1972), van Heuven (1980), and Wester (1985), follows that of te Winkel. It states that Dutch spelling is a code for the pronunciation and is captured by the phonological principle; that is, abstract representations of morphemes. In many cases, conditioned spelling variants are derived from the phonological syllable and prosodic structure, according to Booij (1995), but in some cases they are not, which causes Dutch orthography to be inconsistent. The second account defended by Kerstens (1981) and Zonneveld (1980) presents an objection to the assumption that Dutch spelling is primarily derived from its pronunciation. They argue that Dutch spelling is more adequately described by an autonomous rule system that takes the abstract spelling of morphemes as the basic code for spelling. Nunn's hybrid model combines a set of phoneme–grapheme conversion rules, an implication of the assumption that spelling is a basic code for the pronunciation, with a set of autonomous spelling rules, called autonomous, because they are defined as letter-based processes, rather than as rules that refer to the pronunciation of words.

Earlier it was postulated that the set of Dutch words with respect to its spelling is best described in terms of two distinct orthographies, one for native words and one for non-native words (both written in the Roman alphabet). Following Nunn (1998), the distinction between native and non-native words is made on the basis of the extent to which the spelling of loan words have been adapted to the Dutch linguistic system. Nunn defined the Dutch linguistic system on the basis of a set of formal criteria, described in detail in her work. A description of this set is beyond the purpose of this chapter. Suffice it to say that the extent to which words are adapted appears to be a good predictor of their origin. In the remainder of this section the spelling system of native words is described first, followed by the one for non-native words.

Spelling of Native-Dutch Words

The set of native-Dutch words has 35 native phonemes and 39 native graphemes. The native phonemes are further divided in 19 consonants and 16 vowels; the consonants comprise

5 plosives (p, b, t, d, k), 7 fricatives (f, v, s, z, x, ɣ, h), 3 nasals (n, m, ŋ), 2 liquids (l, r), and 2 glides (w, j); the vowels comprise 5 tense or short vowels (ɪ, ɛ), 7 lax or long vowels (i, y, u, e, ø, o, a), 3 diphthongs (ɛi, œy, ɑu), and the schwa [ə]; and the native graphemes comprise 23 monographs (a, e, i, o, u, ij, b, d, f, g, h, j, k, l, m, n, p, r, s, t, v, w, z), 14 digraphs (aa, ee, oo, uu, ie, oe, ei, ui, au, ou, eu, ng, uw, and ch), and 2 trigraphs (ouw, auw). Although phoneme–grapheme consistency and grapheme–phoneme consistency in the Dutch language are both higher than their counterparts in English, there is substantial deviation from a strict one-to-one correspondence in the Dutch, native-spelling system. Table 9.1 presents the list of all possible native-Dutch graphemes that match the set of native-Dutch phonemes.

As already noted, te Winkel's approach accounts for most of the spelling variations in native-Dutch words and is captured by the first part of the model, that is, the set of phoneme–grapheme conversion rules. The conditioned spelling variants are the remaining ones to be dealt with, and they appear to be adequately captured by the set of autonomous spelling rules developed by Nunn (1998). Next we present two examples of autonomous spelling rules to illustrate solutions for conditioned spelling variants. We chose vowel reduction and consonant doubling because they illustrate rather poignantly the problems of beginning spellers with the type of words to which these rules apply (see the section on Reading and Spelling in Dutch).

Vowel reduction (i.e., degemination) occurs in words with lax vowels. Generally the spelling rule for words with lax vowels prescribes a double letter (i.e., a geminate), for example, the word *raam* [ram] (*window*) has a lax vowel and is thus spelled with two a's. The plural version of *raam* is *ramen* [ram] (*windows*), which still contains a lax vowel, but its vowel is reduced to a single a. This is the result of a spelling rule that states that vowels in open syllables reduce to one.

Consonant doubling (i.e., gemination) occurs in polysyllabic words with tense vowels. Monosyllabic words with tense vowels are generally followed by a single consonant; for example, the word *ster* [stɛr] (*star*) has a single, final consonant r. The plural version of *ster* is *sterren* [stɛrən] (*stars*), and still contains a tense vowel, but the r needs to be doubled to guarantee this reading. This is the result of the spelling rule that states that consonants are doubled in case of a closed syllable. These rules, and the rules developed by Nunn have a lot more applications and implications. For those who are interested, we strongly recommend the work by Nunn (1998).

Thus, to determine the spelling of native-Dutch words, first establish a spelling based on the set of phoneme–grapheme conversion rules for native words. Subsequently adjust this spelling, if necessary, according to the set of autonomous spelling rules. Application of this implemented hybrid model on a corpus of 45,000 words showed that Nunn's system correctly predicted 95% of native-Dutch words. It required 35 phoneme–grapheme conversion rules for native words (with a limited set of exceptions) and 13 relatively complex autonomous spelling rules (with a fair number of exceptions) pertaining to both native and non-native words. See Fig. 9.1 for an illustration.

Spelling of Non-Native-Dutch Words

The set of non-native phonemes and graphemes comprises, in fact, those phonemes and graphemes that do not occur in the list of native-Dutch phonemes and their relations to graphemes presented in Table 9.2. The letters or graphemes, c [s], q [k], x [ks], and y [i] that are present in Dutch words cause them to be uniquely non-native.

For the description of the spelling of non-native words, two main ideas have been put forward in the literature. The first, developed and defended by te Winkel (1865), says that the spelling of non-native words is captured by the principle of etymology. In te Winkel's (1865) own words, "The spelling of foreign and bastard words is given and needs not to be determined by new and specific rules. The spelling of the main part is given by the foreign

TABLE 9.1
Sound–Letter Couplings in Native-Dutch Words

Sound	Letters	Examples
[p]	p, pp, b, 0[a]	(trɑp) *trap*, [kɑpər] *kapper*, [wɛp] *web*, [kɔmpt] *komt*
[b]	b, bb, p	(bɑl) *bal*, [ɣɑbər] *gabber*, [ɔbduk] *opdoek*
[t]	t, tt, d	(tɑk) *tak*, [ɔtər] *otter*, [hœyt] *huid*
[d]	d, dd, t	(dun) *doen*, [ɑdər] *adder*, [œydbrɛŋ] *uitbreng*
[k]	k, kk	(kɑl) *kaal*, [ɑkər] *akker*
[f]	f, ff	(fɛl) *fel*, [ɔfər] *offer*
[v]	v, f, w	(vel) *veel*, [ɑvdun] *afdoen*, [vret] *wreed*
[s]	s, ss	(sɔk) *sok*, [wɪsəl] *wissel*
[z]	z, s	(zɑk) *zaak*, [ɑzbɑk] *asbak*
[x]	ch, g	(sxol) *school*, [krɑx] *kraag*
[ɣ]	g, gg, ch	(weɣə) *wegen*, [wɛɣə] *wegge*, [lɑɣbœy] *lachbui*
[h]	h	(hɛlp) *help*
[n]	n, nn	(nort) *noord*, [lɪnə] *linnen*
[m]	m, mm, n	(moj) *mooi*, [ɛmər] *emmer*, [ɪmpɛrk] *inperk*
[ŋ]	ng, n	(ɑŋəl) *angel*, [bɑŋk] *bank*
[l]	l, ll	(lœyk) *luik*, [ɑləs] *alles*
[r]	r, rr	(rɑm) *raam*, [bɔrəl] *borrel*
[w]	w, uw, 0	(wer) *weer*, [ew] *eeuw*, [muwə] *moeë*
[j]	j, i, 0	(jɑr) *jaar*, [mɑj] *maai*, [zejə] *zeeën*
[ɪ]	i	(pɪt) *pit*
[ɛ]	e	(pɛt) *pet*
[ɔ]	o	(pɔl) *pol*
[ɣ]	u	(pɣt) *put*
[ɑ]	a	(jɑs) *jas*
[i]	ie, i	(rit) *riet*, [miɑu] *miauw*
[ɣ]	uu, u	(mɣr) *muur*, [nɣ] *nu*
[e]	ee, e	(ler) *leer*, [etə] *eten*
[ø]	eu	(løk) *leuk*
[u]	oe	(rum) *roem*
[o]	oo, o	(rot) *rood*, [lopər] *loper*
[a]	aa, a	(kas) *kaas*, [adəm] *adem*
[ɛi]	ij, ei	(wɛis) *wijs*, [trɛin] *trein*
[œy]	ui	(rœyk) *ruik*
[ɑu]	ou(w), au(w)	(hɑut) *hout*, [lɑu] *lauw*, [klɑutər] *klauter*, [snɑu] *snauw*
[ə]	e, i, ij, u, 0	(də) *de*, [nodəx] *nodig*, [olək] *olijk*, [dɔkəm] *Dokkum*, (ɑrəm) *arm*

[a] 0 indicates that the sound is not represented by a grapheme in the letter string.

spelling and the spelling of the word ending is given by ordinary Dutch spelling rules" (p. 192). This principle maintains that the spelling of non-native words is in fact arbitrary or, in linguistic terms, irregular. Neijt (1994) investigated the possibility, suggested by te Winkel, that the spelling of non-native words in Dutch might be predicted by application of foreign spelling rules. The answer was negative. Thus te Winkel's opinion with respect to non-native words implies that their spelling cannot be computed and needs to be looked up.

The second and contrasting opinion is that the spelling of non-native words actually contains a fair degree of regularity, in fact, more than could be expected on the basis of the finding that their spelling cannot be derived from foreign spelling rules. Nunn (1998), in accordance

Step 1: Apply phoneme-grapheme conversion rules

a) Write [i] as IE in the last syllable of non-native morphemes. For example, BALIE [bali], (*counter*), ACTIEF [ɑktif], (*active*), or ARTIEST [ɑrtist], (*artist*), except in Latinate month names, prefixes, the suffix -ISCH and some random examples such as TAXI, ALIBI, FIS, etc.

b) Write [i] as I elsewhere. For example LIMONADE [limonadə], (*lemonade*) VITAAL [vital], (*vital, vigorous*).

Step 2: Apply autonomous spelling rules

c) Change IE into I in an unstressed syllable before a vowel. For example, OLIËN [oliən], (*oils or to oil*) or NEURIËN [nøriən], (*to hum*).

d) Change morpheme final I into IE before a consonant-initial native suffix, as in TAXIEDE [tɑksidə], (*taxied*), except before the plural or genitive suffix–S where an apostrophe is added, as in SKI'S [skis], (*skis*).

FIG. 9.1.   An illustration of Nunn's hybrid model for the sound [i] in both native- and non-native-Dutch words.

TABLE 9.2
Sound–Letter Couplings in Non-Native-Dutch Words

Sound	Letter	Sound	Letter
[i:]	y in *analyse* [analysis]	[y:]	u in *centrifuge* [spin-drier]
[u:]	ou in *rouge* [blusher]	[ɛ:]	e in serre [sun lounge]
[ø:]	eu in *freule* [lady]	[ɔ:]	o in *roze* [pink]
[ɑ:]	a in pass [pass]	[ê]	in in mannequin [model]
[ɶ̃]	um in *parfum* [perfume]	[ô]	ond in *plafond* [ceiling]
[g]	g in goal [goal]		

with former accounts by Booij (1995) and Wester (1985), started with the definition of a set of phoneme–grapheme conversion rules applicable to non-native words and subsequently supplemented these with the set of autonomous spelling rules.

The example presented in Fig. 9.1 also applies to non-native-Dutch words, and the model for non-native-Dutch words is analogous to the model for native-Dutch words. First establish the spelling based on the set of phoneme-grapheme conversion rules for non-native words and then adjust this spelling, if necessary, according to the set of autonomous spelling rules. The non-native hybrid model correctly predicted 73% of non-native-Dutch words, which required 38 phoneme–grapheme conversion rules for non-native words (with a moderate set of exceptions) and the set of 13 autonomous spelling rules pertaining to both native and non-native words. Note that only 25% of the spelling of non-native words could be predicted properly if the spelling rules for native words were used.

READING AND SPELLING IN DUTCH

The preceding discussion suggests, on the one hand, that Dutch spelling is too complex to call it regular or transparent. On the other hand, the fact that a limited set of spelling rules, albeit complicated, resolves many of the ambiguities precludes labelling it irregular or opaque. In the final part of our chapter, we discuss some aspects of Dutch orthography that give rise to reading errors and some features that bring about spelling errors. This discussion is limited to the reading and spelling of isolated words, except for a short treatment of grammatically determined spelling.

Reading

As already stated, the Dutch language largely consists of two different orthographies, one for native words and one for non-native words. Most native-Dutch words contain highly consistent grapheme-to-phoneme relations, which makes reading native words fairly straightforward, provided one has been familiarized with the set of grapheme–phoneme relations and one does not suffer from dyslexia. In the Netherlands, most words in the reading-instruction books used in first grade are native and highly consistent.

Systematic investigations of reading errors in young Dutch readers are limited to two linguistic studies (Caesar, 1971, cited in van Heuven, 1980; Rutjens, 2000) and two psycholinguistic studies (Bakker, 1965; Reitsma, 1992) on native-Dutch words mainly. Psycholinguistic studies are usually based on preconceptions regarding the source of the reading (and spelling) errors, whereas linguistic analyses simply describe the errors. Because we are interested in the relation between the Dutch spelling system and types of reading errors, our discussion focuses on the linguistic studies. Moreover, because no sufficient information regarding the reading of non-native Dutch words is available, our discussion is limited to the reading of native-Dutch words.

Caesar's list (1971, cited in van Heuven, 1980) contains 12 categories, which contain examples of linguistic units that present difficulties in the initial reading stages. The categories most clearly related to the preceding discussion are the reading of digraphs, both consonants (Ch and Ng) and vowels (eu, ie, oe, etc.), reading of trigraphs[2] (aai, oei), reading of words in which the final voiced phoneme is pronounced voiceless (recall that d in *tand* is pronounced [tɑnt]), reading of the schwa written as E or IJ, particularly when these occur in unstressed or final syllables, and finally reading words in which a single letter a, usually pronounced [ɑ], represents the lax vowel [a].

Rutjens's study (2000) is the most general, systematic, and unbiased investigation of reading errors in young readers. She presented 20 children without reading problems (mean age 120 months) and 20 children with dyslexia (mean age 123 months) with the first 58 (mostly native-Dutch) words of the *Eén-minuut-test* [One-minute test] of Brus and Voeten (1973). The *Eén-minuut-test* is a frequently used and well-documented reading test, that involves reading aloud a graded list of unrelated words. She also presented them with the first 58 pseudowords of the *Klepel* (van den Bos, lutje Spelberg, Scheepstra, & de Vries, 1994). The *Klepel* is a standardized reading test for pseudowords; it is derived from and structurally similar to the *Eén-minuut-test*. What makes her study particularly interesting is the fact that she described each reading error as precisely as possible. For example, if the word *deuk* (døk) [dent] was pronounced *duik* (dœyk) [dive], she notated that eu becomes ui, or when the pseudoword *rapones* was pronounced *raponse*, she notated that es, pronounced [əs], becomes se, pronounced [sə]. Interestingly, the percentage of reading errors on the word-reading test was relatively low: 6.3% of the words were misread, of which readers with dyslexia misread 4.9% and

---

[2] Van Heuven (1980) calls these letter clusters trigraphs, a convention not adopted by Nunn (1998).

readers without dyslexia 1.4%. The percentage of reading errors on the pseudoword-reading test was much higher: 32.9% of the pseudowords were misread, of which readers with dyslexia misread 21.2% and readers without 11.7%. Although the absolute number of reading errors was five times higher in the pseudoword-reading test than in the word-reading test, a substantial amount of overlap regarding error type occurred. Because no qualitative differences (only quantitative, confirming results reported by Bakker in 1965) between readers with and without dyslexia emerged, we focus our attention on the distribution of reading errors over the two tests. For the sake of simplicity, we also refrain from the distinction between errors made on the word-reading test and those on the pseudoword-reading test.

In both tests, 227 different types of reading errors occurred, and the majority of errors (73%) occurred in three distinct categories and predominantly in the pseudoword-reading test. That is, 24% of the errors were due to deletion of one letter, 29% to addition of one letter, and 20% were made against the structure of words. An error in the structure of a word was defined as the erroneous application of rules, for example the misreading of the single vowel in an open syllable. Children often pronounced the single a of *ramen* as [ɑ], whereas it should be read as [a]. They also often misapplied the grapheme–phoneme rule pertaining to the e or IJ in final or unstressed position. They often read 'e' as [ɛ] and 'ij' as [ɛi] rather than as schwa [ə]. A substantial number of the remaining 27% of reading errors pertained to digraphs (both double and mixed vowels). The children either substituted a digraph with another digraph (e.g., ei became ie, ui became uu, or oo became ee) or they substituted a digraph with a single letter (*e.g., eu became u or UI became* U).

Thus, misapplication of autonomous spelling rules appears to contribute mostly to the variety of reading errors, with the addition and deletion of single letters ignored. Erroneous application of phoneme-to-grapheme conversion rules is also a source of error, but to a lesser extent. If, however, the absolute number of errors is taken into consideration, we have to conclude that reading in Dutch is actually not a real problem. After all, in reading extant words, young readers without dyslexia misread less than 2% of the Dutch, mostly native words.

Spelling

To understand specifics of Dutch orthography, it is important to distinguish not only between native and non-native words, but also between lexically-based spellings and grammatically based spellings. Lexically-based spellings refer to the unique spelling of words that can be established without the context in which the words appear, except the class of homophones. A homophone pair comprises two words that have identical pronunciation, but different spelling, for example, the pair 'deer' and 'dear' are English homophones. Dutch orthography also contains a limited set of homophones, for example, zij [she] and zei [said] pronounced [zɛi] or lach [laugh] and lag [lied], pronounced [lɑx]. Grammatically based spelling refers to the spelling of verbs and adjectives of which the spelling is determined by the grammatical context in which the word appears. Dutch verb spelling is based on a relatively complex rule-based system that we touch upon following the treatment of lexically based spellings.

Spelling instruction in the Netherlands usually starts when a child is 7 years old, halfway through Grade 1. Initially, the emphasis lies on the application of the principle of received pronunciation, also referred to as the phonological principle. Recall that the sound-to-spelling relations are less consistent in the Dutch spelling system than are the spelling-to-sound relations. In fact, in native-Dutch words, only 9 sound–letter couplings are unique; the remaining 26 native phonemes have at least two, often three, and sometimes four different written possibilities (see Table 9.1). The existence of multiple possibilities for each phoneme seems to make spelling a relatively difficult task. However, the fact that each phoneme has a corresponding, dominant grapheme alleviates the task somewhat.

Shortly after being familiarized with the phonological principle, first graders are introduced to the principle of etymology. They learn that for many phonemes more than one grapheme exists. A large number of Dutch words contain phoneme–grapheme ambiguities because of etymological reasons. Beginning spellers, presented with words that consist of dominant phoneme–grapheme couplings often spell these words correctly (Jansen & Luurtsema, 1986; Reitsma & Geelhoed, 2000), but after the introduction of the etymological principle (i.e., the problem of multiple graphemes for one phoneme) children's spelling contains many errors. These errors are predominantly phonological, that is, the speller chooses an incorrect, but possible, grapheme for a particular phoneme, and the result is a pseudohomophone. For example, *beil* is a pseudohomophone or a wrongly spelled version of the word bijl [bɛil] [axe]. Spelling errors in which the pronunciation of the word is not retained, for example *bijk* instead of *bijl*, are unusual (for a review see Bosman & Van Orden, 1997). Thus, to be able to spell a word with an ambiguous phoneme–grapheme relation, one has to memorize that relationship; the remaining letters can be determined by application of the phoneme–grapheme conversion rules. For example, all words that contain either [ei] or [ɑu] have a written representation of what that particular grapheme has to be remembered; it cannot be derived from its pronunciation. The phoneme [ɛi] has two written representations, ij in *bijt* [*bite*] and ei in *geit* [goat], and the phoneme [ɑu] has four, au in *au* [ow/ouch], auw in *gauw* [quick], ou in *kou* [cold], and finally ouw in *mouw* [sleeve].

At the end of first grade, the children learn about words for which the spelling is determined by two rules that enable the beginning speller to deal with the morpho-phonemic property of the Dutch spelling system: the morphological principle and the combination of the principles of uniformity and analogy. A study by Reitsma and Geelhoed (2000) showed that these additional rules initially complicate the spelling process. They investigated the performance of 1,276 Dutch children from first and second grade in spelling 52 monosyllabic words. The children could spell 30 words correctly, provided they applied dominant phoneme–grapheme rules, for example, *duur* [dyr], [expensive] and *vlieg* (vlix) [fly]. The remaining 22 words deviated from the dominant phonological principle {examples are *paard* (part), [horse] and *warm* [wɑrəm], [*warm*]}. In the case of (part), the final [t] is written with d, and thus deviates from the dominant phoneme–grapheme rule, but can be solved correctly if the principle of uniformity is applied (see preceding discussion). The word [wɑrəm] may be pronounced with a schwa inserted before the [m], which is not represented in the spelling of *warm*. Reitsma and Geelhoed (2000) showed that first graders spelled words with dominant phoneme–grapheme relations better than they did words that deviated from this principle, whereas second graders performed equally well on the two word types. This is in agreement with work by Jansen and Luurtsema (1986), who reported on the spelling errors of 300 children in first grade, and they confirm the claim that the additional rules initially cause spelling problems for Dutch children.

Empirical investigation of the spelling behavior of Dutch spellers regarding words that either deviate strongly from dominant phoneme–grapheme conversion rules or words that require the application of often complex (autonomous) spelling rules, except the rule-based system for verbs and adjectives (see subsequent discussion), has not been reported in the literature. A quick glance at Dutch spelling-instruction books, however, clearly suggests the difficulty of the Dutch spelling system. Spelling is practised until the end of elementary school and often extends right into high school, whereas instruction in technical reading is usually completed in second grade. An example of a complex spelling rule Dutch beginning readers are confronted with is vowel reduction. Recall that, vowel reduction (*raam* becomes *ramen* as plural), also known as the 'vowel-thief' rule, states that in polysyllabic words with a long or lax vowel followed by a single consonant the vowel is spelled with just one letter. The amount of time devoted in practising this rule in first and second grade is a good indication of its complexity.

Empirical research on the acquisition of non-native Dutch spelling is not available either, but again spelling-instruction material shows that all these words are practised throughout the school years. Often the complex rules that underlie the spelling of non-native words are not explained; students are simply asked to memorize the spelling. Interestingly, there is a method, called overpronunciation, that supports the learning of clearly non-native words, but it is not part of systematic spelling practice, nor is it a strategy that students discover spontaneously (Ormrod & Jenkins, 1989). Overpronunciation is a strategy in which students are taught to pronounce a foreign word according to native grapheme–phoneme conversion rules. For example, the spelling of the non-native-Dutch word *sergeant* [sɛrʒɑnt] [sergeant] is better remembered after it is divided into three syllables and pronounced according to dominant, native grapheme–phoneme relations, that is, [sɛr] [ʁe] [ɑnt]. The study by Ormrod and Jenkins (1989) in English and the one by Schiffelers, Bosman, and Van Hell (2002) in Dutch demonstrated the effectiveness of this strategy. Schiffelers et al. showed that Dutch children from regular elementary schools as well as children in special education profited greatly from the application of this technique. It appears that fixing 'the broken relationship' between phonemes and graphemes (in fact, changing inconsistent words into consistent words) enhances spelling performance.

After the introduction of foreign languages (English for everybody and for a large number of students also 3 or 4 years of French and German), students become familiar with other rule systems, which sometimes helps and other times hinders Dutch spelling performance. In some cases, the foreign spelling is retained, as in *bureau* from French, whereas in other words it is not, for example, the Dutch non-native word *artiest* (French word *artiste*). This situation is similar to the differences between American and British spelling (e.g., behavior vs. behaviour).

The final part of this section on learning to spell is devoted to grammatically determined spelling, that is, spelling of verbs. The proper spelling of Dutch verbs depends on the sentence context in which they appear. One of the difficulties in the spelling of verbs pertains to cases in which the stems of so-called weak verbs end with a d or t. The stem is the initial element of a verb's infinitive or that part of a verb used as predicate. For example, the stem of the verb verbranden [vərbrɑndən] [to burn] is *verbrand*, of *wedden* [wɛdən] [to bet] it is *wed*, the stem of the verb *kaarten* (kartən) [to play cards] is *kaart*, and of *praten* (pratən) [to talk] it is *praat*. The first-person present tense is identical to the stem; thus *ik verbrand* [I burn], *ik wed* [I bet], *ik kaart* [I play cards], and *ik praat* [I talk], respectively, and also *ik lach* [I laugh] from *lachen* [to laugh]. The rule for the formation of the second- and the third-person singular present tense is this: Take the stem and put a t at the end, except when the stem already ends with a t; thus, *jij* [you] or *hij/zij* [he/she], *verbrandt* [burns], *wedt* [bets], *lacht* [plays], and the exception *praat* [talks]. This rule causes a lot of verb homophones: *verbrand* sounds identical to *verbrandt*, and *wed* sounds identical to *wedt*.

In forming the past tense additional complexities arise. The past tense in the first-, second-, and third-person singular of weak verbs is the stem plus de or te, and the first-, second-, and third-person plural is the stem plus *den* or *ten*; thus, *ik verbrandde* [I burnt] and *wij verbandden* [we burnt], *ik wedde* [I bet] and *wij wedden* [we bet], *ik lachte* [I laughed] and *wij lachten* [we laughed], and *ik praatte* [I talked] and *wij praatten* [we talked]. Note here that some of the plural forms in the past tense sound identical to the infinitive, but are not always written identically, again causing the emergence of homophones. For example, *wij verbrandden* and *verbranden* sound identical, as do *praatten* and *praten*, and thus are homophones of each other. The past tense of the plural forms of *wedden*, however, is identical in both sound and spelling to the infinitive *wedden*. To complicate matters even further, Dutch speakers often omit the final [n] in words, which causes additional homophones. For example, *verbranden* and *verbrandden* are true homophones of each other, but they also sound nearly identical to *verbrandde*.

Although verb spelling is fully rule based, it is undeniably a rather difficult aspect of Dutch orthography. Empirical research by Assink (1984, 1985, 1990), Sandra, Frisson, and Daems

(1999), and van Diepen and Bosman (1999) proved that difficulties associated with Dutch verb spelling perseveres right into adulthood. Bosman (1989) showed that university students still made about 10% errors in a two-choice verb-spelling task. Assink (1985) maintains that the verb-homophone problem accounts for the majority of spelling errors found in Dutch written materials.

EPILOGUE

In short, learning to read Dutch is more or less completed in second grade, whereas learning to spell lasts throughout high school, because Dutch orthography hardly presents obstacles for reading, but contains a fair number of difficulties for spelling. We suggested earlier, in line with the explanation put forward by Bosman and Van Orden (1997), that this asymmetry between reading and spelling is the result of the higher level of consistency of grapheme-to-phoneme relations (important in the case of reading) than of phoneme-to-grapheme relations (important in the case of spelling). A high level of consistency generally speeds up the learning process.

To alleviate the difficulties that arise as a result of the relative inconsistency of phoneme-to-grapheme relations, we discuss two suggestions. The first possibility concerns an increase of the consistency by means of reforming spelling. The Dutch government twice decided on a spelling reform; the first official one occurred in 1954 and the most recent one in 1995. In both cases, the number of changes were relatively minor, but both events caused heated debates in Dutch society (see, for an impression, Geerts, van den Broek, & Verdoodt, 1977; Molewijk, 1992; Neijt & Nunn, 1997). In the 1960s and 1970s, a group of politically involved Dutch citizens proposed a more drastic spelling change, but it did not make it. They believed that a strict phonological spelling of Dutch would ease the task of learning to spell. This is most likely true, but would have altered the image of Dutch orthography dramatically, demonstrated by the following examples: *tejater* instead of *theater* [tejatər) [theatre]; *krieties* instead of *kritisch* [kritis], [critical]; *polietsie* instead of *politie* [politsi] [police]; *luuksjeus* instead of *luxueus* [lykʃøs] [luxurious].

The other possibility that may help to ease the pain of learning to spell is to explicate the underlying, implicit structure of the spelling system. Nunn's (1998) recent investigation of the system that governs Dutch orthography appears to be a successful enterprise. After all, her set of phoneme–grapheme conversion rules combined with a set of autonomous spelling rules captures almost all native-Dutch words (95%) and the majority of non-native-Dutch words (73%). Stated differently, her study proved that Dutch orthography contains a fair degree of regularity and (statistical) structure, which is the result of a set of rules that can, in principle, be taught. Unfortunately, however, the limited set of rules underlying Dutch orthography are so complex that it seems unlikely that spelling instruction is actually simplified. Applying the spell checker of common word processors is probably more efficient, a well-tried and tested method by the authors of this paper.

ACKNOWLEDGEMENTS

We are greatly indebted to Nicoline van der Sijs and Anneke Nunn for providing invaluable etymological and linguistic information on the Dutch language. We also thank Anneke Nunn for allowing us to use Fig. 9.1 and the contents of Tables 9.1 and 9.2. Finally, we thank Romi de Jong, Norma Montulet, and Reynier Molenaar for their critical comments on earlier versions of this paper.

REFERENCES

Albright, R. W. (1958). *The international phonetic alphabet: Its Background and development.* Bloomington, IN: Indiana University Press.

Assink, E. M. H. (1984). Het in kaart brengen van spellingproblemen [The mapping of spelling problems]. *Tijdschrift voor Taalbeheersing, 4,* 264–276.

Assink, E. M. H. (1985). Assessing spelling strategies for the orthography of Dutch verbs. *British Journal of Psychology, 76,* 353–363.

Assink, E. M. H. (1990). Learning to spell. In P. Reitsma & L. Verhoeven (Eds.), *Acquisition of reading in Dutch* (pp. 65–76). Dordrecht, The Netherlands: Foris Publications.

Bakker, D. J. (1965). Leesstoornissen: een foutenanalyse [Learning difficulties: An analysis of errors]. *Nederlands Tijdschrift voor de Psychologie, 20,* 173–183.

Booij, G. E. (1995). *The phonology of Dutch.* Oxford, UK: Clarendon.

Booij, G. E., Hamans, C., Verhoeven, G., Balk, F., & van Minnen, C. H. (1979). *Spelling* [Spelling]. Groningen, The Netherlands: Wolters-Noordhoff.

Bosman, A. M. T. (1989). [Verb spelling in Dutch University students]. Unpublished raw data.

Bosman, A. M. T., & Mekking, T. (2005). *Statistical structure of spelling-sound and sound-spelling relations in Dutch words.* Manuscript in preparation.

Bosman, A. M. T., & Van Orden, G. C. (1997). Why spelling is more difficult than reading. In C. A. Perfetti, L. Rieben, & M. Fayol, (Eds.), *Learning to spell. Research, theory, and practice across languages* (pp. 173–194). Hillsdale, NJ: Lawrence Erlbaum Associates.

Brus, B. Th., & Voeten, M. J. M. (1973). *Een-Minuut-Test* [One-minute test]. Nijmegen, The Netherlands: Berkhout.

Cohen, A., & Kraak, A. (1972). *Spellen is spellen is spellen. Een verkenning van de spellingsproblematiek* [To spell is to spell is to spell. An investigation of the spelling issue]. den haag, The Netherlands: Martinus Nijhoff.

Coulmas, F. (1996). *The Blackwell encyclopedia of writing systems.* Oxford, UK: Blackwell.

Geerts, G., van den Broeck, J., & Verdoodt, A. (1977). Successes and failures in Dutch spelling reform. In J. A. Fisham (Ed.), *Advances in the creation and revision of writing systems* (pp. 179–245). Paris: Mouton.

Jansen, M. G. H., & Luurtsema, R. (1986). De moeilijkheidsgraad van spelwoorden bij beginnende spellers [The difficulty of spelling words in beginning spellers]. *Pedagogisch Studiën, 63,* 243–251.

Kerstens, J. (1981). Abstracte spelling [Abstract spelling]. *De Nieuwe Taalgids, 74,* 29–44.

Molewijk, G. C. (1992). *Spellingverandering van zin naar onzin (1200-heden)* [Spelling change from sense to nonsense (1200-present)]. Den Haag, The Netherlands: (Sdu Uitgeuers).

Neijt, A. (1994). Van orthografie naar ortografie [From orthography to orthografy]. In A. Neijt, I. Roggema, & J. Zuidema (Eds.), *De spellingcommissie aan het woord* (pp. 59–72). Den Haag, The Netherlands: Sdu Uitgeuers.

Neijt, A., & Nunn, A. M. (1997). The recent history of Dutch orthography. Problems solved and created. *Leuven Contributions in Linguistics and Philology, 86,* 1–26.

Nunn A. M. (1998). *Dutch orthography. A systematic investigation of the spelling of Dutch words.* Den Haag, The Netherlands: Holland Academic Graphics.

Ormrod, J. E., & Jenkins, L. (1989). Study strategies for learning spelling: Correlations with achievement and developmental changes. *Perceptual and Motor Skills, 68,* 643–650.

Reitsma, P. (1992). Invloed van leesfrequentie op fouten als teken van de ontwikkeling van een orthografisch geheugen [The effect of reading frequency on errors indicates the development of orthographic memory]. *Nederlands Tijdschrift voor de Psychologie, 47,* 223–234.

Reitsma, P., & Geelhoed, J. (2000). Aanvankelijk leren spellen: een voorspelling van goede antwoorden [Learning to spell: Predicting correct responses]. *Pedagogische Studiën, 77,* 337–347.

Rutjens, E. (2000). *Onderzoek naar het pseudowoord-deficiet en het type leesfouten bij dyslectische kinderen.* [A study of the pseudoword deficit and the type of reading errors in children with developmental dyslexia]. Unpublished masters' thesis, University of Nijmegen, The Netherlands.

Sandra, D., Frisson, S., & Daems, F. (1999). Why simple verb forms can be so difficult to spell: The influence of homophone frequency and distance in Dutch. *Brain and Language, 68,* 277–283.

Schiffelers, I., Bosman, A. M. T., & van Hell, J. G. (2002). Uitspreken-wat-er-staat: een effectieve spellingtraining voor woorden met inconsistente foneem-grafeem relaties. [Overpronunciation: An effective spelling training for words with inconsistent phoneme-grapheme relations]. *Tijdschrift voor Orthopedagogiek, 41,* 320–331.

Siegenbeek, M. (1805). *Verhandeling over de spelling der Nederduitsche taal, ter bevordering van eenparigheid in dezelve* [Essay on the spelling of the Duutsch language, encouragement to uniformity]. Amsterdam: J. Allart.

Simon, D. P., & Simon, H. A. (1973). Alternative uses of phonemic information in spelling. *Review of Educational Research, 43,* 115–137.

Stone, G. O., Vanhoy, M., & Van Orden, G. C. (1997). Perception is a two-way street: Feedforward and feedback phonology in visual word recognition. *Journal of Memory and Language, 36,* 337–359.

te Winkel, L. A. (1863). *Ontwerp der spelling* [Spelling design]. Leiden, The Netherlands: D. Noothoven van Goor.

te Winkel, L. A. (1865). *De grondbeginselen der Nederlandsche spelling, regeling der spelling voor het woordenboek der Nerderlandsche taal.* [Basic principles of Dutch spelling, regulation of the spelling for the dictionary of the Dutch language]. Leiden, The Netherlands: D. Noothoven van Goor.

te Winkel, L. A., & de Vries, M. A. (1866). *De grondbeginselen der Nederlandsche spelling. Ontwerp der spelling voor het aanstaande Nederlandsch woordenboek* [Basic principles of Dutch spelling. Design of the spelling of the forthcoming Dutch dictionary]. Leiden, The Netherlands: D. Noothoven van Goor.

van den Bos, K. P., lutje Spelberg, H. C., Scheepstra, A. J. M., & de Vries, J. R. (1994). *Klepel: een test voor de leesvaardigheid van pseudowoorden* [Klepel: A test for pseudoword-reading skill]. Nijmegen, The Netherlands: Berkhout.

van der Sijs, N. (1996). *Leenwoordenboek. De invloed van andere talen op het Nederlands* [Loan-word dictionary. The effect of other languages on Dutch]. Den Haag, The Netherlands: Sdu Uitgeuers.

van der Sijs, N. (2001a). *Chronologisch woordenboek* [Chronological dictionary]. Amsterdam: L. J. Veen.

van der Sijs, N. (2001b). Waffles, booze and Santa Claus. *The Netherlands. A practical guide for the foreigner and a mirror for the Dutch* (pp. 66–73). Amsterdam: Prometheus.

van der Wal, M. (1992). *Geschiedenis van het Nederlands* [History of Dutch]. Utrecht, The Netherlands: Uitgeverij Het Spectrum.

van Diepen, M., & Bosman, A. M. T. (1999). Hoe spel jij gespelt? Werkwoordspelling door leerlingen van de basisschool en de middelbare school [Dutch verb spelling in students in primary school and in high-school students]. *Tijdschrift voor Orthopedagogiek, 38*, 176–186.

van Heuven, V. J. (1980). Aspects of Dutch orthography and reading. In J. F. Kavanagh, & R. L. Venezky, *Orthography, reading, and dyslexia* (pp. 57–73). Baltimore, MD: University Park Press.

van Kruysbergen, N., Bosman, A. M. T., & Stone G. O. (1998). Statistical analysis of the bidirectional inconsistency of spelling and sound in Dutch. *Abstracts of the X Congress of the European Society for Cognitive Psychology.*

Wester, J. (1985). Language technology as linguistics: A phonological case study of the Dutch spelling. In H. Bennis & A. van Kemenade (Eds.), *Linguistics in the Netherlands* (pp. 205–212). Dordrecht, The Netherlands: Foris Publications.

Ziegler, J. C., Stone, G. O., & Jacobs, A. M. (1996). Statistical analysis of the bidirectional inconsistency of spelling and sound in French. *Behavior Research Methods, Instruments and Computers, 28*, 504–515.

Zonneveld, W. (1980). Autonome spelling [Autonomous spelling]. *De Nieuwe Taalgids, 73*, 518–537.

10

Literacy Acquisition in Spanish

Javier S. Sainz
Universidad Complutense de Madrid

This chapter briefly describes the nature of the Spanish language as a linguistic type and discusses the difficulties that readers face concerning the way phonologic, morphologic, and orthographic units are aligned and recognized in reading. Particular attention is paid to the syllable-based decomposition of Spanish words. Contrary to most cross-linguistic studies that underestimate the complexity of Spanish orthography on ignoring the role of suprasegmental units in reading, evidence is reviewed that shows that actual performance depends on the materials readers are actually given. Regardless, observations of low performance in reading-comprehension tests, popular assessment scales, and studies that show high performance for Spanish readers keep using nonrepresentative reading material and lexical candidates for which no conflicting word-recognition processes emerge. Thus old prejudices about the shallow nature of Spanish orthography are confirmed in most studies. The role of bottom-up and top-down processes in lexical selection is discussed to account for the way that competing lexical entries become active in multiword displays.

MORPHOPHONOLOGY AND ORTHOGRAPHY
OF SPANISH SCRIPT

The form of a language is the means of expressing a series of conceptual, cognitive, or mental categories and relationships in terms of which we conceive the world described by the language. Underlying human natural languages is a universal event grammar, or tectogrammar, that ensures the intertranslatability of languages. Nonetheless, the implementation of this universal grammar, the phenogrammar, is specific to each language, and thus there are different alternatives for describing experience and assigning meaning to linguistic expressions (Moreno, 1994a). Hawkins (1983) shows that the structural order of linguistic expressions, or configurationality (Jelinek, 1984; Maracz & Muyksen, 1989), obeys a complex conditional structure organized around the two basic universal cognitive linguistic categories—event–verb and entity–object—and the manner in which they are conceptually related. Within this conditional structure, a solution is adopted by each language in response to a particular aspect of the problem of how to transpose the structural order of ideas into the linear order of linguistic discourse (Tesniere, 1966/1976) by concatenation of lexical units. The primitive units of word-level concatenative algebras are lexemes and morphemes. The concatenation of lexemes and morphemes to build words is governed by a lexical grammar, and this constitutes the level at which the morphology and orthography of a language are expressed.

The Spanish Language as a Linguistic Type

The principle that organizes linguistic discourse is verb–object cohesion (Tomlin, 1986, p. 74). The preverbal or postverbal object position is an iconic expression of the representation of the semantic relationship established between verb and object. A cross-linguistic comparison of European languages reveals structural similarities and differences relevant to the study of the computational complexity of linguistic processing (Bechert, Bernini and Buridant, 1990; Givón, 1990). If we turn to the manner in which linguistic components occur or are concatenated in the chain of discourse, languages can be classified according to the order of components into free-word-order languages and closed-word-order languages (Comrie, 1981/1989; Siewierska, 1988). Languages with a free arrangement of their components are morphologically complex when compared with the closed-word-order languages, which are morphologically simple and dependent on the relative position assumed by the components in the chain of discourse. In free-word-order languages, such as Spanish—as opposed to English—the dependency relationships of components in discourse are primarily represented by the morphological relationships between components at the syntagmatic and syntactic levels. The phonetic differentiation between lexeme and morpheme correlates with polysyllabism and monosyllabism (Skalicka, 1935/1979). In inflective languages, the morphemes are generally monosyllabic and lexemes polysyllabic; as for agglutinant languages, there is a greater proportion of monosyllabic lexemes. In Spanish, as an inflective language, we can observe a clear syllabic differentiation between lexemes and morphemes and a notable differentiation between nouns and verbs.

The elements that give meaning to the expressions of a language shape the lexicon. In accordance with the schema proposed in Fig. 10.1, the units of the lexicon are common or

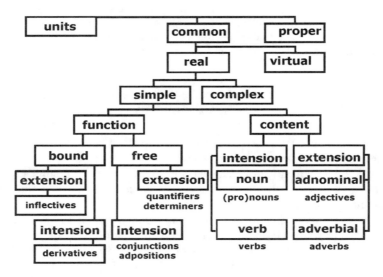

FIG. 10.1.   Units of the lexicon and intensional and extensional classes. Component processes of word recognition—lexical access and processing—are included.

proper, depending on whether they introduce into the discourse classes—or collections—of objects or individuals, respectively. As for the lexicon's common entries or nouns, they are items primarily made up of phonemes; the proper entries or nouns identify individuals in a language and are items that are composed to a lesser extent of phonemes. The structure of the lexicon is expressed through the set of real or existing common entries in a language; virtual entries are structural generalizations of the entries recognized by the speaker of a language.

Real entries can be continuous or discontinuous and, in turn, simple or complex. Simple or atomic entries are organized in general classes of (a) function and (b) content. Compound or molecular entries result from the combination of simple or atomic entries. Lexemes are the smallest units with extralinguistic meaning—or content meaning—and are structured in stems. The stem is defined by a series of lexical allomorphs or allostems with a common nucleus of linguistic meaning. This homonym nucleus is produced phonologically through metaphony in a different way in different lexical entries. For example, the stem *bon** [the quality of being good] is present in the lexical entries *buen* [good], and *buen-o* [good] and in *bon-dad* [goodness]. Morphemes are the smallest units with intralinguistic meaning, or function meaning; morphemes can be conceived only insofar as they contribute to specifying dependency relationships between the thematic elements of discourse. Units of content are linguistically heteroreferent units, and they hold independent meanings and are grammatically autonomous; units of function are linguistically self-referent, have dependent meanings, and are not grammatically autonomous. Units of function can be bound or free, depending on whether their concatenation with a lexeme is obligatory. Inflective and derivative morphemes are bound units. Bound morphemes are classified according to their position with respect to the stem in prefixes, suffixes, infixes, and circumfixes. Circumfixes are discontinuous morphemes, whereas prefixes, suffixes, and infixes are continuous. Infixes are morphemes that break the continuity of a stem, as in the case of *ro-m-p-er* [to break], its past participle being *roto* [broken]. Inflective morphology expresses the forms in which a stem can be expressed, whereas derivative morphology expresses relations that affect lexemes, modifying their lexical class.

Morphology is the mechanism by which lexemes acquire their reference in a context of use on permitting the construction of a referential representation in a linguistic context. The use of a lexeme in a linguistic context requires structural changes. Inflective rules have extensional properties because they are sensitive to the function or sense that stems take on within the chain of discourse; inflective rules are sensitive to the formal, distributional, or both, properties of the lexical elements in the chain of discourse. Hence inflective rules respond to the lexical class of the words to which they are applied. In a language such as Spanish, in which nouns and verbs are sharply differentiated, the inflective rules for nouns and verbs are different. Inflective morphemes imply no change in the way a word is assigned to a lexical class: Inflective morphemes are intracategorical or tautocategorical. In contrast to the strong agglutinant languages, Spanish, as an inflective language, is weak agglutinant; there is therefore a clear distinction between lexemes and morphemes, whereas homosemy and homonymy are uncommon.

Phonological and Orthographic Similarity

The writing systems associated with a language suffer from two fundamental weaknesses: lack of distinctiveness and lack of uniformity. Defects that become all the more notorious when the oral and the written languages undergo development independently of each other, resulting in a lack of correspondence between oral and written linguistic patterns. No existing alphabet or writing system wholly reflects all of the phonetic distinctions. Moreover the combinations of letters as symbols representing oral language cannot capture the acoustic, phonetic, and articulatory nuances that result from the adaptation of sounds when they are concatenated in the chain of discourse. In Spanish the intervocalic *d* in the word *dedo* [finger] is fricative or

Acoustic features	p	b	f	t	d	θ	tʃ	s	k	g	x	m	n	ɲ	ʎ	l	r̄	r
Consonant/Vowel	+	+	+	+	+	−	+	+	+	+	+	+	+	+	+	+	+	+
Compact/Diffuse	−	−	−	−	−	−	+	+	+	+	+	−	−	+	+	−	o	o
Grave/Acute	+	+	+	−	−	−	−	−	+	+	+	+	−	−	o	o	o	o
Nasal/Oral	−	−	−	−	−	−	−	−	−	−	−	+	+	+	−	−	−	−
Continuant/Interrupted	−	o	+	−	o	+	−	+	−	o	+	o	o	o	+	+	−	−
Strident/Mellow	−	−	+	−	−	+	−	+	−	−	+	o	o	o	o	o	o	o
Fortis/Lenis	+	−	+	+	−	−	+	+	+	−	+	+	−	o	o	o	+	−
Voiced/Voiceless	−	+	−	−	+	−	−	−	−	+	−	+	+	+	+	+	+	+

NB: + the leftmost acoustic feature is implemented; - the rightmost acoustic feature is not implemented; o means that either feature can be implemented

FIG. 10.2. Acoustic features of the Spanish consonant system (adapted from Martinez Celdrán, 1989, pp. 104).

spirant, phonetically distinct from the first *d*, which is occlusive. The same occurs in the word *baba* [slime], in which the intervocalic *b* is fricative or spirant, whereas the first is occlusive. Nonetheless, these phonetic variations do not imply changes in meaning and are in complementary distribution. When users write, they must recognize phonetic, acoustic, and articulatory variants as the same written symbol—a problem known as the recognition problem. Solving this problem implies achieving correspondence between patterns in different modalities, usually one oral and another written, so that the segmental units of one pattern correspond to the segmental units of the other—a problem known as the alignment problem. Figure 10.2 shows the consonant system of Spanish, defined by 18 consonant sounds, according to the system of acoustic properties from Jakobson and Halle (1956/1974) and adapted to Spanish by Quilis (1981). The features that characterize phonemes are grouped into a hierarchical structure such that some features are subordinate and others subordinating (Kenstowicz, 1994). As Sagey (1986) and Kim (1987) suggest, the unequal usage of phonological contrasts in different languages and their relative weight in the lexical system of each language express the facility with which the speaker recognizes such contrasts and the way in which they are articulated as features in phonological oppositions.

Segmental Phonology

The phonemes of a phonological system are established in accordance with the criteria of (a) contrastiveness, the minimal segmental units of sound that distinguish between otherwise identical speech patterns; (b) concurrence, the positional recurrence of segmental units in linguistically distinct contexts—a minimal contrastive pair is a pair of distinctive phonemes in the same linguistic context; and (c) structural similarity of sounds that a single phoneme generates—the phonic instantiations of a single phoneme define "a phonological (similarity) space" delimited by the phonemes that are contiguous in that space, which bring about a change in meaning (Hawkins, 1984, p. 34). The differences reflected in the phonological contrasts of a language have their roots in the lexicon and are expressed through the lexical system: Any process of categorization depends on the existence of template patterns in the lexical system, exploiting properties that are cognitively distinguishable according to the criteria of contrastiveness, concurrence, and acoustic, phonetic, and articulatory homogeneity. Phonemes are essentially probabilistic units, reflecting sound discrimination criteria that ensure differentiation between lexical entries. Similarly, letters are symbols that implement structural differences between lexical entries, by means of which it is possible to retrieve and discriminate between different entries. Figure 10.3 shows the structure of the consonant phonological system in Spanish,

Consonant	Supralaryngeal						Laryngeal
	Manner of articulation			Place of Articulation			
	Nasal	Lateral	Continuous	Labial	Coronal	Dorsal	
p			−	+			−
b			−	+			+
f			+	+			−
t			−	−			−
d			−	−			+
θ			+	−			−
ch			−		+		−
s			+		+		o
k			−			+	−
g			−			+	+
x			+			+	−
m	+			+			+
n	+				+		+
ɲ	+					+	+
ll		+				+	+
l		+			+		+
rr		−	+		+		+
r		−	−		+		+

NB: + the referred acoustic feature is implemented; − the referred acoustic feature is not implemented; o means that either feature can be implemented

FIG. 10.3. Hierarchical structure of the Spanish consonant phonological system.

following the hierarchical tree of features that discriminate primarily between place and manner of articulation.

The distribution and relative frequencies of phonemes in the Spanish consonant phonological system, their phonetic variants or allophones, and their standard orthographic correspondences are shown in Fig. 10.4(a).

As shown in Figs. 10.4(a) and 10.4(b), by use of capital letters in the allophone column, a phonological opposition can, in certain contexts, lose its distinctive features so that the features that bring about this contrast are neutralized or disappear (Akamatsu, 1988).

Suprasegmental Phonology

Segmental analysis is not always enough to identify a lexical entry. When the fundamental frequency is applied to an utterance, the suprasegmental feature of tone identifies the intonation or prosodic structure of the utterance. Like intonation, stress is revealed at a syntactic level and cannot be defined as an intrinsic property of the segmental units of segmental phonology. In

Phoneme	Freq	Allophone	Graphemes	Spanish Name
/p /	2.77	[p] onset position in a syllable	p	/pe/
	0.03	[B] rime within a syllable		
/b /	2.37	[b] after pause or nasal [ß] any other position	b; v	/be/ /uße/
	0.03	[B] neutralized in rime position		
/f /	0.55	[f]	f	/efe/
/t /	4.53	[t] onset position in a syllable	t	te/
	0.31	[D] neutralized in rime position		
/d /	4.24	[d] after pause or nasal [∂] any other position	d	/de/
	0.31	[D] neutralized in rime position		
/ θ /	1.45	[θ]	c + (e, i); z	/ θe/ / θeta/
/tʃ /	0.37	[tʃ]	ch	/ tʃe/
/s /	8.32	[s]	s	/ese/
/k /	3.98	[k] onset position	c + (a, o, u, l, r); qu + (e, i); k	/θe/ /ku/ /ka/
	0.28	[G] neutralized in rime position		
/g /	0.94	[g] after pause or nasal [x] any other position	g + (a, o, u, l, r); gu + (e, i);	/xe/
	0.28	[G] neutralized in rime position		
/x /	0.57	[x]	g + (e, i); j	/xe/ /xota/
/m /	3.06	[m] onset position	m	/eme/
/n /	2.78	[m] before labial [subject to changes depending on the phoneme following]	n	/ene/
	4.86	[N] neutralized in rime position		
/ɲ/	0.25	[ñ]	ñ	/eɲe/
/ʎ/	0.38	[ʎ]	ll; y	/eʎe/ /i greek/
/l /	4.23	[l][changes depending on the phoneme following]	l	/ele/
/r̄/	0.43	[rr]	r, after pause, nasal or lateral; rr, otherwise	/double r/
/r /	3.26	[r] in any position except after pause, nasal or lateral	r	/erre/
	1.93	[R] neutralized in rime position		

(a)

FIG. 10.4. Distribution of the Spanish (a) consonant system and (b) vowel system.

Phoneme	Freq	Allophone	Grapheme	Spanish Name
/a /	12.19	[nasal a] before nasal [a] in any other case	a	a
/e /	14.67	[nasal e] before nasal [e] in any other case	e	e
/i /	7.38	[nasal i] before nasal [reduced i] in /ai//ei/ /oi/ [j] in /ia/ /ie/ /io/ [i] in any other case	i, y	i
/o /	9.98	[nasal o] before nasal consonant [o] in any other case	o	o
/u /	3.33	[nasal u] before nasal consonant [reduced u] in /au/ /eu/ /ou/ [w] in /ua/ /ue/ /uo/ [u] in any other case	u	u

(b)

FIG. 10.4. *Continued*

addition to the suprasegmental features of intonation and stress, which identify representative functions at linguistic and cognitive levels also present in Spanish, are the suprasegmental phenomena of quantity and compensatory lengthening, and, to a lesser extent, that of vowel harmony. From a cognitive viewpoint, intonation allows us to differentiate between speech acts and propositions; from a linguistic viewpoint, intonation delimits linguistic utterances. Stress in shallow orthographies, such as Italian or Spanish, serves both a contrastive and a distinctive function (Colombo & Tabossi, 1992; Harris, 1983/1991). The relational nature of stress in Spanish is expressed through the weak–strong dominant metric structure of the explosive syllable structure (Liberman & Prince, 1977). The metric structure of Spanish identifies this language as one with bounded metrical feet.

Syllable stress can be expressed as (a) an intensity stress, by means of an increase in the amplitude of the sound wave; (b) a tonic stress, in which the tone of the accentuated segment is increased or varied; and (c) a quantity stress, by means of a relative increase in the duration of the stressed syllable relative to that which is not stressed. The stress in Spanish is realized by an unequal combination of these mechanisms (Gil Fernández, 1988, p. 130). The normative pattern of accentuation in Spanish is, according to Quilis (1981, pp. 333–336), with the stress on the penultimate syllable. Of words, 79.5% are paroxytone: these words are stressed on the next-to-the-last syllable. Oxytones, which account for 17.68% of words, are stressed on the last syllable. The proparoxytones, words with dactylic stress, are stressed on the antepenultimate syllable, and make up 2.76% of all words. The oxytones are derived from paroxytones that have lost their final syllable. According to Harris (1983/1991), words that are stressed on the third last syllable have dactylic stress because in terms of metrics they contain an extra syllable, known as an extrametrical syllable, confirming the idea that accentuation in Spanish is fixed on the penultimate syllable. Stress, though, also serves a representational function in Spanish, first, because the contrast between words that contain a stressed syllable (63.44%) and words that do not (36.56%) marks the distinction between content words and function words, and second, because it allows us to distinguish between nouns and verbs, and between different entries within these categories, by means of their inflective markers. Thus the word *titulo* expresses a verb, the first-person indicative of the verb *titular* [to title] and means "I title." The word *título*, on the other hand, expresses the corresponding noun [a title], and *tituló* is the third-person-singular form of the past tense of the same verb *titular*. The accent expresses differences that clearly affect the morphological analysis of lexical entries.

Syllables as Structural Units

Spoken language is a continuous stream of transitions between closed and open articulatory positions. Syllables comprise and determine the phonological system of a language (Cutler, Mehler, Norris, & Segui, 1986); the closed–open sequence defines an explosive syllable, the open–closed sequence an implosive syllable, and a sequence comprising a single, open articulatory unit defines a null transition. These simple sequences can be combined to form complex sequences. In general, a syllable consists of onset and rime, and the rime in turn consists of nucleus and rime. As Kurylowicz (1973) suggests, the formal structure of the syllable mirrors the formal structure of the sentence. The nucleus, or subordinating element of a syllable, is the only phoneme that can form a syllable in its own right. In Spanish this nucleus always consists of a vowel with a contextually unambiguous orthography. The onset and the rime are complex elements that assume a subordinate relationship with respect to the syllabic nucleus. Assigning syllable structure to a phonic chain is the result of a formally well-defined assignment function in Spanish (Moreno, 1994b, p. 593), with the following parameters:

1. Each of the vocalic segments is assigned the function of nucleus.
2. The consonant immediately preceding is assigned the function of onset.
3. The consonant immediately after is assigned the function of rime.
4. A consonant immediately before the onset is assigned to the onset.
5. A consonant immediately after the rime is assigned to the rime.
6. The function of rime is assigned to nucleus and rime.
7. The function of syllable is applied to the sequence of onset and rime.

The phonic predictability of an orthographic syllable and the orthographic predictability of a phonic syllable are theoretically perfect. The syllable is an efficient predictor of the relationships between spelling and sound. The syllable with structure CCVCC—*trans*, from the word *transporte*—corresponds to the metric structure S(w[w,s],s[s,w{w,s}]) following the rules of metric structure assignment (Harris, 1983/1991, p. 122) that determines the succession of relatively strong and weak constituents in stress patterns. The syllable is the axis around which phonological oppositions are defined.

THE ROLE OF ORTHOGRAPHY IN
SPANISH LITERACY ACQUISITION

Learning to read is a process of finding correspondences between series of graphic and phonic patterns, such that the representations obtained from processing a symbol in one modality are analogous to the representations obtained from processing a symbol in the other. Alphabetical writing might simply be seen as the result of a speech digitizing process, entirely congruent with the process a learner must follow in order to generate a speech pattern from a visually retrievable series of symbols, structured in terms of time and space. This apparently correct proposition is certainly flawed if we accept that, in the associative relationships linking graphical patterns with lexical entries, speech patterns act as natural and mandatory intermediaries. The hypothesis that reduces reading to the enunciation of a written message is incongruent with (a) the existence of writing systems that are not strictly phonological in nature or that are morphologically based (Leong, 1989); (b) the existence of writing systems common for a wide range of diverse oral languages, but inadequate to accurately express all their sound differences (Goswami, 1999; Morais, 1995); and (c) the existence of word-recognition conflicts whose origins lie in competitive phonological and morphological segmentation processes or conflicts in the elaboration of the message content that cannot be resolved through the oral synthesis of an orthographic pattern alone. The notion of a system of grapheme–phoneme conversion rules is the consummate expression of this conceptual reductionism. The reader's goal is not only to enunciate the word or synthesize a sound derived from a graphical stimulus, but also to discriminate between this pattern and any other orally congruent with the same physical stimulus but incongruent with the information provided by the text.

Phonologic and Orthographic Parsing: What Prevails in Reading?

As is the case at other levels of linguistic analysis, alphabetical writing is a compromise between the economy obtained by the repetition of a finite set of symbols in different combinations and the redundancy that comes through the use of a finite symbol set without exploiting every combinatorial possibility. Because not every possible combination is utilized, the reader is afforded redundant cues with which to identify a word and discriminate between it and similar lexical entries. How much redundancy and economy is borne in any language depends on how its lexicon is actually structured, on how different or similar their lexical entries are from one another. The practical problem for the instructor is to present a number of orthographic patterns that are sufficient enough for the learner to generalize phono-orthographic correspondences to new patterns, complete with all of the relevant orthographic distinctions represented and covering all of the phonological distinctions from the language in question. The ease with which the teacher draws up a sufficient and complete sample of phonological–orthographic models depends in turn on the internal coarticulation of the phonological and orthographic systems.

The role of phonological parsing and coding in reading has long been the subject of a considerable debate. A first issue revolves around the role played by phonological representations in the activation of a lexical entry and in the retrieval of its lexical content. Those who assume a major role for sound encoding associate the process of phonological mediation with visual word recognition and contend that reading proceeds straightforwardly from spelling to sound to meaning (van Orden, 1987; van Orden, Pennington, & Stone, 1990). In sharp contrast, those who assume a minor role for sound encoding interpret the phonological representation as a by-product of a process that directly links an orthographic pattern to its corresponding lexical entry by means of a set of lexical access cues. Mild versions of these extreme views contend that both mechanisms are in place: Although skilled readers generally proceed through "direct access" in visual word recognition, beginners and poor readers cannot bypass phonology as skilled readers usually do.

A second issue concerns the nature of the phonological representation involved in visual word recognition, whether it is derived directly from a lexical entry or assembled on the basis of spelling-to-sound correspondences. Whereas the first issue concerns the role of phonological representations in reading, the second concerns the very existence and nature of the two independent codes for lexical access. Dual-route models assume that the recognition of printed words relies on two types of codes: an abstract lexical orthographic–graphemic code and a nonlexical phonemic code. The critical issue for both single-route and dual-route models is whether prelexical codes exist and whether these nonlexical codes are actually used to access the lexicon. Compelling evidence for the existence of nonlexical phonological codes should be provided if dual-route models are to be supported. In the case of languages with an opaque and deep orthography, such as English and French, readers are supposed to recognize visual words through the activation of orthographic lexical codes; in the case of languages with a transparent and shallow orthography, such as German, Serbo-Croatian, Italian, and Spanish, readers are said to rely on the prelexical phonemic codes. In general, according to dual-route models, languages might differ in the relative use of the independent mechanisms depending on the relative regularity of letter–sound correspondences.

Lexical Structure Constraints in Reading Acquisition

As a shallow transparent orthographic language, Spanish, a language with a regular but context-sensitive mapping from orthography to phonology, can be viewed as a natural laboratory to test whether phonological representations mediate lexical access and whether they can be conceived as a direct route to meaning. The critical issue is whether different reading mechanisms are in use in languages with shallow and deep orthographies (Goswami, Gombert, & de Barrera, 1998).

Spanish spelling-to-sound correspondences could be that of a transparent language, but Spanish morphology could be that of an opaque language. As a consequence, we can find asymmetries in reading acquisition across languages. The shallow spelling-to-sound corre-spondences and deep morphology in Spanish cannot be dissociated from one another when the objective in training a new reader is not for the reader to synthesize speech from a written pattern, but rather for the reader to understand language. Defior, Martos, and Cary (2002) have shown that whereas morphology-based reading development is better for older Portuguese readers than for older Spanish readers, Spanish novice readers are overall better readers than Portuguese novice readers, despite the fact that both languages qualify as transparent shallow orthographies.

Computational costs to translate a letter pattern into a phonological pattern by which phono-logical word forms become active can vary across languages either for different assembly and retrieval mechanisms or for the nature and distribution of information cues that become active in reading. The issue for the researcher is both to choose a representative sample of lexical patterns in any language and to minimize lexical differences across different orthographic systems. When the hypothesis of different processing mechanisms that exist for different or-thographic systems is put to test, no difference arises across deep and shallow orthographies in readers who are dyslexic or who have learning disabilities in a wide variety of languages (Ziegler, Perry, Ma-Wyatt, Ladner, & Schulte-Korne, 2003). Reading can be productively ana-lyzed as a prototypical pattern-recognition situation in which readers exploit multiple sources of information including orthographic structure, spelling-to-sound correspondences, and word frequency. No matter how differently these multiple cues can be expressed in any language, the same word-recognition mechanisms may still be in use. Formal equivalence of processing mechanisms in the human mind is the underlyng hypothesis of the very existence of typological differences across languages.

Segmental Units in Word Recognition and Reading

Although it seems obvious that readers as well as speakers have to decompose words to elab-orate the information that a word contains, one of the most controversial issues within speech perception and reading concerns both the nature of the segments and the segmentation process itself. Empirical evidence suggests minimal availability of component-level information be-fore word recognition (Sainz, 1999, Sainz, Villalba, & Gutierrez, 2003). The opacity or lack of transparency in the process of word recognition is a by-product of the relational coding process that assimilates the letters of a word into a structural description. Models of visual word recognition are unrealistic if they assume, even for the sake of convenient computational implementation, that readers read a string of separate letters.

To study whether different reading mechanisms are associated with different language orthographies, some research has been conducted in Spanish that shows the stringent role played by syllables in word recognition and reading (Alvarez, de Vega, & Carreiras, 1997; Jimenez, Alvarez, Estevez, & Hernandez-Valle, 2000). Intrasyllabic segmental units, such as onsets and rimes but not consonant clusters, seem to have a negligible effect in a transparent orthography, in sharp contrast with English (Goswami, 1999; Treiman, 1994; Treiman & Chafetz, 1987). In Spanish, both typical and nontypical readers do not differ in using correspondences based on onsets and rimes (Jimenez et al., 2000). Notwithstanding, as occurs in English with intrasyllabic segmental units (Mutter, Hulme, Snowling, & Taylor, 1997), the theoretical status of syllables in Spanish remains controversial: Whereas each syllable is computed during the processing of a written word, its actual role depends on the word it contributes to (Sainz et al., 2003) and its positional frequency (Alvarez et al., 1997; Jimenez, Guzman & Artiles, 1997). Even though a sound pattern can be unambiguously obtained from syllable-based parsing of a word—what seems to convey to the transparent and shallow nature of Spanish orthography—the critical issue is whether lexical regularity can guarantee lexical access and selection in any context. Both the actual and the evolutionary forms of Spanish orthography reveal conflicts arising from the phonologically unmotivated orthography of many homophone patterns that activate different lexical entries for their different spellings. The overconfidence of readers in relying on syllable-based decoding strategies is the main cause underlying word parsing and comprehension impairments as reading skills develop (Defior et al., 2000).

Whereas some attention has been paid to lexical regularity in Spanish, lexical consistency and neighborhood density have not received the attention they deserve. For English words, there is minimal evidence of competitive influences on lexical retrieval that is due to higher-frequency neighbors. In contrast, such effects are more common in such languages as French and Spanish, perhaps because they embody a more consistent relationship between orthography and phonology (Andrews, 1996, 1997). In a series of experiments conducted to test the predictions of the prelexical activation hypothesis in Spanish, Sebastián-Gallés (1991), in sharp contrast to Tabossi (1989) in previous tests of this hypothesis, included pseudowords as targets in word naming and lexical decision tasks. Pseudowords were constructed in a way that maximizes orthographic similarity between words and pseudowords. Sebastián-Gallés observed that pseudowords were actually perceived as the words they are based on but did not find any evidence for the activation of prelexical codes. Their results are congruent with the hypothesis that there is no processing difference across languages that is due to orthography. Cutler, Sebastián-Gallés, Soler-Vilageliu, and van Ooijen (2000) conducted a series of spoken-word-recognition tasks in Dutch and in Spanish, in which listeners were required to turn nonwords into real words by changing either a vowel or a consonant. Both Dutch and Spanish listeners responded significantly faster and more accurately when required to change vowels as opposed to consonants. Cutler et al. (2000) contend that vowel information appears to constrain lexical selection less tightly—it allows more potential lexical candidates—than does consonant information: "Listeners find it easier to change a vowel than a consonant to construct a lexical hypothesis from a nonword input, regardless of the relative number of distinctiveness of the phonemes in their native language" (p. 753). The imbalance of number of vowels and consonants between Dutch and Spanish made no difference in their results. Berent and Perfetti (1995) proposed a model of phonological assembly that postulates a multilinear representation that segregates consonants and vowels in different planes. One methodological implication of their model is that regularity effects are not necessary evidence for phonological assembly; in fact, regularity effects might be an expression of how difficult is for the listener or reader to construct a lexical hypothesis from an input pattern. Although this evidence emerges in oral language, it arises equally in written language: Migration errors on word targets are observed that depend on the existence of lexical competing candidates in both English and Spanish, regardless of differences in orthography (Sainz, 1999). Consistency and neighborhood density effects do not reveal in Spanish the existence of different and specific reading mechanisms for shallow and deep orthographies, but they do show the different constraints imposed by lexical structure and experimental task demands.

Reading Acquisition in Spanish-Speaking Children

In the process of teaching a child to read, the task of the teacher is to provide the child initially with a set of temporally sequenced words, drawn from the learner's oral vocabulary, that in accordance with the phonotactic structural complexity of the lexicon allow him or her to generalize the sound they represent onto any other word that shares some segment with them. The combinatorial properties of the units into which linguistic discourse is divided should exploit the human cognitive system's ability to label relationships at different levels of resolution: lexemes, morphemes, and syllables and other units are expressions of a type of relationship the system can recognize as segments of a lexical pattern (Jusczyk, 1997). Thus the identity of a lexical entry, far from being defined by the particular units into which speech is divided, comes instead from the combinatory restrictions imposed on these units.

In an ordinary classroom, teaching progresses in relation to the achievement level of the average pupil. Besides a preliterate year in kindergarten, at the age of 5 years, in which every letter is presented along with its sound, most children need less than 2 more years to properly master reading in Spanish. Before the end of the second year, at the average age of 7 years, most children are able to correctly enunciate a word of any orthographic complexity provided that no learning impediment exists. Additional training is provided for the readers to master reading and recognize orthographic cues in text reading such as differences in orthography, word stress, sentence prosodic contour, and text punctuation. The dominant role of syllable-based parsing in reading-tuition causes that most readers do not recognize the lexical structure of many words. A syllable-based instructional method has a detrimental effect on reading comprehension if no additional reading tuition is provided, because lexical access often requires morpheme decomposition that competes with syllable-based parsing.

Most instructional methods employed by Spanish teachers conceive of reading as the result of a bottom-up operating mechanism by which orthographic patterns are converted into speech patterns through the operation of phonological rules on syllable-based visual word-parsing units. Although every letter does not make an equally salient contribution to the visual patterns or constrain word recognition as effectively as every other letter, no role is assigned to its relative positional frequency in the lexicon. Reading instructional methods seem to ignore how every letter contributes to the identity of a lexical entry, how the relationships it contracts within the lexicon contributes to lexical selection and reading. Little importance is given to previous knowledge in discriminating a lexical entry from any other competing lexical candidates. The teacher strives to achieve an objective in which a novice reader is able to enunciate the word regardless of the actual complexity of stimulus features being taken by the reader as cues for lexical selection and access. However, the elementary components that a word is composed of are not immediately and spontaneously retrievable: Whenever a stimulus is encoded in a structural description, it works as a cue pattern for retrieving the most similar preexisting memory representation to which it was associated in the past. Even in Spanish, in which spoken units are completely predictable from written syllable units, no lexical entry can be identified without a comparison of that entry with every other accessed in the lexicon according to its orthographic similarity. Neither in deep nor shallow orthographies a lexical entry can be predicted by the sole activation of phonology-based units. Syllable-based reading tuition methods have mostly contributed to divert teacher's attention from orthography to phonology, this way ignoring the role played by lexicon structure in word recognition.

Incidence of Word-Recognition Deficits in Spanish Readers

No empirical epidemiological study has been conducted so far to estimate the incidence of reading difficulties and dyslexia across the Spanish population; thus the incidence of reading disabilities could be estimated only indirectly. Because reading and learning disabilities and dyslexia have been commonly associated with deficits in word-recognition processes, an estimate of reading difficulties could be obtained from readers' performance in tasks involving lexical access and lexical processing in cross-language comparison studies. However, longitudinal comprehensive studies of how reading skills develop are lacking in Spanish. In a less ambitious cross-linguistic study, Aro and Wimmer (2003) tested whether different orthographies lead readers to develop different decoding strategies in word recognition. Readers' performances are examined under similar reading conditions and comparable reading material and always include monosyllabic and bisyllabic patterns, words, and pseudowords; pseudowords were constructed by changing the first letter from number words presented as well. Aro and Wimmer observed that "the attainment of high reading accuracy was a much more protracted process for English children than for the children reading more regular orthographies. At the end of Grade 1, reading accuracy levels were already around 85% for the German, Dutch, French, Spanish and Finnish children and above 90% for the Swedish children, leaving little room for further improvement in all these orthographies" (p. 627). In this study, the Spanish-speaking participants obtained a stable measure of 91% of the pseudowords correct by the end of the second year. No data are provided concerning word reading in this article. Although many agree that a pseudoword-reading test constitutes the most accurate test of a reading disability (Siegel, 1989), assuming a standard deviation of 7%–8%, only 3 out 120 Spanish-speaking readers tested in this study would score less than 74% of correct responses on pseudoword reading. Under these conditions and the material used, open to criticisms, Aro and Wimmer's study does not detect readers with disabilities, at least in shallow transparent orthographies.

Cuetos, Rodriguez, and Ruano (1996) developed a reading-skills assessment test, named Prolec—proreading—that is the first that includes standardized error rates on letter naming and letter–sound recognition, same–different pseudoword and word comparison, lexical decisions, and pseudoword and word reading selected by length and use frequency. Thematic-role assignment in active and passive sentences, phrase parsing, and sentence- and text-comprehension tasks are also included as complementary subtests. Lower performances in the test scales have recently been taken as defining criteria of reading disability. Unfortunately, the actual version of the test includes measures on neither many of the phenomena of lexical access and processing (Sainz, 1999), such as neighborhood density, lexical consistency, lexical type, context and homophone effects, nor on reading strategies and spelling, all of which are relevant for reading assessment. Measures of cognitive components, specifically those involved in object naming and attentional processing, are also lacking. Despite the relevance of these missing features, Prolec has proved to be a significant improvement in reading assessment of Spanish readers. The total actual scores obtained with Prolec in a sample of 403 readers drawn from primary schools correlate with scores freely provided by their teachers: 0.53. Although most readers assessed by Prolec perform generally well in any scale, they do not perform as well in text comprehension: The error rate in text comprehension is four times greater than in any other subtest, revealing that, although readers succeed in enunciating a word, they fail in extracting information from more complex linguistic uses, a result of the prevalence of syllable-based tuition methods in Spanish. As shown in the Aro and Wimmer's study (2003), negligible differences in reading performance appear to emerge in Prolec among children after second grade.

In a recent pilot study that forms part of a large-scope longitudinal study conducted by our team in the Applied Psycholinguistics Unit, 120 first-grade children were tested twice a year to examine the temporal course of word-recognition development and reading acquisition (Mousikou & Sainz, 2002). Preliminary results of hit rates and oral reading latency for first graders are presented in Table 10.1.

TABLE 10.1
Reading Assessment of First Graders in a Pilot Study (Preliminary Data)

| | 72–80 Months Old | | | | 80–86 Months Old | | | |
| | Hit Rates | | Reading Latency | | Hit Rates | | Reading Latency | |
Lexicality	Words	Pseudowords	Words	Pseudowords	Words	Pseudowords	Words	Pseudowords
Mean	61	63	68.03	62.80	68	67	50.40	45.15
SD	38	38	0.41	0.39	38	38	0.39	0.39
Orthography	Complex	Simple	Complex	Simple	Complex	Simple	Complex	Simple
Mean	61	63	65.37	65.37	64	70	46.53	48.91
SD	38	38	0.39	0.39	38	37	0.39	0.39
Lexical Type	Content	Function	Content	Function	Content	Function	Content	Function
Mean	60	64	65.37	65.37	68	68	52.98	42.95
SD	38	38	0.39	0.39	38	38	0.39	0.39
Word Length	Short	Large	Short	Large	Short	Large	Short	Large
Mean	63	61	57.97	73.70	68	67	45.15	50.40
SD	38	38	0.39	0.41	38	38	0.38	0.39

Notes: Hit rates: average proportions; Oral reading latency: average production latency per character, in milliseconds.

As can be seen in this table, consistent significant differences, mainly in oral reading latencies, emerge in lexicality and word length in both testing periods, and in lexical type in the second one, but not in orthography. Besides being faster and more efficient in reading after 6-months training, children tend to take advantage of some cues to improve their performance. A more complete throughout analysis of the temporal course of how readers use these word cues to decide on a pattern is needed. Reading performance measures have been obtained in experimental research that provide a view of what difficulties readers with disabilities face in word recognition in a shallow orthography.

THE ROLE OF ATTENTION IN WORD RECOGNITION AND READING

The perceptual processing of words has so far been treated as the result of a bottom-up mechanism in which previous knowledge exerts no influence; what the system knows about words, their units, their structural and distributional properties, and their constraints, plays no role in the identification of a lexical candidate as a legitimate lexical entry.

Psychological theory on attention distinguishes among location-based, feature-based, and object-based forms of selection. These approaches cannot be viewed as mutually exclusive alternatives, and almost every model acknowledges that each of these three mechanisms play some kind of role. Location-based attention tends to select both relevant and irrelevant stimuli at the attended location. Under a strict interpretation of this view, the grouping of stimuli into objects should not influence the allocation of attention. In contrast, however, more recent evidence has illustrated the importance of perceptual groups, and in particular whole objects, in guiding selection. A critical implication is that attention to one part or attribute of an object will entail selection of the whole object at the expense of other objects in the scene. Words can be seen in this respect as objects, as information packages, or bundles of cues. Although location and feature information cannot be ignored, the recursive use of the same alphabetic characters determines that location-based and feature-based organization would rarely efficiently select just one of the active competing words available from the lexicon (Sainz, Villalba, Mousikou, & Jorge-Botana, 2002).

The decisions that lead to the identification of a lexical entry are inevitably the result of a forced-selection process, which assigns as default the entry that best matches the available cues. Word recognition is a self-terminating discrete process (Grosjean, 1980). No word cue is left dangling after a reader selects a lexical entry according to the information at hand. This probabilistic approach means that a reader is making a lexical decision by selecting from the available entries the one that best fits incoming information; the lexical selection of an entry depends on the features that distinguish it from other lexical entries competing for selection and on the cues that allow it to be distinguished from any other in a specific context. The theoretical framework is largely derived from the biased-competition model of Desimone and Duncan (1995). The selection of one word rather than another is the result of the competition and cooperation between the lexical entries comprising the active cohort, to determine which of them will receive further processing. While lexical selection is taking place, both phonological and orthographical representations become involved in cooperation and competition processes, subject to the attentional resources available and task demands (Sainz, Mousikou, & Jorge-Botana, 2003).

Multiple stimuli presented simultaneously are not processed independently, but rather interact with each other in a mutually suppressive way (for a review, see Andrews, 1997). If readers are presented with two distinct but similar orthographic patterns and then asked to identify the one in which a particular letter is displayed, performance is worse than if a single word had been used. Likewise, if readers are presented with two different word strings evoking two semantic associates and then asked to make a lexical decision on a particular orthographic pattern, they simultaneously compute the similarity of both orthographic patterns and the similarity of the phonological representations for which they served as cues. Attention may resolve the problem of competing multiple-word stimuli by counteracting the suppressive influences of nearby distracters, enhancing information processing of the attended target and suppressing interfering information arising from the stimulus display. Success at suppressing irrelevant information depends on the way competing stimuli are internally structured.

Attentional Processes and Dyslexia in a Shallow Orthography

To study interference effects in the production of lexical substitution errors, Villalba and I (Sainz & Villalba, 2003) conducted a series of experiments by using a variant of a migration error paradigm, employed in earlier studies (Sainz, 2002; Sainz, Gutierrez, & Villalba, 2002; Sainz & Villalba, 2003; Sainz, Villalba, & Gutierrez, 2003; Sainz, Villalba, & Mousikou, 2002), in which the target to be recognized from among a set of distracters differs from its competing alternatives by just a single letter. Participants were both dyslexic and typical readers. To determine whether this interference effect stems from phonological retrieval mechanisms or recoding mechanisms, an attempt was made to identify the cues available to a reader during word recognition in which orthographic and phonological cues compete with each other.

The stimuli employed were words of four phonic units or four letters. As can be seen in Table 10.2, as well as the usual variables in this kind of design, the critical independent variables were (a) the orthographical plausibility of distracters in the stimulus set, plausible (Series 1–4

TABLE 10.2

Sample of an Experimental Series for Migration Error

	Stimulus Set		Response Set		
Series	Distracter	Target	Homophone	Migration	Simple
1	VASO	PASA	BASA	PASO	BESO
2	BASA	PASA	VASO	PASO	BESO
3	ZERA*	PERO	CERO	PERA	MERO
4	BELO*	PELA	VELA	PELO	CELO
5	KODA**	MODO	CODO	MODA	BODA
6	ZEDA**	SEDE	CEDE	SEDA	DEDO
7	ZITO**	PITA	CITA	PITO	MITO
8	VULA**	MULO	BULO	MULA	CULO

Notes: Pseudowords marked with an asterisk are orthographically plausible; pseudowords marked with two asterisks are orthographically implausible.

of the stimulus set) and implausible (Series 5–8); and (b) the lexical status of the distracter, word (Series 1 and 2 of the stimulus set) and pseudoword (Series 3 and 4). Orthographically plausible stimuli were phonological words with compatible orthography; implausible stimuli were phonological words with incompatible orthography. The homophone distracter and the migration distracter represent possible response alternatives associated respectively with the processing of the distracter and the target in the stimulus stage. In each trial the participant was presented with a target stimulus and a response set that always included the target stimulus and three context distracters. The participant was asked to locate the target from among the distracter set by pressing the key corresponding to the position in which the target was previously presented. Presentation of the target was automatically postmasked after a period that varied according to the participant's overall efficiency, a maximum error rate of 40% between trials, so that the processing time tends toward an asymptote of display time—exposure threshold—that is constant for each reader and comparable for all readers in the sample.

The key to the differences between these responses lies in the role played by attention and the manipulation of the experimental variables of orthographical plausibility and lexicality. Because the target is postcued, the participant can benefit from the simultaneous presentation of target and distracter only when the distracter is a pseudoword; the target is always a word. In these instances, participants may ignore this part of the stimulus signal, which allows them to choose the target. However, when distracter and target are both words, the participant must make this choice mentally in order to decide which is the target. If letters are processed as cues for the words activated in the lexicon, the presence of a letter implies a set of constraints. These constraints arise from the contribution that the letter makes to the words it can form part of. The results provide evidence that dyslexic readers, unlike typical readers, ignore orthographic cues to eliminate competing pseudohomophones.

The most relevant finding of this experiment is that related to the interaction between lexical context of stimulus and orthographic plausibility. Figure 10.5 demonstrates this effect. Dyslexic readers ignore the orthographic cues for eliminating competitive pseudohomophones, whereas typical readers take advantage of these cues to dramatically improve their performance, especially when lexical consultation permits them to distinguish between plausible and implausible

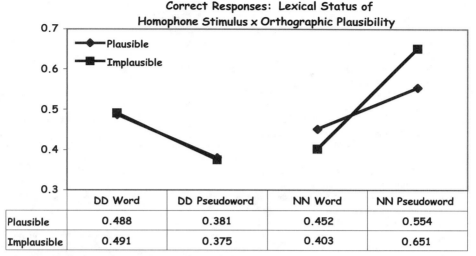

	DD Word	DD Pseudoword	NN Word	NN Pseudoword
Plausible	0.488	0.381	0.452	0.554
Implausible	0.491	0.375	0.403	0.651

NB: DD = Dyslexic readers; NN = Normal or typical readers.

FIG. 10.5. Success rates at target identification for a sample of typical and dyslexic readers, according to lexical status and orthographic plausibility of the distracter.

orthographic patterns. Letters are apparently necessary but insufficient units for the identification of a lexical entry to take place, because letters contribute to word identification only insofar as they are subject to a composition process. Their value depends on their frequency distribution in the segmental units where they occur and on their capacity to discriminate between alternative meanings expressed in the different entries of the lexical system (Sainz, 1999). Lexical substitution errors occur when, in the reader's mind, the cues offered by the linguistic stimulus are shared by lexical entries that compete with the target. The process can be conceived of as the result of mechanisms that compute similarity between lexical candidates and actual entries. The concurrence of orthographically plausible or implausible pseudowords has the effect of dramatically reducing the efficiency with which dyslexic readers recognize the target.

REFERENCES

Akamatsu, T. (1988). *The theory of neutralization and the archiphoneme in functional phonology.* Amsterdam: Benjamins.

Alvarez, C., de Vega, M., & Carreiras, M. (1997). La sílaba como unidad de activación léxica en la lectura de palabras trisílabas [The syllable as a processing unit in reading of trisyllable words]. *Psicothema, 10,* 371–386.

Andrews, S. (1996). Lexical retrieval and selection processes: Effects of transposed-letter confusability. *Journal of Memory & Language, 35,* 775–800.

Andrews, S. (1997). The effect of orthographic similarity on lexical retrieval: Resolving neighborhood conflicts. *Psychonomic Bulletin & Review, 4,* 439–461.

Aro, M., & Wimmer, H. (2003). Learning to read: English in comparison to six more regular orthographies. *Applied Psycholinguistics, 24,* 621–635.

Bechert, J., Bernini, G., & Buridant, C. (1990). *Toward a typology of European languages.* Berlin: Mouton de Gruyter.

Berent, I., & Perfetti, Ch.A. (1995). A rose is a REEZ: The two-cycles model of phonology assembly in reading English. *Psychological Review, 102,* 146–184.

Colombo, L., & Tabossi, P. (1992). Strategies and stress assignment: Evidence from a shallow orthography. In R. Frost & L. Katz (Eds.), *Orthography, phonology, morphology, and meaning* (pp. 319–340). Amsterdam: North-Holland.

Comrie, B. (1981/1989). *Universales del lenguaje y tipología lingüística* [Language universals and language typology]. Madrid: Gredos.

Cuetos, F., Rodriguez, B., & Ruano, E. (1996). *Batería de Evaluación de los procesos lectores de los niños de Educación Primaria* (PROLEC) [Assessment of reading skills test for children]. Madrid: Técnicos Especialistas Asociados.

Cutler, A., Mehler, J., Norris, D., & Segui, J. (1986). The syllable's differing role in the segmentation of French and English. *Journal of Memory and Language, 25*, 385–400.

Cutler, A., Sebastián-Gallés, N., Soler-Vilageliu, O., & van Ooijen, B. (2000). Constraints of vowels and consonants on lexical selection: Cross-linguistic comparisons. *Memory & Cognition, 28*, 746–755.

Defior, S., Martos, F., & Cary, L. (2002). Differences in reading acquisition development in two shallow orthographies: Portuguese and Spanish. *Applied Psycholinguistics, 23*, 135–148.

Desimone, R., & Duncan, J. (1995). Neural mechanisms of selective visual attention. *Annual Review of Neuroscience, 18*, 193–222.

Gil Fernández, J. (1988). *Los sonidos del lenguaje* [The sounds of language]. Madrid: Sintesis.

Givón, T. (1990). *Syntax. A functional typological introduction* (Vol. II). Amsterdam: Benjamins.

Goswami, U. (1999). The relationship between phonological awareness and orthographic representation in different orthographies. In M. Harris & G. Hatano (Eds.), *Learning to read and write: A cross-linguistic perspective* (pp. 134–156). Cambridge, UK: Cambridge University Press.

Goswami, U., Gombert, J. E., & de Barrera, L. (1998). Children's orthographic representations and linguistic transparency: Nonsense word reading in English, French, and Spanish. *Applied Psycholinguistics, 19*, 19–52.

Grosjean, F. (1980). Spoken word recognition processes and the gating paradigm. *Perception and Psychophysics, 28*, 267–283.

Harris, J. W. (1983/1991). *La estructura silábica y el acento en Español. Análisis no lineal* [Syllable structure and stress in Spanish: A non-lineal analysis]. Madrid: Visor.

Hawkins, J. (1983). *Word order universals*. New York: Academic Press.

Hawkins, P. (1984). *Introducing phonology*. London: Routledge.

Jakobson, R., & Halle, M. (1956/1974). *Fundamentos del lenguaje* [Fundamentals of language]. Madrid: Ayuso.

Jelinek, E. (1984). Empty categories, case, and configurationality. *Natural Language and Linguistic Theory, 2*, 39–76.

Jimenez, J. E., Alvarez, C. J., Estevez, A., & Hernandez-Valle, I. (2000). Onset-rime units in visual word recognition in Spanish normal readers and children with reading disabilities. *Learning Disabilities Research & Practice, 15*, 135–141.

Jimenez, J. E., Guzman, R., & Artiles, C. (1997). Efectos de la frecuencia silábica posicional en el reconocimiento visual de palabras y aprendizaje de la lectura [Effects of positional syllable frequency in visual word recognition and learning to read]. *Cognitiva, 1*, 3–27.

Jusczyk, P. (1997). *The discovery of spoken language*. Cambridge, MA: MIT Press.

Kenstowicz, M. (1994). *Phonology in generative grammar*. London: Basil Blackwell.

Kim, K. H. (1987). *The phonological representation of distinctive features: Korean consonantal phonology*. Seoul, Korea: Hanshing Publishing.

Kurylowicz, J. (1973). *Esquissess linguistiques* (Vol. I). Munich: Wilhelm Fink.

Leong, C. K. (1989). Reading and reading difficulties in a morphemic script. In P. G. Aaron & R. H. Joshi (Eds.), *Reading and writing disorders in different orthographic systems* (pp. 267–282). Norwell, MA: Kluwer Academic.

Liberman, M., & Prince, A. (1977). On stress and linguistic rhythm. *Linguistic Inquiry, 8*, 249–336.

Maracz, L., & Muyksen, P. (1989). *Configurationality. The tipology of asymmetries*. Dordrecht, The Netherlands: Foris.

Martinez Celdrán, E. (1989). *Fonética (con especial referencia a la lengua castellana)*. [Phonetics (with a special emphasis on Castillian Spanish)]. Barcelona: Teide.

Morais, J. (1995). Do orthographic and phonological peculiarities of alphabetically written languages influence the course of literacy acquisition? *Reading and Writing: An Interdisciplinary Journal, 7*, 1–7.

Moreno, J. C. (1994a). *Curso universitario de lingüística general. Tomo I. Teoría de la gramática y sintaxis general* [Handbook of general linguistics. I. Grammatical theory and syntax]. Madrid: Sintesis.

Moreno, J. C. (1994b). *Curso Universitario de Lingüística General: Tomo II. Semántica, pragmatica, morfología y fonología* [Handbook of general linguistics. II. Semantics, pragmatics, morphology and phonology]. Madrid: Síntesis.

Mousikou, P., & Sainz, J. S. (2002). Predictores longitudinales de competencia lectora: Un estudio preliminar [Longitudinal predictors of reading performance: A preliminary study]. Oviedo, Spain: Sociedad Española de Psicologia Experimental.

Mutter, V., Hulme, C., Snowling, M., & Taylor, S. (1997). Segmentation, not rhyming, predicts early progress in learning to read. *Journal of Experimental Child Psychology, 65*, 370–396.

Quilis, A. (1981). *Fonética acústica de la lengua Española* [Acoustical phonics of Spanish]. Madrid: Gredos.

Sagey, E. C. (1986). *The representation of features and relations in non-linear phonology*. Cambridge, MA: MIT Press.

Sainz, J. S. (1999). Tracking dyslexia in the research lab: Processes-based diagnosis, and social and educational management of reading disabilities. In I. Reinelt, & G. Gerber, *Trends in dyslexia* (pp. 47–68). Vienna: University of Vienna Press.

Sainz, J. S. (2002, September). *Orthographic and lexical constraints in a transparent orthography: The case of adult dyslexia*. Paper presented at the Sixth Congress on Imparare: Questo é il problema. La disslesia nelle ortografie trasparenti, San Marino, Italy.

Sainz, J. S., Gutierrez, A., & Villalba, C. (2002). La dislexia del disléxico adulto: El curso temporal del efecto de interferencia asociativa. [Dyslexia in adult dyslexic readers: The temporal course of an associative interference effect]. In V. Santiuste, I. Andrés, & A. I. Peña (Eds.), *Actas del II Congreso de Educacion Especial y Atención a la Diversidad en la Comunidad de Madrid* (pp. 163–184). Madrid: Comunidad de Madrid, Consejeria de Educacion.

Sainz, J. S., Mousikou, P., & Jorge-Botana, G. (2003, September). *Conjoining letters into words: Brain response correlates of lexical and attentional mechanisms in lexical substitution errors*. Paper presented at the Congress of the Federation of European Psychophysiology Societies, Bordeaux, France.

Sainz, J. S., & Villalba, C. (2003). Orthographic plausibility effects on letter migration in dyslexic and normal readers (Submitted).

Sainz, J. S., Villalba, C., & Gutierrez, A. (2003). Illusory words: Orthographic and lexical constraints in letter migration. In M. Joshi & B. Kaczmarek (Eds.), *Literacy acquisition, assessment, and intervention: The role of phonology, orthography, and morphology*. Amsterdam: IOS Press.

Sainz, J. S., Villalba, C., & Mousikou, P. (2002, June). *Illusory word- and illusory object-conjunctions: Are the same brain mechanisms in use?* Paper presented at the 2002 Annual Meeting of the Society for the Scientific Study of Reading, Chicago.

Sainz, J. S., Villalba, C., Mousikou, P., & Jorge-Botana, G. (2002, November). *Mecanismes cerebrals en la substitució de paraules: Observacions en el reconeixement de paraules y objectes* [Brain mechanisms in word substitutions: Comparing word and object recognition]. Paper presented at Quarta Jornada Sobre Dislèxia, Girona, Spain.

Sebastián-Gallés, N. (1991). Reading by analogy in a shallow orthography. *Journal of Experimental Psychology Human Perception and Performance, 17*, 471–477.

Siegel, L. S. (1989). IQ is irrelevant to the definition of learning disabilities. *Journal of Learning Disabilities, 22*, 469–479.

Siewierska, A. (1988). *Word order rules*. London: Croom Helm.

Skalicka, V. (1935/1979). *Typologische studien*. Braunschweig, Germany: Vieweg.

Tabossi, P. (1989). *Reading in a language with shallow orthography*. Paper presented at the Fifth Symposium on Escuelas de Logopedia y Psicologia del Lenguaje, Salamanca, Spain.

Tesniere, L. (1966/1976). *Elements de syntaxe structurales*. Paris: Kliencksieck.

Tomlin, R. S. (1986). *Basic word order. Functional principles*. London: Croom Helm.

Treiman, R., & Chafetz, J. (1987). Are there onset- and rime-like units in written words? In M. Coltheart (Ed.), Attention and performance XII: The psychology of reading (pp. 281–298). London: Erlbaum.

Treiman, R. (1994). Sources of information used by beginning spellers. In G. D. A. Brown & N. C. Ellis (Eds.), Handbook of spelling: Theory, process and intervention (pp. 75–91). Chichester, England: Wiley.

Van Orden, G. C. (1987). A ROWS is a ROSE: Spelling, sound, and reading. *Memory & Cognition, 15*, 181–198.

Van Orden, G. C., Pennington, B. F., & Stone, G. O. (1990). Word identification in reading and the promise of subsymbolic psycholinguistics. *Psychological Review, 97*, 488–522.

Ziegler, J. C., Perry, C., Ma-Wyatt, A., Ladner, D., & Schulte-Korne, G. (2003). Developmental dyslexia in different languages: Language-specific or universal? *Journal of Experimental Child Psychology, 86*, 169–193.

11

Beginning Reading Acquisition in Brazilian Portuguese

Cláudia Cardoso-Martins
Universidade Federal de Minas Gerais, Brazil

The purpose of this chapter is to describe early reading acquisition in Brazilian Portuguese. In particular, the chapter discusses the extent to which Ehri's (1992, 2002) phase theory, which has been formulated on the basis of children learning to read English, can be extended to children learning to read a relatively transparent writing system. The chapter begins with a brief overview of the Brazilian Portuguese writing system, followed by a description of Ehri's theory. Finally, I review the results of an investigation of the course of early reading acquisition in Brazilian Portuguese by both typical readers and children with reading disabilities.

THE PORTUGUESE WRITING SYSTEM

In a completely regular alphabetic writing system, each letter would represent one and only one phoneme, and each phoneme would be represented by one and only one letter. This is hardly the case in the Portuguese writing system. Like English, the Portuguese orthography represents sounds at a morphophonemic level and therefore is not completely regular. For example, it is often the case that the same letter represents more than one phoneme (the letter *c*, for instance, can represent either the phoneme /k/ or the phoneme /s/). Likewise, the same phoneme is often represented by different letters or graphemes (e.g., the phoneme /s/ can be represented by the graphemes *ss, sc, x, ç, xc, c, z,* and *s*). In most cases, choice of the right grapheme is dictated by contextual rules or morphological and syntactic considerations. In some cases, on the other hand, the choice is totally arbitrary and has to be learned by rote. However, this arbitrariness creates a problem only for spelling. I believe it is fair to say that, for a majority of words, the Portuguese orthography is consistent as far as reading is considered.

Perhaps the major difference between the Portuguese and the English writing systems is in the vowel system, which has been depicted as exceptionally ambiguous in English (Venezky, 1970). Brazilian Portuguese has 12 vowel sounds (7 oral, 5 nasal) and only 5 vowel letters: *a, e, i, o,* and *u*. Despite fewer letters, regularities of the system make vowel letter–sound correspondences relatively simple. For example, representation of the nasal vowels consists of the corresponding oral vowel letters followed by a nasal consonant (*m* or *n*) or presence of the nasal accent "~." Stress constitutes another important disambiguating cue in the representation of the vowel in Brazilian Portuguese. For example, in stressed syllables, the letter *e* represents the phonemes /e/ or /ɛ/, and the letter *o* represents the phonemes /o/ or /ɔ/; in unstressed syllables, the letters *e* and *o* usually stand for the sounds /e/ and /o/, respectively. In final unstressed syllables, however, the /e/ and /o/ sounds are always reduced. In most variants of Brazilian Portuguese, the *e* in this position sounds like /i/ and the *o* sounds like /u/, which are usually represented by the letters *i* and *u*, respectively. However, because both the letter *i* and the letter *u* occur very rarely in final, unstressed syllables, the representation of the reduced vowels /e/ and /o/ as the letters *e* and *o*, respectively, in this position does not pose much difficulty.[1]

It is true that beginners often ignore these cues. For example, they sometimes spell the reduced /e/ and /o/ sounds with the letters *i* and *u*, respectively (e.g., writing *patu* instead of *pato* [duck]). Likewise, they often pronounce the unstressed letters *e* and *o* as either /e/ and /o/ or /ɛ/ and /ɔ/. In most cases, however, the resulting pronunciation is close enough to the target pronunciation to allow recognition of the word. This probably explains why elementary school teachers also pronounce the vowels *e* and *o* in final, unstressed syllables as /e/ and /o/, respectively, in their lessons about grapheme–phoneme correspondences in Portuguese.

In summary, although the Portuguese alphabetic system is somewhat inconsistent as far as spelling is concerned, mapping from grapheme to phoneme is quite regular in Portuguese, considerably more so than in English. Reading acquisition in Portuguese may thus offer a good test of the generality of reading-acquisition models, most of which have been developed on observations of children leaning to read English. In the next section I present a brief summary of one such model—Ehri's phase theory—and discuss whether it can be extended to account for beginning reading acquisition by Brazilian Portuguese-speaking children.

THE ACQUISITION OF WORD-READING ABILITY: EHRI'S PHASE THEORY

According to several stage models of reading acquisition (e.g., Frith, 1985; Gough & Hillinger, 1980; Gough, Juel, & Griffith, 1992; Marsh, Friedman, Welch, & Desberg, 1981), when children start to learn to read they do not process letter–sound relations in words. Instead, children begin learning to read by remembering a visually salient cue in or around the word such as the golden arches behind the label of McDonald's restaurants. Frith (1985) called this the logographic stage, in analogy to logographic writing systems in which symbols stand for meanings or whole words. Children are believed to learn to read quite a few words in this way (e.g., Gough & Hillinger, 1980; Seymour & Elder, 1986). Nonetheless, the logographic strategy presents two major limitations. First, it can be unreliable and words with similar spellings are often confused. In addition, it does not enable children to read unfamiliar words. These limitations are overcome during the next stage, when children start to learn to read by recoding letters into sounds and then blending the sounds. This strategy corresponds to the alphabetic stage in Frith's model and to Gough and Hillinger's cipher stage. In Frith's model, the alphabetic stage is superseded by the orthographic stage, which is characterized by the ability to recognize words directly, that is, without recourse to phonological recoding.

Stage models of reading acquisition face several difficulties. One major problem concerns the assumption that each new stage is built on the preceding stages. However, there is little, if

---

[1] In fact, there are no Brazilian Portuguese paroxytone or proparoxytone words with a final *u*. The *u* that occurs in final, unstressed syllables is always followed by an *s* (e.g., *ônibus*).

any, evidence that the logographic strategy plays any role in the development of later reading skills (Ehri, 2002). In addition, stage models can hardly account for the fact that, at any given moment, children may use more than one process to read words. Such considerations led Ehri to propose that a phase model is more appropriate to describe the development of the ability to read words. In Ehri's theory, children progress through four phases, each characterized by a predominant, although by no means exclusive, process: (a) prealphabetic, (b) partial alphabetic, (c) full alphabetic, and (d) consolidated alphabetic.

One main distinguishing feature of Ehri's theory is the partial alphabetic phase. Gough and Hillinger (1980) suggested that children rely on the logographic or prealphabetic strategy as long as it works, that is, as long as it enables them to distinguish novel words from the other words they already know. Eventually, however, when their reading vocabulary becomes sufficiently large, the logographic strategy collapses, giving way to the more reliable alphabetic strategy. In Ehri's account, on the other hand, the partial alphabetic strategy does not result from limitations of the logographic strategy per se. Instead, it is a natural consequence of children's increasing knowledge about the names and sounds of the letters. Provided that children have some ability to segment words into their constituent sounds, knowledge of the alphabet impels them to learn to read by forming connections between the letters they see in print and the sounds they can detect in the pronunciation of words. Initially, however, children are able to process only some of the letters and sounds in words, perhaps the first letter–sound or the first and final letter–sound relations. For example, on seeing and hearing the word "jail," children may notice that the letters J and L correspond to the sounds /dʒe/ and /l/ that they can detect in the pronunciation of "jail." This realization enables beginners to use visual–phonological information to create an access route in memory so that the next time they see the word's spelling, they can obtain both its meaning and pronunciation from memory. Nonetheless, the representation of the word is still incomplete, something like J__L, which explains why beginners may often confuse the word with words that are visually similar such as, for example, the word "jelly" (Ehri, 2002). This characteristic of the partial alphabetic phase accounts for beginners' difficulty in reading unfamiliar words.

According to Ehri's characterization of the partial alphabetic phase, initially the word reading process does not entail phonological recoding, but is instead based on the remembered association among one or a few letters in the word and the word's pronunciation and meaning. The main modification of earlier models is that the feature or features that subserve direct access to the mental lexicon are not purely visual, but rather are visual and phonological. Ehri (1992) has labeled this form of reading partial alphabetic or phonetic cue to distinguish it from the full graphophonic processing that is characteristic of the full alphabetic phase.

For most children, explicit instruction on print–speech correspondences at the sublexical level seems necessary for movement into the full alphabetic phase. One advantage of the ability to learn to read by processing and remembering complete graphophonic connections is that word reading becomes much more accurate. In addition, in contrast to partial alphabetic readers, full alphabetic readers are able to read novel, unfamiliar words by phonologically recoding letters into sounds and then blending the sounds. Indeed, it is this ability that allows full alphabetic readers to compute complete graphophonic connections and, as a result, to store complete alphabetic representations of words in memory.

The full alphabetic phase eventually gives way to the consolidated phase. As children's reading vocabularies increase, multiple words sharing letter patterns are retained in memory. Recurring correspondences between these letter patterns and blends of phonemes in pronunciations become noticed and remembered (for example, the connection between the letter pattern "ight" and the phoneme blend /aɪt/ in words like "light", "fight", "night", etc.). These patterns become consolidated units in memory and expand readers' knowledge of the orthographic system. Readers reaching the consolidated alphabetic phase can thus operate with multiletter units that correspond to syllables or parts of syllables in words (e.g., the "ight" in the preceding example). One advantage of operating with such units is that they enhance the regularity of the mappings between print and speech (e.g., Treiman, Mullennix, Bijeljac-Babic, & Richmond-Welty, 1995). Multiletter units also are economical, in the sense that they reduce the number of print–speech connections that are needed to store word spellings in memory.

An important question concerns the generality of Ehri's phase theory, particularly of her earliest two phases, to children learning to read more regular orthographies than English. As subsequently described, Wimmer and Hummer (1990) suggested that children learning to read more transparent writing systems may skip the earliest phases and launch straight into the full alphabetic phase.

Wimmer and Hummer (1990) investigated the reading abilities of Austrian children learning to read in German. At the time of Wimmer and Hummer's assessment, the children had been exposed to only about 6 months of reading and spelling instruction. In contrast to children learning to read in English who reveal logographic or partial alphabetic word reading (e.g., Gough et al., 1992; Seymour & Elder, 1986), the beginning readers in Wimmer and Hummer's study showed clear signs of relying on the full alphabetic strategy. For example, almost all children in their study could read pseudowords, that is, words that do not exist and therefore can be read only by phonological recoding.

As described previously, reliance on either the logographic or the partial alphabetic strategy often results in refusals to try to read unfamiliar words or in errors consisting of familiar words that are visually similar to the target words. In contrast, recoding errors often result in pronounceable pseudowords. An analysis of the German children's reading errors suggested that they were relying on the alphabetic strategy in learning to read. The majority of their reading errors consisted of pseudowords that shared many letter–sound correspondences with the target words.

Wimmer and Hummer interpreted these results in terms of the relatively regular nature of the German writing system. They suggested that more transparent writing systems may encourage children to learn to read by recoding individual letters into sounds from the beginning of reading acquisition. There is, however, an alternative explanation for Wimmer and Hummer's findings. As is generally the case in Austria, the students in Wimmer and Hummer's study were learning to read through a *phonics* approach, that is, an approach that explicitly teaches reading by phonemic mediation. It is not therefore surprising that they relied on the alphabetic strategy to learn to read words from the outset. Indeed, there is evidence that the method of reading instruction has an impact on the strategies beginners use to read words in English. For example, Seymour and Evans (1994) found that, when instruction emphasized grapheme–phoneme relations, children learning to read in English displayed early decoding competence in both reading and spelling.

In what follows, I review evidence indicating that Brazilian Portuguese-speaking children go through a partial alphabetic phase, at least when not directly instructed in phonics, provided they have sufficient knowledge of letter names and sounds. First, evidence from experimental studies in which a paired-associate word-learning procedure was used is described. Then I describe the results of a longitudinal study comparing the strategies children use to learn to read words in different reading instruction schemes.

IS THERE A PARTIAL ALPHABETIC PHASE IN LEARNING TO READ PORTUGUESE?: EVIDENCE FROM EXPERIMENTAL STUDIES

According to phase theory, children should move to the partial alphabetic phase as soon as they begin to learn the names and sounds of the letters. The reason for this is that letter–sound cues provide the tools for remembering how to read words, and these tools are much more effective than prealphabetic or logographic strategies. In a series of studies, an investigation was made of whether Brazilian Portuguese-speaking children might take advantage of whatever knowledge they have of letter names and sounds to learn to read by processing and remembering alphabetic cues in words.

De Abreu and Cardoso-Martins (1998) first tested this prediction in a sample of 4- to 5-year-old preschool children who could not read any words. Two groups of children participated in the study: children who knew most letter names and children who knew very few names. Following Ehri and Wilce's (1985) procedure, we asked the children to learn to read two types of simplified spellings: phonetic spellings, in which the letters corresponded to sounds in the pronunciation of the words (e.g., CRVA for the word *cerveja* /sexveʒa/ [beer]), and visual spellings, in which the letters did not correspond to sounds in the pronunciation of the words but were visually more salient. We managed to make the visual spellings more salient by varying the size and position of the letters in the spellings (e.g., XQκO for the word *cerveja*). In addition, in contrast to the phonetic spellings, no letter occurred more than once in the visual spellings.

Children learned to read the phonetic and visual spellings on separate days. Each word-learning task began with a training trial in which the children were told the pronunciation of the spellings. After that, they were given a series of trials to read the spellings. Correct responses were reinforced and incorrect responses were corrected. As predicted by phase theory, the children who knew the names of the letters learned to read the phonetic spellings more easily than they did the visual spellings. The opposite held for the children who knew only a few letter names, that is, they learned the visual spellings more easily than they did the phonetic spellings.

We also asked the children to spell the phonetic and visual spellings. The children who knew few letter names could hardly remember any letters, for either the visual or the phonetic spellings. In contrast, the children who knew the names of the letters reproduced the phonetic spellings more accurately than they did the visual spellings. The superiority of the phonetic spellings was, in great part, due to their remembering the initial letter, confirming Ehri's suggestion that initially children can process and remember only a few letter–sound relations in words.

We have recently extended these results to a sample of children with Down's syndrome (DS). DS presents an interesting context for testing the hypothesis that knowledge of letter names impels children to learn to read by processing and remembering letter–sound relations in words. The reason has to do with the complex pattern of impairments that is characteristic of the syndrome (e.g., Pennington, Moon, Edgin, Stedron, & Nadel, 2003).

DS is a developmental disorder caused by the presence of an extra chromosome 21. Affected individuals show substantial delays in all cognitive functions, but some functions are more impaired than others. Language is particularly impaired. As a matter of fact, children with DS score below what would be expected on the basis of their mental age on several grammatical and phonological measures. In contrast, they usually do relatively well on visual and spatial memory tasks. Despite their language difficulties, children with DS can learn to read relatively well, with some children being able to read words at a level commensurate with their chronological age (Buckley, 1985; Cardoso-Martins, Pennington, & Moon, 2004). Buckley (1985) has suggested that children with DS do as well as they do because they are able to capitalize on their relatively good visual and spatial skills to learn to read visually. If Buckley is correct, children with DS should learn to read visually salient spellings more easily than they do phonetic spellings, regardless of their knowledge of letter names, sounds, or both.

To test this hypothesis, Cardoso-Martins, Michalick, and Pollo (2004) asked children with DS to learn to read simplified visual and phonetic spellings similar to the spellings used by

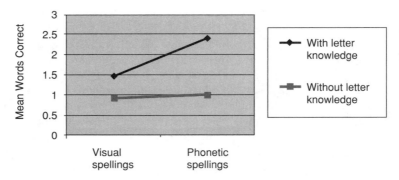

FIG. 11.1.   Mean number of spellings read correctly per trial by children with DS as a function of letter name knowledge and spelling type.

De Abreu and Cardoso-Martins in their study with typically developing preschoolers. Twenty-five children with DS participated in the study. Twelve children were assigned to the high knowledgeable group. They knew the names of at least 17 letters ($M = 20.17$ out of 24, $SD = 2.69$). The remaining children knew between 0 and 7 letter names ($M = 4.54$, $SD = 2.67$), and were assigned to the group with low letter-name knowledge.

As is evident from Fig. 11.1, the results supported phase theory: Despite the phonological deficits characteristic of DS, the children who knew the names of the letters found the phonetic spellings easier to learn than they did the visual spellings. In contrast, the children who did not know the names of the letters showed little evidence of word reading with either type of spelling. For them, both the phonetic and the visual spellings were equally very difficult to learn.

In the studies already mentioned, we chose words that made the connections between the letters and sounds in the phonetic spellings very noticeable. In effect, the name of the first letter could be clearly heard at the beginning of the pronunciation of the word for every single phonetic spelling. In some of the spellings, this also was true for the other letters. For example, the names of the letters C /se/, V /ve/ and A /a/ appearing in the spelling *CRVA* can be clearly detected in the pronunciation of the word it stood for, *cerveja* /sexveʒa/ [beer]. It is therefore possible that we made it very easy for the children to learn to read the phonetic spellings by processing letter–sound relations. It is unlikely, however, that this is the sole reason. As a matter of fact, in a recent study (Cardoso-Martins, Resende, & Rodrigues, 2002), we showed that preschoolers who knew the names of the letters could process letter–sound relations to learn to read spellings in which the letters corresponded to phonemes, not to letter names, for example, the spelling *SPT* for /sapato/, in which the letters *S*, *P*, and *T* stand for sounds contained in the names of the letters, /ɛsi/, /pe/, and /te/, respectively. Children found these spellings easier to learn than they did visually salient spellings whose letters bore no relationship to sounds in the pronunciation of words.

Similar results have been found for nonliterate Brazilian adults. Cardoso-Martins, Rodrigues, and Ehri (2003) showed that, as preschool children did, nonliterate adults found it easier to learn to read simplified phonetic spellings in which the letters stood for phonemes than to learn to read simplified visual spellings. As was the case of the children in the study by Cardoso-Martins et al. (2002), the nonliterate adults had some knowledge of the alphabet and could use it to derive partially phonetic spellings for words.

Cardoso-Martins et al. (2003) also assessed their participants' ability to identify common environmental signs displaying varying degrees of contextual information. The nonliterate adults did not show any signs of using letter knowledge to read or remember words in environmental signs, in contrast to their performance on the word-learning tasks. They read the signs only when presented in their full context, for example, the label Coca-Cola shown on a bottle of Coca-Cola, not when printed in isolation. The adults also failed to notice altered letters in the signs, even when asked to look for something wrong in them.

It seems surprising that the nonliterate adults did not use their letter knowledge to read or remember environmental signs. Possibly, processing of letter cues may be an unnecessary step when print is embedded in a sufficiently rich and distinctive context as is the case with most environmental print. Perhaps more surprising is the fact that neither the children nor the adults who participated in the studies by Cardoso-Martins et al. (2002, 2003) could read any words whatsoever. One possibility is that it may be harder to learn to read on the basis of partial letter–sound information in Portuguese than in English. Because Portuguese is more transparent than English and has fewer vowel types, it is possible that the spellings of words are less unique and distinctive than in English. Consider, for example, the spellings of the words *bola*, *bala*, *bolo*, *bota*, *bolha*, *dado*, *dedo*, *data*, all of which are common in reading books for children. Compared with beginners learning in English, children learning to read in Portuguese may thus need to be able to process and remember a greater number of letter–sound relations in words to read on the basis of partial alphabetic cues.

In our experiments (De Abreu and Cardoso-Martins, 1998; Cardoso-Martins et al., 2002, 2003), participants were required to learn to read only six phonetic spellings, all of which started with a different letter. The ease of this task may explain why they succeeded despite not having started to read yet. Very likely our participants were relying mainly on the initial letter–sound relation to remember how to read the phonetic spellings. Once the word-learning tasks were over, we asked participants to spell the two types of spellings. In all studies, participants remembered significantly more initial letters than either middle or final letters in the phonetic spellings, suggesting the importance of initial letters for the word-learning process.

In summary, we may have made it very easy for the children and adults who participated in our studies to use their knowledge of the alphabet to learn to read by processing and remembering letter–sound cues in print. Before we can conclude that Portuguese-speaking children learn to read by processing partial letter–sound relations in words, we need evidence that children use this mechanism to learn to read words in the real world.

METHOD OF READING INSTRUCTION AND BEGINNING READING ACQUISITION IN PORTUGUESE

If phase theory can be generalized to children learning to read in Portuguese, we would expect that beginners should not wait until they are able to phonologically recode all letters in words before they start reading words by remembering letter–sound relations. Given that the partial alphabetic strategy is more accurate and reliable than the logographic strategy, they should start to use it to read words as soon as they learn about letter names and sounds, especially when faced with the task of learning to read without being simultaneously instructed on print–speech relations at the sublexical level.

To test this hypothesis, I (Cardoso-Martins, 2001) conducted a longitudinal study to examine the strategies that 5- to 6-year-old Brazilian beginning readers use to learn to read words. Some of the children had received instruction in a whole-word program and some in a phonics program. The two groups of children were enrolled in kindergarten classes in two large private schools (henceforth called Whole-Word school and Phonics school) attended by children from upper-middle-socioeconomic-status (SES) families.

The children in the Whole-Word school ($N = 31$) started to learn to read through a whole-word approach. During the first few months of reading instruction, they learned to read a few words in isolation and in small texts. No attempt was made to teach print–speech relations at the sublexical level. Instead, children were encouraged to associate the whole printed word with its pronunciation. Systematic instruction on print–speech relations at the sublexical level started approximately 3 months after the beginning of instruction in reading.

The children in the Phonics school ($N = 30$) were exposed to systematic instruction on print–speech relations at the sublexical level from the start. For these children, such training proceeded at the level of the phoneme. Grapheme–phoneme correspondences were introduced slowly, one at a time, and were used to sound out words from the very beginning of reading instruction.

Children's reading and spelling abilities, as well as their level of phonological awareness, were assessed at the beginning of the school year and at different points during the school year. Only the results of the reading and spelling assessment that occurred toward the middle of the school year, that is, immediately before the beginning of systematic instruction on print–speech relations at the sublexical level for the children in the Whole-Word school, are subsequently described. Even though children in neither school had started to read at the beginning of the study, they knew some letter names ($M = 11.90$ out of 23, $SD = 6.12$, for the children in the Whole-Word school and $M = 9.97$, $SD = 5.97$, for the children in the Phonics school). According to phase theory, at least some of the children in the Whole-Word school should therefore be capable of using their letter knowledge to process letter–sound relations in learning to read words. However, because they were learning to read through a whole-word approach, I did not expect them to show evidence of full alphabetic skills, but they should show evidence of phonetic cue reading.

Children's reading strategies were investigated in two main ways. First, I compared the children's ability to read familiar words with their ability to read matched unfamiliar words and pseudowords, that is, words containing the same letter–sound relations appearing in the familiar words. Second, I investigated the nature of the children's reading errors. If the children were relying on the logographic strategy or on Ehri's phonetic cue strategy, then they should not be able to read unfamiliar words or pseudowords. Instead, these words should lead to refusals or to misreadings sharing some letters with the target words. In contrast, if children were relying on a full alphabetic strategy, reading refusals should be infrequent and nonword responses might be evident as a result of decoding attempts that fall short of the real words.

Table 11.1 presents the mean proportion of words read correctly for the familiar words, unfamiliar words, and pseudowords, separately for the two schools. As is evident from this table, the two groups of children seemed to be relying on different strategies to learn to read.

TABLE 11.1

Mean Proportion of Correct Responses (and Standard Deviations) in the Reading
Tasks as Functions of the Type of Reading Instruction

	Reading Task		
School	Familiar Words	Unfamiliar Words	Pseudowords
Whole-Word	.74 (.13)	.05 (.10)	.02 (.07)
Phonics	.59 (.26)	.31 (.29)	.41 (.35)

TABLE 11.2
Mean Proportion of Errors Classified as Refusals and Nonwords as Functions
of Reading Task and Type of Reading Instruction

School	Frequent Words		Infrequent Words		Pseudowords	
	Refusals	Nonwords	Refusals	Nonwords	Refusals	Nonwords
Whole-Word	.73 (.23)	.04 (.08)	.63 (.33)	.14 (.20)	.63 (.30)	.20 (.22)
Phonics	.25 (.34)	.46 (.33)	.29 (.38)	.48 (.34)	.22 (.34)	.58 (.38)

Even though they did not differ with regard to the proportion of familiar words that were read correctly, the children in the Phonics school read significantly more unfamiliar words and pseudowords than the children did in the Whole-Word school.

In fact, in the Whole-Word school, whereas most of the children could read the majority of the familiar words, 23 children (70%) could not read any unfamiliar words, and as many as 28 (87.5%) could not read any pseudowords. These results contrasted sharply with the results for the children in the Phonics school. Only nine (30%) and four children (13%) could not read any of the unfamiliar words and pseudowords correctly, respectively, suggesting that, in contrast to the children in the Whole-Word school, the children in the Phonics school were learning to read words by phonological recoding. Analysis of reading errors also suggested that the phonics children were using the full alphabetic strategy to learn to read. Indeed, most of their reading errors consisted of nonwords. In contrast, the majority of the reading errors of the children in the Whole-Word school consisted of refusals. As is evident from Table 11.2, this was true for both words and pseudowords.

Participants were also asked to spell the unfamiliar words. Individual spellings were categorized according to four different levels that varied as functions of the number of letter–sound relations represented. The first level corresponded to spellings that did not reveal any understanding that print represents sounds. Refusals to spell a word were also coded as Level 1.

Spellings coded as Level 2 revealed the beginning of the understanding that letters represent sounds. A variety of spellings were coded as Level 2. For example, spellings representing at least one sound in the target word with an appropriate letter, even if not conventionally correct, were coded as Level 2. In many instances, it was the first or the last sound in the word that was represented in Level 2 spellings (e.g., I for *esqueleto* /iske'letu/ [skeleton]). Quite often, more than one sound was appropriately represented (e.g., EI for *chefe* /'ʃɛfɪ/ [chief]). However, in all cases, the number of sounds represented did not exceed the number of sounds not represented or the number of sounds misrepresented.

Like Level 2 spellings, Level 3 spellings did not represent all the sounds in the word. However, unlike in level 2 spellings, in level 3 spellings the number of sounds appropriately represented exceeded the number of sounds not represented or misrepresented (e.g., *ZBU* for *zebu* /ze'bu/). Finally, spellings representing all sounds in the pronunciation of the target word with appropriate letters, even if not conventionally correct (e.g., *DEDU* for *dedo* /'dedu/ [finger]) were coded as Level 4 spellings.

The results in Table 11.3 show that the children in the Phonics school were able to analyze a larger number of segments in the spoken words than were the children in the Whole-Word school. While Levels 3 and 4 predominated among the former children, the reverse was true for Level 1 and especially Level 2 among the children in the Whole-Word school.

TABLE 11.3

Mean Number of Spellings (and Standard Deviations) at Each Spelling Level
as Functions of Type of Reading Instruction (max. = 10)

Spelling Level	Whole-Word School	Phonics School
1	2.93 (3.16)	0.86 (1.68)
2	5.37 (2.55)	1.00 (1.31)
3	1.47 (1.19)	3.21 (1.68)
4	0.23 (0.50)	4.93 (2.70)

Were the Children in the Whole-Word School Phonetic Cue Readers?

The relatively low incidence of Levels 3 and 4 spellings among the children in the Whole-Word school is consistent with the hypothesis that these children were not learning to read by processing and remembering full grapheme–phoneme relations in words. However, the relatively large number of Level 2 spellings found among them raises the possibility that they were not learning to read words by means of a logographic or visual strategy alone. As described before, Level 2 spellings evinced the beginning of the understanding that print represents sounds. Because the children in the Whole-Word school could use this understanding to spell words, it is possible that they also used it to learn to read words. To test this possibility, I correlated the number of spellings coded as Level 2 with the number of familiar words read. I limited the sample to Whole-Word schoolchildren who could not read any unfamiliar words and pseudowords.[2] This correlation was significant, $r(21) = 0.38$, $p < .05$. Further evidence that children in the Whole-Word school were phonetic cue readers was obtained by a correlation of their ability to detect rhyme at the beginning of the school year with their ability to read familiar words at the middle of the school year. The correlation was significant for the Whole-Word children, $r(21) = 0.55$, $p < .01$, and also for children in the Phonics school $r(29) = 0.71$, $p < .001$.

In summary, the results suggest that the strategies beginners use to learn to read words may, to a large extent, depend on the method of reading instruction, even for a relatively regular writing system such as Brazilian Portuguese. As in Wimmer and Hummer's study (2000), the children who learned to read through the phonics approach gave every sign that they were relying on the full alphabetic strategy to learn to read words from the beginning of reading acquisition. A little less than 3 months after the beginning of reading instruction, they could read at least some of the unfamiliar words and pseudowords. In addition, their reading errors consisted mainly of nonwords, and most of their responses on the spelling task consisted of partial or full alphabetic spellings.

In contrast, the performance of children who started learning to read through the whole-word approach was quite different. Most could not read any unfamiliar words or pseudowords 3 months after the beginning of reading instruction. This occurred despite the fact that all unfamiliar words and pseudowords contained familiar letter–sound correspondences, that is,

---

[2] The children who read at least one unfamiliar word or pseudoword were excluded from this analysis because this performance indicated that they could use the alphabetic strategy to learn to read. Any significant correlation between the Whole-Word schoolchildren's ability to read the familiar words and their score on the spelling task could therefore result from the fact that a few of them were already using phonological information to learn to read.

correspondences appearing in the words the children had learned to read in the classroom. Furthermore, the great majority of their reading errors consisted of refusals. This pattern of results is similar to the one reported for children learning to read English through a whole-word approach (see, e.g., Seymour & Elder, 1986) and suggest that, in the absence of explicit instruction on print–speech relations at the sublexical level, beginners do not learn to read by phonologically recoding, even in a relatively consistent writing system. For most children, explicit instruction on print–speech relations at the sublexical level is necessary for beginners to learn to read by phonological recoding letters into sounds.

As discussed before, results are consistent with Ehri's phase theory. Even though children are not explicitly taught about print–speech relations at the sublexical level, they nonetheless learn to read words by processing letter–sound relations, provided they know the names or sounds, or both, of the letters, and provided they can detect the sounds the letters typically represent in the pronunciation of words. As Ehri has found for English-reading beginners at the partial alphabetic phase, it is likely that the graphophonic information that beginning readers of Portuguese use is very limited in scope. Most Level 2 spellings consisted of spellings representing only one or two sounds in the target word. Quite frequently, the letters represented were those whose names could be heard in the pronunciations of the target words. This accounts for the relatively high proportion of spellings in which only vowel sounds were represented. In contrast to the names of the consonants, the names of the vowels can generally be heard in the pronunciation of Brazilian Portuguese words (Cardoso-Martins et al., 2002). Incomplete knowledge of the graphophonic system also accounts for Whole-Word students' inability to read the unfamiliar words or pseudowords.

WHAT IS THE NATURE OF EARLY READING DIFFICULTIES IN BRAZILIAN PORTUGUESE?

According to phase theory, for children (or adults, for that matter) to become fluent readers and spellers, they have to be able to take complete alphabetic representations of words and store them in and obtain them from memory. Evidence indicates that the ability to form full graphophonic connections requires phonemic segmentation skills. As it has been amply documented in the literature (e.g., Rack, Snowling, & Olson, 1992), phonological deficits, especially deficits in phoneme awareness, are rampant among children with reading disabilities. Thus we would expect readers with disabilities to have difficulty moving into the full and consolidated alphabetic phases.

Ehri and Saltmarsh (1995) compared the strategies that English-speaking children with reading disabilities and typical readers use to learn to read words. Three groups of children participated in their study: advanced beginners, novice beginners, and children with learning disabilities. The beginning readers were in Grade 1, whereas the children with reading disabilities were in Grades 2–4. Participants learned to read a set of simplified spellings (e.g., *perfum* for perfume, *dusen* for dozen, *latr* for lantern, and then were tested for their ability to detect single-letter alterations in the spelling of the words. Some of the alterations resulted from their substituting one letter in the target spelling with a phonetically equivalent letter (e.g., *duzen* vs. *dusen*) or a phonetically nonequivalent letter (e.g., *pervum* vs. *perfum*), whereas others consisted of their adding or removing a letter (e.g., *latrn* vs. *latr*). Alterations could occur at the beginning, middle, or end of the words.

Results suggested that the children with reading disabilities learned to read the words by processing and remembering partial letter–sound cues. Whereas the beginning readers, especially the advanced beginning readers, were sensitive to spelling alterations in various positions, including changes involving letters in the middle of words, the children with reading disabilities were sensitive only to changes occurring at the beginning or end of the words. An examination of children's nontarget responses to the altered spellings provided further evidence that they had stored only partial alphabetic representations of the words in memory. According to Ehri and Saltmarsh (1995), over half of these students' nontarget responses to the altered spellings consisted of misreading them as other real words, most of which were other similarly spelled words in the list.

To what extent do children with reading disabilities who are learning more transparent orthographies exhibit the same difficulties? In a series of studies, Wimmer, Landerl, and their colleagues at the University of Salzburg (e.g., Landerl & Wimmer, 2000; Wimmer, Mayringer, & Landerl, 2000) showed that, in contrast to English-speaking children, German-speaking dyslexic students (defined on the basis of a slow reading rate) show high reading accuracy for real words and pseudowords alike. They also exhibit high scores on phoneme-segmentation tasks. Their main problem consists of a deficit in reading fluency and a poorly developed orthographic lexicon. On the face of their relatively good phonemic-segmentation and phonological recoding skills, the difficulties presented by German-speaking dyslexic children, particularly their poor memory for spellings, look disconcerting. According to phase theory, children capable of forming full connections between letters and sounds should be able to become skilled readers and spellers.

Wimmer and his colleagues suggest that German-speaking dyslexic children's poor orthographic memory might result from poor storage of spelling pronunciations. They based this claim on their finding that German-speaking dyslexic children showed difficulties in learning new phonological word forms (Mayringer & Wimmer, 2000). Another possibility has to do with the age of the dyslexic children that Wimmer studied. Most of the students were at the end of either third or fourth grade. In another study, Wimmer (1996) found that during their first year at school German dyslexic students showed poor phonological recoding abilities and poor phonological segmentation skills. Therefore it may be that the older German dyslexic students, during earlier years, built much of their reading vocabularies on the basis of partial alphabetic information and only later, by Grades 3 or 4, learned about grapheme–phoneme correspondences and how to read words by fully recoding letters into sounds. I subsequently discuss the possibility that Brazilian Portuguese-speaking children who show difficulties in learning to read during their first year in school may be processing and remembering only partial alphabetic information to learn to read.

Cardoso-Martins and Guerra (2004) investigated this hypothesis in a sample of 46 7-year-old low-SES Brazilian children enrolled in three first-grade classes of a public school in a major Brazilian city. Literacy and phonological skills were assessed at the beginning of the school year. Toward the end of the school year, we assessed children's progress in learning to read and spell. Only a subsample of the children were included in the analysis reported in the following paragraphs. We selected children who could not read any common words at the beginning of the school year or who read fewer than two words, and then we divided them into two groups, those who made little progress during the school year and those who learned to read reasonably well. We considered that a child had made reasonable progress if, by the end of the school year, he or she could read at least half of a list of 30 pseudowords. Eight children met this criterion and were assigned to the group of successful readers. The 18 children who read two or fewer pseudowords were assigned to the group of unsuccessful students.

The children were asked to read, besides pseudowords, a list of frequent and a list of infrequent (low-frequency) words in children's books. As expected, the successful students were capable of reading most of the frequent and infrequent words ($M = 28.87$ out of 30, $SD = 1.46$, for the frequent words and $M = 25.00$ out of 30, $SD = 3.29$, for the infrequent words). In contrast, there was much variation among the children who read fewer than two pseudowords. We therefore divided these children into two groups as a function of their ability to read the frequent words: students who read 11 or more frequent words correctly ($N = 7$) and students who read fewer than 10 frequent words ($N = 11$). The former (henceforth good word readers) read, on average, 16.86 ($SD = 4.81$) frequent words and 4.00 ($SD = 2.77$) infrequent words. The majority of the other children (the poor word readers) could not read any frequent or infrequent words. Here I focus on results for the successful students and for the unsuccessful students who made some progress in learning to read words. Of interest is whether the unsuccessful but good word readers were relying on partial alphabetic cues to learn to read.

To obtain information about alphabetic knowledge and memory for spellings of words, we assessed children's ability to spell the same set of frequent and infrequent words, and we classified the children's responses into five levels. Levels 1–3 were identical to Levels 1–3 described previously. Level 4 consisted of spellings that were orthographically wrong but phonetically plausible, given letter–sound correspondences in Portuguese. Level 5 corresponded to orthographically correct spellings. We reasoned that if the good word readers were relying on partial letter–sound relations to learn to read, they should show a relatively low incidence of phonetically and orthographically correct spellings, but they should exhibit a relatively large number of partial alphabetic spellings (i.e., spellings coded as Level 2 and Level 3). Furthermore, among the successful students, the incidence of orthographically correct spellings should outnumber the incidence of phonetic spellings, but only for the frequent words. This is because the successful students should have been able to form complete representations of the spellings of the frequent words as a result of their relatively good phonological recoding skills plus exposure to the words. In contrast, no such difference should be found for the unsuccessful students, for either the frequent or the infrequent words.

Table 11.4 lists the number of spellings in each of the five spelling levels, separately for the frequent and infrequent words and for the successful and unsuccessful students. As predicted, the successful students showed a significantly larger number of phonetic and orthographically correct spellings than did the unsuccessful students for both the frequent and infrequent words,

TABLE 11.4

Mean Number of Spellings (and Standard Deviations) at Each Spelling
Level as Functions of Reading Ability and Type of Word

		Reading Ability	
Words	Spelling Level	Unsuccessful but Good Word Readers ($N = 7$)	Successful Readers ($N = 8$)
Frequent	1	4.23 (5.68)	0.25 (0.46)
	2	8.71 (6.90)	0.00 (0.00)
	3	7.57 (3.73)	4.12 (1.73)
	4	3.86 (2.48)	9.00 (3.85)
	5	5.43 (3.55)	16.62 (3.81)
Infrequent	1	6.86 (7.22)	0.75 (1.49)
	2	11.57 (9.18)	0.12 (0.35)
	3	10.14 (11.29)	11.87 (4.29)
	4	1.29 (2.21)	10.62 (3.20)
	5	0.14 (0.38)	6.62 (2.20)

suggesting that they were capable of fully segmenting words into their sound constituents. Furthermore, the orthographically correct spellings outnumbered the phonetic spellings for the frequent words, suggesting that they had been able to store full alphabetic representations of the familiar words in memory. In contrast, the unsuccessful students showed a relatively large number of partial alphabetic spellings, especially spellings coded as Level 2. Similar results were obtained when only the words that were read correctly were included in the analysis. That is, the proportion of correctly read words that were also spelled correctly was significantly higher for the successful than for the unsuccessful students.

Except for a few children, the pattern of reading errors of the good word readers differed from the pattern of reading errors that Cardoso-Martins (2001) found among the children in the Whole-Word school. Most of the good word readers actually tried to decode the words they could not recognize by sight. However, they were often unsuccessful because they lacked complete knowledge of the alphabetic system. In effect, most of their errors resulted from incorrect pronunciations of the graphemes in the words.

It makes sense that the good word readers attempted to recode the words. They were tested after approximately 9 months of learning to read from a program that included explicit instruction of print–speech relations at the sublexical level, and many of them were receiving remedial instruction on how to read by recoding letters into sounds. In contrast, the whole-word children in Cardoso-Martins's (2001) study were tested after only 3 months of learning to read. Furthermore, by the time they were tested, they had not received explicit lessons on print–speech relations at the sublexical level.

An important question concerns the reasons for the difficulties presented by the unsuccessful students. One possibility is that they did not receive sufficiently good instruction. This cannot be the sole reason, however, given that the unsuccessful students were enrolled in the same classrooms as the successful students. Another possibility is that the unsuccessful students had difficulties in processes that are important for learning to read. The unsuccessful students who were classified as *poor* word readers performed significantly worse than the successful readers on several phonological and literacy skills at the beginning of the school year. However, no significant difference was found between the successful students and the unsuccessful students who were *good* word readers on any one of those measures. Nor did these two groups differ in our measures of intelligence. We are now investigating whether the successful and unsuccessful students differed with regard to home environmental variables and how these variables could have an impact on early reading acquisition.

The children who participated in Cardoso-Martins and Guerra's study were extremely poor. To give an idea, monthly income was less than $240 for a large majority of families, and over half of the mothers had completed less than 6 years of education. Very likely these factors played an important role.

Michalick (2004) has recently suggested that difficulty moving into the full alphabetic phase also seems to characterize upper-middle-SES Brazilian children who experience problems in learning to read. Michalick assessed the reading and spelling skills of a group of upper-middle-SES children judged by their teachers as having made poor progress in learning to read after approximately 8 to 9 months of reading instruction. Relative to students from the same classrooms who seemed to be progressing well, the poor readers performed very poorly on phoneme awareness tasks. They also failed to read pseudowords, despite the fact that at least some of them were made of very simple CV syllables (e.g., *nila, lita, teba*). Furthermore, as in Cardoso-Martins and Guerra's study, here the poor readers showed a significantly larger number of spellings coded as partially alphabetic than did the good readers, whereas the reverse occurred for the number of spellings coded as phonetic. From these findings, Michalick argued that, in contrast to the good readers, the poor readers had not progressed into the full alphabetic phase and were learning to read on the basis of partial alphabetic cues.

In both Michalick's and Cardoso-Martins and Guerra's studies, the unsuccessful students clearly differed from the successful students in terms of their reading ability. It is important that future studies investigate the strategies that poor readers use to learn to read vis-à-vis the strategies used by younger children of similar reading ability. Likewise, it is important that longitudinal studies be conducted to assess the fate of early difficulties in learning to read in Brazilian Portuguese. As suggested previously, it is possible that the difficulties shown by older dyslexic children in learning to read more transparent writing systems can be traced to a long-lingering partial alphabetic phase. Another possibility is that readers with learning disabilities do not take advantage of their alphabetic skills to form full connections between letters seen in printed words and phonemes detected in their pronunciations. Even though they may eventually acquire phonemic segmentation skills and master grapheme–phoneme correspondences (e.g., Wimmer et al., 2000), they may continue to rely on partial alphabetic cues to learn to read. As a matter of fact, the readers with learning disabilities in Ehri and Saltmarsh's (1995) study were sensitive to fewer spelling alterations than were the novice beginners, even though the two groups apparently had equivalent knowledge of the English writing system. In addition, even when Ehri and Saltmarsh statistically controlled for the effect of differences in word-reading ability among their three groups of children, the readers with learning disabilities took more trials to learn to read all spellings than either group of beginning readers. It will be interesting to see if similar results occur for children learning to read more transparent orthographies.

FINAL REMARKS

The results strongly suggest that Ehri's phase theory can be extended to children learning to read more transparent writing systems. In particular, children learning to read Brazilian Portuguese seem to go through a partial alphabetic phase, provided that they are required to learn to read in the absence of simultaneous instruction on print–speech relations at the sublexical level and provided that they know the names and sounds of the letters. Furthermore, results suggest that difficulty moving into the full alphabetic phase may be at the core of early reading disability in Brazilian Portuguese. The differences between the results obtained by me and my colleagues and those of Wimmer and his colleagues at the University of Salzburg can probably be explained in terms of differences in the educational, social, and cultural experiences of Austrian and Brazilian children. Differences in the ages of the children tested are likely to be important as well. As mentioned previously, Wimmer (1996) has suggested that German-speaking dyslexic children may show difficulties in learning to read by phonological recoding during their first year at school, even though these difficulties are no longer observed by the time they are in third or fourth grade.

The fact that there are important similarities in early reading acquisition in English and Brazilian Portuguese does not imply that there are not important differences as well. The results of the studies described in this chapter suggest, however, that these differences are likely to be quantitative rather than qualitative. For example, as mentioned previously, it is possible that the partial alphabetic phase plays a relatively unimportant role in learning to read in Brazilian Portuguese, at least for typically developing children. In my longitudinal study (Cardoso-Martins, 2001), the ability of the children in the Whole-Word school to read the familiar words in the middle of the school year did not correlate with their reading and spelling ability at the end of the school year, by which time they clearly could read words by fully recoding graphemes into phonemes.

I suggest that characteristics of the Portuguese orthography may make phonetic cue reading more difficult in Portuguese than in English. This may help explain why the poor word readers in Guerra and Cardoso-Martins's study made hardly any progress in learning to read throughout the course of the school year. Perhaps the low distinctiveness of word spellings in Portuguese together with these children's depressed phonological and literacy skills at the beginning of the school year prevented them from learning to read by processing and remembering partial alphabetic cues. Whatever the explanation, this group provides a sad testimony to the fact that exposure to a relatively regular writing system, even in the context of reading instruction that emphasizes print–speech relations at the sublexical level, is no guarantee of success in learning to read.

ACKNOWLEDGMENTS

Linnea Ehri, Erlaine L. Guerra, Brett Kessler, Mirelle Michalick, Bruce F. Pennington, and Tatiana C. Pollo read the first draft of this chapter and made valuable comments. The author is also grateful to the Conselho Nacional de Ciência e Tecnologia (CNPq, Brazil) and to the Coordenação de Aperfeiçoamento de Pessoal de Nível Superior (CAPES, Brazil), for their support of the work described in this chapter.

REFERENCES

Buckley, S. (1985). Attaining basic educational skills: Reading, writing and number. In D. Lane & B. Stratford (Eds.), *Current approaches to Down's syndrome* (pp. 315–343). Nova York: Praeger Press.

Cardoso-Martins, C. (2001). The reading abilities of beginning readers of Brazilian Portuguese: Implications for a theory of reading acquisition. *Scientific Studies of Reading, 5*, 289–317.

Cardoso-Martins, C., & Guerra, E. L. (2004). Características da dificuldade inicial de aprendizagem da leitura em Português: Evidência de crianças de baixo nível sócio-econômico [Characteristics of early reading difficulties in Portuguese: Evidence from low SES children]. Manuscript in preparation.

Cardoso-Martins, C., Michalick, M. F., & Pollo, T. C. (2004). O Papel do Conhecimento do Nome das Letras no Início da Aprendizagem da Leitura: Evidência de Indivíduos com Síndrome de Down (The Role of Letter-Name Knowledge on Beginning Reading Acquisition: Evidence from Individuals with Down Syndrome). Manuscript submitted for publication.

Cardoso-Martins, C., Rodrigues, L. A., & Ehri, L. C. (2003). Place of environmental print in reading development: Evidence from nonliterate adults. *Scientific Studies of Reading, 7*, 335–355.

Cardoso-Martins, C., Pennington, B., & Moon, J. (2004). Components of Reading Ability in Down Syndrome. Manuscript in preparation.

Cardoso-Martins, C., Resende, S. M., & Rodrigues, L. A. (2002). Letter name knowledge and the ability to learn to read by processing letter-phoneme relations in words: Evidence from Brazilian Portuguese-speaking children. *Reading and Writing, 15*, 409–432.

De Abreu, M., & Cardoso-Martins, C. (1998). Alphabetic access route in beginning reading acquisition in Portuguese: The role of letter-name knowledge. *Reading and Writing: An Interdisciplinary Journal, 10*, 85–104.

Ehri, L. (1992). Reconceptualizing the development of sight word reading and its relationship to recoding. In: P. Gough, L. Ehri, & R. Treiman (Eds.), *Reading acquisition* (pp. 107–143). Hillsdale, NJ: Lawrence Erlbaum Associates.

Ehri, L. (2002). Phases of acquisition in learning to read words and implications for teaching. In R. Stainthorp & P. Tomlinson (Eds.), Psychological Aspects of Education: Current Trends. Number 1. *British Journal of Educational Psychology* Series II.

Ehri, L., & Saltmarsh, J. (1995). Beginning readers outperform older disabled readers in learning to read words by sight. *Reading and Writing, 7*, 295–326.

Ehri, L., & Wilce, L., (1985). Movement into reading: Is the first stage of printed word learning visual or phonetic? *Reading Research Quarterly, 20*, 163–179.

Frith, U. (1985). Beneath the surface of developmental dyslexia. In K. Patterson, J. Marshall, & M. Coltheart (Eds.), *Surface dyslexia: Neuropsychological and cognitive studies of phonological reading* (pp. 301–330). Hillsdale, NJ: Lawrence Erlbaum Associates.

Gough, P., & Hillinger, M. (1980). Learning to read: An unnatural act. *Bulletin of the Orton Society, 30*, 179–196.

Gough, P., Juel, C., & Griffith, P. (1992). Reading, spelling and the orthographic cipher. In P. Gough, L. Ehri, & R. Treiman (Eds.), *Reading acquisition* (pp. 35–48). Hillsdale, NJ: Lawrence Erlbaum Associates.

Landerl, K., & Wimmer, H. (2000). Deficits in phoneme segmentation are not the core problem of dyslexia: Evidence from German and English children. *Applied Psycholinguistics, 21*, 243–262.

Marsh, G., Friedman, M., Welch, V., & Desberg, P. (1981). A cognitive-developmental theory of reading acquisition. In G. Mackinnon & T. Waller (Eds.), *Reading research: Advances in theory and practice* (pp. 199–221). San Diego, CA: Academic Press.

Mayringer, H., & Wimmer, H. (2000). Pseudoname learning by German-speaking children with dyslexia: Evidence for a phonological learning deficit. *Journal of Experimental Child Psychology, 75*, 116–133.

Michalick, M. (2004). Um estudo neuropsicológico da dislexia específica de evolução entre crianças aprendendo a ler em português [A neuropsychological study of developmental dyslexia among Portuguese-speaking children]. Manuscript in preparation.

Pennington, B. F., Moon, J., Edgin, J., Stedron, J., & Nadel, L. (2003). The neuropsychology of Down syndrome: Evidence for hippocampal dysfunctions. *Child Development, 74*, 75–93.

Rack, J., Snowling, M., & Olson, R. (1992). The nonword reading deficit in developmental dyslexia: A review. *Reading Research Quarterly, 27*, 28–53.

Seymour, P. H. K., & Elder, L. (1986). Beginning reading without phonology. *Cognitive Neuropsychology, 3*, 1–36.

Seymour, P. H. K., & Evans, H. M. (1992). Beginning reading without semantics: A cognitive study of hyperlexia. *Cognitive Neuropsychology, 9*, 89–122.

Treiman, R., Mullennix, J., Bijeljac-Babic, R., & Richmond-Welty, E. D. (1995). The special role of rimes in the description, use, and acquisition of English orthography. *Journal of Experimental Psychology: General, 124*, 107–136.

Venezky, R. L. (1970). *The structure of English orthography*. The Hague, The Netherlands: Mouton.

Wimmer, H. (1996). The early manifestation of developmental dyslexia: Evidence from German children. *Reading and Writing: an Interdisciplinary Journal, 8*, 171–188.

Wimmer, H., & Hummer, P. (1990). How German-speaking first graders read and spell: Doubts on the importance of the logographic stage. *Applied Psycholinguistics, 11*, 349–368.

Wimmer, H., Mayringer, H., & Landerl, K. (2000). The double-deficit hypothesis and difficulties in learning to read a regular orthography. *Journal of Educational Psychology, 92*, 668–680.

12

Literacy Acquisition in Greek: Research Review of the Role of Phonological and Cognitive Factors

Costas D. Porpodas
University of Patras

This chapter presents a review of empirical research about the role of phonological and cognitive factors in reading and spelling Greek orthography. Although spoken Greek has changed considerably during historical times, written Greek has remained essentially unchanged throughout its long history. As a result, a number of inconsistencies exist between its spoken and written forms. Because of the differences between the oral and the written forms of the language, Greek language is now written, not as it is pronounced, but as it was probably pronounced almost 25 centuries ago. Greek, like English, is a morphophonemic script but is much more transparent than English in the representation of phonology. On the basis of the existing data derived from empirical research and in view of the nature of the Greek spelling system, it could be argued that Greek children tend to find learning to read easier than learning to spell. However, this does not mean that all children acquire reading and spelling skills easily. This is reflected in the reading performance of dyslexic readers, which, unlike as happens in the English language, is relatively accurate but slow. The most important index of the reading performance of Greek children seems to be their reading speed rather than their reading accuracy.

INTRODUCTION

Understanding the ways in which young children acquire literacy and process reading and spelling seems to be of interest not only to the researcher who focuses on the cognitive and linguistic processes of literacy acquisition and development, but also to those who teach young children to read and spell. Furthermore, the issue of how Greek children acquire literacy and process reading and spelling seems to be of interest to reading theorists and educationists alike. This is justified on the grounds that the Greek language has its own orthographic identity which is distinct from other orthographies.

In view of the preceding statements, the aim of this chapter is to present a review of the empirical research about the role of phonological and cognitive factors in reading and spelling in Greek. For this purpose, the chapter begins with a section on the main features of the Greek writing system and the identity of its orthography. Then a brief overview of phonology and literacy acquisition in shallow and deep orthographies is presented. Finally, a summarized review is presented referring to the main research findings concerning the role of phonological and cognitive factors in reading and spelling in Greek.

THE GREEK WRITING SYSTEM AND ITS ORTHOGRAPHY

The Development of the Greek Alphabet

Available evidence suggests that the Greek writing system was perhaps the first one in which symbols were used to represent all the sounds of the language. Although it is not known when exactly the Greek alphabetic system was developed, it has been calculated that it must have happened not later than the 8th century BC but not earlier than the 11th century BC. Based on existing evidence, according to which the Greek alphabet was used in the 8th century BC (in *Dipilos script—Nestor's cup*), the hypothesis dating the developent of the Greek alphabet to the 10th century BC seems highly probable (Coulmas, 1989).

From the Phoenician alphabet (which did not have letters to represent vowels), the Greeks developed a writing system in order to represent vowels and consonants: "Transforming a consonant script into a full alphabet with letters for both consonants and vowels clearly is a significant step because the script can more easily and more faithfully map the relevant sounds of language. Not being confined any more to consonants only, the alphabet is no longer the script of a particular language or of the language of a particular type" (Coulmas, 1989, pp. 162–163).

The invention of letters for the representation of phonemes seems to have been the most decisive step in the history of writing, which facilitated the one-to-one phoneme–grapheme representation. As a result, for the first time in human history, there was a development that led from logograms through syllabic signs to the decomposition of syllables into signs for consonants and vowels (Gelb, 1963). From this point of view, the Greek alphabet is worthy of the name "alphabet." Indeed, the principle of one letter to one sound is celebrated as the very foundation of western culture and thinking: "By the meaningless sign linked to the meaningless sound we have built the shape and meaning of western man" (McLuhan, 1962, p. 65).

Bearing in mind the principles characterizing the development of the Greek alphabet, the linguist Florian Coulmas (1989) makes this point:

> In principle the Greek alphabet was suitable for representing all the phonemes of the Greek language. It was undoubtedly the simplest and most flexible writing system developed so far, since with it any word could be spelled out without recourse to the cumbersome device of classifiers, logograms, or syllable signs. However, the Greek alphabet underwent considerable changes from the earliest attested documents to the classical period. An important feature whose representation changed significantly was vowel quality. While in the early documents vowel length was not marked, in the classical system only *alpha* and *iota* continued to be used for both short and long vowels. Short /e/ was differentiated from /e:/. The *omega* "big o", Ω and ω, was introduced to distinguish /o:/ from *omikron* "little o", /o/. Vowel length could thus be marked for /o/ and /e/, but the Greek alphabet took no note of and neither did it develop distinct symbols for long as opposed to short /i/, /a/ and /u/. The representation of /u/ which was first expressed by Old Phoenician *waw* also changed as this sound came to be realized as /u:/ in many contexts. The /u/ sound was therefore represented by combining *omikron* and *ypsilon*. (pp. 164–165)

However, that was not the final form of the Greek alphabet. As Coulmas (1989) mentions:

> Further modifications of the archaic alphabet followed later as supplementary signs were intro- duced for the aspirated stops /ph/ and /kh/—that is, φ and χ respectively, and for the double consonant /ps/, ψ. After these supplementary letters, no further additions were made, but in other

respects the Greek script of these early documents was not complete. Word boundaries were not marked, and there were no punctuation marks. Neither was there a distinction between capital and small letters. Moreover, while the Greek alphabet was one unitary system, it was not used in a uniform way. There was, in other words, no standardized orthography. The Classical Greek alphabet achieved its standardized form only late in the fifth century BC. (p. 165)

The Greek Orthography

During its long history from antiquity to the present day, the *spoken form* of the Greek language (as is the case in many other languages) has undergone some evolutionary and developmental changes. Those changes can be observed in the phonetic identity of words, in morphology, in syntax, and in the pronunciation of new words. However, in comparison with other Indo-European languages, the changes that the Greek language has undergone through the centuries could be regarded as moderate. As a result, many aspects of the spoken form have remained almost unchanged throughout its long history. Among the aspects that have remained constant are the pronunciation of many words, many grammatical forms, various elements used in the construction of new words, some elements of syntax, and a great number of morphemes (Tombaidis, 1987).

On the other hand, the *written form* of the Greek language did not follow those (even moderate) changes of the spoken language and has remained essentially unchanged throughout its long history. As a result of the differences in the changes between the oral and the written forms, the Greek language is now written, not as it is pronounced today, but as it was probably pronounced almost 25 centuries ago. Therefore, between its spoken and written forms, a number of inconsistencies exist. Some of those inconsistencies are as follows (Tombaidis, 1987; Triantaphyllidis, 1913; Zakestidou & Maniou-Vakali, 1987):

1. Some phonemes are written with different letters or letter combinations:
   * The phoneme [i] is written with the letters η, ι, υ, ει, οι, υι (e.g., *συνειρμικός/ sinirmikos /, οικιστής /ikistis /, υιικός /iikos /*).
   * The phoneme [o] is written with the letters ο, ω (e.g., *όμως /omos/, ώμος /omos /*).
   * The phoneme [e] is written with the letter ε and the letter combination αι (e.g., *φαί νεται /fenete /*).
   * The phoneme [u] is written with the letter combination ου (e.g., *ουρανού /uranu /*).
   * The phoneme [s] is written with the letters σ, ς, σσ (e.g., *σύσσωμος /sisomos/*).
2. Some letters, depending on the context, represent different phonemes:
   * The letter υ is pronounced as [i] (e.g., *κύβος /kivos/*), [f] (e.g., *ευχαριστώ /efharisto/*), [v] (e.g., *αύριο /avrio /*), or it is almost silent (e.g., *εύφορος /eforos/*).
   * The letter τ is pronounced as [t] (e.g., *κάτω /kato /*) or as [d] (*πέντε /pede/*).
3. In some cases some letters are not pronounced and they are almost voiceless:
   * The letter υ (e.g., *Εύβοια / Evia /*).
   * The double consonants λλ, κκ, ββ, μμ, and so forth (e.g., *κάλλος /kalos /, λάκκος /lakos/, Σάββατο /Savato/, γράμμα /grama/*).
   * The letter π in the consonant cluster μπτ (e.g., *πέμπτη /pemti/*).

As a result of this situation, modern Greek spelling cannot be characterized as totally phonetic but rather as a *historic orthography*, which reflects the initial phonetic identity and etymology of words (Babiniotis, 1980, p. 95).

Greek, like English, is a *morphophonemic* script but is much more transparent than English in its representation of phonology. The English spelling system has variable and inconsistent grapheme–phoneme relationships that are due to many irregular spellings and it is considered as *deep* orthography, with higher level morphological constraints (Chomsky & Halle, 1968). The Greek spelling system, however, is much more consistent in grapheme–phoneme correspondences (approaching a 1:1 relationship between graphemes and phonemes) and can be characterized as a *shallow* orthography in which, as a rule, pronunciation is predictable from print. The grapheme–phoneme inconsistencies existing in Greek (which are mainly due to digraph spelling patterns) are to a large extent rule governed and apply in almost every case in which the particular spelling pattern occurs. It would be expected therefore that the existing systematic relationship between individual letters and individual phonemes would enable Greek children to develop a fully specified orthographic lexicon in which representations would be underpinned at the phonemic level. Consequently, it would also be expected that, in learning to read the Greek language, children would build on the nature of their writing system and they would learn to read by a sequential decoding process.

In spelling, however, Greek is *phonologically opaque* as there is a one-to-many phoneme–grapheme mapping and therefore spelling cannot always be predictable from phonology. Therefore, in a number of cases in which the spelling of a word is derived from its initial or etymological basis, a word's phonemic structure can be represented by more than one graphemic alternative. Because most of such spelling patterns are explained through reference to etymological and grammatical knowledge, spelling can be assisted by a gradual learning process of the rules based on morphology and lexical information.

PHONOLOGY AND LITERACY ACQUISITION IN DEEP AND SHALLOW ORTHOGRAPHIES

Learning to Read

In view of the existing differences in the orthographic systems and their classification as *deep* or *shallow* orthographies, it could be assumed that the degree to which a writing system represents phonology is highly likely to be related to the way in which the word-recognition process takes place. This is in fact what Katz and Frost (1992) suggested in their *orthographic depth hypothesis*. According to this hypothesis, a reader of a deep orthography is likely to be led (by the nature of the orthography) to process words by using *morphological* information from the visual-orthographic structure of the written word. However, the reader of a shallow orthography is likely to be encouraged by the high degree of transparency in the representation of phonology and process words by using the *phonological* information. Evidence from literacy acquisition in deep and shallow orthographic systems, like the English and Greek, can be used to test the validity of this hypothesis.

Extensive investigation of reading acquisition in the English language has resulted in the formulation of various theoretical accounts (for a brief review see Seymour & Duncan, 2001). The common characteristic of the early developed *cognitive developmental stage models* (Frith, 1985; Marsh, Friedman, Welch, & Desberg, 1981) was the idea that the young children's acquisition of reading passes through three different stages. The first is the *logographic* stage, in which a child reads on the basis of a whole-word strategy by associating the whole visual pattern of the word with its pronunciation. At this stage, the child is expected to read successfully only a set of frequently encountered words. The unfamiliar words either cannot be read or should be approached by guessing on the basis of contextual cues. The logographic strategy is regarded as a natural and necessary first step in the acquisition process until the child reaches 7 years of age when, according to Piagetian framework, a transition of the child's cognitive development from the preoperational stage to the stage of concrete operations occurs. As a result of this and on the basis of the development of phonological awareness of speech structure, the young reader enters the *alphabetic* stage, during which he or she develops a decoding strategy (phonological recoding) on a sequential basis. At this stage, the child recognizes the constituent letters of the word, uses his or her knowledge of the associations between different letters and their sounds, blends together the constituent sounds, and forms the pronunciation of the word. Finally the child reaches the *orthographic* stage, during which she or he can read words by using letter groups.

The stage model of reading acquisition was supported by subsequent research on the English language (Byrne, 1991; Harris & Coltheart, 1986; Seymour & Elder, 1986). The outcome of all this research was the belief that the young reader of English is bound to use the logographic strategy as the first step in the learning-to-read process.

However, studies of literacy acquisition in a few other languages have cast doubts on the hypothesis of the importance of this logographic process and the underestimation of the role of alphabetic strategy in the acquisition of reading skills. In the German language, Wimmer's extensive work with Austrian children has demonstrated that, in learning to read and spell German, the children apply mainly a phonological recoding and not a logographic strategy (Wimmer & Hummer, 1990; Wimmer, Landerl, Linortner, & Hummer, 1991). Similarly, Mannhaupt, Jansen, and Marx (1997) found that, 10 weeks after beginning school, German first graders did not rely on logographic reading. They concluded that, in learning to read German, children do not seem to use any other reading strategy before the alphabetic process. Sprenger-Charolles and Bonnet (1996), in a longitudinal study aimed at evaluating the reading strategies used by French children, found that first graders did not use logographic strategies in learning to read French. In the Greek language, Porpodas (in press) evaluated the reading strategies used by first graders after 16 weeks of schooling and literacy instruction, and found that good as well as weak readers were relying widely on the alphabetic process. This was interpreted as indicating that the logographic strategy is unlikely to play an important role in the process of learning to read Greek.

From a longitudinal study, Seymour and Evans (1992) concluded that the logographic strategy could be a result of the teaching method employed in the school and not a natural and necessary first step in literacy acquisition. Stuart and Coltheart (1988) suggested that if children have acquired the phonological skills then their reading process is alphabetical from the beginning. Similarly Ehri (1992) pointed out the importance of phonological cues in the first stages of reading and supported the notion of phonological recoding (based on phonemic and alphabetic knowledge) for reading acquisition. In view of the shortcomings of the *stage models* of literacy acquisition, Philip Seymour of the University of Dundee, UK, from his many extensive and detailed studies, developed the "dual foundation model" of reading acquisition (Seymour, 1997, 1999). The model is developed in terms of phases that are not necessarily sequential but that can overlap in a cumulative manner. Seymour proposes four main phases:

Phase O: Preliteracy. This phase refers to the prereading period. Because of the nature of their language (and especially the poorly defined structure of the syllable), in this phase, English prereaders lack explicit linguistic awareness. In Greek, however, which is characterized by a well-articulated and open syllabic structure, prereaders are expected to approach the task of learning to read with a satisfactory level of explicit phonological awareness at the syllable level (Porpodas, 1989a, 1990).

Phase 1: Foundation literacy. The basic hypothesis is that literacy acquisition requires the knowledge of the visual forms of the letters and their association with the corresponding sounds of speech. Based on that knowledge, two foundation processes are developed: a *logographic foundation* and an *alphabetic foundation*. The logographic foundation is thought to be a process for the representation and recognition of words, on the basis of their partial representation. The alphabetic foundation involves ". . . a simple decoding procedure by which individual letters are converted to sounds and the sounds are synthesized to form a pronunciation. . . . The establishment of an alphabetic decoding mechanism creates a demand for an explicit meta-awareness of the *phonemic* segments out of which speech is constructed (Seymour & Duncan, 2001, p. 292). The degree of development and use of the logographic or the alphabetic foundation process depends on the nature of the language under process and the teaching methods used. For these reasons the development of a distinct logographic foundation seems unlikely in learning to read Greek (Porpodas, in press), and therefore Greek children are assumed to approach reading by using an alphabetic process.

Phases 2 and 3: Orthographic and morphographic literacy: In Seymour's model,

> These frameworks are envisaged as abstract structures in which elements of orthography are organized in a manner which reflects their relationship with sound and meaning. At the *orthographic* level the elements consist of the vowel and consonant graphemes organized into a structure which reflects the subdivision of the syllable into a three-part onset–peak–coda format or a two-part onset–rime format. At the *morphographic* level, the elements are likely to consist of whole syllables, or, more obviously as free and bound morphemes. (Seymour & Duncan, 2001, p. 293).

Because Greek is a consistent orthography the focus of the reading process on rime-level spelling sound parts will not add any advantage in processing Greek (Goswami, Porpodas, & Wheelwright, 1997). In addition, because Greek contains polysyllabic words in which most syllables have an open CV or CCV structure, the morphographic phase (in which syllabic units can be combined) seems to be more important for the development of reading. Therefore, according to Seymour, Greek children can progress rapidly through Phases 1 and 2 and approach Phase 3 with an inventory of well-defined syllabic units in place. This was confirmed by Porpodas (2001) in a study of first-grade Greek children.

In summing up, it could be argued that the most decisive step in the process of learning to read seems to be the acquisition of *phonological recoding*, that is, "the ability to translate printed words independently into their spoken equivalents" (Share, 1995, p. 156). From the preceding account, it could be assumed that Greek children should not face many difficulties in acquiring phonological recoding as a procedure for accurate word recognition. Based on the consistency of orthography, the grapheme–phoneme recoding is expected to be reliable, provided that the lexical item presented conforms to the code (as is normally the case) or that the basics for the rule-read words have been learned. Success in phonological recoding is enhanced by the fact that Greek children are normally taught with an analyticosynthetic phonics method that directly facilitates phonological recoding as a means of word recognition.

Empirical evidence supports this hypothesis for Greek language (Porpodas, 2001, in press). In his studies Porpodas evaluated the reading strategies used by first graders after a period of schooling and literacy instruction and found that good as well as weak readers were relying widely on the alphabetic process.

Learning to Spell

As in the case of reading, most of the existing research on spelling has been conducted on the English language. On the basis of that research, it could be argued that learning to spell involves the employment of visual, phonological, semantic, grammatical, and orthographic knowledge and skills (Bruck & Treiman, 1990; Gough, Juel, & Griffith,1992; Henderson & Beers, 1980; Marsh et al., 1981; Waters, Bruck, & Malus-Abramowitz, 1988).

The theoretical accounts concerning the learning of spelling in English have taken the form of developmental stage models. Such models have been proposed by Brown (1990), Frith (1980, 1985), and Marsh et al. (1981). A close comparison of these models reveals that they share two common characteristics. The first characteristic is that all these models postulate that spelling develops in a series of stages or periods. The second characteristic is that spelling development postulates a period in which spelling is based on a coding strategy of phonological analysis that is called a *phonetic* stage by Brown (1990), an *alphabetic* stage by Frith (1985), and *sequential and hierarchical encoding* by Marsh et al. (1981). The phonological analysis strategy of spelling development is followed by a period in which the spelling strategy is based on lexical analogies, during which visual memory plays a primary role. At this period spelling of a word is produced because it "looks right" (Brown, 1990), it is "independent of sound" (Frith, 1985), or because there is a shift from the phonemic encoding strategy to a strategy based on analogy (Marsh et al., 1981). The most widely used methodology to determine the strategies used by children in their effort to spell has been the analysis of spelling errors. As Read (1986) has pointed out, children's misspellings "provide a window on their spelling processes, their notions of writing and their judgments of speech sounds" (p. 2). Such an analysis shows to what extent children apply information about grapheme–phoneme conversion in spelling. The way to distinguish that is by classifying spelling errors into two main categories. The first is the phonetic or phonological or legal misspelling, in which the misspelled word is phonetically accurate and "sounds like" the target word. In this case, the child is assumed to have employed the phonological rules successfully and consequently has correctly analyzed the spoken word into phonemes and has represented each phoneme with a grapheme. The second category is the nonphonetic or nonphonological or illegal misspelling, which is thought to indicate the use of a rote memorization of the word or an unsuccessful use of the phonological rules (see Cook, 1981, for a review).

The investigation of spelling in consistent orthographic systems has shown that, in German, spelling performance of primary first-grade children was strongly based on the knowledge of phonological information (Wimmer & Hummer, 1990). In the Greek language, there is also some evidence indicating that the Greek children are highly likely to process spelling not by "reading out" the word's orthographic form from memory but by deriving it on the basis of their knowledge about spelling–sound correspondences (Porpodas, 1989a, 1989b, 1989c, 2001).

RESEARCH REVIEW INTO THE ROLE OF PHONOLOGICAL AWARENESS, SPEECH PERCEPTION, AND WORKING MEMORY IN LITERACY ACQUISITION IN GREEK

The Role of Phonological Awareness

The relationship between phonological awareness and success in literacy acquisition in Greek was first investigated by Porpodas in the 1980s. (Porpodas, 1989b, 1990, 1991, 1995a, 1999). The main findings of those investigations could be summarized as follows: First, syllabic awareness is much easier than phonemic awareness at the prereading stage. Second, children, who at the prereading stage had aquired phonological awareness at a satisfacory level, had achieved a better level of literacy development at the end of the first primary year, as compared with their classmates whose level of phonological awareness was low at the prereading stage. However, another interesting observation was that, by the end of the second primary year, the difference in literacy development between those two groups of children became smaller.

The last point was also observed in the only systematic training study of phonological awareness that has been conducted so far in Greek. More particularly, in that training study, Porpodas and Palaiothodorou (1999a, 1999b) not only provided evidence for a causal relationship between phonological awareness and literacy acquisition but, in addition, found that the advantage in literacy acquisition gained in the primary first grade had disappeared by the end of the primary third grade. (A similar finding has also been reported in the Finnish language by Niemi, Poskiparta, & Vauras, 2001). In addition, in the previously mentioned training study in Greek, it was shown that the effect of phonology was specific to literacy acquisition, as there was no evidence of any effect on the learning of mathematics.

The issue of the relationship between phonological awareness and literacy acquisition of Greek has recently become the focus of interest of more researchers. More particularly, the prereaders' greater capability in aquiring syllabic than phonemic awareness of Greek was also reported by Aidinis and Nunes (2001). These researchers also found that the children were experiencing less difficulty in the phonemic analysis of the initial than of the final phonemes of each word. Along the same lines, Nikolopoulos and Porpodas (2001), Chitiri and Porpodas (2003), Tafa (1997), and Papoulia-Tzelepi (1997) found a strong relationship between phonological awareness and litaracy acquisition in Greek.

Finally, the strong role of phonological awareness deficit (and especially at the phonemic level) in dyslexia in the Greek language has been reported by Porpodas (1995b, 1996, 1997) and Porpodas and Dimakos (2003).

The Phonological Representations Hypothesis and the Role of Speech Perception

The *phonological representations hypothesis* (Goswami, 2000) was used for further investigating the causal role of developmental deficit hypothesis in developmental dyslexia. According to this hypothesis, the quality of segmental organization of representations supporting spoken word recognition and production should be related to speech perception parameters (Joanisse, Manis, Keating, & Seidenberg, 2000) and phonological memory skills (Porpodas, 1999). In addition, it should be reflected in the level of difficulty encountered in retrieving the phonological codes of representations from the mental lexicon and an awareness of the phonological structure of those representations as well as the ability to manipulate them (Swan & Goswami, 1997a, 1997b). It is therefore expected that this skill is likely to determine the level of reading and spelling ability.

This hypothesis was investigated in Greek by Panteli (2004) and Panteli and Porpodas (2004). In that research, a battery of tasks was used for assessing auditory perception of non-speech stimuli, auditory discrimination, perception of rhythm in acoustic signals, phonological short-term memory, word-finding ability, and phonological awareness skills. The results obtained so far seem to indicate that the dyslexic children's deficit in phonological processing arises from a lack of distinctness of phonological representations. This difficulty in forming precise representations of the phonological structure of words seems to be partly explained in terms of difficulties in the perception of the rhythm of acoustic signals.

The Role of Working Memory

The decisive role of working memory in reading acquisition has been well documented in the literature (e.g., Baddeley, 1986; Baddeley, Eldridge, & Lewis, 1981; Hulme, 1981). In the case of reading Greek, Porpodas (1991) has found a direct relationship between the level of phonetic representation in short-term memory at the preschool level and the reading level achieved at the end of primary first grade. In addition, Porpodas (1993) investigated the role of short-term memory storage of linguistic information in the process of reading. The main finding of that research was that the functional difficulties of the articulatory loop of working memory seem to inhibit the learning of reading.

LEARNING TO READ AND SPELL GREEK:
CONCLUDING REMARKS

On the basis of the existing data derived from empirical research and in view of the nature of the Greek spelling system, it could be argued that Greek children (with or without learning difficulties) tend to find learning to read easier than learning to spell. However, this does not mean that all children acquire the reading skill easily. On the contrary, some have to struggle to acquire phonological recoding skills in word reading. This is reflected in the beginning readers' and the dyslexic children's reading performance in which, contrary to what happens in the English language, the most notable deficit of their reading performance seems to be the processing time rather than the reading accuracy (Porpodas, 1995a, 1995b, 1996, 1997; Porpodas & Karantzis, 1995). This means that the ability to decode almost every word may finally be achieved by many poor readers but at the expense of reading time.

REFERENCES

Aidinis, A., & Nunes, T. (2001). The role of different levels of phonological awareness in the development of reading and spelling in Greek. *Reading and Writing: An Interdisciplinary Journal, 14*, 145–177.

Babiniotis, G. (1980). *Theoretiki glossologia.* Athens.

Baddeley, A. D. (1986). *Working memory.* Oxford, UK: Oxford University Press.

Baddeley, A. D., Eldridge, M., & Lewis, V. J. (1981). The role of subvocalization in reading. *Quarterly Journal of Experimental Psychology, 33*, 439–454.

Brown, A. (1990). A review of recent research in spelling. *Educational Psychology Review, 2*, 365–397.

Bruck, M., & Treiman, R. (1990). Phonological awareness and spelling in normal children and dyslexics: The case of initial consonant clusters. *Journal of Experimental Child Psychology, 50*, 156–178.

Byrne, B. (1991). Experimental analysis of the child's discovery of the alphabetic principle. In L. Rieben & C. Perfetti (Eds.), *Learning to read: Basic research and its implications* (pp. 75–84). Hillsdale, NJ: Lawrence Erlbaum Associates.

Chitiri, F., & Porpodas, C. (2003). *Phonological awareness and its relations to learning of reading and spelling as well as to linguistic ability and comprehension of Greek.* Patras, Greece: Laboratory of Cognitive Analysis of Learning, Language and Dyslexia, University of Patras.

Chomsky, N., & Halle, M. (1968). *The sound pattern of English.* New York: Harper & Row.

Cook, L. (1981). Misspelling analysis in dyslexia: Observation of developmental strategy shifts. *Bulletin of the Orton Society, 31*, 123–134.

Coulmas, F. (1989). *The writing systems of the world.* Oxford, UK: Basil Blackwell.

Ehri, L. C. (1992). Reconceptualizing the development of sight word reading and its relationship to recoding. In P. Gough, L. Ehri, & R. Treiman (Eds.), *Reading acquisition* (pp. 107–143). Hillsdale, NJ: Lawrence Erlbaum Associates.

Frith, U. (1980). Unexpected spelling problems. In U. Frith (Ed.), *Cognitive processes in spelling* (pp. 495–515). London: Academic Press.

Frith, U. (1985). Beneath the surface of developmental dyslexia. In K. E. Patterson, J. C. Marshall, & M. Coltheart (Eds.). *Surface dyslexia* (pp. 301–330). London: Lawrence Erlbaum Associates.

Gelb, I. (1963). *A study of writing* (Rev. ed.). Chicago: University of Chicago Press.

Goswami, U. (2000). Phonological representations, reading development and dyslexia: Towards a cross-linguistic theoretical framework. *Dyslexia, 6*, 133–151.

Goswami, U., Porpodas, C., & Wheelwright, S. (1997). Children's orthographic representations in English and Greek. *European Journal of Psychology of Education, 12*, 273–292.

Gough, P., Juel, C., & Griffith, P. (1992). Reading, spelling and the orthographic cipher. In P. Gough, L. Ehri, & R. Treiman (Eds.), *Reading acquisition* (pp. 35–48). Hillsdale, NJ: Lawrence Erlbaum Associates.

Harris, M., & Coltheart, M. (1986*). Language processing in children and adults: An introduction.* London: Routledge.

Havelock, E. (1986). Orality, literacy and star wars. *Written Communication* 3/4, 411–420.

Henderson, E., & Beers, J. (Eds.). (1980). *Developmental and cognitive aspects of learning to spell: A reflection of word knowledge.* Newark, DE: International Reading Association.

Hulme, C. (1981). *Reading retardation and multi-sensory teaching.* London: Routledge & Kegan Paul.

Goswami, U. (2000). Phonological representations, reading development and dyslexia: towards a cross-linguistic theoretical framework, *Dyslexia, 6*, 133–151.

Joanisse, M. F., Manis, F. R., Keating, P., & Seidenberg, M. S. (2000). Language deficits in dyslexic children: Speech perception, phonology and morphology, *Journal of Experimental Child Psychology, 77*, 30–60.

Katz, L., & Frost, R. (1992). Reading in different orthographies: The orthographic depth hypothesis. In R. Frost & L. Katz (Eds.), *Orthography, phonology, morphology and meaning* (pp. 67–84). Amsterdam: North-Holland.

Mannhaupt, G., Jansen, H., & Marx, H. (1997). Cultural influences on literacy development. In C. K. Leong & R. Malatesha Joshi (Eds.), *Cross-language studies of learning to read and spell: Phonologic and orthographic processing* (pp. 161–173). Dordrecht, The Netherlands: Kluwer.

Marsh, G., Friedman, M., Welch, U., & Desberg, P. (1981). A cognitive-developmental theory of reading acquisition. In G. E. MacKinnon & T. G. Waller (Eds.), *Reading research: Advances in theory and practice* (Vol. 3, pp. 199–221). New York: Academic Press.

McLuhan, M. (1962). *The Gutenberg galaxy*. Toronto: University of Toronto Press.

Marsh, G., Friedman, M., Welch, U., & Desberg, P. (1981). A cognitive-developmental theory of reading acquisition. In G. E. MacKinnon & T. G. Waller (Eds). *Reading Research: Advances in Theory and Practice, Vol. 3*. N. York: Academic Press.

Niemi, P., Poskiparta, E., & Vauras, M. (2001). Benefits of training in linguistic awareness dissipate by Grade 3. *Psychology, 8*, 330–337.

Nikolopoulos, D., & Porpodas, C. (2001, April). *Pre-cursors of reading and spelling in the regular Greek orthography*. Paper presented at the 5th British Dyslexia Association International Conference, University of York, UK.

Panteli, M. (2004). *Phonological representation and the role of speech perception in normal and dyslexic readers of Greek*. Doctoral dissertation. University of Patras, Greece. Manuscript in preparation.

Panteli, M., & Porpodas, C. (2004). *The role of speech perception in reading and spelling of Greek by dyslexic and non-dyslexis children*. Patras, Greece: University of Patras. Manuscript in preparation.

Papoulia-Tzelepi, P. (1997). Analysis of phonological awareness in the preschool children. *Glossa, 41*, 20–41.

Porpodas, C. D. (1989a).The phonological factor in reading and spelling of Greek. In P. G. Aaron & R. M. Joshi (Eds.), *Reading and writing disorders in different orthographic systems* (pp. 177–190). Dordrecht, The Netherlands: Kluwer.

Porpodas, C. (1989b). The relation between phonemic awareness and reading and spelling of Greek words in the first school years. In M. Carretero, M. Pope, R. J. Simons, & J. Pozo (Eds.), *Learning and instruction* (Vol. 3, pp. 203–217). Oxford, UK: Pregamon.

Porpodas, C. D. (1989c). Spelling by first grade children in relation to linguistic and memory abilities. *Psychologica Themata, 2*, 201–214.

Porpodas, C. (1990, April). *Linguistic awareness and learning to read Greek*. Paper presented at the 9th World Congress of Applied Linguistics, Halkidiki, Greece.

Porpodas, C. (1991, August). *Linguistic awareness, verbal short-term memory and learning to read Greek*. Paper presented at the 4th European Conference for Research on Learning and Instruction, Turku, Finland.

Porpodas, C. (1993). Phonetic short-term memory representation in children's reading of Greek. In R. Malatesha Joshi & C. K. Leong (Eds.), *Reading disabilities: Diagnosis and component processes*. Dordrecht, The Netherlands: Kluwer.

Porpodas, C. (1995a, July). *Learning to read and spell Greek: Their relation to phonological awareness and memory factors*. Paper presented at the IV European Congress of Psychology, Athens.

Porpodas, C. (1995b, July). *Toward a method for the diagnosis and treatment of dyslexia in the Greek language*. Paper presented at the IV European Congress of Psychology, Athens.

Porpodas, C. D. (1996, May). *Reading and dyslexia in the Greek language: Research evidence for an explanation based on phonological awareness—Educational implications*. Paper presented at the 5th Panhellenic Conference of Psychological Research, University of Patras, Greece.

Porpodas, C. D. (1997, May–June). *Dyslexia: A cognitive perspective*. Paper presented at the 6th Panhellenic Conference of Psychological Research, Panteion University, Athens, Greece.

Porpodas, C. (1999). Patterns of phonological and memory processing in beginning readers and spellers of Greek. *Journal of Learning Disabilities, 32*, 406–416.

Porpodas, C. (2001). Cognitive processes in first grade reading and spelling of Greek. *Psychology: The Journal of the Hellenic Psychological Society—A special issue devoted to Research on Reading, Spelling and Dyslexia in Europe, 8*, 384–400.

Porpodas, C. (in press). Cognitive strategies in learning to read Greek: Doubts regarding the importance of the logographic process. In A. Kantas, Th. Veli, & A. Hantzi (Eds.), *Societally significant applications of psychological knowledge*. Athens: Ellinika Grammata.

Porpodas, C., & Dimakos, J. (2003). *Two case-studies of Greek dyslexic children*. Patras, Greece: Unit of Dyslexia, University of Patras, Greece.

Porpodas, C., & Karantzis, J. (1995, July). Working memory in children with and without reading and arithmetic difficulties. Paper presented at the IV European Congress of Psychology, Athens.

Porpodas, C., & Palaiothodorou, A. (1999a, August). *Phonological training and reading and spelling acquisition.* Paper presented at the 4th European Conference on Psychological Assessment, University of Patras, Patras, Greece.

Porpodas, C., & Palaiothodorou, A. (1999b, September). *A training study on phonological awareness and its effect on learning to read and spell the Greek language.* Paper presented at the European Conference on Developmental Psychology, Spetses, Greece.

Read. C. (1986). *Children's creative spelling.* London: Routledge.

Seymour, P. H. K. (1997). Foundations of orthographic development. In C. A. Perfetti, L. Rieben, & M. Fayol (Eds.), *Learning to spell* (pp. 319–337). Hillsdale, NJ: Lawrence Erlbaum Associates.

Seymour, P. H. K. (1999). Cognitive architecture of early reading. In I. Lundberg, F. E. Tonnessen & I. Austad (Eds.), *Dyslexia: Advances in theory and practice* (pp. 59–73). Dordrecht, The Netherlands: Kluwer.

Seymour, P. H. K., & Duncan, L. (2001). Learning to read in English. *Psychology: The Journal of the Hellenic Psychological Society—Special issue: Research on reading, spelling and dyslexia in Europe, 8,* 281–299.

Seymour, P. H. K., & Elder, L. (1986). Beginning reading without phonology. *Cognitive Neuropsychology, 3,* 1–36.

Seymour, P. H. K., & Evans, H. M. (1992). Beginning reading without semantics: A cognitive study of hyperlexia. *Cognitive Neuropsychology, 9,* 89–122.

Share, D. L. (1995). Phonological recoding and self-teaching: *Sine qua non* of reading acquisition. *Cognition, 55,* 151–218.

Sprenger-Charolles, L., & Bonnet P. (1996). New doubts on the importance of the logographic stage: A longitudinal study of French children. *Cahiers de Psychologie Cognitive/Current Psychology of Cognition, 15*(2), 173–208.

Stuart, M., & Coltheart, M. (1988). Does reading develop in a sequence of stages? *Cognition, 30,* 139–181.

Swan, D., & Goswami, U. (1997a). Picture naming deficits in developmental dyslexia and the phonological representations hypothesis. *Brain & Language, 56,* 334–353.

Swan, D., & Goswami, U. (1997b). Phonological awareness deficits in developmental dyslexia and the phonological representations hypothesis. *Journal of Experimental Child Psychology, 66,* 18–41.

Tafa, E. (1997). *Reading and writing at the preschool education.* Athens: Ellinika Grammata.

Tombaidis, D. (1987). *A concise history of the Greek language.* Athens: Publishing Organisation for School Textbooks.

Triantaphyllidis, M. (1913). *Our orthography.* Athens: Estia.

Waters, G., Bruck, M., & Malus-Abramowitz, M. (1988). The role of linguistic and visual information in spelling: A developmental study. *Journal of Experimental Child Psychology, 45,* 400–421

Wimmer, H., & Hummer, P. (1990). How German-speaking first graders read and spell: Doubts on the importance of the logographic stage. *Applied Psycholinguistics, 11,* 349–368.

Wimmer, H., Landerl, K., Linortner, R., & Hummer, P. (1991). The relationship of phonemic awareness to reading acquisition: More consequence than precondition but still important. *Cognition, 40,* 219–249.

Zakestidou, S., & Maniou-Vakali, M. (1987). Orthographic problem in grades 1 and 2 of the high school. *Nea Paideia, 42,* 80–93; *43,* 98–110.

13

The Acquisition of Written Morphology in Greek

Terezinha Nunes
Oxford Brookes University

Athanasios Aidinis
Aristotle University of Thessaloniki

Peter Bryant
Oxford Brookes University

We tested the hypothesis that children do not learn how to spell simply by memorizing words by rote but they also use morphological knowledge to generate the appropriate spellings of words. We put this hypothesis to the test by administering real words and pseudowords to Greek children from grades 2 through 5. The Greek language lends itself nicely to testing this hypothesis. The reason is that many words in the Greek writing system end with similar sounds but are spelled differently, depending on their morphological nature. For example, take the phoneme /o/. This sound is spelled as "o" at the end of singular neuter nouns but as "ω" at the end of first-person-singular verbs. Thus here, and in many other cases in Greek, there is a good rule for deciding which of the two (or more) alternative spellings for the same sound is appropriate. The rule is based almost entirely on morphology. Morphological knowledge therefore can be expected to facilitate the acquisition of correct spelling. If rote memory played a role in spelling, Greek children should do well in spelling real Greek words but poorly in spelling pseudowords, which cannot be spelled from memory. The children's performance showed a high degree of correlation between real word-spelling scores and pseudoword-spelling scores. It appears that Greek children use morphological knowledge for spelling and therefore can spell even pseudowords reasonably well. The study also presents some evidence that there is a connection between morphological awareness and the acquisition of morphological skills. This study used word-ending spelling as a measure of written morphological skills because many Greek words have the same word-ending sound but are spelled differently depending on their morphological status. Methods for assessing morphological awareness in Greek were developed and the correlation between children's performance on these tasks and their progress in using morphology was analyzed. A strong relationship between morphological awareness and written morphological skills was found.

The aim of the studies reported in this chapter is to document the acquisition of written morphology in Greek and to examine whether morphological awareness is a factor in the acquisition of written morphological skills.

Previous work on the acquisition of written morphology indicates that it is not acquired by children early in life. Studies of the representation of written morphology in French are now quite numerous (Brissaud & Bessonnat, 2001; Brissaud & Sandon, 1999; Fayol, Thevenin, Jarrousse, & Totereau, 1999; Lefrançois, 2002) and converge in showing that this skill is not easily acquired. Fayol and his colleagues studied the acquisition of plurals, which are not marked in spoken French but are marked in written language. They observed that it is difficult for children in the first two years of primary school not only to represent plurals in writing but also to interpret the cues given by written plurals in reading. Brissaud and Bessonnat, studying a more complex case of written morphology, argued that there are many different spellings for the same sounds in French, which are pronounced the same way but spelled differently (e.g., er, é, és, ée, ées) for morphological reasons. Their studies showed that the acquisition of this written morphology is not complete even by the time young people enter secondary school. Similar results were obtained in Canada by Lefrançois (2002).

Research on Portuguese spelling has also investigated the distinction between morphemes that sound the same but have different meanings. Similar to French, Portuguese written morphology is also acquired rather late (Rosa, 2002).

Different forms of representations of morphology in written English have been studied— for example, the use of the suffix "ed" to mark the past tense (Nunes, Bryant, & Bindman, 1997), the difference between nouns ending with "ian" and "ion" (Nunes & Bryant, 2004), and the difference between the words that end with a spelling of x or ks representing the sounds /ks/ (Bryant, 2002). In all of these cases, phonology does not always determine the choice of correct spellings. Endings of regular verbs in the past in English are not pronounced as /ed/; they are sometimes pronounced /t/ (as in "kissed"), sometimes /d/ (as in "killed"), and sometimes /id/ (as in "wanted"). In these instances, children must learn to use the ending that flouts letter–sound correspondence. The ending sounds /ən/ in "magician" and "destination" are the same but they are spelled differently because they end in different suffixes. "Magician" is formed with a derivational suffix for agentives (magic–magician) whereas "destination" is an abstract noun and not an agentive. Similarly, the spelling of the final sound /ks/ in "socks" and "box" is determined by the grammatical status of the words: Singular nouns ending in /ks/ sounds are spelled with "x" whereas the same end sound in plural nouns results from the addition of the suffix "s" to the singular form of the noun (sock+s).

The work by Nunes, Bryant, and colleagues has gone beyond the descriptive level and attempts to investigate the processes that support the acquisition of written morphology. Through a combination of longitudinal studies (Nunes et al., 1997) and intervention studies (Nunes, Bryant, & Olsson, 2003), they have been able to show that children's awareness of morphology acts as a causal factor that facilitates the acquisition of written morphology. Levin, Ravid, & Rapaport (1999) reached similar conclusions regarding the role of morphological awareness in the acquisition of written morphology in Hebrew.

The studies reported here provide further evidence that written morphology in Greek is also slow to be mastered and that awareness of morphology may be implicated in the process of acquisition of written morphology.

THE GREEK ORTHOGRAPHY

Modern Greek is a heavily inflected language. It is also a language with few vowel sounds. The result is that several different inflectional morphemes either sound the same or share the same vowel sound. An example is the /o/ ending, which indicates the neuter singular ending in some nouns and adjectives but indicates the first-person-singular present-tense ending in some verbs. In this case, and in all other cases in which different inflections share a sound, the spelling of the common sound varies between morphemes. To take the example of the /o/ ending, this sound is spelled as "o" at the end of singular neuter nouns and as "ω" at the end of first-person-singular verbs. Thus here, and in many other cases in Greek, there is a perfectly good rule for deciding which of the two (or more) phonologically legitimate alternative spellings for the same sound is the right one, and the rule is entirely based on morphology. In spite of having the same sound, different inflections require different spellings.

Our studies focus on the choice of the correct spelling for words and pseudowords for which more than one phonologically acceptable spelling exists. Our hypothesis is that children do not simply memorize the particular spelling of words that end in sounds that can be spelled in more than one way. Rather, they use morphological knowledge to generate the appropriate spellings. Thus our studies use spelling of real words in addition to pseudowords, which cannot be spelled from memory. We also hypothesize that morphological awareness is the basis for the acquisition of this morphological knowledge but the evidence that is provided here is only correlational.

STUDY 1: SPELLING WORDS WITH THE SAME-ENDING SOUND IN DIFFERENT WAYS

The aim of this study is to describe the acquisition of written morphology in Greek by examining how children spell the endings of words that have more than one morphological representation. When the same sound should be spelled in different ways for morphological reasons, three alternative patterns are possible: (a) the children might use only one spelling form for the same-ending sounds even though the word endings belong to different morphological categories; (b) they might use different endings but do so indiscriminately; or (c) they might be able to use written morphology correctly, using different spellings depending on the morphological class. The first pattern would suggest that the children are generating spellings on the basis of phonology and perhaps use a strict grapheme–phoneme correspondence for spelling. Thus if they know any one grapheme that represents a phoneme, they ignore other possible spelling patterns. The second pattern would suggest that the children do not use a rigid grapheme–phoneme correspondence rule for spelling and know that there are alternative spellings for the same sound. However, they do not know which spelling pattern goes with which morphological unit. The third pattern would suggest that the children have acquired a knowledge of written morphology and make use of it when they spell similar sounding word endings.

We examined the spellings of children from four different grades in order to describe the rate of acquisition of written morphological skills. We wanted to examine the plausibility that spelling involves generalization and not simple rote memory, and so we used pseudo-words for spelling. In order to obtain normative data, we also used real words.

Method

Participants

A total of 435 children from state-supported schools in Katerini in Northern Greece participated in the study.[1] The children in these schools come from a wide range of socioeconomic levels. Four levels of age and grade were studied: The mean age of children from Grade 2 was 7 years, 1 month; the mean age of children from Grade 3 was 8 years, 1 month; the mean age of children from Grade 4 was 9 years, 2 months; and the mean age of children from Grade 5 was 10 years, 1 month. The study took place during the months of October and November, which are the last months of the first trimester of the school year.

---

[1] Only partial results of this study are reported here. For full results, see Aidinis, 1998.

Design

The spelling task contained words with three different end sounds; two of them have two phonetically acceptable spellings and the third end sound can be spelled in four different ways. A between-subjects design was used to compare spelling performance across words versus pseudowords. The children were sampled from 20 classrooms, and the classes were randomly assigned to either the word- or the pseudoword-spelling task.

Materials and Procedure

In the word-spelling task, the children were asked to spell words with low frequency taken from the textbooks used in their classrooms (Aidinis, 1998). The words ended in /o/, /e/, or /i/ sounds. The /o/ ending words are spelled with "o," if they are neutral nouns and with "ω" if they are verbs. The /e/ ending words are spelled with "ε" if they are verbs in the first-person-plural present-tense active voice, and with "αι" if they are verbs in the third-person-singular present-tense passive voice.

The /i/ ending words we used could have four different spellings, each representing the whole of an inflection or part of an inflection: "η" for feminine nouns and adjective inflections in the singular, nominative case; "ι" for neutral noun inflections in the singular, nominative case; "οι" for masculine nouns and adjective inflections in the plural, nominative case; and "ει" for part of the verb inflection in the third-person-singular present-tense passive voice. The task contained 8 words of each type and thus a total of 64 words.

The target words were presented in random order to the children in the context of a sentence. The sentence was already written on the answer sheet but the target word was left out of the sentence. The examiner said the word, then said the sentence that had the word in it, and then repeated the word. The children's task was to write the target word down on the answer sheet. The pseudoword task was constructed based on the same structure as that of the real spelling words and was presented in the same manner. All pseudowords were constructed with phonologically acceptable syllables. They were presented in the context of the sentences that were used in the real word-spelling task. The tasks are presented in the appendix.

The spelling tests were administered in the children's classroom; the second author, a native speaker, and the classroom teacher were present. The researcher presented the task; both the teacher and the researcher made sure that the children were working independently and had completed spelling the word before the next word was presented.

Results

The analysis of results was carried out in two different steps. The first analysis investigated patterns of performance across words with the same end sound. The second analysis examined the data to see whether the children were using a generalizable strategy by comparing the spelling patterns of real words with the spelling patterns of pseudowords.

Different Spelling Patterns Across Same-Ending Stimuli

It is quite possible that children start by representing each sound with one spelling only and adopt alternative spellings later on, as they advance in the learning process. The importance of testing whether children are single-letter users is that the use of the same letter across morphological categories would indicate the absence of morphological awareness. In order to categorize the children as users of a single spelling, it was necessary to set a criterion for the classification. We decided that if the children spelled 80% of the words the same way, regardless of the differences in their spelling, they would be considered single-pattern users.

TABLE 13.1
Percentage of Children in Each Grade Level by Spelling Pattern in the Task of Spelling Words

End Sound	Spelling Pattern	Grade Level			
		2	3	4	5
/o/	One pattern only	26.5	3	2	0
	Two patterns indiscriminately	51.9	51.8	28.6	12.5
	Correct written morphology	21.6	45.2	69.4	87.5
/e/	One pattern only	55	16	10	2
	Two patterns indiscriminately	45	67.5	54.6	46.7
	Correct written morphology	0	16.5	35.4	51.3
/i/	One pattern only	16	3	3	1
	Two or more patterns indiscriminately	67.5	39.7	17.5	10.8
	Four patterns; only two systematically correct	2	12	10.2	3.5
	Four patterns; only three systematically correct	10	26.8	21.3	10.8
	Correct written morphology	4.5	18.5	48	73.9

The criterion of using the same spelling in *all* stimuli would have been too strict because the children might have seen some of the words recently and reproduced these from memory. Applying this criterion to the spellings of different end sounds meant that 15 of the 16 words ending in /o/ or /e/ had to be spelled with the same ending for the children to be classified as single-pattern users; in the case of words ending in /i/, the same criterion meant that 26 of the 32 words would have to be spelled with the same ending (when only 6 words would have been spelled with any other ending). Table 13.1 presents the percentage of single-pattern users by grade and by end- sound. These percentages decreased sharply with grade level from as high as 55% of single-pattern users in Grade 2 to about only 1% or 2% by Grade 5.

The second possible pattern of spelling across words with the same sound is that the children might use more than one spelling pattern, but they do so indiscriminately. This spelling pattern would suggest that the children know that the sound has alternative representations but that they do not have a basis for choosing between these alternatives. In other words, they do not use morphological knowledge to disambiguate the alternative spellings. In order to categorize the children as users of more than one pattern while doing so indiscriminately, the criterion of 80% correct was used: The children who did not reach this level of performance were classified as not using the different endings appropriately whereas the children who reached this level of performance were classified as using written morphology adequately. The percentages of children who used two spelling patterns but did so indiscriminately for the different end sound by age level are also presented in Table 13.1.

Together, the children classified as single-letter users and indiscriminate users of two patterns for the sounds /o/ and /e/ account for 78% to 100% of the children in Grade 2 (for /o/ and /e/ sounds, respectively) and 55% to 85% of the children in Grade 3 (for /o/ and /e/ sounds, respectively). These spelling patterns are not compatible with the consistent use of written morphology by children in these grade levels.

Thus only a minority of the children in Grades 2 and 3 was able to use written morphology to represent the /o/ and /e/ sounds correctly. Although the results improve considerably in Grades 4 and 5, performance is not at ceiling level for words ending in /o/ and /e/. Table 13.1 presents the percentages of children who were classified into each of these spelling patterns by grade level.

The results for the spelling of words with /i/ end sounds are in many ways similar, although they vary in the detail of the classification because four instead of two different spellings are possible for the /i/ sound. The children were classified as (a) single-pattern users, (b) indiscriminate users of two or more patterns, (c) users of all four patterns with systematic correct use of only two, (d) users of all four patterns with systematic correct use of only three, (e) users of complete representation of morphology. The first two patterns accounted for more than 80% of the spellings in Grade 2 and almost 50% of the spellings in Grade 3. In spite of the greater complexity in correctly choosing from among the four different possible spellings, about almost 70% of the children in Grade 4 and 85% of the children in Grade 5 chose the correct spelling, indicating the use of written morphology for spelling. These results are quite consistent with those for the /o/ and /e/ end sounds, showing a marked increase in the use of written morphology only from Grade 4 onwards.

Generalization to Pseudowords

Table 13.2 presents a parallel analysis regarding the spelling patterns used across pseudoword endings for the same sounds. It can be seen that a similar developmental trend can be discerned from the data presented in Table 13.2: The number of users of a single spelling for the same sound in different word types decreases sharply after Grade 2, the number of indiscriminate users of different spellings decreases sharply after Grade 3, and only children in Grades 4 and 5 display spelling patterns that are consistent with the acquisition of written morphology. Although the overall performance is lower for pseudowords compared with that for real words, the children did vary the spellings of pseudowords according to their morphological category as determined by the position in which they appeared in the sentence. For the pseudowords ending in /o/, about 55% of children in Grade 4 and 65% children in Grade 5 showed a good discrimination of when to use "o" and when to use "ω." Although results are weaker for the discrimination between different words ending in the /e/ and /i/ sounds, there is still evidence for the use of a knowledge of written morphology in these cases.

Table 13.3 presents the mean number of correctly spelled endings by grade level, type of stimulus, and spelling condition. Because the means and standard deviations were highly

TABLE 13.2
Percentage of Children in Each Grade Level by Spelling Pattern in the Task
of Spelling Pseudowords

		Grade Level			
End Sound	Spelling Pattern	2	3	4	5
/o/	Single letter	24.3	6.5	1	2.7
	Two patterns indiscriminately	55.1	54.6	42.6	32.8
	Correct written morphology	20.6	38.9	56.4	64.5
/e/	Single letter	72	24	14	9
	Two patterns indiscriminately	27	68.5	62.2	58.3
	Correct written morphology	1	7.5	23.8	32.7
/i/	Single letter	15	2	2.5	2
	Two or more patterns indiscriminately	73	59.2	37.5	33.5
	Four patterns; only two systematically correct	5.5	9.3	10.3	9
	Four patterns; only three systematically correct	5.5	26.8	39.4	42.7
	Correct written morphology	1	2.7	10.3	12.8

TABLE 13.3
Mean Correct (and Standard Deviations) and Number of Participants for the Spelling Tasks
by Grade and Condition

| | Grade Level | | | |
Condition	2	3	4	5
Words	30.57	43.34	53.67	57.55
	(7.67)	(10.23)	(9.46)	(7.8)
	n = 51	n = 53	n = 55	n = 55
Pseudowords	32.13	44.91	48.14	49.47
	(7.72)	(10.86)	(10.15)	(9.84)
	n = 53	n = 55	n = 58	n = 55

correlated, a logarithmic transformation was applied to the scores. All analyses here are applied
to the transformed scores.

To determine whether the spelling of pseudowords was significantly inferior than the spelling
of words, a between-subjects analysis of variance was carried out with grade (four levels) and
stimulus type (word versus pseudoword) as the main terms, and number of correct spellings of
word endings as the dependent variable. Both main terms were significant but post hoc tests
showed that scores for words and pseudowords did not differ significantly in Grades 2 or 3.
Thus, in general, although the results of the analysis of spelling patterns suggest that children
do use morphology in spelling pseudowords, the older children (Grades 4 and 5) also use a
great deal of word-specific knowledge in spelling.

STUDY 2: THE CONNECTION BETWEEN GRAMMATICAL
AWARENESS AND THE ACQUISITION
OF WRITTEN MORPHOLOGY

It is now widely recognized that children's awareness of sounds is intimately related to their
ability to learn to read and spell the alphabetic writing system. Using an analogous reasoning,
Nunes, Bryant, and their colleagues have argued that children's awareness of grammar and
morphology in their oral language is causally related to the acquisition of written morphological skills. Because morphemes involve simultaneously meaning (for example, a morpheme
may indicate plurality), a fixed form (in the example, the morpheme "s"), and grammar ("s"
is used in English only for nouns), morphological awareness cannot be separated from grammatical awareness. Nunes, Bryant, and colleagues provided strong evidence for this argument
in English, but similar evidence from other languages is still unavailable.

Morphological Awareness and the Acquisition
of Written Morphological Skills

The study reported here makes some progress in showing that there is a connection between
morphological awareness and the acquisition of written morphology. Methods for assessing
morphological awareness in Greek were developed and the correlation between children's
performance in these tasks and their progress in using written morphology was analyzed.

Method

Participants

The 214 children who participated in the word-spelling task in Study 1 were administered tasks that assessed their morphological awareness.

Design

In order to investigate the connection between morphological awareness and the use of written morphology, the children were given three morphological awareness tasks and two verbal subtests (vocabulary and lexical analogies) of the Athina Test, which is a measure of children's general verbal ability (Paraskevopoulos, 1996). This measure was used to partial out the effects of verbal intelligence in regression analyses in order to test whether there is a specific connection between morphological awareness and the acquisition of written morphology.

Materials and Procedure

The spelling task was described in Study 1. For the purposes of this analysis, each ending sound was scored separately; the scoring of each spelling task was based on only the correct choice of pattern to represent the last sound for the word.

Two of the measures of morphological awareness were designed following the paradigm created by Nunes et al. (1997)—the Sentence Analogy Task and the Word Analogy Task; the third measure, which is referred to as the Productive Morphology Task, was based on the paradigm created by Berko (1958).

In the Sentence Analogy Task we provide an example to the child, in which one puppet "says" a sentence and the second one repeats it, with a change made in the tense of the verb. Then the first puppet "says" a second sentence; the child is asked to help the second puppet find the response and make the same change to the sentence. Here is an example:

First puppet:	"George helps Helen."
Second puppet:	"George helped Helen."
First puppet:	"Maria drinks her milk."
Second puppet:	(The child has to tell the examiner what the second puppet will say)

Each item was scored as 0 or 1.

We use the same paradigm in the Word Analogy Task but we apply it to words. The first puppet "says" a word, the second one says a related word, to which a specific morphological change has been applied; then the first puppet "says" another word and the child is asked to provide the response for the second puppet. Here is an example:

First puppet:	"Beauty."
Second puppet:	"Beautiful."
First puppet:	"Taste."
Second puppet:	(The child has to tell the examiner what the second puppet will say)

Each item was scored as 0 or 1.

In the Productive Morphology Task, we show the children pictures and provide them with pseudowords embedded in sentences that are related to the pictures. They are then asked to complete a sentence in which the word must be changed for the meaning to be correct. Here is an example of this task:

Examiner: "This is a lokia."
Examiner: "Now here is another lokia. Look, there are two of them. There are two . . . ?"
(Child has to complete the sentence.)

Each item was scored as 0 or 1. The tasks are presented in the appendix.

The verbal ability tasks include a vocabulary test and a lexical analogies task. The vocabulary task consists of 35 words; the child is asked to explain what each word means with the question "what does . . . mean?" or "what is a . . . ?" Each response is scored 0, 1, or 2, according to the level of the explanation. The lexical analogies task consists of 24 questions. In each question, there are two sentences; the last word in the second sentence is missing. The child is asked to supply the missing word. For example, "animals have legs, cars have . . . ?" Each item is scored as 0 or 1. The use of this task as a control in regressions is important as it assesses the child's ability to make verbal analogies that are not dependent of morphological knowledge.

Results and Conclusions

The correlations between the three spelling tasks and the three measures of morphological awareness are presented in Table 13.4. The correlations vary between moderate and high and are all significant. Because the correlations between the three spelling tasks were moderate or high, it was decided to merge the scores into a single value for use in the regression analyses.

Three fixed-order multiple regressions were carried out to test the hypothesis that there is a specific connection between children's grammatical and morphological awareness and their knowledge of written morphology. In all of the analyses, the outcome variable was the children's total score on the spelling tasks. Age and the score in the verbal ability tasks were entered at the first and second steps in the regression analyses. The final step in each regression analyses was the score in one of the measures of grammatical awareness. The results are summarized in Table 13.5.

The analyses showed that each of the measures of grammatical awareness made a significant contribution to the prediction of the scores in the use of written morphology after controlling for age and verbal ability. These results are very encouraging because they suggest that there is a specific relation between children's awareness of grammar and morphology and the acquisition of written morphology. The fact that one of the verbal ability tasks was a measure of lexical analogies makes the controls used in these regressions very stringent because not only general verbal ability was controlled for but also the ability to make verbal analogies.

Our demonstration of a strong link between the strength of Greek children's awareness of morphology and their ability to spell inflectional morphemes is consistent with earlier research,

TABLE 13.4
Correlations Between Scores in the Spelling Tasks and Grammatical Awareness Tasks ($N = 214$)

	Spelling of Final /e/	Spelling of Final /i/	Word Analogy	Sentence Analogy	Productive Morphology
Spelling of final /o/	.54	.84	.69	.71	.54
Spelling of final /e/		.56	.51	.50	.44
Spelling of final /i/			.71	.77	.57
Word analogy				.87	.67
Sentence analogy					.66

Note: All correlations are significant at the .001 level.

TABLE 13.5
Results for the Three Fixed-Order Multiple Regression Analyses With Use of Written
Morphology as the Outcome Variable

	B	SE B	Beta	r^2 change	F change[a]
Steps common to all three analyses:					
1. Age	.21	.001	.719	.518	228.07
2. Verbal ability	.13	.002	.476	.104	57.82
Third step in each of the analyses:					
3a. Sentence analogy	.601	.095	.413	.060	39.70
3b. Word analogy	.610	.157	.285	.025	15.05
3c. Productive morphology	.017	.006	.155	.014	8.04

[a] All results were significant at the .001 level.

cited above, on children learning to spell Hebrew words and English words. Educators and psychologists do need to take morphological awareness into account.

APPENDIX
WORDS AND NONWORDS USED IN THE SPELLING TASK

1. Feminine Nouns and Adjectives—Singular Nominative Ending with -η/i/

Words	Nonwords
η τσέπη [pocket]	η λάφαρη
η κατάψυξη [freezer]	η ατόση
η διαφήμιση [advertisement]	η καρμόχη
η αποθήκη [storeroom]	η δοχομπή
η άταχτη [naughty]	η ταλάκη
η ανήσυχη [worried]	η φοδρόμη
η υπέροχη [marvelous]	η νταρισή
η μαρμάρινη [marble]	η περόλη

Η τσέπη μου τρύπησε. [I've worn a hole in my pocket.]
Η κατάψυζη του ψυγείου μας χάλασε. [Our freezer was broken.]
Μου άρεσε η διαφήμιση για τα παιχνίδια. [I liked the advertisement for toys.]
Η αποθήκη μας θέλει καθάρισμα. [Our storeroom has to be cleaned.]
Η Μαρία ήταν άταχτη στο σχολείο. [Maria was naughty at school.]
Η μητέρα ήταν ανήσυχη. [The mother was worried.]
Η μακαρονάδα της μητέρας μου ήταν υπέροχη. [My mother's pasta was marvelous.]
Υ πάρχει μια μαρμάρινη σκάλα στο σπίτι της γιαγιάς μου. [There is a marble staircase in my grandmother's house.]

2. Neuter Nouns—Singular Nominative Ending with -ι /i/

Words	Nonwords
το βαγόνι [wagon (railway)]	το τσαλόπι
το ατσάλι [steel]	το αγκόφι
το ραβδί [stick]	το λοκρί
το μονοπάτι [path]	το μαλοφούρι

το πηγούνι [chin]   το λοσί
το χωνί [funnel]   το πεφάρι
το χαντάκι [ditch]   το φεκότι
το σανίδι [floorboard]   το ραχάκι

Το βαγόνι μας ήταν το νούμερο 25. [Our wagon was number 25.]
Το ατσάλι είναι ένα σκληρό μέταλλο. [Steel is a very hard metal.]
Το ραβδί της μάγισσας έσπασε. [The witch's stick was broken.]
Αντό το μονοπάτι είναι επικίνδυνο. [that path is dangerous.]
Το πηγούνι του Πέτρου ήταν βρώμικο. [Petros's chin was dirty.]
Το χωνί ήταν πολύ μεγάλο. [The funnel was very big.]
Το χαντάκι ήταν πολύ βαθύ. [The ditch was very deep.]
Το σανίδι έσπασε. [This floorboard is broken.]

3. Masculine Nouns and Adjectives—Plural, Nominative Ending with -οι/i/

Words	**Nonwords**
οι λοστρόμοι [boatswain]	οι κρομάλοι
οι άγουροι [unripe]	οι κάχουροι
οι επικίνδυνοι [dangerous]	οι ελέχυτοι
οι διάδρομοι [corridors]	οι λόροι
οι κόποι [hard work]	οι φερισοί
οι θερινοί [summery]	οι αστόλεροι
οι τολμηροί [daring]	οι λαρινοί
οι μύθοι [myths]	οι μάποι

Οι λοστρόμοι είναι πολύ χρήσιμοι. [The boatswains do a good job.]
Οι άγουροι ανανάδες δεν είναι νόστιμοι. [Unripe pineapples are not tasty.]
Οι επικίνδυνοι ληστές φόβισαν τη γειτονιά μας. [People in our neighborhood are afraid of the dangerous thieves.]
Οι διάδρομοι του ξενοδοχείου ήταν πολύ μεγάλοι. [The corridors in the hotel were very long.]
Οι κόποι της Μαρίας ανταμείφθηκαν. [Maria's hard work was rewarded.]
Όλοι οι θερινοί κινηματογράφοι έκλεισαν. [All the open-air cinemas closed down.]
Οι τολμηροί πειρατές ανέβηκαν στο πλοίο. [The daring pirates got on the boat.]
Οι μύθοι του Αισώπου μου αρέσουν πολύ. [I like Aesop's myths very much.]

4. Verbs—Active Voice, Third-Person-Singular Ending with -ει/i/

Words	**Nonwords**
λερώνει [dirty]	κεσώνει
αντέχει [stand up]	αμπέρει
θερίζει [reap]	πεσάφει
αστράφτει [alight]	λορίζει
παριστάνει [take off]	σταλένει
διορθώνει [correct]	βαρίζει
τακτοποιεί [tidy up]	σαδώνει
πατνεύει [praise]	ράιτει

NUNES, AIDINIS, BRYANT

Ο Σάκης <u>λερώνει</u> εύκολα τα ρούχα του. [Sakis often <u>dirties</u> his clothes.]
Η αρκούδα <u>αντέχει</u> στο κρύο. [The bear <u>stands up</u> to the cold weather.]
Ο αγρότης <u>θερίζει</u> το χωράφι του. [The farmer <u>reaps</u> his land.]
Φοβάμαι όταν <u>αστράφτει.</u> [I am afraid whenever I <u>set it alight.</u>]
Ο Γιώργος <u>παριστάνει</u> το δάσκαλο. [Giorgos <u>pretends to be</u> the teacher.]
Ο δάσκαλος <u>διορθώνει</u> τα διαγωνίσματα. [The teacher <u>corrects</u> our papers.]
Η μητέρα <u>τακτοποιεί</u> το σπίτι. [The mother <u>tidies up</u> the house.]
Ο δάσκαλος <u>παινεύει</u> τους καλούς μαθητές. [The teacher <u>praises</u> the good students.]

5. Neuter Nouns—Singular Nominative Ending with -o/o/

Words	Nonwords
το φουγάρο [chimney]	το μέλτο
το ελατήριο [spring]	το χάμαρο
το πόμολο [door handle]	το ρασητό
το βουητό [hum]	το βάκαλο
το μεροκάματο [a day's work]	το πεσαρείο
το περιοδικό [magazine]	το κόροσο
το δοχείο [vessel]	το σαλιβό
το μαντείο [oracle]	το φήριο

<u>Το φουγάρο</u> του εργοστασίου φαίνεται από το σπίτι μου. [I can see the factory's <u>chimney</u> from my house.]
<u>Το ελατήριο</u> του ρολογιού μου χάλασε. [<u>The spring</u> of my watch broke down.]
<u>Το πόμολο</u> της πόρτας είναι επίχρυσο. [<u>The door handle</u> is golden.]
<u>Το βουητό</u> από την τηλεόραση με ενοχλούσε. [<u>The hum</u> from the television was annoying.]
Ο πατέρας λέει ότι <u>το μεροκάματο</u> δεν φτάνει. [The father says that <u>a day's work</u> is not enough.]
Α υτό <u>το περιοδικό</u> βγαίνει κάθε εβδομάδα. [That <u>magazine</u> comes out every week.]
<u>Το δοχείο</u> ήταν γεμάτο με λάδι. [<u>The vessel</u> was full of oil.]
Τα παιδιά παίζουν <u>το μαντείο</u>. [Children play the <u>oracle</u>.]

6. Verbs—Active Voice, First-Person-Singular Ending with -ω /o/

Words	Nonwords
ψηλώνω [grow taller]	μοτάνω
διασχίζω [cross]	καροδείλω
κυκλοφορώ [walk]	ραπαδώνω
ξεριζώνω [uproot]	φαραστίζω
κλειδώνω [lock]	μορόπτω
οφείλω [owe]	καπαροδώ
ζεσταίνω [warm]	μαφρώνω
προτείνω [suggest]	αδαλώ

Κάθε χρόνο <u>ψηλώνω</u> όλο και περισσότερο. [Every year <u>I grow up</u> a bit.]
Για να πάω στο σχολείο <u>διασχίζω</u> ένα μεγάλο δρόμο. [On my way to school I <u>cross</u> a big road.]
Συνήθως δεν <u>κυκλοφορώ</u> το βράδυ. [I usually do not <u>walk</u> in the streets at night.]
Εγώ <u>ξεριζώνω</u> τα χόρτα του κήπου μας. [I <u>uproot</u> the greens of our garden.]

Όταν φεύγω από το σπίτι, <u>κλειδώνω</u> το συρτάρι μου. [When I leave home, I <u>lock</u> my drawer.]

<u>Οφείλω</u> 100 δραχμές στην αδερφή μου. [I <u>owe</u> 100 drachmas to my sister.]

<u>Ζεσταίνω</u> τα χέρια μου στη σόμπα. [I <u>warm</u> my hands at the stove.]

<u>Προτείνω</u> να πάμε στο γήπεδο είπε ο Κώστας. [<u>Let's</u> (<u>I suggest to</u>) go to the football ground, Kostas said.]

7. Verbs—Active Voice, First-Person-Plural Ending with -ε /ε/

Words	**Nonwords**
φορτώνουμε [load]	αμετώνουμε
αραιώνουμε [water down]	οφαρούμε
νοικιάζουμε [rent]	καλειδίζουμε
σπρώχνουμε [push]	ποχτάρουμε
καταστρέφουμε [destroy]	σακαρίζουμε
πουλάμε [sell]	λαμορούμε
ανυπομονούμε [look forward to]	χοκαρώνουμε
αφιερώνουμε [dedicate]	καμποσάφουμε

Εμείς <u>φορτώνουμε</u> τα μήλα στο αυτοκίνητο. [We <u>load</u> the apples on the truck.]

Τον συμπυκνωμένο χυμό τον <u>αραιώνουμε</u> με νερό. [We <u>watered down</u> the concentrated juice.]

Εμείς <u>νοικιάζουμε</u> ένα διαμέρισμα. [We <u>rent</u> a flat.]

Κάθε πρωί <u>σπρώχνουμε</u> το αυτοκίνητο για να ξεκινήσει. [Every morning we <u>push</u> our car in order to start it.]

Το παιχνίδι στον κήπο δεν επιτρέπεται γιατί <u>καταστρέφουμε</u> τα λουλούδια της μαμάς. [We are not allowed to play in the garden because we <u>destroy</u> mother's plants.]

Στο μαγαζί μας <u>πουλάμε</u> χαλιά. [In our store we <u>sell</u> carpets.]

<u>Ανυπομονούμε</u> να έρθουν οι διακοπές. [We <u>look forward</u> to the holidays (to come).]

<u>Αφιερώνουμε</u> τη νίκη μας στο σχολείο μας, είπαν τα παιδιά. [<u>We dedicate</u> our victory to our school, the children said.]

8. Verbs—Passive Voice, Third-Person-Singular Ending with -αι /ε/

Words	**Nonwords**
κρέμεται [hang]	δροκάλεται
κατάγεται [come from]	κοσαρέχεται
παραδέχεται [admit]	ρελάται
καίγεται [burned]	ογάνεται
ταλαιπωρείται [have trouble]	βουκαλείται
φωτίζεται [lighten]	λαγατίζεται
μεταδίδεται [spread]	καλαπίδεται
ονειρεύεται [dream]	τοδέμεται

Το ρολόι <u>κρέμεται</u> στον τοίχο. [The clock <u>is hanging</u> on the wall.]

Ο δάσκαλός μας <u>κατάγεται</u> από την Μακεδονία. [Our teacher <u>comes from</u> Macedonia.]

Ο Γιώργος <u>παραδέχεται</u> πως έκανε λάθος. [Giorgos <u>admits</u> he has made a mistake.]

Το σπίτι του Γιάννη <u>καίγεται</u>. [Giannis's house <u>is burning.</u>]

Ο πατέρας μου <u>ταλαιπωρείται</u> κάθε μέρα με τη συγκοινωνία. [My father <u>has troubles</u> every day with the transport.]

Το δωμάτιο <u>φωτίζεται</u> με μία λάμπα. [The room <u>is lit</u> by one lamp.]
Η ανεμοβλογιά <u>μεταδίδεται</u> εύκολα. [Chicken pox <u>spreads</u> easily.]
Ο Πέτρος <u>ονειρεύεται</u> να γίνει γιατρός. [Petros <u>is dreaming</u> of becoming a doctor.]

THE THREE MORPHOLOGICAL AWARENESS TASKS

A. Word Analogy Task

Practice trials:

1. βάφω, βάψιμο [paint, painting]
   γράφω, γράψιμο [write, writing]
2. δένω, έδεσα [tie, tied]
   τρέχω, έτρεξα [run, ran]
3. χαρούμενος, χαρά [happy, happiness]
   χαμογελαστός, χαμόγελο [smiling, smile]

όμορφη, ομορφιά [beautiful (she), beauty]
νόστιμη, νοστιμιά [tasty (she), taste]
λύνω, έλυσα [untie, untied]
βάφω, έβαψα [paint, painted]
λέω, είπα [say, said]
κατεβαίνω, κατέβηκα [come down, went down]
κοιτάζω, κοίταγμα [look, look, glance]
τσακίζω, τσάκισμα [shatter, shattering]
μαγειρεύω, μάγειρας [cook, cook]
ράβω, ράφτης [stitch, tailor]
κάνω, έκανα [do, done]
έρχομαι, ήρθα [come, came]
μαγεύω, μαγεμένος [bewitch, bewitched]
κουρδίζω, κουρδισμένος [wind (up), winded (up)]
νίκησε, νικητής [won, winner]
ζήλεψε, ζηλιάρης [envied, envious]
ακούω, ακούγομαι [hear, be heard]
κρατώ, κρατιέμαι [hold, be held]
τολμηροί, τόλμη [mettlesome (they), mettle]
ήσυχοι, ησυχία [quiet (they), quiet]
διαβάζω, διαβάζει [read, reads]
θέλω, θέλει [want, wants]
ταξιδεύω, ταξίδι [travel, travel]
κλειδώνω, κλειδί [lock, key]
πειράζω, πειράζετε [tease (I), tease (you plural)]
ρωτώ, ρωτάτε [ask (I), ask (you plural)]
αδικία, άδικος [injustice, unjust]
κακία, κακός [wickedness, wicked]
συχνά, συχνάζω [frequently, go somewhere frequently]
αντίκρυ, αντικρίζω [facing (adv.), face]
γιατρός, γιάτρεψε [doctor, cured]
χτίστης, έχτισε [builder, built]

B. Sentence Analogy Task

Practice trials:

1. Η γάτα τρώει ψάρια. [The cat eats fish.]
   Η γάτα έφαγε ψάρια. [The cat ate fish.]
   Ο Γιώργος σκάβει τον κήπο. [Giorgos hoes the garden.]
   Ο Γιώργος έσκαψε τον κήπο. [Giorgos hoed the garden.]
2. Εγώ πλένω το αυτοκίνητο. [I wash the car.]
   Εγώ θα πλύνω το αυτοκίνητο. [I will wash the car.]
   Εγώ διαβάζω εφημερίδα. [I read the newspaper.]
   Εγώ θα διαβάσω εφημερίδα. [I will read the newspaper.]

Ο Γιώργος <u>βοηθά</u> την Ελένη. [George <u>helps</u> Helen.]
Ο Γιώργος <u>βόηθησε</u> την Ελένη. [George <u>helped</u> Helen.]
Η Μαρία <u>πίνει</u> το γάλα της. [Maria <u>drinks</u> her milk.]
Η Μαρία <u>ήπιε</u> το γάλα της. [Maria <u>drank</u> her milk.]
Ο Μάριος <u>μίλησε</u> με το δάσκαλο. [Marios <u>talked</u> to the teacher.]
Ο Μάριος <u>μιλάει</u> με το δάσκαλο. [Marios <u>talks</u> to the teacher.]
Η Κατερίνα <u>άπλωσε</u> τα ρούχα. [Katerina <u>hung out</u> the washing.]
Η Κατερίνα <u>απλώνει</u> τα ρούχα. [Katerina <u>hangs out</u> the washing.]
Ο Νίκος <u>παίζει</u> μπάλα. [Nikos <u>plays</u> football.]
Ο Νίκος <u>θα παίξει</u> μπάλα. [Nikos <u>will play</u> football.]
Η γιαγιά <u>ράβει</u> μια μπλούζα. [The grandmother <u>stitches</u> a blouse.]
Η γιαγιά <u>θα ράψει</u> μια μπλούζα. [The grandmother <u>will stitch</u> a blouse.]
Ο πατέρας <u>βάφει</u> το δωμάτιο. [The father <u>paints</u> the room.]
Ο πατέρας <u>έβαψε</u> το δωμάτιο. [The father <u>painted</u> the room.]
Εγώ <u>θέλω</u> νερό. [I <u>want</u> water.]
Εγώ <u>ήθελα</u> νερό. [I <u>wanted</u> water.]
Το παιδί <u>έγραψε</u> ορθογραφία. [The child <u>wrote</u> his spellings.]
Το παιδί <u>γράφει</u> ορθογραφία. [The child <u>writes</u> his spellings.]
Εγώ <u>ήξερα</u> το δρόμο. [I <u>knew</u> the road.]
Εγώ <u>ξέρω</u> το δρόμο. [I <u>know</u> the road.]
Εσύ <u>θυμάσαι</u> το καλοκαίρι. [You <u>remember</u> the summer.]
Εσύ <u>θυμήθηκες</u> το καλοκαίρι. [You <u>remembered</u> the summer.]
Εσύ <u>σηκώνεσαι</u> στις 7. [You <u>wake up</u> at 7.]
Εσύ <u>σηκώθηκες</u> στις 7. [You <u>woke up</u> at 7.]
Εμείς <u>κοιμηθήκαμε</u> νωρίς. [We <u>went to sleep</u> early.]
Εμείς <u>κοιμόμαστε</u> νωρίς. [We <u>go to sleep</u> early.]
Εμείς <u>χαρήκαμε</u> πολύ. [We <u>were</u> very <u>happy</u>.]
Εμείς <u>χαιρόμαστε</u> πολύ. [We <u>are</u> very <u>happy</u>.]
Αυτοί <u>θα ζωγραφίσουν</u> ένα σπίτι. [They <u>will draw</u> a house.]
Αυτοί <u>ζωγραφίζουν</u> ένα σπίτι. [They <u>draw</u> a house.]
Οι γείτονές μας <u>θα ψήσουν</u> σουβλάκια. [Our neighbors <u>will grill</u> souvlakia.]
Οι γείτονές μας <u>ψήνουν</u> σουβλάκια. [Our neighbors <u>grill</u> souvlakia.]
Η μαμά <u>κρύβει</u> το γλυκό. [The mother <u>hides</u> the jam.]
Η μαμά <u>θα κρύψει</u> το γλυκό. [The mother <u>will hide</u> the jam.]
Ο Χρήστος <u>απαντά</u> τις ερωτήσεις. [Christos <u>answers</u> the questions.]
Ο Χρήστος <u>θα απαντήσει</u> τις ερωτήσεις. [Christos <u>will answer</u> the questions.]
Εμείς <u>θα ακούσουμε</u> το τραγούδι. [We <u>will listen</u> to the song.]
Εμείς <u>ακούμε</u> το τραγούδι. [We <u>listen</u> to the song.]

Εμείς <u>θα δούμε</u> τηλεόραση. [We <u>will watch</u> television.]

Εμείς <u>βλέπουμε</u> τηλεόραση. [We <u>watch</u> television.]

Κάθε πρωί <u>πλένω</u> το πρόσωπό μου. [Every morning I <u>wash</u> my face.]

Κάθε πρωί <u>πλένομαι</u>. (passive voice) [Every morning I <u>wash</u> my face.]

Εγώ <u>χτενίζω</u> τα μαλλιά μου. [I <u>brush</u> my hair.]

Εγώ <u>χτενίζομαι</u>. (passive voice) [I <u>brush</u> my hair.]

Ο γεωργός <u>οργώνει</u> το χωράφι. [The farmer <u>ploughs</u> the field.]

Το χωράφι <u>οργώνεται</u> από τον γεωργό. [The field <u>is ploughed</u> by the farmer.]

Ο αέρας <u>ξεριζώνει</u> το δέντρο. [The wind <u>uproots</u> the tree.]

Το δέντρο <u>ξεριζώνεται</u> από τον αέρα. [The tree <u>is uprooted</u> by the wind.]

Ο Κώστας <u>ξυρίζεται</u>. [Kostas <u>shaves</u> himself.]

Ο Κώστας <u>ξυρίζει</u> τα γένια του. [Kostas <u>shaves</u> his beard.]

Η Μαρία <u>λούζεται</u>. [Maria <u>gives herself a shampoo</u>.]

Η Μαρία <u>λούζει</u> τα μαλλιά της. [Maria <u>shampoos</u> her hair.]

Το σπίτι <u>γκρεμίζεται</u> από τον εργάτη. [The house <u>is demolished</u> by the worker.]

Ο εργάτης <u>γκρεμίζει</u> το σπίτι. [The worker <u>demolishes</u> the house.]

Το τραπέζι <u>ετοιμάζεται</u> από τη μητέρα. [The dinner <u>is prepared</u> by the mother.]

Η μητέρα <u>ετοιμάζει</u> το τραπέζι. [The mother <u>prepares</u> the dinner.]

C. Productive Morphology Task

I. Singular–Plural

1. Αυτή είναι μία λοκία. Τώρα υπάρχει ακόμα μία λοκία. Κοίτα υπάρχους δύο. Είναι δύο. (λοκίες) [This is a lokia. Now there is another lokia. Look, there are two of them. There are two *lokies*.]

2. Αυτό είναι ένα καφάτο. Τώρα υπάρχει ακόμα ένα καφάτο. Κοίτα υπάρχουν δύο. Είναι δύο ———. (καφάτα) [This is a kafato. Now there is another kafato. Look, there are two of them. There are two *kafata*.]

3. Αυτός είναι ένας αχόνος. Τώρα υπάρχει ακόμα ένας αχόνος. Κοίτα υπάρχουν δύο. Είναι δύο ———. (αχόνοι) [This is an achonos. Now there is another achonos. Look, there are two of them. There are two *achoni*.]

4. Αυτό είναι ένα λιράφι. Τώρα υπάρχει ακόμα ένα λιράφι. Κοίτα υπάρχουν δύο. Είναι δύο ———. (λιράφια) [This is a lirafi. Now there is another lirafi. Look, there are two of them. There are two *lirafia*.]

II. Present–Past

1. Αυτός είναι ένας κύριος που ξέρει να χαδώνει. Τώρα χαδώνει. Εχθές έκανε το ίδιο πράγμα. Τι έκανε λοιπόν εχθές; Εχθές ———. (χάδωσε) [This is a man who knows how to chadoni. Now he chadoni. He did the same thing yesterday. What did he do yesterday? Yesterday he *chadose*.]

2. Αυτός είναι ένας κύριος που ξέρει να μανίζει. Τώρα μανίζει. Εχθές έκανε το ίδιο πράγμα. Τι έκανε λοιπόν εχθές; Εχθές ———. (μάνισε) [This is a man who knows how to manizi. Now he manizi. He did the same thing yesterday. What did he do yesterday? Yesterday he *manise*.]

3. Αυτή είναι μία κυρία που ξέρει να αρωνά. Τώρα αρωνά. Εχθές έκανε το ίδιο πράγμα. Τι έκανε λοιπόν εχθές; Εχθές ———. (αρώνησε) [This is a lady who knows how to arona. Now she arona. She did the same thing yesterday. What did she do yesterday? Yesterday she *aronise*.]

III. Present–Future

1. Αυτός είναι ένας κύριος που ξέρει να καρώνει. Τώρα καρώνει. Αύριο θα κάνει το ίδιο πράγμα. Τι θα κάνει λοιπόν αύριο; Αύριο ———. (θα καρώσει) [This is a man who knows how to karoni. Now he karoni. He will do the same thing tomorrow. What will he do tomorrow? Tomorrow he *will karosi.*]

2. Αυτός είναι ένας κύριος που ξέρει να ντραβίζει. Τώρα ντραβίζει. Αύριο θα κάνει το ίδιο πράγμα. Τι θα κάνει λοιπόν αύριο; Αύριο ———. (θα ντραβίσει) [This is a man who knows how to dravizi. Now he dravizi. He will do the same thing tomorrow. What will he do tomorrow? Tomorrow he *will dravizi.*]

3. Αυτή είναι μία κυρία που ξέρει να λαναρεί. Τώρα λαναρεί. Αύριο θα κάνει το ίδιο πράγμα. Τι θα κάνει λοιπόν αύριο; Αύριο ———. (θα λαναρήσει) [This is a lady who knows how to lanari. Now she lanari. She will do the same thing tomorrow. What will she do tomorrow? Tomorrow she *will lanari.*]

IV. Third person singular–Third person plural

1. Αυτή είναι μια κυρία που ξέρει να πακεύει. Τώρα κάνει το ίδιο μαζί με ένα φίλο της. Τι κάνουν τώρα και οι δύο; Και οι δύο ———. (πακεύουν) [This a lady who knows how to pakevi. Now she is doing the same thing with her friend. What are they both doing? They *pakevoun.*]

2. Αυτή είναι μια κυρία που ξέρει να καλαίνει. Τώρα κάνει το ίδιο μαζί με μια φίλη της. Τι κάνουν τώρα και οι δύο; Και οι δύο ———. (καλαίνουν) [This a lady who knows how to kaleni. Now she is doing the same thing with her friend. What are they both doing? They *kalenoun.*]

3. Αυτή είναι μια κυρία που ξέρει να φαραχεί. Τώρα κάνει το ίδιο μαζί με μια φίλη της. Τι κάνουν τώρα και οι δύο; Και οι δύο ———. (φαραχούν) [This a lady who knows how to farachi. Now she is doing the same thing with her friend. What are they both doing? They *farachoun.*]

V. Possessive (singular and plural)

1. Αυτή είναι η βοκούρα που έχει μία ομπρέλα. Ποιανής είναι η ομπρέλα; Η ομπρέλαείναι———. (της βοκούρας) [This is a vokoura who owns an umbrella. Whose umbrella is it? The umbrella is *vokoura's.*]

2. Αυτός είναι ο αρούφος που έχει ένα σάντουιτς. Ποιανού είναι το σάντουιτς; Το σάντουιτς είναι———. (του αρούφου) [This is an aroufo who owns a sandwich. Whose sandwich is it? The sandwich is *aroufo's*]

3. Αυτός είναι ο παχατής που έχει ένα καπέλο. Ποιανού είναι το καπέλο; Το καπέλο είναι ———. (του παχατή) Τώρα είναι δύο παχατές. Και οι δύο έχουν καπέλα. Ποιανών είναι τα καπέλα; Τα καπέλα είναι ———. (των παχατών) [This is a pachatis who owns a hat. Whose hat is it? The hat is *pachatis'*. Now there are two pachates. They both own hats. Whose hats are they? The hats are *pachatises'*.]

VI. Derived agentives

1. Αυτή είναι μια κυρία που ξέρει να λοκίζει. Πώς θα έλεγες κάποια που η δουλειά της είναι να λοκίζει; ———. (λοκίστρια) [This is a lady who knows how to lokizi. What would you call a lady whose job is to lokizi? *Lokistria.*]

2. Αυτός είναι ένας κύριος που ξέρει να καλάβει. Πως θα έλεγες κάποιον που δουλειάτου είναι να καλάβει; ———. (καλάφτης) [This is a man who knows how to kalavi. What would you call a man whose job is to kalavi? *Kalaftis*.]

3. Αυτός είναι ένας κύριος που ξέρει να χαρώνει. Πως θα έλεγες κάποιον που δουλειά του είναι να χαρώνει; ———. (χαρωτής) [This is a man who knows how to charoni. What would you call a man whose job is to charoni? *Charotis*.]

4. Αυτός είναι ένας κύριος που ξέρει να φαλίζει. Πως θα έλεγες κάποιον που δουλειά του είναι να φαλίζει; ———. (φαλιστής) [This is a man who knows how to falizi. What would you call a man whose job is to falizi? *Falistis*.]

REFERENCES

Aidinis, A. (1998). *Phonemes, morphemes and literacy development: Evidence from Greek.* Unpublished PhD Thesis, University of London, London.

Berko, J. (1958). The child's learning of English morphology. *Word. 14*, 150–177.

Brissaud, C., & Bessonnat, D. (2001). *L'orthographe au collège. Pour une autre approche.* Genoble: CDRP de l'académie de Grenoble.

Brissaud, C., & Sandon, J.-M. (1999). "L'acquisition des finales homophones en /E/ à l'école élémentaire et au collège, entre phonographie et morphographie", *Langue française, 124*, 40–57.

Bryant, P. (2002). Children's thoughts about reading and spelling. *Scientific Studies of Reading, 6*, 199–216.

Fayol, M., Thevenin, M. G., Jarrousse, J. P., & Totereau, C. (1999). From learning to teaching to learning French written morphology. In T. Nunes (Ed), *Learning to Read: An Integrated View from Research and Practice* (pp. 43–64). Dordrecht: Kluwer.

Lefrançois. P. (2002). Les stratégies de résolution de problèmes orthographiques des étudiants universitaires. Paper presented at the Genoble, November.

Levin, I., Ravid, D., & Rapaport, S. (1999). Developing morphological awareness and learning to write: A two-way street. In T. Nunes (Ed.), *Learning to Read: An Integrated View from Research and Practice* (pp. 77–104). Dordrecht: Kluwer.

Nunes, T., Bryant, P., & Bindman, M. (1997). Morphological spelling strategies: developmental stages and processes. *Developmental Psychology, 33*, 637–649.

Nunes, T., Bryant, P., & Olsson, J. (2003). Learning morphological and phonological spelling rules: an intervention study. *Reading and Writing, 7*, 289–307.

Nunes, T., & Bryant, P. (2004). Morphological awareness improves spelling and vocabulary. *Literacy Today, 38*, 18–19.

Paraskevopoulos, I. N. (1996). Αθηνά Τεστ Δυσκολιών Μάθησης (Athina test for learning disabilities). Αθήνα: Ελληνικά Γράμματα (Athens: Ellinika Grammata).

Rosa, J. (2002). The acquisition of written morphology in Portuguese. Paper presented at the annual Developmental Conference of the British Psychological Society (Developmental Section), University of Sussex. September, 2002.

14

How Language Characteristics Influence Turkish Literacy Development

Aydın Yücesan Durgunoğlu
University of Minnesota, Duluth

Languages around the world vary greatly in their structure as well as in how they represent the spoken language in their written form. Commonalities and differences in literacy development across the languages can help us distinguish between universal and language-specific aspects of this vital cognitive process. In this chapter, I focus on the properties of oral and written Turkish and how these properties affect literacy development of children as well as that of adults. Turkish, a member of the Altaic language family, is quite different from the Indo-European languages that have been studied most frequently in literacy research. It can therefore provide us with a different window to literacy development.

STRUCTURE

Morphology

Turkish, like Finnish, is an agglutinative language with many iterative loops that can technically produce words of infinite length. In the following example of an iterative loop, notice how many times the plural suffix *ler/lar* is used: The word *tabak* [plate] can be made plural, *tabaklar* [plates], by the addition of the suffix *-lar*. This can be transformed into another noun, *tabaklardaki* [that present on those plates], and finally pluralized again *tabaklardakiler* [those present on those plates]. To add another layer of complexity, morphemes can change form as a function of vowel harmony. In the previous example, one of the two different forms of the plural suffix *ler/lar* was used depending on the nature of the preceding vowel. This is discussed in more detail in the next section on phonology.

Although iterative loops can be a challenge, Turkish morphemes have a certain order of attachment, such as verb-tense suffix preceding the person suffix. Hence what is also needed is knowledge on the probabilistic information of when and how a suffix can be used especially in iterative contexts. Of course, as the words get more and more inflected, the number of possible suffixes that can be attached to that structure is reduced considerably.

For languages with complex morphological structures, Hankamer (1992) suggested a left-to-right parsing mechanism. According to that model, the root is searched in the lexicon, which presumably also includes information on its grammatical category (see lexicofunctional grammars). The grammatical category then determines the suffixes that can follow. At every step, the possible choice of suffixes is narrowed down.

There is some evidence that left-to-right word parsing can exist even in morphologically simpler languages. For example, Hudson and Buijs (1995) found that, in Dutch, pseudoprefixed words were recognized more slowly than were prefixed words, but pseudosuffixed words were not different from real-suffixed words. These pattern differences have led the authors to suggest that the nature of processing may be different for prefixed versus suffixed words, and affix stripping may be valid for prefixes, but a left-to-right processing may be more likely for suffixes. In languages like Turkish that have only suffixes, left-to-right processing may be the only alternative.

When it comes to word order, Turkish is a left-branching language (Kornfilt, 1990); governed elements precede their governors, objects precede verbs, postpositional objects precede the postposition (*ev* [house], *eve* [to the house]), and adjective modifiers precede the modified head (*mavi ev* [blue house]). The typical word order of Turkish is subject–object–verb. However, word order is relatively flexible because, unlike in English, in Turkish, instead of the location of the words, the inflections signal the word functions such as subject or object. In the following example, *aslan* is "lion" and *adam* is "man": *Aslan adamı ısırdı* and *Aslanı adam ısırdı* mean "The lion bit the man" and "The man bit the lion," respectively. In both sentences the subject is unmarked whereas the object takes the case marker. This implies, of course, that both listeners and readers have to attend to the word endings very carefully to understand the intended meaning.

Another reason for paying special attention to word endings is that Turkish, like Spanish, is a subject-drop language. The pronoun can be dropped from the sentence because the verb inflection carries the person information. For example, *Ben gittim* [I went] can be expressed as only *gittim*, dropping the pronoun *ben* [I] because the verb *gittim* has the following parts: *git* [go], *-ti* (past tense), and *-m* (first-person singular). That can be compared with *gittik* [we went] with a different person marking.

The flexible word order of Turkish also necessitates paying close attention to how the words are strung together because the word closer to the verb is the topic of emphasis (Erguvanlı-Taylan, 1987). In these two sentences *Ali İzmir'e gitti* [Ali to İzmir went] versus *İzmir'e Ali gitti* [to İzmir Ali went], different concepts are emphasized. The first sentence highlights the location: It was İzmir (not another city) to which Ali traveled. The second sentence, on the other hand, highlights the person: It was Ali (not another individual) who traveled to İzmir. Hence flexible word order may place a greater burden on memory compared with fixed-order languages, because remembering the exact order of words is quite important in comprehension as the intended emphasis depends on the location of the words in relation to the verb.

One of the structures of language that is acquired by children relatively late in Turkish, compared with English, is relative clauses (Aksu-Koç & Slobin, 1986). Relative clauses require embedding two simple sentences. For example, the two sentences "The child read the book" and "The child did not like the movie" can be expressed more eloquently when one sentence is embedded as a clause within the other: "The child who read the book did not like the movie." In Turkish, the creation of the same structure is made more difficult because of two factors: First, the verb in the clause needs to be nominalized in Turkish sentences. Second, there are no markers—such as who, that, which—highlighting the beginning of the clause. The two sentences *Cocuk kitabı okudu* [Child the-book read] and *Cocuk filmi beğenmedi* [Child the-movie like-not-past-tense suffix] are combined as *Kitabı okuyan çocuk filmi beğenmedi* [The-book reading child the-movie like-not-past-tense suffix]. Once the verb is nominalized, it takes the inflections of nouns rather than verbs.

Phonology and Orthography

Turkish has 8 vowels and 20 consonants[1] as will be subsequently discussed. The language reform in 1928 replaced the Arabic script with the Latin script and implemented a very systematic, transparent writing system to represent this phonological structure. There is an invariant one-to-one mapping between phonemes and their spellings, making both decoding and spelling relatively easy.

One important characteristic of Turkish phonology is vowel harmony. Turkish has an eight-vowel system (a, e, i, ı, o, ö, u, ü) in which all possible combinations of the distinctive features, front–back, high–low, and rounded–unrounded, are observed (Kornfilt, 1990).

	− back		+ back	
	− round	+ round	− round	+ round
+ high	i	ü	ı (undotted)	u
− high	e	ö	a	o

Vowel harmony is a left-to-right process operating sequentially along syllables. Any of the eight vowels may appear in the first syllable of a word, but each following vowel is conditioned by the vowel immediately preceding it (Underhill, 1976). Thus the following vowel assimilates to the preceding vowel in backness and rounding. Although there are many exceptions to the vowel harmony rule, most exceptions occur in borrowed words. However, even if a second vowel does not harmonize with the previous one, usually because it is a borrowed word, the second vowel creates its own harmony domain and the following third vowel matches the second one. For example, *kitap* [book], a word without vowel harmony, will have -*lar* rather than -*ler* as the plural suffix, thus matching the second vowel.

Vowel harmony becomes a very important feature in word formation when Turkish morphology is considered. As discussed before, Turkish is an agglutinating language with suffixes marking voice, aspect, modality, mood, person, and number in nouns and derivation, negation, tense, person, and so forth, in verbs. As a result of vowel harmony, Turkish suffixes have an extremely variable nature. For example, the nominal and participle suffix -dik (indicating past-tense first-person plural) has 16 different surface forms (Underhill, 1976). Variation in suffixes is very common and may result in vowel dropping in the suffix. For example, the suffix meaning "my" has the form-*im* in ev*im* (meaning "my house"), but -*m* in anne*m* (meaning "my mother").

There are 20 consonants in the language. With the exception of borrowed words, there are no consonant clusters in the beginning of words. In fact, when these borrowed words are pronounced, and sometimes even when they are written, the cluster is broken with a vowel, as in the case of *tren* [train], pronounced as /tiren/. However, consonant clusters such as -ft, -nt, and -rk are allowed at the ends of syllables, for example, *çift-lik* [farm], *kent* [city], and *Türk-çe* (Turkish language).

Syllables are the salient unit of articulation, and they determine the boundaries within words, sometimes even overriding morphemic boundaries. Turkish has fewer syllable types than English, with 98% of all Turkish syllables belonging to one of the four simple syllable forms (V, VC, CV, and CVC). The most frequent syllable form, by far, is the CV, as over

---

[1] There are 20 consonants, but 21 letters. The "silent g," written as "ğ," lengthens the preceding vowel, but it is not a phoneme by itself.

50% of all Turkish syllables have that form. This makes Turkish words very easy to break into syllables, and therefore Turkish may lend itself more readily than English to an awareness of syllables. Because the common syllable types do not include consonant clusters (with the exception of CVCC previously discussed), phonemes within the syllable are also expected to be easier to identify than in English.

EFFECTS OF THESE CHARACTERISTICS ON LITERACY DEVELOPMENT

The characteristics of morphology, phonology, and orthography already discussed facilitate the development of phonological awareness and decoding. However, some linguistic characteristics such as very long and highly inflected words, embedded clauses, and flexible word order can contribute to difficulties in comprehension.

Phonological Awareness

Being a speaker of Turkish requires constant monitoring and manipulation of subword linguistic units. In fact, even young children do this very well, as evidenced by the lack of vowel harmony violation errors in their speech. The critical characteristics of Turkish that are expected to lead to an earlier and more sophisticated development of phonological awareness are (a) the simple syllable structure in which the syllables and their constituent phonemes are easily identifiable, (b) the necessity to manipulate the phonemic units of words and subword structures in order to meet the requirements of vowel harmony, and (c) the complex morphemic structure with postinflections.

Indeed, in a study comparing beginning readers of English and Turkish, there were significant differences between the two groups of children (Durgunoğlu & Öney, 1999). Four groups of children, from Grades Kindergarten (KG) and 1 in Turkey (TR) and the United States (US) were given four different phonological awareness tasks: tapping syllables, tapping phonemes, deleting the initial phoneme, and deleting the final phoneme. The materials for both language groups were identical nonwords pronounceable in both languages.

On the phoneme- and syllable-tapping tasks, there was a significant Language × Linguistic Unit × Grade interaction (see Table 14.1). The TR group showed a significant Linguistic Unit × Grade interaction on the tapping data. Both KG and first-grade children manipulated syllables equally well (see also Cossu, Shankweiler, Liberman, Katz, & Tola, 1988; Goswami, 1999). However, first-grade children could tap phonemes more accurately than KG children could. There was no such interaction in the US data. US first graders were better than KG children on both syllable- and phoneme-tapping tasks. Moreover, in contrast to the TR results, for both US groups syllable tapping was not easier than phoneme tapping. Because a syllable is a more salient unit in Turkish, the syllable-tapping task will be easy for both KG and first-grade TR children. It is interesting to note that, on the syllable-tapping task, not only the TR first graders, but also the TR kindergartners performed at higher levels than did US first graders. However, hearing phonemes is a more advanced skill that develops later for both TR and US children, possibly as a result of instruction.

On the initial- and final-phoneme deletion tasks, there was a significant Language × Grade × Linguistic Unit interaction, indicating that the TR group performed the deletion tasks more accurately than did the US group, but this difference was especially pronounced on the deletion of final phonemes. For the TR group, both KG and first-grade children had similar levels of high performance on the phoneme deletion task if it involved deleting the final phoneme of a nonword. On the initial-phoneme deletion, first graders performed well, but KG children had

TABLE 14.1

Mean number correct (Standard Deviations in Parentheses) for Turkish
and American Kindergarten (KG) and First-Grade Children on Phonological Awareness Tasks

Task[a]	Turkish		American	
	KG	1	KG	1
Syllable tapping	7.48 (1.2)	7.80 (0.5)	5.08 (2.1)	6.00 (1.0)
Phoneme tapping	5.37 (2.3)	7.52 (1.1)	5.04 (1.7)	6.05 (1.4)
Initial-phoneme deletion	5.17 (4.7)	11.10 (2.6)	5.12 (4.6)	8.63 (3.7)
Final-phoneme deletion	10.02 (3.8)	11.75 (0.7)	5.16 (4.8)	8.84 (3.9)

[a]For the tapping tasks, max. = 8; for the deletion tasks, max. = 12.

low levels of performance. Because Turkish requires final-phoneme manipulation as inflections are added to the end of a word, the children gain experience and hence can perform this task effortlessly, even in kindergarten. Initial-phoneme deletion, on the other hand, involves a less-practiced skill and can be performed well only after children have gained proficiency in reading and writing.

For the US group, the deletion of the initial phoneme was similar to the deletion of the final phoneme. The only significant effect was for grade, showing that first graders performed this task more accurately than did the KG students. As summarized in Table 14.1, unlike their TR counterparts, the US children in KG were not very accurate in deleting final phonemes. As they became literate, both final- and initial-phoneme deletion accuracies improved.

Another issue to consider is how the characteristics of spoken language affect development of phonological awareness. In several studies of English-speaking children (e.g., (Chaney, 1994; Metsala & Walley, 1998), the level of productive phonology has been linked to phonological awareness levels. Metsala and Walley suggest that, as oral vocabulary develops, children become familiar with many words and their neighborhood and lexical structures, leading to an awareness of phonemes. This implies that patterns more common in the particular language of a child should be easier to manipulate than unfamiliar patterns. In the Durgunoğlu and Öney (1999) study, the familiarity of nonwords (as determined by the number of rhyming neighbors) was predicted to relate to the phonological awareness performance. To test this hypothesis, each group's performance was compared on familiar and unfamiliar nonwords as a function of grade on initial-phoneme deletion task. First, the nonwords were grouped according to their familiarity in English. Both KG and first-grade students in the US group manipulated familiar English nonwords better than they did unfamiliar English nonwords. The TR group showed no difference in performance. When the nonwords were reclassified according to their familiarity levels in Turkish, there was still the same main effect of grade, but there was no effect of familiarity for the US group. The TR group (more specifically, KG students), on the other hand, now showed an influence of familiarity. First graders manipulated both familiar and unfamiliar items equally accurately. These results illustrate a specific instance of how the characteristics of the home language can affect the development of phonological awareness.

Word Recognition and Spelling

Two factors make it likely for word recognition and spelling to develop rapidly in beginning readers of Turkish. The first factor is the systematic, transparent orthography (Öney & Goldman, 1984). The second factor is the speedy development of phonological awareness, as already discussed. The rapid development of phonological awareness skills have been shown to facilitate decoding skills as indicated by training studies conducted with English-speaking children (see Adams, 1990 for a review). Likewise, several studies indicate that spelling and word recognition progress rapidly in both adult and child beginning readers of Turkish. In one study, we tested the decoding performance of a group of first graders in October, February, and May on the same set of words and pseudowords (Öney & Durgunoğlu, 1997). First, the word- and pseudoword-recognition performances were highly correlated (.97 in October, .92 in February, and .85 in May). Likewise, word- and pseudoword-spelling performances were highly correlated (.89 and .72, for October and May, respectively). These correlations imply that the same strategies are used for reading and writing of both words and pseudowords, with the most likely candidate being the spelling–sound correspondences.

As predicted, the word- and pseudoword-recognition performances increased rapidly and steadily through the year, 26% in October, 72% in February, and 93% in May. The same pattern was also observed for spelling performance, with 20% spelling accuracy increasing to 93% in May. In the Durgunoğlu & Öney (1999) study another kind of evidence for rapid decoding proficiency was observed when the letter- and word-recognition performances of KG and first-grade children in Turkey and the United States were analyzed. Children in both communities were at ceiling levels in letter recognition at the end of first grade, although the TR kindergartners started with a lower level of letter recognition. On the word-recognition task, the TR kindergartners had very low levels of decoding (14%), but decoding proficiency reached 100% for first graders. The growth rate was smaller in the US, with a 22% accuracy in KG, and 82% in first grade.

In another study, average and less-skilled readers of Turkish in Grades 2, 3, and 4 were compared (Öney & Durgunoğlu, 2002). Even for less-skilled readers in Grade 2, with reading comprehension accuracy of 37%, the word-recognition level was 74%. (For the average readers in the same grade, the accuracy rates were 87% and 71% for word recognition and comprehension, respectively.)

Finally, the facilitatory effects of the transparent orthography are also observed with adult beginning readers. We have developed an adult literacy program in Turkey called Functional Adult Literacy Program (FALP) that has now reached about 47,000 participants in 13 provinces (Durgunoğlu et al., 2002). This program lasts only 3 months, providing 120 hr of instruction to participants with no or very limited schooling. However, FALP relies on the explicit teaching of phoneme–grapheme correspondences through direct instruction of decoding skills, exploiting the high correspondence between letters and sounds in the Turkish writing system. In addition, there is explicit instruction to develop phonological awareness. Even with adults, who traditionally have more difficulty with literacy acquisition, word-recognition and spelling performances show significant gains after only 90 to 120 hr of instruction (Durgunoğlu, 2000; Durgunoğlu, Öney, & Kuşcul, 2003).

Role of Phonological Awareness in Decoding

Numerous studies have shown the importance of phonological awareness in literacy development, especially in word-recognition and spelling processes. These studies, conducted with monolingual speakers of many different languages, indicate that high levels of phonological awareness enable the children to understand how the written language represents the spoken language. The same pattern is observed in Turkish literacy development. Along with the knowledge of letter names, awareness of phonemes correlated with decoding proficiencies (Durgunoğlu & Öney, 1999; Öney & Durgunoğlu, 1997, 2002). Syllable manipulation seems to develop readily because of the language characteristics, and hence syllable manipulation tasks were not good predictors of decoding performance, whereas phoneme manipulation tasks were (Durgunoğlu

TABLE 14.2
Predictors of the Outcome Measures After 90 Hours of Instruction for Adult Literacy
Participants of the FALP

| | Postcourse | | | |
| | Spelling | | Work Recognition | |
Step	R^2 (%)	Beta	R^2 (%)	Beta
1 Precourse word recognition			41	.320*
1 Precourse spelling	20.2	.229**		
2 Postcourse phonological awareness	+ 24.4	.511**	+ 12.6	.370**
3 Postcourse letter recognition	+ 0.3	.061	+ 3.2	.214**
Total variance explained	44.9		56.8	

*$p < .09$;   **$p < .05$.

& Öney, 1999; Öney & Durgunoğlu, 1997). The effects of phoneme manipulation were also observed for a longer period of time. However, interestingly, initial-phoneme deletion, rather than final-phoneme deletion, correlated with word-recognition performance of the KG children. A possible explanation is that final-phoneme manipulation was accomplished easily because of much practice these children had, given the nature of the language that they spoke. Focusing on single phoneme changes at the ends of words is a proficiency that develops very early in all children. Therefore this skill did not distinguish between more-skilled and less-skilled decoders.

For adult beginning readers, there was also a significant correlation between level of phonological awareness and word-recognition and spelling accuracy. Both at the beginning of the course without any instruction as well as after 90 hr of instruction, adult literacy participants showed significant correlations between phonological awareness and decoding tasks (Durgunoğlu & Öney, 2002). Table 14.2 summarizes the multiple-regression analyses showing the predictors of adult literacy acquisition after 90 hr of instruction. For both spelling and word-recognition measures at the end of instruction, phonological awareness was a significant predictor even when preexisting levels of those proficiencies were taken into consideration. Given that the adult literacy participants have low but widely varying levels of word-recognition and spelling skills at the beginning of the course, even after the preexisting differences are considered, phonological awareness is still a strong predictor of decoding performance. In fact, for adult participants, as subsequently summarized in Table 14.4 in the subsection on reading comprehension, phonological awareness was a significant predictor of even reading comprehension. Of course, this may be partly due to the short duration of the course.

SOURCES OF POSSIBLE READING DIFFICULTIES

Complex Morphology

Because Turkish is an agglutinating language, with suffixes and multisyllabic words occurring often, reading and writing such complex words can be a challenge for beginning readers. Turkish readers need to have a sense of how the suffixes follow each other. They also need to have an implicit knowledge of the probability of one suffix following another one or the root. In addition, they need to focus on the vowel harmony of the suffixes. However, two sources help a reader faced with this complexity. First, as more suffixes are added to a word, the probability of possible suffixes that can follow are reduced considerably. Therefore longer words are probabilistically simpler in suffix complexity. Second, syllable structure is well defined and syllabification rules can override morphological boundaries, thus providing the readers and spellers with a decoding tool that does not rely on morphological knowledge. There is some evidence showing that both of these sources are helpful for the readers of Turkish.

In a counterintuitive finding, second- and fourth-grade Turkish children were just as accurate in correcting the errors or supplying the correct suffixes for complex, multisyllabic words as they were for simple, short words (Durgunoğlu, 2002). In that experiment, children read a paragraph about an imaginary animal with a pseudospecies name (e.g., *mev*). There were two versions of the story: In one version there were blanks, and children supplied the correctly inflected form of the pseudoword. In the other version of the story, the pseudowords were given with incorrect inflections and they were underlined in the text. Children were asked to correct these incorrectly inflected items. The crucial manipulation was the complexity of the target pseudoword in its base form. The pseudospecies name was given in its simple nominal form (*mev*, Level 1) or in its plural form (*mevler* = *mevs*, Level 2) or in its plural, possessive form (*mevlerimiz* = our *mevs*, Level 3). Hence the base form of the target pseudowords could range from 3 (e.g., *mev*) to 12 letters (e.g., *pelitlerimiz*). The meaning of the paragraph was not affected by the complexity manipulation.

Given the paragraph context, the target pseudowords needed some case suffixes, for example, the suffix –*e*, meaning "to." For Level 1, this would produce *meve* [to mev], for Level 2, *mevlere* [to *mevs*], and, for Level 3, *mevlerimize* [to our *mevs*]. In other words, the children needed to supply or correct the suffix on either a short, simple pseudoword (e.g., *mev*) or a longer, more complex pseudoword (e.g., *mevlerimiz*). Results showed that the morphologically complicated forms of target pseudowords were completed or corrected just as accurately as morphologically simple forms of the target items. Although the complex pseudowords were multisyllabic and much longer, their lower number of probable suffixes overcame these disadvantages and facilitated the suffix correction and completion performance. More interestingly, children tended to make simple forms more complex before supplying or correcting the suffix, rather than vice versa. These accuracy data indicate that children found the orthographically more complex forms easier to handle, possibly because of their reduced number of possible suffixes.

As for the help of syllables in reading and writing morphologically complex words, in the FALP curriculum for adult literacy participants, we included explicit instruction on how to syllabify complex words (Durgunoğlu et al., 2002). There were basically three rules to follow: First the participants were asked to mark the vowels, which gives them the number of syllables. Then they put a line between two consonants that were together. Finally, if there were any vowels left, they put a line after the vowel. As an example, the word *kaldırım* [sidewalk] was syllabified with the following three steps: (a) ka̲ldırı̲m, (b) ka̲l/dırı̲m, (c) ka̲l/dı̲/rı̲/m. (If a single letter is left, it is attached to the previous vowel yielding: ka̲l/dı̲/rım.)

Although I have not conducted any formal studies on the effectiveness of this instruction, informal observations in the classrooms as well as my own teaching of a FALP course suggested that syllables do simplify the decoding of complex words. More interestingly, I have observed some participants saying the syllables under their breath when they are attempting to spell these complex words.

Reading Comprehension

As already discussed, phonological awareness and decoding develop rapidly in both young and adult readers of Turkish because of the transparent orthography and the special characteristics of phonology and morphology. However, reading comprehension is still a problem.

TABLE 14.3

Multiple-Regression Analyses on Children's Reading-Comprehension Performances

Model	Step	Average Readers		Less-Skilled Readers	
		R^2 (%)	Beta	R^2 (%)	Beta
1	1. Grade	30.4	.220	27	.377*
	2. Listening comprehension	+ 17.8	.512*	+ 20	.523*
	3. Decoding	+ 1	.112	+ 0	.007
	4. Digit memory	+ 0	− .007	+ 1	− .135
	Total variance	49		48	
2	1. Grade	30.4	.195	27	.084
	2. Listening comprehension	+ 17.8	.519*	+ 20	.447*
	3. Decoding	+ 1	.116	+ 0	.058
	4. Lexical access	+ 0	− .040	+ 7	− .456*
	5. Digit memory	+ 0	− .009	+ 2.6	− .203
	Total variance	49		56.6	

*p < .05.

For example, in Grade 4, less-skilled readers had 91% accuracy in word recognition, but their comprehension level was 81%, whereas the average readers were at 98% on both measures (Öney & Durgunoğlu, 2002). These statistics indicate that, not surprisingly, variables other than decoding are a source of difficulty in reading comprehension. Demographic data indicated that, of the 61 average readers in Grades 2–4 in that study, 85% had parents with professional or semiprofessional jobs, whereas this percentage was only 38% for the 59 children in the less-skilled group. These socioeconomic-status (SES) influences suggest that, replicating the pattern discovered in many communities, the language and literacy practices in middle-SES homes provide an advantage for the students.

In terms of the cognitive variables, the reading-comprehension performance of average and less-skilled readers were analyzed separately by use of multiple regressions. As summarized in Table 14.3, two different analyses were conducted for both average and less-skilled readers. In the first analysis the following four predictors were entered into the equation in the following order: grade, listening comprehension, decoding (word recognition + spelling) and digit memory. (Digit memory, assessing the recall of progressively longer digit strings, was included as a possible predictor because, as discussed before, the long suffixes, nominalized relative clauses, and flexible word order of Turkish may place a large burden on memory.) The four variables explained 49% and 48% of the variance for average and less-skilled readers, respectively. For average readers, grade, although entered first, was not a significant variable. The only significant predictor of reading comprehension was listening comprehension. Interestingly, decoding or digit memory was not significant either. With the systematic Turkish orthography, decoding was not a significant factor in reading comprehension. The influence of memory as assessed by the digit span task may already have been subsumed in the listening-comprehension performance as these two tasks were significantly correlated.

For less-skilled readers, grade and listening comprehension were both significant predictors. However, after scrutinizing the correlations among variables, we noticed that grade was strongly correlated with the efficiency of lexical access. (In the lexical access task, the time it took for the children to rapidly name the color patches, objects, and digits was measured.) Therefore we considered the possibility that speed of lexical access rather than grade was the underlying

TABLE 14.4

Predictors of the Reading-Comprehension Performance for Adult Literacy
Participants of the FALP After 90 Hours of Instruction

Step	R^2 (%)	Beta
1. Precourse listening comprehension	18.6	.124
2. Postcourse word recognition	+ 22.8	.227*
3. Postcourse phonological awareness	+ 9.3	.468**
Total variance explained	50.7	

$^*p < .09, {}^{**}p < .05.$

predictor. A new regression analysis included the following five variables given in the following order: grade, listening comprehension, decoding, lexical access, and digit memory. These results are summarized at the bottom of Table 14.3 as Model 2. For the average readers, adding the lexical access variable did not change the overall pattern. As in the first analysis, listening comprehension was the only significant predictor.

For the less-skilled readers, the pattern changed significantly when lexical access was added to the equation. Now the five variables explained 57% of the variance in reading comprehension. Listening comprehension was still a significant predictor, but grade was not. Even though it was added after three variables (grade, listening comprehension, and decoding), lexical access was a significant predictor.

To summarize, for young readers of Turkish, decoding was not the bottleneck for reading comprehension. Instead, the rapid-naming task, how fast concepts are accessed from memory, and listening comprehension predicted reading comprehension performance. Listening comprehension, of course, involves many components working in concert. These components include using background knowledge and syntactic knowledge as well as organizing the new material and integrating it with existing knowledge (Oakhill, 1994).

When it comes to adult beginning readers of Turkish, the picture on reading comprehension was quite different. The adult participants of FALP had world experiences, relatively good background knowledge, and a good command of their spoken language. However, their decoding skills were quite weak. As summarized in Table 14.4, following only 90 hr of instruction, the reading-comprehension performances of adult beginning readers were predicted by decoding and phonological awareness, even though the existing listening-comprehension level was entered first into the equation. Of course, as their decoding skills develop more fully, adult participants are also likely to reach a point at which listening comprehension is the strongest predictor of reading comprehension, reflecting the higher-order processes that affect comprehension.

CONCLUSION

In this chapter, the goal was to highlight certain distinctive characteristics of Turkish and relate these characteristics to the literacy acquisition of both adults and children. The transparent orthography, vowel harmony, agglutinating morphology with the complex suffixation, saliency and clear structure of syllables, and flexible word order are some of the distinctive properties of the Turkish language. Given these characteristics of the language, literacy acquisition is marked by rapid development of phonological awareness and decoding. However, replicating the pattern discovered with other languages, listening comprehension, and rapid access of concepts from memory provided challenges for less-skilled readers, especially as predictors of reading comprehension.

REFERENCES

Adams, M. J. (1990) *Beginning to read*. Cambridge, MA: MIT Press.

Aksu-Koç, A. & Slobin, D. I. (1986). The acquisition of Turkish. In D. I. Slobin (Ed.) *The Crosslinguistic study of language acquisition, Volume 1* (pp. 839–878). Hillsdale, NJ: Erlbaum and Associates.

Chaney, C. (1994). Language development, metalinguistic awareness and emergent literacy skills of 3-year-old children in relation to social class. *Applied Psycholinguistics, 15*, 371–394.

Cossu, G., Shankweiler, D., Liberman, I. S., Katz, L., & Tola, G. (1988). Awareness of phonological segments and reading ability in Italian children. *Applied Psycholinguistics, 9*, 1–16.

Durgunoğlu, A. Y. (2000). Adult literacy: Issues of personal and community development. Final report submitted to the Spencer Foundation.

Durgunoğlu, A. Y. (2002). Recognizing morphologically complex words in Turkish. In E. Assink & D. Sandra (Eds). *Recognizing complex words*. Kluwer.

Durgunoğlu, A, Y. & Öney, B. (1999). A cross-linguistic comparison of phonological awareness and word recognition. *Reading & Writing, 11*, 281–299.

Durgunoğlu, A. Y., & Öney, B. (2002). Phonological awareness in literacy development: It's not only for children. *Scientific Studies of Reading, 6*, 245–266.

Durgunoğlu, A. Y., Öney, B., & Kuşcul, H. (2003). Development and evaluation of an adult literacy program in Turkey. *International Journal of Educational Development, 3*, 17–36.

Durgunoğlu, A. Y., Öney, B., Kuşcul, H., Dağıdır, F. Z., Aslan, F., Cantürk, M., & Yasa, M. (2002). *Functional Adult Literacy Program, Level I*. Istanbul: Mother Child Education Foundation, 3rd edition.

Erguvanlı-Taylan, E. (1987). The role of semantic features in Turkish word order. *Folia Linguistica, 21*, 215–227.

Goswami, U. (1999). The relationship between phonological awareness and orthographic representation in different orthographies. In M. Harris, & G. Hatano (Eds.). *Learning to read and write: A cross-linguistic perspective* (pp. 134–156). Cambridge: Cambridge University Press.

Hankamer, J. (1992). Morphological parsing and the lexicon. In W. Marslen-Wilson (Ed.). *Lexical representation and process*. (pp. 392–408). Cambridge, MA: MIT Press.

Hudson, P. T. W. & Buijs, D. (1995). Left-to-right processing of derivational morphology. In L. B. Feldman (Ed.). *Morphological aspects of language processing*. (pp. 383–396), Mahwah, NJ: Lawrence Erlbaum Associates.

Kornfilt, J. (1990). Turkish and Turkic Languages. In B. Comrie (Ed.), *The world's major languages* (pp. 619–644). New York: Oxford University Press.

Metsala, J. L., & Walley, A. C. (1998). Spoken vocabulary growth and the segmental restructuring of lexical representations: Precursors to phonemic awareness and early reading ability. In J. L. Metsala & L. C. Ehri (Eds.). *Word recognition in beginning reading* (pp. 89–120). Mahwah, NJ: Erlbaum and Associates.

Oakhill, J. (1994). Individual differences in children's text comprehension In M. A. Gernsbacher (Ed.). *Handbook of psycholinguistics* (pp. 821–848). San Diego: Academic Press.

Öney, B., & Durgunoğlu, A. Y. (1997). Learning to read in Turkish: A phonologically transparent orthography. *Applied Psycholinguistics, 18*, 1–15.

Öney, B., & Durgunoğlu, A. Y. (2002). Beginning reading in Turkish and its difficulties. Manuscript in preparation.

Öney, B., & Goldman, S. (1984). Decoding and comprehension skills in Turkish and English: Effects of the regularity of grapheme-phoneme correspondences. *Journal of Educational Psychology, 76*, 557–568.

Underhill, R. (1976). *Turkish grammar*. Cambridge, MA: MIT Press.

15

Literacy Acquisition and Dyslexia in Hungarian

Valéria Csépe

*Research Institute for Psychology of the Hungarian
Academy of Sciences*

The aim of this chapter is to describe general and specific features of the Hungarian language that may influence reading acquisition and to give an overview of difficulties in learning to read and spell faced by children and adults. A short description of Hungarian phonology, morphology, and syntax will help us to understand why and how dyslexic readers show deficits in a language that has a relatively transparent and shallow orthography. The first part of this chapter describes the Hungarian orthography. The second part focuses on phonology and gives an overview of the vowel and consonant system as well as that of the phonotactics. The third part focuses on the agglutinative nature of Hungarian morphology in which grammatical relations are expressed by means of affixes. An additional feature of Hungarian language is the free word order. Finally, experimental findings—behavioural and brain measures—that address the general and specific features of the Hungarian language that may influence reading acquisition are presented along with an overview of difficulties in reading and spelling faced by dyslexic children and adults.

GENERAL INTRODUCTION

Hungarian belongs to a small subgroup of the Finno-Ugric branch of Uralic (also called Ural-Altaic or Uralic-Zukaghir) languages, called Ob-Ugric. The nearest subgroups of the branch are Kanthy and Mansi that are spoken in tiny areas of Russia. Well-known relatives from the Finnic branch are Finnish (see Lehtonen's chapter in this book), Estonian, and Saami. Hungarian is different from other European languages; it is also atypical among the members of the Uralic family and has no close neighbors. Its lexicon well reflects the country's history, with loan words from Slavic, Iranian, Turkish, German, Italian, French, and English languages. The earliest literary pieces date back to the 13th and 14th centuries. During the 15th century, there was a literary renaissance, but it soon declined because of different historical events. Strong language-standardization efforts occurred during the 18th and 19th centuries, and, as a consequence of these changes, a century-long period of literary growth occurred. Because of the vigorous standardization efforts, the dialectical variations of the language have remained minimal. The existing dialectical variations mainly involve differences between urban and rural versions of the spoken language.

HUNGARIAN ORTHOGRAPHY

Hungarian has 14 vowels and 25 consonants. The Hungarian alphabet is Latin based and uses accents and diacritics for marking special characteristics. Written Hungarian contains 26 letters whereas spoken Hungarian, similar to English and many other languages, makes use of more than 26 distinct sounds.

In English this discrepancy is dealt with by use of the same letter or letter strings to stand for different sounds depending on meaning (the 'e' in *record* when used as a verb or as an adjective) or context of preceding or following letters (the 'i' in *five* and *fit*). In contrast to English, the Hungarian writing system deals with the discrepancy just described in a different way and makes use of a rather consistent one-to-one mapping (with one minor exception) between written letters and articulated sounds.

Hungarian Vowels

The Hungarian orthography employs accents on 7 of the 14 vowels. However, 5 of these 7 are the long-duration versions of the same vowel sound, and the remaining 2 are distinct vowel sounds of long duration differing in formant structure from their 'counterparts' that are written without accent. That means Hungarian language uses nine distinct vowel sounds, five of which have short and long pronunciation (see Table 15.1).

Hungarian Consonants

The classical Hungarian alphabet does not include four foreign letters, q, w, x, and y, but they are now included in the full Hungarian alphabet. The Hungarian writing system uses $7 + 2$ digraphs (consonant pairs read out as a single sound) and they should be treated as a single letter during reading, similar to the 'th' in English. The digraph 'ly' is an archaic form with the sound /j/ and is pronounced as the 'y' in *you* or *beyond*. There are two other digraphs not used in contemporary Hungarian writing but are used to write some words of Turkish origin (see Table 15.2).

The Role of Sound Duration in Written Hungarian

Vowel as well as consonant duration plays an important role in spoken Hungarian; in writing, distinct accents and double consonants (geminates) are used to mark duration. Accent marks

TABLE 15.1
Vowels Used in the Hungarian Writing System

Duration	Distinct (According to Formant Structure) Sounds								
Short	a	-	e	-	i	o	ö	u	ü
Long	-	á	-	é	í	ó	ő	ú	ű

TABLE 15.2
Consonants Used in the Strict Hungarian Alphabet

Letters or Letter Combinations With Distinct Sounds													
Graphs	b	c		d			f	g		h	j	k	l	
Digraphs			cs		**dz**	**dzs**		gy						**ly**

Distinct Sounds													
Graphs	m	n		p	r	s		t		v	z		
Digraphs			ny			sz		ty			zs		

Note: Digraphs printed in bold represent three archaic forms, two of which (dz and dzs) are used in a small number of words of Turkish origin. The arrow marks the only violation of the one-to-one letter-sound rule.

on vowels as well as consonant geminates also change the meaning of words, as shown in the subsequent small sample list. The Hungarian writing system does not use vowel geminates for marking vowel duration.

- **öt** = five / **őt** = him or her
- **fel** = up / **fél** = fears
- **alma** = apple / **álma** = his or her dream
- **kor** = age / **kör** = circle
- **kert** = garden / **kért** = asked for something
- **mulat** = enjoys himself or herself / **múlat** = lets time pass
- **hal** = fish / **hall** = hears
- **új** = new / **ujj** = finger
- **erre** = here to/ **ere** = his or her vessel

Digraphs used in Hungarian may contribute to reading problems in some cases. For instance, when three digraphs (cs, sz, zs) occur in compound words (e.g., *vaszár* [iron lock]) they should be pronounced as two separate sounds. Other digraphs and accented vowels are considered to represent single sounds. For example, 'cs' is pronounced as 'ch' (as in 'much') and not 'c' + 'z'.

It may seem that the Hungarian orthography is not that simple as it is often described, but once the nearly one-to-one letter–sound correspondences are learned, even non-word reading becomes easy. However, the agglutinating nature of the language that results in many compound words can lead to problems for beginning readers and poor readers. A strict hyphenation is helpful in reading out compound words that have more than six syllables.

PHONOLOGY

As can be seen from the description of orthography, Hungarian has a rich system of vowels and consonants. Stress is always on the first syllable, and words have a clear syllabic structure.

Vowels

As already mentioned, long vowels have a longer duration and their pronunciation is usually tenser than that their shorter counterpart. There are two exceptions (the 'e' vs. 'é' and the 'a' vs. 'á' pairs) that represent qualitative differences (see Abondolo, 1992, for a detailed description in English). One of the interesting features of spoken Hungarian is that vowel length is independent of suprasegmental factors such as stress. Moreover, vowels are interconnected according to vowel harmony (for details see Abondolo, 1992; Benkő & Imre, 1972). This means that suffixes existing in two or in some cases even in three different forms have to be chosen and they have to agree with the last vowel of the stem. The neutrality of the short and long /i/ sound in regard to vowel harmony makes the rule application a bit more complicated.

Consonants

Consonants vary according to voicing and place of articulation. Consonant length has a distinctive role in differentiating for meaning and the duration is independent of vowel length as well as of suprasegmental factors. Viable assimilations are either full or partial. In Hungarian, many morpheme-specific assimilation rules are to be taken into account, and the lack of this knowledge often leads to spelling and reading errors.

Assimilation Rules

The agglutinative nature of Hungarian can lead to phonological inconsistencies occurring frequently at the stem–suffix conjunctions. The origin of the assimilation is different from other languages, in which word-final or word-initial segments are mainly modified by onsets or codas of the surrounding words. Assimilation is a rather strong form of context-dependent variation in all languages, though its frequent and strong occurrence in Hungarian is due to phonemic variations associated with morphology.

In a recent study (Mitterer, Csépe, & Blomert, 2004) Hungarian words and non-words having suffixes and pronounced according to viable and unviable liquid assimilation were presented to Hungarian and Dutch listeners as identification and discrimination tasks. The results indicated that viably changed forms are difficult to distinguish from canonical forms independent of experience with the assimilation rules. Data revealed that auditory processing contributes to perceptual compensation for assimilation, whereas language experience has only a minor role to play. The results showed that the perception of assimilation is context sensitive, independent of lexical status as well as of experience with the Hungarian assimilation rules.

In a second study (Mitterer, Csépe, Honbolygó, & Blomert, 2004), the processing of utterances that changed in viable and unviable ways was investigated by measurement of the mismatch negativity (MMN) component of event-related brain potentials (ERPs). Because the MMN is very sensitive to acoustic changes it is broadly used for measuring the functions of the acoustic sensory memory (Csépe, 1995; Csépe & Molnár, 1997). One of the many advantages of using the MMN ERP component is that it is not only sensitive to differences in the acoustics, but it is also sensitive to differences in perception.

As expected, the MMN to unviable deviants was larger than that to viable pronunciations. Our results indicated that acoustic details of the assimilated utterance play a pivotal role in processing the variations in utterances. Although lexical processing and language experience are pivotal for achieving a stable speech recognition of one's native language, it seems that compensation for assimilation is acquired by means of basic perceptual processes, and these processes are independent of higher-level influences. However, we may assume that an explicit knowledge of the assimilations of morphophonemic origin may play a crucial role in acquiring skilled reading and good spelling in writing. Theories on compensation for assimilation have to account for the fact that compensation is independent of language experience and not subject to a top-down influence of the lexical information. The fact that Hungarian dyslexic people have special difficulties in liquid assimilation, even if they do not show difficulties in phonology, suggests that their sight word representation may be disturbed by frequent variations of the word forms. These variations may be overcome if a good representation for morphology, including the representation of stem variations, is developed before the age of 14 years.

MORPHOLOGY

Hungarian has a rich inflectional morphology with complex noun and verb forms, and grammatical relations are expressed by means of affixes and suffixes. Grammatical gender does not exist in Hungarian.

Nouns

Declension of nouns is derived from stems by a combination of inflectional suffixes (stem + number + person + case). That means that nouns are inflected for number, person, and case. Any of the inflectional suffixes may be substituted by zero suffixes when singular number is used, when possessor is absent, or when nominative case is used. The following example demonstrates the possible variations:

képe-ø-m-re   **kép**-ø-ø-re   **kép**e-k-ø-re   **kép**e-i-m-re
onto my picture   onto picture   onto pictures   onto my pictures

As can be seen in this example, Hungarian language has a complex and even complicated system for noun-stem alternations. For example, stems with final 'a' or 'e' are lengthened before most suffixes and when 'á' and 'é' are used. To make the complex rules even more complex, Hungarian has a special stem form called an *oblique stem*. The oblique stem differs from the nominative singular by an additional stem final vowel or consonant or even by a deletion. This phenomenon may contribute to problems during morphology acquisition as well as in identifying stems.

The case system consists of 17 distinct cases and uses even more forms to mark them. Seven of these distinctions are primarily grammatical (nominative, accusative, dative, etc.) marking the relations of subject, direct object, indirect object, possessor, and instrumental; the remaining 10 are locative and express various spatial and temporal aspects. For example, distinctions such as movement into an interior, an immediate proximity, onto a surface, up to a point, and no further are expressed by tiny little suffixes.

Verbs

Verbs are conjugated and consist of three parts. The stem is followed by a tense and mood suffix (present, past, conditional, and subjunctive) and then by a suffix that indicates person and number. The subjunctive suffix also can be used to mark imperatives. The suffixes that mark person are numerous; there are forms that agree with the subject in person and number and also with objects only in person and definiteness.

In verb conjugation, personal suffixes play a central role because, in case of emphasis on the person, a free pronominal subject is present. Personal suffixes express person with nouns, pronouns, and postpositions as well as with verbal personal endings. Two forms of conjugations are used according to the definiteness of the verb's complement. Two tense features are used for distinguishing past and non-past. The past-tense marker is 't', and this is lengthened in third-person singular when preceded by a vowel. Future tense is denoted by an auxiliary word with a personal ending and followed by an infinitive (for further details in English, see Campbell, 1991).

From the three mood categories—indicative, subjunctive, and imperative—the imperative and subjunctive forms are very important in orthography and therefore in reading and spelling. The marker following some root final consonants results in a different phonetically realized sound that is not always shown in the orthography (see Benkő & Imre, 1972). These morphophonemic irregularities of Hungarian orthography can lead to particular difficulties (for further details see Pléh, 1990).

The rich marking system used in Hungarian is further complicated by allomorphic variations that are not always indicated phonologically, though it avoids homonymy. However, homonymous forms are not fully avoided, and they not only change verbs to nouns but they change past tense to present tense (Pajzs, 1996).

As can be seen from this short description, morphology plays a special role in Hungarian, and studying morphological awareness may help us to understand the nature of deficits that contribute to difficulties in acquiring literacy.

Sentence Structure

In contrast to English, in Hungarian word order is not fixed. Word order is not a matter of stringing together parts according to the categories of subject, object, and verb, but rather is determined by topic and focus. The topic sets the scene and is mainly based on information that is known or assumed. Focus refers to key information that is essentially said about the topic. In Hungarian, topic comes first in a sentence and constituents in focus come immediately before the verb. Acoustic cues such as stress, elongation, and pause that are used in spoken utterances are associated with items in focus.

The Hungarian sentence structure shares some characteristics of the subject–object–verb (SOV) languages as well as those of the SVO languages. The basic syntactical forms that use different orders of the constituents can be changed. We have to bear in mind that these word orders are canonical and represent simple declarative sentences. Moreover, we have to add that Hungarian is a "pro-drop" language in the sense that the subject position of the verb is left empty and is often implicit. This characteristic feature is often used in garden path sentences.

LITERACY ACQUISITION IN HUNGARIAN

Because written Hungarian represents one of the shallow orthographies, it may be thought that it would be one of the easiest writing systems to learn. However, because of the agglutinating nature as well as the acoustic characteristics of the language, some individuals experience difficulty in learning to read.

Nevertheless, acquiring a knowledge grapheme–phoneme correspondence in Hungarian is simpler than it is in English. Furthermore, word-recognition skills can be acquired in more than one way. In English, one of the most critical questions raised in this regard is whether grapheme coding is best acquired implicitly through training on whole words or through explicit instructions on grapheme–phoneme correspondence. There are behavioural data to show that extensive training with whole words can improve reading (Thompson, & Cottrel, & Fletcher-Flynn, 1996; Thompson, Fletcher-Flynn, & Cottrel, 1999). However, two aspects of this type of improvement are not clear. First, we do not know what is acquired through the whole-word training, an implicit knowledge of the correspondences or recognition of the visual pattern of the words. Second, it is possible that the improvement of alphabetical knowledge by means of whole-word training may be valid only for English, and such a training may not be as effective with a transparent language.

According to the dual-route model of Coltheart and his co-workers (1993, 2001), two distinct routes can be used for reading written words, a lexical one that links orthography and meaning, and a phonological route that relies on grapheme-phoneme conversion. In the following subsection I argue that, in a shallow orthography such as Hungarian, explicit phonological training is essential for beginning readers to develop alphabetical knowledge and to acquire reading and spelling skills.

Different Types of Reading Instructions Used in Hungary

The introduction of standardized teaching methods based on phonics goes back to the beginning of the 20th century. The first official teaching method made use of an initial stage of explicit learning of grapheme–phoneme correspondences based on syllabication. Syllables, short words, and hyphenated bisyllabic words were used for initial training; this stage was followed by training on non-hyphenated words of increasing length. As a consequence of this method, Hungarian children read fluently after 3 months and those who experienced difficulties in reading could be identified quite early. The use of phonics also meant that reading acquisition was embedded in a language-focused training program that consisted of speech–sound discrimination and identification, phonological manipulations (deletion, segmentation, blending), and oral language exercises. One of the early methods was called "phonomimics" (Róza Czukrász, 1903) that paid special attention to speech–sound discrimination and segmentation. While this method was implemented, hand movements were associated with sounds.

Because of a general school reform, alternative teaching methods were introduced, and up to the 1980s four different methods were officially approved. However, now in 2005, 14 different methods are used and they could be classified under three approaches: phonics, whole word, or some combination of the two. One variety of the whole-word method, called global program, switches to letter–sound correspondence training after only 87 sight words are taught. It should be noted that Finnish also has a shallow orthography similar to Hungarian, but in Finland, the whole-word method has never been introduced.

It may seem difficult to understand why a nearly one-nation country whose writing system uses discrete letters for discrete sounds and constructs words of complex morphological structures through agglutination is so liberal in trying out many different types of teaching methods. In Hungary there is still an ongoing discussion on the merits of phonics versus whole-word instruction.

In 1992, the percentage of poor readers diagnosed (Csabay, 1994) as dyslexic increased dramatically to 30%–35%. Csabay has even introduced terms such as 'genuine dyslexia' and 'pseudo-dyslexia', the former characterized by reading problems of constitutional origin, probably biological, and the latter a problem that is related to inadequate teaching methods or some other environmental factors.

The Role of Phonological Awareness in Hungarian

As shown by many recent studies, abnormalities in processing words is one of the core deficits of dyslexia and there is a high level of correlation between phonological deficit and reading–spelling skills. According to the phonological deficit hypothesis, dyslexia is characterized by poor phonological awareness (PA; for a review see Goswami, 1999, 2003).

In Hungary, tests of PA are not in general use. However, one of the first research reports on the possible role of PA in reading acquisition was published by Kassai and Kovács-Vass (1991). In a 2-years follow-up study, verbal short-term memory and syllabic awareness were tested in 260 children at the end of kindergarten and at the end of Grade 1. Syllabic awareness was judged by a syllable-counting task, in which rhyming and non-rhyming word strings were used. Both groups of children were divided into two subgroups (low- and high-achievement groups) according to their preschool syllable-counting performance. In the rhyming task, four CVC words (*bor, kor, por, sor* [wine, age, dust, raw]) were used, each with different meaning and different initial phonemes. The authors meant to measure the memory capacity, although they really used a combined measure of capacity and phonemic awareness and memory loading. The authors report that correlations were found between short-term memory performance and reading and between syllabic awareness and reading. Although the overall performance of the two subgroups improved up to the end of the first grade, the initial difference of the two subgroups did not diminish. The observed lower error rate in first grade reflects the rise of phonemic awareness that was much less developed before reading was taught. The ceiling effect seen in the error rates of the rhyming task reported by Kassai and Kovács-Vass (1991) in preschoolers is in agreement with the belief (Goswami, 2000) that phonemic awareness does not develop until children are exposed to reading. However, syllabic awareness is a good predictor of phonemic awareness and both correlate well with reading. An interesting but less discussed finding of the authors was that 91% percent of the good performers but only 36% of the poor performers had a well-developed expressive vocabulary (Peabody Picture Vocabulary Test).

WHOLE-WORD READING VERSUS PHONICS

Before analyzing the deficits that characterize dyslexic reading patterns, let me list some arguments for using phonics as an initial training method for teaching to read Hungarian.

In one of our recent studies (Csépe, Gyurkócza, Szűcs, & Lukács, 2002), speech–sound discrimination of children from first and second grades was measured and compared with changes in the MMN ERP component in order to judge the quality of phonemic representation. Speech–sound discrimination was measured in a same–different judgment task consisting of isolated vowels and CV syllables with voicing and place of articulation contrasts. We measured the assumed change of the phoneme representation by using the MMN elicited by deviating stimuli in a passive "oddball" paradigm.

The latency of the MMN in the good-performer phonics group (see the slightly enlarged F3 recording in Fig. 15.1) showed a highly significant decrease that reflects faster processing of the contrast, probably because of a better representation of the phonemic contrast. Although the poor-performer phonics group showed a smaller and less distinct MMN in the first grade, the rise of a robust MMN (Fig. 15.1) was observed in the group in the second grade. The latency of this MMN was similar to that of the good-performer group from the first grade. Figure 15.2 shows the MMN responses of the group taught through the whole-word method. It can be seen in the figure that the MMN does not differ between the first and second group, so that we may assume that this method does not use the syllabic awareness and does not contribute to a better representation mediated by the development of phonemic awareness. The lack of representational changes in the phoneme clusters may have negative consequences for both subgroups of the whole-word group, though the real losers are those who enter school with poor discrimination skills. Our MMN data show that phonemic representation and reading have a bidirectional relationship; that is, not only does awareness influence reading acquisition but reading instruction leads to further development of phonemic segmentation.

In a recent study (Csépe, Szűcs, & Lukács, 2002), the role of different reading instructions on reading skills was investigated. A computerized reading task that measured reading speed and accuracy was administered to 75 children. The task consisted of four different lists; content words, function words, number words, and non-words. The test was developed in collaboration with other European countries (Seymour, 1998) to investigate 'Learning disabilities as a barrier

MMN changes in the Phonics group

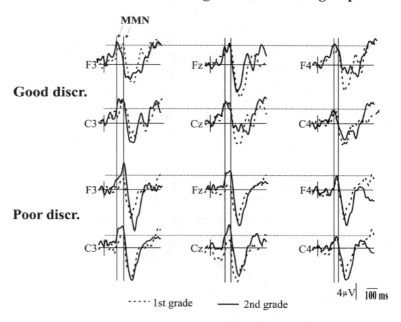

FIG. 15.1.   Changes of the MMN in the same group of children receiving the phonics type of reading instruction in the first and second grades. Good discr., Poor discr.: Subgroup of children with good and poor performances in phoneme discrimination tasks, respectively.

MMN changes in the Whole Word group

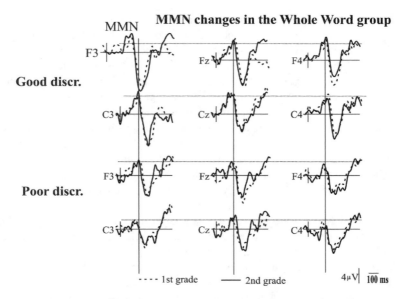

FIG. 15.2.   Changes of the MMN in the same group of children receiving the whole-word type of reading instruction in the first and second grades. Good discr., Poor discr.: Subgroup of children with good and poor performances in phoneme discrimination tasks, respectively.

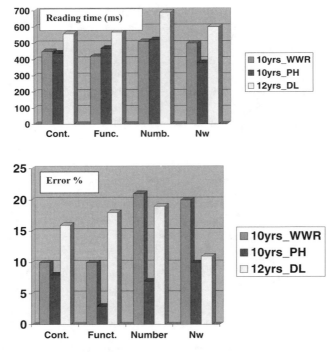

FIG. 15.3.   Reading performance (reading time, error %) of children 10 and 12 years old shown for different word classes. Cont., content words; Func., function words; Numb., number words; Nw., non-words; WWR, whole-word reading group; PH, phonics group; DL, dyslexic children's group.

to human development'. Two thirds of the children were good readers (10 years of age; third grade). Twenty-five children from the good-reader group had been taught reading through a global method (i.e., whole word) and 25 through phonics. The remaining 25 children who were 12 years old and were in fifth grade were diagnosed as dyslexic at the time of the assessment. Their word and non-word reading was characterized by few errors but their reading comprehension of sentences was 1.5 years below average; they were also slow readers.

As can be seen in Fig. 15.3, the reading time did not differ between the whole-word and phonics groups for any class of real words but there was a difference in reading non-words. From this point of view, the whole-word method is as good as phonics. However, the number of reading errors produced by the phonics group was half that of the whole-word group. The whole-word group read less accurately, though with the same speed as the phonics group. The most unexpected finding of the study was that the whole-word group performed worse in reading non-words than did the dyslexic group, and their performance in reading low-frequency words (such as number words) was similar to that of the dyslexic group. It appears that the whole-word method does not help in the development of skills crucial for phonemic representation and segmentation in a transparent orthography.

A qualitative change in language skills seems to occur between the ages 5 and 7 years; to a large extent, this change is due to school experience. A significant increase in the ability to recognize two-syllable words in a noisy environment also occurs in 7-year-olds (Gósy, 1994). Although the largest improvement in linguistic skills takes place during the kindergarten years, development of decoding skills occurs during the first 2 years of school. The more transparent the language is, the more children profit from phonics instruction. I do share the opinion of Share (1995), who argues that explicit phonological instruction is essential for the beginning reader to develop alphabetical knowledge and become a skilled reader. Although I do agree with Perfetti (1992), who thinks that explicit phonemic knowledge is not a prerequisite for reading acquisition, the fact is that, for Hungarian readers, phonics is the method that best fits the shallow orthography, eventually leading to better reading performance. In Hungary, phonological training, explicit phonics instructions, and syllable segmentations are almost exclusively used in dyslexia intervention and reeducation classes for children with delayed language. This practice is based on the belief that, for Hungarian readers, phonics is the best method of reading instruction.

DIFFICULTIES IN LITERACY ACQUISITION

The Role of Phonological Awareness

As we saw earlier, even children who are not at risk for dyslexia may show deficits in low-level linguistic processes such as sound discrimination, phonemic manipulations, and other phonological operations. Two of our basic questions are how reading difficulties in Hungarian are related to PA and what is the best way to assess PA skills.

No standardized tests of phonological awareness are available in Hungarian; the tests that had been used in a few studies are not similar to those in English. A PA test was therefore developed by our research group (Csépe, Szűcs & Lukács, 2002; Lukács & Csépe, 2004). The tasks used in this test were selected from several previous studies of phonological awareness (e.g., Bertelson, de Gelder, & van Zon, 1997; Ellis, 1989; Høien, 1998; Seymour, 1998). The following tasks were used in the Hungarian Phonological Awareness Test (HPAT).

Rhyme judgement task: The child is presented with two spoken words (e.g., *csukló–padló* [wrist–floor] or *párna-doboz* [pillow–box]), and he or she is required to decide whether the two words rhyme and end with the same sound.

Syllable counting: The child is presented with a picture depicting an easily recognizable word. The child's task is to count the number of syllables in the word that represents the picture, marking the syllables by clapping the hands. Words in this task contain 10 one–four syllables plus four practice items.

Phoneme blending: A row of three pictures is presented, and the phonemes that are in the words that represent the pictures are pronounced with 0.5-s interval between the sounds. The child has to point to the picture that matches the word.

Phoneme counting: The task is to count the phonemes in words. The required response is either to tell the number of the speech sounds heard or to indicate the number of sounds by making pencil marks.

Initial phoneme judgement: The child is required to decide whether pairs of spoken words begin with the same sound (*kenyér–körte* [bread–pear]) or not (*répa–vonat* [carrot–train]).

Initial-syllable matching: The experimenter pronounces a word and shows three pictures to the child. The child is to point to the picture whose name starts with the same syllable as the word uttered by the experimenter (the cue is, e.g., *tehén* [cow] and the child has to choose from pictures of an apple [*alma*], a telephone [*telefon*], and a coat [*kabát*] (*telefon* is the correct answer).

In our study, 80 children of 6–10 years of age (from Grades 1–4) with and without reading difficulties were tested. In addition to the PA test, tests of working memory (WM) , a Hungarian non-word-repetition task, and the forward digit-span task were also administered to these children. To our surprise, a ceiling effect for PA was found already in the first grade. Moreover, no difference was found between the at-risk and the non-risk children for all PA tasks but one, the rhyme judgement subtest. The at-risk and not-at-risk groups investigated showed no difference in the non-word-repetition task, but the digit-span performance of the at-risk group was significantly lower than that of the not-at-risk group. This ceiling effect found can be explained in different ways. First, as was already mentioned in the reference to the findings of Kassai and Vass-Kovács (1991), syllabic awareness is well developed in Hungarian preschoolers, probably because of the clear structure of spoken Hungarian as well as to the syllabication exercises, such as counting, clapping, temporal extension, used in kindergarten classes.

Because dyslexic children differ from controls more in speed than in accuracy, deficits in phonological processes can be caught only if complex tasks are used. One of these "complex tasks" is the Spoonerism task (see Ramus, 2003), which taps phonological skills as well as WM. Therefore we have introduced two new PA tasks. One task requires the identification of a real word after the suprasyllabic part of the target word is omitted. The other task requires the child to construct a new word by combining syllables from two different words. The latter task is similar to the Spoonerism task, even though syllables, not phonemes, are changed here.

In addition to practice trials, the PA tasks contain two sections. In the first section, children have to create a new word by leaving out a part of another word (deletion task). In the second section, the children have to change a phoneme, replace it with another phoneme, and then say what the new word is (change task). None of the tasks uses any visual material so that successful completion of the task requires both phonological short-term memory and PA. Potentially strong effects of syllabication were controlled by the selection of units to be deleted or exchanged that did not correspond to the natural linguistic categories of the Hungarian language.

Figure 15.4 shows the results obtained from the at-risk (first and second grades), dyslexic (third and fourth grades), and control groups. As can be seen in the graphs, the first-grade dyslexia group starts with a very low score on both tasks, and the controls are better in the deletion task than in the change task. Whereas no significant change between the first and the fourth grade is shown by the controls in the deletion task, dyslexic children show improvement that decreases the gap between the two groups. The opposite trend can be seen in the change task. First graders in the control group start with a rather low performance but gradually improve up to the fourth grade. Little or no change is seen between the first-grade at-risk children and fourth-grade dyslexic children, and this stagnation leads to an increasing gap between the groups. Moreover, in dyslexics children, a stronger correlation between the WM

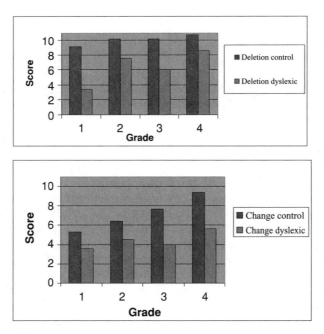

FIG. 15.4.   Performance of dyslexic and control children in two difficult phoneme awareness tasks (deletion and change). First graders of the dyslexic group were children at risk who were visiting special classes organized for early intervention.

and PA measures is seen, suggesting involvement of memory capacity on these tasks. In first graders, the capacity measure (digit span) is the more predictive PA whereas in fourth graders the phonological loop function (non-word repetition) is a better predictor of PA. It is quite possible that a language with rich morphology and sentences with free word order may rely on different memory processes more than non-agglutinating languages do.

LANGUAGE-SPECIFIC OR GENERAL ACOUSTIC DEFICITS IN DYSLEXIA

As already noted, the MMN component of ERPs elicited by various stimulus contrasts gives a fine-grained picture of the processing of speech and non-speech stimuli.

In previous studies (Csépe, Szűcs, & Lukács, 2001; Csépe, Gyurkócza et al., 2002) we investigated 64 dyslexic children 7–14 years of age and 64 gender- and age-matched controls. The aim of the experiments was to clarify whether the speech–sound representation as measured by the MMN is related to the phonological representations responsible for reading difficulties.

The MMN was measured to tone, vowel, and CV contrasts (for the method see Csépe, Osman-Sági, Molnár, & Gósy, 2001) and the results were compared with discrimination performance, PA measures, and reading scores. Statistical analysis of the latency and amplitude values of the MMN elicited by the three stimulus types showed a significant difference between control children and dyslexic children in phoneme discrimination performance. The highest amplitude differences and hemispheric variations were found when consonants (voicing and place of articulation) were used as contrasting features. The CV-elicited MMN provided a reliable measure for differentiating between control children and dyslexic children (Fig. 15.5). As can be seen, 9-year-old dyslexic children and the age-matched control children did not show differences in MMN to pitch differences of pure tones, either in latency or amplitude. On the contrary, the MMN to voicing (/ba:/ versus /pa:/) and to place of articulation (/ba:/ versus /pa:/) showed dramatically smaller amplitude and longer latency in dyslexic children than in control children. As shown in Fig. 15.5, the MMN for place of articulation occurs with very low amplitude to contrasts in voicing. Dyslexic children differ from control children in their performance, suggesting a basic processing deficit in phonemic representation. Moreover, in those children who showed extreme difficulties in reading, a deficiency in vowel processing was also found. Therefore we may conclude that an underdeveloped phonology, in conjunction with a weak working memory, contributes to reading difficulties even in a transparent language.

Deficits in Morphology and Sentence Processing

There is a possibility that, in transparent orthographies, language-specific difficulties can occur in a later stage of literacy acquisition than that in less transparent systems. As was shown by the Hungarian studies previously mentioned, simple measurements of PA fail to tap the main deficits characteristic of the second stage of development in skilled reading. Therefore we may assume that, after the rather easy rules of letter–sound correspondences and syllable blending in Hungarian are acquire, literacy development relies more on higher-level rule extraction and segmentation processes rather than on coding–decoding operations. It seems that the development of a well-functioning sight-word vocabulary as well as the maintenance of the two routes—the lexical and the phonological—of reading is affected by processes that may be related to morphological and syntactical features of the language.

In a recent study of 211 dyslexic readers, Kovács-Vass and Kovács-Fehér (2003), investigated dyslexic and non-dyslexic readers 14–18 years of age. The tasks used were looking for performance differences in morphological judgments (error finding in texts containing affix and suffix violations), word and sentence segmentation, text comprehension, homonym

Amplitude (μV)

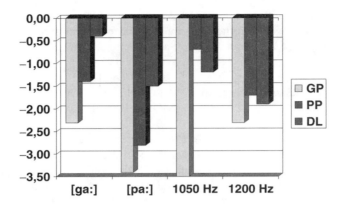

Latency (ms)

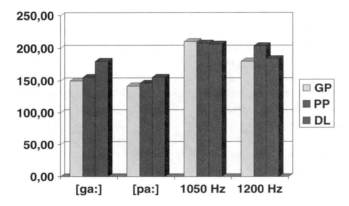

FIG. 15.5.   Changes of amplitude and latency of the MMN to consonant and pure tone contrasts. GP, Subgroup of children with good performance in phoneme discrimination tasks; PP, subgroup of children with poor performance in phoneme discrimination tasks; DL, dyslexic children.

discrimination, and reasoning. As the authors expected, the performances of the dyslexic readers were inferior to those of non-dyslexic readers in all five tasks. The most striking difference between dyslexic and control readers was found in the morphological violation judgment as well as in the segmentation tasks. Furthermore, the 211 dyslexic readers investigated showed a deficit in comprehending homonyms, suggesting a deficit in semantic accessing. It seems that dyslexic readers over 14 years old have most difficulties in morphology and syntax processing stemming from problems in segmentation. An interesting finding was that the difference between the dyslexic and the control readers did not increase with age, and this is probably due to the special training dyslexic children received in this school. Therefore I suggest that a general deficit in segmentation skills and working memory contributes to disturbances in phonology in younger children and a deficit in morphology and syntax contributes to reading difficulties in teenagers. These deficits may be language specific. In Hungarian, this specific character is due to the combination of a transparent orthography and agglutinative morphology.

If we compare the results on morphological segmentation difficulties with the typical problems of younger children whose main problem is phonological segmentation, we may conclude that segmentation skills are one of the most important skills for literacy acquisition in Hungarian. This assumption is in agreement with that of Bitan and Karni (2002), who suggest that the segmentation skills are crucially important in literacy acquisition and these skills do not develop spontaneously from extensive exposure to whole words. It is clear from most of the Hungarian data that extensive and explicit training may lead to knowledge of segmentation, phonology, and morphology. However, it is quite probable that rules useful in one particular aspect may not transfer to other language domains.

It still is a big question of how sight-word vocabulary develops in an agglutinating language. It is of particular importance to test whether the complex word forms used in Hungarian are obtained by means of the lexical route, the phonological route, or a combination of the two. Lexical accessing means that many forms are stored as sight words. Thus a free morpheme will have one entry and its bound form will have another entry. For example, the word 'play' will have one lexical entry and the word 'played' will have another entry, and the word 'playing' yet another entry. Obviously this will increase the cognitive and memory load tremendously. Alternatively, participation of the phonological system can play a role in segmenting complex words into root words and their affixes. This would appear to be a more efficient system of storage and retrieval. Regardless of the validity of these two models, the size of sight vocabulary increases and children over 14 years old do not seem to have problems even with the very long words.

At this point, it has to be noted that there are data (Adamik-Jászó, 1994) that show the whole-word reading instruction is not conducive for teaching Hungarian children to read and spell. Therefore one of my main arguments is that explicit phonemic knowledge is a prerequisite for the acquisition of reading in transparent orthography such as Hungarian. On the other hand, it is quite clear that phonological training can be helpful in the first stage of learning to read. In the second stage of reading acquisition, other processes such as the growth of sight-word vocabulary, morphological awareness, segmentational learning, and syntax sensitivity become crucial.

The Role of Sight-Word Vocabulary

In a recent study, Csépe, Szűcs, and Honbolygó (2003) used the technique of visual ERPs to evaluate the processes of lexical access and selection and early semantic access in young native Hungarian students as well as dyslexic students. This study made use of the well-known lexical-decision paradigm in which ERPs elicited by words, number words, and pseudowords were measured. Subjects had to judge whether the letter string seen was meaningful or meaningless.

Our hypothesis was that the sensory processing stages of the lexical access are reflected in the ERP components that occur during the first 200 ms after stimulus onset, whereas lexical selection and semantic access occur later. The aim of the study was to evaluate this three-phase process of lexical access. Because of the transparency of the Hungarian orthography good readers could easily read pseudowords because no special rules are required for translating orthography into phonology. The experimental design allowed us to judge on compensation strategies used by dyslexic adult. Although common words were chosen as meaningful lexemes, a rarely used semantic difference was introduced, that is, lexical decision was required for words versus pseudowords and number words versus pseudowords. We assumed that reading number words might differ from that of words (nouns) for two reasons. First, numbers have a different external representation, namely digits; second, number words have weaker representation as sight words than high-frequency words.

Our results suggest that, in good readers, additional activity occurs in the sensory or selection stage of lexical access when words of low frequency such as number words are read. The most significant processing differences found between words and number words occurred in a later stage of processing during semantic access. Our results also show that young adults with dyslexia might develop a compensation strategy for reading words of different frequency, which is indicated by additional activity associated with the later stage of processing. As was revealed by the ERP changes, lexical access was fast and accurate in good readers. Unlike when English words are read, when Hungarian words were read the early components of ERPs did not differ between words and non-words.

The behavioural data suggest that, after the first stage of acquisition, further development of sight-word vocabulary relies on the interaction among vocabulary knowledge, memory capacity, and morphology. Future research on morphological awareness could help us to understand why many dyslexic readers do not reach the second stage of word processing and fail to become skilled readers.

ACKNOWLEDGEMENT

Experimental studies of the research group described in this paper were supported by research grants given by the Hungarian Research Fund (OTKA T 33008 and 047381) principal investigator: Valéria Csépe).

REFERENCES

Abondolo, D. (1987). Hungarian. In B. Comrie (Ed.), *The world's major languages* (pp. 577–592). New York: Oxford University Press.

Abondolo, D. (1992). Hungarian. In W. Bright (Ed.), *International encyclopedia of linguistics, Vol. 2* (pp. 182–187). New York: Oxford University Press.

Adamik-Jászó, A. (1994). Actual problems of teaching to read, a historical overview [in Hungarian]. *Fejlesztő Pedagógia, 4–5*, 44–54.

Benkő, L., & Imre, S. (1972). *The hungarian language*. Budapest: Akadémiai Kiadó.

Bertelson, P., de Gelder, B., & van Zon, M. (1997). Explicit speech segmentation and syllabic onset structure: Developmental trends. *Psychological Research, 60*, 183–191.

Bitan, T., & Karni, A. (2002). Alphabetical knowledge from whole words training: Effects of explicit instruction and implicit experience on learning script segmentation. *Cognitive Brain Research, 16, 3*, 323–337.

Campbell, G. L. (1991). *Compendium of the world's languages, Vol. 1*. London: Routledge.

Coltheart, M., Curtis, B., Atkins, P., & Haller, M. (1993). Models of reading aloud: Dual-route and parallel-distributed-processing approaches. *Psychological Review, 100*, 589–608.

Coltheart, M., Rastle, K., Perry, C., Langdon, R., & Ziegler, J. (2001). DRC: A dual route cascaded model of visual word recognition and reading aloud. *Psychological Review, 108*, 204–256.

Csabay, K. (1994). Pseudo-dyslexia as an epidemic of recent years [in Hungarian]. *Fejlesztő Pedagógia, 4–5*, 39–40.

Csépe, V. (1995). On the origin and development of mismatch negativity (invited review). Mismatch negativity as an index of central auditory function [Special issue]. *Ear and Hearing, 16*(1), 90–104.

Csépe, V., Gyurkócza, E. E., Szűcs, D., & Lukács, Á. (2002). Development of and training of speech sound representation—What mismatch negativity is good for? [in Hungarian]. *Pszichológia, 1*, 3–21.

Csépe, V., & Molnár, M. (1997). Towards the clinical application of the mismatch negativity evoked potential component. *Audiology and Neuro-Otology, 2*, 354–369.

Csépe, V., Osman-Sági, V., Molnár, M., & Gósy, M. (2001). Impaired speech perception in aphasic patients: Event-related potential and neuropsychological assessment. *Neuropsychologia, 39*, 1194–1208.

Csépe, V., Szűcs, D., & Honbolygó, F. (2003). Number-word reading as challenging task in dyslexia? An ERP study. *International Journal of Psychophysiology, 51*, 69–83.

Csépe V., Szűcs, D., & Lukács, Á. (2001). Does it matter how we do learn to read? Different training, different comparison, changing mismatch negativity [in Hungarian]. In Cs. Pléh, J. László, & A. Oláh (Eds.), *Learning, initiative, creation* (pp. 198–213). Budapest: ELTE Eötvös Kiadó.

Csépe, V., Szűcs, D., & Lukács, Á. (2002). Speech perception and the language system [in Hungarian]. In I. Czigler, L. Halász, & L. M. Marton, (Eds.), *From general to particular* (pp. 109–131). Budapest: Gondolat Kiadói Kör - MTA Pszichológiai Kutatóintézet.

Czukrász, R. (1903). *First book of the Hungarian child* [in Hungarian]. Cited in Adamik-Jászó, 1994.

Ellis, N. (1989). Reading development, dyslexia and phonological skills. *The Irish Journal of Psychology, 10*, 551–567.

Goswami, U. (1999). Orthographic Analogies and Phonological Priming: A Comment on Bowey, Vaughan, and Hansen. *Journal of Experimental Child Psychology, 72, 3,* 210–219.

Goswami, U. (2000). Phonological representations, reading development and dyslexia: Towards a cross-linguistic theoretical framework. *Dyslexia, 6,* 133–151.

Goswami, U. (2003). Phonology, learning to read and dyslexia: A cross-linguistic analysis. In V. Csépe (Ed.), *Dyslexia: Different brain, different behavior* (pp. 1–40). Dordrecht, The Netherland: Klüwer Academic.

Gósy, M. (1994). Development of speech perception [in Hungarian]. *Fejlesztő Pedagógia, 4–5,* 10–17.

Høien, T. (1998). Components of phonological awareness. In Åke Olofsson & Sven Strömqvist. (Eds.), *European Comission, COST A8—Cross-linguistic studies of dyslexia and early language development* (pp. 93–108). Luxembourg: Office for Official Publications of the European Communities 1998–IV.

Kassai, I., & Kovács-Vass, E. (1991). Phonological processing and dyslexia. In R. Satow & B. Gatherere (Eds.), *Literacy without frontiers* (pp. 7–11). Proceedings of the 7th European and 28th UK Reading Association Annual Conference Oxford: Oxford University Press.

Kovács-Vass, E., & Kovács-Fehér, Zs. (2003). Reading performance of dyslexics in high school [in Hungarian]. In M. Köpf (Ed.), *Ten years of teaching dyslexics in high school* (pp. 4–11). Budapest: Öveges József Gimnázium.

Mitterer, H., Csépe, V., & Blomert, L. (2004). How are assimilated word forms recognized? Evidence from Hungarian liquid assimilation. Manuscript submitted for publication.

Mitterer, H., Csépe, V., Honbolygó, F. & Blomert, L. (2004). The automatic processing of assimilated word forms indexed by the MMN. Manuscript submitted for publication.

Pajzs, J. (1996). *Disambiguation of suffixal structure of Hungarian words using information about part of speech and suffixal structure of words in the context* (Research report of Copernicus Project 621). Budapest: Research Institute of Linguistics, HAS.

Perfetti, C. A. (1992). The representation problem in reading acquisition. In P. B. Gough, L. C. Ehri & R. Treiman (Eds.), *Reading acquisition* (pp. 145–174). Hillsdale, NJ: Lawrence Erlbaum Associates.

Pléh, Cs. (1990). Word order and morphophonological factors in the development of sentence understanding in Hungarian. *Linguistics, 28,* 1449–1469.

Ramus, F. (2003). Developmental dyslexia: specific phonological deficit or general sensorimotor dysfunction. *Current Opinion in Neurobiology, 13, 2,* 212–218.

Seymour, P. H. K., (1998). Relation between phonological awareness and reading acquisition. In Åke Olofsson, & Sven Strömqvist (Eds.), *European Comission, COST A8—Cross-linguistic studies of dyslexia and early language development* (pp. 119–125). Luxembourg: Office for Official Publications of the European Communities 1998–IV.

Share, D. L. (1995). Phonological recoding and self-teaching: Sine qua non of reading acquisition. *Cognition, 55,* 151–218.

Thompson, G. B., Cottrel, D. S., & Fletcher-Flynn, C. M. (1996). Sublexical orthographic–phonological relation early in the acquisition of reading: the knowledge sources account. *Journal of Experimental Child Psychology, 62,* 190–222.

Thompson, G. B., Fletcher-Flynn, C. M., & Cottrel, D. S. (1999). Learning correspondence between letters and phonemes without explicit instructions. *Applied Psychology, 20,* 21–50.

16

Developmental Dyslexia: Evidence from Polish

Agnieszka A. Reid
Independent Researcher

This chapter has two aims. The first is to contribute to the cross-linguistic comparisons of dyslexia and literacy skills by a review of studies on Polish across three research perspectives: the role of orthography in literacy acquisition, the role of phonological awareness in literacy skills, and the role of neuropsychological deficits in dyslexia. The second is to gain some insights into dyslexia. Because Polish has a consistent grapheme-to-phoneme correspondence, it is expected that the prevalence of reading difficulties would be low in Polish. Contrary to this, the prevalence of reading disorders in Polish is approximately as high as in languages with lower grapheme-to-phoneme correspondences. The reading of Polish dyslexic people is characterised by significantly lower reading rates and a higher number of reading errors than those of the control group. The longitudinal studies show that reading rate and accuracy deficits persist into adulthood. These findings suggest that orthography plays a rather minor role in reading by Polish dyslexic people, perhaps because its role is diminished by the severity and the nature of impairment of dyslexic readers. Because Polish has a low phoneme-to-grapheme correspondence, spelling problems are predicted. Reviewed studies support this because dyslexic readers make significantly more spelling errors than do the control population. Although errors in Polish spelling share several common features with orthographies such as English, misspellings caused by incorrectly producing digraphs, errors in denoting nasal phonemes, and leaving out diacritics seem peculiar to Polish. Studies on phonological awareness show that it is a good predictor of literacy acquisition in Polish control and dyslexic populations. The findings from neuropsychological studies have revealed that Polish dyslexic people, in contrast to control groups exhibit striking deficits, including visual magnocellular, auditory, motor, and cerebellar deficits. The results from the neuropsychological studies suggest that these deficits may play an important role in the literacy deficits of people with dyslexia. Regarding the second aim, this review revealed that it is not clear how the phonological deficit theory can account for certain reading and spelling errors. It is suggested that swapping the order of letters within a word when reading and pseudohomophone errors in spelling may be perhaps accounted for by a visual magnocellular deficit. It is further suggested that the slow reading speed and persisting higher number of reading and spelling errors in dyslexia can possibly be accounted for, at least in part, by the cerebellar deficit theory.

INTRODUCTION

We are currently witnessing a strong increase of interest in the underlying causes of dyslexia,[1] as well as increased attempts to develop appropriate remediation treatments for this disorder. Furthermore, the perspective based on the monolingual–English approach, which has been prevalent for many years, is starting to take into consideration other languages.

Two aims were set for this chapter: (a) to review studies on dyslexia in Polish to contribute a typologically distinct data point to the cross-linguistic comparisons, and (b) to gain some insights into the nature of dyslexia. I concentrate here on three main areas of Polish research. I start with the role of orthography in literacy acquisition in dyslexia; I then move on to research on phonological awareness in control and dyslexic readers; and finally I concentrate on investigations of dyslexia within the neuropsychological approach.

Dyslexia is a condition running in families, which makes reading and spelling acquisition very difficult, despite average or above-average IQ, conventional instruction, and sociocultural opportunity. Most of the work on dyslexia has been done on English, for which three major current theories of dyslexia have been formulated—the phonological deficit theory (PDT), the magnocellular deficit theory (MDT), and the cerebellar deficit theory (CDT). It has become clear, however, that English is a rather idiosyncratic language. It is characterised by inconsistent grapheme-to-phoneme and phoneme-to-grapheme correspondences. As languages vary in the characteristics of their orthographic systems, it is questionable whether the results from English can be generalised onto other languages with different degrees of orthographic consistency; only when cross-linguistic comparisons are made can specific influences of orthography on reading and spelling in dyslexia be separated from the universal influences of orthography. Relatively recently, cross-linguistic research has started to emerge, trying to explore the effects of different orthographic systems on reading and spelling processes in dyslexic and non-dyslexic populations (e.g., Aaron & Joshi, 1989; Caravolas & Volin, 2001; Frost, Katz, & Bentin, 1987; Goswami, 2000; Goulandris, 2003; Gupta & Vaid, 2002; Harris & Hatano, 1999; Lamm, 2002; Landerl, 2003; Landerl, Wimmer, & Frith, 1997; Matejcek, 1998; Morchio, Ott, & Pesenti, 1989; Paulesu et al., 2001; Pavlidis & Giannouli, 2002; Reid, 2002; Reid & Szczerbiński, 2002; Szczerbiński, 2001, 2003; Wimmer, 1996; Wydell & Butterworth, 1999; Zhou & Marslen-Wilson, 2000).

According to the PDT (e.g., Lundberg & Hoien, 2001; Rack, Snowling, & Olson, 1992; Snowling, 1981, 2000, 2001; Vellutino & Scanlon, 1987) people with dyslexia have poorly specified phonological representations of words that are due to a highly specific linguistic phonological deficit. It is claimed that the phonological deficit is manifested by problems such as segmenting words into phonemes, keeping strings of sounds or letters in short-term memory, repeating back non-words, reading and writing non-words, and problems with manipulating phonemes. As the PDT focuses on the phonological and orthographic systems of a language it presents an appropriate theoretical framework for the investigation of these systems cross-linguistically. In the first part of this chapter, I take the PDT as a starting point and review data on Polish, a language that, in contrast to English, is characterised by a consistent grapheme-to-phoneme correspondence and a relatively inconsistent phoneme-to-grapheme correspondence, and I address the issue of what role orthography plays in literacy acquisition in Polish dyslexia.

A large proportion of the scientific work within the PDT in English has been research on phonological awareness. Similar to English, in all alphabetic languages investigated so far, phonological awareness has been found to be a strong predictor of literacy skills. In the second part of this chapter I concentrate on the role of phonological awareness in Polish—a language for which grapheme-to-phoneme correspondence is consistent on the phoneme level

---

[1] The term *dyslexia* is used for simplicity to denote *developmental dyslexia* throughout this chapter.

and therefore also on the rime and the syllable levels. I ask whether phonological awareness predicts literacy acquisition and what is the predictive power of different levels of phonological representation in Polish control and dyslexic populations.

Most of the research within the neuropsychological approach has been carried out within the theoretical framework of the MDT and CDT. The MDT (e.g., Stein, 2001; Stein & Talcott, 1999; Stein, Talcott, & Witton, 2001; Talcott, Hansen, Elikem, & Stein, 2000a; Talcott et al., 2000b) claims that dyslexic people have an impaired visual and/or auditory magnocellular system (with spared parvocellular system), and this is responsible for their problems with literacy. In visual perception, the magnocellular system is concerned with where a given object is. It consists of magnocells (the largest cells in the brain) that detect rapid changes in stimuli. Visual magnocells are important in the perception of flicker as well as in the control and movement of the eyes. The auditory magnocells are specialised for tracking rapid frequency and amplitude changes in acoustic signals (Trussell, as cited in Stein & Talcott, 1999, p. 70). The parvocellular system in visual perception is concerned with what a given object is. It consists of parvocells that are responsible for perception of fine detail and colour. It must be born in mind, however, that it is an oversimplification to think of these systems as being completely distinct because their functions overlap and there are a number of interconnections between them (Evans, 2001). The investigations within the magnocellular theory focus mainly on studies in which control and dyslexic readers' literacy skills are investigated in the context of their performance on psychophysical tests that tap into the function of the visual and auditory magnocellular system. Three main types of evidence are cited in support of an impaired visual magnocellular system: unsteady binocular fixation, reduced motion sensitivity, and reduced contrast sensitivity. According to Stein (2001) the magnocellular system helps to keep the two eyes fixated to converge on each world during reading. Many dyslexic people have unsteady binocular fixation and hence experience unstable perceptions of print (Stein et al., 2001). They complain that letters seem to move around on the page, so that it is difficult to work out their order (Stein et al., 2001). Studies on motion sensitivity assess this function by determining what proportion of randomly moving dots have to move coherently for a participant to perceive the dots as moving together rather than randomly. A number of studies have reported that dyslexic people have an elevated threshold for motion sensitivity as compared with that of the control group (e.g., Hansen, Stein, Orde, Winter, & Talcott, 2001; Talcott et al., 2000b). As the magnocellular system is most sensitive to low contrasts, studies investigating contrast sensitivity predict that dyslexic people will have problems with detecting low contrasts. The claim has been made that there is support for this prediction; however, a recent literature review by Skottun (2000) suggests that although the results from some studies support the predictions of the MDT, the results from the majority of contrast sensitivity studies do not.

CDT (e.g., Fawcett & Nicolson, 2001; Nicolson & Fawcett, 1990, 2000; Nicolson, Fawcett, & Dean, 1995, 2001) was originally formulated as an automatisation deficit theory. It was supported by the finding that under optimal conditions dyslexic children could balance as well as the control group. However, in a dual task, in which participants were asked to balance and count backwards at the same time, the control group balanced automatically, whereas dyslexic children did not (Nicolson & Fawcett, 1990). More recently, the automatisation deficit in dyslexia has been linked to impaired function of the cerebellum and evidence has been accumulated in support of this theory. It includes abnormal performance on the postural stability test (Fawcet & Nicolson, 1998), the eye-blink conditioning test (Nicolson, Daum, Schugens, Fawcett, & Schulz, 2002), and the time-estimation test (Nicolson et al., 1995). Also significant differences in the numbers of large and small cerebellar neurons in dyslexic people and the control group were found (Finch, Nicolson, & Fawcett, 2002), as revealed by histological investigations using the same techniques and brain specimens of dyslexic people as those of Galaburda and colleagues (e.g., Galaburda, Menard, & Rosen, 1994). A significantly increased proportion of large neurones and fewer small neurones were found in the cerebellar cortex and inferior olive in the brains of dyslexic people, but not in the dentate nucleus, which suggests that impairment in dyslexia may originate from the input route by means of the climbing fibres from the inferior olive to the cerebellum. As the climbing fibres are considered to be the source of error signals for cerebellar processing (Mar, 1969), this finding is consistent with data that suggest that dyslexic children have particular difficulty in error elimination in the learning process (Nicolson & Fawcett, 2000).

On the basis of the findings which suggest cerebellar impairment in dyslexia, a hypothetical causal chain linking cerebellar impairment, problems with phonology, and reading and spelling deficits was proposed (Fawcett & Nicolson, 2001; Nicolson et al., 2001). According to the causal chain the literacy difficulties arise from several routes. The central route involves the impaired cerebellum, which leads to impaired articulatory skills, which in turn causes impaired sensitivity to the phonological structure of a language, manifested in impaired phonological awareness, which finally leads to reading and spelling deficits. Also, slower articulatory skills lead to reduced effectiveness of the short-term memory, and this can cause problems in language acquisition. The other important aspect of cerebellar impairment is reflected in the requirement for more resources for articulation, leaving fewer resources for processing of sensory feedback. Within this causal chain, cerebellar impairment can be interpreted as the underlying cause of the phonological impairment described within the framework of the PDT. The strength of the CDT lies in that it is the only theory that accounts within one theoretical framework for a wide range of difficulties exhibited by dyslexic people beyond literacy problems, such as problems with automatising skills, difficulty in error elimination, and difficulties with complex movements (incoordination).

The research on Polish dyslexia within the neuropsychological approach has a long tradition. In the third part of this chapter I review earlier studies that used neuropsychological tests and recent studies carried out within the MDT and the CDT. I ask whether more light can be shed by these studies onto the underlying causes of dyslexia.

THE ROLE OF ORTHOGRAPHY IN LITERACY ACQUISITION IN POLISH DYSLEXIA

As the impact of orthography on reading and spelling in dyslexia can be fully studied only cross-linguistically, I focus in this chapter on Polish. As I rely on the distinctive characteristics of Polish orthography, I start with a brief description of this system. For other linguistic characteristics of Polish, see Grzegorczykowa, Laskowski, and Wróbel (1998), Szober (1969) and Zagórska-Brooks (1975).

Characteristics of the Polish Orthographic System

The Polish language is a member of the Slavonic branch of the Indo-European language family. It belongs to the western subgroup of the North Slavonic languages, which also includes languages such as Czech and Slovak.

The Polish alphabet is based on Roman script and consists of 35 letters (Polański, 1997). There are 23 basic letters[2]: *a* [a], *b* [b], *c* [t͡s], *d* [d], *e* [ɛ], *f* [f], *g* [g], *h* [x], *i* [i], *j* [j], *k* [k], *l* [l], *m* [m], *n* [n & ŋ], *o* [ɔ], *p* [p], *r* [r], *s* [s], *t* [t], *u* [u], *w* [v], *y* [ɨ], and *z* [z]; 3 letters that

---

[2] Corresponding phonetic transcription, according to Karaś and Madejowa (1977), given in square brackets, denotes the sounds of the letters and not the names of letters.

occur only in words that are foreign borrowings: *q*, *v*, and *x*; and 9 letters with diacritics: *ą* [ɔ̃], *ć* [t͡ɕ], *ę* [ɛ̃], *ł* [w], *ń* [ɲ], *ó* [u], *ś* [ɕ], *ź* [z], and *ż* [ʒ]. Polish is also characterised by seven letter groups (digraphs): *ch* [x], *cz* [t͡ʃ], *dz* [d͡z], *dź* [d͡z], *dż*, [d͡ʒ], *sz* [ʃ] and *rz* [ʒ]. Nine letters denote vowels and 33 letters and digraphs denote consonants.

Polish has a consistent grapheme-to-phoneme correspondence. Every letter string, be it a real word or a non-word, can be read in Polish in only one way. In the majority of cases one grapheme maps onto one phoneme. There are, however, cases in which two different graphemes map onto the same phoneme, for example, *h* and *ch* map onto [x], *u* and *ó* map onto [u], *ż* and *rz* map onto [ʒ], *ć* and *ci* map onto [t͡ɕ], *ś* and *si* map onto [ɕ], and *ź* and *zi* map onto [z]. Some digraphs map onto one phoneme: *cz* maps to [t͡ʃ], *ch* to [x], *dz* to [d͡z], *dź* to [d͡z] *dż* to [d͡ʒ], *rz* to [ʒ] and *sz* to [ʃ]. Also graphemes and digraphs such as *b*, *d*, *w*, *ż*, *ź*, *dź* and *dż* can represent two sounds. For instance, the grapheme *b* can represent the phoneme [b] as in **b**rama (brama) [gate] or the phoneme [p] as in *dąb* (dɔmp) [oak tree]. This is due to the process of final devoicing in which voiced obstruents become voiceless at the end of a word. The process of devoicing occurs also in the middle of words, if a voiced phoneme follows a voiceless one (e.g., *krzak* (kʃak) [a bush]) and at the beginning of words if the voiced initial phoneme is followed by a voiceless phoneme (e.g., **w**styd (fstɨt) [shame]). These processes of devoicing are default phonological processes; hence the alternatives are disambiguated automatically, and the voicing and devoicing rules do not have to be acquired by the reader consciously. In rare cases some letters map onto zero sound. For instance, '*ł*' is mute in some forms of the past tense and in some past participles, e.g., *mógł* (muk) [he could] and *wszedł* (fʃet) [he entered]. Usually graphemes with two sound values owe this duality to the morphological principle in Polish spelling that tends to preserve the spelling of morphemes (affixes, stems, and roots) despite their different phonological realisations. For instance, in words such as *płazy* (pwazɨ) [amphibians] and *płaz* [pwas] [amphibian], orthography preserves the grapheme '*z*' in both cases, but it is realised as the phoneme [z] in the first word but as [s] in the second word. An example of the same morphological principle in English, which typically results in silent letters, can be found in words such as *bombard* and *bomb*, in which in both cases the grapheme *b* is preserved, but it is realised as the phoneme [b] in *bombard* (bɒmˈbaːd), but as a silent letter in *bomb* [bɒm].

More than one phonemic realisation of a grapheme is very rare. Polish nasal vowels are the exception–each grapheme can denote six phonemes. For instance, the grapheme *ą* can denote the following phonemes: [ɔ̃] as in *mąż* [husband], [ɔm] as in *dąb* [ɔn] as in *oglądać* [to see], [ɔɲ] as in *krzyknąć* [to shout], [ɔŋ] as in *drąg* [a pole], and [ɔ] as in *wziął* [to take, third-person singular, past tense]. This, however, is also governed by a default rule of assimilation, just as devoicing. Words with an exceptional reading, such as the English *pint*, do not exist. However, there are some foreign borrowings that are not read according to Polish phonotactic rules; for instance the word *jaz* [jazz], according to Polish phonotactic rules, should be read as (jas), but instead is read as (d͡ʒɛs), but foreign borrowings constitute a small minority of Polish words.

In contrast, Polish has a rather low phoneme-to-grapheme consistency. The majority of Polish words have several phonologically plausible spellings, but only one way of spelling is orthographically accurate. For instance, a word denoting a river (ʒɛka) can be spelt in two different ways as *rzeka* or *żeka*,[3] but only the first way of spelling is correct; or to take an extreme example, a word denoting a turtle (ʒuwf) can be spelt in seven different ways as *żółw*, *rzółw*, *żułw*, *żółf*, *rzułw*, *żułf*, and *rzułf*, but only the first way of spelling is correct. The alternative ways of spelling, marked with asterisks, are regarded as serious orthographic errors. With the exception of cases in which spelling has to be remembered on an item basis,

---

3 '*' denotes an incorrect orthographic form.

there are several principles that can be applied to checking the correct spelling. These include morphological principle, phonotactic principle, a set of complex morpho-syntactic rules, and the grapho-tactic and grapho-statistic constraints of Polish (Szczerbiński, 2001).

As already discussed, the morphological principle keeps the spelling of roots, stems, and derivational affixes constant, despite changes in their surface phonological realisations. The phonotactic principle governs, for instance, the spelling of palatal consonants. Polish palatal consonants (*ć, dź, ń, ś,* and *ź*) are marked by diacritics before consonants and word final (e.g., *pić* (p̩it͡ɕ) [to drink]), but if they are followed by a vowel, palatelity is marked by the vowel *i*, (e.g., *picie* (p̩it͡ɕɛ) [drinking]). Complex morpho-syntactic rules govern joined or separate spelling of certain particles with words. For instance the particle *nie* [no] is spelled jointly with deverbal nouns (e.g., ***nie**ufność* (ɲɛufnɔɕt͡ɕ) [distrust]), but separately with inflected verbs (e.g., ***nie** ufam* (ɲɛ ufam) [I do not trust]). Graphotactic constraints define which combination of Polish graphemes is legal (e.g., *krz* is legal, but **kż* is illegal). Grapho-statistic constraints define which combinations of Polish graphemes are the default (e.g., *krz-*), which are rare (e.g., *ksz-*), and which do not occur at all and are therefore illegal (e.g., **kż-*).

Predictions for Reading and Spelling in Polish

If orthography plays an important role in reading, then consistency of grapheme-to-phoneme correspondences should facilitate reading. Some evidence in support of this hypothesis comes from experiments that have used simplified orthography (Downing, 1967), cross-linguistic experimental comparisons of dyslexic children's reading (e.g., Landerl et al., 1997), and the data on literacy acquisition comparing English and other European languages (including Finnish, Greek, Italian, Spanish, German, Norwegian, Icelandic, Dutch, Swedish, Portuguese, French, and Danish).[4]

According to the PDT, because of the impairment of the phonological representations of words in people with dyslexia, the orthograhy-to-phonology mappings are compromised. This results in people with dyslexia having 'coarse-grained' orthography-to-phonology mappings that are sufficient for building only associations between whole-word froms and their pronunciations, but are not adequate for developing fine-grained links between the graphemes and phonemes of words (Snowling, 2000). On the basis of these assumptions, the PDT predicts that dyslexic people would have reading difficulties that manifest themselves in low speed and low accuracy of reading. Consistent grapheme-to-phoneme correspondence, however, as found in Polish should reduce reading problems in Polish dyslexic people. The prevalence of reading disorder therefore should be relatively low in Polish.

As noted earlier, in Polish, unlike the high grapheme-to-phoneme correspondence, there is a relatively low phoneme-to-grapheme relationship. If phoneme-to-grapheme correspondence is important for spelling, then the low consistency of this relationship in Polish predicts that spelling would be relatively difficult. Some support for this comes from an investigation of orthographic skills in pupils without learning difficulties in Polish grammar schools, vocational schools, and grammar schools for working pupils carried out by Polański (1973). The results revealed that, although the majority of orthographic errors made by pupils without learning difficulties in their teens and adulthood were secondary (not serious), they also made serious orthographic mistakes. The latter were defined as erroneous usage of graphemes and digraphs, such as *ż, rz, ó, u, h* and *ch*, erroneous usage of the morpheme *nie* [no] with personal verb forms, spelling of verb prefixes separately, and spelling prepositions jointly with nouns or other

---

[4] P.H.K. Seymour, personal communication, 29 October 2000.

inflected words (Polański, 1973). The majority of errors resulted in phonologically plausible and (usually) grapho-tactically legal, yet orthographically incorrect, spellings.

According to the PDT dyslexia is characterised by coarse-grained mappings between the phonological form of a word and its orthographic form (e.g., Snowling, 2000). On the basis of this assumption the PDT predicts that dyslexic people should have a spelling deficit. With the results for typical readers kept in mind, a spelling deficit in Polish dyslexic people should manifest itself quite strongly as measured by accuracy of spelling because of both the inconsistent phoneme-to-grapheme correspondence and the coarse-grained mappings between phonology and orthography. The PDT would also predict that a spelling deficit would be relatively frequent in Polish dyslexic people (Szczerbiński, 2003).

As I focus here on developmental dyslexia I close the sections on reading and spelling with a discussion of this disorder from a developmental perspective.

Reading in Polish Dyslexia

In this section I review studies on reading in Polish dyslexic people by examining whether the predictions specified in the preceding section hold true. I start with the prevalence of dyslexia in Polish, then discuss speed of reading, followed by reading accuracy, after which I turn to discussing the types of reading errors that compromise dyslexic people's reading. I finish with a discussion of these findings within the PDT and the role of orthography in reading from the cross-linguistic perspective.

Bogdanowicz (1985) found that 10% of fourth-grade[5] Polish children (end of introductory education, 10 years of age) and 10% of zeroth graders[6] had reading problems characteristic of dyslexia. The results on the prevalence of reading disorder are in line with Spionek's (1963) earlier findings in Polish. These results show that reading disorder is relatively frequent and therefore incongruent with the prediction made on the basis of consistent grapheme-to-phoneme correspondence in Polish.

Moving onto findings on the speed of reading in dyslexia, in follow-up studies Bogdanowicz (1991, 1997) found that Polish dyslexic children significantly differed from the control group in speed of reading (measured in number of words per minute, hereafter wpm). Fourth and eighth graders' reading (14-year-olds; the end of primary school education in Poland at the time the study was conducted) was investigated with Konopnicki's Test of Reading Speed (Konopnicki, 1961) (which measures wpm), whereas zeroth graders' reading was tested with Bogdanowicz's Reading Test for zeroth-grade pupils. The results revealed that the zeroth-grade control group were able to read 55 wpm, whereas dyslexic children only 1 wpm. The fourth-grade control group read 114 wpm, whereas fourth-grade dyslexic children only 51 wpm. The difference between the speed of reading between dyslexic children and the control group was significant for the eighth graders as well. Similar results were reported by Krasowicz (1997) for third-grade dyslexic children (9 years of age) and by Wszeborowska-Lipińska (1995) for dyslexic teenagers.

These findings show that reading speed is impaired in Polish dyslexic children. They clearly demonstrate that the consistent grapheme-to-phoneme correspondence in Polish does not seem to alleviate speed problems in dyslexia, in contrast to the predictions. The Polish findings regarding speed of reading of younger and older dyslexic readers are consistent with data on Czech second- to seventh-grade dyslexic children (Matejcek, 1998) and German 7- to

---

[5] The term *grade* is used throughout this chapter to denote a year at a Polish primary school.

[6] Polish primary school starts with a non-obligatory reception class—the so-called zeroth grade that children start at the age of 6 years. They start first grade at the age of 7 years.

12-year-old dyslexic children (e.g., Landerl, 2001, 2003; Landerl et al., 1997; Wimmer, 1993, 1996). The findings on the older Polish dyslexic readers are also consistent with Italian findings, in which three case studies of 11- to 12-year-old boys were reported (Morchio et al., 1989) and with findings on English 12-year-old dyslexic children (e.g., Landerl et al., 1997). These results suggest that dyslexia can significantly impair speed of reading across languages, whether a language has a consistent or an inconsistent grapheme-to-phoneme correspondence.

It was also predicted that dyslexic people would make more reading errors than the control group. The consistent Polish grapheme-to-phoneme correspondence, however, should markedly reduce the occurrence of reading errors made by dyslexic people. In contrast to this prediction, however, the studies consistently show that Polish dyslexic readers make significantly more reading errors than the control group (Bogdanowicz, 1997; Jaklewicz, 1980; Spionek, 1981; Trzeciak, 1980; Wszeborowska-Lipińska, 1995). These results are in line with findings on Czech readers. It was reported (Matejcek, 1998) that Czech dyslexic sixth and seventh graders read with less precision and reliability than normal second graders. These results are also consistent with the findings from the three case studies of Italian 11- to 12-year-old boys (Morchio et al., 1989). In contrast, they seem to be less consistent with the findings on German readers, in which the majority of studies (e.g., Wimmer, 1993; Wimmer, Mayringer & Landerl, 1998) reported that slow reading speed is the main problem of German dyslexic children. Note, however, that in a more recent populational study (Wimmer, Mayringer & Landerl, 2000) reading accuracy problems were reported in a small subsample of children with a double (phonological and naming) deficit.

A more recent study on Polish (Szczerbiński, 2003) indentified a group of low-accuracy dyslexic readers and a group of slow-speed dyslexic readers. The chronological-age control group was selected from a sample of second- and third-grade children and the reading-level control group from the first-grade children. The reading-level control group was matched on accuracy and speed of word reading, respectively. Low-accuracy dyslexic children had an alphabetic decoding deficit. Both groups of dyslexic children had difficulty with phonological awareness and rapid serial (or automatised) naming, but whereas low-accuracy dyslexic readers were worse on phonological awareness than on naming, the low-speed dyslexic readers showed the reverse pattern. Szczerbiński's (2003) results are congruent with the earlier findings on reading in Polish dyslexia. However, in contrast to the earlier studies, Szczerbiński's results suggest that speed and accuracy of reading may be impaired to different degrees in dyslexic readers. According to the author, the poor-accuracy dyslexic reader group seems to experience mainly a phonological awareness deficit, whereas the low-speed dyslexic readers experience mainly difficulty in forming and using name–symbol associations, thereby compromising the automaticity of word recognition, which is congruent with the double-deficit theory (Wolf & Bowers, 1999).

The types of reading error made by Polish dyslexic readers may be an important source of insight into which processes are compromised in Polish dyslexic readers and whether they occur in orthography with a consistent grapheme-to-phoneme correspondence. I now focus on this issue in some detail.

A variety of reading errors have been found in Polish dyslexic readers. All the reported reading errors can be classified as phonologically inaccurate errors according to the framework of PDT. The errors included swapping the order of letters in a word, the so-called dynamic inversion (e.g., reading *szufalda* instead of szuflada [a drawer, nominative singular]) (Bogdanowicz, 1997; Spionek, 1981[7]); reading words from right to left (e.g., reading od

---

[7] One needs to be cautious when interpreting the errors reported by Spoinek (1981) because the dyslexic children in her sample exhibited not only dyslexia, but also (either in the past or during the time of investigations) speech impairment. According to the author, quantitative analysis of their reading and spelling problems revealed that they did not simply reflect their speech impairment, but were characteristic of auditory and visual deficits.

[from] instead of *do* [to][8]) (Bogdanowicz, 1997); distortion of words, so that they could not be recognised as existing words (e.g., reading **hne* instead of *chętnie* [willingly]) (Jaklewicz, 1980; Spionek, 1981; Trzeciak, 1980); distorting word endings (Trzeciak, 1980); confusing graphemes with similar graphic structures—*l/t/ł, o/a, u/w/y, m/n* and *J/I* (e.g., reading **tala* instead of *lala* [a doll]) (Bogdanowicz, 1997; Trzeciak, 1980); shortening of words by not reading the initial or final graphemes (Jaklewicz, 1980); and leaving out consonants or vowels (e.g., reading **sponie* instead of *spodnie* [trousers]) (Spionek, 1981). It seems, however, that this classification of reading errors within the PDT does not capture crucial characteristics of some reading errors, such as confusing graphemes with similar graphic structures, reading words from right to left, and swapping the order of letters in a word.

The PDT account of dyslexic people's reading errors in Polish reported in the preceding section is that they occur because dyslexic people have problems with decoding the phonology of words from their orthographic forms and have coarse-grained orthography to phonology mappings. The shortcoming of this account is that it is not clear exactly what impairment determines the deficit in developing the mappings between orthography and phonology. It is also not clear how the PDT can account for such reading errors as confusing graphemes with similar graphic structures, reading words from right to left, and swapping the order of letters in a word. The PDT could argue that these types of error occur because of the impaired phonological representation of words. However, an explanation along these lines would perhaps predict a much less regular pattern of reading errors, such as omitting letters or replacing letters. In contrast, the reported errors seem to be characterised by some regularity, that is, the position of two graphemes is exactly interchanged or letters are decoded correctly, but in the wrong order. Reading errors of this type were also reported for English dyslexic readers (e.g., Orton, 1937). Swapping the order of letters was reported for Italian dyslexic readers (Morchio et al., 1989), whereas confusing graphemes with similar graphic structures and swapping the order of letters and syllables were reported for Czech dyslexic readers (Matejcek, 1998). This indicates that they are not peculiar to Polish orthographic and phonological systems, but occur in opaque orthographies, such as English, as well as in transparent orthographies. One way of accounting for these types of error is to hypothesise a problem on the level of visual processing. I will come back to this issue in the section on the insights into dyslexia from the neuropsychological studies.

A relatively high prevalence of reading disorder, significantly reduced speed, and significantly higher number of reading errors in Polish dyslexic people as compared with those of the control group, in a language with a consistent grapheme-to-phoneme correspondence, indicate that the role of orthography in reading in Polish dyslexia is less than was initially hypothesised, at least for the examined populations of people with dyslexia. It can be suggested that this turns out to be the case because the complexity of Polish orthography has been underestimated. Although it is possible, the cross-linguistic results just discussed suggest that this is not necessarily the case because some of the errors, such as swapping the order of letters within a word and confusing graphemes with similar structure, seem not to rely on any specific characteristic of an orthographic system and indeed have been reported for inconsistent and consistent orthographies.

Although the reading-speed data on German dyslexia (e.g., Landerl et al., 1997; Wimmer, 1993, 1996) are consistent with findings from Polish dyslexia (and Czech and Italian dyslexia), the data on reading accuracy seem to be less consistent. They suggest that reading accuracy problems in German dyslexia are resolved by the end of the second grade of reading instruction. This is certainly not the case in the reviewed studies on Polish dyslexia (and Czech and Italian dyslexia). It is not clear what the underlying cause of these differences is, because German,

---

[8] This particular example can be also classified as a dynamic inversion error.

as well as Polish, Czech, and Italian, is characterised by a consistent grapheme-to-phoneme correspondence.

It has currently become apparent that meaningful cross-linguistic comparisons are difficult to make because of the potential involvement of many confounding variables. Therefore there could be many reasons why the German results on reading accuracy are less congruent with the reviewed results on Polish, Czech, and Italian. Three potential reasons for the observed differences should be noted. It could be that Polish dyslexic readers (and Czech and Italian dyslexic readers) come from more severely impaired dyslexic populations than German dyslexic readers. It is also feasible that Polish dyslexic readers (and Czech and Italian dyslexics) may come from a dyslexic population characterised by a different profile of impairment that would lead to differences in the exhibited symptoms, or indeed they could have both of these characteristics—a higher severity and a different profile of impairment.[9] Future cross-linguistic research on dyslexia involving the role of orthography in reading (and also in other literacy skills) will need to address the issue of severity and profile of impairment in dyslexia to ensure meaningful comparisons.

I now move on to studies on spelling in Polish dyslexic children.

Spelling in Polish Dyslexia

It was hypothesised that if phoneme-to-grapheme correspondence is important for spelling, then the low consistency of this relationship in Polish predicts that spelling in Polish would be relatively difficult. It was further hypothesised on the basis of the PDT that a spelling deficit in Polish dyslexic people should manifest itself quite strongly as measured, for instance, by accuracy of spelling. Finally, it was predicted that the spelling deficit would be relatively frequent in Polish dyslexic people (Szczerbiński, 2003).

I now focus on examining whether there is support for the predictions specified in the preceding section. The prevalence of spelling disorder in Polish dyslexic people is reviewed first, and then the accuracy of spelling is discussed; the subsection ends with a report on the types of spelling errors. I finish with a discussion of these findings within the PDT.

It was reported (Szurmiak, 1974) that the occurrence of a spelling deficit in a representative sample of Polish dyslexic children from the first to the fourth grades was 10%. An epidemiological study by Jaklewicz (1980) and Bogdanowicz (1985) investigated spelling with tests of spelling to dictation, spelling from memory and copying, and found that 13%–17% of fourth-grade children had a spelling disorder. These figures are comparable with the results for reading disorder, although of somewhat smaller magnitude, reported by the same authors. The results on the prevalence of a spelling deficit therefore lend support for the prediction that a spelling disorder would be relatively frequent in dyslexic people in a language with inconsistent phoneme-to-grapheme correspondence, such as Polish.

Regarding spelling accuracy in dyslexia, the studies consistently show that dyslexic people made significantly more spelling errors than people from the control population (Bogdanowicz, 1985; Lewandowska & Bogdanowicz, 1982; Szurmiak, 1974; Wszeborowska-Lipińska, 1995). In some cases there was a considerable discrepancy between the performances of control and dyslexic children. For instance, Szurmiak (1974) reported a case of a third-grade dyslexic child who made 23 spelling mistakes in writing to dictation, whereas the mean of spelling mistakes

---

[9] It is worth noting that such an account is congruent with the existence of populations of dyslexic readers with different profiles of impairment within the same language. Possible examples of this are the data of Morchio et al. (1989) on Italian 11- to 12-year-old boys, which suggest that Italian dyslexic readers make markedly more reading errors than do typical readers, and data on Italian university students (Paulesu et al., 2001), which suggest a relatively mild reading impairment. However, as there are potentially many confounding variables (including age), this comparison could be only suggestive.

for the third graders in this study was 3. The results on spelling accuracy in Polish dyslexia support the prediction that a spelling deficit should manifest itself quite strongly.

Similar to reading errors, spelling errors may be a valuable source of insight into what processes might be compromised in dyslexic people and what types of spelling error occur in Polish orthography. A variety of spelling errors made by Polish dyslexic children in writing to dictation has been reported. Some of the errors were of the same type as errors reported for reading; hence the section on reading should be consulted for examples of these errors. Broadly speaking, the reported Polish spelling errors can be classified within the PDT framework into two categories: phonologically inaccurate errors (the same category as described for the reading errors) and phonologically accurate errors. Phonologically inaccurate errors are characterised by errors in the phonemic features of a word. Phonologically accurate errors, on the other hand, are characterised by the correct phonemic form of a word, but incorrect orthographic form. The phonologically inaccurate spelling errors included leaving out letters[10] (e.g., writing *nazwa instead of nazywa [he/she/it names]) (Spionek, 1981; Szurmiak, 1974); leaving out endings of words (e.g., writing *obrazkam instead of obrazkami [pictures, instrumental, plural]) (Szurmiak, 1974; also see note 10); adding letters (e.g., writing *pomyliyły instead of pomyliły [they mistook, nonpersonal gender]) (Jaklewicz, 1980; Spionek, 1981; Szurmiak, 1974; also see note 10); difficulties with digraphs (e.g., writing *warkoce instead of warkocze [plaits]) (Szurmiak, 1974); confusing letters corresponding to phonetically similar phonemes (e.g., d/t, w/f, sz/cz and l/j) (e.g., writing *Torota instead of Dorota [Dorothy], *forek instead of worek [a sack]) (Jaklewicz, 1980; Szurmiak, 1974; also see note 10); confusing letters with similar shape, an error that is characterised by great instability (this means that a given error is made by the same person on some occasions, but not on others, even within the same passage) (Jaklewicz, 1980; Spionek, 1981; Szurmiak, 1974; also see note 10); changing the order of letters, an error that is also characterised by great instability (Spionek, 1981; Szurmiak, 1974; also see note 10); distorting words so that they could not be recognised as existing words (Spionek, 1981; also see note 10); 'mirror image' letter errors, for example, confusing b/d (Jaklewicz, 1980; also see note 10); reversing words (e.g., writing od [from] instead of do [to]), another error that is characterised by great instability (see note 10); errors in the structure of words (e.g., writing words together, *mapsa, instead of separately, ma psa [he/she/it has a dog], or separately, *na zbierać, instead of together, nazbierać [to collect, perfective] (see note 10); and leaving out diacritics (e.g., writing a instead of ą, e instead of ę, as in for instance *pak instead of pąk [a bud]) (Wszeborowska-Lipińska, 1995; also see note 10).

The phonologically accurate, but orthographically incorrect, spelling errors included errors in denoting nasal phonemes (e.g., writing om instead of ą, en instead of ę, oł instead of ął, as in for instance *wzioł instead of wziął [he took]); orthographic errors resulting in pseudohomophones, defined as words that are orthographically incorrect but phonologically accurate (e.g., writing *żeka instead of rzeka [a river] and *wiewiurka instead of wiewiórka [a squirrel]) (Jaklewicz, 1980; Wszeborowska-Lipińska, 1995; also see note 10); difficulties in differentiating between soft consonants (e.g., writing ś instead of si, as in *Maryśa instead of Marysia [Mary, diminutive] and in *śę instead of się [oneself]) (Szurmiak, 1974; also see note 10); and errors in denoting phonemes that from voiced become voiceless (e.g., writing *chlep instead of chleb [bread]) (Nowak, 1989; also see note 10). In parallel with the reading errors, this classification of spelling errors does not seem to capture crucial characteristics of some spelling errors, such as confusing graphemes with similar graphic structures, reading words from right to left, and swapping the order of letters in a word.

Dyslexic people's spelling errors such as distorting words so that they cannot be recognised as existing words (dysphonetic errors, according to Snowling's [2000] typology) (e.g.,

---

[10] M. Bogdanowicz, personal communication, June 2002.

writing *bagid instead of blanket), errors of minor phoneme-to-grapheme correspondence with the overall phonetic sequence preserved (semiphonetic errors) (e.g., writing *banket instead of blanket), and phonetic errors that are characterised by incorrect orthographic but correct phonological form (e.g., writing *blankit instead of blanket) were reported for English (Snowling, 2000). Spelling errors such as changing the order of letters (dynamic inversion), confusing letters with similar shape, and reversing words were reported for English dyslexic readers (e.g., Orton, 1937); dynamic inversion was also reported for Italian (Morchio et al., 1989) and Czech dyslexic readers (Caravolas & Volin, 2001). This suggests that these errors have a more universal character and occur in consistent as well as in inconsistent orthographies. On the other hand, errors such as difficulties with digraphs, errors in denoting nasal phonemes, and leaving out diacritics seems to be peculiar to the Polish orthographic system.

Similar to the PDT's account of dyslexic people's reading errors, the PDT's account of their spelling errors has shortcomings. First, it is not clear exactly what impairment determines the deficit in developing the mappings between phonology and orthogrphy. Second, as described, errors such as changing the order of letters, confusing letters with similar shape, and reversing words are characterised by great instability. For instance, the spelling of a given word is not constant but its letters may vary between dextral order (towards the right) and sinistral order (towards the left, so that *was* is spelled as *saw*). If the phonological representation of a given word is impaired, then one would predict that its spelling would be mostly impaired and not sometimes spelled correctly and sometimes incorrectly, even within the same passage. Third, spelling errors, such as errors in denoting nasal phonemes, pseudohomophone errors, errors in denoting phonemes that from voiced become voiceless suggest that their phonological representation is uncompromised, but their orthographic representation is impaired. This indicates that spelling errors of this type may not be determined by phonological deficit, but rather by a deficit in orthographic processing. I come back to this issue in the section on insights into dyslexia from the neuropsychological studies.

The Developmental Perspective of Reading and Spelling in Polish Dyslexia

As dyslexia is a disorder that lasts a lifetime, in closing the section on reading and spelling, I focus briefly on the developmental perspective of this disorder.

Bogdanowicz (1991, 1997) reported that reading difficulties reflected by the low reading speed found in zeroth graders (measured with Bogdanowicz's Reading Test for zeroth-grade pupils) persisted in the majority of cases through fourth to eighth grade (measured with Konopnicki's Test of Reading Speed [1961]). Furthermore, reading errors, such as confusing letters, reading words from right to left, and swapping the letter order within words were made significantly more often by dyslexic eighth graders than by the control group (Bogdanowicz, 1997). These results are confirmed by two other studies (Lewandowska & Bogdanowicz, 1982; Jaklewicz; 1980). Lewandowska and Bogdanowicz (1982) reported a follow-up study of a group of participants who were diagnosed with dyslexia when they were 8- to 11-years-old. The results revealed that the difficulties in reading as measured with Konopnicki's Test of Reading Speed (1961) persisted into adulthood in the majority of cases. Jaklewicz (1980) reported a follow-up study of a representative sample of participants with dyslexia (examined at the fourth grade and at a mean age of 21 years). Her results suggest that problems with reading persist throughout development—the reading of the majority of participants with dyslexia when tested in adulthood was below the seventh-grade level (as measured with Konopnicki's Test of Reading Speed [1961]). The reading of these dyslexic participants was also characterised by reading errors, such as swapping the order of letters within a word and distorting words.

A similar picture emerged for spelling. A follow-up study (Lewandowska & Bogdanowicz, 1982) reported that problems with spelling identified in dyslexic teenagers persisted into adulthood. The most common spelling errors made by dyslexic adults included errors in the phonetic form of a word (3.2 errors per person on average) and orthographic errors (3.5 errors per person on average). Errors involving the graphical form of a word occurred rarely (0.8 errors per person on average). The comparison of the spelling data for dyslexic teenagers and adults from this longitudinal study revealed that the number of phonetic errors did not change, the number of errors involving the graphical form of a word decreased, and the number of orthographic errors increased.

I now move on to the second area of research—the investigation of phonological awareness in Polish.

PHONOLOGICAL AWARENESS

In contrast to the western literature on literacy acquisition in control and dyslexic populations, for which research on phonological awareness has been extremely popular, the Polish literature has started to emerge relatively recently. According to the PDT, dyslexic people are impaired on phonological awareness, which is causally related to reading and spelling ability (Snowling, 2000). In support of this claim phonological awareness was found to be a strong predictor of literacy skills in all alphabetic languages studied so far. The role played by different units of phonological representation, such as phonemes and rhymes, was investigated. It was found that the phoneme level successfully predicts reading acquisition in all the alphabetic languages studied so far, such as English (e.g., Goswami & Bryant, 1990), German (Wimmer, Landerl, Linortner, & Hummer, 1991) and Greek (Porpodas, 1993). Rhyme, on the other hand, was found to be a strong predictor of literacy acquisition in English (e.g., Bradley & Bryant, 1983; Goswami, 1991), but not in languages with consistent grapheme-to-phoneme correspondence, such as Norwegian and Swedish (Hoien, Lundberg, Stanovich, & Bjaalid, 1995; Lundberg, Olofsson, & Wall, 1980). It was suggested (Goswami, 2000) that rhyme is a strong predictor in learning to read English because the English grapheme-to-phoneme correspondence is relatively consistent at the level of rhyme compared with the level of vowel phoneme. The findings on the role of rhyme in literacy acquisition in English, however, remain controversial (Seymour Duncan, & Bolik, 1999; Snowling, 2000). The 'large-unit' theories (e.g., Bradley & Bryant, 1983; Goswami, 1991) emphasise the importance of rhyme at the initial stages of literacy acquisition, whereas the 'small-unit' theories (e.g., Duncan, Seymour & Hill, 1997; Seymour et al., 1999) suggest that this role emerges only later and is relevant primarily to orthographic spelling. Here I focus on studies on phonological awareness in Polish, exploring the predictive power of phoneme, syllable, and rhyme in literacy acquisition.

Studies by Krasowicz-Kupis, Bryant, and Bogdanowicz (1999) and Szczerbiński (2003) addressed phonological awareness in the context of literacy acquisition in Polish children. Krasowicz-Kupis et al. (1999) ran an extensive 3-year longitudinal study that addressed the question of which phonological factors underlay Polish children's progress in learning to read in their first, second, and third year at school. In this study children's phonological skills were measured four times (when the children were 6-years and 6-months, 7-years, 8-years, and 9-years old) at three levels: phonemic, syllablic, and intrasyllabic. Four tasks were used to investigate the phonemic level: phoneme discrimination (the child had to judge whether pairs of words–pseudowords sounded the same), phoneme analysis (the child heard a word and had to pronounce its sounds—constituent phonemes—separately), phoneme blending (the child heard phonemes pronounced separately and was asked to put them together into a word or pseudoword), and phoneme deletion (the child heard a word and was asked to say that word without the first sound). The investigation of the syllabic level consisted of three types of task—syllable analysis (separating syllables in the word), syllable blending (synthesis of syllables heard in the correct order), and syllable deletion (removing the first or the last syllable in the word). Finally, the intrasyllabic level was tested with four tasks: rhyme oddity (the child had to say which of the words did not rhyme), alliteration oddity (the child had to say which of the words did not start in the same way), rhyme production (the child had to produce a word that rhymed with the target word), and alliteration production (the child had to produce a word that started the same way as the target word).

The results revealed that all the phoneme scores successfully predicted reading at the end of the first year and at the end of the second year and some of the phoneme scores were also significant predictors of reading at the end of the third year. The results still held when intelligence was controlled. This outcome is in line with findings for other alphabetic languages. Interestingly, the syllable deletion task was a significant predictor of reading in the first and the second year, and the syllable analysis and blending tasks predicted reading in all three years. The strong predictive power of syllable awareness in Polish may be due to Polish being a syllable-timed language and the fact that the majority of Polish words are polysyllabic. Finally, it was found that rhyme was the poorest predictor. It predicted the reading scores in the first and the second year, but not in the third year. Furthermore, the correlation of rhyme with reading in the first and second year was weaker than the correlation with the other phonological tasks. The weak predictive power of rhyme is in line with findings for other languages with consistent grapheme-to-phoneme correspondence and also English (on account of the small-unit theories). In Polish, similar to other languages with consistent grapheme-to-phoneme correspondence on the phoneme level, there must be less demand on a system to represent phoneme-to-grapheme correspondence on the rhyme level. The findings of Krasowicz-Kupis et al. (1999) suggest that phonemes, syllables, and rhymes all contribute to reading acquistion, but the phonemic level of representation has the strongest contribution. A more recent study (Szczerbiński, 2003) has also reported data on phonological awareness in Polish. Phonological awareness was measured with tests of phoneme analysis, phoneme blending, phoneme replacement, and alliteration detection and revealed that it is a good predictor of reading in an unselected group of first to third grade Polish children.

As far as phonological awareness in Polish dyslexia is concerned, the phonemic level has been investigated most. For instance, a study by Nowak (1989) investigated phonemic aware-ness in children with reading and spelling difficulties. A battery of tests was used that included three subtests: phoneme discrimination, phoneme analysis, and phoneme blending. The re-sults revealed that dyslexic participants performed significantly worse than the control group on every test. The participants' reading, spelling, and pronunciation were also investigated. Nowak's (1989) results showed that there was a significant correlation between the ability to auditorily differentiate similar sounding words and the score on the spelling test; the ability of phoneme analysis and the score for writing to dictation; and the ability of phoneme blending and the score on the reading test. Nowak's (1989) findings show that Polish dyslexic children exhibit problems with phonological awareness and that this correlates with their literacy skills.

Another study by Wszeborowska-Lipińska (1995) investigated phonological awareness in a large sample of dyslexic teenagers by using Wepman-Matejcek's 'Chinese Language' Test[11] adapted for Polish by Bogdanowicz and Haponiuk. The results revealed that 71% of dyslexic participants had serious problems with distinguishing phonemes and 80% of dyslexic participants had deficits in phoneme analysis and phoneme synthesis for which non-word material was used. A study mentioned earlier (Szczerbiński, 2003) reported that a selected group of Polish second- and third-grade dyslexics had difficulty with phonological awareness tasks, such as vowel and consonant replacement.

---

[11] This test is currently known as *Nieznany Język* [Unknown Language] (M. Bogdanowicz, personal communication, June 2002). It taps into phonological abilities, such as phoneme differentiation, analysis, synthesis and identification (naming phonemes that are different in the pair), syllable analysis and synthesis, and auditory memory. All subtests involve non-words.

Summary of the Findings From the Phonological Awareness Studies

In summary, the reviewed studies on phonological awareness in Polish indicate three outcomes. First, phonological awareness is a good predictor of literacy skills in Polish control and dyslexic populations, which is in line with the results for other alphabetic languages with consistent and inconsistent grapheme-to-phoneme correspondence. Second, the strength of predictive power of the different phonological levels of representation differ, with the phonemic level being the strongest predictor, syllable being a strong predictor, and rhyme being the poorest predictor. The poorest predictive power of rhyme is congruent with findings for other languages with consistent grapheme-to-phoneme correspondence. It is also in line with the conclusions on the role of rhyme in early reading acquisition in English within the framework of small-unit theories (e.g., Duncan et al., 1997; Seymour et al., 1999). Third, dyslexic readers are significantly worse than the control group on phonological awareness tasks, which correlates with their poor literacy skills.

Shortcomings of the Phonological Awareness Studies

The studies on phonological awareness, however, are not without problems. First, most of the standard tasks used to probe phonological processing, such as phoneme analysis and alliteration production tasks, involve more than just phonological processing. Phoneme analysis involves short-term memory and phonological processing, whereas the alliteration production task involves short-term memory, retrieval from the lexicon (the long-term memory), executive functions, and phonological processing. Therefore, if dyslexic people perform poorly on these tasks, it is not clear, whether it is due to phonological impairment or impairment of other processes or indeed both. Second, as the reviewed data on phonological awareness come mainly from off-line, metalinguistic judgement tasks it is questionable whether they tap into the same unconscious phonological processes that are crucial for reading and spelling and not other conscious operations that are not normally involved.

I now move on to the last group of Polish studies that address dyslexia within the neuropsychological approach.

RESEARCH ON POLISH DYSLEXIA WITHIN THE NEUROPSYCHOLOGICAL APPROACH

Studies that have investigated dyslexia within the neuropsychological approach have a long tradition in the Polish literature. They have focused on testing auditory, visual, and motor functions as well as on patterns of laterality. The studies used a range of tests tapping into neuropsychological functions.[12] Investigations on the level of integration of perceptual and motor functions have also been carried out. More recent studies have concentrated on visual magnocellular and cerebellar impairments. The majority of investigations have ensured that

---

[12] A brief description of the most commonly used tests is given for clarity. Stambak's Rhythmic Structures Reproduction Test (Jaklewicz, 1980) was usually used for investigating the auditory function. In this test participants have to reproduce a sequence of taps against a surface of a table with a pencil. The sequences differ from each other by the number of taps and different occurrence of two breaks (short and long) that separate the taps. Bender-Santucci's Graphic Test of Perceptual Organisation (Bogdanowicz, 1991; Jaklewicz, 1980) was usually used to investigate visual processing. In this test the participants are asked to reproduce two-dimensional figures with an increasing level of difficulty. The test that was usually used to investigate kinaesthetic and motor abilities was Stambak's Lines Test (Jaklewicz, 1980). In this test participants have to draw vertical lines in appropriate cells within a grid. Zazzo's tasks (Zazzo, 1974) were usually administered to examine the pattern of hand, eye, and foot functional dominance.

dyslexic people had average or above-average intelligence, underwent neuropsychological investigation, and had normal hearing and vision (as measured with standard methods).

One of the earliest studies investigating neuropsychological functions in Polish children with difficulties in acquiring reading and writing was reported by Spionek (1963). A large sample of 100 children (7–12 years of age) was selected from a group of children referred to a specialist clinic in Warsaw. Spionek (1963) found that 91% of the children had an auditory deficit, 70% had an a visual deficit, and 68% had a motor deficit. Of the children, 83% showed development of their auditory function to be 2 years or more behind the norm, 52% in a visual function, 48% in a kinaesthetic-motor function. Of the sample, 56% had deficits in more than one function.

As the results obtained in Spionek's (1963) study were not based on a representative sample the author was prompted to initiate an investigation of reading and writing difficulties in children from first to third grade in mainstream Warsaw primary schools. Only data on the auditory deficit for children from the second grade (8 years of age) with reading and writing difficulties and children without difficulties (the control group) from five Warsaw primary schools were reported (Spionek, 1963). The results revealed that 62% of the children with a reading and writing deficit had a more serious auditory deficit, 18% exhibited a 1-year delay in the auditory function, and 20% did not show any problems. These findings stand in contrast to the data for the control group, in which only 4% of children had a more serious auditory deficit, 8% exhibited a 1-year delay in the auditory function, and 88% did not show any auditory deficits. The results for the representative sample of children with reading and spelling problems (Spionek, 1963) revealed that, although the percentage of children with an auditory deficit was smaller than that of the children referred to the specialist clinic, it was still relatively high—reaching 62% of the sample. Spionek's (1963) studies just reported were the first to reveal that Polish children with reading and spelling difficulties have a range of impairments in perceptual and motor functions.

In a more recent large-scale cross-sectional study Bogdanowicz (1985) examined dyslexic childrens' visual perception, auditory perception (assessed with Stambak's, Wepman-Matejcek's, and Muszyńska-Żarczyńska's[13] tests) and the performance of a kinaesthetic–motor function. The results revealed four outcomes. First, 39% of dyslexic fourth graders and 27% of dyslexic zeroth graders had a visual deficit; second, 69% of dyslexic fourth graders and 71% of dyslexic zeroth graders had an auditory deficit; third, 25% of dyslexic fourth graders and 18% of dyslexic zeroth graders had a kinaesthetic–motor deficit; fourth, often two or three deficits co-occured—35% of zeroth graders and 66% of fourth graders exhibited two or three deficits. Interestingly, it was revealed (Bogdanowicz, 1991, 1997) that if only one deficit was present, it was usually an auditory deficit, rarely a visual deficit, but never a kinaesthetic–motor deficit.

Dyslexic children's patterns of laterality were also investigated (e.g., Bogdanowicz, 1991, 1997) within the framework of two hypotheses: the eye and hand cross-dominance hypothesis and the lack of lateral-dominance hypothesis (Orton, 1937). According to the former hypothesis the eye and hand cross-dominance causes difficulties in reading and writing acquisition. Contrary to the predictions, based on the eye and hand cross-dominance hypothesis, no significant difference was reported in the number of children with eye and hand cross dominance in the control and dyslexic groups (Bogdanowicz, 1991, 1997). According to Orton's (1937) hypothesis, words are processed in the symmetrical centres in both hemispheres, and in the perceptual process two mirror images of a given word are created in each hemisphere. In a mature system with well-established hemispheric dominance the left hemisphere controls the perception of words and suppresses their mirror images in the non-dominant hemisphere. With

---

[13] This test taps into phonological processing abilities, including differentiation, analysis and synthesis of phonemes and syllables.

a lack of hemispheric dominance the left hemisphere does not control perception and so does not suppress the mirror images created in the right hemisphere that cause reading and spelling problems in dyslexia. The results on Polish (Bogdanowicz, 1991, 1997) revealed that although abnormal lateral dominance (in most cases lack of lateral dominance) significantly differentiated dyslexic children (60% had this problem) and the control group (48% had abnormal lateral dominance) in the zeroth grade, this difference was no longer significant by the time the participants attended the fourth grade. The Polish results therefore do not provide support for either of these hypotheses.

The fact that some children who did not exhibit deficits in auditory, visual, or kinaesthetic–motor functions, or in the pattern of laterality, were nevertheless poor readers led Bogdanowicz (1997) to undertake an investigation into other possible sources of reading failure. As reading and spelling are complex processes involving all three functions (auditory, visual, and kinaesthetic–motor that must not only function correctly on their own, but also jointly), Bogdanowicz (1997) investigated the integration of perceptual and motor functions. Six tests were used. Three tests tapped into intrasensory integration, defined as the ability of association of information from the same and different modalities (Bogdanowicz, 1997). Monroe's test (Bogdanowicz, 1997) tapped into visual and auditory modalities, whereas two other tests, Zlab's test and Bogdanowicz's Próby I Test (Bogdanowicz, 1997), investigated visual, auditory and kinaesthetic–motor modalities. Three further tests tapped into intersensory integration defined as the ability of transposition of information from one modality to another modality. Brich-Belmont's test and Koppitz's test (Bogdanowicz, 1997) tapped into auditory and visual modalities, whereas Bogdanowicz's Próby T Test (Bogdanowicz, 1997) tapped into auditory, visual, and kinaesthetic–motor modalities.

In a follow-up study (Bogdanowicz, 1997) children with reading difficulties were tested when attending zeroth grade and fourth grade. A reliably significant difference was found between children with reading difficulties and the control groups in both grades in all the tests used. Significant correlations were also found for scores from individual tests of the integration of perceptual and motor functions and scores for reading ability. In comparison with the results from tests designed to tap into 'single' perceptual and motor functions used in the earlier research (e.g., Bogdanowicz, 1985), the 'integration' tests differentiated participants with reading difficulties better. It should be noted, however, that the single and integration tests were not matched on the level of difficulty, with the latter ones being more difficult.

As already discussed, the data from Stamback's Rhythmic Structures Reproduction Test, Bender-Santucci's Graphic Test of Perceptual Organisation, and Stambak's Lines Test were interpreted as a measure of the performance on a single (auditory, visual, or kinaesthetic–motor) function (Bogdanowicz, 1985; Spionek, 1963). However, as stressed by Bogdanowicz (1997), the tests designed to tap into a single perceptual function are confounded, and they usually also tap into the integration of perceptual and motor functions. This becomes apparent when the tasks employed by these tests are analysed.[14] Therefore if dyslexic people have difficulty with these tests it is not clear whether it is due to problems with single functions or to the integration of functions.

There is much less research on Polish dyslexic teenagers and adults than on dyslexic children, perhaps because it has been generally assumed that developmental dyslexia becomes much less severe or even goes away in adulthood. Two studies should be mentioned here. Jaklewicz (1980) reported that 83% of dyslexic adults had an auditory deficit (as measured with Stamback's

---

[14] Stamback's Rhythmic Structures Reproduction Test taps into not only the auditory function, but also auditory memory and auditory–motor integration. Bender-Santucci's Graphic Test of Perceptual Organisation involves performance of visual function and visual–motor integration. Stambak's Lines Test taps into the performance of the kinaesthetic–motor function and visual–motor integration.

Rhythmic Structures Reproduction Test), 46% had a visual deficit (as measured with Bender-Santucci's Graphic Test of Perceptual Organisation), and 37% had a motor deficit (as measured with Stambak's Lines Test). Wszeborowska-Lipińska (1995) reported investigations of a large sample of dyslexic teenagers from secondary school. Investigations of the perceptual and motor functions showed that 77% of dyslexic participants had a visual perception and a visual–motor coordination deficit. Of dyslexic participants, 57% had a serious visual deficit (visual perception equivalent to that of 12-year-olds).

Recent Neuropsychological Studies

Recent studies in Polish dyslexia (Bednarek & Grabowska, 2001; Reid & Szczerbiński, 2002) have focused on the processing of the visual magnocellular system and cerebellar function.

Bednarek and Grabowska (2001) reported a study that focused on the visual magnocellular system in Polish dyslexic children. Forty-nine 9- to 11-year-old children participated in the study. Dyslexic children ($n = 21$), in contrast to control children ($n = 28$), were 2 years delayed in their reading and spelling. Both groups were matched for IQ (as measured by the Wechsler Intelligence Scale for Children). An experimental task investigating contrast sensitivity in four spatial frequencies for sinusoidal black-and-white horizontal gratings, presented in five different conditions (static, flickering [2 and 8 HZ], and drifting [2 and 8 Hz]), was used to tap into the magnocellular system. In each condition gratings of a given spatial frequency were presented 10 times. A control experiment focused on investigating the analogous colour sensitivity function for red and green gratings, tapping into the parvocellular processing. The presentation duration in both tasks was controlled by the participants, so that they were not under time pressure. Four findings were reported. First, the biggest differences in contrast sensitivity were obtained in the spatial frequency range characteristic for magnocellular processing; second, dyslexic children did not show an increase in contrast sensitivity in dynamic presentation at the low spatial frequency in contrast to the control group; third, the colour sensitivity test did not reveal any group differences; fourth, the dyslexic children were more sensitive to contrast than the control group. The first three findings provide support for a magnocellular deficit in dyslexic children with sparing of the parvocellular system. However, the fourth finding does not seem to provide straightforward support for the MDT. Future investigations need to clarify the nature of contrast sensitivity in dyslexia.

A study by Reid and Szczerbiński (2002) was set up with the conviction that in order to make further progress towards discovering what is and what causes dyslexia, fuller profiles of dyslexic people than the ones obtained so far need to be established by an examination of their phonological, magnocellular, and cerebellar functions (Reid, 2001, in press). Only such an approach will allow for verification of which of the current theories of dyslexia, if any, can account for the deficits of a given dyslexic population.

The authors reported a case study of a Polish developmental dyslexic adult, here called DOZ. DOZ is a right-handed 31-year-old female with a family history of developmental dyslexia who graduated from university. She experienced severe difficulties when learning to read, spell, and do mathematics. DOZ was diagnosed as having developmental dyslexia at the age of 13 years. The structured interview, based on DSM–IV, revealed that DOZ had also attention deficit hyperactivity disorder (ADHD). DOZ's performance on the experimental tasks was compared with those of a control group ($n = 4$) matched for IQ, age, gender, handedness, and education.

The results revealed that DOZ was impaired on most of the phonological tasks as compared with the control group. She had problems with the automatised naming of letters as well as digits and letters (randomly intermixed within the same list). She had severe problems with reading single words and even more with non-words. DOZ had difficulties with spoonerising word pairs, which were indicated by both longer time and lower accuracy. She was also impaired on the phoneme deletion task, as indicated by slower speed. DOZ's performance was somewhat better on the speed of naming pictures, colours, as well as pictures and colours (randomly intermixed within the same list), phoneme deletion accuracy, and semantic fluency. She performed normally on digit naming speed and alliteration fluency. DOZ did not show a reading comprehension deficit, which suggests that she was able to compensate for reading problems by relying on context.

To investigate DOZ's visual magnocellular processing the Coherent Visual Motion Test (Hansen, 1995) was used. It is a psychophysical task that biases towards the processing of the magnocellular system. The test allows one to determine what proportion of randomly moving dots have to move coherently for a participant to perceive the dots as moving together rather than randomly. The Coherent Visual Form Test (Hansen, 1999) was used as a control test for the Coherent Visual Motion Test. This task was designed to bias towards tapping into the function of the parvocellular system. It allows one to determine what proportion of random static line segments have to be arranged in concentric circles for a participant to perceive that the line segments formed concentric circles. The results revealed that DOZ had a magnocellular impairment, but no parvocellular deficit that is congruent with data obtained for English dyslexic adults (e.g., Talcott et al., 2000a).

The study by Reid and Szczerbiński (2002) is the only one, to my knowledge, that has addressed cerebellar impairment in Polish dyslexia. In this study the Postural Stability Test (Fawcet & Nicolson, 1998) was used to tap into DOZ's cerebellar function. This test is based on clinical procedures for establishing cerebellar abnormalities and it involves testing participants' balance with a balance tester. In the original version of the test, the participants are tested four times. They are pushed in their back with the balance tester when blindfolded and standing with their feet together. They have their hands by their side on two trials and their arms straight in front of them on the other two trials. Additionally, the study by Reid and Szczerbiński (2002) introduced the second condition, also used by Nicolson and colleagues, in which the participants had to count backwards, instead of being blindfolded. It has been found that counting backwards as a secondary task can disrupt a skill if it is not fully automatic. The task in both conditions was to stay as still as possible while being pushed by the experimenter. Although DOZ's balance was within the normal range on this test when DOZ was blindfolded, she was consistently worse on every trial when asked to count backwards. This was in contrast to the performance of the control participants, the majority of whom did not exhibit balance instability in the counting backwards and blindfolded conditions. This finding suggests that, as DOZ's balance was disrupted by the secondary task it was not fully automatic. This result is therefore consistent with CDT. The problem with interpreting DOZ's instability in the second condition is that it is not clear whether the impairment is due to lack of automatic balance caused by a cerebellar deficit or an attention problem that arises when two tasks have to be performed in parallel. Further investigations based on more sensitive cerebellar tests, such as the time-estimation test (Nicolson et al., 1995) and the eye-blink conditioning test (Nicolson et al., 2002) will allow for more in-depth investigations of DOZ's cerebellar processing.

Reid and Szczerbiński's (2002) study investigated a much fuller profile of dyslexia than that reported in most studies, except, for instance, a study by Ramus et al. (2003). Reid and Szczerbiński's (2002) study indeed revealed a complex profile of deficits involving phonological, magnocellular and possibly cerebellar impairment, as well as ADHD. The findings suggest that DOZ's phonological and magnocellular impairments cannot be easily attributed to her attentional deficit because whereas she had problems with letter naming speed and with the Coherent Visual Motion Test, she had no problems with the parallel tasks of digit naming speed and the Coherent Visual Form Test. The results can be accounted for by MDT; however, if DOZ's cerebellar deficit turns out to be sound, as investigated by more sensitive tests, DOZ's profile would prove to be complex and not straightforward to account for by any of the current theories of dyslexia. The study underscores the fact that dyslexia can co-occur with other developmental disorders, such as ADHD (Pennington, 1991). Future studies based on a representative sample of dyslexic adults will have to address two issues. First, how representative of the population of dyslexic adults is DOZ's cognitive profile? Second, how does the co-occurence of dyslexia with ADHD influence the cognitive profiles of adults with dyslexia?

Summary of the Results From Neuropsychological Studies

The studies previously reviewed from the neuropsychological approach reveal striking facts about the profiles of Polish dyslexic people. First, a significantly higher number of dyslexic people in comparison with the control group exhibit impairment of auditory, visual, kinaesthetic or all three, motor, functions, or the perceptual–motor integration impairment. These data suggest that dyslexic people are characterised by complex and heterogeneous profiles. Second, the results also suggest that two or three deficits can co-occur in one individual, and this correlates with higher severity of reading impairment, suggesting the additive nature of these deficits. Third, the recent studies that have focused on visual impairment provide some support for the visual magnocellular deficit in dyslexia, at least in a subset of dyslexic people. Finally, the preliminary data possibly also suggest a cerebellar impairment at least in some dyslexic people.

Shortcomings of the Neuropsychological Studies

The Polish studies within the neuropsychological approach have shortcomings. First, the main problem with these investigations, as has already been pointed out, is that it is not clear from the neuropsychological tests used whether the impairment is on the level of a single function or on the level of the integration of these functions, or both. Recent data from Polish studies (Bednarek & Grabowska, 2001; Reid & Szczerbiński, 2002) provide support for the claim that at least a subset of Polish dyslexic people have impairment of the visual magnocellular system. This, however, does not preclude the possibility that they also have impairment of the integration of visual and motor functions. Second, none of the studies within the neuropsychological domain included a reading-level-matched design that provides a better comparison in determining the underlying reading deficits than the standard chronological-age comparison. Third, there is no consensus on the interpretation of the data from the neuropsychological studies. Some authors interpret them as causative of dyslexia (e.g., Bogdanowicz, 1997; Jaklewicz, 1980; Spionek, 1963), whereas others (e.g., Szczerbiński, 2003) interpret them as concomitant. Fourth, none of the studies that investigated visual, auditory, and motor functions employed a design with a statistical control, and therefore it is not clear which one of these deficits shows a specific link with reading and spelling deficits when the relevant variables are controlled for. Fifth, there is a notable lack of longitudinal studies that combine multivariate analysis with longitudinal design in the Polish research on dyslexia (except a study by Krasowicz-Kupis, 1999). A design of this type is of particular importance when one is investigating a developmental disorder, such as dyslexia, because it uniquely allows for monitoring the development of the skills under investigation. Finally, most of the Polish studies except the epidemiological studies carried out by Jaklewicz (1980) and Bogdanowicz (1985) are based on relatively small samples of dyslexic people or on case studies. With increasing evidence that dyslexic people are a heterogeneous population, the reviewed results do not permit strong claims about the underlying causes of dyslexia without carrying out studies on large, representative samples of people with dyslexia that will involve the in-depth investigation of cognitive profiles of dyslexic people (Reid, 2001, in press). It is likely that dyslexic people with different cognitive profiles will be found, possibly leading to the identification of distinct subtypes of dyslexia with different underlying causes.

Insights Into Dyslexia From the Neuropsychological Studies

The currently available data from the neuropsychological approach suggest a link between neuropsychological impairments and dyslexia, and they can possibly shed more light on this disorder.

Insights into reading errors such as changing the order of letters in a word reported for Polish dyslexic people (and for English, Italian, and Czech dyslexic people) can be gained from the studies investigating the visual magnocellular function (Bednarek & Grabowska, 2001; Reid & Szczerbiński, 2002). The visual magnocellular system is responsible for keeping the two eyes fixated to converge on each word during reading, and its impairment results in unsteady binocular fixation producing unstable perceptions of print and difficulty in working out the order of letters in a word (Stein, 2001). Dyslexic people therefore experience reading errors such as swapping the order of letter within words. Two studies that investigated visual magnocellular processing in Polish dyslexic readers (Bednarek & Grabowska, 2001; Reid & Szczerbiński, 2002) found impairment of the visual magnocellular system, with an intact parvocellular system, and therefore lend some support for the explanation of such reading errors in terms of a deficient visual magnocellular system. However, as emphasised earlier, these results are based on a small sample of dyslexic readers and a case study and therefore cannot be generalised onto the dyslexic population.

The pseudohomophone errors in spelling reported for Polish dyslexic people suggest that the phonological representation of target words is uncompromised, but the orthographic representation is impaired. As discussed it is hard to see how this type of error can straightforwardly be accounted for by the PDT. A visual impairment can possibly shed some light on this issue. The MDT (e.g., Stein, 2001; Stein et al., 2001; Stein & Talcott, 1999) argues that the impairment is subtle and is on the level of the visual magnocellular system. There is currently some support for this claim in the English literature. For instance, it was reported (Talcott et al., 2000b) that children's visual motion sensitivity, measured with the Coherent Visual Motion Test (Hansen, 1995), correlates with their ability to spell English words with irregular spelling (e.g., *pint*). A relatively strong correlation between visual motion sensitivity and performance in Olson, Wise, Conners, Rack, and Fulker's (1989) Pseudo-Homophone Test was also found across the whole range of reading abilities (Talcott et al., 2000b). The test of Olson et al. (1989) involves participants' decisions regarding which of the two 'words', presented side by side on a computer screen, is spelled correctly (e.g., *rane* or *rain*). As these words are pronounced in exactly the same way, the decision must be made on the basis of the orthographic representation. Further, it was reported (Talcott et al., 2000b) that good spellers were characterised by high visual motion sensitivity, whereas poor spellers had low visual motion sensitivity. These correlations were significant when overall reading skill and intelligence were controlled for and therefore suggest a specific link between the processing of the visual magnocellular system and orthographic processing. However, the issue of how exactly unimpaired–impaired magnocellular processing affects the development of orthographic representations in the mental lexicon of people from control and dyslexic populations needs to be addressed in future research.

Futher insights into two aspects of reading and spelling difficulties in dyslexia can be made from the preliminary results (Reid & Szczerbiński, 2002), which suggest that at least some Polish dyslexic people may have a cerebellar impairment. First, significantly slower reading in the dyslexic readers than in the control group can be linked to difficulties in making the orthography to phonology connections robust and automatic, and this in turn perhaps can be linked to a cerebellar deficit (Nicolson et al., 2001). Second significantly higher numbers of reading and spelling errors in dyslexic people as compared with control data can perhaps be accounted for by difficulties in eliminating errors in the learning process—a skill that was found to be impaired in dyslexic children (Nicolson & Fawcett, 2000). However, Polish errors (as well as English, Italian, and Czech) that are problematic for the PDT, as previously discussed, also seem difficult to account for within the CDT framework, unless it is assumed that the cerebellum is a part of the magnocellular system, as recently suggested by Stein (2001). Further research, however, is indispensible to determine by exactly what mechanisms an unimpaired–impaired cerebellum is involved in typical and impaired reading and spelling.

CONCLUDING REMARKS

I set two aims in this chapter: (a) to make a contribution to the cross-linguistic comparisons on dyslexia by reviewing studies on Polish dyslexia from the three major research areas, the role of orthography in literacy acquisition, the role of phonological awareness in predicting literacy skill and the role of neuropsychological deficits in dyslexia; and (b) equally important, to gain some insights into the nature of dyslexia.

The reviewed data on Polish suggest that the role of orthography in dyslexic reading is less than was hypothesised, at least for the examined dyslexic populations. This is revealed by significantly slower speed and lower accuracy of reading by dyslexic people as compared with those of the control group in Polish despite its consistent grapheme-to-phoneme correspondence. There is now growing evidence that a similar picture regarding reading emerges from other languages characterised by consistent grapheme-to-phoneme correspondence. However, data from the reviewed studies on German dyslexia seem to be less consistent with these findings, revealing that speed, not accuracy, is the main problem of dyslexic readers. A smaller role of orthography in reading in transparent orthographies and the discrepancies between the results on reading accuracy for different languages with transparent orthographies suggests that the role of orthography may be attenuated by some factors. These may involve differences in severity and the profile of impairment of studied dyslexic populations. To gain meaningful cross-linguistic comparisons of literacy skills, future research will need to address the issues of severity and the profile of impairment in people with dyslexia.

Phonological awareness studies that have only recently gained more popularity in Poland show that phonological awareness is a good predictor of literacy acquisition in Polish control and dyslexic readers. Results from the different levels of phonological representation have revealed that the phonemic level was the strongest predictor and syllable was also a strong predictor, whereas rhyme was the poorest predictor. The results on the phonemic level of representation are in line with findings for other languages. The results on rhyme are congruent with other languages, including English (on the account of the small-unit theories).

The findings from the neuropsychological studies have revealed that Polish dyslexic people in contrast to control groups exhibit striking perceptual and motor deficits. The data from these studies suggest that dyslexic people are characterised by complex and different profiles of perceptual and motor deficits that can account for the observation that dyslexic people appear to be a heterogeneous population. The results from the neuropsychological studies suggest that deficits in perceptual and motor functions may play an important role in the literacy deficits of people with dyslexia.

The studies on literacy acquisition in Polish dyslexia provide important data on reading and spelling errors made by people with dyslexia. It is argued that errors such as reading words from right to left and reading and spelling errors, such as confusing graphemes with similar graphic structure, swapping the order of letters in a word, and spelling errors, such as pseudohomophone errors, cannot straightforwardly be accounted for by the PDT. Insights from the neuropsychological studies suggest that reading errors, such as swapping the order of letters within a word, and spelling errors, such as pseudohomophone errors, may be determined by much more fundamental physiological, not linguistic, causes such as a deficit of the visual magnocellular system. Furthermore, the slow reading speed and significantly higher number of errors in reading and spelling in dyslexia can possibly be accounted for, at least in part, by the CDT. However, the CDT, similar to the PDT, also seems to have difficulties accounting for the Polish (and English, Italian, and Czech) errors, such as swapping the order of letters and reading words from right to left, unless it is assumed that the cerebellum is a part of the magnocellular system.

The results from the reviewed studies from the three major areas of research on Polish dyslexia contribute a typologically distinct data point to the cross-linguistic comparisons. They also provide some insights into dyslexia; however, much still remains to be explained in the nature of this enigmatic developmental disorder.

ACKNOWLEDGEMENT

I thank Marcin Szczerbiński for his helpful comments on the earlier draft of this chapter.

REFERENCES

Aaron, P. G., & Joshi, R. M. (Eds.). (1989). *Reading and writing disorders in different orthographic systems*. Dordrecht, The Netherlands: Kluwer Academic.

Bednarek, D., & Grabowska, A. (2001, September). *Contrast and colour sensitivity in dyslexia*. Poster presented at the Fourteenth Polish conference on the difficulties in reading and writing, Gdańsk University, Gdańsk, Poland.

Bogdanowicz, M. (1985). Badania nad częstością występowania dysleksji, dysortografii i dysgrafii wśród polskich dzieci [Investigations into the frequency of occurrence of dyslexia, dysorthography and dysgraphy in Polish children]. *Zeszyty Naukowe Wydziału Humanistycznego Uniwersytetu Gdańskiego–Psychologia, 7*, 143–156.

Bogdanowicz, M. (1991). Badania katamnestyczne nad rozwojem i edukacją szkolną dzieci z dysleksją i dysortografią [A follow-up study on the development and school education of children with dyslexia and dysorthography]. *Zeszyty Naukowe Wydziału Humanistycznego Uniwersytetu Gdańskiego—Psychologia, 10*, 63–78.

Bogdanowicz, M. (1997). *Integracja percepcyjno–motoryczna. Teoria—diagnoza—terapia [Perceptual–motor integration. Theory—diagnosis—therapy]*. Warsaw, Poland: Centrum Metodyczne Pomocy Psychologiczno-Pedagogicznej Ministerstwa Edukacji Narodowej.

Bradley, L., & Bryant, P. E. (1983). Categorising sounds and learning to read—A causal connection. *Nature (London), 301*, 419–421.

Caravolas, M., & Volin, J. (2001). Phonological spelling errors among dyslexic children learning a transparent orthography: The case of Czech. *Dyslexia, 7*, 229–245.

Downing, J. (1967). *Evaluating the initial teaching alphabet*. London: Cassell.

Duncan, L. G., Seymour, P. H. K., & Hill, S. (1997). How important are rhyme and analogy in beginning reading. *Cognition, 63*, 171–208.

Evans, B. J. W. (2001). *Dyslexia and vision*. London: Whurr.

Fawcett, A. J., & Nicolson, R. I. (1998). *The dyslexia adult screening test (DAST)*. London: The Psychological Corporation.

Fawcett, A. J., & Nicolson, R. I. (2001). Dyslexia: The role of the cerebellum. In A. J. Fawcett (Ed.), *Dyslexia: Theory and good practice*. London: Whurr.

Finch, A. J., Nicolson, R. I., & Fawcett, A. J. (2002). Evidence for a neuroanatomical difference within the olivo-cerebellar pathway of adults with dyslexia. *Cortex, 38*, 529–539.

Frost, R., Katz, L., & Bentin, S. (1987). Strategies for visual word recognition and orthographical depth: A multilingual comparison. *Journal of Experimental Psychology: Human Perception and Performance, 13*, 104–115.

Galaburda, A. M., Menard, M. T., & Rosen, G. D. (1994). Evidence for aberrant auditory anatomy in developmental dyslexia. *Proceedings of the National Academy of Science of the USA, 91*, 8010–8013.

Goswami, U. (1991). Learning about spelling sequences: The role of onsets and rimes in analogies in reading. *Child Development, 62*, 1110–1123.

Goswami, U. (2000). Phonological representations, reading development and dyslexia: Towards a cross-linguistic theoretical framework. *Dyslexia: An International Journal of Research and Practice, 6*, 133–151.

Goswami, U., & Bryant, P. E. (1990). *Phonological skills and learning to read*. Hillsdale, NJ: Lawrence Erlbaum Associates.

Goulandris, N. (2003). *Dyslexia in different languages: Cross-linguistic comparisons*. London: Whurr.

Grzegorczykowa, R., Laskowski, R., & Wróbel, H. (Eds.). (1998). *Gramatyka współczesnego języka polskiego [Grammar of contemporary Polish]*. Warsaw, Poland: Wydawnictwo Naukowe PWN.

Gupta, A., & Vaid, J. (2002, June). *Reading strategies of Hindi-speaking children with developmental dyslexia*. Paper presented at the International Conference on Multilingual and Cross-Cultural Perspectives on Dyslexia, Washington, DC.

Hansen, P. (1995). The coherent visual motion test [Computer software]. Oxford, UK: University of Oxford.

Hansen, P. (1999). The coherent visual form test [Computer software]. Oxford, UK: University of Oxford.

Hansen, P. C., Stein, J. F., Orde, S. R., Winter, J. L., & Talcott, J. B. (2001). Are dyslexics' visual deficits limited to measures of dorsal stream function? *NeuroReport, 12*, 1527–1530.

Harris, M., & Hatano, G. (Eds.). (1999). *Learning to read and write: A cross-linguistic perspective*. Cambridge, UK: Cambridge University Press.

Hoien, T., Lundberg, L., Stanovich, K. E., & Bjaalid, I. K. (1995). Components of phonological awareness. *Reading and Writing, 7*, 171–188.

Jaklewicz, H. (1980). *Badania katamnestyczne nad dysleksją—dysortografią [A follow-up study on dyslexia—dysorthography]*. Praca habilitacyjna. Gdańsk, Poland: Instytut Medycyny Morskiej i Tropikalnej.

Karaś, M., & Madejowa, M. (1977). *Słownik wymowy polskiej [Dictionary of Polish pronounciation]*. Warsaw, Poland: Państwowe Wydawnictwo Naukowe.

Konopnicki, J. (1961). *Problem opóźnienia w nauce szkolnej [A problem of retardation in school learning]*. Cracow, Poland.

Krasowicz, G. (1997). *Język, czytanie, dysleksja [Language, reading, dyslexia]*. Lublin, Poland: Agencja Wydawniczo-Handlowa A. Dudek.

Krasowicz-Kupis, G. (1999). *Rozwój metajęzykowy a osiągnięcia w czytaniu u dzieci 6–9-letnich [Metalinguistic development and reading achievement in 6–9-year-old children]*. Lublin, Poland: Wydawnictwo Uniwersytetu Marii Curie-Skłodowskiej.

Krasowicz-Kupis, G., Bryant, P., & Bogdanowicz, M. (1999). The role of children's awareness of phonemes, syllables and rhymes in learning to read. Unpublished manuscript, Maria Curie–Skłodowska University, Lublin, Poland.

Lamm, O. (2002, June). *Surface Dyslexia: Is it a lexical-semantic deficit?* Paper presented at the International Conference on Multilingual and Cross-Cultural Perspectives on Dyslexia, Washington, DC.

Landerl, K. (2001). Word recognition deficits in German: More evidence from a representative sample. *Dyslexia: An International Journal of Research and Practice, 7*, 183–196.

Landerl, K. (2003). Dyslexia in German-speaking children. In N. Goulandris (Ed.), *Dyslexia in different languages: Cross-linguistic comparisons* (pp. 15–32). London: Whurr.

Landerl, K., Wimmer, H., & Frith, U. (1997). The impact of orthographic consistency on dyslexia: A German–English comparison. *Cognition, 63*, 315–334.

Lewandowska, B., & Bogdanowicz, M. (1982). Trudności w czytaniu i pisaniu oraz zaburzenia funkcji percepcyjno-motorycznych u dzieci z dysleksją i dysortografią. Wyniki badań katamnestycznych [Reading and spelling difficulties and disorders of perceptual-motor functions in children with dyslexia and dysorthography. Results from a follow-up study]. *Zeszyty Naukowe Wydziału Humanistycznego Uniwersytetu Gdańskiego – Psychologia, 4*, 5–18.

Lundberg, I., & Hoien, T. (2001). Dyslexia and phonology. In A. Fawcett (Ed.), *Dyslexia: Theory and good practice* (pp. 109–123). London: Whurr.

Lundberg, I., Olofsson, A., & Wall, S. (1980). Reading and spelling skills in the first school years predicted from phonemic awareness skills in kindergarten. *Scandinavian Journal of Psychology, 21*, 159–173.

Mar, D. (1969). A theory of cerebellar cortex. *Journal of Physiology (London), 202*, 437–470.

Matejcek, Z. (1998). Reading in Czech. Part II: Reading in Czech children with dyslexia. *Dyslexia: An International Journal of Research and Practice, 4*, 155–168.

Morchio, B., Ott, M., & Pesenti, E. (1989). The Italian language: Developmental reading and writing problems. In P. G. Aaron & R. M. Joshi (Eds.), *Reading and writing disorders in different orthographic systems* (pp. 143–161). Dordrecht, The Netherlands: Kluwer Academic.

Nicolson, R. I., Daum, I., Schugens, M. M., Fawcett, A. J., & Schulz, A. (2002). Abnormal eyeblink conditioning for dyslexic children. *Experimental Brain Research, 143*, 42–50.

Nicolson, R. I., & Fawcett, A. J. (1990). Automaticity: A new framework for dyslexia research? *Cognition, 35*, 159–182.

Nicolson, R. I., & Fawcett, A. J. (2000). Long-term learning in dyslexic children. *European Journal of Cognitive Psychology, 12*, 357–393.

Nicolson, R. I., Fawcett, A. J., Berry, E. L., Jenkins, I. H., Dean, P., & Brooks, D. J. (1999). Association of abnormal cerebellar activation with motor learning difficulties in dyslexic adults. *The Lancet, 353*, 1662–1667.

Nicolson, R. I., Fawcett, A. J., & Dean, P. (1995). Time estimation in developmental dyslexia: Evidence for cerebellar involvement. *Proceedings of the Royal Society: Biological Sciences, 259*, 43–47.

Nicolson, R. I., Fawcett, A. J., & Dean, P. (2001). Developmental dyslexia: The cerebellar deficit hypothesis. *Trends in Neurosciences, 24*, 508–511.

Nowak, J. E. (1989). *Pedagogiczne problemy słuchu fonematycznego u uczniów z trudnościami w czytaniu i pisaniu* [*Pedagogical problems with phonematic hearing in pupils with reading and spelling difficulties*]. Bydgoszcz, Poland: Wydawnictwo Uczelniane Wyższej Szkoły Pedagogicznej.

Olson, R. K., Wise, B., Conners, F., Rack, J., & Fulker, D. (1989). Specific deficits in component reading and language skills—Genetic and environmental influences. *Journal of Learning Disabilities, 22*, 339–348.

Orton, S. T. (1937). *Reading, writing and speech problems in children*. New York: Norton.

Paulesu, E., Démonet, J. F., Fazio, F., McCrory, E., Chanoine, V., Brunswick, N., Cappa, S. F., Cossu, G., Habib, M., Frith, C. D., & Frith, U. (2001). Dyslexia: Cultural diversity and biological unity. *Science, 291*, 2165–2167.

Pavlidis, G., & Giannouli, V. (2002, August). *What can spelling errors tell us about the causes and the treatment of dyslexia? Why and how can they accurately differentiate Greek from English speaking-USA dyslexics?* Paper presented at the International Research and European Policy Conference on Dyslexia, Uppsala, Sweden.

Pennington, B. F. (1991). *Diagnosing learning disorders: A neuropsychological framework*. New York: Guilford.

Polański, E. (1973). *Badania nad ortografią uczniów* [*Investigations of pupils' orthography*]. Katowice, Poland: Wydawnictwo Uniwersytetu Śląskiego.

Polański, E. (1997). *Nowy słownik ortograficzny PWN z zasadami pisowni i interpunkcji* [*A new PWN dictionary of orthography with rules of spelling and punctuation*]. Warsaw, Poland: Wydawnictwo Naukowe PWN.

Porpodas, C. (1993). The relation between phonemic awareness and reading and spelling of Greek words in the first school years. In M. Carretero, M. Pope, R. J. Simons, & J. I. Pozo (Eds.), *Learning and instruction, Vol. 3* (pp. 203–217). Oxford, UK: Pergamon.

Rack, J. P., Snowling, M. J., & Olson, R. K. (1992). The nonword reading deficit in developmental dyslexia: A review. *Reading Research Quarterly, 27*, 29–53.

Ramus, F., Rosen, S., Dakin, S. C., Day, B. L., Castellote, J. M., White, S., & Frith, U. (2003). Theories of developmental dyslexia: Insights from a multiple case study of dyslexic adults. *Brain, 126*, 841–865.

Reid, A. A. (2001, September). *What is developmental dyslexia? Can any hypothesis give an answer which accounts for the available data?* Poster presented at the Fourteenth Polish Conference on Reading and Writing Difficulties, Gdańsk, Poland.

Reid, A. A. (2002, June). *Reading impairment in shallow orthography: Evidence from Polish developmental dyslexia*. Poster presented at the International Conference on Multilingual and Cross-Cultural Perspectives on Dyslexia, Washington, DC.

Reid, A. A. (in press). Dysleksja rozwojowa: Czy przy pomocy jednej z głównych hipotez wyjaśnić można jej istotę i przyczyny? [Developmental dyslexia: Can any of the major hypotheses account for the available data?] In M. Bogdanowicz (Ed.), *Proceedings of the Fourteenth Polish Conference on Reading and Writing Difficulties*. Gdańsk, Poland: Wydawnictwo Harmonia.

Reid, A. A., & Szczerbiński, M. (2002, August). *A case study of a Polish developmental dyslexic: Theoretical implications*. Poster presented at the International Research and European Policy Conference on Dyslexia, Uppsala, Sweden.

Seymour, P. H. K., Duncan, L. G., & Bolik, F. M. (1999). Rhymes and phonemes in the common unit task: Replications and implications for beginning reading. *Journal of Research in Reading, 22*, 113–130.

Skottun, B. C. (2000). The magnocellular deficit theory of dyslexia: The evidence from contrast sensitivity. *Vision Research, 40*, 111–127.

Snowling, M. J. (1981). Phonemic deficits in developmental dyslexia. *Psychological Research, 43*, 219–234.

Snowling, M. J. (2000). *Dyslexia* (2nd ed.). Oxford, UK: Blackwell.

Snowling, M. J. (2001). From language to reading and dyslexia. *Dyslexia: An International Journal of Research and Practice, 7*, 37–46.

Spionek, H. (1963). Trudności w nauce czytania i pisania u dzieci a poziom funkcjonalny sprawności ich analizatorów [Children's reading and spelling difficulties and the functional level of efficiency of their analyzers]. *Psychologia Wychowawcza, VI*(3), 197–209.

Spionek, H. (1981). *Zaburzenia rozwoju uczniów a niepowodzenia szkolne* [*Pupils' developmental disorders and school failures*] (3rd ed.). Warsaw, Poland: Państwowe Wydawnictwo Naukowe.

Stein, J. F. (2001). The magnocellular theory of developmental dyslexia. *Dyslexia: An International Journal of Research and Practice, 7*, 12–36.

Stein, J. F., & Talcott, J. B. (1999). Impaired neuronal timing in developmental dyslexia—the magnocellular hypothesis. *Dyslexia: An International Journal of Research and Practice, 5*, 59–77.

Stein, J. F., Talcott, J. B., & Witton, C. (2001). The sensorimotor basis of developmental dyslexia. In A. J. Fawcett (Ed.), *Dyslexia: Theory and good practice*. London: Whurr.

Szczerbiński, M. (2001). *Learning to read and spell single words: A case study of a Slavic language*. Unpublished doctoral dissertation, University College, London.

Szczerbiński, M. (2003). Dyslexia in Polish. In N. Goulandris (Ed.), *Dyslexia in different languages: Cross-linguistic comparisons* (pp. 68–91). London: Whurr.

Szober, S. (1969). *Gramatyka języka polskiego* [*Polish grammar*] (11th ed.). Warsaw, Poland: Państwowe Wydawnictwo Naukowe.

Szurmiak, M. (1974). Próby rozwiązania problemu reedukacji dzieci dyslektycznych na terenie Krakowa—Nowej Huty [Attempts to solve the problem of re-education of dyslexic children in Kraków—Nowa Huta]. *Kwartalnik Pedagogiczny, 4*, 135–152.

Talcott, J. B., Hansen, P. C., Elikem, L. A., & Stein, J. F. (2000a). Visual motion sensitivity in dyslexia: Evidence for temporal and motion energy integration deficits. *Neuropsychologia, 38*, 935–943.

Talcott, J. B., Witton, C., McLean, M., Hansen, P., Rees, A., Green, G., & Stein, J. F. (2000b). Dynamic sensory sensitivity and children's word decoding skills. *Proceedings of the National Academy of Sciences (USA), 97*, 2952–2957.

Trzeciak, G. (1980). Wyrównywanie trudności w czytaniu i pisaniu: Sprawozdanie z badań [Ameliorating reading and writing difficulties: A research report]. *Zagadnienia Wychowawcze, 4–5*, 134–145.

Vellutino, F. R., & Scanlon, D. M. (1987). Phonological coding, phonological awareness, and reading ability: Evidence from a longitudinal and experimental study. *Merrill Palmer Quarterly, 33*, 321–364.

Wimmer, H. (1993). Characteristics of developmental dyslexia in a regular writing system. *Applied Psycholinguistics, 14*, 1–34.

Wimmer, H. (1996). The early manifestation of developmental dyslexia: Evidence from German children. *Reading and Writing, 8*, 171–188.

Wimmer, H., Landerl, K., Linortner, R., & Hummer, P. (1991). The relationship of phonemic awareness to reading acquisition: More consequence than prediction but still important. *Cognition, 40*, 219–249.

Wimmer, H., Mayringer, H., & Landerl, K. (1998). Poor reading: A deficit in skill-automatization or a phonological deficit? *Scientific Studies of Reading, 2*, 321–340.

Wimmer, H., Mayringer, H., & Landerl, K. (2000). The double-deficit hypothesis and difficulties in learning to read a regular orthography. *Journal of Educational Psychology 92*, 668–680.

Wolf, M., & Bowers, P. G. (1999). The double-deficit hypothesis for the developmental dyslexias. *Journal of Educational Psychology, 91*, 415–438.

Wszeborowska-Lipińska, B. (1995). Młodzież ze specyficznymi trudnościami w czytaniu i pisaniu [Adolescents with specific reading and writing difficulties]. *Psychologia Wychowawcza, 3*, 223–234.

Wydell, T. N., & Butterworth, B. (1999). A case study of an English–Japanese bilingual with monolingual dyslexia. *Cognition, 70*, 273–305.

Zagórska-Brooks, M. (1975). *Reference grammar*. The Hague, Netherlands: Mouton.

Zazzo, R. (1974). *Metoda psychologicznego badania dziecka* [Psychological method of testing a child]. Warsaw, Poland: PZWL.

Zhou, X., & Marslen-Wilson, W. D. (2000). The relative time course of semantic and phonological activation in reading Chinese. *Journal of Experimental Psychology—Learning, Memory and Cognition, 26*, 1245–1265.

17

Word Reading in Bulgarian Children and Adults

Armina Janyan and Elena Andonova
New Bulgarian University

This chapter addresses developmental differences in single-word reading in terms of vocal response times and the impact of different word characteristics on processing in the orthographically transparent Bulgarian language. A comparison of results of studies of adults and children (8–9 years of age) showed that children's word reading was equally dependent on sublexical and experiential–conceptual word characteristics, whereas adults' processing rate was predicted by experiential–conceptual and semantic word characteristics without much influence from sublexical word properties. The results demonstrated that reading development and linguistic experience have a strong impact on word processing. Correlation and factor analyses indicated theoretically and methodologically important issues. In particular, word frequency appeared to be related to conceptual characteristics of the word's referent whereas object familiarity may represent a conceptual and experiential characteristic that correlates with semantic and lexical properties of a word. Finally, the study underscored the usefulness of multivariate analyses and the inclusion of a large number of word characteristics at different levels of word structure that serve to enhance our understanding of the peculiarities of processing in single-word-reading tasks.

INTRODUCTION

The Bulgarian language is alphabetically codified in the Cyrillic script. The current form of the script for Bulgarian has been reached after a series of alterations throughout the past nine centuries, the most recent one being the orthographical reform in 1945, which attempted to create a more optimal phoneme–grapheme correspondence. The Bulgarian alphabet consists of 30 letters, and the Bulgarian phonological system consists of 42 phonemes (36 consonantal and 6 vowel phonemes). There is a one-to-one fit between the six vowels and six letters of the alphabet. Twenty letters represent consonantal phonemes; many of these have a soft (palatalized) and a nonsoft version. Three letters stand for the single expression of combinations of sounds, and one letter is not pronounced but serves to indicate softness in the preceding consonant.

Generally speaking, there are two types of spelling rules in Bulgarian: phonetic and etymological. Most words are spelled phonetically, for example, *pakema* (paketa) [rocket/racket], *mon* (τοπ) [cannon], and so forth. Some words, however, are spelled so that their etymological and morphological connections with related forms are made transparent. This can be seen in cases of consonantal assimilation (voicing and devoicing) and in assimilation by place of articulation. For example, devoicing occurs when a voiced consonant is at the end of a word or precedes a voiceless consonant. In addition, vowel reduction is a common phenomenon in the Bulgarian phonological system. Under stress, the system consists of six vowels; yet in unstressed syllables, it reduces to three vowels only.

As a whole, the Bulgarian writing system presents more difficulties for children learning to write (especially in view of assimilation and vowel reduction) than does learning to read. Having said that, the Bulgarian language lacks definite rules for stress, which means that the accent of every word must be learned individually and that most words (being multisyllabic) require adequate access to the lexeme representation before they can be read out correctly despite the generally close grapheme–phoneme fit. A study of letter identification in short printed Bulgarian words by dyslexic children and control children (Matanova, 2001) shows that syllable length affects their accuracy. That is, individual letters are better identified in one-syllable than in two-syllable words, a difference in performance that is especially pronounced in the dyslexic participant group.

This study has two main aims. First, we examine and compare factors that influence single-word reading in terms of reaction time (RT). Second, we compare performances on the same task between children and adults in order to track down possible developmental changes. In addition, the studies are carried out in Bulgarian, a language with a high level of orthographic transparency, which is a contribution to the existing cross-linguistic literature. In view of the first aim, we used a large number of word characteristics that reflect different degrees of the word's structure and function. For instance, we examined the influence of different measures such as word length, the frequency with which a word occurs in the language, and word imageability on word reading. Recent studies of word reading pay attention not only to word frequency but also to the age of word acquisition, concept or object familiarity, and word imageability (e.g., Morrison & Ellis, 2000; Yamazaki, Ellis, Morrison & Lambon Ralph, 1997). Most studies on visual word processing have obtained little or no evidence of the influence of semantic–conceptual factors such as imageability, concreteness, and object–concept familiarity on word reading (e.g., Brysbaert, Lange & Van Wijnendaele, 2000; Monaghan & Ellis, 2002; Morrison & Ellis, 2000; Yamazaki et al., 1997). Rather, the results suggest that word frequency and age of acquisition (AoA) may be the most powerful predictors of word-reading time, although there is an ongoing debate in the literature as to whether the frequency effect is an artifact of AoA as well as to whether the AoA effect is independent of frequency or whether it is a cumulative effect (e.g., Brysbaert et al., 2000; Lewis, Gerhand & Ellis, 2001; Zevin & Seidenberg, 2002). However, most researchers agree that these two word characteristics are typically correlated (e.g., highly frequent and imageable words tend to be learned first) so that results may frequently confound these variables. On the other hand, some effects may be canceled under certain conditions. For instance, in a recent experiment conducted by Monaghan and Ellis (2002), the frequency effect disappeared with spelling–sound-consistent stimuli, although it affected word-reading response latency with inconsistent stimuli. As it appears, under certain conditions some word characteristics may become more important than others. Thus, when a large number of word characteristics that potentially influence RT measures are taken into account, it is next to impossible to achieve adequate control over these variables and to trace their influence on processing latency. However, it seems that one useful solution is multivariate analysis such as the one used by Bates, Burani, D'Amico, and Barca (2001) for picture naming and word reading in Italian adults. To deal with the collinearity among the many variables, they applied a factor analysis (principal components analysis), extracting from a large set of variables a small number of factors that combined connected variables into subsets, with each variable having a certain weight within each factor. These factors were then included in a regression analysis to determine their unique contribution to RT variance. We consider this type of analysis to be particularly useful it in the present study.

A potentially confounding variable in word-reading studies is the grammatical class of the word stimuli that are used. In many cases, it is either ignored or the stimuli are described generically as "words" without specification of their grammatical class (e.g., see the stimuli lists in Brysbaert et al., 2000; Monaghan & Ellis, 2002; Zevin & Seidenberg, 2002). With the exception of traditionally researched differences in the processing of open and closed classes of words (e.g., Brown, Hagoort & ter Keurs, 1999), recent studies have shown differential processing of two grammatical classes, nouns and verbs. This grammatical class distinction has gained increasing importance in research on lexical access, especially in relation to neurological studies suggesting that different neural systems may play a critical role in the production and comprehension of nouns and verbs (e.g., Damasio & Tranel, 1993; Daniele, Giustolisi, Silveri, Colosimo, & Gainotti, 1994; Gainotti, Silveri, Daniele, & Giustolisi, 1995). Electrophysiological studies also suggest that nouns and verbs have distinct neural generators in the intact brain (e.g., Koenig & Lehmann, 1996; Pulvermüller, Lutzenberger, & Pressl, 1999). Two recent studies (Colombo & Burani, 2002; Laudanna, Voghera & Gazzellini, 2002) that directly addressed visual processing of nouns and verbs in terms of response latency indicated that the two classes may be influenced by different variables at different levels of processing.

In the present study, only grammatically unambiguous nouns are used as word stimuli. In addition to the variables previously described briefly that potentially affect word reading, we examine a wide range of predictor variables, including a number of subjectively rated measures. First, we include animacy because many neurological studies have found a category-specific deficit manifested in the differential processing of living versus nonliving semantic categories (e.g., Caramazza & Shelton, 1998; Devlin, Gonnerman, Andersen, & Seidenberg, 1998). We also take into account in our analyses three different subjective measures of AoA (pictorial–conceptual, auditory–spoken, and visual–written) and variation in the estimate of the approximate age of conceptual and lexical development, respectively. To the best of our knowledge, this has not been undertaken before. These three different measures would enable us to achieve a better understanding of the degree of variability in subjective AoA ratings depending on the modality of presentation and task instruction and an insight into the possible confounding factors associated with this measure. Note that Yamazaki et al. (1997) obtained independent contributions of spoken and written AoA measures to Japanese Kanji word-reading RTs, which clearly shows that reading RTs were sensitive to both measures of AoA. Thus using three different measures of AoA and adding animacy and concreteness ratings to the list of word characteristics is expected to help us to understand the semantic–conceptual and lexical factors involved in word reading.

The second aim of this study is to compare word-reading processing in Bulgarian adults and children. The Bulgarian language presents a high degree of transparency and regularity of the orthography-to-phonology mapping. According to the dual-route and most computational models of visual word processing (Seidenberg, 1995), orthographically regular (transparent) words may be read and processed without lexical access (or access to the semantic and grammatical information of a word). Experimental studies have found that neither frequency and AoA nor imageability affect reading RTs of regular words (e.g., Ellis & Monaghan, 2002; Monaghan & Ellis, 2002; Strain, Patterson, & Seidenberg, 2002). However, this may be particularly valid for experienced adult readers. In spite of the existence of a great amount of literature on the development of literacy skills, surprisingly few studies have compared the influence of lexical and sublexical features on children's and adults' word processing, and even fewer studies have taken semantic variables into consideration (Ellis & Monaghan, 2002; Morrison & Ellis, 2000; Yamazaki et al., 1997). One such study of spoken word recognition was carried out by Garlock, Walley, and Metsala (2001). However, the study used only errors as dependent variables and a mixed set of stimuli of different grammatical classes as independent variables. To the best of our knowledge, one of the few timed experimental developmental studies reported so far is the one conducted by D'Amico, Devescovi, and Bates (2001), in which they compared data from Italian adults and children in an object-naming task, using a number of semantic, lexical, and sublexical factors. Adults' and children's RTs were similarly affected by AoA, the frequency of the target word, and picture complexity, but in different ways. Children named pictures that depicted animals significantly faster than they did all other categories whereas adult RTs for these objects were rather slow in comparison with those for other categories. The authors explained this finding in terms of recency and frequency effects of children's usual "communication" with animal toys and the like.

Thus it is still an open question of whether word processing effects examined in terms of RTs in children can be replicated in adults. First, not surprisingly, children's reading RTs would be significantly slower than those of adults. In addition, and more specifically, according to Seidenberg and Plaut (1998), for experienced fast subjects, frequency and spelling–sound consistency effects are smaller than for less experienced, slower individuals. Thus we can hypothesize that the more automated reading is, the smaller the influence of lexical and sublexical factors would be on word-reading speed. In this case, both age groups may show the same pattern of factor dependence, but in adults (with more automated reading) the influence of these predictive factors' may be weaker than it is in children.

On the other hand, older adults may have verbal representations that are more lexically holistic rather than clustered around sublexical factors. Then we could expect that the influence of lexical factors' on word reading may increase with age whereas the influence of sublexical factors may decrease. This is exactly what Spieler and Balota (2000) found in their experiment. As far as children and adults are concerned, the differences in their word reading may be similar to differences seen in younger and older adults. That is, a richer and more developed language system and a greater reading experience may lead to a stronger influence of lexical (and possibly semantic) factors on reading than do sublexical ones, whereas children's poorer experience in language use and reading may lead to more dependence on superficial–sublexical factors than on deeper lexicosemantic factors.

Another consideration in undertaking this study concerns the character of word reading in Bulgarian. Probably one of the fundamental ways in which orthographic systems differ is the degree of correspondence between written and spoken units. According to the orthographic depth hypothesis (Seidenberg, 1995), the degree of use of phonological information in reading depends on the degree of transparency of the orthography–phonology relationship. Thus, in a shallow or transparent–consistent orthographic systems such as Serbo-Croatian (and presumably, Bulgarian), a word is read through the nonlexical route (subword level), without semantic activation necessarily, whereas in a deep or opaque–inconsistent orthographic system such as Hebrew, a word is read through the lexical route (word level), which assumes the need for semantic activation. Hence, according to the dual-route model, word reading in Bulgarian may involve no activation of semantic information. However, except for form–form (written–spoken) mappings, other dimensions of transparency are present in languages as well. For example, word stress patterns in Bulgarian are of a less transparent (predictable) nature than those in English or French. Variation in the degree of transparency of form–function mappings may be less obvious, yet also significant. Besides the degree of grammatical class ambiguity of a word, the relationship between the form and the function of a word or morpheme may differ according to the degree of experience (including sensory–motor experience) with a word and its referent. These experiential word characteristics can yield subjective ratings that provide useful and reliable information. Thus, given that these and other word characteristics may influence word processing in one way or another, it would be unjustified to assume that reading in Bulgarian, because of its highly transparent orthography, is not influenced by semantic–conceptual factors.

In summary, two possibilities are explored here with respect to the degree of reading and linguistic experience: Either children's data on word reading will replicate that of adults or children and adults will differ in their patterns of impact of lexicosemantic factors, on the one hand, and sublexical factors, on the other hand. In that case, we may find a double dissociation between the two kinds of factors and the two age groups, with sublexical factors being more important for children and lexicosemantic factors being more influential in adults' performance.

METHOD

Participants: Forty adults (22 women and 18 men) participated in the experiment. All were monolingual university students with normal or corrected-to-normal vision and were native speakers of Bulgarian. Their age ranged from 18 to 39, years, the mean age being 24.2 years. Participants received course credit or were paid for their participation. Forty children (22 girls and 18 boys) with a mean age of 8.81 years also participated in the study. Their age ranged from 8.1 to 9.4 years. All were monolinguals, native speakers of Bulgarian, attending primary school in Sofia. None of them had visual problems or language disorders (as determined by teachers' reports). Participants received small gifts for their participation.

Stimuli: A total of 219 word stimuli were selected from the responses obtained from an online object-naming task that used 520 pictorial stimuli to elicit the responses (Bates et al., 2003). Fifty university students participated in the experiment. The dominant or target response to a picture was the name produced by the highest number of participants. Items for the word-naming study were selected from a larger database according to the following criteria: (a) picture-naming consensus should be higher than 80%, (b) the number of alternative names should be fewer than or equal to six alternatives for each picture, (c) the target–dominant response should consist of one word only, and (d) the target–dominant response should be a culturally appropriate word for Bulgarian speakers and within the vocabulary of 8–9-year-old children.

Predictor Variables: All targets derived from the norming study were subjected to six different tests aimed at obtaining ratings for word characteristics that affect processing time:

1. Subjective frequency ratings on a scale from 1 to 7 (1: lowest word frequency) were collected for all targets from 40 university students;
2. Imageability ratings for the selected stimuli were collected by use of the procedure and instruction published in Paivio, Yuille, and Madigan (1968), on a 7-point scale (1: lowest imageability). For this purpose, 40 university students were asked to rate words depending on the ease or difficulty with which these words arouse mental images;
3. Familiarity with the object denoted by a given word was also established by use of a 7-point scale subjective rating procedure (1: lowest familiarity). Forty university students participated in the familiarity rating experiment;
4. Concreteness ratings were obtained from 40 university students on a 7-point scale (1: most abstract);
5. Animacy ratings were collected on a 7-point scale (1: least animate). Forty university students participated in this experiment;
6. Three types of AoA ratings were collected: written–visual, auditory, and pictorial, according to the modality of stimuli presentation. The instructions asked for an estimate of

the AoA of the word (in the visual and auditory modalities) or of the concept associated with the given object (in the pictorial modality). For this purpose, a 7-point scale was used (7 for the earliest acquired items, i.e., under 2 years of age, and 1 for the latest acquired items, i.e., over 13 years old). The AoA data were collected from 90 university students in a within-participants' design with 30 participants' ratings per item in each modality.

None of the students who participated in the subjective rating tasks were included in the timed word-reading experiment.

In addition to the subjective ratings collected as just described, word stimuli were coded along a number of dimensions. Animacy was coded as a binary variable, (1 for animate entities, i.e., persons and animals, and 0 for inanimate ones). Word length was coded in three ways: number of characters, number of phonemes, and number of syllables. Morphological complexity was coded as presence (1) or absence (0) of compounding. Position of stress was coded in terms of the ordinal number of the corresponding syllable. From the procedure used in Bates et al. (2001) and in Bates, Devescovi, Pizzamiglio, D'Amico, and Hernandez (1995), the presence or absence of frication on the initial consonant was also coded (1 for presence, 0 for absence). All stimuli were grammatically unambiguous nouns in their singular form. Table 17.1 summarizes the means and standard deviations for each of the word characteristics.

TABLE 17.1
Characteristics of Word Stimuli for 219 Items

Scalar Variables	Mean	Minimum	Maximum	SD
Length in characters	5.69	3	13	1.75
Length in phonemes	5.69	3	13	1.74
Length in syllables	2.32	1	5	0.79
Stress position	1.68	1	4	0.74
Frequency	4.42	2.48	6.73	0.98
Imageability	6.15	3.75	6.82	0.35
Object familiarity	6.05	5.15	6.63	0.30
Concreteness	5.94	3.65	6.74	0.55
Animacy (rating)	3.03	1.45	6.38	1.67
Pictorial AoA	5.22	3.97	6.50	0.56
Visual AoA	5.19	2.97	6.47	0.62
Auditory AoA	5.22	3.06	6.45	0.60

Binary Coded Variables	Coding	Number of Items	Items (%)
Initial fricative	no = 0	170	76.63
	yes = 1	49	22.37
Word complexity	simple = 0	212	96.80
	compound = 1	7	3.20
Animacy binary	inanimate = 0	174	79.45
	animate = 1	45	20.55

Procedure: Adult participants were tested in a soundproof room in one session. Stimuli were presented randomly. The session started with 10 practice trials. Each trial started with a fixation cross "+" positioned at the center of the screen for a duration between 500 and 800 ms. Immediately after the fixation cross disappeared, the stimuli appeared in uppercase letters (30-point Geneva BG font) at the center of the screen. The stimulus remained on the screen until the verbal response was made. The intertrial interval was chosen to vary randomly between 1,200 and 1,700 ms.

Children were tested individually in one session, in a quiet room at their primary school. Four randomized orders were constructed to allow the experimenters to monitor children's errors more efficiently. The session started with six practice trials. Each trial started with a fixation cross "+" positioned at the center of the screen for 500 ms. Immediately after the fixation cross disappeared, the stimuli appeared in uppercase letters at the center of the screen (the same font and size as in the adult study). In contrast to the adult experimental procedure, the experimenter advanced to the next trial manually when she was sure that the child was attending to the task. Here a stimulus remained on the screen for 5 s or until the verbal response.

In both experiments, participants were instructed to read the word on the screen as fast and as clearly and as accurately as possible. RT was measured from the onset of each stimulus. A Carnegie Mellon button box recorded voice-onset RT and controlled stimuli presentation and timing. A Power Macintosh 6400/200 equipped with the PsyScope software (Cohen, MacWhinney, Flatt, & Provost, 1993) controlled order of presentation and size of the stimuli.

Results and Discussion

Trials with technical errors (voice-key failure, subject hesitations such as "um"; 0.9% for adults and 5.6% for children) and reading–mispronunciation errors (0.2% for adults and 4.6% for children) were excluded from the analyses. On examination of the data distribution, responses with RTs longer than 1 s for adults and 2.5 s for children (0.7% for adults and 2.1% for children) were excluded from the analysis. The analyses were run on mean RT $\pm$ 2 *SD*, thus removing 4.6% of adults' data and 5.7% of children's data. The data were averaged by items over subjects. A total of 93.7% (adults) and 82.0% (children) of the originally collected RT data were included in further analyses.

Comparing Performance by Children and Adults

Table 17.2 summarizes the descriptive statistics of RTs for children and adults. A one-way analysis of variance indicated that adults had a significant overall advantage over children:

TABLE 17.2
Descriptive Statistics for RTs (in ms) for Children and Adults

Participants	Mean	Minimum	Maximum	SD
Children	865	608	1190	108
Adults	553	481	682	32

TABLE 17.3

Correlations of Adults' and Children's RTs With Each Other and With 15 Predictors

Variable	RT Adults	RT Children
RT adults		0.63***
Length in characters	0.49***	0.66***
Length in phonemes	0.49***	0.66***
Length in syllables	0.29***	0.52***
Stress position	n.s.	0.34***
Initial fricative	0.61***	0.16*
Word complexity	n.s.	0.17*
Frequency	−0.23**	−0.36***
Imageability	−0.23**	−0.24***
Object familiarity	−0.22**	−0.35***
Concreteness	n.s.	n.s.
Animacy (rating)	−0.19**	−0.18**
Animacy binary	n.s.	n.s.
Pictorial AoA	−0.32***	−0.44***
Visual AoA	−0.38***	−0.55***
Auditory AoA	−0.39***	−0.53***

$*p < 0.05; **p < 0.01; ***p < 0.001;$ n.s., nonsignificant

$F(1,436) = 1687.23; p = 0.00$. As expected, children were slower in this task (by 312 ms) than adults. The RT range was quite wide for children's and narrow for adults' data.

Correlations Among Predictors

Table 17.3 summarizes the correlations of overall RTs in the two age groups and of the 15 predictor variables with RTs in each of the age groups. The correlation between the two groups' RT was highly significant, though its coefficient ($r = .63$) revealed only a moderately close relationship between word-naming speed in adults and children, which shows that different factors may influence the two processes and RTs in somewhat different ways.

   The various measures of length (number of characters, phonemes, and syllables) affected both RTs, slowing down both adults and children. Length had a stronger influence on children's RT than that of adults. The position of the stressed syllable affected only children's RT, which may indicate that articulation planning in children was dependent on positional–structural characteristics more than in adults. Frication on the initial consonant slowed down adults' RT more than children's, possibly reflecting differences in articulation experience. Another plausible explanation suggested by D'Amico et al. (2001) and Bates et al. (2001) is that the shorter the RT is, the easier early stages of motor planning are detectable. A third explanation is that longer RTs may diminish or even cancel the impact of word-initial frication (white noise) as an artifact of measurement. Although small in number, compound items slowed down children's RT—but not adults' RT—which shows a tendency for children to process morphologically complex words in a more analytic or decomposed manner than the more holistic approach of adults to familiar (even if morphologically complex) items. Frequency, imageability, and object-familiarity ratings all affected the two RTs in the expected direction, speeding up the reading process, similarly with the three types of AoA measures. Neither binary coded animacy nor subjectively rated concreteness affected RTs. Subjectively rated animacy, however, had the effect of speeding up both groups of subjects. As regards concreteness, the constraints on the picture-naming targets (a subset of which was selected for this study) restrict our stimuli to predominantly highly concrete and picturable referents.

In sum, the correlation analysis showed that the factors that influenced children's and adults' RTs differed indeed, as expected from the relatively moderate value of the overall correlation coefficient for the two dependent measures. RTs of both adults and children were more or less similarly affected by the number of phonemes or characters. This was not true of other form-based factors. In fact, children's RTs were correlated with stress position but not those of adults, thus revealing children's sensitivity to suprasegmental structure. In addition, compounding affected RTs of children, not those of adults. Thus children's RTs exhibited a more complex relationship to structural factors than did adults' in that both suprasegmental phonology and morphological complexity were obviously involved in children's processing. The developmental process appears to involve a trend toward a more synthetic–holistic, rather than analytic, approach in visual word processing.

On examination, two of the semantic factors based on subjective rating measures correlated with RTs in both age groups, that is, imageability and animacy. It is worth reiterating that animacy correlated significantly with the speed of word naming only when it was based on subjective ratings and not when it was used as a binary coded variable (animate–inanimate). Thus the use of more sophisticated (psychologically plausible) measures has received appropriate justification here. In addition, object familiarity is also significantly correlated with RTs in both age groups. To the best of our knowledge, this kind of correlation has only rarely been demonstrated before (Morrison & Ellis, 2000; Yamazaki et al., 1997). Object familiarity is perhaps better viewed as a conceptual rather than a purely lexicosemantic factor. Its inclusion here gives us an understanding of potentially nonverbal factors that may affect the reading process. The nature of this variable becomes clearer in the analysis of correlations among predictors in the next section and in the subsequent factor analysis.

The analysis of correlations of predictor variables with RTs provides a useful initial insight into the nature of the processes and factors involved in reading single nouns. However, as many of the predictor variables are highly correlated, we now turn to the examination of those relationships in more detail. Table 17.4 presents the correlation analysis of the 15 predictor variables with each other. Examination of the form-based (sublexical) predictors of length measured in number of characters, phonemes, and syllables, revealed a strong positive correlation among them.[1] Two other structural, nonsemantic, variables, namely word compounding (morphological complexity) and stress position (a suprasegmental phonological characteristic), were also correlated with all of the form-based measures previously listed. On the other hand, virtually all of the semantic–conceptual variables of imageability, familiarity, concreteness, and animacy were not found to correlate with the form–structure-based measures, thus revealing a considerable degree of mutual independence between form-related and meaning-related systems in the materials.[2]

Imageability, object familiarity, and concreteness all exhibited a strong positive correlation among themselves. Animacy, on the other hand, was negatively correlated with familiarity and uncorrelated at all with concreteness and imageability. Furthermore, animacy ratings were highly correlated with the binary variable of animacy ($r = .87$), thus providing reassurance that the two measures are valid and reliable. Thus three conclusions on the semantic–conceptual variables can be drawn: (a) three factors, namely imageability, object familiarity, and concreteness showed a reliable corelationship; (b) animacy in this study has

---

[1] The two "segmental" measures of length—in characters and in phonemes—correlated absolutely, which reflects the extremely high degree of orthographic transparency in Bulgarian in general and in the materials here in particular.

[2] The only exception was a weak negative correlation between object familiarity and stress position, i.e., more familiar items tended to be named by words with an earlier stress.

TABLE 17.4
Correlations Among Predictor Variables

Variable	1	2	3	4	5	6	7	8	9	10	11	12	13	14
1. Length in characters	–													
2. Length in phonemes	1.0***	–												
3. Length in syllables	.84***	.85***	–											
4. Stress position	.57***	.58***	.62***	–										
5. Initial fricative	.14*	.14*	n.s.	n.s.	–									
6. Word complexity	.34***	.35***	.29***	.36***	.15*	–								
7. Frequency	n.s.	n.s.	n.s.	n.s.	n.s.	n.s.	–							
8. Imageability	n.s.	n.s.	n.s.	n.s.	n.s.	n.s.	.57***	–						
9. Object familiarity	n.s.	n.s.	n.s.	-.15*	n.s.	n.s.	.80***	.59***	–					
10. Concreteness	n.s.	n.s.	n.s.	n.s.	n.s.	n.s.	.19**	.38***	.18**	–				
11. Animacy (rating)	n.s.	n.s.	n.s.	n.s.	n.s.	n.s.	-.29***	n.s.	-.33***	n.s.	–			
12. Animacy Binary	n.s.	n.s.	n.s.	n.s.	n.s.	n.s.	-.36***	n.s.	-.42***	n.s.	.87***	–		
13. Pictorial AoA	-.22**	-.22**	n.s.	-.20**	n.s.	n.s.	.47***	.42***	.53***	n.s.	.14*	n.s.	–	
14. Visual AoA	-.35***	-.35***	-.22**	-.20**	n.s.	n.s.	.51***	.48***	.57***	n.s.	.17*	n.s.	.77***	–
15. Auditory AoA	-.34***	-.33***	-.22**	-.23**	n.s.	n.s.	.48***	.47***	.56***	n.s.	n.s.	n.s.	.75***	.92***

*$p < 0.05$; **$p < 0.01$; ***$p < 0.001$; n.s., nonsignificant

been relatively independent of the other semantic measures except for object familiarity; (c) object familiarity itself may have the mechanisms of experiential learning more than purely semantic–conceptual characteristics. However, we have yet to establish whether these classic semantic measures play an independent role in speeding up word naming. Finally, object familiarity is frequently not examined in this task, although it obviously shows a great degree of correlation with all semantic measures just listed. The question remains, however, whether this effect derives from the "umbrella" nature of the variable or whether there are certain specific semantic variables that object familiarity travels together with more naturally than with others, that is, whether it is closer in its nature to experiential (or statistical learning) influences (such as word frequency), or whether it is better viewed as a truly semantic factor on a par with animacy and concreteness. The answers to these questions can be examined by means of a factor analysis, which is described in the next subsection.

Having examined the covariability of form-based and semantic predictors, we now turn to the experiential measures of word frequency, on the one hand, and AoA, on the other hand. To begin with, the two kinds of measures are moderately highly correlated (correlation coefficients in the .47–.51 range), a result that violates no previous expectations in the field. Frequency— subjectively rated in Bulgarian—is obviously strongly correlated with imageability, object familiarity, and less strongly, but still in positive direction, with concreteness. It is negatively correlated with both measures of animacy. One peculiarity, though, is the lack of correlation between word frequency and the various length measures; apparently, the materials used in the study make an exception to Zipf's law, postulating a negative correlation between the frequency and length. Similar results were obtained by Zevin and Seidenberg (2002), and Bates et al. (2001).

Next we turn to the examination of the three measures of AoA in our study. First, they correlate negatively with all measures of length (in characters, phonemes, and syllables, with one interesting exception, as discussed further), a result that hints at the possibility that, in this study at least, Zipf's law can be applied to word length's being correlated reliably with different developmental stages of lexical acquisition rather than with the more age-neutral frequency measure. AoA ratings were also positively correlated with the semantic variables of imageability, object familiarity, and subjectively rated animacy. As a reminder, the higher values in AoA reflect an earlier chronological age, that is, more highly imageable words and words referring to more animate and familiar referents were acquired earlier in life.[3] Finally, although concreteness correlated with imageability, frequency, and familiarity, it did not correlate with either AoA or animacy ratings, thus showing a different pattern.

Before we consider an analysis of factors, taking into account the collinearity of variables, a final note is due here on the differential effects of the AoA ratings in the three modalities — auditory, visual, and pictorial. As a whole, visual and auditory measures of AoA were highly positively intercorrelated ($r = .92$), whereas their correlation with pictorial AoA was weaker ($r = .77$ and $r = .75$, respectively). Importantly, of the three, only AoA measured in the pictorial modality did not correlate with length of syllables. In addition, the correlation between pictorial AoA and the other length measures was considerably smaller than that of visual and auditory AoAs. These results demonstrate the differential impact of presentation modality and task instruction on AoA measurements.

Factor Analysis

To reduce the number of predictor variables and to avoid—as much as possible—potential con- founds that accompany the examination of intercorrelated variables, a factor analysis (principal

---

[3] With the exception of a lack of correlation between auditory AoA and animacy ratings.

TABLE 17.5
Results of Factor Analysis Across Predictor Variables (Varimax Normalized)

	Factors				
Variable	*1*	*2*	*3*	*4*	*5*
Length in characters	−0.15	0.93	0.07	0.12	−0.01
Length in phonemes	−0.15	0.94	0.06	0.12	−0.01
Length in syllables	−0.05	0.92	0.02	−0.03	−0.001
Stress position	−0.11	0.75	−0.10	−0.11	0.14
Initial fricative	0.004	0.02	0.02	0.95	0.11
Word complexity	0.001	0.44	−0.04	0.39	0.13
Frequency	0.69	−0.02	0.45	0.07	0.25
Imageability	0.62	0.08	0.06	−0.002	0.55
Object familiarity	0.75	−0.02	0.48	0.002	0.20
Concreteness	0.05	0.08	−0.01	0.06	0.91
Animacy (rating)	0.08	−0.05	−0.94	−0.02	−0.02
Animacy binary	−0.02	0.04	−0.95	0.02	0.05
Pictorial AoA	0.87	−0.10	−0.11	0.01	−0.11
Visual AoA	0.90	−0.22	−0.14	−0.03	0.03
Auditory AoA	0.89	−0.21	−0.12	−0.01	0.01
Variance explained	38.5%	34.7%	22.8%	11.0%	12.9%

components) was conducted on the 15 predictor variables. The results of the factor analysis are presented in Table 17.5.

The analysis revealed five factors with eigenvalues greater than 1. The first factor is a combination of frequency, imageability, object familiarity, and the three measures of AoA; this factor accounted for 38.5% of the variance. Thus the first factor combined semantic–conceptual features such as imageability and object familiarity with more experience-based measures such as frequency and AoA. The second factor accounted for 34.7% of the variance and loaded on all length measures (characters, phonemes, and syllables), stress position, and a bit of word complexity. The third factor accounted for 22.8% of the variance and united both types of animacy measures and a relatively modest object familiarity and frequency load. This result is not surprising as both types of animacy correlated negatively with frequency and familiarity ratings (cf. Table 17.4). Therefore, here also, the semantic and conceptual features of animacy and object familiarity were combined with the frequency measure, that is, frequency may be not purely a lexical feature of the word but may also contain conceptual characteristics. Support for this view comes from a cross-language picture-naming study (Bates et al., 2003). Their results of cross-language correlations of frequency and its cross-language impact on picture-naming RT suggest that word frequency may reflect processes not only at the lexical but at the conceptual level as well. This possibility is discussed also by Johnson, Paivio, and Clark (1996), who note that it is still unknown whether frequency has an effect on the stages during or after picture identification, that is, whether frequency is a purely lexical characteristic or whether it contains conceptual attributes as well. They also suggest that the subjective frequency measure may contain more conceptual characteristics than printed word frequency. The fourth factor accounted for 11% of the variance and was formed mainly by word-initial frication. Finally, the fifth factor accounted for 12.9% of the variance and united the semantic word characteristics of concreteness and imageability.

TABLE 17.6
Regression of Factor Scores on Adults' and Children's RTs

Factor	Adults		Children	
	Variance (%)	Partial Correlation	Variance (%)	Partial Correlation
Total (joint variance)	42.6		54.1	
Factor 1: AoA, familiarity, frequency and imageability	13.0	−0.43***	8.5	−0.39***
Factor 2: Form–structure	n.s.	n.s.	8.2	0.39***
Factor 3: Animacy	n.s.	n.s.	n.s.	n.s.
Factor 4: Initial fricative	14.9	0.45***	n.s.	n.s.
Factor 5: Concreteness and imageability	2.0	−0.19**	n.s.	n.s.

$^{**}p < 0.01$; $^{***}p < 0.001$; n.s., nonsignificant

Altogether, we observe that experiential variables stick together with conceptual ones. Furthermore, semantic variables do not necessarily travel together at all, that is, concreteness and imageability are combined in one factor but animacy is on its own. It appears from this analysis that concreteness has more in common with the ease of producing mental images than with the living versus nonliving taxonomy.

Regression Analysis With Factors as Variables

Because the preliminary analysis demonstrated an interconnection among factors, a ridge regression analysis was applied to avoid possible multicollinearity effects in the regression analysis. Thus a stepwise ridge regression analysis was conducted on RTs to examine the independent contribution of each of the five factors when it was entered into the equation on the last step. The results of this analysis are presented in Table 17.6.

The five factors together accounted for 42.6% of adults' RT variance and for 54.1% of children's RT variance. These percentages are relatively high in comparison with those of other studies (e.g., Bates et al., 2001; Spieler & Balota, 2000; Yamazaki et al., 1997). Three factors made significant unique contribution each to adults' RTs. Factor 1 (AoA, frequency, object familiarity, and imageability) was responsible for 13.0% of the RT variance with a highly significant negative partial correlation ($r = -.43$; $p < .001$). Thus high values of these predictor variables had a strong facilitating effect on word reading in adults. This result confirms the findings from the analysis of correlations of the predictor variables with RT (cf. Table 17.3). Factor 4 (word-initial frication) added 14.9% to the overall RT variance by increasing RT values ($r = .45$). Finally, semantic Factor 5 (concreteness and imageability) facilitated processing ($r = -.19$), contributing 2.0% to the overall variance. The direction of influence of the latter two factors, that is, frication and semantic characteristics, is not surprising. Evidence for this comes from studies discussed in the previous subsection and from the results of the correlation analysis. Concreteness, however, stands out here in its combination with imageability in Factor 5, as its correlation with RTs did not reach significance in the previous analysis (cf. Table 17.3). All in all, the findings of this analysis confirm expectations concerning the impact of the various predictors included in this study. What is striking is the relative contribution of each of the five factors. Thus the effects of length and animacy, for example, although reaching significance in the correlation analysis, turned out to be negligible when entered on the last step in a regression analysis. The two overwhelming factors in the regression results for adults' RTs are, on the one hand, the composite measure of AoA, frequency, imageability, and object familiarity, and, on the other hand, word–initial frication. The latter may have different interpretations, as we suggested earlier, that are mostly not informative about word processing.

In the case of children's RTs, two of the five factors made a significant contribution (Table 17.6). Factor 1 (AoA, object familiarity, frequency, and imageability) accounted for 8.5% of the RT variance; it facilitated the word-reading process ($r = -.39$). Factor 2 (form–structure) made a unique contribution to the RT variance (8.2%) by slowing down processing ($r = .39$). The results of the regression analysis for children's RTs are altogether compatible with the results of the correlation analysis of predictors with RTs. This applies to Factor 1 (AoA, object familiarity, frequency and imageability) and Factor 2 (form–structure). As in adults, animacy did not contribute to the overall RT variance. However, unlike adults, for children, Factor 4 (frication) and Factor 5 (concreteness and imageability) did not emerge as independent influences either. The absence of contribution of Factor 4 is not surprising because the correlation between RT and frication was much smaller for kids than for adults (cf. Table 17.3). However, although imageability and concreteness behave in the same way for both age groups in the correlation analysis (cf. Table 17.3), Factor 5 did not reach significance in children's data.

On the whole, the regression analysis showed a partial overlap in the individual contribution made by the factors in the two age groups, that is, Factor 1 (AoA, object familiarity, frequency, and imageability), although smaller in children, significantly contributed to both RT variances, showing the experiential nature of reading. Animacy was not independently important for either group. However, the form–structural factor was a significant predictor of children's RTs suggesting that children, unlike adults, are still highly dependent on form–surface and structural features in word reading. The absence of contribution from form–structure and the presence of contribution on behalf of a semantic factor in adults is an indication that, unlike children, they take a more holistic approach in word processing. Finally, the frication factor, most probably, shows that white noise produced by frication is highly detectable in short RTs (adults) and fades in significance in long RTs (children). Some evidence in support of this suggestion comes from Bates et al. (2001) and D'Amico et al. (2001). In word naming (i.e., with shorter RTs), Bates et al. (2001) obtained a contribution from word–initial frication to the RT variance and did not obtain it in picture naming (i.e., with longer RTs). Similarly, D'Amico et al. (2001) obtained no contribution from frication in relatively long picture naming RTs (for both adults and children).

CONCLUSION

The present study addressed developmental differences in single-word reading in terms of RTs and the influence of various word–related factors in the orthographically transparent Bulgarian language. The results of the regression analysis data collected show that, although in adults sublexical word characteristics such as length play no independent role, in the less experienced age group of 8–9-year-old children sublexical segmentation draws more attentional resources during processing. Thus children appear to be more form focused and structure sensitive. In the same vein, lexical and semantic word characteristics were stronger predictors of RT in adults and accounted for more unique variance in adults than in children. This finding is consistent with the findings of Spieler and Balota (2000), that in the early stages of learning to read, readers pay more attention to individual letters and other sublexical characteristics (see also Bourassa & Treiman, 2001; Treiman, 2000) and less attention to lexical and semantic–conceptual word characteristics. As reading and language skills improve, individuals may rely less and less on form–surface levels of word structure and more on functional, lexicosemantic, conceptual factors, having developed more unitized representations of words and more familiarity with words and their internal structure. Thus children's results are not only quantitatively different from those of adults, but the two profiles are actually qualitatively different. That is, the results showed a double dissociation between the two age groups and the two kinds of characteristics, form–structure–based (length, stress position, and some word complexity) and semantics (concreteness and imageability), whereas, at the same time, they also shared a common factor that united experiential, conceptual, and some semantic characteristics, thus showing the importance of learning experience.

Our main results of correlational patterns and factor analysis show that experiential and semantic–conceptual word characteristics are tied together. Moreover, the results suggest that frequency may be viewed as reflecting not only lexical but also conceptual characteristics. As for animacy, it appears to correlate with experiential and conceptual characteristics. Finally, the three different types of AoA measures are not only compatible but they also supplement each other by revealing the influence of presentation modality and instruction on ratings.

In conclusion, the study demonstrates the possibility and utility of using RT as a dependent measure in developmental studies. The comparison between the two age groups suggests that children and adults have different reading strategies. Although children rely on their (albeit limited) experience, they still focus on the surface features of a word and have not yet developed the adults' holistic approach. Results also indicate that reading in an orthographically transparent language can activate semantic processes in adults. This finding poses a theoretical challenge to the current computational models of reading (and visual word recognition). This study's second methodological contribution (other than using a design with a large number of variables and subjective ratings) is the demonstration of the use of factor and regression analyses in dealing with the multicollinearity of predictors in word reading. Finally, the study suggests that it is useful to view cognitive processes during reading and reading development in a more integrated manner, taking into account many word characteristics at different levels of word structure in order to have a more complete picture of word representation and processing.

ACKNOWLEDGEMENTS

We are grateful to the administration and young participants of primary school No 151 in Sofia, Bulgaria. We also thank our experimenters Dona Astakova, Valja Vladimirova, and Velina Balkanska for their help in gathering the data. This study was partially supported by a NATO grant on "Comparative studies of language development and reading in four languages."

REFERENCES

Bates, E., D'Amico, S., Jacobsen, T., Székely, A., Andonova, E., Devescovi, A., Herron, D., Lu, C.-C., Pechmann, T., Pléh, C., Wicha, N., Federmeier, K., Gerdjikova, I., Gutierrez, G., Hung., D., Hsu, J., Iyer, G., Kohnert, K., Mehotcheva, T., Orozco–Figueroa, A., Tzeng, A., & Tzeng, O. (2003). Timed picture naming in seven languages. *Psychonomic Bulletin and Review, 10*, 344–380.

Bates, E., Burani, C., D'Amico, S., & Barca, L. (2001). Word reading and picture naming in Italian. *Memory and Cognition, 29*, 986–999.

Bates, E., Devescovi, A., Pizzamiglio, L., D'Amico, S., & Hernandez, A. (1995). Gender and lexical access in Italian. *Perception and Psychophysics, 57*, 847–862.

Bourassa, D. C., & Treiman, R. (2001). Spelling development and disability: The importance of linguistics factors. *Language, Speech, and Hearing Services in Schools, 32*, 172–181.

Brown, C. M., Hagoort, P., & ter Keurs, M. (1999). Electrophysiological signatures of visual lexical processing: Open– and closed–class words. *Journal of Cognitive Neuroscience, 11*, 261–281.

Brysbaert, M., Lange, M., & Van Wijnendaele, I. (2000). The effect of age–of–acquisition and frequency–of–occurrence in visual word recognition: Further evidence from the Dutch language. *European Journal of Cognitive Psychology, 12*, 65–85.

Caramazza, A., & Shelton, J. R. (1998). Domain–specific knowledge systems in the brain: The animate–inanimate distinction. *Journal of Cognitive Neuroscience, 10*, 1–34.

Cohen, J. D., MacWhinney, B., Flatt, M., & Provost, J. (1993). PsyScope: A new graphic interactive environment for designing psychology experiments. *Behavioral Research Methods, Instruments and Computers, 25*, 257–271.

Colombo, L., & Burani, C. (2002). The influence of age of acquisition, root frequency, and context availability in processing nouns and verbs. *Brain and Language, 81*, 398–411.

D'Amico, S., Devescovi, A., & Bates, E. (2001). Picture naming and lexical access in Italian children and adults. *Journal of Cognition and Development, 2*, 71–105.

Damasio, A., & Tranel, D. (1993). Nouns and verbs are retrieved with differently distributed neural systems. *Neurobiology, 90*, 4957–4960.

Daniele, A., Guistolisi, L., Silveri, C. M., Colosimo, C., & Gainotti, G. (1994). Evidence for a possible neuroanatomical basis for lexical processing of nouns and verbs. *Neuropsychologia, 32*, 1325–1341.

Devlin, J. T., Gonnerman, L. M., Andersen, E. S., & Seidenberg, M. S. (1998). Category–specific semantic deficits in focal and widespread brain damage: a computational account. *Journal of Cognitive Neuroscience, 10*, 77–94.

Ellis, A. W., & Monaghan, J. (2002). Reply to Strain, Patterson, and Seidenberg (2002). *Journal of Experimental Psychology: Learning, Memory, and Cognition, 28*, 215–220.

Gainotti, G., Silveri, C. M., Daniele, A., & Giustolisi, L. (1995). Neuroanatomical correlates of category–specific semantic disorders: A critical survey. *Memory, 3*, 247–264.

Garlock, V. M., Walley, A. C., & Metsala, J. L. (2001). Age–of–acquisition, word frequency, and neighborhood density effects in spoken word recognition by children and adults. *Journal of Memory and Language, 45*, 468–492.

Johnson, C. J., Paivio, A., & Clark, J. M. (1996). Cognitive components of picture naming. *Psychological Bulletin, 120*, 113–139.

Koenig, T., & Lehmann, D. (1996). Microstates in language–related brain potential maps show noun–verb differences. *Brain and Language, 53*, 169–182.

Laudanna, A., Voghera, M., & Gazzellini, S. (2002). Lexical representations of written nouns and verbs in Italian. *Brain and Language, 81*, 250–263.

Lewis, M. B., Gerhard, S., & Ellis, H. D. (2001). Re-evaluating age–of–acquisition effects: Are they simply cumulative–frequency effects? *Cognition, 78*, 189–205.

Matanova, V. (2001) *Dyslexia.* Sofia: Sophi-R.

Monaghan, J., & Ellis, A. W. (2002). What exactly interacts with spelling–sound consistency in word naming? *Journal of Experimental Psychology: Learning, Memory, and Cognition, 28*, 183–206.

Morrison, C. M., & Ellis, A. W. (2000). Real age of acquisition effects in word naming and lexical decision. *British Journal of Psychology, 91*, 167–180.

Paivio, A., Yuille, J. C., & Madigan, S. (1968). Concreteness, imagery, and meaningfulness value for 925 nouns. *Journal of Experimental Psychology Monograph Supplement, 76*, Part 2, 1–25.

Pulvermüller, F., Lutzenberger, W., & Pressl, H. (1999). Nouns and verbs in the intact brain: Evidence for event–related potentials and high–frequency cortical responses. *Cerebral Cortex, 9*, 497–506.

Seidenberg, M. (1995). Visual word recognition: An overview. In J. Miller & P. Eimas (Eds.), *Speech, language, and communication* (pp. 137–178). San Diego: Academic Press.

Seidenberg, M. S., & Plaut, D. C. (1998). Evaluating word–reading models at the item level: Matching the grain of theory and data. *Psychological Science, 9*, 234–237.

Spieler, D. H., & Balota, D. A. (2000). Factors influencing word naming in younger and older adults. *Psychology and Aging, 15*, 225–231.

Stevens, J. (1996). *Applied multivariate statistics for the social sciences.* Mahwah, NJ: Lawrence Erlbaum Associates.

Strain, E., Patterson, K., & Seidenberg, M. S. (2002). Theories of word naming interact with spelling–sound consistency. *Journal of Experimental Psychology: Learning, Memory, and Cognition, 28*, 207–214.

Treiman, R. (2000). The foundations of literacy. *Current Directions in Psychological Science, 9*, 89–92.

Yamazaki, M., Ellis, A. W., Morrison, C. M., & Lambon Ralph, M. A. (1997). Two age of acquisition effects in reading of Japanese Kanji. *British Journal of Psychology, 88*, 407–421.

Zevin, J. D., & Seidenberg, M. S. (2002). Age of acquisition in word reading and other tasks. *Journal of Memory and Language, 47*, 1–29.

18

Early Phonological Skill as a Predictor of Reading Acquisition in Latvian

Ieva Sprugevica and Ingrida Paunina
University of Latvia

Torleiv Høien
Dyslexia Research Foundation

The grapheme–phoneme relationship in Latvian language is reasonably straightforward even though there are some exceptions. This state of regularity is attained by extensive use of diacritical marks. This chapter reports a study that examined the effectiveness of some measures of phonological skills (phonemic awareness), rapid naming, and short-term memory in predicting later reading skills. Of these independent variables, phonemic awareness assessed at kindergarten level turned out to be the only significant predictor of word decoding and sentence comprehension at first and second grade levels. The predictive power of short-term memory and rapid naming turned out to be insignificant. The study also compared the outcome of traditional methods of data analysis with that of the method of growth-curve analysis and found that both yielded comparable results.

INTRODUCTION

Letters with diacritical marks are characteristic of Latvian writing. The extensive use of diacritical marks perhaps makes letters well matched with Latvian phoneme designation. For instance, compared with the German language, in which the phoneme [š] is indicated by three letters (*sch*), in Latvian, the same phoneme is represented by a single letter [*s*] with an attached circumflex (*š*). Similarly, vowel length is marked by a horizontal bar placed above the letter. Exceptions to this one letter–one phoneme correspondence are the diphthongs, for which a phoneme is formed by a combination of two vowel letters.

Letters are pronounced as the phonemes they represent, irrespective of their position between other letters. For instance, the letter *a* designates the phoneme [a] and is read as such as shown in the following examples—the adjective ***mazs*** [*mas:*], the verb *lasa* [*las:a*], and the noun ***reklāma*** [*reklāma*]. It can, therefore, be claimed that in Latvian a straight-forward relationship exists between writing and reading. It should, however, be noted that the grapheme-phoneme relationship is not perfect; the few phonetic alterations which arise in the flow of speech are not reflected in spelling. The main reason for such a discrepancy between pronunciation and spelling is the phenomenon of assimilation and reduction of the articulation sounds that occur in morphemic junctions such as *aiztikt* [*aistikt*], *labs* [*laps*], *mežs* [*meš* . The most characteristic cases of positional alterations are: assimilation of consonants in terms of sonority—voiced noise consonants *b, d, ǧ, g, dz, dž, z, ž* before voiceless noise consonants alternate with voiceless noise consonants within pairs: *snigt* [*snikt*], *iztikt* [*istikt*], but voiceless noise consonants before voiced noise consonants alternate with voiced ones: *atgūt* [*adgūt*]; affricate *c* origination from the impact of the ending *ts, ds* and the preceding morpheme: *pats* [*pac*], *gads* [*gac*]. These articulatory changes are not reflected in the spelling. Vocalization of the consonants *j* and *v* is also not reflected in spelling. Furthermore, the traditional Latvian orthography does not reflect:

1) the difference between narrow *e, ē* [*e, ē*] and broad *e, ē* [*e O, ē O*] in writing,

Narrow *e, and ē* are determined by the associated palatalized consonants such as *ķ, ǧ, č, dž, š, ž, ņ,* and *ļ*. However, in some cases, an alternation of narrow and broad *e, ē* is regulated by non-positional conditions since the sound changes due to assimilation are nowadays lost or transformed: *tēOvs* (from an earlier form **tēOvas*), *nest* (< **nesti*), an adverb *rēti* (< **rētai*).

2) Latvian orthography also does not reflect the difference between phonemes [*uo*], [*o*] and [*ō*]; These sounds are designated with one letter *o* (Bergmane & Blinkena, 1986). In spite of the homographic nature of such spelling, meaning of the words is made clear from the context. Thus, the noun **soda** [sōda] and the verb **soda** [suoda] are spelled the same way but the two words have different meaning. The norm is that words of Lettish origin and earlier borrowings, and words of foreign origin are read as [*uo*] but words that have entered the language more recently are read as [*o*] or [*ō*].

It seems that the above mentioned exceptions could make the spelling easier, as different phonemes are represented by one and the same letter. Therefore, it is not necessary while spelling to distinguish precisely what sound the writer has heard.

PHONOLOGICAL SKILLS AND THE ACQUISITION OF READING SKILLS IN LATVIAN

In this section, we describe a research project which examined the relationship between early phonological skills (phonemic awareness, rapid naming, and short-term memory) and later word reading and sentence reading skills in Latvian children.

The prediction of success or failure in reading acquisition based on early assessments of prereading skills has been the focus of many studies (for a review, see Snow, Burns, & Griffin, 1998). There is now a substantial body of evidence indicating that phonological skills, especially phonological awareness, is one of the best predictors of reading performance of children (Stanovich, Cunningham, & Cramer, 1984). Even when the variance seen in prior word reading skill is partialled out, early phonological awareness still predicts significant variance in subsequent word and nonword reading ability as well as in reading comprehension (Torgesen, Wagner, & Rashotte, 1997).

There is also evidence that other cognitive–linguistic skills, such as rapid naming and short-term memory, are additional predictors of reading achievement (e.g., Badian, 1994, 1995, 2000; Bowers, 1995; Catts, 1993; Scanlon & Vellutino, 1997). However, in a study that controlled for variance in initial reading ability (the autoregressive effect), rapid naming did not turn out to predict any unique variance in reading performance (Torgesen, Wagner, Rashotte, Burgess, & Hecht, 1997).

The child's ability to memorize and repeat verbal information has also been found to be a good predictor of reading achievement. It is well known that reading ability and short-term memory are significantly correlated (for reviews, see Baddeley, 1986; Wagner & Torgesen,

1987), and Scarborough (1998) also refers to several studies which indicate that verbal short-term memory significantly predicts later reading ability.

A practical limitation in many follow-up studies has been the tendency to use word decoding as the dependent variable rather than reading comprehension (e.g., Wagner, Torgesen, & Rashotte, 1994). The ultimate aim of reading instruction is, of course, reading comprehension; but clearly, efficient word decoding is a necessary prerequisite for achieving this aim. The relative impact of early predictors, then, will differ depending on which predictor is being looked at and which aspect of reading is being predicted.

When investigating early predictors of reading achievement, most studies have used traditional correlation analyses (Hecht, Burgess, Torgesen, Wagner, & Rashotte, 2000; O'Connor & Jenkins, 1999). Some studies, however, have addressed the relationship between early predictors and the growth curve which is an indicator of reading development (Olson, Wise, Johnson, & Ring, 1997; Torgesen, Wagner, Rashotte, Burgess, & Hecht, 1997). Growth-curve analysis provides information about the parameters of the best fitting curve of individual reading development. By further statistical analyses such as hierarchic regression analysis, the individual slope value can be used as a dependent variable when studying which predictor factors are most powerful in explaining the growth of reading development.

In the present study, we have restricted the time window of reading acquisition from the end of preschool to the middle of Grade 2 with four occasions of measurement. Children's reading performance in terms of both word recognition and comprehension, was assessed four times at regular intervals from kindergarten to Grade 2.

The aim of the current study was thus to examine early measures of phonological skills (phonemic awareness, rapid naming) and short-term memory in predicting later reading skills. Based on previous research as well as theoretical considerations, these skills were assumed to be of critical importance for reading development. We also compared the outcome of traditional methods of data analysis with that of the method of growth curve analysis. Our prediction study was carried out in Latvian which is a language with a far more regular orthography than English.

METHOD

Participants

The initial sample consisted of 70 kindergarten children, 39 girls and 31 boys, with an age range from 6 to 7 years ($M = 6$ years and 8 months, $SD = 4.4$ months). The children were randomly selected from four different kindergarten classes in the city of Riga, and the first assessment was carried out at the end of kindergarten (in May 2000). Only children from monolingual Latvian-speaking families were included in the study. The assessments were repeated twice a year (in May and December) during a period of 1.5 years. At the end of the study, only 53 of the original 70 children were still available for testing.

In Latvia, children in kindergarten classes usually receive instruction in enabling skills such as letter recognition, letter–sound correspondences, and sound blending. Although the practice may vary somewhat from kindergarten to kindergarten, it is not uncommon that some instruction in word recognition is also given.

Tests

Two different types of tests were used in assessing these children. The predictor tests measured cognitive–linguistic abilities among children in kindergarten, whereas subsequent reading ability was assessed by tests of word decoding and reading comprehension at four different times during the follow-up study. The cognitive–linguistic tests included phonemic awareness tasks, rapid naming, and verbal short-term memory.

Two different tasks were used to assess phonemic awareness: phoneme segmentation and phoneme deletion. The *phoneme segmentation test* assessed the child's ability to identify phonemes in orally presented words. The test included two practice items with feedback support and 20 experimental items without feedback. The words varied from short and phonologically regular words at the beginning of the test to longer and phonologically complex words at the end (from four to nine phonemes). All words were a part of the children's receptive vocabulary. Experienced preschool teachers constructed the word list based on their knowledge of the typical vocabulary of kindergarten children. One of the experimenters read the word aloud with normal speed and articulation. The children had to segment the word into its constituent phonemes and provide the sounds aloud. The performance score was the number of words segmented correctly. The *phoneme deletion test* assessed the child's ability to identify and delete the first or the last phoneme of the target word and provide the pronunciation of the nonword that remained after this deletion. The test had two practice items with feedback support and 20 experimental items without feedback. The words varied in length from 3 to 10 phonemes, and all of them were selected from the vocabulary used by children at this age. For the first half of the items in the list, the children were asked to delete the initial phoneme; for the remaining half, they had to delete the final phoneme. The performance score was the total number of correct responses after deletion. In further statistical analyses the two phonemic scores were transformed into a composite score for phonemic awareness.

Two subtests were used to assess rapid naming. The *object-naming test* assessed the child's ability to quickly retrieve the phonological representation of five familiar objects: an apple, a house, a tree, a sun, and a star. The drawings of each object occurred several times in random order on a sheet of paper (the total number of pictures on the sheet was 80). The children were given a practice task with feedback for all five drawings before the real testing started. The performance score was the total number of objects named correctly during a testing time of one minute. The *color-naming test* was similar to object naming, but instead of naming objects, the task here was to name colors. The test consisted of five color patches: black, green, blue, red, and yellow, which occurred several times in random order on a sheet of paper (the total number of items on the sheet was 180). Each of the children got a practice task with feedback including all five colors before the test items were presented. The performance score was the total number of color patches the child correctly named during a testing time of 1 min. In further statistical analyses the two test scores were transformed into a composite score for rapid naming.

Verbal short-term memory was assessed by a *digit-span test* and by a *letter-span test*. The strings of digits were presented orally with a time interval about 0.5 between each digit. The child had to repeat back the digits in each string in correct order. The strings started with only two digits, and one digit was added for each new digit string. The test continued until the child made a mistake in two strings in a row. The child got two practice items with feedback support before the test items were presented. The performance score was the number of digits in the longest string reported correctly.

The letter-span test was similar to the digit-naming test, but instead of digits, strings of consonant letters were used as stimuli. Again, two practice items with feedback support were provided before the test strings were presented. The performance score was the number of letters in the longest string repeated back correctly. In the further statistical analyses the two the scores were transformed into a composite score for short-term memory.

Reading ability was assessed by two tests: A *word decoding test* and a *sentence-reading test*. In the word-reading test, the task was to read 80 words aloud. The words varied in length (from 2 to 15 letters) and in phonological–orthographic complexity.

All words were written in lowercase letters on a sheet of paper and presented in a 12-point font. Two practice items with feedback support were provided, but no feedback was given for the test items. The performance score was the number of words correctly read.

The children were presented with two practice sentences and 80 experimental sentences with five pictures below each sentence. The task was to read each sentence silently and choose one of the five alternative pictures corresponding to the target sentence. The children were given 10 min to perform the test, and the score was the total number of pictures correctly marked. The sentences varied in length, and the syntactical structure of the sentences was all in active form. In this study, sentence reading was used as a measurement of reading comprehension. However, it has to be recognized that reading single sentences is a much simpler task than reading and interpreting paragraphs of texts. Sentence reading therefore assesses only elementary reading comprehension processes, and this limitation has to be taken into account when one is interpreting the results.

Procedure

All tests were administered to the children individually by trained research assistants. The tests were presented in the following order: phoneme segmentation, phoneme deletion, rapid object naming, color naming, short-term memory, word decoding, and sentence reading. The test results were recorded on specially prepared scoring sheets, on which the research assistants were required to mark each child's response. Each assistant did the scoring individually in accordance with a clear description of how to score the different tests. In the kindergarten classes, the tests were carried out during a period of 2 weeks, and there were two test sessions for each child. In the elementary classes, the children were assessed three times: In December and May in Grade 1, and in December in Grade 2. The tests were individually administered during a period of 2 weeks.

RESULTS

Descriptive data on the various tests are presented in Table 18.1. Mean raw score, standard deviation, and range of scores are given for each assessment.

Despite the fact that on the phoneme tests (segmentation and phoneme deletion) and the word-reading test, a few children had a ceiling effect, the tests still provide information sufficient to discriminate among the children. The sentence-reading test, however, discriminated well across the four assessments. The intercorrelation matrix (Bonferroni corrected) is presented in Table 18.2. The data were collected from the kindergarten assessments.

The correlations between tests within a conceptual category (e.g., digit span and letter span) are generally high and justify the composite scores used in the further analyses. An analysis of variance was performed to study the growth in word-reading performance from kindergarten to the middle of Grade 2 ($N = 53$). The analysis showed a significant increase in word-reading ability, $F(3, 52) = 75.974$, $p < .001$, and a supplementary polynomial contrast analysis demonstrated that the profile of the developmental curve was both linear, $p < .001$, and quadratic, $p < .001$. Moreover, the development in sentence-reading performance showed a clear and significant increase, $F(3, 52) = 76.706$, $p < .001$, with a linear slope, $p < .001$.

TABLE 18.1
Descriptive Statistics for Kindergarten, Middle of Grade 1, End of Grade 1, and Middle of Grade 2

Task	Max. Possible	Kindergarten			Beginning of the First Grade			End of the First Grade			Second Grade		
		Mean	SD	Range	Mean	SD	Range	Mean	SD	Range	Mean	SD	Range
Phonemic awareness													
Phonemic segmentation	20	8.9	4.8	0–20	12.8	4.8	1–20	16.0	3.0	7–20	15.9	2.5	10–20
Phonemic deletion	20	12.3	4.3	1–20	16.0	3.9	2–20	17.5	2.3	10–20	17.8	1.7	13–20
Rapid naming													
Object naming test	180	45.8	10.4	27–70	54.2	10.8	32–79	58.4	11.1	37–89	62.6	11.1	37–96
Color naming test	180	48.1	11.5	20–75	55.0	12.5	33–85	59.6	11.5	41–86	65.6	12.1	37–93
Verbal short–term memory													
Digit span test	9	4.2	1.0	2–6	4.1	1.0	2–6	4.6	1.0	3–7	4.8	1.1	3–7
Letter span test	9	3.7	0.9	2–7	3.9	0.9	2–6	4.0	0.9	2–6	4.2	0.8	2–6
Reading tasks													
Word reading (accuracy)	60	45.8	10.4	3–60	53.1	8.5	3–60	55.5	3.9	44–60	55.5	3.8	40–60
Sentence reading	80	19.4	9.4	5–50	31.7	12.2	4–57	38.6	11.6	20–73	47.7	12.1	25–78

Note: $N = 53$.

TABLE 18.2
The Intercorrelations Among Tasks at the Kindergarten Level (Bonferroni Corrected)

Task	1	2	3	4	5	6	7	8
1. Segmentation	1.000							
2. Deletion	0.423***	1.000						
3. Color naming	0.195	0.383*	1.000					
4. Object naming	0.162	0.363	0.849**	1.000				
5. Digit span	0.431*	0.325	0.435**	0.360*	1.000			
6. Letter span	0.341	0.215	0.416**	0.384*	0.667***	1.000		
7. Word reading	0.598***	0.515***	0.315	0.329	0.454**	0.383*	1.000	
8. Sentence reading	0.167 (ns)	0.231 (ns)	0.208 (ns)	0.132 (ns)	0.188 (ns)	0.218	0.224 (ns)	1.000

Note. $^* = p < .05,^{**} = p < .001,^{***} = p < .001$; ns, nonsignificant.

Predicting Word- and Sentence-Reading Ability: The Traditional Approach

To investigate the contribution of the phonological factors on word- and sentence-reading ability, multiple-regression analyses were performed with word and sentence reading as dependent variables, and with phonemic awareness, rapid naming, and short-term memory as independent variables.

In the first regression analysis the factor scores on the phonological skills in kindergarten were used as predictors, whereas the performance scores in word reading at three different points of time (middle of Grade 1, end of Grade 1, and middle of Grade 2) were used as dependent variables. The results are presented in Table 18.3.

The analysis revealed that phonemic awareness was the only powerful and significant predictor, explaining 27.4% of unique variance in word reading in the middle of Grade 1 ($p < .01$) and 9.3% of the variance at the end of the Grade 1 ($p < .05$). The phonemic factor did not

TABLE 18.3
How Phonological Skills in Kindergarten Predict Later Word and Sentence Reading

Reading Variable	Predictor	Beginning of First Grade, Unique R^2	End of First Grade, Unique R^2	Second Grade Samples, Unique R^2
Word Reading Test	Phonemic factor	.274**	.093*	.006 (ns)
	Naming factor	.002 (ns)	.056 (ns)	.001 (ns)
	Memory factor	.003 (ns)	.017 (ns)	.022 (ns)
Sentence Reading Test	Phonemic factor	.159*	.087 (ns)	.133*
	Naming factor	.008 (ns)	.011 (ns)	.000 (ns)
	Memory factor	.006 (ns)	.000 (ns)	.000 (ns)

Note. $^*p < 0.05,^{**} p < 0.01$; ns, nonsignificant.

predict word reading in the middle of Grade 2. The other predictor variables (rapid naming and short-term memory) did not predict variance in word reading at any stage in the word-reading development.

A follow-up regression analysis was performed to see if phonemic awareness could explain unique variance in word reading even when differences in word reading in kindergarten (the autoregressive effect) were controlled for. Not surprisingly, variance in early reading ability was the most powerful predictor, explaining 24.3% of the variance in word reading in the middle of Grade 1 ($p < .01$). However, it is important to note that phonemic awareness still accounted for unique 4.9% of the variance in word reading ($p < .05$). At the end of Grade 1 the autoregressive effect predicted significantly 18.3% of the variance in word reading at the end of Grade 1 ($p < .01$), whereas phonemic awareness did not contribute to explain additional variance. The same statistical approach was used to assess how phonological skills may predict sentence reading (see Table 18.3).

The hierarchical regression analysis revealed that phonemic awareness accounted for 15.9% of the variance in sentence reading in the middle of Grade 1 ($p < .01$), but the factor did not account for significant variance at the end of Grade 1. Somewhat surprising was the finding that the phonemic factor nevertheless accounted significantly for 13.3% of the variance in sentence reading in the middle of Grade 2. Neither rapid naming nor short-term memory had any predictive power at any time of sentence-reading assessment.

When sentence-reading scores in kindergarten were forced into the regression analysis as the first predictor (the autoregressive factor), this factor did not account for any variance in sentence reading in the middle of Grade 1. However, the phonemic awareness still explained 3.7% of the variance in sentence reading ($p < .05$), whereas naming and memory did not account for any significant variance in sentence reading.

Predicting Word- and Sentence-Reading Ability: Growth-Curve Analysis

We also examined whether an assessment technique based on the progress across the whole time period of testing (growth potential) is a more illuminating procedure than the traditional prediction technique. The b values (the slope coefficients) for each child were calculated. Then regression analyses were performed by use of phonemic awareness, rapid naming, and short-term memory scores in kindergarten as predictor variables, with the b values as dependent variables. The results are displayed in Table 18.4.

TABLE 18.4

How Phonological Skills Predict the Regression Slopes of Word and Sentence Reading

Slope	Predictor	Unique R^2
word reading	Phonemic factor	.152***
	Naming factor	.046 (ns)
	Memory factor	.088 (ns)
sentence reading	Phonemic factor	.007 (ns)
	Naming factor	.010 (ns)
	Memory factor	.002 (ns)

Note. *** $= p < 0.001$; ns, nonsignificant

In the first analysis, the *b* values for word reading growth were entered as dependent variables. The analysis showed that the phonemic factor predicted significantly 15.2% of the variance in the slope ($p < .05$), whereas memory and naming did not explain any significant variance in the slope. In a follow-up analysis, the *a* values were forced into the regression analysis as the first factor. This analysis showed that the autoregressive factor accounted for 25.2% of the variance in the *b* slope ($p < .001$), whereas phonemic awareness explained an additional 7.8% of the variance ($p < .05$).

When the *b* values for sentence-reading growth were used as dependent variable, the results on the regression analysis revealed that none of the predictor factors contributed significantly to explain variance in *b* values. Even the sentence-reading scores in kindergarten (the autoregressive effect) did not significantly predict any variance in the *b* slope for sentence reading.

DISCUSSION

In this study, children were followed from kindergarten to the middle of Grade 2 with regular assessments. Two different procedures were applied to examine the predictive power of the preschool phonological skills. The first method determined how these skills (phonemic awareness, rapid naming, and verbal short-term memory) predicted word- and sentence-reading scores at three different times—in the middle of first Grade, at the end of the Grade 1, and in the middle of Grade 2. The second approach analyzed individual growth curves on word reading and sentence reading from kindergarten untill the middle of Grade 2, that is, the progress across the whole period of the testing. The same explanatory variables were employed in both approaches.

Phonemic awareness in kindergarten explained above one fourth of the variance in word reading half a year later, and about 9% of the variance at the end of Grade 1. Even when the autoregressive effect was controlled for, phonemic awareness accounted for unique variance at the middle of Grade 1 and again at the end of Grade 1. Our findings thereby provide further evidence on the importance of phonemic awareness for acquiring efficient reading ability (for a review, see Stanovich, 2000).

The predictive power of phonemic awareness as assessed in kindergarten decreased as a function of time. By the middle of Grade 2, phonemic awareness did not predict any variance in word reading. Obviously many factors determine the children's progress in reading, and phonemic awareness is only one of them. Children enter school and are given systematic instruction in reading, and this probably helps their sensitivity to phonemes too. Therefore the decrease in predictive power over time does not mean that the relationship between phonemic awareness and reading ability at any one given point in time is necessarily less important than we have come to see in recent years.

The importance of the phonemic awareness factor for reading acquisition was also confirmed when sentence reading was used as a dependent variable. It is important to note that phonemic awareness explained unique variance in both measurements in Grade 1 and in the middle of Grade 2. Clearly phonemic awareness is also important for reading comprehension. However, we have to consider that the sentence test used in this study was very simple and that the results might have been different if more complex texts were used.

The lack of predictive power of short-term memory and rapid naming was somewhat surprising in light of many research reports (Bowers, 1995; Scarborough, 1998; Wagner et al., 1994; Wolf, 2001). However, the autoregressive effect and the phonemic awareness factor might have accounted for most of the available variance to be explained.

When growth-curve analysis was used, phonemic awareness was the only phonological factor that significantly accounted for variance in the reading slope, The main finding was that growth-curve analysis showed that phonemic awareness in general has a significant impact on early word reading, a finding that adds further evidence to the critical role of phonemic awareness as an initial enabling skill in early reading acquisition.

As noted earlier, the phonemic factor did not explain any significant variance in the b slope for sentence reading. This unexpected result may be caused by unreliability connected with the sentence-reading scores in kindergarten. As shown in Table 18.1, the mean value for sentence-reading is not higher than the value expected from pure guessing (choosing one among four alternatives). Therefore the result should be interpreted with caution. A major theoretical as well as practical issue is to explain why some children acquire reading skills quickly whereas other children make slow progress.

In conclusion, the traditional prediction method, which utilizes correlation statistics, and growth-curve analysis are complementary procedures that provide a more complete picture of the predictive power of initial enabling skills. Whichever strategy is used, our results clearly indicate that phonemic awareness is the single most powerful predictor of early reading in a written language with a regular orthography such as Latvian.

ACKNOWLEDGEMENTS

This research was supported by grants from the Faculty of Psychology, University of Bergen, the Nordic Research Council and The Dyslexia Research Foundation, Stavanger, Norway.

REFERENCES

Adams, M. J., & Bruck, M. (1995). Resolving the "great debate." *American Educator, 19,* 7–20.

Baddeley, A. (1986). *Working memory.* New York: Oxford University Press.

Badian, N. A. (1994). Do dyslexic and other poor readers differ in reading-related cognitive skills? *Reading and Writing: An Interdisciplinary Journal, 6,* 45–63.

Badian, N. A. (1995). Predicting reading ability over the long term: The changing roles of letter naming, phonological awareness and orthographic processing. *Annals of Dyslexia, 45,* 79–96.

Badian, N. (Ed.). (2000). *Prediction and prevention of reading failure.* Baltimore, MD: York Press.

Bergmane, A., & Blinkena, A. (1986). *Latviešu rakstības attīstība.* Riga: Zinātne.

Blachman, B. A. (1984). Relationship of rapid naming ability and language analysis skills to kindergarten and first-grade reading achievement. *Journal of Educational Psychology, 76,* 610–622.

Bowers, P. (1995). Tracing symbol naming speed's unique contributions to reading disabilities over time. *Reading and Writing: An Interdisciplinary Journal, 7,* 1–28.

Bowers, P., & Wolf, M. (1993). Theoretical links among naming speed, precise timing mechanisms and orthographic skill in dyslexia. *Reading and Writing: An Interdisciplinary Journal, 5,* 69–85.

Catts, H. (1993). The relationship between speech-language impairments and reading disabilities. *Journal of Speech and Hearing Research, 36,* 48–58.

Hecht, S. A., Burgess S. R., Torgesen, J. K., Wagner, R. K., & Rashotte, C. A. (2000). Explaining social class differences in growth of reading skills from beginning kindergarten through fourth-grade: The role of phonological awareness, rate of access, and print knowledge. *Reading and Writing: An Interdisciplinary Journal, 12,* 99–127.

Lundberg, I., Olofsson, A., & Wall, S. (1980). Reading and spelling skills in the first school year predicted from phonemic awareness skills in kindergarten. *Scandinavian Journal of Psychology, 21,* 159–173.

O'Connor, R., & Jenkins, J. (1999). Prediction of reading disabilities in kindergarten and first grade. *Scientific Studies of Reading, 3,* 159–197.

Olson, R., Wise, F., Johnson, M., & Ring, J. (1997). The etiology and remediation of phonological based word recognition and spelling disabilities: Are phonological deficits the "hole story"? In B. Blachman (Ed.), *Foundations of reading acquisition and dyslexia. Implications for early intervention.* London: Lawrence Erlbaum Associates.

Scanlon, D. M., & Vellutino, F. R. (1997). Instructional influences on early reading success. *Perspectives. The International Dyslexia Association, 23,* 35–37.

Scarborough, H. (1998). Early identification of children at risk for reading disabilities: Phonological awareness and some other promising predictors. In B. K. Shapiro, P. J. Accordo, & A. J. Capute (Eds.), *Specific reading disability: A view of the Spectrum* (pp. 77–121). Timonium, MD: York Press.

Snow, C. E., Burns, M. S., & Griffin, P. (1998). *Preventing reading difficulties in young children*. Washington, DC: National Academy Press.

Stanovich, K. E. (2000). *Progress in understanding reading. Scientific foundations and new frontiers*. New York: Guilford.

Stanovich, K. E., Cunningham, A. E., & Cramer, B. (1984). Assessing phonological awareness in kindergarten children: Issues of task comparability. *Journal of Experimental Child Psychology, 38,* 175–190.

Torgesen, J. K., Wagner, R. K., & Rashotte, C. A. (1997). Prevention and remediation of severe reading disabilities: Keeping the end in mind. *Scientific Studies of Reading, 1,* 217–234.

Torgesen, J. K., Wagner, R. K., Rashotte, C. A., Burgess, S., & Hecht, S. (1997). Contributions of phonological awareness and rapid automatic naming ability to the growth of word-reading skills in second- to fifth-grade children. *Scientific Studies of Reading, 1,* 161–185.

Wagner, R. K., & Torgesen, J. K. (1987). The nature of phonological processing and its causal role in the acquisition of reading skills. *Psychological Bulletin, 101,* 217–234.

Wagner, R. K., Torgesen, J. K., & Rashotte, C. (1994). Development of reading-related phonological processing abilities: New evidence of bidirectional causality from a latent variable longitudinal study. *Developmental Psychology, 30,* 73–87.

Wolf, M. (Ed.). (2001). *Dyslexia, fluency, and the brain*. Timonium, MD: York Press.

19

If John Were Ivan, Would He Fail in Reading?

Elena L. Grigorenko
Yale University, USA, and
Moscow State University, Russia

The purpose of this chapter is twofold: first, to describe the structures capturing the relationships among sounds, letters, syllables, words, and phrases in Russian; second, to capitalize on this information and put forward a predictive model aimed at depicting how and when, given the characteristics of Russian language, weaknesses in mastering reading are manifested in Russian children and adults. Correspondingly, the first section of the chapter summarizes relevant important characteristics of Russian as a linguistic entity and the way Russian is taught in schools. The second section presents hypotheses regarding how these characteristics are relevant to the manifestation of reading difficulties in Russian.

THE RUSSIAN LANGUAGE: GENERAL DESCRIPTION

A typical school program for the Russian language is spread over 11 years. It focuses on the following parts: phonology, graphics of language, orthoepics and accentology (pronunciation), orthography, morphology, lexicology, phraseology, syntax, and punctuation. Phonology covers issues of phoneme–grapheme correspondence in Russian; graphics of language addresses issues of acceptability of representation of Russian letters; orthoepics and accentology address issues of norms of pronunciation of words in Russian; orthography deals with rules of spelling and word segmentation (hyphenation); morphology analyzes the structure of words and explores issues of word formation; lexicology is concerned with vocabulary structure; phraseology addresses issues of word agreement and building meaningful word chains; and syntax and punctuation are concerned with large word chains and sentences. Here I briefly review only select relevant components of studies of Russian: phonology, graphics, orthoepics and accentology, orthography, morphology, lexicology, and phraseology. These components are relevant for understanding the way difficulties arise in acquiring reading skills in Russian.

Phonology

Russian is an alphabetic language containing 33 letters, which are categorized into three groups: (1) letters that do not symbolize sounds (*ь* and *ъ*), (2) letters that symbolize two sounds (*e, ё, ю* and *я*), and (3) letters that correspond to only one sound (the other 27 letters). There are 10 vowels and 21 consonants in Russian. In addition to the variety of the sounds produced by the alphabetic letters, the richness of Russian phonology is attained through combinations of letters, in which the same letter can signify multiple sounds as well as through a variety of contexts in which a letter can appear so that its sound is changed by surrounding letters. For example, the Russian consonant *c* can symbolize six sounds: [с] (*суд*), [с'] (*сюсюкать*), [з] (*сдать*), [з'] (*сделать*), [ш] (*сшить*), and [ж] (*сжечь*) (Rozental', Golub, & Telenkova, 1998).

The Russian vowels (*и, у, е, ы, а, о, э, ю, я, ё*) are differentiated by the place of articulation (placement and degree of elevation of the mouth), the involvement of lips, and the degree of openness of the mouth.

The Russian consonants, as they appear in the alphabet, are divided into two large groups, voiced (*б, в, г, д, ж, з*) and voiceless (*п, ф, к, т, ш, щ, с, х, ц, ч*). However, when embedded in a word and surrounded by other letters, many Russian consonants can transform themselves—from voiced to voiceless and from voiceless to voiced. Specifically, when voiced consonants appear at the end of the word or before voiceless consonants, they can become voiceless themselves. For example, the voiced consonant *д* sounds like a voiceless consonant *т* in the word *молодь* [fry]. Similarly, the voiced consonant *з* sounds like the voiceless consonant *с* in the word *сказка* [fairy tale]. On the contrary, when appearing before voiced consonants, voiceless consonants sound like voiced consonants (e.g., *т* sounds like *д* in *молотьба* [harvest] and *с* sounds like *з* in *просьба* [request]).

In addition, almost every consonant in Russian can appear in two different forms, hard and soft. For example, the letter *м* sounds like a hard phoneme [м] in the word *мал* (small) and like a soft phoneme [м'] in *мял* to crumble). The letter *б*, in turn, symbolizes four different sounds, [б], [б'], [п], and [п'], depending on the surrounding letters (*булка* [bagel], *белка* [squirrel], *куб* [cube], and *Обь* [a river in Russia], respectively).

Such a "migration" between voiced and voiceless sounds in Russian creates obstacles for the beginning reader and speller. For example, because the word *подкова* (horseshoe) is correctly read as *поткова*, so that *д* sounds like *т*, it is often mistakenly spelled as *поткова*. Similarly, because the word *нож* (knife), when pronounced correctly, sounds like *нош*, many mistakes arise when *нож* is spelled. Correspondingly, the pronunciation of words with consonants changing from voiced to voiceless and vice versa is error prone, although the majority of such changes in pronunciation are strictly rule driven.

As in English, in Russian, one sound can be signified by a combination of letters. For example (Savko, 2001, pp. 17–18), the combination of letters *сч, зч*, and *жч* signifies the sound associated with the letter *щ* (only longer), as in *счёт* [bill], *счастье* [happiness], *извозчик* [carrier], and *мужчина* [man]. The combination of letters *тц, дц, тс*, and *тьс* signifies the sound associated with the long version of the sound associated with the letter *ц*, as in *отца* [father], *тридцать* [thirty] *умывается* [is washing], and *договориться* [to agree]. The combinations of letters *тс* and *дс* produce the sound corresponding to the sound of the letter *ц*, as in *братский* [brotherly] and *городской* [urban]. Finally, the sound associated with the letter combination *нн* is that of the sound produced by the letter *н*, as in *удивленный* [surprised].

Stress (or the degree of prominence of a syllable) in Russian is very important. Two characteristics of Russian stress are relevant here. First, stress in Russian can appear on any syllable of a word—first, last, or middle (*éль* [spruce], *тетрадь* [notebook], or *корá* [bark], respectively). Second, in morphological derivatives from one root, stress in Russian can move (e.g., *óгниво*, *огóнь, огонькá*—words formed with the root *fire*). This very dynamism of Russian provides the basis for differentiation between strong and weak phonetic positions. If the syllable is stressed, the vowel in that syllable is said to be in a strong position; correspondingly, if the syllable is not stressed, the position of the vowel is weak. When in a strong position, the sound is clear and well pronounced; in a weak position, the sound is less pronounced, can change, and can be reduced. There are two types of vowel reduction in Russian. The quantity reduction refers to decreased length and strength of a vowel in an unstressed syllable, as with the vowels *u, ы,* and *y.* The quality reduction refers to weakening of the sound of vowels in an unstressed syllable. For example, the vowels *a* and *o* can sound like [∧] if they appear in the first syllable before the stressed syllable; or like [ъ], if they appear in the second syllable before the stressed syllable or in the syllable following the stressed syllable. The vowels *a, o,* and *э* sound like [$u^э$] after soft consonants in the first syllable before the stressed syllable, but like [ы] if they occur in the second syllable before the stressed syllable or in the syllable following the stressed syllable.

Similarly, there are strong and weak positions of consonants. The consonants are in the strong position before the vowels *a, o, y,* and *и,* and in the weak position, for example, at the end of a word.

In sum, both vowels and consonants in the Russian language are extremely context dependent. But not only that—the fluctuation of stress and the change of sound can get very confusing! For example, the same vowel, occurring in the same root, can sound different depending on the morphological modifications of the root and the fluctuation of the stress. Thus, in morphologically related words that generate from the same root, the same letter can sound very different, depending on the location of the stress and surrounding letters. For example, the words *домовóй, домá, дóм,* and *нá дом* have the same root, *дом* [house], but the vowel *o* generates four different sounds [ы], [∧], [ó], and [ъ], respectively (Rozental' et al., 1998). Similarly, consonants can change their sound if they are not stressed: For example, *гу[б]а* and *гу[п]ka* are words with the same root, but in the second word the consonant *б* changes its sound to [п].

Graphics

Graphics addresses the issues of graphical representation of Russian letters—what is acceptable and unacceptable in written Russian. The specifics of Russian graphics are closely related to Russian phonology. Namely, the presence of two silent letters (*ь, ъ*) and four vowels (*ю, я, е, ё*) that are associated with double sounds creates much confusion for a beginning reader—in some cases there are more letters than sounds (*уголь* [угол'] [coal]) whereas in others there are more sounds than letters (*ёлка* [jолка] [fir tree]).

Orthoepics

The dominant pronunciation of words in Russian is based on what is known as Moscow dialect, which originated in the 18th century. By that time, Moscow had become the true center of Russia, where various northern and southern dialects were combined and integrated. Moscow norms were dispersed to other regions of the country and rooted there (primarily through the bureaucratic machinery of the centralized government in Moscow).

Pronunciation in modern Russian can be classified into categories based on two dimensions. First, there are full and condensed pronunciations: Full pronunciation is characteristic of speech that is well structured, well articulated, and not constrained by time, whereas condensed pronunciation is characterized by lack of clear pronunciation, significant reduction of vowels and consonants, and severe time constraints. Second, there are stylistic characteristics of Russian: One can adopt high, neutral, or everyday styles of pronunciations.

Orthography

In its earlier forms, the Russian language was much more phonologically transparent—the written language closely resembled the spoken language. However, in the 12th through 17th centuries, the phonology of the Russian language underwent a number of transformations, and the result of these processes was a dissociation between the spoken and written languages.

Although there were some early attempts to systematize Russian orthography (e.g., the publications by M. Smotritsky in the 17th century), the fundamental work describing the rules of written Russian appeared in the 18th century (e.g., the publications by V. Trediakovskii and M. Lomonosov). The first schoolbooks of Russian orthography were published in the 19th century (e.g., Ya. Grot's *Russian Orthography*). It is fair to say that by the end of the 19th century, Russian orthography existed in its most complex form, with a number of mismatches between the written and spoken forms of Russian. Being aware of the unnecessary complexity of written Russian, a number of linguists, at the beginning of the 20th century, started a movement in support of a revision of Russian orthography, which was realized in the reform of 1918. The modern version of Russian orthography is based on the work of D. Ushakov's *The Rules of Russian Orthography*—the first systematic and complete handbook of rules of Russian orthography.

Currently, Russian orthography includes rules that determine the written representation of words and morphemes, joint or separate representations of parts of the words or structural units of language, usage of capital letters, and division and hyphenation of words. In this chapter, however, I review briefly only the most general rules of Russian orthography that relate to the written representation of words and morphemes. Words and morphemes are based on a number of major principles, of which the most important are *morphological, phonological, orthographical, traditional, phonetic*, and *differentiating* (Savko, 2002, pp. 238–241).

The *morphological* principle of Russian orthography is its dominant rule because it drives the spelling of the majority of Russian words. This principle presumes the consistent spelling of all morphemes (i.e., roots and affixes) independent of the pronunciation of the words in which these morphemes are embedded. For example, although the letter *o* in the words *вода, заводь, водный*, and *вод* is pronounced differently in each word, that is, as four different phonemes, it is always spelled consistently with the letter *o* because all these words share the same root, *вод*-(signifying water).

The *phonological* principle assumes that the same letter can signify different phonemes when it is present in strong and weak positions, but when such words are written, they should be written with the letter that signifies the phoneme when it appears in the strong position. For example, the letter *д* in a word with the root-*вод* (signifying water) can sound like *д* or soft *д* or as *т* or soft *т*. This principle clearly causes a number of spelling mistakes in relevant words (e.g., the word *заводь* is often misspelled as *завоть*). However, the phonological principle requires that, in all words with the root *од*-, this root is always spelled with the letter *д*, irrespective of the way the word sounds. The phonological principle supposes that the spelling of the phoneme in question should be verified by placing this phoneme in a strong position (e.g., *заводь–вода*).

The *traditional* principle refers to the spelling of certain words along the established tradition, either historical or commonly accepted. Such words do not contain affixes (i.e., the morphological principle is not applicable) and cannot be verified by finding words with the same root (i.e., the phonological principle is not applicable). The spelling of such words should be memorized (e.g., *барабан* [drum], *чувство* [feeling], *периферия* [periphery]).

The *phonemic* principle guides the spelling of words in which the spelling mimics the pronunciation of the word (e.g., *безвинный* [guiltless]—the voiced sound [з] is pronounced before the voiced sound [в]; *беспокойный* [uneasy]—the voiceless sound [с] is pronounced before the voiceless sound [п]).

The *differentiating* principle rules the spelling of words that sound the same or similar but have different meanings (e.g., when a *dancing party* is meant, the corresponding Russian word is spelled as балл, but when *grades* or *scores* are meant, the corresponding word is spelled as бал; the Russian verb for *to burn* is spelled ожёг and the Russian noun for *a burn* is spelled ожог).

In addition to the principles just listed, there are other principles in Russian orthography that guide the rules for writing complex words containing multiple components and dashes indicating the differences between different words and parts of the same word.

Morphology

If a phoneme is the basic meaningful sound, then a morpheme is the meaning unit. Morphemes are divided into two large groups—roots (i.e., the essential part of the word) and affixes (prefixes, suffixes, postfixes, interfixes, and endings).

In Russian, the process of word formation (derivation) is stage based. For example, consider the following formation of word family groups from the word вихрь [whirlwind] (Savko, 2002, p. 90). The first group of words includes as derivatives a noun, an adverb, an adjective, and a verb. The second group originates from modification of the derivative verb вихрить [to whirl] and consists of verbs only:

вихрь→

(1) { вихор-*ёк*
     { вихр-*ем*
     вихр-*ев*-ой
     вихр-*и*-ть→

(2) { вихрить-*ся*
   { *из*-вихриться
   за-вихрить

Modern Russian language utilizes three main types of word formation: morphological, lexical–semantic, and lexical–syntactic (Savko, 2002). Each of these types can be further subdivided into specific clusters of word formation.

The *morphological* type is further subdivided into groups based on the types of morphemes that are involved in the word formation. Specifically, the *prefix* subtype refers to the manipulation with prefixes (e.g., делать [to do]—*пере*делать [to redo]; граница [border]—*за*граница [abroad]; волосатый [hairy]—*без*волосый [hairless]). The *suffix* subtype refers to the word formation that engages suffixes (e.g., лес [forest]—лес*ник* [forester]; рис [rice]—рис*ов*ый [rice, adj.]; умеренный [moderate]—умеренн*ость* [moderation]). The *prefix–suffix* type assumes the simultaneous use of both prefixes and suffixes in word formation (e.g., локоть [elbow]—*под*локот*ник* [elbow rest]; пощада [mercy]—*бес*пощад*ный* [merciless]; кидать [to throw]—*под*кинуть [to throw (a ball) up]). The *postsuffix* type assumes the use of postsuffix morphemes (e.g., греть [to warm up]—греться; целовать [to kiss]—целоваться). The *prefix–postsuffix* word formation assumes manipulations with a word prefix and postsuffix (e.g., пить [to drink]—*с*питься; греть [to warm up]—*пере*греться). The *suffix–postsuffix* type utilizes both suffixes and postsuffixes simultaneously (e.g., дым [smoke]—дым*и*ться; струя [stream]—струиться). The *prefix–suffix–postsuffix* type of word formation capitalizes on using simultaneously all three morphemes, prefix, suffix, and postsuffix (e.g., вина [fault]—*про*вин*и*ться, цена [price]—*обес*цен*ива*ть). The *no-affix* (also known as the null-affix) word formation types assume the generation of words without any affixes (e.g., *сиреневый* [lilac, color]—*сирень* [lilac, flower]; *правдивый* [truthful]—*правда* [truth]). The *word-addition* type assumes the word formation by the addition of two or more words together to generate a new word (e.g., *ракетоносец* [missile carrier], *путеводитель* [guidebook]). There is also a type of word formation that assumes the use of *word addition* and *suffixes* simultaneously (e.g., *большеглазый* ← *большой* [big] + *глаз* [eye] + *е*; *узколобый* ← *узкий* [narrow] + *лоб* [forehead] + *о*). It is important to note that a number of processes can take place during word formation. Specifically, there could be (a) a change of phonemes (e.g., *глухой* [deaf] → *глушить* [to stun]; *квасить* [to make sour] → *квашение* [the process of making sour]; *продукт* [product] → *продукция* [production]); (b) the minimization of the basis (e.g., *дергать* [to pull] → *дернуть* [to pull]; *далекий* [distant] → *даль* [distance]; *глубокий* [deep] → *глубина* [depth]); and (c) the inference of morphemes with identical sounds (e.g., Минск + ск → минский; такси + ист → таксист).

In what follows is one of the most frequently observed manifestations of the morphological principle—the generation of word agreements, also referred to as inflectional morphology (Kozyreva, 2001). Word agreement refers to the situations in which words are linked in phrases in such a way that their meaning is unambiguous. To accomplish this certainty of meaning, endings in adjectives, verbs, and nouns are all expected to correspond to each other. Moreover, the majority of endings in Russian change systematically, based on the invariant structures that establish rules of word agreement. For example, consider agreements between nouns of different gender and the adjective *Russian*:

народ русск*ий* [Russian nation]
речь русск*ая* [Russian stove]
слово русск*ое* [Russian word]
люди русск*ие* (Russian people)

Note that the ending of the adjective *русский* (Russian) changes depending on the type of noun with which the words are used. Similarly, the morphological principle rules the agreements between nouns of different gender and the verb *to squeak*:

скрипе*л* ступ [a chair squeaks]
скрипе*ла* скамейка [a bench squeaks]
скрипе*ло* кресло [an armchair squeaks]
скрипе*ли* ворота [gates squeak]

By the rules, the verb *скрипть* (to squeak) should have endings that unambiguously relate this verb to the subject or object described.

The *morphological–syntactic* type of word formation is based on a move from one type of word to another. For example, the adjective *столовая* [table, as in tableware] can change to the noun *столовая* [dining hall]. Similarly to English, the adjective *будущее* [future, as in future tense] can change into the noun *будущее* [the future]. The meaning and type of such words can be determined only through the context.

The *lexical–semantic* type of word formation assumes the division of a word with multiple meaning into words—homonyms. For example, the word *спутник* carries the meaning of the word *partner* if the word *спутник* is used in the context of talking about a person, and the meaning of the word *sputnik* [a spacecraft] if the word *спутник* is used in the context of space exploration.

Finally, the *lexical–syntactic* type of word formation is based on combining words of different types that change from a phrase into a single word. For example, the descriptive phrase *с ума сшедший* [someone who lost his or her mind] can be transformed into the word *сумасшедший* [mentally ill]. Similarly, the expression *быстро растворимый* [quickly dissolving] can be substituted with the adjective *быстрорастворимый* [instant].

Lexicology

Studies of Russian lexicology include studies of Russian vocabulary (for a more detailed discussion of this topic and more examples, see Rozental' et al., 1998). The unit of lexicology is a word. Lexicology is interested in describing, establishing the etiology of, and understanding the epistemology of words, their meanings, and connections between words. Lexicology studies (a) typologies of lexical meanings in Russian, based on semantic (i.e., relating to the meaning of the word), derivational (i.e., relating to the issues of word formation), and connectional (i.e., relating to various connections between the target word and other words in the language) properties of the word; (b) words with multiple meanings; and (c) groups of words—homonyms, synonyms, and antonyms.

Traditionally, Russian vocabulary (lexicon) includes three main types of words and word constructions (Savko, 2002): general Slavic (i.e., words that originated before the 6th century C.E. and are common to all Slavic languages—Russian, Ukrainian, Byelorussian, Polish, Bulgarian, Czech, Slovenian, and so on), Eastern Slavic (also referred to as Old Russian, i.e., originating between the 7th and 14th centuries C.E. and common to old Eastern Slavic languages—Russian, Ukrainian, Byelorussian), and Russian (i.e., words that originated in the Russian language after its separation from Old Russian, between the 15th century and modern times).

The Russian lexicon is remarkably rich, as Russian includes, by many accounts, one of the highest numbers of words among the world's languages. There are a number of *types of lexical meanings* in Russian. Specifically, in terms of word nomination, word meaning is described as direct, capturing the main meaning of the word, and indirect, capturing the secondary and tertiary meanings of the word. For example, historically the main meaning of the word *стол* was a *throne*, but now the main meaning of the word is a *table* (a piece of furniture). However, the word *стол* has a number of indirect meanings (e.g., *письменный стол*—desk, *операционный стол*—operating podium, *стол станка*—lathe, *платить за комнату со столом*—to pay for room and board, *справочный стол*—information desk).

In terms of the degree of their semantic motivation, words are described as unmotivated (nonderivative, first order), whose meaning is not dependent on the meaning of the morphemes in the word, and motivated (derivative, second order), whose meaning can be determined by the meaning of their componential morphemes (affixes). For example, the word *стол* [table] is an unmotivated word, but the words *столовый, настольный, столоваться*, and *престол* are all motivated, as they were formed by modification of the root *стол* with meaningful affixes, each of which adds a certain semantic coloring to the word.

In terms of their capacity to form phrases with other words, words can be described as free and nonfree. Inclusion into phrases of free words is constrained only by the semantic meaning of the word; for example, the word *есть* [to eat] can be combined with any other word that signifies anything edible. Inclusion into phrases of nonfree words is constrained by the semantic meaning and morphology of the word. For example, the word *одержать* [to gain] contains the prefix *о-*, which signifies, in part, success in overcoming obstacles; therefore, even without a reference to semantic meaning of the word *одержать*, this word cannot be combined with the word *поражение* [defeat]. In addition, nonfree words are characterized by the presence of stable idioms, from which other phrases cannot be reassembled (e.g., in the idioms *заклятыйвраг* [sworn enemy] and *закодычный друг* [coded friend], the elements of the phrases cannot be exchanged, as the resulting phrases *заклятый друг* and *закодычный враг* do not capture the intended meaning).

Functionally, words are broadly divided into two categories—nominal (i.e., labeling events, things, and so on) and expressive–synonymic (i.e., assigning expressivity and emotion to events, things, and so on). For example, the descriptor *невысокий человек* [short person] is nominal, but when this descriptor is substituted with an expressive synonymous word *коротышка* [squab], the descriptor gains emotional connotation. Russian is characterized by the richness of its expressive vocabulary.

Finally, words are divided into categories describing their semantic networks with other words. Specifically, words are described as autonomous (i.e., characteristic of words retaining their dominant meaning independent of other words in Russian lexicon), comparative (i.e., characteristic of words describing polar qualities or opposite dimensions), and determined (i.e., characteristic of words whose meaning is dependent on the meaning of other words).

Another area of lexicology is studies of *words that carry multiple meanings*. In Russian, there are many words with multiple meanings; in fact, the majority of words in the Russian lexicon are polysemantic (Rozental' et al., 1998). A particular meaning of the word relevant for a given usage is mostly derived from the context. Multiple meanings of words are differentiated by frequency of usage, with the most frequently used meaning presented first in dictionaries and referred to as the main meaning; other meanings of the word are referred to as derivative meanings.

In addition, words with multiple meanings might form multiple pairs of antonyms so that a particular meaning of the word is paired with a particular antonym (e.g., *вредный* [unhealthy]–*полезный* [healthy] and *вредный* [bad]–*хороший* [good]). Moreover, it is possible that the antonym pair itself has multiple meanings (e.g., in the antonym pair *длинный* [long]–*короткий* [short] both words have multiple meanings; correspondingly, this antonym pair changes its meaning depending on the context in which it appears). Clearly, such accumulation of meanings can be an obstacle in acquiring proficiency of comprehension for the beginning reader. In addition, Russian has synonymous pairs of antonyms (e.g., *большой* [big]–*маленький* (small); *большой* [big]–*крошечный* [very small]). In such cases, one pair of antonyms, the one that contains a stylistically neutral pair of words, is referred to as a dominant pair of antonyms (e.g., *большой–маленький*). Typically nondominant synonymous pairs of antonyms contain words capturing stylistic peculiarities (e.g., *большой–крошечный*, in which the word *крошечный* modifies the meaning of the antonym pair, stressing a particularly small size of the second member of the pair of objectives that are being compared).

In terms of distinguishing *groups of words*, Russian lexicology classfies words into homonyms, synonyms, antonyms, and paronyms.

Homonyms—words that sound similar but have totally different meanings—are widely distributed in Russian. A very nice and playful example of how homonyms work in Russian comes from the following piece of children's poetry:

Смотрит зайка *косой*,
Как девчонка с *косой*
Еа речною *косой*
Травы косит *косой*
                    —M. Mitreikin (cited in Kozyreva, 2001, p. 11)

The four italicized words in this piece of poetry are all homonyms: squint, braid, split, and scythe, respectively. To appreciate how widely spread homonyms are in Russian, consider the following chain of words: *горе* [grief], *сгорать* [to burn out], *прогорать* [to burn through], *горный* [mountain, adj.] *горка* [mountain, noun], *гореть* [to burn], *горюшко* [tragedy], *горевать* [to grieve], *пригорок* [knoll], *пригорюнился* [to become sad], *гористая* [mountainous], and *горючий* [combustible]. To a novice in Russian, all these words sound as if they have the same root (*гор*); in fact, these words were derived from three different roots.

There are many typologies of homonyms (Rozental' et al., 1998), but here I exemplify only two of them. The first typology divides homonyms into complete and incomplete ones. The second typology divides homonyms into roots and derivatives.

Complete homonyms are words that belong to the same part of speech (e.g., nouns, verbs, adjectives), sound the same, have completely overlapping grammatical forms, and are spelled the same, but have different meanings. An example of such a pair of words is *ключ* [key] and *ключ* [brook]. Incomplete homonymy relates to words whose sound and spelling overlap only in certain grammatical forms. For example, the word *завод* can mean *factory* (e.g., *автомобильный завод* [automobile factory]) as well as *winding mechanism* (e.g., *завод у часов* [watch with a winding mechanism]). However, not all grammatical forms of these words correspond with each other. Specifically, the second word *завод* does not have a plural form, but the first one does (*заводы*).

Root homonyms are those words that have first-order (root) overlap, i.e., no other affixes are present in the word (for definitions and examples, see Rozental' et al., 1998). Examples of such words are *мир* [peace] and *мир* [universe] and *брак* [defective goods] and *брак* [marriage]. Derivative homonyms are words that originated in the process of word formation and therefore have morphological affixes (for definitions and examples, see Rozental' et al., 1998, p. 30): *сборка* (as in *сборка автомобиля*—car assemblage) and *сборка* (as in *сборка на платье*—dress gathers) and *строевой* (as in *строевой офицер*—combatant officer) and *строевой* (as in *строевой лес*—timber).

Other types of homonymy include (a) homoforms, words whose sounds overlap only in one (or a few) grammatical forms (e.g., *три* сыр на тёрке [to grate cheese] and *три* сестры [three sisters]); (b) homophones, words that sound the same, but are spelled differently (e.g., *лук* [bow] and *луг* [meadow], *молот* [hammer] and *молод* [young], *вести* [news] and *везти* [to drive]; and (3) homographs, words that are written in the same way, but are pronounced differently (e.g., *замо́к* [lock] and *за́мок* [castle]).

In all its different types, homonymy introduces a serious complication to the morphological principle of spelling in Russian. Consider the following chain of words: *летательный аппарат* [flying machine], *знаменитый лётчик* [famous pilot], *летний вечер* [summer evening], and *погода лётная* [flying weather] (Kozyreva, p. 6). Two underlined roots are spelled *лет* and pronounced [l'et] and two other roots are spelled *лёт* and pronounced [l'ot]. In fact, three of the words (*летательный, лётчик, лётная*) originate from the same root (*лет*), signifying the relatedness of these words to the action of flying, whereas the word *летний* indicates the season (*лето* [summer]). Here, the Russian language tricks a novice reader twice—the words that are derived from the same root do not look similar because of the rule of vowel substitution often utilized in the language, whereas the word derived from a different root sounds just the same as one of the three words originating from the same root.

The following list of words exemplifies homonymy's challenge even more, contrasting meaning and spelling of homophones. All words with italicized letters sound the same, but differ in spelling (Kozyreva, 2001, pp. 13–14): отв*а*ри картофель [boil potatoes], but отв*о*ри ворота [open the gates]; сп*е*ши на занятия [hurry to your class], but сп*и*ши упражнение [copy this exercise]; пол*о*скать белье [to rinse laundry], but пол*а*скать ребенка [to caress a child]; зап*и*вать лекарство [to take (water or milk) with one's medicine], but зап*е*вать песню [to break into song]; прим*е*рять костюм [to try a suit on], but прим*и*рять друзей [to make friends reconcile]; зал*е*зать в долги [to get into debt], but зал*и*зать рану [to lick the wound]; выш*е*л из комнаты [left a room], but, выш*и*л шёлком [embroidered in silk]; пос*и*деть на скамейке [to sit on a bench], but пос*е*деть от старости [to turn gray]. Thus spelling in Russian relies deeply on both the knowledge of morphology and lexicology.

Another very important group of words in the Russian lexicon is that of *synonyms*—words that differ in their sounds but are close in their meanings (for more detail, see Alektorova et al., 2002). The number, richness, and diversity of synonyms in a language are considered to be one of the fundamental characteristics of the language. In turn, the large number of synonyms in a language is due, at least in part, to the morphological richness and complexity of the language. Specifically, because Russian is morphologically complex, large numbers of synonyms are a characteristic feature of the Russian language. Consider the following examples (Alektorova et al., 2002, p. 5). Russian contains a number of adjectives that signify a small object (quantity, amount), for example, *небольшой, маленький, малый, крошечный, крохотный, микроскопический, миниатюрный, карликовый*, and *чуточный*. Similarly, there is a rather long synonymous row for the signification of a large object: *большой, громадный, огромный, гигантский, исполинский*, and *колоссальный*. Russian verbs also commonly have multiple synonyms; for example, the verbs *истратить, растратить, издержать, расточить, израсходовать, прожить, спустить, промотать, убухать, растранжирить, ухлопать*, and *разбазарить* all signify one action—to give money (or something valuable) in exchange for something.

Synonyms rows are characterized by the presence of one so-called rod word (also referred to as the key word or the dominant word). Such a word is the most frequently used and most stylistically neutral of all the words in the row. Words with multiple meanings typically belong to various synonymous rows. For example the word *тихий* enters the following synonymous rows: *тихий* [quiet], *негромкий, слабый* (as used with the word *голос* [voice]); *тихий* [calm], *смирный, кроткий* (as used with the word *человек* [person]); *тихий* [peaceful], *спокойный, безмятежный* (as used with the word *сон* [sleep]). Such multimeaning words may or may not serve as dominant words in all or some of their synonymous rows.

There are multiple classifications of synonyms, but once again, for the sake of brevity, I review only some of them.

Ideographic (also referred to as semantics; Rozental' et al., 1998) synonyms refer to words that capture different shades of the semantic field, for example, *изгиб, извилина,* and *излучина.* All three words signify a curved surface but can be used within different contexts and capture semantic fields of different magnitude, with *изгиб* being the most inclusive semantic category (e.g., *изгиб реки* [river curve], *изгиб ветви* [bend of a tree branch], *изгиб руки* [arm curve]), *извилина* being less inclusive (e.g., *извилины мозга* [convolution], *извилины пути* [winding route]), and *излучина* being typically used only with the word *river* (*излучина реки* [river curve]) (Alektorova et al., 2002, p. 8).

Stylistic synonyms are words capturing different stylistic aspects of the text. For example, the verbs *топать* [to stamp] and *идти* [to walk] capture the same meaning of moving forward on foot, but their stylistic coloring is very different.

Finally, *contextual* (also referred to as semantic–stylistic; Rozental' et al., 1998) synonyms are words that serve as synonyms only in specific contexts. For example, the word *пришпорить* [to spur] can serve as a synonym to the words *ускорить* [to speed up] and *подхлестнуть* [to urge forward] in specific selected contexts (e.g., in a piece of poetry, as in Alektorova et al., 2002, p. 9).

Now consider yet another large group of words important for the description of the Russian lexicon, that of antonyms—words that differ in sound and meaning (for more detail, see Vvedenskaia, 2002). The largest number of antonyms is observed among adjectives and nouns. Although there are verb, adverb, and pronoun antonyms, their number is small. Typically, antonyms are divided into two large classes, words with opposite meanings that are derived from the same root (e.g., *правда–неправда* [truth–lie]; *людный–безлюдный* [crowded–empty]) and words with opposite meaning derived from different roots (*день–ночь* [day–night], *друг–враг* [friend–enemy]).

Same-root antonyms are formed with the help of different morphological affixes. The majority of same-root antonyms are created with prefixes; in fact, Russian has prefixes whose function is to assist in making antonym words, both traditionally Russian (e.g., *без(с)-*, *не-* for nouns and adjectives and *в-* and *вы-*, *при-* and *у-*, *от-* and *за-* for verbs) and adapted from foreign languages (e.g., *контр-*, *анти-*, *а-* for nouns and adjectives).

The final group of words distinguishable in the Russian lexicon that I briefly describe in this chapter is *paronyms*, words that are derived from the same root and whose sound is very similar, but whose meaning is different (e.g., *главный* [main]–*заглавный* [title, adj.]; *опечатки* [typos]–*отпечатки* [prints]). The knowledge of paronyms is extremely important for the development of correct spoken and written language expressions in Russian. Here, a lack of mastery results in agrammatism, or failure to use proper Russian grammar. For example, consider the following sentences (examples from Rozental' et al., 1998, p. 56).

Мать *одела* (надела) на ребенка пальто.) (1)
В вестибюле гостиницы сидели *командировачные* (командированные). (2)

Here, the italicized words indicate paronyms to the words in parentheses, the correct words. In the first sentence, the semantic difference between the correct word and its paronym is slight, so that the two words indicate the same action (to put something on, as in the sentence, "The mother put a coat on a child"); although the used paronym is grammatically incorrect, the meaning of the sentence is preserved even with the wrong word in it. In the second sentence, however, the paronym and the word that should have been used in the sentence have totally different meanings (i.e., the word *командированные* refers to people who are on a business trip, whereas its paronym *командировачные* refers to the per diem allowed for business trips), resulting in the sentence not only being agrammatical, but also meaningless. (The sentence should be translated as "Business travelers sat in the hall of the hotel.") Thus, correct usage of paronyms is a characteristic of grammatically correct, well-cultured oral and written language; on the contrary, the lack of knowledge of paronyms reflects a deprived linguistic education.

At the conclusion of this section of the chapter, I hope it is apparent to the reader that one of the main characteristics of Russian lexicology is its polysemantic nature. In other words, given the size of homonymic, synonymic, and antonymic groups of words, isolated Russian words often carry multiple meanings that are undecipherable without relating to the context in which the word appears. Consequently, spelling of isolated words might be multioptional. Moreover, again because of the sheer number of homonyms, synonyms, and antonyms in Russian, meanings of phrases and even sentences in Russian can be ambiguous when context is not available. All these peculiarities of Russian make learning the language a challenge.

Phraseology

I conclude my summary of the main characteristics of Russian language by describing Russian phraseology, which deals with complex units of language that consist of more than a single word. Russian, like English, has a large collection of phraseological structures. Consider the following few examples:

словно по волшебству [as if by magic]
трещать как сорока [chatter like a magpie]
грехи молодости [wild oats]
вмешиваться в чужие дела [have an oar in every man's boat]

Similar to words, there are synonymous and antonymous groups of phraseological structures, which both enrich the Russian language and make it ever more complex.

The correct and fluent usage of phraseological structures in Russian adds liveliness and color to the language. However, this very usage is liable to errors, as most phraseological structures do not tolerate any change and require precise reproduction of the original phrase. Specifically, phraseological structures cannot be shortened; words in the phrase cannot be substituted with synonyms or paronyms; grammatical forms of words cannot be changed; two or more phraseological structures cannot be blended together; and the meaning of the phrase should be preserved (Rozental' et al., 1998).

WHICH CHARACTERISTICS OF RUSSIAN ARE SERIOUS OBSTACLES TO THE MASTERY OF READING?

The brief summary of the features of the Russian language just provided was intended to set up the context for understanding what difficulties can be encountered (or have been observed to be encountered) by a beginning reader of Russian. In this part of the chapter, capitalizing on the work of a number of Russian colleagues (e.g., Efimenkova, 1991; Iastrebova, 1984; Ivanenko, 1984; Kozyreva, 1997; Rakhmanova, 1987; Sadovnikova, 1983; Spirina, 1985; Triger, 1972), I try to link the information presented in Section 19.1 to specific illustrations and examples of other than optimal mastery of written Russian.

As is likely the case in the instruction of reading and writing all over the world, the knowledge acquired in Russian school grades is expected to form the basis of future skills. Russian national standards for the primary grades (Grades 1–3) assume mastery of alphabetic sounds and letters, syllables, frequent words, and simple sentences. At the level of sounds and letters, the course is aimed at the acquisition of understanding of sounds, their phonological characteristics, sounds in weak (unstressed) and strong (stressed) positions, letter–sound correspondences, and the skill of performing a phonological analysis of simple words. At the word level, a child, by the end of third grade, is expected to determine what part of speech a given word is (noun, verb, adjective, and so on) and to master rules of word agreement (e.g., establishing case-based agreement between nouns and adjectives). At the sentence level, the child is expected to construct and analyze simple sentences, communicate meanings of sentences in his or her own words, and classify major types of sentences (e.g., statements, questions, exclamations).

In addition, the primary grade course of Russian includes extensive introduction to phonology, orthography, morphology, and lexicology. Specifically, children are familiarized with the main principles of Russian orthography (phonological, traditional, and morphological). Reading, writing, and spelling are taught simultaneously within one subject matter titled "Russian Language." Table 19.1 provides an abridged overview of components of the course on Russian language in the primary grades and indicates the domains of acquisition known to be especially difficult for weak students.

Clearly, given the amount of rules and exceptions that a primary school student needs to master within the first three years of schooling, many things can go wrong. Yet Russian can be characterized as a relatively easy language in certain aspects and as a relatively difficult language in other aspects. For example, Russian is considered to be relatively phonologically transparent, because the majority of its letters and letter combinations correspond to a limited number of sounds. However, Russian is considered to be orthographically quite complex because its sounds can be transcribed in multiple ways.

This dichotomy is shown in Figs. 19.1 and 19.2. In the context of *reading familiar words* (Fig. 19.1), word decoding in Russian is usually easy. Typically, if the child knows the word he

TABLE 19.1
Where Can It Go Wrong in Russian?

Domain of Mastery	Criteria to Be Reached	Expected Areas of Difficulty	Examples From Students' Work (Correct spelling is shown in parentheses)
		Grade 1	
Phonology	Phonological analysis of words	Counting sounds, letters, and syllables	
Orthography	Mastery of alphabet	Soundless letters ь and ъ	
Graphics	Sound and letter correspondence	Double-sound letters (е, ё, ю, and я)	
Accentology		Soft consonants ч and щ	
Morphology	Mastery of open and closed syllables	CVCC, CCVC syllables and their junctions	
Beginning lexicology	Spelling of sound combinations	Combinations жи, ши, ча, ща, чу, щу, чк, чн	чяшка (чашка) чюдом (чудом)
		Hushing sounds	што (что) жолтый (жёлтый)
	Prosody of reading	Lack of prosody due to lack of automatization	
	Normative accentology and pronunciation	Flexible position of stress	ожыл–ожил (ожила)
	Graphics of Russian alphabet	Separation between capital and small letters	
	Spelling of grade-appropriate single words (6–8 words in a dictation)		
	Connected text dictation (20–25 words)	Stressed and unstressed vowels	
	Introduction of morphological principle	Voiced and voiceless consonants	
	Expected rate of reading 15–20 words/min		
	Introduction of synonyms and antonyms		
	Vocabulary building		
	Written summaries of the material read (30–40 words)		
		Grade 2	
Morphology	Mastery of accentology and orthoepics	Determining the stressed syllable(s)	бутьте (будьте)
Lexicology	Phonology	Voiced-voiceless pairs of consonants	плате (платье)
	Understanding of the role of letters ь and ъ	Determining the function without an associated sound	лёт (льёт) вехал (въехал)

(Continued)

TABLE 19.1
(Continued)

Domain of Mastery	Criteria to Be Reached	Expected Areas of Difficulty	Examples From Students' Work (Correct spelling is shown in parentheses)
	Understanding the role of doubled consonants	Determining the phonological function	клас (класс) утренний (утренний) одиннадцатое (одиннадцатое) юнность (юность) пано (панно) сделаных (сделанных) старинные (старинные) несмотри (не смотри)
	Understanding word structure Mastering grade-appropriate word formation Introduction of inflectional morphology	Negative particle не with verbs Feminine and masculine nouns with hushing sounds at the end Feminine, masculine, and neutral endings in adjectives	уж (уж) дальная (дальняя) серце (сердце) грусный (грустный) чудесный (чудесный)
	Mastery of combinations of letters with omitted sounds	Д, Т, СН combinations	
	Spelling of grade-appropriate single words (10–12 words in a dictation) Connected text dictation (55–60 words) Vocabulary building Written summaries of the material read (60–75 words)		
		Grade 3	
Morphology Lexicology	Analyses of phonologically complex words Mastery of inflectional morphology	Mistaken syllabolization Words with hidden (nontransparent) roots Cases in nouns Cases in adjectives	Себирье (Сибири) ножём (ножом) сторожом (сторожем) полотенцом (полотенцем) сирене (сирени) дороги (дороге) большём (большом) свежим (свежем)

Mastery of derivational morphology

Unstressed vowels in roots

л<u>е</u>сток (*листок*)
к<u>о</u>залось (*казалось*)
в<u>и</u>ть (*ведь*)
<u>а</u>гароды (*огороды*)
р<u>а</u>сточек (*росточек*)
пр<u>е</u>оде (*природе*)
м<u>е</u>нуту (*минуту*)
х<u>а</u>рош (*хорош*)
с<u>а</u>бой (*собой*)
гр<u>е</u>бов (*грибов*)
н<u>а</u>чиные (*ночные*)
к<u>а</u>рой (*корой*)
мол<u>а</u>д<u>а</u>жонам (*молодёжё нам*)
пож<u>и</u>лают (*пожелают*)
п<u>а</u>том (*потом*)
озн<u>о</u>чала (*означала*)
посв<u>е</u>щена (*посвящена*)
к<u>а</u>гда (*когда*)
в<u>е</u>сит (*висит*)
р<u>а</u>сли (*росли*)
зар<u>а</u>сли (*заросли*)

Endings with the letter *и*
Unstressed prefixes
Unstressed suffixes
Prefixes with voiced and voiceless consonants

птиц<u>и</u> (*птицы*)
п<u>а</u>розила (*поразила*)
путешеств<u>а</u>вать (*путешествовать*)
со<u>з</u>дали (*создали*)
ра<u>с</u>казала (*рассказала*)
ра<u>с</u>телают*ся* (*расстилаются*)

Mastery of personal pronouns

Prepositions and pronouns

евоные (*его*)
<u>ко</u>мне (*ко мне*)
<u>с</u>вами (*с вами*)

Mastery of the morphological principle
Spelling of grade-appropriate single words (12–15 words in a dictation)
Connected text dictation (70–85 words)
Written summaries of the material read (90–100 words)

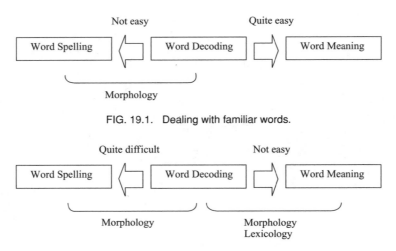

FIG. 19.1. Dealing with familiar words.

FIG. 19.2. Dealing with unfamiliar words.

or she is decoding it is relatively easy. What is not so trivial, however, is knowing how to spell the word. Here, unfortunately, common sense and rules of phonological spelling work only occasionally. As already indicated, Russian spelling is anything but transparent. In short, for familiar words, if one knows how to spell it, one knows how to sound the word out. Knowing how the word sounds, however, does not necessarily mean knowing how to spell it. What is really instrumental here is the knowledge of morphology, as Russian orthography is driven primarily by the morphological principle.

In the context of dealing with *unfamiliar words* (Fig. 19.2), the situation, however, is quite different. Decoding unfamiliar words (and nonwords) can be quite challenging to both the beginning reader and the poor reader. The issue here is that, although not so frequent in common words, there are some combinations of letters, especially silent letters (e.g., the лн combination) or with substituted sounds (e.g., the сч combination), for which the pronunciation is ambiguous even when the spelling is known. In decoding and understanding such words, a knowledge of morphology and lexicology appears to be very helpful. As for spelling, although guided by *many* rules, Russian spelling is much more rule based than otherwise. Thus, once again, morphology can be quite helpful in spelling unfamiliar words.

The situation becomes even more difficult for a beginning reader or a poor reader when the transition from a single word to word phrases and sentences occurs (see Fig. 19.3). At this level, no doubt, the demands become much greater, because a child needs not only to decode and understand single words, but also to link them into combinations by using the rules of inflectional morphology and preserving the demand of word agreement that is so crucial in Russian. Moreover, understanding meanings of phrases and sentences can be easily hindered by multiple meanings of many words in Russian and similarities of words formed through the rules of derivational morphology. This situation is exactly where most beginning and poor readers start to have difficulties—at the junction of the transition from dealing with words to dealing with sentences and connected text.

To summarize, my brief analysis of major characteristics of the Russian language suggests that one can expect variation in mastery in multiple, if not all, relevant domains. First, although more phonologically transparent than English, Russian contains a number of letters and letter combinations for which the phoneme–grapheme links are not straightforward. Second, although the typical situation is such that, when a word is seen, especially if it is a familiar word, decoding the word is easy, the backward movement from the sound of the word to its

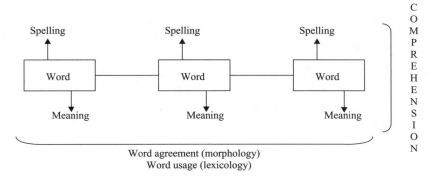

FIG. 19.3. Dealing with sentences.

orthographical representation can be very difficult. There are many aspects of the language that create this difficulty, the most obvious of which is the existence of silent letters, which do not have sound representations of their own, but significantly modify the sound of other letters that appear next to them. Third, because the stress is fluid in Russian and its placement can be different for various morphological derivatives of the root, mastering accent is critical; however, there is a great deal of normal variation in children's and adults' usage of stress, often resulting in the formation of agrammatical Russian constructions. Fourth, Russian morphology is one of the central pieces of the language, as many roots are used over and over in different derivational formats. Once again, there is much intraindividual variation in the mastery of morphology and use of its rules in spelling and writing in Russian. Finally, and especially critical with regard to comprehension of higher-than-word units of the language, the mastery of lexicology is important. The polysemantic nature of Russian vocabulary makes this language heaven for experts and hell for novice writers and readers.

ACKNOWLEDGMENT

Preparation of this chapter was supported by a Fogarty International Research Collaboration Award and a research award from the International Dyslexia Association. I am thankful to Robyn Rissman for helpful editorial comments.

REFERENCES

Alektorova, L. P., Vvedensakaia, L. A., Zimin, V. I., Kim, O. M., Kolesnikov, N. P., & Shanskii, V. N. (2002). *Slovar' sinonimov russkogo iazyka* [Dictionary of synonyms in Russian]. Moscow: Astrel'.

Efimenkova, L. N. (1991). *Korrektsia ustnoi i pis'mennoi rechi uchashchikhsia nachal'nykh klassov* [Oral and written speech correction in primary-grade students]. Moscow.

Iastrebova, A. B. (1984). *Korrektsiia narushenii rechi u uchashickhsia obsheobrazovatel'noi shkoly* [Correction of speech disturbances in children in public schools]. Moscow.

Ivanenko, S. F. (1984). *Formirovanie vospriatiai rechi u detei pri tiazhelykh narusheniakh proiznoshenia* [Speech perception in children with severe speech and disorder]. Moscow.

Kozyreva, L. M. (1997). *Logopedicheskaia rabota v klassakh korrektsii* [Speech and language correction in children with special needs]. Smolensk.

Kozyreva, L. M. (2001). *Sekrety prilagatel'nykh i tainy glagolov* [Secrets of adjectives and mysteries of verbs]. Yaroslav, Russia: Akademia Razvitia.

Rakhmanova, T. N. (1987). Osobennosti postroenia predlozhenii v rechi mladshikh shkol'nikov s ZPD [Peculiarities of sentence formation in children with mental retardation]. *Defectologia, 6.*

Rozental', D. E., Golub, I. B., & Telenkova, M. A. (1998). *Sovremennyi russkii iazyk* [Modern Russian language]. Moscow: Airis-Press.

Sadovnikova, I. N. (1983). *Narushenie pis'mennoi rechi u mladshikh shkol'nikov* [Disturbances of writing in primary-grade children]. Moscow.

Savko, I. E. (2002). *Ves' shkol'nyi kurs russkogo iazyka* [A complete overview of school courses in the Russian language]. Minsk: Sovremennyi Literator.

Spirina, L. F. (1985). *Ucheteliu o detiakh s narusheniami rechi* [For teachers about children with speech disorders]. Moscow.

Triger, R. D. (1972). Nedostatki pis'ma u pervoklassnikov s ZPR [Difficulties in writing in primary-grade children with mental retardation]. *Defectologia, 5.*

Vvedenskaia, L. A. (2002). *Slovar' antonimov russkogo iazyka* [Dictionary of Russian antonyms]. Moscow: Astrel'.

20

Reading in Arabic Orthography: Characteristics, Research Findings, and Assessment

Salim Abu-Rabia and Haitham Taha
University of Haifa

Arabic is a Semitic language with a unique orthography that just recently has attracted scholars' attention, but a study of Arabic orthography can shed light on its unique characteristic features and the role these features play in the reading processes of regular, dyslexic, and nondyslexic poor readers. This chapter presents the Arabic orthography and some related research findings concerning the following: reading accuracy, reading comprehension, reading and spelling errors of dyslexic and regular readers, and bilingual readers. In addition, the chapter discusses some issues relating to reading instruction and intervention. The Arabic research findings are reviewed and discussed in terms of the findings from other orthographies such as English.

ARABIC ORTHOGRAPHY

Written Arabic is an alphabetic system based on 28 letters, with 25 consonants and 3 long vowels. Most Arabic letters have more than one written form, depending on the letter's position in the word: initial, middle, or terminal. However, the essential shape of the letter is maintained in all cases (Abd El-Minem, 1987). In addition, the letters are divided into categories according to basic letter shapes, and the difference between them is the number of dots on or below the letter. Dots appear with 15 letters: 10 have one dot, 3 have two dots, and 2 have three dots. In addition to the dots, there are diacritical marks that contribute to phonology. Even though Arabic words are a combination of consonants and vowels, skilled and adult readers are expected to read texts without short vowels. This places heavy reliance on context for reading. Beginning readers are therefore introduced to reading through text that has short vowels. Vowelized Arabic can be considered shallow orthography whereas unvowelized Arabic can be considered deep orthography. Reading accuracy in Arabic requires vowelizing word endings according to their grammatical function in the sentence, which requires advanced phonological and syntactical ability (Abu-Rabia, 2001). Silent-reading comprehension is less demanding, because the reader can rely on orthography, morphology, and other resources (Abu-Rabia, 2002).

Arabic Morphology

Arabic morphology is composed of two types of structures: derivational and inflectional.

Derivational Morphology.   All words in Arabic are based on phonological patterns built on roots that are consonantal patterns. Roots are triliteral or quadriliteral, that is, they have three or four consonants. However, the root is not a phonological unit but an abstract entity. The phonological pattern is constructed of the following entities:

1. Short vowels built onto roots. The phonological process does not break the orthographic order of the consonantal root;
2. Vowel letters, which are inserted between the root consonants. Here, the phonological pattern of the infixes breaks the orthographic order of the consonantal root;
3. Vowel letters that may occur as prefixes or suffixes. The root facilitates initial lexical access and the combination of roots and phonological patterns conveys specific semantics.

The derivational morphology has two types of word patterns: verbal word patterns and nominal word patterns. There are 15 high-frequency verbal word patterns in Arabic. Each verbal word pattern determines the inflectional pattern of the word (Abd El-Minem, 1987; Al-Dahdah, 1989; Wright, 1967). The verb pattern conveys basic semantics by means of verb roots, and it can change the meaning of a new word created from that root; different verb patterns built on the same root may have different semantic values (Abd El-Minem, 1987). There are nine nominal word patterns. There is semantic consistency in all these different nominal word patterns (Bentin & Frost, 1995), but some of these are more common than others. The derivations of nouns are constructed in two ways, one by addition of nominal patterns of the base roots and one by changing the past tense to the present tense by applying a phonological pattern to the latter (Abd El-Minem, 1987; Al-Dahdah, 1989; Wright, 1967).

Inflectional Morphology.   In contrast to the derivational process, in which the basic constituents are roots and word patterns, the inflectional morphological system in Arabic is constructed by attaching prefixes and suffixes to real words. The system of inflectional morphology of verbs is systematic and marks for person, number, gender, and tense. In the past tense, inflectional morphology indicates person, number, and gender through the addition of suffixes to the basic verb pattern (third-person masculine singular). Inflectional morphology denotes future and present tenses according to person, number, and gender. The imperative mood is formed for person, number, and gender by the addition of prefixes and suffixes (Abd El-Minem, 1987; Al-Dahdah, 1989; Wright, 1967). The inflectional morphological system of nouns considers gender and number.

Most verbs and the majority of nouns are constructed out of roots of three consonants, occasionally two or four. Roots are built in phonological patterns to create specific words; these patterns may be a series of consonants or a series of vowels and consonants. As for roots and morphemic word patterns, most words in Arabic are constructed of two morphemes: The combination of a root and a word pattern creates the particular word. Different morphemes convey different types of information: The root conveys more information than the phonological pattern because it provides the core meaning of the word (Abu-Rabia, 2001, 2002); the word patterns usually convey information on word class.

In sum, the combination of morphological units in Arabic is not linear, but relies on the intertwining of two independent morphemes (the root and the word pattern). The order of root letters depends on the word pattern and its way of intertwining with the root. The word pattern can be built of prefixes, suffixes, and infixes, whose intertwining with the root can break the order of the root letters.

Diglossia

Ferguson (1959) defined *diglossia* as a stable linguistic state that includes different spoken dialects and a totally different literary language version, which is usually grammatically more complicated, as distinct from the spoken dialects, and includes a respectable written literature. This literary version is officially studied in schools (and is not acquired naturally without formal learning). Furthermore, it is the formal written language and is not the language of day-to-day conversation. Ferguson (1959) considered Arabic a case of diglossia. Somech (1980) described the diglossia of the Arabic language as two language worlds: the elite, educated, and highly civilized world, which is expressed through literary Arabic, and the common oral world, which is expressed through spoken Arabic.

Furthermore, according to Harris and Hodges (1981), the term diglossia is used to refer to "the presence of a high and low style or standard in a language, one of formal use in writing and some speech situations and one for colloquial use" (p. 88). Note, however, that this definition of Arabic diglossia is not universally accepted (see, e.g., El-Hassan, 1977).

Ayari (1996) concurs with the preceding definition of diglossia and adds that this diglossic situation of the Arab world interferes with children's Arabic-reading acquisition. Because, from the first grade, Arab children are required to study literary Arabic, which is a different language from spoken Arabic, they often encounter difficulties. He adds that, unfortunately, preschool children are not exposed to literary Arabic because there is a virtual consensus in the Arab world that literary Arabic is difficult for them and that they should not be exposed to it before Grade 1. Parents, teachers, and educators share this belief. Consequently these children encounter literary Arabic in the first grade of primary school almost as a second language. According to Ayari (1996), this means that children are required to cope simultaneously with reading and writing in a second language (i.e., literary Arabic). Ayari (1996) nevertheless adds that early exposure of these children to literary Arabic during their preschool period is the proper pedagogy to enhance their Arabic-reading skills.

A recent study by Abu-Rabia (2000) tested the effect of Arab children's early exposure to literary Arabic on their reading acquisition. Participants in the study were 282 children, 135 from Grade 1 and 147 from Grade 2. Of the participants, 144 children constituted the experimental group and were exposed to literary Arabic throughout their preschool period. The 138 participants in the control group were exposed not to literary but to spoken Arabic during that period. These two groups of children were tested for reading comprehension at the end of Grade 1 and Grade 2. The results generally indicated that children exposed to literary Arabic had better reading comprehension skills than the comprehension skills of children exposed only to spoken Arabic.

STUDIES OF READING ACCURACY

Abu-Rabia (1997a) and Abu-Rabia and Siegel (1995) developed the argument that the Arabic language with its writing system is distinct in nature from any orthography based on the Latin alphabet, such as English. More research is needed in the field of Arabic orthography to understand the development and nature of reading, which will result in a comprehensive reading theory. Abu-Rabia and Siegel (1995) tested skilled and poor native Arabic readers on reading vowelized and unvowelized isolated words and sentences. The differences between poor and highly skilled readers in reading unvowelized isolated words were not statistically significant. We interpreted these results as deriving from the homographic nature of Arabic words, that is, without the posting of short vowels on words, the orthography becomes deep rather than shallow, as is the case when short vowels are posted above, in, and under the letters.

Furthermore, a study by Abu-Rabia (1997a) indicated that word naming as a method is not suitable as a testing paradigm for Arabic because Arabic is commonly homographic and adults and good readers read their texts (newspapers and books) without short vowels; they read the consonants and guess the vowels. Thus presenting a list of words without short vowels would be nonsense for the Arabic reader, because many of the words would be visually identical yet could carry several different meanings (Abu-Rabia, 1997a; Abu-Rabia & Siegel, 1995).

Accordingly, Abu-Rabia (1996) tested the importance of vowels in reading accuracy in Arabic among highly skilled Arabic readers aged 17–18 years. Each participant individually was asked to read aloud vowelized and unvowelized paragraphs, and vowelized and unvowelized lists of words. The results showed that vowels were a significant facilitator of word recognition in Arabic orthography. Moreover, Abu-Rabia (1998) tested the effect of Arabic vowels on reading accuracy in four different reading conditions: narrative, informative, poetic, and Koranic texts. Three texts of each style were presented in three reading conditions: correctly vowelized, unvowelized, and wrongly vowelized. The results indicated that vowels had a significant effect on reading accuracy of poor and skilled readers in each reading condition.

Consistent with the preceding results, Abu-Rabia (1997b) tested Arabic vowels and their influence on the reading accuracy of poor and skilled native Arabic speakers reading narrative stories and newspaper articles. The participants were 109 10th-grade native-Arabic speakers, 39 of them poor readers and 70 skilled readers. They read newspaper articles and narrative stories in four reading conditions for each text type; vowelized text, unvowelized text, vowelized word naming, and unvowelized word naming. The results indicated that vowels in Arabic orthography were important variables for facilitating word recognition in poor as well as in skilled readers.

Additionally, a study carried out by Abu-Rabia (1997c) tested the effect of vowels and context on reading accuracy of poor and skilled native-Arabic readers in reading paragraphs, sentences, and words. Central to this study was the hypothesis that reading theory today should consider additional variables, such as vowels and sentence context, when explaining the reading process in Arabic orthography. The participants were 77 native-Arabic speakers, 34 of them poor readers and 44 skilled readers. They had to read 15 paragraphs, 60 sentences, and 210 isolated words. There were three reading conditions: fully vowelized, partially vowelized, and unvowelized texts. The results indicated that vowels were important variables for facilitating word recognition in both poor and skilled readers of Arabic. All of the preceding studies tested reading accuracy, and all of them variously involved isolated words, paragraphs, and texts of different kinds. The results indicated a clear pattern whereby vowels and context affected reading accuracy of poor as well as skilled readers.

Clearly the significant effect of vowels is due to their providing phonological information for reading. In addition, we assume that phonological information helps to code written language in working memory, which will be helpful in retaining information longer and thus facilitate reading comprehension. Thus the connectionist approach (Seidenberg & McClelland, 1989; Van Orden, Pennington, & Stone, 1990) may explain the role of context and vowels in reading Arabic—namely, the contribution of phonological information by the vowels is a very important resource in word recognition in Arabic. Furthermore, the sentence context is also a very important source of information for word recognition in reading vowelized and unvowelized Arabic regardless of reading level, age, and reading materials.

STUDIES OF READING COMPREHENSION

All the foregoing reading tests examined reading accuracy as a function of vowels and context among readers of different ages and reading levels and with different reading materials. None of these studies tested the effect of vowels on reading comprehension. Yet such a test is important because the material skilled and advanced readers encounter is unvowelized Arabic text.

Abu-Rabia (1999) tested the effect of vowels on the reading comprehension of second- and sixth-grade native-Arabic-speaking children. Two groups of native-Arabic speakers were randomly selected, one from two elementary schools in the Haifa area and the other from two elementary schools in Nazareth. Both groups in both experiments read Arabic texts in two forms, vowelized and unvowelized; the older group ($n = 74$) answered 10 multiple-choice comprehension questions about each story and the younger ($n = 71$) answered 7 multiple-choice comprehension questions. The results indicated that vowels were a significant facilitator of reading comprehension in both age groups.

Similarly, Shimron and Sivan (1994) evaluated whether the orthography of readers' first or second language affected their reading time and comprehension. Subjects were highly skilled bilinguals in Hebrew (a Semitic language like Arabic) and English. The results indicated that the comprehension of Hebrew voweled texts was significantly better than the comprehension of Hebrew unvoweled texts. However, the reading time of voweled and unvoweled texts revealed no significant differences. The high performance on vowelized Hebrew texts was probably due to facilitation of phonological processing affecting working memory in a way that improves text comprehension. In our opinion, the preceding conclusion may also explain the role of vowels in reading aloud and reading comprehension of Arabic texts.

It was proposed in the Arabic reading comprehension study (Abu-Rabia, 1999) that word recognition and reading comprehension of Arabic script is accomplished through information derived from vowels and context (Seidenberg & McClelland, 1989; Van Orden et al., 1990). Furthermore, in the reading of voweled Arabic, the short vowels contribute phonological in-formation that facilitates word recognition and ultimately comprehension. Because Arabic is a highly homographic language and is presented unvoweled for skilled and adult readers, con-text may be considered a crucial facilitator of word recognition and reading comprehension (Stanovich, 1980). Usually the presence of short vowels is helpful in disambiguating homo-graphs in Arabic texts, but when short vowels are not present, sentence context becomes a crucial factor for disambiguating homographs.

Another recent study by Abu-Rabia (2001) examined the effect of vowels and context on reading accuracy of skilled adult native-Arabic speakers in Arabic and in Hebrew, their second language. Their reading comprehension of Arabic and Hebrew texts was also tested as a function of vowels. The participants read fully vowelized and unvowelized lists of Arabic words and vowelized and unvowelized paragraphs in Arabic. The same was done in Hebrew. They were also given two stories, one in Arabic and one in Hebrew, in two reading formats: fully vowelized and unvowelized. The results indicated that vowelization in Arabic and in Hebrew positively affected the participants' reading comprehension, even though they were adults and highly proficient in Arabic and in Hebrew. Furthermore, the reading accuracy results did not correlate with the silent-reading results. These results were explained through the morphology of the Semitic languages, yet another variable to be considered in the quest for explanations of the process of reading Arabic, Hebrew, or both. Ben-Dror, Bentin, and Frost (1995) found that the morphology of Hebrew explained the poor reading of children with reading disabilities even more than did the phonology. The results of Ben-Dror et al. (1995) can be used to explain the results of Abu-Rabia's study (2001). The participants' reading-accuracy results and silent-reading results did not correlate because the two reading processes are different and demand different resources. The reading-aloud tasks require phonology and grapheme–phoneme conversion. Silent-reading comprehension, however, may require visual–orthographic identification of roots of words for initial lexical access more than phonological representation.

READING AND SPELLING ERROR ANALYSIS OF DYSLEXICS AND NORMAL READERS

A recent study conducted by Abu-Rabia and Taha (2004) compared the reading and spelling errors committed by dyslexic native-Arabic speakers with those of their age-matched peers and reading-level-matched peers. There were 20 dyslexic readers from fifth grade, 20 typical readers from fifth grade, and 20 younger typical readers who were matched with the dyslexic group according to their reading level. The three groups were screened by the Progressive Matrices test (Raven, 1959) to test the nonverbal thinking level; Wechsler's Intelligence Scale for Children (1974) to test children's ability to figure out the shared characteristics between two words; and visual perception with the Motor free visual perception test revised (MVPT-R) (Colarusso & Hamill, 1996) to assess spatial skills. Finally, a reading test was also administered to these children; participants were tested on reading vowelized isolated words, vowelized pseudowords, vowelized text, and on spelling vowelized isolated words, vowelized pseudowords, and vowelized text. The following error categories were observed in reading across the groups:

1. *Nonsemantic semiphonetic* (Snowling, Defty & Goulandris, 1996): These are errors that result from mispronunciation of words. The output usually is a nonword. In this case, the readers are unable to read correctly strings with short vowels on and under the letters. This causes reliance on the orthography. For example, سُوق [market] was read as سَوق, a nonword. However, both words share the same letters but not the same short vowels.

2. *Semantic and nonmorphological semiphonetic* (Beland & Mimouni, 2001): These are errors that result from the mispronunciation of the word; however, the target word is read as another word that is visually and orthographically similar to the target word, but the short vowels are posted on different letters. For example, the word ذَهَب [went] was read as ذَهْب [gold]; the word تُوعْمِنْ [believes] was read as تُوعَمْنْ [to keep safe].

3. *Semantic dysphonetic* (Boder, 1973; Snowling et al., 1996): These errors are a result of a substitution of one or more phonemes. The result is reading the target word incorrectly and substituting a totally different word for it. For example, ألأَيّام [the days] was read as ألأَيْتَام [the orphans].

4. *Nonsemantic dysphonetic* (Snowling et al., 1996): These errors are a result of mispronunciation of the orthographic units of words, which occurs when the reader substitutes phonemes while relying on visual–orthographic guessing. The result is usually a nonword. For example, the word سَنَوات [years] was read as سَوْنَوات [*sawnawat*], a nonword.

5. *Morphological errors* (Beland & Mimouni, 2001): These are reading errors that are related morphologically and semantically to the target word. For example, the word تَنْتَظِر [waiting] was read as يَنْظُر [looking], and the word ولد [boy] was read as أولاد [boys].

6. *Addition of functional words*: These errors occur when readers add unnecessary function words, such as في [in], إلى [to], من [from], and أل [the].

7. *Visual-letter confusion*: These errors are made as a result of confusing letters of similar shapes. A mismatch between graphemes and phonemes is the result.

8. *Irregular pronunciation rules*: These errors are made when readers pronounce letters that are silent. For example, the rule not to pronounce أل [the] before the sun or the moon letters is not followed.

TABLE 20.1
Means and Standard Deviations of Types of Errors of the Three Groups on Reading Texts

Type of Error	Dyslexic Group		Age-Matched Group		Reading-Level-Matched Group	
	M	SD	M	SD	M	SD
Nonsemantic–semiphonetic	2.50	1.63	0.05	0.22	3.40	1.85
Semantic and nonmorphological–semiphonetic	2.70	2.04	0.686	0.45	2.20	1.36
Semantic–dysphenetic	3.30	2.08	0.70	0.87	1.30	1.20
Nonsemantic–dysphonetic	1.90	1.55	0.05	0.22	0.70	1.03
Morphological errors	22.25	1.55	1.55	1.14	17.85	7.32
Addition of functional words	2.3	1.26	0.12	0.37	1.5	1.5
Visual letter confusion	0.3	0.66	—	—	0.05	0.22
Irregular pronunciation rules	1.40	1.76	—	—	1.20	1.44
Semantic sentence guessing	1.05	0.50	0.15	0.37	0.50	0.82
Semantic errors	0.55	1.05	0.15	0.34	0.50	1.00
Omitting functional words	1.55	1.31	0.10	0.30	1.30	2.47

9. *Semantic sentence guessing*: This type of error is made as a result of semantic guessing of the sentence based on the visual–orthographic structure of the sentence. For example: في يوم الاحد [on Sunday] was read as في أحد الايّام [once upon a time].

10. *Semantic errors* (Beland & Mimouni, 2001): This type of error is made when the target word is substituted with another word that is related semantically to the target word. For example, the word لبَيتها [to her house] was read as لدارها [to her home].

11. *Omitting functional words*: Errors that are made when function words are omitted.

Error Analysis in Text Reading

This subsection focuses on error analysis only in text reading and spelling.[1] The dyslexic readers made significantly more mistakes than did the other two groups: Dyslexics group ($M = 39.85$, $SD = 7.20$); age-matched group ($M = 3.3$, $SD = 2.1$); and the young reading-level-matched group ($M = 30.50$, $SD = 8.62$). These differences were statistically significant, $t(38) = 3.724$, $p < 0.05$ and $t(38) = 21.80$, $p < 0.05$, respectively.

Table 20.1 presents means and standard deviations of the groups' error types. The dyslexic group made significantly more morphological errors than did the other two groups. The morphological errors were more common in all groups than were the other types of errors (see Table 20.1 and Fig. 20.1).

The multivariate analysis of variance (MANOVA) indicated significant effects for all error categories at the level of $p < 0.05$, except for the semantic error type, which did not reach statistical significance.

The Tukey post hoc comparisons between the dyslexic readers and their reading-level-matched peers on text reading indicated a nonsignificant effect on all types of errors, except for semantic–dysphonetic, nonsemantic–dysphonetic, and morphological errors ($p < 0.05$, all

---

[1] For a thorough analysis and discussion of Arabic reading and spelling error analysis please see the special issue of *Reading and Writing: An Interdisciplinary Journal* (2004) *vol. 17* about dyslexia in Semitic languages.

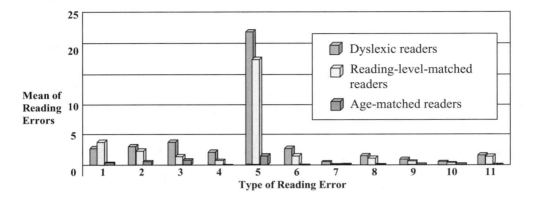

1– Nonsemantic–semiphonetic
2– Semantic and nonmorphological semiphonetic
3– Semantic–dysphonetic
4– Nonsemantic–dysphonetic
5– Morphological
6– Addition of functional words
7– Visual-letter confusion
8– Irregular pronunciation rules
9– Semantic sentence guessing
10– Semantic
11– Omitting functional words

FIG. 20.1.   Mean of errors of all groups in reading texts.

differences being significant). However, the differences were statistically significant ($p < 0.05$) when the dyslexic readers were compared with their age peers on all types of errors, except for the semantic errors.

The spelling error analysis revealed the following profile:

1. *Phonetic errors* (Snowing et al., 1996): These types of spelling errors are made when the writer is unable to translate specific phonemes of a certain word into graphemes. This mismatch between orthography and phonology occurs when the writer cannot rely on lexical processing alone. For example, the word يُحَضّر [to attend] has the letter that represents the sound *d*, but there is another similar representation to this letter, that is, ض [d], which ultimately leads to a different but incorrect word. Further, some phonetic errors are also made when the short vowels are confused with long vowels: بَ [BA] confused with بَا [BAH]. Some of these errors occur at the end of words when writers have to vowelize the ends of words. Usually they confuse the short vowel with the long vowel (e.g., the word مدرسة [school] ends with a short phoneme *tun*, but it is misspelled with the long vowel مدرسَن [school], which is pronounced *madrasatoon* with long *oon*). In addition, colloquial Arabic can interfere with spelling if children hear the literary word but write it the way they speak it in their daily life.

2. *Semiphonetic errors* (Snowling et al., 1996): These errors occur when the orthography of a word does not represent the target word phonologically because of lack of internal specific representation, but the major orthographical–phonological chunk of the word is preserved. These errors are caused when phonemes are omitted, added, or substituted. For example, the word وظيفه [job] was written as وظّفه [gave him a job].

3. *Dysphonetic errors* (Boder, 1993; Snowling et al., 1996): This type of error occurs when the words are spelled incorrectly when the spelled orthographic chunk does not represent most of the phonemes of the target words. Namely, there is no correct grapheme–phoneme

correspondence and no internal lexical representation. For example, the word فكره [idea] was read as رفرت, pronounced *rifrat*, a nonword. It is more of a pseudohomophone but does not carry any meaning in Arabic.

4. *Visual-letter confusion errors*: The spelling errors were caused because children confuse letters with similar visual shapes : // ن, ت, ب, ث // ص, ض // ط, ظ //. For example, the word تذكَرَت [she remembered] is spelled ندكرت, which is a nonword, because of substituting the letter ت [t] with the letter ن [n].

5. *Irregular spelling rules*: These errors are caused because of lack of mastery of the spelling rules of Arabic. For example, أل التّعريف [the] is not pronounced when it precedes the "sun" letters; however, it is represented in writing. Further, the consonant is presented in a word according to the vowel and letter that precedes it. Thus there are different ways of spelling a consonant in a word: سائل [liquid], مسؤول [responsible], and أين [where].

6. *Word omission*: Errors in which children omit whole words.

7. *Function words omission*: Errors in which children omit function words that precede words.

The dyslexic readers made significantly more spelling errors, $M = 27.65$, $SD = 11.52$, than did the other two groups, the reading-level-matched, $M = 20.45$, $SD = 9.02$, $t(38) = 2.2$, $p < 0.05$, and the age-matched groups, $M = 1.80$, $SD = 2.14$, $t(38) = 9.87$, $p < 0.05$ (see Table 20.2 and Fig. 20.2).

Both groups, the dyslexic readers and the young reading-level-matched readers, made more phonetic spelling errors than any other type of error: dyslexic readers 56.45% and reading-level-matched readers 65.32%. The differences between the two groups on the phonetic error type was not statistically significant. However, the age-matched readers made significantly fewer errors compared with the dyslexic readers, $t(38) = 8.92$, $p < 0.05$. The MANOVA indicated significant effects for error categories at the 0.05 level of significance, but the function word errors did not reach significant significance. The Tukey post hoc comparisons between the dyslexic readers and their reading-level-matched peers indicated nonsignificant effects for almost all types of errors, except for dysphonetic and irregular spelling rules ($p < 0.05$). However, comparison of the dyslexic readers with the age-matched peers indicated significant differences on almost all types of errors ($p < 0.05$), except for visual-letter confusion and function words omission.

TABLE 20.2
Means and Standard Deviations of Text Spelling Errors Among the Three Groups

Type of Error	Dyslexic Group		Age-Matched Group		Reading-Level-Matched Group	
	M	SD	M	SD	M	SD
Phonetic	15.60	7.11	1.15	1.38	13.40	6.21
Semiphonetic	2.75	1.74	0.15	0.49	2.00	1.41
Dysphonetic	2.65	3.15	—	—	0.40	0.75
Visual letter confusion	0.65	0.87	0.10	0.31	0.90	0.96
Irregular spelling rules	4.75	2.25	0.30	0.57	2.70	1.53
Word omission	0.60	0.94	—	—	0.35	0.67
Functional words omission	0.65	0.88	—	—	0.70	2.10

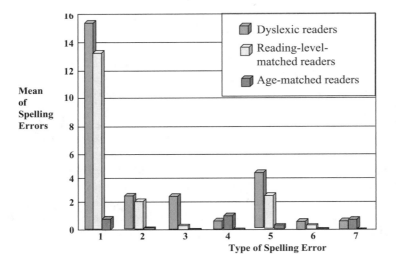

1— Phonetic
2— Semiphonetic
3— Dysphonetic
4— Letter confusion
5— Irregular spelling rules
6— Word omission
7— Functional word omissions

FIG. 20.2.   Mean of spelling errors of all groups in texts.

The results of this study indicate that similar reading and spelling error profiles were observed among the dyslexic group and the reading-level-matched group, and these profiles were different those of from the age-matched group. This is in addition to the clear influence of the Arabic orthography and its morphology on reading and spelling. However, some of the performances of the dyslexic group and the reading-level-matched group were different and inconsistent. This can be attributed to the phonological lag that characterizes those readers with reading problems and not the typical reading-level-matched group (Snowling, 2001).

The results indicate that the reading-level-matched group committed significantly more errors on the nonsemantic–semiphonetic category than did the dyslexic group. However, the dyslexic readers made significantly more semantic dysphonetic errors. The dysphonetic errors involve inaccurate pronunciation of words: The readers disregard short vowels posted on words, causing the pronunciation to sound only partially like the expected sound according to the suggested orthographic pattern in reading texts, words, and nonwords. It seems that, because of a severe phonological deficit in applying grapheme–phoneme rules in decoding words, dyslexic readers tend more to rely on visual strategies for word recognition (Snowling, 1987). Thus the dyslexic group's semantic–dysphonetic errors are significantly greater than the errors of the reading-level-matched group, because the latter made more semiphonetic errors because of their reliance on phonological decoding strategies. Morphological errors dominated in all groups.

The error patterns observed between the dyslexic group and the reading-level-matched group indicate that the Arabic orthography clearly demands visual word-recognition strategies, especially because most of the error patterns were shared by all readers: the dyslexic group and the reading-level-matched group. This indicates that the reading process in Arabic orthography involves strong morphological dimensions along with decoding processes based on phonological decoding (grapheme–phoneme conversion rules), along with a clear lexical dimension, which is also based on correct and precise pronunciation of Arabic. The mastery of these reading dimensions is a developmental issue that characterizes the Arabic reader.

Morphological errors occur during phonological decoding, along with heavy reliance on visual–orthographic identification. Similarly, according to Beland and Mimouni (2001), words that are visually and phonologically similar have a high potential of being related to the same root. Further, spoken Arabic and literary Arabic are rich with morphological structures; such structures are stored in the phonological lexicon in regard to pronunciation and in the orthographic lexicon in regard to identification of root consonants and their combinations. When the phonological lexicon is activated by means of retrieved orthographic knowledge from the orthographic lexicon after visual identification of a word, and when the phonological decoding processing is not applied or is partially applied, the phonological lexicon is activated according to the registered information that has been retrieved from the phonological lexicon. As a result, partial phonology and partial lexical orthography partially trigger the lexical phonology, which includes the phonological combinations of root pronunciations. Further, the retrieved inaccurate lexical phonology that was stimulated by partial orthographic and phonological sources of the printed word does not represent the exact pronunciation of the target word, raising the possibility of morphological, nonsemantic–semiphonetic, and dysphonetic errors. Similarly, Snowling (1987) argues that reliance on partial phonological and orthographic knowledge, along with contextual cues, is the strategy that characterizes reading-disabled and poor readers.

The findings of our study (Abu-Rabia & Taha, 2004) can be summed up in two points: (a) readers with learning disabilities revealed error profiles that resembled the error profiles of the reading-level-matched peers (Olson, 1994); and (b) the nature of Arabic orthography contributed to errors of a specific nature among the readers with learning disabilities and the reading-level-matched peers. Spelling performance is also influenced by factors such as diglossia, morphology, and vowel phonology.

These error profiles enabled us to understand the developmental profiles of reading and spelling among these native-Arabic-speaking children. Our study (Abu-Rabia & Taha, 2004) has some implications for the field of Arabic reading and spelling acquisition: (a) Early exposure to literary Arabic should help overcome the diglossia effect, (b) it should equip children from early ages with a morphological knowledge of Arabic, and (c) it should equip children from early ages with a knowledge of vowelized reading and vowelized writing.

STUDIES OF BILINGUAL NATIVE ARABIC LEARNERS

Arab minorities in Israel are required to learn three languages. Arab children speak Arabic, their first language (L1) in their homes and neighborhoods and receive their schooling in it. Because the Arab minority live in Israel, they need to learn Hebrew, the language of the dominant group, as their second language (L2). A knowledge of Hebrew is essential for their daily survival. They must also be educated in English because it is international in scope and the common written and spoken language of academic life. Arab students study English as their third language (L3) from fourth grade on.

A study by Abu-Rabia and Siegel (2003) tested the language skills of Israeli Arab high school students. It was designed to examine aspects of learning English and Hebrew by native-Arabic speakers. The interdependence hypothesis, proposed by Cummins (1979, 1981), may be relevant here as it holds that cognitive academic language proficiency (CALP) is transferred from one language to another. This hypothesis predicts that reading instruction in one language leads to a general language proficiency, which is strongly related to literacy in the second language even though specifics, such as orthography, develop separately. Cummins postulates that an underlying CALP is common across languages, which creates high transferability of cognitive, academic, and literacy-related skills. This proposition is supported by a number of studies. Skutnabb-Kangas and Toukomaa (1976) found that Swedish proficiency of Finnish immigrant children in Sweden was a function of their level of proficiency in Finnish at the time they started school. For 10-year-olds, with a relatively high proficiency in L1 (i.e., Finnish), there were no negative consequences in their language development. However, 7-year-olds, whose L1 proficiency was less advanced, showed negative effects in their L2 (Swedish) development. The conclusion of Skutnabb-Kangas and Toukomaa was that the degree of L1 development had a significant influence on L2 development.

Abu-Rabia and Siegel (2003) examined the relationships among reading, writing, phonological, syntactic, orthographic, and memory skills in the three languages (Arabic, Hebrew, and English). The children were native-Arabic speakers and received all their school instruction in Arabic. They studied Hebrew as a second language and English as a third.

The authors examined some processes that are significant in the development of skills in reading English that have not been studied in Arabic. These were phonological and syntactic awareness and orthographic and working memory processes. From their performance on the Hebrew word-identification test, the participants were divided into two groups, skilled and less skilled readers. Students' scores on the Hebrew, Arabic, and English tests were similar to their scores on the Arabic word-identification test. There was a significant difference between the skilled and less skilled readers in all tasks in all the languages: multivariate Wilks for Arabic tests $F(8, 29) = 2.4$, $p < .025$ (see Table 20.3); multivariate Wilks for Hebrew tests

TABLE 20.3
Means and Standard Deviations of Skilled and Less Skilled Arab Readers on Arabic Tests

Arabic Tests	Less Skilled (N = 35)	Skilled (N = 35)	F	p
Word identification				
Mean	78.29	89.31	26.54	.001
SD	(12.56)	(1.62)		
Word attack				
Mean	29.29	34.00	44.74	.001
SD	(3.49)	(2.29)		
Working memory				
Mean	3.71	4.71	6.46	.01
SD	(1.54)	(1.74)		
Spelling				
Mean	38.31	41.51	7.40	.008
SD	(6.16)	(3.25)		
Orthography				
Mean	14.66	15.37	3.0	n.s.
SD	(1.88)	(1.55)		
Oral cloze				
Mean	18.29	19.17	5.62	.01
SD	(1.86)	(1.20)		
Phonological				
Mean	16.46	20.77	6.42	.02
SD	(.92)	(.60)		
Visual				
Mean	24.14	24.83	1.87	n.s.
SD	(1.57)	(2.51)		

Note. n.s. = not significant.

TABLE 20.4
Means and Standard Deviations of Skilled and Less Skilled Arab Readers on Hebrew Tests

Hebrew Tests	Less Skilled (N = 35)	Skilled (N = 35)	F	p
Word identification				
Mean	63.32	80.58	17.51	.001
SD	(13.54)	(9.67)		
Word attack				
Mean	25.24	32.24	24.78	.001
SD	(5.71)	(3.45)		
Working memory				
Mean	3.26	5.60	10.78	.002
SD	(3.70)	(2.04)		
Spelling				
Mean	30.88	37.23	15.76	.001
SD	(7.03)	(5.15)		
Orthography				
Mean	10.94	11.45	.85	n.s.
SD	(1.88)	(1.55)		
Oral cloze				
Mean	13.18	16.20	10.20	.002
SD	(4.68)	(2.88)		
Phonological choice				
Mean	14.06	17.6	9.39	.007
SD	(1.87)	(1.32)		
Visual				
Mean	22.65	22.23	.95	n.s.
SD	(2.64)	(2.04)		

Note. n.s. = not significant.

$F(8, 28) = 7.36$, $p < .001$ (see Table 20.4) and multivariate Wilks for English tests $F(8, 27) = 12.65$, $p < .001$ (see Table 20.5; see Tables 20.6 and 20.7 for univariates for all tests in all languages).

The participants were also divided into two skilled and less skilled reader groups, based on their performance on the English word-identification test. The same cutoff score rationale was used. Their performances on the English, Hebrew, and Arabic tests were similar to those based on the Arabic and Hebrew word-identification scores. There was a significant effect for group; skilled and less skilled readers, in all tests of all languages: multivariate Wilks for Arabic tests $F(8, 29) = 3.70$, $p < .001$; multivariate Wilks for Hebrew tests $F(8, 27)$ 12.60, $p < .001$; multivariate Wilks for English tests $F(8, 27) = 4.48$, $p < .001$ (see Tables 20.6 and 20.7 for univariates for all tests in all languages).

The results of Abu-Rabia and Siegel (2003) indicate that exposure to different orthographies is clearly not an impediment to the development of reading skills. These data provide support for trilingual education. All the children who participated in this study came from Arabic-speaking homes and received their school instruction in Arabic. They also received instruction in Hebrew (from Grade 3) and English (from Grade 4) for about 3–4 hours a week. Although the exposure to the three languages was not equal, participants, defined as skilled readers on the basis of their performance on the Arabic word-identification test, performed significantly better than did the less skilled readers in all tests across languages.

TABLE 20.5
Means and Standard Deviations of Skilled and Less Skilled Arab Readers on English Tests

English Tests	Less Skilled (N = 35)	Skilled (N = 35)	F	p
Word identification				
Mean	64.37	74.16	4.75	.03
SD	(18.53)	(13.20)		
Word attack				
Mean	23.85	28.670	7.32	.02
SD	(9.28)	(5.78)		
Working memory				
Mean	3.07	5.30	5.63	.004
SD	(1.04)	(1.12)		
Spelling				
Mean	15.96	21.24	10.26	.002
SD	(6.21)	(5.62)		
Orthographic choice				
Mean	11.52	11.32	.11	n.s.
SD	(2.42)	(1.80)		
Oral cloze				
Mean	10.37	14.92	9.72	.003
SD	(6.39)	(3.66)		
Phonological choice				
Mean	14.56	20.03	18.19	.001
SD	(1.87)	(2.03)		
Visual				
Mean	21.04	21.92	.33	n.s.
SD	(3.25)	(3.76)		

Note. n.s. = not significant.

TABLE 20.6
Performance Contrasts for Good and Poor Readers of Hebrew, Univariate *F* Tests With Degrees
of Freedom for Arabic Tests (1, 67), Hebrew Tests (1, 62), and English Tests (1, 60)

Tests	Arabic (F)	Hebrew (F)	English (F)
Word attack	8.00**	34.79**	29.59***
Working memory	7.61**	81.57**	5.79*
Spelling	n.s.	18.12***	13.78***
Orthographic choice	n.s.	n.s.	n.s.
Oral cloze	3.28*	24.42***	54.29***
Phonological choice	n.s.	4.32*	5.45*
Orthographic knowledge	n.s.	18.53***	8.71**
Word identification	6.09*	33.50***	85.23

Notes. n.s. = not significant. $^* p < .05$; $^{**} p < .01$; $^{***} p < .001$.

TABLE 20.7
Performance Contrasts for Good and Poor Readers of English, Univariate F Tests With Degrees
of Freedom for Arabic Tests (1, 68), Hebrew Tests (1, 63), and English Tests (1, 62)

Tests	Arabic (F)	Hebrew (F)	English (F)
Word attack	24.69***	36.14***	16.16***
Working memory	5.64*	7.40***	5.16*
Spelling	7.38**	34.26***	12.05***
Orthographic choice	n.s.	n.s.	n.s.
Oral cloze	6.34*	18.88***	23.33***
Phonological choice	5.55**	9.03**	4.05*
Orthographic knowledge	n.s.	16.34***	14.04***
Word identification	19.86*	29.36***	32.34***

Notes. n.s. = not significant. $^* p < .05$; $^{**} p < .01$; $^{***} p < .001$.

However, is orthographic skill dependent on the type of orthography to be learned? Initial reading instruction in Hebrew and Arabic is conducted with vowelized text. However, vowelized texts are gradually phased out by about the fourth grade. The participants in this study had not had contact with vowelized Arabic or Hebrew texts for many years. They read the consonants and guessed the vowels. Many of the participants in this study reported difficulties in reading voweled Arabic and Hebrew tests. These results indicate a language-specific pattern and the importance of orthographic experience.

The phonological awareness measures indicated partial correlations across languages. Significant correlations were found between Arabic and Hebrew in tests of phonological awareness and word attack. The correlations of these tests among Arabic, Hebrew, and English were partially significant, which may be due to the nature of these different orthographies. This result contradicts results obtained by Durgunoglu, Nagy, and Hacin-Bhatt (1993), Tunmer, Herriman, & Nesdale (1988), and Yopp (1988) on the importance of the phonemic awareness transfer from L1 to L2 regardless of orthographic depth. However, our results are in agreement with the moderate phonological transfer reported by Verhoeven (1994). It appears that transfer of phonological skills may be positive between two or more related orthographies, such as Arabic and Hebrew, but be negative or nil between two unrelated orthographies, such as English and Arabic.

Overall, the results of Abu-Rabia and Siegel's study support Cummins's interdependence hypothesis, but suggest that different orthographies may differ in the degree of their dependence on visual orthographic, and phonological processes. In addition, proficiency in reading and spelling in L1, L2, and L3 (Arabic, Hebrew, and English, respectively) may also be related the degree of exposure to print and also motivation to learn each specific language.

ISSUES IN ASSESSMENT AND PEDAGOGY

There are some important facts that have to be considered in testing reading in Arabic children:

1. The homographic nature of the Arabic language should be taken into consideration in testing and data analysis. It was noted earlier that almost every second or third word in

unvowelized Arabic can be read in more than one way. For this reason, only vowelized words should be used in word-naming tasks.

2. Because vowelization of Arabic facilitates reading isolated words and texts, materials in Arabic should be presented in full vowelization even for skilled readers.

3. Sentence context has positive and significant effects on reading regardless of reading level. Thus the ability to use sentence context should be included as an indicator of reading skill.

4. It is essential to differentiate between reading accuracy and reading comprehension. These are different processes that demand different resources. Research reveals that *reading accuracy* in Arabic orthography does not correlate very well with reading comprehension. To locate reading problems, testing should focus on *reading accuracy* in read-aloud tasks.

5. Teaching Arabic should focus on context, phonology, and orthography. Phonological instruction should start from a very early age. Morphological and vocabulary instruction should also start early.

6. The orthography of Arabic does not impede the process of acquiring skills in additional language systems.

7. Context and phonology (short vowels) are highly interwoven, as vowelization of ends of words serves a grammatical function. Reading unvowelized sentences or texts and indicating the vowelization of ends of words is not only an indication of phonological ability but is also a syntactic ability.

8. We recommend using irregular and low-frequency words in testing instead of using pseudowords. From our experience, creating pseudowords in Arabic is somewhat problematic because of the great dialectical variants of Arabic.

9. We should also consider the degree of morphological density of Arabic words in test construction. This morphological load is cognitively demanding and requires long eye fixations for morphological decomposing.

10. Children should be read to in literary Arabic from a very early age. This type of intervention will reduce the negative effects of diglossia on reading and writing acquisition.

REFERENCES

Abd El-Minem, I. M. (1987). *Elm al-Sarf*. Jerusalem: Al-Taufik Press.

Abu-Rabia, S. (1995). Learning to read in Arabic: Reading, syntactic, orthographic and working memory skills in normally achieving and poor Arabic readers. *Reading Psychology: An International Quarterly, 16*, 351–394.

Abu-Rabia, S., & Siegel, L. S. (1995). Different orthographies, different context effects: The effects of Arabic sentence context in skilled and poor readers. *Reading Psychology: An International Quarterly, 16(1)*, 1–19.

Abu-Rabia, S. (1996). The role of vowels and context in reading of highly skilled native Arabic readers. *Journal of Psycholinguistic Research, 25(6)*, 629–641.

Abu-Rabia, S. (1997a). The need for cross-cultural considerations in reading theory: The effects of Arabic sentence context in skilled and poor readers. *Journal of Research in Reading, 20*, 137–147.

Abu-Rabia, S. (1997b). Reading in Arabic orthography: The effect of vowels and context on reading accuracy of poor and skilled native Arabic readers in reading paragraphs, sentences, and isolated words. *Journal of Psycholinguistic Research, 26*, 465–482.

Abu-Rabia, S. (1997c). Reading in Arabic orthography: The effect of vowels and context on reading accuracy of poor and skilled native Arabic readers. *Reading and Writing: An Interdisciplinary Journal, 9*, 65–78.

Abu-Rabia, S. (1998). Reading Arabic texts: Effects of text type, reader type and vowelization. *Reading and Writing: An Interdisciplinary Journal, 10*, 105–119.

Abu-Rabia, S. (1999). The effect of vowels on the reading comprehension of second- and sixth-grade native Arab children. *Journal of Psycholinguistic Research, 28*, 93–101.

Abu-Rabia, S. (2000). Effects of exposure to literary Arabic on reading comprehension in diglossic situation. *Reading and Writing: An Interdisciplinary Journal, 13*, 147–157.

Abu-Rabia, S. (2001). The role of vowels in reading Semitic scripts: Data from Arabic and Hebrew. *Reading and Writing: An Interdisciplinary Journal, 14*, 39–59.

Abu-Rabia, S., (2002). Reading in a root-based morphology language: The case of Arabic. *Journal of Research in Reading, 25,* 299–309.

Abu-Rabia, S., Share, D., & Mansour, M. (in press). Word recognition and basic cognitive processes among reading-disabled and normal readers in Arabic languages. *Reading and Writing: An Interdisciplinary Journal.*

Abu-Rabia, S., & Siegel, L. S. (2002). Reading, writing, orthographic, phonological, syntactic and memory skills in bilingual Arabic–English speaking Arab children in Canada. *Journal of Psycholinguistic Research, 30,* 437–455.

Abu-Rabia, S., & Siegel, L. S. (2003). Reading and writing skills in three orthographies. *Reading and Writing: An Interdisciplinary Journal, 16,* 611–634.

Abu-Rabia, S., & Taha, H. (2004). Reading and spelling Arabic error analysis of dyslexic native Arabic children. *Reading and Writing: An Interdisciplinary Journal, 17,* 651–689.

Al-Dahdah, A. (1989). *The grammar of the Arabic language in tables and lists* [in Arabic]. Beirut: Maktabat Lebanon.

Ayari, S. (1996). Diglossia and illiteracy in the Arab world. *Language, Culture and Curriculum, 9,* 243–253.

Beland, R., & Mimouni, Z. (2001). Deep dyslexia in the two languages of an Arabic–French bilingual patient. *Cognition, 82,* 77–126.

Ben-Dror, I., Bentin, S., & Frost, R. (1995). Semantic, phonologic, and morphological skills in reading disabled and normal children: Evidence from perception and production of spoken Hebrew. *Reading Research Quarterly, 30,* 876–893.

Bentin, S., & Frost, R. (1995). Morphological factors in visual word identification in Hebrew. In L. Feldman (Ed.), *Morphological aspects of language processing* (pp. 217–292). Hillsdale, NJ: Lawrence Erlbaum Associates.

Boder, E. (1973). Developmental dyslexia: A diagnostic approach based on three typical reading-spelling patterns. *Developmental Medicine and Child Neurology, 15,* 663–687.

Colarusso, R. P., & Hammill, D. D. (1996). *Motor free visual perception test revised.* Los Angeles CA: Academic Therapy Publications.

Cummins, J. (1979). Linguistic interdependence and the educational development of bilingual children. *Review of Educational Research, 49,* 221–251.

Cummins, J. (1981). The role of primary language development in promoting educational success for language minority students. In California State Department of Education, *Schooling and language minority students: A theoretical framework.* Los Angeles: Evaluating, Dissemination and Assessment Center, California State University.

Cummins, J. (1989). *Empowerment of minority children.* Sacramento, CA: California Association for Bilingual Education.

Durgunoglu, A. Y., Nagy, W. E., & Hacin-Bhatt, B. J. (1993). Cross-language transfer of phonological awareness. *Journal of Educational Psychology, 85,* 453–465.

El-Hassan, S. A. (1977). Educated spoken Arabic in Egypt and the Levant: A critical review of diglossia and related concepts. *Archivum Linguisticum, 8,* 112–132.

Ferguson, C. H. (1959). Diglossia. *Word, 15,* 325–340.

Frith, U. (1985). Beneath the surface of developmental dyslexia. In K. E. Patterson, J. C. Marshall, & M. Coltheart (Eds.), *Surface dyslexia* (pp. 301–330). London: Lawrence Erlbaum Associates.

Harris, T. L., & Hodges, R. E. (1981). A *dictionary of reading and related terms.* Newark, DE: International Reading Association.

Lennox, C., & Siegel, L. (1993). Visual and phonological spelling errors in subtypes of children with learning disabilities. *Applied Psycholinguistics, 14,* 473–488.

Marsh, G., Freidman, M., Desberg, P., & Welch, V. (1980). Development of strategies in learning to spell. In U. Frith (Ed.), *Cognitive processing in spelling* (pp. 57–72). London: Academic Press.

Morton, J. (1989). An information processing account of reading acquisition. In A. Galaburda (Ed.), *From reading to neurons* (pp. 43–66). Cambridge, MA: MIT Press.

Olson, R. K. (1994). Language deficits in "specific reading disability." In M. A. Gernsbacher (Ed.), *Handbook of psycholinguistics* (pp. 895–916). San Diego, CA: Academic Press.

Raven, C. J. (1959). *Coloured progressive matrices.* Oxford, UK: Oxford Psychologists Press.

Seidenberg, M. S., & McClelland, J. L. (1989). A distributed, developmental model of word recognition and naming. *Psychological Review, 96,* 523–568.

Shimron, J. & Sivan, T. (1994). Reading proficiency and orthography: Evidence from Hebrew and English. *Language Learning, 44,* 5–27.

Skutnabb-Kangas, T., & Toukomaa, P. (1976). *Teaching migrant children's mother tongue and learning the language of the host country in the context of the sociocultural situation of the migrant family.* Helsinki: The Finnish National Commission for UNESCO.

Snowling, M. (1987). *Dyslexia: A cognitive developmental perspective.* Cambridge, UK: Gomeh Scientific Publications.

Snowling, M. (2001). From language to reading and dyslexia. *Dyslexia, 7,* 37–46.

Snowling, M. J., Goulandris, N., & Defty, N. (1996). A longitudinal study of reading development in dyslexic children. *Journal of Educational Psychology, 88,* 653–669.

Somech, S. (1980). *The problem of language in modern Arabic literature.* Teaching Contemporary Arabic Series. Tel Aviv: Ministry of Education and Culture, Curriculum Center, Tel Aviv University.

Stanovich, K. E. (1980). Toward an interactive-compensatory model of individual differences in the development of reading fluency. *Reading Research Quarterly, 16*, 32–71.

Symour, P. H. K. (1990). Developmental dyslexia. In M. W. Eysenck (Ed.), *Cognitive psychology: An international review* (pp. 135–196). Chichester, UK: Wiley.

Tunmer, W. E., Herriman, M. L., & Nesdale, A. R. (1988). Metalinguistic abilities and beginning reading. *Reading Research Quarterly, 33*, 134–158.

Van Orden, G. C., Pennington, B. F., & Stone, G. O. (1990). Word identification in reading and the promise of subsymbolic psycholinguistics. *Psychological Review, 97*, 488–522.

Verhoeven, L. (1994). Transfer in bilingual development: The linguistic interdependence hypothesis revisited. *Language Learning, 44*, 381–415.

Wechsler, D. (1974). *Wechsler intelligence scale for children, revised.* New York: Psychological Corporation.

Wright, W. (1967). *A grammar of the Arabic language.* Cambridge, UK: Cambridge University Press.

Yopp, H. K. (1988). The validity and reliability of phonemic awareness tests. *Reading Research Quarterly, 23*, 159–177.

21

Hebrew Orthography and Literacy

Dorit Ravid
Tel Aviv University

The purpose of this chapter is to present an overview of the nature of Hebrew orthography and its relationship to literacy acquisition as seen in Israel. This chapter provides a linguistic and psycholinguistic analysis of different facets of Hebrew orthography by reviewing studies of spelling and reading acquisition in Hebrew and describes the impact of Hebrew typology on emergent literacy and beyond.

INTRODUCTION

Modern Hebrew at the turn of the new millennium is a century-old language that still carries with it the traces of its 4,000-year-old past in its morphology and orthographic system. Hebrew-speaking children have to contend with the remnants of ancient rules in language acquisition, on the one hand, and in the development of literacy, on the other. This chapter presents relevant background facts about the Hebrew language and its speakers, readers, and writers. It then focuses on the Hebrew orthography with its unique Semitic features and main problems, traces its acquisition, and shows how its learners make use of phonological and morphological information available from oral usage. Special attention is paid to the differences between the representation of various phonological and morphological categories and their consequences for literacy acquisition and consolidation.

Hebrew has an alphabetical orthography with 22 letters, most of which denote consonants alone, and an ancillary system of 13 vowel diacritic marks termed *nikud* (literally, pointing). Hebrew is written from right to left, either with no vocalization marks and consequent under-specification of vowels, or with full vowel specification when including vocalization marks. Thus the sentence *kotvim ivrit mi-yamin li-smol* [(they) write Hebrew from-right to-left[1]] may be written in the nonvocalized version as כותבים עברית מימין לשמאל, which is the universal

---

[1] Spoken Hebrew (broad phonemic transcription) appears in italics with gloss following in square brackets.

form of written Hebrew, or in the vocalized version, which is used only for special purposes, with full vowel specification as כּוֹתְבִים עִבְדִית מְיָמִין לְשָׂמֹאל. Side by side with Hebrew script, this chapter makes use of capital Latin letters standing for Hebrew graphemes to facilitate presentation of orthographic matters. For example, this is the Latinized orthographic version of the preceding sentence: KWTBYM 9BRYT MYMYN LŠMAL.[2] Five of the Hebrew letters have double forms—regular and word final; for example, M is spelled ם at word-final position and מ elsewhere.[3] Three letters have alternative forms with an apostrophe, marking recent loan palatal consonants, for example, ז Z with an apostrophe, 'ז, is pronounced ž.

Having briefly presented this essential basic information about written Hebrew, we can now proceed to an in-depth introduction about the language, its orthography, and its readers and writers.

HEBREW MORPHOLOGY

Hebrew is a highly synthetic Semitic language with a rich morphology (Berman, 1987; Ravid, 1990). Morphological density is expressed in a variety of grammatical and lexical semantic notions systematically expressed in morphological form, on the one hand, and in numerous and diverse morphophonological structures, on the other. The bulk of content words in Hebrew—all verbs and most nouns and adjectives—are at least bimorphemic, constructed of the typically Semitic *nonlinear* structure (McCarthy, 1982). This is a combination of the consonantal *root*, for example, *s-g-r* [close], and a vocalic pattern that may be preceded by, followed by, or both preceded and followed by a consonant, for example, the abstract noun pattern *miCCéCet*. These two are combined by interdigitating the root consonants in their designated sites in the pattern as in *misgéret* [frame] (Berman, 1997; Ravid, 1990, 2003). Combining the same root *s-g-r* [close] with other patterns yields past tense *sagar* [closed], passive *nisgar* [was closed], causative *hisgir* [extradite], and adjectival *sagur* [closed], as well as *sgira* [closing], *sgirut* [introvertness], and *séger* [closure].

A second type of morphological structure in Hebrew is *linear*, a concatenation of a stem (typically a word) and a prefix or a suffix, for example, *sagár-ti* [(I)-closed]. Several lexical noun categories are expressed by linear suffixes, for example, *iton-ay* [journal-ist], *iton-ut* [journal-ism] (Berman, 1987, 1997; Schwarzwald, 2002). All obligatory and optional grammatical markings of number, gender, and person on nouns, adjectives, and verbs are expressed linearly, for example, *kadur-im* [ball-s], *atsuv-ot* [sad, Pl, Fm].[4]

Hebrew nouns and adjectives are obligatorily inflected for gender and number, for example, *ha-maxbarot ha-adumot*, "the-notebooks, Fm the-red, Fm, Pl = the red notebooks." Verbs are obligatorily inflected for gender, number, person, and tense, for example, *ha-maxbarot ha-adumot kol ha-zman ne'elamot*, "the red notebooks keep disappearing, Fm, Pl." Prepositions are also obligatorily inflected for gender, number, and person, for example, *ha-maxbarot ha-adumot kol ha-zman ne'elamot lax*, "the red notebooks keep disappearing to-you, Fm = you keep losing your red notebooks." In addition, Hebrew has optional bound inflectional forms such as possessive markers on nouns (e.g., *armona*, "palace-hers = her palace") and an accusative inflection on transitive verbs (e.g., *re'itiv*, "I-saw-him") (Berman, 1978; Ravid, 1995a; Schwarzwald, 2002).

---

[2] To make Hebrew script more accessible to non-Hebrew speakers, I use Latin capitals to transcribe Hebrew characters. The digit 9 is used to designate the letter ע, standing for the voiced pharyngeal fricative.

[3] Except in loan words and in strings not considered established "words," e.g., *ma'am*, "VAT," spelled M9M מע"מ rather than מע"ם.

[4] The following linguistic conventions are used in this chapter: -s stands for the English plural marker; Pl. = Plural; Fm. = Feminine.

Hebrew derivational morphology is rich and varied, with a large array of derivational affixes of various structures and with an extremely complex root, stem, and affix allomorphy. Nouns and adjectives express an array of nominal meanings, ranging over agent, attributive, diminutive, instrument, place, collective, action, and abstract nominals. Consider, for example, the variety of meanings deriving from basic "take in, abstract" in the morphological family of root *k-l-t: koltan* [receptor], *maklet* [receiver], *miklat* [shelter], *kélet* [input], *haklata* [recording], *taklit* [record], *muklat* [recorded], and *kalit* [easily remembered]. Verbs express transitivity relations such as causativity, passive voice, reflexivity, change of state, and reciprocity. Consider, for example, the semantic clusters created by verbs related through their roots as in *nirdam–hirdim* [fell asleep–caused to sleep]; *katav–hixtiv–huxtav–hitkatev* [wrote–dictated–was dictated–corresponded]; and *lavaš–nilbaš–hilbiš–hitlabeš* [put on–was worn–dressed somebody–dressed oneself] (Clark, 1993).

The wealth of morphological structures in Hebrew is reflected in its written form, as shown in the next section, and this reflection promotes morphological perception and strategies in Hebrew speakers, readers, and writers, as predicted by Olson's script-as-model theory of literacy (Olson, 1994).

HISTORICAL SOURCES OF HEBREW STRUCTURE AND ORTHOGRAPHY

Hebrew has one of the longest written records known to us, deriving from ancient historical periods during which classical Hebrew was a spoken, living language (Kutscher, 1982). Classical Hebrew (1100 B.C.E.–250 C.E.) is usually divided into two distinct and consecutive periods: biblical and mishnaic Hebrew (Rabin, 1972). Biblical Hebrew was a derivative of Canaanite (a northwestern Semitic language), the language spoken in the Land of Israel during the time of the First Temple from the beginning of the second millennium B.C.E. until the middle of the first millennium B.C.E. (Bergsträsser, 1982; Driver, 1976). It is recorded in written form in the Hebrew Bible (the Old Testament) and in various inscriptions (Kautzsch, 1910). A postbiblical form of the language, referred to as mishnaic Hebrew, was used in the Land of Israel side by side with another northwestern Semitic language, Aramaic, up to approximately the middle of the first millennium C.E. (Bendavid, 1971). For about 1,500 years, until the 20th century, Hebrew was dormant, no longer a spoken native language, but used extensively in writing in the Jewish Diaspora for liturgical, religious, cultural, scholarly, and scientific purposes, serving as the *lingua franca* of Jews speaking different languages in the world (Kutscher, 1982; Schwarzwald, 2001). Moreover, Hebrew continued to change during this time, acquiring new lexical items and grammatical forms, which are used extensively nowadays in modern Hebrew (Ben Hayyim, 1985; Ravid & Zilberbuch, 2003).

The major sources of written records about classical Hebrew are the Hebrew Bible and the Mishna, with some additional sources such as the Dead Sea scrolls and numerous inscriptions. These provide us with a wealth of information about Hebrew orthography. The unique characteristic of Semitic script is best expressed by the 19th-century scholar W. Gesenius in the classical text edited by Kautzsch (1910, p. 5):

> No system of writing is ever so perfect as to be able to reproduce the sounds of a language in all their various shades, and *the writing of the Semites* has one striking fundamental defect, viz. that only the consonants (which indeed form the substance of the language) are written as real letters.

One of the theories for the omission of vowels in Hebrew writing is the extreme prominence of Semitic consonants as carrying the main lexical content of the word. Another theory claims that

Semitic writing started out as a syllabary and later on became purely consonantal (Coulmas, 1989). This consonantal character of written Hebrew is as real today as in ancient times, though facilitating systems representing vowels were added in the course of history. Such a skeletal orthography necessitates heavy reliance on morphological, syntactic, and discourse context cues (Shimron, 1993).

As a result of early sound changes in the evolution of north Semitic languages, long vowels in word-final position came to be represented in Semitic writing by "weak" consonantal signs, that is, graphemes representing semivowels (e.g., Y ׳ and W ו representing y and w, respectively). This came to be known as *plene* or full writing, and later on it spread to medial positions as well (Coulmas, 1989). With the increased influence of Greek in the Middle East in post-Alexandrian times and the growing number of loan words whose meaning could not be inferred from the context, Semitic writing was no longer transparent enough for efficient reading. The consonantal letters AHWY (Hebrew אהוי) thus took on an additional value in mishnaic Hebrew, to indicate vowels between consonant letters in a manner similar to Greek and Latin, and came to be known in this role as *matres lectionis* [mothers of reading] (Bendavid, 1971). This system facilitated consonantal reading, but was not precise and consistent enough.

In the seventh and eighth centuries C.E., fuller and more consistent systems of vowel marking were developed in Hebrew. These were competing systems of diacritics, which represented vowels, consonantal spirantization, and gemination, as well as the musical cantillation of the reading tradition (Bergsträsser, 1982; Khan, 1997; Rendburg, 1997). The diacritic system, which is still used in Hebrew today, was developed under the influence of the Nestorian system of Syrian by the Tiberian Masoretes (tradents), and is known as the Tiberian pointing system (*nikud*, also called vocalization, voweling, punctuation). This system is the major source of our knowledge about classical Hebrew phonology, and especially about its vowels. The Tiberian system consists of seven diacritics placed mainly under (and also above and within) letters, to which an eighth (schwa ∂) was added to mark vowel absence or a reduced nonhigh vowel before the accent (Bolozky, 1997). The schwa also participates in a composite diacritic called *ḥataf*, representing an auxiliary vowel (Blau, 1971; Ravid & Shlesinger, 2001). Tiberian *nikud* represented the vowels of its contemporary phonology at the end of the first millennium fully and accurately (see Table 21.2 in the next section).

MODERN HEBREW: DEMOGRAPHIC AND PHONOLOGICAL FEATURES

Modern Hebrew was revived twice: First, in the middle of the 19th century, Hebrew was standardized into a single *written* language constructed from a variety of previous periods (biblical, mishnaic, medieval) together with contributions from other European languages as well as from Yiddish. Then, at the beginning of the 20th century, Hebrew was revived as a *spoken* language, mostly in prestate Israel. Modern Hebrew had served as the sole language of teaching at all levels of education by 1914, and by 1920 was already being spoken as a mother tongue by a first generation of native Hebrew speakers (Fellman, 1973). At the time this chapter is being written, the beginning of the 21st century, a fourth generation of Israelis is acquiring Hebrew as its first language.

The Hebrew-speaking community in Israel, now numbering about 5 million people, has always constituted an extreme case of an immigrant society, and as a result modern Hebrew has undergone swift and radical changes since its revival (Ravid, 1995a). Immigration waves came in more or less every decade in the 20th century, and in 1948 600,000 Israelis took in double their number in Jewish refugees from communities in Europe, Asia, and Africa. Immigration to Israel continued throughout the second half of the 20th century, culminating in a million immigrants, mainly from the former Soviet Union in the 1990s (Emmons, 1997; Shuval, 1996). Although immigrant adults do not always achieve proficiency in Hebrew and contribute to the intense "languages in contact" situation, their children invariably join the widening circles of native speakers (Donitsa-Schmidt, 1999; Olshtain & Horenczyk, 2000). Modern Hebrew is thus the only common means of communication among Jewish Israelis. On the one hand, this situation has brought on a consolidation of the colloquial vernacular of spoken Hebrew all Israelis share; on the other hand it also means a continuous pressure for the language to change and adapt itself at the spoken level. This means the gap between spoken and written language increases with crucial implications for the interface of spoken language, orthography, and literacy in the Hebrew-speaking population in Israel (Ben Rafael, Olshtain, & Gajst, 1994; Levin et al., 2002).

Although modern Hebrew morphology remains essentially biblical and its syntax mainly mishnaic, modern Hebrew phonology is very different from the classical phonology because of extensive neutralizations (or mergers) of previously distinct phonemes (Bolozky, 1997; Ravid, 1995a). These discrepancies between classical and modern Hebrew underlie some of the reading and writing challenges facing Hebrew readers and writers.

Consonants.   Several sets of classical consonants have merged in modern Hebrew, resulting in the loss of several phonological distinctions and with important consequences for orthography and literacy (Laufer & Condax, 1981; Schwarzwald, 2001; Weinberg, 1966). I subsequently enumerate the main differences between classical and modern Hebrew consonants. These are also taken up again further in the discussion of homophony and opacity in Hebrew orthography.

1. Of the historical set of six stops spirantizing by regular phonetic rule (*p, b, t, d, k, g* spirantizing into *f, v, θ, ð, x, r*), only three stop–spirant pairs are left in modern Hebrew (*p–f, b–v, k–x*), and they alternate according to complex morphophonological conditions (Bolozky, 1997; Ravid, 1995a). This is a fundamental and pervasive feature of modern Hebrew phonology. For example, the first radical of root *p-z-r* [scatter] occurs as *p* in *pizur* [scattering] and as *f* in *mefazer* [scatters]. Hebrew speakers perceive the three pairs of alternating phonemes as signifying unified segments (Ravid & Bar-On, 2001).

2. The Semitic class of *emphatic* consonants no longer exists in modern Hebrew. Subsequently, the voiceless emphatic coronal stop *t* and the voiceless coronal stop *t* have merged, as did the voiceless emphatic velar stop *q* and the voiceless velar stop *k* (the stop alternant of *x*).

3. The semivowel *w* is now a full-fledged consonant *v*, and it has merged with *v*, the spirant alternant of *b*.

4. The Semitic class of gutturals and pharyngeals, traditionally termed *groniyot* (glottal stop *ʔ*, glottal fricative *h*, pharyngeal fricatives *ḥ* and ʿ), has been eroded in modern Hebrew. Most speakers pronounce both *ʔ* and ʿ as glottal stops or else omit them (Bolozky, 1997). The precise enunciation of *h* is restricted to formal spoken Hebrew; in other cases it is deleted. The standard pronunciation of *ḥ* is now *x*, and it has merged with the fricative alternant of *k*. A minority of Hebrew speakers with a Mideastern accent retain the pharyngeal fricatives *ḥ* and ʿ in their speech. For details, see Ravid (1995a).

A new phonological system with several consonant neutralizations and a weakened guttural–pharyngeal class has emerged in modern Hebrew (Bolozky, 1997; Ravid, 1995a). However, all of the ancient consonantal distinctions are still reflected in the Hebrew orthographic system in the form of distinct graphemes. Table 21.1 summarizes consonantal homophony in standard

TABLE 21.1

Consonantal Neutralizations and Resulting Homophony in Hebrew, With Corresponding
Graphemic Values

Classical Hebrew Consonant	Modern Hebrew Consonant	Hebrew Grapheme	Corresponding Latin Grapheme
w	v	ו	W
v	v	ב	B
b	b	בּ	B
q	k	ק	Q
k	k	כ	K
ħ	x	ח	Ḥ
x	x	כ	K
ṭ	t	ט	Ṭ
t	t	ת	T
h	h/ʔ/0	ה	H
ʔ	ʔ/0	א	A
ʕ	ʔ/0	ע	9

spoken Hebrew and its interface with the orthography, resulting from the mergers previously described.

Vowels.   Comparing modern vowels with classical vowels is more complex than tracing consonant neutralizations. First, vowels are more susceptible to historical change than consonants. This is because consonants are perceived categorically, and fluctuations in their articulatory implementation are likely to be filtered out by listeners. Therefore listeners' perceptions of consonants remain stable and robust even in the face of unstable productions, and the diffusion of incipient change is prevented. Vowels, in contrast, are perceived continuously, and therefore listeners are not as consistent and as confident in their decisions as to vowel identity. Thus a change from one vocalic category to another is not blocked as easily as in the consonantal domain (Berg, 1998, pp. 202–204). Second, scholars are not in a position to decide how accurately Masoretic text reading with the Tiberian diacritic system actually reflects the pronunciation of classical Hebrew (Bergsträsser, 1982; Blau, 1971; Kautzsch, 1910). Although Masoretic readers were extremely conservative in their reading tradition, some vocalic allophones recorded in the Tiberian system may have developed after the classical period. There was also much local variation in the realization of the vowels in Tiberian Hebrew (Rendburg, 1997).

Vowel mergers have resulted in no less homophony than consonant mergers. First, modern Hebrew has five canonic vowels (*a, e, i, o, u*) compared with seven full classical vowels and four reduced ones (Bolozky, 1997; Schwarzwald, 2001). Second, classical Hebrew vowels were matched one-to-one by corresponding vowel diacritics, but these no longer carry distinct phonological values. Table 21.2 summarizes vowel homophony in standard spoken Hebrew and its interface with the orthography—both with diacritic signs as well as with the four graphemes with the double role of marking consonants and vowels (AHWY אהוי) in their *matres lectionis* vowel function.

Every language, especially one with such a long history as Hebrew, undergoes phonological change, and obviously changes in the orthography always lag behind those in speech. However, the modern Hebrew neutralizations of historical phonological distinctions just delineated have critical, though different, implications for the oral and written behavior of Hebrew

TABLE 21.2
Vowel Neutralizations and Resulting Homophony in Hebrew, With Corresponding Graphemic
Values in Diacritics (With the Letters G ג and A א Used to Demonstrate Diacritic Values)
and in the Four Graphemes Denoting Vowels

Classical Hebrew Vowel	Modern Hebrew Vowel	Hebrew Diacritic Sign	Hebrew Diacritic Name	Hebrew matres lectionis Grapheme Denoting Vowel
å	a	ָ	qamats	ה, א A, H
a	a	ַ	pattah	
ă	a	ֲ	hataf-pattah	
e	e	ֵ	serey	ה, א A, H
ε	e	ֶ	segol	ה, א A, H
ě	e	ֱ	hataf-segol	
i	i	גִ גֵ	hiriq	י Y
o	o	גֹ גו	holam	ו W
ă	o	ָ	qamats qatan	W
u	u	ֻ	qubuts	W
u	u	ֻ	shuruq	W
ə	e / 0	ְ	schwa	

users. Consonant and vowel neutralizations have blurred the phonological underpinnings of Hebrew morphology, which are closely related to the historical phonological system. This is one of the main sources for child language errors, some of which persist to middle childhood and adolescence and also mark current Hebrew sociolects (Ravid, 1995a, 1995b). But literacy, with attendant knowledge of written Hebrew, reintroduces these distinctions through the orthographic system and consequently reveals the underlying morpho(phono)logical system.

Consider first the two verbs *shafxa* [she spilled] (root *š-p-x*) and *patxa* [she opened] (root *p-t-x*), sharing exactly the same form in the past-tense third-person-singular feminine pattern *CaCCa*. They take, however, different vowels in singular feminine present-tense pattern *niCCéCet*, namely, regular *nishpéxet* [is being spilled, Fm] versus irregular *niftáxat* [is being opened, Fm] with a lower vowel pattern *a-a*. This is because final homophonous *x* in these roots derives from different historical consonants: The final *x* in root *š-p-x* is the spirantized alternant of *k*, spelled K כ, and it has regular behavior; whereas the final *x* in root *p-t-x* is the neutralized form of pharyngeal *ħ*, spelled Ħ ח, which attracts the irregular low vowel pattern despite currently being homophonous with the other *x*. This is a source of opacity in early child Hebrew: Young children often fail to lower the vowel where required, saying, for example, *niftéxet* for *niftáxat* [is opening, Fm] (Ravid, 1995a). But the distinction between the two *x*s and the reason for their different behaviors become apparent later on with the onset of literacy and growing familiarity with the writing system that marks them with two different graphemes, K כ and Ħ ח.

As a second example, consider the behavior of the homophonic words *davar* [thing] and *davar* [mailman] under pluralization: *davar* [thing] – *dvarim* [things]; *davar* [mailman] – *davarim* [mailmen]. These two nouns sound exactly the same, but behave differently: In both words, the addition of the plural suffix –*im* creates a new stressed syllable at the end of the word. However, in *davar* [thing], pluralization results in vowel reduction, whereas in plural *davarim* [mailmen] no vowel reduction takes place, and the vowel *a* is retained. This difference reflects a classical Hebrew rule based on the difference between the historical vowels represented by diacritics *qamats* and *pattah*, respectively, which have now merged into a single *a* (Table 21.2): The morphophonological behavior of these Hebrew words continues to follow the differential paths dictated by their past identities (Ravid & Shlesinger, 2001). For native Israelis untutored in historical Hebrew grammar—practically the whole population— this difference in the behavior of the two homophonic words is unmotivated and leads to nonreduction and overreduction of vowel errors in both child and adult language, such as *matsofim* for *metsofim* [floaters] and *sbonim* for *sabonim* [soap cakes] (Ravid 1995a, 1995b). Although these errors gradually decrease with age and schooling, this decrease is not related to learning *nikud*, as vowel representation by diacritics is not a widespread shared-knowledge domain in Hebrew, as I subsequently elaborate. This is one example of the instability of word-internal Hebrew vowels, which persists in various forms into adulthood, and is subsequently discussed in relation to spelling vowels in Hebrew (Ravid, 1990; Ravid & Kubi, 2003).

Another way of looking at the impact of the phonological discrepancy between historical and current Hebrew consonants and vowels is from the perspective of the acquisition of writing and reading skills. In this respect, consonant and vowel neutralization have different implications for reading and for writing. Consonant neutralization poses no difficulty for novice *readers* who do not find homophonous graphemes problematic in any way; but it is the main (though not the only) source of *spelling* errors in grade school, as consonant mergers entail homophonous graphemes (e.g., *k* can be spelled either by K ‏כ‎ or Q ‏ק‎). However, as I subsequently show, the distinct graphemic values of long-lost phonological distinctions reflect current systematic morphological information, which is very helpful in overcoming homophony and restricting such spelling errors to novice writers. In contrast, vowels and their inconsistent written representation constitute a key issue in the controversy relating to different methods of *reading* instruction in Israel, focusing specifically on the use of *nikud* diacritics. For Hebrew *writers*, however, *nikud* marking is a nonissue, whereas writing the *matres lectionis* graphemes AHWY ‏אהוי‎ is a source of spelling errors continuing long into adolescence (Ravid & Kubi, 2003).

Given this background, I now turn to a detailed description of current Hebrew orthography, with two foci of inquiry: phonology—the representation of consonants and vowels; and morphology—the representation of morphological constructs in Hebrew orthography. The interface of these two linguistic facets is particularly significant in Hebrew literacy acquisition.

MODERN HEBREW ORTHOGRAPHIC VERSIONS

There is general agreement that Hebrew orthography is alphabetical, with the typical phoneme–grapheme relationship between consonants and Hebrew letters. It is a mainly consonantal orthography, reflecting its fundamental Semitic root-based underpinnings: 18 of the 22 letters indicate consonants alone, whereas the four *matres lectionis* ‏אהוי‎ AHWY have a double consonant–vowel function (Coulmas, 1989). As a result, in line with claims that the ancient Semitic script may have been a syllabary (Gelb, 1963), experienced readers of nonvocalized modern Hebrew may be using syllabary shortcuts to overcome vowel opacity by referring to morphophonemic structures (see subsequent discussion).

Modern Hebrew officially employs two versions of the same orthography, one shallow and transparent and another deep and opaque. The full, transparent, and shallow version is the *vocalized* orthography, which represents both consonants and vowels. This version provides precise, in many cases redundant, phonological information about the written Hebrew word. The main information is vocalic: In addition to the full representation of all consonants by 22 letters, the five vowels *a,e,i,o,u* are represented by 9 diacritic vocalization *nikud* marks, combining to form 13 marks (Table 21.2). Thus each modern Hebrew vowel has at least two, in some cases three, corresponding written signs. For example, the vowel *e* is represented by the marks *serey, segol*, and *hataf-segol* appearing under the letters, as in the examples *séfer* [book], spelled סֵפֶר, and *emet* [truth], spelled אֱמֶת. However, precise vocalization of a Hebrew word represents much more than its superficial phonology: The occurrence of specific *nikud* marks in the Hebrew word is governed by the classical Tiberian system, which still underlies Hebrew morphophonological behavior (Baayen, 1985). Thus, for example, all words belonging to a certain morphological pattern have exactly the same *nikud* pattern, with allomorphic modifications allowing for root types. For example, instrument nouns of the pattern *maCCeC*, *maklet* [receiver] (מַקְלֵט), *mashpex* [funnel] (מַשְׁפֵּךְ) *mavreg* [screwdriver] (מַבְרֵג), and *maxshev* [computer] (מַחְשֵׁב), all take the same *nikud* pattern, reflecting their phonological and morphological affinity. The historical phonological differences between *nikud* marks standing for the same current vowel are no longer in existence, but they continue to correspond to general morphophonological principles in Hebrew. Thus for example the first vowel *a* in *tsalaf* [caper] and *tsalaf* [sniper] is spelled with two different *nikud* diacritics (צָלָף vs. צַלָּף), corresponding to different behavior in plural formation: Vowel reduction in *tslafim* [capers] versus vowel retention in *tsalafim* [snipers] (Ravid & Shlesinger, 2001).

Diacritic marks also distinguish between the stop and spirant versions of the letters B,K,P, ב,כ,פ (Table 21.1). Thus *kotev* [is writing] is spelled כּוֹתֵב with a dot (termed *dagesh*) inside the letter K כ to mark the stop *k*, whereas *yixtov* [will write] is spelled יִכְתֹּב without the *dagesh*, to mark the spirant *x*. The *dagesh*, like vowel marks, expresses lost phonological dimensions, such as gemination, and again its precise distribution in the Hebrew word is subject to Tiberian morphophonology.

In sum, the vocalized version gives Hebrew readers and writers specific phonological information about the fully vocalized word. A straightforward hypothesis, assuming that full phonological information is superior to underspecificity in psycholinguistic terms, would predict that Hebrew users prefer vocalized texts in reading and writing. But the facts say differently. The vocalized version with *nikud* marking is restricted to two contexts: (a) initial reading and writing instruction, and consequently texts for novice readers—children's books and texts for new immigrants; and (b) to ensure precise reading as in the case of biblical and poetic texts, and to disambiguate specific words in standard nonvocalized texts. Despite its phonological underspecification, the nonvocalized orthography is the default version of written Hebrew, used across the board for literacy activities, including school instruction from about 4th grade onwards (Share & Levin, 1999).

The universally used orthographic version of Hebrew, the *nonvocalized* orthography, represents all consonants by all letters, whereas vowels are partially and ambiguously represented by *matres lectionis*, AHWY אהוי, which serve a double function as designators of consonants and vowels. For example, both initial consonantal (or rather, semivowel) *y* and final vowel *i* in the word *yalduti* [childish] are represented by the letter Y י in the written string YLDWTY ילדותי. The stop–spirant distinction is not marked in the nonvocalized version. Vowel representation by AHWY is far from consistent and systematic, as shown by Table 21.3. Two vowels (*a,e*) are both represented by two letters (A, H, ה, א) and are almost never marked word internally (except cases in which A א stands for a root letter). Therefore written strings such as *géver* [man] and *gavar* [overpowered] belonging to the frequent patterns *CéCeC* and *CaCaC* (Ravid, 1990; Schwarzwald & Cohen-Gross, 2000) do not contain any vowel letters and appear in their bare consonantal form as GBR גבר. Not only are strings such as this homophonous; they also promote thinking of words as consonantal roots by demoting the perceived status of internal vowels (Schiff & Ravid, 2004). Two other vowels (*o, u*) are represented by one letter (W ו), and *i* is marked by the letter Y י. These three are marked both word internally and in final position, for example, *kotev* [is writing] spelled KWTB כותב and *pakid* [clerk] spelled PQYD פקיד, although Y י is subject to further, more subtle constraints (see subsequent discussion).

TABLE 21.3

AHWY (Hebrew אהוי) in Their Dual Function as Consonant and Vowel Designators

Grapheme	Hebrew Form	Consonant	Vowel	Constraints on Occurrence as Vowel Designator
A *Alef*	א	?	*a,e*	Word final only (unless root letter)
H *He*	ה	*h*	*a,e*	Word final only
W *Vav*	ו	*v* (historically, *w*)	*o,u*	Word internal and word final
Y *Yod*	י	*y*	*i*	Word internal and word final

Taken together, *matres lectionis* AHWY אהוי fall into two groups: AH אה and WY וי, differing in their vocalic values, orthographic distribution, and morphological functions.

Consonants are the more stable part of the written Hebrew word, as each and every consonant is represented in writing, whereas vowels are underrepresented, especially in the word-medial position. Note, for example, the 11-letter written string WKŠBMKTBYYK וכשבמכתבייך pronounced *uxšebemixtaváyix* [and-when-in-your Fm, Pl-letter-s]: All nine consonants are represented in this written string, including the root morpheme *k-t-b* [write] and affixal elements—two conjunctions, a preposition, a pattern prefix, and a genitive suffix; but only two (*u* and *i*) of the seven vowels in the word are represented in writing.

AHWY אהוי are not really alternative but rather are complementary ways of marking vowels in written Hebrew, as they are not discarded in vocalized script. In fact, all AHWY אהוי are obligatory at word-final position in both orthographic versions, whereas Y י and W ו are marked in many cases in word-internal positions, so that the actual additional phonological information in vocalized script is mostly vowels *e* and *a*, and stop – spirant alternation.

Vowels may thus be represented in four different ways in written Hebrew:

1. *By vocalization diacritic marks in vocalized script.* For example, *a* is represented twice in the vocalized written string סַפָּר *sapar* [hairdresser] by two diacritic marks.
2. *By zero marking in nonvocalized script.* For example, *a* is represented twice in the nonvocalized string SPR ספר denoting *sapar* [hairdresser] by zero marking.
3. *By the graphemes AHWY in nonvocalized script.* For example, *i* and *u* are represented in the nonvocalized string SYPWR סיפור *sipur* [story] by Y י and W ו, respectively.
4. *By a combination of vocalization marks and AHWY in vocalized script.* For example, *yafe* [pretty] is spelled יָפֶה; The string יָפֶ without final H ה, though vocalized, is incorrect.

MORPHOLOGICAL UNITS IN WRITTEN HEBREW

The rich and varied morphological constructs of Hebrew are systematically and consistently reflected in its orthography. To understand morphological patterning in written Hebrew, it is best to conceive of the written Hebrew word as consisting of two layers: the core, which contains root letters and internal vocalics, and the envelope, which comprises function letters. For example, consider the words in Table 21.4, derived from roots *k-r-n* [shine] and *m-s-r* [transmit, hand over], in their normal nonvocalized forms.

Note that all the words in Table 21.4 contain at least the three root letters QRN קרנ or MSR מסר, which form the internal part of the word, its core. All 22 Hebrew letters may represent

TABLE 21.4

Root Letters and Function Letters in the Written Hebrew Word

Word	Gloss	Hebrew Written Form	Written Form
Root *q-r-n*	"Shine"	קר"נ	QRN
karanta	you, Sg, shone	קרנת	QRNT
hikrinu	they screened	הקרינו	HQRYNW
kéren	beam, N	קרן	QRN
makrena	projector	מקרנה	MQRNH
hakrana	screening	הקרנה	HQRNH
krina	emission	קרינה	QRYNH
karnit	cornea	קרנית	QRNYT
Root *m-s-r*	"hand over"	מס"ר	MSR
masarti	I handed over	מסרתי	MSRTY
nimsera	she was handed over	נמסרה	NMSRH
hitmaser	devoted himself	התמסר	HTMSR
méser	message	מסר	MSR
timsóret	transmission	תמסורת	TMSWRT
hitmasrut	self-devotion	התמסרות	HTMSRWT
tamsir	handout, N	תמסיר	TMSYR
mimsar	relay, N	ממסר	MMSR

root radicals. The Semitic root, which underlies most of the Hebrew lexicon, is represented in consistent orthographic form even when alternating phonologically (see preceding section), thus preserving its morphological unity. Moreover, in speech the root is a discontinuous unit, interdigitated by vowels, but in writing it often appears as an intact continuous sequence, enhancing its unity. These features contribute to the root's being the phonological, semantic, and orthographic core of the written Hebrew word (Frost, Forster & Deutsch, 1997; Ravid, 2003). Of the 22 letters in the Hebrew alphabet, 11 letters (ANY ŠLMH KWTB אני שלמה כותב) consistently represent nonroot morphemes (verbal and nominal pattern affixes, linear derivational suffixes, and inflectional suffixes indicating tense, number, gender, and person) in addition to representing root elements (Ravid, 2001).

Morphemic function letters always appear in the external envelope of the written Hebrew word, that is, to the right and to the left of the orthographic root. For example, *hakrana* HQRNH הקרנה [screening] is framed by H and H, which indicate the action nominal pattern *haCCaCa*; *timsóret* TMSWRT תמסורת [transmission] is framed by T and T, which indicate the abstract noun pattern *tiCCóCet*. Other examples are listed with their particular details in Table 21.4. No function elements appear within the core of the written Hebrew word, except for vowels *i, o, u*, marked by letters WY וי (recall that *a* and *e* are not allowed written representation word internally): But note that these vocalics do not carry separate morphological information, as they constitute part of the whole pattern (as does W ו in *timsóret* TMSWRT תמסורת [transmission] and Y י in *hikrin* HQRYN הקרין [shone], for example). This layered structure of written morphological constructs in Hebrew has important implications for reading and for writing, as experienced Hebrew readers will know that the lexically meaningful part of the word is represented in its middle, whereas letters framing the word carry grammatical and categorial meaning.

In addition to morphemic function letters in its envelope, the written Hebrew words may be prefixed by a series of *attached* function letters designating syntactic constructs, phrasal and clausal clitics (Spencer, 1991; Ravid, 2001). These letters fall into three subsets[5]: (a) *conjunctions ve-* [and], spelled W ו, and the relative marker *she-* [that] spelled Š ש; (b) *definite articles ha-* [the], spelled H ה; and (c) *prepositions me-* [from], spelled M מ; *be-* [in], spelled B ב; *ke-* [as], spelled K כ; and *le-* [to], spelled L ל. For example, *umehabayit* [and-from-the-house] is spelled WMHBYT ומהבית. Attached function letters thus extend the external envelope of the written word.

Having presented the structure of Hebrew orthography and the linguistic constructs it reflects, we can now turn to an overview of literacy acquisition in the context of these factors.

EMERGENT ORTHOGRAPHIC KNOWLEDGE

Both general and Hebrew-specific features emerge early on in children's writing, as evidenced in a number of studies on early writing development in Hebrew-speaking preschoolers by Levin and her colleagues (see summary in Share & Levin, 1999). For example, Tolchinsky-Landsmann & Levin (1985) found that, by 5 years of age, most children used the right-to-left Hebrew-specific direction. Referential and phonological strategies (i.e., representing referent size and length in phonological units) are typical of Israeli preschool writing, with the phonological strategy becoming more dominant with age (Levin, Korat & Amsterdamer, 1996; Levin & Tolchinsky-Landsmann, 1989; Tolchinsky-Landsmann & Levin, 1987). It is interesting to note that the most advanced preschoolers already used a morphological strategy whereby they used more signs for phonologically longer bimorphemic words, for example, *etsim* [trees] suffixed by the plural marker *–im* (Levin & Korat, 1993).

Five writing levels were identified by Levin et al. (1996) in Hebrew-speaking children's emergent orthographic acquisition in the age range of 4–7 years: *scribbling*, nonorthographical productions indistinguishable from drawing; *pseudowriting*, arbitrary signs in writinglike form; *random letters*, Hebrew letters unrelated to the phonological string represented; *phonetic writing*, essentially breaking the graphophonemic code that associates graphemes with phonemes (cf. Goswami, 1999; Treiman, 1993), evidenced by letters representing phonological units in the spoken word; and *orthographic writing,* which involves incorporating orthography-specific and morphological components into the spelling (Ellis, 1994; Jones, 1991; Treiman, Zukowski & Richmond-Welty, 1995). Writing at the last level occurred only in the oldest children in the sample (7-year-olds), whereas all other levels occurred in all age groups (Levin et al., 1996; Share & Levin, 1999). There is evidence that Israeli children go through parallel development in learning to read: from using nonlinguistic pragmatic–contextual information in 4-year-olds, to relying on logographic, phonetic and alphabetical strategies in 5-year-olds, combined with growing phonemic awareness and letter–sound knowledge (Share & Gur, 1999). Language-specific features, such as writing direction, exercise their unique impact on the acquisition of writing, as evidenced by a recent study on neglect dyslexia (Friedmann & Nachman-Katz, 2004).

A particularly helpful strategy in the very initial stages of learning to read and write Hebrew is knowledge of letter names, most of which are full-sized words with typical Hebrew

---

[5] The link between attached function letters and the next word is not only orthographic: All of them, except for *she-* [that], spelled Š, have morphophonological allomorphs depending on their environment (e.g., *ve-* [and] also has the forms *vi-* and *u-*). The spelling (e.g., W) does not change because the difference is in the accompanying vowel that is not represented in nonvocalized spelling. Mastery of all possible allomorphs is part of literate language knowledge in Hebrew (Ravid, 1996).

morphophonemic structure (e.g., *gimel* for G ג). Levin, Patel, Margalit, and Barad (2002) asked Hebrew-speaking kindergartners and first graders to provide orally initial or final letters of spoken words, to spell words in writing, and to select a written word out of two as standing for an oral word. Their study provides rich converging evidence that letter names in Hebrew provide scaffolding to the alphabetic principle and to a mental model of the orthography. For example, children succeeded more in providing the initial letter or in spelling it if the word started with a letter-name sequence, e.g., *kaftor* [button], spelled with K כ (letter name: *kaf*). This was true even in the case of partial letter names, for example, *ta* in *taf*, the letter name of T ת, helped spell *talmid* [student] TLMYD תלמיד.

Given this background, the main focus from now on is on the interface of phonological, morphological, and orthographic features of Hebrew with literacy development at the phonetic and the orthographic levels.

ORTHOGRAPHIC FEATURES AND THE DEVELOPMENT OF HEBREW LITERACY

Three knowledge domains are necessary for the acquisition of writing and reading skills in Hebrew (and, in different measures, for other alphabetical systems; cf. Blanche-Benveniste & Chervel, 1974): mapping phonology onto graphemic segments; becoming familiar with the internal conventions of the orthographic system; and learning about morphological regularities in the spelling system (Ravid & Gillis, 2002). The first two domains are learned in kindergarten and first grade and are consolidated in the earlier grades of primary school, whereas integration of morphological knowledge takes place in later grade school. Moreover, the three domains interact in different ways in learning to read and to write, and in learning about the written representation of consonants and vowels.

Novice Reading and Writing

Breaking the graphophonemic code and learning about the internal properties of the orthographic system are basic and critical in formal literacy. From the very beginning, even though learning to read and learning to write are obviously related (Levin, Share & Shatil, 1996), they take place at different paces and are affected by different properties of Hebrew orthography.

Since the 1980s, Israeli scholars have made a particular contribution to general understanding of writing development in preschoolers and in the early grades of primary school and its importance in the context of emergent and early literacy (e.g., Levin & Korat, 1993; Tolchinsky-Landsmann & Levin, 1985). Levin, Share, and Shatil (1996) tested 349 Israeli children in kindergarten on writing, concepts of print and vocabulary, and again in first grade on spelling and reading. They found that kindergarten writing made a unique contribution to achievement in first grade above and beyond other types of language and literacy knowledge. The results of these studies were disseminated by education leaders in the teacher population, with the result that many kindergartens now actively encourage writing activities (Teubal, 2002).

One critical feature of Hebrew orthographic conventions that novice readers and spellers have to learn is the attached function letters (four prepositions, two conjunctions, and the definite article) prefixing written words. Studies have shown that adult Hebrew readers are sensitive to the syntactic functions of these letters (Koriat, Greenberg, & Goldshmid, 1991). In one study, attached function letters in texts presented to adult students were separated by a hyphen from the main word (e.g., H-ZMN ה-זמן for *ha-zman* [the time], instead of HZMN הזמן),

with the idea that this would enhance morphological transparency and would increase reading rate. However, in fact the opposite effect was observed—reading slowed down (Loewenstein & Kozminsky, 1999). This indicates to what extent orthographic conventions are embedded in the decoding mechanism of Hebrew readers. Novice spellers learn early on that these function letters should be attached to the next word. Seidman (2000) tested children twice, in kindergarten and in first grade, on writing sentences containing attached function letters, for example, *aba ve-ima nas'u le-eylat* [daddy and-mommy went to-Eilat], spelled ABA WAMA NS9W LAYLT אבא ואמא נסעו לאילת. Correct function letter attachment was performed in kindergarten only 10% of the time, but 8 months later, in the middle of first grade, performance increased to 70%. An analysis of syntactic functions showed that both kindergartners and first graders were more successful at attaching prepositions (e.g., in, to) to the next word than conjunctions (and, that) and the definite article. A likely explanation is that sentential conjunctions were perceived as having a more independent and separate standing than prepositions, which form part of a Prepositional Phrase.

The Strange Developmental History of *Nikud*

A second unique feature of Hebrew writing is vowel representation by *nikud* diacritics. Neither the consonantal nor the vocalic homophony described in the section modern Hebrew Demographic and phonological features constitutes an obstacle to early decoding success in Hebrew, as children find it easy to assign the same reading to multiple signs. Share and Levin (1999, p. 96) note that the most conspicuous fact about learning to *read* Hebrew in school is the rapid mastery of decoding skills. A number of reports confirm that accurate reading of real and nonce vocalized Hebrew words (i.e., with *nikud* diacritics) in first grade is already about 80% (Geva & Siegel, 1991; Geva, Wade-Woolley & Shany, 1993; Haimowitz, 2003; Shatil, Share & Levin, 2000). The most obvious explanation of this fact is the transparency of the vocalized system and the fact that it provides full phonological information about both consonants and vowels (Frost, 1992; Shimron, 1993).

Nevertheless, using *nikud* diacritics is currently at the center of an educational controversy in Israel. Concern about reading comprehension abilities in the upper grades of primary school and junior high school has recently led to an investigation of reading instruction methods used in Israeli first grades, and especially phonic versus "whole-language" methods (Shapira, 2001). Phonic methods, which emphasize a meticulous bottom-up building of phonological–orthographic skills, teach reading (and writing) by using *nikud* vocalization marks, thus providing novice readers with the fullest information about both consonants and vowels in the word. More "holistic" methods attribute reading success to children's ability to guess the meaning from large text units; they deemphasize the role of grapheme–phoneme correspondence and use full words, sentences, and texts in early reading instruction, omitting *nikud* marks. Antiphonic proponents in Israel claim that focusing on phonological nonmeaningful units such as syllables, nonce words, and even single words—in which *nikud* vocalization is crucial for decoding—is technical rather than ecologically valid and does not promote real text comprehension later on (Teubal, 2002; Wahl, 2002). At this time, reports by leading Israeli researchers clearly support using *nikud* marks in the context of reading instruction, starting with focus on phonological awareness and letter names in kindergarten and followed by formal phonics-oriented methods in first grade (Levin, 2002; Shapira, 2001).

Nikud diacritics play an interesting—even paradoxical—role in Hebrew literacy development. For the initial stages of reading, vocalization seems to be very helpful (Navon & Shimron, 1984). This is because it provides full phonological information about the written word and renders it orthographically shallow so that the semantic value of a word is reached easily and efficiently (Frost, 1992). Research on reading Arabic, another mainly consonantal Semitic language that uses diacritics to disambiguate homophonous strings, also indicates a facilitating effect of pointing on readers, mediated by context (Abu-Rabia, 2001). With this in view, all reading materials for novice readers (children and nonnative speakers alike) are presented with *nikud.* However, this widespread and well-justified use of *nikud* in initial reading instruction is mitigated by two developmental inconsistencies: reading and writing.

Reading. Making progress in reading and achieving reading comprehension requires more abilities than does phonological decoding of single words and always involves aban-doning vocalized script (Ravid, 1996; Ravid & Shlesinger, 2001; Shimron, 1999). Studies on reading vocalized and nonvocalized Hebrew words indicate that single pointed words are read faster than nonpointed words, but when words are presented in context, the effect of pointing diminishes (Koriat, 1985; Navon & Shimron, 1984). In a recent study, Shimron (1999) found that pointing did not have a powerful effect on grade schoolers' memories and interacted with task conditions and reader skills. As they progress in grade school, children stop relying on *nikud* diacritics in their reading texts (Share & Levin, 1999). This process starts as soon as they are able to decode Hebrew words, as literacy-promoting notices, notes, forms, newspapers, and signs at home, in school, and on the street, including television subtitles, are almost always nonvocalized. Most written materials used in grade school are nonvocalized by fifth grade. This poses a special problem for children with dyslexia and other forms of linguistic impairments, as their orthographic lexicons are not well established (Friedmann & Gvion, 2002). Toward junior high school, formal knowledge of *nikud* becomes required in Hebrew language instruc-tion, which focuses to a large extent on morphophonological processes (Avinun, 1996; Ravid, 1995a). At this time, teachers report problems in which knowledge of *nikud* is necessary: By the end of grade school the overwhelming majority of the children do not know the names of *nikud* marks, and many of them do not know how to pronounce them in nonce or rare words (Ravid, 1996; Ravid & Shlesinger, 2001). It is only in high school, as a result of intense refocus on metamorphological manipulation of written and spoken isolated words, that *nikud* marks regain prominence and knowledge in students.

Ravid conducted two experiments on reading *nikud* marks in children, adolescents, and adults. Ravid (1996) examined reading inflected words in 75 Hebrew-speaking first graders, fourth graders, and college students in two conditions—vocalized and nonvocalized. They were asked to read aloud 20 literate forms of words in which some of the vowels differed from their colloquial spoken forms (e.g. *xitsim* [arrows] rather than the colloquial *xetsim*). Reading the *nikud* marks accurately resulted in a form different from that of the colloquial one. Adults' reading in both conditions was the most accurate of all three groups and with the fewest self-repairs, indicating mastery of the orthographic system including *nikud.* First graders read vocalized words more accurately, though also with more self-repairs, than did fourth graders. This reflected novice readers' close attention to *nikud* marks and inability to access lexical semantics through addressed reading. Fourth graders not only read *nikud* less accurately than did first graders, they also performed equally in both vocalized and nonvocalized conditions, relying on their oral representations in reading without attention to *nikud* diacritics.

Ravid and Shlesinger (2001) tested 100 participants in five age groups (5th, 7th, 9th, and 11th graders, and adult students) on reading aloud the same words in three conditions—twice without *nikud* marks, and once more with *nikud* marks. Once again, vocalization indicated that these words differed from their colloquial spoken forms. Results showed that all study groups read the nonvocalized words as inaccurately on the first two conditions. On the third, vocalized, condition, reading accuracy in the two older groups (11th graders and adults) improved, whereas the three younger groups performed equally badly in all three conditions. These two studies attest to the ability of older, more literate Hebrew users to elicit phonological information from *nikud* compared with the "blindness" of grade schoolers to this information. The use and the knowledge of *nikud* in reading do not simply increase with age and schooling. Rather, it is learned, lost, and relearned throughout childhood and adolescence. First graders use *nikud* functionally as scaffolding on the way to literacy; older grade schoolers ignore it; adolescents reacquire facts about *nikud* for metalinguistic purposes.

Writing.   In contrast to the U-shaped developmental curve of using *nikud* diacritics in reading, the situation in writing is simpler: At no point in development do Hebrew nonexpert writers use *nikud.* At the very time preschoolers and first graders are relying heavily on vocalized script in learning to read, they almost completely shun *nikud* in writing (Levin & Korat, 1993). In a recent study (Haimowitz, 2003), kindergartners and first graders were asked to write the same syllables with different vowels (e.g., *ro, ra, re*), and words ending with vowels carrying familiar and obligatory morphological information such as verb and adjective inflection (e.g., *halxu* [they walked], *xola* [she is sick]) and inflected prepositions (e.g., *ito* [with him]). In the first task, which required children to mark the vocalic difference between syllables, kindergartners used inappropriate *nikud* marks (e.g., marking *a* for *e*) 33.75% of the time, and appropriate *nikud* marks 3.75% of the time. In first grade there was appropriate marking 75% of the time. In the second task, writing words with vowels, none of the kindergartners used appropriate *nikud*, whereas first graders used it 35%–48% of the time, depending on the vowel. Thus children are reluctant to use *nikud* in writing during emergent and formal literacy training—at the time when it is very prominent in reading—unless forced to by a complete lack of context. In later years even this sparse usage of *nikud* in writing declines. Grade schoolers never employ it in their written texts (Berman & Ravid, 1999), and even educated adults (e.g., kindergarten teachers) are unwilling to write using *nikud.* Texts with *nikud* are produced only by highly trained individuals with specialized knowledge in formal Hebrew grammar.

The developmental history of *nikud* in Hebrew readers and writers is puzzling. Why should a system that renders the orthography transparent and consequently more readable be completely shunned in writing and discarded early on in reading?

The principal reason is its redundancy. For nonnovice Hebrew readers, vocalization is predictable from the morphological, orthographic, syntactic, and discourse contexts, with very narrow margins for error. Hebrew pattern morphology places heavy restrictions on possible vowel combinations both structurally (Cohen-Gross, 2000) and semantically (Ravid, 1990). Syntax further eliminates possible vowel combinations, for example, passive morphology in active contexts. Veteran readers make semantic decisions by using structural cues indicating content versus function words and relying on their knowledge of phrase and clause structure. Orthographic conventions of placing *matres lectionis* AHWY אהוי on the type of vowels that cannot be represented by them and on attached function letters (see above) provide more precise information about the word. Finally, ambiguity can be resolved by larger context cues (Shimron, 1999). Thus educated adults find *nikud* necessary only in extreme cases of extreme ambiguity or foreign words. This idea is supported by a wide range of studies that point at the centrality of morphological structure and meaning in reading and writing Hebrew (Ben-Dror, Bentin, & Frost, 1995; Frost, 1995; Frost et al., 1997; Ravid, 2001, 2003). For all of these reasons, *nikud* is superfluous for non-novice Hebrew readers who shed the need for vocalization as soon as addressed reading is achieved (Shimron, 1999).

However, literate Hebrew users not only discard *nikud* in many cases, they are also averse to using it. This seems strange in view of the fact that vocalization adds important information to the written string and makes it orthographically transparent. I propose that *nikud*, although an essential tool for novice readers, interferes with normal processing of Hebrew texts later on. Nonnovice readers process written information fast and efficiently by addressed reading—that is, top-down processing—by using morphological and syntactic cues. Processing *nikud* diacritics requires processing of a different kind—assembled or bottom-up reading. This hinders the normal process of information processing during reading. In fact, letters and *nikud* diacritics are two different notational systems, with letters occupying most visual and cognitive space, whereas *nikud* provides secondary, categorial, often redundant information about the word and occupies a small part of visual space. It requires additional processing power to process both types of information simultaneously, which is available only to literate adults, and especially to highly analytic language experts. Processing vocalized text slows down contextual reading and forces the reader to pay attention to features that are not semantically crucial in Hebrew, such as internal vowels (Ravid, 1990, 1996; Ravid & Kubi, 2003).

GAINING ORTHOGRAPHIC MASTERY IN GRADE SCHOOL AND BEYOND

Spelling takes a different route than reading, though the underpinnings of Hebrew structure and orthography govern development along similar lines. Unlike accurate decoding of short sequences, which takes place early on in grade school, the shift from phonetic to orthographic (i.e., correct) spelling takes much longer. This is because even vocalized Hebrew, like most orthographies, is not entirely shallow, that is, it does not represent phonological information fully and accurately (Frost, 1992). As we have already seen, homophonous graphemes, which provide alternative spellings for the same grapheme, occur in Hebrew mainly in the consonant system. As shown in Table 21.1, there are two types of one-to-many relationships between current Hebrew consonants and letters: First, a number of phonemes are expressed each by two graphemes, reflecting historically distinct segments. For example, *t* is spelled as either ט Ŧ or as ת T (Bolozky, 1997). Conversely, three letters denote two distinct sounds, a stop and a spirant, for example, the letter B indicates both the phonemes *b* and *v*. Altogether there are 13 homophonous Hebrew letters, which together designate 6 phonemes:

$$t = \text{Ŧ ט T ת} \qquad ?/0 = \text{A א H ה 9 ע}$$
$$k = \text{K כ Q ק} \qquad v = \text{W ו B ב}$$
$$x = \text{K כ H ח} \qquad s = \text{Š שׂ S ס}$$

Early spelling errors typically occur within the 13 homophonous letters, which constitute the major source of consonantal spelling errors in Hebrew found in the writing of Hebrew-speaking grade schoolers up to sixth grade (Eylon, 1992). Consonantal spelling errors specifically derive from two homophony conditions: *identity* and *similarity*. Most homophonous letters represent identical sounds, for example, K ק – Q כ both stand for *k*, and W ו – B ב both stand for *v*. For example, the word *merkava* [carriage] was erroneously spelled by a third grader as MRQWH מרקוה instead of MRKBH מרכבה (Ravid, 2001). The three gutteral-pharyngeals A א / H ה / 9 ע (sometimes accompanied by Y י) stand for similar, rather than identical, sounds, which are often interchanged in speech or omitted completely (Ravid, 1995a). As a result, they are also often confused or deleted in writing, for example, *hevin* [understood] erroneously spelled as ABYN אבין instead of the correct HBYN הבין. Such errors persist throughout grade school and sometimes beyond.

This might lead us to expect that novice Hebrew spellers make the same amount of spelling errors across the board in homophonous letters, with the factor of word frequency an aid in remembering word shapes and spelling patterns. In fact, spelling errors in Hebrew are critically affected not only by phonological and orthographic considerations, but also by morphological distinctions. In a series of studies Ravid and her associates have shown that morphology and its representation in different classes of words and of morphemes are important factors in the development of Hebrew orthographic spelling.

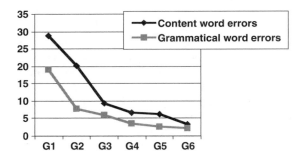

FIG. 21.1. Percentages of erroneously spelled content words and grammatical words in grade schoolers' compositions, by grade (data from Ravid, 2001).

Let us turn first to the evidence showing that content words are more difficult than grammatical words. Ravid (2001) analyzed 378 compositions by children from Grades 1–6. All the words in each composition were counted and classified into content words (nouns, verbs, adjectives, and manner adverbs) and grammatical words (pronouns, prepositions, conjunctions, quantifiers, etc.). Spelling errors were located and counted in both word types. There was a general decline in errors with grade, but content word errors were more numerous than errors in grammatical words and took longer to disappear (Fig. 21.1). One reason is that content words have a high type frequency, whereas the token frequency of each word is low, and the frequency of different lexical classes varies according to register and genre. This means that there is a lower chance of encountering them in print and working out a systematic analysis of their spelling to begin with, depending on the topic and the context. In contrast, grammatical words, a small, closed class occurring obligatorily in any kind of text, have a low type and high token frequency. This makes for numerous occurrences of the same word, which are thus likely to create deep memory traces in spellers early on. Moreover, content words are longer and more likely to contain roots whose spelling is unpredictable, whereas grammatical words are usually shorter and often fused with function suffixes (e.g., *kamó-xa* [like-you]) whose spelling is predictable.

Second, there is converging evidence from a number of my studies using different methodologies that homophonous root letters are more problematic in spelling development than homophonous function letters. First, in the same study just described (Ravid, 2001) the 15,997 homophonous root letters and 6,618 homophonous function letters in the children's compositions were analyzed for spelling errors. There were seven times as many root letters errors (694) as function letter errors (91); function letter errors almost disappeared by second grade, and root letter errors declined gradually from third grade onward. A second study described in Ravid (2001) was a dictation of 36 items to 72 grade schoolers (Grades 2–4). Here, too, root letter errors exceeded function letter errors in all grades, and by Grade 4, there were 3 times as many root letter errors than function letter errors (Fig. 21.2).

These results have been replicated since in a number of studies. For example, Ravid and Bar-On (2001, in press) conducted a series of experiments in which children and adolescents were given dictations with and without spelling primes. Figure 21.3 presents the amount of homophonous root and function letter errors in the no-prime condition. Here, too, there were twice as many errors in root letters in third and fourth grade, but by fifth grade this difference was much smaller. In a cross-linguistic study of Hebrew and Dutch, Gillis & Ravid (2001) compared success in spelling homophonous root and function letters in Hebrew with homophonous stem and function letters in Dutch (see Fig. 21.4). Whereas Hebrew showed the expected patterning of root and pattern spelling, Dutch showed an opposite patterning—correct

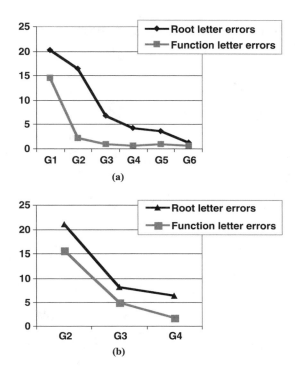

FIG. 21.2. (a) Percentages of erroneously spelled root letters and function letters, by grade (data from study 1, Ravid, 2001); (b) Percentages of erroneously spelled root letters and function letters, by grade (data from study 2, Ravid, 2001).

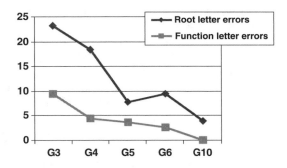

FIG. 21.3. Percentages of erroneously spelled root letters and function letters, by grade (data from Ravid & Bar-On, 2001).

stem letter spelling came earlier and was easier than spelling function letters, although stem spelling is idiosyncratic and function letter spelling is guided by clear rules in Dutch. This difference in learning patterns between the two languages is attributed to the typological differences between Hebrew, which is a morphologically rich language, and Dutch, which is morphologically sparse. Children learning these two languages are assumed to be attuned from early on to meaning-carrying constructions in their language. Paying close attention to morphological constructions, their meanings and permutations, in Hebrew entails using

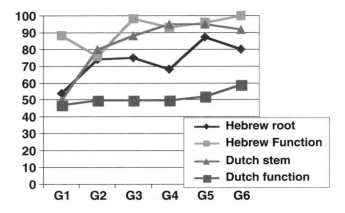

FIG. 21.4. Percentages of correctly spelled root letters and function letters in Hebrew and stem and function letters in Dutch, by age group (data from Gillis & Ravid, 2001).

morphological strategies in learning to read and write (see also Ravid & Gillis, 2002, for a detailed explanation).

The development of orthographic spelling thus typically takes place across the grade school years. Most function letters are already spelled correctly by third to fourth grade, whereas correct spelling of root letters is a long and protracted process that is delayed to the end of grade school (sixth grade). This of course relates to normal development: In children with special needs, especially those who have specific difficulties in language, root letter errors linger on and are harder to eradicate. However, this Hebrew-specific patterning of root and function spelling errors is not violated even in children with Specific Language Impairment (SLI) (Lapidot, 2003).

Root spelling lags behind the spelling of function letters, but it too consolidates across the grade school years together with the increase in density and accessibility of systematic morphological knowledge and awareness (Karmiloff-Smith, 1992). A study by Weil and Fromowitz (1998) focuses on the relationship between oral and written perception of the root morpheme in 48 third-grade girls who were asked to spell words with homophonous root segments and then to provide words with analogous structures. For example, "which word does *tahaluxa* [parade] remind you of"? Morphological responses consisted of words with the same root (third graders are not able to give pattern responses; see Ravid & Malenky, 2001); nonorthographical responses relied either on phonologically or semantically similar words. A reverse relationship was found between participants' spelling and morphological ability: the fewer spelling errors in root letters, the more morphological root responses. Moreover, follow-up interviews of participants with the highest and lowest numbers of morphological responses revealed different understanding of word structure. Weak students' explanations of their own choices were almost exclusively associative for both semantic and morphological response types. For example, to explain the choice of semantic *tmuna* [picture] for target *mazkéret* [souvenir], one weak student said "because a souvenir can be a picture." But "high" participants responded in ways indicating their ability to analyze a given word into its root and pattern structure.

A number of studies indicate that Israeli grade schoolers rely on morphophonological cues in learning to spell root letters. These cues are more elusive and less straightforward than semantic cues, and therefore take more time and exposure to written language to detect. Nevertheless, evidence has been accumulating that grade schoolers make increasing use of morphophonology in spelling. For example, homophonous root segments historically deriving from low guttural and pharyngeals attract lower vowels, unlike homophonous root letters from other origins, which retain the default vowel pattern. Compare, for example, the spelling of the homophonous root segment *x* in *mélex* [king], spelled MLK מלך, with *mélax* [salt], spelled MLH מלח. The first word retains the default *CéCeC* pattern, indicating that *x* should be spelled by K כ ; whereas in the second one *x* is preceded by a lower vowel, a clear sign of its pharyngeal origins, and therefore should be spelled with H ח. Ravid (2002) tested children across grade school levels (first–sixth grades) on spelling of words with such homophonous segments. Results indicate that even the youngest spellers in first grade find marked H ח that attracts lower vowels easier to spell correctly than כ K, and that toward third grade the morphophonological cues start making sense, resulting in more correct spelling of the unmarked segment as well.

Another morphophonological phenomenon that assists spellers in recovering the homophonous segment is stop–spirant alternation. In such cases, the homophonous segment that displays stop–spirant alternation can be distinguished from the one that does not. For example, *v* has two possible spellings, W ו and B ב, and *k* can be spelled by either Q ק or K כ. The second of both pairs displays stop–spirant alternants *b–v* and *k–x*, whereas the first one stays constant (*v* and *k*, respectively). This differing morphophonological behavior is a reliable cue for spelling. Again, this is rather sophisticated knowledge, which requires exposure and attention to both spoken and written cues. Therefore it is not available at the very beginning of learning to spell—but it does become available toward the middle of grade school (Gillis & Ravid, 2001).

Finally, voicing assimilation sometimes interferes with phonological identification and may lead to spelling errors in root letters. For example, root *z-k-r* [remember] may sound *s-k-r* as a result of assimilation of voiced *z* to voiceless *k*, rendering *mazkéret* [souvenir] as *maskéret* in casual speech. As a result, MZKRT מזכרת may be spelled erroneously as MSKRT מסכרת, masking the identity of root *z-k-r* [remember]. A strong memory trace of the root and a good ability to analyze a given word into its root and pattern structure help in overcoming assimilation interference and in correct spelling. Evidence shows that, by third grade, children's ability to overcome voicing assimilation that masks root identity is almost perfect (Shany, Zeiger, & Ravid, 2001).

Findings by different Israeli scholars clearly support the idea that morphological and orthographic knowledge in Hebrew are fundamentally related. Levin, Ravid, and Rapaport (1999, 2001) tested 40 native Hebrew-speaking children in a longitudinal study from kindergarten to first grade on three late-emerging oral morphological constructions and on writing noun – adjective strings. They found a clear correlation between spoken morphology and writing ability: Spoken morphology and writing were found to correlate concurrently in kindergarten and in first grade, and predictively from kindergarten to first grade. In addition, each domain made an additional unique contribution to the change in the other from kindergarten to first grade. From a different perspective, Schiff (2002) tested reading of nonvocalized nouns in which the final letter H ה served different functions for second, fourth, and sixth graders. In half of the words the letter H ה constituted part of the nominal pattern, as in *braxa* [blessing] (pattern *CCaCa*), spelled BRKH ברכה; whereas in the other half it designated the bound possessive third-person feminine inflection, as in *znava* [her tail], spelled ZNBH זנבה. Schiff found that the younger participants found the inflected words, in which the H ה renders the word more morphologically complex, more difficult to read accurately than the words in which the same letter designated an integral part of the word; whereas 6th graders were able to read both types of words with equal ease. In a related study Schiff (2003) tested 150 second, fourth, and sixth graders on reading nouns with these two structures. She found morphological effects on reading latency and accuracy as well as different learning patterns for the two constructions. Although reading accuracy increased with grade in both constructions, inflections took longer to read and elicited more correct responses than did derivations, but with age latency became longer. In derivations, in contrast, latency became shorter with time. Ben-Dror et al.

(1995) tested fifth graders with reading disabilities together with an age-matched group and a vocabulary-matched (third-grade) group on phonological, semantic, and morphological skills. The children with reading disabilities made the most mistakes and were the slowest to respond; and the most conspicuous difference between the groups was in the morphological test, most markedly in derivational morphology.

SPELLING VOWELS

Beyond the problem of *nikud*, vowel spelling constitutes the most problematic area in Hebrew writing from the onset of literacy to adulthood. Recall that vowels are not only undermarked in graphemic format, but they also map ambiguously and inconsistently onto the four *matres lectionis* AHWY אהוי (Tables 21.2 and 21.3). A number of studies showed repeatedly that consonants emerge earlier and are spelled more correctly than vowels in young children's writing (Haimowitz, 2003; Levin et al., 1999, 2001; Share & Levin, 1999). Vowel writing is inconsistent across the board in Hebrew spellers because it often requires formal linguistic and historical Hebrew knowledge that is beyond the abilities of 99% of Hebrew readers and writers (Ravid & Shlesinger, 2001; Schwarzwald, 2001). The most problematic of all are vowels that appear within the internal part of the word and mainly carry sparse phonological rather than morphological value. A subset of these are formally required in *plene* nonvocalized spelling and deleted in vocalized spelling, so that Hebrew users cannot form a consistent representation of the spelling of the word, e.g., Y ' in *siper* [told], spelled both as SYPR סיפר and SPR ספר (Schiff & Ravid, 2004).

A series of studies indicate that representing internal vowels constitutes an area of instability for spellers of all ages. Ravid (2002) found that young grade schoolers tend to overmark Y ' incorrectly (e.g., MYBHNYM מיבתנים rather than MBHNYM מבתנים). Alkaslassi (2003) found that adults systematically delete internal vowels incorrectly in nonvocalized writing (e.g., SPR ספר for *siper* [told]). Ravid & Kubi (2003) elicited spelling errors from children, adolescents, and adults in two conditions. First, participants were given a dictation of a story. In the second condition, participants were given the same text and asked to write it using deliberate spelling errors. All spelling errors in the dictations were counted and classified with phonological (consonants and vowels) and morphological (root and function letters) criteria. The most frequent "natural" errors that lasted long into high school were errors in internal vowel letters YW יו; whereas the overwhelming majority of the deliberate errors were consonantal root errors, switching, for example, K כ for Q ק or T ת for Ŧ ט. Schiff and Ravid (2004) presented vocalized and nonvocalized words in sentential context to Hebrew readers. Nonvocalized rootlike strings with illegal spelling (e.g., MKR מכר for *mukar* [familiar]) were identified faster than those with legal spelling (e.g., MWKR מוכר) despite being inappropriate in the context.

These findings indicate to what extent Hebrew speakers and writers regard the consonantal root as a unified entity across phonology, semantics, and orthography. Root representation in writing is the consistent, stable, consensual facet of Hebrew orthography, and violating it is considered a real "spelling error" typical of children and illiterate persons. In contrast, internal vowel letters carry little if any morphological value because none of the meaning-carrying Hebrew affixes is word internal. Internal vowels may carry phonological information alone, as in loan words (e.g., *minimali* [minimal]). In most cases, internal vowels constitute part of the word pattern, for example, *CiCeC* or *CiCuC*, but in such cases it is not the individual vowel that carries meaning but rather the full pattern. At any rate, pattern meaning is categorial rather than lexical and is less coherent semantically than that of roots (Ravid, 1990, 2003). Moreover, Hebrew speakers often accept two *spoken* versions of the same word with differing vocalic patterns (e.g., both *madad* and *méded* for [index]), another indication of the relative instability of vowels compared with consonants in Hebrew. Consequently, the status of internal vowel representation is unstable and a range of alternative spellings is acceptable to mature and literate speakers and writers. In fact, although consonantal errors disappear from the spelling of the majority of normally developing children by the end of grade school, vowel errors linger on in the writing of adolescents and adults and are not regarded as real "spelling errors" (Ravid & Kubi, 2003). In a recent academic paper written by a native Hebrew graduate who had never been diagnosed with any language problems, I found 24 vowel letter errors, including spelling the loan word *minimali* [minimal] as MNMLY מנמלי instead of MYNYMLY מינימלי, and deleting the vowel root letter W ו in *lavo* [to come], spelled LBA לבא instead of LBWA לבוא.

Consonant and vowel spelling patterns testify to the strong and constant links between classical Hebrew and modern Hebrew, two versions of a Semitic language with a rich morphology and a mainly consonantal orthography.

REFERENCES

Abu-Rabia, S. (2001). The role of vowels in reading Semitic scripts: Data from Arabic and Hebrew. *Reading and Writing, 14*, 39–59.

Alkaslassi, N. (2003). Marking vowels in gradeschoolers' texts. Unpublished master's thesis, Cognitive Studies Program, Tel Aviv University, Tel Aviv, Israel.

Avinun, S. (1996). *Hebrew word-formation for highschool* [in Hebrew]. Tel Aviv: Center for Educational Technology.

Baayen, H. (1985). Tiberian Hebrew within the framework of lexical phonology. *Working Papers in Linguistics, 21*. Amsterdam: Vrÿe Universiteit.

Bendavid, A. (1971). *Biblical Hebrew and Mishnaic Hebrew* [in Hebrew]. Tel Aviv: Dvir.

Ben-Dror, I., Bentin, S., & Frost, R. (1995). Semantic, phonologic and morphologic skills in reading disabled and normal children. *Reading Research Quarterly, 30*, 876–893.

Ben Hayyim, Z. (1985). The historical unity of Hebrew. In M. Bar-Asher (Ed.), *Studies in Language I* [in Hebrew]. Jerusalem: The Hebrew University.

Ben Rafael, E., Olshtain, E., & Gajst, I. (1994). Aspects of identity and language acquisition among immigrants from the Commonwealth of Independent States [in Hebrew]. Jerusalem: Research Institute for Innovation in Education, School of Education, The Hebrew University of Jerusalem.

Berg, T. (1998). *Linguistic structure and change*. New York: Oxford University Press.

Bergsträsser, G. (1982). *Hebräische Grammatik* (M. Ben Asher, Trans.). Jerusalem: Hebrew University, Magnes.

Berman, R. A. (1978). *Modern Hebrew structure*. Tel Aviv: University Publishing Projects.

Berman, R. A. (1987). Productivity in the lexicon: New-word formation in Modern Hebrew. *Folia Linguistica, 21*, 225–254.

Berman, R. A. (1997). Israeli Hebrew. In R. Hezron (Ed.), *The Semitic languages* (pp. 312–333). London: Routledge.

Berman, R. A., & Ravid, D. (1999, September). *The oral/literate continuum: Developmental perspectives*. Final Report submitted to the Israel Science Foundation. Tel Aviv: Tel Aviv University.

Blau, Y. (1971). *Hebrew phonology and morphology* [in Hebrew]. Tel Aviv: Ha-Kibbutz Ha-Meuchad.

Blanche-Benveniste, C., & Chervel, A. (1974). *L'orthographe*. Paris: F. Maspero.

Bolozky, S. (1997). Israeli Hebrew phonology. In Alan S. Kaye & Peter T. Daniels (Eds.), *Phonologies of Asia and Africa* (pp. 287–311). Winona Lake, IN: Eisenbrauns.

Clark, E. V. (1993). *The lexicon in acquisition*. Cambridge, UK: Cambridge University Press.

Cohen-Gross, D. (2000). The syllabic structure of Modern Hebrew. In O. Schwarzwald, S. Blum-Kolka & E. Olshtain (Eds.), *The Raphael Nir book: Studies in communication, linguistics and language teaching* (pp. 359–369) [in Hebrew]. Jerusalem: Carmel.

Coulmas, F. (1989). *The writing systems of the world*. Oxford, UK: Blackwell.

Donitsa-Schmidt, S. (1999). *Language maintenance or shift: Determinants of language choice among Soviet immigrants in Israel*. Unpublished doctoral dissertation, Ontario Institute for Studies in Education of the University of Toronto.

Driver, G. R. (1976). *Semitic writing: from pictograph to alphabet* (Rev. ed.). London: Oxford University Press.

Ellis, N. C. (1994). Longitudinal studies of spelling development. In G. D. A. Brown & N. C. Ellis (Eds.), *Handbook of spelling: Theory, process and intervention* (pp. 155–177). Chichester, UK: Wiley.

Emmons, S. (1997). Russian Jewish immigration and its effect on the state of Israel. *Indiana Journal of Global Legal Studies, 5*, 341–356.

Eylon, A. (1992). Spelling errors in gradeschool children, and developing a computer-assisted program for correcting intervention for improving spelling ability [in Hebrew]. Unpublished doctoral dissertation, School of Education, Tel Aviv University.

Fellman, J. (1973, May). Concerning the 'revival' of the Hebrew language. *Anthropological Linguistics*, 250–257.

Friedmann, N., & Gvion, A. (2002). Modularity in developmental disorders: Evidence from SLI and peripheral dyslexias. *Behavioral and Brain Sciences, 25*, 756–757.

Friedmann, N., & Nachman-Katz, I. (2004). Neglect dyslexia in a Hebrew- reading child. *Cortex, 40*, 301–313.

Frost, R. (1992). Orthography and phonology: The psychological reality of orthographic depth. In P. Downing, S. Lima, & M. Noonan (Eds.), *The linguistics of literacy* (pp. 255–274). Amsterdam: Benjamins.

Frost, R. (1995). Phonological computation and missing vowels: Mapping lexical involvement in reading. *Journal of Experimental Psychology: Learning, Memory, and Cognition, 21*, 398–408.

Frost, R., Forster, K., & Deutsch, A. (1997). What can we learn from the morphology of Hebrew? A masked-priming investigation of morphological representation. *Journal of Experimental Psychology, Learning, Memory, and Cognition, 23*, 829–856.

Gelb, I. J. (1963). *A study of writing*. Chicago: University of Chicago Press.

Geva, E., & Siegel, L. (1991, July). *The role of orthography and cognitive factors in the concurrent development of basic reading skills in bilingual children*. Paper presented at the meeting of the International Society for the Study of Behavioral Development, Minneapolis, MN.

Geva, E., Wade-Woolley, L., & Shany, M. (1993). The concurrent development of spelling and decoding in two different orthographies. *Journal of Reading Behavior, 25*, 383–406.

Gillis, S., & Ravid, D. (2001). Language-specific effects on the development of written morphology. In S. Bendjaballah and W. U. Dressler (Eds.), *Morphology 2000* (pp. 129–136). Amsterdam: Benjamins.

Goswami, U. (1999). The relationship between phonological awareness and orthographic representation in different orthographies. In M. Harris & G. Hatano (Eds.), *Learning to read and write: A crosslinguistic perspective* (pp. 134–156). Cambridge, UK: Cambridge University Press.

Haimowitz, S. (2003). *Learning to use vowels and consonants in written Hebrew*. Unpublished master's final project, the Department of Communications Disorders, Tel Aviv University.

Jones, N. K. (1991). Development of morphophonemic segments in children's mental representations of words. *Applied Psycholinguistics, 12*, 217–239.

Karmiloff-Smith, A. (1992). *Beyond modularity: A developmental perspective of cognitive science*. Cambridge, MA: MIT Press.

Kautzsch, E. (1910). *Gesenius' Hebrew grammar*. Revised by A. E. Cowley. Oxford, UK: Clarendon.

Khan, G. (1997). Tiberian Hebrew phonology. In Alan S. Kaye & Peter T. Daniels (Eds.), *Phonologies of Asia and Africa* (pp. 85–102). Winona Lake, IN: Eisenbrauns.

Koriat, A. (1985). Reading without vowels: Lexical access in Hebrew. In H. Bouma & D. G. Bouwhuis (Eds.), *Attention and performance, Vol. 10. Control of language processes* (pp. 227–242). Hillsdale, NJ: Lawrence Erlbaum Associates.

Koriat, A., Greenberg, N. S., & Goldshmid, Y. (1991). The missing-letter effect in Hebrew: Word frequency or word function? *Journal of Experimental Psychology: Learning, Memory and Cognition, 17*, 66–80.

Kutscher, E. Y. (1982). *A history of the Hebrew language*. Jerusalem: Magnes.

Lapidot, S. (2003). *Spelling and oral morphology in gradeschoolers with SLI*. Unpublished master's thesis, School of Education, Tel Aviv University, Tel Aviv, Israel.

Laufer, A., & Condax, I. (1981). The function of the epiglottis in speech. *Language and Speech, 24*, 24–39.

Levin, I. (2002). *Towards reading and writing; Report of the special committee* [in Hebrew]. Jerusalem: Ministry of Education.

Levin, I., & Korat, O., (1993). Sensitivity to phonological, morphological, and semantic cues in early reading and writing in Hebrew. *Merrill-Palmer Quarterly, 39*, 213–232.

Levin, I., Korat, O., & Amsterdamer, P. (1996). Emergent writing among kindergartners: Cross-linguistic commonalities and Hebrew-specific issues. In G. Rijlaarsdam, H. van der Bergh, & M. Couzijn (Eds.), *Current trends in writing research: Theories, models and methodology* (pp. 398–419). Amsterdam: Amsterdam University Press.

Levin, I., Patel, S., Margalit, T., & Barad, N. (2002). Letter names: Effect on letter saying, spelling and word recognition in Hebrew. *Applied Psycholinguistics, 23*, 269–300.

Levin, I., Ravid, D., & Rapaport, S. (1999). Developing morphological awareness and learning to write: A two-way street. In T. Nunes (Ed.), *Learning to read: An integrated view from research and practice* (pp. 77–104). Amsterdam: Kluwer.

Levin, I., Ravid, D., & Rapaport, S. (2001). Morphology and spelling among Hebrew-speaking children: From kindergarten to first grade. *Journal of Child language, 28*, 741–769.

Levin, I., Share, D. L., & Shatil, E. (1996). A qualitative-quantitative study of preschool writing: Its development and contribution to school literacy. In M. Levy & S. Ransdell (Eds.), *The science of writing* (pp. 271–293). Hillsdale, NJ: Lawrence Erlbaum Associates.

Levin, T., Shohamy, E., Spolsky, B., Levi-Keren, M., Inbar, O., & Shemesh, M. (2002). *Scholastic achievements of immigrant children*. Report submitted to the Israeli Ministry of Education.

Levin, I., & Tolchinsky-Landsmann, L. (1989). Becoming literate: Referential and phonetic strategies in early reading and writing. *International Journal of Behavioral Development, 12*, 369–384.

Loewenstein, M., & Kozminsky, E. (1999). The effect of morphological transparency of written Hebrew on the efficiency of reading [in Hebrew]. *Script, 1*, 127–142.

McCarthy, J. (1982). Prosodic templates, morphemic templates, and morphemic tiers. In H. van der Hulst & N. Smith (Eds.), *The structure of phonological representation, Part I*. Dordrecht, The Netherland: Foris, 191–223.

Navon, D., & Shimron, Y. (1984). Reading Hebrew: How necessary is the graphemic representation of vowels? In L. Henderson (Ed.), *Orthographies and reading: Perspectives from cognitive psychology, neuropsychology, and linguistics*. London: Lawrence Erlbaum Associates.

Olshtain, E., & Horenczyk, G. (Eds.). (2000). *Language, identity and immigration*. Jerusalem: The Hebrew University & Magnes Press.

Olson, D. (1994). *The world on paper*. Cambridge, UK: Cambridge University Press.

Rabin, H. (1972). *History of the Hebrew language*. Jerusalem: World Zionist Association.

Ravid, D. (1990). Internal structure constraints on new-word formation devices in Modern Hebrew. *Folia Linguistica, 24*, 289–346.

Ravid, D. (1995a). *Language change in child and adult Hebrew: A psycholinguistic perspective*. New York: Oxford University Press.

Ravid. D. (1995b). The acquisition of morphological junctions in Modern Hebrew. In H. Pishwa & K. Maroldt (Eds.), *The development of morphological systematicity: A cross linguistic perspective* (pp. 55–77). Tübingen, Germany: Gunter Narr.

Ravid, D. (1996). Accessing the mental lexicon: Evidence from incompatibility between representation of spoken and written morphology. *Linguistics, 34*, 1219–1246.

Ravid, D. (2001). Learning to spell in Hebrew: Phonological and morphological factors. *Reading and Writing, 14*, 459–485.

Ravid, D. (2002). Spelling errors in Hebrew: A developmental perspective [in Hebrew]. *Megamot, 32*, 29–57.

Ravid, D. (2003). A developmental perspective on root perception in Hebrew and Palestinian Arabic. In Y. Shimron (Ed.), *The processing and acquisition of root-based morphology* (pp. 293–319). Amsterdam: Benjamins.

Ravid, D., & Bar-On, A. (2001). The Semitic root in language acquisition. *GALA (Generative Approaches to Language Acquisition), 2001 Proceedings*. Lisbon, Portugal: University of Lisbon, Cidade Universitária - Faculdade de Letras.

Ravid, D., & Bar-On, A. (In press). Manipulating written Hebrew roots across development: The interface of semantic, phonological and orthographic factors. *Reading & Writing*.

Ravid, D., & Gillis, S. (2002). Teachers' perception of spelling patterns and children's spelling errors: A cross-linguistic perspective. In M. Neef, A. Neijt, and R. Sproat (Eds.), *Consistency in writing systems* (pp. 71–95). Tübingen, Germany: Niemeyer Verlag.

Ravid, D., & Kubi, E. (2003). What is a spelling error? The discrepancy between perception and reality. *Faits de Langue [special issue]. The dynamics of scripts: A multidisciplinary approach, 22*, 87–98.

Ravid, D., & Malenky, D. (2001). Awareness of linear and nonlinear morphology in Hebrew: A developmental study. *First Language, 21*, 25–56.

Ravid, D., & Shlesinger, Y. (2001). Vowel reduction in Modern Hebrew: Traces of the past and current variation. *Folia Linguistica, 35*, 371–397.

Ravid, D., & Zilberbuch, S. (2003). Morpho-syntactic constructs in the development of spoken and written Hebrew text production. *Journal of Child Language, 30*, 1–24.

Rendburg, G. A. (1997). Ancient Hebrew phonology. In Alan S. Kaye & Peter T. Daniels (Eds.), *Phonologies of Asia and Africa* (pp. 65–83). Winona Lake, IN: Eisenbrauns.

Schiff, R. (2002). They look similar, but they are different: Reading two morphological structures of Hebrew nouns. *First Language, 22*, 305–322.

Schiff, R. (2003). The effects of morphology and word length on the reading of Hebrew nominals. *Reading and Writing, 16*, 263–287.

Schiff, R., & Ravid, D. (2004). Vowel representation in written Hebrew: Phonological, orthographic and morphological contexts. *Reading and Writing, 17*, 245–265.

Schwarzwald, O. R. (2001). *Modern Hebrew. Languages of the world / materials* 127. Munich: Lincom Europa.

Schwarzwald, O. R. (2002). *Modern Hebrew morphology*. Tel Aviv: The Open University.

Schwarzwald, O. R., & Cohen-Gross, D. (2000). The frequent nominal patterns in Hebrew [in Hebrew]. In M. Horwitz (Ed.), *Contemporary journalistic Hebrew* (pp. 148–161). Tel Aviv: Mofet Institute, Reches.

Seidman, O. (2000). *Morphological and phonological perception and the development of writing from kindergarten to first grade*. Unpublished master's thesis, Department of Communications Disorders, Tel Aviv University.

Shany, M., Zeiger, T., & Ravid, D. (2001). Development and validation of Diagnostic tools for assessing basic processes in reading and spelling [in Hebrew]. *Script, 2*, 167–203.

Share, D. L., & Gur, T. (1999). How reading begins: A study of preschoolers' print identification strategies. *Cognition and Instruction, 17*, 177–213.

Share, D. L., & Levin, I. (1999). Learning to read and write in Hebrew. In M. Harris, and G. Hatano (Eds.), *Learning to read and write* (pp. 89–111). Cambridge, UK: Cambridge University Press.

Shapira, R. (2001). *Report of the Committee on Reading Instruction*. Jerusalem: The Parliamentary Education Committee and the Ministry of Education.

Shatil, E., Share, D. L., & Levin, I. (2000). On the contribution of kindergarten writing to Grade 1 literacy: A longitudinal study in Hebrew. *Applied Psycholinguistics, 21*, 1–21.

Shimron, J. (1993). The role of vowels in reading: A review of studies of English and Hebrew. *Psychological Bulletin, 114*, 52–67.

Shimron, J. (1999). The role of vowels signs in Hebrew: Beyond word recognition. *Reading and Writing, 11*, 301–319.

Shuval, J. (1996). Editorial: Two waves of Russian immigration: Comparative reference groups. *Israel Journal of Psychiatry and Related Science, 33*, 2–4.

Spencer, A. (1991). *Morphological theory*. Oxford, UK: Blackwell.

Teubal, H. (2002). An ecological approach to early literacy. In P. Klein & D. Givon (Eds.), *Language, learning and literacy in early childhood* (pp. 257–278). Tel Aviv: Ramot, Tel Aviv University Press.

Tolchinsky-Landsmann, L., & Levin, I. (1985). Writing in preschoolers: An age-related analysis. *Applied Psycholinguistics, 6*, 319–339.

Tolchinsky-Landsmann, L., & Levin, I. (1987). Writing in four to six year olds: Representation of semantic and phonological similarities and differences. *Journal of Child Language, 14*, 127–144.

Treiman, R. (1993). *Beginning to spell*. Oxford, UK: Oxford University Press.

Treiman, R., Zukowski, A., & Richmond-Welty, E. D. (1995). What happened to the "n" of *sink*? Children's spelling of final consonant clusters. *Cognition, 55*, 1–38.

Wahl, A. (2002). Approaches to reading. In P. Klein & D. Givon (Eds.), *Language, learning and literacy in early childhood* (pp. 279–303). Tel Aviv: Ramot, Tel Aviv University Press.

Weil, A., & Fromowitz, F. (1998). Awareness of spoken and written roots in 3rd graders [in Hebrew]. Unpublished seminar paper, Department of Communications Disorders, Tel Aviv University.

Weinberg, W. (1966). Spoken Israeli Hebrew: Trends in departure from classical phonology. *Journal of Semitic Studies, 11*, 40–68.

22

Persian Orthography and Its Relation to Literacy

Bahman Baluch
Middlesex University

Persian orthography, which is a modified version of the Arabic script, is used for transcribing the Persian (Farsi) language, which is the major language spoken in Iran. Persian is also one of the two (Farsi and Urdu) major languages spoken in Afghanistan, and the main language in Tajikestan, a former central Asian republic of the former Soviet Union. However, the Persian spoken in these countries and the script used to transcribe the spoken language, particularly in Tajikistan, have been influenced by local factors and borrowed words. The focus of this chapter is on the Persian spoken in the present-day Iran and its relationship with the orthography, henceforth referred to as Persian orthography. In particular, the emphasis is on how literacy acquisition by Persian beginner (and skilled) readers may be affected by peculiarities of Persian orthography. Arguably, very little systematic research has been conducted on cognitive processes involved in the reading of Persian. It is hoped that this article will stimulate such research. After presenting factors that influence literacy acquisition in Persian, we take up the question of whether there should be changes to Persian orthography.

INTRODUCTION

This chapter is divided into two sections: The first section deals with the Persian orthography and the nature of its phonological and morphological structure. These features are reviewed from a historical perspective followed by a discussion of how these historical changes have affected modern Persian. The second section deals with literacy acquisition and the nature of reading problems encountered by beginner and skilled readers. More specifically, we also examine the relationship between the written and spoken forms of language, potential difficulties the Persian orthography might present for the reader in the process of literacy acquisition, and the development of skilled reading. In the concluding part of this section, the question of whether introducing changes in the Persian orthography would minimize some of the difficulties being experienced by readers is raised.

PERSIAN, ITS ORTHOGRAPHY, MORPHOLOGY, AND PHONOLOGY

Modern Persian is derived from Indo-Iranian, one of the branches of the Indo-European languages. As shown in Fig. 22.1, the Indo-European language group split into Indo-Iranian and Indic language groups, from which most of the languages of India are derived. This development is estimated to have taken place around 1500 B.C.E. (Khanlari, 1979, 1995).

The old Persian, dating back to around 551 B.C.E. was written in cuneiform, the wedge-shaped characters used throughout much of the Middle Eastern countries. Around the historical period known as the middle Persian (around 331 B.C.E.) the Persians created their own writing system, known as *Pahlavi*, which remained in use until the Islamic conquest of the seventh century. What is referred to as modern Persian script is a transcription of Persian by a modified version of the Arabic script and therefore dates from the seventh century, marked by the Arabic conquest of Persia. Modern Persian is spoken by over 50 million people in Iran and another 5 million in Afghanistan. In Iran it is generally referred to as Farsi, but in Afghanistan as Dari. A variety of Persian called Tajik is spoken in Tajikistan; however, it is written in the Cyrillic alphabet (Khanlari, 1979, 1995).

The Persian Alphabet and Its Peculiarities

The Persian alphabet comprises 32 letters, the original 28 Arabic letters and an addition of four letters that represent Persian phonemes that are not represented by Arabic letters. The additional four letters are graphically identical to Arabic letters but differ only with the addition of dots to the Arabic letters. Examples are the Arabic letters ر /re/ and ز /zeh/ and the invented Persian letter ژ /jeh/. Furthermore, the addition of a stroke on the top of the Arabic letter ک /keh/ and the Persian invented letter گ /geh/ distinguishes these letters from the original Arabic letters. However, the rules of transcription and letter shapes for the invented letters follow that of Arabic writing. Indeed, it is a noticeable feature of the Arabic alphabet and invented Persian letters that there are only eight basic forms for letters. Other letters are simply a variant of one of these basic forms, with the difference of dot(s) in almost all cases. The following is the list of

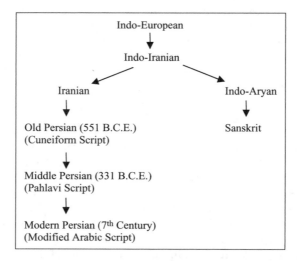

FIG. 22.1. Schematic presentation of the development of historical roots of the Persian language and script.

basic letter forms on which other letters of the alphabet are created with the addition of dot(s) above or below the basic letter shape: ب /beh/, ح /he/, د /dâl/, ز /re/, س /se/, ص / sât/, ع /eyin/, ط /tâ/.

Persian, like all Semitic scripts (Arabic and Hebrew), is written from right to left. Most letters are written in a joined fashion, rather like English cursive handwriting. However, some letters, depending on their position in the word, are never joined to a following letter. Although there are no uppercases or lowercases in Persian letters, there are many letters that have different shapes depending on their position in the word and whether or not they should be written connected to another letter. For example, the letter غ /geh/ takes on different forms depending on its position as initial غ or middle غ or final غ Word-final forms mark the word boundaries. Even though the transcription of Persian letters in cursive format is helpful in marking word boundaries, readers may experience difficulty in deciding word boundaries when they encounter letters that do not join other letters. The letters ا /alef/, د /dâl/, ذ /zâl/, ر /re/, ز /ze/, ژ /jeh/, and و /vâv/ have only one form, regardless of their position within the word. Like English, most words are separated by a space. However, in view of the cursive form of written Persian, if the first word ends in one of the characters that is left unjoined to a preceding letter (e.g., the word /mozd/) [wages], transcribed as ضد, the end of the word may not be as predictable as most other words in the text.

The Vowels and Diacritics

The number of vowels has been reduced from eight in old Persian to six (â, a, e, i, o, u) in modern Persian. Three vowels (a, e, and o), generally known as short vowels, are simply represented by diacritic superscript or subscript marks attached to the letters of the alphabet. The other three vowels are the long vowels (â, i, u) and are conveyed by letters of the alphabet (see Fig. 22.2 for examples of Persian words with vowels letters and diacritics).

There is a direct, one-to-one relationship between letters of the alphabet and phonemes in Persian. Moreover, Persian script, insofar as grapheme–phoneme correspondences are concerned, in its fully vowelised format is a highly regular orthography. For this reason, it is similar to Roman orthographies such as Turkish. However, similar to English, in Persian a phoneme may be presented by more than one letter of the alphabet. In addition, in practice, diacritic vowels are used in writings used by beginning readers and religious writings; vowels are almost always omitted from general text. Long vowels are never omitted from written text (see Fig. 22.2 for examples). This creates ambiguities, namely phonological, semantic, and visual–orthographic (Baluch, 1990, 1992).

Phonological and semantic ambiguity results when the reader is faced with a string of consonantal letters. For example, the consonantal string /krm/ can be pronounced with different vowel combinations resulting in five possible pronunciations and meanings /*kerm*/ [worm], /*karam*/ [generosity], /*kerem*/ [cream], /*krom*/ [chrome], and /*karm*/ [vine]. The manner in which a reader may eventually retrieve the correct pronunciation (and meaning) has been the subject of the research that is discussed in a subsequent section of this chapter. Adding to the confusion is the

	Persian Spelling	Transcription	Meaning
Vowel letter/â/	سال	/sal/	year
Diacritic /a/	سزد	/sard/	cold
No diacritic	سرد	/srd/	cold

FIG. 22.2. Examples of Persian words with vowel letters, diacritic vowels, and with no diacritics specified.

many meanings that one could still infer by adding the (absent) stress assignment (see next subsection). For example, in the preceding string, depending on stress assignment, one may read /karam/ to mean 'generosity' or with the stress assignment on the /a/ to mean 'I am deaf'.

Another possible source of ambiguity is visual. The absence of vowels in written Persian makes the words somewhat shorter. Thus there are fewer visual cues as to the identity of the word. Indeed, research on English has shown a direct relationship between word length and visual word recognition (see Weekes, 1997).

Stress Assignment and Colloquial Ambiguity

The rules of stress assignment and intonations in Persian have been discussed elsewhere (see, e.g., Lazard, 1992). What is important to note is that, although understanding these rules may contribute to phonological disambiguation of written Persian, by itself it falls short when faced with problems caused by colloquial ambiguity. The change in the spoken version, what is known as a 'Tehrani accent', has resulted in complete changes in stress assignments to a large corpus of words. For example, the word /miguyand/ [they say] undergoes a complete vowel change in colloquial language by being pronounced as /migan/; the stress assignment to the verb /xastan/ [to want] when used in written correct format would be /mixaham/ [I want]; with a Tehrani accent the stress is on the initial and final syllables resulting in /mixam/. Labelled as diglossia, the possible psychological impact of this dissociation between written and spoken language has been the subject of investigation (see, e.g., Hudson, 1992).

The Persian Morphological System

In spite of the fact that a considerable portion of the Persian lexicon is derived from Arabic roots, including the Arabic plural patterns, Persian morphology and orthography do not match perfectly. Persian morphology is an affixal system consisting mainly of suffixes and a few prefixes. Thus when it relates to Arabic words, two kinds of spellings and morphological processes are encountered by the reader. Figure 22.3 shows how the Arabic root system (a consonant string) is used for deriving nouns by the insertion of certain vowel patterns and the way it differs from a similar process in Persian.

In the preceding example, the Arabic plural form for ketâb is /kotob/, obtained by the root derivation system. In Persian, the plural for the lexical word /ketâb/ can be given as it is in (/kotob/), or it can be obtained just by the addition of the Persian plural morpheme /hâ/ = /ketâb+hâ/. Any new Persian word, however, can be pluralized only by the addition of the plural morpheme. In addition, because the plurals formed by the Arabic morphological system constitute a small portion of the Persian vocabulary (about 5%; Khanlari, 1995), it is not necessary to include them in the morphology; they are listed instead in the dictionary as irregular forms.

Root letter string	Arabic word/ meaning/spelling	Arabic plural/spelling
/k-t-b/	/ketâ b/ "book" كتاب	كتب
Root letter string	Persian word/meaning/spelling	Persian plural/spelling
/k-t-b/	/ketâ b/ "book" كتاب	كتابها

FIG. 22.3. Example of the root consonant string /ktb/ and the morphological processes in Arabic and Persian.

Persian word/ meaning	with suffix y/meaning	
/mard/ "man"	/mardy/	"a man" Noun+Indefinite marker
	/mardy/	"the man" Noun+Relative clause linking enclitic
	/mardy/	"you are man" Noun+Copula (second, singular)
	/mardy/	"manliness" Noun+derivational morpheme

FIG. 22.4.   Examples of morphological ambiguity in Persian depending on stress assignment.

Although the presence of suffixes may seem more helpful to Persian readers in the absence of short vowels, there are still many examples of morphological ambiguity. For example, the root word written as /mrd/, when pronounced with the /a/, reads as /mard/ [man]. When the suffix *y* is added and read with the short vowel, it reads as /mardy/ [a man] (see Fig. 22.4 for examples). In addition, the same spelling also can give rise to the morphological ambiguities depending on stress assignment, as shown with an example in Fig. 22.4.

The Role of the *Ezafeh* Morpheme

An issue not discussed in the past by researchers on Persian is the difficulties that readers may encounter in determining phrase boundaries, especially the boundaries of noun phrases. Determining phrase boundaries is difficult because Persian is a verb-final language and there are no markers to distinguish the subject or the objects in a sentence (with the exception of the specific object marker *râ*). For example, in English one adds the suffix to the phrase 'John's book' to indicate that the book belongs to John. In Persian, a phrase to indicate that a book belongs to, say, Ali, would be written as /ktâb/ /ali/ and reads as 'book ali'. What is missing is the *ezafeh* morpheme, usually an unwritten vowel pronounced in the latter example as /e/, which is a short vowel and is therefore not written in text. The *ezafeh* only appears in written text after the vowels /â/ and /u/. Thus, without any clear markers to determine the phrase boundaries, and without the ezafeh (in most cases) to link the phrase constituents, Persian readers may face difficulty in determining meaning and end of phrases.

Summary

In today's Iran, a modified version of Arabic script is used to transcribe the spoken language. Both Arabic and modified Arabic used to transcribe Persian are argued to be phonologically opaque because short vowels are omitted from the script. It may also be argued to be visually opaque as most letters differ only with the presence or absence of dots. However, although in then fully vowelised format Persian and Arabic are highly regular in the direction of grapheme–phoneme correspondences, the same is not true for phoneme–grapheme relationships. Thus there is considerable ambiguity that is due to which letter should be used in relation to a specific phoneme.

Adding to these there are further problems that are due to the importation of Arabic script to fit an Indo-European language. Most noticeable are the irregularities of the imported Arabic words and the use of both Persian and Arabic morphological processes in the derivation of various variants of the root morpheme. Moreover, in view of the grammatical nature of Persian and the absence of morpheme *ezafeh* there is clear difficulty in determining phrase boundaries. Added to this is also the issue of the possible impact on literacy dissociation of colloquial Persian, the 'Tehrani accent', and the standard Persian.

THE IMPACT OF PERSIAN ORTHOGRAPHY
ON LITERACY ACQUISITION

Introduction

In this section the issue of cognitive processes involved in literacy acquisition of Persian is reviewed. The question pursued here is the extent to which the peculiarities outlined in the previous section, in relation to Persian orthography, affect literacy acquisition. According to the recent statistics by the office of National Statistics of the Islamic Republic of Iran, the literacy rate is 76% and the illiterate population stands at 10.6 million.

Of the main orthographic and phonological factors that may be thought to affect literacy in Persian one may identify the grapheme–phoneme regularity, the phoneme–grapheme ambiguity, and the absence of short vowels in written text. These peculiarities of Persian have been the subject of limited investigation (Arab-Moghaddam & Senechal, 2001; Baluch, 1990, 1993; Gholamain & Geva, 1999). Other factors such as the preponderance of dots to differentiate letters, letter similarity, and variety of letter shapes, the omission of stress symbols, the absence of the marker *ezafeh* as indication of phrase boundary, the morphological structure of Persian, and the issue of diglossia have yet to be investigated.

Grapheme–Phoneme Regularity and Literacy

One of the most noticeable aspects of Semitic scripts, and in particular Persian orthography, is the regularity of grapheme- (letter-) to-sound relationships. The issue of whether such regularity may have an impact on learning to read has been investigated in greater length among orthographies other than Persian that differ in the manner in which they represent the phonology of the spoken language (see, for example, Geva, 1995). The term 'orthographic depth' is used to distinguish orthographies on a continuum ranging from shallow to opaque (Baluch, 1993; Baluch & Besner, 1991; Frost, Katz, & Bentin, 1987). Implicit in this is the assumption that some alphabetic scripts labelled as shallow, like Persian, Hebrew and Arabic, and the Roman scripts like Turkish and Italian, have simple grapheme–phoneme relationships whereas other scripts like English, labelled as deep, have more complicated grapheme–phoneme structures. In terms of literacy acquisition, the argument goes that shallow orthographies are easier to acquire than deep orthographies because 'the development of word-based processes in different languages might vary as a function of orthographic regularity' (Gholamain & Geva, 1999, p. 184). This script-dependent hypothesis has found support from various studies on deep and shallow orthographies that have shown that shallow orthographies have lower incidents of reading disability than do deep orthographies (e.g., Goswami, Schneider & Scheurich, 1999; Lindgren, de-Renzi, & Richman, 1985; Wydell & Butterworth, 1999). There is also evidence that word recognition in terms of oral naming is easier in shallow orthographies such as vowelised Hebrew (Geva, 1995), and Turkish (Oney & Golden, 1984; Oney, Peter, & Katz, 1997; Raman, 1999).

However, an alterative hypothesis, the 'central-processing hypothesis', maintains that skilled reading depends on the efficient functioning of working memory, naming speed, and lexical processes. If these cognitive and linguistic skills are deficient, the individual is likely to experience difficulties in the acquisition of literacy skills, regardless of the orthography involved (e.g., Bowers, 1995; Bowers, Golden, Kennedy, & Young, 1994). There is of course a possibility of a compromise between these two positions, namely, that there are some basic mechanisms that have to be in place for efficient functioning of reading performance, such as an efficient working memory. What enhances the functioning of this system is how transparent the orthography of a given language is (see, for example, Baluch, 1990; Geva, 1995; Baluch & Danaye-Tousie, 2005).

Evidence From Persian

An extensive study by Gholamain and Geva (1999) examined the linguistic, cognitive, and basic reading skills of 70 Persian children from immigrant families in Canada in Grades 1 to 5. These children were learning to read concurrently English and Persian. Gholamain and Geva (1999) argued that, because Persian has a reliable one-to-one grapheme–phoneme correspondence, it should be much easier for the children to master the grapheme–phoneme correspondence rules and therefore be able to read and decode Persian words with a relatively greater degree of accuracy in the early grades than might be the case for reading English. If confirmed, this hypothesis, of course, would support the script-dependent hypothesis. Indeed, in line with this prediction, it was found that with only 3 hr of Persian literacy instructions per week, once the children had mastered the rules they were able to decode even unfamiliar complex Persian words. However, Gholamain and Geva (1999) also reported data in support of the central-processing hypothesis in that they found that children who performed better on measures of reading and cognitive skills in English, their primary language, were more likely to perform better in Persian, their second language. In particular, the role played by working memory and rapid automatised naming was highly correlated between the two languages.

There is, however, a methodological question regarding the research just described and indeed any research using bilingual participants, namely, there are the possible effects of learning strategies used in one language being generalised to a second language. The immigrant Persian children studied in Gholamain and Geva (1999) were learning Persian as a second language in Canada. For example, Mumtaz and Humphreys (2001) reported that Pakistani children learning Urdu (which, like Persian, is transcribed by a modified version of the Arabic script) and English make errors that are more indicative of over-generalisation of strategies used in one language to a second language.

There is very little, if any, published work that has examined the development of reading skills among monolingual Persian children learning to read and write in their homeland. Two unpublished master's dissertations are the only sources of data that could shed some light on reading performance of monolingual Persian children. Amini (1997) studied 120 normal and dyslexic first- and second-grade elementary school children on a battery of 20 cognitive tests. Amini concluded that there are greater similarities between factors affecting poor reading in Persian than those reported in the literature on reading English. She argued that her data on Persian children are more in line with the central-processing hypothesis. The problem with Amini's study is that there are no reports on how the batteries of tests used in her study were developed and validated for her investigation.

Shirazi's (1996) master's dissertation on monolingual Persian children may also be taken as a further support for the central-processing hypothesis. Shirazi's research was aimed at 67 Persian children, 35 girls and 32 boys 6–7 years old.

Shirazi administered the tests of rapid naming, phonological awareness, verbal working memory span, and oral reading to first-grade children in a school in Tehran during the first month of their reading instruction, and later tested the same children 3 months later. Shirazi reported that there is a significant relationship between phonological awareness and oral reading speed. She further argued that accuracy in reading and improvement in phonological awareness are highly related to each other. Moreover, those children performing significantly better on phonological awareness were also ranked higher on their reading performance by their teacher. Although Shirazi's sample is small and probably not representative of the children in Iran, it is nevertheless a good attempt to develop a Persian version of cognitive tests used in western countries to conduct research on Persian readers.

Phoneme–Grapheme Ambiguity and Literacy

The regular grapheme–phoneme correspondences in Persian may facilitate oral reading performance; however, the same is not true about the ability to spell. This is because, in Persian, the same phoneme may be represented by more than one grapheme (polygraphy). Thus the expectation is that, in order to decide on the use of the correct grapheme for the word's spelling, Persian readers may have to rely on their lexical knowledge. Therefore a major problem encountered in children's spelling is letter substitution.

Azzam (1989) reported many errors by Arab children in using the correct letters when engaged in a spelling task; for example, the errors made on the choice between the letters ز and ذ, both of which are pronounced /ze/. One reason for the errors made by Arab children may be due to the extensive reliance on phonological strategies when dealing with the spelling task. This is because at the grapheme–phoneme level there is a very transparent relationship in Arabic. Hence children experiencing regularities at grapheme–phoneme level for oral reading may be less likely to use their lexical knowledge for spelling words and hence the kind of errors reported in Azzam's (1989) study. The question is whether the same is true for readers of Persian. Cossu (1995) examined possible discrepancies between reading and spelling strategies for Italian children. Cossu (1995) argued that, because Italian is transparent in both grapheme–phoneme and phoneme–grapheme correspondences, this should encourage parallel strategies and similar level of performance. Cossu (1995), however, reported that reading accuracy is significantly better than spelling accuracy for first- and second-grade Italian children. This indicates that although Italian is a very transparent script it does not necessarily encourage parallel strategies in reading and spelling.

Oney et al. (1997) compared reading and spelling performance of English and Turkish readers in first, second, and fifth grades and found that orthographic transparency determines the degree to which readers use phonology during word recognition and suggests that readers become less dependent on phonological mediation with experience and that this reduction is more rapid for readers of opaque orthographies. Thus for reading English the fact that both grapheme–phoneme and phoneme–grapheme correspondences are opaque there is a greater reliance on non-phonological strategies, whereas for readers of transparent Turkish this non-reliance may take longer.

Evidence From Persian

In an extensive study, Arab-Moghaddam and Senechal (2001) examined orthographic and phonological processing skills in bilingual Persian–English children, targeting a relatively large sample of 55 bilingual children living in Canada. They argued that because Persian is polygraphy but not polyphony, whereas English is both polygraphy and polyphony, it should encourage different phonological and orthographic strategies in literacy acquisition of the two languages. In the case of oral reading, Arab-Moghaddam and Senechal (2001) found that both phonological and orthographic skills were predictors of good performance in both English and Persian. However, Arab-Moghaddam and Senechal (2001) reported that, first, Persian children were better able to spell words in English than they did in Persian, and, second, the orthographic skills were a key predictor of their spelling ability. The argument put forward was that the nature of the Persian orthography encourages children to adopt different strategies when spelling words. Spelling words in Persian is inefficient if an analytic strategy is used, and perhaps the realisation that this is an inappropriate strategy comes in at a later stage compared with that of English.

Phonological Ambiguity Due to the Omission of Short Vowels

As outlined in the section titled "The Vowels and Diacritics," the short vowels in Persian are used only for beginner readers. Thus the reader is faced with a string of mainly consonantal spelling (Baluch, 1990, 1992). The expectation is that, by the time the diacritic marks are omitted, the reader has developed appropriate strategies for cognitive processes in reading and a well-established visual orthographic lexicon (Baluch, 1992). However, the fact that vowels are absent from written text may indeed cause ambiguity of various degrees for readers of Persian.

Evidence From Persian

Baluch and Shahidi (1991) studied naming of words with consonantal spelling and matched words with vowel letters by Persian children with the mean age of 8.4 years. The children were taught to read under the traditional system of first learning to read words with the use of diacritics followed by omission of diacritics. The results showed that there were significantly more errors made to opaque words (e.g., بچه /bch/, pronounced as /baceh/ [child]) compared with transparent words (e.g., بازی /bâzi/ [play]). Moreover, the time taken to name a list of words with consonantal spelling was significantly slower than the time in naming a list of words with vowel letter spellings.

Baluch (1990, 1993) reported similar findings when the oral naming of consonantal words and vowel letter words was examined by skilled adult Persian readers (see Table 22.1).

For vowel letter spellings, even of a high-frequency nature, there was a 65-ms difference in oral naming than for consonantal spellings, a difference that was even greater for low-frequency words. Moreover, a consonantal word with multiple meanings was named significantly slower than a consonantal word with a unique spelling. These findings demonstrate significant difficulty in naming consonantal spelling by use of phonological processes.

TABLE 22.1

Mean Reaction-Time Latencies, Standard Deviations (in Parentheses), and Error Percentages to High- and Low-Frequency Persian Words and to Opaque-Ambiguous and Opaque-Unique Persian Words

Spelling Type	Opaque	Transparent	Difference
High Frequency			
Mean (*SD*)	615 (137)	550 (122)	65
Error (%)	5.8	2.5	3.3
Low Frequency			
Mean (*SD*)	652.5 (151)	565.9 (110)	86.6
Error (%)	14.6	4.16	10.4
	Opaque (Polysemous)	*Opaque (Monosemous)*	*Difference*
Mean (*SD*)	600 (124)	551 (94)	49
Error (%)	4.16	2.8	1.36

Abu-Rabia (1997) came to similar conclusions in relation to reading Arabic. Abu-Rabia (1997) investigated the effect of vowels on reading accuracy of poor and skilled native Arabic readers in Israel. The materials used were narrative stories and newspaper articles. His subjects read Arabic narrative stories and newspaper articles under four reading conditions: vowelised text, unvowelised text, vowelised word naming, and unvowelised word naming. The results showed that vowels and text contexts were important variables that facilitate word recognition in poor as well as skilled readers in Arabic orthography. Vowels speeded word naming and context facilitated disambiguation of polysemous words.

The question may then be raised as to the costs and benefits of having the diacritics omitted from text for both beginning and skilled readers (Baluch, 1992).

Other Possible Factors That Affect Literacy Acquisition of Persian

Greater letter similarity and confusion in distinguishing between different letter shapes and their identity, the absence of *ezafeh* as markers of word boundary, and diglossia in Persian, that is, the strong dissociation of standard written Persian and colloquial Persian (Tehrani accent), are other sources of ambiguity encountered by Persian readers.

The greater letter similarities of Arabic have been noted by Azzam (1989). She reported that Arab readers have difficulty distinguishing between different letters (e.g., ز and ظ) and between consonantal and vowel letters (vowel diacritic و and vowel letter و). Moreover, Azzam reported on the errors made by Arab children in reading words with letters that change shape depending on their position in the word. She reported that children were confused when reading long vowel /a/ with alef ا or yeh ى for instance, children may read متا rather than متى

In relation to diglossia, Abu-Rabia (2000) examined the influence of exposure to literary Arabic on reading comprehension in Arabic-speaking children. He concluded that exposure of preschool children to literary Arabic in diglossic situations enhances their reading ability in the first and second grades. Ravid (1996) came to similar conclusions when examining reading performance of both children and adult readers of Hebrew. There is no reported research of a similar kind in Persian.

CONCLUDING REMARKS

In short, the arguments put forward in this section of this chapter suggest that perhaps the only beneficial aspect of Persian orthography, insofar as literacy acquisition is concerned, is a relatively easier task enjoyed by Persian beginning readers in oral naming. The ambiguity at phoneme–grapheme level and the absence of short vowels, in addition to a host of yet uninvestigated factors associated with Persian orthography, may be other significant sources that affect literacy acquisition.

A final note that may be made here is whether some changes should be introduced into Persian orthography. More than a couple of decades ago Nickjoo (1979) highlighted some of the key features of the Persian scripts, namely, letter similarities, phoneme–grapheme ambiguity, absence of vowels, and many variants of the position-dependent letters. Nickjoo (1979) argued that such peculiarities of written Persian have implications for literacy and argued for the abolition of the Persian alphabet and the creation of a Latinised version of Persian. Nevertheless, Nickjoo (1979) acknowledged that the political and religious considerations may be a serious hindrance for any such reform. Similar political and religious considerations were also heavily present in relation to the transformation of Turkish writing system. However, in 1931, Kamal Ataturk, the father of modern Turkey, with the help of the slogan "the

Turkish language has been a prisoner for centuries and is now casting off its chains" set in motion a change of Turkish script from Arabic to Roman (Raman, 1999). Moreover, an attempt was made to make the correspondence as reliable and as transparent as possible. Although the political and religious debates may be the key factors affecting decisions on whether to change the Persian alphabet, there is also an interesting possibility for a more scientific argument to enter the equation. Because a generation of Turkish readers have now experienced reading in the Romanised script, a comparison of literacy acquisition by both beginning and skilled readers of Turkish and Persian language may shed more light as to the possible impact of orthography change on literacy acquisition.

REFERENCES

Abu-Rabia, S. (1997). Reading in Arabic orthography: The effect of vowels and context on reading accuracy of poor and skilled native Arabic readers. *Reading and Writing, 9*, 65–78.

Abu-Rabia, S. (2000). Effects of exposure to literary Arabic on reading comprehension in a diglossic situation. *Reading and Writing, 13*, 147–157.

Amini, M. (1997). *Differences between normal and dyslexic children in reading and writing Persian texts.* Unpublished master's dissertation, College of Rehabilitation Sciences, Tehran, Iran.

Arab-Moghaddam, N., & Senechal, M. (2001). Orthographic and phonological processing skills in reading and spelling in Persian/English bilinguals. *International Journal of Behavioral Development, 25*, 140–147.

Azzam, R. (1989). Orthography and reading of the Arabic language. In P. G. Aaron & R. M. Joshi (Eds.), *Reading and writing disorders in different orthographic systems* (pp. 203–218). Dordrecht, The Netherlands: Kluwer Academic.

Baluch, B. (1990). Word recognition in Persian. *Baranoosh Scientific Quarterly, 1*(1), 3–6.

Baluch, B. (1992). Reading with and without vowels: What are the psychological consequences? *Journal of Social and Evolutionary Systems, 15*, 95–104.

Baluch, B. (1993). Lexical decisions in Persian: A test of the orthographic depth hypothesis. *International Journal of Psychology, 28*, 19–27.

Baluch, B., & Besner, D. (1991). Visual word recognition: Evidence for strategic control of lexical and nonlexical routines in oral reading. *Journal of Experimental Psychology, Learning, Memory and Cognition, 17*, 644–651.

Baluch, B., & Danaye-Tousie, M. (2005, January). *Developmental dyslexia as a function of opaqueness and transparency of a word's spelling: Evidence from Persian.* Presented at the meeting of the Experimental Psychology Society, London.

Baluch, B., & Shahidi, S. (1991). Visual word recognition in beginning readers of Persian. *Perceptual and Motor Skills, 72*, 1327–1331.

Bowers, P. G. (1995). Tracing symbol naming speed's unique contributions to reading disabilities over time. *Reading and Writing, 7*, 189–216.

Bowers, P. G., Golden, J., Kennedy, A., & Young, A. (1994). Limits upon orthographic knowledge due to processes indexed by naming speed. In V. W. Berninger (Ed.), *The varieties of orthographic knowledge, 1: Theoretical and developmental issues* (pp. 173–218). Dordrecht, The Netherlands: Kluwer Academic.

Cossu, G. (1995). Acquisition of reading and written spelling in a transparent orthography: Two non parallel processes? *Reading and Writing, 7*, 9–22.

Frost R., Katz, L., & Bentin, S. (1987). Strategies for visual word recognition and orthographical depth: A multilingual comparison. *Journal of Experimental Psychology: Human Perception and Performance, 13*, 104–115.

Geva, E. (1995). Orthographic and cognitive processing in learning to read English and Hebrew. In I. Taylor & D. R. Olson (Eds.), *Scripts and literacy: Reading and learning to read alphabets, syllabaries and characters* (pp. 277–291). Dordrecht, The Netherlands: Kluwer Academic.

Gholamain, M., & Geva, E. (1999). Orthographic and cognitive factors in the concurrent development of basic reading skills in English and Persian. *Language Learning, 49*, 183–217.

Goswami, U., Schneider, W., & Scheurich, B. (1999). Picture naming deficits in developmental dyslexia in German. *Developmental Science, 2*, 53–58.

Hudson, A. (1992). Diglossia: A bibliographic review. *Language in Society, 21*, 611–674.

Khanlari, P. N. (1979). *The history of Persian language (Vol. 1).* New Delhi, India: New Delhi Press.

Khanlari, P. (1995). *Tarikh-e Zaban-e Farsi* [History of the Persian Language]. Tehran, Iran: Simorgh Press.

LaBerge, D., & Samuels, S. J. (1974). Toward a theory of automatic information processing in reading. *Cognitive Psychology, 2*, 293–323.

Lazard, G. (1992). *A Grammar of Contemporary Persian.* Costa Mesa, CA: Mazda Publishers.

Lindgren, S. D., de-Renzi, E., & Richman, L. C. (1985). Cross-national comparisons of developmental dyslexia in Italy and the United States. *Child Development, 56*, 1404–1417.

Mumtaz, S., & Humphreys, G. W. (2001). The effects of bilingualism on learning to read English: Evidence from the contrast between Urdu–English bilingual and English monolingual children. *Journal of Research in Reading, 24*, 113–134.

Nickjoo, M. (1979, May). A century of struggle for the reform of the Persian script. *The Reading Teacher*, 926–929.

Oney, B., & Goldman, S. R. (1984). Decoding and comprehension skills in Turkish and English: Effects of the regularity of grapheme-phoneme correspondences. *Journal of Educational Psychology, 76*, 557–567.

Oney, B., Peter, M., & Katz, L. (1997). Phonological processing in printed word recognition: Effects of age and writing system. *Scientific Studies of Reading, 1*, 65–83.

Raman, I. (1999). *Single word naming in a transparent orthography*. Unpublished Ph.D. thesis, Middlesex University, England.

Raman, I., Baluch, B., & Sneddon, P. (1996). What is the cognitive systems preferred route for deriving phonology from print? *European Psychologist, 1*, 221–227.

Ravid, D. (1996). Accessing the mental lexicon: Evidence from incompatibility between representation of spoken and written morphology. *Linguistics, 34*, 1219–1246.

Shirazi, T. S. (1996). Phonological awareness as an important predictor of reading acquisition in Persian speaking children. Unpublished master's dissertation, University of Rehabilitation and Social Welfare, Tehran, Iran.

Weekes, B. S. (1997). Differential effects of number of letters on word and nonword naming latency. *Quarterly Journal of Experimental Psychology: Human Experimental Psychology, 50A*, 439–456.

Wydell, T. N., & Butterworth, B. (1999). A case study of an English-Japanese bilingual with monolingual dyslexia. *Cognition, 70*, 273–305.

23

Literacy Acquisition in Korean Hangul: Investigating the Perceptual and Phonological Processing of Good and Poor Readers

Jeesun Kim and Chris Davis
The University of Melbourne

In this chapter we explore the role that the Korean alphabetic–syllabic writing system (Hangul) may play in the development of literacy by specifically considering its influence on good and poor readers. This discussion is presented in the context of research programs that have tried to determine whether a particular orthographic system may play a role in acquiring literacy. It must be recognized that different writing systems are often associated with different cultures that differ in the emphasis they place on the importance of literacy and education. In addition, the learning environments and teaching methods also differ from society to society. Given that so many factors can vary across different language contexts, the approach that we have taken has been to develop profiles of good and poor readers and to compare them across different languages. That is, we start by examining perceptual processes and move up to tasks that involve language processing. Somewhat surprisingly, it turned out that the performance of good and poor readers on perceptual tasks appears to vary from language to language whereas the association between poor reading skill and poor phonological processing is more constant.

THE KOREAN HANGUL WRITING SYSTEM

Korean Hangul has moved away from a writing convention based on considerations of phonemic transparency to one that emphasizes morphophonemics (see Kim-Renaud, 1997; Perfetti, 2003). If Korean orthography followed a phonemic system, then in a Hangul stem with a final consonant followed by a vowel, the intervocalic consonant would be shifted to the following syllable. For example, to maximize phonological transparency, the stem "flower" /k'ot/ would be written 꼳 (see the appendix for a list of Hangul letters and sounds). The form "flower" + agent marker /i/ (/k'o.chi/), would be written 꼬치. In writing it this way, the morphological derivation will be obscured. In modern Korean however, the existence of the two morphemes is preserved by denoting "flower" as 꽃 and "flower" + agent marker as 꽃이 (see below for more on how Hangul letter are written together).

377

In the following sections, we outline the different levels over which the Korean orthographic system might make a difference in learning and processing written text. We describe these processes from a bottom-up perspective for the sake of convenience although it must be remembered that reading and writing are interactive processes.

THE ROLE OF SCRIPT FORMAT IN READING DEVELOPMENT

In this section we present a general outline of some features of the Korean alphabet and then describe how these might play a role in reading development.

The Korean Alphabet

The invention of the writing system is traditionally ascribed to King Sejong (ca.1418–1450) and his advisors. It was named Hangul by Chu Si-gyŏng (1876–1914). Korean Hangul is based on a design principle that gives importance to the letter shapes. Originally the writing system consisted of 28 basic letters, with each letter formed very simply and distinctly (see the appendix for a chart of Hangul vowels and consonants). Currently, Korean has 14 basic consonants and 10 basic vowels. The construction of these characters was intended to relate the sounds they represented, with each of the five basic letter formats standing for a consonant pronounced depending on the place of articulation; the remaining consonants were derived from these by adding strokes (e.g., a line is added for aspiration, see Fig. 23.1). Each letter is visually distinctive and is composed of one to four strokes, mostly vertical or horizontal straight lines and one circle character, with vowels and consonants having distinct shapes. Consonants and vowels are written in a fixed CVC order.

Visual Format

Given the properties of written Korean just described, one reason why a mild visual deficit may not lead to poor reading ability is because of the distinctiveness of the letters, their syllabic arrangement (see subsequent discussion), and their intrinsic consonant and vowel ordering. These features of Hangul may also facilitate visual grouping, a process thought to be faulty in dyslexic readers (Lewis & Frick, 1999).

The Partial-Alphabetic Principle and the Role of Hangul

Many features of Hangul make letter-to-sound mapping easy to learn and at the same time make letter recognition a relatively simple task (i.e., "graphemic awareness" also needs to be considered in learning grapheme-to-phoneme correspondences). First, letter names have a

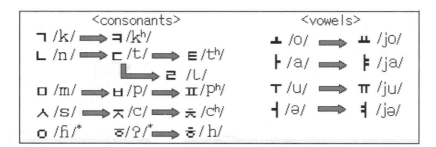

FIG. 23.1.   The design of Hangul consonant letters as based on the Hunmin *chŏng'ŭm* (훈민정음) 1446. *Letter is now obsolete.

consistent link with letter sounds because the names of the vowels match their pronunciation; for example, 아 /a/ is the name of ㅏ and its sound ("ㅇ" does not have any sound as an initial consonant in a syllable). The consonant letter names all consist of two syllables (CV and CVC) such that the first syllable starts with the letter sound with the vowel /i/, and the second syllable ends with the sound for the letter with the value it has as a final consonant in a syllable. There is constraint on what sound a consonant can have in a syllable- or word-final position. For example, the letter name of ㄱ /k/ is 기역 (i.e., 기 + 역), ㄴ /n/ is 니은, ㄷ /t/ is 디귿.

The Hangul alphabet is unique in that the consonantal letters were designed to partially indicate the shapes of the articulators, that is, it is a featural writing system (see Kim, 1997; Sampson, 1985). For example, the letters for the sounds /n/ and /t/ are similar because the sounds have a similar place of articulation. They differ in that the letter for /t/ has an extra top stroke to indicate the blocking of the nasal passage. Hangul consonants are divided into five classes corresponding roughly to the place of articulation (bilabial, apical, sibilant, velar, and laryngeal). These consonants are represented by stylized depictions of the articulations involved. For instance, the symbols for /n/ or /t/ show the tongue tip raised up to touch the front of the palate, whereas the symbol for /k/ indicates that the back of the tongue touches the rear of the palate.

Consistency of Letter and Sound Mappings

Another factor that has long been considered to play a substantial role in both learning to read and spell is the degree of regularity or phonological transparency of the writing system (e.g., Cossu, Shankweiler, Liberman, Katz, & Tola, 1988). In general, the mapping of grapheme to phoneme in Hangul is transparent except for sound alternations that are often predictable from context. However, as mentioned in the previous subsection, there are circumstances under which different phonemes are realized in different sound environments, although the core referent remains the same, for instance, 옷 /ot/ [clothes]; 옷안 /o.tan/ [garment lining]; 옷에 /o.se/ [on clothes]; 옷속 /os.s'ok/ [inside clothes]; 옷농 /on.noŋ/ [clothes chest]; 옷만 /on.man/ [clothes only]. What is interesting is that the spelling of the base morpheme (clothes) remains the same (옷), even though this form has different phonological realizations, depending on context. This situation also applies to a variety of morphophonological rules, for example, palatalization, 솥이 "sot^h-i" [cauldron + nom) → /so.c^{h}i/; neutralization of coda obstruents, 부엌 "pu-ek^h" [kitchen] → /pu-ək/; liason, 앞이 "ap^h-i" [front + nom] → /a.p^{h}i/; aspiration of lenis obstruents adjacent to /h/, 법학 "pep.hak" [study of law] → /pə.p^{h}ak/; tensification of lenis obstruents, 법대 "pep.te" [law school] → /pəp.t'ɛ/; nasalization of obstruents, 국민 "kuk-min" [citizens] → /kuŋ.min/; simplification of coda clusters, 값진 "kaps-cin" [precious] → /kap.c'in/; nasalization of labiolabial plosives, 집문 "cip-mun" [house gate] → /cim.mun/; and lateralization of /n/, 진리 "cin-li" [truth] → /cil.li/.

Another instance of a mismatch between orthography and phonology arises because of the constraint that, out of the 19 consonant phonemes, only 8 can occur in the final position in a syllable or a word. In all then, the relationship between initial phonemes and graphemes is almost entirely regular, but the relationship between final phonemes and graphemes is regulated by the morphophonological properties of the language. Thus initially it should be easier to learn to pronounce and spell word-initial segments compared with word-final ones. Moreover, when a language has a pervasive agglutinative morphology, as does Korean, the regularities of affix types can provide cues to an understanding of semantic properties that are useful for reading and writing.

Syllabic Structure and Representation

There are other properties that relate print and sound beside the regularity of grapheme-to-phoneme mapping. For instance, the "granularity" or coarseness of what sound (e.g., syllable,

FIG. 23.2.   An example of the syllable format. Note that vertical vowels are written next to consonants whereas the horizontal vowels are written underneath.

word) is represented by an orthographic unit is important. In terms of the granularity, Korean Hangul presents a unique case, for it is an alphabetic syllabary, with alphabetic *jamo* (e.g., consonant–vowel graphemes representing phonemes, ㅎ, ㅏ, ㄴ, ㄱ, ㅜ, ㄱ, ㅇ, ㅡ) organized into *eumjeol*, orthographic syllables (한, 국; see also Fig. 23.2). That is, when written together, Hangul alphabetic characters are grouped into square blocks that represent syllables, with each block separated with a larger space between *eojeol* (words), that is, a sequence of *eumjeols* is grouped into *eojeol* (한국의 열). Although it is not clear whether the syllabic aspects of the orthographic representation will have a moderating influence on phonological processing problems in beginning Korean readers, one study has shown that it does have an influence on the processes involved in reading aloud. In a study that investigated students learning Korean, Kim and Sohn (1986) showed that oral reading time was, on average, more than two times faster when the script was written in the standard syllable-block format compared with when it was written in a linear format (like Roman script).

Number of Sounds and Their Structure

The final property of Korean that we consider with regard to possible language-specific effects on reading development concerns the idea that orthographic processing is constrained by phonological structure. The first thing to point out is that the phonological structure of Korean is more restricted than that of English. For example, in Korean, there are no clusters at the beginning of the syllable and there are only a limited number of consonant clusters in word-final positions. There is also a constraint regarding which consonants can appear in syllable-final position. Syllables consist of initial, medial, and final letters, in which initial letters are consonants or a null character; medials are vowels or diphthongs; and final letters are one or two consonants or left empty. That is, a phonological syllable can consist of (C1) (S) V (C3), where the parentheses designate optionality; C1 is any of the consonants sounds shown in the appendix other than the velar nasal /ŋ/; S is one of the semivowels (/w, j/); and C3 is an unreleased variant of any of the lenis stops /p/, /t/, /k/, one of the three nasals /m/, /n/, /ŋ/, or the liquid /l/ or /s/ only before a word or suffix beginning /s, s/. Compared with English, this more restricted set of phonemes may be of help to beginning Korean readers.

There are of course a number of other properties of Korean phonology that may influence literacy acquisition. For instance, work by Yoon, Bolger, Kwon, and Perfetti (1999) suggests that, unlike English readers, Korean readers are not sensitive to rime units. Rather, it is argued that Korean readers are sensitive to the syllable body (onset plus vowel). It is suggested that because these preferences are also found in judgments of spoken words then the difference between languages must be at the linguistic level, at which the two languages have different syllable structures. Given that phonological structure can guide orthographic intuitions, the particular syllable structure of Korean may mean that Korean readers may not be very sensitive to phonological segments (particularly in the rime). Results germane to this prediction are described in the next section.

In sum, the following properties of Hangul may make reading Korean different from that of other languages: visual format, featural cues, phonological transparency, and syllable structure. The following section reviews the research of Kim and her colleagues (Kim & Davis, 2004a, 2004b; Kim, Davis, Burnham & Luksaneeyanawin, 2004; Kim & Yi, 1999) who have investigated the performance of good and poor Korean readers on processing tasks that ranged from making simple perceptual discriminations to pronouncing words and nonwords.

There are two aspects of these studies of good and poor readers that are important to note. The first is that the selection of the reader groups was based on reading tests that examined a range of reading skills (comprehension, syntax, and word knowledge), so the poor readers were poor in a number of skills. The second noteworthy feature is that performance measures used for studying the Korean readers were also obtained for good and poor readers of other languages such as English and Thai.

GOOD AND POOR KOREAN READERS

In the Kim and Davis (2004a) study, good and poor Korean readers were selected by the following procedure. From a pool of more than 140 students at a school, teachers selected those children whose performance in school suggested a reading problem ($n = 45$). All the children ($N = 140$) in the classes of these teacher-selected children were subsequently given two standardized pen and paper tests to determine reading performance and nonverbal IQ. The first test consisted of a sentence completion test (a Cloze task), a word reasoning task, and a test of vocabulary (a synonym judgment task). The nonverbal IQ test was similar to Ravens progressive matrices. The readers, 10 good and 10 poor, were selected so that the poor reader's combined reading test scores were 1.5 SD below those of the population mean but their nonverbal score did not differ from the population mean. Both the reading and nonverbal scores of the good reader group did not differ from the population mean, so the term "good" reader does not mean above average, but is used simply to contrast it from the "poor" reader group. Also, the overall performances of the two reading groups were not different on a test of sustained attention (Beale, Mathew, Oliver & Corballis, 1987).

To assess the role of basic sensory processing mechanisms in reading performance, tasks were selected that measured the detection of dynamic visual and auditory stimuli (e.g., stimuli that require the perception and discrimination of a dimension that changes in time). The basic visual task was one that tested the perception of coherent dot motion with random-dot kinematograms (RDKs). In this task, participants were asked to judge the direction of movement of a field of white dots on a black background. Studies of English readers have shown that poor readers are less sensitive than control readers are to coherent motion stimuli (e.g., Cornelissen, Richardson, Mason, Fowler & Stein, 1995; Eden et al., 1996; Everatt, Bradshaw & Hibbard, 1999; Slaghuis & Ryan, 1999).

The ability to perceive incoming stimuli as dynamic groups was determined by the Ternus (1938) procedure. In this procedure, an illusion of movement is induced by a rapid display of two frames of three horizontally aligned equidistant squares. As with the RDK task, a number of studies have shown that poor readers of English are less sensitive to movement as they require longer ISIs (Inter Stimulus Interval) to report group movement than do typical readers (Davis, Castles, McAnally & Gray, 2001; Slaghuis & Ryan, 1999; Winters, Patterson & Shontz, 1989).

The results of our study showed that the performances of Korean poor readers did not differ from that of the good Korean readers in either the RDK task or the Ternus task. However, both Thai and English poor readers were worse compared with the Korean readers on these tasks.

Given that this group of Hangul poor readers had no demonstrable visual problems, then is it possible they had auditory processing ones? The task chosen to measure the reader's ability to process rapidly changing auditory stimuli was a discrimination task that required the children to make a same or different judgment about the pitch of two tones. To assess reader's capacity to perceive auditory grouping, an auditory analog of the Ternus task was employed. This auditory measure was based on the phenomenon of auditory stream segregation (Bregman, 1990, 1993). In the streaming procedure, a sequence of alternating high- and low-pitch tones is presented. When the presentation rate is slow, these sounds can be perceived as a connected series of tones. However, as the presentation rate is increased, the perception changes to that of two separate sound streams, one with higher and the other with lower pitch. Helenius, Uutela, and Hari (1999) and Sutter, Petkov, Baynes, and O'Connor (2000) have demonstrated that poor readers perceive segregated streams at longer presentation rates than do typical readers. Habib (2000) has suggested that the demonstration that dyslexic adults perceive auditory stream segregation at much slower rates is equivalent to the presumed sensory persistence that underlies visual processing deficits.

As a group, the Korean poor readers did show some problems with performing the tone-matching task, but only when the ISI between tones was 60 ms or less. However, this difference between the reading groups did not occur for the auditory streaming task, as the poor readers' segregation thresholds did not differ from those of the good readers. An inspection of the individual threshold scores, showed that a few of the poor readers had much higher thresholds than the rest. In all then, perceptual problems did not appear to be associated with the reading problems of Korean poor readers. Indeed, the correlations between any of the perceptual performances and reading measures were weak. This absence of noticeable perceptual problems presents a contrast to many published studies of poor readers of English.

The level of skill in processing the phonological elements of a language has been shown to be a predictor of learning to read in English (Adams, 1990). More recently, Goswami (1999) has shown that indicators of phonological awareness also are predictive of reading acquisition in other languages (although the degree of predictability for any particular level of phonological information, phonemes, syllables, onsets, or rimes appeared to depend on the characteristics of the language in question). It was of interest therefore to determine the level of phonological awareness of Korean readers given the alphabetic-syllabic properties of Hangul. To this end, Kim and Davis used two measures of phonological processing (the accuracy of word and nonword-naming performance and the accuracy of performance in an odd-one-out task) and manipulated the test materials to try and determine the level and type of phonological information that was accessible. Two other studies (Kim & Yi, 1999; Kim & Davis, 2004b) used these tests with an additional set of experiments (naming and dictation) that were carried out on a sample of good and poor readers selected with the same procedure as that previously outlined.

As a preliminary measure of phonological short-term memory, the digit spans of both good and poor readers were estimated. In both studies by Kim and Davis, the combined digit spans (forward and backward) of the poor readers were significantly lower than those of the good readers, with the difference in scores being similar to that reported by Paulesu and colleagues (2001) for French, Italian, and British good and poor readers. The finding that the poor readers performed worse on a short-term memory task supports the idea that poor reading is associated with some sort of processing deficit, particularly because the Korean poor readers were not selected on the basis of having phonological impairments but rather on general tests of reading skill.

Naming Words and Nonwords

In the naming task, monosyllabic words and nonwords were presented one at a time either on postcards (Kim & Davis, 2004a; Kim & Yi, 1999) or on a computer monitor, with naming latency being recorded by a voice key (Kim & Davis, 2004b). The word items were highly familiar and would have been known to the participants of the studies. Because in Korean only eight consonant phonemes occur in syllable- and word-final position, two different types of words were selected, a set of words in which the syllable-final letters had their full phonological value and a set in which the sound of the syllable-final letter was unexpressed (rule items). In different sets of experiments, several types of nonwords were used. One contrast involved whether the nonword existed in the written language or not. That is, existing nonwords were syllables that were not words (an English example would be the "acle" in "miracle") and nonexisting syllables, those syllables that do not appear in Korean but are nonetheless pronounceable (again an English example "dilk"). A final type of nonword was also used, those that were bound morphemes (those that could not stand alone as words but still had meanings, e.g., "vive").

The naming results for the word stimuli showed that there was no difference (in response latencies or errors) between the words in which the match between the final consonant sound and the orthography was rule based and those that had the standard letter sound match. However, there was an effect of final syllable contrast for existing nonwords, but only for the poor reader group (with poor readers making 6% more errors on the rule nonwords). There was no effect on normal versus rule-assigned pronunciation for the poor readers on the nonexisting nonword set. This may have been due to general uncertainty in the poor reader group as they made almost 20% errors for both rule and nonrule types.

Overall, there was a trend for faster and more accurate naming of the words compared with the nonword stimuli. However, for the existing nonwords, reading skill modulated the size of the difference. For the good readers, there was no difference between words and existing nonwords for naming time or accuracy, whereas for the poor readers, there was a near-significant trend for the nonwords to take longer and to elicit more errors. Both groups of readers were slower and made more errors on the nonexisting nonwords compared with the words. Furthermore, these nonexisting nonwords took longer to begin to pronounce and generated more errors than did the existing nonwords. That even the good readers made more errors on the nonexisting nonwords compared with the existing nonwords suggests that syllable-level processing may well be the default strategy in reading Korean. This is because the essential difference between these types of nonwords is whether the syllable exists in the language or not. That is, if only grapheme-to-phoneme level processing determined the naming response, then a difference between the nonexisting and exiting nonwords would not be expected.

To summarize the results of this study, Korean poor readers showed a trend to be slower than the Korean good readers in beginning to name the word stimuli, but they did not make many errors. When faced with existing nonwords, poor readers were slower than the good readers but again had similar error rates as the good readers (except for the final consonant rule words for which the poor readers made more errors). When faced with the nonexisting nonwords, the poor readers made many more errors than the good readers.

Auditory Exposure

Before leaving the single-item-naming studies, we consider the results of an experiment in which the participants were first exposed to the sounds of the nonword items. In this experiment, Kim and Davis (2004b) used a procedure developed by McKague, Pratt, and Johnston (2001). In this procedure, participants are first familiarized with the sounds of nonwords that are introduced in a word game. In the game, participants are instructed to repeat each item after the experimenter unless the item was from a prespecified category (e.g., animals, fruits, or colors) in which case they respond by saying the category name. The game was repeated for each category, so that each nonword was heard five times. Another group of participants played the same game except that they did not articulate the nonwords. A number of days after playing the game, participants were then presented with the nonword items in written form and required to read them out. Good and poor readers were tested on both regular and irregular final consonant rule nonwords (see preceding discussion). As it turned out, only the good readers benefited from prior exposure to the sounds of the nonword. This beneficial effect was slightly greater for the irregular final consonant nonwords.

In summary, the results from single-item naming have parallels with other studies that have shown that poor readers either are slower at naming nonwords (e.g., for German, Wimmer, 1996) or make more errors (e.g., in English, Davis et al., 2001). The Korean poor readers showed a trend to be slower than the Korean good readers in beginning to name the word stimuli, but they did not make more errors. When faced with existing nonwords, poor readers were slower than the good readers but again had similar error rates (except for the final consonant rule words for which the poor readers made more errors). When faced with the nonexisting nonwords, the poor readers made more errors than the good readers. Further, poor readers did not benefit from hearing the nonwords in a training session.

The Odd-One-Out Task

The odd-one-out task was designed to test the sensitivity of the good and poor readers to the phonological features of words. The task consisted of having to decide which one of four spoken words was different from the others. Two types of lists were constructed, one in which the odd-sounding word could be determined by analysis at the level of the syllable and the other in which the task could be accomplished by a phonological analysis. That is, in one set, three of the four words had the same second syllable and the fourth word did not share any syllable (e.g., so-ri, bo-ri, *na-mu*, ko-ri). In the next set of test items, the last phoneme of the first syllable (e.g., mo-ki, bo-ki, ko-ki, s*a*-ki) was different in one out of four words. Each test consisted of 10 sets of words. The lists were read out twice so that the structure of the items would be clear. In the studies by Kim and Davis (2004a,b), it was found that good and poor readers made more errors on the phoneme-level trials compared with the syllable ones. When the two groups of readers were compared, poor readers made more errors overall. There was also an interaction between these two main effects, indicating that the poor readers made significantly more errors on the phoneme-level trials than they did on the syllable-level ones. The finding that poor readers did worse on a task that requires some level of phonemic analysis again suggests that difficulties in phonological processing are associated with poor reading skills in Korean also.

Spelling Dictation Task

Kim and Davis (2004b) tested the ability of good and poor readers to derive an orthographic form given a spoken word by using a dictation task. The dictation test consisted of nine short Korean sentences that ranged from 5 to 10 syllables (two to five words). The sentences included word phrases (the word and its participle) whose spelling differed from their pronunciation because of the application of a phonological rule or where there was potentially more than one spelling (because of the restriction on final consonant phonemes). For example, the spellings included double consonants, silent consonants, and cases in which there was a mismatch between the orthography and phonology. To lessen any effects of memory load, first, the whole sentence was read out and then each word phrase of the sentences was read out and the children wrote this down before the next word phrase was read.

In general, the readers from the good reader group had no difficulty with this task. Poor readers had the most difficulty in cases in which there was a double-consonant coda (e.g., 값, 닒다, 싫다), with almost all children committing at least one error. These errors either consisted of using a single consonant (that had the value of the expressed phoneme) or in getting one of the two consonants wrong. There were also two items for which there were single silent consonants (e.g., the ㅎ /h/ in 좁다랗다, 좋다). For one of these words, almost all the poor readers made an error (with the majority of these consisting of the wrong letter being written). By contrast, there were no errors for the other word, a word that had a very high frequency of occurrence (the word 좋다 [like]). Words whose written form has a different syllable structure were also often misspelled. Once again, however, many of the poor readers were able to correctly spell familiar and high-frequency word phrases.

The results of the phonological awareness tasks indicated that Korean poor readers had problems in phonological processing. The results from the dictation task indicate that they also had problems in word specific knowledge and handling morphophonological variations. It is clear that phonological processing skill contributes to both reading and spelling, although success in both domains requires more than phonological processing per se.

CONCLUSIONS

We began this chapter by considering the role that perceptual processes may play in reading and how these might be influenced by the properties of the written and spoken language. In terms of visual processing, it was suggested that properties of Hangul orthographic format might moderate the influence of visual processing problems because in a sample of poor Korean readers no indication of any visual processing deficits was found.

The results of the tests that assessed auditory processing of sounds that occur in quick succession showed some evidence that Korean poor readers experienced some difficulty. It could be that, for a small percentage of poor readers, initial problems in accurately processing rapidly changing auditory stimuli resulted in degraded auditory representations of the sounds standing for letters and that this affected phoneme segmentation and thereby the learning of the relationship between speech and print.

In contrast to the auditory processing data, the phonological tests administered showed a strong association with the reading scores, and the difference between the performances of the good and the poor readers was striking. This suggests that Korean poor readers may lack the skill of rapidly obtaining and organizing phonologically coded information and this may be deleterious for the processing of words (particularly those encountered only infrequently).

In general then, the results of the studies of good and poor readers of Hangul reviewed in this chapter are consistent with a framework that views reading as a learning process that is constrained by the properties of the language and the shape and form of the script.

ACKNOWLEDGMENTS

This research was supported by a postdoctoral fellowship to the first author from the National Academy of Education (Spencer Foundation). We also acknowledge the support from Australian Research Council in the writing up of this manuscript.

REFERENCES

Adams, M. J. (1990). *Beginning to read: Thinking and learning about print.* Cambridge, MA: MIT Press.

Beale, I. L., Mathew, P. J., Oliver, S., & Corballis, M. C. (1987). Performance of disabled and normal readers on the continuous performance test. *Journal of Abnormal Child Psychology, 15,* 229–238.

Bloom, P. (2000). *How children learn the meanings of words.* Cambridge, MA: MIT Press.

Bregman, A. S. (1990). Auditory scene analysis: the perceptual organization of sounds. Cambridge, MA: MIT Press.

Bregman, A. S. (1993). Auditory scene analysis: Hearing in complex environments. In S. McAdams & E. Bigand (Eds.), *Thinking in sound: The cognitive psychology of human audition* (pp. 10–36). Oxford, UK: Clarendon.

Cornelissen, P., Richardson, A., Mason, A., Fowler, S., & Stein, J. (1995). Contrast sensitivity and coherent motion detection measured at photopic luminance levels in dyslexics and controls. *Vision Research, 35,* 1483–1494.

Cossu, G., Shankweiler, D., Liberman, I. S., Katz, L., & Tola, G. (1988). Awareness of phonological segments and reading ability in Italian children. *Applied Psycholinguistics, 9,* 1–16.

Davis, C., Castles, A., McAnally, K., & Gray, J. (2001). Lapses of concentration and dyslexic performance on the Ternus Task. *Cognition, 81,* B21–B31.

Eden, G. F., VanMeter, J. W., Rumsey, J. M., Maisog, J. M., Woods, R. P., & Zeffiro, T. A. (1996). Abnormal processing of visual motion in dyslexia revealed by functional brain imaging. *Nature (London), 382,* 66–69.

Everatt, J., Bradshaw, M. F., & Hibbard, P. B. (1999). Visual processing and dyslexia. *Perception, 28,* 243–254.

Goswami, U. (1999). The relationship between phonological awareness and orthographic representation in different orthographies. In M. Harris & G. Hatano (Eds.), *Learning to read and write: A cross-linguistic perspective* (pp. 134–156). New York: Cambridge University Press.

Habib, M. (2000). The neurological basis of developmental dyslexia: An overview and working hypothesis, *Brain, 123,* 2373–2399.

Helenius, P., Uutela, K., & Hari, R. (1999). Auditory stream segregation in dyslexic adults. *Brain, 122,* 907–913.

Kim, C.-W. (1997). The structure of phonological units in Han'gŭl. In Y. K. Kim-Renaud (Ed.), *The Korean alphabet: Its history and structure* (pp. 145–160). Honolulu: University of Hawaii Press.

Kim, C.-W. & Sohn, H. (1986). A phonetic model for reading: Evidence from Korean. *Studies in the Linguistic Sciences, 16,* 95–105.

Kim, J., Davis, C., Burnham, D., & Luksaneeyanawin, S. (2004). The effect of script on poor reader's sensitivity to dynamic visual stimuli. *Brain and Language, 91,* 326–335.

Kim, J., & Davis, C. (2004a). Characteristics of poor readers of Korean Hangul: Auditory, visual and phonological processing. *Reading and Writing, 17,* 187–218.

Kim, J., & Davis, C. (2004b). The effect of auditory exposure on Korean good and poor reader's nonword naming. Manuscript in preparation.

Kim, J., & Yi, K. (1999). How kids read nonwords: A study of poor readers. Paper presented at the May 1999 Conference of Korean Cognitive Science, Seoul.

Kim-Renaud, Y. K. (1997). The phonological analysis reflected in the Korean writing system. In Y. K. Kim-Renaud (Ed.), *The Korean alphabet: Its history and structure* (pp. 161–192). Honolulu: University of Hawaii Press.

Lewis, J. P., & Frick, R. W. (1999). Row blindness in Gestalt grouping and developmental dyslexia. *Neuropsychologia, 26,* 274–282.

McKague, M., Pratt, C., & Johnston, M. B. (2001). The effect of oral vocabulary on reading visually novel words: a comparison of the dual-route cascaded and triangle frameworks. *Cognition, 80,* 239–270.

Paulesu, E., Démonet, J. F., Fazio, F., McCrory, E., Chanoine, V., Brunswick, N., Cappa, S. F., Cossu, G., Habib, M., Frith, C. D., & Frith U. (2001). Dyslexia: Cultural diversity and biological unity. *Science, 291,* 2165–2167.

Perfetti, C. A. (2003). The universal grammar of reading. *Scientific Studies of Reading, 7,* 3–22.

Sampson, G. (1985). *Writing sytems: A linguistic introduction.* London: Hutchinson.

Slaghuis, W. L., & Ryan, J. F. (1999). Spatio-temporal contrast sensitivity, coherent motion, and visible persistence in developmental dyslexia. *Vision Research, 39,* 651–668.

Sutter, M. L., Petkov, C., Baynes, K., & O'Connor, K. N. (2000). Auditory scene analysis in dyslexics. *Neuroreport, 11,* 1967–1971.

Ternus, J. (1938). The problem of phenomenal identity. In D. W. Ellis (Ed.), *A sourcebook of Gestalt psychology.* London: Routledge and Kegan Paul.

Wimmer, H. (1996). The nonword reading deficit in developmental dyslexia: Evidence from children learning to read German. *Journal of Experimental Child Psychology, 61,* 80–90.

Winters, R. L., Patterson, R., & Shontz, W. (1989). Visual persistence and adult dyslexia. *Journal of Learning Disabilities, 22,* 641–645.

Yoon, H. K, Bolger, D. J., Kwon, O. S., & Perfetti, C.A. (April, 1999). *Grapheme-phoneme processes in English and Korean.* Paper presented at the annual meeting of the Society for the Scientific Study of Reading, Montreal.

APPENDIX: HANGUL VOWELS AND CONSONANTS

Consonants		Simple Vowels		Compound Vowels	
Hangul	IPA	Hangul	IPA	Hangul	IPA
ㄱ	k, g	ㅏ	a	ㅘ	ʷa
ㅋ	kʰ	ㅓ	ə	ㅝ	ʷə
ㄲ	kˡ	ㅗ	o	ㅟ	ʷi, y
ㄷ	d, t	ㅜ	u	ㅙ	ʷɛ
ㅌ	tʰ	ㅡ	ɨ	ㅞ	ʷe
ㄸ	tˡ	ㅣ	i	ㅚ	ʷe, ø
ㅂ	p, b	ㅔ	ɛ	ㅑ	ja
ㅍ	pʰ	ㅖ	ij	ㅕ	jə
ㅃ	pˡ	ㅢ		ㅛ	jo
ㅈ	c, ɟ			ㅠ	ju
ㅊ	cʰ			ㅒ	jɛ
ㅉ	cˡ			ㅖ	je
ㅅ	sʰ				
ㅆ	sˡ				
ㅎ	h				
ㅇ*	ŋ				
ㄴ	n				
ㄹ	l, ɾ				
ㅁ	m				

*This sound applies only when the letter appears in the final position of a syllable. It has a null value in the initial position.

24

The Kagunita of Kannada—Learning to Read and Write an Indian Alphasyllabary

Prathibha Karanth
M. V. Shetty College of Speech & Hearing

Much of the empirical research as well as theoretical models on reading processes have been based mainly on alphabetic orthography, most notably English. More recently doubts have been raised regarding the applicability of findings from alphabetic writing systems to readers of writing systems that are nonalphabetic in nature. At the same time, apart from some limited work on morphosyllabic scripts, little is known about the nature and processing of other nonalphabetic writing systems. This chapter presents the features of Kannada, a Dravidian language used in Southern India, characterized by an alphasyllabic script, along with research findings and their implications for literacy instruction.

INTRODUCTION

Kannada is one of the four major literary languages of the Dravidian family of languages and belongs to its southern branch. It is spoken today by about 50 million people in Karnataka, one of the four southern states of India, and is the official language of the state. It has a range of regional, social, and stylistic variations. The three major regional varieties identified are the old Mysore or Mysore dialect, coastal or Mangalore dialect, and northern or Dharwar dialect. In addition to these variations, there are several varieties that are characteristic of particular castes or social classes.

Kannada is diglossic. The formal or literary variety of the language differs from the spoken or colloquial variety. The major difference between spoken and written Kannada lies in the extensive reduction and deletion of short vowels in the spoken language. The literary or formal variety is used in written language, including school texts, journals, and literary work. The colloquial or informal variety is spoken and is now increasingly used in plays, magazines, and short stories. The Kannada lexicon has several borrowed words from many sources, chief among them being Sanskrit, Hindi-Urdu, and English. Loan words show three levels of "nativization," corresponding roughly to the historical depth of the various sources of borrowing, with Sanskrit being the most assimilated, English the least, and Persio-Arabic standing somewhere in between. Several types of compound words are also present.

There has been considerable interest in Kannada data during the past two decades from both the linguistic and the psycholinguistic–neurolinguistic points of view. (For more details on Kannada from the linguistic point of view see Bright, 1958; Ramanujan, 1963; Schiffman, 1983; and Sridhar, 1990.) Apart from the mainstream work of linguistic scholars in Kannada, there has also been some amount of psycholinguistic and neurolinguistic research in Kannada, since the 1970s, perhaps because of, the geographical location of institutions such as the Central Institute of Indian Languages, the All India Institute of Speech & Hearing, the Regional Institute of Education, The Institute of Kannada Studies, and the Department of Psychology within the campus of the University of Mysore. This chapter presents the features of Kannada, a Dravidian language used in Southern India, characterized by an alphasyllabic script; along with research findings and their implications for literacy instruction in Kannada.

KANNADA

Phonology of Kannada

Kannada has 43 phonemes (Upadhyaya, 1972). The basic Kannada vowel system consists of five short and five long vowels. The basic Kannada consonant system consists of 33 consonants consisting of stops (voiceless and voiced pairs, the aspirated versions of the same, and corresponding nasals), affricates, fricatives, laterals, flaps, and continuants.

The phonemes are represented by 50 graphemes in the *kagunitha* or the "syllable matrix" of Kannada and are described in a later section. Pitch is not distinctive in the language. Intonation and stress have not been studied much in Kannada. It is generally assumed that stress does not play an important role in Kannada except occasionally for emphasis. Similarly some common patterns of intonation have been identified but not much is documented about such patterns in Kannada as yet.

Morphology and Syntax of Kannada

Morphophonemic processes include both assimilatory and dissimilatory processes such as retroflexion, deretroflexion, and devoicing. Other alterations such as vowel shortening, vowel raising, vowel fronting, metathesis, coalescence and split, deletion, insertion, and reduplication are present and are covered by a set of morphophonemic rules called the *sandhi*. The diglossia of written and spoken Kannada can be seen as largely being due to these morphophonemic changes. For instance, Bright (1970) suggests that literary Kannada represents an earlier historical stage of modern spoken Kannada, and, in most cases, "the forms of literary Kannada can be safely posited as the morphophonemically basic forms of the current spoken varieties" (p. 141).

Structurally, Kannada, like most other Dravidian languages, is a polysyllabic agglutinating language with numerous inflections. It is richly inflected with syntactic markers that are suffixed to the noun and verb stem, making Kannada a richly inflected language with fairly extensive case and complex verbal systems. It has a basic subject–object–verb (SOV) constituent order. However, the word order is fairly free, as noun phrases are marked for case and verbs (in most cases) for agreement with subject in number, gender, and person. Subjects and objects are often dropped. The basic principle of the Kannada syntax is that all modifiers (including most subordinate clauses) precede the modified entities. With a few exceptions, subordination invariably involves nonfinite clauses, of which there are several types. Finiteness is a function of agreement, not tense. There is a separate negative conjugation of the verb. The burden of the syntax is carried by participles, both relative and verbal, gerunds, infinitives, compound and conjunct verbs, and postpositions (Schiffman, 1983; Sridhar, 1990).

Nature of the Kannada Script

The current orthographies of India are all said to have derived from the Indic scripts of Kharosti and Brahmi, which appeared around the fourth and third centuries B.C.E. There is disagreement about whether they, in turn, were the offshoots of the Indus valley script from the third millennium B.C.E. or a derivative of a semitic prototype. Over the past 2,000 and odd years with development and regional diversification, Brahmi became the ancestor not only of the several scripts of India but also several from neighboring countries such as Sri Lanka, Tibet, Myanmar, Thailand, Laos, Cambodia, and some regional scripts of Indonesia and Philippines, serving languages of more than one family such as the Indo-Aryan, Dravidian, and others.

Because these scripts share characteristics of both alphabets and syllabaries they have been referred to by a variety of descriptive labels such as "alphabet," "syllabary," "semisyllabary," and "abugida," among others. However as suggested by Bright (2000) they are perhaps best seen as constituting the most typical and most widespread specimens of the alphasyllabic scripts. Alphasyllabaries are types of scripts that are distinct and separate from both alphabets and syllabaries, though not unrelated to them. Alphabets have distinct graphemic elements for consonants, vowels, graphic units, and subunits that correspond to individual phonemes rather than to words and syllables. In the syllabaries the primary graphic unit is a syllable, which is indivisible in the sense that the component parts cannot stand alone. Alphasyllabaries share characteristics of both alphabets and syllabaries because, as in the syllabaries, their primary graphic unit is an indivisible syllable but as in the alphabets they have distinct subunits that correspond to individual phonemes (Daniels, 2000; Salomon, 2000).

Like alphabets, the Indic scripts distinguish two types of symbols: consonants and vowels. The vowels are represented by a diacritic when in combination with a consonant and by an independent grapheme when they are not in combination with a consonant. However, in all consonant symbols there is an inherent vowel, rendering the term "alphabet" inappropriate. The basic written unit, called *akshara* in India, consists of one of three possibilities: (a) an independent vowel, (b) a consonant symbol with inherent or attached diacritic vowel, or (c) two or three consonants plus a vowel forming a "graphic syllable" (McCawley, 1997). It is this feature of the writing system that has led to its being called a syllabary by some. However, the structure of the Indian *aksharas*, unlike syllables in other syllabaries such as the Japanese *kana* (most, but not all, of which are unique), clearly have shared graphic elements that are easily distinguishable and represent distinct phonemes.

All the writing systems of the two major groups of languages in India, the Indo-Aryan and the Dravidian, share a common underlying script. It is relevant that all Indian scripts, be they languages of Indo-Aryan origin such as Hindi or those of Dravidian origin such as Kannada, have originated from the Brahmi script with a comparatively short evolutionary history, so that the basic system is common to all of them. In this system, the syllable, and not the phoneme (except in the case of independent vowels, subsequently described), is the smallest basic unit of writing. Each vowel has a distinct grapheme (primary form) and a diacritic or secondary form. Each consonant has a distinct grapheme and is presented in conjunction with the short vowel "a" in the base syllabary (the *akshara mala* or string of letters). When a CV syllable with a vowel other than "a" is written, the part of the grapheme that represents the consonant is combined with the diacritic or secondary form of the other vowel. Thus the substantial part of the letter (*akshara*) is the consonant that precedes the vowel; the vowel itself being indicated by a diacritic (secondary form of the vowel) attached to the consonant. The independent (primary) form of the vowel is used only when it forms a morpheme by itself or as an independent syllable when it is not combined with a preceding consonant, that is, when it is in the word-initial position. All consonants too have secondary forms, and when more than one consonant precedes the vowel, forming a single syllable with it, these secondary characters are combined into a single compound graphosyllable according to specific rules. However, because the composition of the graphosyllable is rule governed, it is possible to identify the distinct phonemic composition of each graphosyllable. As in most other writing systems, there are exceptions to the general rules but these are few in number.

All Indic scripts exhibit what are considered definitive characteristics of an alphasyllabic script. They are best described as alphasyllabaries for the following reasons: They have the syllable as the smallest graphic unit with the unmarked consonantal grapheme understood to have an automatic or inherent vowel; vowels other than the inherent one are indicated by the addition of an extra marker, and vowels that do not follow a consonant are represented by independent graphemes.

Orthography of Kannada

The southern group of Indian scripts that serve the Dravidian languages are smaller in number compared with the northern group, which is used for representing languages belonging to the Indo-European group. The important southern scripts include the ones that represent the Dravidian languages of Tamil, Telugu, Malayalam, and Kannada.

Kannada is the spoken language of about 50 million people in the southern Indian state of Karnataka. With the literacy level in the state being 67% one could assume that approximately over 35 million people know how to read and write Kannada. The earliest written record of Kannada is said to be an inscription dating back to 450 c.e. Although the form of the Kannada letters has changed marginally over the past 1,500 years, the base form of the letters and the organization of the syllabary have remained pretty much the same. The manner in which the letters of Kannada, like all other Indic scripts, are arranged is clear evidence of the conscious design of re-creating the script along segmental phonemic lines as it follows purely phonological principles. The letters are classified in accordance with places of articulation: vowels and diphthongs first, then consonants—that is, consonants with an inherent /a/. First come the primary vowels /a/, /i/, and /u/. Next come the secondary vowels, comprising the midvowels /e/ and /o/, short and long. The semivowel /r/, referred to by some as the syllabic /r/, which is primarily used in borrowings from Sanskrit, finds a place between the primary and secondary vowels. Diphthongs /ai/ and /au/ also occur, each having its own grapheme. An additional nasal symbol (*anusvaara*) that can replace all nasals when they occur before a consonant and the *visarga*, a glottal fricative occurring before a consonant, were needed to accommodate Sanskrit loan words. The seven additional graphemes are because of the two vowel graphemes /r/ and / r:/ being incorporated to accommodate the Sanskrit words containing these vowels, which are seldom used. The palatal nasal /n/ has a separate grapheme, though it is an allophone of /n/.

The Kannada syllabary (see Table 24.1) as noted earlier, has 50 letters representing 43 phonemes. These letters–graphemes or *aksharas* do not have separate names; the sounds they represent are their names. Further, unlike alphabets such as English, they do not have different cases such as uppercase and lowercase. There is no distinction such as cursive versus print, and there are no italic typefaces.

Vowels: The traditional order of letters begins with vowels (see Table 24.2). The canonical form order proceeds from each short vowel to the corresponding long vowel.

Next in order come two symbols that are written only after vowels and are sometimes listed in combination with /a/. In addition to characters representing the basic Kannada vowels, diphthongs, and consonants, these additional characters are generally used to accommodate

TABLE 24.1
Kannada Syllabary

ವರ್ಣವಾಲಿ

ಸ್ವರಗಳು *(Vowels)*	ವ್ಯಂಜನಗಳು *(Consonants)*

ಅ ಆ ಇ ಈ ಉ ಊ ಋೠ   ಕ ಖ ಗ ಘ ಙ
ಎ ಏ ಐ ಒ ಓ ಔ ಅಂ ಅಃ   ಚ ಛ ಜ ಝ

ಟ ಠ ಡ ಢ ಣ
ತ ಥ ದ ಧ ನ
ಪ ಫ ಬ ಭ ಮ
ಯ ರ ಲ ವ ಶ ಷ ಸ ಹ ಳ

TABLE 24.2
Vowels of Kannada

Primary Form	ಅ	ಆ	ಇ	ಈ	ಉ	ಊ	ಋ	ೠ
	a	a:	i	i:	u	u:	r	r:
Secondary Form	⌐	ಾ	ಿ	ೀ	ು	ೂ	ೃ	ೄ
Primary Form	ಎ	ಏ	ಐ	ಒ	ಓ	ಔ	ಅಂ	ಅಃ
	e	e:	al	o	o:	au	am	aha
Secondary Form	ೆ	ೇ	ೖ	ೊ	ೋ	ೌ	ಂ	ಃ

Sanskrit loan words. The first is a nasal feature called *anusvaara*, written as /o/ and transliterated as /am/. It is most often used for a nasal consonant homorganic with a following stop; for example, /*kamba*/ [pillar] is usually written not with a conjunct consonant symbol for /m/, "ಕಮ್ಬ" but rather as "ಕಂಬ." After *anusvaara* in the sequence comes an element called *visarga*, occurring principally in Sanskrit words. It is written as /:/, transliterated as "h," and usually pronounced as "ha," for example, *punaha*. The *visarga* is included to accommodate Sanskrit words; it represents a glottal fricative before a consonant. Note that the semivowel–syllabic /r/, the *anusvaara*, and the *visarga* are included in the *akshara mala* of Kannada to facilitate the writing of borrowed Sanskrit words.

For each of the 10 vowels there are two characters, a primary form and secondary form (the secondary forms or allographs of vowels do not necessarily have any visual similarity with the respective vowel in the alphabet). To write a syllable that consists of a vowel and no consonant, the primary form is used. To write a syllable in which the vowel is preceded by one or more consonants, the secondary form is used. The primary and secondary written forms for a vowel in general look quite different: For example, the primary form for /a/ is ಅ but its secondary form is ೃ. Similarly, the diphthongs /ai/ and /au/ also have primary and secondary forms in written Kannada.

Consonants: The basic Kannada consonant system (see Table 24.3) consists of 34 consonants. Each consonant is represented by a basic consonantal symbol. The short vowel /a/ is considered inherent in all consonantal graphemes. These consonants are presented in groups of five, each set representing an articulatory position (velars–gutturals, palatals, cerebral palatals,

TABLE 24.3
Consonants of Kannada

ಕ	ಖ	ಗ	ಘ	ಙ
ka	kha	ga	gha	nga
ಚ	ಛ	ಜ	ಝ	ಞ
ča	čha	d̆a	d̆ha	nya
ಟ	ಠ	ಡ	ಢ	ಣ
t	ṭ	da	ḍa	ṇa
ತ	ಥ	ದ	ಧ	ನ
ṭ	ṭa	ḍa	ḍha	na
ಪ	ಫ	ಬ	ಭ	ಮ
pa	pha	ba	bha	ma
ಯ	ರ	ಲ	ವ	ಶ
ya	ra	la	va	ʃa
ಷ	ಸ	ಹ	ಳ	
ʃha	sa	ha	ḷa	

dentals, and labials), with the voiceless and voiced pairs, the aspirated versions of the same, and finally the corresponding nasal. The canonical order of these proceed horizontally within each row. Among the nasals, velar /n/ and palatal /n/ are associated with Sanskrit and are relatively rare in Kannada. There follow, again in order from the back of the mouth toward the front, the oral sonorants and the voiceless sibilants. Finally comes a miscellaneous category of sounds not classified in terms of articulation, comprising /ha/ and /ḷa/.

Syllables: Any graphosyllable of Kannada consists of a vowel, preceded by zero, one, two, or three consonants; that is, the possible syllable structures are V, CV, CCV, or CCCV. A vowel occurring independently or in the word-initial position is written not with a diacritic but with an independent symbol. Written representations of consonants without vowels are possible but are rarely found in Kannada writing. They are generally found in grammar texts illustrating morphophonemic rules or in writing loan words. CCCV syllables are also rare in Kannada and are generally to be found in loan words. Also, although the number of possible CCV syllables is more than 10,000, only about 300 geminations and CCV clusters actually occur in current Kannada texts.

1. V syllables: As described earlier, a syllable that is just a vowel is written with the primary orthographic form of the vowel.

2. CV syllables: *Aksharas*, other than those that represent vowels, encode syllables. The graphic shape of letters explicitly indicates both the consonant and the vowel that constitute the syllable concerned. The basic shape for each set of syllables beginning with the same consonant reflects the consonant, and vowels are denoted by additions to the consonantal base. The primary orthographic form of a consonant denotes not a consonant phoneme, but a CV syllable, the vowel being the vowel /a/. If one wishes to write a CV syllable for which the vowel is not /a/, then the secondary form of this vowel character must be added to the primary orthographic form of the consonant character. These various possibilities are illustrated in Table 24.4 with the consonant /k/.

The entire range of possible CV syllables in Kannada, the *Kagunita* is presented in Table 24.5.

Most CV syllables are formed by the retention of the original consonantal symbol (C + short /a/) and the addition of the diacritic or secondary form of the other vowel, as seen in Table 24.4.

TABLE 24.4
Set of CV Syllables for /k/ in Kannada

Consonant /k/

Base form in Kannada /ಕ್ /	ಅ	ಆ	ಇ	ಈ	ಉ	ಊ	ಋ	ೠ	ಎ	ಏ	ಐ	ಒ	ಓ	ಔ	ಅಂ	ಅಃ
Secondary graphemes of vowels in Kannada	ా	ి	ీ	ు	ూ	ృ	ౄ	ె	ే	ై	ొ	ో	ౌ	ం	ః
	a	ā	i	ī	u	ū	r	r̄	e	ē	ai	o	ō	au	am	a:
VC combinations	ಕ	ಕಾ	ಕಿ	ಕೀ	ಕು	ಕೂ	ಕೃ	ಕೄ	ಕೆ	ಕೇ	ಕೈ	ಕೊ	ಕೋ	ಕೌ	ಕಂ	ಕಃ
Kannada graphemes for	ka	kā	ki	kī	ku	kū	kr	kī	ke	kē	kai	ko	kō	kau	kam	ka:

TABLE 24.5
CV syllables

ಕ	ಕಾ	ಕಿ	ಕೀ	ಕು	ಕೂ	ಕೆ	ಕೇ	ಕೈ	ಕೊ	ಕೋ	ಕೌ	ಕಂ	ಕಃ
ಗ	ಗಾ	ಗಿ	ಗೀ	ಗು	ಗೂ	ಗೆ	ಗೇ	ಗೈ	ಗೊ	ಗೋ	ಗೌ	ಗಂ	ಗಃ
ಚ	ಚಾ	ಚಿ	ಚೀ	ಚು	ಚೂ	ಚೆ	ಚೇ	ಚೈ	ಚೊ	ಚೋ	ಚೌ	ಚಂ	ಚಃ
ಜ	ಜಾ	ಜಿ	ಜೀ	ಜು	ಜೂ	ಜೆ	ಜೇ	ಜೈ	ಜೊ	ಜೋ	ಜೌ	ಜಂ	ಜಃ
ಟ	ಟಾ	ಟಿ	ಟೀ	ಟು	ಟೂ	ಟೆ	ಟೇ	ಟೈ	ಟೊ	ಟೋ	ಟೌ	ಟಂ	ಟಃ
ಡ	ಡಾ	ಡಿ	ಡೀ	ಡು	ಡೂ	ಡೆ	ಡೇ	ಡೈ	ಡೊ	ಡೋ	ಡೌ	ಡಂ	ಡಃ
ಣ	ಣಾ	ಣಿ	ಣೀ	ಣು	ಣೂ	ಣೆ	ಣೇ	ಣೈ	ಣೊ	ಣೋ	ಣೌ	ಣಂ	ಣಃ
ತ	ತಾ	ತಿ	ತೀ	ತು	ತೂ	ತೆ	ತೇ	ತೈ	ತೊ	ತೋ	ತೌ	ತಂ	ತಃ
ದ	ದಾ	ದಿ	ದೀ	ದು	ದೂ	ದೆ	ದೇ	ದೈ	ದೊ	ದೋ	ದೌ	ದಂ	ದಃ
ನ	ನಾ	ನಿ	ನೀ	ನು	ನೂ	ನೆ	ನೇ	ನೈ	ನೊ	ನೋ	ನೌ	ನಂ	ನಃ
ಪ	ಪಾ	ಪಿ	ಪೀ	ಪು	ಪೂ	ಪೆ	ಪೇ	ಪೈ	ಪೊ	ಪೋ	ಪೌ	ಪಂ	ಪಃ
ಬ	ಬಾ	ಬಿ	ಬೀ	ಬು	ಬೂ	ಬೆ	ಬೇ	ಬೈ	ಬೊ	ಬೋ	ಬೌ	ಬಂ	ಬಃ
ಮ	ಮಾ	ಮಿ	ಮೀ	ಮು	ಮೂ	ಮೆ	ಮೇ	ಮೈ	ಮೊ	ಮೋ	ಮೌ	ಮಂ	ಮಃ
ಯ	ಯಾ	ಯಿ	ಯೀ	ಯು	ಯೂ	ಯೆ	ಯೇ	ಯೈ	ಯೊ	ಯೋ	ಯೌ	ಯಂ	ಯಃ
ರ	ರಾ	ರಿ	ರೀ	ರು	ರೂ	ರೆ	ರೇ	ರೈ	ರೊ	ರೋ	ರೌ	ರಂ	ರಃ
ಲ	ಲಾ	ಲಿ	ಲೀ	ಲು	ಲೂ	ಲೆ	ಲೇ	ಲೈ	ಲೊ	ಲೋ	ಲೌ	ಲಂ	ಲಃ
ವ	ವಾ	ವಿ	ವೀ	ವು	ವೂ	ವೆ	ವೇ	ವೈ	ವೊ	ವೋ	ವೌ	ವಂ	ವಃ
ಶ	ಶಾ	ಶಿ	ಶೀ	ಶು	ಶೂ	ಶೆ	ಶೇ	ಶೈ	ಶೊ	ಶೋ	ಶೌ	ಶಂ	ಶಃ
ಸ	ಸಾ	ಸಿ	ಸೀ	ಸು	ಸೂ	ಸೆ	ಸೇ	ಸೈ	ಸೊ	ಸೋ	ಸೌ	ಸಂ	ಸಃ
ಹ	ಹಾ	ಹಿ	ಹೀ	ಹು	ಹೂ	ಹೆ	ಹೇ	ಹೈ	ಹೊ	ಹೋ	ಹೌ	ಹಂ	ಹಃ
ಳ	ಳಾ	ಳಿ	ಳೀ	ಳು	ಳೂ	ಳೆ	ಳೇ	ಳೈ	ಳೊ	ಳೋ	ಳೌ	ಳಂ	ಳಃ

The exceptions to this general rule are the following: The head strokes are absent from all consonants when the vowel /a:/, / i/, or/ i:/ is attached. There are a few exceptions that do not follow the general pattern in Kannada: When /m:/ and /y:/ occur with the vowels /o/ and /o:/ the consonants take reduced forms /mo/ and /yo/. To maintain the distinction between /m/ 'ಮ' and /v/ 'ವ' the sequence /vo/ is written as 'ವೂ'. When attached to the consonants /p/, /ph/, and /v/ 'ಪ' 'ಫ' 'ವ' the vowels /u/ /u:/ take special forms that start beneath the consonant, for example, /pu/ ಪು and /pu:/' 'ಪೂ' . This means that /ma/ ಮ can be interpreted only as /ma/ because /vu / is 'ವು'. In Kannada these special vowel forms are also used for /o/ and /o:/ (Purushotama, 1994).

Children are required to learn all possible combinations of CV syllables even though they may not all be used; in fact of the more than 10,000 possible, only about 300 are used in current texts.

3. CCV syllables: Any sequence of consonants within a word is written by the addition of a reduced or conjunct version of the later consonant or consonants to the shape of the first consonant. Such a combination still forms a single *akshara*. Most such combinations are formed by the reduction of consonant symbols other than the first one in the sequence to an altered form, adjoined beneath the first consonant. A vowel following a consonant combination is adjoined to the first of the consonants. There can be clusters of up to five consonants, and there are no graphic closed syllables. Consequently anything can theoretically be written with a combination of individual consonant signs (Daniels, 2000).

The consonants occur in clusters, especially in words borrowed from Sanskrit; these may involve both initial and medial sequences of two or three consonants. In Kannada, with two exceptions (described later), one writes CCV syllables as follows: The first consonant is written in its primary form, and below this the second consonant is written in its secondary or conjunct form, the vowel character being indicated by the first consonant; for example, "ಅ" /a/ is the independent vowel "a," "ತ" / ta / is the consonant symbol for "t" with the inherent vowel "a," "ಅತ್ತ" / atta / is the word "there," in which the first *akshara* is the independent vowel "a," and the second is a composite CCV syllable "tta" consisting of the consonant "t" in its primary and secondary forms and the inherent vowel "a." In contrast, "ಅತ್ತೆ" /atte/ [aunt], although sharing all other features with the word /atta/ has /e/ as the final vowel instead of /a/, and this is indicated by the secondary form of the vowel /e/ being added to the consonant /t/ instead of the secondary form of /a/.

There are two exceptions to the rule of syllable formation in Kannada. In the first the semivowel /r/ is often handled in a special way; the /r/ is written with /ɛ/ to the right of the consonant which follows it thus:

/Karnataka/ → /ka/ /na/ /r/ /ta/ /ka/
/ಕರ್ನಾಟಕ/ →/ ಕ/ /ನಾ/ /ɛ/ /ಟ/ /ಕ/

A second exception occurs in the use of the nasal *anusvaara*. If the first member of the consonant cluster is O, representing the nasals, the second consonant is written in its primary form and immediately following (not under) the O, for example, ಗಂಗ /Ganga/ [Ganges].

The use of the *anusvaara* has had different interpretations. Whereas some see it as an indication of the nasalization of a vowel (in this example nasalization of /a/) others interpret it as representing the nasal in a homorganic consonantal cluster (in this case the cluster /nga/).

Geminating consonants or clustering consonants is a relatively easy task, as the symbols for consonant conjuncts are often visually similar to the consonant grapheme. Even here though, there are seven allographs that do not resemble the consonants, as pointed out by Purushotama (1994).

4. CCCV syllables are not common in Kannada and are generally to be found in loan words. In these cases, the first consonant is written in its primary orthographic form with appropriate indicators of the final vowel. The secondary form of the second consonant is written immediately below this and the secondary form of the third consonant is written further below as in *shaastra* [scripture] ಶಾಸ್ತ್ರ; *shaastri* [pundit] ಶಾಸ್ತ್ರಿ; where ್ is the secondary form of /t/ and ್ is the secondary form of /r/. The two exceptions already described with reference to CCV syllables hold true here too.

5. CCCCV syllables are extremely rare but possible and consist mostly of loan words from other languages. As pointed out by Daniels (2000, p. 79), "Indic orthography employs graphic syllables that can contradict phonological syllables by combining all consonants in a cluster—tautosyllabic or heterosyllabic—into a single visual unit."

As mentioned earlier, a gap exists between the written style and the spoken style (diglossia) of many modern Indian languages including Kannada (Coulmas, 1989). In modern spoken Kannada, the aspirated versions of the stop consonants are seldom produced, and these graphemes are often used only in the written representation of words borrowed from Sanskrit. Where conjunct consonants are involved the *akshara* does not actually correspond to a spoken syllable; thus *bhakta* "ಭಕ್ತ" would be syllabified as bhak + ta in pronunciation but it is written with the two *aksharas* bha + kta /ಭ / + /ಕ್ತ /.

Only during the twentieth century have serious attempts been made to bring the written language closer to colloquial speech. The written varieties of most literary languages of India are still far removed from the vernacular. Written language and spoken language are functionally distinct; as a result, there are structural differences between the spoken form and written forms of all languages used in writing. Phonological representations reflect "reading pronunciations" used in relatively formal situations. Pronunciations used in informal, colloquial speech vary greatly depending on social and geographical dialect.

The great number of letters or *aksharas* and their combinations in CCV and CCCV syllables in Indian scripts such as Kannada render them visually complex, and those who are unfamiliar with the script often baulk at the thought of having to master these complex-looking letters. However, given the rule-governed nature of the writing system, albeit with some exceptions, this process is not as difficult as it may seem. In reality, the early reader is required to master only the first set of 16 vowel symbols and 34 CV syllables of the base syllabary. In the second stage, the reader masters the range of CV syllables across all consonant–vowel combinations, which are 294 in number, but given that they are clearly rule governed, it is actually an extension of the stage of learning the base syllabary (see Table 24.5). Finally, in the third stage, the reader learns to combine two or more consonants vertically for complex consonantal syllables and here again he is guided by the visual similarity of the conjunct forms of the second or third consonant in the syllable. Once these rules are mastered, the Indian writing systems become highly transparent, given the close correspondences between what is said and written. These features of the Indian writing systems, such as Kannada, provide a contrasting picture to the processing of alphabetic writing systems such as English.

READING AND READING DISORDERS IN KANNADA

Historically, scholars in India have claimed that specific reading difficulties in healthy, normal children reported in English-speaking societies were largely a by-product of the vagaries of the alphabetic script. The transparency of the alphasyllabaries of India with its close graphemic–phonemic correspondence was cited as the reason for the apparent nonexistence of specific difficulties in learning to read. This viewpoint is not unique to India and its scripts but has also received support from other eastern countries with transparent writing systems, such as the Japanese syllabaries (Makita, 1986, Mann, 1986).

At the same time, this reportedly low incidence of specific reading difficulties among Indian children was attributed by western scholars to the lack of awareness of and sensitivity to the phenomenon among Indian schoolteachers who struggled to cope with large numbers of children in overcrowded classrooms. However, among others, Stevenson, Stigler, Lucker, and Lee (1982) have questioned the hypothesis that orthographies could be the determining feature for the incidence of reading difficulties across cultures.

The documentation of learning disability (LD), reading disability in particular, among Indian children during the past couple of decades is threatening to bring in a replay of the LD revolution of the West, albeit 50 years late. Interestingly, the initial identification of LD among Indian children has emerged largely from the urban schools in which English is the medium of instruction. Although at first glance this may seem to support the argument that these reading difficulties are consequent to the alphabetic English orthography, it could also be interpreted to support the counterargument that the identification has occurred in the urban schools because of their increasing awareness of these conditions.

The issue of reading and reading disorders in countries such as India is further complicated by the overbearing presence of other social factors. For instance, the number of languages spoken by a child and his or her relative fluency in them and in the language in which he or she is taught to read and write are important variables. Similarly, the literacy level of the parents and the extent of preschool exposure to literacy varies widely among children, not to mention the conditions prevalent in schools, that is the number of children per classroom, the teacher–student ratio, and other environmental factors in the school. These issues confound the identification of the child with a reading disability to a far greater extent than in the West, leading to fierce arguments on operational definitions of LDs and reading disabilities among researchers.

A recent survey on LDs in Indian children from the state of Kerala (where Malayalam, another Dravidian language similar to Kannada, is the language of the state) by Suresh and Sebastian (2003), who used a broad definition of LDs, indicated an incidence of about 10% in a large unselected population. However, these figures do not represent reading difficulty alone.

In a selected sample of poor and good readers in Kannada, from urban and rural schools in and near Mysore, Ramaa (1993) arrived at an incidence of 14 dyslexic children among 550 by using an exclusionary criteria based on several assessment procedures. Because reliable studies of incidence of dyslexia in children learning to read Kannada are not easy to come by, one could extrapolate incidence figures on the basis of this study. A total of 57 children out of 550 were identified as poor readers without any other extraneous causes. Of these, 14 were identified as dyslexic based on the discrepancy criteria. If incidence figures were extrapolated on the basis of this study we would arrive at an overall incidence of 10.36% for poor readers, with those identified as dyslexic being 2.51%. The latter is clearly much lower than that quoted in the West and would appear to support the notion that incidence of dyslexia is lower among children reading Indian alphasyllabaries like Kannada as compared with that in the West.

Others have documented reading difficulties in children learning to read and write Kannada. Purushotama (1994), although noting that palindromes and spelling problems are unlikely to occur, documented other kinds of errors in children learning to read Kannada. In his study on good and poor Kannada readers, he observed that simultaneous–sequential processing strategies did not differentiate good and poor readers in Kannada, unlike that reported in English. Poor readers in Kannada were poorest in rules of orthography and were not able to follow rules for construction of complex syllables. Poor readers confused letters and were unable to make out the salient features of the letter not only from brief exposures but also following long exposures.

Transpositions, palindromes, and letter reversals are reported to have been far fewer than in English. At times, the children wrote the spoken forms instead of the written forms—an equivalent of phonetic writing in English perhaps, except that in Kannada "the illegality" and failure to convey accurate semantic reference, by these "misspelt" words would not be as severe as in English.

As already noted, there has been some psychoneurolinguistic work in Kannada, particularly on reading. This research has thrown up some interesting findings that are not entirely in consonance with the existing literature on the processing of the alphabetic scripts like English. In addition it has raised some questions regarding the universal applicability of notions such as "spelling," which play an important role in learning to read and write alphabetic scripts like English. Some of these issues based on empirical research on Kannada readers are subsequently discussed.

Models of Reading Acquisition

Karanth and Prakash (1996) undertook a 3-year longitudinal study of 48 typical, healthy children learning to read Kannada, from kindergarten, through Grades 1 and 2, within the general framework of one of the more widely accepted current western models of literacy acquisition, that of Frith (1985). Literacy acquisition, in these children, was studied in terms of a sequence of stages involving logographic, alphabetic, and orthographic phases of development, as suggested by Frith. They did not find any evidence for the first logographic stage in which the children were expected to both "read" and "write" certain commonly seen words through a holistic process without deciphering the constituent units. Similar findings have been reported by Mythra (1991). In contrast, the second stage, termed the alphabetic stage by Frith, which could perhaps be equalized to the mastery of the alphasyllabary in Kannada readers, because this is when they master the grapheme-phoneme correspondence (GPC) rules of the language, was not only present, but encompassed the entire period of the study extending from upper kindergarten to Grade 2. Further, within this stage, there were distinct substages that corresponded directly to the complexity of the graphosyllables. In the third stage, termed the orthographic stage, the child is said to instantly analyze words into units at the morphemic level without phonological conversion. Karanth and Prakash did not find evidence for the use of morphemic reading in Kannada, even during the third year when the children were in Grade 2. Further, at no stage of their study was there evidence for writing setting the pace for reading, as suggested by Frith.

It is noteworthy that the importance of logographic reading in other transparent orthographies such as German has been questioned (Wimmer & Goswami, 1994; Wimmer & Hummer, 1990). Similarly, Liow (1999) did not find support for the stages of reading acquisition proposed by Frith in her study of bilingual children in Singapore.

Phonological Awareness

Not unexpectedly, given the importance it has been accorded by reading researchers in the West, phonological awareness is another area of research that has received considerable attention from reading researchers in Kannada. Similar to reading acquisition, here too the nature of the script has emerged as an important variable. In a series of studies on phonological awareness in children and adults (literate and nonliterate), whose primary language–script was Kannada, it was established that phonological awareness is neither as evident in nor as crucial for successful reading, supporting the theoretical position that, in alphabetic scripts, phonological awareness is more a concomitant of than requisite for successful reading. On tasks such as rhyme recognition, syllable deletion, phoneme deletion, and phoneme oddity, the different subgroups—children learning to read alphasyllabaries, monoliterates in alphasyllabaries (those who had learned to read only an alphasyllabary like Kannada), nonliterate adults, and biliterate adults (those who knew how to read Kannada and English)—performed well in rhyme-recognition and syllable deletion tasks but with a few exceptions only the biliterates (with exposure to the alphabetic script of English) performed well on the phoneme segmentation tasks. For more details on this work see P. Karanth (1998), Prakash, Rekha, Nigam, and Karanth (1993), Prakash and Rekha (1992), Prakash (2003), and Prema and Karanth (2003).

Orthographic Principles

Several researchers have emphasized the crucial role that orthographic principles play in the acquisition of reading in Kannada. Karanth and Prakash (1996) designed a task called the SHWA test to assess children's knowledge of the underlying phonemic–alphabetic principles of the Kannada syllabary. The task required the subject to combine a given visual symbol for an imaginary phoneme, which is nonexistent in Kannada, with different vowels and write them down as graphemes on the basis of their knowledge of the Kannada syllabary. Several children from among the group of children studied over 3 years, from upperkindergarten to Grade 2, developed an insight into the phonemic–alphabetic principles of the Kannada script by the third year, as evidenced in their success in the SHWA test. Interestingly, at the same time, with a few exceptions, the group as a whole failed to master the tasks of phoneme oddity and phoneme stripping even at the end of the second grade, after 3 years of exposure to and training in reading. Success in the SHWA test—the test for sensitivity to the underlying phonemic–alphabetic principles of the Kannada syllabary—was seen in children in Grade 2 during the third year of reading instruction at the age of 9 years. It is noteworthy that this mastery over the orthographic principle was sudden, abrupt, and nearly complete in nature rather than a slow cumulative process. This phenomenon indicates the possibility of a sudden awareness of the phonemic–alphabetic principle of grapheme construction underlying the superficially syllabic nature of the script. This insight also seemed to differentiate good readers from poor readers in Kannada. The SHWA test has since been expanded (Prema & Karanth, 2003) and was also tested in several other Indian scripts such as Tamil and Malayalam, confirming the earlier result. The sensitivity to the orthographic principles underlying the alphasyllabaries is apparently a crucial factor in the acquisition of reading in these writing systems. The paramount importance of orthographic principles, in the learning of scripts like Kannada, was also emphasized by Purushotama (1994).

Rapid Reading

Reaction-time measures for rapid reading of briefly exposed single words has been an important area of empirical reading research in the west. The substantial amount of empirical research in this area has established, for instance, that reading of high-frequency words and imageable, concrete words are more rapid in skilled readers compared with the reading of low-frequency, nonimageable, abstract words and nonwords. This kind of information has been used extensively in developing and vetting the neuropsychological models of reading. Attempts to establish similar norms in the alphasyllabic Kannada writing system in experimental studies on rapid reading, by Karanth, Mathew, and Kurien (2004), suggest that reading rates for high-frequency words, and low-frequency words, concrete words, and abstract words of the same length and graphemic complexity are not significantly different. Significant differences were seen between high- and low-frequency words only when the words were orthographically complex with two consonantal clusters. This was also true for the concrete–abstract word pairs. Reading time for nonwords was, on the whole, parallel with that of words, that is, the longer the nonword, the longer the time taken. However, there was a slight but nonsignificant difference between words and nonwords at all lengths and complexity, indicating that familiarity is a factor, though not a significant factor. As to the irregular graphemes of Kannada, words written with the nasal *anusvaara* were read faster than those with geminates suggesting that the *anusvaara* words were processed as though they had fewer phonemes than the corresponding geminates. That is, the results suggested that the *anusvaara*, which nasalizes the following consonant, is processed as a feature of the consonant rather than as a separate phoneme, despite having a separate grapheme. These results suggest that in alphasyllabaries like Kannada, with close sound-to-symbol correspondence, semantic variables such as word type (concrete vs. abstract) or word frequency may not have as important a role in rapid reading as has been noted for opaque scripts, such as English.

Spelling

Learning to spell accurately is an important stage in the acquisition of reading in scripts such as English, and teachers pay much attention to this skill. However, the notion of spelling prevalent in opaque nonalphabetic scripts like English and French cannot be easily applied to transparent scripts with high grapheme phoneme correspondence like Kannada. In Kannada, spelling is reading, albeit with a slightly speeded production in the latter task, for all letter names are also letter sounds. Spelling practice is therefore not an important part of learning to read and write Kannada, nor are there many spelling difficulties seen in Kannada readers. The most common instances of spelling errors seen are those that have to do with the irregular *arka* and *anuswaara* or in the instances in which the written and spoken forms of words diverge.

DEVELOPMENTAL AND ACQUIRED DYSLEXIAS IN KANNADA

Developmental Dyslexia

Studies of reading difficulties in children learning to read Kannada are rare. However, two recent studies (Purushotama, 1994; Ramaa, 1993) have highlighted the difficulties some children experience in learning to read Kannada. These studies suggest that, as reported in the West, about 10% of children have difficulty in reading because of factors such as deficits in auditory sequential memory, visual–verbal association, and word analysis and synthesis skills. Within this group, about 25%–30% who have visual–verbal association difficulties and poor word analysis show the greatest amount of reading difficulties in Kannada and may be classified as dyslexic.

Comparisons of the relative reading difficulties faced by children in learning to read two scripts have lent support to the hypothesis that the same individual can have different degrees of difficulty with different scripts, all other factors being equal. P. Karanth (1992) documented case reports of developmental dyslexic readers whose difficulties in making spelling–sound correspondences manifested as a more severe reading disorder in English as compared with the more transparent but visually complex Kannada.

It is also likely that, given the transparent nature of the Kannada script coupled with the agglutinative nature of the language, although the errors at the word level in reading Kannada may not be as high as it is in scripts like English with its irregular words, those at the phrasal level will probably be greater in scripts like Kannada, given that the suffixes, prefixes, and morphophonemic changes carry much of the syntactic burden. Such observations have been made by Aaron (1982), who found that about 10% of children learning to read in Tamil (another Dravidian language similar to Kannada) have sequential difficulties as seen in their omission of suffixes and inflections. Similar difficulties have been seen with adult acquired dyslexia. There is therefore a need to go beyond the word level in studying reading skills, particularly in inflected languages such as Kannada.

Acquired Dyslexia

Parallel to the study of reading and reading disorders of children learning to read Kannada, there has been a smaller body of clinical research related to the acquired dyslexias. Much of this work has centered on identifying the subtypes of acquired dyslexias such as "pure," "surface," and "deep" in Kannada compared with that reported in the western literature. The presence of bilingual–multilingual/ biscriptal–multiscriptal subjects with acquired brain damage, one of whose languages is the alphasyllabic Kannada and the other the alphabetic English, has provided ideal testing grounds for the hypothesis that the nature of the script is an important variable in the manifestation of the different types of reading disorders. For a detailed description of the data and a discussion of the relevance of this data for the models of the acquired disorders of reading see Karanth (2004).

EDUCATIONAL IMPLICATIONS AND FUTURE DIRECTIONS

Teaching to Read in Kannada

Reading can be achieved by different strategies. Different scripts enhance different strategies. This has relevance to the teaching of reading. Methods for teaching any one script need not necessarily be ideal for another. India has had a strong oral tradition, which has overridden and intertwined with the written. The oral tradition, based on verbatim repetition, has also been traditionally used for teaching the syllabary. Traditionally, the separate components of each phoneme in a written syllable are not dealt with independently except at a much later stage in grammar school.

Kannada and most other Indian scripts are generally taught syllabically. The script is introduced in stages from the beginning to the end. The child begins by tracing the vowel forms (primary V) and consonants (CV − C+/a/) and naming them. It must be remembered that the Kannada reader does not learn the consonant component and the vowel component separately and then combine it to form a syllable. Instead, having first learned the basic syllabary with the primary forms of the vowels and the consonants in combination with the vowel /a/, the reader is taught the entire syllabary containing all possible CV combinations, by rote, pretty much like the multiplication tables are taught.

Hence *kagunita*—the "multiplication of the ka." The separate components of each phoneme in a written syllable are not dealt with independently except at a much later stage in grammar school. Gradually, the child starts reading words given alongside pictures in the text. The child then quickly moves on to short phrases and simple sentences, again presented alongside suitable pictures. Throughout this process, the syllabic strategy is emphasized.

However, the teaching of reading in India has, during the twentieth century, been influenced to a great extent by western literature on the topic, and we have had our share of the protagonists of the "whole-word" and "phonic" approaches and the ongoing battles between the camps. The traditional letter-type teaching of Kannada is reported to have been discouraged during the days of the Madras presidency in 1932 (S. Karanth, 1992) and the phonic and whole-word methods of teaching introduced from 1930 to 1950. S. Karanth, pointed out the difficulties that will face the child in breaking the letter in to consonant and vowel components and then combining them. He advocated a combination of the letter reading and whole-word processes by introducing words within the vocabulary of children and highlighting the letters that these words are composed of. Consequently the letters are not introduced in the order given in the syllabary but are dependent on children's early vocabulary. He emphasized that the words should be within the child's vocabulary and cited the difficulties in introducing compound clusters and graphemes for aspirated letters. S. Karanth (1992) produced a series of early readers for children in the early stages of reading acquisition on lines similar to those used in the primers for adult education for the UNESCO Group Training Scheme for Fundamental Education (S. Karanth, 1954).

The teaching of reading calls for script-specific methods. The advantages and disadvantages that different types of scripts pose, such as ease of reading phonetically versus reading comprehension, need to be studied further and given adequate attention when reading is taught in different scripts. Better understanding of the factors involved in processing different scripts will be relevant not only for models of reading and teaching of reading, but also for management of developmental dyslexia and rehabilitation procedures for acquired dyslexias.

REFERENCES

Aaron, P. G. (1982). The neuropsychology of developmental dyslexia. In R. N. Malatesha & P. G. Aaron (Eds.), *Reading disorders: Varieties and treatments* (pp. 5–67). New York: Academic Press.

Boder., E. (1971). Developmental dyslexia: A diagnostic screening procedure based on three characteristic patterns of reading and spelling. In B. Bateman (Ed.), *Learning disorders.* Seattle, WA: Special Child Publications.

Boder., E. (1973). Developmental dyslexia: A diagnostic approach based on three atypical reading-spelling patterns. *Developmental Medicine and Child Neurology, 15,* 663–687.

Bright, W. O. (1958). *An outline of colloquial Kannada.* Monograph Series, No. 22, Poona, India: Deccan College.

Bright, W. O. (1970). Phonological rules in literary and colloquial Kannada. *Journal of the American Oriental Society, 90,* 140–144.

Bright, W. (2000). A matter of typology: Alphasyllabaries and abugidas. In C. W. Kim, E. H. Antonsen, W. Bright, & B. B. Kachru. (Eds.), *Studies in the linguistic sciences: Literacy and writing systems in Asia,* 63–72. Urbana-Champaign, IL: University of Illinois.

Coulmas, F. (1989). *The Writing Systems of the World.* Oxford, UK: Blackwell.

Daniels, P. T. (2000). On writing syllables: Three episodes of script transfer. In C. W. Kim, E. H. Antonsen, W. Bright, & B. B. Kachru (Eds.), *Studies in the linguistic sciences: Literacy and writing systems in Asia,* 73–86. Urbana-Champaign, IL: University of Illinois.

Frith, U. (1985). Beneath the surface of developmental dyslexia. In K. E. Patterson, J. C. Marshall, & M. Coltheart (Eds.). *Surface dyslexia: Neuropsychological and cognitive studies of phonological reading,* 301–330. London: Lawrence Erlbaum Associates.

Karanth, K. S. (1954). *Jo:gi KHanda U:ru.* Mysore, India: UNESCO Group Training Scheme for Fundamental Education.

Karanth, K. S. (1992). *O:duva A:Ta.* Bangalore, India: Sapna Book Stall Publishers.

Karanth, P. (1992). Developmental dyslexia in bilingual biliterates. *Reading and Writing, 4,* 297–306.

Karanth, P. (1998). Literacy and language processes—Orthographic and structural effects. In Marta Kohl de Oliviera & J. Valsiner (Eds.), *Literacy in human development,* 145–160. New York: Ablex.

Karanth, P. (2004). *Cross-linguistic studies of acquired disorders of reading: Implications for reading models, disorders, acquisition and teaching.* Dordrecht, The Netherlands: Kluwer.

Karanth, P., Mathew, A., & Kurien, P. (2004). Orthography and reading speed: Data from native readers of Kannada. *Reading & Writing, 17,* 101–120.

Karanth, P., & Prakash, P. (1996). *Developmental investigation on onset, progress and stages of literacy acquisition: Its implication for instructional processes.* Research Project (F.2-17/89/eric/1147). Report submitted to and Funded by the National Council of Educational Research and Training, New Delhi.

Liow, S. R. (1999). Reading skill development in bilingual Singaporean children. In M. Harris & G. Hatano (Eds.), *Learning to read and write: A cross-linguistic perspective* (pp. 196–213). New York: Cambridge University Press.

Makita, K. (1968). The rarity of reading disability in Japanese children. *American Journal of Orthopsychiatry, 8,* 599–614.

Mann, V. A. (1986). Phonological awareness: The role of reading experience. *Cognition, 24,* 65–92.

McCawley, J. M. (1997). Hangul and other writing systems. In *Literacy & Hangul: Proceedings of International Conference (Memory of the 600th Anniversary of King Sejong)* (pp. 5–16). Seoul: Ministry of Culture & Sports, International Association for Korean Language Education.

Mythra, J. (1991). *Logographic reading skills in children.* Unpublished master's dissertation, University of Mysore, Mysore, India.

Prakash, P. (2003). Early reading acquisition. In P. Karanth & J. Rozario (Eds.), *Learning disability in India: Willing the mind to learn,* 62–76. New Delhi: Sage.

Prakash, P., & Rekha, B. (1992). Phonological awareness and reading acquisition in Kannada. In A. K. Srivastava (Ed.), *Researches in child and adolescent psychology,* 47–52. New Delhi: National Council for Educational Research and Training (NCERT).

Prakash, P., Rekha, D., Nigam, R., & Karanth, P. (1993). Phonological awareness, orthography and literacy. In R. Scholes (Ed.), *Literacy: Linguistic and cognitive perspectives.* Hillsdale, NJ: Lawrence Erlbaum Associates.

Prema, K. S., & Karanth, P. (2003). Assessment of learning disability: Language based tests. In P. Karanth & J. Rozario (Eds.), *Learning disability in India: Willing the mind to learn,* 138–149. New Delhi: Sage.

Purushotama, G. (1994). *A framework for testing Kannada reading.* Mysore, India: CIIL Silver Jubilee Publication Series.

Ramaa, S. (1993). *Diagnosis and remediation of dyslexia: An empirical study in Kannada—An Indian language.* Mysore, India: Vidyasagar.

Ramanujan, A. K. (1963). *A generative grammar of Kannada.* Unpublished doctoral dissertation, Indiana University, Bloomington.

Salomon, R. G. (2000). Typological observations on the Indic script group and its relationship to other alphasyllabaries. *Studies in the Linguistic Sciences, 30*, 87–103.

Schiffman, H. (1983). *A reference grammar of spoken Kannada*. Seattle, WA: University of Washington Press.

Shankarabhat, D. N. (1978). *KannaDa Va: KyagaLu—A:ntarika Racane Mattu Arthavyavaste* [Kannada sentences: Syntax and semantics]. Mysore, India: Geeta Book House.

Stevenson, H. W., Stigler, J. W., Lucker, G. W. and Lee, S. (1982). Reading disabilities: The case of Chinese, Japanese and English. *Child Development*, 11164–11181.

Sridhar, S. N. (1990). *Kannada*. London: Routledge.

Suresh, P. A., & Sebastian S. (2003). Epidemiological and neurological aspects of learning disabilities. In P. Karanth & J. Rozario (Eds.), *Learning disability in India: Willing the mind to learn*, 30–43. New Delhi: Sage.

Upadhyaya, U. P. (1972). *Kannada phonetic reader*. Mysore, India: CIIL.

Wimmer, H., & Goswamy, U. (1994). The influence of orthographic consistency on reading development: Word recognition in English and German children. *Cognition, 51*, 91–103.

Wimmer, H., & Hummer, P. (1990). How German speaking first graders read and spell: Doubt in the importance of the logographic stage. *Applied Psycholinguistics, 11*, 349–368.

www.censusindia.net/office of the Registrar General India: New Delhi.

25

Literacy in Kiswahili

Katie J. Alcock
Lancaster University

Kiswahili is a little-studied but widely spoken language with its origins in East Africa. This chapter introduces the topic of literacy in Kiswahili by summarising some information about the language and its history. Following this, work on the development of reading and spelling in Kiswahili is reviewed. Learning to read Kiswahili is generally a rapid, all-or-nothing process. However, spelling development is not so straightforward, even in this regularly spelled language, because a variety of factors other than the phoneme–grapheme relationship contribute to spelling. This chapter concludes with an illustration of how the study of this language can illuminate our knowledge of literacy development in languages other than English.

INTRODUCTION

Kiswahili belongs to the Bantu group of languages, a group found throughout Eastern, Southern, and Central Africa. Kiswahili is spoken as a first language in coastal, urban, and inland Tanzania and in coastal and inland Kenya; it is a *lingua franca* throughout East Africa including Uganda, Rwanda, Burundi, and parts of the former Zaire.

In Bantu languages, prefixes denote grammatical classes. For example, the *Ki-* prefix in *Kiswahili* denotes an adjective similar to ' ish' in "English." However, when referring to people or places, different prefixes are used. The Swahili people are therefore the *Waswahili*. Literature in English often simply uses 'Swahili' to denote the people and culture, and this convention is followed in this chapter, with 'Kiswahili' reserved for the language.

Some Phonological Features

The phonological structure of Kiswahili makes it a relatively easy language to transcribe and also to learn to read and write. There are five vowel sounds, and most of the syllables are open (i.e., end in a vowel); there are few consonant clusters. Stress is predictable because in all the words the emphasis is placed on the penultimate syllable. Orthography is perfectly regular from grapheme to phoneme; each grapheme maps onto only one phoneme, with some digraphs (such as SH[1] for /ʃ/).

The transcription from phoneme to grapheme, however, is not perfectly regular for two reasons. First, Kiswahili has a complex grammatical system in which many parts of a sentence must share markings that refer to grammatical class (a feature of the language similar to grammatical gender as it exists in many European languages). Some grammatical affixes are phonologically equivalent but are spelled differently. For example:

Mti alioona

m-	*ti-*	*a-*	*li-*	*o-*	*ona*
class 3 prefix	'tree'	Class 1 subject prefix	Past-tense marker	Relative pronoun marker class 3	'see'

'The tree which he saw'

Ndege aliyoona

n-	*dege*	*a-*	*li-*	*yo-*	*ona*
Class 9 prefix	'tree'	Class 1 subject prefix	Past-tense marker	Relative pronoun marker class 9	'see'

'The airplane which he saw'

In these two examples the second words—*alioona* and *aliyoona*—are pronounced exactly the same, but the grammatical difference (the agreement of the relative pronoun marker with a class 3 referent—*mti* [tree] versus a class 9 referent—*ndege* [airplane]) is marked in the spelling.

Second, dialect differences make some phonological distinctions that are preserved in the orthography but are irrelevant for beginning spellers. For example, younger speakers of Kiswahili often confuse /l/ and /r/ and in some dialects /θ/ (spelled TH) is pronounced /s/ and /ð/ (spelled DH) is pronounced /z/ (Nurse & Spear, 1985).

History of Literacy in Kiswahili

The Swahili people were originally a coastal East African people who conducted trade with the Arabic peninsula from approximately 800 C.E. (Nurse & Spear, 1985). This trade and contact had a great influence on Kiswahili vocabulary—it has one of the highest proportions of loan words of any Bantu language (Frederiksen & Chitepo, 1992; Legère, 1992). From at least the 18th century, Kiswahili was written in Arabic script (Whiteley, 1993), and literacy and verbal fluency were prized throughout the pre-colonial period. Poetry also flourished (Biersteker, 1996), and the earliest surviving manuscript, the *Epic of Heraklios*, by Bwana Mwengo, is dated 1728. Knappert (1979) suggests that the nature of this manuscript indicates that earlier versions of this work were in existence. An early manuscript is shown in Fig. 25.1.

---

[1] In this chapter the following conventions will be followed: English words that are examples and English translations of foreign words, will be in inverted commas ("dog"). Kiswahili and other foreign words will be in italics (*mbwa*, "dog"). Spellings and orthographic representations will be in capitals (*mbwa* is sometimes spelled BWA). Phonological representations will be between slash marks (*mbwa*, pronounced /ˈmbwa/).

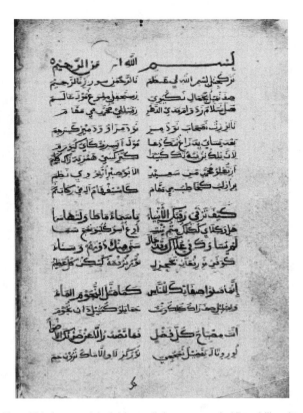

FIG. 25.1. *Hamziyya*: This is one of the oldest religious poems in Kiswahili, written in Arabic script, praising the prophet Mohammed. The translation into Kiswahili dates from 1792.

During the latter part of the 19th century, East Africa was colonised by Britain and Germany, and missionaries started the transcription and description of Kiswahili (Tabouret-Keller & International Group for the Study of Language Standardization and the Vernacularization of Literacy, 1997, p. 70). Books on religion as well as vernacular non-religious texts were published (Steere, 1870a, 1870b). During this period, the first children's books (mainly Sunday school texts, e.g., *Kusoma kwa Watoto, kwa siku ya Jumapili, [Sunday School Services in Swahili]*; Christian Knowledge Society, 1901) were also produced; the emphasis was on Christian literature. Later in the colonial period, the transcription of Kiswahili, which had previously varied according to region and missionary group, was standardised by a colonial committee (Inter-territorial Language [Swahili] Committee to the East African Dependencies & Johnson, 1939). Literacy in Arabic script, in some cases without literacy in Roman script, remained common. Following independence, all the East African nations emphasised basic literacy development and for the most part chose the vernacular language as the medium of instruction. In many parts of Tanzania, Kiswahili is not the original vernacular language, but a political movement was instituted to promote Kiswahili as a spoken and written national language (Tabouret-Keller & International Group for the Study of Language Standardization and the Vernacularization of Literacy, 1997). Because of this, the prevalence of spoken Kiswahili, and therefore literacy in Kiswahili, is much higher in Tanzania than in other East African nations.

Literacy in general, however, is not particularly advanced in the region compared with that of developed nations. Currently, it is estimated that, in Tanzania, 65% of 7- to 13-year-old children attend primary school. Of these, only 10% are in their age-appropriate grades; many children start school late. In a set of data collected as part of a previous study (Jukes et al., 2002), it was found that, on average, there was a delay of 3 years in starting school. Because many children in the schools are over the compulsory schooling age, more than 65% of children obtain at least some primary education. This has resulted in an estimated literacy rate of 84% for adult men and 67% for adult women. In Kenya, which also uses Kiswahili, the corresponding figures are slightly higher, at 89% for men and 76% for women. Secondary schools are available to only a small proportion of the population, with approximately 5% of Tanzanian and about 30% of Kenyan children having access to secondary school education (UNICEF & Bellamy, 2001).

The majority of schools in East Africa are poorly resourced and staffed. Class sizes are up to 100, even in the early years of primary school, and there are frequently insufficient desks, very few books, and families often cannot afford school supplies. Teachers' pay is very low–around $50 per month–and teachers are frequently absent, in order to tend to their own small businesses or even to encourage parents to pay for extra tuition outside school hours.

Teaching style tends to be traditional and rigid, although the phonic approach involving classroom drill of letter sounds is also currently fashionable in the West. Ngonyani (1992) suggests that one of the major problems for schoolchildren is the unsuitability of textbooks. The first page of the first reading book used in Grade 1 in Tanzania is shown in Fig. 25.2.

Kusoma

leo tunasoma kitabu
sote tunasoma a e i o u
tunasoma ba be bi bo bu
tunasoma herufi zote
tunasoma silabi na maneno
tunafurahi kusoma kitabu
kitabu chetu ni kizuri

FIG. 25.2.   The first page of the first reading book encountered by children when they enter Grade 1 in Tanzanian primary schools. The translation is as follows: 'Reading. Today we are reading a book. We all read a e i o u. We read ba be bo bu. We read all the letters. We read syllables and words. We are happy to read a book. Our book is nice.'

Surprisingly, given the many inadequacies of the education system, children seem to learn to read fairly rapidly (Alcock et al., 2000), and features of the language may explain this.

LEARNING TO READ KISWAHILI

There has been little previous work on the acquisition of literacy skills in Kiswahili. Most previous educational research has focussed on the debate surrounding the use of Kiswahili versus English or other local languages as the medium of instruction in primary and secondary schools. Frederiksen and Chitepo (1992) compared text analysis and recall in Kiswahili-speaking children who were being educated in an English medium primary school with a second group who had Arabic instruction in a religious school. Text comprehension and recall were better in Kiswahili than in either English or Arabic, even though Kiswahili was not the medium of instruction for the first group of children. Children also tended to interpret texts literally, inferring little, which was thought to be due to the type of response expected of children in both secular primary schools and religious schools.

Detailed investigation of reading development in Kiswahili (Alcock et al., 2000) was motivated by the need to develop a reading test suitable for administration by teachers with the equivalent of secondary education, and for use with large numbers of primary school children, as part of a study examining the impact of health on cognitive development (Jukes et al., 2002).

Oral, single-word-reading tests are commonly used in opaque languages such as English. These may not be very useful for regularly spelled languages. This may be because children learning to read such languages seem to proceed very rapidly from the state of not knowing how to read to the state of being able to decode all the words in the language. Hence the classic type of reading test used in English, such as the Wide Range Achievement Test (WRAT; Jastak & Jastak, 1965), which involves reading single words out loud in an untimed format with accuracy-based scoring, can yield a bimodal distribution of scores consisting of non-readers who can read no words and readers who can read all words. This was investigated in the first of the two studies reported here.

Study 1

The first study examined data obtained from existing reading tests, both standardised and teacher-created reading tests. Both kinds of reading tests involved oral reading of single words. One test was an adaptation of the WRAT (Jastak & Jastak, 1965). On this test, as well as on the teacher-created tests, children's scores fell into a bimodal distribution, with all children's scores at the extremes and none in the centre of the distribution. The scores of 67 children on the adaptation of the WRAT are shown in Fig. 25.3.

Study 2

New reading tests were therefore developed in order to avoid various problems: children reading aloud words that they cannot understand, children with non-zero knowledge of letters scoring at floor level, and all children with any word-reading knowledge at all scoring at ceiling level.

The revised tests consisted of three levels: a letter/pseudoletter discrimination task, a word/pseudoword discrimination task, and a silly/sensible sentence discrimination task. In each test, children were asked to place a tick mark ($\checkmark$) on a sheet of paper if each of the letters/words/sentences made sense and a cross mark ($\times$) if the item was a silly/not real letter/word sentence. In Kiswahili these marks are known as 'correct' and 'wrong' marks, respectively, and even children who cannot write letters can usually form these marks. The distribution of

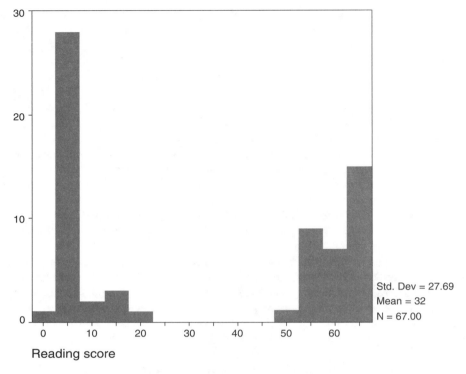

Reading score

FIG. 25.3.   Score distribution of a Kiswahili adaptation of the WRAT single-word oral reading test.

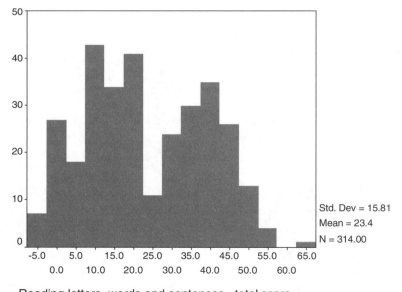

Reading letters, words and sentences – total score

FIG. 25.4.   Score distribution on letter, word, and sentence discrimination test.

scores for 314 children on all three tasks is shown in Fig. 25.4. It can be seen that the aim of removing ceiling and floor effects has been achieved. The distribution is not wholly normal; this is probably because when the scores were totalled on the three tests (letter, word, and sentence reading) children who scored the maximum score (24) on the letter- and word-reading tasks usually did not score zero on the sentence-reading task.

Discussion

The design of the three tests is such that children must read the words (on the word-reading task) and the sentences (on the sentence-reading task) for meaning; this, of course, requires decoding skills. The task demands and the distribution of scores make us confident that these tests are measures of both comprehension and decoding.

Given these results we can ask various questions, including this: How generalisable are the data from Kiswahili to other languages?

It is possible that some particular features of Kiswahili lead to this all-or-nothing decoding phenomenon. In particular, it may be that the invariant simple syllable structure (only open syllables and very few consonant clusters) and completely predictable stress pattern lead children to rapid development of decoding skills. For example, skilled beginning readers in Spanish displayed a similar pattern (Signorini, 1997), being able to read aloud 75% of pseudowords (compared with 94% of words, suggesting that they are almost as capable of decoding pseudowords as words). Unskilled beginning readers were able to read only 17% of pseudowords, suggesting a bimodal distribution very similar to that found in our (Alcock et al., 2000) data.

Although we have not carried out cross-linguistic comparisons, there is a large amount of data from other languages that suggests that this unequal distribution of reading skill is not an isolated phenomenon. Nevertheless, it is possible from these data to draw a few conclusions about the development of reading in Kiswahili and other regularly spelled languages. Thorstad (1991) carried out a comparative study of reading development in regular and non-regular orthographies, looking at initial teaching alphabet (i.t.a.), Italian, and traditional English orthographies. The analysis showed that children learning to read in either of the regular orthographies, (i.e., Italian or i.t.a.) read earlier than those learning traditional English orthography. Their data also concur with our findings (especially on the translation of the WRAT and the school-administered reading tests) that children who can decode a few words can also decode most of the words; development of decoding accuracy is rapid and develops in an all-or-nothing fashion in regularly spelled languages. After learning to decode words, children may increase their speed of decoding, but there does not seem to be a period during which they can decode some but not all words, or familiar but not unfamiliar words.

An examination of languages that are also regularly spelled but do not have such a simple phonological structure as Kiswahili (or, arguably, Spanish or Italian) can give us more information about the common processes in these languages. In Turkish, for example, which has more consonant clusters than Kiswahili, including many closed syllables, beginning readers were found to read pseudowords and real words equally well (Oeney & Durgunoglu, 1997). Like the beginning Italian readers just discussed (Thorstad, 1991) these beginning readers were able to learn very rapidly to read both words and pseudowords: In October of their first-grade year, they could read 26% of words and pseudowords and by February were able to read 72% of these items (though no breakdown of distribution is reported), reaching a ceiling level of 93% by May (Oeney & Durgunoglu, 1997). An ongoing study of Malay, which has some consonant clusters, some diphthongs, some closed syllables, and no accent on any syllable in a word, suggests that children learning to read this language can also decode words they do not yet understand once they have cracked the code (S. Rickard Liow, April, 2000, personal communication).

Likewise, in Greek, which has a large number of consonant clusters, Harris and Giannouli (1999; Giannouli & Harris, 1997) found that, at the end of first grade, given sufficient time to read, children could read all words, familiar and unfamiliar, as well as pseudowords.

In languages such as Spanish and Turkish, for which a comparison between skilled and unskilled beginning readers has been done, a bimodal distribution has been found in reading skills of familiar words, unfamiliar words, and pseudowords, as in our data for Kiswahili. The levels of performance for skilled and unskilled (or early and late first grade) beginning readers on such words are very similar in proportion in every language—less than 25% for unskilled readers and at ceiling for skilled readers by the end of first grade. In Italian, and in English taught with i.t.a., rapid acquisition of the ability to decode almost all words by the end of first grade is also reported. Our data from Kiswahili therefore seem to be in agreement with the findings of studies of other regularly spelled orthographies, regardless of syllable structure.

LEARNING TO SPELL KISWAHILI

Learning to spell in Kiswahili also seems to resemble learning to spell in other regularly spelled languages. As is true with many of these languages, although decoding the written word is a relatively straightforward task, spelling often lacks the complete one-to-one phoneme-to-grapheme correspondence of reading (Bryant, Nunes, & Aidinis, 1999; Harris & Giannouli, 1999). This has been demonstrated in observational studies of children's spontaneous spellings and in experimental studies. Many other languages share this feature of Kiswahili that the grapheme-to-phoneme link is more consistent than the phoneme-to-grapheme association. For this reason, children learning to spell even regularly spelled languages may have problems if one phoneme is represented by more than one grapheme.

Treiman (1993) suggests that there are a number of types of information that children must take into account when they learn to spell; these include phonological, orthographic, and grammatical information. This hypothesis is also applicable to regularly spelled languages such as Kiswahili. For example, in languages in which the phoneme-to-grapheme route is largely regular but double letters exist that are not represented in the phonological form of the word, as in Greek, children need to learn the orthographic information necessary to represent these double letters (Harris & Giannouli, 1999). Likewise, dialect variations can present an additional challenge for beginning spellers (Treiman, Goswami, Tincoff, & Leevers, 1997). Some regularly spelled languages, such as Portuguese, use different orthographic representations for different grammatical morphemes (Bryant et al., 1999), which means children must also take this type of information into account when spelling in such languages. The type of phonological information that challenges beginning spellers includes consonant clusters (Treiman & Cassar, 1996; Treiman, Zukowski, & Richmond-Welty, 1995), which exist in regularly spelled languages also. All of these factors could prove troublesome for beginning Kiswahili spellers.

Two studies of Kiswahili beginning spellers have been carried out, one of which involved quantifying all types of errors made in free spelling and using a group spelling test and the other of which concentrated on specific, potentially difficult, word forms.

Study 1: Description of Spelling Errors

In this study (Alcock & Ngorosho, 2003), two procedures were used to examine children's spelling. First, 41 children in Grades 2 through 6 in two primary schools were asked to write a message and draw a picture on the occasion of the author's leaving the research project. These children were allowed to write freely on the chosen topic, and their productions varied from a few words to long greetings with suitable local metaphors. A sample can be seen in Fig. 25.5.

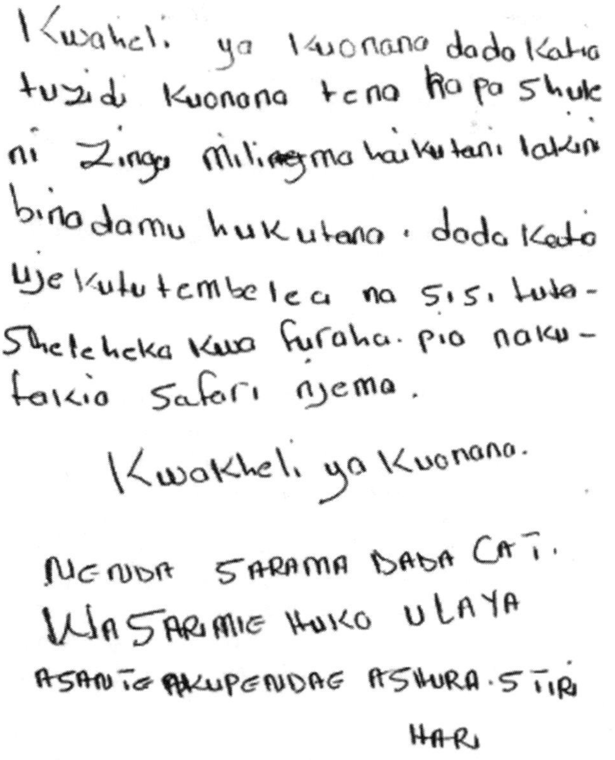
Kwaheli ya kuonana dada Katia
tuzidi kuonana tena hapa shule
ni Zinga Milimama haikutani lakini
binadamu hukutana. dada Kato
uje kututembelea na sisi. tuta-
Sheleheka kuwa furaha. pio naku-
takia safari njema.
Kwakheli ya kuonana.
NENDA SARAMA DADA CATI.
WASARIMIE HUKO ULAYA
ASANTE AKUPENDAE ASHURA. STIRI
HARI

FIG. 25.5. Sample of child's writing. The text reads (correct transcriptions of errors in sqare brackets): KWA HELI [*kwaheri*] YA KUONANA DADA KATIE TUZIDI KUONANA TENA HAPA SHULENI ZINGA MILIMA HAIKUTANI LAKINI BINADAMU HUKUTANA. DADA KATIE UJE KUTUTEMBELEA NA SISI TUTASHELEHEKA [*tutashereheka*] KWA FURAHA. PIA NAKUTAKIA SAFARI NJEMA. KWAKHELI [*kwaheri*] YA KUONANA. NENDA SARAMA [*salama*] DADA CATIE WASARIMIE [*wasalimie*] HUKO ULAYA ASANTE AKUPENDAE [*akupendaye*] ASHURA STIRIHARI: 'Goodbye and see you again sister Katie. We should see each other more again here at the school in Zinga. Mountains do not meet but people can meet. Sister Katie you should come to visit us and we will rejoice with happiness. Also I wish you a good journey. Goodbye and see you again. Go in peace sister Katie. Greet them where you are going in Europe. Thank you, one who loves you, Ashura Stirihari.

Second, 188 children in Grades 2 and 3 in five different schools were given a spelling test consisting of 50 words of graded difficulty. This was an adaptation of the WRAT spelling test. This test involved the tester's reading aloud a single word, placing the word in the context of a sentence, followed by the single word again.

Results

Children's errors were classified according to phonological errors. In the first data set, children could write as many or as few words as they wished, and children could therefore avoid words they found difficult. Errors in this data set are reported for each error type as the percentage of all errors made, as it is not possible to report errors in proportion to the opportunities children had to spell specific words. In the second data set children were encouraged to attempt all words, regardless of how difficult an individual word was for the individual child. The following categories of errors were noted:

Errors involving L/R
Errors involving Y or W
Errors involving H
Errors involving TH or DH (the orthographic representations of /θ/ and /ð/, respectively)
Errors involving nasal consonants—omission, substitution, or deletion
Errors involving other consonants—mainly in which a single feature (place, voicing, etc.)
    is changed
Errors involving vowels (mainly substitution of a single vowel, or replacing a double vowel
    with a single letter or vice versa[2]).

These errors can be broken down as follows:

Features of Dialect.   In the dialect of Kiswahili spoken by the children in the study, it is common to drop /h/. This was reflected in children's spelling as well. In the first data set, 11% of the errors consisted of omission of the H; in the second set of data, the corresponding figure was 20%. In the first data set 5% of errors were due to the addition of an H, and in the second data set children added H on an average of 0.37% words only.

Likewise, although in standard Kiswahili /l/ and /r/ are different phonemes, in the dialect spoken by children these are often used interchangeably. Some older adults in the area speak another language related to Kiswahili as their first language, and this and some related languages do not distinguish between the two phonemes; in any case, this is a contrast learned late for children learning to speak other languages, including English (Grunwell, 1982). In the first data set, 48% of errors were L/R substitutions and in the second data set 34.5% of words containing /r/ were spelled with L and 15.9% of words containing /l/ were spelled with R. This was therefore one of the most difficult distinctions for children to learn to spell.

Another dialectical feature is the tendency to pronounce /θ/ (spelled TH) as /s/ and /ð/ (spelled DH) as /z/. Children rarely attempted these words in the first data set but in the second data set one of each type of word was included. Of words that have /ð/, 61% were spelled with Z, and of words that have /θ/, 56% were spelled with S. Smaller numbers of words were spelled with D (for /ð/), T or F (for /θ/); these types of words are also very difficult for children. Such words are, it is true, less frequent in the language than words spelled with other digraphs, but words spelled with DH occur with at least one third the frequency of words with the well-spelled digraph CH[3].

Morphological Information.   Children were very poor in spelling L and R but one morphological feature of Kiswahili seems to help them. In Kiswahili, bound morphemes can contain /l/ but never /r/. In the second data set, children were significantly more likely to spell L successfully when it was part of a bound morpheme than when it was part of a root morpheme (Wilcoxon $Z = -3.7096$, $df = 187$, $p = .002$), and there was a tendency for children who were better spellers to be even better in applying this rule (Mann–Whitney $U = 3603.50$, $df = 1$, $p = .052$). Hence children are able to use morphological information to help them to spell better, and this use of grammatical information is one of the specific skills that better spellers have acquired and that distinguishes them from poor spellers.

---

[2] In Kiswahili double vowels are articulated separately, so that *za* ([of], agreeing with noun class 10) has one syllable whereas *zaa* ([give birth]) has two, with stress on the first syllable.

[3] Although no frequency norms exist for Kiswahili, in a dictionary sample of 10,000 word forms (Kamusi Project, 1999), 206 words containing /ð/ (spelled DH), 42 word forms containing /θ/ (spelled TH), 907 word forms containing /ʃ/ (spelled SH), and 563 word forms containing /tʃ/ (spelled CH) were found.

As already described, some words have a /j/ in their phonological representation but the spelling of the word with or without a Y depends on the grammatical class. Likewise some words that have /w/ in their phonological representation may or may not have W in their spelling. In the case of W in which the phonological /w/ transition is between morphemes, the word will be less likely to have the W in the spelling than that in which the transition is within the morpheme. In the first data set, errors of additions of Y or W represented 11.7% of the errors. In the second data set Y omissions represented 7.3% of the errors and W omissions represented 3.2% of the errors. Children appeared to understand the common placing of Y or W within a bound morpheme as in the first data set, but Y and W were added more frequently at morpheme boundaries (K–W chi-square $= 25.972$, $df = 2$, $p < .001$). As children got older the proportion of Y or W additions at root morphemes compared with bound morphemes decreased significantly (chi-square $= 7.969$, $df = 4$, $p = .047$). In the second data set W was more likely to be added at a morpheme boundary than in a root morpheme; however better spellers were less likely to commit such errors (Mann-Whitney $U = 3062.00$, $df = 1$, $p < .001$). Here again, better spellers seemed to use specific types of grammatical information to spell words.

Phonological Information. Consonant clusters are particularly hard for beginning spellers, as has been shown in other languages also (Treiman, 1991). Kiswahili has very few consonant clusters but the ones that exist consist of a nasal consonant followed by another consonant, such as the Kiswahili word *banda* [shed]. Children learning to spell Kiswahili found these clusters also particularly challenging. The nasal consonants in these clusters were more likely to be spelled incorrectly than were nasals that were not in clusters. Nasals in clusters in Kiswahili can either be syllabic or nonsyllabic, although this is not expressed in the spelling, and syllabic nasals were easier than nonsyllabic nasals (Wilcoxon $Z = 4.675$, $p < .001$). This suggests that one of the problems with nasal consonants that occurs in clusters may be their low saliency. In summary, children were found to make a wide variety of errors, many of which correspond to the types of errors seen in English and other languages.

Study 2

In Study 2 (Alcock & Ngorosho, 2004) we investigated further the difficulty children have in spelling consonant clusters that include nasal consonants. In Study 1, we found that if a consonant cluster contains a nasal consonant before a non-nasal consonant, the nasal consonant is more likely to have an error than either the second consonant of the cluster or a nasal consonant alone. If the nasal consonants were syllabic, however, they were not more difficult than were the non-nasal consonants in the clusters.

Kiswahili does not have many clusters, but unlike most European languages, in Kiswahili these consonant clusters can occur at the beginning of the word (for example, *ndimu* [lime]). In English and other European languages these types of consonant clusters (nasal followed by another consonant) are also difficult for beginning spellers (van Bon & Uit-De-Haag, 1997) and this could be due to children thinking that the nasal is part of the vowel rather than that it is a separate phoneme (Treiman et al., 1995).

It was therefore hypothesised that factors affecting the saliency of the nasals—such as whether the nasal cluster was stressed, whether the nasal was syllabic, and whether the nasal cluster was at the beginning or in the middle of the word—might affect how difficult the nasals are for beginning spellers. In addition, the comparison of errors on clusters at the beginnings and in the middle of the words can address the issue of whether having no preceding vowel might help children to correctly spell the nasals.

Study 2 included two experiments, each designed to investigate differing aspects of the nasal clusters that might affect spelling.

Experiment 1.   In Experiment 1, words were chosen with initial or medial nasal consonant clusters, of which some clusters were stressed and some clusters were unstressed, some were initial and some were medial, and some contained syllabic nasals and some contained non-syllabic nasals. Thus the effects of stress, position in the word, and syllabicity were examined.

Experiment 2.   In Experiment 2, all of the nasals studied were syllabic nasals. Initial and medial and stressed and unstressed nasal clusters were compared with each other. The finding in the first study, that nasal consonants in a cluster were harder to spell than the other consonant in the cluster and than single nasal consonants, was replicated in Study 2, in both Experiment 1 and Experiment 2. Unlike in the first study, this also applied to the syllabic nasal consonants in clusters. In the first study, syllabic nasals in clusters were not examined systematically and there were not as many tokens of this type of cluster, so the data from the second study are more likely to reflect the true picture.

Also in both experiments in the second study, children misspelled nasals in initial and medial positions, suggesting that some factor other than processing the nasals as part of a preceding vowel must be at work. In Experiment 1, examination of the possible saliency of nasals in clusters revealed that some nasals that are more salient—syllabic nasals—were easier to spell than comparable non-syllabic nasals.

However, other evidence in Experiment 1 did not support the hypothesis that saliency of the nasal is important. Nasals in initial, stressed, nonsyllabic clusters were more poorly spelled than those in medial nonsyllabic clusters—despite the fact that not all of the latter were stressed and that initial nasals might be supposed to have greater saliency. The nasals in initial nonsyllabic clusters were also in shorter words—and although the shorter words were on the whole spelled with fewer errors, a cluster in a short word hindered spelling more than a cluster in a longer word.

Experiment 1 contained both syllabic and non-syllabic nasals in clusters, but some potential combinations of stress, word length, and cluster position were not represented in the words used in this experiment, partly because only some types of words are possible in Kiswahili.

In Experiment 2, however, the types of words chosen represented both initial and medial and both stressed and unstressed nasal and other consonant clusters, and all the nasals were syllabic. Hence the comparisons made were more systematic. Again, however, evidence for saliency of the nasal in a cluster assisting spelling was not found. Initial nasals in clusters were harder to spell than medial consonants in clusters; stressed nasals in clusters were harder to spell than unstressed nasals in clusters. The initial, stressed nasals were those in the shortest words, but were the hardest to spell, although they might be the most salient. The apparently contradictory nature of this evidence can be explained if the concept of *phonetic density* is taken into account.

Phonetic density is defined as the ratio between the number of vowels and consonants in a word. When errors in spelling clusters were analysed on the basis of this criterion, it was found that phonetic density could account for the difficulty of spelling nasals in clusters in the words used in both experiments. This may explain why clusters in shorter words were harder to spell than those in longer words.

Returning to a comparison of spelling development in other languages, the problem with spelling nasals in clusters in Kiswahili can illuminate the spelling of clusters in other languages. Most studies in other languages have not examined the interaction between length and clusters (i.e., phonetic density) in spelling. However, one of the features of English is that it has a high proportion of consonant clusters and therefore has a high phonetic density. It is possible that it is phonetic density, as well as the opaque nature of the spelling system, that makes English difficult to spell.

Although in other languages beginning spellers often omit the first consonant of a medial cluster (Treiman & Cassar, 1996; Treiman et al., 1995) for initial consonant clusters (Stemberger & Treiman, 1986) the pattern is the opposite to that found here. The first consonant of the cluster is represented, and the second is more commonly misspelled or omitted (Treiman, 1991).

It has been suggested that this is a universal feature of the phonology of languages—that the initial consonant in a word-initial consonant cluster is better represented than the second consonant (Stemberger & Treiman, 1986). The pattern for initial consonant clusters is therefore the reverse of that found in Kiswahili, in which the initial (nasal) consonant has more errors than the other consonant in the cluster.

Although the saliency of the nasal in a consonant cluster is not the only factor that determines its spelling, it does seem to have some explanatory power given that syllabic nasals in clusters are easier to spell than non-syllabic nasals in clusters. Nasals do not occur as the first consonant of a word-initial consonant cluster in many languages, but they are intrinsically low in phonetic saliency, and when they do occur as the first consonant in consonant clusters, low phonetic saliency makes them difficult to spell. This further suggests that the difficulty in some languages with spelling the second consonant of word-initial consonant clusters is not that the consonant is non-initial, but that being non-initial gives the consonants lower phonetic saliency.

CONCLUSIONS

Data from Kiswahili therefore suggest that literacy development in this non-European language, taught in a school system that is severely underresourced, can still be compared with literacy development in other languages. Like other regularly spelled languages, learning to read Kiswahili is much easier than learning to spell it. This is no doubt due to a number of factors, including the less-than-perfect phoneme–grapheme correspondence in the face of a highly predictable grapheme–phoneme correspondence, but is also due to factors such as these:

Differential criteria used by teachers and testers in scoring children's reading and spelling performance: If a child slightly mispronounces a word he or she reads out loud (e.g., "hot" as /ot/), he or she is less likely to be marked as incorrect than if the same word were spelled as OT.

Children's difficulty in analysing consonant clusters: This kind of difficulty is found in other languages also, and data from Kiswahili has illuminated children's problems with consonant cluster representation in ways that are difficult to do in other languages.

For example, the inverse—and highly unexpected—relationship between length of word and difficulty of spelling consonant clusters may give us some clues about why English words, which are often very short and very dense in terms of the number of consonants per vowel, are difficult for children to spell. Certainly there are many other factors that influence spelling. What we can conclude, however, is that, in Kiswahili as in previously studied languages, learning to read and learning to spell use different sources of information.

REFERENCES

Alcock, K. J., & Ngorosho, D. (2003). Learning to spell a regularly spelled language is not a trivial task—Patterns of errors in Kiswahili. *Reading and Writing, 16*, 635–666.

Alcock, K. J., & Ngorosho, D. (2004). Learning to spell and learning phonology: The spelling of consonant clusters in Kiswahili. Cognitive Development submitted Nov 2004.

Alcock, K. J., Nokes, K., Ngowi, F., Musabi, C., McGregor, S., Mbise, A., Mandali, R., Bundy, D., & Baddeley, A. (2000). The development of reading tests for use in a regularly spelt language. *Applied Psycholinguistics, 21*, 525–555.

Biersteker, A. J. (1996). *Kujibizana: questions of language and power in nineteenth- and twentieth-century poetry in Kiswahili* (4th ed.). East Lansing, MI: Michigan State University Press.

Bryant, P., Nunes, T., & Aidinis, A. (1999). Different morphemes, same spelling problems: Cross-linguistic developmental studies. In M. Harris & G. Hatano (Eds.), *Learning to read and write: A cross-linguistic perspective* (pp. 112–133). New York: Cambridge University Press.

Christian Knowledge Society. (1901). *Kusoma kwa Watoto, kwa siku ya Jumapili* [Sunday school services in Swahili]. London: Author.

Frederiksen, C. H., & Chitepo, T. (1992). Text understanding among Swahili-speaking children in coastal Kenya. In K. Legère (Ed.), *The role of language in primary education in eastern Africa with special reference to Kiswahili.* Bonn, Germany: Deutsche Stiftung fur internationale Entwicklung/Zentralstelle fur Erziehung, Wissenschaft und Dokumentation.

Giannouli, V., & Harris, M. (1997). *The relationship of phonemic awareness to reading and spelling in Greek preschool and primary school children.* Paper presented at European Developmental Psychology Conference, University of Rennes, France.

Grunwell, P. (1982). *Clinical phonology.* London: Croom Helm.

Harris, M., & Giannouli, V. (1999). Learning to read and spell in Greek: The importance of letter knowledge and morphological awareness. In M. Harris & G. Hatano (Eds.), *Learning to read and write: A cross-linguistic perspective* (pp. 51–70). New York: Cambridge University Press.

Inter-Territorial Language (Swahili) Committee to the East African Dependencies, & Johnson, F. (1939). *A standard English–Swahili dictionary (founded on Madan's English-Swahili dictionary).* London: Oxford University Press H. Milford.

Jastak, J., & Jastak, S. (1965). *The Wide Range Achievement Test.* Wilmington, DE: Guidance Association.

Jukes, M. C., Nokes, C. A., Alcock, K. J., Lambo, J. K., Kihamia, C., Ngorosho, D., Mbise, A., Lorri, W., Yona, E., Mwanri, L., Baddeley, A. D., Hall, A., & Bundy, D. A. (2002). Heavy schistosomiasis associated with poor short-term memory and slower reaction times in Tanzanian schoolchildren. *Tropical Medicine and International Health, 7*, 104–117.

Kamusi Project (1999). *Internet living Swahili dictionary.* Available on-line at http://www.yale.edu/swahili.

Knappert, J. (1979). *Four centuries of Swahili verse: A literary history and anthology.* London: Heinemann Educational.

Legère, K. (1992). *The role of language in primary education in eastern Africa with special reference to Kiswahili.* Bonn, Germany: Deutsche Stiftung fur internationale Entwicklung/Zentralstelle fur Erziehung, Wissenschaft und Dokumentation.

Ngonyani, D. S. (1992). A weak reading foundation: some inadequacies of Tanzanian Primary School language textbooks. In K. Legére (Ed.), The role of language in primary education in eastern Africa with special reference to Kiswahili. Bonn: Deutsche Stiftung fur internationale Entwicklung/Zentralstelle fur Erziehung, Wissenschaft und Dokumentation.

Nurse, D., & Spear, T. T. (1985). *The Swahili: Reconstructing the history and language of an African society, 800–1500.* Philadelphia: University of Pennsylvania Press.

Oeney, B., & Durgunoglu, A. Y. (1997). Beginning to read in Turkish: A phonologically transparent orthography. *Applied Psycholinguistics, 18*, 1–15.

Signorini, A. (1997). Word reading in Spanish: A comparison between skilled and less skilled beginning readers. *Applied Psycholinguistics, 18*, 319–344.

Steere, E. (1870a). *A handbook of the Swahili language as spoken at Zanzibar.* London: Society for Promoting Christian Knowledge.

Steere, E. (1870b). *Swahili tales: as told by natives of Zanzibar.* Nendeln, Switzerland: Kraus Reprint.

Stemberger, J. P., & Treiman, R. (1986). The internal structure of word-initial consonant clusters. *Journal of Memory & Language, 25*, 163–180.

Tabouret-Keller, A., & International Group for the Study of Language Standardization and the Vernacularization of Literacy. (1997). *Vernacular literacy: A re-evaluation.* Oxford, UK: Clarendon.

Thorstad, G. (1991). The effect of orthography on the acquisition of literacy skills. *British Journal of Psychology, 82*, 527–537.

Treiman, R. (1991). Children's spelling errors on syllable-initial consonant clusters. *Journal of Educational Psychology, 83*, 346–360.

Treiman, R. (1993). *Beginning to spell: A study of first-grade children.* New York: Oxford University Press.

Treiman, R., & Cassar, M. (1996). Effects of morphology on children's spelling of final consonant clusters. *Journal of Experimental Child Psychology, 63*, 141–170.

Treiman, R., Goswami, U., Tincoff, R., & Leevers, H. (1997). Effects of dialect on American and British children's spelling. *Child Development, 68*, 229–245.

Treiman, R., Zukowski, A., & Richmond-Welty, E. D. (1995). What happened to the "n" of sink? Children's spellings of final consonant clusters. *Cognition, 55*, 1–38.

UNICEF, & Bellamy, C. (2001). *The state of the world's children 2002*. New York: UNICEF.

van Bon, W. H. J., & Uit-De-Haag, I. J. C. A. (1997). Difficulties with consonants in the spelling and segmentation of CCVCC pseudowords: Differences among Dutch first graders. *Reading and Writing, 9*, 363–386.

Whiteley, W. H. (1993). *Swahili: The rise of a national language* (1st ed.). Aldershot, Hampshire, UK: Gregg Revivals.

26

Reading Chinese

Him Cheung, Catherine McBride-Chang, and
Bonnie Wing-Yin Chow
The Chinese University of Hong Kong

In this chapter we overview research on learning to read Chinese. We first describe Chinese orthography and then summarize past findings on adults' cognitive processing of written language. Next, we review studies on Chinese children's reading acquisition. Finally, we outline previous work on Chinese reading impairment. There are a number of unique features of written Chinese that have important implications for reading and learning to read.

CHINESE ORTHOGRAPHY

The basic unit of written Chinese is the character, the total number of which in modern usage has been estimated at around 4,600 (Chen, Song, Lau, Wong, & Tang, 2003). A character is a visual–spatial unit occupying a fixed amount of space in print, analogous to the English letter in this respect. Nevertheless, rather than being a sound symbol, each character functions as a lexical morpheme carrying a meaning. In other words, characters are primarily meaning symbols, although they can contain phonetic cues; combining them results in words. Because characters are equally spaced, no visual word boundaries can exist (Chen, 1992, 1996).

Actually, the concept of a "Chinese word" is rather fuzzy, even among native speakers (Chen, 1993). Chinese readers all know what a character is; their identification of characters would agree perfectly with one another, because characters are equally spaced. However, Chinese readers' agreement on word identity is typically less than satisfactory, perhaps because Chinese words are not marked by spaces in print. Nevertheless, words do play a role in reading comprehension; Chinese readers are simply unaware of their identity (Chen, 1993).

Many Chinese characters are polysemous: A polysemous character can take on different meanings; that is, it corresponds to several distinct morphemes. Which meaning of a polysemous character should be selected and emphasized depends on word context. For example, the character 華 means "Chinese" in the word 華人 [Chinese people], but means "luxurious" in the word 華麗. Furthermore, the meaning of a character does not always contribute to the meaning of the word that carries it. For example, the character 飛 means "fly"; one Cantonese–Chinese word that contains this character is 飛仔, which means "gangster." Gangsters certainly have nothing to do with flying. Words containing characters that do not bear obvious semantic relations to the words themselves are known as opaque words; those that share semantic relations are referred to as transparent words.

Calling characters the "basic" unit of written Chinese does not mean that they are nonanalyzable. Actually, smaller components can be identified. Compound or complex characters are characters that can be analyzed into radicals, conveying either phonetic or semantic information. About 85% of characters in modern usage belong to this category (Zhu, 1988). Phonetic radicals are themselves characters; they are therefore pronounceable and can hint at how the overall compound character should be pronounced. Semantic radicals are not necessarily characters; some of them are nonpronounceable stroke patterns suggesting to what semantic category the referent of the overall character should belong. For example, the characters for "table" (柏), "chair" (椅), and "cabinet" (櫃) all share the semantic radical standing for "wood" (木), because the objects being referred to are instances of the "furniture" category, which is strongly associated with "wood." Finally, some radicals can be decomposed into smaller stroke patterns, which are canonical figural combinations of strokes. Stroke patterns do not necessarily carry meaning.

The character constitutes the smallest pronounceable unit in written Chinese. Each character is pronounced as a syllable. Smaller phonological units, such as the phoneme, are not represented in the script. This is why phonetic radicals must themselves be characters (that makes them pronounceable), and why they can only provide subtle cueing for the sound of the overall character, rather than representing subsyllabic sound components (simply because these components are not represented anywhere in the script).

Phonetic radicals are not always reliable in cueing compound character pronunciation. According to the estimation of Zhou (1978), only about 39% of compound characters contain phonetic radicals that serve the sound-cueing function effectively (Mandarin pronunciation). For this reason, Chinese script has been considered highly opaque, in contrast with transparent systems such as Italian and Serbo-Croatian, in which phonemes are reliably represented by graphemes.

Currently two systems of Chinese characters are used. Traditional characters are adopted in Taiwan and Hong Kong, whereas simplified characters are used in Mainland China and Singapore. Simplified characters were first released for official and everyday use by the Mainland Chinese Government in 1956. To date, there have been few studies on possible differences in the processing of the two scripts.

One obvious advantage of adopting the logographic principle (i.e., graphemes directly representing meaning) in written Chinese is that it greatly facilitates communication among people speaking different Chinese languages. China is a vast country in which some 200 closely related languages are spoken. We call these languages collectively "Chinese," yet most of them are mutually unintelligible because of phonological, lexical, and syntactic differences. Because the emphasis of written Chinese is on representing meaning by means of graphemes, adoption of the script greatly alleviates communication problems that are due to pronunciation differences between language groups.

COGNITIVE PROCESSING OF WRITTEN CHINESE IN ADULTS

Given the many unique features of the Chinese script, character and word recognition and their subsequent processing have recently attracted a lot of research attention. Researchers are concerned with the implications of these script-specific features for the development of general theories of reading. One interesting issue in character recognition has to do with the prominence of direct phonological activation during initial character reading. Because Chinese characters have been viewed as morphosyllabic units in which the expression of meaning is relatively important, some researchers argue for a nonprominent role of direct phonological access from orthography. Chen (1992, 1996) provided an exposition of this theoretical view and how it has come out of the unique features of the Chinese script. Note that the hypothesized pattern, that phonological activation is less dominant than orthographic and semantic access, stands in contrast with what has been typically assumed in English reading (e.g., Frost, 1998; Lukatela & Turvey, 1991; Perfetti, Zhang, & Berent, 1992; van Orden, 1987). For example, in an early study, Chen, Yung, and Ng (1988) required their participants to search among several candidates for the character that was different from the rest in terms of its component graphemes, phonemes, or meaning, as specified by a cue. Results showed that phonemic search was slower than both graphemic and meaning search, thus indicating a certain degree of indirectness of phonological activation in character reading. Chen, Flores-d'Arcais, and Cheung (1995) failed to establish that homophonic foils influenced semantic categorization more than did nonhomophonic words. Hence phonological access does not appear to be obligatory and unavoidable in Chinese reading.

Wong and Chen (1999) adopted the eye-movement approach to examine how different types of manipulations would affect eye-fixation patterns. Manipulation was done by the replacement of a target character in a short passage with either an orthographically or a phonologically similar character, thus rendering the word containing the target ill-formed. Disruptions in fixation duration were measured. Results indicated that orthographic manipulation produced early and reliable disruptions in fixation, whereas the effect of phonological manipulation was late and much less robust. The authors therefore concluded that orthography plays a more dominant role than does phonology in reading Chinese. This conclusion was later reinforced by the eye-movement findings of Feng, Miller, Shu, and Zhang (2001), which showed early phonological activation in English but not in Chinese reading. Use of phonological information in reading Chinese was not evident until a late stage at which the reader needed to recover reading from errors.

Using the priming technique, both Shen and Forster (1999) and Chen and Shu (2001) were able to establish clear orthographic effects, whereas phonological effects were consistently absent. Chen (2002) examined the relations among reading efficiency, indicated by reading accuracy and speed, and a host of reading strategy indices, including how likely the reader was to use orthographic–lexical, semantic, phonological, and lexical decomposition information during reading. Results showed that the phonological index was predictive of *slow* reading, especially with low-frequency lexical items. These findings all lead to the conclusion that phonological activation in Chinese reading is less dominant than orthographic processing. Hence meaning access in the Chinese script should not depend critically on phonology (see also Hoosain, 2002).

On the other hand, Perfetti and his colleagues argue that, in processing characters, phonology plays the most dominant role. Evidence for this position has come from a series of laboratory studies (e.g., Perfetti et al., 1992; Perfetti & Tan, 1998; Perfetti & Zhang, 1991, 1995; Tan & Perfetti, 1997, 1999). Findings from this research group contrast with what has been found elsewhere (e.g., Chen & Shu, 2001; Shen & Forster, 1999), in that very early and robust phonological effects in Chinese reading were consistently demonstrated and have been difficult to replicate in other studies (Chen & Shu, 2001; Zhou & Marslen-Wilson, 1999, 2000; Zhou, Marslen-Wilson, Taft, & Shu, 1999). At present, there is no sign that the debate about the relative prominence of orthographic or phonological information for expert Chinese reading can be easily resolved.

Another issue in Chinese reading that is of particular interest has to do with the prominent role of the character in reading cognition. The point becomes clear if we compare characters with written English words. Each written English word is a spatially marked visual unit; it can, however, represent multiple syllables and morphemes. In contrast, a character is always pronounced as a syllable and represents a single morpheme. Hence the character constitutes a salient visual, phonological, and semantic unit all at the same time. What, then, are the psychological implications? One assumption is that one gains access to visually presented multiple-morpheme (multiple-character) words by means of the activation of their component characters, due to the prominence of characters as a reading unit. In other words, the level of morphemic (character) representation is critical in visual word recognition.

This prediction was confirmed by Peng, Liu, and Wang (1999), who reported that the lexical-decision times of two-character words were sensitive to both word- and character-occurrence frequencies. Furthermore, activation of individual morphemes played a more important role in the recognition of transparent (character meaning obviously related to word meaning) than in the recognition of opaque words (character meaning unrelated to word meaning). Hence character representation is as important as word representation; the contribution of character representation is qualified by the semantic relation between the word and its component characters. These conclusions are echoed and reinforced in a review by Taft, Liu, and Zhu (1999). The authors argue that morphemic (character) activation plays an important role in the recognition of multiple-morpheme Chinese words. The involvement of morpheme-level activation differs in processing transparent versus opaque words (see also Taft, Huang, & Zhu, 1994; Taft & Zhu, 1995, 1997; Zhang & Peng, 1992).

Zhou et al. (1999) adopted the priming paradigm with a visual lexical-decision task to examine the interaction among orthographic, morphological, and phonological information in reading two-character Chinese words. Priming effects were observed when the prime and the target shared a common character, which either did or did not represent the same morpheme across the prime and the target contexts. On the other hand, no priming was obtained when the shared component was a homophonic morpheme, realized orthographically as different characters across the prime and the target contexts. Therefore characters as an orthographic–morphemic unit constitute a critical level of representation in Chinese visual word recognition.

Using the eye-movement method to investigate Chinese reading cognition, Chen and his colleagues obtained data showing both similarities and differences between reading English and Chinese texts. One focus of this line of inquiry has to do with the special status of the character in Chinese reading comprehension. Chen, Lau, and Wong (1998) coded passages at the character, word, sentence, and text levels; the resultant measures were entered into multiple-regression equations as independent variables predicting eye-fixation times. The most reliable predictors turned out to be certain character-level variables, such as character complexity and frequency. Word-level variables were relatively unimportant. Wong and Chen (1999) and Feng et al. (2001) reported that character-level eye movements were more stable and less affected by manipulation of linguistic information than were word-level movements. This finding speaks to the central role of character processing in Chinese reading comprehension.

In summary, we highlight two major findings concerning skilled adult readers' processing of written Chinese. First, orthographic sensitivity is particularly important in expert readers' character recognition. The role of phonology in adults' Chinese reading is relatively limited. Second, the character plays a special role in Chinese reading, because it is at the same time a salient visual, phonological, and morphemic unit. Character processing contributes significantly to the comprehension of words and connected texts. The prominence of characters has more to do with the fact that they represent morphemes rather than syllables.

LEARNING TO READ CHINESE

Studies of Chinese character-recognition development can be grouped into at least two categories. First, there are some studies that have considered the cognitive abilities underlying basic Chinese character recognition. These studies link cognitive developmental constructs to early character recognition. This research focuses primarily on the importance of theoretical constructs such as visual and phonological processing for initial character recognition. The second group of studies focuses on developmental comparisons of Chinese children's analyses of characters themselves, once children have already acquired some character-recognition skills. Such studies focus particularly on the extent to which children apply knowledge of phonetic or semantic radicals to learning to read or write new characters. Despite considerable differences in the contexts in which Chinese characters are learned across regions, some consensus on the development of Chinese character recognition, both as linked to theoretical constructs and to children's analytic abilities in processing characters and character components, has emerged. We begin with a consideration of how very early Chinese character recognition appears to develop. Here, we focus on some constructs demonstrated to have importance for character acquisition. These include visual skills, phonological awareness, rapid naming speed, and morphological awareness.

Very early in the process of literacy acquisition, Chinese children become aware of print. For example, Chan and Louie (1992) demonstrated that Hong Kong Chinese children distinguished Chinese characters from pictures by the age of 3 years. This early awareness of print as distinct from pictures is similar to that observed in other cultures (Gibson & Levin, 1975; Gombert & Fayol, 1992). By the age of 4 years, Chinese children also show more accurate detection of characters presented in correct perceptual orientation as opposed to their mirror images (Miller, 2002). In this study, children were asked to indicate whether a given character was in a correct or incorrect orientation; the characters presented were unfamiliar to the children. Their responses were compared with those of similarly aged American peers without experience in Chinese. Results suggest a general perceptual orientation to Chinese that emerges very early because of general experience with the script but not specific reading experience.

Chinese character recognition places a relatively large burden on children's visual processing skills. Because, relative to alphabetic scripts, more visual information is contained in Chinese, visual skills may be particularly important for early learning of this orthography (e.g., Hoosain, 1991). This visual information may be in a different form than that required for alphabetic script processing. In alphabets, for example, perhaps the most salient visual information is the length of words. In contrast, in Chinese, the visual–spatial layout is constant. That is, for every character, an identical square space is allocated. Thus, for Chinese, number and types of strokes within each character is most salient (e.g., Seidenberg, 1985).

Previous researchers (e.g., Ehri & Wilce, 1985; Ho & Bryant, 1997) have referred to a logographic period of early reading. In initial experiences with print, children may focus on a visually salient cue to help them to read a word. This cue might be a single (usually first) letter in many alphabetic orthographies; it could even be a more distributed visual configuration, as in Hebrew (Share & Gur, 1999). For Chinese, it appears that most children focus on prominent visual features of Chinese characters to distinguish them initially. For example, a longitudinal study conducted by Ho and Bryant (1999) showed that the Constancy of Shape subtest of the Frostig Developmental Test of Visual Perception in 3-year-old Hong Kong children predicted Chinese character recognition 1 year later, once children's age, IQ, and their mothers' education level were statistically controlled. Ho and Bryant (1999) pointed out that Chinese character recognition is based on the identification of a set of recurring stroke patterns that appear in different characters in different sizes and locations, and this requires visual skills very similar to those of the Constancy of Shape task. A number of studies have now demonstrated that various visual processing skills are associated with reading both in correlational (e.g., Huang & Hanley, 1995; Lee, Stigler, & Stevenson, 1986; Siok & Fletcher, 2001) and longitudinal research (e.g., Ho & Bryant, 1997, 1999). We (McBride-Chang, Chow, Zhong, Burgess, & Hayward, in press) recently demonstrated that children's knowledge of visual–spatial relations (Gardner ,1996) is particularly important for early character recognition in both traditional and simplified script. In this study, we also found that visual skills were more strongly linked to character recognition and better developed for readers of simplified script. These results are in line with those found by Chen and Yuen (1991), who attributed the greater number of visual errors made in character recognition in simplified compared with traditional script to reduced visual distinctiveness in simplified script. Overall, the importance of visual processing skills for reading has been downplayed in the reading acquisition literature up to this point. An important developmental issue for future research on reading acquisition is how various visual skills might be expected to affect early character recognition. Although a great deal has been written about the importance and levels of phonological awareness within and across orthographies (e.g., Adams, 1990; Goswami, 1999), researchers have relatively little information on the unique and shared importance of various visual processing skills (e.g., visual memory, visual perception, visual matching) to reading development.

A second area of exploration in acquisition of Chinese character recognition is the role of phonological awareness. As in all orthographies, an important goal of initial character recognition is to map orally learned vocabulary onto script. Thus early speech–sound sensitivity may be helpful in ensuring that Chinese characters are mapped onto clearly specified oral referents. Ho and Bryant (1997) demonstrated the importance of speech–sound sensitivity in young Hong Kong children in a longitudinal study. Ho and Bryant (1997) showed that children's prereading phonological skills uniquely predicted the children's reading performance in Chinese 2 and 3 years later after controlling for the effects of age, IQ, and mother's education. This research was crucial in demonstrating the importance of early phonological awareness for subsequent Chinese reading.

In Chinese, the most important unit of speech for the task of reading is the syllable, because every syllable maps onto a single character. Thus some awareness of the syllable as an oral referent that can be manipulated may help children to learn to map syllables onto the characters they are taught. Across several studies of children in both Hong Kong (McBride-Chang & Ho, 2000; McBride-Chang & Kail, 2002; McBride-Chang, Shu, Zhou, Wat, & Wagner, 2003) and other parts of China (McBride-Chang & Zhong, 2003; McBride-Chang, Chow et al., in press), a task of syllable deletion was among the best predictors of Chinese character recognition among children of ages 3–6 years. In this task, children are asked orally to take away a syllable from a two- or three-syllable phrase. An analogous task in English would be to ask a child to say "big teacup" without saying "tea".

Phoneme awareness may also play a role in learning to read in Chinese, but this role is strongly restricted by the teaching method to which children are exposed. Phonemes are particularly important to the extent that they are taught to children as a coding system to facilitate character recognition, particularly in Pinyin, used in China. However, onsets and rimes of characters may also have some salience to Chinese children (Siok & Fletcher, 2001). For example, some Chinese dictionaries are organized according to onsets and rimes, as represented by characters (Siok & Fletcher, 2001). Previous studies have demonstrated that awareness of onsets and rimes (Siok & Fletcher, 2001) or phonemes (Huang & Hanley, 1997) is correlated with Chinese character recognition as well. Nevertheless, given the fact that phonemic awareness is not necessary for Chinese reading, it is likely that the importance of phonological awareness wanes with age. Although syllable awareness appears to be a strong predictor of early character recognition, syllable awareness develops naturally and is attained by most children by the age of 6 years or so (Treiman & Zukowski, 1991). In contrast, phonemic awareness does not develop naturally and may never develop in the absence of explicit teaching about phonemes (Bowey & Francis, 1991). Thus, although phonological awareness is a strong predictor of reading over a long period of time in children learning to read alphabetic orthographies, the same may not be true for Chinese.

Another construct that has proved useful in predicting Chinese character recognition is rapid automatized naming (RAN). In this type of task, children are presented with rows of nameable things, either linguistic symbols, such as numbers, radicals, or letters, or pictures, such as blocks of colors or objects. They are asked to name these rows of things as quickly as possible, and the speed with which they name them aloud is a good indicator of their reading ability. This task has reliably distinguished good from poor readers in a number of studies (Ho & Lai, 1999; Shu, Meng, & Lai, in press). It is also a unique predictor of Chinese character recognition in young children (McBride-Chang & Kail, 2002). Although RAN is clearly a good predictor of reading across orthographies, its theoretical relevance for the development of Chinese character recognition is unclear. The issue here is what cognitive constructs relevant to reading are captured by RAN tasks. Some of the importance of RAN tasks is that they measure phonological coding in lexical access (Wagner & Torgesen, 1987). RAN tasks also have a strong speeded element (McBride-Chang & Kail, 2002). Speed of processing is influenced both by individual and developmental differences among children, and children who are generally faster tend to excel in various cognitive tasks (Kail, 1995).

Manis, Seidenberg, and Doi (1999) also note an "arbitrariness" element of RAN tasks. Such tasks require children quickly to label pictures or symbols with verbal labels. The names of these pictures or symbols are arbitrary in language, and facility with arbitrarily pairing names with symbols may help children to learn to read more effectively. This may be particularly true for Chinese reading, because Chinese orthography is relatively inconsistent in symbol–sound mappings. For example, in English, letter–phoneme patterns, though sometimes inconsistent (e.g., "k" often makes the /k/ sound but sometimes is silent, as in "know"), are often fairly regular in their mappings. In contrast, Chinese has less consistent mappings of phonetic radicals to syllables (e.g., Shu, et al., 2003). Thus, although learning the meanings of semantic radicals and noticing consistencies in the sounds made by phonetic radicals across Chinese characters are somewhat helpful in learning to recognize new characters (by meaning, by sound, or both), they do not guarantee success in character acquisition in the way that learning letter sounds might facilitate subsequent English word recognition (Li & Rao, 2000). Instead, perhaps greater tolerance for arbitrary mapping of oral language to characters is particularly important in learning to read Chinese.

A final cognitive construct that facilitates learning to read Chinese is morphological awareness. We define morphological awareness here as awareness of and access to the meaning system of language. Morphological awareness is gaining increased attention in the reading acquisition literature (e.g., Mann, 2000), but its importance for reading and the ways in which it is measured likely differ markedly depending on the language in which it is measured.

A focus on meaning in relation to reading acquisition may be particularly important for learning to read Chinese, because the semantic radical of a Chinese character usually gives some indication as to its meaning. For instance, the semantic radical "氵" stands for water, and characters with this radical usually represent something related to water, such as 河 [river] and 湖 [lake]. In contrast, in alphabetic languages, although explicit learning of some root words (e.g., "love," "manage," "accept"), prefixes (e.g., "un," "dis," "mis") or suffixes (e.g., "ing," "able," "ful") may help children to read new words, there is no clear expectation of a meaning component to a given word, as there often is in Chinese compound characters. In addition, phonological and semantic letter sequences may be confounded in English in a way that they are not in Chinese. For example, the "under" in "understand" does not have the same meaning as the "under" in "underrepresented." In contrast, in Chinese, the semantic radical holds a special position within most Chinese compound characters.

Shu and Anderson (1997) were the first to demonstrate the importance of semantic radicals for learning to read. Subsequent researchers have also demonstrated that children make use of semantic radicals to help them to read and write new characters from early primary school, despite the fact that they are rarely explicitly taught about these radicals (Chan & Wang, 2003; Tsai & Nunes, 2003). Wu and colleagues (Wu, Anderson, Li, Chen, & Meng, 2002) followed up on this work by testing a teaching program that focused on explicitly teaching semantic (and phonetic) radicals to children. Results indicated that such training facilitated children's reading-related skills.

Given the importance of morphological awareness for learning to read Chinese, recent research has focused on the extent to which morphological awareness measured in the absence of print predicts character recognition. We (McBride-Chang, Shu et al., 2003) tested this in a study of kindergarten and second graders in Hong Kong. We measured two aspects of morphological awareness in these children. First, children's abilities to distinguish among homophones the correct meaning intended were tested. Because Chinese has many homophones, an important task for learning to read may be to figure out which character maps onto which of multiple speech syllables that sound identical. We did this by having children select from among three pictures the one that best represented the meaning of the homophone used. For example, three pictures showing a basketball (*laam4 kau4*), a boy (*laam4 haai4*), and the color blue (*laam4 sik1*) were presented, and the child was asked to select from the three pictures the one that corresponded best to the meaning of boy and girl (*laam4 leoi5*, which is a common phrase in Cantonese). The target morpheme was *laam4* and the target picture was that with the boy. We called this morpheme identification. Second, we tested children's abilities to combine familiar words in unfamiliar ways to build new meanings. This was done with stories. For example, "When the sun goes down at night, we call this a sunset. What would we call it if the moon went down at night?" (correct answer = moonset). This ability was termed morphological construction. Results of this study were that, among kindergartners, both morpheme identification and morphological construction uniquely predicted Chinese character recognition, even controlling for children's naming speed, speed of processing, vocabulary knowledge, and phonological awareness. Among second graders, only the morphological construction variable contributed uniquely to Chinese character recognition once these other reading-related tasks were included in an equation. We tested children from Beijing on these skills as well and found some support for the importance of morphological awareness. In particular, among both kindergartners and second graders, morphological construction was a unique and strong predictor of Chinese character recognition, controlling for other reading-related tasks.

To summarize very early Chinese character acquisition, these constructs just reviewed must be considered. Developmentally, visual skills are likely important for initial character recognition, though very little research has been done on this so far. Practically speaking, early phonological awareness and speeded naming tasks are useful as indicators of who might be at risk for early reading problems. Although phonological awareness is important for early reading, its importance for reading past early primary school is unclear, because Chinese reading does not require phonemic awareness, a relatively difficult skill, as it does in alphabetic orthographies. Finally, morphological awareness is theoretically and practically important for early Chinese character recognition. However, the importance of morphological awareness is clearest in studies of how children make use of semantic radicals. Few studies to date have examined the construct of morphological awareness measured in the absence of print in relation to early reading ability.

The second group of developmental studies on Chinese reading is more descriptive in nature. Research along this line examines how children make use of certain structural characteristics inherited in the script for both comprehension and production. The majority of these studies focus on children's processing of compound characters containing phonetic and semantic radicals. Convergent results indicate that from a young age on children learning the script are generally able to take advantage of the information contained in these radicals and process them in predictable ways. First, children appear to be sensitive to the positional distributions of phonetic versus semantic radicals. The two types of components are not randomly positioned. For instance, phonetic radicals are more likely to be found on the right-hand side in left–right structured characters. In contrast, semantic radicals usually appear in the left-hand position. Note, however, that the actual positions of radicals depend on their identities. Some phonetic radicals must appear on the left, whereas some semantic radicals must appear on the right. Chan and Nunes (1998) required their young Chinese participants, aged 4 to 9 years, to create names for novel objects. Both phonetic and semantic radicals were provided for name construction. At around the age of 6 years, children were already capable of putting these radicals into their legal positions when creating object names. Using a similar method, Chan and Wang (2003) replicated the result in both Hong Kong and Beijing children, who had learned to read the traditional and simplified Chinese scripts, respectively. Names that involved characters containing illegally positioned radicals, that is, noncharacters, were especially likely to be rejected as suitable object labels. Shu and Anderson (1999) required first, second, fourth, and sixth graders to make lexical decisions on character items. The authors focused on analyzing children's proportion of false-alarm responses to three types of stimuli. Well-formed items contained real radicals in their legal positions, but the overall items were not actual characters. Ill-formed components items contained pseudoradicals in their legal positions, whereas ill-formed structure items contained real radicals in their illegal positions. Results showed that false alarms were proportionally much less likely for ill-formed structure items than were the other two types of illegal items. The effect was already observable in children in second grade. Hence children's sensitivity to the relative positions of phonetic and semantic radicals starts developing at a very early stage.

Second, young children are sensitive to the cueing function of phonetic radicals. Ho and Bryant (1997) showed that, when asked to read aloud pseudocharacters or illegal characters in which the radicals are legally positioned, young children were likely to take the pronunciation of the phonetic radical as that of the whole character. When asked to read aloud real characters, children used the same strategy, and hence in many cases they committed errors (i.e., in irregular compound characters in which the phonetic radical did not sound the same as the overall character). Ho, Wong, and Chan (1999) replicated such a tendency to use the sound-cueing function provided by phonetic radicals in first graders. Chan and Nunes (1998) reported the same processing tendency among older children (third and fourth graders). Wang and Guthrie (2002) reported that it was quite common for fifth graders to commit reading (aloud) errors because they identified the pronunciations of unknown compound characters by using the sounds of their phonetic radicals. The trend was especially marked among skilled readers. In a primed naming study, Wu, Zhou, and Shu (1999) asked third and sixth graders to respond to target characters that were homophonic to the phonetic radicals of prime compound characters, but not to the compound characters themselves. Significant priming effects were observed for both third and sixth graders. Therefore third graders are already capable of analyzing compound characters and obtaining the pronunciation of their phonetic radicals.

Third, young children are sensitive to the cueing function of semantic radicals. Shu and Anderson (1997) showed that children around 8 years of age started to use the meaning of semantic radicals to interpret the meaning of newly learned compound characters. Ho et al. (1999) and Chan and Nunes (1998) all noticed the use of semantic radicals for overall character meaning interpretation in even younger children. Chan and Wang (2003) asked 5-, 6-, 7-, 8-, and 9-year-olds to select single-character names for novel objects. Character names contained semantic radicals that were either consistent or inconsistent with the semantic categories to which the objects belonged. Results showed that children, especially the older ones, preferred character names carrying consistent radicals over those containing inconsistent radicals, even when both types of semantic radicals were appearing in their "correct" legal positions.

Fourth, children in their early primary years are capable of combining knowledge in phonetic and semantic radicals to read and interpret compound characters in a sensible way. Ho, Yau, and Au (2003) obtained a variety of measures in kindergartners, first, and third graders (mean ages = 5.7, 6.7, and 8.6, years, respectively). These variables included word reading, word spelling (i.e., dictation), semantic radical judgement, phonetic reading, pseudocharacter reading, and pseudocharacter spelling. The phonetic reading and pseudocharacter reading tasks tapped the child's knowledge of phonetic radicals, whereas the semantic radical judgment task measured the child's knowledge of semantic radicals. The pseudocharacter spelling task required the child to make use of his or her full orthographic knowledge, because both the sound and the meaning of pseudocharacters had to be computed when the child attempted to spell them. Results indicated that children progressed steadily from kindergarten through Grade 3 in word reading, word spelling, semantic radical judgment, and phonetic reading. Children did not make effective use of phonetic radicals to identify the pronunciations of pseudocharacters until Grade 3, as shown in their pseudocharacter reading performance. Finally, children started exhibiting substantial orthographic knowledge in pseudocharacter spelling in Grade 1. These findings are in agreement with the pseudocharacter reading and writing results obtained by Tsai and Nunes (2003). These authors tested second to fifth graders (aged 7–10 years) and reported that even the youngest participants were able to benefit from their knowledge in phonetic and semantic radicals when asked to identify pseudocharacter pronunciations and write pseudocharacters to match meaningful pictures.

Blöte, Chen, Overmars, and van der Heijden (2003) taught Chinese and Dutch children (aged 10 years) the meaning and sound of some pseudocharacter components and tested them on their reading of novel pseudocharacters. In these children there were both good and poor readers. Results showed that both the Chinese and the Dutch children were able to combine their phonological and semantic knowledge in reading new pseudocharacter items. Specifically, there were differences in the ability to make use of such knowledge in pseudocharacter reading between good and poor Chinese readers only; no corresponding differences were observed in the Dutch children. The authors thus concluded that being able to combine phonological and semantic cues constitutes a very special skill required for good Chinese reading.

In summary, Chinese children at around the age of 6 years are already sensitive to the cueing functions of phonetic and semantic radicals in compound characters. They are also acquainted with the legal positions of these radicals. Such orthographic knowledge develops steadily from kindergarten through the early primary years and sets the stage for children's subsequent reading development.

DEVELOPMENTAL DYSLEXIA IN CHINESE

Although most children learn to read and write quite easily, some encounter great difficulties in reading and writing. Of all learning difficulties, reading problems are perhaps the most predominant (Leong, 2002). Different terms have been used by different professionals to describe children's difficulty in reading. For example, "developmental dyslexia," "specific learning disabilities," and "specific learning differences" are commonly accepted. We use the term "developmental dyslexia" in the following paragraphs to refer to children's reading difficulties.

Historically, it was believed that developmental dyslexia existed only among children who used alphabetic languages that emphasized phonological skills (e.g., Gough, 1996; Makita, 1968). According to this view, many thought that developmental dyslexia did not exist among Chinese because Chinese characters were learned as logograms. Although relatively few cases of developmental dyslexia are reported among Chinese people, there has been a growing consensus that developmental dyslexia exists in the Chinese population. For instance, Stevenson, Stigler, Lucker, and Lee (1982) reported that the proportions of children with reading disabilities were comparable among American, Chinese, and Japanese children. Developmental dyslexia is a problem not only with alphabetic readers but also with nonalphabetic readers (Ho, Law, & Ng, 2000). With increasing focus on the existence of the disorder in Chinese, tools to help identify Chinese developmental dyslexia have been developed and utilized. Although diagnosis of developmental dyslexia is done by medical professionals and special education scholars, teachers play important roles in helping to identify pupils who are suspected of having reading difficulties. In Hong Kong, the Hong Kong Specific Learning Difficulties Behavior Checklist for Primary School Pupils and the Observation Checklist (OCT) are tools that aid primary school teachers in the early identification of developmental dyslexia, and the Hong Kong Test of Specific Learning Difficulties in Reading and Writing, which was the first local assessment tool of the disorder and was published in 2000, is utilized by psychologists in the diagnosis in the territory (Lee, 2002). As there has not yet been a well-published diagnosis test for developmental dyslexia in Taiwan, 13 instruments for testing different cognitive abilities from related research work are used as generally accepted diagnosis tools in the territory (Lue, 2002).

With the assessment tools, the identification of children with developmental dyslexia in the Chinese population has been greatly facilitated. Yang (1994) estimated that 3.26% of school-age children in the Mainland China had developmental dyslexia (cited in Chen, Yang, & Tang, 2001a). Although no research data have yet been available on the prevalence rate in Hong Kong, the number of students diagnosed as having developmental dyslexia by educational psychologists has increased in recent years. There were 144 students who were assessed as having developmental dyslexia in the school year 1997–1998 but the number increased to 948 in the school year 2001–2002 in Hong Kong (Lee, 2002). Ho and Ma (1999) suggested that relatively few cases of developmental dyslexia have been assessed in the Chinese population because Chinese parents and teachers often lack knowledge about developmental dyslexia and often attribute children's poor reading performance to their laziness or to poor learning motivation. The increasing number of diagnosed cases of developmental dyslexia may reflect improved understanding of the disorder in the territory.

COGNITIVE DEFICITS EXPERIENCED BY CHINESE DYSLEXIC CHILDREN

Although understanding of developmental dyslexia has been increasing, a universal definition of this disorder has not yet been accepted. One possible reason for this is that there is not a universal pattern of deficits established in every dyslexic reader. Different characteristics of languages may contribute to different types of deficits experienced by dyslexic readers (e.g., Ho, Chan, Tsang, & Lee, 2002; Woo & Hoosain, 1984). For example, dyslexic readers who use a phonologically transparent script, such as German, or an orthography without grapheme–phoneme relations, such as Chinese, might be less affected by problems in phonological skills (Wydell & Butterworth, 1999). In the past, Chinese children tended to be classified as dyslexic primarily because of difficulties with comprehension and less because of problems in sight-reading of isolated words (Woo & Hoosain, 1984). Over 50 years ago, Ai (1949; cited in Woo

& Hoosain, 1984) estimated that Chinese dyslexic children who had difficulties in identifying meaning accounted for double those who had difficulties in identifying sounds.

Current research evidence on Chinese dyslexic readers has identified several underlying cognitive deficits in these children, including weakness of visual–orthographic skills, phonological awareness, verbal memory, and naming speed. For example, Chen, Yang, and Tang (2001b) found three primary subtypes of Chinese developmental dyslexia among 80 Chinese dyslexic children. These subtypes were those with a prominent in linguistic process deficiency (35%), those primarily demonstrating a visual–space process deficiency (36%), and mixed (29%). The Chinese dyslexic children performed significantly worse than did the average readers of the same age, but similarly to the typical readers who were 2 years younger, on most of the cognitive tasks, which suggests that their reading problem is caused by a certain level of delay rather than deviance (Ho et al., 2002). Ho and colleagues (2002) compared the relative prevalence of different types of cognitive deficits among 30 Chinese dyslexic children. Rapid naming was the most dominant type of cognitive deficit (60% for deficits in naming color and 53% for naming digits), followed by orthographic processing deficits (38.9%) and visual processing deficits (36.7%), whereas phonological awareness and memory deficits (15.3%) were the least dominant type among the four cognitive skills examined (Ho et al., 2002). It was also found that most of the Chinese dyslexic children experienced more than one kind of cognitive deficit. Among 30 Chinese dyslexic children, 20% had single deficit, 23% had double deficits in which about half had visual or naming deficits, and over 50% had three or more deficits (Ho et al., 2002). There seem to be multiple causes for reading difficulties of Chinese children. These deficits are discussed individually in the following subsections.

Visual–Orthographic Deficits

Owing to the lack of reliable grapheme–phoneme correspondences of the Chinese characters, many educational professionals believe that visual skills are particularly important in learning to read Chinese, and children with poor visual skills may encounter problems in reading Chinese. Chinese children in Hong Kong who are suspected to have developmental dyslexia are often assessed on visual skills tasks along with other intelligence, reading, and writing tests (Ho et al., 2000). Early research particularly supported a visual deficit view. For instance, Woo and Hoosain (1984) found that 8.5-year-old Chinese children with developmental dyslexia showed inferior performance in all of the five subtests (eye–motor coordination, figure–ground, constancy of shape, position in space and spatial relationships) of the Frostig Developmental Test of Visual Perception, but not in the Auditory Association Test of the Illinois Test of Psycholinguistic Abilities, compared with typical readers of the same age. The dyslexic children also made more visual-distractor errors in Chinese character recognition than did the average readers, but not more phonological-distractor errors (Woo & Hoosain, 1984). From the findings, Woo and Hoosain (1984) concluded that Chinese dyslexic children had a disability in basic visual perceptual functions, and this disability in visual processing was the primary cause of developmental dyslexia.

Phonological Awareness Deficits

Despite the fact that visual deficits have sometimes been considered to be a core problem encountered by Chinese dyslexic children, there has been growing research that provides evidence of the importance of phonological skills in reading Chinese and the influence of phonological skill deficits for Chinese dyslexic children.

Ho and Ma (1999) found that 8-year-old Chinese dyslexic readers used the phonetic component of Chinese characters for sound cues in reading, though they relied less on the cues than did the typical readers, and they had difficulty in learning to read both familiar and unfamiliar phonologically irregular Chinese characters. Consistent with their findings, Ho et al. (2000) indicated that Chinese dyslexic children aged 7–10 years could use the phonetic components in reading Chinese pseudocharacters, but their performance in reading Chinese pseudocharacters was poorer compared with that of the typical readers of the same age. These findings showed that Chinese dyslexic children do not have great difficulties in appreciating that the phonetic component offers sound cues in character reading. However, they have relatively poor knowledge of phonetics and encounter difficulties in learning the exceptions.

Other findings support the conclusion that poor readers have limited phonological awareness. From the testing of 32 Chinese dyslexic second graders and 32 typical readers of the same age, The dyslexic children performed worse than did the typical readers on initial phoneme deletion, sound categorization, and tone detection (Huang & Zhang, 1997, cited in Ho, 2003). Chinese dyslexic children, whether with or without writing difficulties, have inferior phonological skills compared with those of typical readers of the same age, and those with both reading and writing difficulties have greater problems with phonological skills than do those with reading difficulties alone (Ho et al., 2000). Apart from this research evidence, clinical observations of 30 Chinese children showed that about one-third of those with early language and phonological problems were later found to have reading and writing disabilities (Lam & Cheung, 1996, cited in Ho et al., 2000).

Verbal Memory Deficits

Verbal memory is another skill that has been found to be important for reading acquisition in Chinese (e.g., Hu & Catts, 1998). Stevenson et al. (1982) demonstrated that general information, verbal memory, and memory for words were the cognitive skills that best discriminated low and typical fifth-grade Chinese readers. In other studies, Chinese dyslexic children performed worse in verbal memory tasks, such as tasks of digit memory and memory for text (Zhang, Zhang, Chang, & Zhou, 1998) and tasks of word repetition and nonword repetition (Ho & Lai, 1999) compared with typically achieving children. Chinese dyslexic children seem to have difficulties in keeping sounds in their short-term memory generally, particularly unfamiliar speech sounds (Ho et al., 2000). These difficulties are likely to hinder the development of lexical skills, adversely affecting their development of stable graphic–sound associations and their acquisition of verbal vocabulary, and these problems in turn impair typical reading development. (e.g., Gathercole & Baddeley, 1989, 1990, 1993). Ho and colleagues suggested that verbal memory appears to be one of the most prominent problems faced by Chinese dyslexic children, followed by phonological awareness and naming speed (Ho et al., 2000; Ho & Lai, 1999).

Naming-Speed Deficits

Wolf, Miller, and Donnelly (2000) pointed out that naming-speed deficits were the problems experienced by the majority of children with developmental dyslexia across all languages and ages. Ho and Lai (1999) found that Chinese dyslexic children named digits, colors, pictures, and Chinese characters more slowly than did typically achieving children of the same age both at the basic level of name retrieval (as tested in the discrete-trial format) and at the complex level that required scanning and sequencing strategies (as tested in continuous format), and they concluded that Chinese dyslexic children seemed to have some generalized deficit in the speed of access to the lexicon that hindered their reading development. The rapid naming task may be useful in testing and diagnosing Chinese dyslexic children (Ho et al., 2002).

TRAINING FOR CHINESE CHILDREN WITH
DEVELOPMENTAL DYSLEXIA

To train Chinese dyslexic children, the education authority in Hong Kong is using the Data Pac: Chinese Reading Package, which employs a visual memory approach in teaching reading (Ho & Ma, 1999). This package involves daily teaching and assessment by parents at home, and it was effective in improving children's performance in reading, writing, and dictation, especially with parents' involvement (Hui, 1991).

Although the focus is on visual strategies in training Chinese dyslexic children, research has shown that their reading performance can also be improved by training their phonological strategies. Ho and Ma (1999) demonstrated that direct teaching of the script–sound regularities in Chinese and using the phonetic component of a Chinese character for sound cues could help Chinese dyslexic readers to read better. However, as this training program, which focused on teaching regular character reading, improved the children's reading of regular characters but not of irregular ones, it is suggested that more emphasis should be put on teaching the irregular characters and developing ways to improve phonological memory skills (Ho & Ma, 1999).

Training for Chinese dyslexic readers that focuses on speeded-naming skills is rare in the territory despite the importance of speeded-naming skills in Chinese reading acquisition. Given the importance of speeded naming for reading fluency, training that emphasizes speeded-naming skills, such as the RAVE-O (Retrieval, Automaticity, Vocabulary Elaboration, Orthography) reading intervention program in western countries (e.g., Wolf, 1997), might be a fruitful focus for Chinese dyslexic readers.

In summary, developmental dyslexia does exist in Chinese. Although it is quite clear that difficulty in phonological skills is a core problem of the disorder, the question of which cognitive deficits are the most fundamental to Chinese developmental dyslexic readers has not yet been answered by research findings. The early view supporting visual deficits and neglecting other cognitive deficits, especially phonologically based ones, is facing challenges. Research evidence has shown that other cognitive skills, such as speeded-naming and phonological processing skills, may be important contributors to early reading success and failure in Chinese. More research data on developmental dyslexia in Chinese are needed.

CONCLUSION

We have shown that written Chinese is unique in many ways: For example, it follows the logographic principle for meaning representation. Its basic operating constituent, the character, takes on the multiple identities of being a visual, phonological, and morphemic unit. A remarkable number of characters, known as compound characters, contain radicals that function as impressionistic sound and meaning cues. In addition, the Chinese word is not a prominent unit. These unique features bear important implications for skilled and inexperienced readers' cognitive processing, learning, and difficulties in mastering of the script.

ACKNOWLEDGMENT

The writing of this chapter was partially supported by RGC grant 4325/01H from the Hong Kong government to C. McBride-Chang.

REFERENCES

Adams, M. J. (1990). *Beginning to read.* Cambridge, MA: MIT Press.

Blöte, A. W., Chen, P., Overmars, E., & van der Heijden, A. H. C. (2003). Combining phonological and semantic cues in reading pseudocharacters: A comparative study. In C. McBride-Chang & H.-C. Chen (Eds.), *Chinese children's reading development* (pp. 127–140). New Haven, CT: Greenwood.

Bowey, J. A., & Francis, J. (1991). Phonological analysis as a function of age and exposure to reading instruction. *Applied Psycholinguistics, 12,* 91–121.

Chan, L., & Louie, L. (1992). Developmental trend of Chinese preschool children in drawing and writing. *Journal of Research in Childhood Education, 6,* 93–99.

Chan, L., & Nunes, T. (1998). Children's understanding of the formal and functional characteristics of written Chinese. *Applied Psycholinguistics, 19,* 115–131.

Chan, L., & Wang, L. (2003). Linguistic awareness in learning to read Chinese: A comparative study of Beijing and Hong Kong children. In C. McBride-Chang & H.-C. Chen (Eds.), *Chinese children's reading development* (pp. 91–106). New Haven, CT: Greenwood.

Chen, H. B., Yang, Z. W., & Tang, X. L. (2001a). Cognitive function of Chinese children with reading disorder. *Chinese Mental Health Journal, 16(1),* 49–51.

Chen, H. B., Yang, Z. W., & Tang, X.L. (2001b). Subtypes of reading disorders in Chinese children. *Chinese Mental Health Journal, 16*(1), 52–54.

Chen, H.-C. (1992). Reading comprehension in Chinese: Implications from character reading times. In H.-C. Chen and O. J. L. Tzeng (Eds.), *Language processing in Chinese* (pp. 175–205). Amsterdam: Elsevier.

Chen, H.-C. (1996). Chinese reading and comprehension: A cognitive psychology perspective. In M. H. Bond (Ed.), *The handbook of Chinese psychology* (pp. 43–62). Hong Kong: Oxford University Press.

Chen, H.-C., Flores-d'Arcais, G. B., & Cheung, S.-L. (1995). Orthographic and phonological activation in recognizing Chinese characters. *Psychological Research/Psychologische Forschung, 58,* 144–153.

Chen, H.-C., Lau, W. Y. L., & Wong, K. F. E. (1998). *Reading Chinese: Implications from character reading times and eye movements.* Paper presented at the First International Workshop of Writing Language Processing, Sydney, Australia.

Chen, H.-C., & Shu, H. (2001). Lexical activation during the recognition of Chinese characters: Evidence against early phonological activation. *Psychonomic Bulletin and Review, 8,* 511–518.

Chen, H.-C., Song, H., Lau, W. Y., Wong, K. F. E., & Tang, S. L. (2003). Development characteristics of eye movement in reading Chinese. In C. McBride-Chang & H.-C. Chen (Eds.), *Chinese children's reading development* (pp. 157–169). New Haven, CT: Greenwood.

Chen, M. J. (1993). A comparison of Chinese and English language processing. In J. Altarriba (Ed.), *Cognition and culture: A cross-cultural approach to cognitive psychology. Advances in psychology* (pp. 97–117). Amsterdam: North-Holland/Elsevier Science.

Chen, M. J., & Yuen, J. C.-K. (1991). Effects of pinyin and script type on verbal processing: Comparisons of China, Taiwan, and Hong Kong experience. *International Journal of Behavioral Development, 14,* 429–448.

Chen, M. J., Yung, Y. F., & Ng, T. W. (1988). The effect of context on the perception of Chinese characters. In I. M. Liu, H.-C. Chen, & M. J. Chen (Eds.), *Cognitive aspects of the Chinese language* (pp. 27–39). Hong Kong: Asian Research Service.

Chen, Y.-P. (2002). Reading efficiency and reading strategies. In H. S. R. Kao., C.-K. Leong, & D.-G. Gao (Eds.), *Cognitive neuroscience studies of the Chinese language* (pp. 143–155). Hong Kong: Hong Kong University Press.

Ehri, L. C., & Wilce, L. S. (1985). Movement into reading: Is the first stage of printed word learning visual or phonetic? *Reading Research Quarterly, 20,* 163–179.

Feng, G., Miller, K., Shu, H., & Zhang, H. (2001). Rowed to recovery: The use of phonological and orthographic information in reading Chinese and English. *Journal of Experimental Psychology: Learning, Memory, and Cognition, 27,* 1079–1100.

Frost, R. (1998). Toward a strong phonological theory of visual word recognition: True issues and false trails. *Psychological Bulletin, 123,* 71–99.

Gardner, M. F. (1996). *Test of Visual-Perceptual Skills (Non-Motor): Revised manual.* Hydesville, CA: Psychological and Educational Publications.

Gathercole, S. E., & Baddeley, A. D. (1989). Evaluation of the role of phonological STM in the development of vocabulary in children: A longitudinal study. *Journal of Memory and Language, 28,* 200–213.

Gathercole, S. E., & Baddeley, A. D. (1990). Phonological memory deficits in language disordered children: Is there a causal connection? *Journal of Memory and Language, 29,* 336–360.

Gathercole, S. E., & Baddeley, A. D. (1993). *Working memory and language.* Hove, UK: Lawrence Erlbaum Associates.

Gibson, E. J., & Levin, H. (1975). *The psychology of reading.* Cambridge, MA: MIT Press.

Gombert, J. E., & Fayol, M. (1992). Writing in preliterate children. *Learning and Instruction, 2,* 23–41.

Goswami, U. (1999). The relationship between phonological awareness and orthographic representation in different orthographies. In M. Harris & G. Hatano (Eds.), *Learning to read and write: A cross-linguistic perspective* (pp. 134–156). New York: Cambridge University Press.

Gough, P. B. (1996). How children learn to read and why they fail. *Annals of Dyslexia, 46*, 3–20.

Ho, C.S.-H. (2003). Reading acquisition and developmental dyslexia in Chinese: A cognitive perspective. In N. Goulandris (Ed.), Dyslexia in different languages: Cross-linguistic comparisons (pp. 277–296). London: Whurr Publisher Ltd.

Ho, C.S.-H., & Bryant, P. (1997). Phonological skills are important in learning to read Chinese. *Developmental Psychology, 33*, 946–951.

Ho, C.S.-H., & Bryant, P. (1999). Different visual skills are important in learning to read English and Chinese. *Educational and Child Psychology, 16(3)*, 4–14.

Ho, C.S.-H., Chan, D.W.-O., Tsang, S.-M., & Lee, S.-H. (2002). The cognitive profile and multiple-deficit hypothesis in Chinese developmental dyslexia. *Developmental Psychology, 38*, 543–553.

Ho, C.S.-H., & Lai, D.N.-C. (1999). Naming-speed deficits and phonological memory deficits in Chinese developmental dyslexia. *Learning and Individual Differences, 11*, 173–186.

Ho, C.S.-H., Law, T.P.-S., & Ng, P.M. (2000). The phonological deficit hypothesis in Chinese developmental dyslexia. *Reading and Writing, 13*, 57–79.

Ho, C.S.-H., & Ma, R.N.-L. (1999). Training in phonological strategies improves Chinese dyslexic children's character reading skills. *Journal of Research in Reading, 22*, 131–142.

Ho, C.S.-H., Wong, W.-L., & Chan, W.-S. (1999). The use of orthographic analogies in learning to read Chinese. *Journal of Child Psychology and Psychiatry, 40*, 393–403.

Ho, C.S.-H., Yau, P.W.-Y., & Au, A. (2003). Development of orthographic knowledge and its relationship with reading and spelling among Chinese kindergarten and primary school children. In C. McBride-Chang & H.-C. Chen (Eds.), *Chinese children's reading development* (pp. 51–71). New Haven, CT: Greenwood.

Hoosain, R. (1991). *Psycholinguistic implications for linguistic relativity: A case study of Chinese.* Hillsdale, NJ: Lawrence Erlbaum Associates.

Hoosain, R. (2002). Speed of getting at the phonology and meaning of Chinese words. In H. S. R. Kao., C.-K. Leong, & D.-G. Gao (Eds.), *Cognitive neuroscience studies of the Chinese language* (pp.129–142). Hong Kong: Hong Kong University Press.

Hu, C.-F., & Catts, H.W. (1998). The role of phonological processing in early reading ability: What we can learn from Chinese. *Scientific Studies of Reading, 2*, 55–79.

Huang, H.-S., & Hanley, J.R. (1995). Phonological awareness and visual skills in learning to read Chinese and English. *Cognition, 54*, 73–98.

Huang, H.-S., & Hanley, J.R. (1997). A longitudinal study of phonological awareness, visual skills and Chinese reading acquisition among first graders in Taiwan. *International Journal of Behavioral Development, 20*, 249–268.

Hui, E. K.-P. (1991). Using Data Pac for Hong Kong Chinese children with reading difficulties. *Educational Psychology in Practice, 7*, 180–186.

Kail, R. (1995). Processing speed, memory, and cognition. In F.E. Weinert & W. Schneider (Eds.), *Memory performance and competencies: Issues in growth and development* (pp.71–88). Hillsdale, NJ: Lawrence Erlbaum Associates.

Lee, S. H. (2002, October). *Information sheet on educational services for students with specific learning difficulties.* Paper presented at the International Conference of the Hong Kong Society of Child Neurology and Developmental Paediatrics, Hong Kong.

Lee, S. Y., Stigler, J. W., & Stevenson, H. W. (1986). Beginning reading in Chinese and English. In B.R. Foorman and A.W. Siegel (Eds.), *Acquisition of reading skills: Cultural constraints and cognitive universals.* Hillsdale, NJ: Lawrence Erlbaum Associates.

Leong, C. K. (2002, October). *Developmental dyslexia with reference to Chinese: What we have learnt and yet to learn.* Paper presented at the International Conference of the Hong Kong Society of Child Neurology and Developmental Paediatrics, Hong Kong.

Li, H., & Rao, N. (2000). Parental influences on Chinese literacy development: A comparison of preschoolers in Beijing, Hong Kong, and Singapore. *International Journal of Behavioral Development, 24*, 82–90.

Lue, W. P. (2002, October). *Overview of services for Taiwan's children with SLD.* Paper presented at the International Conference of the Hong Kong Society of Child Neurology and Developmental Paediatrics, Hong Kong.

Lukatela, G., & Turvey, M. T. (1991). Phonological access of the lexicon: Evidence from associative priming with pseuodohomophones. *Journal of Experimental Psychology: Human Perception and Performance, 19*, 166–178.

Makita, K. (1968). The rarity of reading disability in Japanese children. *American Journal of Orthopsychiatry, 38*, 599–614.

Manis, F. R., Seidenberg, M. S., & Doi, L. M. (1999). See Dick RAN: Rapid naming and the longitudinal prediction of reading subskills in first and second graders. *Scientific Studies of Reading, 3*, 129–157.

Mann, V. A. (2000). Introduction to special issue on morphology and the acquisition of alphabetic writing systems. *Reading and Writing: An Interdisciplinary Journal, 12*, 143–147.

McBride-Chang, C., & Ho, C.S.-H. (2000). Developmental issues in Chinese children's character acquisition. *Journal of Educational Psychology, 92*, 50–55.

McBride-Chang, C., & Kail, R. (2002). Cross-cultural similarities in the predictors of reading acquisition. *Child Development, 73*, 1392–1407.

McBride-Chang, C., Shu, H., Zhou, A., Wat, C. P., & Wagner, R. K. (2004). Morphological awareness uniquely predicts young children's Chinese character recognition. *Journal of Educational Psychology, 95*, 743–75.

McBride-Chang, C., & Zhong, Y.-P. (2003). A longitudinal study of the effects of phonological awareness and speed of processing on early Chinese character recognition. In C. McBride-Chang & H.-C. Chen (Eds.), *Chinese children's reading development* (pp. 37–49). New Haven, CT: Greenwood.

McBride-Chang, Chow, B.W.-Y., C., Zhong, Y.-P., Burgess, S., & Hayward, W. (in press) Chinese character acquisition and visual skills in two Chinese scripts. *Reading and Writing*.

Miller, K. F. (2002). Children's early understanding of writing and language: The impact of characters and alphabetic orthographies. In W. Li, J.S. Gaffney, & J.L. Packard (Eds.), *Chinese children's reading acquisition: Theoretical and pedagogical issues*. London: Kluwer Academic.

Peng, D., Liu, Y., & Wang, C. (1999). How is access representation organized? The relation of polymorphemic words and their morphemes in Chinese. In J. Wang, A. Inhoff, & H.-C. Chen (Eds.), *Reading Chinese script: A cognitive analysis* (pp. 65–89). Mahwah, NJ: Lawrence Erlbaum Associates.

Perfertti, C. A., & Tan, L. H. (1998). The time course of graphic, phonological, and semantic activation in Chinese character identification. *Journal of Experimental Psychology: Learning, Memory, and Cognition, 24*, 101–118.

Perfetti, C. A., & Zhang, S. (1991). Phonological processes in reading Chinese characters. *Journal of Experimental Psychology: Learning, Memory, & Cognition, 17*, 633–643.

Perfetti, C. A., & Zhang, S. (1995). Very early phonological activation in Chinese reading. *Journal of Experimental Psychology: Learning, Memory, & Cognition, 21*, 24–33.

Perfetti, C. A., Zhang, S., & Berent, I. (1992). Reading in English and Chinese: Evidence for a "universal" phonological principle. In R. Frost & L. Katz (Eds.), *Orthography phonological, morphology, and meaning* (pp. 227–248). Amsterdam: North-Holland.

Seidenberg, M. S. (1985). The time course of phonological code activation in two writing systems. *Cognition, 19*, 1–30.

Share, D. L., & Gur, T. (1999). How reading begins: A study of preschoolers' print identification strategies. *Cognition and Instruction, 17*, 177–213.

Shen, D., & Forster, K. I. (1999). Masked phonological priming in reading Chinese words depends on the task. *Language and Cognitive Processes, 14*, 429–459.

Shu, H., & Anderson, R. (1997). Role of radical awareness in the character and word acquisition of Chinese children. *Reading Research Quarterly, 32*, 78–89.

Shu, H., & Anderson, R. C. (1999). Learning to read Chinese: The development of metalinguistic awareness. In J. Wang, A. Inhoff, & H.-C. Chen (Eds.), *Reading Chinese script: A cognitive analysis* (pp. 1–18). Mahwah, NJ: Lawrence Erlbaum Associates.

Shu, H., Meng, X.-Z., & Lai, A. C. (2003). Lexical representation and processing in Chinese-speaking poor readers. In C. McBride-Chang & H.-C. Chen (Eds.), *Chinese children's reading development* (pp. 199–213). New Haven, CT: Greenwood.

Siok, W. T., & Fletcher, P. (2001). The role of phonological awareness and visual-orthographic skills in Chinese reading acquisition. *Developmental Psychology, 37*, 886–899.

Stevenson, H. W., Stigler, J. W., Lucker, G. W., & Lee, S.-Y. (1982). Reading disabilities: The case of Chinese, Japanese and English. *Child Development, 53*, 1164–1181.

Taft, M., Huang, J., & Zhu, X. (1994). The influence of character frequency on word recognition responses in Chinese. In *Advances in the Chinese language processing* (Vol. 1, pp. 59–73). Taiwan: Department of Psychology, National Taiwan University.

Taft, M., Liu, Y,. & Zhu, X. (1999). Morphemic processing in reading Chinese. In J. Wang, A. Inhoff, & H.-C. Chen (Eds.), *Reading Chinese script: A cognitive analysis* (pp. 91–113). Mahwah, NJ: Lawrence Erlbaum Associates.

Taft, M., & Zhu, X. (1995). The representation of bound morphemes in the lexicon: A Chinese study. In L. Feldman (Ed.), *Morphological aspects of language processing*. Hillsdale, NJ: Lawrence Erlbaum Associates.

Taft, M., & Zhu, X. (1997). Submorphemic processing in Chinese. *Journal of Experimental Psychology: Learning, Memory, and Cognition, 23*, 761–775.

Tan, L. H., & Perfetti, C. A. (1997). Visual Chinese character recognition: Does phonological information mediate access to meaning? *Journal of Memory and Language, 37*, 41–57.

Tan, L. H., & Perfetti, C. A. (1999). Phonological activation in visual identification of Chinese two character words. *Journal of Exprimental Psychology*. Learning, Memory and Cognition, 25(2), 382–393.

Treiman, R., & Zukowski, A. (1991). Levels of phonological awareness. In S. A. Brady & D. P. Shankweiler (Eds.), *Phonological processes in literacy: A tribute to Isabelle Y. Liberman.* Hillsdale, NJ: Lawrence Erlbaum Associates.

Tsai, K. C., & Nunes, T. (2003). The role of character schema in learning novel chinese characters. In C. McBride-Chang & H.-C. Chen (Eds.), *Chinese children's reading development* (pp. 109–125). New Haven, CT: Greenwood.

van Orden, G. C. (1987). A ROWS is a ROSE: Spelling, sound and reading. *Memory & Cognition, 15,* 181–198.

Wagner, R. K., & Torgesen, J. (1987). The nature of phonological processing and its causal role in the acquisition of reading skills. *Psychological Bulletin, 101,* 192–212.

Wang, J. H.-Y., & Guthrie, J. T. (2002). Differences in Chinese character identification between skilled and less skilled young readers. In H. S. R. Kao, C.-K. Leong, & D.-G. Gao, *Cognitive neuroscience studies of the Chinese language.* Hong Kong: Hong Kong University Press.

Wolf, M. (1997). A provisional, integrative account of phonological and naming-speed deficits in dyslexia: Implications for diagnosis and intervention. In B.A. Blachman (Ed.), *Foundations of reading acquisition and dyslexia: Implications for early intervention.* London: Lawrence Erlbaum Associates.

Wolf, M., Miller, L., & Donnelly, K. (2000). Retrieval, automaticity, vocabulary, elaboration, orthography (RAVE-O): A comprehensive, fluency-based reading intervention program. *Journal of Learning Disabilities, 33,* 375–386.

Wong, K. F. E., & Chen, H.-C. (1999). Orthographic and phonological processing in reading Chinese text: Evidence from eye fixations. *Language and Cognitive Processes, 14,* 461–480.

Woo, E. Y. C., & Hoosain, R. (1984). Visual and auditory functions of Chinese dyslexics. *Psychologia, 27,* 164–170.

Wu, X., Anderson, R. C., Li, W., Chen, X., & Meng, X. (2002). Morphological instruction and teacher training. In W. Li, J. S. Gaffney, & J. L. Packard (Eds.), *Chinese children's reading acquisition.* London: Kluwer Academic.

Wu, X., Zhou, X., & Shu, H. (1999). Sublexical processing in reading Chinese: A development study. *Language and Cognitive Processes, 14,* 503–524.

Wydell, T. N., & Butterworth, B. (1999). A case study of an English–Japanese bilingual with monolingual dyslexia. *Cognition, 70,* 273–305.

Yang, H. M. (1994). *Word perception and eye movements in Chinese reading.* Unpublished doctoral dissertation, University of Illinois at Urbana-Champaign.

Zhang, B. Y., & Peng, D.-L. (1992). Decomposed storage in the Chinese lexicon. In H.-C. Chen & O. J. L. Tzeng (Eds.), *Language processing in Chinese* (pp. 131–149). Amsterdam: North-Holland.

Zhang, C.-F., Zhang, J.-H., Chang, S.-M., & Zhou, J. (1998). A study of cognitive profiles of Chinese learners' reading disabilities [in Chinese]. *Acta Psychologica Sinica, 30,* 50–56.

Zhou, X., & Marslen-Wilson, W. (1999). Phonology, orthography, and semantic activation in reading Chinese. *Journal of Memory and Language, 41,* 579–606.

Zhou, X., Marslen-Wilson, W. (2000). The relative time course of semantic and phonological activation in reading Chinese. *Journal of Experimental Psychology: Learning, Memory, and Cognition, 26,* 1245–1265.

Zhou, X., Marslen-Wilson, W., Taft, M., & Shu, H. (1999). Morphology, orthography, and phonology in reading Chinese compound words. *Language and Cognitive Processes, 14,* 525–565

Zhou, Y. G. (1978). Xian dai han zi zhong sheng pang de biao yin gong neng wen ti [To what degree are the "phonetics" of present-day Chinese characters still phonetics?]. *Zhong Guo Yu Wen, 146,* 172–177.

Zhu, D. X. (1988). Dynamic account of the functions of phonetic radicals in modern Chinese character. In X. Yuen (Ed.), *Written language and culture.* Beijing: Beijing Guanming Daily Publishing House.

II

Literacy Acquisition From
Cross-Linguistic Perspectives

27

Theoretical Framework for Beginning Reading in Different Orthographies

Philip H. K. Seymour
University of Dundee

This chapter outlines an inclusive framework for discussion of literacy acquisition in different languages. Learning to read proceeds through a common series of phases in which an increasingly complex model of the writing system is constructed through an interaction with linguistic awareness. This involves the formation of implicit and explicit representations of morphological and phonological segments of spoken language. Learning an alphabet of symbols (Phase 0) is a common prerequisite. Foundation processes of sight-word recognition and elementary decoding (Phase 1) differ significantly among languages, depending on teaching methods and the balance of transparent and complex spellings in beginning reading materials. Subsequent learning (Phases 2 and 3) of the orthography (syllable-level mapping of sounds and symbols) and morphography (morpheme-level representation) depends on linguistic factors, especially the clarity of syllabic structure and the depth of the orthography. These factors influence the time needed to progress through each phase, the underlying cognitive architecture, and the linguistic units that are prioritised.

INTRODUCTION

It is often noted that a preponderance of empirical and theoretical research focuses on the English language. This has led to a presumption that theoretical models of learning to read in English have a general reference. I recall being told, during a visit to Norway in the late 1980s, that Frith's (1985) stage model had been officially adopted as descriptive of learning to read in Norwegian. I remember thinking; Wait a minute, surely Frith's (excellent and influential) paper refers to reading in English. Isn't Norwegian rather different and might not Norwegians engage in a different process of learning?

Learning to read is in essence a matter of establishing mappings between visual symbols and the spoken form and semantics of a language. Languages differ in their phonological and morphological structures, and these aspects may influence the way in which literacy is acquired. Equally, the languages have different writing systems (orthographies) that vary in the way in which speech and meaning are represented and, indeed, in the consistency and logic of the relationship. We can distinguish between logographic systems, such as Chinese, in which combinations of signs represent words or concepts; syllabaries, such as the Japanese *kana,* in which symbols stand for the syllables of the language; consonantal scripts, such as Arabic or Hebrew; and alphabetic scripts in which letters represent the vowel and consonant phonemes that are the building blocks for syllables and words. These latter scripts may be subdivided into shallow orthographies, in which the correspondence between letters (graphemes) and phonemes is coherent and consistent (Finnish, for example); and deep orthographies, in which the correspondences are variable, inconsistent, sometimes arbitrary, and subject to lexical and morphological influences (English, for example) (Katz & Frost, 1992).

Reading is also a product of the activity of the brain and sensory systems. Learning involves the construction of the necessary neurological structures and is dependent on genetic endowment and on environmental factors (nutrients, toxins) that affect brain development in the pre- and post-natal periods and in infancy and early childhood. These aspects are probably approximately constant across cultures and languages but may be not entirely so. Social deprivation is known to retard literacy acquisition (see, for example, Duncan & Seymour, 2000b), and this effect could, in part, be related to diet or alcohol and tobacco abuse. It is also possible that language characteristics are themselves an influence on the way in which the brain develops to encompass the task of learning to read and spell. Paulesu et al. (2000) recently investigated adult readers of English and Italian in a study involving both behavioural measures (accuracy and speed of word and nonword reading) and functional brain imaging. English and Italian are both written alphabetically but Italian is a shallow orthography whereas English is a deep orthography. Reading in Italian was more efficient than reading in English and appeared to activate different brain regions, an area concerned with phonemic processing in Italian and an area concerned with lexical and semantic processing in English.

Reading also depends on educational factors. Each society has its own conventions regarding the age at which children begin their schooling, when the formal teaching of literacy is initiated, whether or not there is informal encouragement of literacy in the home or kindergarten, and, most importantly, how literacy is taught. There is a long-standing contrast between analytic methods, which emphasise the correspondence between symbols and sounds, and wholistic methods, which emphasise whole words as symbols for concepts and the use of context in unravelling the meaning of text. To a certain extent the teaching method that is favoured is conditioned by the nature of the orthography. In a shallow alphabetic orthography, in which there is a strong and reliable correspondence between letters and sounds, it seems natural to teach reading by synthetic phonic methods by which letters are decoded to sounds and then combined to form larger units, such as syllables. This approach is obviously not appropriate for a logographic script such as Chinese, in which it is essential for children to learn which signs correspond to which concepts. In deep alphabetic orthographies, such as English, a combined method by which children learn basic alphabetic decoding procedures and at the same time master a 'sight vocabulary' of familiar words may be preferred. These differing approaches to instruction may therefore reinforce the contrasts between the orthographies and encourage the formation of different reading processes.

THEORETICAL FRAMEWORK

A theoretical framework for literacy acquisition in different orthographies needs to acknowledge the universal features of the process while at the same time permitting options and variations that can accommodate different language structures and educational methods. In this chapter, I consider whether the foundation literacy framework developed by Seymour and

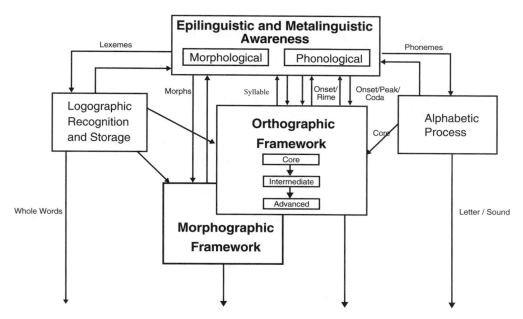

FIG. 27.1. Schematic representation of dual-foundation framework for literacy acquisition (from Seymour & Duncan, 2001).

colleagues (Seymour, 1990, 1993, 1997; Seymour & Duncan, 2001) can be adapted for this purpose. The framework derives from earlier analyses of reading acquisition, including stage models (Frith, 1985; Marsh, Friedman, Welch, & Desberg, 1980), decoding models (Gough & Hillinger, 1980), accounts of 'sight-word' learning (Ehri, 1992), as well as contemporary connectionist approaches (Plaut, McClelland, Seidenberg, & Patterson, 1996; Seidenberg & McClelland, 1989).

A diagrammatic representation of the framework is displayed in Fig. 27.1 (Seymour & Duncan, 2001). The underlying assumption is that literacy acquisition involves a developmental interaction between two cognitive systems, an orthographic system (encoding the characteristics of written language) and a linguistic system (representing features of oral language). The linguistic system is subdivided into two components, a phonological system, which is concerned with the representation of segments of speech, and a morphological system, which is concerned with the representation of meaning, lexical identity, and grammatical structure. There are various assumptions regarding the orthographic and linguistic systems and their interaction, which are briefly explained.

Linguistic Awareness System

It is widely acknowledged that 'linguistic awareness' is critical for the acquisition of literacy. This insight dates back to the work of Mattingly (1972) and others in the 1970s, in particular the suggestion that reading is a 'secondary' language skill that requires the development of an awareness of the structure of the 'primary' language used in spoken communication. The linguistic system is organised in terms of segments of language. Within the phonological component these segments correspond to the syllables of the language and sub-syllabic entities, for example onset, peak, and coda structures, rimes (V+C) and head bodies (C+V), and vowel and consonant phonemes. In the morphological component the segments are words (lexemes) and free and bound morphemes, including stems, inflections, prefixes, and derivational suffixes.

It is assumed that the representations of linguistic units held in the phonological and morphological components can exist at two levels. The first level is held to be implicit and to underpin the natural use of spoken communication in a manner that is inaccessible to consciousness or mental manipulation. This level corresponds to the 'primary' use of language and was designated as *epilinguistic* by Gombert (1992). The second level is explicit in the sense that the units may be isolated and cognitively manipulated, and may be objects of conscious awareness. This corresponds to the 'secondary' use of language and is commonly referred to as *metalinguistic* (Gombert, 1992).

The assumption is that all linguistic units defined within the phonological and morphological components may exist at the implicit (epilinguistic) level and that the formation of such representations is part of the natural process of spoken language development. In line with Gombert's suggestions, it is held that the formation of an explicit (metalinguistic) representation of a given unit is not part of natural development but is instead a special change that is brought about by the need to satisfy a particular challenge or demand. One such demand is the task of learning to read and write, which may create a need to elevate the representations of specified linguistic units to the metalinguistic level. Of course, there may be other demands that arise during language use. These could include participation in language games (secret languages such as Pig Latin, which require isolation and exchange of linguistic units) and educational activities that highlight particular units.

Orthographic System

The second major component of the framework is the orthographic system. This contains representations of the visual symbols used in the writing system of a language and the mapping of these symbols onto speech (phonology) and meaning (morphology, semantics). The assumption is that this system develops towards increasing levels of complexity and sophistication over time. It is conceptually convenient to subdivide the development into a series of phases. These phases are not thought to be temporally distinct, as in traditional stage models, but to overlap in time. A phase is defined in terms of the main emphasis in development that occurs during a given period, and it is broadly true that the work of an early phase has to proceed to a certain level of mastery before the next higher phase can proceed successfully. Four main developmental phases are proposed:

Phase 0: Alphabet Knowledge.   The basis of all subsequent literacy development is a knowledge of the symbols employed by the writing system and their correspondence with the sounds of the spoken language.

Phase 1: Foundation Literacy.   This is a preliminary phase during which the basic elements of (a) familiar sight-word recognition and storage (logographic process) and (b) sequential decoding (alphabetic process) are established.

Phase 2: Orthographic Literacy.   During this phase, a framework for definition of legitimate spellings of syllables is assembled and structured around linguistic units, especially onset–peak–coda or onset–rime elements. This is viewed as an internal reorganization that builds on structures established during the foundation phase, including stored word exemplars and letter–sound correspondences.

Phase 3: Morphographic Literacy.   The focus of the third phase is on the formation of representations of complex words in which syllables are combined, stress is assigned, and free and bound morphemes are identified and combined.

In Fig. 27.1, these hypothetical phases are associated with the elaboration of distinct ortho-graphic structures:

At Phase 0, a structure for recognition and storage of the elements of the alphabet is formed together with pointers to speech forms (names of the symbols, or their sounds, not shown in the diagram).

During Phase 1, the foundation processes are given a preliminary and simplified form: This includes a decoding mechanism (referred to as the alphabetic process in Fig. 27.1), a proce-dure for referring to symbols in an array in strict sequence, deriving associated sounds, and combining the elements in speech. If necessary, a second process, specialised for recognition of whole-words, may develop. This is referred to as the logographic process and is presumed to encode whole-word forms, perhaps on the basis of partial information, and normally in terms of the elements making up the alphabet of the writing system. If this happens, the be-ginnings of reading will involve the construction of a *dual foundation* containing functionally distinct logographic and alphabetic processes, as shown in Fig. 27.1. However, it is possible for development to proceed on the basis of a single foundation. This would most usually be the alphabetic decoding process, although it is theoretically possible to envisage development based on a single logographic process. The methods used in the teaching of beginning reading will affect the way in which foundation development proceeds, with strict phonic and synthetic methods favouring the alphabetic process, exclusively whole-word approaches favouring the logographic process, and mixed approaches favouring parallel development of the dual (logo-graphic + alphabetic) foundation.

Phase 2 involves the initial step in the construction of an abstract internal representation of the spelling system. This is referred to as the *orthographic framework* in Fig. 27.1. The assumption is that this is a syllable-based organization that represents the conventions for spelling whole syllables as coordinated representations that are formulated in terms of the underlying linguistic segments—usually onset, peak, and coda structures. This differs from the representations held in the alphabetic foundation process by replacing a sequence of dis-crete elements with a linguistically based and coordinated representation. It also differs from the content of the logographic foundation by being an abstraction of the general principles of the spelling system rather than a store of discrete lexical units. This is the sense of the term *framework*, the idea being that the spellings of all possible syllables in the language are repre-sented by reference to the set of possible onset structures (initial-consonant groups), the set of possible peak structures (vowels, monophthongs, and diphthongs), and the set of possible coda structures (final-consonant groups). The framework incorporates orthographic knowledge of features that exist above the level of discrete letter–sound associations, including aspects such as letter doubling, contextual determination, and multiletter groups (complex graphemes). The construction of the representation is held to be contingent on the prior establishment of the foundation processes, with the alphabetic process providing the basis for the standard spelling of the onset, peak, and coda elements and the logographic process providing a store of exem-plars that may be repeatedly searched by a process of abstraction of general principles. This process is closely analogous to the learning described in connectionist models of orthographic development (Seidenberg & McClelland, 1989). A difference is that, in the present account, the exemplars used in the abstraction process are available in a logographic store, so that learn-ing is not immediately dependent on real-time encounters with words in external texts. The development of the orthographic framework may itself be an elaborate process that is extended in time, so that some straightforward and simple features are established first (core structure) and more complex, variable or contextual features later on. A key feature of the framework is that the knowledge it contains is generalisable rather than specific.

In Phase 3 a further level of representation is formed in which syllabic or other segments can be combined to form complex (multisyllable, multimorpheme) words. This level takes account of conventions that operate across syllables, for example, whether or not intervocalic consonants are doubled in bisyllables and the assignment of stress. One possibility is that the segments combined at this level are free and bound *morphemes*, that is, word stems and elements such as prefixes, inflectional suffixes, and derivational suffixes. For this reason, the term *morphographic framework* is used in Fig. 27.1. The presumption is that the Level 3 framework builds on the Level 2 orthographic framework and incorporates in addition conventions regarding the written forms of morphologically complex words, for example, rules for adding suffixes to stems.

Interaction With Linguistic Awareness

The demand for the formation of explicit (metalinguistic) representations is expected to alter as development proceeds through these phases. For example, in Phase 1, the introduction of the alphabetic principle and decoding procedures may create a demand for the establishment of explicit *phonemic* representations. In Phase 2, there is a requirement for an organization defined in terms of syllables and the internal structure of the syllable, that is, metalinguistic representations of *onset* and *rime*, or *onset*, *peak*, and *coda*. Finally, in Phase 3, there is a requirement for the coordination of syllabic and morphological elements that may require a metalinguistic representation of *morphemes*. The assumption is that these explicit representations come into existence as and when particular units become important within the developing orthographic system. The further assumption is that metalinguistic representations build on pre-existing implicit (epilinguistic) representations. If so, limitations in the quality of the epilinguistic representation of a particular unit may constrain the capacity to form a metalinguistic representation of that same unit. This would be expected to impede the developing interaction between the linguistic and orthographic systems and to delay or interfere with literacy acquisition.

Application of the Framework to Differing Languages and Writing Systems

The proposal is that this framework is applicable to literacy acquisition in all languages and orthographies. Hence beginning readers in all languages advance through these four overlapping phases of orthographic development, and the process is characterised by an ongoing interaction between orthography and the epilinguistic and metalinguistic levels of linguistic awareness. The differences between languages affect aspects such as

- the learning time needed to traverse a given phase;
- the cognitive structures that are formed, for example, whether a dual or a unitary foundation is required;
- the linguistic units that are emphasised at each level.

These variations will be in part determined by the nature of the phonology and morphology of the spoken language and in part by the nature of the orthography, especially the elements contained in the alphabet, the consistency of the correspondence system, and the degree of lexical or morphological influence on spelling. Variations may also arise in response to differing instructional approaches, especially the balance between analytic phonic approaches and whole-word or meaning-based approaches.

Delayed or incomplete reading development (dyslexia) is expected to occur in all languages. This will stem from internal neurological variations, deriving from genetic or other influences on brain development, which affect the adequacy (neural resourcing) of the cortical and sub-cortical regions that support the linguistic awareness and orthographic systems and their sensory and motor pathways. However, the manifestation of the dyslexia might be expected to differ between languages, depending on the way in which orthographic development occurred and the phases of learning that were most affected.

METHODOLOGICAL CONSIDERATIONS

It is possible to conduct cross-linguistic comparisons of reading acquisition and dyslexia within this framework. This undertaking requires that equivalent methodologies for the investigation of orthographic competence and linguistic awareness be devised for different languages and orthographies. To date, this has not been attempted on a comprehensive scale, although there are several published studies of comparisons of subsets of orthographies for readers at differing stages of development (Frith, Wimmer, & Landerl, 1998; Goswami, Gombert, & de Barrera, 1998; Goswami, Porpodas, & Wheelwright, 1997; Seymour, Aro, & Erskine, 2003; Wimmer & Goswami, 1994).

The following subsections describe what appear to be the essential requirements for a fully comprehensive investigation:

Samples

The study will involve children from the pre-school and primary school age ranges who are in the process of establishing a basic competence in literacy. Because socio-economic circumstances are known to affect literacy acquisition, this factor should be controlled, ideally by the avoidance of sampling from schools and districts that are subject to social deprivation. The sample should consist of children who are receiving an educational programme that is standard for the society in question and delivered by schools that are recognized as efficient and effective. A description of the teaching methods will be required that details literacy-related and other activities in the kindergarten and the primary school and sets out the programme of instruction, including aspects such as the age at which children begin to learn, when and how the alphabet is introduced and taught, and the schedule of literacy instruction, especially the relative degrees of attention to decoding and sight-word acquisition and the linguistic units (syllables, rimes, phonemes, etc.) that are emphasised.

A measure of general ability is required for control purposes, perhaps a non-verbal test of intelligence, such as the *Ravens Matrices*, which can be applied in an equivalent way irrespective of language differences. If there are standardised measures of reading and spelling attainment, these should be applied at the end of each academic year as a means of tracking progress relative to the local norms and expectations. Other control measures, such as short-term memory (digit span), naming speed, and simple or choice reaction time may be included for purposes of comparison across samples.

Linguistic Awareness

In the earlier discussion it was argued that the linguistic awareness system contains representations of segments of spoken language that are classifiable as phonological units (syllables, rimes, onsets, codas, consonant and vowel phonemes) or as morphological units (lexemes, functors, word stems, free and bound morphemes). In each case, the units may exist at different levels of clarity, accessibility, and manipulability, which are referred to as implicit (epilinguistic) and explicit (metalinguistic). There is an important distinction regarding the status of the linguistic awareness system pre- and post-literacy. In the pre-literacy period no orthographic structures exist, and linguistic awareness reflects mainly a natural competence in communication based on implicit (epilinguistic) representations. These representations are important as the basis for subsequent developments and may differ between languages in ways that could be significant. With the beginnings of literacy, the linguistic awareness system undergoes profound and irreversible changes. This is because of the two-way interaction with the developing orthographic systems, which has the effect of elevating particular units to explicit (metalinguistic) status.

What is required for a cross-linguistic investigation therefore is a set of agreed procedures that may be used to assess the availability of the relevant phonological and morphological segments at the implicit (epilinguistic) level and at the explicit (metalinguistic) level. These procedures need to have a common format and need to be applied in each language group to pre-literate and post-literate children who are located at successive phases of orthographic development. The obvious questions are these: What are the appropriate procedures for assessing awareness of a range of linguistic units at the implicit (epilinguistic) level? And what are the appropriate procedures for assessing the accessibility of these same units at the explicit (metalinguistic) level? The proposal is that procedures that are suitable for the assessment of the implicit (epilinguistic) level are those that involve natural uses of language, rather broad or global judgements of similarity and difference, and, perhaps, some playful activities such as rhyming. Procedures that are effective in assessing the explicit (metalinguistic) level are those that clearly require the isolation and manipulation of segments of sound or meaning (e.g., deletion, addition, or transposition of elements).

Illustrative Data

These suggestions can be illustrated by reference to studies of the development of linguistic awareness carried out at the University of Dundee in Scotland. One such study was a longitudinal investigation of beginning reading that extended across the pre-school kindergarten period, when the children were aged about 4 years, into the first 2 years of the primary school (ages 5 and 6+ years) (Duncan & Seymour, 2000a). Part of the focus of this study was on *rime* units that, on theoretical grounds, were thought likely to play a critical part in early reading development (Goswami & Bryant, 1990). This expectation followed from the argument that linguistic awareness may develop according to a large-to-small unit schedule, beginning at the level of the syllable and then proceeding through an intermediate level of onset and rime and eventually to a small unit level of the phoneme (Metsala & Walley, 1998; Treiman & Zukowski, 1991). According to this view, young children may arrive at the task of learning to read with an awareness of large units such as the syllable or the rime already in place, and this awareness may be an effective basis for beginning reading.

Rime awareness was investigated by two sets of techniques: (a) The implicit (epilinguistic) level was assessed with the natural task of giving rhymes on demand and a judgemental task of identifying the odd-man-out in a set of words, two of which shared a rime (e.g., win, pen, fin) (Bradley & Bryant, 1983). (b) The explicit (metalinguistic) level was assessed with a new procedure, the common unit identification task, in which children were presented with pairs of spoken words and were asked to report the segment of sound shared by the two words, which, under some conditions, was a rime unit (e.g., 'goat . . . boat' → 'oat') (Duncan, Seymour, & Hill, 1997).

The important conclusion was that the epilinguistic and metalinguistic levels of representation of rime units are not the same thing. One clear finding was that children might display excellent epilinguistic awareness of rime, demonstrated by high scores on the rhyming and oddity tasks, while at the same time displaying an absence of metalinguistic awareness of this same unit, shown by an inability to isolate and report the common segment in a pair of words such as 'goat' and 'boat'. In fact, the task of reporting the common rime unit remained difficult for a majority of children throughout the first 2 years of primary school. It was only the most advanced readers who proved able to perform the task successfully by the end of their second school year (Duncan, Seymour, & Hill, 2000).

A further conclusion was that the epilinguistic representation did not exert a controlling or directing influence over the way in which children learned to read. The longitudinal study included pre-school interventions, one of which was directed towards the training of rhyme awareness. This intervention was successful in improving sensitivity to rhyme, and this was shown in gains in capacity to perform rhyme production and rhyme oddity tasks. However, this enhanced expertise in epilinguistic rhyming did not result in accelerated reading progress in primary school (Duncan & Seymour, 2000a). Further, an analysis of the orthographic units used in reading failed to support the expectation that expert rhymers would base their early attempts at reading on onset and rime segments in written words. Instead, the data suggested that initial progress in reading was based on small units (grapheme–phonemes), probably in direct response to the teaching of the letter–sounds and the alphabetic principle, and that this was an overriding effect that occurred irrespective of the level of epilinguistic awareness of rime demonstrated in pre-school before the onset of reading (Duncan et al., 1997; Duncan & Seymour, 2000a).

A striking finding was that metalinguistic awareness of small units (phonemes) emerged in parallel with the growth of alphabetic literacy. This was shown by applications of the common unit task in which the shared segment was an initial or final phoneme (e.g., 'boat . . . bin' → 'buh'). Identification of these small shared segments improved sharply during the first school year and approached ceiling at a time when a majority of the children remained unable to perform the task at the level of the larger rime unit. A conclusion is that learning to read in an alphabetic orthography induces the formation of explicit (metalinguistic) representations of the phoneme. This development will, of course, be contingent on teaching approaches that include an emphasis on letter–sound learning and decoding (as was the case in the primary schools in Dundee that participated in the study), and would not be expected to occur under teaching regimes that focused exclusively on whole-word (logographic) learning.

In more recent studies, Lynne Duncan and Pascale Colé and colleagues have compared English- and French-speaking children at the pre-school and early primary school ages on tasks assessing metaphonological awareness of syllable structures and boundaries (Duncan, Colé, Seymour, & Magnan, 2004). A common unit procedure was used in which children were presented with pairs of spoken bisyllables and asked to report the common segment. The common unit was a whole syllable in some instances but a smaller unit (a rime or initial phoneme) in others. English-speaking pre-readers were unable to perform this task. By contrast, French-speaking pre-readers, aged 4 or 5 years, performed the task of reporting common syllables almost perfectly. In an additional task, spoken bisyllabic words were presented under the instruction to segment the utterance into two parts. Pre-readers in both languages were able to perform this task. However, whereas French children were entirely consistent in placing the division at a juncture corresponding to the application of the maximal onset principle of syllabification, this was not true of English-speaking children, who located the boundary in many different places.

These data imply that there are differences in the phonological component of the linguistic awareness systems developed by French-speaking and English-speaking children in the period before they learn to read. For French speakers these representations include a precise segmentation into clearly defined syllabic units. This structure is absent from the representations of English-speaking children. It is important to note that this distinction refers to the explicit (metalinguistic) level of representation because it is present in the common unit task that requires isolation and manipulation of syllabic segments. In Gombert's framework, establishment of a metalinguistic representation of a unit is normally held to be a response to some kind of special 'demand' imposed by language use and communication. If so, it may be that producing and listening to the French language, perhaps supported by activities involving syllabification, induce an explicit awareness of syllables and syllable boundaries.

The results from the French–English comparison also support the conclusion that the emergence of explicit phonemic awareness is contingent on the introduction of alphabetic literacy instruction. One consequence is that the timing of the appearance of metalinguistic awareness of phonemes can be expected to vary between languages in line with socio-educational variations in the *ages* at which alphabetic reading is formally taught. In the UK, formal instruction begins at the age of 5 years, whereas, in France, the starting age is 6 years, and both societies favour the teaching of alphabetic competence (letter–sounds, decoding) from the outset of learning. Metalinguistic awareness of phonemes was assessed with the common unit task in which the shared segment was the initial-consonant phoneme of two bisyllabic words. Capacity to isolate and report back this segment appeared at 5 years of age in English-speaking children, in line with the previous findings by Duncan et al. (1997), but not until 6 years of age in French-speaking children. This is not a difference in phonological capacity but a consequence of the difference in the age at which reading is taught.

Orthographic Development

It was argued earlier that orthographic development may be analysed into a series of phases that are distinguished in terms of the type of learning which is emphasised—the elements of the alphabet in Phase 0, simple decoding and familiar sight-word learning in Phase 1, internalisation of orthographic structure in Phase 2, and the assembly of multisyllables and morphologically complex forms in Phase 3. The requirement for a cross-linguistic study is that formally equivalent procedures for the assessment of the knowledge associated with each phase should be devised for each language and applied to beginning readers of primary school age.

Phase 0: There should be a test of capacity to identify the elements of the *alphabet* of each language, to give names or sounds for each symbol, and to produce the written forms. This may include alternative forms (e.g., upper- and lower-case characters) or alternative alphabets (for example, *hiragana* and *katakana* symbols in Japanese). Fluency should be measured by reaction times for labelling or speed of reading lists of symbols.

Phase 1: This requires two test procedures: (a) a test of simple decoding, and (b) a test of familiar sight-word identification. Both procedures can be treated as a measure of reading (vocal response to visual presentation) and as a measure of spelling (written response to dictation). The *decoding* test involves arrays of symbols drawn from the alphabet. They are unfamiliar forms (nonwords) that are 'simple' in the sense that they are decodable by association of individual symbols with their predominant sounds, that is, those that are defined in alphabet books and directly taught to children in school. They do not contain complex orthographic features, such as multiletter graphemes, or phonological complexities, such as consonant clusters or diphthongs. The *sight-word* test is based on familiar forms. These are words that commonly occur in young children's vocabulary and in the reading texts used in school. They may be classified as 'simple' if they can be read on the basis of the elementary symbol–sound associations or as 'complex' if they contain features that violate or deviate from the elementary correspondences. Both tests yield measures of accuracy and fluency (reaction time) as well as qualitative data in the form of types of error responses. Ideally, the assessment should be applied longitudinally so that the growth in competence in simple decoding and sight-word identification can be traced over time and the rate of gain function plotted for each language.

Phase 2: The assessment of the internalisation of orthographic knowledge requires tests of reading and spelling of real words and legal nonwords (pseudowords). The words should be drawn from the middle- to lower-frequency range with respect to the vocabularies and reading materials of primary school children. It may be best if the words are monomorphs and if they are drawn from a particular class, for example, content words of average concreteness. The source of this set will need to be a database of words that occur in primary school children's texts in each society. This corpus has to be classified with respect to features such as word frequency, word length, morphological structure, syllabic structure, and, most important, *orthographic complexity*. One way of approaching this is along the lines suggested for the foundation level. It should be possible, for each language, to identify a set of standard symbol–sound correspondences that are the basis of the early teaching of the alphabet. Words that are written with these standard correspondences on a one symbol–one sound basis can be described as 'simple'. All words that depart from this pattern are described as 'complex'. Obviously, the proportions of words in the database falling into these two categories will vary according to the orthographic depth of each writing system. Further, the complex features, such as symbol combinations, doubling of elements, contextual influences, and variable or inconsistent correspondences, will differ in form and incidence between languages. However, it should be possible to devise for each language lists of words that contain simple spellings in contrast to a sampling of words containing examples of whatever types of complexity can be found. The list may also need to take account of phonological complexity, that is, monosyllables, insofar as these occur, and multisyllables, and the presence of initial and final-consonant, clusters, again insofar as these occur. We would therefore envisage the construction, for each language, of a word list that is internally structured in terms of orthographic complexity (simple vs. various forms of complexity) and phonological complexity. The nonword lists can be constructed so as to follow the format of the word lists, and will accordingly also involve differences in phonological complexity as well as simple versus complex orthographic structure. Again, the data of interest are accuracy levels for reading and spelling these items, reaction times, and qualitative descriptions of error types. The investigation needs to sample the early and middle ranges of the primary school and could be conducted longitudinally or, more conveniently, in a cross-sectional design to reveal the rate of gain in orthographic competence for each language.

Phase 3: Morphographic competence can be assessed with lists of morphologically complex words and corresponding pseudowords. For this purpose, words from the children's text-based vocabularies that are identifiable as multimorphs should be analysed into stem and affix components (prefixes, suffixes, etc.). These elements need to be classified with respect to their orthographic simplicity, especially how far each element has a simple phonologically transparent spelling and how far there is a deviation that is motivated by morphological considerations. Again, the incidence of lexically or morphologically motivated spellings of stems or affixes can be expected to vary between languages according to the differences in orthographic depth. The list might be expected to consist of morphologically complex words that differ in orthographic simplicity, together with a parallel set of pseudowords which are constructed by recombination of the stem and affix components contained in the word list. The words and nonwords may be presented for reading and spelling. In addition, it may be helpful to test the efficiency of direct access to semantics in the context of a decision task, for example, lexical decisions for discrimination between morphologically complex words and plausible nonwords. The lists should be applied at the middle to later primary school age range. The data consist of accuracy, reaction times, and error patterns and should display rates of gain for each language.

Illustrative Data

Although no comprehensive study of learning to read in different orthographies has as yet been carried out within this framework and methodology, there has been a recent attempt to examine contrasts within a subset of European orthographies. This was initially undertaken within the

TABLE 27.1

Hypothetical Classification of European Languages Relative to the Dimensions of Syllabic
Complexity (Simple, Complex) and Orthographic Depth (Shallow to Deep)

		Orthographic Depth				
		Shallow............:...........................:.......................:...............*Deep*				
Syllabic Structure	**Simple**	Finnish	Greek Italian Spanish	Portuguese	French	
	Complex		German Norwegian Icelandic	Dutch Swedish	Danish	English

Source. Seymour, Aro, and Erskine (2003).

context of a European network, the COST (Coopération de Sciences et Technologies) Action A8 (1994–1999), 'Learning Disorders as a Barrier to Human Development', which supported joint endeavours by literacy and dyslexia researchers from most European countries (Niessen, Frith, Reitsma, & Öhngren, 2000). This is now being followed up in an extended project coordinated at the University of Dundee in Scotland with support from national research councils and the European Science Foundation.

Table 27.1 details the European languages that participated in the COST A8 study. These are organised according to the outcome of a review of the phonological and orthographic structures of each language that was undertaken by the consortium. This suggested the importance of (a) a *phonological* contrast between languages having a simple syllabic structure characterised by a predominance of open CV syllables and a low incidence of initial- or final-consonant clusters and languages having a complex syllabic structure with many consonant clusters and closed syllables; and (b) an *orthographic* depth variation reflecting differences in the complexity and consistency of letter–sound correspondences. It can be noted that this classification was based on an intuitive evaluation of reports by informants regarding the characteristics of each language and not on the kind of computational analysis of databases of children's textual vocabularies recommended in the section on methodology.

The COST A8 project addressed the beginnings of reading (foundation literacy, Phases 0 and 1). The samples consisted of first-grade primary school children who were learning under standard teaching conditions in each country. The groups differed in age in line with educational policies affecting the age of starting primary school (5 years old in the UK; 6 years old in most societies; 7 years old in Germany and some Scandinavian countries). In addition, Primary 2 samples were tested in English, French, and Danish. Foundation literacy was operationally defined in terms of indicators of (a) letter–sound knowledge, (b) reading sets of very familiar content and function words such as occur in beginning reading materials, and (c) decoding unfamiliar nonwords of one syllable or two syllables. The items were presented as vertical lists for reading aloud, and errors were recorded as well as the time to complete the list. The data were collected towards the latter half of the first school year.

Letter–sound knowledge (Phase 0) was assessed by requiring children from each language group to give the sounds (or names) of the letters of their alphabet. Overall, letters were read with an accuracy of over 90% and at a rate of about 1 s/item. Performance was not consistently affected by age or the variations in syllabic complexity and orthographic depth set out in Table 27.1. However, the English-speaking group of Scottish primary school children, although as accurate as others (94% correct), had the slowest rate of reading, at 1.88 s/item. One possibility is that 5-year-old children lack the maturity to achieve fluent, automatised letter processing as rapidly as older children.

The assessment of the logographic (word-identification) process involved the reading of very common content and function words such as occur in children's beginning reading materials. In most European orthographies, familiar word reading was very accurate (>95% correct) and fluent (1.6 s/item). Performance was significantly poorer in Portuguese, French, and Danish (approximately 75% correct), and far lower in English (34% in Primary 1, 76% in Primary 2). These are the orthographies that are classed as deep in Table 27.1, suggesting that acquisition of a sight vocabulary of familiar words is indeed delayed by orthographic depth. The results for English are grossly different from those of other languages. Seymour et al. (2003) analysed the regression of word-reading accuracy and speed against reading age, estimated from the British Abilities Scale (BAS) word-recognition sub-test, in the Primary 1 and 2 samples. This indicated that a reading age in excess of 7 years was needed before word identification in English matched the accuracy and fluency levels achieved in the majority of languages before the end of the first school year. Given that the BAS scale starts with the beginning of reading at 5 years of age, this implies that the establishment of an effective sight vocabulary needs 2+ years of reading experience in English as against less than 1 year in many European languages.

The alphabetic process (decoding) was assessed by measures of accuracy and speed of reading very simple nonwords. The monosyllables were two- or three-letter items such as 'op' and 'fip' in English and equivalent forms in the other languages. The bisyllables were three- or four-letter items, such as 'uba' and 'afen'. The nonwords contained no consonant clusters and no orthographically complex forms and could be decoded on a one-letter, one-phoneme basis. In the majority of languages decoding was accurate (90% correct for monosyllables, 80% for bisyllables). Among simple syllable languages, performance was poorer in French and Portuguese than in Finnish, Greek, Italian, or Spanish. In the complex syllable languages, there was a higher error rate in Danish than in the other languages, and a huge effect in English. The differences were also reflected in the fluency measure. There was evidence that decoding was in general poorer in complex syllable languages than in simple syllable languages. The difficulties were greater in Danish and English than in French and Portuguese, and, among the easier orthographies, accuracy was slightly higher in the simple syllable set (92% vs. 89%), and there was a clear advantage in speed (1.97 vs. 2.81 s/item). There also appears to be a strong effect of orthographic depth on decoding. French has a deeper orthography than Spanish, and, despite the equivalence of the age at which learning commences, Grade 1 nonword reading was less accurate and slower (85% vs. 95% correct, 4.13 vs. 1.44 s/item). Danish is written in a deeper orthography than German, and this again associates with large differences in accuracy and speed (54% vs. 94% correct, 4.58 vs. 1.45 s/item). The most extreme disadvantage occurs in English. Although the Scottish Primary 1 children were ahead of age expectation, they read only 29% of nonwords correctly and were extremely dysfluent (6.69 s/item). Primary 2 children, aged 6.56 years on average, read only 64% of nonwords at a rate of 3.17 s/item, well below the children for all other languages tested (except for the Danish Grade 1 group). Seymour et al. estimated that the reading age needed to match the level of the majority of European languages was above 7.5 years, implying that the English-speaking groups needed 2 years of learning, or more than twice as much time as most other languages, to establish a most minimal and basic decoding function.

It is clear from these results that there are wide differences among alphabetic orthographies in the speed with which the basic (foundational) elements of literacy are acquired. Acquisition is slower in the deeper orthographies than in the shallow orthographies and is accompanied by much greater *variability* in the rates of progress of individual children. This effect is illustrated in Fig. 27.2 (from Seymour et al., 2003), which displays, for words and nonwords, the mean accuracy levels and the extent of normal variation (defined as within ±1.75 *SD* of the mean) for the

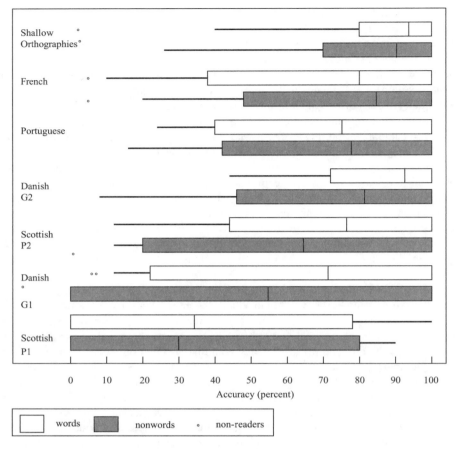

FIG. 27.2.   Individual variability in word- and nonword-reading accuracy by readers of shallow and deep European orthographies (from Seymour, Aro, & Erskine, 2003).

group of shallow European orthographies (topmost bar graphs). In these orthographies, the bulk of children score above 80% for words and above 70% for nonwords. Outlying cases occur but tend to score above 40% for words and above 30% for nonwords. Non-readers (scoring <10%) are seldom, if ever, found. The figure also reports the variability for the French and Portuguese Grade 1 groups. Here, the normal range extends down to 40%–50% and the tail approaches the non-reader zone. In English and Danish, the normal variation among Primary 1 children covers almost the whole range of possible scores and includes appreciable numbers of non-readers.

The COST A8 study did not extend to an investigation of the orthographic or morphographic phases of development. However, previous bilateral comparisons between older readers of English and shallow orthographies have supported the conclusion that the relative difficulty of English is a long-term effect. For example, Wimmer & Goswami (1994) compared reading of digits, number names, and nonwords created from the onsets and rimes of number names by 7-, 8-, and 9-year-old children in German and English. Nonword reading was significantly slower and more error prone in English at all three age levels. Frith et al. (1998) reached similar conclusions by using structurally equivalent sets of one-, two-, and three-syllable nonwords. Analogous findings are reported for comparisons of English with Spanish by Goswami et al. (1998) and for English with Greek by Goswami et al. (1997).

CROSS-LANGUAGE DIFFERENCES IN THE COURSE
OF READING ACQUISITION

It is now possible to set out some speculations regarding the way in which differences in phonology, orthographic depth, and educational methods might result in differing patterns or rates
of development by children learning to read in differing languages and educational systems.
These speculations can be formulated by reference to the structural framework presented
in Fig. 27.1 and the characterisation of acquisition as a progression through a series of cumulative phases, each involving an interaction between linguistic awareness and developing
orthographic structure.

Pre-Literacy (Phase 0–1)

A first possibility is that there may be language-based differences that are present before
literacy is acquired and that affect subsequent acquisition. This pre-literate period might be
referred to as Phase 0–1. At this point, the only component of the model that is present is
the linguistic awareness system. This will contain primarily implicit (epilinguistic) representations of phonological and morphological components that are important in the local linguistic
context. An assessment of these representations by use of global judgemental procedures such
as same–different matching or odd-word-out detection is likely to support a preference for
large units, such as syllables, over small units, such as phonemes. As already noted, there are
arguments to support a three-level large-to-small progression of syllable → onset–rime →
phoneme that might be a universal feature of epilinguistic development. However, it seems
possible that this is mainly a property of monosyllables and that the priority of the rime may
be less evident when multisyllables are considered.

Given that the epilinguistic organization is supposed to underpin subsequent metalinguistic development, it is possible that a weakness at this level is a marker for children who
are 'at risk' for reading failure. However, in Duncan and Seymour's (2000a) longitudinal
study, the pre-literacy scores for rhyming and rhyme or alliteration oddity detection were
very widely distributed, making it impossible to identify the children who later developed
reading difficulties. Consequently, although cross-language comparisons of pre-literate epilinguistic awareness might reveal differences, it is uncertain whether these should be treated
as evidence of differences in capacity to acquire literacy. A likely determinant is the age of
the children when epilinguistic competence is measured. The duration of Phase 0–1 is determined by national policies regarding the age at which children are taught to read. Danish pre-
readers, aged 6 years, are likely to perform better on these tasks than British pre-readers, aged
4 years.

The most critical pre-literate measure may be the test for the presence of *meta*linguistic
representations. The comparison of French and English by Duncan et al. (2004) indicated that
pre-literate French-speaking children have explicit representations of syllables whereas pre-
literate English-speaking children lack these representations. It is currently unclear whether
this distinction is related to the contrast between simple and complex syllable structures, as
set out in Table 27.1, or whether it relates more directly to the emphasis on the syllable as the
unit of timing in language production. Either way, it seems likely that the presence or absence
of metarepresentations of the syllable in pre-literate children is a relevant contrast between
languages. This difference is detectable by application of the common unit task with syllables
as the shared segment.

A speculation is that the presence of a metarepresentation of the syllable before the onset
of literacy is a positive feature that can be expected to assist subsequent literacy acquisition.

Alphabet Learning (Phase 0)

The first requirement for learning to read in any orthography is the learning of the alphabet. There will be socioeducational differences between cultures that affect the *age* at which this learning occurs. A hypothesis, based on the results of the European study by Seymour et al. (2003) is that this age variation may not be too important. However, the lack of fluency shown by Scottish first graders raised the possibility that 4–5-year-olds may have difficulty in automatising their letter–sound knowledge.

There are differences between orthographies with reference to the symbols making up the alphabet, especially whether they correspond to syllables, as in the Japanese *kana* scripts, or to vowel or consonant phonemes. However, from the standpoint of the learner, there is a common requirement to associate arbitrary (non-representational) visual forms with spoken labels, usually monosyllables. For example, children learn to associate letters with their names (b → 'bee') or with their 'sounds' (b → 'buh'). The time required for this learning will depend on educational factors, particularly on how the symbols of the alphabet are scheduled by the teacher, and also on factors such as (a) the size of the alphabet or (b) the extent of internal confusability (e.g., visually similar forms such as 'b' vs. 'd', 'n' vs. 'u', etc.). These factors will create differences in the duration of Phase 0 in different languages.

A first indication of dyslexia may be a difficulty in acquiring the alphabet. Duncan & Seymour (2000a) found that poor acquisition of letter knowledge in the first year of primary school was the first usable indication of later difficulties. Seymour and Evans (1999) studied a sample of English-speaking dyslexic children who all had low reading ages (<7 years). Many children in this group had weak letter knowledge relative to typically developing children of equivalent reading age. A small subgroup knew only part of the alphabet after 2 or more years in school and had difficulty in learning in response to systematic instruction. These were described as instances of *literal dyslexia*. Follow-up investigations suggested a very poor prognosis for subsequent reading acquisition. This form of dyslexia could, in principle, occur in the learning of any orthography that depends on an alphabet of symbols.

Foundation Literacy (Phase 1)

Both the duration and the format of Phase 1 are expected to vary widely depending on language characteristics, orthographic depth, and educational methods. As already noted, two functions, referred to as (a) the alphabetic (decoding) function and (b) the logographic (sight-word) function, are held to emerge during this phase. There will be language differences affecting whether one or both of these functions are implemented as well as the time required for establishing each function.

Alphabetic (Decoding) Function

It is expected that this function will be established by readers of all orthographies that are based on principles of phonographic symbol–sound correspondence (syllabaries, consonantal scripts, alphabetic scripts). The function is dependent on prior learning of the alphabet (Phase 0). Age of onset will normally be contingent on education, especially the point at which the teaching of systematic directional decoding and blending is introduced, and may be marked by overt 'sounding' of symbols in attempts at reading.

Establishment of the function might be inferred when decoding of simple unfamiliar forms (nonwords) can be successfully carried out. Progress is likely to be most rapid in syllabic systems, especially if pre-literate metarepresentations of the syllable are established, and somewhat slower in alphabetic systems that require abstraction of phonemic segments from syllabic letter labels (e.g., 'b' → 'bee' → /b/). Seymour et al. (2003) reported differences in efficiency of decoding between simple and complex syllable languages (Table 27.1) and suggested that the embedding of simple correspondences in phonologically complex consonant clusters might be a delaying factor. The orthographic environment is also important. Decoding develops more slowly in a deep orthography than in a shallow orthography. This could occur because the correspondences are encountered in inconsistent contexts. Alternatively, it is possible, as argued by Seymour et al. (2003), that progress is delayed when attention and learning resources are divided between two functions. The assumption is that deep orthographies, such as English, induce the formation of a dual (alphabetic + logographic) foundation whereas shallow orthographies, such as Finnish, permit a focus on a single (alphabetic) foundation.

The development of the decoding function is expected to involve an interaction with linguistic awareness. In the case of a syllabary, this will involve the formation of a metarepresentation of the syllable (unless this has already been formed in the pre-literate period, Phase 0–1). For alphabets, the establishment of the decoding function will normally result in the emergence of explicit representations of the phonemes of the language, marked by a capacity to perform metalinguistic tasks such as deletion, addition, transposition, or common unit identification, in which phonemes have to be isolated and manipulated.

A difficulty in establishing the basic decoding function might result from an inability to meet the demand to form metarepresentations of phonemes. This could be traceable to an insufficiency in the epilinguistic organization formed before literacy. Thus Seymour & Evans (1999) identified some dyslexic children who appeared to have a selective difficulty in learning to decode, shown by much poorer performance in reading simple CVC nonwords relative to the ability to read orthographically complex familiar words. The teaching of the decoding procedure posed special problems in these cases, which were referred to as instances of *alphabetic dyslexia*. This type of difficulty could, in principle, occur in all languages that employ an alphabetic orthography. However, the presence of factors that inhibit the normal development of decoding, such as complex syllable structure and, most obviously, a complex and inconsistent orthographic environment, would be expected to interact with the dyslexic difficulty and to exaggerate the effects. This is suggested by the differences in individual variability between shallow and deep European orthographies (Fig. 27.2). Hence the consequences of an inability to form explicit phonemic representations may be more dramatic and severe when learning is divided between the alphabetic and logographic functions than when it is focused on a single function.

Logographic (Sight-Word) Function

The formation of a distinct logographic foundation is likely to be required in all orthographies that use more or less arbitrary symbols to signify whole words or morphemes. This refers most obviously to the Oriental orthographies (Chinese, Japanese *kanji* system). In these languages, a specialised logographic function is required for learning the forms of the written characters and their reference to concepts and spoken words. The present argument is that *some* phonographic orthographies may also require the development of a logographic process. These are held to be those alphabetic writing systems that exhibit a degree of complexity and inconsistency that exceeds a threshold level of depth. Orthographic depth might be viewed as a continuous variable, measurable by some appropriate metric of complexity, as suggested in the classification of European orthographies in Table 27.1. However, it is possible that the depth variation is dichotomous in its cognitive effects. Seymour et al. (2003) considered that their results for familiar word and simple nonword reading were consistent with a discontinuous account of this kind. The majority of orthographies produced similar levels of good performance in word and nonword reading and a narrow range of individual variation. There then appeared to be an abrupt change to a subset of orthographies in which acquisition was substantially more difficult and characterised by a large amount of individual variation. Seymour et al. suggested that this threshold separated English, Danish, French, and Portuguese (the *deep* alphabetic orthographies) from the other languages in the sample (the *shallow* orthographies). It is hypothesised that the deep orthographies require the development of a dual (logographic + alphabetic) foundation whereas, for shallow orthographies, a unitary (alphabetic) foundation suffices. The reason for the establishment of the dual process is that too high a proportion of words encountered early in learning violates the alphabetic principle of one letter–one sound. It becomes necessary to build up a store of word forms that can be recognised and reproduced in addition to establishing a basic decoding procedure.

The function of the logographic process is to learn to discriminate between written words on the basis of identifying features while at the same time building up a store of word forms. These representations may be partial or complete. Seymour and Elder (1986) showed how beginning readers of English who were learning according to a logographic (whole-word) method discriminated words from a sight vocabulary on the basis of letters and shapes. Ehri (1992) has argued that these features may be letter–sounds and that partial representations tend to favour the initial and final positions at first, gradually developing in an ends-in direction. According to this view, the logographic process in phonographic scripts is based on knowledge of the alphabet and is contingent on prior completion of alphabet learning in Phase 0.

The establishment of the logographic foundation might be inferred when a majority of the words encountered by children in their beginning reading texts can be identified and read aloud. There will be differences between languages in the learning time needed to reach this point. It is expected that the rate of learning will depend on (a) the degree of arbitrariness in the symbol–sound/morpheme mapping, (b) on the extent to which support is provided by an adjacent decoding function, and (c) on the structural relationship between the decoding and logographic processes. Thus learning will be slowest when an arbitrary set of logographs is presented without parallel teaching of decoding. This could be true of isolated learning of Chinese characters or the learning of English by exclusively whole-word teaching methods. In practice, learning of Chinese characters is usually supported by the *pin yin* alphabetic transcription, just as the Japanese *kanji* are supported by the learning of the syllabic *kana* scripts. In these cases, a transparent method of labelling the phonology of each logograph is provided, and this could improve rates of learning by giving rapid and independent access to the names of new characters. However, the two systems are structurally unrelated. Hence we would say that in these languages the logographic and alphabetic foundations are fully distinct and independent processes. This is not the case in alphabetic orthographies such as English, in which the two functions share a dependency on a common set of symbols and the principles underlying the decoding mechanism reduce the arbitrariness of the logographic learning task. It follows that logographic learning should proceed faster in deep alphabetic orthographies than in the Oriental orthographies. At the same time, the rate of learning will be affected by the degree of alphabetic consistency present in the word set. According to the principles suggested by Ehri (1992), it is expected that learning will be facilitated for words that contain simple and standard letter–sound correspondences and retarded for words that violate these correspondences. By the same argument, logographic learning should be slower for deep alphabetic orthographies having a high proportion of words containing complexities and deviant spellings than for a deep orthography containing fewer such words.

The development of the logographic process is expected to produce an interaction with linguistic awareness, mainly affecting the morphological component through sharpening the concept of what constitutes a 'word' in the language (metalexical representations). Some children may suffer a selective difficulty in developing a logographic process. Seymour and Evans (1999) observed that the lexicality effect (difference between familiar words and simple nonwords) was positive in some typical readers (word-reading accuracy much higher than nonword-reading accuracy) and negative in others (nonwords considerably better than words). These latter children, referred to as having *logographic dyslexia*, appeared to encounter a real difficulty in establishing a sight vocabulary and seemed unable to remember familiar words from one occasion to the next. The basis is unclear, but could reflect difficulties in the global (as opposed to analytic) processing of symbol arrays and could, in theory, arise in any orthography that favours the implementation of the logographic process.

Orthographic Literacy (Phase 2)

Phase 2 is envisaged as a process by which the legitimate orthographic forms of monosyllables are represented in an abstract format. This is comparable with the process simulated in the connectionist models (Plaut et al., 1996; Seidenberg & McClelland, 1989). It is a process of internal learning and reorganization that depends on (a) the establishment of the foundation process(es) (Phase 1), and (b) subsequent reading experience. Hence the onset of the phase may differ between languages as a consequence of differences in the commencement and duration of Phase 1.

Orthographic literacy involves the construction of an internal model of conventions and variations in the way in which the syllables of the language can be written. It might be viewed as the assembly of an increasingly complex and subtle framework that expresses the way in which the onset, peak, and coda elements of the syllable may be spelled, including features such as the use of multisymbol structures (complex graphemes), various kinds of contextual influence, as well as alternative variants and inconsistencies. Some of these aspects may be directly taught, for example, letter combinations that commonly represent consonant or vowel phonemes, in which case there will be an instructional effect on the growth of orthographic literacy. Many aspects will probably not be taught and must be inferred or abstracted from experience with the written language, as is modelled in the connectionist account (Seidenberg & McClelland, 1989).

The time required for establishing this system is expected to vary according to phonological factors such as syllabic structure. The rate of development will be faster if the set of possible syllables is small rather than large and if syllable boundaries are clear rather than ambiguous. If a syllable is defined by the presence of a peak (vowel), an (optional) onset (initial-consonant group), and an (optional) coda (final-consonant group), then the size of the set will reflect the number of vowel forms, the number of onsets, and the number of legitimate codas. These values will be small in those languages, such as the Romance languages, which have few possible onsets and mainly open syllables, and higher in the Germanic and other languages that have a much larger range of possible onset and coda clusters.

The time needed to construct the orthographic framework will also be affected by orthographic complexity and depth. The process is trivial in a syllabary in which the written symbols already specify whole syllables. It will be very rapid and straightforward in shallow alphabetic orthographies in which the syllables are few in number and mainly open CV structures. The rate of learning can be assumed to become slower as syllable complexity is increased by the addition of consonant clusters, as multiletter spellings are introduced for vowels and consonants (complex graphemes), and as variability, inconsistency, and idiosyncracy increase. In a language such as English there are numerous monosyllabic words that contain high degrees of phonological and orthographic complexity, making the formation of an orthographic framework for the spelling of monosyllables an arduous and long-drawn-out affair. This is not the case for other languages in which the proportion of monosyllabic words may be very small and the syllables are encountered largely as components of multisyllables.

The abstraction of an orthographic framework is expected to involve an interaction with linguistic awareness. This should be largely a matter of emphasising the sub-syllabic structures of the onset (initial consonants), peak (vowel), and coda (final consonants). In closed syllable languages, the rime (vowel + final consonant) structures will be relatively numerous and complex and may reflect consistencies in spelling, as occurs within the special domain of English monosyllables (Treiman, Mullennix, Bijeljac-Babic, & Richmond-Welty, 1995). Insofar as this occurs, there may be a demand for the formation of rime units as objects of metalinguistic awareness during orthographic development. This should be marked by improvements in capacity to perform explicit phonological tasks, such as common unit identification, in which rime units are targets (Duncan et al., 2000). The capacity to make this shift will, in turn, depend on pre-literate implicit (epilinguistic) awareness of rime. Thus Duncan et al. found that early measures of implicit rhyming, using the oddity task, were selectively related in fixed-order multiple-regression analyses to later post-literate measures of explicit rhyme awareness, using the common unit task. These developments appear less likely to occur in simple syllable languages and shallow orthographies, such as Greek, in which monosyllabic words are few in number and the rime is not a focus for enhanced spelling consistency (Goswami et al., 1998).

In the deeper orthographies, the construction of the framework is held to require a merging of information initially established in the alphabetic and logographic foundation processes. This occurs in those cases in which there are two types of script involved, as in the Japanese *kanji* and *kana*, and in cases such as English in which distinct decoding and sight-word functions are envisaged. Broadly, the orthographic framework draws its onset–peak–coda structure from the alphabetic function and abstracts complex and special features of spelling by repeated scanning and reviewing of the word forms stored by the logographic function. It follows that delayed development (dyslexia) could result from deficiencies in one or other or both of the foundation processes, probably producing somewhat different outcomes. Equally, it is possible that the orthographic framework could itself be underresourced in terms of the available neural elements.

Phase 3: Morphographic Level

The morphographic level is hypothesised as a structure in which syllable-sized segments may be combined to form complex multisyllabic words. A distinction may be made between monomorphemic multisyllables and morphologically complex forms that are analysable into free and bound morphemes. The organisation of the morphographic level is uncertain but could consist of whole-word forms or combinations of syllables or combinations of morphemes. The organisation specifies the combinations of elements that are legitimate and orthographic conventions that are required (for example, consonant doubling at the boundary between syllables; spelling changes associated with the addition of a suffix to a stem). The time required for establishing this system is likely to depend on the number of combinations that are possible (i.e., the size of the vocabulary of multisyllables or multimorphs) as well as the lengths of the words that may be constructed. A syllable-based representation might be preferred in shallow orthographies. For example, Finnish has a very complex agglutinative morphology in which stems are combined with large arrays of bound morphemes that are nonetheless written in a phonologically transparent manner. In deep orthographies, in which spellings may signal lexical identity as well as morphological structure, often in conflict with phonological principles, an organization based on morphemes may be most appropriate. Stress assignment may be regular or variable and may or may not be marked by diacritics in the writing system. In English, most bisyllables have first syllable stress but some have second syllable stress, which is not marked orthographically, suggesting the need for a lexical- or morpheme-based organisation.

The morphographic framework builds on the structures established during Phase 2. Further, if there are orthographic conventions for combining syllables or morphemes, and if there are particular spellings for word stems or affixes, then additional input is required from the logographic store of word forms in which examples of morphologically complex words will be stored in an unanalysed format. This will be the main process involved for a logographic script such as Chinese, in which the elements making up compound characters need to be grouped according to conventions for specifying semantic or phonetic radicals. Building the framework will involve an interaction with linguistic awareness. Where a morphological organisation is favoured, this will typically require a sharpening of the representation of elements of morphological structure (prefixes, stems, suffixes), resulting in the emergence of explicit (metalinguistic) representations of these structures. In general, it is speculated that the time required for building the morphographic framework will be greater in languages in which lexical and morphological features are implicated in the spelling system than in shallow orthographies that require simply the combination of syllabic segments that are already established.

It follows from these comments that dyslexia could arise at the morphographic level for a variety of reasons. Development would be undermined if the underlying orthographic framework was imperfect or, in the case of deep orthographies, if the logographic store of word forms was impoverished. The interaction with linguistic awareness would not work properly if there were difficulties in forming metarepresentations of syllables, or morphemes. Again, the framework itself might be in some way underresourced, and this could affect capacity for fluent coordination of segments.

CONCLUSIONS

The goal of this chapter was to outline a theoretical framework that might be useful in discussions of similarities and differences among languages and orthographies in the ways in which children acquire literacy and dyslexic problems may arise. It is argued that this can be achieved by the analysis of acquisition into a succession of phases that involve the formation of orthographic structures as well as interactions with linguistic awareness. Educational factors, such as age of school starting and methods of teaching, are partial determinants of the course and rate of literacy acquisition. The main argument has been that linguistic differences, especially aspects of syllable structure and variations in orthographic depth, may be crucial in determining how the structures are formed and the amount of learning necessary for successful progression through each phase.

REFERENCES

Bradley, L., & Bryant, P. E. (1983). Categorising sounds and learning to read—A causal connection. *Nature (London)*, *301*, 419–521.

Duncan, L. G., Colé, P., Seymour, P. H. K., & Magnan, A. (2004). Differing sequences of metaphonological development in French and English. Manuscript submitted for publication.

Duncan, L. G., & Seymour, P. H. K. (2000a). Phonemes and rhyme in the development of reading and metaphonology: The Dundee longitudinal study. In N. A. Badian (Ed.), *Prediction and Prevention of Reading Failure* (pp. 275–297). Parkton, MD: York Press.

Duncan, L. G., & Seymour, P. H. K. (2000b). Socio-economic differences in foundation-level literacy. *British Journal of Psychology, 91*, 145–166.

Duncan, L. G., Seymour, P. H. K., & Hill, S. (1997). How important are rhyme and analogy in beginning reading? *Cognition, 63*, 171–208.

Duncan, L. G., Seymour, P. H. K., & Hill, S. (2000). A small to large unit progression in metaphonological awareness and reading? *The Quarterly Journal of Experimental Psychology (Section A), 53*, 1081–1104.

Ehri, L. C. (1992). Reconceptualizing the development of sight word reading and its relationship to recoding. In P. Gough, L. C. Ehri, & R. Treiman (Eds.), *Reading acquisition* (pp. 107–143). Hillsdale, NJ: Lawrence Erlbaum Associates.

Ehri, L. C. (1997). Learning to read and learning to spell are one and the same, almost. In C. A. Perfetti, L. Rieben, & M. Fayol (Eds.), *Learning to spell: Research, theory, and practice across languages* (pp. 237–269). Hillsdale, NJ: Lawrence Erlbaum Associates.

Frith, U. (1985). Beneath the surface of developmental dyslexia. In K. E. Patterson, J. C. Marshall, & M. Coltheart (Eds.), *Surface dyslexia: Neuropsychological and cognitive studies of phonological reading* (pp. 301–330). Hillsdale, NJ: Lawrence Erlbaum Associates.

Frith, U., Wimmer, H., & Landerl, K. (1998). Differences in phonological recoding in German- and English-speaking children. *Scientific Studies of Reading, 2,* 31–54.

Gombert, J. E. (1992). *Metalinguistic development.* London: Harvester Wheatsheaf.

Goswami, U., & Bryant, P. E. (1990). *Phonological skills and learning to read.* Hillsdale, NJ: Lawrence Erlbaum Associates.

Goswami, U., Gombert, J. E., & de Barrera, L. F. (1998). Children's orthographic representations and linguistic transparency: Nonsense word reading in English, French and Spanish. *Applied Psycholinguistics, 19,* 19–52.

Goswami, U., Porpodas, C., & Wheelwright, S. (1997). Children's orthographic representations in English and Greek. *European Journal of Psychology of Education, 12,* 273–292.

Gough, P. B., & Hillinger, M. L. (1980). Learning to read: An unnatural act. *Bulletin of the Orton Society, 30,* 180–196.

Katz, L., & Frost, R. (1992). Reading in different orthographies: The orthographic depth hypothesis. In R. Frost & L. Katz (Eds.), *Orthography, phonology, morphology, and meaning* (pp. 67–84). Amsterdam: North-Holland.

Marsh, G., Friedman, M., Welch, V., & Desberg, P. (1981). A cognitive-developmental theory of reading acquisition. In G. E. MacKinnon & T. G. Waller (Eds.), *Reading research: Advances in theory and practice, Vol. 3* (pp. 199–221). New York: Academic Press.

Mattingly, I. G. (1972). Reading, the linguistic process, and linguistic awareness. In J. F. Kavanagh & I. G. Mattingly (Eds.), *Language by ear and by eye: The relationship between speech and reading* (pp. 133–147). Cambridge, MA: MIT Press.

Metsala, J. L., & Walley, A. C. (1998). Spoken vocabulary growth and the segmental restructuring of lexical representations: Precursors to phonemic awareness and early reading ability. In J. L. Metsala & L. C. Ehri (Eds.), *Word recognition in beginning literacy* (pp. 89–120). Mahwah, NJ: Lawrence Erlbaum Associates.

Niessen, M., Frith, U., Reitsma, P., & Öhngren, B. (2000). *Learning disorders as a barrier to human development 1995–1999.* Evaluation Report. Technical Committee, COST Social Sciences.

Paulesu, E., McCrory, E., Fazio, F., Menoncello, L., Brunswick, N., Cappa, S. F., Cotelli, M., Cossu, G., Corte, F., Lorusso, M., Pesenti, S., Gallagher, A., Perani, D., Price, C., Frith, C. D., & Frith, U. (2000). A cultural effect on brain function. *Nature Neuroscience, 3,* 91–96.

Plaut, D., McClelland, J. L., Seidenberg, M. S., & Patterson, K. E. (1996). Understanding normal and impaired reading: Computational principles in quasi-regular domains. *Psychological Review, 103,* 56–115.

Seidenberg, M. S., & McClelland, J. L. (1989). A distributed developmental model of word recognition and naming. *Psychological Review, 96,* 523–568.

Seymour, P. H. K. (1990). Developmental dyslexia. In M. W. Eysenck (Ed.), *Cognitive psychology: An international review* (pp. 135–196). Chichester, UK: Wiley.

Seymour, P. H. K. (1993). Un modèle de développement orthographique à double fondation. In J.-P. Jaffré, L. Sprenger-Charolles, & M. Fayol (Eds.), *Lecture-écriture: Acquisition. Les actes de la villette* (pp. 57–79). Paris: Nathan Pedagogie.

Seymour, P. H. K. (1997). Foundations of orthographic development. In C. A. Perfetti, L. Rieben, & M. Fayol (Eds.), *Learning to spell* (pp. 319–337). Hillsdale, NJ: Lawrence Erlbaum Associates.

Seymour, P. H. K. (1999). Cognitive architecture of early reading. In I. Lundberg, F. E. Tønnessen, & I. Austad (Eds.), *Dyslexia: Advances in theory and practice* (pp. 59–73). Dordrecht, The Netherlands: Kluwer.

Seymour, P. H. K., Aro, M., & Erskine, J. M. (2003). Foundation literacy acquisition in European orthographies. *British Journal of Psychology, 94,* 143–174.

Seymour, P. H. K., & Duncan, L. G. (2001). Learning to read in English. *Psychology: The Journal of the Hellenic Psychological Society, 8,* 281–299.

Seymour, P. H. K., & Elder, L. (1986). Beginning reading without phonology. *Cognitive Neuropsychology, 3,* 1–36.

Seymour, P. H. K., & Evans, H. M. (1999). Foundation level dyslexias: Assessment and treatment. *Journal of Learning Disabilities, 32,* 394–405.

Treiman, R., Mullennix, J., Bijeljac-Babic, R., & Richmond-Welty, E. D. (1995). The special role of rimes in the description, use, and acquisition of English orthography. *Journal of Experimental Psychology: General, 124,* 107–136.

Treiman, R., & Zukowski, A. (1991). Levels of phonological awareness. In S. A. Brady & D. P. Shankweiler (Eds.), *Phonological processes in literacy: A tribute to Isabelle Y. Liberman* (pp. 67–83). Hillsdale, NJ: Lawrence Erlbaum Associates.

Wimmer, H., & Goswami, U. (1994). The influence of orthographic consistency on reading development: Word recognition in English and German children. *Cognition, 51,* 91–103.

28

Orthography, Phonology, and Reading Development: A Cross-Linguistic Perspective

Usha Goswami
University of Cambridge

In this chapter, I attempt to provide a theoretical cognitive description of the connection between phonological awareness and reading development across languages. The sequence of phonological development, which depends largely on speech and language acquisition factors, seems to be similar across orthographies. This is discussed in the first section of the chapter. In contrast, solutions to the 'mapping problem' of how sounds are related to symbols appear to differ among orthographies. When orthographies allow 1:1 mappings between symbols and sounds, children learn to read relatively quickly. When orthographies have a many:one mapping between sound and symbol (feedback inconsistency), or between symbol and sound (feedforward inconsistency), children learn to read more slowly. This is discussed in the second section of this chapter. My basic argument is that the linguistic relativity of orthographic and phonological structures is central to any theoretical description of reading and its development.

INTRODUCTION

In this chapter, I attempt to provide a plausible theoretical description at the cognitive level of the connection between phonological awareness and reading development across languages. I propose that the development of reading is founded on phonological processing. Children come to the task of learning to read with varying degrees of phonological awareness, and so reading acquisition is never a purely 'visual' task. However, as languages vary in their phonological structure and also in the consistency with which phonology is represented in orthography, cross-language differences in the development of certain aspects of lexical representation and in the development of phonological recoding strategies should be expected across orthographies.

These differences can be studied empirically and can be described by a 'psycholinguistic grain-size' theory of reading and its development (Goswami, Ziegler, Dalton, & Schneider, 2001; Ziegler & Goswami, 2005). According to this theory, although the sequence of phonological development may be language universal, the ways in which sounds are mapped to letters (or other orthographic symbols) may be language specific. The sequence of phonological

463

development appears to depend largely on speech perceptual and language acquisition factors, which seem to be similar across orthographies. In contrast, solutions to the 'mapping problem' of how sounds are related to symbols appear to differ with orthographic consistency. When orthographies allow 1:1 mappings between symbols and sounds (e.g., Spanish), children learn to read relatively quickly. When orthographies have a many: one mapping between sound and symbol (feedback inconsistency, which is very characteristic of French, as in *pain–fin–hein*) or between symbol and sound (feedforward inconsistency, very characteristic of English, e.g., cough–rough–bough), children learn to read more slowly. This is discussed in the second section of this chapter. My basic argument throughout is that the linguistic relativity of orthographic and phonological structures is central to any theoretical description of reading and its development.

PHONOLOGICAL DEVELOPMENT: LANGUAGE UNIVERSAL?

Psycholinguistic grain-size theory (PGST) proposes that there is a general developmental progression in phonological representation, or in the process of making implicit phonological knowledge explicit, across all languages so far studied. Following Metsala and Walley's (1998) lexical restructuring theory, PGST assumes that there is a general pressure in all languages for segmental specificity as more and more vocabulary items are acquired. Metsala and Walley argued that early vocabulary items were represented as holistic phonological representations, but that, as the child acquired more and more words, segmental restructuring occurred, so that syllables were represented as were, eventually, phonemes. Extending this idea, PGST argues that, before literacy, phonological restructuring occurs, largely at the syllable and onset–rime level (note that because many words have single-phoneme onsets and some have single-phoneme rimes, PGST assumes that some phonemic information is represented by preliterate children). However, PGST argues that the acquisition of literacy causes a profound change in the lexical restructuring process. Alphabetic literacy is critical for the full representation of phonemes. To paraphrase Frith (1998), once an alphabetic code is acquired, phonological awareness is never the same again.[1]

There are at least three sources of evidence for the idea that the sequence of phonological development is language universal before literacy. These are (a) cross-language studies of phonological awareness in which identical tasks are used with children at the same developmental stage, (b) studies in single languages in which identical tasks are used with children at the same developmental stage, and (c) studies looking for cross-language differences in phonological development on the basis of contrasting phonological structure.

Cross-Language Studies of Phonological Awareness

Although there are surprisingly few cross-language studies of phonological awareness, the studies that have been conducted support the idea that the development of phonological awareness of syllables, onsets, and rimes precedes the development of phonological awareness of phonemes. The strongest research design uses the same tasks in different languages, so that task demands are equated across language. For example, Liberman, Shankweiler, Fischer and Carter (1974) and Cossu, Shankweiler, Liberman, Katz, and Tola (1988) gave the *tapping* task to American and Italian children, and Bradley and Bryant (1983) and Wimmer, Landerl, and

---

[1] Frith (1998) compared the acquisition of an alphabetic code to a virus: 'This virus infects all speech processing, as now whole word sounds are automatically broken up into sound constituents. Language is never the same again' (p. 1051).

Schneider (1994) gave the *oddity* task to English and German children. A particularly strong research design is to give children who speak different languages the same items, so that (for example) a Chinese-speaking child might be making a rhyme-oddity decision about both English and Chinese words, whereas an English-speaking child might be making a rhyme-oddity decision about both Chinese and English words. Such a study was recently reported by Siok and Fletcher (2001).

Taking the tapping task first, Liberman at al. (1974) asked American children aged from 4 to 6 years to tap once for words that had either one syllable or phoneme (*dog, I*), twice for words that had two syllables or phonemes (*dinner, my*), and three times for words that had three syllables or phonemes (*president, book*). Syllabic awareness was shown by 46% of the 4-year-olds, 48% of the 5-year-olds, and 90% of the 6-year-olds. The 4- and 5-year-olds were pre-readers, and the 6-year-olds had been learning to read for about a year. Phonemic awareness was shown by 0% of the 4-year-olds, 17% of the 5-year-olds, and 70% of the 6-year-olds. Liberman et al. concluded that whereas syllabic awareness was present in pre-readers, phonemic awareness was dependent on learning to read. Cossu et al. (1988) found a similar developmental pattern in Italian children. Cossu and colleagues studied a group of 4-year-olds, a group of 5-year-olds, and a group of 7- to 8-year-olds, the former two groups being preschoolers and the latter group being in school. Syllable awareness was shown by 67% of the 4-year-olds, 80% of the 5-year-olds, and 100% of the school-age sample. Phoneme awareness was shown by 13% of the 4-year-olds, 27% of the 5-year-olds, and 97% of the school-age sample. Italian children, like English-speaking children, seem to have good syllable awareness before receiving literacy teaching. Phoneme awareness, however, develops largely in response to learning an alphabetic orthography.

The oddity task pioneered by Bradley and Bryant (1978) is usually described as a measure of onset–rime awareness (see Kirtley, Bryant, MacLean & Bradley, 1989). In this task children have to select the 'odd word out' on the basis of either the initial, medial, or final sound (e.g., bus, bun, *rug*; *pin*, bun, gun; top, *doll*, hop). The initial sound-oddity task can be solved on the basis of the onset, and the medial, and final sound-oddity tasks can be solved on the basis of the rime. Bradley and Bryant (1983) reported that preschool English children (aged 4 and 5 years) were above chance in both the onset and the rime versions of the task. Performance was on average 56% correct with onsets and 71% correct with rimes. Wimmer et al. (1994) found a similar developmental pattern for German children. Preschool German children (aged 6 years) were on average 44% correct with onsets and 73% correct with rimes. In the study with Chinese children reported by Siok and Fletcher (2001), Chinese first-grade children were on average 44% correct with onsets and 54% correct with rimes. Performance in terms of language did not differ significantly, with an average level of 51% correct for Chinese items across both tasks compared with 47% correct for English items (an unfamiliar language). Preschoolers were not studied, but a comparable study by Ho and Bryant (1997) found that Chinese pre-readers performed on average 68% correct in the rhyme-oddity task. Hence onset and rime awareness appears to be present before literacy instruction across languages. The finding for the Chinese children with the English items suggests that such awareness may exist at an abstract as well as at an item-specific level. More cross-language studies need to be conducted to test this hypothesis.

Studies in Single Languages Using Identical Phonological Awareness Tasks

The tapping task (or a variant of the tapping task, phoneme counting) has also been used in many studies in single languages at the syllable and the phoneme levels. These studies all find the same developmental pattern. Syllable awareness is relatively good before literacy, whereas phoneme awareness is relatively poor. For example, Hoien, Lundberg, Stanovich, and Bjaalid (1995) gave syllable- and phoneme-counting tasks to Norwegian preschoolers. For the syllable task, the children had to make pencil marks for each syllable in a word (e.g., 'telephone' = three marks). For the phoneme task, the children had to make pencil marks for each phoneme in a word. The children performed at 83% correct in the syllable task and 56% correct in the phoneme task. Wimmer, Landerl, Linortner, and Hummer (1991) gave syllable-counting and phoneme-counting tasks to German preschoolers. Performance was 81% correct in the syllable version of the task and 51% correct in the phoneme version of the task. French kindergarterners were tested on syllable and phoneme counting by Demont and Gombert (1996). The children performed at 69% correct in the syllable version of the task in kindergarten, compared with 2% correct in the phoneme version. When the same children were tested at the end of first grade, performance levels were 77% correct (syllable level) and 61% correct (phoneme level). Durgunoglu and Oney (1999) gave syllable- and phoneme-tapping tasks to Turkish kindergartners and first graders. The children performed at 94% correct in the syllable version of the task in kindergarten compared with 67% correct in the phoneme version. At the end of Grade 1, performance levels were 98% correct (syllable level) and 94% correct (phoneme level). Finally, Harris and Giannoulis (1999) gave Greek kindergarten and first-grade children a syllable-counting task and a phoneme-counting task. At the beginning of kindergarten, the children were performing successfully on 85% of the syllable trials compared with 0% of the phoneme trials. By early first grade, performance was 98% correct with syllables and 50% correct with phonemes. By the end of first grade, the children were 100% correct in both tasks. In all of these languages therefore phonological awareness of syllables was markedly superior to awareness of phonemes before literacy. However, rapid progress in phonemic awareness followed the onset of literacy instruction.

Studies Looking for Cross-Language Differences in Phonological Awareness

The data discussed so far support the hypothesis that the sequence of phonological development is the same across languages. Children learning languages as different as Chinese, English, and Italian appear to show good syllabic and onset–rime awareness before learning to read. Good phonemic awareness appears to emerge only when the child is being taught an alphabetic code. This general developmental sequence does not preclude the existence of language-specific deviations, however. A plausible source of cross-language differences in the development of phonological awareness is differences in the phonological structure of languages.

Languages differ in a variety of measures of phonological structure, of which at least two have been postulated as possible sources of developmental differences in phonological awareness. One of these is sonority profile. Vowels are the most sonorant sounds in speech, followed in decreasing order by glides (e.g., /w/), liquids (e.g., /l/), nasals (e.g., /n/), and obstruents (e.g., /p/). Languages differ in the sonority profile of their syllables. For example, whereas the majority of syllables in English end with obstruents (almost 40%), the majority of syllables in French either end in liquids or have no coda at all (almost 50%). Hence differences in coda awareness in English versus French might be expected, with French children showing more accurate phonological representations for syllables ending in very sonorant sounds and English children showing more accurate phonological representations for syllables ending in less sonorant sounds. A second measure of phonological structure that could plausibly be a source of cross-language differences in phonological development is phonological neighbourhood. We have been examining the effects of both sonority profile and phonological neighbourhood on the development of phonological awareness in recent work (De Cara & Goswami, 2000,

2002; De Cara, Goswami & Fayol, 2001; Goswami & De Cara, 2000). For reasons of space, I focus here on the effects of phonological neighbourhood only.

As noted earlier, PGST follows Metsala and Walley's (1998) lexical restructuring theory in taking seriously the idea that the representation of different levels of phonological structure with development is initially item specific. That is, children may have lexical representations for some words in their vocabularies that specify segmental information at the phoneme level, whereas they may have lexical representations for other words that specify onset–rime or syllable-level information only. Metsala and Walley (1998) suggested a number of factors that might determine which words have more finely grained segmental representations. These included age of acquisition, word frequency, overall vocabulary size, the rate of expansion of vocabulary, and phonological neighbourhood. Of these factors, age of acquisition, word frequency, and vocabulary size and rate of expansion might be expected to have *similar* effects on phonological development across languages. The general idea would be that words that are acquired early and used more frequently experience more pressure for segmental representation in order to increase the efficiency of lexical access and output. A priori, however, phonological neighbourhood might be expected to exert *differential* effects on phonological development across languages. This is because the nature of a word's neighbours in a particular language may differ depending on other aspects of phonological structure (e.g., proportion of open versus closed syllables, sonority profile).

The most frequently used measure of phonological neighbourhood comes from the speech-processing literature. This literature defines a phonological neighbour as a word that can be created from the target by the addition, deletion, or substitution of a single phoneme. For example, if the target word is 'cot', then its neighbours include 'scot' (addition) and 'cat' (substitution). This similarity metric yields three psycholinguistic classes of neighbour, *rime* neighbours like 'pot', *onset–vowel* neighbours like 'cough', and *consonant* neighbours like 'kit'. On a phoneme-based similarity metric, all of these words are considered to be equal neighbours of the target word 'cot'. The overall pattern of similarity relations for a particular language will then depend on how frequent each type of neighbour is within the mental lexicon. For example, the word 'cot' is said to reside in a *dense* neighbourhood because it has 49 phonological neighbours (Luce & Pisoni, 1998). Of these, 24 are rime neighbours (49%), 15 are onset–vowel neighbours (31%), and 10 are consonant neighbours (20%). A word like 'crib' is said to reside in a sparse neighbourhood, because it has only 15 phonological neighbours; of these, 7 are rime neighbours (47%), 7 are onset–vowel neighbours (47%), and 1 is a consonant neighbour (6%). These two examples are approximately representative of the similarity relations across the whole lexicon of English monosyllables. For all English monosyllables, 54% of neighbours are rime neighbours, 29% are onset–vowel neighbours, and 17% are consonant neighbours (De Cara & Goswami, 2002). Rime neighbours clearly dominate the phonological similarity structure of English. This in itself might help to explain the salience of onset–rime segmentations of English syllables as language develops (e.g., Bradley & Bryant, 1983; Treiman, 1985).

An obvious question is whether the phonological similarity structure of other languages also shows a predominance of rime neighbours. If phonological awareness emerges partly from implicit processing of interitem phonological similarity relations as vocabulary grows, a premise that is at the heart of lexical restructuring theory, then the characteristics of the phonological lexicon in different languages would be expected to affect the development of phonological awareness in those languages. To compare patterns of phonological similarity relations across languages, we therefore computed the prevalence of rime neighbours, onset–vowel neighbours, and consonant neighbours in English, German, and French. The English analyses were based on the monosyllabic words in the Luce and Pisoni (1998) database and were carried out by Bruno De Cara; the German analyses were based on all the monosyllabic

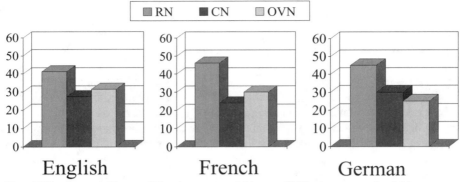

Note. RN = rime neighbours, CN = consonant neighbours, OVN = onset-vowel neighbours.
English: Analysis from De Cara & Goswami, 2001, 3069 words. French: Analysis from R.
Peereman, 1766 wds; German: Analysis from J. Ziegler, 1422 wds

FIG. 28.1. Phonological neighbourhood statistics for English, French, and German obtained with
the Ph± 1 similarity metric.

German words in CELEX and were carried out by Jo Ziegler, and the French analyses were
based on all the monosyllabic words in BRULEX and were carried out by Ronald Peereman.
These data are presented in Fig. 28.1.

It is clear from Fig. 28.1 that rime neighbours predominate in all three languages. Quite
unexpectedly for us, the phonological structures of English, French, and German turned out
to be very similar in terms of phonological similarity relations. Phonological neighbourhood
characteristics make the rime a very salient psycholinguistic unit in all of these languages.
Further, our analyses showed that rimes predominate, particularly in dense neighbourhoods.
In English, 58% of all neighbours are rime neighbours in dense neighbourhoods (dense N),
and French and German showed the same pattern. In these European languages, therefore,
words in dense neighbourhoods might experience more pressure for early lexical restructuring
to the rime level than words in sparse neighbourhoods (sparse N). This should have consequent
effects on the emergence of phonological awareness. For example, children might show more
accurate representations of the rimes of words in dense neighbourhoods. They might therefore
be more accurate in making rime judgements about words from dense neighbourhoods than
about words from sparse neighbourhoods, and words in dense rime neighbourhoods might
also show advantages in other phonological processing tasks such as short-term memory tasks.
Such predictions have so far been tested only in English.

In a series of experiments conducted with Bruno De Cara, Jenny Thomson, and Ulla
Richardson, I have been exploring the effect of varying phonological neighbourhood density on phonological awareness and phonological short-term memory in beginning readers
and in older children with dyslexia. For example, De Cara and Goswami (2003) used the
rime-oddity task described earlier to test whether 5-year-old children would show a processing advantage for words from dense neighbourhoods. The children were asked to make
rhyme judgements about word triples like 'hot, lot, wait' (dense N) and other word triples
matched for familiarity and vowel quality like 'mud, thud, good' (sparse N). Most of the children were pre-readers. De Cara and Goswami (2003) found significant density effects for the
5-year-olds with good vocabularies only, irrespective of reading ability. The 'high vocabulary'
children were more accurate at recognising rimes from phonological neighbourhoods with
many rhyming words than at recognising rimes from phonological neighbourhoods with few
rhyming words. This suggests that there might be a close connection between the emergence

of phonological awareness and vocabulary size, as hypothetically a larger vocabulary should serve to highlight the structural similarity relations in English phonology. Given the similarity of the phonological structure of French and German to English according to the neighbour-hood metric (at least for monosyllables), comparable patterns of phonological development might be expected in these languages. Such patterns, of course, are consistent with the broad developmental sequence of syllable and onset–rime awareness preceding literacy. At present, available analyses of phonological similarity relations across languages allow the prediction that certain items (e.g., words in dense N) might be restructured to the onset–rime level be-fore others. Further research within this framework is required for establishing whether any language-specific *deviations* from the general sequence of phonological development can be predicted for any particular language.

MAPPING SOUNDS TO LETTERS: UNIVERSAL DILEMMA, LANGUAGE-SPECIFIC SOLUTIONS?

All children learning to read are faced with a 'mapping problem'. They need to learn how sounds are represented by letters or by other symbols. This mapping is critical, because it allows access to the many words already in the child's phonological lexicon. Finding a straightforward mapping between orthography and phonology enables self-teaching to occur by means of phonological recoding—the *sine qua non* of successful reading acquisition (e.g., Share, 1995). Most children first tackle the task of learning to read at the age of around 5, 6, or 7 years, an age at which their spoken lexicons are relatively large. For example, it has been estimated that a 6-year-old child comprehends around 14,000 different words (Dollaghan, 1994). Further, I have already discussed some evidence that vocabulary growth in itself fosters the development of phonological awareness (e.g., N density effects). The phonological representations of many of the words known by the pre-reading child will be segmented to at least the onset–rime level. The child now needs to relate these units of sound to units of print.

Classically, it has been assumed that the child has 'two routes' to choose from in forming such relations for an alphabetic orthography. The child can either learn to associate entire letter strings with entire spoken words (the so-called 'visual' or 'lexical' route to reading), or the child can learn the sounds of alphabetic letters (or groups of letters) and map these sounds to spoken words (phonological recoding, the sub-lexical route to reading). However, as pointed out by Brown and Ellis (1994), use of the latter route imposes a non-trivial learning problem. The grain sizes available in the child's phonology and in an alphabetic orthography are quite different. The available phonological units for the preliterate child are at 'large' grain sizes—whole words, syllables, onsets and rimes. The available orthographic units—individual letters—map onto phonemes, which are not yet represented phonologically. Initially at least, there is no shared grain size. The 'easy' orthographic units (single letters) are phonologically difficult, whereas the phonologically 'easy' units are orthographically difficult. (One exception to this might be a non-alphabetic script like Japanese, which has a syllabic orthography. Here the phonological units represented in the child's lexicon—syllables—map directly to orthographic units. The mapping problem can be solved at a large grain size. Because these mappings are sub-lexical, there is a theoretical advantage for learning to read Japanese over learning to read a script like Chinese, which represents phonology at the lexical level and hence imposes a far greater memory load.)

The incompatible levels of representation in the orthographic and phonological domains highlighted by Brown and Ellis (1994) for alphabetic orthographies provide the starting point for our (Ziegler & Goswami, 2005) PGST with respect to orthographic learning. PGST pro-poses that the dynamic process of orthographic–phonological convergence onto shared grain sizes will have language-specific aspects. The basic premise is that developing high-quality phonological representations at small grain sizes (phonemes) will be the key factor in successful reading acquisition in all alphabetic languages, because these small grain sizes map onto graphemes. However, PGST argues that the relationship between phonological awareness at the different levels of syllable, onset–rime, and phoneme and progress in reading and spelling will differ depending on the phonology of the language that is being learned and the orthographic units that this phonology makes salient. Differences in phonological structure, differences in the consistency of various grain sizes in the orthography, and differences in the linguistic salience of different psycholinguistic units would all be expected to affect this process.

One example of how such factors might affect reading acquisition in language-specific ways comes from a consideration of orthographic *consistency*. Alphabetic writing systems differ with regard to how consistently letters map onto sounds. In relatively consistent orthographies, such as Greek, Italian, or German, letters or letter groups usually map to the same sound in different words. In relatively inconsistent orthographies such as English, the relation between letters and sounds is very variable. Some letters or letter clusters can be pronounced in more than one way, and some sounds can be spelled in more than one way (Berndt, Reggia, & Mitchum, 1987; Ziegler, Stone, & Jacobs, 1997). The consistency of the language that the child is learning to read and to spell would be expected to have an effect on how rapidly the child was able to acquire sub-lexical recoding procedures at the smallest grain size.

Further, orthographic consistency should also affect how rapidly the child can become explicitly aware of phonemes and restructure their phonological representations of words to represent segmental information. Although some orthographies should facilitate this development (e.g., Italian), others may hinder it (e.g., English), and some do not represent phonemic information at all (e.g., Chinese). PGST therefore predicts developmental differences in the grain size of lexical representations and reading strategies across orthographies. Children learning to read orthographically consistent languages should show relatively rapid reading acquisition, because letters always provide consistent information about phonemes, making the mapping problem easier to solve. Rapid development of phonemic awareness would be expected in orthographically consistent languages. Children learning to read orthographically inconsistent languages should show slower reading acquisition. Exclusive reliance on a grapheme–phoneme recoding strategy will not be successful in such languages, necessitating the deployment of larger sub-lexical units like rimes and also of whole words. This need to focus on multiple grain sizes should affect the development of phonemic awareness, which is expected to be slower in orthographically inconsistent languages.

Another example of how factors such as phonological structure and differences in the consistency of various grain sizes might affect reading acquisition in language-specific ways comes from a consideration of basic phonological structure. Languages like Italian and Spanish have many simple or open (consonant–vowel or CV) syllables. For these languages, onset–rime segmentation is equivalent to phonemic segmentation for many words (e.g., *casa, mama*). The normally developing Italian or Spanish child who has organized the spoken lexicon in terms of the intrasyllabic units of onset and rime *before* reading is thus well placed to acquire alphabetic literacy. Because phonemes and onset–rimes are equivalent for many words, the child's phonological lexicon already represents phonemic information (e.g., for words like *casa* and *mama*, the onset-rimes are /c/ /a/ /s/ /a/ and /m/ /a/ /m/ /a/, and these are also the phonemes). This makes the mapping problem easier on the phonological side. As these languages additionally have orthographic consistency (the same letter always maps to the same phoneme), shared grain sizes with orthography are relatively easy to find. For Italian and Spanish children, PGST predicts that lexical representations can be rapidly restructured to the phoneme level. This process should be somewhat slower in a language like German, which has orthographic consistency but a more complex syllable structure. The German child who has organised the spoken lexicon in terms of the intrasyllabic units of onset and rime before reading will have represented less phonemic information and will thus be slightly less well placed to acquire alphabetic literacy.

Overall, PGST predicts that the ease with which reading acquisition and phonemic restructuring are accomplished should vary with (a) the phonological structure of the spoken language and (b) the consistency with which the orthography of that language represents phoneme-level information. Different reading strategies should develop in response to differences in orthographic structure. Reading acquisition and phonemic restructuring will also vary with individual differences in children's phonological sensitivity, but a discussion of this is beyond the scope of this chapter (see Goswami, 2003, for details). Available data suggest that there are indeed language-specific differences in the rate at which children learn to read and the ease with which phonemic restructuring is accomplished. Available data also suggest that readers of different orthographies indeed adopt different solutions to resolve the mapping problem. Regarding individual differences, it is possible that children with phonological difficulties (such as dyslexic children or children with specific language impairment) may never attain automaticity in grapheme–phoneme mapping, regardless of orthography (see Goswami, 2003). I turn now to the available evidence.

Reading Acquisition and Phoneme Awareness in Different Orthographies

Children learning to read consistent orthographies such as Italian, Spanish, Turkish, Greek, and German appear to acquire reading at a faster rate than children learning to read inconsistent orthographies such as English. Reading accuracy, and reading speed, for words and nonwords appear to be greater in more consistent writing systems. Accordingly, phonemic awareness skills seem to develop more rapidly in children learning consistent orthographies.

Cross-Language Studies of Reading Acquisition

When word and nonword reading is studied in individual languages, children who are learning to read consistent orthographies typically show very good levels of decoding, even in the first year of learning to read. For instance, Porpodas, Pantelis, & Hantziou (1990) gave Greek schoolchildren lists of real words and nonwords to read aloud at the end of Grade 1. The children read on average 90% of the real words correctly compared with 89% of the nonwords. Similar results were reported by Cossu, Gugliotta, & Marshall (1995) for Italian children. Italian children at the end of first grade read on average 94% of real words correctly compared to 82% of nonwords. Very different results are usually found when children who are learning to read inconsistent orthographies are given similar tests. For instance, Frith, Wimmer, and Landerl (1998) gave English children lists of words and nonwords to read at the end of Grade 2. The children scored no more than 70% in word reading and 45% in nonword reading. Such results for nonwords appear to be typical rather than exceptional for English children (e.g., 51% accuracy in monosyllabic nonword reading for 9-year-olds in Goswami, Gombert, & de Barrera, 1998; 45% accuracy in reading nonwords derived from the number words for 9-year-olds in Wimmer & Goswami, 1994).

These patterns of word and nonword reading clearly support the hypothesis that reading and phonological recoding strategies at the grapheme–phoneme level are acquired at a faster rate in consistent orthographies. However, comparisons among monolingual studies must be treated with some caution, as typically item characteristics and participant characteristics differ widely from one study to another. The ideal way to test the hypothesis that the acquisition of reading accuracy for words and nonwords is faster in more consistent writing systems is to match participants across languages for key characteristics and to match word and nonword items as well. Two examples of such studies are now given. In one study (Goswami et al., 1998), children learning to read English, French, and Spanish were matched for standardised reading ability, real word reading, and digit decoding speed, and were then given nonwords to decode that were generated according to the same constraints in the three languages. In the second (Frith et al., 1998), children learning to read English and German were given identical words and nonwords to decode, a manipulation that was possible because of the phonological similarity between English and German.

To look specifically at grapheme–phoneme decoding strategies across languages, Goswami et al. (1998) generated nonwords that could be decoded only by using grapheme–phoneme correspondences. The nonwords were constructed so that neither rime orthography nor rime phonology were familiar to the children (e.g., English: *zoip*, *koog*; French: *loun*, *loave*; Spanish: *muet*, *niet*). This meant that all the constituent graphemes in each word had to be decoded sequentially and blended into an unfamiliar phonological string. For monosyllables, the English 7-year-olds decoded on average 12% of these simple nonwords accurately compared with 53% for the French 7-year-olds and 94% for the Spanish 7-year-olds. By a reading age of 9 years, the English children decoded on average 51% of these nonwords correctly compared with 73% for the French children and 92% for the Spanish children. In general, the Spanish children read more quickly than the English and French children. These differences in decoding accuracy and speed reflect the relative consistencies of the orthographies. In the highly consistent Spanish orthography, the children were virtually performing at ceiling at 7 years. In the less consistent French orthography, the 7-year-old readers could decode about half of the nonwords. In the least consistent orthography (English), the 7-year-olds found the decoding task extremely difficult. Grapheme–phoneme recoding skills were clearly developing in English and French as reading age improved, but at a slower rate, as the relative differences in performance between orthographies were maintained across the languages. This supports the notion that grapheme–phoneme recoding skills are taking longer to develop in children who are learning to read inconsistent orthographies.

The study by Frith and her colleagues (1998) was able to utilise an ideal manipulation for studying grapheme–phoneme decoding strategies across languages. Frith et al. (1998) were able to use exactly the same word and nonword items with their English and German participants. For example, words like 'ball', 'park', and 'hand' exist in both languages in identical form. However, there is a dramatic difference in orthographic consistency. The grapheme 'a' receives the same pronunciation in all three words in German, but has a different pronunciation in each word in English. By deriving nonwords from these identical real words (e.g., ball–*grall*), Frith et al. were able to compare word and nonword reading of the same items in English and German 7-, 8- and 9-year-olds.

Frith et al. reported that the German children's reading performance was close to ceiling after as little as 1 year of reading instruction. In contrast, the reading accuracy of the English children was much lower and did not reach comparable levels until the children had experienced 3 years of reading instruction. When reading identical nonwords (e.g., *grall–Grall*), for example, the 7-year old English-speaking children made errors in the region of 55% compared with 15% for their German peers. In both language groups, performance improved with age, but differences were still marked at the age of 9 years. A significant difference in nonword reading was even found when only those German- and English-speaking children whose word-reading performance was 100% correct were compared. The selected German children made only 8% errors with nonwords based on these real words (as in *Grall–Ball*), whereas their English-speaking counterparts made 22% errors. This comparison is particularly revealing, because it suggests that English and German children are relying on phonological recoding processes that operate at different psycholinguistic grain sizes. This idea is subsequently discussed further.

Cross-Language Studies of Phonemic Awareness

As noted earlier, PGST suggests that phonemic awareness develops largely in response to learning about letters. Before literacy, the development of phonological awareness is thought to be based on the implicit processing of interitem phonological similarity relations (such as rhyme) as vocabulary grows. With the acquisition of alphabetic literacy, however, a big change occurs. The need to solve the mapping problem drives the developing reading system to systematically represent phoneme-level information. This should be easier when letters convey highly consistent information about phonemes (e.g., Italian) than when letters convey highly inconsistent information about phonemes (e.g., English).

As in the case of reading acquisition, monolingual studies provide suggestive rather than conclusive data in support of this hypothesis. For example, many studies in single languages have administered phoneme-counting tasks to children during their first year of being taught to read and write, as noted earlier. Most of these studies report high levels of correct performance for children learning to read consistent orthographies and somewhat lower levels of correct performance for children learning to read inconsistent orthographies. The performance levels reported for children in first grade who are learning to read different consistent orthographies are 100% correct for Greek children (Harris & Giannoulis, 1999; Porpodas, 1999), 97% correct for Italian children (Cossu et al., 1988), 94% correct for Turkish children (Durgunoglu & Oney, 1999), 92% correct for German children (Wimmer et al., 1991), and 83% correct for Norwegian children (Hoien et al., 1995). In contrast, performance levels for children learning less consistent orthographies are usually less impressive. In a study of French children, Demont and Gombert (1996) reported 61% success in a phoneme-counting task at the end of first grade. Representative success levels reported for English children in phoneme-counting tasks are 70% correct (Liberman et al., 1974), 71% correct (Tunmer & Nesdale, 1985), and 65% correct (Perfetti, Beck, Bell, & Hughes, 1987).

It is interesting to note that the pattern of performance found across languages mirrors the statistical distribution of spelling–sound and sound–spelling inconsistency across these languages (see Ziegler & Goswami, 2005). Greek, Italian, and Turkish are highly consistent both from spelling to sound (an orthographic pattern is always pronounced the same way) and from sound to spelling (a phonological pattern is usually spelled the same way). In these languages, phonemic awareness is close to ceiling. In German, spelling–sound consistency is high but there is a fair amount of inconsistency in spelling (i.e., sound–spelling inconsistency). Interestingly, German children were not at ceiling in phoneme awareness, but at around 90% correct. French children obtained even lower scores, a pattern that is again mirrored in the statistical data because, unlike spelling–sound relations, sound–spelling relations are highly inconsistent in French (Ziegler, Jacobs, & Stone, 1996). Finally, a low level of performance for the English children is expected because in English both spelling–sound and sound–spelling relations are notoriously inconsistent (see Berndt et al., 1987; Ziegler et al., 1997). The idea that learning to spell is as—if not more—important for the development of phonemic awareness as learning to read has been around for a long time (see Goswami & Bryant, 1990; Treiman, 1993 for reviews). However, the growing availability of lexical database statistics now allows fine-grained predictions about the development of phonological awareness in different orthographies depending on sound–spelling (feedback) as well as spelling–sound (feedforward) inconsistencies.

Solutions to the Mapping Problem in Different Orthographies

As outlined earlier, PGST argues that differences in orthographic structure across languages will in themselves affect solutions to the problem of mapping sounds to letters in different languages. The result will be the development of phonological recoding processes that operate at different psycholinguistic grain sizes. PGST argues that one explanation for the often large differences found in reading accuracy and reading speed across orthographies in studies such as those already discussed is that they reflect fundamental differences in the nature of the phonological recoding and reading strategies that are developing in response to the orthography. Children who are learning to read more orthographically consistent languages, such as Greek, German, and Spanish, should rely heavily on grapheme–phoneme recoding strategies, because grapheme–phoneme correspondences are relatively consistent and there is pressure to use smaller grain sizes if this is possible. Children who are learning to read less orthographically consistent languages, like English, cannot use smaller grain sizes as easily, because inconsistency is much higher for smaller grapheme units than for larger units like rimes–bodies (Treiman, Mullennix, Bijeljac-Babic, & Richmond-Welty, 1995). As a consequence, English-speaking children will need to supplement grapheme–phoneme recoding strategies with 'large-unit' strategies such as the use of spelling patterns for rhymes ('reading by analogy'; see Goswami, 1986) and the recognition of whole words. Inconsistent orthographies like English may by their very nature push readers into developing both 'small-unit' and 'large-unit' decoding strategies in parallel.

There are a number of sources of evidence for the idea that different decoding strategies develop in response to differences in orthographic structure. For example, from her studies of reading acquisition in English, Frith (1985) suggested that reading was initially based on a 'logographic' strategy in which words were recognised as wholes. There has since been much debate over whether there is ever a 'logographic' stage in the acquisition of consistent orthographies (e.g., Wimmer et al., 1991; also see Treiman, this volume). The current consensus is that there is not. In consistent orthographies, children appear to use grapheme–phoneme decoding strategies from the earliest phases. Other sources of data relevant to the idea that different decoding strategies develop in response to differences in orthographic structure include comparisons of psycholinguistic effects such as lexicality and pseudohomophone effects in different orthographies, and investigations of children's reliance on large-unit (analogy) and small-unit (phoneme-based) phonological recoding strategies in different orthographies. I give three examples of such studies.

The Use of Analogy Strategies in Different Orthographies

If children who are learning to read an inconsistent orthography like English need to supplement grapheme–phoneme recoding strategies with recoding strategies at larger grain sizes, then 'rhyme analogy' effects should be more marked in English than in consistent orthographies like Greek. Rhyme analogy effects (see Goswami, 1986) are assumed to be based on the use of large units in reading. For example, an English-speaking child who has to decode a nonword like *dake* or *taffodil* can either use grapheme–phoneme recoding, generating the sound of each letter in the nonwords and blending the sounds together, or can make an analogy from a real word sharing the spelling pattern of the nonword after the onset, for example using 'cake' to read *dake*, and 'daffodil' to read *taffodil*. On the other hand, if a nonsense syllable like *dake* is spelled *daik*, then the English-speaking child has to use a grapheme–phoneme recoding strategy in order to generate a pronunciation for the nonword, as the large unit is unfamiliar—there are no real English words spelled with the rime pattern *aik*. If the trisyllable *taffodil* is written as *tafoddyl*, again, grapheme–phoneme recoding is the only feasible reading strategy. Matched nonwords of this nature can be used to test for the reading system's utilisation of large-unit strategies in any one orthography. If matched nonwords like *dake* and *daik* are generated in a principled way in different orthographies, then a comparison of reading accuracy and reading speed for the two types of nonword can provide a relative index of the reliance on large-unit strategies across orthographies. In orthographies in which children develop phonological recoding strategies at multiple grain sizes, a decoding advantage for the large-unit nonwords with familiar orthographic segments would be predicted. Children who have developed large-unit decoding strategies such as analogy would be expected to apply them to large-unit nonwords. In contrast, for orthographies in which children rely on small-unit (grapheme–phoneme) recoding strategies, there should be no difference in reading accuracy for the two kinds of nonword. Both can be read equally efficiently by use of a small-unit strategy.

Nonwords with familiar versus unfamiliar orthographic patterns at the large-unit level were used in a cross-language comparison of phonological recoding strategies in English and Greek by Goswami, Porpodas, and Wheelwright (1997). They gave children with a reading age of 7, 8, or 9 years in the two orthographies (the children were matched for reading age, real word knowledge, and digit reading speed) both kinds of nonword to decode in different lists. Because of the very small number of monosyllables in Greek, the comparisons were made at the bisyllabic (*ticket–bicket–bikket, toffee–loffee–loffi*) and trisyllabic (*daffodil–taffodil–tafoddyl*) level. The prediction was that the English-speaking children would show a greater difference between the large-unit (*loffee*) and small-unit (*loffi*) nonwords than the Greek children, because the English children were assumed to be learning decoding strategies at a variety of grain sizes.

The results showed that the Greek children could read both types of nonword with ease. The Greek 7-year-olds recoded 92% (bisyllables, e.g., *loffee*) and 85% (trisyllables, e.g., *taffodil*) of the large-unit nonwords correctly and 84% (bisyllables, e.g., *loffi*) and 95% (trisyllables, e.g., *tafoddyl*) of the small-unit nonwords correctly. There were no significant differences in reading accuracy between the large-unit and the small-unit nonwords at any age. In contrast, the English children showed significant differences in reading accuracy between the large-unit and small-unit nonwords at all ages. For example, the English 7-year-olds read 51% of the large-unit bisyllables correctly (e.g., *loffee*) compared with 39% of the small-unit bisyllables (e.g., *loffi*). For the trisyllables, the English children read 27% of the large-unit nonwords correctly (e.g., *taffodil*) compared with 7% of the small-unit nonwords (e.g., *tafoddyl*). These patterns suggest that English children rely on large-unit decoding strategies more than Greek children. Greek children have developed very efficient phonological recoding strategies at the grapheme–phoneme level, even by the age of 7 years. At this age, the Greek children decoded 95% of the most difficult nonwords accurately (the small-unit trisyllables). They did so very slowly, taking on average 3 s per nonword, suggesting the use of letter-by-letter recoding procedures. In contrast, the English 7-year-olds decoded only 7% of small-unit trisyllabic nonwords accurately. They also read these long nonwords extremely slowly, taking on average 3.5 s per nonword.

Pseudohomophone Effects in Consistent and Inconsistent Orthographies

Another source of evidence for the idea that inconsistent orthographies foster the development of phonological recoding strategies at multiple grain sizes comes from the comparison of psycholinguistic marker effects, such as lexicality or pseudohomophone effects, across orthographies. For example, pseudohomophone effects in nonword reading are usually taken as evidence of the influence of phonological information at the whole-word level on the phonological recoding process. If a nonword like *brane* is named faster than an orthographically matched nonword like *brate*, it is assumed that the phonological information associated with the lexical entry for the real word 'brain' assisted in the naming process. Conversely, pseudohomophone effects in lexical decision tasks are usually taken as evidence for the automatic activation of phonology during silent reading. It is assumed that it takes longer to reject *brane* as a candidate word than *brate* because the phonology of *brane* automatically activates the lexical representation for 'brain' and impedes a lexical decision.

These complementary effects of pseudohomophones in lexical decision and naming can be used cross linguistically to test the psycholinguistic grain-size hypothesis. If children learning to read inconsistent orthographies are developing phonological recoding strategies at multiple grain sizes, then they should show greater effects of whole-word phonology when naming pseudohomophones than children who are learning to read consistent orthographies. For example, English children should name a pseudohomophone like *faik* more accurately than an orthographically matched nonword like *dake*. German children should not show this pattern. German children should read the pseudohomophones and the matched nonwords with equal accuracy, because they are relying on phonological recoding at the smallest grain size, that of grapheme–phoneme correspondences. Alternatively, if the task is lexical decision rather than naming, the opposite effects should be found. Now it should be the German children who show pseudohomophone effects, because of their automatic use of grapheme–phoneme recoding strategies when reading. German children should find it more difficult to reject a pseudohomophone like *faik* than an orthographic control like *dake*. English children, however, should find it as easy to reject *faik* as *dake*. The unfamiliar spelling pattern of *faik* at the large-unit level should provide a simple basis for rejection.

In a recent study, we (Goswami et al., 2001) gave pseudohomophones and matched orthographic control nonwords to English and German children aged 7, 8, and 9 years who were matched for standardised reading ability. We found exactly the pattern previously predicted. The English children showed a significant pseudohomophone advantage in naming in comparison with the orthographic control nonwords, whereas the German children did not. Conversely, the German children showed a significant pseudohomophone advantage in lexical decision in comparison with the orthographic control nonwords, whereas the English children did not. Clearly phonological recoding was involved in reading in both languages. The absence of pseudohomophone effects in German naming did *not* mean that the German children relied less on phonological information when reading. This was demonstrated by the very large pseudohomophone effect in lexical decision. The difference between orthographies does not seem to lie in the overall 'amount' of phonological versus orthographic activation. Rather, the findings suggest differences in the efficiency and grain size of the sub-lexical recoding processes that are developing in each orthography. Both English and German children need to develop efficient phonological recoding strategies, but the strategies themselves may need to differ in terms of grain size in order to meet the requirements of the orthography that is being read.

Large-Unit and Small-Unit Strategies in Consistent and Inconsistent Orthographies

A further test of the idea that children who are learning to read inconsistent orthographies like English develop large-unit (whole-word and rhyme analogy) phonological recoding strategies in parallel with small-unit (grapheme–phoneme) phonological recoding strategies because of the nature of the orthography comes from a recent experiment that we conducted on sub-lexical strategy switching. The term 'strategy' is not used here in an explicit sense. The phonological recoding strategies that English children are assumed to be developing at multiple grain sizes are conceptualised by PGST as an implicit response to orthographic structure rather than an explicit, conscious choice about how to read (a discussion of the issue of direct teaching of large-unit versus small-unit strategies and how this might affect reading behaviour is beyond the scope of this chapter). Nevertheless, if it is correct to assume that the English orthography is forcing English-speaking children to develop phonological recoding strategies at multiple grain sizes, then reading should be more efficient when words are grouped in ways that encourage a focus on a single grain size. For example, if large-unit nonwords like *dake* ('cake') are presented blocked with other large-unit nonwords in one list, and small unit nonwords like *daik* are presented blocked with other small-unit nonwords in another list, decoding might be more accurate than if both types of nonword were presented mixed together in the same list. Goswami et al. (2003) recently investigated strategy switching costs in English versus German by using a design of this nature.

In our experiment (Goswami, Ziegler, Dalton, & Schneider, 2003), English and German 7-, 8-, and 9-year-old readers matched for reading age were given monosyllabic, bisyllabic, and trisyllabic nonwords to read that were either presented blocked by large versus small unit or that were presented mixed together in the same list. If a block of nonwords contains familiar large-unit patterns only (large-unit nonwords, like *dake*), then the exclusive application of a large-grain-size strategy should be very successful. If, in another block, all nonwords contain only unfamiliar large-unit patterns (small-unit nonwords, like *daik*), then decoding should be most successful if an exclusively small-grain-size strategy is applied. Accordingly, if both types of nonwords are mixed within a particular block, continual switching between small-unit and large-unit processing should result, incurring a switching cost. This makes the interesting prediction that decoding accuracy for both large-unit and small-unit nonwords should be better in English if they are presented blocked by grain size than if they are presented mixed together within the same lists. In contrast, children who are learning to read an orthographically consistent language like German should be unaffected by a switching cost of this type. These children should always use small-grain-size sub-lexical recoding strategies, and so there should be no accuracy cost when they are reading mixed lists.

Our results were in line with these predictions. We found significant blocking effects for the English children, but no blocking effects for the German children. The youngest English readers (7-year-olds) showed blocking effects for both the large-unit and small-unit lists (i.e., reading accuracy for the identical nonwords was greater in the blocked lists than in the mixed lists). The older English readers (8- and 9-year-olds) showed blocking effects for the large-unit lists only, at the monosyllabic level. Blocking seemed to help the English children to focus on one grain size of processing, and this particularly increased decoding accuracy for large-unit items like *dake* (rhyme analogies to 'make', 'cake', 'bake', etc.). The German readers did not show these blocking effects. Hypothetically, this was because they already relied on general and efficient decoding at the small-unit (grapheme–phoneme) level. Note that this experiment utilises an 'ideal' strategy manipulation, as our conclusions are not based on absolute processing differences between different groups of items (e.g., large-unit nonwords versus small-unit nonwords). Instead, identical items are presented in both blocked and mixed lists. Further, the large-unit and the small-unit nonwords being used required the same output phonology and articulatory preparation. Hence any differences between languages cannot be attributed to articulatory or motor factors. Similarly, any phonological priming between identical large-unit and small-unit phonological forms will be equivalent across languages. Thus any *differences* that may be found between languages cannot be attributed to phonological priming. The simplest explanation of the presence of blocking effects for the English children and the absence of blocking effects for the German children is that whereas the German children always use a small-grain-size strategy for decoding nonwords, English children use phonological recoding strategies at multiple grain sizes.

CONCLUSION

In this chapter, I have provided a selective review of the cross-language database on phonological development and reading acquisition according to the psycholinguistic grain-size theory of reading development that I have been developing with Jo Ziegler (e.g., Goswami et al., 2001; Ziegler & Goswami, 2005). PGST is based on the fact that languages vary in phonological structure and in the consistency with which that phonology is represented in orthography.

This fact means that there will be developmental differences in the grain size of lexical representations and reading strategies across orthographies. Phonological development appears to follow a language-universal sequence, with phonological awareness at large grain sizes (syllables, onsets, and rhymes) developing before literacy and awareness at smaller grain sizes (phonemes) developing in response to learning to read and spell an alphabetic orthography. PGST predicts that the beginning reading system will thus experience dual pressure, functional pressure towards smaller units that are orthographically less complex (i.e., graphemes), and linguistic pressure towards bigger units that are phonologically more accessible. Initially, this dual pressure might cause only the easiest units from both functional and linguistic domains to be present (for example, onsets that are single phonemes). PGST predicts that one should naturally find evidence for both small- and large-size units in reading depending on task constraints, stimulus selection, methods of reading instruction, or language.

One advantage of PGST is that it takes into account what happens before reading. This constrains the theory in important ways. It means that phonological structure in different languages and children's phonological knowledge of this structure need to be accorded central roles if reading and reading development are to be fully understood. As we have seen, there is currently insufficient cross-language data available to determine whether the sequence of phonological development is truly language universal, perhaps affected mainly by the speech-processing constraints that are innate to human brains, or whether there are language-specific deviations. A second advantage of PGST is that it offers a unified framework for understanding reading and reading development in different orthographic writing systems. Previous theories of reading have been strongly biased by research results from English. Yet English seems to be the exception rather than the rule in a variety of respects (e.g., consistency of orthography, development of phonological recoding procedures, manifestation of developmental dyslexia). Thus some of the most sophisticated processing architecture for reading may in fact develop only for English. Brains are basically the same across languages. Orthographies are not. This is why it makes sense to propose that different psycholinguistic units will develop for reading in response to different orthographies.

REFERENCES

Berndt, R. S., Reggia, J. S., & Mitchum, C. C. (1987). Empirically derived probabilities for grapheme-to-phoneme correspondences in English. *Behavior Research Methods, Instruments, and Computers, 19*, 1–9.

Bradley, L., & Bryant, P. E. (1978). Difficulties in auditory organisation as a possible cause of reading backwardness. *Nature, 271*, 746–7.

Bradley, L., & Bryant, P. E. (1983). Categorising sounds and learning to read: A causal connection. (*Nature, London*), 310, 419–421.

Brown, G. D. A., Ellis, N. C. (1994). Issues in spelling research. In G. D. A. Brown and N. C. Ellis (Eds.), *Handbook of spelling: Theory, process and intervention* (pp. 3–25). Chichester, UK: Wiley.

Cossu, G., Shankweiler, D., Liberman, I. Y., Katz, L., and Tola, G. (1988). Awareness of phonological segments and reading ability in Italian children. *Applied Psycholinguistics, 9*, 1–16.

Cossu, G., Gugliotta, M., & Marshall, J. C. (1995). Acquisition of reading and written spelling in a transparent orthography: Two non-parallel processes? *Reading and Writing, 7*, 9–22.

De Cara, B., & Goswami, U. C. (2000, November 23–25). *Sonorité, transparence orthographique et développement des représentations phonémiques.* Paper presented at the Colloque International Psychologie Cognitive et Apprentissage de la Lecture, Tunis, Tunisia.

De Cara, B., & Goswami, U. (2002). Statistical analysis of similarity relations among spoken words: Evidence for the special status of rimes in English. *Behavioural Research Methods and Instrumentation, 34*, 416–423.

De Cara, B., & Goswami, U. (2003). *Phonological neighbourhood density effects in a rhyme awareness task in 5-year-old children. Journal of child Language*, 30, 695–710.

De Cara, B., Goswami, U. C., & Fayol, M. (2001, September 5–8). *Phonological development and spelling across orthographies: Role of sonority and sound-spelling consistency.* Paper presented at the Twelfth Conference of the European Society for Cognitive Psychology (ESCOP), Edinburgh.

Demont, E., & Gombert, J. E. (1996). Phonological awareness as a predictor of recoding skills and syntactic awareness as a predictor of comprehension skills. *British Journal of Educational Psychology, 66*, 315–332.

Dollaghan, C. A. (1994). Children's phonological neighbourhoods: Half empty or half full? *Journal of Child Language, 21*, 257–271.

Durgunoglu, A. Y., & Oney, B. (1999). A cross-linguistic comparison of phonological awareness and word recognition. *Reading & Writing, 11*, 281–299.

Frith, U. (1985). Beneath the surface of developmental dyslexia. In K. Patterson, M. Coltheart, and J. Marshall (Eds.), *Surface dyslexia* (pp. 301–330). Cambridge, UK: Academic Press.

Frith, U. (1998). Editorial: Literally changing the brain. *Brain, 121,* 1051–1052.

Frith, U., Wimmer, H., & Landerl., K. (1998). Differences in phonological recoding in German- and English-speaking children. *Scientific Studies of Reading, 2,* 31–54.

Goswami, U. (1986). Children's use of analogy in learning to read: A developmental study. *Journal of Experimental Child Psychology, 42,* 73–83.

Goswami, U. (2003). Phonology, learning to read and dyslexia: A cross-linguistic analysis. In V. Csepe (Ed.), *Dyslexia: Different brain, different behaviour* (pp. 1–40). Dordrecht, The Netherlands: Kluwer Academic.

Goswami, U., & Bryant, P. E. (1990). *Phonological skills and learning to read.* London: Lawrence Erlbaum Associates.

Goswami, U., & De Cara, B. (2000). Lexical representations and development: The emergence of rime processing. In A. Cutler, J. McQueen, & R. Zondervan (Eds.), *Proceedings of the Workshop on Spoken Word Access Processes* (pp. 99–102). Nijmegen: Max-Planck Institute of Psycholinguistics.

Goswami, U., Gombert, J. E., & de Barrera, L. F. (1998). Children's orthographic representations and linguistic transparency: Nonsense word reading in English, French, and Spanish. *Applied Psycholinguistics, 19,* 19–52.

Goswami, U., Porpodas, C., & Wheelwright, S. (1997). Children's orthographic representations in English and Greek. *European Journal of Psychology of Education, 3,* 273–292.

Goswami, U., Ziegler, J. C., Dalton, L., & Schneider, W. (2001). Pseudohomophone effects and phonological recoding procedures in reading development in English and German. *Journal of Memory and Language, 45,* 648–664.

Goswami, U., Ziegler, J. C., Dalton, L., & Schneider, W. (2003). Nonword reading across orthographies: How flexible is the choice of reading units? *Applied Psycholinguistics, 24,* 235–47.

Harris, M., & Giannoulis, V. (1999). Learning to read and spell in Greek: The importance of letter knowledge and morphological awareness. In M. Harris & G. Hatano (Eds.), *Learning to read and write: A cross-linguistic perspective* (pp. 51–70). Cambridge, UK: Cambridge University Press.

Ho, C. S. H., & Bryant, P. (1997). Phonological skills are important in learning to read Chinese. *Developmental Psychology, 33,* 946–951.

Hoien, T., Lundberg, L., Stanovich, K. E., & Bjaalid, I. K. (1995). Components of phonological awareness. *Reading & Writing, 7,* 171–188.

Kirtley, C., Bryant, P., MacLean, M., & Bradley, L. (1989). Rhyme, rime, and the onset of reading. *Journal of Experimental Child Psychology, 48,* 224–245.

Liberman, I. Y., Shankweiler, D., Fischer, F. W., & Carter, B. (1974). Explicit syllable and phoneme segmentation in the young child. *Journal of Experimental Child Psychology, 18*, 201–212.

Luce, P. A., & Pisoni, D. B. (1998). Recognising spoken words: The neighbourhood activation model. *Ear & Hearing, 19,* 1–36.

Metsala, J. L., & Walley, A. C. (1998). Spoken vocabulary growth and the segmental restructuring of lexical representations: Precursors to phonemic awareness and early reading ability. In J. L. Metsala & L. C. Ehri (Eds.), *Word recognition in beginning literacy* (pp. 89–120). Mahwah, NJ: Lawrence Erlbaum Associates.

Perfetti, C. A., Beck, I., Bell, L., & Hughes, C. (1987). Phonemic knowledge and learning to read are reciprocal: A longitudinal study of first grade children. *Merrill-Palmer Quarterly, 33,* 283–319.

Porpodas, C. D. (1999). Patterns of phonological and memory processing in beginning readers and spellers of Greek. *Journal of Learning Disabilities, 32,* 406–416.

Porpodas, C. D., Pantelis, S. N., & Hantziou, E. (1990). Phonological and lexical encoding processes in beginning readers: Effects of age and word characteristics. *Reading and Writing, 2,* 197–208.

Share, D. L. (1995). Phonological recoding and self-teaching: Sine qua non of reading acquisition. *Cognition, 55,* 151–218.

Siok, W. T., & Fletcher, P. (2001). The role of phonological awareness and visual-orthographic skills in Chinese reading acquisition. *Developmental Psychology, 37,* 886–899.

Treiman, R. (1985). Onsets and rimes as units of spoken syllables: Evidence from children. *Journal of Experimental Child Psychology, 39,* 161–181.

Treiman, R. (1993). *Beginning to spell. A study of first-grade children.* New York: Oxford University Press.

Treiman, R., Mullennix, J., Bijeljac-Babic, R., & Richmond-Welty, E. D. (1995). The special role of rimes in the description, use, and acquisition of English orthography. *Journal of Experimental Psychology: General, 124,* 107–136.

Tunmer, W. E., & Nesdale, A. R. (1985). Phonemic segmentation skill and beginning reading. *Journal of Educational Psychology, 77,* 417–527.

Wimmer, H., & Goswami, U. (1994). The influence of orthographic consistency on reading development: Word recognition in English and German children. *Cognition, 51*, 91–103.

Wimmer, H., & Hummer, P. (1990). How German speaking first graders read and spell: Doubts on the importance of the logographic stage. *Applied Psycholinguistics, 11*, 349–368.

Wimmer, H., Landerl, K., Linortner, R., & Hummer, P. (1991). The relationship of phonemic awareness to reading acquisition. More consequence than precondition but still important. *Cognition, 40*, 219–249.

Wimmer, H., Landerl, K., & Schneider, W. (1994). The role of rhyme awareness in learning to read a regular orthography. *British Journal of Developmental Psychology, 12*, 469–484.

Ziegler, J. C., & Goswami, U. (2005). Reading acquisition, developmental dyslexia & skilled reading across languages: A psycholinguistic grain size theory. *Psychological Bulletin, 131*, 3–29.

Ziegler, J. C., Jacobs, A. M., & Stone, G. O. (1996). Statistical analysis of the bidirectional inconsistency of spelling and sound in French. *Behavior Research Methods, Instruments, & Computers, 28*, 504–515.

Ziegler, J. C., Stone, G. O., & Jacobs, A. M. (1997). What's the pronunciation for -OUGH and the spelling for /u/? A database for computing feedforward and feedback inconsistency in English. *Behavior Research Methods, Instruments, & Computers, 29*, 600–618.

29

Literacy Acquisition in Japanese–English Bilinguals

Nobuhiko Akamatsu
Doshisha University

The primary goal of this chapter is to provide an overview of research findings on the orthographic effects of Japanese as a first language (L1) on reading acquisition in English as a second language (ESL). The first section, reflecting the historical background of the Japanese writing system, illustrates four types of scripts that are all used in modern Japanese text: *kanji*, *hiragana*, *katakana*, and *romaji*. The second and third sections briefly review Japanese modern literacy education and recent English education. Major research findings of Japanese orthographic effects on second-language (L2) reading acquisition are reviewed in the fourth section. It focuses on three aspects in which the Japanese learners of ESL may experience L1 effects in the course of L2 reading acquisition: (a) the type of information dominantly used in word recognition, (b) metaphonological ability, and (c) efficiency in processing the constituent letters in an English word.

THE JAPANESE WRITING SYSTEM

Japanese is often described as one of the most difficult languages to learn because of its unique writing system. The uniqueness derives from two types of orthographic systems cofunctioning in one writing system: logography and syllabary. The logographic writing system is known as *kanji*, which originated from Chinese characters. The syllabic writing system is called *kana*, a simplified form of *kanji* characters. There are two types of *kana*: *hiragana* (cursive *kana*) and *katakana* (square *kana*); therefore there are three different types of scripts (i.e., *kanji*, *hiragana*, and *katakana*) in the Japanese writing system. Furthermore, the Roman alphabet, called *romaji*, is sometimes used to write road signs, acronyms, and translations for foreigners. Each of these scripts (*kanji*, *hiragana*, *katakana*, and *romaji*) plays its own distinctive functions in the Japanese writing system.

Kanji

Chinese civilization played a crucial role in the sociocultural characteristics of early Japan. In particular, contact with the Chinese language, by means of not only the Chinese but also the Koreans, led to Japan's cultural and technological progress (Loveday, 1996). The Korean immigrants in the fourth century, for example, brought Buddhism, Buddhist literature written in Chinese, and new technologies such as pottery and ironware. The advanced technologies and the new culture brought by the Korean immigrants earned the Japanese people's respect toward Chinese culture, resulting in Japan's tendency to imitate China as a model. When the Japanese government started to compose the constitution of Japan, for example, they adapted the format of the Chinese law. Because there was no writing system in early Japan, the Chinese characters were also used for writing Japanese.

Chinese characters were introduced to Japan in several historical phases between the 5th and 14th centuries, and the Japanese adopted them each time (Taylor & Taylor, 1995). The "Han characters" (*han-zi* in Chinese; *kan-ji* in Japanese) associated with the Han Dynasty period in China seems to predominate such borrowing (Kess & Miyamoto, 1999). Although *kanji* originates from Chinese characters, both Japanese and Chinese languages differ in their phonology, syntax, and vocabulary. In other words, Chinese characters were chosen for the Japanese script not because of linguistic commonalities between Chinese and Japanese languages, but because of the value of the Chinese characters, that is, the only medium through which the Japanese could learn advanced technologies and new culture. Thus the adaptation of Chinese characters to represent the Japanese language created somewhat unique, yet complex, features in *kanji*, for example, the emergence of multiple phonological representation and homophony.

A majority of *kanji* characters have two types of phonological representations: the *on*-reading (*on-yomi*) and the *kun*-reading (*kun-yomi*). The *on*-reading is the pronunciation derived from the original Chinese pronunciation and reflects the historical, dialectical, and phonological features of the original Chinese characters. Accordingly, those characters introduced from China more than once in several historical periods have multiple *on*-readings, reflecting phonological changes of their original Chinese characters. The *kun*-reading, on the other hand, is based on the Japanese translation of the original Chinese character. This was possibly due to the fact that each Chinese character corresponds to a concept or a meaning that can be translated into spoken Japanese, thereby making possible the association between Chinese characters and the sounds of the Japanese language. Furthermore, unlike in an alphabetic writing system, the components of Chinese characters generally do not indicate their phonological representations; therefore it might be easy to associate Chinese characters with the Japanese pronunciation (Loveday, 1996).

Another feature of *kanji*, which resulted from the adoption of Chinese characters, is that the Japanese language has a great many homonyms. This is partly because of the way in which the *on*-reading was created. The spoken Chinese has tones, or contrasting intonations, that play an important role as allophonemes; a change in the tone therefore results in a different meaning, even though the word preserves the same pronunciation. Japanese, however, does not have counterparts to the Chinese tones, and the tone features were ignored when the Japanese adopted the Chinese characters and created their *on*-readings. As a result, there are a great number of homonyms in Japanese.

In the 13-volume *Great Sino-Japanese Dictionary*, there are approximately 50,000 different *kanji* characters; however, most of them are seldom used by the Japanese people (Taylor & Taylor, 1995). The use of *kanji* has changed over time, and the number of different *kanji* characters that are used in modern Japan is estimated to be between 3,200 and 5,100, depending on the type of text or topic (Tajima, 1989). For example, the number of different *kanji* characters used in newspapers and magazines is approximately 3,300 whereas the corresponding number for Japanese literature is approximately 5,000. This does not mean, however, that the Japanese must remember 3,300 *kanji* characters to be able to read newspapers or magazines; according to Tajima (1989), the most frequently used 2,000 *kanji* can account for 99.6% and 98.6% of all the *kanji* characters used in newspapers and magazines, respectively. The fact that 2,000 *kanji* characters can cover most news items may reflect a declining tendency in the use of *kanji* for writing Japanese.

Morioka (1991), who surveyed the number of words written in *kanji* in newspapers that were printed between 1879 and 1968, pointed out that the use of *kanji* characters in newspapers dropped almost 30% in 90 years. This decline of *kanji* in print appears to go hand in hand with an increase of words written in *kana*, simplified forms of *kanji* characters. Morioka suggested that few, if any, Sino-Japanese words with the *on*-reading were affected by the replacement of *kanji* with *kana*; the script for Japanese native words with the *kun*-reading was changed from *kanji* to *kana*.

Kana

Kana, the Japanese original script, was developed in the process of adapting the Chinese characters into the Japanese, and the problems resulting from linguistic differences between Chinese and Japanese necessitated the development of *kana* in the Japanese writing system. According to Yoshino (1988), there were four stages in the adaptation process: (a) The ideographic value of the Chinese characters was lost when Japanese proper names were written in *kanji*, (b) word order shifted from the Chinese format to the Japanese format, (c) function words in Japanese (e.g., particles, auxiliaries) that did not have counterparts in Chinese were added and written in *kanji*, and (d) both *kanji* and *kana* became standard systems of written Japanese.

The oldest document that contained Japanese proper names was written in the early sixth century. In that document, a Japanese proper name was written with several *kanji* characters whose pronunciation respectively matched the syllables in the name. The semantic features of those *kanji* characters, however, had nothing to do with the pronunciation of the names; only the phonetic value of the Chinese characters was adopted. This particular use of Chinese characters as phonetic symbols is seen as the first step to the creation of *kana*.

The second and third steps in the development of *kana* were related to major problems that the Japanese faced in writing text in *kanji* only: Chinese and Japanese differ in word order and the use of grammatical morphemes. Until the late sixth century, writing text in *kanji* meant translating Japanese into Chinese; Japanese word order and grammatical morphemes were ignored in written text. During the early seventh century, however, the Japanese began to write text in *kanji*, following the Japanese grammar. Furthermore, at the end of the seventh century, Japanese grammatical morphemes (e.g., particles, auxiliaries) were also added to the written text, with certain *kanji* characters used as phonetic signs. Because there are few, if any, particles and auxiliaries in Chinese, such function words needed to be added in the Japanese text. Written Japanese became closer to spoken Japanese, and the Japanese began to treat writing not as translation, but as their communication tool. This shift from the Chinese grammar to Japanese grammar in writing was very significant in terms of the Japanese identity of the written text.

The *kanji* system used only for phonetic symbols, disregarding their semantic features, is called *manyo-gana*. *Manyo-gana* were first used to write Japanese proper names; soon they were also used for writing Japanese grammatical morphemes. Which *kanji* character to use for *manyo-gana*, however, was not standardized, but depended on each writer, resulting in each Japanese syllable being represented by multiple *manyo-gana* symbols. According to Taylor and Taylor (1995), by the end of the eighth century, over 970 *manyo-gana* were chosen to represent approximately 90 syllables of the Japanese language of the day. During this early period, *manyo-gana* consisted of both simple and complex Chinese characters. Complex

TABLE 29.1

Examples of Kanji Origins of *Hiragana* and *Katakana*

Kanji	Hiragana	Kanji	Katakana
武	む (mu)	毛	モ (mo)
乃	の (no)	加	カ (ka)
太	た (ta)	多	タ (ta)
安	あ (a)	阿	ア (a)
以	い (i)	伊	イ (i)
奈	な (na)	奈	ナ (na)
世	せ (se)	世	セ (se)

manyo-gana, however, gradually declined in number for practical reasons, and only simple *manyo-gana* (i.e., *kanji* characters with a small number of strokes) remained. Although during this early period many *manyo-gana* characters represented one Japanese syllable, documents written by the end of the ninth century contained one *manyo-gana* for each syllable, and over time these selected *manyo-gana* became simplified to form two types of syllabic scripts: *hiragana* (cursive *kana*) and *katakana* (square *kana*) (Chikushima, 1982) (see Table 29.1).

Although *hiragana* can be found in only a limited number of formal documents written during these early years, it is believed that *hiragana* had been widely used by the end of the ninth century. The scantiness of historical documents containing *hiragana* reflects the fact that *hiragana* were preferably used for writing colloquial Japanese, mainly in poems, personal letters, and diaries, which were not meant to be preserved or publicized.

"*Kata*" of *katakana* means "imperfect" or "immature." The reason why *katakana* are called "imperfect script" is related to the reason for creating *katakana*. *Katakana* were first considered as symbols rather than letters. This was because *katakana* were created for the practical reason of fast writing. *Katakana*, invented from *manyo-gana*, were treated as abbreviations (e.g., "b/n" for "between.").

Both *hiragana* and *katakana* independently evolved over a period of thousand years, resulting in many variant shapes of *kana*. This was because different *manyo-gana* were simplified to create *kana* signs representing the same syllables. In 1900, the government finally standardized both *kana* scripts to eliminate the variations in shapes. Both *kana* were modernized and standardized again in 1947, with the introduction of the family registration law, which tried to regulate the use of *kanji* and *kana* scripts for personal names (Chikushima, 1982).

Today the *kana* system consists of 46 basic symbols and 25 symbols with diacritics, and the basic *kana* symbols represent five vowels (a, i, u, e, o), 40 consonant–vowel (CV) combinations, and one nasal sound /n/. Each *kana* symbol represents a speech unit that corresponds to one *mora*, a single beat, and the relationship between each *kana* symbol and its corresponding *mora* is highly consistent.

In modern text, *hiragana* and *katakana* each play distinctive roles. *Hiragana* are generally used for grammatical morphemes such as function words and verb or adjective endings. *Katakana*, on the other hand, are mainly used to write modern European loan words, onomatopoeia, the names of uncommon animals and plants, and the names of uncommon chemical substances (Taylor & Taylor, 1995). *Katakana* are also used as a kind of visual italics to draw the attention of the reader (Kess & Miyamoto, 1999).

Romaji

In modern Japanese writing, the Roman alphabet called *romaji* [Roman letters] are used to write specific words, such as road signs (e.g., STOP), abbreviations for measures of length or amount (e.g., m for *meter*; 1 for *liter*), acronyms (e.g., *JR* for *Japan Railway*), and English translations for foreign tourists (e.g., railway station designations). The titles of some popular magazines are also written in *romaji*. There is no standardized rule for when to use *romaji*; because of the distinctive appearance of *romaji* in the mixture of *kanji* and *kana*, the words written in *romaji* seem to be more stylish and impressive than the same words written only in *katakana* or *hiragana*. For the same reason, media advertising tends to use *romaji* often, resulting in increased exposure of the Japanese people to the Roman alphabet.

The increase in exposure to *romaji* appears to affect Japanese literacy acquisition. English words that used to be written in *katakana* are now often written in the original Roman alphabet, and even young children nowadays recognize many of the English letters. This may lead one to consider that "[romaji] is no longer regarded as an alien form of writing, exotic and incomprehensible to the average Japanese" (Kess & Miyamoto, 1999, pp. 112). The use of *romaji*, however, is still much less widespread than that of the other three scripts (i.e., *kanji*, *hiragana*, and *katakana*). Therefore one should be cautious in treating *romaji* as equal to *kanji* and *kana* systems.

In general, modern Japanese texts consist of *kanji*, *hiragana*, *katakana*, and *romaji*. According to Hayashi (1982), the frequency of occurrence of these characters in text is *kanji*, approximately 46%, *hiragana*, 35%, *katakana*, 6%, and *romaji*, 0.4%. As already mentioned, *hiragana* are mostly used for writing grammatical morphemes (e.g., postpositions after nouns, adjective, and verb endings) whereas *katakana* are mostly used for writing loan words from English and other European languages. The majority of content words such as roots of nouns, adjectives, and verbs are written in *kanji*. Thus, to understand Japanese literacy acquisition, it is critical to have a knowledge of how *kanji* contribute to Japanese vocabulary.

JAPANESE VOCABULARY

Japanese words can be classified into four types: (a) *wago* (Japanese native words), (b) *kango* (words of Chinese or Sino-Japanese origin), (c) *gairaigo* (loan words from languages other than Chinese), or (d) *konshugo* (mixed words, e.g., *wago* + *kango*, *kango* + *gairaigo*, etc.). *Wago* are written in *hiragana* or *kanji* in their *kun*-reading whereas *kango* are written only with *kanji* in their *on*-reading. *Gairaigo* are written in *katakana*, and *konshugo* are written with a mixture of *hiragana*, *katakana*, and *kanji*. *Kango* are basically words of Chinese origin, and therefore they are read in the *on*-reading, that is, the Chinese pronunciation of the characters. However, *kango* are not necessarily pure loan words from Chinese. The Japanese created many compound words by combining two or three *kanji* characters. These compound words are typically pronounced through the *on*-reading of each *kanji* character; the meanings of the words are obtained by summing up the meaning of each *kanji* character. For example, the compound word 自動車 [automobile] consists of three kanji characters, "auto" (自), "move" (動), and "wheel" (車), and it is pronounced "ji-doo-sha."

A particularly productive period of *kango* (i.e., authentic-looking compound words that are written in *kanji* characters only) occurred from the end of the 19th century to the beginning of the 20th century, when Japan abolished the national isolation policy and needed to find a way of dealing with new intellectual and scientific concepts from western civilization. Morioka (1991) and his colleagues carried out research on English–Japanese dictionaries published in the *kango*-creation phase to investigate how the new intellectual, scientific, and technological

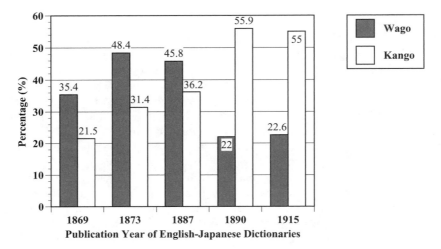

FIG. 29.1.   The percentage of *wago* and *kango* among the words listed in English–Japanese dictionaries published between 1869 and 1915.

terms imported from western civilization affected Japanese vocabulary. The total number of translated words that were listed in the five English–Japanese dictionaries selected for the investigation increased by more than twofold, from 815 words in the *Satsuma English–Japanese Dictionary* (1869) to 2,134 words in the *Inoue English–Japanese Dictionary* (1915). During this period, the ratio of *kango* among the translated words exceeded that of *wago* (see Fig. 29.1). This appears to indicate that *kango* were superior to *wago* as the vocabulary for introducing new concepts. Furthermore, the dominance of *kango* over the other types of words (i.e., *wago*, *gairaigo*, and *konshugo*) was also evident in the vocabulary of specialized disciplines such as mathematics, mineralogy, and philosophy (Morioka, 1991).

The National Language Research Institute (NLRI) initiated more recent research on the classification of Japanese vocabulary. They surveyed the distribution of *wago, kango, gairaigo*, and *konshugo* in 90 magazines published in 1961 (NLRI, 1962–1964). The surveyed magazines contained approximately 420,000 words in total, consisting of 30,000 different words. Results showed that, among the running words, *wago* represented the largest percentage (53.9%), followed by *kango* (41.3%), *gairaigo* (2.9%), and *konshugo* (1.9%). When word type was used as the criterion, however, the largest percentage of the words was *kango* (47.5%); *wago* had the second largest percentage (36.7%), followed by *gairaigo* (9.8%), and *konshugo* had the lowest (6.0%). This seems to reflect the fact that *kango* still dominates the modern Japanese vocabulary in number. With respect to the gap in the percentage of *wago* between the running words and the word type, Sugito (1989) suggested that "[it] is because wago include a great number of the fundamental words which are used frequently in all contexts, for example words like *suru* (to do), *iru* (to be), and *aru* (to be)" (p. 120).

LITERACY EDUCATION IN JAPAN

Children begin their Japanese literacy education officially in elementary school, at the age of 6 years. As one can imagine, it takes a long time to learn to read and write Japanese because of the complex nature of the Japanese writing system. In particular, *kanji* heavily contribute to the lengthening of acquisition of literacy, which is often a lifelong process. *Kana*, on the other hand, does not require such time-consuming learning. Normally preschoolers are exposed to print even before kindergarten, and some kindergarteners start their school life with some knowledge of *kana*; Japanese children normally begin to read *hiragana* approximately by the age of 4 years. In 1967, the NLRI carried out research on literacy acquisition of children aged 4 to 6 years (NLRI, 1972). Approximately 2,200 kindergarteners participated in the study; the age range of the younger children was 4.7–5.7 years ($M = 5.1$) and that of the older children was 5.7–6.7 ($M = 6.1$). Results showed that, by the age of 4 years, 33.6% of the children could read more than 60 *hiragana*, and 16.4% of the children could read all 71 *hiragana*; 9.3% of the children could not read any *hiragana*. By the age of 5 years, the number of the children who could read all the *hiragana* increased: 40.2% of the children read all the *hiragana* correctly. Only 1.1% of the children could not read any *hiragana* at all (NLRI, 1972). It was also found that the 5-year-olds who read all 71 *hiragana* could read simple *kanji* characters, such as ⼀ [one], 子 [child], 山 [mountain], and 川 [river]. With respect to the ability to write *hiragana*, no preschooler could write all the *hiragana* correctly. By the age of 5 years, 56.7% of the children wrote more than 21 *hiragana* correctly, and 26% wrote more than 41 *hiragana* correctly. However, there were only 3.6% who could write more than 60 *hiragana* correctly.

In elementary school, Japanese children officially start to learn *hiragana* and *katakana*. Because most first graders have already known most *hiragana* by the time they start their elementary school life, the focus of literacy education in the first three grades is on the acquisition of *katakana* and *kanji* characters. *Kanji* are especially carefully chosen for literacy education so that children can learn *kanji* systematically.

Historically, systematic *kanji* education was introduced in 1904. All the textbooks used in elementary schools were written and published by the government, so that every child in the country would learn the same *kanji* characters. However, in 1947, two years after Japan was defeated in World War II, the educational regulations were revised, and the use of national textbooks in schools was discontinued. This abolition of national textbooks necessitated the development of a guideline for teaching *kanji* characters.

From 1952 to 1955, in designing the literacy curriculum of elementary school, the Ministry of Education carried out a survey on schoolchildren's literacy acquisition, and selected 881 *kanji* characters from the 1,850 *Toyo Kanji*[1] (Temporary Kanji; NLRI, 1988). The selected *kanji* were then allocated to each grade on the basis of the frequency and familiarity of *kanji* characters, the importance of basic radicals and phonetics, and ease of memorization (Sato, 1988). In 1968, reflecting the public view that children should know more *kanji*, the Ministry of Education added 115 *kanji* characters to the list and assigned them to each grade. In 1988, 10 more *kanji* characters were added, and in all a total of 1,006 *kanji* were selected for elementary education (see Table 29.2).

As Table 29.2 shows, *kanji* characters taught in elementary school and class meetings for its literacy education decreased after World War II. This decrease may have reflected the postwar national movement or thought to restrict the use of *kanji* (NLRI, 1994). The mean length of time for studying per *kanji* character, however, remained almost constant (see Fig. 29.2).

The Ministry of Education provided, along with the *kanji* list, guidelines for *kanji* instruction for each grade. For example, for the first graders, the guideline suggests that the instruction focus on the ideographic nature of *kanji* because the first graders tend to see *kanji* as pictographs only. For the second, third, and fourth graders, the focus of the *kanji* instruction gradually shifts

---

[1] In 1946, the Japanese government, with the intention of promoting the use of less complex *kanji* characters in public, selected 1,850 characters as *Toyo Kanji* [Temporary Kanji]. The list of these *kanji* was called "temporary" because "it was considered to be a temporary measure until a Roman alphabet replaced all other scripts in Japan. It severely restricted the use of Kanji" (Taylor & Taylor, 1995, p. 298). Later, a more liberal list of common *kanji* was called for, and, in 1981, 1,950 kanji characters known as *Joyo Kanji* [Common Kanji] were chosen.

TABLE 29.2

Number of *Kanji* Characters Taught and Literacy Class Meetings in Each Grade Between 1904 and 1992

Year		Grade 1	Grade 2	Grade 3	Grade 4	Grade 5	Grade 6	Total
1904	A	10	73	161	256	152	202	854
	B	340 (10)	420 (12)	525 (15)	525 (15)	350 (10)	350 (10)	2,510
1910	A	34	119	268	351	313	275	1,360
	B	340 (10)	420 (12)	490 (14)	490 (14)	350 (10)	350 (10)	2,440
1918	A	49	173	307	343	262	232	1,366
	B	340 (10)	420 (12)	420 (12)	420 (12)	315 (9)	315 (9)	2,230
1933	A	82	234	336	298	215	197	1,362
	B	340 (10)	420 (12)	420 (12)	420 (12)	315 (9)	315 (9)	2,230
1941	A	129	276	244	225	234	193	1,301
	B	272 (8)	315 (9)	280 (8)	280 (8)	245 (7)	245 (7)	1,637
1947	A	50	98	150	144	133	109	684
	B	170 (5)	210 (6)	210 (6)	245 (7)	245 (7)	280 (8)	1,360
1961	A	46	105	187	205	194	144	881
	B	238 (7)	315 (9)	280 (8)	280 (8)	245 (7)	245 (7)	1,603
1971	A	46	105	187	205	194	144	881
	B	238 (7)	315 (9)	280 (8)	280 (8)	245 (7)	245 (7)	1,603
1980	A	76	145	195	195	195	190	996
	B	272 (8)	280 (8)	280 (8)	280 (8)	210 (6)	210 (6)	1,532
1992	A	80	160	200	200	185	181	1,006
	B	306 (9)	315 (9)	280 (8)	280 (8)	210 (6)	210 (6)	1,601

Notes. Row A lists the number of *kanji* characters taught in each grade at elementary school. Row B lists the number of class meetings for literacy education in each grade in elementary school. Values enclosed in parentheses represent the number of class meetings per week. Each class was 45 minutes long. This table is based on the data from the NLRI (1994).

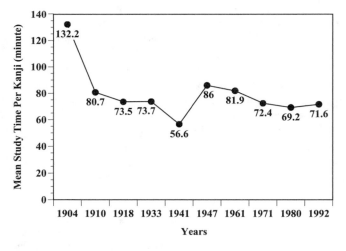

FIG. 29.2. Study time (in minutes) per kanji character at elementary school between 1904 and 1992.

from reading to writing; the children are expected to increase vocabulary by not only reading but also writing *kanji*. Recent guidelines also recommend that the children understand the nature of *kanji*, including the historical background of *kanji* in Japan and the basic knowledge of orthographic and phonological components in *kanji* characters. *Kanji* education continues until middle school, and the curricula for *kanji* education in middle school are designed as systematically as those of primary school. For example, according to the guideline issued in 1981, 250 to 400 *kanji* are designated in each grade, and, by the end of middle school, the students learn to read and write approximately 950 *kanji* characters. Thus, with the 1,006 *kanji* designated for primary school, all the 1,945 *Joyo Kanji* (*kanji* for common use) selected by the government are taught by the ninth grade, when the children are 15 years old. Past the ninth grade, however, *kanji* are not particularly taught in the curriculum; the students are expected to learn new *kanji* not only in Japanese class, but also in other classes such as history, science, and classic Chinese. In these subjects, it is quite common that the students encounter unfamiliar *kanji* that are not included in the 1,945 *Joyo Kanji*.

A large-scale, questionnaire-based survey carried out by the NLRI in 1987 illustrates how *kanji* instruction is positioned in literacy education in primary and secondary schools (NLRI, 1994). Results highlighted the teachers' common recognition that *kanji* instruction plays a very important role in literacy education.[2] In light of the ability of reading and writing *kanji*, 52.7% of the primary school teachers prioritized writing in literacy education whereas 54.7% of the secondary school teachers taught both reading and writing *kanji* to the same degree. It was also found that about half of the primary school teachers and three fourths of the secondary school teachers taught *kanji* that were not listed on the *Joyo Kanji* list. The higher the grade was, the more non-*Joyo Kanji* were introduced in class.

Another NLRI survey, which investigated the primary school children's reading and writing abilities of *kanji*, reveals that Japanese primary school students have fairly good, but by no means perfect, knowledge of *kanji* (NLRI, 1988). Overall, the students were better at reading than at writing, and the mastery level of both *on*-readings and *kun*-readings was lower than that of either *on*-readings or *kun*-readings. The mean percentage of reading *kanji* in either the *on*-reading or the *kun*-reading was 92.7% whereas that in both readings was 76.0%. The mean ratio of writing kanji with the *on*-reading or the *kun*-reading was 66.2% whereas that with both readings was 53.5%. More specifically, the students in each grade showed higher than 90% accuracy in reading *kanji* in either the *on*-reading or the *kun*-reading. In reading *kanji* in both the *on*-reading and the *kun*-reading, however, the accuracy rates ranged from 58.2% to 87.0%; children in higher grades tended to show a higher percentage of accuracy. With respect to the writing ability of *kanji*, the accuracy rates in writing *kanji* with both the *on*-reading and the *kun*-reading remained constant, around 50%, in each grade. The accuracy rates in writing *kanji* with either the *on*-reading or the *kun*-reading, on the other hand, ranged between 57.6% and 88.3%; children in the lower grades tended to show a higher percentage of accuracy.

ENGLISH EDUCATION IN JAPAN

Since the late 19th century, when Japan emerged from its national isolation, English has been the most popular foreign language (FL) in Japan. When Japan opened its door to the world after a 350-year closure, English was seen as a means of importing advanced science and technology from western civilization. The important role of English for Japan's modernization

---

[2] Approximately one third of the teachers (33.9% for primary school; 27.8% for secondary school) recognized that *kanji* instruction is extremely important in literacy education. There were only 4.7% (primary school) and 5.9% (secondary school) teachers who paid little attention to *kanji* instruction.

was realized and emphasized (e.g., Okakura, 1911; Uchimura, 1899/1984), which led to the inclusion of English in the Japanese curriculum.

Harold Palmer is one of the educators who had a remarkable influence on English education in Japan. Palmer, an advisory committee member in the Ministry of Education, emphasized the practical aspect of English as a tool of communication and promoted the oral method (Palmer, 1921). He disagreed with the idea that English education in Japan should focus on reading books for the information or knowledge of the civilization and culture of western countries. He argued that the Japanese should acquire English as a thinking tool for formulating and exchanging ideas and thoughts with people from different cultures. His emphasis on spoken English and the instructional approach he chose (i.e., the oral method), however, were not supported by other educators because most Japanese had little opportunity for using English for communication with foreigners (Katayama, Endo, Sasaki, & Matsumura, 1994). Learning to read English therefore became the focus of English education in Japan, and the translation method was, and still is, widely used at school.

Almost one century has passed since Palmer's recommendation that English should be taught as a thinking and communication tool, and now Japan seems to regret that its English education has paid little attention to Palmer's suggestions. In 1996, the Ministry of Education published a special report, *Education in Japan: Towards the 21st century*, and recommended that English be taught for the sake of communication (Ministry of Education, 1996). The report proposed several general guidelines for education in Japan, and English education is discussed under the issue of global education for international understanding. The guidelines for English education particularly emphasize the needs for (a) offering English education at public elementary schools, (b) improving teacher-training programs, and (c) updating English instructor's teaching techniques.

In light of early English education, private primary schools have started already to offer English, although the time allocated for English education varies. Public primary schools, however, have not yet officially included English education in their curricula. In 1996, to investigate the possibility of teaching English in elementary schools, the Ministry of Education selected one model school in each prefecture. In 2002, reflecting the results of the surveys on English education of the model schools, the Ministry of Education, Culture, Sports, Science, and Technology[3] (MEXT) revised the guidelines and suggested that English conversation could be taught as an extracurricular activity.[4] According to the guidelines, the main objectives of early English education are (a) helping the students become familiar with foreign cultures and (b) motivating the children to further learn English in secondary school. Accordingly, the class activities are based on songs, games, and skits that use simple phrases for basic conversation. As of April 2003, approximately half of the public primary schools offer English classes.

Since 1987, the Japanese government has run the Japan Exchange and Teaching Program (JET program) and hired native speakers of English called AETs (assistant English teachers) or ALTs (assistant language teachers) on a 1-year contract basis.[5] ALTs mainly teach speaking and listening with the Japanese teachers of English in a team-teaching style, in junior high and high schools, and now in elementary school. ALTs are also expected to participate in extracurricular activities such as sports days, school festivals, and various club activities after school. The JET Program is now seen as a significant part of Japan's English education, especially in light of

---

[3] Since January 6, 2001, because of its structural reform, the Ministry of Education has been called the Ministry of Education, Culture, Sports, Science, and Technology.

[4] This extracurricular activity is officially geared toward the third to sixth graders (ages 9 to 12 years), and three class meetings (45 minutes each) per week are allocated.

[5] The increase in the number of ALTs appears to reflect the emphasis on oral communication skills in English education. The number of ALTs in 1986 was 813, and that in 2000 was 5,444; it increased almost seven times in 15 years. Most ALTs come from the United States, the United Kingdom, Canada, Australia, and New Zealand.

helping not only the students but also the Japanese teachers of English become exposed to English on a communicative basis.

Despite the fact that early English education has recently been promoted by the government, many Japanese students start to learn English only at the age of 12 years, when they enter junior high school. Most students spend three additional years studying English in high school, and many of them continue to learn English for 2 years at university. Japanese students therefore normally study English for 6 to 8 years. Learning English for 6 to 8 years may appear to be long enough to acquire a high level of English proficiency. Nonetheless, the ranking of the Japanese in the Test of English as a Foreign Language (TOEFL) scores fall short of such expectations. The mean TOEFL score of approximately 100,000 Japanese testees was 501, and Japan ranked 33 on the TOEFL World List of 39, and 18 among 21 Asian countries (Educational Testing Service, 1999). Because the TOEFL measures grammatical knowledge and listening and reading abilities, the relatively low ranking of Japan on the TOEFL score may imply that Japan's English education needs to be far more communication oriented; it also indicates that teaching reading and grammar, which has been prioritized in the curriculum since the beginning of English education in Japan, may not be good enough.

Recent movements of emphasizing communication in English education do not necessarily devalue reading skills and grammatical knowledge. Reading is still seen as one of the most useful skills in English education in Japan (Katayama et al., 1994). In teaching reading, the translation method is widely used; explaining grammar rules and introducing new vocabulary takes up most of the teaching time. Compared with teaching approaches for oral communication, those for reading English have not changed much in Japan. This may suggest that the findings in L2 reading research have not had much effect on the teaching methods for EFL reading in Japan. Regrettably, new approaches for teaching EFL reading, which are based on recent L2 research findings, do not seem to have been fully utilized yet in Japan.

THE EFFECTS OF JAPANESE (L1) ON READING ACQUISITION IN ENGLISH (L2)

In learning a foreign language, the notion of "nativelike" has attracted quite a few people's attention. L2 learners are normally interested in how *naturally* they can manage the target language, and FL instructors seek for a better teaching approach to help the learners become *proficient* in the target language. What hinders L2 or FL learners from speaking and writing like "native users" has been always an important issue. In addition to some physiological and affective factors, the learners' L1 is seen as one of the critical factors in the acquisition of a FL. Especially when the target language is orthographically different from the learner's L1, particular L1 orthographic features are considered to affect reading acquisition in the L2 or FL (Koda, 1996). According to recent cross-linguistic studies on L2 word recognition, there are three factors that may affect the Japanese learners of ESL. These are (a) the type of information used in word recognition, (b) metaphonological ability, and (c) efficiency in processing the constituent letters in English words.

Dominant Information in Word-Recognition Processing

In L1 reading research, orthographic depth, which refers to the degree to which print corresponds to its sound, has been used to support the proposal that word–recognition procedures may vary according to different writing systems (Frost, 1994). The basic notion is that language differs in how consistently orthographic information in a word provides its corresponding phonological representation.

An orthography that represents its phonology in a straightforward manner is called a *shallow* or *transparent* orthography (e.g., Spanish, Turkish). Because of the transparent relationships between spelling and pronunciation, in a shallow orthography, phonological information is considered to be dominantly used even at a prelexical level of word recognition (e.g., Carello, Turvey, & Lukatela, 1992). In contrast, in a *deep* orthography (e.g., English, French), non-phonological, orthographic information is seen to play a more important role in processing printed words (Frost & Bentin, 1992). This is because, in a deep orthography, the relationship between spelling and phonology is relatively opaque and not straightforward, and therefore the accurate phonological representation of a word is not always guaranteed from its spelling.

In L2 reading research, studies that apply the basic concepts of the orthographic depth hypothesis argue for the transfer of specific L1 word–recognition procedures to L2 reading. Koda (1988), for example, comparing Spanish and Arabic learners of English (shallow L1 orthography) with the Japanese (deep L1 orthography), investigated whether the difference in L1 orthographic depth affects the type of information that plays a dominant role during L2 word-recognition processing. She found that the Japanese ESL learners were more adversely affected by the absence of visual information in the lexical decision task, whereas such unavailability of visual information had less impact on the Spanish and Arabic ESL learners. She suggested that ESL readers whose L1 is orthographically opaque or deep (e.g., Japanese) were more dependent on orthographic information in recognizing L2 words than those with relatively shallow L1 orthography (e.g., Arabic, Spanish). Similar L1 effects were also observed in more cognitively demanding tasks such as reading L2 passages.

Providing English passages containing keywords written in either pseudowords (pronounceable condition) or Sanskrit symbols (unpronounceable condition), Koda (1990) examined whether L1 orthographic depth affects L2 reading strategies. She found that the inaccessibility of phonological information in a word (i.e., Sanskrit symbols) slowed the reading performance of the Spanish and Arabic groups (L1—shallow orthography). The Japanese group (L1—deep orthography), on the other hand, was not disrupted by the Sanskrit keywords in text, suggesting that the Japanese were not dependent on phonological information, but rather relied on visual information in recognizing English words. Koda suggested that this dependence on visual information by the Japanese ESL learners reflected the reading strategies that they had developed in the course of acquiring their L1 deep orthography.

Metaphonological Ability

Along with orthographic depth, a representational unit is considered one of the L1 orthographic properties that affects L2 word recognition. A representational unit refers to a minimal linguistic component that is represented by a grapheme; orthographic systems vary in the representational unit. In logographies such as *kanji*, for example, the representational unit is normally a morpheme or word, whereas in an alphabetic language (e.g., English) it is a phoneme. An important conception deriving from the view of representational units is that the underlying processes in word recognition could vary, depending on the nature of the representational unit of the written language. Furthermore, the difference in a representational unit may relate to individual differences among L2 readers with differing L1 orthographic backgrounds (e.g., Holm & Dodd, 1996; Huang & Hanley, 1994; Read, Zhang, Nie, & Ding, 1986).

Holm and Dodd (1996) investigated two groups of Chinese readers' ability to manipulate speech sounds in an English word. One group comprised ESL learners from the People's Republic of China who learned to read their L1, Chinese, by using *pinyin* (an alphabetic–based written form of Chinese). The other group comprised ESL learners from Hong Kong who had not been exposed to alphabetic symbols. Holm and Dodd found that the Chinese people with more exposure to alphabetic print could manipulate speech sounds at a phonemic level better than those who had little, if any, exposure to alphabetic scripts. Holm and Dodd speculated that the Chinese group's experience of alphabetic symbols (*pinyin*) in their L1 reading acquisition provided the Chinese group with better metaphonological abilities than those of the Hong Kong group.

Wade-Woolley (1996) also explored the effects of L1 orthographic features on L2 metaphonological abilities by using a phoneme deletion task. Two groups of low–intermediate ESL learners with differing L1 backgrounds (Russian and Japanese) and native speakers of English (comparison group) participated in her study. In the experiment, each participant was orally provided with a total of 30 monosyllabic pseudowords whose structures were either CVC (e.g., "sipe" /saip/) or CCVC (e.g., "snize" /snaiz/), and asked to delete (a) the first phoneme from the CVC items (CVC condition), (b) the first phoneme from the CCVC items (CC1 condition), and (c) the second phoneme from the CCVC items (CC2 condition). The phonemes to be deleted were all common in the L1s of the ESL participants; however, there was a difference in familiarity toward the syllable structures between the two ESL groups.

The two syllable structures used in the phoneme deletion task (i.e., CVC and CCVC) are not common in Japanese. The CCVC structure is not permissible, and the CVC is found only with the nasal sound /n/ in the second consonant of the CVC. For the Russians, on the other hand, both syllable structures are common in their L1. Thus, assuming that L1 phonological features, in this case, the features in L1 syllable structure, would affect L2 metaphonological ability, one could predict that phonological processing such as eliminating a phoneme would be more cognitively demanding for the Japanese than for the Russians. This is exactly what Wade-Woolley found in her study, except for one condition: the CC1 condition (deletion of the first phoneme from the CCVC items).

The performance of the Japanese ESL participants in the phoneme deletion task was significantly slower and less accurate than that of the English and Russian participants. More specifically, the Japanese responded significantly more slowly and less accurately on CVC and CC2 items (i.e., deleting the first phoneme from CVC items and the second phoneme from CCVC items) than did the Russian and the control groups. Nonetheless, no differences were found among the groups in both response time and accuracy in deleting the first phoneme from a CCVC item.

Efficiency in Processing the Constituent Letters

Cross-linguistic studies on the efficiency of word processing in ESL demonstrate the influence of the orthographic nature of L1 on L2. For instance, Brown and Haynes (1985) measured various types of visual and word-processing abilities of L2 readers with differing L1 backgrounds (i.e., Spanish, Arabic, and Japanese). In perceiving and discriminating words, letter strings, and abstract figures in the same–different matching tasks, the Japanese ESL learners were the fastest and the most accurate performers of the three groups. In translating alphabetic symbols into spoken units, however, the Japanese ESL learners had more difficulty than the Arabic or the Spanish learners. Brown and Haynes assumed that this disadvantage of the Japanese ESL learners in amalgamating the constituent letters of a word into the corresponding pronunciation might be related to the way in which the Japanese learners perceive English words. The Japanese group depended relatively more on sight-word processing and less on grapheme-to-phoneme conversion than did the Arabic and the Spanish groups.

Akamatsu (1999) also argued that the Japanese ESL learners are less efficient in processing constituent letters in a L2 word than learners whose L1 is alphabetic in nature. Focusing on the effects of case-alternated words (e.g., cAsE aLtErNaTiOn) on word recognition, he investigated whether L1 orthographic features affect the manner in which L2 readers recognize English words. In a naming task, he provided monosyllabic English words printed in either normal case or alternated case to highly proficient ESL readers with various L1 backgrounds (Chinese, Japanese, and Persian) and measured the impact of case alternation on word-recognition speed and accuracy. The results revealed that, with respect to word-recognition speed, the Chinese and the Japanese were more adversely affected by case alternation than were the Iranians. Considering the impact of visual distortion (i.e., case alternation) on word recognition as an index of efficiency in processing the sequence of constituent letters in a word, Akamatsu proposed that L2 readers with nonalphabetic L1 backgrounds were less efficient in processing the component letters in an English words than were those with an alphabetic L1 background. Furthermore, he suggested that this relatively less efficient word-recognition ability of the Chinese and Japanese L2 readers reflected their L1 literacy experience, which normally lacks amalgamating intraword components of a word in the sound-retrieval processes.

The Japanese ESL readers were also found to be relatively less efficient in processing the constituent letters in an English word during text reading (Akamatsu, 2003). The Chinese, Japanese, and Iranian ESL readers were provided 12 passages of text (110 to 150 words) varying in text difficulty; half were printed in a normal manner and the other half in alternated case. They were asked to read each passage silently and answer the comprehension questions afterwards. Results showed that the effect of case alternation on both reading time and comprehension was robust; however, there was a difference in the impact of case alternation on reading time only between the Chinese–Japanese groups and the Iranian group. Specifically, the Chinese and the Japanese ESL readers were more significantly slowed down by case alternation than were the Iranian ESL readers. Akamatsu suggested that, because Chinese and Japanese do not share the same orthographic characteristics as English, the Chinese and the Japanese ESL readers are less efficient in processing constituent letters of words in text than the Iranian ESL readers, whose L1 (i.e., Persian) shares alphabetic orthographic features with English.

CONCLUSION

Major cross-linguistic studies of Japanese–English show that recognition of English words by Japanese students is affected by the orthographic features of Japanese. Specifically, (a) the Japanese ESL learners are inclined to be more heavily dependent on holistic visual information for word recognition, probably because of the nature of *kanji* (i.e., deep orthography), in which the accurate phonological information of a word is not always obtainable. (b) The Japanese L2 learners are also weak in their ability to manipulate speech sounds at a phonemic level; they are particularly poor at segmenting CV units. This impairment is assumed to be due to the nature of the Japanese syllabic script, *kana*, most of which are in the form of CV combinations. Moreover, (c) the Japanese ESL readers are relatively inefficient in amalgamating the constituent letters in an English word into its corresponding phonological representation. This inefficiency is considered to reflect the Japanese learners' L1 literacy experience that lacks such amalgamation processes in sound retrieval (Akamatsu, 1998, 2003).

These findings regarding Japanese–English bilingual readers converge with the findings of other studies on L1 orthographic effects on L2 reading and word recognition (e.g., Chikamatsu, 1996; Koda, 2000; Mori, 1998; Muljani, Koda, & Moates, 1998). These studies suggest that word-processing skills or strategies cultivated in a first language, L1, are transferred to L2 reading and that the nature of L1 orthographic properties (e.g., orthographic depth, representational units) has a major impact on the cognitive processes that are used in reading a second written language, L2. Nevertheless, this does not necessarily imply that L2 learners whose L1 is orthographically different from the target language encounter insurmountable difficulty in acquiring particular L2 reading skills or strategies. These research findings that investigated Japanese–English bilinguals' reading performance simply suggest that some qualitative differences in their ability to recognize written English words could be attributed to the nature of the Japanese orthography.

REFERENCES

Akamatsu, N. (1998). L1 and L2 reading: The orthographic effects of Japanese on reading in English. *Language, Culture, and Curriculum, 11*, 9–27.

Akamatsu, N. (1999). The effects of first language orthographic features on word recognition processing in English as a second language. *Reading and Writing: An Interdisciplinary Journal, 11*, 381–403.

Akamatsu, N. (2003). The effects of first-language orthographic features on second-language reading in text. *Language Learning, 53*, 207–231.

Brown, T., & Haynes, M. (1985). Literacy background and reading development in a second language. In H. Carr (Ed.), *The development of reading skills* (pp. 19–34). San Francisco: Jossey-Bass.

Carello, C., Turvey, M., & Lukatela, G. (1992). Can theories of word recognition remain stubbornly nonphonological? In R. Frost & L. Katz (Eds.), *Orthography, phonology, morphology, and meaning* (pp. 211–226). Amsterdam: Elsevier Science.

Chikamatsu, N. (1996). The effects of L1 orthography on L2 word recognition: A study of American and Chinese learners of Japanese. *Studies in Second Language Acquisition, 18*, 403–432.

Chikushima, H. (1982). Kana. In S. Ohno & S. Kutani (Series Eds.), *Nihongo no sekai* [The world of the Japanese language]: *Vol. 5*. Tokyo: Chuokoron.

Educational Testing Service (1999). *TOEFL: Test and score data summary (1999–2000 edition)*. Princeton, NJ: Author.

Frost, R. (1994). Prelexical and postlexical strategies in reading: Evidence from a deep and a shallow orthography. *Journal of Experimental Psychology: Learning, Memory, and Cognition, 20*, 116–129.

Frost, R., & Bentin, S. (1992). Reading consonants and guessing vowels: Visual word recognition in Hebrew orthography. In R. Frost & L. Katz (Eds.), *Orthography, phonology, morphology, and meaning* (pp. 27–44). Amsterdam: Elsevier Science.

Hayashi, O. (1982). *Tosetsu nihongo* [The Japanese language in graphs]. Tokyo: Kadokawa Shuppan.

Holm, A., & Dodd, B. (1996). The effect of first written language on the acquisition of English literacy. *Cognition, 59*, 119–147.

Huang, H., & Hanley, J. (1994). Phonological awareness and visual skills in learning to read Chinese and English. *Cognition, 54*, 73–98.

Katayama, Y., Endo, E., Sasaki, A., & Matsumura, M. (Eds.). (1994). *Sin eigoka kyoiku no kenkyu* [New teaching methodology of English in Japan] (New ed.). Tokyo: Taishukan.

Kess, J., & Miyamoto, T. (1999). *The Japanese mental lexicon: Psycholinguistic studies of kana and kanji processing*. Amsterdam: Benjamins.

Koda, K. (1988). Cognitive process in second language reading: Transfer of L1 reading skills and strategies. *Second Language Research, 4*, 133–156.

Koda, K. (1990). The use of L1 reading strategies in L2 reading: Effects of L1 orthographic structures on L2 phonological recoding strategies. *Studies in Second Language Acquisition, 12*, 393–410.

Koda, K. (1996). L2 word recognition research: A critical review. *The Modern Language Journal, 80*, 450–460.

Koda, K. (2000). Cross-linguistic variations in L2 morphological awareness. *Applied Psycholinguistics, 21*, 297–320.

Loveday, L. (1996). *Language contact in Japan*. Oxford, UK: Oxford University Press.

Ministry of Education. (1996). *21 seiki wo tenboshita wagakuni no kyoiku no arikata ni tsuite* [Education in Japan: Towards the 21st century]. Special issue of *Ministry of Education, Sports and Culture*. Tokyo: Gyosei.

Mori, Y. (1998). Effects of first language and phonological accessibility on Kanji recognition. *The Modern Language Journal, 82*, 69–82.

Morioka, K. (1991). *Kindaigo no seiritsu* [Realization of modern Nappanee vocabulary] (Rev. ed.). Tokyo: Meijishoin.

Muljani, D., Koda, K., & Moates, D. R. (1998). The development of word recognition in a second language. *Applied Psycholinguistics, 19*, 99–113.

National Language Research Institute (NLRI). (1962–1964). *Zasshi kyuujusshu no yoogo yooji* [Vocabulary and Chinese characters in ninety magazines of today] (Vols. 1–3). Tokyo: Tokyo Shoseki.

National Language Research Institute (NLRI). (1972). *Yoji no yomikaki noryoku* [Reading and writing ability in pre-school children]. Tokyo: Tokyo Shoseki.

National Language Research Institute (NLRI). (1988). *Jido seito no joyo kanji no shutoku* [Acquisition of joyo kanji by school children]. Tokyo: Tokyo Shoseki.

National Language Research Institute (NLRI) (1994). *Acquisition and teaching of joyo kanji.* [Joyo kanji no shutoku to shido]. Tokyo: Shuei Shuppan.

Okakura, Y. (1911). *Eigo kyoiku* [English education]. Tokyo: Kenkyusha.

Palmer, H. (1921). *The oral method of teaching languages*. Cambridge, UK: Heffer & Sons.

Read, C., Zhang, Y.-F., Nie, H.-Y., & Ding, B.-Q. (1986). The ability to manipulate speech sounds depends on knowing alphabetic writing. *Cognition, 24*, 31–44.

Sato, K. (Ed.). (1988). *Kanji Kyoiku* [Kanji education]. Tokyo: Meiji Shoin.

Sugito, S. (1989). Lexical aspects of the modernization of Japanese. In F. Coulmas (Ed.), *Language adaptation* (pp. 116–126). Cambridge, UK: Cambridge University Press.

Tajima, K. (1989). Computer and kanji. In K. Sato (Series ed.) *Kanji koza* [Lectures on kanji]: *Vol. 11. Kanji to kokuji mondai* [Kanji and the problems of the national language] (pp. 229–257). Tokyo: Meijishoin.

Taylor, I., & M. Taylor (1995). *Writing and literacy in Chinese, Korean and Japanese*. Amsterdam: Benjamins.

Uchimura, K. (1899/1984). *Gaikokugo no kenkyu* [The study of foreign languages]. Tokyo: Nanundo.

Wade–Woolley, L. (1996). *Language transfer in second language readers: Evidence and implications for metaphonological processing*. Unpublished doctoral dissertation, University of Toronto, Toronto, Ontario, Canada.

Yoshino, M. (1988). *Kanji no fukken* [Appreciation of the use of kanji]. Tokyo: Nicchu Shuppan.

30

Learning to Spell in Different Languages: How Orthographic Variables Might Affect Early Literacy

Marketa Caravolas
University of Liverpool

This chapter is divided into three sections. First, the main characteristics of alphabetic orthographies as well as some relevant distinguishing features of the orthographies are examined. Next, a summary of studies of English spelling development, which has provided the backdrop for much of the cross-linguistic work, is presented. Finally, the cross-linguistic evidence pertaining to the potential effects of orthographic depth on various aspects of spelling development is discussed.

INTRODUCTION

As is true of many aspects of literacy research, much more is known about the development of spelling in English than in other languages. Although the cognitive processes involved in learning to spell are not yet fully understood in any language, numerous English-based studies have now documented various aspects of the skill including the main developmental phases (Ehri, 1997; Frith, 1980; Gentry, 1982; Henderson & Beers, 1980), a detailed inventory of the various types of difficulties posed by the English spelling system (Treiman, 1993; Treiman, Zukowski, & Richmond-Welty, 1995), as well as developmental models of the cognitive processes and component skills underpinning spelling performance (Caravolas, Hulme, & Snowling, 2001; Rittle-Johnson & Siegler, 1999). What clearly emerges from these and many other studies is that learning to spell in English is a complex, long-term process that is founded on phoneme analysis ability, letter knowledge, and phoneme-grapheme recoding skills (Caravolas et al., 2001), but that eventually requires the integration of knowledge about the morphological (Bryant, Nunes, & Bindman, 1997; Treiman, Cassar, & Zukowski, 1994) and orthographic (Cassar & Treiman, 1997; Ehri, 1997) structure of words as well. An important question, and the main focus of this chapter, concerns the extent to which the descriptions and explanations of spelling development in English generalize to other alphabetic orthographies.

The evident complexity of the skill—at least in English—and the great diversity of alphabetic writing systems and their associated languages and cultures make obvious the fact that there will be no simple answer to this question. Nevertheless, despite their many potential differences, alphabetic orthographies do share one critical characteristic: They are all based on the alphabetic principle, the idea that graphemes (defined here as the minimal letter strings used in correspondence with phonemes) represent phonemes in spoken language. Within the context of literacy acquisition, this shared characteristic is not trivial. On the contrary, it is broadly acknowledged that an understanding of the alphabetic principle is the cornerstone of alphabetic literacy e.g. (Byrne, 1998; Goswami & Bryant, 1990; Liberman, Shankweiler, Liberman, Fowler, & Fischer, 1977). Thus to the extent that different orthographies adhere to the alphabetic principle, learners of those orthographies should rely on similar knowledge and component skills, at least in learning those aspects of spelling that exploit the principle. Cross-linguistic studies should enable us to determine whether alphabetic spelling development does indeed involve some cognitive universals, and if so, to pinpoint what they are.

As already noted, however, most alphabetic orthographies do not adhere strictly to the alphabetic principle, and they may diverge from it in different ways (subsequently outlined). It is plausible therefore that the extent to which and the ways in which writing systems deviate from simple one-to-one phoneme–grapheme and grapheme–phoneme correspondences will be reflected specifically in learners' use of different types of knowledge and strategies. Hence cross-linguistic studies should also enable us to identify the language-specific cognitive components and processes involved in learning to spell. A full explanation of the language-general and language-specific aspects of alphabetic spelling development poses a daunting task that awaits much future research across a wide range of alphabetic languages. Nevertheless, overtures have been made. Spelling development has been examined in a number of languages including French (Alegria & Mousty, 1994; Fayol, Hupet, & Largy, 1999; Pacton, Perruchet, Fayol, & Cleeremans, 2001; Sénéchal, 2000) and Spanish (Justicia, Defior, Pelegrina, & Martos, 1999); although they were not specifically designed for cross-linguistic comparison and primarily focused on how children learn orthographic inconsistencies, they make valuable contributions to the elaboration of a general model of spelling development. In addition, several cross-linguistic studies, subsequently described, have been carried out in which the effects not only of the orthographic but also of the phonological features of a child's input language on spelling have been investigated. Specifically, spelling data from learners of Czech (Caravolas & Bruck, 1993), French (Bruck, Genesee, & Caravolas, 1997; Caravolas, Bruck, & Genesee, 2003), and German (Landerl & Wimmer, 2000; Wimmer, Mayringer, & Landerl, 1998) were compared directly with data from learners of English.

The chapter is divided into three main sections. First, the main characteristics of alphabetic orthographies, as well as some relevant distinguishing features of the orthographies examined in the present chapter, are outlined and contrasted. Next, a summary of studies of English spelling development, which have provided the backdrop for much of the cross-linguistic work, is presented. Finally, the cross-linguistic evidence pertaining to the potential effects of orthographic depth on various aspects of spelling development is examined.

GENERAL CHARACTERISTICS OF ALPHABETIC ORTHOGRAPHIES

An ideal alphabetic orthography should contain a set of isomorphic one-to-one grapheme–phoneme (or *spelling–sound*) and phoneme–grapheme (or *sound–spelling*) correspondences. In theory, a system such as this would enable spellers to accurately spell any word in their language on the basis of merely two skills: phonemic segmentation ability and knowledge of the letter–sound inventory of the language. A small minority of languages, such as Finnish, Turkish, and Serbo-Croatian, approximate such writing systems. The majority of alphabetic orthographies, however, also encode information other than the phonemic content of words. Deviations from the alphabetic ideal may result in the presence of inconsistent (many-to-one spelling–sound and sound–spelling correspondences), irregular, and/or opaque (silent letters) spellings. Consequently, to become proficient spellers, learners typically require other types of linguistic and orthographic knowledge; these are subsequently summarized.

First, many alphabetic orthographies preserve some *morphological* information about words at the expense of phoneme–grapheme consistency. For example, in the words "h*ea*l" and "h*ea*lth," two different vowel phonemes, /i/ and /ɛ/, are represented by a single vowel letter string reflecting their morphological relationship. Languages with complex phonological systems (i.e., ones in which morphologically related words frequently have phonologically different stems), such as English and French, tend to have deep orthographies whereas languages with simpler phonologies (i.e., ones that maintain phonologically similar word stems for morphologically related words but are extensively inflected), such as Czech, tend to have transparent orthographies (see Katz & Frost, 1992, for an excellent exposé on this topic). A second source of inconsistency in many writing systems is the presence of *foreign words* that may have been imported into the language along with their original spellings (for example, the Anglicized words *chateau* and *connoisseur* have retained their original French spellings). Generally speaking, such imported words exist as exceptions within the adoptive orthographic system. Third, writing systems may retain *historical spellings* that reflect archaic word pronunciations, such as the spellings of *knee* and *walk*, which retain graphemes that once represented articulated sounds, but as a result of phonological change have become redundant. In French, such spellings are prevalent and give rise to a complex system of "silent morphology." For example, many verb inflections are written (e.g., ils par*lent*; *tu* man*ges*) but are not pronounced (/il parlə/; /ty mãʒə/). When letters have no correspondence in speech, they produce opacity in the spelling system. Opacity is more frequent in systems that have not been reformed recently, such as English and French.

To the extent that they are present within orthographies, the preceding factors all reduce spelling–sound and sound–spelling consistency and regularity. Consequently, most writing systems are constrained to greater or lesser degrees by orthographic rules that may (a) relate morphological relationships, (b) relate grammatical relationships, or (c) determine the permissible positions and sequencing of graphemes (i.e., graphotactic rules). From the learner's point of view, all else being equal, the greater the number of rules, exceptions, and sources of inconsistency, the more slow and difficult the learning process is likely to be.

Phoneme–Grapheme Consistency in English, French, and Czech.   As already described, the sources of inconsistency within writing systems can be quite diverse, reflecting differences in the historical developments as well as in the linguistic structure that they encode. It is nevertheless possible to compare orthographies on a number of criteria that indicate their complexity in terms of phonographic consistency. These include the ratio of phonemes to letters of the alphabet, the number of graphemes, and measures of feedforward (spelling–sound) and feedback (sound–spelling) consistency (see summary in Table 30.1).[1] Unfortunately, with the possible exception of the phoneme-to-letter ratio, it is still quite difficult to obtain comparable statistics because scholars do not always agree on the best way to define graphemes. Consistency estimates are unavailable for most orthographies, and where they do exist, they are not always derived from the same computational principles or models. Until such data become

---

[1] Words are *feedforward* consistent when only one pronunciation is possible for the orthographic unit under consideration (e.g., grapheme, rime, body). They are *feedback* consistent when only one spelling is possible for the representation of the phonological unit under consideration (phoneme, onset, rime, coda, body) (Peereman & Content, 1999).

TABLE 30.1

Summary of Orthographic Consistency Indicators in English, French, and Czech

Indicator	English	French	Czech
Number of phonemes	44 = 20V + 24C	38 = 19V + 19C	39 = 13V + 26C
Number of letters	26 = 6V + 20C	26 = 6V + 20C	37 = 6V + 25C
Phoneme-to-letter ratio	1.7 : 1	1.5 : 1	1 : 1
Number of graphemes	~ 210[a]	~ 165[b]	42[c]
(unconditional)	(106V + 104C)	(120V + 45C)	(14V + 28C)
Context-dependent GPC rules	Many	Many	Few
Feedforward consistency	Low	High	Very High
Feedback consistency	Low	Low	High

Notes. [a] Estimate obtained from Carney (1994); [b]estimate obtained from Ziegler et al. (1996); [c]number obtained from Hlavsa et al. (1998).

available, researchers must rely on fairly rough indicators of consistency and preferably look for converging evidence from multiple measures such as those reported in Table 30.1.

As can be seen in Table 30.1, the ratio of phonemes to letters is higher in English (1.7:1) and French (1.5:1) than in Czech (1:1). Although this is a very basic indicator of sound–spelling consistency, it does suggest that so-called deep orthographies have fewer letters than speech sounds, which in turn suggests that they require letter combinations for representing at least some phonemes.[2] A second indicator of consistency is the number of plausible letters and letter strings, in effect graphemes, that may represent the inventory of phonemes in a language. Again, the relevant numbers reported in Table 30.1 must be considered only as rough indicators because each estimate was obtained from a different source, some based on polysyllabic words (Carney, 1994; Hlavsa, 1998), others only on monosyllables (Ziegler, Jacobs, & Stone, 1996). Thus graphemes may have been defined with slightly different criteria in each language. Nevertheless, the trend is replicated such that English has more graphemes than French and both have many more graphemes than Czech. Moreover, spelling manuals and formal descriptions of each orthography reveal that English and French contain many more position- and context-dependent rules for spelling phonemes than does Czech, thus confirming greater graphemic isomorphism in the latter orthography than in the former (Carney, 1994; Hendrich, Radina, & Tláskal, 1991; Hlavsa, 1998; Palková, 1997).

The most informative and precise measures are those of feedforward and feedback consistency, usually extracted from large lexical corpora. Typically, feedback consistency estimates reflect the proportion of words in which a given unit (e.g., a rime like /it/) occurs with a given spelling (e.g., *eet*) relative to the total number of words that contain that particular unit (e.g., feet, beet, seat, mete, etc.); feedforward consistencies are similarly computed in terms of the number of possible pronunciations for a given grapheme (Peereman & Content, 1999). However, here again, methodological differences often preclude direct comparisons in within-language as well as between-language studies because consistencies are not always computed in the same way or for the same sublexical units. Such disparities can lead to considerably different estimates. For example, whereas a seminal study by Hanna, Hanna, Hodges, and Rudorf (1966) concluded that the English spelling system is 50% regular (or consistent), more recent and computationally more sophisticated estimates show that even the least consistent class of graphemes, the vowel, is considerably more consistent (predictable) than .50 if the adjacent

---

[2] This is confirmed by the fact that English and French both contain many digraphs (and letter doublets) whereas Czech has one digraph (and only exceptionally uses doublets).

phoneme in the syllable and its position are taken into account (Kessler & Treiman, 2001). More specifically, the spelling of an American–English vowel is on average .65 consistent if one considers the onset phoneme that precedes it, and it is .74 consistent if one considers the ensuing coda phoneme.

Cross-linguistic consistency analyses have been carried out for English and French, which indicate that whereas French (.88) (Ziegler, et al., 1996) is more consistent than English (.67) (Stone, Vanhoy, & Van Orden, 1997) in the feedforward direction, especially for vowels, the two languages are equally inconsistent in the feedback direction (.20 and .24 for French and English, respectively).[3] No published consistency estimates exist for Czech; however, it seems safe to conclude that, compared with English and French, this writing system is highly (though not perfectly) consistent in both directions, but like most alphabetic orthographies it is more consistent in the spelling–sound than in the sound–spelling direction, making it easier to read than to spell (see Table 30.1). An important feature of Czech pertains to the spelling of vowels (the most inconsistent units in English and French): For all but 3 of the 13 vowel phonemes, spellings are 100% predictable regardless of their position and context in words; the 3 remaining vowels are highly predictable when positional and morphosyntactic rules are taken into account (Hlavsa, 1998). Similarly, the spelling of consonants is almost perfectly predictable if morphological rules regarding consonant voicing are taken into account. To summarize, the range of measures in Table 30.1 suggests that phoneme spellings, and those of vowels in particular, are far more consistent in Czech than in English and French.

Consistency Effects on Skilled Reading and Spelling.   Consistency has been found to affect word recognition as well as spelling performance among skilled adults such that the speed and accuracy of each skill decrease as the degree of feedforward and feedback consistency, respectively, decreases, especially in low-frequency words (Kreiner, 1996; Peereman, Content, & Bonin, 1998; Stone et al., 1997). Several cross-linguistic studies of word recognition have demonstrated that, *ceteris paribus*, readers of relatively transparent orthographies recognize words more quickly and accurately than do readers of deep orthographies (Frost, Katz, & Bentin, 1987; Lukatela & Turvey, 1990; but see Besner & Smith, 1992, for an opposing view). Whether similar cross-linguistic effects of sound–spelling consistency exist in skilled spelling performance has yet to be investigated.

Does orthographic depth, as defined by consistency, influence how learners of different writing systems *acquire* literacy skills, and more specifically how they learn to spell? Before this question is addressed, a brief review of what is known about spelling development in English is warranted. Spelling development has been studied most extensively in English, and it is the language of comparison in most cross-linguistic studies.

SPELLING DEVELOPMENT IN ENGLISH

The process of spelling development in English has been described in three (Frith, 1980) to five phases (Bissex, 1980; Ehri, 1997) that span the first four to five years of formal schooling. These include first the *precommunicative (logographic)* phase, during which children produce drawings, scribbles, or a few select letters that bear no systematic linguistic relationship to spoken language. During the second *semiphonetic* phase, spellings are partially phonologi-cally accurate. For example, the word "dog" may be spelled as *dk*, the word "you" may be spelled as *U*. Children are next said to progress to the third *phonetic (alphabetic)* phase when their spellings become generally phonologically accurate (e.g., they now spell the simple word

---

[3] Note that these proportions reflect consistency estimates for rime units (vowel plus ensuing consonants in a syllable).

"*dog*" correctly but may misspell the word "*cake*" as the phonologically plausible but or-thographically implausible string *keik*). In the fourth, *transitional* phase, spellings become phonologically accurate with some application of orthographic conventions (e.g., "cake" may now be spelled with the orthographically plausible, although conventionally incorrect, spelling *caik*). Finally in the fifth *correct (orthographic)* phase, words are spelled according to con-vention. Although these phases have been observed by numerous authors, it is now clear that the developmental sequence is not discrete but rather progresses more or less in "overlap-ping waves" (cf. Rittle-Johnson & Siegler, 1999). Thus children may simultaneously produce spellings typical of *several stages* and they may rely on *various strategies* while attempting to spell words at any given time. For example, they may use phoneme segmentation, letter-name strategy, rote recall of whole words (e.g., "school") or parts of words (Steffler, Varnhagen, Friesen, & Treiman, 1998). It is also evident that children possess some knowledge about the patterns in their orthography in very early stages of learning to spell and long before they consistently produce conventional spellings. For example, Cassar and Treiman (1997) have shown that school beginners are able to recognize some illegal spelling patterns (e.g., *ckat, *mmom). Another set of findings has revealed that young English spellers are sensitive to the *morphological* information in word structure (e.g., Bryant et al., 1997; Treiman et al., 1994) and this again, long before they can reliably produce this information in their own spellings. What is important, despite this variability, is that children generally progress from a one-letter-to-one-sound "sounding-out" strategy to encoding larger grapheme units roughly in the order described by the 3/5-phase models (Rittle-Johnson & Siegler, 1999).

In a longitudinal study of spelling development among English-speaking children, Caravolas et al. (2001) found that only two skills, phoneme awareness and letter knowledge, predicted phonological (also referred to as "invented") spelling skills in the first year of schooling, and in turn, phonological spelling predicted reading ability at this stage. Reading did not predict phonological spelling ability. As of the end of the first year, however, reading became an increasingly strong predictor of later conventional spelling skills in the second and third years of schooling. On the basis of these results, the authors proposed that phoneme awareness and letter–sound knowledge enable children to learn the basic mappings between graphemes and phonemes. These primitive mappings provide the child with a kind of "phonological scaffold" (indexed by phonological spelling) of words. The extent to which children can represent this scaffold determines their future ability to map more complex, conventional graphemes to phonological representations by means of reading and spelling experiences.

ORTHOGRAPHIC DEPTH AND SPELLING DEVELOPMENT

The English-based findings raise interesting questions regarding the universality of the compo-nents and developmental phases of spelling development in other alphabetic writing systems. However, it is useful first to consider a cross-linguistic theoretical framework within which the questions can be addressed. The main proponent of a "developmental orthographic depth hypothesis," Heinz Wimmer has argued that orthographic depth does affect early literacy acqui-sition in a number of ways. First, he proposes that transparent orthographies confer an advantage on learners because, unlike in deep orthographies, graphemes reliably correspond to phonemes. This regularity and consistency are said to help children quickly learn the letter–sound corre-spondences of their language, which in turn boosts their "phonological assembly" or decoding skills, as well as their phoneme analysis skills. Thus learners of transparent orthographies pre-sumably learn the skills that form the basis of alphabetic literacy more quickly than do learners of deep orthographies (Wimmer, Landerl, Linortner, & Hummer, 1991). Moreover, Wimmer and colleagues (1991) have argued that an additional benefit of transparent orthographies is that learners' success in reading does not depend as heavily on phonological awareness skills as it does in English; that is, the effect of regular and consistent spelling–sound correspondences is sufficiently powerful to raise children's phonological skills after a few months of reading experience, regardless of their prereading levels of ability. Data consistent with these hypotheses have been reported in a number of cross-linguistic studies in which children learning Czech (Caravolas & Bruck, 1993), Turkish (Oney & Goldman, 1984), Italian (Cossu, Shankweiler, Liberman, Katz, & Tola, 1988), French (Bruck, et al., 1997; Goswami, Gombert, & de Barrera, 1998) German (Wimmer & Goswami, 1994) and Spanish (Goswami, et al., 1998) showed either better phoneme awareness, word recognition, or nonword-decoding skills than did matched English-speaking children by the first or second year of schooling.

However, much less cross-linguistic work has focused on spelling development, and certainly no comprehensive longitudinal study of spelling development has been published on learners of a language other than English. Nevertheless, a sufficient number of studies have been carried and suggest preliminary answers to several questions. First, one can ask whether alphabetic spelling development in all languages depends on the same foundation skills that enable the preliterate child to grasp the alphabetic principle and to eventually build an orthographic lexicon, as in English. If so, then letter knowledge and phoneme awareness should be critical precursors of phonological and conventional spelling ability across alphabetic writing systems.

Three studies suggest that this is the case. Öney and Durgunoglu (1997) found letter knowledge and two measures of phonemic awareness to be significant concurrent predictors of word and nonword spelling among Turkish first graders. In a longitudinal study with German-speaking first-grade children, Wimmer et al. (1991) reported that nonword-spelling ability at the end of the year was best predicted by letter knowledge and phoneme awareness measured at school entry. Interestingly, they found, in line with the results of Caravolas et al. (2001), that reading ability and nonverbal IQ measured at the beginning of the year did not predict spelling ability 7 months later. A point reiterated in these studies with Turkish and German children, however, is that, unlike in English, the relationship between these foundation skills and reading and spelling is relatively short lived. That is, neither predictor appeared to be reliable beyond the earliest stages of learning primarily because children quickly reach mastery levels in letter knowledge and phonemic awareness tasks as well as in phonological spelling. However, both studies assessed only children in first grade, and neither study directly compared its pattern of results with an English-speaking cohort of children. Thus it is not certain whether in transparent orthographies early achievements in letter knowledge and phoneme awareness predict spelling ability only in the first year of schooling, nor whether, given the same tasks within the same time frame, the English correlational patterns would have been different.

Evidence to suggest that a long-term relationship between letter knowledge and phoneme awareness exists in languages other than English was obtained in a longitudinal, cross-linguistic study of 66 French– Canadian and 73 English–Canadian children. These two groups were followed from kindergarten to the end of Grade 3 (the participants and range of tasks administered in kindergarten and first grade are described in Bruck et al., 1997, the third-grade spelling tests are described in Caravolas et al., 2003). Over the course of the study, both language groups were assessed on a parallel battery of phonological awareness, reading, spelling, IQ, and other tests. At the end of third grade, the two groups had spent the same amount of time in formal schooling and were matched in age (English children were 8.9 years old and the French 9.0 years old), IQ, broad cultural experience, and Socioeconomic status. The groups were taught by different reading methods, however: The English group received whole-language tuition whereas the French group was taught by a structured, syllabic method (akin to phonics). Relevant to the present discussion is the result of simultaneous regressions that, for both language groups, kindergarten measures of letter knowledge accounted for significant variation, over and above IQ, in word spelling ability 3 years later. Moreover, the proportion of variance explained was virtually identical in English ($R^2 = .19$) and French ($R^2 = .20$). Phoneme awareness scores in kindergarten did not predict third-grade spelling, but this was due to floor effects as the children were given a task, phoneme deletion, that is rather difficult for preschoolers. Phoneme awareness performance in Grade 1 did reliably predict Grade 3 spelling in both language groups, although it accounted for more variance in the English group ($R^2 = .39$) than in the French group ($R^2 = .18$). Thus the two skills fundamental to alphabetic literacy seem to play important roles in spelling development in English as well as in French; however, in line with the claims about Turkish and German, the relationship between phoneme awareness and spelling appears to be stronger in English than in French. To gain a fuller understanding of how orthographic depth influences the long-term relationships between these two skills and spelling, however, more large-scale longitudinal studies are needed in different languages that assess the predictive strength of similar variables and that control for IQ, and a host of other potentially relevant variables.

Another hypothesis pertains to the effect of orthographic depth on the rate of spelling development. If consistency in sound–spelling correspondences has the same effect on spelling that spelling–sound consistency is said to have on reading, then children learning an orthography with high feedback consistency should learn to spell more quickly than those learning a feedback inconsistent orthography. Accordingly, Czech children should learn to spell more quickly than English children. But how is learning influenced in "intermediate" systems such as French and German, in which feedforward consistency is quite high but feedback consistency is less so (much less so in the case of French)? Wimmer and Landerl (1997) have put forward the interesting hypothesis that orthographies with high spelling–sound consistency may confer advantage on spelling development even if they have relatively low feedback consistency, as in French and German. This effect is said to operate by means of reading experience, which, as previously explained, promotes both grapheme–phoneme recoding and phoneme segmentation skill; in turn, phoneme segmentation skill might promote the spelling acquisition process, at least in the early, preconventional stages of learning, when spelling is achieved primarily by sequential sound–letter recoding.[4] If this indirect effect does in fact operate on spelling development, then German and French children should also learn phonological spelling skills faster than do English children. In addition, if, as suggested by Caravolas et al. (2001), phonological spelling ability enables learners to create phonological scaffolds onto which more complex conventional graphemes can be mapped, then more consistent and transparent orthographies should also promote faster acquisition of conventional spelling skills.

The first hypothesis, that sound–spelling consistency affects the rate at which children develop early phonological spelling skills, finds support in a direct cross-linguistic by Caravolas and Bruck (1993). One aim of their study was to investigate whether Czech children would show a faster rate of learning phonological spelling than English children, in particular of complex syllable onsets that are known to be very difficult units for the latter group, but that are very common in Czech. They compared 30 Czech and 30 English–Canadian Grade 1 children on two phonological awareness tasks and on a nonword-spelling test.

---

[4] A similar hypothesis regarding the reciprocal effects of feedforward and feedback consistency on word recogntion is currently debated in the skilled reading literature. Stone et al. (1997) recently reported that, when feedforward consistency was held constant, their English-speaking participants read words with lower *feedback* consistency more slowly, suggesting that both types of information are processed during reading and presumably also during spelling. However, in a study with French adults, Peereman et al. (1998) found that although feedback consistency influenced spelling performance it had no effect of on word recognition when subjective frequency (a variable Stone et al. did not control) of the words was controlled. Thus it is currently not clear whether the differences between these two studies are due to differences in reading and spelling processes in the two languages or whether the finding of Stone et al. is artifactual.

The groups were well matched for age (English = 7.1 years, Czech = 7.3 years); however their schooling experience naturally differed in some ways. The English children had spent at least 1 year in kindergarten, during which time they experienced informal instruction in letter names, sight-word reading, and invented spelling. The Czech children had attended kindergarten classes for approximately 3 years but had experienced no instruction in any of the preliteracy skills taught to the English children, although they were read to by their teachers on a daily basis. Thus, on entry into first grade, the English children were at somewhat of an advantage. The spelling test of interest here consisted of 16 nonwords, 8 of which contained complex syllable onsets (CCVC) and 8 contained complex codas (CVCC). The items were equated for syllable structure and for phonemic content of each syllable with the provision that all phoneme sequences were legal in both languages. In terms of the plausible spellings, 7 of the 16 items could be represented with the same graphemes in both languages (e.g., /semp/, /sont/); 9 of the 16 items differed in terms of digraphs and diacritics but were equated for number of symbols required (e.g., /ʃ/= sh in English and š in Czech; /u/= oo, u_e, oe in English and ů, ú in Czech). The children's spellings were scored in a lenient way such that any grapheme that could plausibly represent a phoneme in the target language, regardless of positional and contextual constraints, was deemed acceptable. The results showed an overall 20% advantage for the Czech group across syllable types, although it was greater on items with complex onsets (Czech group mean was 65% whereas the English group mean was 36%). Thus, despite the fact that the Czech children began first grade with less preschool exposure to preliteracy skills than the English children, they nevertheless produced more phonologically accurate nonword spellings after 8 months of schooling. This study also suggested that not only orthographic depth but also phonological input affected the Czech children's spelling performance. That is, groups of prekindergarten, kindergarten, as well as the first-grade children had better phoneme awareness skills than their English counterparts. Nevertheless, the results are in line with an orthographic depth account.

Data from the cross-linguistic French-English study conducted by Bruck and her colleagues make it possible to assess whether any evidence exists to suggest that spelling–sound consistency can also influence spelling development. Recall that French is more consistent in the feedforward direction than English, but the two orthographies are equally inconsistent in the feedback direction. The two participant groups already described were tested on nonword and word spelling in Grade 3. Parallel spelling tests of 25 and 26 words were created in English and French, respectively, and the same number of nonwords was derived from the words in each language. In both language versions, half of the words were monosyllables, one quarter were bisyllables, and one quarter were trisyllables. The word sets were designed to contain spelling patterns that are normally taught in first to third grade in each language, all words contained regular spelling patterns and were closely matched for syllable structure and number of graphemes (in words) and phonemes (in nonwords). The word spellings were simply scored as correct or incorrect according to convention. All nonword spellings were assessed according to a constrained system in which any grapheme that could possibly represent a given phoneme, given its position and context in the word, was deemed acceptable (for a detailed description of the stimulus characteristics and scoring techniques see Caravolas et al., 2003).

Analyses of the percentages of phonologically acceptable nonword spellings revealed a 30% advantage for the French group (75% vs. 43%). Thus, still in third grade, English children have considerable difficulty in representing the phonological structure of words, a skill that Czech (and German and Turkish) children seem to master by the end of first grade. Although not at ceiling, the French children clearly experience much less difficulty than their English peers. By aggregating across all word lengths, however, this comparison may provide an inaccurate estimate of English children's abilities. English has a preponderance of monosyllabic words and a high proportion of two-syllable words, but relatively few three-syllable words. In contrast

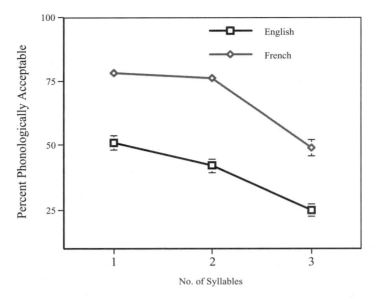

FIG. 30.1. Percentage of phonologically acceptable spellings of one-, two-, and three-syllable non-words by English and French third grade children.

French has a preponderance of two-syllable words and one- and three-syllable words are not infrequent. Consequently it was possible that the English children performed disproportionately less well on three-syllable items, with which they have little experience, but as well as their French peers on one and two syllable items. An analysis by syllable number showed that this was not the case (see Fig. 30.1). Although both groups clearly performed better on monosyllables than on three-syllable items, the French group showed a clear advantage on all nonword lengths relative to the English group, and no decrement in performance from monosyllabic to bisyllabic items. The English group's performance decreased significantly at every increment in syllable number. These data are consistent with the hypothesis that spelling–sound consistency affects phonological spelling ability, however, as was demonstrated by the preceding analyses and by Caravolas et al. (2003), linguistic variables such as typical word length, syllable structure, and lexical stress also played a role in shaping these children's spelling performances.

The word-spelling data also made it possible to explore the hypothesis that differences in phonological spelling ability, as indexed here by nonword spelling, may lead to associated differences in the acquisition of conventional spelling skills. It is logically plausible that children who have poorly developed phonological (nonword) spelling skills nevertheless perform well on real word spelling, particularly if they adopt whole-word memorization or "direct" visually mediated strategies to learn real word spellings. However, if a word-spelling advantage for the French children, parallel to that observed in nonword spelling, were obtained this would be consistent with the hypothesis that phonological spelling development drives conventional spelling development; of course, no causal connections could be inferred from the present data. A two-way (language group by syllable number) repeated measures analysis of variance revealed a pattern very similar to that obtained in the nonword-spelling analysis (see Fig. 30.2). Again the French children showed a 30% advantage overall, although the between-group gap in accuracy became larger as word length increased. Thus again, the English children were more strongly affected by word length than the French children and their word spelling skills were less well developed.

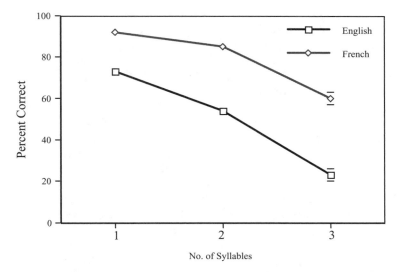

FIG. 30.2. Percent of correct spellings of one-, two-, and three-syllable words by English and French third-grade children.

Wimmer and Landerl (1997) investigated whether differences in sound–spelling consistency of vowels influenced German-speaking Austrian and British–English children's learning of conventional vowel spellings. Although both orthographies have worse sound–spelling consistency than spelling–sound consistency, German is said to be more feedback consistent than English. In that study, second-, third-, and fourth- grade children were asked to spell the vowels in words that were similar in phonological structure and meaning in the two languages. Aggregating across age groups, the authors found that, for 19 of 29 words, the German-speaking children spelled vowels more accurately than the English children, whereas the reverse was true for five words. An interesting finding was revealed by analyses of the children's errors. In line with the hypothesis that sound–spelling consistency influences how children learn conventional spellings, Wimmer and Landerl found that when the English children erred, they produced many more variants of the target spelling than did the German-speaking children. This suggests that the greater number of graphemic alternatives of English interfere with children's learning of the conventional spellings of words. In addition, there was some indication that the English children had greater difficulty not only with conventional spelling but also with the representation of the phonological structure of the words. That is, they omitted or added graphemes much more frequently than the German children. Thus both results are consistent with those found in the other cross-linguistic comparisons. Unfortunately, none of the results were reported by grade level and so it is not possible to draw conclusions about any between-language differences in the rate of learning over the course of development.

DISCUSSION

Together, the preceding cross-linguistic studies clearly show that the early development of spelling skills is slower in English than it is in other relatively more transparent orthographies and languages. Although the studies included somewhat different age groups, different spelling tasks, and focused on different aspects of spelling ability, English-speaking children consistently performed less well than their non-English-speaking peers. The main causal factor considered in this chapter was orthographic complexity, particularly as manifested through sound–spelling and spelling–sound consistency. Of course, many other factors may contribute to the between-language differences observed in the preceding studies, not least cultural variables that influence home literacy and educational practices in different countries. These are discussed shortly, but first a summary of the hypotheses and the general findings may be useful.

The first question asked whether the skills that enable children to learn the alphabetic principle and to establish the foundations necessary for spelling development are the same across alphabetic languages. Although limited in number, studies with Turkish, German, and French children showed that, as in English, letter knowledge and phoneme awareness were significant predictors of spelling ability over and above IQ. However, whereas letter knowledge was found to be an equally strong predictor of spelling, there was some suggestion that the influence of phoneme awareness may be shorter in duration and less strong in more transparent orthographies than in English. These results suggest that alphabetic literacy is founded on the same core skills across languages, even though orthographic (and other) factors may rapidly interact with and influence the learning process. Second, the potential effect of orthographic consistency on the rate of spelling development was considered. A finding that is easy to reconcile with a consistency effect was that, by the end of first grade, Czech children—whose orthography is more consistent both in the sound–spelling and in the spelling–sound direction— were better nonword spellers than English-speaking children. A less obvious finding, but one that fits with the view that spelling–sound consistency also influences spelling development, was that French-speaking children in third grade were also better nonword spellers than their English peers. As nonword spelling provides a good measure of children's ability to construct phonological representations or scaffolds of words in their language, learners of transparent orthographies seem to develop this skill sooner than learners of English. Finally, Caravolas et al. (2001) found that, in English, phonological spelling ability predicted later conventional spelling ability. Therefore the possibility that more consistent and transparent orthographies promote faster acquisition of conventional spelling skills was also investigated. Two studies suggested that this might be the case. French- and German-speaking children were found to have better word-spelling skills in the third and fourth years of schooling than did English-speaking children. Moreover, error analyses revealed that, at least in part, the between-language differences are due to the relative inconsistency of English spellings.

The variable of primary interest in this chapter was orthographic complexity. However, this is certainly not the only, nor perhaps the main, variable that plays a role in spelling development. In fact, several of our studies have shown that various linguistic factors such as phonotactic constraints, syllable structure (Caravolas & Bruck, 1993, 2000), and lexical stress (Caravolas et al., 2003) also drive between-language differences in spelling performance. A task for future studies will be to determine how linguistic variables interact with orthographic ones in shaping alphabetic spelling development.

Another variable of importance, and one that poses a particular problem for cross-linguistic studies, is the method of literacy instruction and general educational practice in different countries. Certainly the method of instruction often presents an unavoidable confound. However, the problem is not insurmountable, and its importance in explaining between-language differences may be overestimated. For example, in several of the preceding studies, the English children were taught to read and write by the whole-language method, whereas all of the non-English groups had received structured phonics or syllabic method instruction. It is true that, for English-speaking children (and presumably more so for learners of transparent orthographies), phonics instruction tends to produce better spelling results than does whole language (Bruck, Treiman, Caravolas, Genesee, & Cassar, 1998). Interestingly, the English third graders who participated in the French–English study described earlier were also compared with a group of American–English children who had been taught to read and write by means of structured phonics (Bruck et al., 1998). The groups were matched on reading ability and parental education. The American children were asked to spell the same list of words and nonwords as the Canadian–English children in the French–English study. If method of literacy instruction were the only, or the primary, cause of the French–English differences, then the American children should attain more or less the same levels of spelling accuracy as the French children. However, relative to the Canadian–English children, the advantage of the American phonics-taught children was of 14% on word and 9% on nonword spelling (both significant differences) whereas the advantage of the French children was of 30% on words and nonwords alike. It should also be noted that in most of the cross-linguistic studies reported, English-speaking children typically do have an advantage in terms of preliteracy instruction. In most European countries and in Québec French schools, preschool education up to the first grade *discourages* instruction in letter knowledge, invented spelling, and sight-word reading. These are common practices in most British, American, and English–Canadian preschool and kindergarten programmes. Yet, despite this putative preschool advantage, no benefits have yet been observed in the first year of formal schooling. Although method of instruction must be considered in explaining any between-group differences, it should not preclude cross-linguistic studies from taking place.

As pointed out in the introduction, the study of spelling development in languages other than English is in its infancy. Cross-linguistic studies of spelling development are even more rare. Thus the studies just reviewed are but first steps and provide only preliminary insights into the spelling process across languages. A great deal remains to be done in terms of setting comparable research questions and devising similar methods and test batteries across investigations in different languages. Also, to gain a truly cross-linguistic perspective, comparisons will need to be made not only with English as the base language, but also with languages that are perhaps more similar in their linguistic roots and cultures. Ultimately it will be the combination of detailed within-language studies and well-controlled cross-linguistic comparisons that will produce a general understanding of spelling development.

REFERENCES

Alegria, J., & Mousty, P. (1994). On the development of lexical and nonlexical spelling procedures of French-speaking normal and disabled children. In G. B. a. N. Ellis (Ed.), *Handbook of spelling: Theory, process and invervention* (pp. 211–226). Chichester, UK: Wiley.

Besner, D., & Smith, M. (1992). Basic processes in reading: Is the orthographic depth hypothesis sinking? In R. Frost & L. Katz (Eds.), *Orthography, phonology, morphology, and meaning* (pp. 45–66). Amsterdam: Elsevier Science.

Bissex, G. L. (1980). *GNYS at work: A child learns to write and read.* Cambridge, MA: Harvard University Press.

Bruck, M., Genesee, F., & Caravolas, M. (1997). A cross-linguistic study of early literacy acquisition. In B. Blachman (Ed.), *Foundations of reading acquisition and dyslexia: Implications for early intervention.* Mahwah, NJ: Lawrence Erlbaum Associates.

Bruck, M., Treiman, R., Caravolas, M., Genesee, F., & Cassar, M. (1998). Spelling skills of children in whole language and phonics classrooms. *Applied Psycholinguistics, 19*, 669–684.

Bryant, P. E., Nunes, T., & Bindman, M. (1997). Children's understanding of the connection between grammar and spelling. In B. Blachman (Ed.), *Foundations of reading acquisition and dyslexia: Implications for early intervention.* Mahwaw, NJ: Lawrence Erlbaum Associates.

Byrne, B. (1998). *The foundation of literacy: The child's acquisition of the alphabetic principle.* Hove, UK: Psychology Press.

Caravolas, M., & Bruck, B. (2000). Vowel categorization skill and its relationship to early literacy skills among first-grade Québec-French children. *Journal of Experimental Child Psychology, 76*, 190–221.

Caravolas, M., & Bruck, M. (1993). The effect of oral and written language input on children's phonological awareness: A cross-linguistic study. *Journal of Experimental Child Psychology, 55*, 1–30.

Caravolas, M., Bruck, M., & Genesee, F. (2003). Similarities and differences between English- and French-speaking poor spellers. In N. Goulandris (Ed.), *Dyslexia in different languages,* (pp. 157–180). London: Whurr.

Caravolas, M., Hulme, C., & Snowling, M. (2001). The foundations of spelling ability: Evidence from a 3-year longitudinal study. *Journal of Memory and Language, 45,* 751–774.

Carney, E. (1994). *A survey of English spelling.* London: Routledge.

Cassar, M., & Treiman, R. (1997). The beginnings of orthographic knowledge: Children's knowledge of double letter in words. *Journal of Educational Psychology, 89,* 631–644.

Cossu, G., Shankweiler, D., Liberman, I., Katz, L., & Tola, G. (1988). Awareness of phonological segments and reading ability in Italian children. *Applied Psycholinguistics, 9,* 1–16.

Ehri, L. C. (1997). Learning to read and learning to spell are one and the same, almost. In C. Perfetti, L. Rieben, & M. Fayol (Eds.), *Learning to spell: Research, theory and practice* (pp. 237–269). Mahwah, NJ: Lawrence Erlbaum Associates.

Fayol, M., Hupet, M., & Largy, P. (1999). The acquisition of subject-verb agreement in written French: From novices to experts' errors. *Reading and Writing, 11,* 153–174.

Frith, U. (1980). Unexpected spelling problems. In U. Frith (Ed.), *Cognitive processes in spelling* London: Academic Press.

Frost, R., Katz, L., & Bentin, S. (1987). Strategies for visual word recognition and orthographical depth: A multilingual comparison. *Journal of Experimental Psychology: Human Perception and Performance, 13,* 104–115.

Gentry, J. R. (1982). Analysis of developmental spelling skills in GNYS AT WORK. *The Reading Teacher, 36,* 192–200.

Goswami, U., & Bryant, P. E. (1990). *Phonological skills and learning to read.* London: Lawrence Erlbaum Associates.

Goswami, U., Gombert, J.-E., & de Barrera, L. F. (1998). Children's orthographic representations and linguistic transparency: Nonsense word reading in English, French, and Spanish. *Applied Psycholinguistics, 19,* 19–52.

Hanna, P. R., Hanna, J. S., Hodges, R. E., & Rudorf, E. F. (1966). *Phoneme–grapheme correspondences as cues to spelling improvement.* Washington, DC: US Department of Health, Education, and Welfare.

Henderson, E. H., & Beers, J. W. (Eds.). (1980). *Developmental and cognitive aspects of learning to spell: A reflection of word knowledge.* Newark, NJ. International Reading Association.

Hendrich, J., Radina, O., & Tláskal, J. (1991). *Francouzská Mluvnice* [French Grammar]. Prague: Státní Pedagogické Nakladatelství.

Hlavsa, Z. (1998). *Pravidla českého Pravopisu* [The Rules of Czech Orthography]. Prague: Academia.

Justicia, F., Defior, S., Pelegrina, S., & Martos, F. (1999). Sources of error in Spanish writing. *Journal of Research in Reading, 22,* 198–202.

Katz, L., & Frost, R. (1992). The reading process is different for different orthographies: The orthographic depth hypothesis. In R. Frost & L. Katz (Eds.), *Orthography, phonology, morphology and meaning* (pp. 67–84). Amsterdam: Elsevier Science. Publishers.

Kessler, B., & Treiman, R. (2001). Relationships between sounds and letters in English monosyllables. *Journal of Memory and Language, 44,* 592–617.

Kreiner, D. S. (1996). Effects of word familiarity and phoneme–grapheme polygraphy on oral spelling time and accuracy. *Psychological Record, 46,* 49–70.

Landerl, K., & Wimmer, H. (2000). Deficits in phoneme segmentation are not the core problem of dyslexia: Evidence from German and English children. *Applied Psycholinguistics, 21,* 243–262.

Liberman, I. Y., Shankweiler, D., Liberman, A. M., Fowler, C., & Fischer, F. W. (1977). Phonetic segmentation and recoding in the beginning reader. In A. S. Reber & D. Scarborough (Eds.), *Toward a psychology of reading.* Hillsdale, NJ: Lawrence Erlbaum Associates.

Lukatela, G., & Turvey, M. T. (1990). Phonemic similarity effects and prelexical phonology. *European Journal of Cognitive Psychology, 18,* 128–152.

Öney, B., & Durgunoglu, A. Y. (1997). Beginning to read in Turkish: A phonologically transparent orthography. *Applied Psycholinguistics, 18,* 1–15.

Oney, B., & Goldman, S. R. (1984). Decoding and comprehension skills in Turkish and English: Effects of the regularity of grapheme–phoneme correspondences. *Journal of Educational Psychology, 76,* 557–567.

Pacton, S., Perruchet, P., Fayol, M., & Cleeremans, A. (2001). Implicit learning out of the lab: The case of orthographic regularities. *Journal of Experimental Psychology: General, 130,* 401–426.

Palková, Z. (1997). *Fonetika a fonologie češtiny* [Czech phonetics and phonology]. Prague: Karolínum.

Peereman, R., & Content, A. (1999). Lexop: A lexical database with orthography-phonology statistics for French monosyllabic words. *Behavior Research Methods, Instruments and Computers, 31,* 376–379.

Peereman, R., Content, A., & Bonin, P. (1998). Is perception a two-way street? The case of feedback consistency in visual word recognition. *Journal of Memory and Language, 39,* 151–174.

Rittle-Johnson, B., & Siegler, R. S. (1999). Learning to spell: Variability, choice and change in children's strategy use. *Child Development, 70,* 332–348.

Sénéchal, M. (2000). Morphological effects in children's spelling of French words. *Canadian Journal of Experimental Psychology, 54,* 76–85.

Steffler, D., Varnhagen, C. K., Friesen, C. K., & Treiman, R. (1998). There's more to children's spelling than the errors they make: Strategic and automatic processes for one-syllable words. *Journal of Educational Psychology, 90*, 492–505.

Stone, G. O., Vanhoy, M., & Van Orden, G. C. (1997). Perception is a two-way street: Feedforward and feedback phonology in visual word recognition. *Journal of Memory and Language, 36*, 337–359.

Treiman, R. (1993). *Beginning to spell: A study of first-grade children.* New York: Oxford University Press.

Treiman, R., Cassar, M., & Zukowski, A. (1994). What types of linguistic information do children use in spelling? The case of flaps. *Child Development, 65*, 1310–1329.

Treiman, R., Zukowski, A., & Richmond-Welty, E. D. (1995). What happened to the "n" of sink? Children's spellings of final consonant clusters. *Cognition, 55*, 1–38.

Wimmer, H., & Goswami, U. (1994). The influence of orthographic consistency on reading development: Word recognition in English and German. *Cognition, 54*, 91–103.

Wimmer, H., & Landerl, K. (1997). How learning to spell German differs from learning to spell English. In C. A. Perfetti, L. Rieben, & M. Fayol (Eds.), *Learning to spell: Research, theory and practice across languages* Mahwah, NJ: Lawrence Erlbaum Associates.

Wimmer, H., Landerl, K., Linortner, R., & Hummer, P. (1991). The relationship of phonemic awareness to reading acquisition: More consequence than precondition but still important. *Cognition, 40*, 219–249.

Wimmer, H., Mayringer, H., & Landerl, K. (1998). Poor reading: A deficit in skill automatization or a phonological deficit? *Scientific Studies of Reading, 2*, 321–340.

Ziegler, J. C., Jacobs, A. M., & Stone, G. O. (1996). Statistical analysis of the bidirectional inconsistency of spelling and sound in French. *Behavior Research Methods, Instruments, & Computers, 28*, 504–515.

31

Reading Acquisition in Different Orthographies: Evidence from Direct Comparisons

Karin Landerl
University of Salzburg

This chapter surveys research on reading acquisition in different orthographies. Direct comparisons of reading acquisition in English and other orthographies show that the acquisition of the basic strategy of phonological decoding takes considerably longer in English than in many other orthographies. The main reason for this difference is the particularly low consistency of grapheme–phoneme correspondences in English. Other factors such as the method of reading instruction, age of school entry, or cultural differences play only a minor role. The higher grapheme–phoneme correspondence consistency of German probably also explains why the power of phonological awareness to predict later reading skills is lower in German than is reported for English and why the problems of dyslexic children are less marked in consistent than in inconsistent orthographies. Despite orthographic differences, reading is probably based on the same neurological mechanisms in all alphabetic orthographies.

INTRODUCTION

Mark Twain, the famous American novelist, tried hard to learn German. But when the keeper of a museum in Heidelberg told him that his German was "very special, probably unique" and should be added to a collection of curiosities, he came to the conclusion that "a gifted person ought to learn English (barring spelling and pronunciation) in thirty hours, French in thirty days, and German in thirty years. It seems manifest, then, that the latter tongue ought to be trimmed down and repaired. If it is to remain as it is, it ought to be gently and reverently set aside among the dead languages, for only the dead have time to learn it" (Twain, 1880).

As a native speaker of German, I can certainly understand how Mark Twain came to his conclusion, given that the linguistic structure of German is clearly more complex than that of English (or French). German has a comparatively rich morphology, both with respect to inflectional as well as derivational processes; word order is less restricted than in English, and the assignment of grammatical gender to each noun must seem completely arbitrary and is almost impossible to acquire for nonnative speakers. The grammatical simplicity of English in combination with a huge vocabulary resulting from many intakes from various languages (starting with having both Germanic and Romance influences when Anglo-Saxon and Norman communities lived in England) are probably among the many reasons why English (and not German) is a world language. However, there is a major drawback of having English as an international language, and Mark Twain was well aware of that: We all have to learn to "spell and pronounce" English orthography, which is among the most complex (or may be *the* most complex) alphabetic writing systems of the world. In this chapter, convincing evidence is presented and discussed that shows that Mark Twain's quote can be reversed for reading and spelling acquisition: It takes thirty hours to learn to read German, thirty days to learn French, and thirty years to learn English. And maybe one could even say that it is English orthography that is in urgent need of repair.

This chapter surveys studies on reading development in different orthographies. The main focus is on comparing studies on English, the orthography on which by far the most reading research has been carried out, with findings on German. German is ideal for direct comparisons with English because the two languages are very closely related. Many words occur in both languages (e.g., hand–*Hand;* summer–*Sommer;* discussion–*Diskussion*). Therefore it is possible to present English and German readers with more or less the same reading material and observe differences and similarities in reading skills and strategies.

German is a much more typical example of an alphabetic orthography than English. As in many other orthographies, the correspondences between spoken and written words are more consistent and predictable than in English. For example, the letter *a* is consistently pronounced as /a/ in the German words *Hand, Hass, Ball,* and *Garten,* whereas the pronunciation is different for each of the English equivalents, *hand, hate, ball,* and *garden.* Inconsistencies like the various pronunciations of the letter sequence *ough* in *through, thorough, cough,* and *enough* do not occur in German (and in most other alphabetic orthographies). A central research question is therefore whether findings on the phonologically nontransparent English orthography can be generalized to other orthographies.

The empirical evidence that is presented in the following sections clearly suggests that reading acquisition in the English writing system proceeds more slowly than in any other orthography that has been looked at so far. It could also be shown that the manifestations of developmental dyslexia are more apparent in English than in German. Furthermore, research suggests that well-developed phonological processing skills are more relevant for working out the correspondences between spoken and written words in English than in phonologically more transparent languages. The reason for this finding is certainly not that children learning phonologically transparent orthographies do not need phonological processing skills, but rather that the acquisition of a phonologically transparent orthography itself promotes phonological processing skills so that individual differences that might have been there before the onset of reading acquisition are evened out.

ALPHABETIC WRITING SYSTEMS

The basic principle of alphabetic writing systems is that letters or letter clusters—called graphemes—represent speech sounds. The speech sounds that ought to be represented by an alphabet are the phonemes of a language, that is, the smallest sound units that cause a change in meaning (e.g., <u>v</u>an vs. <u>f</u>an). Finnish is a "perfect" alphabetic orthography so to speak, as one letter stands for one phoneme. The consistency from letters to speech sounds is as high as that from speech sounds to letters. Homophonic spellings, that is, different spellings for the same phonological word form (e.g., *to, two, too*) or—even worse—irregular spellings that do not conform to the standard grapheme–phoneme correspondence (GPC) rules (e.g., *yacht, sword*) do not occur in this phonologically highly transparent writing system. Finnish does not even have multiletter graphemes. Multiletter graphemes (like English *th* or *sh*) are one way to solve the problem that there are often more phonemes in a language than letters in the orthography.

Orthographies that—like Finnish—are characterized by high consistency between graphemes and phonemes are called "shallow" (Liberman, Liberman, Mattingly, & Shankweiler, 1980) because they represent the linguistically shallow level of phonology. English, on the other hand, is termed a "deep" orthography because it is rather a representation of the linguistically deeper level of morphology than of the phonological structure of the spoken language. English spellings allow us to perceive the morphological relatedness of words like *sign* and *signature* or *heal* and *health*, although the pronunciation of the identical morphemes is very different. Quite often this consistency on the morphemic level can be achieved only at the expense of phonemic consistency. The consistency of both GPCs and phoneme–grapheme correspondences (PGCs) is low in English compared with that of most other orthographies.

According to the orthographic depth hypothesis (Katz & Frost, 1992) readers of shallow orthographies rely more strongly on phonological decoding processes than do readers of deep orthographies. If we want to determine the influence of orthographic depth on reading processes, the ideal comparison would obviously be between Finnish and English, the extremes on both sides of the continuum. However, English is one among many Indo-European languages whereas Finnish belongs to the few Finno-Ugric languages. The two languages are very different with respect to vocabulary, grammar, and even phonology. Hardly any common word exists in both languages. Finnish is an agglutinating language, that is, grammatical specification is achieved by the addition of suffixes to the word stem, one suffix for each grammatical function. In addition to a very simple orthography, Finnish is also characterized by a very simple phonology with mainly open syllables. Consonant clusters are very exceptional and occur only in foreign words. Thus, if we compare reading words or texts in English and Finnish, we have to be aware that words might have the same semantics, but will be very different with respect to their phonological (and orthographic) word form (probably longer but less complex in Finnish than in English). And if we construct very simple nonwords, for example with four-letter length and a CVCV sequence, we automatically put the English readers at a disadvantage because this phonological structure is much less common than in Finnish.

THE METHOD OF DIRECT COMPARISON: WHY ENGLISH–GERMAN IS IDEAL

On the continuum of orthographic depth, German is somewhere in between Finnish and English. The most striking difference between English and German is that German has highly consistent and predictable GPCs, also termed as high feedforward consistency for vowels as well as consonants (see Landerl & Thaler, 2005). Irregular word spellings exist only for foreign words, which are quite often English (e.g., *computer, skateboard, Walkman*). Thus, with respect to GPCs, German can be categorized as a shallow orthography.

However, German is much less consistent in the direction from phoneme to grapheme, also termed as feedback consistency. Although in reading there is almost always only one possible translation of a certain grapheme into a phoneme, in spelling one has to chose among various possible translations of a phoneme into a grapheme. German (just as English) has a considerable number of homophonic spellings, e.g., *mehr–Meer* [more–sea], *viel–fiel* [a lot–fell], *Lied–Lid* [song–eyelid], *Wal–Wahl* [whale–election]. Thus, with respect to spelling, German is rather at the deep end of the continuum of orthographic depth, although PGCs are still more predictable than in English. Interestingly, this divergence of orthographic depth for reading and spelling is typical for many alphabetic orthographies, for example, French, Spanish, Swedish, Dutch, or Greek.

Therefore the main difference between English and German lies in the consistency of GPCs. In many other respects, the two orthographies are highly similar. Apart from *ä, ö, ü,* and *ß,* which are used only in German, the two orthographies use the same letter set. Both orthographies make use of multiletter graphemes (e.g., English *fish, beast, jacket,* German:. *Fisch, Biest, Jacke*). Silent letters also occur in both English and German (e.g., English: *hate;* German: *Zahl*). As both English and German are Germanic languages, it is not surprising that phonological word structure is comparable. Many onset and end clusters exist in both languages (e.g., *blood–Blut; green–grün; street–Straße; hand–Hand, beast–Biest; lift–Lift*). However, German allows more complex clusters than English. Good examples are the words *knee–Knie, sword–Schwert,* and *psychology–Psychologie,* in which English has only orthographic reflections of ancient or foreign pronunciations whereas every grapheme of the onset cluster is pronounced in German. In particular, in word-final position German allows very heavy consonant sequences that quite often result from the addition of another morpheme, for example, *du kämpfst* [you fight], in which the *–st* is an inflectional morpheme for marking second-person singular. Finally, many words, so-called "cognates" (de Groot & Nas, 1991) exist in both languages. Thus one can select sets of words in English and German that are identical in meaning, highly similar or identical with respect to spelling, and highly similar or indeed identical (apart from typical language accent) in pronunciation. With respect to nonword reading, the danger of creating sound sequences that are typical for one orthography but highly atypical (or even impossible) in the other orthography is much lower than when two dissimilar languages are compared. These are the type of stimuli that were used in a whole line of research that looked at language differences in reading acquisition, reading strategies in competent adult readers, and in cases of developmental dyslexia. The results of this research are reported in the following sections.

READING ACQUISITION

Frith, Wimmer, and Landerl (1998) compared word- and nonword-reading skills in 7- to 12-year-old children reading English and German. In a first experiment, 7-, 8- and 9-year-old native speakers of each language were confronted with list-reading tasks. The words were short (one and two syllabic) and familiar words that are highly similar in the two languages (e.g., *boat–Boot, word–Wort*). The nonwords were derived from these words by exchange of the consonantal onsets (e.g., *wuest* was derived from *word* and *guest* and equivalently, *Wast* was derived from *Wort* and *Gast*). By this method of nonword construction, it could be ensured that (a) the nonwords did not include any orthographic or phonological sequences that are unfamiliar or even illegal in one of the two languages and (b) the nonwords (just as the words) were highly similar for both language groups.

The report by Frith et al. (1998) noted differences between the two language groups with respect to both reading accuracy and speed. While even the youngest group of German readers read with high accuracy for both words (8% errors) and nonwords (15% errors), the youngest group of English readers had marked difficulties with words (30% errors) and even more so with nonwords (53% errors). A clear decrease of reading errors was evident for the English children of increasing age. By the age of 9 years, English children's word-reading accuracy was as high as that of the German children of that age group; however, there was still a reliable difference in nonword-reading accuracy, with only about 5% errors for the German, but still about 20% errors for the English sample. German-speaking children read the word lists faster than the English children (1.01 vs. 2.56 s per item on average), and the difference was even larger for nonwords (1.41 vs. 4.10 s). English-speaking children showed greater improvement in reading speed with age than German-speaking children, and this was particularly marked for nonwords. A further interesting observation from this study was that the variability of reading skills was clearly higher among the English than the German samples—a finding that was replicated in a number of other studies.

In a second experiment, individual trial presentations for words and nonwords are reported for groups of 8- and 12-year-old English and German readers. In this study, words and nonwords up to three-syllable length were presented and for the shorter one- and two-syllable items, high- and low-frequency words could be distinguished (all three syllable words were of low frequency compared with the shorter items). Once again the German-speaking 8-year-olds clearly outperformed the age-equivalent English group, but by the age of 12 years the English readers had largely caught up with their German peers. German-speaking 8-year-olds read one- and two-syllable words and nonwords with high accuracy (less than 10% errors) and showed little effect of lexicality and word frequency. In contrast, these effects were strong for their English-speaking peers. There was hardly any language difference in the case of the high-frequency words (English: 9% errors; German: 5% errors). However, the disadvantage of the English-speaking compared with the German-speaking children was considerable for low-frequency words (28% vs. 9% errors) and nonwords (23% vs. 7% errors). The higher proportion of errors in low-frequency words compared with that of nonwords is readily explained by the fact that the nonwords were scored leniently, that is, every possible pronunciation of a certain grapheme was counted as correct, whereas for the low-frequency words only one pronunciation, that is, the adequate word, was accepted. The three-syllable words and nonwords posed a particular problem to the younger group of English readers, but not to their German peers (53% vs. 12% errors). The 12-year old readers of both language groups performed at ceiling on these short items as well as on the three-syllable words. However, accuracy for the three-syllable nonwords was still somewhat lower for 12-year-old English (22% errors) compared with German readers (12% errors).

Finally, a nonword-reading task is reported in which identical three-syllable nonwords with a simple CVCVCV structure were presented to both language groups. It should be noted that such a simple sound structure is atypical for both German and English words; however, such a structure without any consonant clusters should make sounding out comparably easy from a linguistic point of view. It was obvious that the German readers indeed found these items easy, performing at ceiling for both age groups. The English children, however, once again showed marked problems with 30% errors among the 8-year-olds and still about 8% errors among the 12-year-olds, clearly indicating that the sounding-out skills of these children are far from perfect.

The analysis of reading latencies for correct responses largely confirmed the findings on accuracy: German 8-year-olds read faster and showed less marked effects of lexicality and word frequency than their English peers for the short one- and two-syllable items. For three-syllable items, German readers were once again faster than English readers, but here the lexicality effect was equally strong for both language groups. By the age of 12 years, English and German participants read with the same speed and showed a similar effect of lexicality.

Another observation in this study was that the variability of reading errors was higher among the English than among the German readers. In particular, misreadings of vowel graphemes were very typical for the English readers but occurred only infrequently consistency among German readers. The most likely explanation for this finding is the difference of GPC for vowels in English (especially low) and German (as high as for consonants). Younger English readers also showed a stronger tendency to incorrectly respond with an existing word whereas German misreadings most often resulted in a nonword pronunciation.

The general superiority of the German compared to the English readers is even more surprising given the fact that English children start school more than a year earlier than children in Germany and Austria and thus had at least one more year of formal reading instruction. The conclusions from this detailed study were that the low orthographic consistency of English necessitates the use of complex and error-prone strategies in phonological decoding, like breaking up letter sequences into onsets and rimes or searching the lexicon for similar words that would allow reading by analogy. On the other hand, the high consistency of German allows phonological decoding into syllables on-line.

Wimmer and Goswami (1994) also compared word- and nonword-reading skills in 7-, 8- and 9-year-old English- and German-speaking readers. They developed a very simple list-reading paradigm that should once again ensure that English and German readers were presented with highly similar stimuli. In one condition, children had to name a list of Arabic digits (2, 4, 7). In this condition, visual input was identical for the two language groups and pronunciation of these numbers was also highly similar. In the second condition, children were given the corresponding number words to read (two–zwei; four–vier; seven–sieben). In the third condition nonwords were presented that were—just as in the Frith et al. (1998) study—created by exchange of the consonantal onsets of the number words (e.g., English: nour from nine and four; or German: nier from neun and vier). Once again the nonwords were highly similar in the two languages and by deriving them from existing words the authors made sure that no illegal letter or sound sequences occurred.

Wimmer and Goswami (1994) did not find any relevant language differences for the first two conditions, naming of Arabic digits and naming of number words. Similar performance on Arabic digits indicates that there are no major differences between English and German readers in general articulation speed and confirms that the pronunciations of the number words in the two languages are comparable. Similar performance in the number-word-reading condition is somewhat unexpected given the marked differences that Frith et al. (1998) found for young English and German readers in their word-reading skills. Wimmer and Goswami presented only words from one semantic category (numbers), and it is likely that the English children in their study could make up for differences in word-recognition skill by partial phonological decoding and guessing of a number word that started with or included the translated phonemes.

In agreement with Frith et al. (1998), Wimmer and Goswami also found marked differences with respect to nonword-reading skills. In all three age groups, German children read the nonwords more accurately and faster than their English peers. As a matter of fact, the youngest group of 7-year-old German readers made a lower number of nonword reading errors than the oldest group of 9-year-old English readers. Therefore once again it is confirmed that the process of left-to-right decoding is more easily acquired by German compared with English readers.

The paradigm developed by Wimmer and Goswami (1994) was also applied in the context of a European cooperation of reading researchers (European Co-operation in the field of Scientific and Technical Research, COST A8: Learning disorders as a barrier to human development). The task was translated into seven different languages (English, German, Dutch, Swedish, French, Spanish, and Finnish) and presented to children in Grades 1–4 in each country. Interestingly, Aro and Wimmer (2003) report for this cross-language comparison that nonword-reading accuracy was very high (between 80% and almost 100% correct) for all but one language group (i.e., English) even in Grade 1. The English children, however, were able to reach a similarly high level of accuracy only in Grade 4. In Grade 1, the English readers produced acceptable pronunciations for only about half of the nonwords, and in Grades 2 and 3 reading accuracy was still comparably low, with about 70% correct.

The findings of this study suggest that consistency of GPCs is more relevant for acquisition of decoding skills than word length. Among the orthographies compared in the Aro and Wimmer study, English was the one with the lowest and Finnish the one with the highest orthographic consistency. On the other hand, the Finnish nonwords were clearly longer than the nonwords in all other orthographies. All Finnish number words are at least bisyllabic, so the nonwords derived from high-frequency number words also had two, or sometimes even three, syllables. This was in contrast to all other languages, in which the nonwords were mainly monosyllabic with only few bisyllabic exceptions. The results clearly showed that the higher number of syllables did not have any negative effect on Finnish readers as their reading accuracy was just as high as accuracy for all other consistent orthographies, even in Grade 1, and even reading speed was comparable.

Another comparative study of reading acquisition in European orthographies (Seymour, Aro, & Erskine, 2003) also suggests that the acquisition of basic reading skills takes a few months up to 1 year in consistent orthographies, but 3–4 years in the inconsistent English orthography. Seymour et al. looked at the development of basic word- and nonword-reading skills in 13 different orthographies. Two features were of special interest in that study: Syllable structure and orthographic depth. Languages with simple syllable structure had a predominance of open syllables and few consonant clusters (Finnish, Greek, Italian, Spanish, Portuguese, and French), whereas languages with complex syllable structure were those that have a predominance of closed syllables and many consonant clusters (German, Norwegian, Icelandic, Swedish, Dutch, Danish, and English). Within the two categories of syllabic structure the orthographies were sorted with respect to orthographic depth. It should, however, be noted that the simple syllable structure languages are in general more shallow than the complex syllable structure languages. Finnish is more shallow than German, and, on the other end of the continuum, French is more shallow than English.

Seymour et al. (2003) applied a different method of item selection from the studies discussed so far. For the assessment of word-recognition skills, short high-frequency content and function words were selected. Thus the words were typical for each language, but less comparable across languages than in the studies of Wimmer and Goswami (1994) or Frith et al. (1998), in which an effort was made to select words that exist in the participating languages in similar word form. For the assessment of phonological decoding skills, very simple one- and two-syllable nonwords were constructed for each language. As Seymour et al. were especially interested in the assessment of the foundations of literacy, they did not allow for consonant clusters, but only for CV, VC, or sometimes CVC syllables. Thus, with respect to orthographic structure, the nonwords of this study were more comparable across languages than the nonwords of the Aro and Wimmer (2003) study that were derived from existing words in each language and therefore sometimes had different orthographic structures. However, by prescribing the phonological structure of the nonwords, Seymour et al. accepted that the presented nonwords might have been more familiar to the children of the simple syllable languages than to those acquiring complex syllable languages. The nonwords *id, lat*, and *ti* look perfectly familiar in an Italian context, but the nonwords *ca* and *uli* look rather un-English and may have put the English readers at a certain disadvantage.

The findings of this European comparison are largely in line with the findings of the detailed English–German comparison by Frith et al. (1998): After 1 year of formal reading instruction, only the readers of the rather deep orthographies of Portuguese, French, Danish, and English had problems in reading short familiar words and simple nonwords whereas readers of all other orthographies performed with high accuracy and adequate fluency. Interestingly, although the French and Danish groups at the end of Grade 2 showed similar performance to that of the first graders learning more shallow orthographies, English second graders' performance was still lower. Seymour et al. report a stronger lexicality effect in simple compared with complex syllable languages; however, as already discussed, syllable structure is confounded with orthographic depth in this study. Finally, Seymour et al. replicated the finding of higher variance among readers of deep compared with shallow orthographies. Only among the English and Danish children did appreciable numbers remain unable to read after several months in school, although a few made rapid progress and read within the normal range for the shallow orthographies.

In line with the findings discussed so far, Goswami, Gombert, and de Barrera (1998) report that Spanish first graders who acquire a phonologically transparent orthography could read one- and two-syllable nonwords more or less without mistake whereas reading accuracy of English first graders was particularly low, with only 30% correct. French first graders, who acquire a consistent but rather complex orthographic system, were in between the two other orthography groups, with about 60% correct. Goswami, Porpodas, and Wheelwright (1997) found that for English children nonword-reading accuracy increases if the nonwords contain rhyme segments that exist in real words (*comic–bomic*), indicating that children use orthographic knowledge to work out the nonword pronunciations. For young readers of Greek, a shallow orthography, such a facilitating effect of familiar rhymes was not evident for reading accuracy because the level of accuracy was generally very high; however, a similar effect could be observed for reading speed.

Further convincing evidence for heavier reliance on phonological decoding in consistent than inconsistent orthographies comes from another direct comparison of reading acquisition in German and English (Goswami, Ziegler, Dalton, & Schneider, 2001) that examined the pseudohomophone effect in the two orthographies. English and German children, 7, 8, and 9 years old, were presented with a reading and a lexical decision task with three types of stimuli: real word spellings (e.g., German: *Hund*; English: *fake*), pseudohomophone spellings, that is, invented spellings that sound like existing words (e.g., German: *Hunt*; English: *faik*), and non-word spellings that were either phonologically and orthographically plausible (e.g., German: *Tund*; English: *dake*) or implausible (e.g., German: *Lunss*; English: *koog*). In the reading task, the English children showed a pseudohomophone effect, that is, they were better in reading pseudohomophones (63% correct) compared with nonwords (56% correct). The general inter- pretation of the facilitating effect of pseudohomophonic spellings in reading is that top-down information from the phonological lexicon improves nonword reading (Borowsky & Masson, 1999). For the German sample, however, no such pseudohomophone effect was observed, but children read pseudohomophones and plausible as well as implausible nonwords with equally high accuracy (91%, 93%, and 84% correct, respectively), indicating that these children relied almost exclusively on a bottom-up phonological decoding strategy. This interpretation was also confirmed by the fact that the German children showed a more marked length effect than the English children. A facilitating effect of pseudohomophones might have been evident in faster response times for such stimuli compared with those of other nonwords (Goswami et al., 2001 do not report response times for this task); however, the important fact is that the German children were obviously able to decode all stimuli with equal accuracy, independent of their phonological and orthographic structure.

In a second experiment, the participants had to perform a lexical decision task on the same stimuli. In this kind of paradigm, subjects typically take longer and make more errors in re- jecting pseudohomophones compared with nonwords (e.g., Besner & Davelaar, 1983). This pseudohomophone disadvantage suggests that phonological information is automatically acti- vated even in a task that could in principle be solved on a purely orthographic basis. In contrast to the reading task, Goswami et al. (2001) found a pseudohomophone disadvantage for Ger- man, but not for English. German children quite often accepted pseudohomophone spellings as existing words (40% errors for pseudohomophones, but only 10% for nonwords), whereas English children did not show specific difficulties in rejecting pseudohomophone spellings (be- tween 10% and 20% errors for pseudohomophones and nonwords). The authors conclude that English children appear to be making lexical decisions on the basis of orthographic familiarity, whereas the German children appear to be impeded in their use of orthographic familiarity by automatic phonological decoding.

The findings reported in the last section consistently suggest that the acquisition of basic word- and nonword-reading skills progresses faster in shallow, phonologically transparent orthographies compared with deep, phonologically rather opaque orthographies. It is reasonable to assume that phonologically transparent orthographies allow comparably fast acquisition of an on-line phonological decoding procedure. As long as GPCs are reliable, such a left-to-right decoding procedure is always successful and results either in a correct pronunciation or at least in a sort of hypercorrect pronunciation of the grapheme sequence that will allow access of the correct word in the phonological lexicon. Obviously such a simple left-to-right decoding procedure will not be sufficient in the long run. It is slow and laborious and has to be replaced with more efficient word-recognition processes over time. The fact that even the youngest readers in shallow orthographies show a clear lexicality effect is first evidence that orthographic processes move in very early. However, phonological decoding is a highly reliable backup procedure in shallow orthographies: If a word cannot be recognized it can always be sounded out. Furthermore, phonological decoding functions as a self-teaching mechanism (Share, 1995). Words that are sounded out correctly can be stored in the orthographic lexicon and can from then on be read by direct access of that entry in the lexicon.

Young readers of deep and phonologically opaque orthographies on the other hand cannot resort to this simple sounding out procedure because in many cases it will be misleading and will not result in the correct pronunciation. Thus they will have to use additional strategies right from the start. Seymour et al. (2003) argue that deeper orthographies induce the implementation of a dual foundation of logographic (whole-word) and alphabetic (sound-based) reading strategies, which takes longer to establish than the single foundation required for the learning of shallow orthographies. Goswami (2002) suggests that the low orthographic consistency of English necessitates the use of complex and error-prone strategies in phonological decoding, like breaking up letter sequences into onsets and rimes or searching the lexicon for similar words that would allow reading by analogy.

However, before we accept the explanation of differences in the pace of literacy acquisition in terms of differences in orthographic structure, we have to rule out a number of external factors that were not considered so far. The first factor that comes to mind is whether differences in method of reading instruction might have an influence on the observed language differences. Second, in most European countries formal schooling starts at the age of 6 to 7 years; however, in some countries, for example, Great Britain, schooling starts earlier, around the age of 5 years, whereas in other countries, for example, Finland, formal reading instruction starts particularly late, after children's seventh birthday. Age of school entry might at least partly explain the differences observed between different nations in the pace of reading acquisition. And third, there might be minor or not so minor cultural differences between the participating nations that might have an influence on children's reading development.

INFLUENCE OF READING INSTRUCTION, AGE OF SCHOOL ENTRY, AND CULTURAL BACKGROUND ON READING DEVELOPMENT

Although the most typical teaching approaches among phonologically transparent orthographies are so-called phonics methods with clear emphasis on practicing letter–sound knowledge and blending of phonemes into syllable and word pronunciations (for reading) and segmenting of sound sequences into individual phonemes (for spelling), such approaches are not typical for English. Most English instructional approaches put more emphasis on direct word recognition as this is the only way to deal with the many irregular and exceptional word spellings.

There are, however, some schools in Great Britain that are exceptions and adhere to a very straightforward phonics teaching approach, claiming that even in the phonologically opaque orthography, systematic knowledge about letter–sound correspondences and blending is the best way to acquire literacy skills. In a recent study (Landerl, 2000) such a school was included in a cross-language design. For this study, the paradigm developed by Wimmer and Goswami (1994) was used. The same lists of numerals, number words, and nonwords derived from the number words were presented to groups of English- and German-speaking children who received the dominant method of reading instruction (mixed for English and phonics for German). In addition, the reading tasks were presented to English children receiving explicit phonics teaching. The first finding was that the differences between English and German children's nonword-reading skills observed by Wimmer and Goswami (1994) could largely be replicated. In Grades 1, 2, and 3 English children made reliably more nonword-reading errors than German-speaking children, although in this study nonword-reading accuracy was already comparably high in Grade 4.

The main question was how the English phonics group would perform. If the differences between reading acquisition in English and German are solely due to differences in reading instruction, the English phonics group's performance should be as good as that of the German children. If, however, the differences between reading acquisition in English and German are due to differences in orthographic consistency, performance of the English phonics group should be comparable with that of the English group taught by a standard mixed approach. The findings were as follows: In Grade 4 all three groups performed on a similarly high level of accuracy; that is, by then differences caused by both orthographic consistency and method of reading instruction had leveled off. In Grade 3, the English phonics group made a reliably lower number of nonword-reading errors than the English standard group. In fact, their nonword-reading accuracy was as low as that of the German third graders. This indicates that indeed phonics instruction helps children to fully understand the alphabetic code earlier than with the standard mixed approach. In Grades 1 and 2, however, the picture was reversed: English phonics readers made clearly more nonword reading errors than German-speaking children and did not differ from the equivalent English standard groups. Thus, for the younger readers, the negative influence of the lower consistency was dominant whereas method of reading instruction did not make much difference. This is surprising as one would obviously expect that instructional methods have the strongest influence in the early phases of reading acquisition.

Two reasons for this finding were discussed in Landerl (2000). First a difference in the English phonics group and German children's blending procedure was observed that probably had a relevant influence. The English phonics children were taught to name the sounds of a presented spelling and then blend these sounds into a coherent pronunciation (e.g., /sə/–/e/–/nə/–/sen/). This strategy works very well for short CVC items. For longer items, however, especially the youngest Grade 1 children found it difficult to keep all the sounds in their working memory. Typical errors for the two-syllable nonword *feven* were to reduce the item to a one-syllable pronunciation (/ven/ or /fen/). Another way to perform phonological decoding that is typically applied by young German readers is to blend the sounds successively in a left-to-right fashion. An extreme example of such a successive decoding that might be observed for children in their very first stages of reading acquisition would be /tsə/–/tswə/–/tswe:/–/tswe:n/ for *zwehn*. In this variant of the blending procedure, memory load is considerably smaller because it does not require storing a sequence of unconnected sounds but only the output of the blending procedure that has been performed so far. The second plausible reason for the poor performance of the young English phonics group is age. The English first-grade children had only just turned 6 years old and were more than a year younger than the German-speaking first graders and their general cognitive and linguistic development was clearly less advanced.

It cannot be ruled out that at least some of these children were overcharged by the demands of this complex memory-dependent blending procedure.

Age of school entry is of course a factor that might have a relevant influence on the differences in reading skills found between languages. In Great Britain formal schooling starts earlier, around children's fifth birthday, whereas in most other European countries formal schooling starts when the children are approximately 6 years old or older. Thus the English groups in the two discussed European studies (Aro & Wimmer, 2003; Seymour et al., 2003) were always younger than all other groups. Age of school entry certainly does not completely explain the differences found in these studies. The Danish first graders who also had to cope with a deep and phonologically opaque orthographic system were more than 2 years older than the English first graders and still performed worse than most other participating language groups. Furthermore, in the reported direct English–German comparisons (Frith et al., 1998; Wimmer & Goswami, 1994), children were selected to be of comparable age, which means that in those studies the English children had even more formal reading instruction than the German-speaking children. It is, however, unclear if the early age of school entry in addition to the complexities of English orthography may cause early failure in young children whose linguistic skills are not yet readily developed.

Thus it is interesting to have a look at cross-language comparisons involving other English-speaking nations like the United States or Canada, where age of school entry is also later, after children's sixth birthday. Oney and Goldman (1984) compared reading acquisition in American and Turkish first and third graders. Turkish is a highly consistent and phonologically transparent orthography. The same set of nonwords of three- to nine-letter length were presented to children in both orthographies. Both age groups of the Turkish children read the nonwords without any particular problems; even for the longest nonwords accuracy was higher than 90% for both first and third graders. In contrast, the American first graders read only 85% of the shortest nonwords correctly, and, for the longest nine-letter items, accuracy dropped to only about 40% correct. The American third graders could read the short nonwords with the same accuracy as the Turkish children; however, they still showed a more marked length effect, with only about 80% of the longest nonwords correct. Reading speed was also consistently higher among the Turkish compared with the American groups. Interestingly, reading speed of the American third graders was well comparable with that of Turkish first graders. Thus this study once more confirms that the acquisition of phonological decoding takes a few months in a consistent orthography, but several years in the inconsistent English orthographic system. It is sometimes argued that heavy reliance on phonological decoding prevents young readers from full text comprehension. However, Oney and Goldman found in their comparison that Turkish first graders also outperformed their American peers on a reading comprehension test.

One problem with this direct English–Turkish comparison is that the two languages are very different. This means that presenting identical nonwords as was done by Oney and Goldman may have put one or the other group at a disadvantage. Although the authors made sure that all nonwords conformed to the phonotactic rules of both orthographies, they readily admit that the phonological structure of their nonwords may have been unusually simple for the English readers.

In a recent study, Mann and Wimmer (2002) compared reading acquisition of English-speaking Californian and German-speaking Austrian first and second graders who were comparable with respect to chronological age. They used subsets of the word and nonword lists developed for the European comparison designed by Seymour et al. (2003), which contain short high-frequency words in each orthography and simple CV structured one- and two-syllable nonwords. Interestingly, the young Californian readers performed much better than the young Scottish readers in the Seymour et al. study. At the end of Grade 1, they read 94% of the words correctly, and at the end of Grade 2 the American readers performed at ceiling for the word reading condition. Their word-reading accuracy was equally high as that of the Austrian participants, and there was also no difference with respect to word-reading speed. Even nonword-reading accuracy was very high among the American children with 80% and 85% for first and second graders, but still reliably lower than that of their Austrian peers, who showed accuracy levels of 91% and 93%. Nonword-reading speed was also lower among American compared with Austrian children. Therefore later onset of formal reading instruction of the American compared with British children might indeed facilitate the first steps into literacy. However, it should be noted that in the Mann and Wimmer study even a group of kindergarten children who did not yet have formal reading instruction (but very good letter knowledge) were able to read about half of the words and nonwords. Thus the differences in pace of reading acquisition induced by formal reading acquisition may have been obscured by very good preschool reading preparation among the Californian sample.

The third external factor that deserves discussion is whether cultural differences might contribute to the differences observed in children's reading development. In all reported cross-language studies, children living in different nations were compared with each other. Although common sense suggests that cultural differences among European nations are not dramatic, they are difficult to control in empirical studies. Wales provides an interesting setting for a kind of natural experiment that helps to exclude cultural differences as an influential factor. In Wales many children grow up bilingual learning both English and Welsh. When they come to school, they can chose between English schools and Welsh schools in which English is taught only as a second language. The interesting feature about Welsh is that its orthography is highly consistent. Thus, in Wales we can compare reading acquisition in a deep and a shallow orthography in children who live in the same area and therefore have highly similar cultural backgrounds. The two groups are even matched on method of reading instruction because, in the absence of traditional Welsh reading primers, English primers were simply translated into Welsh when Welsh schooling was introduced. Thus Welsh children receive the mixed approach of phonics and whole-word teaching that is typical in the English context.

Ellis and Hooper (2001) compared reading skills in English- and Welsh-speaking second graders. As the two languages are very dissimilar with respect to phonological as well as ortho-graphic structure, Ellis and Hooper developed English and Welsh word lists that were carefully constructed so that the items were equally representative of both languages, and children of the same age had equal opportunity to experience the parallel items. This was achieved by equating the word lists for frequency of written exposure, but no other aspect. According to the authors, "everything to do with learning opportunity should be matched; everything to do with language should be freed to vary" (p. 574). From the children's performance on these word lists with decreasing frequency, Ellis and Hooper could predict that the average English second grader of their sample would have been able to read down to the 716th word form type of English with a frequency of 118/million, whereas the average Welsh child would have performed more than twice as well by reaching the 1821st word form type with a frequency of 61/million.

Ellis and Hooper (2001) also assessed children's comprehension of the words that they had to read aloud and could show that Welsh children's good decoding skills allowed them to read further beyond their comprehension levels than English children. This is a highly interesting finding as it suggests that learning new words during reading is more likely to take place in the consistent Welsh than in the inconsistent English orthographic system. The Welsh–English comparison by Ellis and Hooper once more confirms that young readers in a consistent orthography are more reliant on an alphabetic decoding strategy than young English readers: Word length determined 70% of reading latency in Welsh but only 22% in English, and Welsh reading errors tended to be nonword mispronunciations whereas English children made more real word substitutions and null attempts.

Recently the paradigm introduced by Ellis and Hooper was extended to Albanian (Hoxhallari, van Daal, & Ellis, 2004). Albanian orthography has a one-to-one correspondence between graphemes and phonemes as well as between phonemes and graphemes, that is, it is one of the few "ideal" alphabetic orthographies with high feedforward and feedback consistency. An Albanian word list with decreasing frequency (analogous to the lists in English and Welsh) was presented to a sample of first graders. Although these children had 1 year fewer of formal reading instruction than the Welsh and English children, they nevertheless read more words than both English and Welsh children. Just as was observed in the Welsh sample, the Albanian readers produced mainly nonword errors. Interestingly, their reading latencies were even more strongly tied to word length than in Welsh. The authors interpret their findings as evidence that "reading acquisition is faster the shallower the orthography." However, it should be admitted that although the English–Welsh comparison by Ellis and Hooper (2001) controlled for many background factors because the children assessed in the two languages actually lived in the same area and attended the same school system, this was not the case for the Albanian sample.

An older study by Thorstad (1991) also shows that orthographic differences are still evident when differences in cultural or social background are ruled out. Thorstad presented 6-year-old English children with a short text. The interesting variation was that one group read the text in standard English whereas the other group had been taught to read the Initial Teaching Alphabet (ITA), a consistent variant of English orthography that was thought to facilitate reading acquisition. Indeed, although the young ITA readers read the 56 words of the text with high accuracy, the children of the standard orthography group could read only 31 words correctly on average. Interestingly, the ITA group did not differ from a group of 6-year-old Italian children who read the same text in translation.

To summarize, although method of reading instruction, age of onset of formal reading instruction, and cultural influences do show effects on the course of reading acquisition, these factors cannot fully explain the differences between orthographies. The available empirical evidence clearly and consistently shows that orthographic depth has a major influence on reading acquisition.

EARLY PREDICTION OF READING DEVELOPMENT BY PHONOLOGICAL TASKS

Research on reading development in English has identified early phonological skills as a strong predictor of later reading development (for reviews see Catts, 1991; Goswami & Bryant, 1990; Pennington, 1991). The theoretical connection between phonological skills and reading development is that alphabetic orthographies represent the phonological units of speech; therefore phonological skills are necessary for understanding the alphabetic principle that the segments of written language, the graphemes, stand for segments of spoken language, that is, phonemes. What do we know about early prediction in orthographies other than English? Does orthographic consistency make a difference to the relevance of early phonological skills? On the one hand, empirical evidence shows that early reading in consistent orthographies is more strongly based on phonological decoding than in English. This could mean that young readers in consistent orthographies are even more dependent on a good understanding of the phonological segments of their language. On the other hand, consistent orthographies provide a much clearer and more systematic representation of the underlying phonological structure than English. It could be that experience with such a consistent representational system in combination with an instructional scheme that is based on GPCs and blending and segmenting of phonemes helps even children with early phonological deficits to improve their phonological skills to a sufficient level to cope with the requirements of reading acquisition. This would mean that differences in phonological skills would be equalized when formal reading instruction comes in and are less predictive for later reading skills than in the inconsistent orthography of English.

Interestingly, only limited evidence on early prediction is available for non-English orthographies. Elbro, Borstrom, and Petersen (1998) report strong prediction of early phonological skills for later reading acquisition in Danish; however, this is only further confirmation for the English findings as Danish is also a deep orthography. Several studies on reading acquisition in Dutch, a consistent orthography, show that preschool phonological skills are predictive in the early phases of reading acquisition, but cease to show a relevant influence after first grade (Bast & Reitsma, 1998; de Jong & van der Leij, 2002; Wesseling & Reitsma, 2000).

Once again, German provides an interesting test case, not only because of the already discussed similarities in language structure and dissimilarities in orthographic consistency, but also because of differences in ideology of preschool education. While in the English context, reading preparation is provided as early as possible and children most often learn the letters in kindergarten or nursery school, the German and Austrian kindergarten system does not provide any letter training at all and, in general, hardly any preparation for the requirements of reading acquisition is given. The philosophy is that learning to read and spell is children's main task in primary school and should not start earlier. Thus one of the main methodological problems with English prediction studies, that the early prediction of phonological skills might in fact be explained by early differences in letter knowledge and reading skills, can be easily ruled out for German.

The differences in early reading preparation became clearly evident in a direct comparison of the relationship of phonological awareness and reading acquisition of U.S. children acquiring English orthography and Austrian children acquiring German orthography (Mann & Wimmer, 2002). Children at the end of kindergarten, Grade 1, and Grade 2 were given tests of phoneme identification ("Which nonword starts like *fish*: *nalo* or *falo*?"), phoneme deletion ("Say *fire* without the first sound"), rapid automatized naming (RAN colors), letter identification, and short tests of word and nonword reading. All items were as similar as possible in the two languages and the two language groups were comparable with respect to age and verbal short-term memory (WISC-III digit span). It turned out that the U.S. kindergarten children already had very good letter knowledge (94% correct) and could identify about half of the presented simple words and nonwords. Not surprisingly, they also showed good phoneme awareness, with 92% correct responses on phoneme identification and 48% correct on phoneme deletion. This was completely different from performance of the Austrian kindergarten children who—as a consequence of the nonexistent reading preparation—knew less than 30% of the presented letters and were nonreaders throughout. Their performance on the phoneme identification task was close to chance level (69% correct), and they had a hard time segmenting the first sound from the rest of the word in the phoneme deletion test (17.5% correct). However, this lack of phonological awareness before the onset of formal reading instruction did not do them any harm. The first and second graders in both languages were at ceiling on both phoneme awareness measures. The two groups were also comparable with respect to accuracy and fluency of word recognition, and for nonwords, the German sample even outperformed the U.S. children.

Mann and Wimmer entered phonological awareness, RAN, and WISC III digit span as predictors into regression analyses for reading accuracy and speed. It turned out that these measures accounted for a greater amount of variance among the U.S. than the Austrian children both for accuracy (70% vs. 27%) and for speed (49% vs. 29%). The only single predictor that entered the analyses for the U.S. children was phonological awareness both for accuracy and for speed. For the Austrian children, no single predictor entered the analysis for reading accuracy and the only reliable single predictor for reading speed was RAN. These differences between early prediction of reading in English and German are in line with the theoretical view that phonological skills might be easier to acquire in German and might therefore not discriminate between good and poor readers as well as it has been shown for English.

DEVELOPMENTAL DYSLEXIA

Direct comparisons of developmental dyslexia in two languages / orthographies are even more difficult and problematic than direct comparisons of normal reading development because, in addition to all the methodological aspects already discussed (differences in phonological and orthographic structure, method of reading instruction, age of onset of formal reading instruction, cultural background), one further critical aspect needs to be considered, that is, how dyslexia is defined. According to ICD-10 Classification of Mental and Behavioural Disorders of the World Health Organization (1992) specific reading difficulties should be diagnosed when there is a serious and specific delay in reading skills assessed by a standardized reading test. English reading tests usually assess accuracy of word recognition by presenting children with word lists with increasing difficulty and determining how many of the words can be read correctly. Reading speed is often not even assessed (Compton & Carlisle, 1994). Because of the generally high reading accuracy in consistent orthographies, this procedure cannot be used. The main diagnostic criterion therefore is usually reading speed.

In a direct comparison of 12-year-old dyslexic children in England and Austria (Landerl, Wimmer, & Frith, 1997) we selected 18 children who had persistent reading problems and showed a serious delay of about 4 years in reading development in each orthography measured by standardized reading tests in each language. These two groups were presented with one-, two-, and three-syllable words that were highly comparable in the two languages, that is, they had identical meaning and were similar with respect to orthography and pronunciation (e.g., *hand–Hand, summer–Sommer, discussion–Diskussion*). From each of the presented words a nonword was derived by exchanging the onsets of the one- and two-syllable words and by rearranging the syllables of the three-syllable words. Thus it was ensured that the nonwords were also highly comparable across the two orthographies (e.g., *hoat–Hoot, sutter–Sutter, ralective–Ralektiv*) and that they did not include any orthographic or phonological segments that did not occur in that language.

In correspondence with the findings of normal reading acquisition, a remarkable difference between the two dyslexic language groups was observed. Whereas the 12-year old German dyslexic children read both words and nonwords with high accuracy and had less than 25% errors even for the most difficult condition of three-syllable nonwords, the English group showed marked accuracy problems. As a matter of fact, their reading accuracy for the easiest condition, the one-syllable words was lower (about 30% errors) than that of the German group for the three-syllable nonwords. The English dyslexic children showed a marked length effect with about 50% errors on the three-syllable words and about 70% errors on the three-syllable nonwords. Another interesting finding was that the English dyslexic children showed a specific nonword-reading deficit (Rack, Snowling, & Olson, 1992), that is, their nonword-reading accuracy for one- and two-syllable items was lower than that of a group of English 8-year-old children who showed the same word-reading accuracy. This shows that phonological decoding is a specific problem of English dyslexic readers that is assumed to be a direct reflection of the phonological deficit underlying their reading problems. Because of the generally high accuracy of German dyslexic readers, such a specific nonword-reading deficit was not evident with respect to accuracy, even though it was found for reading speed. The German dyslexic children read one- and two-syllable nonwords reliably slower than a group of 8-year-old children with typical reading development who were matched on reading speed for words. Thus it seemed that although the German dyslexic children learned to carry out the phonological decoding procedure with high accuracy, the fluency of this process was still not adequate. The nonword-reading fluency deficit of German dyslexic children was confirmed by Wimmer (1996).

With respect to speed of response, the German dyslexic group also outperformed the English dyslexic group. However, their reading fluency was clearly deficient in comparison with that of typical German readers. On average, it took these 12-year-old children about 2 s to work out the correct pronunciation of familiar three-syllable words and almost 3 s to work out the pronunciation of three-syllable nonwords. Obviously this puts them at a serious disadvantage in an orthography in which verbs and compound nouns frequently consist of three or more syllables.

Ziegler, Perry, Ma-Wyatt, Ladner, and Schulte-Körne (2003) recently reported a similar comparison of 10-year-old Australian and German dyslexic children. Both English- and German-speaking dyslexic readers showed a lag of about 3 years in their reading development on standardized reading tests. Children were presented with highly similar one-syllable words and nonwords consisting of three to six letters. Ziegler et al. replicated the finding of a clear advantage of the German-speaking sample with respect to reading accuracy as well as reading speed. Both groups of dyslexic children showed a serious deficit in reading speed, not only compared with that of typical readers of the same age but also compared with that of the reading level control groups, and for both groups this reading speed deficit was more marked for nonwords than for words. Surprisingly though, Ziegler et al. did not find a nonword-reading deficit for the English-speaking children with respect to accuracy that, as previously outlined, is now generally seen as a characteristic feature of dyslexia in English, indicating specific difficulties with phonological decoding (see Rack et al., 1992). It is possible that the English-speaking children in the Ziegler et al. study did not have serious disability—which would mean that in that study the differences between English and German dyslexic readers might have been underestimated.

DIFFERENT ORTHOGRAPHIES—SAME BRAIN MECHANISMS

The survey of research looking at reading acquisition in two or more orthographies clearly shows that orthographies with high consistency of GPCs are easier to acquire than orthographies with low consistency. Even the problems of dyslexic children seem to be less marked in consistent than in inconsistent orthographies. Does that mean that reading in different orthographies is based on different neurocognitive mechanisms? This was one of the research questions raised by a seminal brain-imaging project (Paulesu et al., 2000, 2001). Paulesu and colleagues compared the brain regions involved in word and nonword reading in Italian and English adults. Italian has a highly consistent orthographic system. Overall, the brain activations of the two language groups were highly similar, suggesting that (not surprisingly) readers of alphabetic orthographies use the same neurocognitive systems. However, Paulesu et al. (2000) could observe a reflection of different reading strategies in Italian and English readers in their brain activation: During reading, Italian readers showed greater activation in brain regions, which have been associated with processing phonemes, whereas English readers had greater activation in areas that have been associated with word retrieval during both reading and naming tasks. Obviously this small but significant difference in brain activation is well in correspondence with the behavioral studies showing that readers of consistent orthographies rely more strongly on decoding whereas readers of the inconsistent English orthography seem to rely more on direct recognition.

In a second study, Paulesu and colleagues also compared brain activation in dyslexic readers in the two orthographies (Paulesu et al., 2001). Here the finding was different: Italian and

English dyslexic readers did not show any differences in normal brain activation, but both showed lower activation in certain left hemispheric areas than did the typical readers. These findings suggest that competent readers are able to adapt to certain subtle characteristics of their orthography; however, they also allow the fascinating speculation that dyslexic readers are not able to do so. In other words, whereas typical readers to some extent tune in to the orthography they acquire, dyslexic readers do not. The other conclusion from this brain-imaging project is that, despite all orthographic differences outlined and discussed in this chapter, the neurological basis of reading and dyslexia is probably the same in all alphabetic orthographies.

ACKNOWLEDGEMENT

The author is currently supported by an APART grant of the Austrian Academy of Science.

REFERENCES

Aro, M., & Wimmer, H. (2003). Learning to read: English in comparison to six more regular orthographies. *Applied Psycholinguistics, 24*, 621–635.

Bast, J., & Reitsma, P. (1998). Analyzing the development of individual differences in terms of Matthew effects in reading: Results from a Dutch longitudinal study. *Developmental Psychology, 34*, 1373–1399.

Besner, D., & Davelaar, E. (1983). Suedohomofoan effects in visual word recognition: Evidence for phonological processing. *Canadian Journal of Psychology, 37*, 300–305.

Borowsky, R., & Masson, M. E. J. (1999). Frequency effects and lexical access: On the interpretation of null pseudohomophone base-word frequency effects. *Journal of Experimental Psychology: Human Perception and Performance, 25*, 270–275.

Catts, H. W. (1991). Phonological processing deficits and reading disability. In A. G. Kamhi & H. W. Catts (Eds.), *Reading disabilities: A developmental language perspective* (pp. 67–132). Boston: Allyn & Bacon.

Compton, D. L., & Carlisle, J. F. (1994). Speed of word recognition as a distinguishing characteristic of reading disabilities. *Educational Psychology Review, 6*, 115–139.

de Groot, A. M. B., & Nas, L. J. N. (1991). Lexical representations of cognates and noncognates in compound bilinguals. *Journal of Memory and Language, 30*, 90–123.

de Jong, P. F., & van der Leij, A. (2002). Effects of phonological abilities and linguistic comprehension on the development of reading. *Scientific Studies of Reading, 6*, 51–77.

Elbro, C., Borstrom, I., & Petersen, D. K. (1998). Predicting dyslexia from kindergarten: The importance of distinctness of phonological representation of lexical items. *Reading Research Quarterly, 33*, 36–60.

Ellis, N., & Hooper, A. M. (2001). It is easier to learn to read in Welsh than in English: Effects of orthographic transparency demonstrated using frequency-matched cross-linguistic reading tests. *Applied Psycholinguistics, 22*, 571–599.

Frith, U., Wimmer, H., & Landerl, K. (1998). Differences in phonological recoding in German- and English-speaking children. *Scientific Studies of Reading, 2*, 31–54.

Goswami, U. (2002). Phonology, reading development, and dyslexia: A cross-linguistic perspective. *Annals of Dyslexia, 52*, 141–163.

Goswami, U., & Bryant, P. (1990). *Phonological skills and learning to read.* Hove, UK: Lawrence Erlbaum Assocites.

Goswami, U., Gombert, J. E., & de Barrera, F. L. (1998). Children's orthographic representations and linguistic transparency: Nonsense word reading in English, French, and Spanish. *Applied Psycholinguistics, 19*, 19–52.

Goswami, U., Porpodas, C., & Wheelwright, S. (1997). Children's orthographic representations in English and Greek. *European Journal of Psychology of Education, 12*, 273–292.

Goswami, U., Ziegler, J., Dalton, L., & Schneider, W. (2001). Pseudohomophone effects and phonological recoding procedures in reading development in English and German. *Journal of Memory and Language, 45*, 648–664.

Hoxhallari, L., van Daal, V., & Ellis, N. C. (2004). Learning to read words in Albanian: A skill easily acquired. *Scientific Studies of Reading, 8*, 153–166.

Katz, L., & Frost, R. (1992). The reading process is different for different orthographies: The orthographic depth hyposthesis. In R. Frost & L. Katz (Ed.), *Orthography, phonology, morphology, and meaning* (pp. 45–66). Amsterdam: Elsevier.

Landerl, K. (2000). Influences of orthographic consistency and reading instruction on the development of nonword reading skills. *European Journal of Psychology of Education, 15*, 239–257.

Landerl, K., & Thaler, V. (2005). Reading and Spelling acquisition and Dyslexia in German: In M. Joshi & P. G. Aaron (Eds.), *Handbook of Orthography and Literacy* (pp. 121–134). Mahwah, NJ: Lawrence Erlbaum Associates.

Landerl, K., Wimmer, H., & Frith, U. (1997). The impact of orthographic consistency on dyslexia: A German–English comparison. *Cognition, 63*, 315–334.

Liberman, I. Y., Liberman, A. M., Mattingly, I. G., & Shankweiler, D. L. (1980). Orthography and the beginning reader. In J. F. Kavannagh & R. L. Venezky (Eds.), *Orthography, reading and dyslexia* (pp. 137–153). Baltimore, MD: University Park Press.

Mann, V., & Wimmer, H. (2002). Phoneme awareness and pathways into literacy: A comparison of German and American children. *Reading and Writing, 17*, 653–682.

Oney, B., & Goldman, S. R. (1984). Decoding and comprehension skills in Turkish and English: Effects of the regularity of grapheme-phoneme correspondences. *Journal of Educational Psychology, 76*, 447–568.

Pennington, B. F. (1991). *Diagnosing learning disorders: A neuropsychological framework*. New York: Guilford.

Paulesu, E., Démonet, J. F., Fazio, F., McCrory, E., Chanoine, V., Brunswick, N., Cappa, S. F., Cossu, G., Habib, M., Frith, C. D., & Frith, U. (2001). Dyslexia: Cultural diversity and biological unity. *Science, 291*, 2165–2167.

Paulesu, E., McCrory, E., Fazio, F., Menoncello, L., Brunswick, N., Cappa, S. F., Cotelli, M., Cossu, G., Corte, F., Lorusso, M., Pesenti, S., Gallagher, A., Perani, D., Price, C., Frith, C. D., & Frith, U. (2000). A cultural effect on brain function. *Nature Neuroscience, 3*, 91–96.

Rack, J. P., Snowling, M. J., & Olson, R. K. (1992). The nonword reading deficit in developmental dyslexia. *Reading Research Quarterly, 27*, 29–53.

Seymour, P. H. K., Aro, M., & Erskine, J. M. (2003). Foundation literacy acquisition in European orthographies. *British Journal of Psychology, 94*, 143–174.

Share, D. L. (1995). Phonological recoding and self-teaching: Sine qua non of reading acquisition. *Cognition, 55*, 151–218.

Thorstad, G. (1991). The effect of orthography on the acquisition of literacy skills. *British Journal of Psychology, 82*, 527–537.

Twain, M. (1880). *A tramp abroad*. Hartford, CT: American Publishing Company.

Wesseling, R., & Reitsma, P. (2000). The transient role of explicit phonological recoding for reading acquisition. *Reading and Writing, 13*, 313–336.

Wimmer, H. (1996). The early manifestation of developmental dyslexia: Evidence from German children. *Reading and Writing, 8*, 171–188.

Wimmer, H., & Goswami, U. (1994). The influence of orthographic consistency on reading development: Word recognition in English and German children. *Cognition, 51*, 91–103.

World Health Organization. (1992). The ICD-10 classification of mental and behavioural disorders (10th ed.). Geneva, Switzerland: Author.

Ziegler, J. C., Perry, C., Ma-Wyatt, A., Ladner, D., & Schulte-Körne, G. (2003). Developmental dyslexia in different languages: language-specific or universal? *Journal of Experimental Child Psychology, 86*, 169–193.

32

Learning to Read: The Effect of Orthography

Mikko Aro
University of Jyväskylä and Niilo Mäki Institute

Recent cross-language studies have suggested that the rate of reading acquisition differs in different alphabetic orthographies. These cross-language differences are usually interpreted to reflect variation in orthographic depth, the complexity of the grapheme–phoneme correspondence system. This chapter discusses the cross-language findings, with a specific focus on two recent studies that investigated reading acquisition in several alphabetic orthographies and two studies that examined literacy acquisition in Finnish. It is noteworthy that Finnish is one of the most transparent alphabetic orthographies. The main conclusion from the cross-language studies is that the development of literacy skills in English deviates from the majority of alphabetic orthographies. It is argued that the observed differences in early literacy development are not only quantitative, but also qualitative. This view is further supported by the observations concerning early reading development in Finnish. In summary, the research findings give consistent support for the orthographic depth hypothesis and stress the need for a revision of English-based characterisation of reading development.

INTRODUCTION

The most important models of alphabetic literacy acquisition are presented as general models of learning to read in alphabetic orthographies. The models are, however, typically based on research concerning the acquisition of a single orthography, that of English. This bias is, of course, not the fault of the scholars working in the English-speaking countries, where cognitive psycholinguistics and research in reading acquisition have a long and fine tradition. However, it reflects the fact that the question of orthographic differences in reading acquisition in alphabetic orthographies has been out of the focus of research, and when the question has been addressed, the implicit assumption has been that the non-English findings are somehow less universal than the findings concerning the English orthography.

The purpose of this chapter is to discuss reading acquisition from a cross-linguistic point of view. A specific focus is on Finnish orthography, which lies at one end of the orthographic depth continuum, with English occupying the other end. First, the features of orthographies that are suggested to have an effect on literacy development are briefly described. After a short review of findings concerning literacy development across alphabetic orthographies, a series of four studies that examined orthography effects in literacy acquisition and literacy development in highly transparent Finnish are summarised and discussed. These studies add to the accumulating body of evidence that emphasises the need for a revision of English-based models of reading acquisition and calls for more concentrated research efforts on the language-related aspects of literacy development.

Recent research findings, which suggest there is considerable variation in the rate of reading acquisition among orthographies and that this variation is related to the so-called orthographic depth (transparency, regularity, consistency), have drawn the increased attention of scholars. The relative lack of research addressing the question as to whether the findings can be generalised across orthographies is somewhat surprising, as the knowledge that irregular orthographies pose problems for the learner is not new. The very same problems of reading acquisition in English, which are discussed in this chapter, were the reason for experimenting in the 1960s with the Initial Teaching Alphabet (ITA). In the ITA each phoneme of the English language is consistently represented with one grapheme. As Adams (1990, p. 256) noted, the advantage of ITA as compared with traditional English orthography in beginning reading instruction was demonstrated under a variety of circumstances. Furthermore, the ITA advantage persisted at least through the fifth grade. Downing (1964, pp. 11–14) lists a multitude of even earlier attempts to provide beginners with a more simple and more consistent writing system for learning to read English. The earliest such efforts date back to the 17th century.

Although the question of differences between alphabetic orthographies has not received much attention in the field of reading acquisition, it has attracted more interest in studies of skilled reading and lexical access. The question was first introduced into reading research as a result of findings concerning word-recognition processes in Serbo-Croatian and English (Feldman & Turvey, 1983; Katz & Feldman, 1983; Lukatela, Popadic, Ognjenovic, & Turvey, 1980). The studies revealed that, in Serbo-Croatian, word-recognition processes were biased towards phonemic coding, whereas in English, the orthographic processes were more important. The resulting 'orthographic depth hypothesis', as formulated by Frost, Katz, and Bentin (1987), asserted that '. . . lexical word recognition in shallow orthographies is mediated primarily by phonemic cues generated prelexically by grapheme-to-phoneme translation. In contrast, lexical access for word recognition in a deep orthography relies strongly on orthographic cues, whereas phonology is derived from internal lexicon.' The later formulations of this hypothesis are less stringent in labelling the core processes 'orthographic' or 'phonological' according to the depth of the writing system, as phonological processing has also been shown to be involved in word recognition in deep orthographies (Lukatela & Turvey, 1999). Ziegler, Perry, Jacobs, and Braun (2001) have suggested that the main difference between word recognition in deep and shallow orthographies relates to the varying sizes of the processing units that are necessary for successful decoding, and the varying need to switch between different 'grain-size' levels.

From the point of view of reading acquisition, the orthographic depth hypothesis implies several further hypotheses. Because the grapheme–phoneme correspondences are simple and straightforward in shallow orthographies, the development of phonological recoding—the ability to build word pronunciation on the basis of grapheme–phoneme correspondences—should be rapid. The mastery of phonemic assembly, which is based on grapheme–phoneme correspondences, is sufficient for accurate word recognition. In deep orthographies, grapheme–phoneme correspondences are complex and irregular, and the beginning reader has to supplement (and replace) grapheme–phoneme conversion strategies with recognition of units such as rime and whole word (Ziegler et al., 2001). Therefore the learning process should be more protracted.

ALL ORTHOGRAPHIES ARE BASED ON PHONETIC ASPECTS OF LANGUAGE

Different writing systems (orthographies) can be classified according to the levels of linguistic information that is coded in the script. DeFrancis (1989) points out that all writing systems are based on phonetic aspects of language. This is the case even with Chinese, which is commonly perceived as a script consisting of only semantic coding and is often mislabelled as 'pictographic', 'logographic', or 'ideographic'. He presents a classification system that is based on, first, whether the phonetic components are represented with graphic or alphabetic symbols; second, whether written symbols represent syllables, consonant sounds, or all phonemes of the language; and third, whether the orthographic code also includes non-phonetic clues such as morphological information. The classification according to DeFrancis is given in Table 32.1.

It is worth noting that the classification just described is one of many, and the categories are not discrete. Nevertheless, it accentuates the facts that all orthographies share a phonetic base and that, inside each of the three representational levels (syllabic, consonantal, and alphabetic), orthographies can be classified according to whether morphological information is coded into script or whether the orthography is 'purely' phonetic. This is also the case with alphabetic orthographies. The orthographies that are 'purely' phonetic have consistent grapheme–phoneme correspondences. English is an example of a language in which morphological information is also coded in spelling. This creates inconsistency in grapheme–phoneme correspondences. There are also other alphabetic orthographies that share a similar morphophonemic nature, including Danish, which also has a reputation of poor fit between spelling and sound. Whereas these two orthographies are symmetrical, that is, irregular in both the spelling–to–sound and sound–to–spelling directions, some orthographies are asymmetrical. French is relatively regular from the perspective of reading, whereas it is less so from the point of view of spelling. The same can also be said about German. The Romanic languages are generally thought of as being relatively regular and symmetrical. At present, there exists no common measure for quantifying the transparency of an orthography, although the calculations made for a few orthographies have been published. On the spelling body–rime level, 31% of English monosyllabic words are inconsistent (Ziegler, Stone, & Jacobs, 1997); the corresponding figure for French is 12% (Ziegler, Jacobs, & Stone, 1996). It should be noted that the preceding figures are not calculated

TABLE 32.1

Classification of Orthographies and Examples of Orthographies Falling in These Categories According to DeFrancis (1989)

Graphic Symbols		Alphabetic Symbols			
Syllabic		Consonantal		Alphabetic	
'Phonetic'	'Meaning + Phonetic'	'Phonetic'	'Meaning + Phonetic'	'Phonetic'	'Meaning + Phonetic'
Japanese	Chinese	Phoenician	Egyptian	Greek	Korean
Yi	Mayan	Hebrew		Latin	English
	Sumerian	Arabic		Finnish	

on the basis of grapheme–phoneme correspondences, in which the inconsistencies supposedly are much more frequent.

Because objective measures of consistency are lacking, the term 'regular orthography' has been used somewhat loosely. The 'transparency' of orthographies can best be thought of as a continuum. Within this framework, we know with much certainty that English is one of the most irregular alphabetic orthographies, and Finnish is one of the most regular.

THE OPPOSITES OF THE ORTHOGRAPHIC DEPTH CONTINUUM: ENGLISH AND FINNISH

English is an example of an orthography in which the written script does not fully represent the phonemic structure of spoken language. According to Ehri et al. (2001, p. 253), there are 'about 41' phonemes in English; in the ITA there are 44 characters with a distinct corresponding phoneme (Downing, 1964, p. 15). The number of graphemes is much higher, and many graphemes consist of multiple letters. A phoneme can be marked with a variety of graphemes, depending on the context, and vice versa.

DeFrancis (1989, pp. 201–208) lists a number of factors behind the complex correspondence of spoken and written English. More than half of the words of the present-day English vocabulary are of foreign origin, mostly from Latin or French. Often, the spelling and pronunciation of the loan words were preserved in English. The historical changes of pronunciation in French have resulted in loan words with differing pronunciations in English depending on the time they were borrowed (*chant–chiffon*). One major factor resulting in a gulf between spoken and written language has been the lack of standardisation of the spelling until the middle of the 18th century. Until that time, there was great variation among writers in the spellings of particular words. With the publication of the first dictionary, 'the chaos began to be systematized—not ended, merely codified', as DeFrancis (1989, p. 203) states. In the creation of the dictionary, a principle of preserving historical spellings prevailed. Thus the spellings of the words often reflect their etymology at the expense of pronunciation (e.g., *debt–debitus* [lat.]).

Another feature that affects the inconsistency of spoken and written English relates to the marking of morphemic components. The English spelling system is often characterised as morphophonemic. Whereas the spelling of roots in English is basically phonemic—although in a complicated manner—the spelling of derivatives and compounds tends to be morphemic (Venezky, 1970). The established graphemic form of the base is retained as much as possible, regardless of the phonemic alterations. Thus, in words like 'nation' and 'nationality', the spelling of the root is similar, despite different pronunciations. As another example of this morphophonemic spelling, the regular past-tense ending is spelled -*ed*, although it has three different pronunciations. DeFrancis (1989, p. 207) notes that unique spellings for a considerable number of homophones (e.g., 'sight', 'site', and 'cite') are another reflection of the morphophonemic nature of English orthography.

Whereas English is an example of a morphophonemic alphabetic orthography, Finnish is an example of an almost purely phonemic alphabetic orthography. The grapheme–phoneme correspondences are regular and symmetrical, and the morphophonemic features are few. The number of phonemes is relatively small, and each phoneme is marked with a corresponding single letter, with one exception. (For a more detailed description see Lyytinen, Aro, & Holopainen, 2004; see also Lyytinen et al., in this volume).

The number of standard Finnish consonant phonemes is 13 (/p/, /t/, /k/, /m/, /n/, /l/, /r/, /s/, /h/, /j/, /v/, /d/, and /ŋ/), and the number of vowel phonemes is 8 (/i/, /e/, /ä/, /y/, /ö/, /u/, /o/, and /a/). There are three additional consonant sounds, which are used in recent loan words only (/b/, /g/, and /f/). Each phoneme is marked with the corresponding single letter, except the phoneme /ŋ/, which is marked with the letter *n* when short (in letter combination *nk*) and with the digraph *ng* when long. All phonemes can have two phonemic quantities, long and short, with the exception of /d/, /h/, /j/, and /v/. The long quantity is consistently marked by the doubling of the corresponding letter. With knowledge of the basic letter–sound correspondences and phonemic assembly skill, a reader is able to decode practically any Finnish word or pseudoword.

There are 10 syllable types: CV, CVC, CVV, CVVC, VC, V, VV, CVCC, VVC, and VCC. The longest syllable consists of four phonemes. A syllable—and consequently a word—never begins with a consonant cluster. However, some loan words can have initial clusters. Consonant clusters can appear at the end of the syllables, but never at the end of the word. The syllables are perceptually salient units of the spoken language because the main stress in Finnish is placed on the first syllable and the secondary stress on every second syllable thereafter. In the initial reading materials, the syllables are explicitly marked in the texts and syllabic segmentation is a central feature of early reading and spelling instruction.

Most Finnish words are polysyllabic. The words tend to be long because of highly productive compounding, a rich derivational system, and agglutinative morphology. Whereas Finnish orthography is transparent, the Finnish morphology is complicated and opaque. With different combinations of case (15), plural markers, and a variety of clitics, any noun can have over 2,000 orthographic forms, of which 150 are so-called core forms (Niemi, Laine, & Tuominen, 1994; for an example, see Karlsson, 1996). For Finnish verbs, this figure is even higher. A verb can have 12,000–18,000 forms, when the inflections for tense, mood, and person, and cliticisation are included (Niemi et al., 1994). When derivation and highly productive compounding are taken into account, the number of lexical environments in which a typical Finnish root can exist is vast. Because affixation often affects the stem (e.g., *lammas–lampaan*) the Finnish morphological system is best described as agglutinative–fusional. It should be noted that, irrespective of the morphological complexity of the word, the spelling is consistent with the pronunciation.

From the perspective of literacy acquisition, the Finnish orthography is in many ways optimal. The grapheme–phoneme correspondence system is perfectly regular, and the number of phonemes is small. Thus the number of correspondence rules required for phonological recoding is very small. Because the graphemes are single letters, the written words explicate the otherwise abstract phonemic structure of the words for the reader. Consonant clusters are rare, and the phonemic structure of syllables is simple. These factors should be beneficial for learning to read, as they allow a systematic use of left–to–right phonological recoding, basically at the level of single letters, without the need for complex graphemic parsing. From another point of view, the effectiveness of logographic/orthographic strategies in word recognition is severely handicapped by the previously mentioned features of Finnish morphology. The ability to recognise roots does not suffice, as words are usually inflected and these inflections can also affect the root.

The challenges posed by the Finnish orthography relate to the length of the words and the coding of phonemic length, which, in the case of stop consonants, does not perfectly match the spoken language. It is also worthy of note that the few morphophonological instances of the Finnish orthography that violate the consistency of spelling are also related to phonemic length.

THE MODELS OF READING ACQUISITION
AND THE CROSS-LINGUISTIC FINDINGS

Almost all English-based models of reading acquisition have in common the idea of dual processing routes for word recognition: one route based on the phonological process of letter–sound translation and the other based on sight word recognition. Different models suggest a somewhat differing developmental sequence for these processes. Some models have described a preliminary process of visual word recognition, which is followed by the letter–sound translation processes (Frith, 1985; Gough & Hillinger, 1980). The model put forward by Seymour (e.g., 1997, 1999) described these two processes as parallel, with both required for further orthographic development. Ehri (1992) proposed an integrative theory, in which an interactive relation of these processes is postulated: letter–sound knowledge and partial phonological cues form the basis for visual word-recognition skills.

Consequently this common assumption of dual processing skills as necessary for reading acquisition has led to models of impaired reading acquisition that describe different types of reading problems, depending on which of the two skills is most affected. This distinction has traditionally been reflected in numerous sub-type models of reading disabilities (e.g., Boder, 1973; Lovett, 1987), as well as in the contrast between 'phonological dyslexia' (disorder of grapheme–phoneme translation) and 'surface dyslexia' (disorder of word–specific lexical processing) (e.g., Ellis, 1985). Lately, connectionist approaches have resulted in computational models of word recognition that seem to model well both typical word-recognition skills and the dyslexic performance. These models contradict the item–specific mechanisms postulated in the previously mentioned dual processing models, and suggest that the cognitive system adheres to certain probabilistic principles of computation for implicit learning in quasi-regular domains, such as English orthography (e.g., Plaut, McClelland, Seidenberg, & Patterson, 1996).

Despite the previously described dissociation of the sub-lexical and lexical processes in early reading development in English, there is currently a common consensus that phonological processing skills are the most important skills for reading development. In an extensive review of findings concerning reading acquisition, Share (1995) states that the quintessential problem (*sine qua non*) of reading acquisition is phonological recoding, the ability to independently generate pronunciations for novel orthographic strings. According to this 'self–teaching hypothesis', phonological recoding has a primary role in reading acquisition, and the orthographic or visual-based skills serve a secondary role: The orthographic lexicon develops with increasing reading experience and 'self-teaching'. Phonological recoding is based on the application of grapheme–phoneme correspondence rules and analogical mechanisms and is the basis for the development of orthographic knowledge (Share, 1995). The benchmark measure of phonological recoding skill is, naturally, the pseudoword-reading task. Goswami and Bryant (1990) claimed that onset- and rime-level correspondences, in particular, are central to early reading development. Currently there is an ongoing debate on the question as to whether reading acquisition in English is based primarily on small-unit (phoneme) or large-unit (onsets and rimes) correspondences (see Bryant, 2002; Hulme et al., 2002; Goswami, 2002a).

Most cross-linguistic comparisons of reading acquisition have been pairwise comparisons of English and a supposedly more regular orthography. One of the earliest studies of this kind was carried out by Öney and Goldman (1984). They compared the pseudoword-reading skills of Turkish and American children in first and third grades. The results showed that the Turkish children were more accurate and also faster than the American children in the first grade, accuracy being 94% and 59%, respectively. In the third grade, both groups reached the ceiling, but the Turkish children were still more fluent than American children. Other studies have reported similar differences also in word-recognition skills between Turkish- and English-speaking children (Durgunoğlu & Öney, 1999; Öney, Peter, & Katz, 1997).

Since the study by Öney and Goldman (1984), a number of comparisons have shown a similar difference in phonological recoding skills between English children and children acquiring literacy skills in other orthographies. Most of these studies concern German–English comparisons, and, overall, they show that German-speaking children have better phonological recoding skills than English children. Wimmer and Goswami (1994) reported a clear advantage for German children up till the fourth grade. In her replication, Landerl (2000) showed that the performance of the English children was better with phonics instruction, but still the German children outperformed the English children in first and second grades. Goswami, Ziegler, Dalton, and Schneider (2001) reported large differences in phonological recoding accuracy between German and English children up till the reading age of 9 years. Frith, Wimmer, and Landerl (1998) reported similar differences up until Grade 4, even in sub-samples of children who had good word-recognition skills. A similar difference in phonological recoding has also been reported in a comparison of the pseudoword-reading skills of German and American children in Grades 1 and 2 (Näslund, 1999), and even between dyslexic German and English children with a comparable lag in their reading skills (Landerl, Wimmer, & Frith, 1997).

Reports concerning comparisons of English and other more regular orthographies are few, but the findings are consistent. Thorstad (1991) showed that Italian children outperformed English children in word recognition and spelling. Goswami, Porpodas, and Wheelwright (1997) reported a phonological recoding difference between Greek and English children up until a reading age of 9 years. A similar difference in early pseudoword-reading accuracy has also been reported between English and French and English and Spanish children (Goswami, Gombert, & de Barrera, 1998), as well as English and Welsh children (Spencer & Hanley, 2003).

As Landerl (2000) notes, there is not a single empirical study that shows the reverse finding that English children are better in phonological recoding than children who use any other alphabetic orthography. The same conclusion can be drawn from studies that examined the development of pseudoword-reading skills in a single orthography. The reported pseudoword-reading error rates of English first-grade children have been high, between 40% and 80% (Jorm, Share, MacLean, & Matthews, 1984; Juel, Griffith, & Gough, 1986; Seymour & Elder, 1986; Treiman, Goswami, & Bruck, 1990). These error rates show that the acquisition of efficient phonological recoding skills in English seems to take more than 1 year of reading instruction. Corresponding findings with Finnish, Turkish, Italian, Greek, German, Dutch, and Portuguese children, have shown error rates below 25% for first-grade children (Coenen, van Bon, & Schreuder, 1997; Cossu, Gugliotta, & Marshall, 1995; Holopainen, Ahonen, & Lyytinen, 2001; Öney & Durgunoğlu, 1997; Pinheiro, 1995; Porpodas, 1989, 1999; Wimmer & Hummer, 1990).

In the most regular alphabetic orthographies such as Finnish, Greek, Turkish, and Italian, phonological decoding development seems to be close to ceiling after 1 year of reading instruction (Cossu et al., 1995; Holopainen et al., 2001; Öney & Durgunoğlu, 1997; Porpodas, 1999). It seems clear that the development of phonological recoding skills takes place *during* the first grade. Therefore the few studies that have followed reading acquisition during the first grade are worthy of closer inspection.

Öney and Durgunoğlu (1997) followed the literacy development of a group of Turkish children during the first grade, with assessments in October, February, and May. Because both reading and spelling accuracy in word and pseudoword tasks were highly correlated (.92 to .72), they reported combined scores for both reading and spelling. The most striking finding was the rapid growth in word-reading and spelling skills. In October, the children's accuracy percentage in a reading task was 26%; in February it had increased to 72%; and in May it had reached almost the ceiling level, 93%. Correspondingly, spelling accuracy was 20% in October and 92% in May. The high correlations of word recognition and pseudoword reading and the ceiling level of both the reading and spelling tasks at the end of the school year were interpreted as reflecting the simplicity of the Turkish grapheme–phoneme correspondence system. Cossu (1999) reported a follow–up of Italian first graders with assessments of reading and spelling skills in October, January, March, and May. The results showed the steepest development in accuracy between October and January. By January, reading accuracy was already around 80% and spelling accuracy around 60%. In this study, the development of spelling lagged behind reading throughout the first year, and also a small but consistent lexicality effect in favour of words was seen. Holopainen et al. (2001) assessed the pseudoword-reading accuracy of Finnish first-grade children in January and May and reported accuracy percentages to be 73% and 88%, respectively.

These studies suggest that reading acquisition in Turkish, Italian, and Finnish proceeds at a completely different rate of growth from what has been reported in irregular orthographies, such as English. It is worthy of note that the development of word recognition, phonological recoding, and spelling go hand in hand in Turkish, which is, like Finnish, completely transparent and symmetrical at the level of single letters. The Italian data showed that spelling accuracy seemed to emerge later than reading accuracy. The difference persisted until the second grade in the study by Cossu et al. (1995). The authors interpreted this as reflecting the partial structural independence of these skills. Another possibility could be that context-specific grapheme–phoneme correspondences in Italian require more explicit rule-based knowledge in spelling than in reading, as the phonemic context affecting the correspondence is readily visible to a reader but not to a speller.

PREDICTORS OF READING ACQUISITION

The importance of phonological awareness as a central precursor for later developing reading skills is widely accepted (see Goswami & Bryant, 1990; Wagner & Torgesen, 1987, for reviews). In a quantitative meta-analysis of experimental training studies of phonological awareness, Bus and van IJzendoorn (1999) showed that phonological training reliably enhances both phonological and reading skills. They also concluded that gains produced by means of phonological training are more robust and consistent when phonological awareness and letter–sound correspondences are taught together, claiming that the letters may draw the child's attention to the sounds of spoken words and the visual symbols anchor the phonemes perceptually.

It is easy to understand why access to the phonemic levels of speech is necessary for literacy acquisition and especially for phonological recoding; in alphabetic orthographies, the speech sounds are coded into script at the phonemic level. However, the relationship between phonemic awareness and reading seems to be complex. The findings with adults who are considered illiterate seem to suggest that phonemic awareness is more a product than a prerequisite of alphabetic literacy (Lukatela, Carello, Shankweiler, & Liberman, 1995; Morais, Cary, Alegria, & Bertelson, 1979). This notion is supported by the findings that letter knowledge is highly correlated with phoneme awareness measures (Bowey, 1994; Johnston, Anderson, & Holligan, 1996; Lukatela et al., 1995).

Furthermore, the development of phoneme awareness seems to be more rapid in transparent orthographies than in English. The results from orthographies such as Italian, Turkish, Finnish, Norwegian, Greek, and German show that phonemic awareness is at ceiling level relatively soon after the beginning of reading instruction (Cossu, Shankweiler, Liberman, Katz, & Tola, 1988; Durgunoğlu & Öney, 1999; Høien, Lundberg, Stanovich, & Bjaalid, 1995; Holopainen, Ahonen & Lyytinen, 2003; Porpodas, 1999; Wimmer, Landerl, Linortner, & Hummer, 1991). In a comparison of phonemic awareness in German and American children, Mann and Wimmer (2002) showed that the level of phonemic awareness depends on literacy experience and literacy development. Their results support the view that phonemic awareness does not develop as a function of spontaneous linguistic restructuring as such, but more as a result of literacy exposure. From the cross-linguistic point of view, especially interesting are the findings that suggest that, in more transparent orthographies, phonological or phonemic awareness predicts the very early development of phonological recoding skills and that they do not seem to be very good predictors of reading problems (de Jong & van der Leij, 1999; Holopainen et al., 2001, 2003; Landerl & Wimmer, 2000; Öney & Durgunoğlu, 1997; Poskiparta, Niemi & Vauras, 1999; Wimmer, 1993; Wimmer et al., 1991). On the basis of these findings, it could be hypothesised that phonological awareness is associated with reading acquisition as long as reliable individual differences in reading accuracy exist. This could explain the somewhat contradictory results obtained for different orthographies. Another related factor causing differences might be the varying measures of reading outcome employed. In English studies, pure accuracy measures are often used, whereas, in more regular orthographies, the measures usually include reading speed. It is also worthy of note that relatively few prediction studies have paid any attention to children's literacy skills before school entry. This makes the interpretation of the results more complicated; phonological awareness could have been confounded with children's early literacy experience.

There is evidence to show that reading problems in more transparent orthographies are indicated by reading speed rather than by reading accuracy (e.g., Lundberg & Høien, 1990; Porpodas, 1999; Rodrigo & Jiménez, 1999; Wimmer, 1993; Wimmer, Mayringer, & Landerl, 1998; Yap & van der Leij, 1993; Zoccolotti et al., 1999). There is also evidence that suggests that the development of reading fluency is associated more with early rapid-naming skills than with early phonological awareness measures (Holopainen et al., 2003; Wimmer & Mayringer, 2002; Wimmer, Mayringer, & Landerl, 2000). Wolf, Bally, and Morris (1986) were the first to show that early differences in rapid-naming tasks were predictive of reading skills. Later, the predictive role of naming skills has been shown repeatedly, and rapid-naming skills have shown only modest correlations with phonological awareness measures (see Wolf & Bowers, 1999, for a review).

A SUMMARY OF FOUR STUDIES INVESTIGATING CROSS-LINGUISTIC DIFFERENCES IN READING ACQUISITION AND LITERACY DEVELOPMENT IN FINNISH

Two of the studies summarised here were cross–language comparisons of reading acquisition, in which the main interest was in the development of the phonological recoding skills of children learning to read in different orthographies. Aro and Wimmer (2003) reported a replication and extension of the comparative study by Wimmer and Goswami (1994). The aim was to see whether the original findings of the differences between English and German children can be generalised across other orthographies more regular than English. In the study reported by Seymour, Aro, and Erskine (2003), reading acquisition was compared in 13 different orthographies with varying orthographic depth. The aim was to assess whether orthographic depth already exerts effects from the very beginning of learning to read, with reference to the theoretical model of foundation literacy acquisition developed by Seymour (e.g., 1997, 1999). These cross-linguistic studies were carried out within the context of the COST A8 ('Learning Disorders as a Barrier to Human Development') network of European researchers. These studies would not have been possible without the collaboration of a number of researchers in the respective countries.

Two of the studies were follow-ups of the early literacy development of Finnish children. Aro et al. (1999) followed up the development of six Finnish nonreading children for a period of 13 months. The main research questions addressed the relation between emerging phonological abilities and reading skill and inter-individual variation in the development of these skills. Aro, Tolvanen, Poikkeus, and Lyytinen (2004) reported an intensive follow–up of Finnish children entering the first grade. The purpose of the study was to clarify the development of literacy skills during the first grade, and especially during the early months of reading instruction. Another goal was to investigate whether language-related skills measured at school entry could predict the developing literacy skills.

CROSS-LINGUISTIC STUDIES OF READING ACQUISITION

Aro & Wimmer (2003) applied the method developed by Wimmer and Goswami (1994) to an investigation of the reading skills of German-, English-, Dutch-, Spanish-, French-, Swedish-, and Finnish-speaking children in Grades 1–4. The aim was to see whether the original findings of pseudoword-reading accuracy differences between English and German children generalise across other orthographies more regular than English. The total sample consisted of 759 children. The ages of the language groups differed because of variation in school entry age in the participating countries. English and French children enter school at 5 years of age; Austrian (German), Spanish, and Dutch children at 6 years; and Finnish children (Finnish- and Swedish-speaking participants) at 7 years.

Three list-reading tasks were used: (a) numeral naming, (b) number-word reading, and (c) pseudoword reading. The pseudowords were constructed on the basis of the number words in each language. The errors in numeral naming and number-word-reading tasks were few. In the pseudoword-reading task, the attainment of high accuracy was a much more protracted process for English children than for the children reading more regular orthographies. At the end of Grade 1, the pseudoword-reading accuracy levels were around 85% for the German-, Dutch-, French-, Spanish-, and Finnish-speaking children and above 90% for Swedish-speaking children. The accuracy level of English children at that point was 50%, and they did not attain the high accuracy shown by Grade 1 children in other orthographies until Grade 4. The variance in the performance of English children was large. Out of the entire English group, 23% read less than half of the pseudowords correctly; only 3 of the 649 children in other orthographies matched this figure. The ratio of pseudoword-reading speed and numeral-naming speed was used as an index of recoding speed. It revealed that Finnish, Swedish, and Spanish children were generally the fastest in phonological recoding. The corresponding ratio of number-word-reading speed and numeral-naming speed showed that, for English, German, Dutch, and Spanish first graders, the reading of number words took twice the time of numeral naming, whereas the difference was much smaller for Swedish, French, and Finnish children. Between Grades 1 and 2, there was a rapid progress in number-word-reading speed in all orthographies. However, the larger standard deviations of English, German, and Dutch children reflected a more protracted development in the fluency of number-word reading.

The conclusion was that phonological recoding skill was easily acquired in all the alphabetic orthographies involved in the study, with the exception of English. This finding was interpreted to underline the need for a revision of English-based characterisations of reading development and challenge the notion of phonological recoding skill as a developmental hurdle that is generally difficult to surmount. Apparently, the difficulty of phonological recoding is specific to English, with its complex grapheme–phoneme relations. The problem may be further aggravated by instruction methods that do not explicitly introduce children to word recognition by means of phonemic assembly, and possibly also the young age of the English schoolchildren. The observed differences in reading speed were hypothesised to reflect various orthographic factors in addition to orthographic depth.

Seymour, Aro, and Erskine (2003) sought to extend the cross-linguistic comparisons to a wider range of European orthographies and to determine the stage in reading acquisition at which the effect of orthographic depth becomes evident. The number of orthographies involved was 13 (Finnish, Greek, Italian, Spanish, German, Norwegian, Icelandic, Portuguese, Dutch, Swedish, French, Danish, and English). The children were assessed close to the end of the first grade. For English, Danish, and French, children from Grade 2 were also included. The total sample size was 684 children, and the sample sizes of the first graders varied between 25 and 70 across orthographies. The theoretical context was provided by the foundation literacy framework developed by Seymour (e.g., 1997, 1999). This model proposes that reading is acquired in stages so that basic foundational components are established in Phase 1, and the complexities of orthographic and morphographic structure are internalised in Phases 2 and 3 (see Seymour, this volume). The foundation consists of a logographic process involved in the identification and storage of familiar words and an alphabetic process, which supports sequential decoding. Both of these processes are thought to be dependent on the availability of letter–sound knowledge.

Three types of list-reading tasks were used to assess (a) letter knowledge, (b) very familiar word identification, and (c) pseudoword reading. The constructed pseudowords shared a similar structure across languages.

All groups of children achieved good letter knowledge (90% or better) during the first school year. The variations observed in letter knowledge or in the speed of letter identification were not attributable to language differences. In familiar word reading, the variation between languages was related to orthographic depth. The accuracy of French, Portuguese, and Danish children was reduced in comparison with that of more regular orthographies. However, the most striking feature was the relative delay of English children, who, at the end of second grade, still showed clearly poorer familiar word-reading accuracy than did children reading more regular orthographies at the end of first grade. In nonword reading, the effects of orthographic depth paralleled those found for familiar word-reading. Further, the variability in the rate of progress in word and nonword reading was related to orthographic depth; the standard deviations in both accuracy and speed scores were greatly exaggerated, especially in English and Danish, but also in Portuguese and French samples. In pseudoword reading, a smaller effect of syllabic structure was also observed; the children whose language had simple syllable structures had a small advantage over children with languages with complex syllable structures in both pseudoword-reading accuracy and speed. It was also shown that the lexicality effect was smaller in languages with simple syllable structures.

The study demonstrated that the time required for establishing foundation literacy varies according to orthographic depth. More especially, English and Danish differed greatly from the other language groups. It was estimated that the rate of foundation literacy acquisition is slower by a ratio of about 2.5:1 in English than in most European orthographies. It was suggested that there is an abrupt effect of orthographic depth that requires a different cognitive architecture for developing reading processes. When the complexity of grapheme–phoneme correspondences is above this threshold, the dual process system (alphabetic and logographic foundation) is involved in literacy acquisition, whereas in more regular orthographies, an alphabetic foundation is sufficient.

LITERACY DEVELOPMENT IN FINNISH

Aro et al. (1999) followed up the development of six nonreaders for a period of 13 months. The main questions addressed in the study concerned the relation between emerging phonological abilities and the basic reading skill and the degree of inter-individual variation in the development of phonological manipulation skills. The participants were six nonreading Finnish children whose school entry had been postponed because of underdeveloped social skills and immature group-work abilities. Their ages varied between 7 years and 7 years 9 months at the beginning of the study. The children's phonological abilities were individually assessed every 4 weeks. Altogether, there were 12 assessments. During the follow-up period the children participated in a training program that targeted phonological, visuomotor, and metacognitive skills. The measures of phonological abilities included tasks that assessed rhyme detection, syllable deletion, phoneme identification, phoneme deletion, and phoneme synthesis. The reading criterion used was the ability to read three simple nonword syllables.

When the development of phonological skills was investigated in relation to the time point of mastering the basic reading skill at group level, it was evident that the children showed rhyme-detection and phoneme-identification skills months before learning to read. Syllable-deletion abilities seemed to develop gradually up to the time point when the children learned to read, whereas phoneme-synthesis skill and especially phoneme-deletion skill showed improvement mainly after reading acquisition. Observation of the individual development of phonological skills revealed considerable inter-individual variation in the development of phonological skills. The children achieved basic reading ability with varying sets of phonological abilities. Syllable-deletion and phoneme-identification skills seemed to be the phonological subskills that most consistently preceded reading acquisition, even though they did not seem to predict the time point of learning to read.

It was concluded that the predictive value of phonological abilities was not high at the individual level. On the basis of the findings, it seemed justifiable to ask whether the tests of phonological manipulation skills measure abilities that are cognitively independent and separate from reading skill or whether they merely reflect emerging literacy skills, especially in an orthography in which single letters are consistently related to corresponding phonemes. It was also hypothesised that, in a transparent orthography, phonemic awareness might be more strongly related to letter knowledge, and develop simultaneously.

Aro et al. (2004) carried out an intensive follow–up of Finnish children entering the first grade. The purpose of the study was to investigate the development of literacy skills during the first grade, and especially during the early months of reading instruction. Another goal was to study whether language-related skills measured at school entry predict the way in which literacy skills develop. The participants were 63 children entering the first grade. Their literacy skills were assessed four times during the autumn semester, at 5-week intervals. The fifth assessment was carried out at the end of the first grade, in May. At each of these five assessment points, three reading tasks and a spelling task were used; the reading tasks were similar to those used by Seymour et al. (2003). They assessed (a) letter knowledge, (b) very familiar word identification, and (c) pseudoword reading. In addition to these, letter-writing and pseudoword-spelling tasks were administered. The first assessment at school entry also included an assessment of phonological, rapid-naming, and morphological skills for those children who did not reach a predefined criterion for being able to read. This sub-sample of nonreaders at school entry consisted of 31 children.

On average, the children already knew 16 out of 23 letters at school entry, and over a third of the children read at an accuracy level of 90%. The same level of accuracy in spelling was reached by 17.5% of the children. The variability in literacy skills was large, especially in reading and spelling, in which the distributions were practically dichotomous. The development of reading and spelling accuracy was fast, and individual development was characterised by rapid leaps between successive assessment points. At the end of the school year, the children's accuracy was at ceiling level on all tasks. Until the end of the first grade, the correlation between word- and pseudoword-reading performance remained high, indicating the use of similar processes in both tasks. To examine the development of literacy skills, the relation between the development of reading and spelling accuracy, and their association with reading speed at the end of the grade, the accuracy scores were subjected to a latent growth-curve analysis with categorical variables. The analysis revealed that, in the development of reading and spelling accuracy, there was variation in only the initial level of accuracy (intercept) and not in the type of development (slope). The levels of accuracy in reading and spelling were very highly correlated (.995), showing that the development of these skills is concurrent. The developmental rate of accuracy had only a modest association with reading-speed outcome.

The best predictors at school entry for the development of accuracy in reading and spelling were letter knowledge, phoneme identification, and pseudoword repetition. No school entry language measures had clear associations with reading speed at the end of the school year.

The findings gave strong support for the orthographic depth hypothesis of reading acquisition. In phonological recoding, the Finnish first graders reached the accuracy level of English children at Grade 2 (as reported by Seymour et al., 2003) after 10 weeks of reading instruction. The concurrent development of early reading and spelling skills is thought to reflect the symmetrical, bidirectional regularity of the Finnish orthography. The lack of dissociation between word and pseudoword reading supported the notion that similar alphabetic and serial strategies are used in early reading in Finnish, irrespective of the reading materials.

WHAT DO THESE STUDIES TELL ABOUT READING ACQUISITION AND ORTHOGRAPHIC DEPTH?

The main question addressed in the cross-linguistic studies outlined in the preceding section was whether there are differences in reading acquisition between children trying to break the orthographic code in different languages. The answer to this question is definitely affirmative. In the study reported by Aro and Wimmer (2003), the English-speaking children struggled with the acquisition of phonological recoding skill whereas the French-, German-, Dutch-, Spanish-, Swedish-, and Finnish-speaking children seemed to acquire the skill with little difficulty. At the end of the first grade, the reading accuracy in the just-mentioned more regular orthographies was generally between 85% and 93%, with little room for further improvement in the pseudoword-reading task that was administered. The exception was English, in which the children reached the same high level of accuracy only in fourth grade. The English children were also consistently the slowest in pseudoword reading until the fourth grade. Seymour et al. (2003) demonstrated similar differences in the early reading skills. The acquisition of elementary word-recognition skills, as well as phonological recoding skills, occurred more slowly in Portuguese, French, and Danish than in the majority of the languages, and the delay was greatly exaggerated in English. On the basis of the English findings, it could be estimated that the readers of English require over 2.5 years for achieving the level that was achieved during the first year of reading instruction in the majority of European orthographies involved. Aro and Wimmer reported that the English-speaking children approached 90% accuracy level in phonological recoding 3 years later than children in other orthographies. Generally, the results of these two studies showed an effect of orthographic depth in both familiar word-recognition and phonological recoding tasks and a smaller effect of syllable complexity in phonological recoding.

It is especially remarkable that the effect of orthographic depth was present in simple pseudoword-reading tasks in which the assembly with basic letter sounds would suffice and without any complex graphemes or contextual effects to be taken into account before pronunciation was obtained (Seymour et al., 2003). Similarly, the effect of the syllabic complexity of the orthography was present even in materials with no consonant clusters. Accordingly, in the study by Aro and Wimmer (2003) the responses of English children were scored in an especially lenient manner: Any grapheme–phoneme translation that occurred in real words was accepted. Thus the observed orthographic effects on early literacy cannot be interpreted as by–products of the variation between task requirements in different languages.

These findings give strong support to the notion of qualitative differences between transparent and opaque orthographies in the process of reading acquisition. With reference to the foundation literacy model presented by Seymour (1997, 1999), it can be suggested that literacy acquisition in transparent orthographies is based on a single process of alphabetic assembly. Further, the empirical support for a logographic stage in reading acquisition is vague in transparent orthographies (e.g., Wimmer & Hummer, 1990). In a transparent orthography, the knowledge of grapheme–phoneme correspondences and phonemic assembly are effective and sufficient tools for decoding any kind of word. Thus, the child is prepared for efficient 'self-teaching' (see Share, 1995) and the fast build–up of an orthographic word lexicon from the very early stages of literacy acquisition. In opaque orthographies, the development of alphabetic processing skills is hampered by complex grapheme–phoneme correspondences. Furthermore, the child encounters common words that require the knowledge of complex graphemes, contextual effects on pronunciation, and irregularities. Therefore separate logographic processing skills and word–specific knowledge is required from an early stage. The early literacy development has to be based on two separate processing skills instead of one, which compromises the developmental rate of basic literacy skills.

In cross-linguistic comparisons, the interpretation of the results is complicated by a number of confounding factors that are often impossible to control. The age of school entry and the methods of reading instruction employed vary among countries. There are also a number of cultural and social factors that might exert their effect on the results. However, as was shown by Seymour et al., the overall correlations between age and reading performance were weak or non-significant. No doubt it is safe to say that the young age of British school entrants does not exactly help in the task of acquiring phonological recoding skills, but it can nonetheless be concluded that the effects of orthographic depth discussed in this study are not due to age differences.

Another factor that is often inextricable from the effects of orthography in cross-linguistic studies is the variation in reading instruction methods. In transparent orthographies, reading instruction is typically based on phonics, as it is in Finland. In opaque orthographies, such as English, early reading instruction is usually a mixture of phonics and whole-word methods. The claim that the observed differences in reading acquisition are due to differences in reading instruction methods would, of course, offer a relatively easy solution for the problems of slow reading acquisition in English. Actually, there is evidence to suggest that phonics teaching is beneficial for the development of phonological recoding skills in English (for a review see Snowling, 1996). However, Landerl (2000) showed that English-speaking children, who had received consistent phonics instruction, were nonetheless outperformed by German children in phonological recoding, although they performed better than children receiving standard instruction in English. The most plausible conclusion is that orthographic depth and reading instruction methods are naturally linked. When the orthography allows systematic rule–based teaching of grapheme–phoneme correspondences, that is also the natural choice for a reading instruction method. Correspondingly, in less transparent orthographies, more whole-word-oriented teaching methods may be required because explicit teaching of grapheme–phoneme correspondence rules is difficult.

A third factor that might have an effect on the observed cross-linguistic differences relates to cultural and social differences among countries and, correspondingly, orthographies. In some countries, the kindergarten programs explicitly discourage any school-related activities such as the teaching of letters, whereas in other countries the teaching of letters and print exposure are an essential part of kindergarten activities. It is also possible that the literacy-related activities in families vary between countries as a function of, for example, the quality of the library system or the extent of newspaper circulation. Again, the socioeconomic differences between countries, and the variability of socioeconomic status (SES) within each country might have an effect on literacy acquisition. Duncan and Seymour (2000) have shown that SES has an effect on foundation literacy acquisition in Scotland. The effect of cultural and social differences on reading acquisition can be truly controlled only in multilingual countries in which reading acquisition can be assessed in different orthographic contexts, but within the same educational system and culture. Two Welsh studies fit these criteria (Ellis & Hooper, 2001; Spencer & Hanley, 2003). Both studies showed consistently that children learning to read Welsh, which has a relatively transparent orthography, acquired reading skills at a faster rate than their English-speaking peers.

In summary, it seems highly unlikely that the observed cross-linguistic differences would be caused by factors unrelated to orthographic depth. The findings of Aro and Wimmer (2003) and Seymour et al. (2003) are consistent with the previous comparisons of English and other orthographies. It is interesting to note that the actual outlier in both studies was English (and, to a lesser extent, Danish in Seymour et al., 2003) and that the differences between the other orthographies were relatively small. This might seem counterintuitive if one considers orthographic depth as a continuum. There are at least two possible explanations for the lack of clear differences between more transparent orthographies. One is that the effect of orthographic depth is abrupt rather than graded. Thus there is a threshold of orthographic depth above which the phonemic assembly becomes unreliable and compensating processes are required. From the point of view of beginning reading, it seems probable that this threshold is not related to the number of inconsistent spellings in a language as such, but to the number of explicit grapheme–phoneme rules that enable the assembly of the pronunciation. Another reason for the lack of differences between transparent orthographies can be methodological. One could hypothesise that more demanding reading materials could elicit more subtle differences. After all, in both studies summarised here, reading accuracy was close to ceiling in most orthographies, and in both studies the reading materials included only relatively simple word and pseudoword items. However, because the specific complexities of the orthographies vary greatly, the creation of a comparable set of more demanding items across languages is a challenging task and requires more knowledge of the specific bottlenecks of reading development in different orthographies.

HOW DO THE LITERACY SKILLS DEVELOP IN THE HIGHLY TRANSPARENT FINNISH LANGUAGE?

In the follow-up reported by Aro et al. (2004), a third of the Finnish children performed in reading tasks at the accuracy level of 90% at school entry, that is, before the start of formal reading instruction. Because the methods used in this study allow direct comparison with the results reported by Seymour et al. (2003), it is interesting to take a closer look at how the performance of Finnish children at the beginning of reading instruction compared with the performance of English-speaking children at the end of the first and second grades. On average, Finnish children read pseudowords at school entry more accurately than the English-speaking children at the end of the first grade. Furthermore, they needed only 10 weeks of reading instruction to surpass the pseudoword-reading accuracy level of English-speaking children at the end of the second grade. This difference in the development of pseudoword-reading skill shows convincingly that the task of phonological recoding is an easy one in Finnish and that children do not seem to need much support in gaining an insight into the Finnish orthographic cipher.

Although the difference is striking, it is not unexpected from the point of view of the orthographic depth hypothesis. It is worth pointing out how closely the findings concerning the development of Finnish first graders resembled the findings from the follow-ups of other transparent orthographies, especially Turkish (Öney & Durgunoğlu, 1997). The observed similarities of literacy development seem to parallel the similarities of the orthographies: The Turkish orthography has regular bidirectional correspondences between phonemes and single letters (Raman & Baluch, 2001), similar to Finnish. In both Finnish and Turkish, literacy acquisition was rapid, and many children entered school with decoding skills. There was no dissociation between word and pseudoword reading, as was revealed by the high correlations between these measures, and the development of spelling skills was concurrent with the development of reading. The findings concerning spelling and reading skills are especially interesting. Many transparent orthographies are less transparent in the sound–to–spelling direction and, for accurate spelling, knowledge of phoneme–grapheme correspondences does not suffice: The child needs specific knowledge of orthographic word forms. This orthographic lexicon is built up with reading experience, so accurate spelling is supposed to follow accurate reading. In Finnish and Turkish, a reverse phonological route should be sufficient for accurate spelling because of the bidirectional consistency of grapheme–phoneme correspondences. The effect of orthography on literacy has mostly been studied by use of reading tasks, and the aforementioned hypothesis concerning the dissociation of spelling and reading development as a function of asymmetrical transparency has yet to be studied.

Aro et al. (1999) addressed the question of the relation between phonological skills and emerging reading skills. They showed that phonological skills have a limited predictive value in terms of how early the child will learn to read. The six children acquired a very basic phonological recoding ability with varying sets of phonological skills. Many skills showed improvement shortly before the child could be classified as a reader, or only thereafter. The two skills that most consistently preceded reading ability were syllable deletion and phoneme identification. In summary, the connection between phonological skills and reading ability was uncertain, with a lot of inter-individual as well as intra-individual variation during the follow–up. The difficulty of making causal inferences relating phonological awareness with literacy skills was underlined by the fact that five out of six children consistently gave letter-name responses in the phoneme-identification task.

In the study by Aro et al. (2004) the development in reading and spelling accuracy was best predicted by letter knowledge at school entry. Of the phonological measures, the phoneme-identification and pseudoword-repetition tasks had a small but significant association with the development of accuracy. This is in accordance with a multitude of previous findings. Although the school entry measures had predictive value with regard to the rate of development of pseudoword reading and spelling accuracy, the variation they predicted was somewhat irrelevant, because, at the end of the first grade, practically all children had acquired basic phonological recoding skills. It is perhaps more interesting that no school entry measures were reliably associated with reading fluency, for which there was a large individual variation at the end of the school year. This is in contradiction to the findings of Holopainen et al. (2003), which showed that the only preschool measure reliably associated with reading performance in Grade 4 was rapid-naming speed. It is possible that the reliable variation in reading speed appears only later, when the basic skills have become more automatised for most children. However, the results underline the fact that reading accuracy, as such, is not a sufficient measure of reading proficiency. One interesting question for further studies concerns the nature of the rapid and fluent word-recognition skills in a transparent orthography such as Finnish. It is yet to be determined whether fluent reading is based on lexical processes or on the assembly of larger sublexical units such as morphemes or syllables, or whether fluent reading is based on the automatisation of phonological recoding skills, still at the level of single graphemes.

More conclusive answers concerning the nature of the relation between phonological development and emerging reading skills would possibly require earlier assessment of phonological skills, because, at school entry, children in Finland already have a lot of experience of written language, and they often have close to perfect letter knowledge. Furthermore, the current concepts and measures of phonological awareness are problematic, as phonological awareness has been shown to have at least a reciprocal relationship with literacy experience and literacy instruction. In a transparent orthography, phonological tasks can be easily solved with the help of orthographic knowledge. It could be speculated that the true phonological prerequisites of reading skills lie somewhere under phonological awareness, phonological memory, and naming, which are the current primary candidates for a language-related core deficit of developmental dyslexia. The notion of an underlying deficit in phonological representations seems promising in terms of accounting for the various findings relating to both normal development of reading acquisition and reading disorders across orthographies (see Goswami, 2002b).

CONCLUSIONS

The findings reviewed here should not be interpreted as undermining the role of phonological skills in literacy acquisition. Quite the opposite: The development of early literacy skills in a transparent orthography seems to be completely dependent on the phonological apparatus of the beginning reader. However, it can be concluded that a transparent orthography, like Finnish, treats even a phonologically immature reader in a lenient manner because the grapheme–phoneme correspondences are regular at the level of single letters, thus explicating the alphabetic principle. This does not necessarily mean that a child with reading problems in a transparent orthography fares well in comparison with a child struggling with larger overt reading problems in a less transparent orthography. The rate and content of instruction are usually based on the average performance of the group. The ease with which a typical child acquires literacy is also a challenge for the teachers: Very early reading instruction has to be adjusted to a wide range of individual skills and a wide range of individual needs.

The current evidence shows that many aspects of reading development and also failure in reading acquisition are dependent on the specific orthographic context. Thus far, the orthographic context studied has most often been English. Only by gaining more insight into the differences between orthographies can we specify the universal features of reading acquisition across alphabetic orthographies. Therefore studies that reveal the orthographic complexities affecting reading development in specific orthographic contexts are valuable. Especially important would be studies comparing the phenotype of dyslexia in different orthographies. Currently such attempts are very few in number.

Finally, on the basis of the accumulating evidence concerning the differences in reading acquisition and also in reading problems between English and more transparent orthographies, we should keep in mind the caution expressed by Wimmer and Landerl (1997): '. . . the researchers and teachers working within consistent orthographies are well advised not to base their theories and instructional choices solely on English findings.'

REFERENCES

Adams, M. J. (1990). *Beginning to read: Thinking and learning about print.* Cambridge, MA: MIT Press.
Aro, M., Aro, T., Ahonen, T., Räsänen, T., Hietala, A., & Lyytinen, H. (1999). The development of phonological abilities and their relation to reading acquisition: Case studies of six Finnish children. *Journal of Learning Disabilities, 32,* 457–463, 478.
Aro, M., Tolvanen, A., Poikkeus, A.-M., & Lyytinen H. (2004). The development of reading and spelling skills, and the predictors of accuracy and fluency: An intensive follow-up in a transparent orthography (Finnish). Manuscript submitted for publication.
Aro, M., & Wimmer, H. (2003). Learning to read: English in comparison to six more regular orthographies. *Applied Psycholinguistics, 24,* 619–634.
Boder, E. (1973). Developmental dyslexia: A diagnostic approach based on three atypical reading–spelling patterns. *Developmental Medicine and Child Neurology, 15,* 663–687.
Bowey, J. A. (1994). Phonological sensitivity in novice readers and nonreaders. *Journal of Experimental Child Psychology, 58,* 134–159.

Bus, A. G., & van IJzendoorn, M. H. (1999). Phonological awareness and early reading: A meta-analysis of experimental training studies. *Journal of Educational Psychology, 91,* 403–414.

Bryant, P. (2002). It doesn't matter whether onset and rime predicts reading better than phoneme awareness does or vice versa. *Journal of Experimental Child Psychology, 82,* 41–46.

Coenen, M. J. W. L., van Bon, W. H. J., & Schreuder, R. (1997). Reading and spelling in Dutch first and second graders: Do they use an orthographic strategy? In C. K. Leong & M. Joshi (Eds.), *Cross-language studies of learning to read and spell: Phonological and orthographic processing* (pp. 249–269). Dordrecht, The Netherlands: Kluwer Academic.

Cossu, G. (1999). The acquisition of Italian orthography. In M. Harris & G. Hatano (Eds.), *Learning to read and write: A cross-linguistic perspective* (pp. 10–33). Cambridge, UK: Cambridge University Press.

Cossu, G., Gugliotta, M., & Marshall, J. C. (1995). Acquisition of reading and written spelling in a transparent orthography: Two non-parallel processes? *Reading and Writing, 7,* 9–22.

Cossu, G., Shankweiler, D., Liberman, I. Y., Katz, L., & Tola, G. (1988). Awareness of phonological segments and reading ability in Italian children. *Applied Psycholinguistics, 9,* 1–16.

DeFrancis, J. (1989). *Visible speech: The diverse oneness of writing systems.* Honolulu, HI: University of Hawaii Press.

de Jong, P. F., & van der Leij (1999). Specific contributions of phonological abilities to early reading acquisition: Result from a Dutch latent variable longitudinal study. *Journal of Educational Psychology, 91,* 450–476.

Downing, J. A. (1964). *The i.t.a. reading experiment: Three lectures on the research in infant schools with Sir James Pitman's Initial Teaching alphabet.* Bath, UK: Evans Brothers Ltd.

Duncan, L., & Seymour, P. H. K. (2000). Socio-economic differences in foundation-level literacy. *British Journal of Psychology, 91,* 145–166.

Durgunoğlu, A. Y., & Öney, B. (1999). A cross-linguistic comparison of phonological awareness and word recognition. *Reading and Writing: An Interdisciplinary Journal, 11,* 281–299.

Ehri, L. C. (1992). Reconceptualising the development of sight word reading and its relation to recoding. In P. Gough, L. Ehri, & R. Treiman (Eds.), *Reading acquisition* (pp. 107–143). Hillsdale, NJ: Lawrence Erlbaum Associates.

Ehri, L. C., Nunes, S. R., Willows, D. M., Schuster, B. V., Yaghoub-Zadeh, Z., & Shanahan, T. (2001). Phonemic awareness instruction helps children learn to read: Evidence from the National Reading Panel's meta-analysis. *Reading Research Quarterly, 36,* 250–287.

Ellis, A. W. (1985). The cognitive neuropsychology of developmental and acquired dyslexia: A critical survey. *Cognitive Neuropsychology, 2,* 169–205.

Ellis, N. C., & Hooper, M. (2001). Why learning to read is easier in Welsh than in English: Orthographic transparency effects evinced with frequency-matched tests. *Applied Psycholinguistics, 22,* 571–599.

Feldman, L. B., & Turvey, M. T. (1983). Word recognition in Serbo-Croatian is phonologically analytic. *Journal of Experimental Psychology: Human Perception and Performance, 9,* 288–298.

Frith, U. (1985). Beneath the surface of developmental dyslexia. In K. E. Patterson, M. Coltheart, & J. C. Marshall (Eds.), *Surface dyslexia, neuropsychological and cognitive studies of phonological reading* (pp. 301–330). London: Lawrence Erlbaum Associates.

Frith, U., Wimmer, H., & Landerl, K. (1998). Differences in phonological recoding in German- and English-speaking children. *Scientific Studies of Reading, 2,* 31–54.

Frost, R., Katz, L., & Bentin, S. (1987). Strategies for visual word recognition and orthographical depth: A multilingual comparison. *Journal of Experimental Psychology: Human Perception and Performance, 13,* 104–115.

Goswami, U. (2002a). In the beginning was the rhyme? A reflection on Hulme, Hatcher, Nation, Brown, Adams, and Stuart (2002). *Journal of Experimental Child Psychology, 82,* 47–57.

Goswami, U. (2002b). Phonology, reading development, and dyslexia: A cross-linguistic perspective. *Annals of Dyslexia, 52,* 141–163.

Goswami, U., & Bryant, P. (1990). *Phonological skills and learning to read.* Exeter, UK: Lawrence Erlbaum Associates.

Goswami, U., Gombert, J. E., & de Barrera, L. (1998). Children's orthographic representations and linguistic transparency: Nonsense word reading in English, French and Spanish. *Applied Psycholinguistics, 19,* 19–52.

Goswami, U., Porpodas, C., & Wheelwright, S. (1997). Children's orthographic representations in English and Greek. *European Journal of Psychology of Education, 12,* 273–292.

Goswami, U., Ziegler, J. C., Dalton, L., & Schneider, W. (2001). Pseudohomophone effects and phonological recoding procedures in reading development in English and German. *Journal of Memory and Language, 45,* 648–664.

Gough, P. B., & Hillinger, M. L. (1980). Learning to read: An unnatural act. *Bulletin of the Orton Society, 30,* 179–195.

Høien, T., Lundberg, I., Stanovich, K., & Bjaalid, I.-K. (1995). Components of phonological awareness. *Reading and Writing: An Interdisciplinary Journal, 7,* 171–188.

Holopainen, L., Ahonen, T., & Lyytinen, H. (2001). Predicting delay in reading achievement in a highly transparent language. *Journal of Learning Disabilities, 34,* 401–413.

Holopainen, L., Ahonen, T., & Lyytinen, H. (2003). Development of reading and linguistic abilities: Results from a Finnish longitudinal study. Manuscript submitted for publication.

Hulme, C., Hatcher, P. J., Nation, K., Brown, A., Adams, J., & Stuart, G. (2002). Phoneme awareness is a better predictor of early reading skills than onset–rime awareness. *Journal of Experimental Child Psychology, 82,* 2–28.

Johnston, R. S., Anderson, M., & Holligan, C. (1996). Knowledge of the alphabet and explicit awareness of phonemes in pre-readers: The nature of the relationship. *Reading and Writing: An Interdisciplinary Journal, 8,* 217–234.

Jorm, A. F., Share, D. L., MacLean, R., & Matthews, R. G. (1984). Phonological recoding skills and learning to read: A longitudinal study. *Applied Psycholinguistics, 5,* 201–207.

Juel, C., Griffith, P. L., & Gough, P. B. (1986). Acquisition of literacy: A longitudinal study of children in first and second grade. *Journal of Educational Psychology, 78,* 243–255.

Karlsson, F. (1996). The word-forms of the Finnish noun kauppa 'shop'. Retrieved October 14, 2003, from http://www.ling.helsinki.fi/~fkarlsso/genkau2.html.

Katz, L., & Feldman, L. B. (1983). Relation between pronunciation and recognition of printed words in deep and shallow orthographies. *Journal of Experimental Psychology: Learning, Memory, and Cognition, 9,* 157–166.

Landerl, K. (2000). Influences of orthographic consistency and reading instruction on the development of nonword reading skills. *European Journal of Psychology of Education, 15,* 239–257.

Landerl, K., & Wimmer, H. (2000). Deficits in phoneme segmentation are not the core problem of dyslexia: Evidence from German and English children. *Applied Psycholinguistics, 21,* 243–262.

Landerl, K., Wimmer, H., & Frith, U. (1997). The impact of orthographic consistency on dyslexia: A German–English comparison. *Cognition, 63,* 315–334.

Lovett, M. W. (1987). A developmental approach to reading disability: Accuracy and speech criteria of normal and deficient reading skill. *Child Development, 58,* 234–260.

Lukatela, K., Carello, C., Shankweiler, D., & Liberman, I. Y. (1995). Phonological awareness in illiterates: Observations from Serbo-Croatian. *Applied Psycholinguistics, 16,* 463–487.

Lukatela, G., Popadic, D., Ognjenovic, P., & Turvey, M. T. (1980). Lexical decision in a phonologically shallow orthography. *Memory & Cognition, 8,* 415–423.

Lukatela, G., & Turvey, M. T. (1999). Reading in two alphabets. *American Psychologist, 53,* 1057–1072.

Lundberg, I., & Høien, T. (1990). Patterns of information processing skills and word recognition strategies in developmental dyslexia. *Scandinavian Journal of Educational Research, 34,* 231–240.

Lyytinen, H., Aro, M. & Holopainen, L. (2004). Dyslexia in highly orthographically regular Finnish. In I. Smythe, J. Everatt & R. Salter (Eds.), *International book of dyslexia: A cross language comparison and practice guide* (pp. 81–91). London: Wiley.

Mann, V., & Wimmer, H. (2002). Phoneme awareness and pathways into literacy: A comparison of German and American children. *Reading and Writing: An Interdisciplinary Journal, 15,* 653–682.

Morais, J., Cary, L., Alegria, J., & Bertelson, P. (1979). Does awareness of speech as a sequence of phones arise spontaneously? *Cognition, 7,* 323–331.

Näslund, J. C. (1999). Phonemic and graphemic consistency: Effects on decoding for German and American children. *Reading and Writing: An Interdisciplinary Journal, 11,* 129–152.

Niemi, J., Laine, M., & Tuominen, J. (1994). Cognitive morphology in Finnish: Foundations of a new model. *Language and Cognitive Processes, 9,* 423–446.

Öney, B., & Durgunoğlu, A. (1997). Beginning to read in Turkish: A phonologically transparent orthography. *Applied Psycholinguistics, 18,* 1–15.

Öney, B., & Goldman, S. R. (1984). Decoding and comprehension skills in Turkish and English: Effects of the regularity of grapheme-phoneme correspondences. *Journal of Educational Psychology, 76,* 557–568.

Öney, B., Peter, M., & Katz, L. (1997). Phonological processing in printed word recognition: Effects of age and writing system. *Scientific Studies of Reading, 1,* 65–83.

Pinheiro, A. M. V. (1995). Reading and spelling development in Brazilian Portuguese. *Reading and Writing: An Interdisciplinary Journal, 7,* 111–138.

Plaut, D. C., McClelland, J. L., Seidenberg, M. S., & Patterson, K. (1996). Understanding normal and impaired word reading: Computational principles in quasi–regular domains. *Psychological Review, 103,* 56–115.

Porpodas, C. (1989). The phonological factor in reading and spelling of Greek. In P. G. Aaron & R. M. Joshi (Eds.), *Reading and writing disorders in different orthographic systems.* Dordrecht, The Netherlands: Kluwer Academic.

Porpodas, C. D. (1999). Patterns of phonological and memory processing in beginning readers and spellers of Greek. *Journal of Learning Disabilities, 32,* 406–416.

Poskiparta, E., Niemi, P., & Vauras, M. (1999). Who benefits from training in linguistic awareness in the first grade, and what components show training effects? *Journal of Learning Disabilities, 32,* 437–446, 456.

Raman, I., & Baluch, B. (2001). Semantic effects as a function of reading skill in word naming of a transparent orthography. *Reading and Writing: An Interdisciplinary Journal, 14,* 599–614.

Rodrigo, M., & Jiménez, J. E. (1999). An analysis of the word naming errors of normal readers and reading disabled children in Spanish. *Journal of Research in Reading, 22,* 180–197.

Seymour, P. H. K. (1997). Foundations of orthographic development. In C. Perfetti, L. Rieben, & M. Fayol (Eds.), *Learning to spell* (pp. 319–337). Hillsdale, NJ: Lawrence Erlbaum Associates.

Seymour, P. H. K. (1999). Cognitive architecture of early reading. In I. Lundberg, F. E. Tønnessen, & I. Austad (Eds.), *Dyslexia: Advances in theory and practice* (pp. 59–73). Dordrecht, The Netherlands: Kluwer Academic.

Seymour, P. H. K., Aro, M., & Erskine, J. M. (2003). Foundation literacy acquisition in European orthographies. *British Journal of Psychology, 94,* 143–174.

Seymour, P. H. K., & Elder, L. (1986). Beginning reading without phonology. *Cognitive Neuropsychology, 3,* 1–37.

Share, D. (1995). Phonological recoding and self–teaching: Sine qua non of reading acquisition. *Cognition, 55,* 151–218.

Snowling, M. (1996). Contemporary approaches to the teaching of reading. *Journal of Child Psychology and Psychiatry, 37,* 139–148.

Spencer, L. H., & Hanley, R. (2003). Effects of orthographic transparency on reading and phoneme awareness in children learning to read in Wales. *British Journal of Psychology, 94,* 1–28.

Thorstad, G. (1991). The effect of orthography on the acquisition of literacy skills. *British Journal of Psychology, 82,* 527–537.

Treiman, R., Goswami, U., & Bruck, M. (1990). Not all nonwords are alike: Implications for reading development and theory. *Memory & Cognition, 18,* 559–567.

Venezky, R. L. (1970). *The structure of English orthography.* The Hague: Mouton.

Wagner, R. K., & Torgesen, J. K. (1987). The nature of phonological processing and its causal role in the acquisition of reading skills. *Psychological Bulletin, 101,* 192–212.

Wimmer, H. (1993). Characteristics of developmental dyslexia in a regular writing system. *Applied Psycholinguistics, 14,* 1–33.

Wimmer, H., & Goswami, U. (1994). The influence of orthographic consistency on reading development: Word recognition in English and German children. *Cognition, 51,* 91–103.

Wimmer, H., & Hummer, P. (1990). How German speaking first graders read and spell: Doubts on the importance of logographic stage. *Applied Psycholinguistics, 11,* 349–368.

Wimmer, H., & Landerl, K. (1997). How learning to spell German differs from learning to spell English. In C. A. Perfetti, L. Rieben, & M. Fayol (Eds.), *Learning to spell: Research, theory, and practice across languages.* Mahwah, NJ: Lawrence Erlbaum Associates.

Wimmer, H., Landerl, K., Linortner, R., & Hummer, P. (1991). The relationship of phonemic awareness to reading acquisition: More consequence than precondition but still important. *Cognition, 40,* 219–249.

Wimmer, H., & Mayringer, H. (2002). Dysfluent reading in the absence of spelling difficulties: A specific disability in regular orthographies. *Journal of Educational Psychology, 94,* 272–277.

Wimmer, H., Mayringer, H., & Landerl, K. (1998). Poor reading: A deficit in skill automatization or a phonological deficit? *Scientific Studies of Reading, 2,* 321–340.

Wimmer, H., Mayringer, H., & Landerl, K. (2000). The double-deficit hypothesis and difficulties in learning to read a regular orthography. *Journal of Educational Psychology, 92,* 668–680.

Wolf, M., Bally, H., & Morris, R. (1986). Automaticity, retrieval processes, and reading: A longitudinal study in average and impaired readers. *Child Development, 57,* 988–1000.

Wolf, M., & Bowers, P. G. (1999). The double-deficit hypothesis for the developmental dyslexias. *Journal of Educational Psychology, 91,* 415–438.

Yap, R., & van der Leij, A. (1993). Word processing in dyslexics: An automatic decoding deficit? *Reading and Writing: An Interdisciplinary Journal, 5,* 261–279.

Ziegler, J. C., Jacobs, A. M., & Stone, G. O. (1996). Statistical analysis of the bidirectional inconsistency of spelling and sound in French. *Behavior Research Methods, Instruments & Computers, 28,* 504–515.

Ziegler, J. C., Perry, C., Jacobs, A. M., & Braun, M. (2001). Identical words are read differently in different languages. *Psychological Science, 12,* 379–384.

Ziegler, J. C., Stone, G. O., & Jacobs, A. M. (1997). What is the pronunciation for –ough and the spelling for /u/? A database for computing feedforward and feedback consistency in English. *Behavior Research Methods, Instruments & Computers, 29,* 600–618.

Zoccolotti, P., de Luca, M., di Pace, E., Judica, A., Orlandi, M., Spinelli, D. (1999). Markers of developmental surface dyslexia in a language (Italian) with high grapheme-phoneme correspondence. *Applied Psycholinguistics, 20,* 191–216.

33

Learning to Spell From Print and Learning to Spell From Speech: A Study of Spelling of Children Who Speak Tamil, a Dravidian Language

P. G. Aaron
Indiana State University

R. Malatesha Joshi
Texas A & M University

In the opening segment of this chapter, the spelling performance of children who speak Tamil, a Dravidian agglutinative language, is examined. Tamil orthography can be described as shallow because it has an almost one-to-one correspondence with pronunciation. As can be expected, Tamil-speaking children attending Grades 6 through 12 committed very few spelling errors on a dictation test. The small number of spelling errors was due to certain unique features of the phonology and morphology of the Tamil language. In the later part of the chapter, the question of whether learning English first from textbooks rather than from speech will lead to a reduced number of spelling errors is addressed. The spelling performance of a group of Tamil-speaking children who learn English first as a written language is compared with that of a group of American children who learn English first as a spoken language. It is concluded that learning English first as a written language helps children to avoid spelling errors that are dialectical in nature, but the phonology of native Tamil leads children to commit different kinds of spelling errors. It was also found that Indian children who are exposed to textbook English during the entire schoolday are better spellers of English than Indian children who are exposed to written English only for about an hour per day. The results point to the influence of both speech and print on learning to spell.

INTRODUCTION

Research conducted in recent years has shown that, during the early stages of learning to spell, children tend to represent words by their sounds and letter names rather than by their looks. The research studies that support this view have relied on the developmental trends seen in spelling acquisition as well as comparison of spellings produced by children who speak different dialects of English. Developmentally, children's misspellings reflect their effort to phoneticize the spellings of words that, in orthographies such as English, do not have a systematic correspondence with pronunciation (Treiman, 1993). For instance, a number of studies that examined the spelling performance of elementary school children report that Black English dialect has an influence on the spelling of children who speak that dialect (Carney, 1979; Hugh, 1970; Kligman and Bruce, 1974; Schwab, 1971). Further evidence attesting to the influence of dialect on spelling comes from studies that found that, even among speakers of standard English, dialectical variation is correlated with spelling variation. Treiman, Goswami, Tincoff & Leevers (1997) studied British and American children and found that young children's spelling errors reflect the characteristics of their dialect. Treiman and Barry (2000) further found that the influence of dialect on spelling is not a transient phenomenon because differences similar to the ones seen in children's spellings can also be found in the spellings of British and American college students. These studies show that dialectical variation can be a source of spelling errors and that this can be taken as evidence of the influence of phonology on spelling.

It would follow then that at least some of the spelling errors committed by English-speaking children can be attributed to the speech they hear. If this hypothesis could be extended beyond the boundaries of English-speaking communities, we can expect that the spelling of children who learn English as a second language (ESL children, hereafter) by first reading textbooks rather than by listening to and speaking in English would unlikely be swayed by the idiosyncrasies of English pronunciations. The spelling productions of these ESL children therefore may not contain errors that are products of efforts to phoneticize and regularize "irregular" words that tend to align spelling with pronunciation. In fact, many ESL children pronounce English words the way they are spelled rather than the way native English speakers utter them.

A strong version of this hypothesis would lead to the expectation that children who learn English as a second language from textbooks, being free from dialectical influences, would be better spellers than children for whom English is the native language.

A weak version of this hypothesis would propose that ESL children may not be better spellers than English-speaking children but that there will be differences in the nature of the spelling errors committed by these two groups of children.

Learning English First From Print Rather Than Speech

The educational system in certain parts of India provides an opportunity to test the validity of the hypothesis of whether English that is learned through exposure to print rather than to speech bestows an advantage as far as spelling is concerned. The studies described in this chapter examined the validity of this expectation and were conducted in Tamil Nadu, a state in India.

Under the Indian educational system, children from the state of Tamil Nadu from where data were collected, start school at the age of 5 years; English instruction starts by the time these children reach the sixth grade, when they are about 11 years old. At this stage, education follows a two-track instructional system. For one group of children, English is taught as one of the subject matter areas, usually for about 1 hr per day. All the subject matter areas such as science and social studies are taught in the children's native language, Tamil. In this chapter, we designate these children as the "Tamil medium" group. Children in the second track also start learning English in Grade 6, but all the subject matter areas are taught in English. We designate these children as the "English medium" group. It is important to note that the term "English medium" is somewhat misleading for the following reason. During classroom instruction, the teachers in the school from which the data were collected read to the children in the English medium classes the English passages from the textbook, whatever it is—science, social studies, or math—and then translate the sentences into Tamil. The teachers do not use spoken English for instruction because they themselves can hardly speak fluent English. The difference between these two groups—Tamil medium and English medium—then is that the former group has exposure to written English for about 1 hr per day whereas the latter group is exposed to written English for most of the day. Neither group uses spoken English in the classroom for communication. Admission to the two different tracks of instruction is invariably based on the ability of the English medium children to pay additional tuition fees.

A BRIEF LINGUISTIC DESCRIPTION OF TAMIL LANGUAGE

Phonology of Tamil Language

Tamil belongs to the Dravidian language family, the world's fourth largest linguistic group (Steever, 1987). Even though Tamil is spoken primarily in the southern part of India and in Sri Lanka, emigrants have taken the language to countries such as Singapore, Malaysia, Fiji, Guyana, and Trinidad. It is an agglutinative, suffixal language with nouns inflecting for person, tense, number, and gender (Caldwell, 1875).

Tamil has 10 primary and 8 secondary vowels, 2 diphthongs, and 16 consonants (Arulmani, 2003). The 10 primary vowels are also called "initial" vowels because they have phonemic value and tend to appear in word-initial position (Steever, 1996). The 8 secondary vowels (or noninitials) have no phonemic value in and of themselves, but gain value in combination with the consonants. The secondary vowels appear as ligatures or satellites and precede or follow a primary vowel. Steever (1996) considers these two forms of vowels as two forms of allomorphs. In addition, diacritical marks, which can alter the pronunciation, also are attached to primary vowels and consonants.

Of the 10 primary vowels, 5 are classified as short vowels and 5 as long vowels. The five short vowels are /அ/, /இ/, /உ_/, /எ/, /ஒ/ (/a/, /e/, /u/, /ay/, /o/). The five long vowels are created by the addition of a diacritical mark (e.g., / ஆ /, aa) or by the attachment of a secondary vowel, (e.g., உ_ + ள = / ஊ /oo/). The two diphthongs are /ai/ and /ow/.

Each consonant is represented by a symbol that has an inherent vowel /a/. Thus the letter [ப] is a combination of [p] + [a] and is pronounced /pa/ as in "papa." In English orthography, a vowel is added to a consonant to alter the pronunciation of the grapheme ([p] + [a] = /pa/), whereas in Tamil orthography, such an addition is not necessary as every consonant has an inherent vowel. When the consonant phoneme has to be lengthened or altered, secondary vowels or diacritical marks are added to lengthen the phoneme. For instance, adding the secondary vowel [π] to[ப] (/pa/) makes it [பா] (pau) and is pronounced /pau/ as in the word "Paul." When a diacritical mark [] is added to [ப] it makes it /பு/, as in "put." The inherent vowel in the consonant can be muted by the placement of a dot over the consonant sign that makes it a stop consonant (e.g., [ம] /ma/ becomes [ம்] /m/ as the word-final sound in "mum"). Because of the changeable nature of the consonant sounds, each consonant has a phonemic value rather than a phonetic value.

A noteworthy characteristic of the Tamil language is the presence of retroflex sounds. A person produces a retroflex sound by placing the tip of the tongue against certain place at the roof of the mouth, and the tip of the tongue is then reversed and reverted. Meenakshi (2002) recognizes two tongue positions on the palate, high and low, which produce an "apical" retroflex sound and a "lower" retroflex sound. For instance, the lower retroflex [ழ] /z/ (பழ ம், *pazam* [fruit]) is palatal and the higher retroflex [ள] as in (நாள், *nal* [day]) is apical. An additional alveolar phoneme /l/ [ல] (*kal* [stone]), which is not a retroflex, is also present in Tamil. Confusion among these three consonants can be a potential source of spelling errors. There is no consensus regarding the number of retroflexes in Tamil; Emeneau (1970) lists seven and Zvelebil (1970) identifies four. Most of the spelling errors committed by children involve these four retroflex sounds. The four retroflex sounds are retroflex /rr/ [ற], nasal /mn / [ண], palatal retroflex /z/, [ழ], and apical retroflex /z/ [ள]. Retroflexes do not occur in word-initial positions but are fully recognized in written words even though glossed over in speech.

Spoken Tamil and written Tamil differ from each other in many ways. For instance, word-final nasal retroflex /mn/ is not fully expressed, but glossed over or even omitted in speech. Voiceless consonantal fricative /f/ does not occur in word-initial position but is pronounced as voiceless stop /p/. In addition, spoken Tamil and written Tamil also differ from each other in morphology.

Morphology

As noted earlier, Tamil is an agglutinating language; words contain a linear sequence of morphs starting with the root morpheme onto which suffixes indicating the different grammatical cases are tagged. In general, the inflectional suffix is attached to the lexical root, which is often extended by a derivational suffix. Nouns and verbs are inflected for person, case, number, tense, and gender. Tamil nouns consist of root plus eight case suffix markers. In addition to case markers, additional postpositions are added after the case marker to indicate interrogative and evocative statements. Thus, even though Tamil morphology is transparent, agglutinating, and exclusively suffixal, it can also be considered complex.

When sounds come together across morpheme boundaries, certain changes occur. These are generally morphophonemic in nature and are referred to as *sandhi*, which means "junction." In Tamil, glides are usually inserted between words ending in certain vowels that tend to smoothen the transition between boundaries (Schiffman, 1999). For instance, when the two morphemes இன்பம் [bliss] and கண்டான் [he found] come together, they are combined to form one morpheme இன்பங்கண்டான். However, notice that the word-final consonant [ம்] in the first morpheme changes into [ங்] when the morphemes are combined. Even though there is a sound change, writing the phrase as two morphemes or as a single agglutinated morpheme does not really change the meaning.

Often, sonorants are deleted at morphemic junctions. These changes occur in speech but not in written language. These differences between spoken and written language therefore can be a source of spelling errors.

Written Tamil

Epigraphic records of Ashokan Brahmi writings date Tamil from the second century B.C.E. (Steever, 1987). Tamil orthography is transparent with an almost one-to-one correspondence between the written character and its pronunciation. In this respect, Tamil orthography falls toward the shallow end of the grapheme–phoneme correspondence scale. As noted earlier, each consonant has an inherent vowel and is written as one unit; each consonant therefore represents one syllable. Even when the phonemic value of the consonant is lengthened by the addition of a secondary vowel or a diacritical mark, it still is considered a single character because the secondary phoneme has no inherent value. As a matter of fact, old written Tamil used to physically fuse the consonant and the secondary vowel and write them as a single character. For this reason, Tamil orthography is considered alphasyllabic (Steever, 1996). As noted earlier, certain consonants can be modified by the addition of diacritical marks or secondary vowels that appear as satellites or ligatures to the consonants. The diacritical satellite and ligature signs are sources of spelling errors for Tamil children.

Written Tamil differs markedly from spoken Tamil, an instance of diglossia. As a result, some written consonants are reduced or glossed over in speech. Written Tamil can differ from spoken Tamil in the following respects:

1. Some voiced stops in the written language are devoiced in speech.
2. Word-final nasal sounds may be omitted in speech (*vanthan* → *vantha* [he came]).

3. Palatalization converts /tt/ into /ch/: (*chiritten* → *chirichen* [I laughed]).
4. Cluster reduction is very common in spoken Tamil. The cluster /ndr/ can become /nr/ when /d/ is dropped; /ttr/ can become /tt/ (*vittran* → *vittan* [I sold]).
5. Triliteral consonant is sometimes altered by deletion of a consonant and addition of a vowel (*tattuvam* → *tattva* [tradition]).
6. The diphthong "ai" may be palatalized (*ainthu* → *anchu* [five]).
7. Tamil inanimate nouns are usually unmarked for number in speech; (*oru pustaham*; *rendu pustaham* → [one book; two book]); it is, however, marked in written language (*rendu pusthahangal* [two books]).
8. *Sandhi* was described in the previous section. This refers to changes that occur when sounds come together across morpheme boundaries.

The differences between written Tamil and spoken Tamil can be quite striking and are potential sources of spelling problems for children. It has to be noted, however, that there is a systematic relationship between graphemes and phonemes, making the concept of "irregular words" alien to the Tamil language.

The Nature of Spelling Errors Committed by Tamil-Speaking Children

To answer the question "Do children whose native language is not English but learn English as a textbook language commit fewer spelling errors in English than children whose native language is English?," it is necessary to examine the nature of spelling errors committed by Tamil-speaking children in their own native language. This will allow us to have an understanding of the nature of English spelling errors committed by Tamil-speaking children and use it as a baseline for comparing spelling errors committed by Tamil-speaking and English-speaking children.

Does the Transparent Nature of Tamil Orthography Eliminate Written Spelling Errors?

Study I

A test of dictation was administered to 281 students in Grades 6 through 12. The age of these students ranged from 11 to 17 years. Of these children, 75 were attending English medium classes and the remaining 206 were in the Tamil medium classes. The gradewise distribution of these students is shown in Table 33.1.

The passages chosen for dictation contained 101 of the most commonly occurring words in textbooks of sixth-, seventh-, eighth-, and ninth- grade levels. One of the teachers read the passage to children in every grade and asked them to write down what they heard, taking care not to commit spelling errors. The teacher read these passages at a steady rate with a clear enunciation so that the children could keep up with their writing. The children were told that they could ask the examiner to repeat any phrase or word they missed. The task was administered to one grade at a time by the same teacher. At the end, the written papers were collected and the spelling errors were counted and the errors were classified. The results are given in Table 33.2.

As the data in Table 33.2 show, there was a steady decrement of spelling errors as the grades go up. It appears that there is a significant drop in the errors of the Tamil medium children after Grade 7 and a similar drop at Grade 8 for English medium children. However, the English medium children committed more errors than the children in Tamil medium classes.

TABLE 33.1

Number of Students Who Performed the Dictation Task, Classified According to
Grade and Medium of Instruction

Grade	Tamil Medium	English Medium
6	34	9
7	25	4
8	24	9
9	26	11
10	34	8
11	48	18
12	15	14
Total	206	75

TABLE 33.2

Mean Number of Errors Committed by Students in Different Grades

Grade	Tamil Medium	English Medium
6	4.42	7.96
7	6.18	5.81
8	2.85	8.28
9	3.03	2.62
10	2.36	4.36
11	1.67	3.56
12	1.16	3.28
Overall mean	3.09	5.12

These results are not surprising except that they indicate exposure to visual language (Tamil) contributes to a reduction in spelling errors even in a transparent orthography.

Qualitative analysis of the spelling errors showed that children from both groups committed a large number of errors pertaining to the *sandhi* phenomenon. However, as noted earlier (e.g., இன்பம் கண்டான் → இன்பங்கண்டான்), there is some uncertainty whether these errors should be viewed as spelling errors or as instances arising from the diglossic nature of the language. For our purpose, we disregard errors associated with *sandhi* and do not consider them spelling errors. Leaving aside *sandhi*-related errors, the different kinds of spelling errors that are seen in Tamil are presented in the subsequent list in the order of frequency of their occurrence, with No. 1 showing the most frequently occurring spelling errors and No. 6 showing the least frequently occurring errors.

1. Errors involving the retroflex consonants (திரமை → திறமை பழக → பளக)
2. Errors arising from the omission or substitution of secondary vowels (நாம் → நம்)

3. Errors that are due to the omission of diacritical marks (முடிவு→மடிவு)
4. Errors in the use of "nasals" (நாங்கள்→நான்கள்)
5. Addition and omission of consonants (சாதம்→சாத்தம்; வாய்க்கால்→வாக்கால்)
6. Substitution of consonant (கனி →கணி).

In summary, analysis of the writings of the children who completed the dictation task shows that they make very few spelling errors. Children commit fewer errors as they move up the grades, and by the time they reach the end of high school, they commit practically no spelling errors. This is in agreement with studies that show that spelling errors arise largely from the inconsistencies between pronunciation and spelling. A majority of errors involve confusions arising from the proper use of retroflex consonants followed by failure to properly use secondary vowels and diacritical marks. There are very few errors involving consonants. Overall, compared with English-speaking children, Tamil-speaking children commit considerably fewer spelling errors at all grade levels.

Children from the English medium classes committed more errors compared with the Tamil medium children but showed a similar developmental trend. Here too the overall number of errors committed was relatively small. The spelling performance of these children shows that the degree of grapheme–phoneme correspondence plays an important role in spelling; at the same time, exposure to print also contributes to better spelling.

Special mention has to be made of the agglutinative nature of the Tamil language, which has many multisyllabic morphemic compounds. One may expect that children will fail to add, omit, or substitute morphemic segments and thus commit spelling errors. The results obtained in the present study show that this was not the case. There were hardly any errors in the writings of these children, which can be described as morphemic in nature.

Study II

The objective of this study was to find answers to the following questions:

1. Do children whose native language is not English but who learn English from print commit fewer spelling errors than do children whose native language is English?
2. Are there qualitative differences in the spelling errors committed by Indian children who attend Tamil medium classes, Indian children who attend English medium classes, and American children?
3. Can spelling errors be explained in terms of dialectical differences?
4. Is there is a difference in the spelling performance of Tamil medium children from India who are exposed to written English for about an hour a day and English medium children from India who are exposed to written English the entire school day? Put another way, does the amount of exposure to written English have an influence on the spelling skills of these two groups of children?

Participants.   A list of 20 English function words was administered as a spelling test to two groups of children from India—one group from the Tamil medium classes and another group from the English medium classes. The children tested were from Grades 7–10. The native language of all these children was Tamil. The same list of 20 function words was also administered to American children from Grades 2–5 attending a school in Oklahoma. The native language of all these children was English.

It may be recalled that English is introduced in Grade 6 in India. Therefore, at the time of testing, the Indian children in Grade 7 had been exposed to written English for a period of 2 years. Consequently, Indian children from Grades 8, 9, and 10 had 3, 4, and 5 years of exposure to written English, respectively. American children from Grades 2 through 5 also had exposure to formal written English for a corresponding duration, namely, 2, 3, 4, and 5 years. Of course, the Indian children were chronologically older than the American children, a fact that makes the comparison of spelling production of these children not straightforward. The total number of Tamil medium Indian children, English medium Indian children, and American children studied were 124, 44, and 171, respectively.

Function words were selected to assess the spelling of these children because function words are among the most frequently occurring morphemes, and, as a result, ESL children are likely to have encountered these words many times in spite of their limited exposure to English. Furthermore, function words are universal features of the language whereas lexical morphemes used in textbooks may differ considerably as a result of cultural variations. The spelling test was administered as a group test. Each word was read first by their classroom teacher, who embedded the word in a sentence and uttered the word again. Children then wrote down their responses on a sheet of paper.

Results: Question No. 1.   In Study II, four questions were raised. The first question was this: "Do children whose native language is not English, but learn to spell from print, commit fewer spelling errors in English than children whose native language is English?"

Quantitative analysis was carried out by computing the number of errors committed by children from the different grade levels and then by examining the differences among scores for statistical significance. The results of the quantitative analysis are shown in Table 33.3.

The spelling error scores shown in Table 33.3 indicate that, not surprisingly, children in the Tamil medium group committed significantly more errors than did the English medium Indian children and the American children. This was true for all four grade levels. English medium Indian children from all four grades committed fewer errors than did the American children, with the exception of Grade 3; these differences were statistically significant or were marginally significant.

To analyze the data statistically, the spelling error scores of the three groups of children were subjected to a 3 (groups) $\times$ 4 (grades) analysis of variance. The analysis showed that the differences among the groups as well as the grades were significant: groups: $F(2, 332) = 28.389, p < 0001, \eta^2 = 0.495$; grades: $F(11, 332) = 109.315, p < .0001, \eta^2 = 0.254$. There was also a significant interaction effect: $F(11, 332) = 4.432, p < .005, \eta^2 = 0.04$. Post hoc analysis showed that seventh-grade English medium children committed fewer spelling errors than did second-grade American children who, in turn, performed better than seventh-grade Tamil medium children: $F(2, 76) = 25.225, p < .001, \eta^2 = 0.405$.

There was no significant difference between eighth-grade English medium children and third-grade American children. Children in these two groups performed better than did eighth-grade Tamil medium students: $F(2, 99) = 25.40, p < .001, \eta^2 = 0.344$. English medium Indian children from Grade 9 committed fewer errors than did fourth-grade American children: $t(2, 50) = 2.22, p < .01$; and 10th-grade English medium Indian children committed fewer errors than did fifth-grade American children: $t(2, 48) = 1.54, p < .06$.

Statistical analysis shows that being exposed to spoken English first was associated with more spelling errors as seen in the performance of American children from Grades 2, 4, 5 and 7 than that of English medium Indian children from Grades 7, 9, and 10. The first question therefore can be answered by the statement that children who learn English as a textbook language commit fewer spelling errors than do children whose native language is English.

Results: Question No. 2.   The second question raised in the present study was this: Are there qualitative differences in the spelling errors committed by the three groups of children (Tamil medium, English medium, and American children)?

TABLE 33.3

Mean Number of Spelling Errors Committed by the Three Groups of Children

Parameter	Group of Children		
	Tamil Medium From India	*English Medium From India*	*American– English Children*
Grade	7	7	2
CA (years)	12.6	12.3	7.3
	(*n* = 32)	(*n* = 8)	(*n* = 44)
Mean errors	**12.80**	**3.75**	**8.54**
	(*SD* = 3.28)	(*SD* = 3.10)	(*SD* = 4.05)
Grade	8	8	3
CA (years)	13.4	13.3	8.3
	(*n* = 36)	(*n* = 9)	(*n* = 56)
Mean errors	**9.91**	**4.55**	**4.93**
	(*SD* = 3.78)	(*SD* = 2.74)	(*SD* = 3.29)
Grade	9	9	4
CA (years)	13.2	14.4	9.4
	(*n* = 23)	(*n* = 11)	(*n* = 39)
Mean errors	**9.69**	**1.73**	**3.7**
	(*SD* = 4.95)	(*SD* = 1.73)	(*SD* = 2.84)
Grade	10	10	5
CA (years)	14.3	14.3	10.6
	(*n* = 33)	(*n* = 16)	(*n* = 32)
Mean errors	**4.90**	**1.38**	**2.56**
	(*SD* = 3.34)	(*SD* = 2.06)	(*SD* = 2.71)

Notes. CA = chronological age; *SD* = standard deviation.

Qualitative analysis was carried out addressing two issues: (a) What is the nature of the spelling errors; are the spelling errors phonologically acceptable, phonologically unacceptable, or morphemic substitutions? (b) Are the words misspelled by the three groups of children the same or different?

To address the first issue, all the misspelled words were examined and each misspelling was classified as phonologically acceptable (phonological hereafter), phonologically unacceptable (nonphonological hereafter), or an instance of morphemic substitution. To be phonologically acceptable, the misspelled word, when pronounced, should sound like the target word. Examples of phonologically acceptable misspellings are "which" → *wich, whych*; "any" → *eny, eni*. Examples of phonologically unacceptable misspellings are "which" → *wicht, yuch*; "any" → *inny, anne*. Morphemic substitutions are real words substituted for target words. Examples are "it" → *ate*; "thus" → *this*. There are instances when it is difficult to decide whether the misspelling is a phonologically acceptable error or a semantic substitution. Examples of such ambiguous errors are "once" → *ones*; "off" → *of*. Under those circumstances, these words were classified both as phonologically acceptable and as morphemic substitution errors.

The results of such classifications are shown in Tables 33.4 and 33.5.

The data shown in Tables 33.4 and 33.5 lead to the following conclusions:

TABLE 33.4

Nature of Spelling Errors Committed by Indian Children and American Children From the Different Grades

Group of Children	Grade	Phonological Errors (%)	Nonphonological Errors (%)	Morphemic Substitutions (%)
Tamil med	7	16.9	64.6	18.5
English med	7	41.4	44.8	14.8
American	2	38.4	47.3	14.3
Tamil Med	8	24.4	50.3	25.3
English Med	8	45.7	32.6	21.7
American	3	64.0	28.6	7.4
Tamil Med	9	41.9	35.0	23.1
English Med	9	30.8	46.2	23.1
American	4	57.9	25.7	16.4
Tamil Med	10	33.3	26.3	40.4
English Med	10	45.2	35.5	19.4
American	5	65.6	26.8	7.5

TABLE 33.5

Nature of Spelling Errors Committed by Indian Children and American Children, All Four Grades Combined

Group of Children	Phonological (%)	Nonphonological (%)	Morphemic Substitutions (%)
Tamil Med	28.82	43.90	26.83
English Med	40.35	39.58	19.75
American	56.12	31.58	11.40

1. The two groups of Indian children as well as the American children make more non-phonological than phonological errors during the second year of exposure to printed English. That is, both groups of Indian children from Grade 7 and American children from Grade 2 produce more nonphonological than phonological misspellings.

2. Tamil medium children continue to commit more nonphonological errors during the next grade, but during the following two years (Grades 9 and 10), they too commit more phonological than nonphonological errors. Children in the English medium group are somewhat inconsistent, but, during the final grade studied, they too produce more phonological errors. There is a general increase in the proportion of phonological errors for all groups.

3. When all the four grades were combined, 56.1% of all the spelling errors committed by American children were phonologically acceptable. The corresponding percentage for English medium and Tamil medium Indian children were 40.35 and 28.82, respectively. This may be taken to mean that phonology has greater influence on the spelling production of American children than on that of Indian children.

4. At all grades, Indian children from both groups make more morphemic substitution errors than American children.

TABLE 33.6

Most Frequently Misspelled Target Words and the Percentage of Children Who Misspelled Them

Tamil medium (grade)	Target Word				
	any	*since*	*much*	*could*	*ago*
7	88.46	76.90	92.30	61.53	53.12
8	80.50	77.70	61.60	22.20	22.23
9	69.60	73.91	56.50	21.71	26.12
10	40.90	18.18	38.63	2.27	03.33

English medium (grade)	Target Word			
	yet	*since*	*though*	*off*
7	37.50	37.54	50.50	22.27
8	66.62	33.32	66.65	22.95
9	45.45	9.12	18.18	33.30
10	16.25	12.50	18.75	12.29

American children (grade)	Target Word			
	which	*thus*	*any*	*once*
2	84.36	63.63	87.73	88.64
3	73.20	51.80	44.62	54.19
4	48.71	58.90	32.84	46.90
5	46.90	42.75	9.72	58.59

The second issue raised was whether the words misspelled by all the three groups of children were the same or different. This issue was addressed by listing all the misspellings and then computing the number of children who misspelled each word. The most frequently misspelled words are shown in Table 33.6.

The data shown in Table 33.6 indicate that, when analysis is limited to four or five words that are misspelled most often, there is little commonality of misspellings among the three groups of children. Some words are more difficult to spell for Indian children than others, whereas some other words are more difficult for American children. However, when the less frequently misspelled words were examined, it was noted that some words were misspelled by all the three groups of children equally often.

Results: Question No. 3. Can the spelling errors be explained in terms of dialectical differences? To answer this question, words that were most frequently misspelled by children from each group were identified. The misspellings of each group were then examined and compared with the misspellings produced by the other two groups of children for the same target word. This was done to see if the three groups differ from each other in their misspellings and to see if the source of their misspellings could be identified. For example, the word "yet" was overwhelmingly misspelled as *et, ait*, and *ate* by Indian children whereas it was misspelled as *whet*

TABLE 33.7

Words Most Frequently Misspelled by Tamil Medium Children From the Four Grades, the
Product of Their Misspelling, and the Misspellings Produced by Seventh-Grade English Medium
Children and Second-Grade American Children for the Same Target Words

Target Word	Product of Misspelling	Frequency	Comments
such			
Tamil medium children	sarch	30/66[a]	Initial
(n = 124)	chuch	26/66	[ch] substitution common
English medium children	huch	1/2	Very few errors
(n = 44)	schich	1/2	
American children	sarch	10/13	
(n = 171)	chrch	1/13	[ch] Substitution uncommon
yet			
Tamil medium children	et, eet	36/80	Substituting [a] for [y] is common because [y] does not occur in word-initial position in Tamil.
	ait, at	26/80	
English medium children	ate, aet	11/17	
	ete, et	3/17	
American children	whet	6/12	Substituting [w] for [y] common, but not Substitution with [a]
	yeat	5/12	
could			
Tamil medium children	good	51/65	Morphemic substitution "good" very common.
	cood	7/65	In Tamil, voiced stop /g/ is pronounced as voiceless stop /k/
English medium children	kood, good	5/7	
American children	cud, coud	22/22	No American child spells with an initial [g]
since			
Tamil medium children	sings, sins	69/79	In Tamil, initial /c/ is pronounced /s/
	cins, ceins	10/79	Substitution of [c] for [s] Morphemic substitution common
English medium children	sines, sence	8/9	No [c] substitution
American children	sence, sens	32/37	Only two [c] substitutions
	sins	4/37	Four morphemic substitutions
ago			
Tamil medium children	ako, kao	10/32	Substituting [k] for [g] common
English medium children	aggo, agao	2/2	No [k] substitution
American children	ugo, agoe, aggo	9/11	No American child substitutes [k] for [g]
let			
Tamil medium children	lat, late, lete	36/39	Addition of word-final [e] common
English medium children	lat, lert	3/3	No word final [e]
American children	lat, leat	10 /11	Addition of word-final [e] not common
much			
Tamil medium children	match, mach	30/32	Have difficulty in producing [mu] cluster, which is represented by a single grapheme in Tamil with an herent [a]
English medium children	mach, mush	2/2	
American children	mush, muoch, muce	21/21	Very few [mu] related errors

(Continued)

TABLE 33.7
(Continued)

Target Word	Product of Misspelling	Frequency	Comments
off			
Tamil medium children	*of*	49/58	Tamil has no voiceless fricative /f/; morphemic substitution quite common
English medium children	*of*	5/5	Morphemic substitutions
American children	*of*	4/6	Morphemic Substitution
	oof	2/6	
will			
Tamil medium children	*well, while*	4/9	Easiest word to spell
	vike, wall	3/9	
English medium children	No errors		
American children	*well*	6/8	Easy to spell; many morphemic substitutions
else			
Tamil medium children	les, lse	36/82	Most misspelled words start with [i] or [a] In Tamil, alveolar /l/ is represented by a single grapheme.
	els, esl, ais	28/82	
	yels, yulse	12/82	
English medium children	els, asl	5/12	
	yls	5/12	
	als	2/12	
American children	els, ells	58/69	Only 5 out of 69 misspellings start with [i] or [a]
	als, alls	6/69	
	les, lss	6/69	
any			
Tamil medium children	eny, eney	20/39	Groups do not
	aney, anne	17/39	differ much
English medium children	ainy	1/2	Very few errors
	eny	1/2	
American children	eny, eney	20/38	
	Innye	6/38	
	anney	2/38	

[a]Example: Out of the 60 words misspelled by Tamil medium children, 30 fell into this category of misspelling.

and *yeat* by many American children. This indicates that Indian children had more difficulty with the grapheme [y] than American children, perhaps because, in Tamil, the phoneme /y/ does not occur in the word-initial position and there is no single grapheme in Tamil to represent the phoneme /y/.

The results of such an analysis are shown in Tables 33.7, 33.8, and 33.9.

Information provided in Tables 33.7, 33.8, and 33.9 show that there are noticeable differences in the misspellings produced by the three groups. Some of the differences can be traced to differences in the speech patterns and phonological features of the two languages, Tamil

TABLE 33.8

TABLE 33.8

Words Most Frequently Misspelled by English Medium Indian Children From the Four Grades
and the Misspellings Produced by Tamil Medium Children and Second-Grade American Children
for the Same Target Words

Target Word	Product of Misspelling	Frequency	Comments
though			
Tamil medium children	thoe, tho	68/73	
(n = 124)	doe, go	5/73	
English medium children	thou, thouth, tough	13/16	[th] graph is not difficult
(n = 44)			
American children			
(n = 171)	thowe, tho,	65/71	Error pattern similar to that of English medium children
	do, doe	6/71	
else			
Tamil medium children	les, lse	36/82	Most misspelled words start with [i] or [a]
	els, esl, ais	28/82	
	yels, yulse	12/82	
English medium children	els, asl	5/12	Phoneme /l/ does not occur in word-initial position except in loan words
	yls	5/12	
	als	2/12	
American children	els, ells	58/69	Only 5 out of 69 misspellings start with [i] or [a]
	als, alls	6/69	
	les, lss	6/69	
nor			
Tamil medium children	naar, nour	49/63	
	nore	9/63	
	north	5/63	
English medium children	noar	9/12	Easy word to spell
	nore	3/12	
American children	nore, nowre	72/83	Adding [e] to word ending, a common error
	naur	8/83	
	knor	3/83	
yet			
Tamil medium children	eat	34/68	Represent /y/ sound; hence [a & e] substitutions
	ate, at	31/68	
English medium children	ate, ait	11/18	Tamil does not have a grapheme for /y/
	ete	3/18	
American children	yeat, yate,	7/18	Substitution of [w] for [y] common
	wet	7/18	
	eat	1/18	
since			
Tamil medium children	sings, sins	9/21	In Tamil, initial /c/ is pronounced /s/
	cins, ceins	4/21	Substitution of [c] for [s]; morphemic substitution common
English medium children	sines, sence	8/9	No [c] substitution
American children	sence, sens	32/37	Only two [c] substitutions; four morphemic substitutions
	sins	4/37	
off			
Tamil medium children	of	49/58	Tamil has no voiceless fricative [f]
English medium children	of	5/5	Morphemic substitution common
American children	of	4/6	
	oof	2/6	Of is easy to spell

TABLE 33.9
Words Most Frequently Misspelled by American Children From the Four Grades and the
Misspellings Produced by Tamil Medium and English Medium Indian Children From the
Different Grades for the Same Words

Target Word	Product of Misspelling	Frequency	Comments
which			
American children	wich	67/113	[h] omission 84.3%
(n = 171)	witch	39/113	
Tamil medium children	wicht	29/57	[h] omission 64.9%
(n = 124)	uch, yuh	20/57	
	with	6/57	
	wich, witch	5/57	
English medium children	wicht	2/4	[h] omission 50.0%
(n = 44)	yuch	2/4	
thus			
American children	thuse, thous	83/94	"Thus" is more difficult for American children than for Indian children; morphemic substitutions 9.5%.
	this, these	5/94	
	does	4/94	
Tamil medium children	thes, thuse,	27/55	Mormephic substitutions 47.3%.
	this, these	21/55	
	does	5/55	
English medium children	thuse	5/8	Morphemic substitutions 37.5%
	this, these	3/8	
once			
American children	wuns	30/56	[w] substitution 53%
	onec, ones	23/56	[o] substitution 41%
Tamil medium children	ones, onces, oncer	53/55	[w] substitution 0.0%
English medium children	ones, one	6/6	[w] substitution 0.0%
any			
American children	eney, yny	26/37	Word-initial [e] 64.1%
	inny	9/37	Word-initial [i] 24.5%
	ane	1/37	Word-initial [a] 2.7%
Tamil medium children	eni	22/42	Word-initial [e] 53.3%
	anne	18/42	Word-initial [a] 42.8%
	inny	0/42	Word-initial [i] 0.0%
English medium children	aney	1/2	
	eny	1/2	Very few errors

and English. In the following list, some spelling errors are interpreted in terms of phonological and dialectical features of English and Tamil:

1. Initial [ch] substitution is common in Tamil medium children's spellings (e.g., "such" → "chuch"). Such a substitution is uncommon in American children's spellings.
2. Indian children substitute [a] or [e] for [y] (yet → *ate, eat*). American children tend to substitute [w] for [y]. *In Tamil, /y/ is not represented as a distinct phoneme.*
3. Tamil medium Indian children substitute [g] for [c] (e.g., could → *good*), indicating a general inconsistency in the use of [c] and [g]. American children misspell the word

"could" as *cud*, *culd*, and so forth. *In Tamil phonology, voiced stop /g/ in initial position is produced as allophones of voiceless /k/. (agrahara → akraharam).*

4. Tamil medium Indian children also tend to substitute [k] for [g] (e.g., ago → *ako*). Such a substitution is not seen in American children's spelling. This indicates a general inconsistency in the use of /c/ and /g/ by Indian children. *Tamil phonology does not mark for the glottal /g/ phoneme.*

5. Indian children substitute [c] for [s] (since → cins) *Tamil does not make a distinction between voiced and voiceless /c/.*

6. Tamil medium Indian children have a tendency to add [e] at the word-final position (e.g., let → *lete*, *late*). Such an addition is uncommon in the spellings of English medium Indian children and American children. *In Tamil, the phoneme /t/ is not present.*

7. The digraph [mu] is difficult for Indian children to produce (e.g., much → *mach, match*). Such substitution is generally not seen in the spellings of American children. *The [mu] digraph is represented by a single grapheme in Tamil orthography.*

8. Indian children show a tendency to replace [el] with [l] or [y] (else → *als*; *yls*). Such a substitution is rarely seen in American children's spellings. *The alveolar /el/ is represented in Tamil phonology by a single grapheme.*

9. "Off" is a difficult word to spell correctly for Indian children. *The grapheme [f] has no representation in Tamil orthography.*

10. American children substitute /wi/ for /wh/ (which → wich, witch). Indian children also omit [h], but not to the same extent. The combination of two semivowels or glides /w/ and /h/ can be a source of this difficulty for all children. *Oklahoma dialect may also be an additional contributing factor.*

11. The word "thus" is difficult for American children (54.9%). It is less so for Tamil medium children (44.35%) and English medium Indian children (18.18%). The misspellings of Indian children of this word is primarily due to morphemic substitutions. *The difficulty in spelling "thus" may be due to treating [u] as a neutral vowel, schwa.*

12. American children frequently substitute /w/ for /o/ in "once." *American children tend to confuse between the glide /w/ and other vowel sounds such as /o/. The local Oklahoma dialect may not draw a sharp distinction between these two sounds.*

13. American children spell "any" as *eney* and *yny* and "since" as *sense*, "will" as *well*, and "which" as *wich*. *These spellings may reflect the influence of the local Oklahoma dialect.*

14. All three groups of children have difficulty with liquids (/w/, /y/) but deal with them differently. Indian children substitute /u/ for /oo/ (e.g., soon → *sun*) but American children often omit one /o/ (*sone*). *In Tamil, /oo/ is represented by a single character.*

The information presented in Tables 33.7–33.9 indicate that not only the words most often misspelled by the three groups of children are different but the etiology of their misspellings also differs. However, all three groups experienced difficulties in spelling words such as "any," "will," and "though."

Results: Question 4. Is there is a difference in the spelling performance of Tamil-medium children who are exposed to written English for about an hour a day and English medium children who are exposed to English the entire schoolday? Put another way, does the amount of exposure to written English have an influence on the spelling skills of these two groups of children?

Data from Tables 33.5 and 33.6 show that, at all grade levels, English medium Indian children committed significantly fewer spelling errors than did Tamil medium children. This is taken to mean that exposure to printed language does have a positive influence on the spelling development of children. This is based on the observation that these English medium children can hardly speak English nor are they exposed to spoken English as American children are. Even if the children hear English words and short sentences in the classroom, the teachers pronounce them just as they pronounce Tamil words.

CONCLUSIONS

Linguistic comparisons across linguistic boundaries are difficult because of the many confounding factors that can contribute to differences in the performances of children. One obvious factor is familiarity with the words used in the spelling test. Not knowing a word can lead to phonetic misspellings. However, none of the 20 function words used in the present study was misspelled by all the children in any group. Even a low-frequency word such as "yet" was spelled correctly by more than 35% of Tamil medium children from second grade.

One major confounding feature is the difference in the chronological age between the Indian children and the American children involved in the studies. Can the observation that these Indian children were better spellers be attributed to their being older than the American children?

The data presented in the paper bring us to these conclusions:

1. Phonology does play an important role in spelling. American children tend to produce more phonology-based misspellings than Indian children.
2. Exposure to native speech can be a source of spelling errors. Exposure to native English pronunciation and dialect affects the spelling of American children more than it does the spellings of Indian children.
3. At the same time, phonology of the native language of Indian children is also a source of spelling errors, even though of a different kind.
4. When phonology is not accessible for spelling, children tend to make morphemic substitutions. This may be an explanation of the overproduction of morphemic errors by the Indian children.
5. Visual exposure to written language has a facilitating effect on the acquisition of spelling skill. This statement is based on the observation that Indian children from English medium classes are better spellers than Indian children who are from Tamil medium classes.
6. Neither the complex nature of Tamil morphology nor the diglossic nature of Tamil language is a major source of errors of written language.

ACKNOWLEDGMENTS

The authors sincerely thank Mathuram Thiruthuvakani, Tamil Nadu, India, who collected data on Indian children, and Nancy Hill from Oklahoma, who collected data on American children. This study would not have been possible without their help.

REFERENCES

Arra, C. T., & Aaron, P. G. (2001). Effects of psycholinguistic instruction on spelling performance. *Psychology in the Schools. 38*, 357–363.

Arulmani, S. N. (2003). Reading difficulties in Indian languages. In N. Goulandris (Ed.), *Dyslexia in different languages* (pp. 235–253). London; Whurr.

Beschi, C. J. (1848/1992). *A grammar of the common dialect of the Tamil Language*. (G. W. Mahon, Trans.). Madras, India: Asican Educational Services.

Caldwell, R. (1875). *A comparative grammar of the Dravidian or South Indian family of languages*. Madras, Tamil Nadu, India: University of Madras.

Carney, S. (1979). *The relationship of black non-standard dialect features to a core spelling vocabulary*. ERIC Document No. ED 170700; Clearninghouse No. CS004778.

Castle, J. M., Biach, J., & Nicholson, T. (1994). Getting off to a better start in reading and spelling: The effects of phonemic awareness instruction within a whole language program. *Journal of Educational Psychology, 86*, 350–359.

Emeneau, M. B. (1970). *Dravidian comparative phonology: A sketch*. Annamalai Nagar, Tamil Nadu, India: Annamalai University.

Hugh, R. E. (1970). Dialect and spelling. *Elementary English, 47*, 363–376.

Kligman, D., & Bruce, C. (1974). *Black English and spelling*. ERIC document No. ED108234; Clearinghouse No. CS 202121.

McCardle, P. (1980). *Vernacular Black English and underlying phonological form: Evidence from child spelling*. ERIC document No. ED2111614.

Meenakshi, K. (2002). Retroflex sounds in Indian Languages. *International Journal of Dravidian Linguistics, 31*, 1–16.

Schiffman, H. F. (1999). *A reference grammar of spoken Tamil*. New York: Cambridge University Press.

Schwab, D. (1971). *Black English and rule-based spelling output*. Eric document no. ED 111022, Clearinghouse No. CS 202241

Steever, E. F. (1980). Dialect and spelling. In E. H. Henderson & W. Beers (Eds.), *Developmental and cognitive aspects of learning to spell* (pp. 46–51). Newark, DE: International Reading Association.

Steever, H. (1987). Tamil and the Dravidian Languages. In B. Comrie (Ed.), *The world's major languages* (pp. 725–746). New York: Oxford University Press.

Steever, H. (1996). Tamil writing. In P. T. Daniels & W. Bright (Eds.), *The world's writing systems* (pp. 426–430). New York: Oxford University Press,.

Treiman, R. (1993). *Beginning to spell*. New York: Oxford University Press.

Treiman, R., & Barry, C. (2000). Dialect and orthography: Some differences between American and British spellers. *Journal of Experimental Psychology (Learning, Memory, & Cognition), 26*, 1423–1430.

Treiman, R., Goswami, U., Tincoff, R., & Leevers (1997). Effects of dialect on American and British children's spelling. *Child Development, 68*, 229–245.

Walker, L. (1979). Newfoundland dialect interference in fourth grade spelling. *Alberta Journal of Educational Research, 25*, 221–233.

Zvelebil, K. (1970). *Comparative Dravidian phonology*. The Hague: Mouton.

34

Learning to Spell by Ear and by Eye: A Cross-Linguistic Comparison

R. Malatesha Joshi
Texas A & M University

Torleiv Høien
Stavanger Institute

Xiwu Feng
La Guardia Community College

Rajni Chengappa
University of Mysore

Regina Boulware-Gooden
Neuhaus Education Center

Orthographies vary from each other in terms of grapheme–phoneme correspondence. The grapheme–phoneme relationship can be shallow or deep, and the extent of this relationship is generally referred to as "orthographic depth." We present the results of two studies that examined the spelling performance of non-English-speaking children who had learned English as a second language primarily through textbooks. The results showed that the nature of orthography of the native language of these children influenced their spelling of English words. Results also showed that, regardless of whether English was learned in the spoken form or primarily through books, phonology plays an important role in spelling.

Brains may be similar from one culture to another but orthographies certainly are not
—Coltheart, Patterson, & Marshall (1980)

INTRODUCTION

Recently there has been a resurgence of interest in the literacy acquisition of bilinguals and second-language learners. This is not surprising because bilinguals appear to exceed the number of people who are monolinguals. One of the questions often asked is the influence of the orthographic, phonological, and visual features of the first language (L1) has on the acquisition of a second language (L2). In one study, Durgunoğlu, Nagy, and Hancin-Bhatt (1993) found that children who had high level of phonological awareness in Spanish performed well on reading words and nonwords in English. This led Durgunoğlu et al. (1993) to conclude that "phonological awareness was a significant predictor of performance on word recognition tests both within and across languages" (p. 461). A similar facilitating effect of transfer from Portuguese to English has been found by Da Fontoura and Siegel (1995) and from Italian to English by D'Angiuilli, Siegel, and Serra (2002).

These findings may be true of alphabetic orthographies, but can these be generalized to other types of writing systems such as the morphemic Chinese and syllabic Korean Hangul and some of the alphasyllabic East Asian orthographies?

There is some evidence to support that the type of orthography of L1 can influence word-recognition skills in L2. Holm and Dodd (1996), for example, compared the phonemic awareness and English nonword-reading skills of children from mainland China, who were exposed to Pinyin (an alphabetic-based written form of Chinese) and children from Hong Kong who were not exposed to Pinyin. They found that children from mainland China performed better at segmenting English words as well as at naming English nonwords. Mumtaz and Humpreys (2001) found that Urdu–English bilinguals who were exposed to Urdu (a phonologically regular orthography) as L1 performed better on reading English words and nonwords than did monolingual English-speaking children. Koda (1987, 1989) observed that the Japanese script influenced the learning of English by Japanese who were learning English as a second language, (ESL) and Jackson, Chen, Goldsberry-Shaver, Kim, & Vanderwerff (1999) found that the Chinese script had some influence on the learning of English. In both of these studies, participants performed better on orthographic tasks than on phonological tasks.

Most of these studies have examined the L1 influence on L2 on phonological awareness and reading-related tasks. However, spelling performance might be a better predictor of an individual's knowledge of alphabetic principle because spelling is more demanding than reading and because it is a recall task rather than a recognition task. Shankweiler, Lundquist, Dreyer, and Dickinson (1996) made this suggestion: "Thus, although spelling is, of course, not a component of reading, it provides a valuable indicator of the level of orthographic skill on which all literacy activities ultimately depend. Word recognition and all subsequent higher level processes that take place in reading are constrained by the ability to fluently transcode print into language" (p. 287).

One of the few studies that has compared the transfer of spelling performance from L1 to L2 was conducted by Wang and Geva (2003). They compared the spelling performance of Chinese ESL children with monolingual English-speaking children. It was found that Chinese ESL children in Grade 2 performed poorly on spelling English pseudowords than English monolingual children did, even though there was no difference between the two groups in the spelling of real words. These results were interpreted in terms of the Chinese script, which does not make use of the "assembled phonology" route (Besner & Smith, 1992; Coltheart, Rastle, Perry, Langdon, & Ziegler, 2001). This finding was replicated by Wade-Woolley and Siegel (1997), who also found similar results in which Chinese ESL children did not differ from English-speaking children on spelling of real words but performed poorly on phonological tasks.

In the studies reported in this chapter, we wanted to examine the extent to which exposure to a nonalphabetic orthographies influences the ability to spell English words.

STUDY I

Method

Participants

The participants for the present study were selected from regular classrooms from the following grades in different countries: Grades 3 and 4 from the United States; Grades 5 and 6 from Norway; Grades 7 and 8 from India; and Grades 5 and 6 from China. The children from Norway and China involved in the present study learned English as a second language from Grade 3 on, and children from India started learning English when they entered Grade 5. The common factor shared by all children was that at the time of the present study they had received at least 2 years of formal instruction in English. The orthography of these languages differs from each other in the following way: Norwegian orthography is essentially alphabetic; Chinese orthography

TABLE 34.1

Number of Participants From Different Countries at Various Grade Levels

	Country			
Grade	U.S.	Norway	India	China
3	41			
4	39			
5		93		43
6		72		42
7			36	
8			40	

is predominantly morphemic. Indian children for this study were selected from the state of Karnataka, where Kannada is the predominant language and the script is basically alphabetic–syllabic in nature. (For a detailed description of the nature of the Norwegian, Chinese, and Kannada scripts, please refer to chapters by Hagtvet, Helland, & Lyster; Cheung & McBride-Chang; and Karanth, respectively, in this volume). The number of participants from different countries at various grade levels is shown in Table 34.1. There were approximately an equal number of boys and girls at each grade level.

Procedure

Spelling Test.   All the children were administered a spelling test of 50 English words. These words were selected from the children's textbooks, and hence these words were familiar to the children. The list of words consisted of high-frequency content words such as "father," "world," and "food," and high-frequency function words such as "because" and "between." The list also included irregular words such as "elephant" and "half." The frequency count of these words was based on the guide by Zeno, Ivenz, Millard, and Duvvuri (1995).

The spelling test was administered as a group test. The target word was pronounced and then used in a sentence, and then the target word was repeated and the children were asked to write the target word as best as they could, even if they did not know how to spell the word. All 50 words were dictated first, and, at the end of the test, subjects were asked whether they wanted any word to be repeated. Four trial words were administered to ensure that the subjects understood the task. The classroom teacher administered the test to the U.S. children. The test for Norwegian, Chinese, and Indian subjects was administered by a local person who was fluent in English. The written spellings were analyzed and scored by two examiners.

Results

The written spellings of the children were scored right or wrong by the two examiners. The means and standard deviations of this assessment are shown in Table 34.2.

An analysis of variance (ANOVA) showed that there was a significant difference among the four groups at 0.000 level ($F = 61.727$). The next step was to conduct a post hoc analysis by use of Tukey's honestly significant difference (HSD) method to see whether there were

TABLE 34.2

Number of Words Spelled Correctly by Children From Different Grades
and Different Countries (Standard Deviations in Parentheses)

	Country			
Grade	U.S.	Norway	India	China
3	33.54 (10.87)			
4	40.58 (9.12)			
5		8.92 (8.49)		7.40 (3.58)
6		19.04 (13.42)		11.83 (6.18)
7			11.06 (7.86)	
8			21.33 (9.07)	

any significant differences among children from different grades and different countries. This analysis showed that there was a significant difference between American third graders and the other three orthographic groups. However, there was no significant difference among Chinese fifth graders, Norwegian fifth graders, and Indian seventh graders. From this analysis, it seems that orthography may not influence the acquisition of spelling of English words, irrespective of the L1 background. However, the pattern of performance was different for the next grade. Sixth-grade Chinese children performed significantly worse than the other three groups, but there was no significant difference between eighth graders from India and sixth graders from Norway. This leads to the conclusion that, even though the three groups performed similarly at the third-year of learning English, once the children become more exposed to English, Indian and Norwegian children perform better than their Chinese counterparts.

Because scoring spelling as right or wrong might not give a comprehensive understanding of children's knowledge of English orthography, the spelling of children was scored with Tangel and Blachman's (1995) 7-point scoring criteria. This form of scoring is based on the child's knowledge of phonetic and morphological structure of the word. According to this criterion, no (o) points are given to a random production of a string of letters that bears no relation to the target word; 1 point is given if there is one letter that represents a correct phoneme from the target word, 2 points are given if the first phoneme of the target word is present and another letter that represents another phoneme. A correct spelling receives 6 points. The means and standard deviations of the scores of the participants in the study were computed, and the results are shown in Table 34.3.

The results of ANOVA showed that there was a significant difference among the four orthographic groups at the 0.000 level ($F = 103.17$). Post hoc analysis with Tukey's HSD method showed that there was a significant difference between U.S. third graders and the other three orthographic groups. However, when the degree of phonological approximation to the target word was taken into consideration, Chinese fifth graders performed significantly poorer than the comparable groups from India and Norway. Even though there was no significant difference when the spelling was scored right or wrong among fifth-grade Chinese, fifth-grade Norwegian, and seventh-grade Indian children, there was a significant difference when spelling was evaluated in terms of its phonetic approximation. When Indian and Norwegian children were not sure of the correct spelling, they would make an attempt to spell the word and were successful in producing a few phonetic equivalents, whereas Chinese children tended to skip

TABLE 34.3
Means (and Standard Deviations) of Correct Phonetic Elements

		Country		
Grade	U.S.	Norway	India	China
3	250.71 (46.97)			
4	287.79 (25.12)			
5		156.77 (28.94)		70.35 (30.21)
6		195.07 (30.70)		106.14 (49.12)
7			135.56 (52.94)	
8			192.80 (47.65)	

the word entirely or their misspellings were off the target word when they were uncertain about the word. This could be because the phonological nature of the Norwegian and Kannada orthography might have facilitated the production of an approximation to the target word. For example, take the word "night." The misspellings produced by Norwegian children were *nait, nte, naj it, nigt, and nnet*; spellings produced by Indian children were *nite, nit, niat,* and *niteght*; spellings produced by the Chinese children were *nite, nice, like, light, nike,* and *nine*. Note that, in contrast to Norwegian and Indian groups, the Chinese children tended to produce real words. Similarly, for the word "world," Norwegian children wrote: *word, wold, vold,* and *vorld*; Indian children wrote *word, volte, wold,* and *owed*; but the Chinese children wrote *work, worker, wall,* and *what,* all of which are real words.

From this study, it could be concluded that the nature of orthography and the knowledge that words could be broken down into phonetic elements might facilitate the acquisition of English spelling. Further, an additional exposure of 1 year to English orthography had a greater facilitating effect on Norwegian and Kannada-speaking beginning readers than on Chinese beginning readers.

STUDY II

It has been recognized that phonology plays an important role in the acquisition of spelling skills by children. This conclusion is primarily based on the works of Read (1975) and Treiman (1993). Read analyzed the data from spontaneous production of spelling by precocious preschoolers and concluded that, similar to learning to talk, learning to spell is a creative process. Even though spelling was generally considered as a visual memorization process, Read's work showed that children try to symbolize the sounds that they hear in their spelling. He also noticed that spelling errors committed by children were not random errors but reflected the influence of phonology that underlies spelling. For instance, children often omitted nasal sounds such as /n/ because nasal consonants are acquired much later than other consonants. Hence children had a tendency to leave out "n" in words like "pant" and "snow." Similarly, Treiman's (1993) study of first-grade children showed that their spelling errors indicated the use of sound structure of the spoken language to a great extent. Thus, from the analysis of spelling errors of children, both precocious and normal, we have come to realize that phonology plays an important role in children's spelling.

Another avenue of research that has shed light on the relationship between phonology and spelling is the study of spelling performance of children who speak different dialects. Treiman, Goswami, Tincoff, and Leevers (1997) studied spelling performance of speakers of different dialects of English such as general American English and southern British English and confirmed the earlier finding that phonology of spoken language influences spelling. For instance, British children spelled "car" as *ca* whereas American children spelled car as *cr*; similarly, British children spelled "hurt" as *hut* whereas American children spelled it as *hrt*. Interestingly, adults with different accents (American and Welsh) also produce similar errors, further indicating that phonology plays an important role in the spelling of adults as well (Treiman & Barry, 2000). Further, it has been shown that training in phonemic awareness improves spelling of children (Arra & Aaron, 2001; Ball & Blachman, 1991; Lundberg, Frost & Petersen, 1988).

If phonology plays a major role in spelling, then the nature of spelling errors committed by children whose native language is not English but who learn English first as a written language would be expected to differ from those committed by children who acquire English as a spoken language first. That is, children whose mother tongue is English are likely to be influenced by the English they hear and therefore their misspellings are likely to reflect the influence of phonology. Children who learn English first as a spoken language are therefore likely to "regularize" the spellings of many irregular words whereas children who learn English first as a written language are likely not to "phoneticize" many irregular words.

The school system in India provides an opportunity to evaluate the validity of this hypothesis. In the study reported here, we compared the spelling errors committed by children who learned English first as a spoken language and errors committed by children who learned English first as a written language.

Participants

The participants for the U.S. sample came from an elementary school in the southwestern part of the country, and the sample of Indian children came from the state of Karnataka, South India. There were a total of 36 children in the U.S. sample and 47 children in the Indian sample. Because we were testing children for their spelling ability, we selected the Indian children from Grade 2. These children start learning English from the first grade and are therefore exposed to English for at least 1 year. It has to be noticed that these children are taught to read and write English rather than use it for conversation. Consequently the major difference between the two groups in the study was that American children acquired English as a spoken language at home whereas the Indian children learned English as a formal subject at school. These children spoke Kannada, an alpha-syllabic language at home. Kannada is one of the major Dravidian languages with a linguistic history of nearly 1,500 years and a literary tradition of about 1,200 years. Being a polysyllabic agglutinative language, it has numerous inflections. The orthography of Kannada derives from Brahmi; sometimes a single character represents a single syllable with an almost one-to-one correspondence between graphemes and phonemes. However, each syllable can be analyzed into its consonant and vowel components.

None of the children studied had noticeable mental or physical deficiencies; the average age of the children from both the countries was approximately 7.5 years.

Procedure

The same procedure used in Study I was adopted in administering the spelling test. The test was administered to the Indian children by a local person who was a fluent speaker of English.

TABLE 34.4

Means, Standard Deviations, and the Results of the *t* Test

	U.S. (n = 36)	India (n = 47)	t value
Mean	14.31	12.96	
			1.9 n.s.
Standard deviation	7.95	7.15	

The classroom teacher administered the test to the American children. The written spellings were analyzed by two examiners.

Results

As a first step, the produced spellings were scored as "right" or "wrong." The number of correctly spelled words was calculated and the mean and standard deviation were computed for both groups. A *t* test was computed for determining whether there was any significant difference between the two groups. The results would indicate whether phonology plays an important role because these children from India were not exposed to spoken English language whereas the American children were. The results are shown in Table 34.4.

The next step was to analyze the number of phonetic equivalents each group had produced in their spelling. We accomplished this by analyzing the words according to Tangel and Blachman's (1995) scoring criteria described in Study I. The mean number of correct phonemes in the spellings as well as the standard deviation were computed and were found to be 166.92 ($SD = 46.43$) for the U.S. children and 136.69 ($SD = 43.98$) for the Indian children. The results of the *t* test showed that this difference was significant at the 0.003 level ($t = 9.17$).

Further qualitative analysis of some words revealed interesting findings. Some high-frequency regular words such as "father" and "cold" were spelled equally well by both groups of children. Further, more Indian children spelled the word "elephant" correctly or produced more phonetic equivalents of the word than the U.S. children did. This is understandable because children in this part of India are regularly exposed to the word "elephant" in both spoken and written forms. However, in addition to the word "elephant," Indian children also performed better than did their U.S. counterparts on some irregular words such as "night" and "hair." This could be because Indian children, who are not much influenced by phonology, should memorize these words or have a visual memory for these words. Some of the spelling errors are shown in Table 34.5.

Even though visual exposure appears to have an influence on the spellings of Indian children, the role of phonology cannot be completely ruled out. For instance, for the word "half," the spelling errors produced by American children were *hafe, haf,* and *haff,* whereas Indian children misspelled it as *of* and *off.* This could be because of the difference in the way the words are pronounced by a native of India and native of the United States. The misspellings of two other words are also informative. In spelling the word "knee," many of the Indian children did not produce the silent "k;" similarly, many of the Indian children had omitted the initial "e" in the word *enough.* Both of these are low-frequency irregular words. Some of the spelling errors are shown in Table 34.6.

TABLE 34.5
Sample of Spelling Errors

Word	U.S. Children	Indian Children
Night	nit, niht, nite, nitea, niat nitea, niat, nith, nigt, niightt	nite, night
Hair	haer, haire, har, hir her, hare, hire, haey, harre, hrie, heer, harr	air, hare, hear

TABLE 34.6
Sample of Spelling Errors

Word	U.S. Children	Indian Children
Knee	ke, kney, knew, keen	ne, nee, nea
Enough	enuf, enaf, enfh	naf, nef, neafe, nafa

DISCUSSION AND CONCLUSION

From these analyses, some generalizations could be made. Similar to Study I, when spelling performance was evaluated as "right" or "wrong" in quantitative terms, both groups did equally well. However, when a qualitative analysis was performed, there were differences between American and Indian children. Further, high-frequency words, such as "father" and "cold" were spelled equally well by both groups. Learning English as a written language has an influence on spelling of some phonologically inconsistent words like "night" and "hair." Exposure to print plays a role in spelling, as demonstrated by the superior performance of Indian children on words such as "elephant." Finally, regardless of how English language was learned, whether in its written form or its spoken form, low-frequency irregular words were phoneticized by both groups of children, as shown in spelling of the words "half," "knee," and "enough."

From these two studies, we can conclude that phonology plays an important role in the acquisition of English spelling. However, children who learn English first as a written language tend to spell correctly more high-frequency irregular words compared with children who learn first to speak English and read English later. Further, when children learn English as a second language, the nature of the orthography of their first language appears to influence their English spelling. More importantly, these studies have shown that spelling errors can be scored in more than one way to assess the orthographic knowledge of the individual; scoring only as right or wrong may not give an accurate picture of the individual's spelling skill. As previously shown, when spelling errors were scored as right or wrong, there was no difference among the different groups investigated in the two studies. However, when a qualitative analysis that examined the number of phonetic equivalents was performed, there were significant differences among the different groups used in this study.

ACKNOWLEDGMENT

We wish to thank the school children and classroom teachers who willingly participated in this study.

REFERENCES

Arra, C., & Aaron, P. G. (2001). Effect of psycholinguistic instruction on spelling development. *Psychology in the Schools, 38,* 357–363.

Ball, E. W., & Blachman, B. A. (1991). Does phoneme awareness training in kindergarten make a difference in early word recognition and developmental spelling? *Reading Research Quarterly, 26,* 49–66.

Besner, D., & Smith, M. C. (1992). Basic processes in reading: Is the orthographic depth hypothesis sinking? In R. Frost & L. Katz (Eds.), *Orthography, phonology, morphology, and meaning* (pp. 192–210). Amsterdam: Elsevier Science.

Coltheart, M., Patterson, K., & Marshall, J. (1980). *Deep dyslexia.* London: Routledge & kegan paul.

Coltheart, M., Rastle, K., Perry, C., Langdon, R., & Ziegler, J. (2001). DRC: A dual route cascaded model of visual word recognition and reading aloud. *Psychological Review, 108,* 204–256.

D'Anguilli, A., Siegel, L. S., & Serra, E. (2002). The development of reading in English and Italian in bilingual children. *Applied Psycholinguistics, 22,* 479–507.

Durgunoğlu, A. Y., Nagy, W. E., & Hancin-Bhatt, B. J. (1993). Cross-language transfer of phonological awareness. *Journal of Educational Psychology, 85,* 453–465.

Holm, A., & Dodd, B. (1996). The effect of first written language on the acquisiton of English literacy. *Cognition, 59,* 119–147.

Jackson, N. E., Chen, H.-W., Goldsberry-Shaver, L., Kim., A., & Vanderwerff, C. (1999). Effects of variations in orthographic information on Asian and American readers. *Reading and Writing: An Interdisciplinary Journal, 11,* 345–379.

Koda, K. (1987). Cognitive strategies transfer in second language reading. In J. Devine, P. L. Carnell, & D. E. Eskey (Eds.), *Reading in English as a second language* (pp. 127–144). Washington, DC: Teaching English to Speakers of other languages (TESOL).

Koda, K. (1989). Effects of L1 orthographic representation on L2 phonological coding strategies. *Journal of Psychological Research, 18,* 201–222.

Lundberg, I. Frost, J., & Petersen, O. P. (1988). Long term effects of a pre-school training program in phonological awareness. *Reading Research Quarterly, 28,* 263–284.

Mumtaz, S., & Humpreys, G. W. (2001). The effects of bilingualism on learning to read English: Evidence from the contrast between Urdu–English bilingual and English monolingual children. *Journal of Research in Reading, 24,* 113–134.

Read, C. (1975). *Children's categorization of speech sounds in English*, Research Report No. 17. Urbana, IL: National Council of Teachers of English.

Shankweiler, D., Lundquist, E., Dreyer, L. G., & Dickinson, C. C. (1996). Reading and spelling difficulties in high school students: Causes and consequences. *Reading and Writing: An Interdisciplinary Journal, 8,* 267–294.

Tangel, D., & Blachman, B. (1995). Effect of phoneme awareness instruction on the invented spelling of 1st-grade children: A one-year follow up. *Journal of Reading Behavior, 27,* 153–185.

Treiman, R. (1993). *Beginning to spell.* New York: Oxford University Press.

Treiman, R., & Barry, C. (2000). Dialect and authography: Some differences between American and British spellers. *Journal of Experimental Psychology (Learning, Memory, & Cognition), 26,* 1423–1430.

Treiman, R., Goswami, U., Tincoff, R., & Leevers, H. (1997). Effects of dialect on American and British children's spelling. *Child Development, 68,* 229–245.

Wade-Woolley, L., & Siegel, L. (1997). The spelling performance of ESL and native speakers of English as a function of reading skills. *Reading and Writing: An Interdisciplinary Journal, 9,* 387–406.

Wang, M., & Geva, E. (2003). Spelling performance of Chinese children using English as a second language: Lexical and visual-orthographic processes. *Applied Psycholinguistics, 24,* 1–25.

Zeno, S. M., Ivenz, S. H., Millard, R. T., & Duvvuri, R. (1995). *Educator's word frequency guide.* Brewster, NY: Touchstone Applied Science Associates.

III

Literacy Acquisition:
Instructional Perspectives

35

Knowledge About Letters as a Foundation for Reading and Spelling

Rebecca Treiman
Washington University in St. Louis

Phonological awareness and knowledge about letters are both important for learning to read and spell, but less is known about the development of letter knowledge than about the development of phonological awareness. This chapter reviews the research on young children's knowledge about the visual forms, names, and sounds of letters, showing that it involves more than rote memorization. The chapter begins by considering children's early knowledge about the visual characteristics of writing and the phonological characteristics of letter names. The discussion then turns to children's knowledge about the written word that is most important to them, their own first name, and how children's learning of their name influences their knowledge about the letters within it. I also examine how children use their early acquired knowledge about the names of letters, in concert with their phonological skills, to make inferences about the letters' sounds. Children's knowledge of letter names and sounds, it is argued, helps them form preliminary connections between print and speech. These connections are not sufficient for skilled reading of English, a system that requires more than simple letter–sound correspondences, but they help children take their first steps toward mastery of the writing system.

Children need to possess a number of skills in order to learn to read and write. One important skill is phonological awareness. A child who can divide the spoken words "bat" and "bug" into smaller units and who knows that the two words start with the same sound can understand why both words are written with three letters and why the first letter is the same in both. Indeed, a child's level of phonological awareness at school entry is a good predictor of that child's success in learning to read (e.g., Share, Jorm, Maclean, & Matthews, 1984; for a review see Snow, Burns, & Griffin, 1998). Another skill that is important for literacy is knowledge about letters. Even if a child can segment a complex spoken syllable such as "blast" into its individual sounds or *phonemes*, the child will not be able to write the word unless he or she knows that

/b/ is typically symbolized as *b*, /l/ as *l*, and so on.[1] Children's knowledge about letters and the sounds they represent is, not surprisingly, another good predictor of success in learning to read and spell (e.g., McBride-Chang, 1999; Share et al., 1984; Snow et al., 1998).

Over the past 30 years or so, many researchers have studied phonological awareness and its links to reading and spelling skill (e.g., Brady & Shankweiler, 1991; Sawyer & Fox, 1991). This research has been valuable for several reasons. One reason is its developmental approach. Phonemic awareness, studies have shown, does not emerge full-blown in kindergarten or first grade. It develops gradually, with awareness of syllables and their *onset* (initial consonant or cluster) and *rime* (vowel and any following consonants) subunits typically preceding awareness of phonemes (e.g., Liberman, Shankweiler, Fischer, & Carter, 1974; Treiman, 1992). Another strength of the research on phonological awareness has been its linguistic focus. For example, researchers have shown that children have more difficulty breaking up consonant clusters, such as the /bl/ of "blast," than other phoneme sequences, such as the /bæ/ of "bat" (e.g., Treiman & Weatherston, 1992). Children's difficulties with consonant clusters make sense on linguistic grounds. Indeed, many linguists consider syllable-initial consonant clusters to be units, with initial consonants or consonant clusters forming the onset of the syllable (e.g., Fudge, 1987). As another example of the effects of linguistic factors on phonological awareness, children are more likely to confuse pairs of phonemes that differ in the phonetic feature of voicing (e.g., /b/ and /p/) than phonemes that differ in other ways (Treiman, Broderick, Tincoff, & Rodriguez, 1998). Yet another positive feature of the research on phonological awareness is that it has linked specific phonological difficulties to specific reading and spelling errors. For instance, children's problem in the oral segmentation of consonant clusters may cause them to symbolize a consonant cluster with a single letter in spelling (e.g., *bat*[2] for "blast"), rather than with a sequence of two letters (e.g., Treiman, 1993). Finally, the research on phonological awareness has had valuable implications for instruction. Research-based phonological training programs have yielded improvements in children's phonological awareness and literacy skills (e.g., Byrne, Fielding-Barnsley, & Ashley, 2000).

Although there is a large body of research on children's phonological awareness, relatively little research has examined children's knowledge about letters. This imbalance probably reflects the fact that learning the names and sounds of letters has been considered a matter of

---

[1] Because spelling is not always an unambiguous guide to pronunciation, phonemes are presented in the alphabet of the International Phonetic Association (IPA; 1996, 1999). Spellings are given in italics and pronunciations in IPA symbols surrounded by slash marks, e.g., *cat* is pronounced /kæt/. The values of most IPA symbols agree with those of the corresponding English letter, but the following require special attention. Usage reflects general American pronunciation.

/aɪ/	*ai*sle
/æ/	*a*pple
/ɑ/	w*a*nd, c*a*r
/dʒ/	ba*dg*e
/e/	V*e*gas
/ɛ/	*e*dit
/ə/	cass*e*role
/g/	*g*o
/i/	mach*i*ne
/ɪ/	*i*t
/o/	*o*bey
/ɔ/	da*w*n
/tʃ/	e*tch*
/u/	r*u*de
/ɹ/	*r*un

The mark /ˈ/ precedes a stressed syllable; stress is marked only for words of more than one syllable.

[2] Children's spellings of words are indicated in italic letters here and throughout the chapter.

rote, paired-associate learning (e.g., Windfuhr & Snowling, 2001). If so, it should be a relatively uninteresting topic for researchers to study and a relatively mundane body of knowledge for children to master. The goal of this chapter is to review recent research on children's knowledge about letters, showing that it involves much more than rote memory. I focus on research that has been carried out with middle-socioeconomic-status (SES) children from the United States who are learning English as their first language, the group of children that has been examined in the majority of the studies. Selected studies with other groups of children are also mentioned. I hope to show that a developmental, linguistically based approach can bear fruit in the study of children's letter knowledge, as in the study of phonological awareness. Moreover, certain patterns of performance in reading and spelling make sense given what children know about letters, and the research on letter knowledge has important implications for instruction.

I begin the chapter by considering children's early knowledge about the visual characteristics of writing and the phonological characteristics of letter names. Next, I discuss how children learn about the written word that is most important and most meaningful to them, their own first name. The following sections examine how children use their early acquired knowledge about the names of letters to make inferences about the letters' sounds and how their knowledge of letter names and sounds helps them form preliminary connections between print and speech. I also discuss the need to go beyond simple letter–sound associations in the learning of writing systems such as English. The concluding section considers the interactions between children's letter knowledge and their phonological awareness, as well as directions for future research.

CHILDREN'S EARLY LEARNING ABOUT THE VISUAL CHARACTERISTICS OF WRITING AND LETTERS

Figure 35.1(a) shows a "spelling" of "chair" that was produced by a child of 3 years, 8 months. The visual form is composed of units that, although not recognizable as English letters, have many of the characteristics of English print. For example, the units are arranged roughly horizontally and are separated by spaces. Figure 35.1(b) shows a "no trespassing" message that was written by the same child 7 months later. This flowing, linear form has many of the characteristics of cursive writing. As these examples suggest, children in literate societies learn about the visual characteristics of letters and writing from an early age. Lavine (1977) documented this knowledge by asking children to put cards that had writing on them into a play mailbox and cards that did not have writing on them into another container. Some of the cards displayed linear sequences of units, as in printing; other cards had units that were not on a line. From the age of 3 years, children were more likely to judge the former displays as writing than the latter. Also, displays that contained a variety of units were more often labeled as writing than displays in which the same unit was repeated several times.

Children who are exposed to writing systems other than English also learn about their visual characteristics. For example, Chinese-speaking children from Hong Kong appear to differentiate writing from drawing by the age of 3 years (Chan & Louie, 1992). When asked to write, they tend to use the horizontal and vertical lines and dots that characterize Chinese characters. Circular forms, which are not typical of Chinese characters, appear more often in the children's drawings than in their writings. Children who are exposed to Chinese may arrange their marks in a square pattern, as with conventional Chinese characters, rather than along a line, as with English (Chi, 1988). As another example, young Israeli children may write from right to left, the conventional direction for Hebrew, even when their "letters" are seemingly arbitrary shapes (Levin, Share, & Shatil, 1996).

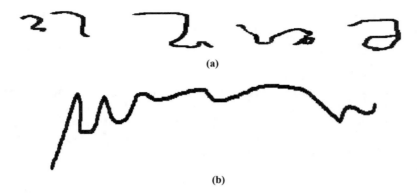

(a)

(b)

FIG. 35.1. (a) "Chair" as written by child of 3 years, 8 months; (b) "No trespassing" as written by the same child at 4 years, 3 months.

CHILDREN'S EARLY LEARNING ABOUT THE PHONOLOGICAL CHARACTERISTICS OF LETTER NAMES

English letters are distinguished not only by their visual properties but also by the phonological properties of their names. In English, all but one of the 26 letter names is a single syllable. The majority of these syllables have two phonemes, with the most common pattern being consonant + vowel. The vowel in consonant + vowel letter names is often /i/, as in /bi/ and /si/. For letters with vowel + consonant names, the vowel is typically /ɛ/, as in /ɛf/ and /ɛs/. The distinctive phonological properties of letter names could help children to identify the letters as a set. No comparable phonological cues are available for other educationally important sets such as numbers and colors, which do not have distinctive phonological forms in English. Many languages have letter names that are similar phonologically (see Treiman & Kessler, 2003), but the letter names in certain languages are less similar than those of English. For example, Hebrew letter names are both monosyllabic and bisyllabic, and they include a variety of vowels.

Anecdotal evidence suggests that English-speaking children begin to learn about the phonological characteristics of letter names from an early age. The child who produced the spelling of "chair" in Fig. 35.1(a), when asked what letters he had written, responded /ɹu/, /di/, /ɑ/. /di/ is a real English letter name, but /ɹu/ and /ɑ/ are not. This child may have known that letter names tend to contain a single syllable. Another child who participated in one of our experiments (Treiman, Tincoff, & Richmond-Welty, 1996) said that "loose" began with the "letter" /li/, that "moon" began with /mi/, and that "group" began with /gɹi/. The letter names that this child invented have the monosyllabic, onset + /i/ structure that characterizes many English letter names.

Treiman, Tincoff, and Richmond-Welty (1997) carried out two experiments to examine preschoolers' knowledge about the phonological structure of letter names. Across the two studies, the children averaged 4 years, 8 months in age. A puppet, which was introduced as being not very knowledgeable about letters, "said" various syllables. The children were asked to judge whether each one was a real letter. The children made more false-positive responses to syllables such as /fi/, which have the onset + /i/ structure that is shared by a number of English letter names, than to syllables such as /fɔ/ and /if/, which sound less like English letter names. The effects were small, in part because some children were never misled by the false letter names, but they were statistically reliable. The results suggest that English-speaking children gain a sensitivity to the phonological structure of letter names as they learn the alphabet. This sensitivity may foster the development of phonological awareness, providing an early example of how knowledge about letters and reading improves knowledge about sounds.

THE SPECIAL ROLE OF THE CHILD'S OWN NAME

The first printed word that most children pay attention to and learn about is their own first name or commonly used nickname. In a study carried out in the United States by Villaume and Wilson (1989), the majority of the 3-year-olds and all of the 4- and 5-year-olds could pick out their own first name when it was presented along with two other names that began with different letters. Hildreth (1936) found that children between the ages of 4 years, 6 months and 4 years, 11 months typically produced some correct letters when asked to print their own first name. Most children produced fully correct spellings by the ages of 5 years to 5 years, 5 months. Children's knowledge of their last name lagged behind their knowledge of their first name, with most of the children tested by Hildreth unable to write their own last name until the age of 6 years, 6 months to 6 years, 11 months. Similar findings have been reported with children in other literate societies. For example, Chan and Louie (1992) found that many 5-year-olds in Hong Kong could write their names correctly.

What do young children learn when they learn to write and recognize their own name? Do they treat their name analytically, in terms of its component letters, or do they consider it a holistic visual pattern? The idea that young children are *logographic* (Frith, 1985) or *prealphabetic* readers (Ehri, 1998) suggests that children treat their names holistically. Logographic readers are thought to attend to the shapes and colors on signs such as those for *Pepsi* and *McDonalds*; they make little or no use of the letters in the words when connecting the visual symbols to their meanings and pronunciations. Supporting this view, young children may not notice if the initial *p* in the *Pepsi* logo has been changed to *x*, stating that it still says *Pepsi* (Masonheimer, Drum, & Ehri, 1984).

However, when children learn about their own names, they do appear to learn about the component letters. Treiman and Broderick (1998) analyzed data from three groups of children: U.S. preschoolers (mean age 4 years, 10 months), U.S. kindergartners (mean age 5 years, 8 months), and Australian children similar in age to the U.S. kindergartners (mean age 5 years, 5 months). The children were asked to say the name of each letter of the alphabet and also, on separate trials, the conventional sound of each letter (e.g., /də/ for *d*, /s/ for *s*). For each letter, we calculated the proportion of correct responses in the letter-name task for children whose name began with that letter. We also calculated the proportion of correct responses to each letter for children whose name did not begin with that letter. Of interest was whether the proportion of correct responses was higher in the name case than in the no-name case. For the first letter of the first name, letter-name knowledge was significantly better in the own-name case than the no-name case, as assessed by a *t* test across the letters of the alphabet. This held true for all three groups of children. That is, children whose first name started with a particular letter were especially likely to know the name of that letter. Similar trends were observed for the letters of the name beyond the first letter, but these trends were not significant. For letter-sound knowledge, no significant difference between the name case and the no-name case was observed, even for the first letter of the first name. There were no significant effects for last names, either for letter-name or letter-sound knowledge. Thus a child named Dan is more likely to know the label for the letter *d* than are his classmates Joe and Sarah. However, Dan is no more knowledgeable about the sound that *d* symbolizes. In learning the spelling of his name, Dan has apparently analyzed the visual string into letter units and has learned the label of especially the first unit. The different results for letter names and letter sounds may reflect the emphasis on letter names in children's experiences with their own first names.

Young children often hear the oral spelling of their own name, as in /di/, /e/, /ɛn/ for *Dan*. These experiences give the child the opportunity to link the spoken labels to the printed letters. Parents and teachers in the United States do not typically label the letters in a child's name by their sounds (e.g., /də/, /æ/, /n/).

To replicate and extend these findings, Treiman and Broderick (1998) carried out a second study with preschoolers whose names began with one of the letters *d*, *j*, *k*, *m*, *r*, or *s*. These letters were chosen largely because they were among the most common name-initial letters in the population of children studied. The children averaged 4 years, 11 months in age, similar to the preschoolers in Treiman and Broderick's first experiment. We asked the children to name each of the six letters under study and also to provide the sound corresponding to each letter. Children who made several errors in the letter-name or letter-sound production tasks were also given a recognition task in which they were asked to select the name or the sound of each letter from two alternatives. The children did better on the first letter of their own name than on the other letters in the tasks tapping knowledge of letter names. In contrast, no significant superiority for the first letter of the child's name was found in either the production or the recognition version of the letter-sound task. These results agree with those of Treiman and Broderick's first study, providing additional evidence for the idea that children's experiences with their own name help them learn to label its initial letter.

The second experiment of Treiman and Broderick (1998) went beyond the first experiment by asking children about the first letter and the first sound of various spoken words. Of interest was whether children would perform well with the first letter of their own name in these tasks. In the first-letter task, children were asked such questions as, "What letter does *doll* start with, *d* or *p*?" A sample question for the first-sound task is "What sound does *jar* start with, /tə/ or /dʒə/?" To succeed on the first-letter task, children must know the phonemes that the letters symbolize. They must also have enough phonological awareness to be able to pick out these phonemes in the spoken targets. Phonological awareness is also required for the first-sound task. No significant advantage for the first letter of the child's own name was found in either the first-letter task or the first-sound task, just as no significant advantage was found in the letter-sound task just described. These findings show that children whose names begin with a particular letter are no more likely than other children to know the sound that this letter symbolizes.

Treiman and Broderick (1998) also asked the children in their second experiment to print each of the six letters under study. We developed a scoring system that considered the strokes and junctures that the child used and the overall form of the letter. Children scored significantly higher on this measure with the first letter of their own name than with the other letters. For example, a child named Dan could write better-quality *d*s than could children named Joe or Sarah.

Overall, the results of Treiman and Broderick (1998) show that children's experiences with their own first names boost their knowledge about the letters within the name, especially the name's first letter. These experiences help children learn about the visual form of the letter and also its conventional label. However, they do not help children learn about the sound that the letter symbolizes. The results suggest that young children treat their printed name as made up of smaller elements, letters. They also treat the oral spelling of their name as made up of smaller elements, letter names. For example, Dan often sees the printed word *Dan* and hears, simultaneously, /di/, /e/, /ɛn/. From such experiences, he links at least the first elements of the written and spoken scripts. The conclusion that children's knowledge about their own name is analytic and letter based from an early age contrasts with the idea that young children rely on a prealphabetic or logographic strategy when they begin to read words (Ehri, 1998; Frith, 1985). Children may adopt a letter-based approach with their own name at a time when they focus on overall shape and color with signs and with other types of print, performing in a more sophisticated way with their own name than with other words. That is, children's names may play a leading role in the development of literacy, just as they do in the development of spoken language (Mandel, Jusczyk, & Pisoni, 1995). The results of Treiman and Broderick further show that a particular factor (experience with one's own name, in this case) can have different influences on children's knowledge about letters' names and children's knowledge about letters' sounds. The two types of knowledge are distinct, although related. They should not be lumped together as "alphabet knowledge" (see also McBride-Chang, 1999).

As mentioned earlier, one valuable feature of the research on children's phonological awareness is that it helps reveal the logic behind certain spelling and reading errors that would otherwise be difficult to explain. A misspelling such as *chruck* for "truck," which might at first appear bizarre, makes sense given that /t/ sounds different before /ɹ/ than in other contexts (e.g., Read, 1975; Treiman, 1985). Just as children's phonological knowledge helps explain certain spelling errors, so their knowledge about their own names helps explain other errors. An example comes from a study of kindergartners' spellings that was carried out by Treiman, Kessler, and Bourassa (2001). We found, as expected from previous research, that some of the erroneous letters in children's spellings of words were motivated by the words' sounds. For example, the first two letters in *chruck* reflect the pronunciation of /t/ before /ɹ/. Other spelling errors seem to have no phonological basis. For instance, one kindergartner wrote "fur" as *yoonyy*, and another wrote "work" as *tctba*. These errors began to make sense when we looked at the names of the children who produced them. Danny wrote *yoonyy* for "fur," using *n* and *y* from his own name. Scott produced *tctba* for "work," using two *t*s and a *c* from his name. Statistical analyses confirmed that letters from the kindergartners' own names were overrepresented in the children's intrusion errors. Given the results of Treiman and Broderick (1998), which were described earlier, one might expect that the own-name intrusions would primarily involve the first letter of the child's own name. However, the kindergartners tended to overuse letters from a variety of positions within their name, with no significant priority for the first letter. Younger children may produce a larger number of intrusions involving the first letter of their own name than other letters, but this remains to be investigated. Treiman and colleagues, in addition to examining the spellings of kindergartners, also looked at spellings produced by first and second graders. Although the kindergartners produced own-name intrusions, the first- and second-grade children did not appear to do so. Thus, the phenomenon of overusing letters from the child's own name is relatively short-lived. Other studies of young children from the United States (Bloodgood, 1999), Israel (Levin et al., 1996), and France (Gombert & Fayol, 1992) provide additional evidence that young children tend to overuse letters from their own names when writing.

Spellings such as *yoonyy* for "fur" and *tctba* for "work" have been thought to mark a *precommunicative* (Gentry, 1982) or *prealphabetic* (Ehri, 1997) stage of writing development. This is a stage during which children string letters together in a random fashion, if indeed they use conventional letters at all. This stage is believed to overlap, in large part, with the postulated logographic stage of reading development (Frith, 1985). However, the results of Treiman et al. (2001) show that young children's spellings are not as random or haphazard as they first appear. There may be a reason why Scott uses a *t* at the beginning of "work," and this reason may have more to do with his familiarity with the letter *t* than with a mistaken belief that the spoken form of "work" begins with /t/. As Treiman and Cassar (1997) also emphasized, we must go beyond phonology to understand why children spell words as they do.

CHILDREN'S USE OF LETTER NAMES IN LEARNING ABOUT LETTER SOUNDS

Treiman and Broderick (1988) found that children in the United States and Australia performed substantially better when asked to provide the names of letters than when asked to provide the letters' sounds. The same result has been found in other studies with similar groups of children (e.g., Byrne, 1992; McBride-Chang, 1999; Worden & Boettcher, 1990). The finding that letter-name knowledge and letter-sound knowledge do not necessarily follow the same developmental course supports the idea that these two skills are not the same. The discrepancy further suggests that children may use their prior knowledge of letters' names to learn and remember the letters' sounds. Rather than memorizing associations such as v–/v/ and m–/m/ in a rote fashion, children may use the letter names, /vi/ and /ɛm/, to induce the sounds. Deriving the letter sounds in this way requires a degree of phonological skill, as children need to detect the letter sound within the letter name.

If children use their knowledge of letter names and their phonological skills to learn letter sounds, then they should find it easier to master the sounds of some letters than of others. The easiest letter–sound correspondences should be those such as v–/v/, in which the sound to which the letter typically corresponds is the onset of the letter's name. As mentioned earlier, children can typically segment spoken syllables into onset and rime units at a fairly young age. Also, consonant + /i/ letter names are common in English. The repeated use of /i/ across a number of letter names, each with a different initial consonant, may make the consonant stand out. The sounds of letters such as m should be somewhat harder to learn. Although the letter's sound is in the name, it is at the end (i.e., part of the rime) rather than at the beginning (i.e., the onset). This may make it harder for children to segment the phoneme from the letter name. Finally, the sounds of letters such as w should be most difficult to learn. The consonantal sound to which w typically corresponds, /w/, is not present in its name, "doubleyou." For the relatively few letters of this kind that exist in English, children may need to memorize the letters' sounds in a rote fashion. Note that this classification of letters depends on their names in a particular culture. In the United States, h is typically labeled /etʃ/ and does not contain the /h/ sound. It thus falls into the most difficult category for U.S. children. In some parts of the English-speaking world, however, h is called /hetʃ/ and so does contain its sound.

To test the hypothesis that children attempt to use the names of letters to learn and remember the letters' sounds, Treiman, Tincoff, Rodriguez, Mouzaki, and Francis (1998) analyzed four sets of data on children's knowledge of letter sounds and letter names. One set of data (Worden & Boettcher, 1990) was collected from 4-, 5-, 6-, and 7-year-olds in California. Another data set came from preschoolers in Detroit, a third from kindergartners in Detroit, and a fourth from kindergartners in Houston. In each study, children had been presented with each letter of the alphabet and asked to name it and provide its sound. We analyzed data from a total of 660 children.

Treiman, Tincoff, et al. (1998) divided letters into three categories—those for which the sound is at the beginning of the name (e.g., v), those for which the sound is at the end of the name (e.g., m), and those for which the sound is not in the name at all (e.g., w). On the letter-sound task, children generally performed best on the first type of letter, intermediate on the second type, and poorest on the third type. This pattern supports the idea that children use their knowledge of letter names and their phonological skills to learn letter sounds. On the letter-name task, performance was similar on beginning, end, and not-in-name letters. This latter finding suggests that the results obtained for letter sounds do not arise from different amounts of experience with the three types of letters. One way to describe the results is to say that the discrepancy between knowledge of letter names and knowledge of letter sounds is smallest for letters such as v, intermediate for letters such as m, and largest for letters such as w. The name-sound discrepancy appears to reflect the difficulty of deriving the letter's sound from its name. It does not appear to reflect the kind of instruction that the children had received. The younger children in the study were not receiving formal instruction about the sounds of letters; such instruction does not typically begin until kindergarten in the United States. The instruction that was provided to the older children differed from classroom to classroom and from school to school; no standard sequence for teaching the letters of the alphabet exists in

U.S. schools. McBride-Chang (1999) reported similar differences in letter-sound knowledge among beginning, end, and not-in-name letters in another study of U.S. kindergartners.

The results of Treiman, Tincoff, et al. (1998) suggest that certain properties of a letter's name affect children's ability to learn its sound. Do properties of the sound itself also have an influence? We carried out additional analyses to test two hypotheses about such effects that were proposed by other researchers. Stuart and Coltheart's (1988) *syllable position hypothesis* states that the earliest letter–sound correspondences to be learned involve sounds that commonly occur at the beginnings and ends of syllables. These tend to be consonants that fall into the linguistic category of *obstruent*, including *fricatives* such as /v/ and *stops* such as /p/. In this view, letter–sound correspondences involving *sonorants* (e.g., /w/, /l/, vowels) should be relatively hard to learn because sonorants often occur in the middles of syllables. Another hypothesis is the *pronounceability hypothesis*. This hypothesis states that stop consonants, which cannot be pronounced without a vowel and whose acoustic realizations often differ depending on the adjacent phoneme, are particularly difficult for children to identify as separate units (Byrne & Fielding-Barnsley, 1990; but see Treiman, Broderick, et al., 1998). According to the pronounceability hypothesis, children should find it difficult to link a consonant such as *p* with its pronunciation. Our analyses did not support either the syllable position hypothesis or the pronounceability hypothesis. These properties of the phoneme itself—whether it is a consonant or a vowel, an obstruent or a sonorant, a stop consonant or a phoneme that can be pronounced on its own—seem to have little influence on children's ability to relate the phoneme to its spelling. More important is whether the phoneme occurs in the name of the letter that is used to represent it and, if so, its position in the letter name.

So far, primarily correlational evidence has been presented that children use their knowledge of letters' names to learn about the letters' sounds. That is, differences in letter-sound knowledge are related to properties of the letters' names. Experimental support for the idea that children use their knowledge of letter names when learning letter sounds comes from a training study that Treiman, Tincoff, et al. (1998) carried out with preschoolers (mean age 4 years, 11 months). We selected children who knew the names of a set of consonant letters but did not yet know most of the letters' sounds. Over the course of several sessions, the children were taught the letters that are used to symbolize the sounds. We asked whether children learned the sound–letter relationships more quickly for some letters than for others. Specifically, the children were requested in a pretest to point to the letter that made a particular sound from among 10 letters. The pretest was followed by a demonstration trial in which children were told the sound that each letter symbolized. This was followed by a training trial in which children were asked to point to the letter corresponding to each sound and were told the correct response if they made a mistake. The second session included another demonstration trial and two more training trials. Finally, a posttest of letter-sound knowledge was given in a third session.

The results of the training study revealed significant differences among cases such as /v/–*v* (sound at beginning of name), /m/–*m* (sound at end of name), and /h/–*h* (sound not in name in American English). Children showed most improvement over the course of the study when the letter's sound was at the beginning of its name. For letters such as *v*, they went from 17% correct on the pretest to 67% correct on the posttest, a substantial improvement. Intermediate in ease of mastery were letters such as *m*, in which the sound is at the end of the letter name. Children went from 6% correct in the pretest to 31% correct on the posttest for such letters, a significant gain but less than that for letters such as *v*. Children had most trouble learning the sounds of letters such as *h*. With such letters, they scored 14% correct on the pretest and 19% correct on the posttest, not a reliable improvement. No significant differences were found between sonorants and obstruents that had the same type of name–sound relationship (e.g., the sonorant /m/ vs. the obstruent /f/, both of which are heard at the end of a letter name). These latter results fail to support the syllable position hypothesis (Stuart & Coltheart, 1998), which states that obstruents are easier to connect to letters than sonorants.

Overall, the results of the training study by Treiman, Tincoff, et al. (1998) show that children find it easier to learn some letter-sound correspondences than others. A relatively small amount of instruction yields substantial improvement for letters like v. This is because children who know v's name and who have a certain amount of phonological skill can notice the sound of the letter at the beginning of the name and remember the sound on that basis. Improvement is slower for letters like m, where the sound is less accessible in the name, and even slower for letters like h, for which the sound is not in the name at all. The results show that children bring their knowledge of letter names and their phonological skills to the task of learning letter sounds. For many English letters, children can put these skills to use in a way that allows them to avoid memorizing the letters' sounds in a rote fashion. Learning the phonemes that letters symbolize may boost children's phonological awareness by helping them notice the phonemes in the letter names. For example, children who could not access the /m/ in /ɛm/ when they first learned the letter name may become able to do so as they learn that m corresponds to /m/.

Further evidence that children use the names of letters to learn about their sounds comes from certain erroneous beliefs that children may hold about letter–sound relationships. Treiman, Weatherston, and Berch (1994, Study 3) found evidence for these beliefs when they asked kindergartners to provide the name and the sound of w and y, as well as other letters. The children were tested twice, once before w and y had been formally taught at school (mean age 6 years) and once 3 months later, after the children had spent about a week learning about w and a week learning about y. This instruction involved writing the letter, learning its name, and identifying its sound in words. The children had a separate booklet of exercises for each letter. This "letter-of-the-week" approach is common in U.S. kindergartens.

Most of the kindergartners could label w and y even before the letters had been taught in school. This outcome fits with the earlier observation that middle-SES children in the United States know the names of many letters before they start school. The children were much less knowledgeable about the letters' sounds. On the first test, the children provided the correct sound for w only 20% of the time. The most common error, which occurred 28% of the time, was to say that w made the sound /də/. This error probably occurs because the name of w, "doubleyou," begins with /d/. Some of the children, apparently knowing that the sounds of many letters are found in the first positions of their names, assumed that w has this property. On the second test, correct responses to w on the letter-sound task increased to 53%. However, /də/ errors were still fairly common, occurring 25% of the time.

Even stronger evidence that children use their knowledge of letter names and their phonological skills to make inferences about the letters' sounds comes from the results for y. On the first test, 58% of the children said that y makes the sound /wə/, /w/ being the first phoneme of the name /waɪ/. Only 13% of the children produced the correct sound for y at this time. Performance was little better on the second test, even though the children had spent a week at school learning about y. Now, 18% of the children responded correctly to y on the letter-sound task and 60% said that it made the sound /wə/. The belief that y maps onto the first phoneme of its name is thus quite persistent, more persistent than the belief that w does so. Errors with y may be particularly lasting because y has a consonant + vowel name, as do many English letters. Indeed, y is the only English letter with a consonant + vowel name for which the initial consonant is not a possible sound of the letter. One factor that may decrease the number of letter name-influenced errors on w is that it is the only English letter whose name has more than one syllable. The unique name of w may alert children that it does not follow the typical name–sound relationships. Also, the length of w's name may make it hard for children to abstract the initial /d/ even if they try to do so. This latter suggestion is supported by the finding that children perform more poorly on phonological awareness tasks when required to isolate the initial consonant of a long word rather than a short word (Treiman & Weatherston, 1992).

The research showing that children use their knowledge of letters' names to make inferences about the letters' sounds has some important implications for instruction. The results suggest that more teaching of letter–sound correspondences is required for letters such as y and w than for letters such as v and p. The common practice of spending a week on each letter, regardless of its difficulty, is not an ideal use of time. In addition, the results point to errors that are likely to occur as children learn the sounds of letters such as y and w. Although teachers need to correct errors such as saying that y makes the sound /wə/, they should realize that these are "good" errors. The errors reveal some understanding of the English letter-name system and some phonological skills.

So far, the evidence that children use the names of letters to learn and remember the letters' sounds comes from tasks in which children must relate individual letters to individual phonemes. However, it is more important for a child to be able to spell a phoneme such as /w/ than to state the sound made by an isolated w. To determine whether similar effects occur in spelling tasks, Treiman, Weatherston, and Berch (1994, Study Two) gave preschoolers (mean age 5 years, 2 months) and kindergartners (mean age 5 years, 11 months) a simplified spelling task. In the initial condition of the study, children were asked the first letter that would be used to spell various spoken syllables. In the final condition, children were asked to say the last letters of various syllables. Some of the syllables began or ended with phonemes such as /v/, the spellings of which are suggested by the initial phoneme of a letter name. Other syllables began or ended with phonemes such as /m/, the spellings of which are suggested by the final phoneme of a letter name. Still other syllables contained phonemes such as /g/, which do not occur in the name of an English letter. In both the initial and final conditions, children performed best with phonemes such as /v/, intermediate with phonemes such as /m/, and most poorly with phonemes such as /g/. These results show that children use their knowledge of letter names when deciding how to spell phonemes. Treiman and Broderick (1998) and Treiman and Tincoff (1997) reported similar differences between letters with consonant + vowel names and letters with vowel + consonant names in spelling tasks.

Children's spelling errors provide further evidence that they use the names of letters when deciding how to spell phonemes. The children in the previously described study by Treiman, Weatherston, and Berch (1994) sometimes said that syllables beginning with /w/ were spelled with an initial y. In another study reported by these authors, kindergartners sometimes spelled common words with initial /w/ with y, as in yrk for "work," yrm for "warm," and yd for "word". These results demonstrate, again, that certain spelling errors that might at first appear bizarre make sense given the knowledge that children bring with them to the spelling task. A teacher who encounters such errors should acknowledge that y is a reasonable attempt to spell /w/, even though it is not correct.

To summarize the results reviewed in this section, children in the United States and a number of other countries typically know the labels of many letters before they fully understand that letters serve as symbols for sounds. These children use the letters' labels, together with their phonological skills, to learn the letters' sounds and decide which letters should be used to symbolize which sounds. The results shed doubt on the idea that children necessarily learn the correspondences between letters and phonemes in a rote, paired-associate fashion (e.g., Windfuhr & Snowling, 2001). Instead, children search for systematic relationships between letters and phonemes, and they benefit from those relationships that make sense given their prior knowledge. In English, the sounds of most but not all letters appear in the letters' names. In some other languages, the relationships between letter names and letter sounds are more systematic than they are in English and so letter-name knowledge should be even more helpful (see Treiman & Kessler, 2003).

CHILDREN'S USE OF LETTER NAMES IN CONNECTING PRINT AND SPEECH

We have seen that English-speaking children use their knowledge of letters' names to make inferences about the phonemes that the letters symbolize. These inferences are often right, as when a child spells /v/ as *v* because /v/ appears at the beginning of the letter name /vi/. However, the inferences are sometimes wrong, as when a child spells /w/ as *y* based on the fact that /w/ begins the letter name /waɪ/. The learning of letter–sound correspondences provides one example of how children use their knowledge of letter names to connect print and speech. As discussed in this section, letter-name knowledge has other influences as well.

Misspellings such as *frm* for "farm" and *hlp* for "help" point to another way in which children use letter names to connect print and speech (Treiman, 1993, 1994). Children who produce such errors symbolize a vowel + consonant sequence not with a vowel letter followed by a consonant letter, as correct in English, but with the single consonant letter whose name matches the entire phoneme sequence. Such errors are particularly common for the vowel + consonant sequence /aɪ/, which is the name of the letter *r*. In one study (Treiman, 1994, Experiment 2), kindergartners (mean age 5 years, 7 months) produced spellings such as *gr* for the nonword /gaɪ/ 61% of the time, and first graders (mean age 6 years, 4 months) did so at a rate of 50%. The children were less likely to produce spellings such as *gf* for /gɛf/ than spellings such as *gr* for /gaɪ/. Differences among various types of letter-name sequences also appear in first graders' classroom spellings of real words (Treiman, 1993). These differences fit with the observation that, in phonological awareness tasks, children find it easier to break up vowel + obstruent sequences such as /ɛf/ than vowel + liquid sequences such as /aɪ/ (Hindson & Byrne, 1997; Treiman, Zukowski, & Richmond-Welty, 1995). Children's use of letter names in spelling is thus linked to their phonological skills. Children are most likely to spell a sequence of phonemes as a whole, using a single known letter name, when the phonemes form a cohesive linguistic unit.

The syllable is another important linguistic unit, and its influence may be seen in spelling as well. Research has shown that children sometimes transcribe an entire syllable that matches the name of a letter with the corresponding letter. For example, children sometimes use a single *b* to symbolize /bi/ when /bi/ forms a syllable, as in the nonword /gəˈbi/ (Treiman & Tincoff, 1997). When the letter-name sequence is part of a larger syllable, as in /gəˈbiv/ or /biv/, such errors tend to be less common. Again, we see a relationship between phonological factors—in this case, the cohesiveness of syllables—and children's use of single letters to symbolize the letters' names.

Letter-name effects are not restricted to children in the United States. Levin, Patel, Margalit, and Barad (2002) found similar phenomena among Israeli children. For instance, the Hebrew word /beˈton/ [concrete] is conventionally spelled with the letters for *b*, *t*, and *n*; vowels are not normally represented with separate letters in Hebrew. Young Israeli children sometimes spell the word with just *b* and the *n*, apparently using *b* to represent its entire name, /bet/, rather than just the /b/.

Omissions of the vowel in the English "farm" and the Hebrew /beˈton/ are errors, and they suggest that children's reliance on letter names can lead them to spelling errors. However, letter names are for the most part helpful during the early years of literacy acquisition (e.g., Treiman & Kessler, 2003). Young children who know the names of letters can appreciate why certain words are written with certain letters. They can begin to grasp that the printed forms of words encode the words' phonological forms. These experiences may help children move away from earlier, incorrect views, such as the idea that the printed forms of words are related to the sizes or shapes of the objects they represent (Levin & Tolchinsky Landsmann, 1989).

Evidence that knowledge of letter names helps children grasp how alphabetic writing represents speech comes from a study in which children were asked what letters would be used at the beginnings or ends of various words (Treiman et al., 1996, Experiment 1). When questioned about initial letters, preschoolers (mean age 5 years, 5 months) were more likely to respond with the correct *b* for letter-name words such as "beach" than for control words such as "bone". When asked about final letters, the children did better on letter-name words such as "deaf" than on control words such as "loaf". These findings suggest that young children use their knowledge about letters' names to form expectations about words' spellings. These expectations are sometimes wrong in English, as when some of the children tested by Treiman et al. said that "seem" began with *c*. However, the expectations are usually correct.

Further support for the idea that letter names help children link spoken and written language comes from the results of a spelling study reported by Treiman (1994, Experiment 2). The preschoolers in this study, who averaged 5 years, 3 months in age and who were selected for their good knowledge of letter names, often produced single-letter spellings such as *r* for /gɑɹ/ and *t* for /tib/. Although these spellings are incorrect, they are more advanced than errors like *l* for /mɪp/. Errors of the latter kind were more common on items that did not contain letter-name sequences than on items that did. Children's more advanced performance on items that contain letter-name sequences suggests that it would be useful to include real words of this kind in early spelling and reading instruction.

Children use the names of letters to connect print and speech when reading as well as when spelling. Evidence comes from a study by Treiman and Rodriguez (1999) in which preschoolers and kindergartners were taught pronunciations for various types of novel words. The words, which were presented as belonging to a puppet's language, exemplified different types of print–speech relationships. In one condition, the name of the first letter of the printed item could be heard at the beginning of its spoken form. For example, *bt* was presented as the spelling of "beet" in this *name condition*. In a second condition, the first letter of the printed item corresponded to its typical phoneme but the entire letter name was not present. In this *sound condition*, for instance, *pl* was presented as a spelling of "pole". A third condition featured pronunciations that were not related to the printed forms of the words on the basis of either letter names or letter sounds. The letters of the printed words in this *visual condition* varied in size and positioning, as when C$_D$ was presented as the spelling of "wife". The words within each set in the visual condition were thus relatively distinctive on a visual basis. Each child learned five words in each condition, with up to eight trials allotted to learn the pronunciations. If young children adopt a logographic approach in learning to read the items, they should perform relatively well in the visual condition. Indeed, Ehri and Wilce (1985) found such a result when they compared a visual condition with a condition that was similar to the sound condition of Treiman and Rodriguez.

The participants in the Treiman and Rodriguez (1999) study included prereaders (mean age 5 years) who could not read simple words like "no" and "stop" when presented out of context. A second group, the novice readers (mean age 5 years, 6 months) could read a few real words. Both the prereaders and the novice readers were relatively knowledgeable about the names of English letters. However, the prereaders knew few of the letters' sounds.

The novice readers tested by Treiman and Rodriguez (1999) learned the items in the name condition more easily than they learned those in the sound condition. Their performance in the visual condition was substantially poorer than their performance in the other two conditions. In other words, the novice readers did better when the spellings of the novel words followed English letter–sound relationships (e.g., *pl* for "pole") than when they did not (e.g., *cd* for "wife"). Importantly, the novice readers derived additional benefit from letter–name links above and beyond letter–sound links. Although the beginning readers could use letter–sound relationships, they had not abandoned the use of letter names.

The prereaders in the Treiman and Rodriguez (1999) study showed a different pattern of performance. They did significantly better in the name condition than in the sound or visual conditions, which were statistically indistinguishable from one another. This outcome suggests that the prereaders did not benefit from correspondences between letters and phonemes.

However, the prereaders did use print–speech relationships that were based on letter names. The prereaders' better performance in the name condition than the visual condition suggests that they did not learn the words in a purely logographic fashion. They derived some benefit from the link between the *b* of the printed *bt* and the /bi/ of the spoken /bit/. This helped them learn and remember the pairs in the name condition.

The finding of Treiman and Rodriguez (1999) that prereaders performed significantly better in the name condition than in the visual condition is surprising given the view that young children approach the task of learning to read in a logographic manner (e.g., Frith, 1985). It is also surprising given the results of Ehri and Wilce (1985), who reported good performance in a visual condition by prereaders. However, the findings of Treiman and Rodriguez have been replicated in another study with prereaders who were even younger and less knowledgeable about letters than those in the original study. In the follow-up study, Treiman, Sotak, and Bowman (2001, Experiment 1) selected prereaders who could produce the names of six or fewer letters of the alphabet. These children were younger than those in the original Treiman and Rodriguez study (mean age 4 years, 3 months), and their overall level of performance in the word-learning task was relatively low. More important, though, the new group of children again showed a significant superiority for the name condition over the sound and visual conditions. Although these children performed quite poorly in the letter-name production task, they had some ability to select the correct name for a letter when given two choices. Apparently, even a relatively small amount of knowledge about letter names helps children make some sense of mappings such as that between the printed *bt* and the spoken /bit/.

Together, the results of Treiman and Rodriguez (1999) and Treiman, Sotak, and Bowman (2001) suggest that even young children can sometimes go beyond a logographic strategy to connect print and speech. We are currently examining the factors that promote an analytic approach to the learning of printed words and those that discourage it, trying to understand why the prereaders in our studies appear to be more analytic than those tested by Ehri and Wilce (1985).

Even if children begin to relate print and speech on the basis of letter names, they must learn to use relationships that are based on letter sounds. Our data suggest that children start to do this as they gain the ability to recognize simple words out of context. Although print–speech relationships that are based on letter names are not an end in themselves, they may form an early bridge between oral and written language. Teachers could help children cross this bridge by introducing them to printed words such as *beet*, *jail*, and *teepee*. These real words are similar to the abbreviations used in the name conditions of Treiman and Rodriguez (1999) and Treiman, Sotak, and Bowman (2001). Children may appreciate that many of the letters in the spellings of such words make sense given the letter names they hear in the spoken words. This may help them understand that print represents speech.

Hebrew-speaking children, like American children, appear to use letter names early on in the process of learning to read. Support for this view comes from a study by Levin et al. (2002) with Israeli kindergartners (mean age 5 years, 10 months). Children were shown the printed form of a word such as /be'ton/ [concrete] and were asked whether the word was /be'ton/ or /kaf'ri/ [rustic]. Both /bet/ and /kaf/ are the names of Hebrew letters, and even young children may be able to recognize that a printed word that starts with the Hebrew *b* is more likely to stand for /be'ton/ than for /kaf'ri/. Indeed, the children performed quite well on letter-name pairs such as these, substantially better than on control pairs. For Hebrew-speaking children, as for English-speaking ones, experiences with words whose spellings make sense on the basis of letter names may help children connect print and speech.

To summarize the results reviewed in this section, children who are familiar with the names of letters, as many children are in literate societies, use this knowledge when linking print to speech (reading) and when linking speech to print (spelling). Children's reliance on letter names sometimes leads to errors, as when an English-speaking child spells "seem" with c rather than s. However, its effects are mostly positive. For young children, letter names provide a more accessible link between print and speech than do letter sounds. As children notice that the letters in printed words sometimes say their names in the words' pronunciations, they begin to understand that the printed forms of words symbolize the words' phonological forms. Printed words do not symbolize properties of the objects that the words represent, such as their size or shape. Once this insight has been achieved, children still have much work to do to learn exactly how print symbolizes speech. However, letter names may provide the earliest connection.

BEYOND SIMPLE LETTER–SOUND ASSOCIATIONS

The evidence discussed so far indicates that children often use their knowledge about the names of letters, together with their phonological skills, to make preliminary links between print and speech. This sets the stage for the learning of associations between letters and sounds, which is essential for continued progress. In highly regular alphabetic systems, such as Finnish, simple letter–sound connections such as those between /d/ and d and /ε/ and e permit the accurate reading and writing of all words. This is not true in English, in which most letters have more than one possible pronunciation and most phonemes have more than one possible spelling. Such considerations have led to the idea that English is a *deep* or inconsistent writing system, in contrast to the *shallow* or consistent system of a language like Finnish (e.g., Frost, 1992). Whole-word memorization is thought to play a major role in the learning of inconsistent systems. For example, because "head" is an exception to the rule that /ε/ is spelled as e, learners must memorize the irregular ea spelling. In this section, I argue that English is less inconsistent than widely believed (see also Kessler & Treiman, 2001, 2003). Many probabilistic patterns are available to readers and spellers who are willing to go beyond simple letter–sound associations and who are willing to use patterns that do not apply in every case. The role of word-specific memorization, in this view, is smaller than commonly thought.

When a phoneme has several possible spellings, a speller can sometimes choose the correct one by considering the smaller meaningful parts (*morphemes*) in the word. For example, the /ε/ of "health" is spelled with ea because "health" is related to "heal". The ea in "heal" stands for /i/; the vowel changes its pronunciation in "health" but the spelling remains the same. Early on, it appears, children begin to appreciate that morphemes often retain their spellings even when their pronunciations change. Treiman, Cassar, and Zukowski (1994, Experiment 4) took advantage of a phenomenon that occurs in American English, *flapping*, to investigate this issue. In flapping, the /t/ of a word like "eat" changes its pronunciation when a suffix such as *-er* is added. In "eater," the first consonant is pronounced as a voiced tap of the tongue or *flap*, differently than it is pronounced in "eat". Young children often spell flaps with d because flaps, like /d/, are voiced. However, if children know that the stem retains its spelling when a suffix is added, they should be less likely to spell the flap of *eater* with a d than to spell the flap of a single-morpheme word like *city* with a d. To find out if they do, we tested kindergartners, first graders, and second graders on two occasions during the school year. The children heard words such as "eater" and "city" and were asked to fill in a blank in these words' spellings with either t or d. Even the kindergartners were more likely to choose the correct t with two-morpheme words like *eater* than with one-morpheme words like "city". This result suggests that the children were beginning to use morphological relations among words to guide their spelling. At the same time, the children were less likely to choose t in two-morpheme words such as "eater" than in stems such as "eat". This difference, which continued through the end of second grade in this study and through fourth grade in a similar study (Treiman, Cassar, & Zukowski, 1994, Experiment 3), suggests that a complete understanding of morphological constancy takes time to develop. Children do not take full advantage of this aspect of the English writing system during the early years of school.

Another factor that can be helpful in deciding how to spell a phoneme is its position in the word or syllable. For example, English /l/ is sometimes spelled as *ll* when it is in the middle or at the end of a word, as in "belly" and "ball". However, initial *ll* is very rare in English. Children show a beginning appreciation of such patterns as early as kindergarten and first grade (Cassar & Treiman, 1997; Treiman, 1993). For instance, the kindergartners who were tested by Cassar and Treiman (Experiment 3) toward the end of their school year (mean age 5 years, 11 months) tended to judge that *luss* looked more like a real English word than *llus* did. This tendency, although statistically significant, was weak at the kindergarten level. As children gain more experience with the English writing system, their knowledge of its patterns grows and deepens and they begin to learn how double letters help signal pronunciation, as in "latter" versus "later". Children who are learning to read and write in French show a similar sensitivity to the position and identity of double letters. This sensitivity appears to reflect their experience with the letter patterns in written words (Pacton, Perruchet, Fayol, & Cleeremans, 2001).

A third factor that can be useful in deciding how to spell a phoneme is the identity of the surrounding phonemes. In English, many of these contextual effects occur within the rime, the unit that consists of the vowel and the following consonants. For example, /ε/ is more likely to be spelled as *ea* in a single-morpheme word when the following consonant is /d/ (e.g., *head*, *spread*) than when it is /k/ or /g/ (*heck*, *egg*). This pattern is probabilistic in that /ε/ is not always spelled *ea* before /d/. Even though the pattern has exceptions, it could be useful to spellers. Indeed, college students are sensitive to this and other effects of context on vowel spelling (Treiman, Kessler, & Bick, 2002). They are more likely to use *ea* when spelling a nonword such as /smεd/ than a nonword like as /smεk/, and they are more likely to misspell "shred" as *shread* than to misspell "trek" as *treak*. College students also use associations that extend beyond the onset–rime boundary. For example, their spelling of nonwords reveals a knowledge that /ɑ/ tends to be spelled differently after /w/ (e.g., *wand*, *want*) than after other consonants (e.g., *pond*, *font*). Thus experienced spellers do not rely on simple, context-free associations between letters and sounds. We are currently carrying out research to determine when and how use of context emerges in children. Are children especially sensitive to patterns within the rime, given their tendency to segment spoken syllables into onsets and rimes, or can they use patterns that extend beyond the rime unit?

Just as children must go beyond simple sound-to-letter relationships in spelling words, so they must go beyond simple letter-to-sound relationships in pronouncing words. A reader of English who expects each letter to always correspond to the same phoneme would encounter many irregular words that need to be memorized. A reader who knows that morphology, position, and context can all affect spelling-to-sound translation is better able to deal with the English system. Researchers have documented some of the statistical regularities that exist in English spelling-to-sound translation (e.g., Kessler & Treiman, 2001; Venezky, 1970). For example, *a* tends to be pronounced as /æ/ when followed by a consonant in a monosyllabic word (e.g., *act*), as /ɑ/ when at the end of a monosyllabic word (*spa*) or when followed by *r* (*card*), as /e/ when followed by *nge* (*change*), and as /ɔ/ when followed by *l* (*bald*). With *a* and other letters, the variation is not random. Readers who can use probabilistic patterns, going beyond context-free letter-to-sound associations, can cope with the complexity of the English system.

English is not the only alphabetic writing system that has been characterized as deep or inconsistent. French, like English, appears to be rather irregular in sound-to-spelling translation. However, it too contains statistical patterns that could help spellers choose the correct option from among the several possibilities. For example, /o/ is more likely to be spelled as *o* than as *au* between /b/ and /ʁ/, but is more likely to be spelled as *au* than as *o* between /p/ and /v/ (Pacton,

Fayol, & Perruchet, 2002). French children begin to follow these patterns as early as second grade. Thus rote memorization may be less important than commonly believed in the learning of French, as in the learning of English. In these and other writing systems, learners must go beyond context-free letter-sound correspondences to achieve reasonable levels of accuracy.

CONCLUSIONS

Knowledge of the alphabet and phonological awareness are two foundations on which literacy learning rests. Typically, they have been considered as separate and very different skills. Alphabet knowledge, it is thought, is largely a matter of rote memorization. Phonological awareness is a linguistic process. The research reviewed in this chapter shows that alphabet knowledge and phonological awareness have a good deal in common. Children in literate societies acquire many skills in both domains well before formal reading instruction begins. An understanding of this early knowledge sheds light on how children learn from the instruction they receive. It also sheds light on the kinds of errors children make and the reasons they make these errors. Young children are not just rote memorizers when learning about the sounds of letters, when learning about the printed forms of their own names, and when learning to read their first few words. Linguistic factors are intimately involved in this learning, just as they are in the development of phonological awareness.

The research reviewed here further suggests that phonological awareness and letter knowledge influence one another as they develop. For example, learning the names of English letters may foster children's phonological awareness by alerting them to the similarities in sound among the letters' names. Learning the letters' sounds may improve children's phonemic awareness by helping them detect a phoneme such as /m/ within a letter name such as /ɛm/. Phonological awareness and letter knowledge are closely related, and they should be examined together.

Theories of how children learn to read and spell must consider the formal and informal learning experiences that are provided to the children, the nature of the writing system that is learned, and the predispositions that the children bring with them. Much of our evidence on these topics comes from studies that have been conducted with middle-SES learners of English from the United States. In the future, it will be important to carry out work with learners from other linguistic and cultural backgrounds. Differences as a function of language and background may reflect characteristics of the children's languages and the children's experiences. However, all children likely bring their knowledge of spoken language and whatever knowledge about print they have acquired before the onset of formal instruction to the tasks of learning to read and spell.

ACKNOWLEDGMENTS

This work was supported, in part, by grants from the National Science Foundation (SBR-9408456, SBR-9807736, BCS-0130763) and the March of Dimes Birth Defects Research Foundation (12-FY98-204, 12-FY99-674, 12-FY00-51).

REFERENCES

Bloodgood, J. W. (1999). What's in a name? Children's name writing and literacy acquisition. *Reading Research Quarterly, 34*, 342–367.

Brady, S. A., & Shankweiler, D. P. (Eds.). (1991). *Phonological processes in literacy: A tribute to Isabelle Y. Liberman.* Hillsdale, NJ: Lawrence Erlbaum Associates.

Byrne, B. (1992). Studies in the acquisition procedure for reading: Rationale, hypotheses, and data. In P. B. Gough, L. C. Ehri, & R. Treiman (Eds.), *Reading acquisition* (pp. 1–34). Hillsdale, NJ: Lawrence Erlbaum Associates.

Byrne, B., & Fielding-Barnsley, R. (1990). Acquiring the alphabetic principle: A case for teaching recognition of phoneme identity. *Journal of Educational Psychology, 82,* 805–812.

Byrne, B., Fielding-Barnsley, R., & Ashley, L. (2000). Effects of preschool phoneme identity training after six years: Outcome level distinguished from rate of response. *Journal of Educational Psychology, 92,* 659–667.

Cassar, M., & Treiman, R. (1997). The beginnings of orthographic knowledge: Children's knowledge of double letters in words. *Journal of Educational Psychology, 89,* 631–644.

Chan, L., & Louie, L. (1992). Developmental trend of Chinese preschool children in drawing and writing. *Journal of Research in Childhood Education, 6,* 93–99.

Chi, M. M. (1988). Invented spelling/writing in Chinese-speaking children: The developmental patterns. *National Reading Conference Yearbook, 37,* 285–296.

Ehri, L. C. (1997). Learning to read and learning to spell are one and the same, almost. In C. A. Perfetti, L. Rieben, & M. Fayol (Eds.), *Learning to spell: Research, theory, and practice across languages* (pp. 237–269). Mahwah, NJ: Lawrence Erlbaum Associates.

Ehri, L. C. (1998). Grapheme–phoneme knowledge is essential for learning to read words in English. In L. C. Ehri & J. L. Metsala (Eds.), *Word recognition in beginning literacy* (pp. 3–40). Mahwah, NJ: Lawrence Erlbaum Associates.

Ehri, L. C., & Wilce, L. S. (1985). Movement into reading: Is the first stage of printed word learning visual or phonetic? *Reading Research Quarterly, 20,* 163–179.

Frith, U. (1985). Beneath the surface of developmental dyslexia. In K. E. Patterson, J. C. Marshall, & M. Coltheart (Eds.), *Surface dyslexia: Neuropsychological and cognitive studies of phonological reading* (pp. 301–330). Hove, UK: Lawrence Erlbaum Associates.

Frost, R. (1992). Orthography and phonology: The psychological reality of orthographic depth. In M. Noonan, P. Downing, & S. Lima (Eds.), *The linguistics of literacy* (pp. 255–274). Amsterdam: Benjamins.

Fudge, E. (1987). Branching structure within the syllable. *Journal of Linguistics, 23,* 359–377.

Gentry, J. R. (1982). An analysis of developmental spelling in GNYS AT WRK. *Reading Teacher, 36,* 192–200.

Gombert, J. E., & Fayol, M. (1992). Writing in preliterate children. *Learning & Instruction, 2,* 23–41.

Hildreth, G. (1936). Developmental sequences in name writing. *Child Development, 7,* 291–303.

Hindson, B. A., & Byrne, B. (1997). The status of final consonant clusters in English syllables: Evidence from children. *Journal of Experimental Child Psychology, 64,* 119–136.

International Phonetic Association. (1996). *Reproduction of The International Phonetic Alphabet.* Retrieved from http://www2.arts.gla.ac.uk/IPA/ipachart.html.

International Phonetic Association. (1999). *Handbook of the International Phonetic Association: A guide to the use of the International Phonetic Alphabet.* Cambridge, UK: Cambridge University Press.

Kessler, B., & Treiman, R. (2001). Relationships between sounds and letters in English monosyllables. *Journal of Memory and Language, 44,* 592–617.

Kessler, B., & Treiman, R. (2003). Is English spelling chaotic? Misconceptions concerning its irregularity. *Reading Psychology, 24,* 291–313.

Lavine, L. O. (1977). Differentiation of letterlike forms in prereading children. *Developmental Psychology, 13,* 89–94.

Levin, I., Patel, S., Margalit, T., & Barad, N. (2002). Letter names: Effect on letter saying, spelling, and word recognition in Hebrew. *Applied Psycholinguistics, 23,* 269–300.

Levin, I., Share, D. L., & Shatil, E. (1996). A qualitative-quantitative study of preschool writing: Its development and contribution to school literacy. In C. M. Levy & S. Ransdell (Eds.), *The science of writing: Theories, methods, individual differences, and applications* (pp. 271–293). Mahwah, NJ: Lawrence Erlbaum Associates.

Levin, I., & Tolchinsky Landsmann, L. (1989). Becoming literate: Referential and phonetic strategies in early reading and writing. *International Journal of Behavioral Development, 12,* 369–384.

Liberman, I. Y., Shankweiler, D., Fischer, F. W., & Carter, B. (1974). Explicit syllable and phoneme segmentation in the young child. *Journal of Experimental Child Psychology, 18,* 201–212.

Mandel, D. R., Jusczyk, P. W., & Pisoni, D. B. (1995). Infants' recognition of the sound patterns of their own names. *Psychological Science, 6,* 314–317.

Masonheimer, P. E., Drum, P. A., & Ehri, L. C. (1984). Does environmental print identification lead children into word reading? *Journal of Reading Behavior, 16,* 257–271.

McBride-Chang, C. (1999). The ABC's of the ABC's: The development of letter-name and letter-sound knowledge. *Merrill-Palmer Quarterly, 45,* 285–308.

Pacton, S., Fayol, M., & Perruchet, P. (2002). The acquisition of untaught orthographic regularities in French. In L. Verhoeven, C. Elbro, & P. Reitsma (Eds.), *Precursors of functional literacy* (pp. 121–137). Dordrecht, The Netherlands: Kluwer.

Pacton, S., Perruchet, P., Fayol, M., & Cleeremans, A. (2001). Implicit learning out of the lab: The case of orthographic regularities. *Journal of Experimental Psychology: General, 130,* 401–426.

Read, C. (1975). *Children's categorization of speech sounds in English* (*NCTE Research Report No. 17*). Urbana, IL: National Council of Teachers of English.

Sawyer, D. J., & Fox, B. J. (Eds.). (1991). *Phonological awareness in reading: The evolution of current perspectives.* New York: Springer.

Share, D. L., Jorm, A. F., Maclean, R., & Matthews, R. (1984). Sources of individual differences in reading acquisition. *Journal of Educational Psychology, 76,* 1309–1325.

Snow, C. E., Burns, M. S., & Griffin, P. (Eds.). (1998). *Preventing reading difficulties in young children.* Washington, DC: National Academy Press.

Stuart, M., & Coltheart, M. (1988). Does reading develop in a sequence of stages? *Cognition, 30,* 139–181.

Treiman, R. (1985). Phonemic awareness and spelling: Children's judgments do not always agree with adults'. *Journal of Experimental Child Psychology, 39,* 182–201.

Treiman, R. (1992). The role of intrasyllabic units in learning to read and spell. In P. B. Gough, L. C. Ehri, & R. Treiman (Eds.), *Reading acquisition* (pp. 65–106). Hillsdale, NJ: Lawrence Erlbaum Associates.

Treiman, R. (1993). *Beginning to spell: A study of first-grade children.* New York: Oxford University Press.

Treiman, R. (1994). Use of consonant letter names in beginning spelling. *Developmental Psychology, 30,* 567–580.

Treiman, R., & Broderick, V. (1998). What's in a name? Children's knowledge about the letters in their own names. *Journal of Experimental Child Psychology, 70,* 97–116.

Treiman, R., Broderick, V., Tincoff, R., & Rodriguez, K. (1998). Children's phonological awareness: Confusions between phonemes that differ only in voicing. *Journal of Experimental Child Psychology, 68,* 3–21.

Treiman, R., & Cassar, M. (1997). Spelling acquisition in English. In C. A. Perfetti, L. Rieben, & M. Fayol (Eds.), *Learning to spell: Research, theory, and practice across languages* (pp. 61–80). Hillsdale, NJ: Lawrence Erlbaum Associates.

Treiman, R., Cassar, M., & Zukowski, A. (1994). What types of linguistic information do children use in spelling? The case of flaps. *Child Development, 65,* 1318–1337.

Treiman, R., & Kessler, B. (2003). The role of letter names in the acquisition of literacy. In R. Kail (Ed.), *Advances in Child Development and Behavior, Vol. 31.* (pp. 105–135). San Diego: Academic Press.

Treiman, R., Kessler, B., & Bick, S. (2002). Content sensitivity in the spelling of English vowels. *Journal of Memory and Language 47,* 448–468.

Treiman, R., Kessler, B., & Bourassa, D. (2001). Children's own names influence their spelling. *Applied Psycholinguistics, 22,* 555–570.

Treiman, R., & Rodriguez, K. (1999). Young children use letter names in learning to read words. *Psychological Science, 10,* 334–338.

Treiman, R., Sotak, L., & Bowman, M. (2001). The roles of letter names and letter sounds in connecting print and speech. *Memory & Cognition, 29,* 860–873.

Treiman, R., & Tincoff, R. (1997). The fragility of the alphabetic principle: Children's knowledge of letter names can cause them to spell syllabically rather than alphabetically. *Journal of Experimental Child Psychology, 64,* 425–451.

Treiman, R., Tincoff, R., & Richmond-Welty, E. D. (1996). Letter names help children to connect print and speech. *Developmental Psychology, 32,* 505–514.

Treiman, R., Tincoff, R., & Richmond-Welty, E. D. (1997). Beyond zebra: Preschoolers' knowledge about letters. *Applied Psycholinguistics, 18,* 391–409.

Treiman, R., Tincoff, R., Rodriguez, K., Mouzaki, A., & Francis, D. J. (1998). The foundations of literacy: Learning the sounds of letters. *Child Development, 69,* 1524–1540.

Treiman, R., & Weatherston, S. (1992). Effects of linguistic structure on children's ability to isolate initial consonants. *Journal of Educational Psychology, 84,* 174–181.

Treiman, R., Weatherston, S., & Berch, D. (1994). The role of letter names in children's learning of phoneme–grapheme relations. *Applied Psycholinguistics, 15,* 97–122.

Treiman, R., Zukowski, A., & Richmond-Welty, E. D. (1995). What happened to the "n" of sink? Children's spellings of final consonant clusters. *Cognition, 55,* 1–38.

Venezky, R. L. (1970). *The structure of English orthography.* The Hague: Mouton.

Villaume, S. K., & Wilson, L. C. (1989). Preschool children's explorations of letters in their own names. *Applied Psycholinguistics, 10,* 283–300.

Windfuhr, K. L., & Snowling, M. J. (2001). The relationship between paired associate learning and phonological skills in normally developing readers. *Journal of Experimental Child Psychology, 80,* 160–173.

Worden, P. E., & Boettcher, W. (1990). Young children's acquisition of alphabet knowledge. *Journal of Reading Behavior, 22,* 277–295.

36

Morphology and Spelling: What Have Morphemes to Do With Spelling?

Peter Bryant
Oxford Brookes University

Hélène Deacon
Dalhousie University

Terezinha Nunes
Oxford Brookes University

Many spelling rules are based on *morphemes*. Such rules abound in English spelling and in other orthographies as well. They are the main reason why we have to study children's ability to learn about morphological as well as about phonological rules in spelling. These rules govern the relationship between spelling on the one hand and inflectional and derivational morphemes on the other. Children initially find some derivational suffixes extremely hard to spell despite the fact that they occur quite frequently. In the process of acquiring knowledge about morphology, children go through a phase when they spell some words worse than they did before, at the same time spelling others better than they did before. Our studies that led us to this conclusion are described in this chapter. In this chapter, we also address the question of how children learn about morphological spellings: Do they learn through formal and informal instruction or through their own discoveries? This implicit–explicit distinction is the next great problem to solve for researchers on children's morphological spelling. It is already clear that children's knowledge of morphemes and of its impact on spelling rules plays a significant and interesting part in their learning to read and to spell. Now we need to know what and how to tell children about these rules.

In many scripts certain sounds can be spelled in more than one way. We write the opening sound of 'fan' in one way and 'phantom' in another, even though they are the same sound. So the writer often has to decide which of two or three or even four possible spellings for a sound is the right one for a particular sound in a particular word. This degree of choice in English and in many other orthographies is one of the main reasons for the mistakes that children make in spelling. When they misspell a sound in a particular word, the spelling that they choose for it is frequently appropriate, though wrong. Children, and sometimes adults too, often choose a spelling for a particular sound in a particular word that really does represent that sound correctly, but does so in different words, for example, *sownd* for 'sound', *reesen* for 'reason'.

Sometimes we have to resort to rote learning to be able to make the right choice among these alternative spellings. How else can anyone possibly know and remember the different spellings for the same vowel sound in 'fight' and in 'bite'? There is no basic rule to tell us why one of these verbs is spelled with an "ight" and the other with an "ite" ending. In other cases, however, there are rules that determine which spelling is the right one and rote learning therefore is in principle unnecessary.

Many of these spelling rules are based on *morphemes*. Such rules abound in English spelling and, as we shall see, in other orthographies as well. They are the main reason why we have to study children's ability to learn about morphological as well as about phonological rules in spelling.

Morphemes are units of meaning. A word like 'list' is a one-morpheme word: It has only one unit of meaning. However, the word 'kissed' contains two morphemes: These are the stem, 'kiss', and the /t/ ending, spelled as 'ed', which is the past-tense suffix. This division of words into constituent morphemes has a radical effect on the way that the two words are spelled. 'List' and 'kissed' rhyme, which means that they have identical end sounds, but this rhyming sound is spelled entirely differently in the two words because the two-morpheme word 'kissed' is given the 'ed' ending to signify that it is a past verb.

The English plural suffix is another good example of the impact of morphology on English spelling. In regular plural words the sound of this suffix ending can be /s/ or /z/, but it is always spelled as /s/. So we spell 'fleas' with an 's' ending to denote that it is a plural word, even though we spell the same end sound quite differently in 'freeze' and in 'please'.

The spelling of words that end in /ks/ provides us with a dramatic example of a simple, and completely consistent, morphological English spelling rule that is based on the difference between one- and two-morpheme words. In singular nouns, which in English have no inflection, the /ks/ ending is always spelled as 'x' or 'xe' (box, axe). In English plural nouns, however, the spelling for this same end sound is always 'cks' or 'ks'/'k(e)s' (socks, books, lakes) because of the hard-and-fast rule that the plural inflection in regular plural nouns must be spelled as 's' to denote that it is a suffix added to the stem.

The rule that this ending is spelled as 'x' in one-morpheme words, but as 'cks' or 'ks' in two-morpheme words, applies as well to present verbs in English. We finish 'I fix' with an 'x', because 'fix' is a one-morpheme verb, in contrast, we put an added 's' on the verbs, 'He picks/ looks/bakes' because these are all two-morpheme verbs in which the final /s/ sound is the third-person-singular inflection and the written final "s" represents the existence of that added morpheme.

These are examples of a difference in English spelling between inflected two-morpheme words and non-inflected one-morpheme words. This happens reasonably frequently in English, because this is a language with relatively few inflections, and therefore with many non-inflected nouns, verbs, and adjectives. In more inflected languages, such as modern Greek, several different inflections share the same sound as each other but are spelled in different ways. Morphological rules determine the spelling of these endings too, but the spelling differences are between different two-morpheme words. For example, there are several different ways of spelling the long /i/ vowel sound in Greek. When this sound is at the end of a word it can signify a masculine-plural (-οι), a feminine-singular (-η), a neuter-singular-nominal or adjectival inflection (-ι) or a third-person-singular verb ending (-ει). Note that these four suffixes sound exactly the same as each other, but are spelled in four entirely different ways, each of which is a legitimate spelling for that sound. The clue to choosing the right spelling for each inflection is therefore entirely morphological.

These examples all involve the presence or absence of inflectional morphemes, but derivational morphemes are probably just as important. Children initially find some derivational suffixes extremely hard to spell despite the fact that they occur quite frequently. Words ending in 'ion,' 'ian,' or 'ness' are frequently misspelled even though these suffixes are very common indeed. No doubt a child who recognises them as distinct morphemes will be in a better position as a result to learn to spell them properly.

There is, too, the well-known phenomenon of derivational constancy, whereby in English and in several other languages the stem of a derived word is spelled in the same way as the word from which it was derived, even when it is pronounced differently. 'Heal' and 'health' and 'muscle' and 'muscular' are two well-known examples.

Derivations affect spellings in other languages too. In Portuguese, for example, the words *princesa* and *pobreza* share the same sounding two-syllable ending, which is pronounced as /eza/ but is spelled differently in the two words because 'esa' symbolises a female title whereas 'eza' signifies an abstract noun.

Sometimes, as far as morphemes are concerned, spelling outstrips speech. This happens when morphological distinctions are represented in writing but not in speech. In English the most famous, and probably the most difficult, example is the use of the apostrophe to represent possession. The phrases 'the boy's drink' and 'the boys drink' sound the same in spoken language but have entirely different meanings, and this difference is represented in writing by the presence in one phrase, and the absence in the other, of an apostrophe.

French boasts a similar phenomenon. The plural ending on nouns, adjectives, and verbs is silent in French, but it appears in writing. We do not hear the 's' on the end of the noun and the adjective in the phrase *les maisons blanches*, or the 'nt' at the end of *ils regardent*, but we spell these endings when we write such words in French. This requirement, as we shall see, causes French-speaking children a great deal of difficulty.

In most of the cases that we have discussed so far, the choice that the speller must make is between two or more perfectly legitimate spellings. Even quite young English-speaking children already know that 'x' and 'cks' are both reasonable ways, in alphabetic terms, of writing the sound /ks/ and Greek-speaking children soon learn that η, οι, ι, and ει are perfectly plausible spellings for the sound /i/. However, there are instances when morphologically based spelling rules actually flout the alphabetic rules that children master, often with great difficulty, in the initial stages of learning to read.

One example is the 'ed' ending for regular past-tense verbs. There are three different sounds for the past-tense affix in regular verbs, but all three are spelled as 'ed'. The spelling of this affix is the same in 'kissed' (/kɪst/), 'filled' (/fɪld/), and 'fitted' (/fɪtɪd/), but the affix is represented by a different sound in each of these words. The three different sounding endings, all spelled as 'ed', are /t/, /d/, and /ɪd/. These three end sounds are always spelled as 'ed' in regular verbs, but are never spelled in this way in any other kind of word. We spell the endings of 'filled' and 'fitted' with an 'ed' but not the endings of 'field' and 'fetid'. It is a consistent and an inflexible morphologically based rule. The rule is in conflict with alphabetic, grapheme–phoneme correspondences, because according to these correspondences the 'ed' spelling sequence represents the sound /d/, but we never actually pronounce the endings of any English regular past verbs in this way.

In every example that we have given so far, the alphabetic grapheme–phoneme correspondence system simply does not provide the writer with a sufficient basis for making the right choice between different spellings. Children have to go beyond phonology to learn about conventional spellings and, as we shall see, this is quite hard for them to do.

WHEN DO CHILDREN LEARN MORPHOLOGICALLY DETERMINED SPELLINGS?

The Time Scale

We need to know when and how children eventually manage to transcend phonology, and also what they learn. There is a simple rule of thumb here, though it has one possible exception.

The rule is that it takes children a long time to learn conventional spellings that are based on morphemic distinctions and where the choice of spellings goes beyond grapheme–phoneme correspondences.

The clearest and most famous illustration of this gap between learning to write alphabet-ically and learning to write conventional, morphologically determined spellings is the well-established phenomenon of invented spelling (Read, 1986). When children begin to write, they depend heavily on grapheme–phoneme correspondences, or at any rate on their own version of these correspondences, and blithely ignore conventional spellings for affixes. The past-tense ending, for example, is quite consistently ignored in children's early writing, as Fig. 36.1, which is a story written by a 7-year-old girl, attests. The works of Read (1986) and of Treiman

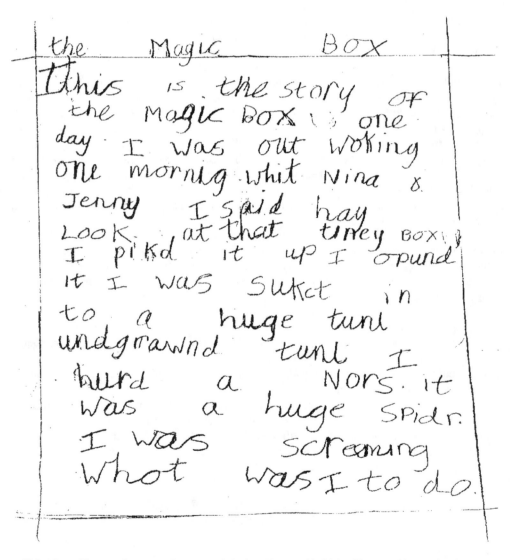

FIG. 36.1.   The opening page of a story written by a 7-year-old girl that illustrates the predominance of phonetic spellings for past verb endings at this age. Note the spellings for 'picked', 'opened', and 'sucked'.

(1993) and of several others have shown quite unambiguously that children make no attempt at first to adopt the conventional 'ed' past-tense ending, but simply write the ending phonetically.

Children's initial avoidance of morphemic distinctions in spelling suggests that they first go through a phase during which they conquer the alphabetic principle, and only later turn to morphology as well. However, both Read and Treiman suggest that there is at least one instance in which this is not so. This concerns the rule that the plural suffix in nouns is spelled as 's' even though the sound of the suffix is often /z/ (e.g., birds, smiles, fishes). The reason for thinking that children understand this rule is that they apparently obey it: For the most part they use the letter 's', and hardly ever the letter 'z', to write the plural ending even when its sound is /z/. However, they might avoid the letter 'z' merely because it is such an uncommon letter anyway. (Shakespeare called it the 'unnecessary letter' with some reason.) One could be certain that children understand the rule that 's' is the right way to spell the plural ending only if they spell the /z/ ending in other, non-plural, words, like 'jazz' for example, differently.

However, a child who puts 's' at the end of 'buns' but 'z' at the end of 'jazz' may not be doing so for morphological reasons, as Nenagh Kemp (2000) has pointed out. She argued that children may learn this distinction on the basis of frequency of certain letter patterns. Her point was that in virtually all non-plural English words ending in /z/, this final end sound is immediately preceded by a vowel (jazz, craze). In contrast, the sound preceding the /z/ or /ɪz/ ending in most plural nouns is a consonant (buns, fishes). This means that children could learn, on the basis of frequency alone, that 'z's do not follow a consonant—that there are no sequences like 'mz', 'nz', or 'lz', and that the 'z' sound should be represented as 's' immediately after these letters.

To obey frequency-based associations in this way would lead to fairly good but not to completely correct spelling. The child who relies on these associations would get the plural endings for nouns whose stems ends in a consonant ('buns') perfectly. This child would also do well with /z/ ending words whose penultimate sound is a short vowel, as there are no English nouns whose stem ends in a short vowel. To put it another way all /z/ ending words in English whose penultimate phoneme is a short vowel are non-plural words (buzz, fizz) and should not be spelled with an "s" at the end.

There is one category of /z/ ending words, however, that would not be spelled very well by anyone following a frequency-based rule. These are the words whose /z/ ending is a long vowel. There are plenty of plural nouns (pleas, fees) and non-plural words (please, seize) in this category, and therefore there is no consistent way of telling, on the basis of frequency alone, whether these words should end in 's' or in some other spelling ('se', 'ze').

Therefore it follows that anyone who bases his or her spelling on frequency-based learning rather than on morphological rules will do well at spelling the plural /z/ sounding endings of nouns whose stem ends in a consonant. They will also spell without too much difficulty the endings of non-plural /z/ ending words, whose penultimate sound is a short vowel. They will, however, make many errors with /z/ ending words whose penultimate sound is a long vowel (craze, ways).

Kemp (Kemp and Bryant, 2003) found exactly this pattern (many more errors with plural and non-plural words whose penultimate sound was a long vowel than with the other two categories) in tasks involving real words and pseudo-words with school children of 5–9 years old. She even found the same pattern, though in not so strong a form, when she gave the same pseudo-word task to adults. Even adults, to some extent at least, followed frequency-based associations in preference to a morphologically based rule. An interesting aspect of Kemp's results was that adults who had been to university did better on this task than those who had not. Going to university, it seems, does wonders for one's knowledge of morphologically based spelling rules.

Kemp's interesting work is a useful warning against concluding too rapidly that children are following a morphological spelling rule when there are other possible explanations for the spelling patterns that they are using. It also demonstrates how elusive these rules seem to be–not only to children but to some adults as well. Certainly much other work shows that children's learning of the conventional spellings for inflectional morphemes takes a great deal of time. The rule about the /ks/ ending that we already mentioned is a clear instance. We have shown (Bryant, 2002) that children of 5–9 years of age often fail to assign 'x' endings to one-morpheme and 's' endings to two-morpheme words that have this final sound. They get better at doing so as they grow older, but even at the age of 9 years their spelling of this final sound is by no means perfect, and they are particularly weak in pseudo-word tasks that are the definitive test of their knowledge of the morphological spelling rule.

Our own work (Nunes, Bryant, & Bindman, 1997) also confirms that English-speaking children are very slow indeed to adopt the past-tense 'ed' ending. We conducted a longitudinal study of 363 children whose ages in the study ranged from 6 to 11 years, and in the course of this study we gave the children spelling tasks involving the words presented in Table 36.1. These were regular past verbs (ending in 'ed') and also non-verbs with similar sounding endings and irregular past verbs that also ended with the same sounds but whose endings were spelled phonetically. Our results with the younger children confirmed that a sizeable number of them simply ignored the 'ed' ending with regular verbs and wrote these endings phonetically. The developmental improvement in the use of this difficult ending was quite marked. However, it was not comprehensive. Many of the oldest children did not put this ending on all the regular verbs, even though these were all frequent and well-known words.

Children are also in striking difficulty with the apostrophe (Bryant, Devine, Ledward, & Nunes, 1997). Younger children (9–10-year-olds) tend to leave it out altogether in genitive

TABLE 36.1

Words That the Children Had to Spell in
the Nunes et al. Longitudinal Study

Regular Past Verbs	
/d/ ending	/t/ ending
called	dressed
covered	kissed
filled	laughed
killed	learned
opened	stopped
Irregular Past Verbs	
found	felt
heard	left
held	lost
sold	sent
told	slept
Non-Verbs	
bird	belt
cold	except
field	next
gold	paint
ground	soft

(possessive) words: Older children (11- and 15-year-olds) put it in more often, but almost as often in the wrong words (plural nominatives) as in the right ones. We return to this pattern of children's spelling getting worse with some words at the same time as it gets better with others later in this chapter.

There is hardly any dispute about children's slowness in learning the correct conventional spellings for words whose spelling depends on their morphemic structure (Nunes et al., 1997; Read, 1986; Treiman, 1993) Nor is there any disagreement that children do eventually find out about these spellings. But it is hard to find a consensus about how they learn about these spellings. This is a subject that researchers have entirely neglected until quite recently.

HOW DO CHILDREN LEARN ABOUT MORPHOLOGICAL SPELLINGS?

Learning to Spell Worse

It is tempting to argue that children learn any topic that they encounter at school just by being taught it and for no other reason. But this is not a good answer to the question of how children learn about morphological spellings, and it is certainly not a complete answer. It is incomplete because there are spelling rules that are not taught at school but that children nevertheless learn about. We deal with one of these, which concerns the difference between English regular and irregular verbs, later on in this chapter.

Another reason for not using teaching as a catch-all explanation of their learning about morphological spelling rules is the shape of the learning. If children were simply learning a rule by being told about it, one would expect them to go directly from a state of not knowing the rule to knowing it. This, as we shall now see, is not the case.

In all the cases that we have been discussing, children have to learn to represent the same sound with different spellings in different words. Typically they start by using one spelling for this and avoiding others. So, as we have seen, they initially spell /d/ and /t/ endings as 'd' and 't', which means that they are right in the case of non-verbs like 'list' and of irregular verbs like 'slept' but wrong with regular past verbs like 'kissed' and 'clapped'. At this stage they clearly lack the morphological rule that past verbs end in 'ed'.

If it were a matter simply of learning the rule by being told it, we would expect that children would change rather suddenly from spelling words like 'kissed' as 'kist' to spelling them correctly, and that at the same time they would continue to spell the endings of non-verbs and of irregular past verbs correctly. But this is not what happens. Our longitudinal study (Nunes et al., 1997) showed that many children take an intermediate step. They begin by avoiding the 'ed' spelling entirely. Then they go on to use this spelling for some words ending in /d/ and /t/, but they use it with the wrong types of words as well as with the right ones. In this intermediate stage they put 'ed's on the ends of some regular verbs but also on the ends of some non-verbs and irregular past verbs.

Figure 36.2 gives an example of a 7-year-old boy's spelling of the words in Table 36.1 together with some other words. The pattern of this boy's spelling is quite typical. He managed not use the 'ed' spelling when it was needed, writing 'filled' as 'filld' and 'dressed' as 'dressd'. However, he did apply the 'ed' ending all over the place, and often in entirely the wrong places. His spelling of 'slept' as 'sleped' and of 'sold' as 'soled' may not seem so surprising, as these are past verbs, even though they are not regular ones. 'Necsed', 'sofed', and 'direced' are much more striking because these are non-verbs, and these misspellings demonstrate that he is probably not using any morphological criterion when he decides how to spell /d/ and /t/ endings even though he has adopted the 'ed' spelling that is the correct conventional spelling for an inflectional morpheme.

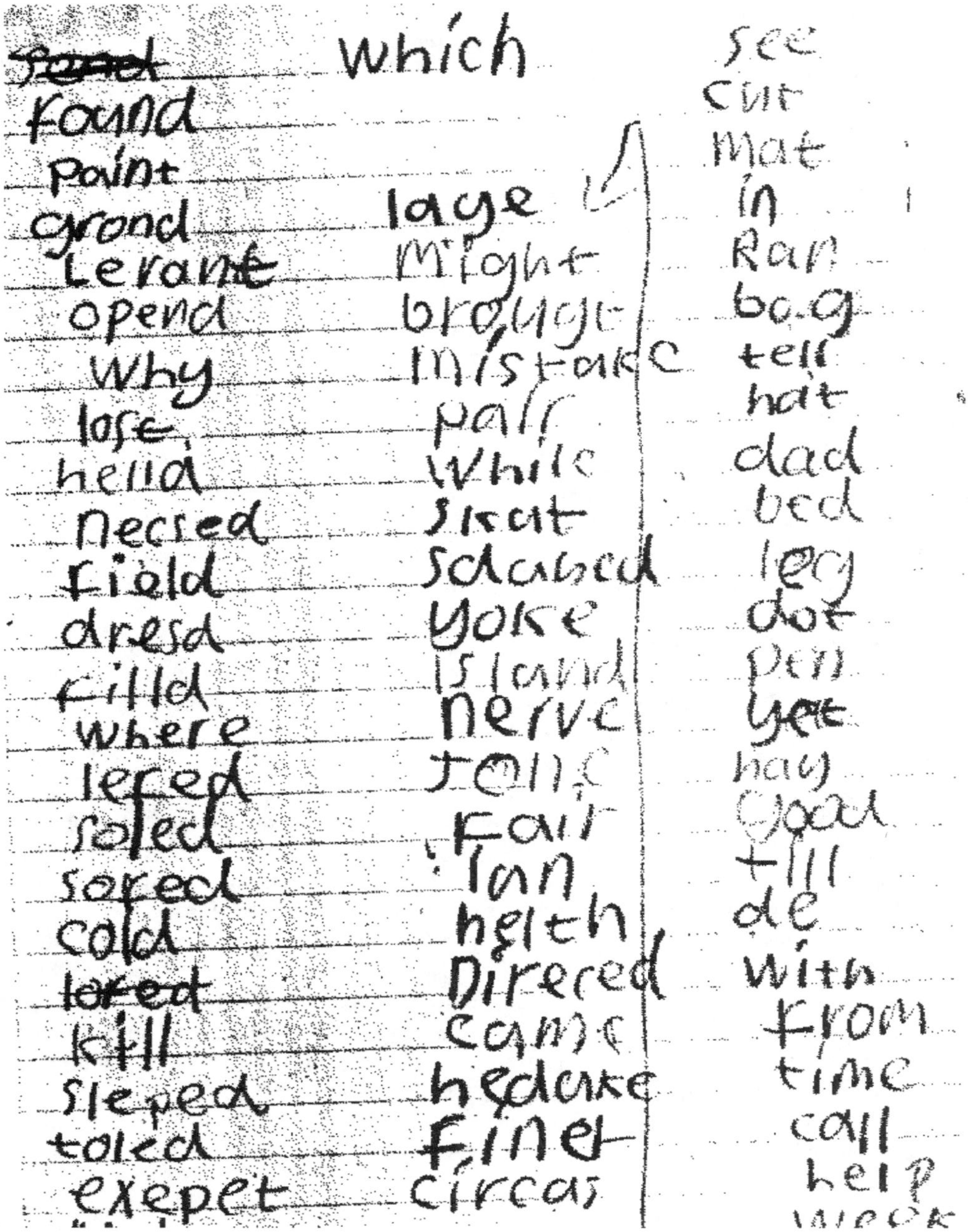

FIG. 36.2.   Examples of misplacements of the '-ed' ending in the spelling of a 7 1/2 -year-old English schoolboy.

These misuses of the 'ed' ending in irregular past verbs and in non-verbs were extremely common. By the end of our study 71% of the children had made this mistake with irregular past verbs and 56% with non-verbs. Our longitudinal data also confirmed that this kind of mistake was the main feature of a genuinely intermediate phase of a three-phase development. First the children did not use the 'ed' spelling; then (the intermediate phase) they used it altogether too generously with non-verbs as well as with past verbs; and finally they used it with past verbs only and eventually just with regular past verbs.

The developmental picture is much the same with English children's spelling of the /ks/ ending (Bryant, 2002). We used the technique of giving children written sentences with a missing word, and then dictating the whole sentence including the missing word, which the child then had to write in. The words they had to write—the missing words—had /ks/ endings, but some were one morpheme (e.g., fox, mix) and others two morpheme (e.g., socks, picks) nouns and verbs.

We also worked with pseudo-words. We dictated sentences like 'Bob *crecks* the windows every morning'. The children had to write the /ks/ ending pseudo-word, and the surrounding sentence provided the context that made it clear whether this pseudo-word represented a one-morpheme or a two-morpheme word.

The pseudo-word task produced clear and surprising results. Six-year-old children hardly ever used the 'x' ending, and so they spelled the endings of the two-morpheme more success-fully than they did the endings of the one-morpheme pseudo-words. Between the ages of 6 and 8 years their use of 'x' increased, but it increased as much with the inappropriate two-morpheme pseudo-words as with the appropriate one-morpheme ones. Thus, here is another example of children getting worse with some words while they get better with others. We must add that 9-year-old children did genuinely improve. They used the 'x' spelling more with the appropriate words and less with inappropriate words than the younger children.

The appearance of new mistakes with /ks/ words between the ages of 6 and 8 years is yet another example in children of a striking, and quite general, developmental sequence in spelling. When children begin to use apostrophes, when they start to give /d/ and /t/ ending words the 'ed' ending, and when they first use both the 'x' and the 's' endings for the /ks/ ending words, their spelling gets better and it gets worse at the same time. They go through a phase of spelling some words worse than they did before at the same time as they are spelling others better than they did before.

This strange and interesting intermediate spelling phase is not at all a purely Anglophone phenomenon. Here are some examples from other languages, starting with the effect of different stress patterns in Portuguese. In most Portuguese words, the stress is on the penultimate syllable, but there are exceptions. One concerns the very frequent final /u/ sound. Most words that end in /u/ do follow the typical pattern of having the stress on the penultimate syllable. In all these words the final /u/ sound is spelled as 'o' (e.g. *gato* meaning 'cat'). Young Portuguese-speaking children initially find this spelling ('o' for /u/) rather difficult because it violates the grapheme–phoneme correspondence of 'u' for /u/ that they learned when they learned about the alphabet. They often make the mistake of writing *gato*, for example, as *gatu*.

There are, however, Portuguese /u/ ending words that have a different, and unusual, stress pattern. In these words the stress is on the last syllable—on the /u/ in fact—and this affects the spelling of that sound. In all these words the final /u/ is spelled as 'u'. *Bambu* is one example and *caju* another.

Nunes, Buarque, and Roazzi (2000) were the first to show that beginning spellers usu-ally write /u/ sounds as 'u' and thus misspell words like *carro* as, for example, *carru*. They found too that, as children grow older, they spell /u/ endings as 'o' more often than before, which means that they get better at spelling words like *carro*. But they also reported the more surprising result they actually become less successful than they were before with words like *bambu* because they now begin to give these the 'o' ending as well: They misspell *bambu* for example as *bambo*.

Later still they manage to distinguish these two kinds of word quite well, and this suggests that they eventually do learn the stress-related rule. This final step is also surprising in a way, because the children in this study had not been taught this complex rule. Their learning of the rule was probably implicit.

We find a rather similar sequence in French children. Michel Fayol and his colleagues (Fayol, Thenevin, Jarousse, & Totereau, 1999; Totereau, Thenevin, & Fayol, 1997) looked at their spelling of the plural morphemes that, as we have remarked, are mostly silent in French. They found that beginning spellers usually omit these plural inflections when writing plural words. Later on they begin to include the 's' plural inflection for nouns and adjectives. However, they also tend to put this ending at the ends of verbs (*Les garcons manges*) as well. When they are older they do begin to adopt the 'nt' plural ending, but at first they sometimes make the opposite mistake: They sometimes put this on plural nouns and adjectives as well (*Les femment mangent*). Eventually they learn that the plural inflection is spelled as 's' in nouns and adjectives and as 'nt' in verbs. This study gives us yet another example of children adopting a new spelling pattern without being clear about the rule for using it and of spelling some words worse at the same time as spelling others better than before during an intermediate phase. The child who puts 'nt' at the end of the noun *femme*, having previously used the correct 's' ending for this word, does not at first know the rule for the new spelling that he or she has just begun to use. It seems that, here as in the other examples, the child must have the experience of using the new spelling, wrong as well as right, before understanding its purpose.

Greek children follow this sequence too. Greek has an extremely regular orthography: One can tell exactly how any Greek word is pronounced from its spelling. However, as we have seen, several sounds in Greek are spelled in more than one way. We have already considered the example of the long /i/ vowel sound, which can be spelled as η, ι, ει, and οι. There are other instances. The /o/ sound is spelled either as 'o' or 'ω' and the /ey/ sound either as 'ε' or as 'αι'. So the Greek child has to choose, and in many instances morphology can help him or her make the choice. Whenever these sounds represent the whole or a part of an inflectional morpheme at the end of a word, there is no ambiguity at all in their spelling. Each inflectional morpheme has its own fixed spelling.

Two studies have shown that Greek children tend at first to adopt one spelling only when there are alternative spellings for the same sound and to apply this preferred spelling quite generally. Aidinis (1998; see also Bryant, Nunes, & Aidinis, 1999) has shown this in a cross-sectional study and Chliounaki and Bryant (2001) in a longitudinal one. Beginning spellers use 'o' rather than 'ω', 'ε' rather than 'αι' and either 'η' or 'ι' rather than 'ει' and 'οι'. (Note their preference for single letters over digraphs.)

Chliounaki's longitudinal study has already established a developmental pattern with which we are becoming quite familiar. Her data cover the spelling of 6-year-old children in their first year at school. In the first of two sessions during that year, Chliounaki found that many of them used one spelling only for sounds like /i/ for which there are alternative spellings. We shall take as an example words ending in /o/. Some words ending in this sound are neuter-singular nouns, and their final sound is spelled as 'o'. Others are first-person-singular verbs, in which case the final /o/ is spelled as 'ω'. Many children in the sample wrote both kinds of words with an 'o' ending and thus were right in the case of singular-neuter nouns but wrong with first-person-singular verbs. Six months later, Chliounaki also found that a high proportion of these children began to use the 'ω' as well as the 'o' at the ends of such words. However, most of these children sometimes applied the new 'ω' spelling not only to first-person verbs, which is correct, but also on occasion to neuter nouns as well, which is quite wrong. They spelled the noun endings worse than before at the same time as they spelled the verb endings better.

So when children adopt new morphologically based spellings they do not always use these new spellings correctly. They do not progress seamlessly from not using a spelling sequence to using it in the correct place. They seem to need an intermediate phase in which they sort out for themselves the underlying rules for the new spellings. So how do they sort it out?

Is Construction the Answer?

The significance of this widespread intermediate phase, in which children start to spell worse than before as well as better than before, needs some discussion. The connecting thread that pulls together the highly disparate examples that we have given is that children adopt new spelling patterns before they understand the rules for these new spellings. It looks as though they have to try these patterns out first in order to understand them properly.

One possible explanation is that children have to construct these rules for themselves. They have, according to this explanation, to experiment with the new spellings themselves before they can understand the rules behind them properly. This is not to say that they have to work things out entirely on their own, without any help from their teachers or their friends. If they are experimenting effectively, they have to pay attention to the outcome of their experiments, and that outcome should take the form of comments and corrections from teachers and others. Therefore other people should play a vital part in the process of construction, but the centre of it is still the child actively trying out new ways of writing and studying the results of their actions.

The idea of construction in children's learning is of course a Piagetian one. One of Piaget's main claims was that children have their own ideas about the rules that govern the world that they live in and try to understand this world through this theory. However, when the children find that their ideas cease to provide coherent explanations for their experiences or solutions to new problems that they encounter, they set about creating a new and more sophisticated hypothesis than the one that they held before.

Piaget's theory was that children start with an inadequate rule and apply it as widely as they can. However, eventually they find that the simple rule does not cover everything that happens to them. Their first response to these encounters with exceptions to their present rule is to adjust and extend the rule to take account of the exceptions. These adjustments then lead them into new experiences, which eventually lead them to abandon the first and inadequate rule and to construct a new and more sophisticated one.

It is not hard to apply this theoretical analysis to the developmental sequence that we have found in children's spelling. First children concentrate entirely on alphabetic rules that are based on grapheme–phoneme correspondences. Next they find that there are other ways of spelling the sounds than are to be found in a simple alphabetic code. They realize that 'ed', for example, is a legitimate, though slightly odd, way of writing /d/ and /t/ endings, and now they alternate between the straightforward alphabetic spelling and the new 'ed' spelling. At this stage (the intermediate phase in the sequence) they are still using a phonologically based rule, that particular sounds are spelled with particular letters, but they incorporate the idea of alternative spellings for the same sound. As a result they will now have experiences and feedback from writing the new 'ed' sequence themselves. These new experiences eventually and rather slowly lead them to take the third step of learning the morphological basis for deciding which alternative is the right one. This is an entirely new kind of rule, and a much more sophisticated one.

Thus, in our analysis, as in Piaget's theories about children's construction of logic, children's attempts to maintain the old rule, almost perversely, provide them with the experiences that they need to learn the new rule. The child who, in the intermediate phase, spells the final /t/ sometimes as 't' and sometimes as 'ed' without any good way of choosing between these two spellings will *as a result* learn a new rule for using both of these spellings.

WHAT DO CHILDREN LEARN ABOUT THE WORDS THEY WRITE?

The fact that children do eventually learn to obey some morphological spelling rules implies that they are able to divide each word into its morphological segments and to assign the right spelling to these segments. Yet very little is known about the extent to which they parse words in this way, or even if they do parse words at all. We carried out two studies (Deacon & Bryant, 2001) to examine whether children parse words into their component morphemes.

In the first study, we asked 6-, 7-, and 8-year-old children to complete words whose final segment was already in front of them. We gave the children two tasks, in which they had to write identical sequences. In one, the two-morpheme task, we asked them to write a two-morpheme word like 'turned', but we gave them the written ending 'ed', and so their job was to complete the word by writing its opening part, 'turn'. In this example the complete word is a two-morpheme word and the child simply had to add one morpheme, the stem, to the other, the affix. Half of the time the word was a derived one and the affix already provided was therefore a derivational one. In the other half, the affix provided was an inflectional one.

In the other task, the one-morpheme task, the children had to write the same sequences, but the complete word contained only one morpheme. This time neither the segment that the child had to write nor the segment already provided represented a morpheme. Thus in one trial the complete word was 'turnip' and the segment that was already provided was 'ip': The child had to write 'turn' in this trial as well, but this time neither this segment nor the segment provided represented a complete morpheme.

If children divide words into morphological segments, the first of these tasks should be easier for them than the second, because each segment—the segment provided and the segment that the child must write—is a distinct morpheme in the first task. In the second task, however, each of these segments is only part of a morpheme, and thus a tendency to divide words into component morphemes will not help.

This study produced a clear difference between the tasks. The two-morpheme task was the easier one for our 6-, 7- and 8-year-old participants: $F(1, 62) = 13.83$, $p < .001$. Despite the fact that they had to write the same letter sequences in each task, the children did better when the segment that they were writing represented a morpheme than when it was only part of a morpheme. This is evidence that children at this age do divide two-morpheme words into morphemes when they are writing these words.

However, our second parsing study suggested that children attempt to divide words along morphological lines, even when it is not appropriate to do so. We looked at the effect of giving children in the same age range a clue that was the first part of the word and asking them to write the whole word. Again we gave the children two-morpheme words like 'turned' in one task and one-morpheme words like 'turnip' in the other. In the two-morpheme task the children were given the first morpheme of the word, 'turn', as a clue. The clue for the one-morpheme task was also 'turn'. In this case it was just the first few letters of the word, not the root of the word. Each clue was hidden in the context sentence that was written on the children's sheet and that was spoken by the experimenter. Just as in the first study, one half of the two-morpheme words were derived and one half were inflected.

We also had a control task in which no clue was provided and the children had to write the whole word. This provided a base measure of the children's spelling of the two- and one-morpheme words. Our analysis compared the children's spelling of the words when they were given the clue to their spelling of these same words when they were not given a clue.

If children use roots to parse two-morpheme words, then the clue should aid more when it represents the stem (two-morpheme task) than when it does not (one-morpheme task). Further, the clue should be helpful with both of the morphemes (the stem and the inflectional or derivational suffix) of the two-morpheme words. Using the root to divide the word should break the two-morpheme words, but not the one-morpheme words, into individual morphemes that the child can then attempt to spell.

Our results were very clear for children's spelling of the initial portion of the one- and two-morpheme words. This was the section that had been given as a clue, such as the 'turn' of 'turned' and 'turnip'. They were better in spelling the first part of both the one- and two-morpheme words when they had been given the clue, regardless of whether this section was a morpheme or not: $F(1, 84) = 27.334$, $p < .001$. Thus children will use roots to divide both one- and two-morpheme words.

The critical test of whether children are parsing words into morphemes comes from children's spelling of the endings of words, such as 'ed' and 'ip'. If children are using the stems to break the words into morphemes, then the clue should help in spelling the endings that are morphemes, but not those that are not morphemes. Only the spelling of the inflectional suffixes improved when children were given the clue: $F(1, 84) = 11.57$, $p < .001$. The clue did not help them in spelling the endings that were not morphemes (the last sections of the one-morpheme words), nor did it help them in spelling the derivational suffixes. We can see that in this study children used the roots to divide inflected words into two morphemes.

Children were not able to divide all of the two-morpheme words into morphemes: They were not successful with the derived words. Many researchers have argued that learning to spell derivations is much more difficult than learning to spell inflections (e.g., Carlisle, 1988; Treiman, 1993). The meaning that is shared between the root and derived form of words is often slightly opaque (as in the connection between the words 'occasion' and 'occasional'). Further, there is often a change in pronunciation between the base and derived form (as occurs between the words 'magic' and 'magician'). These factors might make it more difficult to divide derived words into two morphemes.

In this study, children were using 'turn' to divide the words 'turnip' and 'turned'. Trying to parse both one- and two-morpheme words might lead them to make mistakes with certain words. For example, they might try to use 'low' to divide (and spell) both 'lower' and 'load'. This is the same kind of mistake that we discussed in the earlier sections of this chapter, in which children first try out a spelling without understanding the basis for using it. We need further studies to determine if children might construct their knowledge about when it is appropriate to try to divide words into morphemes. This is an exciting next step that will tell us more about what children are learning about the words that they are writing.

IMPLICIT LEARNING

It is obvious that children who obey morphological spelling rules must draw on their linguistic knowledge in order to do so. But there is a further question to be asked about the nature of this knowledge and of children's use of it. This knowledge, or at any rate their use of this knowledge, could be either explicit or implicit, and we need to know which. The distinction between implicit and explicit knowledge and learning is widespread, and there is plenty of good evidence for the importance of both kinds of knowledge and learning. The distinction is important in studies of children's reading or spelling, because it raises the question of how best to teach children. Should we give them explicit instruction about morphological spelling rules, or should we make sure that they are given the right kind of practice to build up a sufficient stock of implicit knowledge about these rules?

Very little is known either about the degree of explicit knowledge that children have of this type of spelling rule or even about the explicit instruction that they are given about morphemes and spelling. In the current British national curriculum for reading and spelling ("The Literacy Hour") there are arrangements for the specific teaching about some morphological rules, like the spelling of the past-tense ending, but we cannot tell yet whether this translates into children becoming explicitly aware of these rules and consciously using them in reading and writing.

We do, however, have one instance of a morphological rule that children learn at least to some extent, but that is not taught explicitly because the teachers themselves have no explicit knowledge of this rule. This rule—quite a simple one—also concerns the English past-tense ending. Some past verbs end in the sound /d/ or /t/, and yet they seem to break the 'ed' rule, because these /d/ and /t/ endings are spelled phonetically. These are past verbs like 'slept', 'felt', 'went', 'heard', and 'found'. Typically these apparent exceptions are high frequency and therefore quite important words. Children are usually taught that they are exceptions to the general 'ed' rule, which is true at a surface level, but not at a deeper level.

The fact is that, at a deeper level, there is a conditional spelling rule that accounts both for the past verbs whose endings are spelled as 'ed' and for past verbs whose endings are spelled phonetically. This rule is about the relation between the sound of the infinitive and the past stem. In some cases these stems sound exactly the same, as do 'kiss–kissed', 'kill–killed', 'clap–clapped', and 'purr–purred'. In others the sounds of the two stems are different, usually because of a vowel change from the infinitive to the past: Some examples are 'hear–heard', 'sleep–slept', 'feel–felt', 'find–found'. Notice that in the first group all the past verb endings are spelled as 'ed' and in the second group they are spelled simply as 'd' or 't'.

This actually is the rule. Same-sound verbs (those with the same-sounding stem in infinitive and past) have 'ed' endings in the past. Different-sound verbs (those with a different-sounding stem in infinitive and past) do not have the 'ed' ending: Their endings are spelled phonetically. There is barely an exception to this rule. As far as we know the endings of all different-sound past verbs are spelled phonetically, and the endings of nearly all the same-sound words are spelled as 'ed'. There are a few exceptions such as 'pay/paid'.

Although this is a clear and simple rule, it is not widely known and it is not taught in English schools. We interviewed 21 primary school teachers about past-tense endings and all of them answered that most past verbs that end in /d/ or /t/ are spelled as 'ed', but that there are some exceptions to this rule. So their answers were at a surface level, and none of these teachers showed any knowledge of the deeper rule that we have just described. Our attempts to elicit some explicit knowledge of this rule from their pupils were just as fruitless. We are satisfied therefore that neither the children nor their teachers have any conscious knowledge of the deeper rule, despite its economy and its simplicity.

What about the possibility of some implicit knowledge of this untaught rule? We (Bryant, Nunes, & Snaith, 2000) looked for this type of knowledge in a series of experiments, with 8- and 9-year-old children, in which we used pseudo-verbs. In these experiments we always followed the same method, which was to dictate a passage that contained the same pseudo-verb in the present tense or as an infinitive and in the past tense. These passages therefore made it clear whether the stem of this entirely new verb sounded the same or different in the infinitive or in the present tense and the past. In half the passages the stem sounded the same in present and past: 'Harry is a chailer. At the moment he is chailing the teacher's book. He /tʃeɪld/ another one this morning'. In the other half it sounded different: 'Harry is a cheller. At the moment he is chelling the teacher's book. He /tʃɛld/ another one this morning'. If children follow the stem-based rule, they should spell the missing word as "chailed" in the first and as "chaild" in the second passage.

We gave the child a written transcript of this passage except that one word was missing (signified by a gap in the written passage). The missing word, which the child had to write in, was always the past pseudo-verb. We dictated the whole passage including the past pseudo-verb, and the child's task was to put this missing verb in the gap provided as soon as he or she heard the word.

Our questions were simple. Would the children assign the 'ed' ending more to same-sound than to different-sound past pseudo-verbs? By the same token, would they spell the endings of different-sound past pseudo-verbs phonetically more often than the endings of same-sound past pseudo-verbs?

The answers to both these questions were positive. In three different experiments we found that 8- and 9-year-old children do treat the two kinds of pseudo-verbs differently. In all three experiments there was a consistent and significant difference between the two conditions, both in the amount of 'ed' endings (more in same- than in the different-sound past pseudo-verbs) and of phonetically spelled endings (more in different- than in the same-sound past pseudo-verbs).

This result is remarkable. Children learn, though never perfectly, a rule that they cannot articulate, of which they almost certainly have no conscious awareness at all, and that they are never taught at school or anywhere else. This rule, though simple, is much more sophisticated than a mere orthographic association. It is a conditional rule that relies on a combination of morphological and phonological knowledge. Yet children manage to learn about it on their own without any help from other people.

One possible explanation for their ability to do this for themselves is again construction. The children may be constructing this untaught rule for themselves, and the constructive process might be much the same as when they originally learned to use 'ed'. It may be that the active experience of using the 'ed' ending both with same- ('clapped') and with different-sound past verbs ('sleped') gives children the information that they need to learn the conditional rule about the different between same- and different-sound stems.

The result raises another interesting question. What would be the effect of explicit instruction on this untaught, but teachable, rule? It may be that children can learn it only on their own and would not be helped by explicit instruction. On the other hand, explicit instruction may help them to a thorough understanding of a rule that, until now, they have been able to grasp only incompletely. The question is certainly an important one, for it has strong educational implications. We need to know how explicit the teacher ought to be about these morphological rules.

The implicit–explicit distinction is the next great problem to solve for researchers on children's morphological spelling. It is already very clear that children's knowledge of morphemes and of their impact on spelling rules plays a significant and interesting part in their learning to read and to spell. Now we need to know what and how to tell children about these rules.

REFERENCES

Aidinis, A. (1998) Phonemes, morphemes and literacy: Evidence from Greek. Unpublished doctoral thesis, Institute of Education, University of London.

Bryant, P., (2002). Children's thoughts about reading and spelling. *Scientific Studies of Reading, 6*, 199–216.

Bryant, P., Devine, M., Ledward, A., & Nunes, T. (1997). Spelling with apostrophes and understanding possession. *British Journal of Educational Psychology, 67*, 93–112.

Bryant, P., Nunes, T., & Aidinis, A. (1999). Different morphemes, same spelling problems: Cross-linguistic developmental studies. In M. Harris & G. Hatano (Eds.), *Learning to read and write: A cross-linguistic perspective* (pp. 112–133). Cambridge, UK: Cambridge University Press.

Bryant, P., Nunes, T., & Snaith, R. (2000). Children learn an untaught rule of spelling. *Nature (London), 403*, 157–158.

Carlisle, J. F. (1988). Knowledge of derivational morphology and spelling ability in fourth, sixth and eighth graders. *Applied Psycholinguistics, 9*, 247–266.

Chliounaki, K., & Bryant, P. (2001, October). *The link between morphology and spelling: Evidence from Greek.* Paper presented at the Conference on Psychopaedagogics of the Preschool Years, University of Crete.

Deacon, S. H., & Bryant, P. E. (2001). Using 'fair' to spell 'fairly' and 'fairies': Children's use of stems to spell morphologically and orthographically related words. Society for Research in Child Development, Minneapolis, Minnesota, April 19–22.

Fayol, M., Thenevin, M.-G., Jarousse, J.-P., & Totereau, C. (1999). From Learning to teaching to learn French written morphology. In T. Nunes (Ed.), *Learning to read: An integrated view from research and practice* (pp. 43–64). Dordrecht, The Netherlands: Kluwer.

Kemp, N. (2000). *The representation of morphology in children's spelling.* Unpublished doctoral thesis, University of Oxford.

Kemp, N., & Bryant, P. (2003). Do bees buzz? Rule-based and Frequency-based knowledge in learning to spell plural-s. Child Development, *74*, 63–74.

Nunes, T., Bryant, P., & Bindman, M. (1997). Morphological spelling strategies: Developmental stages and processes. *Developmental Psychology, 33*, 637–649.

Nunes, T., Buarque, L., & Roazzi, A. (2000, July). Children's understanding of the role of stress in spelling Portuguese. Paper presented at the Society for the scientific Study of Reading (SSSR) meeting, Stockholm, Sweden.

Read, C. (1986). *Children's creative spelling.* London: Routledge & Kegan Paul.

Totereau, C., Thenevin, M.-G., & Fayol, M. (1997). The development of the understanding of number morphology in written French. In C. A. Perfetti, L. Rieben, & M. Fayol (Eds.), *Learning to spell: Research, theory and practice across Languages* (pp. 97–114). Mahwah, NJ: Lawrence Erlbaum Associates.

Treiman, R. (1993). *Beginning to spell.* New York: Oxford University Press.

37

Metalinguistic Abilities, Phonological Recoding Skill, and the Use of Context in Beginning Reading Development: A Longitudinal Study

William E. Tunmer and James W. Chapman
Massey University

The aim of this longitudinal study was to test a model of the relationships among the major learning tasks, learning strategies, and cognitive prerequisites of beginning reading development. Path analyses were used to examine data collected toward the end of Year 1 (when the mean age of 141 target children was 5 years, 9 months), at the middle of Year 2 (when the mean age of the children was 6 years, 5 months), and at the end of Year 2 (when the mean age of the children was 6 years, 10 months). Results indicated that the ability to use letter–sound patterns and the ability to use sentence context made the strongest independent contributions to variance in early reading achievement; that each of these abilities appeared to influence the development of the other; that the use of letter–sound patterns exerted a stronger influence than the use of sentence context in relation to both early reading development and the reciprocal causation between these two factors; and that when extraneous variables and autoregressive effects were controlled, phonological sensitivity was the major factor influencing the ability to use letter–sound patterns, and grammatical sensitivity was the major factor influencing the ability to use sentence context. The findings suggested that, when beginning readers encounter unfamiliar words in text, they should be encouraged to use letter–sound patterns first and then to use sentence context, but only to confirm hypotheses about what unfamiliar words might be, based on information from decoding attempts.

The purpose of this study was to test the relationships among learning strategies and cognitive prerequisites of beginning reading development in an alphabetic orthography. This model, which is presented in Fig. 37.1, is similar to a model of early reading acquisition developed by David Share and colleagues (Jorm & Share, 1983; Share, 1995, 1999; Share & Stanovich, 1995), according to which "phonological recoding (print-to-sound translation) functions as a self-teaching mechanism enabling the learner to acquire the detailed orthographic representations necessary for . . . fast, efficient, visual word recognition" (Share & Stanovich, 1995, p. 16). Share further claims in his model that the self-teaching operates primarily "when a child is independently reading connected text for meaning" (Share, 1999, p. 100). In agreement with Share, we propose in our model that the central task of beginning reading is learning to read unfamiliar words in meaningful text.

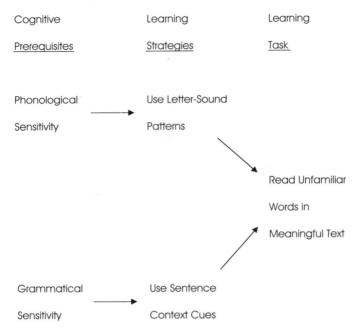

FIG. 37.1.   Proposed conceptual framework specifying the major learning task, learning strategies, and cognitive prerequisites of beginning reading development.

There are two general learning strategies that beginning readers can use to identify unfamiliar words in text. First, they can use letter–sound patterns, which research suggests is the basic mechanism for acquiring word-specific knowledge in alphabetic orthographies, including knowledge of irregularly spelled words (Ehri, 1992, 1997; Gough & Walsh, 1991; Share, 1995; Tunmer & Chapman, 1998). Taking advantage of the systematic mappings between subcomponents of written and spoken words enables beginning readers to identify unfamiliar words that, in turn, results in the formation of sublexical connections between orthographic and phonological representations in lexical memory. These interconnected representations provide the basis for rapid and efficient access to the mental lexicon, which frees up cognitive resources for allocation to comprehension and text integration processes (Adams, 1990; Adams & Bruck, 1993; Ehri, 1992, 1997; Hulme, Snowling, & Quinlan, 1991; Perfetti, 1992).

It is believed that beginning readers can also use sentence context in conjunction with gradually improving phonological recoding skills to identify unfamiliar words in text. The use of sentence context to confirm hypotheses about what unfamiliar words might be, based on incomplete information from partial decoding attempts, results in positive learning trials (i.e., correct identifications) that, in turn, facilitate the development of beginning readers' word-specific orthographic knowledge from which additional spelling–sound correspondences can be induced. An important qualification, however, is that relying heavily on sentence context to *guess* words in text, with little or no use of spelling–sound relationships, will not be an effective learning strategy for beginning readers because the average predictability of the less-familiar, to-be-learned words, most of which are content words, is generally very low (Gough, 1983). Moreover, the use of such an unreliable strategy at the expense of word-level information will impede the development of sublexical connections between orthographic and phonological representations in lexical memory. Contextual information will be useful to beginning readers only if they rely primarily on the alphabetic code to identify unfamiliar words in text with sentence context being used to supplement word-level information, not to substitute for it (Tunmer & Chapman, 1998, 2002, 2004).

Share (1999) argues along similar lines in claiming that self-teaching begins early in the reading acquisition process and depends on three factors: "Letter-sound knowledge, some minimal phonological sensitivity, and the ability to utilize contextual information to determine exact word pronunciations on the basis of partial decodings" (p. 97). However, a major difference between Share's model and ours concerns the ability to use sentence context to supplement word-level information. Although Share believes that the ability to use context to facilitate word identification is an important processing mechanism in learning to read, he does not think that it is "a major determinant of individual differences in reading acquisition" (Share & Stanovich, 1995, p. 7). In contrast, we hypothesize that the ability to use the constraints of sentence context is an important source of individual differences in learning to read, although not as important as the ability to use letter–sound patterns.

We further propose in our model that two cognitive prerequisites are essential. The ability to use mappings between spelling patterns and sound patterns requires sensitivity to the sub-components of spoken words (called *phonological sensitivity*) and the ability to use sentence context to supplement information from partial decodings or to select the correct target from among a set of candidate pronunciations generated from polyphonic or irregular spelling patterns (which are common in English orthography) require sensitivity to the semantic and syntactic constraints of sentence contexts (called *grammatical sensitivity*).

The representation of our model in Fig. 37.1 is oversimplified in at least three ways. First, although all of the hypothesized causal links are unidirectional, the process of learning to identify words itself further develops the skills that provide the basis for growth in reading, a phenomenon referred to as *reciprocal causation*. As Share and Stanovich (1995) argued, a basic knowledge of simple spelling–sound correspondences acquired mostly through direct instruction and the ability to utilize contextual information will provide the means for "acquiring basic orthographic representations and . . . for refining and expanding knowledge of the spelling-sound system" (p. 25). The utilization of the learning strategies proposed in our model (and Share's) is assumed to facilitate the process by which beginning readers induce *untaught* spelling–sound relationships, which leads to improved word-identification skills. In addition, as children become better readers, both the amount and the difficulty of the material they read increase, which leads to further development of vocabulary and syntactic knowledge, both of which should improve beginning readers' ability to use the semantic and syntactic constraints of sentences. Finally, it is also likely that using letter-sound patterns and sentence context to identify unfamiliar words contributes to the further development of phonological and grammatical sensitivity in a reciprocally facilitating manner.

A second oversimplification in the representation of our model is that it does not specify the relative importance of the two learning strategies (spelling–sound relationship and use of sentence context) proposed in the model. As noted earlier, most researchers agree that using spelling–sound relationships to identify unfamiliar words is the basic mechanism for acquiring word-specific knowledge in alphabetic orthographies. In support of this claim is a considerable amount of convergent evidence indicating that with very rare exceptions, progress in learning to read in alphabetic orthographies can occur only if the child acquires phonological recoding ability (Gough & Juel, 1991; Gough & Tunmer, 1986; Hoover & Gough, 1990; Rack, Snowling, & Olson, 1992; Tunmer & Chapman, 1998). Although considered important, the ability to use sentence context to supplement word-level information is hypothesized to play only a secondary role in early reading acquisition. The ability to use letter–sound patterns should therefore exert a stronger influence on reading achievement than the ability to use sentence context.

A third way in which our model is oversimplified is that it does not specify any direct causal links between the two learning strategies (spelling–sound relationship and use of sentence context) proposed in the model. In our earlier research on phonological recoding and the use of context, we reported data suggesting that phonological recoding is necessary for taking advantage of the constraints of sentence context in identifying unfamiliar words in text (Tunmer & Chapman, 1998). Only beginning readers who had begun to acquire a fair amount of letter–sound knowledge were able to make use of context. For children with limited phonological recoding ability, context provided little or no help in identifying unfamiliar words. These findings suggest that the ability to use letter–sound patterns directly influences the ability to use sentence context. However, if using contextual information enables beginning readers to identify partially decoded words, and thus increase their word-specific orthographic knowledge from which additional spelling-sound correspondences can be induced, including perhaps morphophonemic spelling patterns, then the ability to use sentence context may also directly influence the development of phonological recoding ability. This suggests that there may be a reciprocally facilitating relationship between the two factors, with phonological recoding ability exerting the stronger influence.

To examine these issues further we carried out path analyses of data from a longitudinal study of beginning reading to test four hypotheses relating to our proposed model. The hypotheses were (a) that the ability to use letter–sound patterns and the ability to use sentence context would each make strong independent contributions to variance in early reading achievement; (b) that each of these abilities would influence the development of the other; (c) that the use of letter–sound patterns would exert a stronger influence than the use of sentence context in relation to both early reading development and the reciprocal causation between these two factors; and (d) that when extraneous variables and autoregressive effects were controlled, phonological sensitivity would be the major factor influencing the ability to use letter–sound patterns; grammatical sensitivity would be the major factor influencing the ability to use sentence context.

Another issue investigated in this study concerned the measure we developed in our earlier research to assess beginning readers' ability to use sentence context to identify unfamiliar words in text (Tunmer & Chapman, 1998). Children were asked to read aloud 80 words containing irregular or polyphonic spelling patterns (e.g., stomach, post), first in isolation and then, in another test session, in underdetermining contexts that were read aloud by the experimenter (e.g., The football hit him in the *stomach*; the farmer dug a hole for the *post*). Children's ability to read in context words that they were unable to read in isolation was assessed as the ratio of contextual gain to the number of words presented in isolation that were not correctly identified.

On the basis of an examination of different scoring methods used to analyze the data from our earlier study, Allerup and Elbro (1998) argued against the use of the ratio scoring procedure to address the question of whether better readers are, as they put it, "supported more by context than are poorer readers in the initial phases of reading development" (p. 411). Using a log-odds procedure to reanalyze our data, they obtained a monotonically decreasing function for the relation of context use to decoding, whereas we had reported a monotonically increasing function. On the basis of this reanalysis, Elbro (personal communication, 1997) concluded that the data from our original study were "in full accordance with previously published results [showing that] context dependency *decreases* rather uniformly with increasing decoding ability."

There are, however, two major difficulties with Allerup and Elbro's (1998) study. First they misunderstood what the ratio procedure was designed to measure, which is beginning readers' ability to read in context words that they could not read in isolation; that is, their ability to *use* context if they needed to, not the overall extent to which they *relied* on context in reading text. Making this distinction allows the following possibility: skilled readers are better than less-skilled readers in using context to identify unfamiliar words in text because of their superior phonological recoding skills, grammatical sensitivity skills, or both, but they rely less on context than less-skilled readers to read the words of text because of their superior context-free word-recognition ability. Second, Allerup and Elbro (1998) neglected to mention our use of a second scoring procedure that yielded a pattern of results very similar to that obtained with the ratio scoring procedure. Following Rego and Bryant (1993), we also assessed beginning readers' ability to use context by the number of words they read correctly when the first 15 words not correctly identified in isolation were presented in context. In the present study we used both the Rego and Bryant (1993) scoring procedure and the ratio scoring procedure to investigate this issue further.

METHOD

Sample

The sample comprised children who were participating in a 3-year longitudinal study of factors associated with beginning literacy achievement. Children in New Zealand commence school on or around their fifth birthday, and formal reading instruction begins at that time. To control for amount of prior schooling, the children selected for participation in the study had turned 5 years of age during the preceding summer break and therefore had entered school for the first time at the beginning of a new school year. The initial sample comprised 152 new school entrants (90 boys, 62 girls) with a mean age of 5 years, 1 month (range = 4 years, 11 months to 5 years, 3 months). The target children were enrolled in 16 urban schools located in a range of socioeconomic areas. During the course of the study, six additional schools were included because of student transfers. A total of 25 classroom teachers were initially involved in the study, but this number increased as the study progressed. The classroom reading programs of all participating teachers strongly adhered to the whole-language philosophy of teaching reading (for detailed descriptions of the New Zealand version of whole language, see Smith & Elley, 1994; Thompson, 1993; Tunmer & Chapman, 1999, 2002).

Instruments

Several reading and reading-related measures were administered throughout the study, each at developmentally appropriate testing times. For purposes of the present study, data were analyzed from measures administered toward the end of Year 1 (when the mean age of the target children was 5 years, 9 months), at the middle of Year 2 (when the mean age of the children was 6 years, 5 months), and at the end of Year 2 (when the mean age of the children was 6 years, 10 months). These included measures of metalinguistic abilities, oral language skills, learning strategies, and reading achievement.

Phonological sensitivity was assessed at all three testing points by means of a modified version of a phoneme counting task developed by Tunmer, Herriman, and Nesdale (1988). The children were required to use counters to represent the sounds in orally presented pseudowords of varying length. The task was presented in the form of a game in which the children were asked to identify the sounds in "funny sounding names of children who live in far away lands." One demonstration item was given, followed by four practice items with corrective feedback. The test items were then presented with no corrective feedback. Scoring was based on the number of items correctly segmented, giving a total possible score of 24.

Grammatical sensitivity was assessed by means of an oral cloze task administered at all three testing points and a word-order correction task administered at the end of Year 1 and in the middle of Year 2. The oral cloze task was adapted from tasks developed by Tunmer, Nesdale, and Wright (1987) and Siegel and Ryan (1988). Children were asked to supply the missing word in each of 25 orally presented sentences that ranged in length from 3 to 12 words. The missing words included both content and function words, and the location of the missing words varied across items. The sentences were presented by a handheld puppet, and the children were told that the puppet "forgets to say all the words" and that their task was to guess what the missing word was. The experimenter moved the puppet's mouth for all words spoken aloud and stopped for the deleted words. Five practice items with corrective feedback were given, followed by the 25 test items with no corrective feedback. For many deleted words there were alternative words that could be supplied that would yield semantically and syntactically well-formed sentences. Children's responses were therefore scored as correct if the word they provided was appropriate to the sentence context.

The word-order correction task was similar to one used in earlier studies (Tunmer, 1989; Tunmer, Herriman, & Nesdale, 1988; Tunmer, Nesdale, & Wright, 1987). The children were asked to correct orally presented sentences of three to five words in length that contained word-order violations (e.g., "Jane the ball kicked," "Steven swimming was"). The task was presented in the form of a game with a handheld puppet. The children were told that the puppet "can't talk properly" and "says things all jumbled up." The child's task was to use all the same words as the puppet, but to "change the words around so that they sound right." Four demonstration items were given, followed by four practice items with corrective feedback. Twenty-five test items were then presented with no corrective feedback. Items were scored as correct only if the child's response was a correct reordering of the words that were presented.

Reading comprehension and *listening comprehension* were assessed at all three testing points by means of adapted versions of subtests of the Interactive Reading Assessment System (IRAS) developed by Calfee and Calfee (1981). The materials for the reading and listening comprehension subtests consisted of well-formed narrative and expository passages, ordered in difficulty based on word frequency, number of words per sentence, number of sentences, and number of propositions expressed per sentence. Each story was constructed according to the principles of story grammar, and associated with each element was a probe question. A similar procedure was used in constructing the expository passages. The children were presented with the lowest level passage and were asked to read it aloud. If they were able to read the passage within 150 seconds, they were asked to retell as much of the passage as they could. After the children finished the free-recall task, any element that was not adequately recalled was then probed with the corresponding question. If the child recalled half or more of the passage elements under free or cued recall, the next more difficult passage was presented until the child failed to meet this criterion. Listening comprehension was assessed with parallel narrative and expository passages, again with the free- and cued-recall procedures. The starting point for each child was one level above the highest level attempted on the reading comprehension subtest. If the child failed the recall criterion, easier passages were presented until success was achieved. The same scoring procedure was used for both the listening and the reading comprehension subtests. After elements were scored separately for free and cued recall, each element was assigned a single value ranging from 0 to 7, based on responses under both conditions. A critical index was then computed, with the integer portion of the index representing the level of highest success and the decimal portion the ratio of assigned points for combined elements to total possible points for that level.

Verbal working memory was measured at the end of Year 1 by an adapted version of a nonword-repetition task developed by Snowling, Stackhouse, and Rack (1986). This task involved a puppet "saying" 24 nonsense words, which were presented to the children as the names of children who live in a faraway land. The child's task was to repeat each nonword immediately. Each nonword was pronounced very clearly by the experimenter, with the stress pattern of each nonword shown by a similar real word in parentheses. For example, the nonsense word *vetha* was pronounced like the real word "feather." Scoring was based on the number of items pronounced correctly.

A reduced version of a *mispronunciation correction* task developed by Tunmer and Chapman (1998) was used at the end of Year 1 to assess the *potential* contribution of word-level and sentence-level information to reading words containing irregular and polyphonic spelling patterns. The task was presented in the form of a game involving a handheld puppet that said words the "wrong way." The child's task was to try to figure out what the puppet was trying to say. The mispronounced words presented to the children were all formed from the regularized pronunciations of irregularly spelled words (e.g., "stomach" pronounced as *stow-match*) or the incorrect pronunciation of words containing polyphonic spelling patterns (e.g., glove pronounced as *glōve*). There was a total of 40 words that varied in print frequency (10 words from each of four levels of decreasing frequency). The children were administered the task in two sessions that were separated by 1 to 2 weeks. During the first session the mispronounced words were presented in isolation. During the second session the same mispronounced words were presented in underdetermining contexts (e.g., "The football hit him in the *stow-match*," "He lost his *glōve*"). Scoring was based on the number of words correctly identified at each of the four frequency levels under each presentation condition.

Ability to use sentence context was assessed at the middle and end of Year 2 by a task designed by Tunmer and Chapman (1998). The task measured children's ability to read in context words that they were unable to read in isolation. The children were administered the task in two sessions that were separated by 1 to 2 weeks. During the first session, the children were asked to read aloud 80 individually presented words that contained irregular or polyphonic spelling patterns (e.g., bread). During the second session, the children were asked to read aloud the same 80 words, primed by orally presented, underdetermining sentence contexts (e.g., "The children's granny baked some *bread*"). The task was scored in two ways; first, as the ratio of contextual gain (i.e., number of words identified in context minus number of words identified in isolation) to potential improvement (as indicated by the number of words presented in isolation that were not correctly identified), and second, as the number of words read correctly when the first 10 words not correctly identified in isolation were presented in context.

Ability to use letter–sound patterns was measured at all three testing points by an adapted version of a pseudoword decoding task developed by Richardson and DiBenedetto (1985). Thirty monosyllabic pseudowords from Section 3 of their Decoding Skills Test were used to measure knowledge of letter–sound patterns. The task was presented in the form of a game in which the children were asked to try to read the "funny sounding names of children who live in faraway lands." The pseudowords were presented in order of increasing difficulty, ranging from simple consonant–vowel–consonant patterns (e.g., *jit, med, dut*) to blends, digraphs, and vowel variations (e.g., *prew, thrain, fruice*). Two practice items with corrective feedback were given followed by the 30 test items with no corrective feedback. When the child incorrectly pronounced an item, the mispronunciation was recorded with the pronunciation key provided by Richardson and DiBenedetto. The items were scored according to the total number of sounds pronounced correctly in each item, provided the sounds in the item were blended into a single syllable.

Context-free word recognition was assessed at all three testing points by means of the Burt Word Reading Test, New Zealand Revision (Gilmore, Croft, & Reid, 1981). The Burt Word Reading Test is a standardized test in which children are presented with a list of 110 words of increasing difficulty and asked to look at each word carefully and read it aloud. Testing continued until 10 successive words were read incorrectly or not attempted. Scoring was based on the number of words read correctly.

Procedure

All instruments were administered individually to each child by trained research assistants experienced in working with children in the initial years of schooling. During all testing sessions, the research assistants paid particular attention to ensuring that rapport was maintained with the child and that the session did not contain an excessive number of assessments.

RESULTS AND DISCUSSION

Mispronunciation Correction Task (Year 1)

The ability to use sentence context to read unfamiliar words in text was not assessed during the first year of schooling because children's phonological recoding skills were not sufficiently advanced for them to benefit much from underdetermining sentence contexts. As noted earlier, underdetermining, as opposed to predictive, contexts are the more naturally occurring situation in ordinary language use (Gough, 1983). We did, however, administer the mispronunciation correction task in Year 1 to assess the *potential* contribution of sentence context to identifying partially decoded words, which we simulated by presenting to the children, in isolation and in context, the regularized or alternative pronunciations of words containing irregular or polyphonic spelling patterns (e.g., *stow-match* for "stomach;" *glōve* for "glove"). As Share and Stanovich (1995) argued:

> Most irregular words, *when encountered in natural text*, have *sufficient* letter–sound regularity (primarily consonantal) to permit selection of the correct target among a set of candidate pronunciations. That is, even an approximate or partial decoding may be adequate for learning irregular words encountered in the course of everyday reading. Note that for an unskilled novice, even regular words will be "irregular" in the sense of being phonologically underdetermined. (p. 23)

In support of these claims are the results presented in Table 37.1, which show the means of correctly identified words on the mispronunciation correction task as a function of presentation condition and decreasing print frequency. Overall, the mean performance of the children when the regularized or incorrect pronunciations of the target words were presented in isolation was 26.8%, compared with 52.4% when the same mispronunciations were presented in underdetermining contexts (e.g., "He lost his *glōve*"), a difference that was highly significant, $F(1,140) = 724.82$, $p < .001$. These findings are very similar to those reported in an earlier study (Tunmer & Chapman, 1998) of 6- and 7-year-old children (37.2% vs 75.5%). In both studies, presenting the mispronunciations in underdetermining sentence contexts resulted in a twofold increase in the number of words correctly identified, which suggests that sentence context makes an important contribution to the identification of partially decoded words.

TABLE 37.1

Mean Percentages and (Standard Deviations) of Correctly Identified Words on the Mispronunciation Correction Task as a Function of Presentation Condition and (Decreasing) Print Frequency

Presentation Condition	Frequency Level			
	1	*2*	*3*	*4*
Isolation	22.8	32.6	28.2	23.6
	(13.8)	(9.8)	(17.5)	(14.9)
Context	59.0	51.7	51.3	47.6
	(21.4)	(14.8)	(19.3)	(21.2)

Note. Measure taken at end of Year 1.

TABLE 37.2
Intercorrelations, Means, and Standard Deviations for Measures Taken at Middle of Year 2

Variables	1	2	3	4	5	6	7	8	9
Metalinguistic ability measures									
1. Phoneme segmentation		.43	.53	.37	.71	.58	.46	.56	.51
2. Oral cloze			.70	.59	.56	.64	.52	.53	.58
3. Word-order correction				.52	.60	.64	.56	.55	.58
Oral language measure									
4. Listening comprehension					.45	.53	.43	.39	.50
Learning strategy measures									
5. Ability to use letter–sound patterns						.83	.68	.86	.82
6. Ability to use sentence context (PRCG)							.82	.81	.85
7. Ability to use sentence context (PBC)								.66	.71
Reading measures									
8. Context-free word recognition									.91
9. Reading comprehension									
M	15.8	16.6	20.1	4.74	59.9	32.0	3.25	26.6	2.55
SD	6.0	3.5	4.4	2.10	24.1	18.1	2.19	13.7	2.00
Maximum score	24	25	25	7.99	101	100	10	110	7.99

Notes. $N = 134$. All correlations are significant ($p < .01$). PRCG = percent relative contextual gain; PBC = priming by context.

Concurrent Intercorrelations and Path Analyses (Middle and End of Year 2)

Presented in Tables 37.2 and 37.3 are the intercorrelations, means and standard deviations for measures taken at the middle and end of Year 2. The middle of Year 2 measures of grammatical sensitivity (oral cloze and word-order correction) correlated more strongly with each other than with any of the other variables. A factor analysis was therefore performed to generate a grammatical sensitivity factor score. The factor score accounted for 85.1% of the variance, and the factor loading for each measure was .92.

At both testing times phoneme segmentation correlated more highly with the ability to use letter–sound patterns than did the grammatical sensitivity measures, whereas the grammatical sensitivity measures correlated more highly with ability to use sentence context than did phoneme segmentation. In addition, at both testing times ability to use letter–sound patterns (as measured by pseudoword decoding) and ability to use sentence context (as measured by the ratio scoring procedure, or percent relative contextual gain) correlated more strongly with the two reading achievement measures than did any of the other variables.

Of particular interest were the strong positive correlations between ability to use letter-sound patterns and ability to use sentence context at the middle and end of Year 2 (.83 and .80, respectively). Scatterplots of these two variables at both testing points are presented in Figs. 37.2 and 37.3. Similar to what we found in an earlier study (Tunmer & Chapman, 1998), no children performed poorly on the pseudoword decoding task and well on the contextual facilitation task. Only children who had begun to acquire phonological recoding ability were

TABLE 37.3

Intercorrelations, Means, and Standard Deviations for Measures Taken at End of Year 2

Variables	1	2	3	4	5	6	7	8
Metalinguistic ability measures								
1. Phoneme segmentation		.39	.29	.58	.54	.47	.46	.48
2. Oral cloze			.59	.50	.58	.48	.49	.59
Oral language measure								
3. Listening comprehension				.44	.58	.54	.40	.52
Learning strategy measures								
4. Ability to use letter–sound patterns					.80	.64	.86	.87
5. Ability to use sentence context (PRCG)						.84	.71	.82
6. Ability to use sentence context (PBC)							.59	.70
Reading measures								
7. Context-free word recognition								.90
8. Reading comprehension								
M	18.3	18.0	5.70	66.2	40.5	3.86	30.3	3.61
SD	4.7	3.0	1.86	22.0	18.6	2.32	13.3	2.14
Maximum score	24	25	7.99	101	100	10	110	7.99

Notes. $N = 131$. All correlations are significant ($p < .01$). PRCG = percent relative contextual gain; PBC = priming by context.

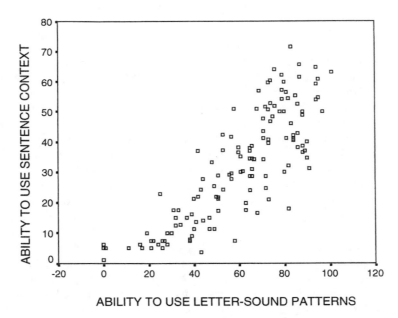

FIG. 37.2. Scatterplot of ability to use letter-sound patterns and ability to use sentence context at middle of Year 2.

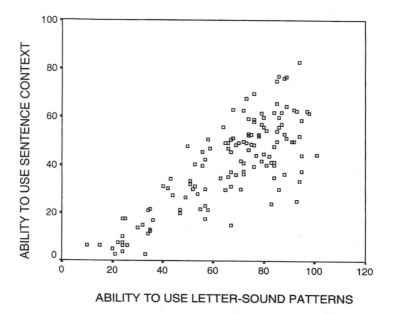

FIG. 37.3. Scatterplot of ability to use letter-sound patterns and ability to use sentence context at end of Year 2.

able to use context to identify unfamiliar words, suggesting that phonological recoding ability is necessary (but not sufficient) for taking advantage of sentence context.

To examine the question of whether percent relative contextual gain should be reanalyzed according to the log-odds procedure recommended by Allerup and Elbro (1998), we compared the results we obtained by using the ratio scoring procedure with those we obtained by using the Rego and Bryant (1993) scoring procedure, which we refer to as priming by context. As shown in Tables 37.2 and 37.3, the scores obtained with the two procedures were strongly and positively correlated (.82 and .84, respectively). When the priming by context scores were converted to percentages, the mean scores of the two measures at each testing point were very similar (32.0% and 32.5% at the middle of Year 2, and 40.5% and 38.6% at the end of Year 2). Moreover, the distributional characteristics of the two measures were similar at each testing point. Finally, an examination of Tables 37.2 and 37.3 revealed that the overall pattern of correlations obtained with each measure was similar, although the magnitudes of the correlations obtained with the ratio scoring procedure tended to be higher, most likely because of the larger number of items scored, which would have improved the psychometric properties of the measure. The similarities between the two measures are perhaps not surprising, given that they essentially measure the same thing; namely, children's ability to read in context words that they were unable to read in isolation, not the overall extent to which they rely on context, as mistakenly assumed by Allerup and Elbro (1998).

To investigate further the pattern of correlations among the measures taken at the middle and end of Year 2, the data were subjected to path analyses. In both analyses we used the scores obtained with the ratio procedure as our assessment of children's ability to use sentence context. Reading comprehension served as our measure of reading achievement at the end of Year 2. However, at the middle of Year 2 we used context-free word-recognition ability as our measure of reading achievement because of the poor distributional characteristics of the reading comprehension scores that were due to floor effects (over a fourth of the children scored 0.0). At both testing points word-recognition ability correlated very highly with reading

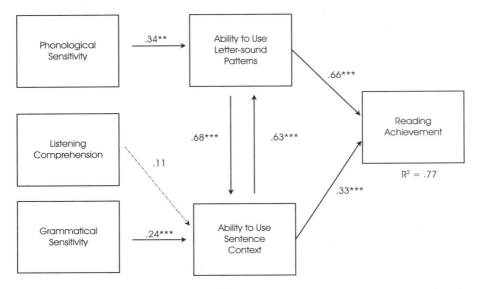

FIG. 37.4. Path model displaying structure of relationships among metalinguistics abilities, learning strategies, and reading achievement at middle of Year 2. (Standardized beta weights are shown on each path; *** $p < .001$.)

comprehension (.91 at the middle of Year 2 and .90 at the end of Year 2). The factor score generated from performance on the oral cloze and word-order correction tasks served as the measure of grammatical sensitivity at the middle of Year 2. Listening comprehension was included in our analyses as an extraneous variable that might exert an influence on reading achievement either directly or indirectly through other variables in the model.

The path model for the measures taken at the middle of Year 2 is presented in Fig. 37.4. The first step in the analysis was to determine which of the five variables made significant independent contributions to variance in reading achievement. As expected, two did, ability to use letter–sound patterns and ability to use sentence context, with ability to use letter–sound patterns exerting the stronger influence of the two. The model is nonrecursive in that the possibility of a two-way influence between letter–sound knowledge and use of context was investigated. When ability to use letter-sound patterns was the criterion variable and all of the remaining variables with the exception of reading achievement were predictor variables, only ability to use sentence context and phonological sensitivity independently influenced performance on the pseudoword decoding task. In contrast, when ability to use sentence context was the criterion variable, only ability to use letter–sound patterns and grammatical sensitivity independently influenced performance on the contextual facilitation task. However, the path from listening comprehension to contextual facilitation approached statistical significance.

A similar path model was obtained with the end of Year 2 measures, but with two exceptions. The path from listening comprehension to contextual facilitation was statistically significant, and grammatical sensitivity directly influenced reading achievement (see Fig. 37.5). In general, the findings from the path analyses are consistent with the suggestions that the abilities to use letter–sound patterns and sentence context are the major learning strategies influencing reading achievement; that ability to use letter–sound patterns exerts the stronger influence of the two; that the two learning strategies may influence the development of the other; that phonological sensitivity is the major factor influencing phonological recoding ability; and that grammatical sensitivity is the major factor influencing ability to use sentence context.

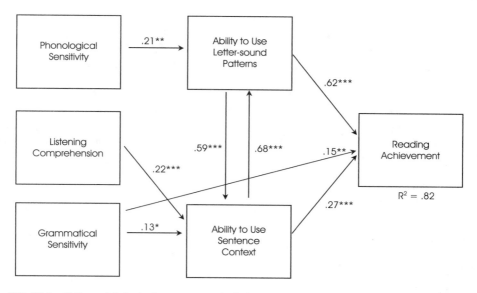

FIG. 37.5.   Path model displaying structure of relationships among metalinguistic abilities, learning strategies, and reading achievement at end of Year 2. (Standardized beta weights are shown on each path; *$p < .05$, **$p < .01$, ***$p < .001$.)

Predictive Correlations and Cross-Lag Relationships (Middle to End of Year 2)

To investigate further the possibility of causal links among the variables specified in our model, we computed the predictive correlations between measures taken at the middle of Year 2 and the learning strategy and reading measures taken at the end of Year 2. As shown in Table 37.4, the predictive correlation between phonological sensitivity and letter-sound knowledge was somewhat stronger than that between grammatical sensitivity and letter–sound knowledge, whereas the opposite pattern was observed between the metalinguistic measures and ability to use sentence context. Listening comprehension more strongly predicted ability to use sentence context ($r = .56$) and reading comprehension ($r = .50$) than ability to use letter–sound patterns ($r = .40$) and context-free word-recognition ability ($r = .35$), most likely because listening comprehension, reading comprehension, and ability to use sentence context depend more on syntactic knowledge than do ability to use letter–sound patterns and context-free word-recognition ability.

The predictive correlations between the learning strategy measures and the measures of reading achievement were particularly strong, ranging from .79 to .86. Presented in Table 37.5 are the standardized beta weights for regression equations with the learning strategy measures at the middle of Year 2 as predictor variables and the reading achievement measures at the end of Year 2 as criterion variables. As indicated in Table 37.5, both learning strategy measures independently influenced later reading achievement (as assessed by word recognition and reading comprehension ability). However, when word-recognition ability at the middle of Year 2 was included in the regression equations to control for autoregressive effects, only letter–sound knowledge made an independent contribution to word-recognition ability, and only ability to use sentence context made an independent contribution to reading comprehension (the beta weight for the relation of letter–sound knowledge to reading comprehension performance approached statistical significance).

TABLE 37.4
Predictive Correlations Among Measures Taken at Middle of Year 2 and Learning Strategy and
Reading Measures Taken at End of Year 2

Predictor Variable (MY2)	Learning Strategy Measures (EY2)		Reading Measures (EY2)	
	Ability to Use Letter–Sound Patterns	Ability to Use Sentence Context	Context-Free Word Recognition	Reading Comprehension
Metalinguistic ability measures				
1. Phonological sensitivity	.68	.61	.56	.60
2. Grammatical sensitivity	.61	.66	.60	.63
Oral language measure				
3. Listening comprehension	.40	.56	.35	.50
Learning strategy measures				
4. Ability to use letter–sound patterns	.92	.81	.86	.85
5. Ability to use sentence context	.81	.86	.79	.85
Reading measures				
6. Context-free word recognition	.84	.73	.97	.92
7. Reading comprehension	.81	.77	.88	.94

Notes. MY2 = middle of Year 2; EY2 = end of Year 2. All correlations are significant ($p < .01$).

TABLE 37.5
Standardized Beta Weights for Regression Equations With Learning Strategy Measures at Middle
of Year 2 as Predictor Variables and Reading Measures at End of Year 2 as Criterion Variables

Predictor Variable (MY2)	Criterion Variables (EY2)	
	Context-Free Word Recognition	Reading Comprehension
Model 1		
Ability to use sentence context	.27***	.44***
Ability to use letter–sound patterns	.63***	.49***
	($R^2 = .75$)	($R^2 = .79$)
Model 2		
Ability to use sentence context	.01	.26***
Ability to use letter–sound patterns	.10**	.12*
Context-free word recognition	.89***	.61***
	($R^2 = .94$)	($R^2 = .87$)

Notes. MY2 = middle of Year 2; EY2 = end of Year 2. * $p < .10$, ** $p < .05$, *** $p < .001$.

Path-analytic procedures were used to investigate further the possibility of a reciprocally facilitating relationship between the two learning strategies postulated in our model. Presented in Fig. 37.6 is the path model displaying cross-lag relationships between ability to use letter-sound patterns and ability to use sentence context at the middle and end of Year 2. In support of our reciprocal causation hypothesis, both cross-lag relationships were statistically significant,

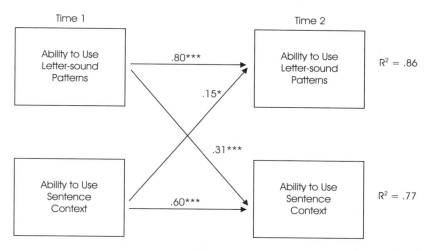

FIG. 37.6. Path model displaying cross-lag relationships between ability to use letter–sound patterns and ability to use sentence context at Time 1 (middle of Year 2) and Time 2 (end of Year 2). (Standardized beta weights are shown on each path; $^{*}p < .05$, $^{***}p < .001$.)

and, as expected, ability to use letter–sound patterns exerted a stronger influence on ability to use sentence context than ability to use sentence context exerted on ability to use letter–sound patterns.

Predictive Correlations and Standardized Beta Weights For Regression Equations (End of Year 1 to Middle and End of Year 2)

Presented in Table 37.6 are the intercorrelations, means, and standard deviations for measures taken at the end of Year 1. As with the middle of Year 2 measures, the oral cloze and word-order correction tasks correlated more strongly with each other than with any of the other variables. A factor analysis was therefore performed to generate a grammatical sensitivity factor score. The factor score accounted for 81.8% of the variance, and the factor loading for each measure was .91.

An important pattern observed in the intercorrelations at all testing points (see Tables 37.2, 37.3, and 37.6) was that the grammatical sensitivity measures correlated more strongly with listening comprehension than did phoneme segmentation, which would perhaps be expected, given that grammatical sensitivity and listening comprehension depend more on syntactic knowledge than does phonological sensitivity. For reasons mentioned earlier, the ability to use sentence context to identify unfamiliar words in text was not assessed during the first year of schooling. However, children's ability to use letter–sound patterns was assessed and was found to correlate more strongly with the two reading achievement measures than any of the other variables.

Presented in Table 37.7 are the predictive correlations between measures at the end of Year 1 and the learning strategy measures at the middle and end of Year 2, and reading comprehension at the end of Year 2. The predictive correlations between the metalinguistic ability measures and the learning strategy and reading comprehension measures were all moderately strong, ranging from .64 to .78, and were consistently larger than those between the oral language measures and the learning strategy and reading comprehension measures. Children's ability to use letter–sound patterns was the strongest predictor of the learning strategy and reading comprehension measures, with correlations ranging from .76 to .86.

TABLE 37.6
Intercorrelations, Means, and Standard Deviations for Measures Taken at End of Year 1

Variables	1	2	3	4	5	6	7	8
Metalinguistic ability measures								
1. Phoneme segmentation		.54	.60	.38	.37	.77	.67	.56
2. Oral cloze			.64	.53	.33	.57	.55	.50
3. Word-order correction				.50	.53	.58	.54	.50
Oral language measures								
4. Listening comprehension					.23	.41	.36	.37
5. Verbal working memory						.39	.36	.33
Learning strategy measure								
6. Ability to use letter–sound patterns							.87	.75
Reading measures								
7. Context-free word recognition								.87
8. Reading comprehension								
M	11.5	14.6	18.1	3.58	17.9	39.1	16.9	1.18
SD	7.4	3.6	4.9	2.08	4.8	27.0	12.3	1.76
Maximum score	24	25	25	7.99	24	101	110	7.99

Note. $N = 141$. All correlations are significant ($p < .01$).

TABLE 37.7
Predictive Correlations Between Measures at End of Year 1 and Learning Strategy Measures
at Middle and End of Year 2 and Reading Comprehension at End of Year 2

Predictor Variable (EY1)	Learning Strategy Measures (MY2)		Learning Strategy Measures (EY2)		Reading Comprehension (EY2)
	Ability to Use Letter–Sound Patterns	*Ability to Use Sentence Context*	*Ability to Use Letter–Sound Patterns*	*Ability to Use Sentence Context*	
Metalinguistic ability measures					
1. Phonological sensitivity	.78	.75	.76	.72	.71
2. Grammatical sensitivity	.65	.72	.64	.71	.68
Oral language measures					
3. Listening comprehension	.40	.45	.37	.47	.45
4. Verbal working memory	.47	.51	.43	.43	.39
Learning strategy measure					
5. Ability to use letter–sound patterns	.86	.82	.82	.76	.84
Reading measures					
6. Context-free word recognition	.81	.78	.78	.67	.87
7. Reading comprehension	.65	.65	.63	.55	.75

Notes. EY1 = end of Year 1; MY2 = middle of Year 2; EY2 = end of Year 2. All correlations are significant ($p < .01$).

TABLE 37.8

Standardized Beta Weights for Regression Equations With Selected Measures at End of Year 1 as Predictor Variables and Learning Strategy Measures at Middle and End of Year 2 and Reading Comprehension at End of Year 2 as Criterion Variables

Predictor Variable (EY1)	Learning Strategy Measures (MY2)		Learning Strategy Measures (EY2)		Reading Comprehension (EY2)
	Ability to Use Letter–Sound Patterns	Ability to Use Sentence Context	Ability to Use Letter–Sound Patterns	Ability to Use Sentence Context	
Metalinguistic ability measures					
1. Phonological sensitivity	.38***	.27***	.37***	.33***	.12*
2. Grammatical sensitivity	.08	.23**	.13	.31***	.17**
Oral language measures					
3. Listening comprehension	.01	.04	.01	.09	.09
4. Verbal working memory	.05	.11*	.03	.04	.04
Reading measures					
5. Context-free word recognition	.48*** ($R^2 = .76$)	.40*** ($R^2 = .75$)	.44*** ($R^2 = .71$)	.21** ($R^2 = .65$)	.67*** ($R^2 = .81$)

Notes. EY1 = end of Year 1; MY2 = middle of Year 2; EY2 = end of Year 2. *$p < .05$, **$p < .01$, ***$p < .001$.

Presented in Table 37.8 are the standardized beta weights for regression equations with Year 1 metalinguistic and oral language measures as predictor variables and Year 2 learning strategy and reading comprehension measures as criterion variables. Context-free word identification at the end of Year 1 was used to control for autoregressive effects rather than reading comprehension because the children performed at floor levels on the latter measure. As expected, phonological sensitivity independently influenced the ability to use letter–sound patterns at the middle and end of Year 2. However, both phonological and grammatical sensitivity independently influenced ability to use sentence context, with phonological sensitivity appearing to exert a somewhat stronger influence. Two factors may account for these findings. First, because phonological recoding ability exerts a relatively strong influence on the ability to use sentence context (see Fig. 37.6), and even appears to be necessary for taking advantage of sentence context (see Figs. 37.2 and 37.3), phonological sensitivity probably affects the ability to use sentence context indirectly through its effects on phonological recoding ability, as suggested by the path models presented in Figs. 37.4 and 37.5. Second, because listening comprehension is more strongly related to ability to use sentence context than to phonological recoding (see Tables 37.2–37.4 and 37.7), and because grammatical sensitivity correlates more strongly with listening comprehension than does phonological sensitivity (see Tables 37.2, 37.3 and 37.6), the inclusion of listening comprehension in the regression equations reduced the magnitudes of the beta weights for grammatical sensitivity more than it did for phonological sensitivity. Of particular importance, both metalinguistic ability measures made independent contributions to reading comprehension at the end of Year 2 even after extraneous oral language measures and autoregressive effects were controlled.

CONCLUSIONS

The central aim of this study was to examine the structure of relationships among the major learning task, learning strategies, and cognitive prerequisites of beginning reading development. Four findings supported the hypothesized causal links specified in our model. First, the ability to use letter–sound patterns and the ability to use sentence context made the strongest independent contributions to variance in early reading achievement. Second, each of these abilities appeared to influence the development of the other. Third, phonological recoding ability exerted a stronger influence than did the use of sentence context in relation to both early reading development and the reciprocal causation between these two factors, and even appeared to be necessary for taking advantage of sentence context. Fourth, phonological sensitivity was the major factor influencing phonological recoding ability, and grammatical sensitivity was the major factor influencing the ability to use sentence context. An important implication of these findings is that when beginning readers encounter unfamiliar words in text, they should be encouraged to use letter–sound patterns first and then to use sentence context, but only to confirm hypotheses about what unfamiliar words might be, based on information from partial decoding attempts.

Our results do not support Allerup and Elbro's (1998) arguments against using the ratio scoring procedure for assessing children's ability to use sentence context to identify unfamiliar words in text. Stated simply, the issue is this: If a good decoder and a poor decoder failed to identify a word presented in isolation, which beginning reader would be more likely to identify the word when presented in context? On the basis of their analysis, Allerup and Elbro claim that it would be the poor decoder, which is surely incorrect.

ACKNOWLEDGMENT

This study is part of a research project fund by the New Zealand Ministry of Education, Contract No. ER/299/5. We are grateful to Julie Russell, Rosemary Manning, and Johanna van Laar-Veth for their professionalism and competence in collecting the data.

REFERENCES

Adams, M. J. (1990). *Beginning to read: Thinking and learning about print*. Cambridge, MA: MIT Press.

Adams, M. J., & Bruck, M. (1993). Word recognition: The interface of educational policies and scientific research. *Reading and Writing: An Interdisciplinary Journal, 5*, 113–139.

Allerup, P., & Elbro, C. (1998). Comparing differences in accuracy across conditions or individuals: An argument for the use of log odds. *The Quarterly Journal of Experimental Psychology, 51A*, 409–424.

Calfee, R. C., & Calfee, K. W. (1981). *Interactive Reading Assessment System (IRAS)*. Unpublished manuscript, Stanford University, California.

Ehri, L. (1992). Reconceptualizing the development of sight word reading and its relationship to recoding. In P. Gough, L. Ehri, & R. Treiman (Eds.), *Reading acquisition* (pp. 107–143). Hillsdale, NJ: Lawrence Erlbaum Associates.

Ehri, L. C. (1997). Sight word learning in normal readers and dyslexics. In B. Blachman (Ed.), *Foundations of reading intervention and dyslexia: Implications for early intervention* (pp. 163–189). Mahwah, NJ: Lawrence Erlbaum Associates.

Gilmore, A., Croft, C., & Reid, N. (1981). *Burt Word Reading Test: New Zealand revision*. Wellington, New Zealand: New Zealand Council for Educational Research.

Gough, P. B. (1983). Context, form and interaction. In K. Rayner (Ed.), *Eye movements in reading: Perceptual and language processes* (pp. 203–211). San Diego, CA: Academic Press.

Gough, P. B., & Juel, C. (1991). The first stages of word recognition. In L. Rieben & C. A. Perfetti (Eds.), *Learning to read: Basic research and its implications* (pp. 47–56). Hillsdale, NJ: Lawrence Erlbaum Associates.

Gough, P. B., & Tunmer, W. E. (1986). Decoding, reading and reading disability. *Remedial and Special Education, 7*, 6–10.

Gough, P. B., & Walsh, M. (1991). Chinese, Phoenicians, and the orthographic cipher of English. In S. Brady & D. Shankweiler (Eds.), *Phonological processes in literacy* (pp. 199–209). Hillsdale, NJ: Lawrence Erlbaum Associates.

Hoover, W., & Gough, P. B. (1990). The simple view of reading. *Reading and Writing: An Interdisciplinary Journal, 2*, 127–160.

Hulme, C., Snowling, M. J., & Quinlan, P. (1991). Connectionism and learning to read: Steps towards a phonologically plausible model. *Reading and Writing: An Interdisciplinary Journal, 3*, 159–168.

Jorm, A. F., & Share, D. (1983). Phonological recoding and reading acquisition. *Applied Psycholinguistics, 4*, 103–147.

Perfetti, C. A. (1992). The representation problem in reading acquisition. In P. Gough, L. Ehri, & R. Treiman (Eds.), *Reading acquisition* (pp. 145–174). Hillsdale, NJ: Lawrence Erlbaum Associates.

Rack, J. P., Snowling, M. J., & Olson, R. K. (1992). The nonword reading deficit in developmental dyslexia: A review. *Reading Research Quarterly, 27*, 29–53.

Rego, L., & Bryant, P. (1993). The connection between phonological, syntactic and semantic skills and children's reading and spelling. *European Journal of Psychology in Education, 8*, 235–246.

Richardson, E., & DiBenedetto, B. (1985). *Decoding skills test.* Parkton, MD: York Press.

Share, D. L. (1995). Phonological recoding and self-teaching: *Sine qua non* of reading acquisition. *Cognition, 55*, 151–218.

Share, D. L. (1999). Phonological recoding and orthographic learning: A direct test of the self-teaching hypothesis. *Journal of Experimental Child Psychology, 72*, 95–129.

Share, D. L., & Stanovich, K. E. (1995). Cognitive processes in early reading development: Accommodating individual differences into a model of acquisition. *Issues in Education, 1*, 1–57.

Siegel, L. S., & Ryan, E. B. (1988). Development of grammatical-sensitivity, phonological, and short-term memory skills in normally achieving and learning disabled children. *Developmental Psychology, 24*, 28–37.

Smith, J. W. A., & Elley, W. B. (1994). *Learning to read in New Zealand.* Auckland, New Zealand: Longman Paul.

Snowling, M. J., Stackhouse, J., & Rack, J. (1986). Phonological dyslexia and dysgraphia—A developmental analysis. *Cognitive Neuropsychology, 3*, 304–339.

Thompson, G. B. (1993). Reading instruction for the initial years in New Zealand schools. In G. B. Thompson, W. E. Tunmer, & T. Nicholson (Eds.), *Reading acquisition processes* (pp. 148–154). Clevedon, UK: Multilingual Matters.

Tunmer, W. E. (1989). The role of language-related factors in reading disability. In D. Shankweiler & I. Liberman (Eds.), *Phonology and reading disability: Solving the reading puzzle* (pp. 91–131). Ann Arbor, MI: University of Michigan Press.

Tunmer, W. E., & Chapman, J. W. (1998). Language prediction skill, phonological recoding ability, and beginning reading. In C. Hulme & R. M. Joshi (Eds.), *Reading and spelling: Development and disorders* (pp. 33–67). Mahwah, NJ: Lawrence Erlbaum Associates.

Tunmer, W. E., & Chapman, J. W. (1999). Teaching strategies for word identification. In G. B. Thompson, & T. Nicholson (Eds.), *Learning to read: Beyond phonics and whole language* (pp. 74–102). New York: Teachers College Press & International Reading Association.

Tunmer, W., & Chapman, J. (2002). The relation of beginning readers' reported word identification strategies to reading achievement, reading-related skills, and academic self-perceptions. *Reading and Writing: An Interdisciplinary Journal, 15*, 341–358.

Tunmer, W. E., & Chapman, J. W. (2004). The use of context in learning to read. In T. Nunes & P. Bryant (Eds.), *Handbook of children's literacy* (pp. 199–212). Dordrecht, The Netherlands: Kluwer Academic Publishers.

Tunmer, W. E., Herriman, M., & Nesdale, A. R. (1988). Metalinguistic abilities and beginning reading. *Reading Research Quarterly, 23*, 134–158.

Tunmer, W. E., & Hoover, W. (1992). Cognitive and linguistic factors in learning to read. In P. Gough, L. Ehri, & R. Treiman (Eds.), *Reading acquisition* (pp. 175–214). Hillsdale, NJ: Lawrence Erlbaum Associates.

Tunmer, W. E., Nesdale, A. R., & Wright, A. D. (1987). Syntactic awareness and reading acquisition. *British Journal of Developmental Psychology, 5*, 25–34.

38

The Case for Teaching Phonemic Awareness and Simple Phonics to Preschoolers

Thomas Nicholson
The University of Auckland

Giok Lian Ng
Advent Links—Southeast Asia Union College

The 24 preschool children examined in the study (mean age 3 years, 11 months) were learning to read English as a second language. They were given phonemic awareness training and were taught simple letter–sound correspondences in small groups, daily for 20 min for a duration of 6 weeks. A control group of children was taught through dialogic reading, for the same duration, in which stories were read to them in an interactive way. The results showed that the phonemic awareness training and simple phonics instruction produced significantly higher phonemic awareness scores compared with the scores of the control group. The performance of the children in the training group on tests of word reading both in lists and connected texts was better when compared with that of children in the comparison group. The phonological training benefited children no matter whether they entered the study with high levels of phonemic awareness or low levels of phonemic awareness.

If you ask parents what is the best thing to do to help preschool children learn to read, they are likely to say, "Read books to them." Yet many researchers nowadays would say that the best thing a parent can do is teach prereading skills such as alphabet knowledge and phonemic awareness, along with some simple phonics skills. A great deal of research is now showing that children on the verge of starting school who lack these skills have considerable difficulties lying ahead of them when they start to learn to read.

Many children start school knowing few if any letters of the alphabet and with little conscious awareness that spoken words are made up of phonemes (i.e., phonemic awareness). They also lack the ability to show even very simple understanding of the alphabetic principle, such as the ability to apply letter–sound correspondences. The prognosis for children who are behind in letter knowledge and phonemic awareness is not good. They are at risk of not learning to read. They are also at risk for emotional and behavioral difficulties, especially if they are from low socioeconomic and minority backgrounds (Levy & Chard, 2001; Nicholson, 2004).

In contrast, many children, particularly those from middle-socioeconomic homes, start school with good prereading skills. They know most of the letters of the alphabet, have some phonemic awareness, and some basic decoding ability. What this means is that, from the first day of school, while some children immediately face a steep learning curve, others have a much easier time. It is not at all easy to quickly close this gap in prereading knowledge. The letters of the alphabet are abstract identities and take a lot of time to learn. It is also difficult to teach children to become consciously aware that a spoken word consists of a series of phonemes. It can be argued that if all children started school with good prereading skills, then there would be a much more level playing field in terms of benefiting from reading instruction. Children who are poorly equipped to begin the task of learning to read will struggle, and most of them will still not be reading even after a year of school (Nicholson, 1999a).

In New Zealand, between 20% and 25% of children have a hard time in learning to read (Kerslake, 2001). A possible reason is the large discrepancy in prereading skills among children when they first start school. This discrepancy was found in a New Zealand longitudinal study of the reading and writing progress of 112 school beginners over a 5-year period (Nicholson, 2003). The children were from low-income and middle-income home backgrounds. The middle-income children made much better progress in reading than did the low-income children, who as a group remained below average for their age throughout the study.

What was noticeable from the outset of this study was that even in the first months of school there were huge gaps in prereading skills between children from these two social backgrounds. For example, out of 88 children in the study from low-income homes, there were 41 (47%) who started school knowing fewer than 5 letters of the alphabet, and only 14 (16%) who knew between 22 and 26 letters. In contrast, out of 23 children from middle-income homes, there were none who knew fewer than 5 letters, and 14 (61%) who knew between 22 and 26 letters (Fig. 38.1).

There were also large differences in phonemic awareness of these children. In the low-income group, 28 (32%) did not score any points on a phonemic awareness test, whereas in the middle-income group only 1 (4%) failed to get a score (Fig. 38.2). In a test of invented spelling, which reflects the ability to relate phonemes to letters, 46 (60%) of the low-income group did not score at all whereas in the middle-income group all the children scored at least some points (Fig. 38.3).

Alphabet Knowledge At School Entry

Alphabet knowledge for low- and high-SES groups

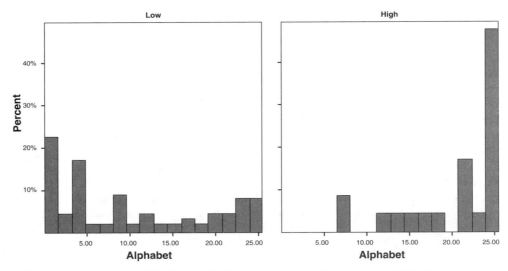

FIG. 38.1. Percentage of distribution of alphabet scores (maximum score = 26) for the low- and high-socioeconomic (SES) groups at the start of their first year of school.

Phonemic Awareness At School Entry

Phonemic awareness scores for low- and high-SES groups

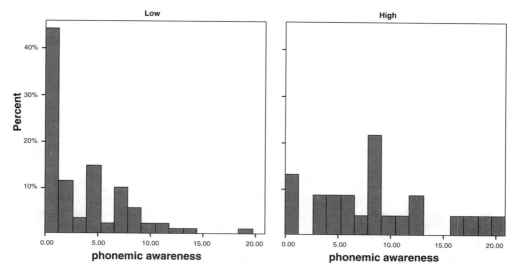

FIG. 38.2.   Percentage of distribution of phonemic awareness scores (maximum score = 42) for the low- and high-SES children at the start of their first year of school.

Invented Spelling At School Entry

Invented spelling point scores for low- and high-SES groups

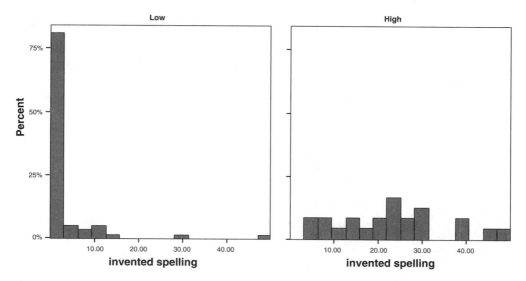

FIG. 38.3.   Percentage of distribution of invented spelling point scores (maximum score = 72) for the low- and high-SES children at the start of their first year of school.

These differences in prereading skills at children's entry to school seem to lead to Matthew effects in which children who are well prepared for reading instruction move ahead quickly, whereas those who are not so well prepared fall behind and stay behind (Juel, 1994; Stanovich, 1986).

HOW DO WE KNOW THAT PRESCHOOL CHILDREN WITH GOOD PREREADING SKILLS HAVE A GOOD PROGNOSIS FOR LEARNING TO READ?

Most researchers will agree that if you had to recommend two skills that will help children most when they start school, it would be knowing the alphabet and having phonemic awareness. With these two skills, preschoolers are able to begin to learn the correspondences between letters and sounds necessary to decode and spell words. Researchers have known for many years that knowledge of the alphabet is a strong predictor of learning to read (Bond & Dykstra, 1967). Children typically learn the names of letters before they learn their sounds (McBride-Chang, 1999; Treiman, 1994). Children use the names of letters as a bridge to learning their sounds for example, using the name "bee" for the letter b to infer the phoneme /b/ (Treiman, 1994; also see Treiman, this volume). In this way, they begin working out the letter–sound relationships needed to learn to read.

Phonemic awareness is awareness that spoken words can be deconstructed into their constituent phonemes. Phonemic awareness is not all or nothing (Nicholson, 1999b, 2000); a child can have a little bit of phonemic awareness if he or she is able to break a word into its onset and rime or tell that the first sound in "fish" is /f/. The child who has complete awareness can segment spoken words into all their phonemes (e.g., f-i-sh).

There is a great deal of correlational evidence to suggest that children with high levels of phonological awareness before starting school have a very good prognosis for later success in reading (e.g., Bradley and Bryant, 1983; Byrne and Fielding-Barnsley, 1991a, 1991b, 1993, 1995; Helfgott, 1976; Juel, 1994; Lundberg, Frost & Petersen, 1988; Lundberg, Olofsson & Wall, 1980; MacLean, Bryant & Bradley, 1987; Nicholson, 2003; Roper, 1984; Share, Jorm, MacLean, & Matthews, 1984; Stanovich, Cunningham, & Cramer, 1984; Tunmer, Herriman & Nesdale, 1988). In support of the long-term importance of phonemic awareness in learning to read, Nicholson (2003) reported that although the correlation between alphabet knowledge and phonemic awareness was very high in the first year of school, the best predictor of reading progress in the second year of school was phonemic awareness alone. This is because most children after a year of school have learned the letters of the alphabet, but even at the end of their second year of school many have still not acquired high levels of phonemic awareness.

The report of the National Reading Panel (2000) in the United States, based on a meta-analysis of training studies in the teaching of phonemic awareness, found that preschool children in particular were likely to benefit from phonological awareness instruction. The report found that the preschoolers benefited more than kindergartners and first- and second-grade children from training in phonological awareness.

Although preschool children have much to gain from phonological awareness instruction, McCutcheon, Abbott, Green, and Beretvas (2002), have reported that preschool teachers are not very knowledgeable about phonological awareness and require training in this area. They instructed a group of 23 kindergarten and first-grade teachers. These teachers and a control group of 20 teachers were followed for a year. The study found that children in the experimental group made greater gains in reading and writing than did children in the control group.

THE ARGUMENT AGAINST TEACHING PREREADING SKILLS

On the other hand, there is the argument that preschools should not teach prereading skills, but should instead focus their efforts on reading to children. Coles (2000) has argued that knowing the names and sounds of the letters of the alphabet and having phonemic awareness is not so much a cause of reading success but a marker of family support. Children with high levels of phonemic awareness come from homes in which there are many books, in which there is a rich language environment, and in which they encounter many experiences with written language through having books read to them. Phonemic awareness, then, may be a result of a home environment rich in literacy 'cultural capital'. If this is the case, then it can be argued that the best way to help children learn to read is provide a literate environment at home and at school by reading books to children and surrounding them with print. Moustafa (1997) writes that "Reading to children helps children learn to read" (p. 72) and that "the primary literacy education task of preschool and the early school years is not teaching children letter-sound correspondences but reading to them" (p. 79). She cites in support of her argument studies that have found positive relationships between being read to at home and learning to read (Heath, 1982; Wells, 1985). Mason (1992) also reviewed several studies that also supported the relation between reading books to preschool children and learning to read.

On the other hand, Scarborough and Dobrich (1994) reviewed research on this topic over a 30-year time period and found only a small correlation ($r = .28$) between reading aloud to preschool children and whether or not they learned to read. Nicholson (1997) asked 57 children from low-income homes (mean age of 7 years) to estimate how many books they had at home. The correlation between reading and the number of books they had at home was low, $r = .22$, whereas the correlation between reading and their level of phonemic awareness scores was higher, $r = .55$. The correlation between reading and their invented spelling scores was even higher, $r = .68$.

Anderson and Matthews (1996) conducted a study of the emergent literacy development of 15 preschoolers from low-income homes over a 1-year period. Storybook reading was emphasized in class, and children took storybooks home at least once each week. At the end of the year only one of the 15 children showed any awareness of written language.

In a training study designed to simulate the experience of being read to, Gibbs and Nicholson (1999) used a "talking book" procedure with 5-year-old school beginners in a small mining town in New Zealand. In the first term of school the sample of 64 children was assigned either to a talking book, in which they listened to stories read to them on audiotape, every day for 5 weeks, or to a control group who looked at the same books but did not get the talking book audio support. The results showed that the talking book group was significantly better than the control group when asked to read the books they had listened to. However, when given new books that they had not heard before, there was no difference in reading between the experimental and control groups. These results indicated that the talking book children had memorized the stories they had listened to, but had not acquired any reading skills as a result of listening to stories being read to them.

It could be objected that talking books at school are not the same as being read a story by the teacher or a parent. Yet there have been several recent studies of the effects of reading storybooks to preschool children showing that children benefit in terms of learning new vocabulary but do not benefit in terms of learning to read words (Arnold & Whitehurst, 1994; Whitehurst et al., 1994a, 1994b).

Nevertheless, the case is not closed about the effects of coming from a literate home environment. Burgess, Hecht, and Lonigan (2002) conducted a 1-year study of 115 preschool children's literacy progress. A survey of the parents of these children, which asked them questions about when they first started reading to their children, how often they read themselves, and so on, showed differences in home literacy practices. The researchers found that these differences predicted growth in reading related skills such as phonological awareness. They concluded that the home literacy environment plays a large part in assisting children's emerging literacy skills. They argued that previous studies did not use measures that were sensitive to changes in literacy knowledge (e.g., alphabet knowledge, measures of phonological sensitivity, ability to identify high-frequency words, and so on), and this might explain the small correlations found by other researchers between home literacy environments and reading.

A COMPARISON STUDY OF THE TEACHING OF PHONEMIC AWARENESS AND READING BOOKS TO PRESCHOOL CHILDREN

To explore this issue further, we carried out a training study to compare the effects of teaching reading directly with the effects of reading books to children. The treatment group was given training in phonemic awareness and simple phonics. The comparison group was read a number of children's stories that included lots of discussion and interaction.

The study was carried out in a child-care center in Singapore. The language of instruction was English. The school curriculum was taught in English, but the children also spent a portion of the morning learning to read in Mandarin and write Chinese script. All children were from middle-socioeconomic backgrounds. None of the children was a native speaker of English. There is strong willingness to learn English among Singapore children because it is an official language of Singapore.

There were 24 children in the study, 13 girls and 11 boys. Their ages ranged from 3 years 6 months to 4 years 5 months, with a mean age of 3 years and 11 months. They were assessed for prereading skills as well as verbal and nonverbal ability. The children were assessed for receptive language in English. The pretest standard scores were below average for their age but the posttest scores of both groups were within the normal range. There was no statistical difference in receptive language between the two groups at pretest and posttest.

The children were placed in matched pairs according to their verbal and nonverbal ability, alphabet knowledge, and phonological sensitivity. They were then assigned randomly to an experimental and a control group. The 12 children in each group were divided into two further subgroups of 6 according to whether their scores on the phonological sensitivity tests were high or low. An analysis of variance showed no statistical differences between the groups for any of the pretest measures, except that children with high phonological sensitivity had significantly higher phonemic scores than the children with low phonological sensitivity. Also, the high phonological ability children were a few months older than the low phonological ability children.

This was a pretest–posttest design with an experimental group and a control group. There were 24 children, with 12 in each of the main groups, and 6 in each subgroup. The children were taught in pairs rather than individually or as a whole group.

The design of the study was as follows:

Phonological Sensitivity	Experimental Group	Control Group
High	N = 6	N = 6
Low	N = 6	N = 6

A timed letter-naming test was used to assess knowledge of letter names as it has been found to be an even stronger predictor of reading performance than untimed letter naming. The Rapid Letter Naming Test (O'Connor, Jenkins, & Slocum, 1995) was used, in which the child named up to 60 letters as rapidly as possible in 1 min. Phonological sensitivity was assessed with a composite test that was sensitive to emerging phonological skills. The assessment tasks included nursery rhyme knowledge (MacLean et al., 1987), rhyme detection and initial- and final-phoneme detection (Byrne & Fielding-Barnsley 1991a). More complex phoneme awareness was assessed with the Gough–Kastler–Roper (GKR) test of phonemic awareness (Nicholson, 1999b, 2005; Roper, 1984).

A standardized test was used to assess receptive vocabulary (Peabody Picture Vocabulary Test—revised; Dunn & Dunn, 1981). Raven's Progressive Matrices (Raven, Court, & Raven, 1990) were used to assess nonverbal ability.

Word reading was assessed with the Burt Word Reading Test (Gilmore, Croft, & Reid, 1981). It has a test–retest reliability of 0.97. Pseudoword reading was assessed with the Bryant Test of Basic Decoding Skills (Bryant, 1975). Because the children were very young, a simple measure of text reading, which used easy-to-decode CVC words, was developed, so as to provide a sensitive indicator of children's emergent reading skills. Three sentences were selected from the popular children's book, *Hop on Pop: The Simplest Seuss for Youngest Use* (Seuss, 1963). The children scored a point for each word correctly read. The maximum possible score for each sentence read correctly was 4, and for the entire text reading exercise, 12.

The experimental group received 30 sessions of phonemic awareness, letter–sound, and simple phonics training, with daily sessions lasting 20 mins, 5 days a week, spread over 6 weeks. Two children were taught at a time in a room in the child-care center. The 30 sessions covered all 26 letter sounds of the alphabet, and the short sounds of the vowels /a/, /e/, /i/, /o/, and /u/.

The skills taught in the 30 sessions included naming of letter sounds, the identification of initial and final phonemes, as well as blending and segmenting. Letter–sound correspondences were emphasized in each lesson. Sandpaper letters were used to familiarize the children with the shapes of the letters (Montessori, 1964).

The identification of the initial and final phonemes was taught by use of posters that had many illustrations of animals and objects beginning or ending with the same phoneme, from a teaching package called Sound Foundations (Byrne & Fielding-Barnsley, 1991b, 1993).

Other activities included the two-picture activity, in which the child had to decide whether the pictures started with the same phoneme, the yes–no activity (Wallach and Wallach, 1976), in which the child had to answer if the picture started with a certain phoneme, and the odd-one-out activity (Bradley & Bryant, 1983), in which the child had to decide which of three pictures did not start or end with the same sound. Children were taught to break words into onsets and rime (e.g., m–at). Where the phoneme was difficult to pronounce, a repetition technique was used (e.g., b–b–b–b–bear), as mentioned in Lewkowicz (1980).

The Elkonin technique (Elkonin, 1973) of using a square to represent a phoneme was used, albeit with the children using letters without first resorting to tokens. The Fun Fit (Nutshell, Products, 1993) alphabet cards were used to facilitate segmenting and blending of letter sounds.

The control group received an alternative training session equal in duration to that of the experimental group. The control group instruction was intended to provide children with the possibility of learning to read by being read to (Moustafa, 1997). Children were taught in pairs. The teaching approach used the technique of interactive reading, in which an adult reads stories and uses open-ended questions to encourage the child's participation (Whitehurst, undated). A total of 12 books were read to the children during those 30 sessions. Some books were read over two sessions, and there were also repeated readings of some books, as chosen by the children.

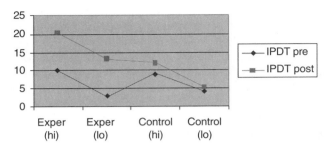

FIG. 38.4.   Pretest and posttest scores on the IPDT.

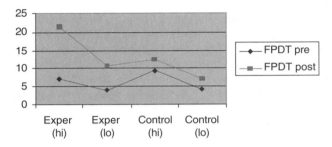

FIG. 38.5.   Pretest and posttest scores on the FPDT.

Results

The results were based on scores from 22 children, after one of the matched pairs was dropped because one of the pair had been receiving reading instruction at home and could already read.

For the initial-phoneme detection task (IPDT) and the final-phoneme detection task (FPDT) the experimental group made significantly greater gains from pretest to posttest than did the control group (see Figs. 38.4 and 38.5).

For the GKR phonemic awareness measure, there was an advantage for the experimental group. The experimental subgroup with good phonological pretest scores had a mean posttest score of 10.00 ($SD = 5.98$). The experimental subgroup with low phonological pretest scores had a mean posttest score of 2.83 ($SD = 1.33$). The control group did not score at all on this measure.

For reading of words there was a significant difference between the two groups (see Fig. 38.6). In the experimental group, the high phonemic awareness subgroup mean was 4.60 ($SD = 2.88$) and the low phonemic awareness subgroup mean was 2.50 ($SD = 1.52$). In the control group, the high phonemic awareness subgroup mean was 0.40 ($SD = 0.89$) and the low phonemic awareness subgroup mean was 0.67 ($SD = 1.21$). Inspection of the individual word-reading scores (see Fig. 38.7) showed that all of the children in the experimental group were able to read at least one word on the Burt word test, whereas 8 out of 11 of the control children were unable to read any of the words. To explore the extent to which the training influenced ability to read regularly spelled words, the words on the Burt test that were successfully read by the children were analyzed according to whether they had regular spellings (e.g., up, sad) or irregular (e.g., of, to). The children's individual scores revealed that 7 out of 11 children in the experimental group were able to read some regular words. Of the seven who did, the number of regular words constituted, for each child, at least half of the total number of words read. This suggested that the effects of the training extended to both regular and irregular words.

Word reading and Dr. Seuss sentences

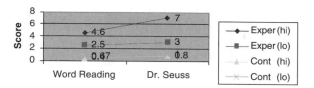

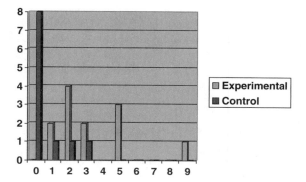

FIG. 38.6. Posttest scores on the word-reading test and the Dr. Seuss sentences.

FIG. 38.7. Distribution of Burt word-reading scores across the experimental and control groups (e.g., 8 children in control group had a score of zero).

For reading of the three sentences from Dr. Seuss text there was also a significant difference favoring the experimental group (see Fig. 38.6). In the experimental group, the high phonemic awareness subgroup mean was 7.00 ($SD = 5.20$) and the low phonemic awareness subgroup mean was 3.00 ($SD = 4.69$). In the control group, the high phonemic awareness subgroup mean was 0.80 ($SD = 1.30$) and the low phonemic awareness subgroup mean was 1.00 ($SD = 1.55$).

The results for pseudoword reading, obtained with the Bryant test, showed an advantage for the experimental group (high ability $M = 3.00$, $SD = 4.64$; low ability $M = 0.50$, $SD = 1.23$). The control group did not score any points at all on this task.

IMPLICATIONS OF THE STUDY

The study outlined in this chapter showed that the combination of instruction in phonemic awareness, letter–sound correspondences, and simple phonics was more effective in terms of children's acquiring elementary reading skills than the "interactive" technique of reading books to this particular group of preschool children.

Results suggested that phonemic awareness training combined with simple letter–sound (CVC) decoding instruction helped these preschoolers, who were second-language learners, to make a start in learning to read. The instruction helped both the children who started the training with high levels of phonological sensitivity as well as children with low levels of sensitivity.

CONCLUSION

Teaching phonemic awareness and initial reading skills to preschoolers gives them a protection factor in terms of learning to read (Nicholson, 2005). Children who start school well prepared in terms of knowing the alphabet, having phonemic awareness, and having some basic understanding of letter–sound correspondences, are more likely to succeed in reading. Although all children are likely to benefit from such instruction, children who are particularly at risk in terms of not acquiring these skills before starting school are those from minority and low-income backgrounds.

Results of the study just outlined, along with other research reviewed in this chapter, suggest that the teaching of prereading skills is certainly possible in preschool, which is where children have an opportunity to learn necessary reading-related skills that will enable them to hit the ground running when they start elementary school. The provision of such instruction at preschool is the best hope for many at-risk children who otherwise are likely to start school way behind other children who are better prepared, and will be unlikely to catch up. This is why there is a strong case for teaching phonemic awareness and other reading-related skills at the preschool level.

REFERENCES

Anderson, J., & Matthews, R. (April, 1996). *Re-examining emergent storybook reading: A sociocultural perspective.* Paper presented at a meeting of the American Educational Research Association, New York.

Arnold, D. S., & Whitehurst, G. J. (1994). Accelerating language development through picture book reading: A summary of dialogic reading and its effects. In D. A. Dickenson (Ed.), *Bridges to literacy: Children, families and school* (pp. 103–128). Cambridge, MA: Blackwell.

Bond, G. L., & Dykstra, R. (1967). The cooperative research program in first grade reading instruction. *Reading Research Quarterly, 2,* 5–142. (Reprinted in 1997 in a special issue of *Reading Research Quarterly.*)

Bradley, L., & Bryant, P. (1983). Categorizing sounds and learning to read: A causal connection, *Nature (London), 30,* 419–421.

Bryant, D. (1975). *Bryant test of basic decoding skills.* New York: Teachers College Press.

Burgess, S. R., Hecht, S. A., & Lonigan, C. J. (2002). Relations of the home-literacy environment (HLE) to the development of reading-related abilities: A one-year longitudinal study. *Reading Research Quarterly, 37,* 408–426.

Byrne, B., & Fielding-Barnsley, R. (1991a). Evaluation of a program to teach phonemic awareness to young children. *Journal of Educational Psychology, 83,* 451–455.

Byrne, B., & Fielding-Barnsley, R. (1991b). *Sound foundations: An introduction to prereading skills.* Sydney, Australia: Peter Leyden Educational.

Byrne, B., & Fielding-Barnsley, R. (1993). Evaluation of a program to teach phonemic awareness to young children. A 1-year follow-up. *Journal of Educational Psychology, 85,* 104–111.

Byrne, B., & Fielding-Barnsley, R. (1995). Evaluation of a program to teach phonemic awareness to young children: A 2- and 3- year follow-up and a new preschool trial. *Journal of Educational Psychology, 87,* 488–503.

Coles, G. (2000). Misreading reading: The bad science that hurts children. Portsmouth, NH: Heinemann.

Dunn, L. M., & Dunn, L. M. (1981). *Peabody Picture Vocabulary Test—Revised.* Circle Pines, MN: American Guidance Service.

Elkonin, D. B. (1973). USSR. In J. Downing (Ed.), Comparative reading. *Cross-national studies of behavior and processes in reading and writing* (pp. 551–580). New York: Macmillan.

Gibbs, C. J., & Nicholson, T. W. (1999). When you've heard it all before and still can't read. *Effective School Practices, 17,* 80–86.

Gilmore, A., Croft, C., & Reid, N. (1981). *Burt Word Reading Test.* Wellington, New Zealand: New Zealand Council for Educational Research.

Heath, S. B. (1982). What no bedtime story means: Narrative skills at home and at school. *Language in Society, 2,* 49–76.

Helfgott, J. A. (1976). Phonemic segmentation and blending skills of kindergarten children: Implications for beginning reading acquisition. *Contemporary Educational Psychology, 1,* 157–169.

Juel, C. (1994). *Learning to read and write in one elementary school.* New York: Springer-Verlag.

Kerslake, J. (2001, June). Annual monitoring of Reading Recovery: The data for 2000. *The Research Bulletin,* No. 12, 65–71.

Levy S., & Chard, D. J. (2001). Research on reading instruction for students with emotional and behavioural disorders. *International Journal of Disability, Development and Education, 48,* 317–326.

Lewkowicz, N. K. (1980). Phonemic awareness training: What to teach and how to teach it. *Journal of Educational Psychology, 72,* 686–700.

Lundberg, I., Frost, J., & Petersen, O. J. (1988). Effects of an extensive program for stimulating phonological awareness in preschool children. *Reading Research Quarterly, 23,* 263–284.

Lundberg, I., Olofsson, A., & Wall, S. (1980). Reading and spelling skills in the first school years predicted from phonemic awareness skills in kindergarten. *Scandinavian Journal of Psychology, 21,* 159–173.

MacLean, M., Bryant, P. E., & Bradley, L. (1987). Rhymes, nursery rhymes and reading in early childhood. *Merrill-Palmer Quarterly 33,* 255–282.

Mason, J. M. (1992). Reading stories to preliterate children: A proposed connection to reading. In P. B. Gough, L. C. Ehri, & R. Treiman (Eds.), *Reading Acquisition* (pp. 215–241). Hillsdale, NJ: Lawrence Erlbaum Associates.

McBride-Chang, C. (1999). The ABCs of the ABCs: The development of letter-name and letter-sound knowledge. *Merrill-Palmer Quarterly, 45,* 285–308.

McCutcheon, D., Abbott, R. D., Green, L. B., & Beretvas, S. N. (2002). Beginning literacy: Links among teacher knowledge, teacher practice, and student learning. *Journal of Learning Disabilities, 35,* 69–86.

Montessori, M. (1964). *The Montessori method.* New York: Schocken Books.

Moustafa, M. (1997). *Beyond traditional phonics. Research discoveries and reading instruction.* Portsmouth, NH: Heinemann.

National Reading Panel (2000). *Teaching children to read: An evidence-based assessment of the scientific literature on reading and its implications for reading instruction.* Washington, DC: National Institute for Child Health and Development. Retrieved December 20, 2002, from http://www.nichd.nih.gov/publications/nrp/report.htm

Nicholson, T. (1997). Closing the gap on reading failure: Social background, phonemic awareness, and learning to read. In B. Blachman (Ed.), *Foundations of reading acquisition and dyslexia* (pp. 381–407). Mahwah, NJ: Lawrence Erlbaum Associates.

Nicholson, T. (1999a). Literacy in the family and society. In G. B. Thompson & T. Nicholson (Eds.), *Learning to read. Beyond phonics and whole language.* New York: Teachers College Press.

Nicholson, T. (1999b). *At the cutting edge: Learning to read and spell for success* (2nd ed.). Wellington, New Zealand: New Zealand Council for Educational Research.

Nicholson, T. (2000). *Reading the writing on the wall: Debates, challenges and opportunities in the teaching of reading.* Palmerston North, New Zealand: Dunmore Press.

Nicholson, T. (2003). Risk factors in learning to read, and what to do about them. In B. Foorman (Ed.), *Preventing and remediating reading difficulties: Bringing science to scale* (pp. 165–193). Timonium, MD: York Press.

Nicholson, T. (2004). Academic underachievement and behaviour: An axiomatic link? In P. Garner, F. Yuen, P. Clough, & T. Pardeck (Eds.), *Handbook of emotional and behavioural difficulties in Education.* London: Sage.

Nicholson, T. (2005). Phonics handbook. London, England: Whurr.

Nutshell Products. (1993). *Fun fit.* Kalbar, Australia: Author.

O'Connor, R. E., Jenkins, J. R., & Slocum, T. A. (1995). Transfer among phonological tasks in kindergarten: essential instructional content. *Journal of Educational Psychology, 87,* 202–217.

Raven, J. C., Court, J. H., & Raven, J. (1990). *Manual for Raven's Progressive Matrices and Vocabulary Scales.* Oxford, UK: Oxford University Press.

Roper, H. D. (1984). *Spelling, word recognition and phonemic awareness among first grade children.* Unpublished doctoral dissertation, University of Texas, Austin.

Scarborough, H. S., & Dobrich, W. (1994). On the efficacy of reading to preschoolers. *Developmental Review, 14,* 245–302.

Seuss, Dr. (1963). *Hop on Pop: The simplest Seuss for easiest use.* New York: Random House.

Share, D. L., Jorm, A. F., MacLean, R., & Matthews, R. (1984). Sources of individual differences in reading acquisition. *Journal of Educational Psychology, 64,* 429–439.

Stanovich, K. E. (1986). Matthew effects in reading: Some consequences of individual differences in the acquisition of literacy. *Reading Research Quarterly, 20,* 360–406.

Stanovich, K. E., Cunningham, A. E., & Cramer, B. B. (1984). Assessing phonological awareness in kindergarten children: Issues of task comparability. *Journal of Experimental Child Psychology, 38,* 175–190.

Treiman, R. (1994). Use of consonant letter names in beginning spelling. *Developmental Psychology, 30,* 567–580.

Tunmer, W. E., Herriman, M. L., & Nesdale, A. R. (1988). Metalinguistic abilities and beginning reading. *Reading Research Quarterly, 23,* 134–158.

Wallach, M. A., & Wallach, L. (1976). Teaching all children to read. Chicago: University of Chicago Press.

Wells, G. (1985). Preschool literacy-related activities and success in school. In D. R. Olson, N. Torrance, & A. Hildyard (Eds.), *Literacy, language, and learning* (pp. 229–255). Cambridge, UK: Cambridge University Press.

Whitehurst, G. J., Epstein, J. N., Angell, A. L., Payne, A. C., Crone, D. A., & Fischell, J. E. (1994a). Outcomes of a emergent literacy intervention in head start. *Journal of Educational Psychology, 86*, 542–555.

Whitehurst, G. J., Arnold, D. S., Epstein, J. N., Angell, A. L., Smith, M., & Fischel, J. E. (1994b). A picture book reading intervention in day care and home for children from low-income families. *Developmental Psychology, 30*, 679–689.

Whitehurst, G. J. (undated). *The Stony Brook emergent literacy curriculum: Materials for teachers, parents, and children; pre-K, Head Start, and kindergarten.* Stony Brook, NY: Author.

39

Alphabetics Instruction Helps Students Learn to Read

Linnea C. Ehri
City University of New York

Alphabetics refers to the system of representing words and phonemes with letters and includes phonemic awareness, grapheme-phoneme correspondences, and spelling patterns. It also refers to the use of alphabetic knowledge to spell words and to read words by sight, by decoding, by analogy, and by prediction. Phonemic awareness (PA) instruction teaches students how to manipulate phonemes in spoken words, with letters sometimes used to support instruction. Systematic phonics instruction teaches the major grapheme-phoneme correspondences and their use to decode and spell words.

Findings of two meta-analyses revealed that both PA instruction and systematic phonics instruction helped children learn to read and spell more effectively than alternative forms of instruction. Both were especially effective for beginners at risk of reading failure. Phonics instruction exerted a greater impact in the early grades (kindergarten and first) when it was the method used to start children out than in the later grades (second through sixth) after children had made some progress in reading, presumably with another method. Findings support Chall (1967) in underscoring the importance of teaching alphabetics early, especially in schools with large numbers of at-risk students who enter school with very little letter knowledge or phonemic awareness.

INTRODUCTION

One of the great mysteries to challenge researchers is how beginners learn to read and comprehend text rapidly with ease. A large part of the explanation lies in how they learn to read individual words. Explaining this is not simple. Skilled readers are able to look at thousands of words and immediately recognize their meanings without any effort by reading the words from memory. In addition, skilled readers can pronounce unfamiliar written words with ease, by transforming letters into sounds or by recognizing resemblances to words they already know how to read. Readers who are skilled at reading words can also generate plausible spellings of unknown words as well as remember the spellings of familiar words. A major task has been to explain how beginners learn to read and spell words this well.

A key ingredient enabling the acquisition of word reading and spelling skill is knowledge of the alphabetic system. This includes the following capabilities: knowing the shapes, names and sounds of letters; having phonemic awareness (PA), which is the ability to manipulate phoneme-size units in speech, especially the skill of segmenting and blending phonemes; recognizing mapping relations between graphemes in the spellings of words and phonemes in their pronunciations; and knowing spelling patterns and their relationship to syllabic units in speech. All of these capabilities constitute alphabetic knowledge, or alphabetics.

Two forms of instruction have been studied extensively as a means of teaching alphabetics explicitly to beginners: instruction in PA and systematic phonics instruction. The purpose of this chapter is to review theory and evidence regarding the contribution of alphabetic knowledge in learning to read. The evidence is drawn from findings reported by the National Reading Panel (NRP). In 1997, the U.S. Congress directed that a panel be convened to assess the status of research-based knowledge on the effectiveness of various approaches for teaching children to read. The panel's work included two meta-analyses, one on PA instruction and one on systematic phonics instruction. The final report was submitted to Congress in April, 2000. Findings regarding alphabetics are included in this chapter. (For more extensive details, see Ehri, Nunes, Willows, Schuster, Yaghoub-Zadeh, & Shanahan, 2001; Ehri, Nunes, Stahl, & Willows, 2001, and National Reading Panel, 2000.)

THE CASE FOR ALPHABETICS

Learning to read involves two basic processes captured in the simple view of reading (Gough & Tunmer, 1986; Hoover & Gough, 1990). One process involves learning to decipher written words. The other involves comprehending the meaning of the print. Children acquire language comprehension skills in the course of learning to speak. This skill enables them to understand written as well as spoken language. However, children do not acquire deciphering skills in the course of learning to speak. This achievement requires special experiences that do not occur when parents hold conversations with their children or even when they read books aloud to their children. Acquisition requires focused instruction that teaches children how to process the alphabetic writing system. When children attain reading skill, they can decipher print in a way that allows their attention to focus on the meaning of the text while the mechanics of deciphering operate unobtrusively and out of awareness. The goal of alphabetics instruction is to enable readers to decipher words accurately and automatically.

Beginners learn to read words in various ways, all of which require knowledge of the alphabetic system (Ehri, 1991, 1994). Readers might read words in any of the following ways:

1. by assembling graphemes into a blend of phonemes, referred to as decoding
2. by pronouncing and blending larger units such as familiar spellings of onsets, rimes, and syllables, a more advanced form of decoding
3. by retrieving sight words from memory
4. by analogizing to words already known by sight, and
5. by using context cues combined with alphabetic cues to predict words.

In each case, the processes differ. As readers attain skill, they learn to read words in all five ways.

One way to read words is to transform letters into sounds and blend them to form pronunciations that match up to familiar real words. This requires knowledge of graphophonemic correspondences (GPCs) and phoneme-blending skill. Some correspondences are harder for children to learn, namely, those that are not present in letter names, for example, short vowels, the consonants h for /h/, w for /w/, y for /y/, and consonant digraphs such as sh, ch, and th. Use of a decoding strategy enables readers to read words they have never seen before. It is slower than sight-word reading (Ehri & Wilce, 1983; Perfetti & Hogaboam, 1975). In reading English, this strategy works sometimes but not always, because many spellings have variable or irregular pronunciations.

A more advanced form of decoding words is to pronounce and blend syllabic units. Knowledge of syllabic chunks may be taught or may arise from the student's experiences reading and writing different words that share common letter patterns and pronunciations. According to Ehri (1998), sequences of GPCs that form syllabic or subsyllabic units (i.e., rime spellings such as -ick or -ump) that recur across words become consolidated into larger units. When readers see new words containing these patterns, they can pronounce the patterns as units without having to subdivide them into graphophonemic correspondences. Examples of common chunks are -ing, -ed, -tion, -ble, and -un. Studies show that words having common letter patterns are easier to decode by readers who are familiar with the patterns (Bowey & Hansen, 1994; Juel, 1983; Laxon, Coltheart & Keating, 1988; Treiman, Goswami, & Bruck, 1990). This skill is especially valuable for reading multisyllabic words.

A different way to read words is by sight. Sight words are words read often enough to be stored in readers' memory. When readers see words they know by sight, the words' spellings, pronunciations, and meanings are activated immediately in their minds without any decoding steps required. Reitsma's (1983) study suggests that even first graders can retain sight words in memory after reading the words as few as four times. Readers' ability to read unusually spelled words instantly without any problem is evidence for this way of reading words, for example, "yacht," "bouquet," "limousine." However, sight-word reading is not limited to strangely spelled, difficult-to-decode words or high-frequency words. With sufficient practice, all words acquire status as sight words.

One property of sight-word reading makes it especially valuable for text reading. When sight words are known well enough, readers can recognize their pronunciations and meanings *automatically* (LaBerge & Samuels, 1974). That is, they can read these words without expending any attention or effort decoding the words. They recognize these words instantly, even when they try to ignore them.

The traditional view is that, to retain sight words in memory, readers memorize visual features of words such as their shapes. However, this is incorrect (Ehri, 1992; Perfetti, 1992; Share, 1999). Rather, sight words are retained in memory when connections are formed between graphemes in the spellings and phonemes in the pronunciations of words. In other words, readers use their knowledge of the alphabetic system to remember how to read words by sight. For example, to remember the word "blunt," readers segment the word's pronunciation into phonemic segments that correspond to letters in the spelling. These connections bond the spelling to its pronunciation in memory. Subsequently, seeing the word activates these connections and enables readers to read the word from memory.

Another way to read words is by analogy (Baron, 1977; Bowey & Hansen, 1994; Cunningham, 1976; Gaskins, et al., 1988; Glushko, 1979, 1981; Goswami, 1986, 1988; Laxon et al., 1988; Marsh, Freidman, Welch, & Desberg, 1981). Readers may read a new word by recognizing how its spelling is similar to a word they already know as a sight word. They access the similar sight word in memory and then adjust the pronunciation to accommodate the new word, for example, reading "fountain" by analogy to "mountain," or "brother" by analogy to "mother." Goswami (1990) has found that beginning readers can use their knowledge of rhyming words to read words by analogy. However, having some decoding skill appears to be required for beginners to analogize by access sight words in memory (Ehri & Robbins, 1992).

One, final way to read unfamiliar words is by predicting the words by using alphabetic cues combined with context cues such as pictures and the preceding text. Readers can use their knowledge about language, their knowledge of the world, and their memory for the text already read to make predictions about the identities of words in text. Some words are easier to predict than others. For example function words such as "to" and "the" are easier than content words. Predicting words based on context cues alone, however, is not very effective and does not explain how readers read most words in text (Stanovich, 1980). Studies of the predictability of words in text indicate that, on average, 25% to 30% of the words can be guessed correctly. However, the most important content words that carry the most meaning are the least predictable, with only 10% guessed correctly (Gough & Walsh, 1991). If readers combine context cues with alphabetic cues, their accuracy reading words is improved (Tunmer & Chapman, 1998, 2001). This way of reading words is evident in the miscues that readers produce when they read text aloud. When words are misread, the words substituted often share initial letters and fit the sentence structure and meaning, indicating that alphabetic knowledge and context influence how the words were read (Biemiller, 1970; Clay, 1968; Goodman, 1976; Weber, 1970).

Review of the various ways to read words reveals that alphabetic knowledge is needed in all cases. There is no way to become a skilled reader of English without acquiring knowledge of GPCs and how to use them to read words. Two types of instruction to teach alphabetic knowledge are reviewed in this chapter. PA instruction is focused on teaching students how to distinguish and manipulate phonemes in spoken words. Although letters may be used as part of this instruction, teaching is centered on phoneme manipulation, not on teaching reading or writing. Phonics instruction is focused on the systematic teaching of letter–sound units, which may include larger phonogram and onset–rime units as well as GPCs, and how to use these units to decode words. Of interest is whether the evidence indicates that these forms of instruction help children learn to read.

THE CASE FOR PHONEMIC AWARENESS INSTRUCTION

In the first meta-analysis, the review considered experiments testing the effectiveness of phonemic awareness instruction.[1] Answers to several questions were sought: Is PA instruction effective in helping children learn to read? Under what circumstances and for which children is it most effective? Were studies showing its effectiveness designed to yield scientifically valid findings? How applicable are these findings to classroom practice?

There are many reasons to evaluate research on PA instruction. PA and letter knowledge have been identified as the two best school-entry predictors of how well children will learn to read during the first two years of instruction (Blachman, 2000; Ehri, 1979; Share, Jorm, Maclean, & Matthews, 1984; Snow, Burns, & Griffin, 1998; Stahl & Murray, 1994; Wagner & Torgesen, 1987). Many experimental studies have been conducted to evaluate the effectiveness of PA instruction in facilitating reading acquisition. Many PA instructional programs have

---

[1] This research was conducted by the Alphabetics subgroup of the National Reading Panel and was supported by the National Institute of Child Health and Human Development. The section on phonemic awareness instruction was adapted from "Phonemic awareness instruction helps children learn to read: Evidence from the National Reading Panel's meta-analysis," by L. Ehri, S. Nunes, D. Willows, B. Schuster, Z. Yaghoub-Zadeh, & T. Shanahan (2001), *Reading Research Quarterly, 36*, 250–287. Copyright 2001 by the International Reading Association. Adapted with permission.

been published and purchased by teachers to teach PA in the belief that this will improve their students' success in learning to read. However, a recent critique by Troia (1999) suggested that some of the studies showing the effectiveness of PA instruction are seriously flawed, indicating the need for closer examination of the evidence.

What is phonemic awareness? Phonemes are the smallest units comprising *spoken* language. Phonemic awareness refers to the ability to focus on and manipulate phonemes is spoken words (Liberman et al.,1974). Researchers have used the following tasks to assess and teach PA:

1. Phoneme *isolation* which requires recognizing individual sounds in words, for example, "Tell me the first sound in *paste*." (/p/)
2. Phoneme *identity* which requires recognizing the common sound in different words, for example, "Tell me the sound that is the same in *bike, boy,* and *bell*." (/b/)
3. Phoneme *categorization* which requires recognizing the word with the odd sound in a sequence of 3 or 4 words, for example, "Which word does not belong? *bus, bun, rug*." (rug)
4. Phoneme *blending* which requires listening to a sequence of separately spoken sounds and combining them to form a recognizable word, for example, "What word is /s/ /k/ /u/ /l/?" (*school*)
5. Phoneme *segmentation* which requires breaking a word into its sounds by tapping out or counting the sounds, or by pronouncing and positioning a marker for each sound, for example, "How many phonemes in *ship*?" (3: /š/ /I/ /p/)
6. Phoneme *deletion* which requires recognizing what word remains when a specified phoneme is removed, for example, "What is *smile* without the /s/?" (*mile*)

To evaluate the adequacy and strength of the evidence, the NRP located all the experimental studies that taught PA to students, that included a control group receiving non-PA instruction or no special instruction and that measured the impact of PA instruction on reading. The NRP meta-analysis differed from a previous PA meta-analysis by Bus and van IJzendoorn (1999). The NRP database included more studies. Also in contrast to Bus and van IJzendoorn, who formed single treatment–control comparisons when studies included more than one PA treatment or more than one control group, in the NRP analysis, these comparisons were kept separate. Having more treatment–control comparisons strengthened the analysis of moderator variables. In addition, the NRP report made use of Troia's (1999) critique, which was not available to Bus and van IJzendoorn. This enabled a more thorough examinination of the relationship between methodological design features and effect size.

Method.   Electronic searches and hand searches of reference lists yielded studies that were further screened to meet several criteria. Studies had to be experiments or quasiexperiments with a control group; they had to be published in a refereed journal; they had to test the hypothesis that instruction in PA improves reading performance over alternative forms of instruction or no instruction; they had to provide instruction in PA that was not confounded with other instructional methods or activities; and they had to report statistics permitting the calculation or estimation of effect sizes.

The final set of studies numbered 52. From these, 96 cases comparing individual treatment and control groups were derived. Different age and grade levels as well as different types of treatment and control groups within a study were treated as separate comparison cases.

The studies in the database were coded for several characteristics. Three outcomes were of primary interest: PA, reading, and spelling. The kinds of measures that were combined into the reading outcome included word reading, pseudoword reading, reading comprehension, oral text reading, reading speed, time to reach a criterion of learning, and miscues. The spelling composite included measures of invented spellings as well as correct spellings of words and pseudowords. Because several studies examined whether PA instruction had an impact on students' performance in math, this outcome was included as well. It was expected that scores in math would not show gains, hence ruling out Hawthorne effects.

There were three reader groups. One group consisted of children who were not distinguished as having any reading problems, referred to as normally achieving (NA) readers. One group consisted of children below second grade who were at risk for developing reading difficulties in the future. Being at risk was indicated by low PA or low reading in 83% of the cases and low socioeconomic status (SES) in 27% of the cases. The third group consisted of comparisons involving students with a reading disability (RD). All RD comparisons involved children between second and sixth grades, except for three from first grade.

PA programs varied in whether they focused on specific PA manipulations. Single-focus studies taught blending, categorization, identity, segmention, or onset–rime. Double-focus studies involved combinations of blending, segmenting, deletion, or categorization. Global treatments taught three or more PA skills. Instruction varied in whether children were taught to manipulate phonemes by using letters or whether attention was limited to phonemes in speech. The instructional delivery unit varied across studies. Students were tutored individually, or taught in small groups, or in whole classrooms. The size of the small groups varied from two to seven students. The identity of instructors varied and included classroom teachers, researchers or their assistants, or computers.

Some features of the experimental methodology were coded: whether assignment to groups was random; whether fidelity to treatment was checked; whether the control group received an alternative treatment; size of the sample. In addition, evaluations of methodological rigor calculated by Troia (1999) were applied to 56 comparisons derived from 28 studies in the database.

The primary statistic used to analyze outcomes was effect size, indicating whether and by how much performance of the treatment group exceeded performance of the control group. The formula to calculate raw effect sizes was the mean of the treatment group minus the mean of the control group divided by a pooled standard deviation. The DSTAT statistical package (Johnson, 1989) was used to determine weighted effect sizes and to test the influence of moderator variables.

An effect size of 1 indicates that the treatment-group mean was one standard deviation higher than the control-group mean, revealing a strong effect of instruction. An effect size of 0 indicates that treatment- and control-group means were identical, showing that instruction had no effect. To judge the strength of an effect size, values suggested by Cohen (1988) are commonly used. An effect size of $d = 0.20$ is considered small, an effect size of $d = 0.50$ moderate, and an effect size of $d = 0.80$ or above large. Translated into more familiar terms, $d = 0.20$ indicates that the treatment has moved the average child from the 50th to the 58th percentile; $d = 0.50$ indicates that the treatment has moved the average child to the 69th percentile; $d = 0.80$ indicates that the treatment has moved the average child to the 79th percentile.

Results.   Mean effect sizes weighted by sample size were calculated on three outcomes measured at the end of training: PA, reading, and spelling. The mean effect size of PA instruction on the acquisition of PA was large, $d = 0.86$, based on 72 treatment–control comparisons. The mean effect size on reading was moderate, $d = 0.53$, based on 90 comparisons. The mean effect size on spelling was moderate, $d = 0.59$, based on 39 comparisons. All values were statistically greater than zero ($p < .05$). In contrast, the mean effect size on math outcomes was small and not significant, $d = 0.03$, $p > .05$, based on 15 comparisons. This indicates that the positive effects of PA instruction were limited to literacy outcomes and cannot be attributed to Hawthorne effects.

Effects of PA instruction were examined for several moderator variables. On the outcome measure of PA, effects were statistically greater than zero across all moderators and their levels, indicating that PA instruction taught PA effectively for all groups under all conditions. On the outcome measure of spelling, all but two effect sizes across moderators were statistically greater than zero. Effects were nonsignificant when computers were the instructors and when the readers were students with RD. Thus, across most levels of the moderator variables, PA instruction improved spelling skills more than alternative forms of instruction or no instruction.

Table 39.1 presents mean effect sizes for reading outcomes. Values of d that were statistically greater than zero are marked with an asterisk. It is apparent that effect sizes across moderator variables were all statistically greater than zero, indicating that PA instruction was effective in boosting reading performance across all types of students and conditions.

Table 39.1 also reports the number of comparisons contributing to mean effect sizes, 95% confidence intervals, and results of statistical tests contrasting levels of each moderator. The table also includes results of homogeneity tests calculating how probable it is that the variance exhibited among effect sizes in a moderator pool would be observed if only sampling error was making them different (Cooper, 1998). "Yes" indicates that the mean effect size is representative of that set. "No" indicates that other moderator variables may explain variance. At the top of the table, it is apparent that, on the immediate outcome measure of reading, the effect size was not homogeneous. Thus there is reason to examine moderator variables that may explain these effects.

In interpreting effects of the moderator variables, caution is urged. When effect sizes are larger for some levels of a moderator than for others, concluding that the moderator caused the difference is problematic. This is because a third hidden factor may be confounded with the moderator and explain the difference. Any conclusions about moderator effects are only tentative and suggestive. Another caution involves concern about the number of comparisons contributing to any effect size. The comparisons contributing to mean effect sizes changed across moderator variables, either because some studies did not report the information or they did not assess that outcome at that test point. Thus one cannot assume that effect sizes represent the whole database. Moreover, one should note that mean effect sizes are less reliable when they are based on fewer comparisons.

From Table 39.1, it is apparent that PA instruction had an impact on reading when measured at the end of instruction. Effects persisted through the first and second follow-up tests (i.e., 2 to 15 months and 7 to 30 months, respectively). PA instruction improved various types of reading, including children's ability to read words and pseudowords as well as their comprehension of text.

The benefits of PA instruction for various types of students was examined. Students at risk (AR) and students with RD are known to have greater difficulty manipulating phonemes in words than NA readers (Bradley & Bryant, 1983; Juel, 1988; Juel, Griffith, & Gough, 1986). Of interest was whether PA instruction could help these students. In acquiring PA, all three groups showed significant effects although effect sizes were larger for NA readers ($d = 0.93$) and AR readers ($d = 0.95$) than for students with RD ($d = 0.62$). This indicates that all types of readers were responsive to the instruction in acquiring PA.

Transfer of PA instruction to reading also occurred in all three groups. Table 39.1 reveals that AR children showed statistically larger transfer effects on reading than did normal and RD students whose effect sizes were moderate and did not differ statistically.

Transfer of PA instruction to spelling differed among the reader groups. Effect sizes were large and did not differ statistically for AR ($d = 0.76$) and NA ($d = 0.88$) readers, indicating that PA instruction strongly benefited spelling for these students. However, the effect size was small and not statistically different from zero for students with RD ($d = 0.15$), indicating that they need more than PA instruction to improve their spelling.

TABLE 39.1
Mean Effect Sizes (*d*) Produced by PA Instruction on Reading Outcomes

Moderator Variables and Levels	No. Cases	Mean d	Homogeneous	95% CI	Contrasts[a]
Characteristics of Outcome Measures					
Time of posttest					
Immediate	90	.53*	No	.47 to .58	Im = 1 > 2
First follow-up	35	.45*	No	.36 to .54	
Second follow-up	8	.23*	No	.11 to .34	
Test of word reading					
Experimenter devised	58	.61*	No	.54 to .69	E > S
Standardized	37	.32*	No	.23 to .42	
Test of pseudoword reading					
Experimenter devised	47	.56*	No	.48 to .64	ns
Standardized	8	.49*	Yes	.29 to .69	
Reading comprehension	20	.34*	No	.21 to .46	
Math achievement	15	.03ns	No	−.11 to .16	
Characteristics of Participants					
Reading level					
At risk	27	.86*	No	.72 to 1.00	A > D = N
Disabled	17	.45*	Yes	.32 to .57	
Normal progress	46	.47*	No	.39 to .54	
Grade					
Preschool	7	1.25*	No	1.01 to 1.50	P > K = 1 = 2
Kindergarten	40	.48*	No	.40 to .56	
First	25	.49*	Yes	.36 to .62	
Second–Sixth	18	.49*	Yes	.35 to .62	
SES					
Low	11	.45*	No	.33 to .58	MH > L
Mid & High	29	.84*	No	.72 to .96	
Language of Instruction					
English	72	.63*	No	.55 to .70	E > O
Other	18	.36*	No	.27 to .46	
Characteristics of PA Instruction					
Skills Taught					
One skill	32	.71*	No	.58 to .84	1 = 2 > 3
Two skills	29	.79*	No	.69 to .89	
Three or more skills	29	.27*	Yes	.19 to .35	
Blend & segment only	19	.67*	No	.54 to .81	BS > 3
3 or more skills	29	.27*	Yes	.19 to .35	
Use of Letters					
Letters manipulated	48	.67*	No	.59 to .75	L > NoL
Letters not manipulated	42	.38*	No	.30 to .46	
Delivery Unit					
Individual child	32	.45*	Yes	.34 to .57	S > I = C
Small groups	42	.81*	No	.71 to .92	
Classrooms	16	.35*	No	.26 to .44	

(Continued)

TABLE 39.1
(Continued)

Moderator Variables and Levels	No. Cases	Mean d	Homogeneous	95% CI	Contrasts[a]
Length of Instruction					
1 to 4.5 hr	17	.61*	Yes	.42 to .79	1= 5 = 10
5 to 9.3 hr	23	.76*	No	.62 to .89	20 < others
10 to 18 hr	19	.86*	No	.72 to 1.00	
20 to 75 hr	25	.31*	No	.22 to .39	
Characteristics of Instructors					
Classroom teachers	22	.41*	No	.33 to .49	RO > CT
Researchers & others	68	.64*	No	.56 to .73	
Computers	8	.33*	Yes	.16 to .49	O > C
Others	82	.55*	No	.49 to .61	
Characteristics of Design					
Random assignment	46	.63*	No	.54 to .72	R > N
Matched	22	.57*	Yes	.43 to .72	M = all
Non-equivalent	20	.40*	No	.31 to .49	
Fidelity checked	31	.43*	No	.34 to .53	N > F
Not checked	59	.59*	No	.51 to .66	
Control Group					
Treated controls	54	.65*	No	.56 to .73	T > U
Untreated controls	36	.41*	No	.33 to .49	
Size of sample					
9 to 22 students	24	.72*	No	.51 to .92	9 = 31 > 56
24 to 30 students	22	.54*	Yes	.37 to .70	24 = 9, 56
31 to 53 students	22	.91*	No	.76 to 1.05	31 > 24
56 to 383 students	22	.40*	No	.33 to .48	
Troia overall ranking of rigor					
High (1–12)	19	1.00*	No	.85 to 1.15	H > M = L
Middle (13–24)	14	.61*	Yes	.47 to .75	
Low (25–36)	23	.58*	No	.46 to .69	

Notes. d = mean effect size; Homogeneous reports results of the statistical test of whether the set of effect sizes was homogeneous; CI = confidence interval; PA = phonemic awareness; ns = results were not statistically significant.
* indicates that d was statistically greater than zero at $p < .05$.
[a] Contrasts signify results of post hoc pairwise statistical tests comparing levels of moderator variables. Symbols are initial letters or numbers referring to levels of moderators.

The effects of PA instruction were examined at various grade levels (see Table 39.1). Most of the second-grade–sixth-grade comparisons (i.e., 14 out of 18) involved students with RD, so findings apply mainly to these students rather than to second–sixth graders in general. PA instruction had an impact on reading to a similar extent for kindergartners, first graders, and second–sixth graders. The effect size for preschoolers was much larger statistically but it was based on fewer comparisons, only seven, given simplified word-recognition tests.

SES levels made a difference. Although both low-SES and mid–high-SES groups showed large effect sizes in acquiring PA (ds of 1.02, 1.07), transfer to reading was statistically greater among mid–high-SES than among low-SES students (see Table 39.1). Because most RD studies did not report the students' SES, these results pertain mainly to normally developing and AR children.

Studies examining PA instruction were conducted not only in English-speaking countries but also in countries where languages other than English are spoken. Results revealed that PA instruction exerted a statistically larger impact on the acquisition of PA by English-speaking students ($d = 0.99$) than by the non-English students ($d = 0.65$). Transfer to reading was also statistically greater for English students than for others (see Table 39.1). However, effect sizes on spelling outcomes did not differ statistically in the two language groups ($d = 0.60$ E vs. 0.55 non-E). One likely explanation of the latter finding is that 94% of the RD comparisons, whose spelling was not affected by PA instruction, were in the English pool, thus suppressing the English spelling effect size. When the effect size was recalculated with the RD comparisons removed, a statistically significant difference emerged: $d = 0.95$ E vs. $d = 0.51$ non-E. One possible reason for the larger effect sizes in English may be that the English writing system is not as transparent in representing phonemes as it is in the other languages, so explicit PA instruction may make a bigger contribution to clarifying phoneme units and their linkage to graphemes in English. This would produce a bigger difference between treatment and control groups in English than in non-English experiments.

Studies varied in the particular PA skills that were taught. Some studies taught single PA skills whereas others taught two skills or multiple skills. Focusing instruction on one or two skills was statistically more effective for teaching PA than was focusing on multiple skills: $d = 1.16, 1.03, 0.70$, respectively. Transfer to reading was statistically greater, in fact twice as great when PA instruction focused on one or two PA skills than when multiple skills were taught (see Table 39.1).

Of the various combinations of phoneme manipulations that might be taught, two are thought to play a central role in learning to read and spell words. Blending phonemes helps children decode unfamiliar words. Segmenting words into phonemes helps children form connections to remember how to read words and also to spell words. A number of studies taught children to blend and segment (B&S) phonemes. To assess its value, the effect size for this treatment was compared to the effect size for the multiple-skills (MS) treatment. Neither approach was more effective than the other for teaching PA ($d = 0.81$ B&S vs. 0.70 MS). However, Table 39.1 shows that teaching students to B&S produced statistically greater improvement in reading than a MS approach did. The same difference was found on spelling outcomes ($d = 0.79$ B&S vs. 0.23 MS). These findings support the special value of B&S instruction.

Another feature of PA instruction expected to be important involved the use of letters to teach PA. In some studies, children used letters to learn to manipulate phonemes in words whereas, in other studies, children only spoke the sounds or they manipulated phonemes with unmarked tokens. Letters were expected to improve children's acquisition of PA because they provide concrete, lasting symbols for sounds that are short-lived and hard to grasp. Results showed that children taught with letters did not acquire stronger PA ($d = 0.89$) than children taught without letters ($d = 0.82$). However, RD students were disproportionately represented across the two sets, with all but one RD comparison in the letter set. Because RD students showed significantly smaller effect sizes in acquiring PA than non-RD students, their presence may have suppressed the effect size for letters. Removal of RD students from the set revealed a statistically significant difference favoring letter instruction ($d = 1.11$) over no letters ($d = 0.83$). These findings indicate that teaching children to manipulate phonemes by using letters is more effective for acquiring PA than teaching them without letters.

Teaching PA with letters was also expected to promote superior transfer to reading and spelling than teaching PA without letters because reading and spelling tasks require students to work with letters and sounds. From Table 39.1, it is apparent that PA instruction with letters produced an effect size that was almost twice as large as the effect size without letters on reading outcomes. The same advantage was evident on spelling outcomes ($d = 0.61$ L vs. 0.34 no L). These findings support the importance of including letters to teach PA.

It is commonly believed that tutoring is the most effective way to deliver instruction because tutors can tailor their teaching to individual needs. However, results of our analysis did not support this. Findings showed that PA was taught most effectively in small groups in which the effect size on PA outcomes was very large ($d = 1.38$) and statistically greater than the effect size for tutoring ($d = 0.60$) and for classrooms ($d = 0.67$). PA instruction delivered to small groups also boosted reading performance more than did tutoring or classroom delivery as evident in Table 39.1. The effectiveness of small groups may have arisen from enhanced attention, social motivation to achieve, or observational learning opportunities for students.

It is common wisdom that greater time spent instructing students yields superior learning. The length of time allocated for PA instruction varied across studies from 1 to 75 hr. Comparisons were grouped into four time blocks to determine whether longer proved better. Analysis of PA outcomes revealed that effect sizes were statistically larger for the two middle time periods lasting from 5 to 9.3 hr ($d = 1.37$) and from 10 to 18 hr ($d = 1.14$) than for the shorter periods ($d = 0.61$) and longer periods ($d = 0.65$). On reading outcomes, programs that were long-lasting yielded a statistically smaller effect size than did shorter programs, as shown in Table 39.1. These findings suggest that PA instruction does not need to be lengthy to exert its strongest effect on reading.

Classroom teachers are the primary purveyors of reading instruction, so it is important to verify that they can teach PA effectively. Results showed that classroom teachers produced a large effect on PA outcomes ($d = 0.78$), although not as large statistically as that produced by researchers ($d = 0.94$). The PA instruction that was delivered by teachers was found to transfer to reading although the effect size was statistically smaller than the effect size produced by researchers (see Table 39.1). Of course, these experiments were designed to evaluate the contribution of PA instruction unconfounded by reading and writing instruction. This fact dictated that neither teachers nor researchers intervened to teach children explicitly how to apply their PA skills in the reading transfer tasks. If transfer occurred, it was unassisted. This contrasts with typical classroom operations, in which teachers not only teach PA but also teach children how to apply it in their reading and give the students practice doing this. Under these circumstances, in which transfer is facilitated through teaching, much bigger effects on reading would be expected.

There were 10 treatment–control comparisons that used computers to teach PA. Findings revealed statistically significant effect sizes on the acquisition of PA ($d = 0.66$) as well as transfer to reading ($d = 0.33$). However, instruction did not transfer to spelling ($d = 0.09$, based on six cases). These findings indicate that computers are effective for teaching PA and for promoting transfer to reading.

Design features were analyzed to see whether positive effect sizes on reading occurred across experiments regardless of how rigorously they were designed. Results were positive. In Table 39.1 it is evident that effects were statistically greater than zero for all moderator levels. The effect size for randomly assigned groups was statistically greater than the effect size for nonequivalent groups. However, effect sizes were statistically larger in studies that did not check on instructors' fidelity to prescribed procedures than in studies that did check.

Bus and van IJzendoorn (1999) reported an unexpected finding involving the type of control group in their PA meta-analysis. Effect sizes were *smaller* in comparisons involving untreated control groups than in comparisons involving treated control groups. In other words, performance of the PA-instructed group surpassed performance of the control group to a lesser extent when the control group received no special alternative treatment than when it did receive a treatment. One would expect the opposite to occur, because Hawthorne effects should inflate the effect size in comparisons in which control groups receive no special attention. In the present study, this finding was partly replicated. As evident in Table 39.1, comparisons using untreated controls showed statistically smaller effect sizes on reading outcomes than comparisons using treated controls. However, on the other outcomes, results were different. On the PA outcome, the two types of control groups yielded about the same effect sizes, which did not differ statistically. On the spelling outcome, studies with untreated controls showed statistically larger effects than studies with treated controls.

These control group results emerged across the general set of studies. We also compared effects within eight studies that included both treated and untreated control groups in the same study. The advantage of looking within studies is that other differences are controlled. On reading outcomes, six studies exhibited larger effect sizes for untreated than treated control groups whereas two showed larger effect sizes for treated controls. Although more in conformance with expectations, this difference fell short of statistical significance on a matched-pair t test ($p > .05$). The fact that studies using untreated controls did not consistently show larger effect sizes than studies using treated controls raises doubt about the commonly held belief that untreated control groups necessarily produce larger effects. It is not the case that Hawthorne effects always prevail. Other factors appear to influence outcomes as well.

In his critique of PA instruction studies, Troia (1999) assessed the methodological rigor of 39 studies, of which 28 were in the NRP database. (Troia's other studies were not included because they did not assess reading as an outcome.) The NRP adopted Troia's summary ratings, grouped comparisons into high, middle, and low rankings, and examined their relationship to effect sizes on reading outcomes. Results in Table 39.1 show that effect sizes for the most rigorous studies were statistically larger than effect sizes for the less rigorous studies. Thus, although Troia found fault with PA studies, his findings do not undermine claims about the effectiveness of PA instruction for helping children learn to read. Troia's concluding plea, that researchers maintain high standards in designing their studies, is supported by effect sizes. The NRP findings suggest that if there is a difference to be found, researchers stand a better chance of detecting that difference when they design strong studies than when they design weak studies threatened by violations to internal and external validity.

Discussion.   Findings of the meta-analysis were uniformly positive. The benefits of PA instruction were replicated multiple times across experiments and thus provide solid support for the claim that PA instruction is more effective than alternative forms of instruction or no instruction in teaching PA and in helping children learn to read and spell. Effects of PA instruction were found to be greater under some circumstances than others. This evidence is suggestive but not conclusive regarding the possible importance of moderator variables. Consideration of findings raises several issues. (For more extensive discussion, see Ehri et al., 2001 and National Reading Panel, 2000.)

According to findings, children who received instruction that focused on only one or two PA skills, most importantly segmenting and blending, exhibited stronger PA and stronger transfer to reading than did children who were taught three or more PA skills. Perhaps when more skills were taught, fewer students mastered those skills. However, given our findings, it may be prudent for teachers who have adopted multiple skills programs to teach one skill at a time until it is mastered before moving on to the next and to teach students how each skill applies in reading or spelling tasks as soon as it is taught.

More important than the number of PA skills to teach may be the question of which skills to teach. It is important to provide PA instruction that is appropriate for children's level of literacy development. Factors influencing the difficulty of PA tasks include the type of manipulation applied to phonemes, the number and phonological properties of phonemes in the words manipulated, whether the words are real or are nonwords, and whether letters are included (Stahl & Murray, 1994). The following tasks are ordered from easy (1) to difficult (6) based on findings of Schatschneider, Francis, Foorman, Fletcher, & Mehta (1999):

1. First-sound comparison: identifying the names of pictures beginning with the same sound
2. Blending onset–rime units into real words
3. Blending phonemes into real words
4. Deleting a phoneme and saying the word that remains
5. Segmenting words into phonemes
6. Blending phonemes into nonwords.

In deciding which PA manipulations to teach, teachers need to consider not only task difficulty but also how students are expected to apply the PA skill being taught. The reason to teach first-sound comparisons is to draw preschooler or kindergarten prereaders' attention to the fact that words have sounds as well as meanings. A reason to teach phoneme segmentation is to help kindergartners or first graders generate more complete spellings of words. The reason to teach phoneme blending is to help first graders combine letter sounds to decode words. Teaching PA effectively includes teaching the applications as well as the skill.

One very striking finding in the meta-analysis was that PA instruction did not enhance spelling skill in older readers with RD whereas it did in AR and NA readers. Other studies have found that readers with RD have special difficulty learning to spell (Bruck, 1993). Even though their reading might be remediated, they still display spelling problems as adults. Perhaps the phonological processing difficulties that children with RD commonly exhibit—difficulty segmenting words into phonemes, difficulty reading nonwords—make spelling especially hard to learn (Rack, Snowling, & Olson, 1992). Alternatively, perhaps PA instruction failed to help older readers with RD with their spelling because the types of words that are spelled in higher grades require knowledge of syllabic and morphemic spelling patterns whereas PA instruction targets phoneme–grapheme knowledge. The NRP findings support the conclusion that remediating spelling in readers with RD is especially difficult and requires an approach that targets spelling explicitly.

The meta-analysis showed that PA instruction brings about improvement in children's reading and spelling acquisition. However, the opposite causal relationship is also supported by other studies showing that children acquire PA in the course of learning to read and spell, even though they are not taught PA explicitly. The process of learning letter–sound relations and how to use them to read and spell enhances children's ability to manipulate phonemes. Studies show that people who do not learn to read in an alphabetic system do not develop much PA (Mann, 1986; Morais, Alegria, & Content, 1986; Read, Zhang, Nie, & Ding, 1986). Children in the control groups who received regular literacy instruction in school made some gains on PA tests in the studies we analyzed. However, effect sizes showed that controls did not gain as much PA as children who received explicit PA instruction. Thus we cannot assume that the full extent of PA needed to facilitate reading will be acquired incidentally in the course of learning to read. It must receive special attention.

The NRP findings indicate that PA contributes significantly to reading and spelling acquisition. However, there is obviously much more that children need to be taught to become competent readers and writers.

THE CASE FOR PHONICS INSTRUCTION

Teaching students to read is a complex task.[2] Children enter school with substantial competence speaking their language. To link their knowledge of spoken language to written language, children must master the alphabetic code, that is, the system of GPCs that link the spellings of words to their pronunciations. Phonics instruction teaches beginning readers the alphabetic code and how to use this knowledge to read words. In systematic phonics programs, a planned set of phonics elements is taught sequentially. The set includes not only the major correspondences between consonant letters and sounds but also short- and long-vowel letters and sounds, and vowel and consonant digraphs (e.g., oi, ea, sh, th). Also it may include blends of letter sounds that form larger subunits in words such as onsets (i.e., consonants that precede the vowel such as "j" in "jump" or "st" in "stop") and rimes (i.e., the vowel and following consonants such as "ump" in "jump" and "op" in "stop").

Over the years educators have disagreed about how beginning reading should be taught. Some have advocated starting with a systematic phonics approach whereas others have argued for a whole-word approach or a whole-language approach. Disagreement has centered on whether teaching should begin with explicit instruction in symbol–sound correspondences, whether it should begin with whole words, or whether initial instruction should be meaning centered with correspondences taught incidentally in context as needed.

The purpose of this review was to determine whether there is experimental evidence showing that systematic phonics instruction helps children learn to read more effectively than unsystematic phonics instruction or instruction teaching little or no phonics. Also of interest was whether phonics instruction is more effective under some circumstances than others and for some students more than others. To assess the evidence, a meta-analysis like the one described in the preceding section was conducted. The NRP searched the literature to locate experimental studies that administered systematic phonics instruction to one group of children and administered another type of instruction involving unsystematic phonics or no phonics to a control group. Studies in the previous meta-analysis evaluating PA instruction were not included in this analysis.

Several different approaches have been used to teach phonics systematically (Aukerman, 1971, 1984; Harris & Hodges, 1995). These include synthetic phonics, analytic phonics, embedded phonics, analogy phonics, onset–rime phonics, and phonics through spelling. These approaches differ in several respects. Synthetic phonics programs use a part-to-whole approach that teaches children to convert graphemes into phonemes (e.g., to pronounce each letter in "stop," /s/-/t/-/a/-/p/) and then to blend the phonemes into a recognizable word). Analytic phonics uses a whole-to-part approach that avoids having children pronounce sounds in isolation to figure out words. Rather, children are taught to analyze letter–sound relations once the word is identified. Phonics-through-spelling programs teach children to segment and write the phonemes in words. Phonics in context teaches children to use letter–sound correspondences along with context cues to identify unfamiliar words they encounter in text. Analogy phonics teaches children to use parts of written words they already know to identify new words. For example, they are taught a set of key words that are posted on the wall (e.g., tent, make, pig) and then are taught to use these words to decode unfamiliar words by pronouncing the shared rime and blending it with the new onset (e.g., rent, bake, jig). Some systematic phonics programs are hybrids that include components of two or more of these approaches.

---

[2] This research was conducted by the Alphabetics subgroup of the NRP and was supported by the National Institute of Child Health and Human Development. The section on phonics instruction was adapted from "Systematic phonics instruction helps students learn to read: Evidence from the National Reading Panel's meta-analysis," by L. Ehri, S. Nunes, S. Stahl, & D. Willows, in press, *Review of Educational Research.* Copyright 2002 by the American Educational Research Association. Adapted with permission.

Phonics programs may differ in several other important ways, for example, in how many letter–sound relations are taught and how they are sequenced, whether phonics generalizations are taught, whether phonemic awareness is taught, what the pace of instruction is, whether learning activities include oral drill–and–practice or reciting phonics rules or filling out worksheets, whether children read decodable text in which the vocabulary is limited mainly to words containing familiar letter–sound associations, whether phonics instruction is embedded in or segregated from the literacy curriculum, whether the teaching approach involves direct instruction in which the teacher takes an active role and students passively respond, or whether a "constructivist" problem-solving approach is used, and how interesting and motivating the instructional activities are for teachers and for students (Adams, 1990; Aukerman, 1981).

Evaluating the effectiveness of systematic phonics instruction has been addressed many times in the literature. The best-known effort was Jeanne Chall's (1967) comprehensive review of beginning reading instruction covering studies up to the mid-1960s, *Learning to Read: The Great Debate*. Her basic finding was that early and systematic instruction in phonics led to better achievement in reading than later and less systematic phonics instruction. This conclusion has been reaffirmed in many research reviews conducted since then (e.g., Adams, 1990; Anderson, Hiebert, Wilkinson, & Scott, 1985; Balmuth, 1982; Dykstra, 1968). In the 1967 review, Chall did not recommend any particular type of phonics instruction, but in the 1983 revision she suggested that synthetic phonics instruction held a slight edge over analytic phonics instruction (Chall, 1983).

At the time of Chall's (1967) original review, the contrast between phonics instruction and the alternative "look–say" methods was considerable. In the look–say approach, children were taught to read words as wholes, and they practiced reading words until they had acquired perhaps 50 to 100 in their sight vocabularies. Only after this, toward the end of first grade, did phonics instruction begin. This was truly a nonphonics approach, because teaching letter–sound relations was delayed for a considerable time.

More recently, whole-language approaches have replaced the whole-word method as the most common alternative to systematic phonics programs. The shift has involved a change from very little letter–sound instruction to a modicum of letter sounds taught unsystematically in first grade. Whole-language teachers are not told to wait until a certain point before teaching children about letter–sound relationships. Typically they provide some instruction in phonics, usually as part of invented spelling activities or through the use of graphophonemic prompts during reading (Routman, 1996). However, their approach is to teach it incidentally in context as the need arises. Observations suggest that, in whole-language classrooms, instruction in vowel letter–sound correspondences occurs infrequently (Stahl, Duffy–Hester, & Stahl, 1998). This contrasts with systematic phonics programs in which the teaching of vowels is central in learning to decode (Shankweiler & Liberman, 1972).

In the present meta-analysis, the effectiveness of systematic phonics instruction was compared with various types of nonphonics or unsystematic phonics instruction given to control groups. Some studies provided whole-language instruction or whole-word instruction to control groups. Another form of control-group instruction involved some type of basal program. In basal programs, teachers are provided with a structured package of books and supplementary materials. They work from a manual that details daily lesson plans based on a scope and sequence of the reading skills to be taught. Students are given workbooks in which to practice skills. Tests are used to place students in the proper levels of the program and to assess mastery of skills (Aukerman, 1981). Basal reading programs of the same era tend to be roughly similar in their characteristics. The basal programs given to control groups in our studies provided only limited or no systematic phonics instruction. Typically they were the programs prescribed in a school or district. A few studies created control groups by utilizing the performance of comparable classes of students enrolled in the same schools the year before the treatment when phonics was not taught systematically. Some studies included more than one control group. Selected for the calculation of effect sizes in the meta-analysis was the group receiving the least phonics instruction. In the following text, control treatments are referred to in various ways, as unsystematic or nonsystematic phonics or no phonics, all of which should be regarded as synonymous.

Of particular interest to the NRP was this question: When should phonics instruction begin? It has been suggested (Chall, 1996) that beginners need to develop foundational knowledge such as concepts about print, phonological awareness, and letter names before formal reading instruction. Expecting students to grapple with synthetic phonics and decoding instruction in kindergarten may be too much. On the other hand, countries such as New Zealand and the United Kingdom have introduced children to reading and writing at the age of 5 years in full-day programs for many years.

In the United States, formal reading instruction typically begins in first grade, so introducing phonics instruction above first grade means that students have already acquired some reading ability, presumably from another method. To exert an impact at this point may be harder because it may require students to change their way of processing print. The database included studies that introduced phonics to students from kindergarten to sixth grade. Of interest was whether phonics instruction was more effective in kindergarten and first grade than in later grades.

Phonics instruction is considered particularly beneficial to children with reading problems because poor readers have exceptional difficulty decoding words, which is a central goal of phonics instruction (Rack et al., 1992). Three types of potential or actual poor readers were distinguished in the meta-analysis: younger children considered *at risk* (AR) of developing reading difficulties; children above first grade whose poor reading was discrepant with their cognitive level, referred to as *reading disabled* (RD); and a miscellaneous group of poor readers, referred to as *low achieving* (LA).

One purpose of the meta-analysis was to examine whether phonics instruction benefits several types of reading behavior. Studies in the database tested children's ability to decode words by giving them regularly spelled words and pseudowords to read. Sight vocabulary was examined by having them children read lists of miscellaneous and irregularly spelled words. Also measures of reading fluency, comprehension, and spelling were included in the meta-analysis.

Method.   Electronic and hand searches of reference lists were used to identify potential studies. Criteria were applied to screen these studies. They had to be experiments or quasi-experiments with a control group and be published in a refereed journal after 1970. Studies had to teach phonics in English. They had to involve interventions that might be found in schools, not short-term laboratory studies teaching very limited alphabetic processes.

From the 38 studies in the database, 66 treatment–control-group comparisons were derived. Different age and grade levels as well as different types of treatment and control-groups within a study provided separate comparisons. Studies were coded for several characteristics including the following: type of phonics program (synthetic, larger subunits, miscellaneous); type of control group; sample size; grade level; reading ability; SES; instructional delivery unit (class, small groups, tutoring); group assignment procedure (random assignment, nonequivalent groups); and existence of pretreatment group differences.

Four types of readers were distinguished:

1. Normally achieving (NA) readers: children who were either not screened for reading ability or were screened to exclude poor readers.
2. At risk (AR) readers: kindergartners and first graders judged to be at risk for future reading difficulties because of poor letter knowledge, poor phonemic awareness, poor reading skills, or enrollment in low achieving schools.

3. Students with a reading disability (RD): children who were below grade level in reading but at least average cognitively and were above first grade in most cases.
4. Low achieving (LA) readers: children above first grade who were below average in their reading and whose cognitive level was below average or was not assessed.

Children's performance on six specific outcomes was analyzed: decoding regularly spelled real words; decoding pseudowords; reading real words that included irregularly spelled words; comprehending text; reading connected text orally; and spelling words correctly or according to developmental criteria (Morris & Perney, 1984; Tangel & Blachman, 1995). Entered into the database were outcomes measured at various times: at the end of training; at the end of the first school year if the program was taught for more than 1 year; after a delay ranging from 4 months to 1 year to assess long-term effects of training. The outcome used in analyses of moderator variables was performance at the end of training or at the end of the first year of training if training extended beyond one year.

As in the PA meta-analysis, the DSTAT program was used to calculate effect sizes and assess statistically the impact of phonics instruction. Effect sizes across the six specific outcomes were averaged to create one overall effect size for each of the 66 comparisons. The overall effect size was interpreted to indicate the general impact of phonics instruction on learning to read. Although one of the six outcomes was a spelling measure, spelling effect sizes contributed only 16% of the values whereas reading measures contributed 84% to the average. Studies have shown that reading words and spelling words are highly correlated, with rs commonly above .70, indicating that both involve the same processes (Ehri, 1997). Thus interpreting the overall effect size as an index of reading is justified.

Results.   Table 39.2, reports the mean effect sizes weighted by sample size (d). It is apparent that effects of systematic phonics instruction on reading were statistically greater than zero and moderate in size, regardless of whether effects were measured at the end of the program or at the end of the first year. These findings indicate that systematic phonics helps children learn to read more effectively than do programs with little or no phonics instruction.

There were six comparisons assessing both immediate and long-term effects of phonics instruction, with delays ranging from 4 months to 1 year after instruction ended. As shown in Table 39.2, the effect size declined but remained statistically greater than zero at follow-up, indicating that the impact of phonics instruction lasted well beyond the end of training.

Inspection of the column of effect sizes associated with moderator variables in Table 39.2 reveals that the vast majority were significantly greater than zero (those marked with an asterisk). This suggests that systematic phonics instruction was effective across a variety of conditions and characteristics.

Phonics instruction facilitated reading acquisition in both younger and older readers. Effect sizes were statistically greater than zero in both cases, but were statistically larger among beginners than among older children, in fact, more than twice as large (see Table 39.2). Effects were moderate and very similar for kindergartners and first graders. These findings support Chall's (1996) claim that phonics instruction exerts its greatest impact early.

In most of the studies, phonics instruction lasted one school year or less. However, there were four treatment–control comparisons conducted with AR readers, for whom phonics instruction began in kindergarten or first grade and continued for 2 or 3 years (Blachman, Tangel, Ball, Black, & McGraw, 1999; Brown & Felton, 1990; Torgesen et al., 1999). Mean effect sizes at the end of each grade level were moderate, and their strength was maintained across the grades: kindergarten $d = 0.46$; first grade $d = 0.54$; second grade $d = 0.43$. This confirms the value of starting phonics early and continuing to teach it for two to three years.

TABLE 39.2

Mean Effect Sizes Produced by Systematic Phonics Instruction

Moderator Variables and Levels	No. Cases	Mean d [a]	Homogeneous[b]	95% CI	Contrasts[c]
Time of Posttest					
End of training	65	0.41*	No	0.36 to 0.47	n.s.
End of training or first year	62	0.44*	No	0.38 to 0.50	
Followup	7	0.28*	Yes	0.10 to 0.46	
End of training[d]	6	0.51*	Yes	0.32 to 0.70	n.s.
Follow-up[d]	6	0.27*	Yes	0.07 to 0.46	
Outcome Measures					
Decoding regular words (DRW)	30	0.67*	No	0.57 to 0.77	DRW=DP;
Decoding pseudowords (DP)	40	0.60*	No	0.52 to 0.67	Both >
Reading miscellaneous words (RMW)	59	0.40*	No	0.34 to 0.46	RMW, SW,
Spelling words (SW)	37	0.35*	No	0.28 to 0.43	RTO, CT
Reading text orally (RTO)	16	0.25*	No	0.15 to 0.36	
Comprehending text (CT)	35	0.27*	No	0.19 to 0.36	
Characteristics of Participants					
Grade levels					
Kindergarten & First	30	0.55*	No	0.47 to 0.62	Kind.–1st >
Second–Sixth (NA, RD, LA[e])	32	0.27*	Yes	0.18 to 0.36	2nd–6th
Lower Grades					
Kindergarten	7	0.56*	Yes	0.40 to 0.73	n.s.
1st Grade	23	0.54*	No	0.46 to 0.63	
Grade and Reading Ability					
Kindergarten AR	6	0.58*	Yes	0.40 to 0.77	1AR > 2–6N,
First NA	14	0.48*	No	0.38 to 0.58	2–6LA, RD
First AR (1AR)	9	0.74*	No	0.56 to 0.91	
Second–Sixth NA (2–6N)	7	0.27*	Yes	0.12 to 0.43	
Second–Sixth LA (2–6LA)	8	0.15n.s.	Yes	−0.06 to 0.36	
RD	17	0.32*	Yes	0.18 to 0.46	
Outcome Measures					
Kindergarten and first graders					
Decoding regular words (DRW)	8	0.98*	No	0.81 to 1.16	DRW > RMW
Decoding pseudowords (DP)	14	0.67*	No	0.56 to 0.78	CT, RTO
Reading miscellaneous words (RMW)	23	0.45*	No	0.37 to 0.53	SW > RTO
Spelling words (SW)	13	0.67*	No	0.54 to 0.79	DP > RTO
Reading text orally (RTO)	6	0.23*	No	0.05 to 0.41	
Comprehending text (CT)	11	0.51*	No	0.36 to 0.65	
Second–Sixth (NA,RD,LA[e])					
Decoding regular words (DRW)	17	0.49*	No	0.34 to 0.65	DRW > SW
Decoding pseudowords (DP)	13	0.52*	Yes	0.37 to 0.66	DP > SW, CT
Reading miscellaneous words (RMW)	23	0.33*	No	0.22 to 0.44	
Spelling words (SW)	13	0.09 n.s.	Yes	−0.04 to 0.23	
Reading text orally (RTO)	6	0.24*	Yes	0.08 to 0.39	
Comprehending text (CT)	11	0.12 n.s.	Yes	−0.04 to 0.28	
Socioeconomic Status					
Low SES	6	0.66*	Yes	0.48 to 0.85	n.s.
Middle SES	10	0.44*	No	0.28 to 0.60	
Varied	14	0.37*	Yes	0.26 to 0.48	
Not Given	32	0.43*	No	0.34 to 0.51	

(Continued)

TABLE 39.2
(Continued)

Moderator Variables and Levels	No. Cases	Mean d [a]	Homogeneous[b]	95% CI	Contrasts[c]
Characteristics of Instruction					
Type of Phonics Program					
Synthetic	39	0.45*	No	0.39 to 0.52	n.s.
Larger phonics Units[f]	11	0.34*	No	0.16 to 0.52	
Miscellaneous	10	0.27*	Yes	0.08 to 0.46	
Instructional Delivery Unit					
Tutor[f]	8	0.57*	No	0.38 to 0.77	n.s.
Small group	27	0.43*	Yes	0.34 to 0.52	
Class	27	0.39*	No	0.31 to 0.48	
Type of Control Group					
Basal	10	0.46*	Yes	0.37 to 0.55	n.s.
Regular curriculum	16	0.41*	No	0.27 to 0.54	
Whole language	12	0.31*	No	0.16 to 0.47	
Whole word	10	0.51*	No	0.35 to 0.67	
Miscellaneous	14	0.46*	Yes	0.28 to 0.63	
Characteristics of the Design of Studies					
Assignment of Participants to Treatment and Control Groups					
Random	23	0.45*	Yes	0.32 to 0.58	n.s.
Nonequivalent groups	39	0.43*	No	0.37 to 0.50	
Existence of Pretreatment Group Differences					
Present	5	0.13n.s.	Yes	−0.08 to 0.35	n.s.
Absent	41	0.47*	No	0.39 to 0.54	n.s.
Present but adjusted	6	0.48*	Yes	0.36 to 0.60	
Not given	10	0.40*	Yes	0.24 to 0.56	
Sample size					
20 to 31	14	0.48*	No	0.26 to 0.70	n.s.
32 to 52	16	0.31*	Yes	0.15 to 0.47	
53 to 79	16	0.36*	No	0.23 to 0.49	
80 to 320	16	0.49*	No	0.41 to 0.57	

[a] Effect sizes were tested statistically. * indicates that an effect size was significantly greater than zero at $p < .05$; n.s. indicates it was not significantly different from zero.

[b] Effect sizes were tested statistically for homogeneity by use of the Q statistic. "Yes" indicates that set was homogeneous and "No" that it was not at $p < .05$.

[c] Pairs of effect sizes for levels of moderators were tested statistically to determined whether they differed from each other at $p < .05$; n.s. means not statistically different.

[d] The same six comparisons contributed effect sizes to both outcomes.

[e] NA = normally achieving readers; RD = students with reading disability; LA = low achieving readers.

[f] This effect size was adjusted to reduce the impact of one atypically large outlier.

[g] Letters in parentheses refer to the type of phonics program: S = synthetic, LU = larger units.

From Table 39.2 it is apparent that effect sizes for all six literacy outcomes were statistically greater than zero, indicating that phonics instruction benefited not only word reading and spelling but also text processing. Effects were statistically stronger on measures of decoding regularly spelled words and pseudowords than on the other four measures, indicating that phonics instruction was especially effective in teaching children to decode novel words, one of the main goals of phonics.

The students who received phonics instruction varied in age and grade in school. Of interest were whether phonics instruction made a contribution across groups and whether its impact was larger when introduced early. Treatment–control comparisons were grouped by grade and reading ability. Table 39.2 shows that effect sizes were statistically significant for all but one group. Mean effect sizes were moderate to large for AR and NA readers in kindergarten and first grades. Effect sizes were significant but smaller for second-grade–sixth-grade NA readers and students with RD. These findings indicate that phonics instruction improves reading ability more than nonphonics instruction does, not only among beginning readers but also among normally progressing readers above first grade and older readers with RD. In contrast, phonics instruction did not enhance reading among LA older readers.

When effects on the six outcome measures were examined separately for younger and older students, results differed. As shown in Table 39.2, phonics instruction produced significant effects on all six measures among beginners, with effects ranging from moderate to large on five measures. Among older readers, a different picture emerged. Effects on decoding were moderate, and effects on reading miscellaneous words were small to moderate. However, effects on spelling and reading comprehension were not statistically greater than zero. Further analysis revealed that the nonsignificant effect on the comprehension outcome arose primarily from the students not classified as having RD. Students with RD revealed a significant effect size on comprehension ($d = 0.27$, based on eight comparisons). These findings indicate more limited benefits of phonics instruction among students beyond first grade.

Effects were examined for three categories of phonics programs. As evident in Table 39.1, all three categories of systematic phonics programs produced effect sizes that were statistically greater than zero, indicating that all types were more effective than nonsystematic or no phonics programs. Although the effect size produced by synthetic phonics was somewhat larger, the difference was not statistically significant.

Another property of systematic phonics instruction examined was the delivery unit. In the analysis, one atypically large effect size in the tutoring set (i.e., Tunmer & Hoover, 1993, $d = 3.71$) was reduced to the next largest effect size in the set ($d = 1.99$). Results revealed that all three forms of instruction produced positive effects that did not differ statistically from each other, indicating that all three forms were equally effective ways to deliver phonics instruction to students (see Table 39.2). The fact that classroom instruction can be as effective as tutoring is important to note, given the expense and impracticality of delivering instruction individually.

The type of instruction administered to control groups varied. In some cases, students received unsystematic or incidental phonics whereas in others students received no phonics. Control groups were categorized as one of five types based on labels or descriptions provided by authors: basal, regular curriculum, whole language, whole word, or miscellaneous. Results revealed that effect sizes favoring the phonics treatment were statistically greater than zero for all types of control groups (see Table 39.2). None of the effect sizes differed statistically from the others. These findings show that systematic phonics instruction produced superior performance in reading compared with all types of unsystematic or no phonics instruction.

Studies in the database varied in methodological rigor. Three features were coded and analyzed to determine whether more rigorous designs yielded larger or smaller effect sizes: use of random assignment; use of larger samples; nonexistence of pretreatment differences between experimental and control groups. From Table 39.2, it is apparent that more rigorous designs involving random assignment and larger samples yielded effect sizes that were as large as, if not larger than, effect sizes for other less rigorous designs. These findings confirm that the positive effects of phonics instruction on reading did not arise primarily from weakly designed studies.

One design feature, that involving the assessment of pretreatment differences, did yield one nonsignificant effect size, as shown in Table 39.2. There were five comparisons in which treatment and control groups differed on pretests, with the phonics group showing higher scores in all cases. The mean effect size on outcomes of these comparisons was not significantly greater than zero, indicating that the phonics groups did not outperform the control groups. Thus, contrary to what one might expect, this favoritism did not contribute at all to the positive findings detected for phonics instruction in other analyses.

Discussion.   Findings of the meta-analysis support the conclusion that systematic phonics instruction helps children learn to read more effectively than does nonsystematic or no phonics instruction. The impact of phonics instruction on reading was significantly greater in the early grades (kindergarten and first grades) when phonics was the method used to start children out than in the later grades (second through sixth grades) after children had made some progress in reading presumably with another method. These results support Chall's (1967) assertion that early instruction in systematic phonics is especially beneficial for learning to read. Although there was some thought that kindergartners might not be ready for phonics instruction (e.g., Chall, 1996; Stahl & Miller, 1989), findings did not support this. Effect sizes resulting from phonics instruction were similar in kindergarten and first grade.

Although systematic phonics instruction produced modest effects in older poor readers, it produced large effects in beginners at risk for developing reading problems. This underscores the special importance of teaching phonics early, especially in schools with large numbers of AR students who enter school with very little letter knowledge or phonemic awareness.

The conclusion that phonics instruction is less effective when introduced beyond first grade may be premature. Several mitigating factors may have reduced effect sizes in the studies examined. The majority of the comparisons involved either LA readers or students with RD. Remediating their reading problems may be especially difficult. Only a few comparisons were conducted with NA older students.

Systematic phonics instruction produced significant effects among children diagnosed as having RD. Small-to-moderate effect sizes were evident on reading-comprehension measures as well as on word-reading measures, indicating that systematic phonics is effective in remediating reading problems in children whose struggle is specific to reading and does not include more general cognitive difficulties.

In contrast, systematic phonics instruction did not benefit LA poor readers. Perhaps LA readers' difficulties arose from other sources such as lack of fluency or poor vocabulary or poor reading comprehension.

Comprehending text successfully requires being able to read most of the words. Phonics programs teach children how to apply the alphabetic system to read words. As a result, phonics instruction should improve text reading. Findings of the meta-analysis confirmed that among beginners and older students with RD, phonics instruction benefited reading comprehension.

Systematic phonics instruction was found to boost spelling skill in beginning readers, very likely because it helps them acquire the alphabetic knowledge they need to begin learning to spell. However, phonics instruction failed to boost spelling among readers above first grade. Interestingly, a similar finding was detected in the meta-analysis of PA instruction (see preceding discussion). It may be that because poor readers experience special difficulty learning to spell (Bruck, 1993), remediation requires specific instruction designed to teach spelling. This may necessitate teaching students about spelling patterns, morphographic roots, and affixes as well as GPCs, plus word memory strategies (Ehri, 1997).

Two types of systematic phonics instruction were examined. Results showed that both a synthetic approach and a larger-unit approach produced effects that were close to moderate in size. In the control conditions, programs taught phonics unsystematically or delayed the introduction of phonics until children had learned to read whole words. Results showed that systematic phonics produced better reading than every type of nonsystematic or nonphonics program. The fact that control groups received limited phonics instruction in some comparisons means that the effect sizes found here may underestimate the full contribution of phonics instruction to reading acquisition.

There has been much controversy about the relative effectiveness of phonics and whole-language programs for helping beginners learn to read (Adams, 1990; Goodman, 1993; Grundin, 1994; McKenna, Stahl, & Reinking, 1994; Stahl, 1999; Taylor, 1998; Weaver, 1998). Some of the studies in our database examined the effectiveness of enriching whole-language instruction with systematic phonics. Results were positive. These findings point to the value of integrating systematic phonics instruction into whole language approaches rather than abandoning whole language practices when beginning reading is taught.

One potential criticism of the analyses is that only published studies were considered. Because negative findings are less apt to be published, the concern is that the pool of studies was biased and unrepresentative of a population of mostly unpublished studies finding no effects. This is unlikely. In the phonics analysis, there were 43 comparisons showing effect sizes greater than or equal to $d = 0.20$. If these significant findings constituted the 5% expected by chance, there would have to be 860 unpublished comparisons showing effect sizes below 0.20. This is unlikely. In a meta-analysis of instructional studies involving students with LD, Swanson and Hoskyn (1998) found that effect sizes on a cognitive–language outcome were significantly larger for published studies than for unpublished studies. However, both effect sizes were statistically greater than zero, indicating that unpublished studies were not lacking in effects. For these reasons, this criticism is unfounded.

There is currently much interest in whether systematic phonics instruction is effective for children who are learning English as a second language (ESL). However, most of our studies either provided no information about this population or intentionally excluded these students from the sample. Results of only one study pertained to ESL students, that by Stuart (1999), who included 86% ESL children in her sample. The effect size she observed was large, indicating that phonics instruction helps ESL kindergartners learn to read more effectively than a whole-language approach does. More research is needed to replicate and extend this finding.

It is important to underscore the place of phonics in a beginning reading program. Systematic phonics instruction by itself does not help students acquire all the processes they need to become successful readers. Phonics needs to be combined with other forms of instruction to create a comprehensive reading program. Other sections of the NRP report (National Reading Panel, 2000) indicated the importance of instruction to teach fluency, vocabulary, and reading comprehension strategies. In a meta-analysis of instructional studies employed with students having LD, Swanson (2000) observed significantly larger effect sizes on reading outcomes when direct skills instruction was combined with comprehension strategy instruction than when each was administered separately to students. By emphasizing all of the processes that contribute to growth in reading, teachers will have the best chance of making every child a reader.

REFERENCES

Adams, M. J. (1990). *Beginning to read: Thinking and learning about print.* Cambridge, MA: MIT Press.

Anderson, R. C., Hiebert, E. F., Wilkinson, I. A. G., & Scott, J. (1985). *Becoming a nation of readers.* Champaign, IL: Center for the Study of Reading.

Aukerman, R. (1971). *Approaches to beginning reading.* New York: Wiley.

Aukerman, R. (1981). *The basal approach to reading.* New York: Wiley.

Aukerman, R. (1984). *Approaches to beginning reading* (2nd ed.). New York: Wiley.

Balmuth, M. (1982). *The roots of phonics: A historical introduction.* New York: McGraw-Hill.

Baron, J. (1977). Mechanisms for pronouncing printed words: Use and acquisition. In D. LaBerge & S. Samuels (Eds.), *Basic processes in reading: Perception and comprehension* (pp. 175–216). Hillsdale, NJ: Lawrence Erlbaum Associates.

Biemiller, A. (1970). The development of the use of graphic and contextual information as children learn to read. *Reading Research Quarterly, 6*, 75–96.

Blachman, B. (2000). Phonological awareness. In M. Kamil, P. Mosenthal, P. Pearson, & R. Barr (Eds.), *Handbook of reading research: Vol. III* (pp. 483–502). Mahwah, NJ: Lawrence Erlbaum Associates.

Blachman, B., Tangel, D., Ball, E., Black, R., & McGraw, D. (1999). Developing phonological awareness and word recognition skills: A two-year intervention with low-income, inner-city children. *Reading and Writing: An Interdisciplinary Journal, 11*, 239–273.

Bowey, J., & Hansen, J. (1994). The development of orthographic rimes as units of word recognition. *Journal of Experimental Child Psychology, 58*, 465–488.

Bradley, L. & Bryant, P. (1983). Categorizing sounds and learning to read: A causal connection. *Nature (London), 30*, 419–421.

Brown, I., & Felton, R. (1990). Effects of instruction on beginning reading skills in children at risk for reading disability. *Reading and Writing: An Interdisciplinary Journal, 2*, 223–241.

Bruck, M. (1993). Component spelling skills of college students with childhood diagnoses of dyslexia. *Learning Disability Quarterly, 16*, 171–184.

Bus, A., & IJzendoorn, M. (1999). Phonological awareness and early reading: A meta-analysis of experimental training studies. *Journal of Educational Psychology, 91*, 403–414.

Castle, J., Riach, J., & Nicholson, T. (1994). Getting off to a better start in reading and spelling: The effects of phonemic awareness instruction within a whole language program. *Journal of Educational Psychology, 86*, 350–359.

Chall, J. S. (1967). *Learning to read: The great debate* (1st ed.). New York: McGraw-Hill.

Chall, J. S. (1983). *Learning to read: The great debate* (2nd ed.). New York: McGraw-Hill.

Chall, J. (1996). *Stages of reading development*. Fort Worth, TX: Harcourt Brace.

Clay, M. (1968). A syntactic analysis of reading errors. *Journal of Verbal Learning and Verbal Behavior, 7*, 434–438.

Cohen, J. (1988). *Statistical power analysis for the behavior sciences* (2nd ed.). Hillsdale, NJ: Lawrence Erlbaum Associates.

Cooper, H. (1998). *Synthesizing research*. Thousand Oaks, CA: Sage.

Cunningham, A. (1990). Explicit vs. implicit instruction in phonemic awareness. *Journal of Experimental Child Psychology, 50*, 429–444.

Cunningham, P. (1976). Investigating a synthesized theory of mediated word identification. *Reading Research Quarterly, 11*, 127–143.

Dykstra, R. (1968). The effectiveness of code- and meaning-emphasis in beginning reading programs. *The Reading Teacher, 22*, 17–23.

Ehri, L. (1979). Linguistic insight: Threshold of reading acquisition. In T. G. Waller & G. E. MacKinnon (Eds.), *Reading research: Advances in theory and practice, Vol. 1* (pp. 63–114). New York: Academic Press.

Ehri, L. (1991). Development of the ability to read words. In R. Barr, M. Kamil, P. Mosenthal, & P. Pearson (Eds.), *Handbook of reading research, Vol. II* (pp. 383–417). New York: Longman.

Ehri, L. C. (1992). Reconceptualizing the development of sight word reading and its relationship to recoding. In P. Gough, L. Ehri, & R. Treiman (Eds.), *Reading acquisition* (pp. 107–143). Hillsdale, NJ: Lawrence Erlbaum Associates.

Ehri, L. (1994). Development of the ability to read words: Update. In R. Ruddell, M. Ruddell, & H. Singer (Eds.), *Theoretical models and processes of reading* (4th ed., pp. 323–358). Newark, DE: International Reading Association.

Ehri, L. C. (1997). Learning to read and learning to spell are one and the same, almost. In C. A. Perfetti & L. Rieben (Eds.), *Learning to spell: Research, theory, and practice across languages* (pp. 237–268). Mahwah, NJ: Lawrence Erlbaum Associates.

Ehri, L. C. (1998). Grapheme-phoneme knowledge is essential for learning to read words in English. In J. L. Metsala & L. C. Ehri (Eds.), *Word recognition in beginning literacy* (pp. 3–40). Mahwah, NJ: Lawrence Erlbaum Associates.

Ehri, L., Nunes, S., Stahl, S., & Willows, D. (2001). Systematic phonics instruction helps students learn to read: Evidence from the National Reading Panel's meta-analysis. *Review of Educational Research, 71*, 393–447.

Ehri, L., Nunes, S., Willows, D., Schuster, B., Yaghoub-Zadeh, Z., & Shanahan, T. (2001). Phonemic awareness instruction helps children learn to read: Evidence from the National Reading Panel's meta-analysis. *Reading Research Quarterly, 36*, 250–287.

Ehri, L. & Robbins, C. (1992). Beginners need some decoding skill to read words by analogy. *Reading Research Quarterly, 27*, 12–26.

Ehri, L. C., & Wilce, L. S. (1983). Development of word identification speed in skilled and less skilled beginning readers. *Journal of Educational Psychology, 75*, 3–18.

Gaskins, I. W., Downer, M. A., Anderson, R. C., Cunningham, P. M., Gaskins, R. W., Schommer, M., & the Teachers of Benchmark School (1988). A metacognitive approach to phonics: Using what you know to decode what you don't know. *Remedial and Special Education, 9*, 36–41.

Glushko, R. J. (1979). The organization and activation of orthographic knowledge in reading aloud. *Journal of Experimental Psychology: Human Perception and Performance, 5*, 674–691.

Glushko, R. J. (1981). Principles for pronouncing print: The psychology of phonography. In A. M. Lesgold & C. A. Perfetti (Eds.), *Interactive processes in reading* (pp. 61–84). Hillsdale, NJ: Lawrence Erlbaum Associates.

Goodman, K. (1976). Reading: A psycholinguistic guessing game. In H. Singer & R. Ruddell (Eds.), *Theoretical models and processes of reading* (2nd ed., pp. 497–508). Newark, DE: International Reading Association.

Goodman, K. S. (1993). *Phonics phacts*. Portsmouth, NH: Heinemann.

Goswami, U. (1986). Children's use of analogy in learning to read: A developmental study. *Journal of Experimental Child Psychology, 42*, 73–83.

Goswami, U. (1988). Orthographic analogies and reading development. *Quarterly Journal of Experimental Psychology, 40*, 239–268.

Goswami, U. (1990). A special link between rhyming skill and the use of orthographic analogies by beginning readers. *Journal of Child Psychology and Psychiatry, 31*, 301–311.

Gough, P., & Tunmer, W. (1986). Decoding, reading, and reading disability. *Remedial and Special Education, 7*, 6–10.

Gough, P., & Walsh, S. (1991). Chinese, Phoenicians, and the orthographic cipher of English. In S. Brady, & D. Shankweiler (Eds.), *Phonological processes in literacy: A tribute to Isabelle Y. Liberman*. Hillsdale, NJ: Lawrence Erlbaum Associates.

Griffith, P. (1991). Phonemic awareness helps first graders invent spellings and third graders remember correct spellings. *Journal of Reading Behavior, 23*, 215–233.

Grundin, H. (1994). If it ain't whole, it ain't language—or back to the basics of freedom and dignity. In F. Lehr & J. Osborn (Eds.), *Reading, language, and literacy* (pp. 77–88). Mahwah, NJ: Lawrence Erlbaum Associates.

Harris, T., & Hodges, R. (Eds.). (1995). *The literacy dictionary*. Newark, DE: International Reading Association.

Holdaway, D. (1979). *The foundations of literacy*. Sydney, Australia: Ashton-Scholastic.

Hoover, W., & Gough, P. (1990). The simple view of reading. *Reading and Writing: An Interdisciplinary Journal, 2*, 127–160.

Johnson, B. (1989). *DSTAT: Software for the meta-analytic review of research literatures*. Hillsdale, NJ: Lawrence Erlbaum Associates.

Juel, C. (1983). The development and use of mediated word identification. *Reading Research Quarterly, 18*, 306–327.

Juel, C. (1988). Learning to read and write: A longitudinal study of fifty-four children from first through fourth grade. *Journal of Educational Psychology, 80*, 437–447.

Juel, C., Griffith, P., & Gough, P. (1986). Acquisition of literacy: A longitudinal study of children in first and second grade. *Journal of Educational Psychology, 78*, 243–255.

LaBerge, D., & Samuels, J. (1974). Toward a theory of automatic information processing in reading. *Cognitive Psychology, 6*, 293–323.

Laxon, V., Coltheart, V., & Keating, C. (1988). Children find friendly words friendly too: Words with many orthographic neighbours are easier to read and spell. *British Journal of Educational Psychology, 58*, 103–119.

Leach, D., & Siddall, S. (1990). Parental involvement in the teaching of reading: A comparison of hearing reading, paired reading, pause, prompt, praise, and direct instruction methods. *British Journal of Educational Psychology, 60*, 349–355.

Liberman, I., Shankweiler, D., Fischer, F., & Carter, B. (1974). Explicit syllable and phoneme segmentation in the young child. *Journal of Experimental Child Psychology, 18*, 201–212.

Lovett, M., Lacerenza, L., Borden, S., Frijters, J., Steinbach, K., & DePalma, M. (2000). Components of effective remediation for developmental reading disabilities: combining phonological and strategy-based instruction to improve outcomes. *Journal of Educational Psychology, 92*, 263–283.

Mann, V. (1986). Phonological awareness: The role of reading experience. *Cognition, 24*, 65–92.

Marsh, G., Freidman, M., Welch, V., & Desberg, P. (1981). A cognitive-developmental theory of reading acquisition. In G. Mackinnon & T. G. Waller (Eds.), *Reading research: Advances in theory and practice, Vol. 3* (pp. 199–221). New York: Academic Press.

McKenna, Stahl, S., & Reinking, D. (1994). A critical commentary on research, politics, and whole language. *Journal of Reading Behavior, 26*, 211–233.

Morais, J., Alegria, J., & Content, A. (1987). The relationships between segmental analysis and alphabetic literacy: An interactive view. *Cahiers de Psychologie Cognitive, 7*, 415–438.

Morris, D., & Perney, J. (1984). Developmental spelling as a predictor of first grade reading achievement. *Elementary School Journal, 84*, 441–457.

National Reading Panel (2000). *Report of the National Reading Panel: Teaching children to read: An evidence-based assessment of the scientific research literature on reading and its implications for reading instruction: Reports of the subgroups*. Rockville, MD: National Institute of Child Health and Human Development Clearinghouse.

Perfetti, C. (1992). The representation problem in reading acquisition. In P. Gough, L. Ehri, & R. Treiman (Eds.), *Reading acquisition* (pp. 107–143). Hillsdale, NJ: Lawrence Erlbaum Associates.

Perfetti, C., & Hogaboam, T. (1975). The relationship between single word decoding and reading comprehension skill. *Journal of Educational Psychology, 67*, 461–469.

Rack, J., Snowling, M., & Olson, R. (1992). The nonword reading deficit in developmental dyslexia: A review. *Reading Research Quarterly, 27*, 29–53.

Read, C., Zhang, Y., Nie, H., & Ding, B. (1986). The ability to manipulate speech sounds depends on knowing alphabetic writing. *Cognition, 24*, 31–44.

Reitsma, P. (1983). Printed word learning in beginning readers. *Journal of Experimental Child Psychology, 75*, 321–339.

Routman, R. (1996). *Literacy at the crossroads*. Portsmouth, NH: Heinemann.

Schatschneider, C., Francis, D., Foorman, B., Fletcher, J., & Mehta, P. (1999). The dimensionality of phonological awareness: An application of item response theory. *Journal of Educational Psychology, 91*, 439–449.

Shankweiler, D., & Liberman, I. Y. (1972). Misreading: A search for causes. In J. F. Kavanaugh & I. G. Mattingly (Eds.), *Language by eye and by ear* (pp. 293–317). Cambridge, MA: MIT Press.

Share, D. (1999). Phonological recoding and orthographic learning: A direct test of the self-teaching hypothesis. *Journal of Experimental Child Psychology, 72*, 95–129.

Share, D., Jorm, A., Maclean, R., & Matthews, R. (1984). Sources of individual diferences in reading achievement. *Journal of Educational Psychology, 76*, 1309–1324.

Snow, C., Burns, M., & Griffin, P. (Eds.), (1998). *Preventing reading difficulties in young children*. Washington DC: National Academy Press.

Stahl, S. (1999). Why innovations come and go: The case of whole language. *Educational Researcher, 28*, 13.

Stahl, S., Duffy-Hester, A., & Stahl, K. (1998). Everything you wanted to know about phonics (But were afraid to ask). *Reading Research Quarterly, 35*, 338–355.

Stahl, S. A., & Miller, P. D. (1989). Whole language and language experience approaches for beginning reading: A quantitative research synthesis. *Review of Educational Research, 59*, 87–116.

Stahl, S., & Murray, B. (1994). Defining phonological awareness and its relationship to early reading. *Journal of Educational Psychology, 86*, 221–234.

Stanovich, K. (1980). Toward an interactive-compensatory model of individual differences in the development of reading fluency. *Reading Research Quarterly, 16*, 32–71.

Stuart, M. (1999). Getting ready for reading: Early phoneme awareness and phonics teaching improves rading and spelling in inner-city second language learners. *British Journal of Educational Psychology, 69*, 587–605.

Swanson, H. L. (2000). What instruction works for students with learning disabilities? Summarizing the results from a meta-analysis of intervention studies. In R. Gersten, E. Schiller, & S. Vaughn (Eds.), *Contemporary special education research: Syntheses of the knowledge base on critical instructional issues* (pp. 1–30). Mahwah, NJ: Lawrence Erlbaum Associates.

Swanson, H. L., & Hoskyn, M. (1998). Experimental intervention research on students with learning disabilities: A meta-analysis of treatment outcomes. *Review of Educational Research, 68*, 277–321.

Tangel, D., & Blachman, B. (1995). Effect of phoneme awareness instruction on the invented spelling of first-grade children: A one-year follow-up. *Journal of Reading Behavior, 27*, 153–185.

Taylor, D. (1998). *Beginning to read & the spin doctors of science: The political campaign to change America's mind about how children learn to read*. Urbana, IL: National Council of Teachers of English.

Torgesen, J., Wagner, R., Rashotte, C., Rose, E., Lindamood, P., Conway, T., & Garvan, C. (1999). Preventing reading failure in young children with phonological processing disabilities: Group and individual responses to instruction. *Journal of Educational Psychology, 91*, 579–593.

Treiman, R., Goswami, U., & Bruck, M. (1990). Not all nonwords are alike: Implications for reading development and theory. *Memory and Cognition, 18*, 559–567.

Troia, G. (1999). Phonological awareness intervention research: A critical review of the experimental methodology. *Reading Research Quarterly, 34*, 28–52.

Tunmer, W., & Chapman, J. (1998). Language prediction skill, phonological recoding ability, and beginning reading. In C. Hulme & R. Joshi (Eds.), *Reading and spelling: Development and disorders* (pp. 33–67). Mahwah, NJ: Lawrence Erlbaum Associates.

Tunmer, W., & Chapman, J. (2001, November). *The relation of metalinguistic abilities, phonological recoding skill, and the use of context to beginning reading development: A longitudinal study*. Paper presented at the NATO Advanced Study Institute on Literacy Acquisition, Assessment and Intervention, Il Ciocco, Tuscany Italy.

Tunmer, W., & Hoover, W. (1993). Phonological recoding skill and beginning reading. *Reading and Writing: An Interdisciplinary Journal, 5*, 161–179.

Venezky, R. (1970). *The structure of English orthography*. The Hague: Mouton.

Venezky, R. (1999). *The American way of spelling*. New York: Guilford.

Wagner, R., & Torgesen, J. (1987). The nature of phonological processing and its causal role in the acquisition of reading skills. *Psychological Bulletin, 101*, 192–212.

Weber, R. (1970). A linguistic analysis of first-grade reading errors. *Reading Research Quarterly, 5*, 427–451.

Weaver, C. (1998). Experimental research: On phonemic awareness and on whole language. In C. Weaver (Ed.), *Reconsidering a balanced approach to reading* (pp. 321–371). Urbana, IL:

APPENDIX A: STUDIES IN THE META-ANALYSIS OF PHONEMIC AWARENESS INSTRUCTION

Ball, E., & Blachman, B. (1991). Does phoneme awareness training in kindergarten make a difference in early word recognition and developmental spelling? *Reading Research Quarterly, 26*, 49–66.

Barker, T., & Torgesen, J. (1995). An evaluation of computer–assisted instruction in phonological awareness with below average readers. *Journal of Educational Computing Research, 13*, 89–103.

Bentin, S. & Leshem, H. (1993). On the interaction between phonological awareness and reading acquisition: It's a two–way street. *Annals of Dyslexia, 43*, 125–148.

Blachman, B., Ball, E., Black, R., & Tangel, D. (1994). Kindergarten teachers develop phoneme awareness in low–income, inner–city classrooms: Does it make a difference? *Reading and Writing: An Interdisciplinary Journal, 6*, 1–18.

Bradley, L., & Bryant, P. (1983). Categorizing sounds and learning to read: A causal connection. *Nature (London), 301*, 419–421.

Bradley, L., & Bryant, P. (1985). *Rhyme and reason in reading and spelling.* International Academy for Research in Learning Disabilities, Monograph Series, *1*, 75–95. Ann Arbor, MI: University of Michigan Press. (1985 publication is a more complete report of 1983 publication.)

Brady, S., Fowler, A., Stone, B., & Winbury, N. (1994). Training phonological awareness: A study with inner–city kindergarten children. *Annals of Dyslexia, 44*, 26–59.

Brennan, F., & Ireson, J. (1997). Training phonological awareness: A study to evaluate the effects of a program of metalinguistic games in kindergarten. *Reading and Writing: An Interdisciplinary Journal, 9*, 241–263.

Bus, A. (1986). Preparatory reading instruction in kindergarten: Some comparative research into methods of auditory and auditory–visual training of phonemic analysis and blending. *Perceptual and Motor Skills, 62*, 11–24.

Byrne, B., & Fielding–Barnsley, R. (1991). Evaluation of a program to teach phonemic awareness to young children. *Journal of Educational Psychology, 83*, 451–455.

Byrne, B., & Fielding–Barnsley, R. (1993). Evaluation of a program to teach phonemic awareness to young children: A 1-year follow-up. *Journal of Educational Psychology, 85*, 104–111. [First follow-up to Byrne & Fielding-Barnsley, 1991]

Byrne, B., & Fielding–Barnsley, R. (1995). Evaluation of a program to teach phonemic awareness to young children: A 2- and 3- year follow-up and a new preschool trial. *Journal of Educational Psychology, 87*, 488–503. [Second follow-up to Byrne & Fielding-Barnsley, 1991]

Castle, J. M., Riach, J., & Nicholson, T. (1994). Getting off to a better start in reading and spelling: The effects of phonemic awareness instruction within a whole language program. *Journal of Educational Psychology, 86*, 350–359. [Experiment 2]

Cunningham, A. (1990). Explicit versus implicit instruction in phonemic awareness. *Journal of Experimental Child Psychology, 50*, 429–444.

Davidson, M., & Jenkins, J. (1994). Effects of phonemic processes on word reading and spelling. *Journal of Educational Research, 87*, 148–157.

Defior, S., & Tudela, P. (1994). Effect of phonological training on reading and writing acquisition. *Reading and Writing: An Interdisciplinary Journal, 6*, 299–320.

Ehri, L., & Wilce, L. (1987). Does learning to spell help beginners learn to read words? *Reading Research Quarterly, 22*, 48–65.

Farmer, A., Nixon, M., & White, R. (1976). Sound blending and learning to read: An experimental investigation. *British Journal of Educational Psychology, 46*, 155–163.

Fox, B., & Routh, D. (1976). Phonemic analysis and synthesis as word–attack skills. *Journal of Educational Psychology, 68*, 70–74.

Fox, B., & Routh, D. (1984). Phonemic analysis and synthesis as word attack skills: Revisited. *Journal of Educational Psychology, 76*, 1059–1064.

Gross, J., & Garnett, J. (1994). Preventing reading difficulties: Rhyme and alliteration in the real world. *Educational Psychology in Practice, 9*, 235–240.

Haddock, M. (1976). Effects of an auditory and an auditory-visual method of blending instruction on the ability of prereaders to decode synthetic words. *Journal of Educational Psychology, 68*, 825–831.

Hatcher, P., Hulme, C., & Ellis, A. (1994). Ameliorating early reading failure by integrating the teaching of reading and phonological skills: The phonological linkage hypothesis. *Child Development, 65*, 41–57.

Hohn, W., & Ehri, L. (1983). Do alphabet letters help prereaders acquire phonemic segmentation skill? *Journal of Educational Psychology, 75*, 752–762.

Hurford, D., Johnston, M., Nepote, P., Hampton, S., Moore, S., Neal, J., Mueller, A., McGeorge, K., Huff, L., Awad, A., Tatro, C., Juliano, C., & Huffman, D. (1994). Early identification and remediation of phonological-processing deficits in first-grade children at risk for reading disabilities. *Journal of Learning Disabilities, 27*, 647–659.

Iversen, S., & Tunmer, W. (1993). Phonological processing skills and the Reading Recovery Program. *Journal of Educational Psychology, 85*, 112–126.

Kennedy, K., & Backman, J. (1993). Effectiveness of the Lindamood Auditory Discrimination in depth program with students with learning disabilities. *Learning Disabilities Research and Practice, 8*, 253–259.

Korkman, M., & Peltomaa, A. (1993). Preventive treatment of dyslexia by a preschool training program for children with language impairments. *Journal of Clinical Child Psychology, 22*, 277–287.

Kozminsky, L., & Kozminsky, E. (1995). The effects of early phonological awareness training on reading success. *Learning and Instruction, 5*, 187–201.

Lie, A. (1991). Effects of a training program for stimulating skills in word analysis in first-grade children. *Reading Research Quarterly, 26*, 234–250.

Lovett, M., Barron, R., Forbes, J., Cuksts, B., & Steinbach, K. (1994). Computer speech-based training of literacy skills in neurologically impaired children: A controlled evaluation. *Brain and Language, 47*, 117–154.

Lundberg, I., Frost, J., & Petersen, O. (1988). Effects of an extensive program for stimulating phonological awareness in preschool children. *Reading Research Quarterly, 23*, 263–284.

McGuiness, D., McGuiness, C., & Donohue, J. (1995). Phonological training and the alphabet principle: Evidence for reciprocal causality. *Reading Research Quarterly, 30*, 830–852.

Murray, B. (1998). Gaining alphabetic insight: Is phoneme manipulation skill or identity knowledge causal? *Journal of Educational Psychology, 90*, 461–475.

O'Connor, R., & Jenkins, J. (1995). Improving the generalization of sound/symbol knowledge: Teaching spelling to kindergarten children with disabilities. *The Journal of Special Education, 29*, 255–275.

O'Connor, R., Jenkins, J., & Slocum, T. (1995). Transfer among phonological tasks in kindergarten: Essential instructional content. *Journal of Educational Psychology, 87*, 202–217.

O'Connor, R., Notari-Syverson, A., & Vadasy, P. (1996). Ladders to literacy: The effects of teacher-led phonological activities for kindergarten children with and without disabilities. *Exceptional Children, 63*, 117–130.

O'Connor, R., Notari-Syverson, A., & Vadasy, P. (1998). First-grade effects of teacher-led phonological activities in kindergarten for children with mild disabilities: A follow-up study. *Learning Disabilities Research and Practice, 13*, 43–52. [Follow-up to O'Connor et al., 1996]

Olofsson, A., & Lundberg, I. (1983). Can phonemic awareness be trained in kindergarten? *Scandinavian Journal of Psychology, 24*, 35–44.

Olofsson, A., & Lundberg, I. (1985). Evaluation of long term effects of phonemic awareness training in kindergarten: Illustrations of some methodological problems in evaluation research. *Scandinavian Journal of Psychology, 26*, 21–34. [Follow-up to Olofsson & Lundberg, 1983]

Reitsma, P., & Wesseling, R. (1998). Effects of computer-assisted training of blending skills in kindergartners. *Scientific Studies of Reading, 2*, 301–320.

Sanchez, E., & Rueda, M. (1991). Segmental awareness and dyslexia: Is it possible to learn to segment well and yet continue to read and write poorly? *Reading and Writing: An Interdisciplinary Journal, 3*, 11–18.

Schneider, W., Kuspert, P., Roth, E., Vise, M., & Marx, H. (1997). Short- and long-term effects of training phonological awareness in kindergarten: Evidence from two German studies. *Journal of Experimental Child Psychology, 66*, 311–340.

Solity, J. (1996). Phonological awareness: Learning disabilities revisited? *Educational & Child Psychology, 13*, 103–113.

Tangel, D., & Blachman, B. (1992). Effect of phoneme awareness instruction on kindergarten children's invented spelling. *Journal of Reading Behavior, 24*, 233–261.

Torgesen, J., Morgan, S., & Davis, C. (1992). Effects of two types of phonological awareness training on word learning in kindergarten children. *Journal of Educational Psychology, 84*, 364–370.

Treiman, R., & Baron, J. (1983). Phonemic-analysis training helps children benefit from spelling sound rules. *Memory and Cognition, 11*, 382–389.

Uhry, J., & Shepherd, M. (1993). Segmentation/spelling instruction as part of a first-grade reading program: Effects on several measures of reading. *Reading Research Quarterly, 28*, 218–233.

Vadasy, P., Jenkins, J., Antil, L., Wayne, S., & O'Connor, R. (1997). Community-based early reading intervention for at-risk first graders. *Learning Disabilities Research and Practice, 12*, 29–39.

Vadasy, P., Jenkins, J., Antil, L., Wayne, S., & O'Connor, R. (1997). The effectiveness of one-to-one tutoring by community tutors for at-risk beginning readers. *Learning Disability Quarterly, 20*, 126–139.

Vellutino, F., & Scanlon, D. (1987). Phonological coding, phonological awareness, and reading ability: Evidence from a longitudinal and experimental study. *Merrill-Palmer Quarterly, 33*, 321–363.

Warrick, N., Rubin, H., & Rowe-Walsh, S. (1993). Phoneme awareness in language-delayed children: Comparative studies and intervention. *Annals of Dyslexia, 43*, 153–173.

Weiner, S. (1994). Effects of phonemic awareness training on low- and middle-achieving first graders' phonemic awareness and reading ability. *Journal of Reading Behavior, 26*, 277–300.

Williams, J. (1980). Teaching decoding with an emphasis on phoneme analysis and phoneme blending. *Journal of Educational Psychology, 72*, 1–15.

Wilson, J., & Frederickson, N. (1995). Phonological awareness training: An evaluation. *Educational & Child Psychology, 12*, 68–79.

Wise, B., Ring, J., & Olson, R. (1999). Training phonological awareness with and without explicit attention to articulation. *Journal of Experimental Child Psychology, 72*, 271–304.

Wise, B., Ring, J., & Olson, R. (2000). Individual differences in gains from computer-assisted remedial reading. *Journal of Experimental Child Psychology, 77*, 197–235.

APPENDIX B: STUDIES IN THE META-ANALYSIS OF SYSTEMATIC PHONICS INSTRUCTION

Blachman, B., Tangel, D., Ball, E., Black, R., & McGraw, D. (1999). Developing phonological awareness and word recognition skills: A two-year intervention with low-income, inner-city children. *Reading and Writing: An Interdisciplinary Journal, 11*, 239–273.

Bond, C., Ross, S., Smith, L., & Nunnery, J. (1995–1996). The effects of the sing, spell, read, and write program on reading achievment of beginning readers. *Reading Research and Instruction, 35*, 122–141.

Brown, I., & Felton, R. (1990). Effects of instruction on beginning reading skills in children at risk for reading disability. *Reading and Writing: An Interdisciplinary Journal, 2*, 223–241.

Eldredge, L. (1991). An experiment with a modified whole language approach in first-grade classrooms. *Reading Research and Instruction, 30*, 21–38.

Evans, M., & Carr, T. (1985). Cognitive abilities, conditions of learning, and the early development of reading skill. *Reading Research Quarterly, 20*, 327–350.

Foorman, B., Francis, D., Fletcher, J., & Schatschneider, C. (1998). The role of instruction in learning to read: Preventing reading failure in at-risk children. *Journal of Educational Psychology, 90*, 37–55.

Foorman, B., Francis, D., Novy, D., & Liberman, D. (1991). How letter-sound instruction mediates progress in first-grade reading and spelling. *Journal of Educational Psychology, 83*, 456–469.

Foorman, B., Francis, D., Winikates, D., Mehta, P., Schatschneider, C., & Fletcher, J. (1997). Early interventions for children with reading disabilities. *Scientific Studies of Reading, 1*, 255–276.

Freppon, P. (1991). Children's concepts of the nature and purpose of reading in different instructional settings. *Journal of Reading Behavior, 23*, 139–163.

Fulwiler, G., & Groff, P. (1980). The effectiveness of intensive phonics. *Reading Horizons, 21*, 50–54.

Gersten, R., Darch, C., & Gleason, M. (1988). Effectiveness of a direct instruction academic kindergarten for low-income students. *The Elementary School Journal, 89*, 227–240.

Gittelman, R., & Feingold, I. (1983). Children with reading disorders—I. Efficacy of reading remediation. *Journal of Child Psychology and Psychiatry and Allied Disciplines, 24*, 167–191.

Greaney, K., Tunmer, W., & Chapman, J. (1997). Effects of rime-based orthographic analogy training on the word recognition skills of children with reading disability. *Journal of Educational Psychology, 89*, 645–651.

Griffith, P., Klesius, J., & Kromrey, J. (1992). The effect of phonemic awareness on the literacy development of first grade children in a traditional or a whole language classroom. *Journal of Research in Childhood Education, 6*, 85–92.

Haskell, D., Foorman, B., & Swank, P. (1992). Effects of three orthographic/phonological units on first-grade reading. *Remedial and Special Education, 13*, 40–49.

Klesius, J., Griffith, P., & Zielonka, P. (1991). A whole language and traditional instruction comparison: Overall effectiveness and development of the alphabetic principle. *Reading Research and Instruction, 30*, 47–61.

Leach, D., & Siddall, S. (1990). Parental involvement in the teaching of reading: A comparison of hearing reading, paired reading, pause, prompt, praise, and direct instruction methods. *British Journal of Educational Psychology, 60*, 349–355.

Leinhardt, G., & Engel, M. (1981). An iterative evaluation of NRS: Ripples in a pond. *Evaluation Review, 5*, 579–601.

Lovett, R., Ransby, M., Hardwick, N., Johns, M., & Donaldson, S. (1989). Can dyslexia be treated? Treatment-specific and generalized treatment effects in dyslexic children's reponse to remediation. *Brain and Language, 37*, 90–121.

Lovett, M., & Steinbach, K. (1997). The effectiveness of remedial programs for reading disabled children of different ages: Does the benefit decrease for older children? *Learning Disability Quarterly, 20*, 189–210.

Lovett, M., Warren-Chaplin, P., Ransby, M., & Borden, S. (1990). Training the word recognition skills of reading disabled children: Treatment and transfer effects. *Journal of Educational Psychology, 82*, 769–780.

Lovett, M., Lacerenza, L., Borden, S., Frijters, J., Steinbach, K., & DePalma, M. (2000). Components of effective remediation for developmental reading disabilities: combining phonological and strategy-based instruction to improve outcomes. *Journal of Educational Psychology, 92*, 263–283.

Lum, T., & Morton, L. (1984). Direct instruction in spelling increases gain in spelling and reading skills. *Special Education in Canada, 58*, 41–45.

Mantzicopoulos, P., Morrison, D., Stone, E., & Setrakian, W. (1992). Use of the SEARCH/TEACH tutoring approach with middle-class students at risk for reading failure. *Elementary School Journal, 92*, 573–586.

Marston, D., Deno, S., Kim, D., Diment, K., & Rogers, D. (1995). Comparison of reading intervention approaches for students with mild disabilities. *Exceptional Children, 62*, 20–37.

Martinussen, R., & Kirby, J. (1998). Instruction in successive and phonological processing to improve the reading acquisition of at-risk kindergarten children. *Developmental Disabilities Bulletin, 26*, 19–39.

Oakland, T., Black, J., Stanford, G., Nussbaum, N., & Balise, R. (1998). An evaluation of the dyslexia training program: A multisensory method for promoting reading in students with reading disabilities. *Journal of Learning Disabilities, 31*, 140–147.

Santa, C., & Hoien, T. (1999). An assessment of early steps: A program for early intervention of reading problems. *Reading Research Quarterly, 34*, 54–79.

Silberberg, N., Iversen, I., & Goins, J. (1973). Which remedial reading method works best? *Journal of Learning Disabilities, 6*, 18–27.

Snider, V. (1990). Direct instruction reading with average first-graders. *Reading Improvement, 27*, 143–148.

Stuart, M. (1999). Getting ready for reading: Early phoneme awareness and phonics teaching improves rading and spelling in inner-city second language learners. *British Journal of Educational Psychology, 69*, 587–605.

Torgesen, J., Wagner, R., Rashotte, C., Rose, E., Lindamood, P., Conway, T., & Garvan, C. (1999). Preventing reading failure in young children with phonological processing disabilities: Group and individual responses to instruction. *Journal of Educational Psychology, 91*, 579–593.

Traweek, K., & Berninger, V. (1997). Comparisons of beginning literacy programs: Alternative paths to the same learning outcome. *Learning Disability Quarterly, 20*, 160–168.

Tunmer, W., & Hoover, W. (1993). Phonological recoding skill and beginning reading. *Reading and Writing: An Interdisciplinary Journal, 5*, 161–179.

Umbach, B., Darch, C., & Halpin, G. (1989). Teaching reading to low performing first graders in rural schools: A comparison of two instructional approaches. *Journal of Instructional Psychology, 16*, 23–30.

Vandervelden, M., & Siegel, L. (1997). Teaching phonological processing skills in early literacy: A developmental approach. *Learning Disability Quarterly, 20*, 63–81.

Vickery, K., Reynolds, V., & Cochran, S. (1987). Multisensory teaching approach for reading, spelling, and handwriting, Orton-Gillingham based curriculum, in a public school setting. *Annals of Dyslexia, 37*, 189–200.

Wilson, K., & Norman, C. (1998). Differences in word recognition based on approach to reading instruction. *Alberta Journal of Educational Research, 44*, 221–230.

40

The Effectiveness of Synthetic Phonics Teaching in Developing Reading and Spelling Skills in English-Speaking Boys and Girls

Rhona S. Johnston
University of Hull

Joyce E. Watson
University of St. Andrews

In three studies we have focussed on examining the effectiveness of different types of phonics teaching methods, that is, synthetic and analytic phonics. The outcome of three studies reported in this chapter leads to the conclusion that synthetic phonics can be used to teach English-speaking children to learn to read at the start of schooling, and its advantages are not just due to the accelerated letter–sound learning that is typical of this approach. Synthetic phonics develops phonemic awareness, and gives rise to word reading, reading comprehension, and spelling skills significantly above children's chronological ages. Furthermore, it is a method of teaching reading that is particularly beneficial for boys. Potential explanations for the superior reading performance of boys over that of girls are presented.

INTRODUCTION

For many years, research has been carried out to examine what skills are associated with learning to read in order to gain insights into how to accelerate literacy attainment. We know that measures of preschool phonological awareness ability correlate with later reading skill (Bradley & Bryant, 1983; Lundberg, Olofsson, & Wall, 1980; Share, Jorm, Maclean, & Matthews, 1984; Stanovich, Cunningham, & Cramer, 1984, Stuart & Coltheart, 1988). However, phonological awareness includes both rhyme and phoneme awareness; we know that pre-readers have limited ability to detect phonemes in spoken words, this being a skill that develops largely through learning to read in an alphabetic language (e.g., Morais, Bertelson, Cary, & Alegria, 1986; Morais, Cary, Alegria, & Bertelson, 1979). One skill that pre-readers are rather better at, however, is awareness of rhyme (Goswami & Bryant, 1990). It has been proposed that children will make better progress in learning to read if their phonological awareness skills, especially rhyme skills, are well developed before they start a reading programme (Fraser, 1997; Goswami, 1999; Maclean, Bryant, & Bradley, 1987).

Some studies have been successful in improving later reading ability by solely training phonological skills, such as rhyme and phoneme awareness, either before school entry

(Lundberg, Frost, & Petersen, 1988) or concurrently with the school's initial reading pro-gramme (Cunningham, 1990; Lie, 1991). However, other studies suggest that children benefit from phonological awareness training only if they are shown how the sounds in the words are represented by letters of the alphabet (Ball & Blachman, 1991; Bradley & Bryant, 1983; Byrne & Fielding Barnsley, 1989, 1991; Fox & Routh,1984; Hatcher, Hulme, & Ellis, 1994, Williams, 1980).

Share (1995) reviews evidence that shows that learning letter–sound correspondences is very important for learning to read, and concludes that phonemic awareness and letter–sound knowledge are both prerequisites for acquiring this skill. He also contrasts the effectiveness of phonemic synthesis and phonemic analysis training. He concludes that reading benefits when phonemic synthesis is trained in conjunction with letter–sound correspondences (Fox & Routh, 1984; Haddock, 1976; Treiman & Baron, 1983; Vellutino & Scanlon, 1987), but that it is not generally benefitted by training in phonemic analysis, even when it is accompanied by letter sound training (Byrne & Fielding-Barnsley, 1989, 1991; Fox & Routh, 1984; Treiman & Baron, 1983). He argues that phonemic analysis may be more important for learning to spell. He concludes, however, that both phonemic synthesis and analysis need to be taught in the context of learning letter sounds. In a meta-analysis of 52 studies, Ehri et al. (2001) similarly concluded that, although phonological awareness training on its own does enhance reading skills, it should not be taught in isolation as it is more effective when letter–sound correspondences and the applications to reading and writing are also taught.

Traditionally phonics, which teaches children the importance of letter–sound correspon-dences in pronouncing unfamiliar words, has been taught starting at the phoneme level. How-ever, reading tuition in the UK has been greatly influenced by Goswami's (1994a) view that reading tuition should build on the phonological awareness skills children have at the start of schooling. She proposes that those who are weak in this area should be given rhyme and alliteration training before starting reading instruction, as these are skills that develop before phoneme awareness. Children can then be shown how to read by making analogies between known sight words and unfamiliar words, focussing on common rimes and onsets. According to this view, as young children have so little awareness of phonemes, except at the beginning of spoken words, letter–sound correspondences should only be taught in the context of onsets (Goswami, 1995). Furthermore, Goswami (1994b) argues that children should not learn by a method in which they are taught initially about the spelling–sound correspondences for all the phonemes in spoken words, as this poses unnecessary difficulties for them.

In our studies we have focussed on examining the effectiveness of different types of phonics teaching methods, that is, synthetic and analytic phonics. In both forms children are taught about the importance of letter–sound correspondences for pronouncing words. However, there are substantial differences between the two methods. In synthetic phonics, children are taught to read right at the start by synthesising the pronunciation of an unfamiliar word by sounding and blending the letters. By contrast, in analytic phonics whole words are presented and pronounced by the teacher, and the children's attention is only subsequently drawn to the information given by letter–sound correspondences.

In the early stages of an analytic phonics scheme, children are generally taught all of the letter sounds in the initial position of words, consonants first, and then vowels, at the pace of one letter sound a week. Each letter is shown at the beginning of a list of words, for example, car, cat, candle, cake, castle, and caterpillar. Typically in Scotland it would not be until the third term of the first year at school that children would be made aware of the importance of letter sound correspondences in all positions of words. At this stage children's attention is drawn to middle sounds, for example, cat, bag, rag, and final sounds of words, for examples, nap, cup, pip, as well as initial sounds. Sounding and blending might also be introduced at this point. In the second and third year at school, children learn more complex structures through lists of similarly spelt words; that is, words with initial consonant blends, for example, 'bl-', 'cr-', 'sp-'; final consonant blends, for example, '-nt', '-ng', '-st'; vowel and consonant digraphs, for example, 'ee', 'oo', 'ch', 'sh'; and silent 'e', for example, 'bake', 'make', 'cube', 'tube'.

Synthetic phonics is typically taught very rapidly. Children learn a small group of letter sounds in the space of a few days and are then shown how they can be combined and recombined to form different words. For example, the letter sounds 'a', 's', 't', 'i', 'p', and 'n' would be taught, and the teacher would generate words on the blackboard such as 'sat', 'tin', 'pat', 'tap', and so forth. The children are not told the pronunciation of the word formed from the letters; they sound each letter in turn and then synthesise the sounds together in order to find the pronunciation of the word for themselves. All of the letter–sound correspondences, including the consonant and vowel digraphs, can be taught in the space of a few months. This approach is widely used in Germany and Austria for the initial teaching of reading, but it is uncommon in Britain.

STUDY 1

We have carried out a number of studies comparing different types of phonics teaching (see Johnston & Watson, 2004, and Watson & Johnston, 1998, for further details). In one study of initial readers, all of the children had just started school at around the age of 5 years and were being taught by the classroom analytic phonics programme advocated by their local education authority, learning one letter sound a week at the beginning of words. We extracted the children from their classrooms for extra tuition in addition to their normal reading programmes. They were taught in groups of four to five, starting 6 weeks after entering school. The children in the three experimental groups were drawn equally from four classes, thereby controlling for minor differences in the implementation of the analytic phonics method used by the classroom teachers. The intervention lasted for 10 weeks, with two 15-min training lessons a week and 19 sessions in all. The same print vocabulary was used for all three programmes. One group was told how these words were pronounced, but they were not taught letter sounds in the training programme, and their attention was not drawn to letter sounds within the words (no-letter training group). A second group learnt letter sounds at the rate of two a week, and their attention was drawn to letter sounds in the initial position of words (accelerated letter learning group). The third group learnt letter sounds at the rate of two a week, and had their attention drawn to letter sounds in all positions of words (synthetic phonics group).

Ninety-two children participated, 46 boys and 46 girls. There were 29 children in the no-letter training group, 33 in the accelerated letter training group, and 30 in the synthetic phonics group. The participants were matched into three groups, on chronological age, sex, vocabulary knowledge (British Picture Vocabulary Scale [BPVS]; Dunn & Dunn, 1982), letter knowledge, emergent reading (Clay Ready to Read; Clay, 1979), phoneme segmentation (Yopp-Singer Test; Yopp, 1988) and rhyme generation ability. See Table 40.1 for means and standard deviations. No differences were found between the groups on these measures. These tasks were administered again at the first post-test, straight after the end of the programme, with the addition of the British Ability Scales (BAS) Word Reading Test (Elliott, Murray, & Pearson, 1977). At the second post-test, 9 months after the end of the intervention, the Schonell Spelling Test (Schonell & Schonell, 1952) and a nonword-naming task were additionally administered. See Table 40.2 for means and standard deviations.

At the first post-test, at the end of the programme, the groups were found to differ on single-word-reading ability (BAS Word Reading Test; Elliott et al., 1977). The synthetic phonics group performed better than the accelerated letter learning and no-letter groups, who did not differ from each other. On the test of emergent reading (Clay, 1979) the groups also differed,

TABLE 40.1

Mean Chronological Age, IQ (BPVS), Reading Age (British Ability Scales), Emergent Reading
(Clay Ready to Read Test), Letter–Sound Knowledge, Phoneme Segmentation (Yopp–Singer
Test), and Rhyme Skills (Standard Deviations in Parentheses), Pre-test, Study 1

Research Group	Age (Years)	BPVS (Standardised Scores)	Emergent Reading (%)	Letter Knowledge (%)	Phonemic Segmentation (%)	Rhyme Skills (%)
Pretest						
No-letter controls,	5.0	94.3	3.7	8.0	2.7	30.5
n = 29	(0.3)	(12.5)	(16.2)	(18.6)	(11.4)	(37.6)
Accelerated letter	5.0	94.6	1.8	5.8	1.8	26.5
controls, n = 33	(0.3)	(15.2)	(10.4)	(16.9)	(10.3)	(38.5)
Synthetic	5.0	95.5	3.6	8.6	1.7	20.6
phonics, n = 30	(0.3)	(14.4)	(13.4)	(21.2)	(9.1)	(27.2)

$F(2,89) = 9.1$, $p < .001$. Newman–Keuls tests showed that the synthetic phonics group read more words correctly than the accelerated letter learning and no-letter groups, who did not differ from each other. The groups also differed in letter knowledge, $F(2,89) = 7.7$, $p < .001$. Newman–Keuls tests showed that the synthetic phonics group read more letters correctly than the accelerated letter learning and no-letter groups, who did not differ from each other. On the Yopp–Singer Test (Yopp, 1988), the difference among groups was not quite significant, $F(2, 89) = 3.0$, $p = .055$. On the test of rhyme production ability, there was also no significant difference among the groups.

The second post-test measures were taken at the start of the second year at school, 9 months after completion of the intervention programme (see Table 40.2 for means and standard deviations). By this time all of the children had learnt about letter sounds in all positions of words in their normal classroom programmes. The groups differed in single-word-reading ability (BAS Word Reading Test; Elliott et al., 1977), $F(2,83) = 5.8$, $p < .004$. Newman–Keuls tests showed that the synthetic phonics group performed better than the accelerated letter learning and no-letter groups, who did not differ from each other. On the emergent reading test (Clay, 1979) the groups also differed, $F(2,83) = 6.9$, $p < .002$. Newman–Keuls tests showed the synthetic phonics group read more words correctly than the accelerated letter learning and no-letter groups, who did not differ from each other. The groups differed in letter-sound knowledge, $F(2, 83) = 3.6$, $p < .05$. Newman–Keuls tests showed that the synthetic phonics group had better letter-sound knowledge than the other two groups, who did not differ from each other. On nonword reading, a main effect of groups was found, $F(2, 83) = 16.5$, $p < .001$. Newman–Keuls tests showed the synthetic phonics group read more nonwords correctly than the accelerated letter learning and no-letter groups, there being no difference between the latter two groups. On the spelling test, there was a main effect of groups, $F(2,83) = 11.1$, $p < .001$. Newman–Keuls tests showed that the synthetic phonics group spelt more words correctly than the accelerated letter learning and no-letter groups, who did not differ from each other. On the Yopp–Singer (Yopp, 1988) phoneme segmentation task, the groups also differed, $F(2, 83) = 13.3$, $p < .000$. Newman–Keuls tests showed that the synthetic phonics group performed better than the accelerated letter learning and no-letter groups, the latter two groups not differing from each other. On the test of rhyme production ability, there was a "between-groups" difference, $F(2,83) = 3.6$, $p < .05$. Newman–Keuls tests showed that the synthetic phonics group performed better than the accelerated letter group, but not better than the no-letter group, and the latter two groups did not differ from each other.

TABLE 40.2

Mean Chronological Age, IQ (BPVS), Reading Age (BAS), Emergent Reading (Clay Ready to Read Test), Letter-Sound Knowledge, Phoneme Segmentation (Yopp–Singer Test), Rhyme Skills, and Nonword Reading (Standard Deviations in Parentheses), First and Second Post-tests, Study 1

Research Group	Age	BPVS	Reading Age	Spelling Age	Emergent Reading	Letter Knowledge	Phonemic Segmentation	Rhyme Skills	Nonwords
First post-test									
No-letter controls, n = 29	5.2	–	5.0	–	8.0	30.4	9.7	47.1	–
	(0.3)		(0.5)		(18.3)	(24.0)	(21.6)	(38.1)	
Accelerated	5.2	–	5.0	–	10.3	37.1	9.0	36.4	–
controls, n = 33	(0.3)		(0.3)		(16.0)	(26.8)	(19.7)	(37.7)	
Synthetic	5.3	–	5.4	–	25.6	51.8	21.2	33.6	–
phonics n = 30	(0.3)		(0.3)		(17.7)	(21.7)	(26.5)	(35.9)	
Second post-test									
No-letter controls, n = 29	6.0	–	5.6	5.6	24.8	68.1	26.8	41.4	14.6
	(0.3)		(0.9)	(0.8)	(24.4)	(22.6)	(36.2)	(44.1)	(26.8)
Accelerated	6.0	–	5.5	5.4	27.3	68.1	25.8	32.5	12.1
controls, n = 33	(0.3)		(0.8)	(0.7)	(30.6)	(24.9)	(36.7)	(38.3)	(24.6)
Synthetic	6.0	–	6.3	6.3	49.9	82.0	69.3	61.6	54.6
phonics n = 30	(0.3)		(1.3)	(0.8)	(28.8)	(20.1)	(36.1)	(44.9)	(40.7)

It was concluded from this study that even when exposure to new print items was controlled for, children taught by a synthetic phonics approach made better progress in reading and spelling than children taught by an analytic phonics approach. This was the case even when letter sounds were taught at the same accelerated pace as in the synthetic phonics programme, in which there was the same new print exposure. These gains were long lasting and could still be found at the start of the second year at school, yet the intervention had lasted for only 9.5 hr. It seems very likely that children who are taught the technique of sounding and blending early on are able to continue to expand their reading vocabulary by using the approach to decode the unknown words they encounter when reading text.

STUDY 2

In Study 1, the intervention was carried out on a group basis, with small groups of four to five children. This raised the question of whether the synthetic phonics approach would be effective in the classroom situation, delivered by classroom teachers. It was also found in Study 1 that synthetic phonics was very effective at increasing children's phonemic awareness skills. A further issue was therefore whether analytic phonics teaching would be found to be as effective in developing reading and spelling skills as synthetic phonics if there was an additional phonological awareness training programme. Altogether 304 children participated in 13 classes in Clackmannanshire in Scotland. Our interventions began shortly after the children started school at around the age of 5 years. Four classes were taught about the relationship between letters and sounds through an analytic phonics approach (analytic-phonics-only group). Another four classes carried out a programme in which, in addition to analytic phonics teaching, segmenting and blending spoken words was taught at the level of both rhymes and phonemes, without the aid of print or letters (analytic phonics + phonological awareness group). In the third programme, five classes of children were taught by a synthetic phonics approach.

It was predicted that the synthetic phonics programme would be the most effective in developing reading, spelling, and phonemic awareness, showing that children can use a grapheme–phoneme conversion level approach right at the start of reading instruction. It was further predicted that the teaching of explicit phoneme and rhyme awareness in the absence of print, in addition to an analytic phonics programme, would confer no advantages in terms of reading and spelling attainment over a control group taught wholly by the analytic phonics method. The programmes lasted for 16 weeks, the children receiving their interventions by means of scripted whole-class programmes that lasted for 20 min a day.

The same pre-tests and post-tests as those for Study 1 were administered. In addition, at the first post-test, a separate analysis was made of ability to read irregular words on the BAS Word Reading Test, and a test of analogy reading skills was made. At pre-test (see Table 40.3 for means and standard deviations), the children in the three groups were found to be matched on all tasks except for knowledge of letter sounds, $F(2, 301) = 3.3, p < .04$; the analytic-phonics-only group knew more letter sounds than the other two groups.

At the first post-test, (see Table 3 for means and standard deviations), it was found that the groups differed in single-word-reading ability (BAS Word Reading Test; Elliott et al., 1977), $F(2, 289) = 30.7, p < .001$; Newman–Keuls tests showed that the synthetic phonics group children had significantly higher reading ages than did the other two groups, who did not differ from each other. The groups also differed on the more sensitive test of emergent reading (Clay, 1979), $F(2, 289) = 27.2, p < .001$; Newman–Keuls tests showed that not only did the synthetic phonics group children perform better than the other two groups, but the analytic-phonics-only group performed better than the analytic phonics + phonological awareness group. There was a group difference in nonword reading,

TABLE 40.3

Mean Chronological Age, IQ (BPVS), Reading Age (BAS Word Reading Test), Spelling Age (Schonell Spelling Test), Emergent Reading (Clay Ready to Read Test), Letter-Sound Knowledge, Phoneme Segmentation (Yopp–Singer Test), Rhyme Skills, and Nonword Reading (Standard Deviations in Parentheses), Pre-test and First Post-test, Study 2

Research Group	Age (Years)	BPVS (Standardised Score)	Reading Age (Years)	Spelling Age (Years)	Emergent Reading (%)	Letter Knowledge (%)	Phonemic Segmentation (%)	Rhyme Skills (%)	Nonwords (%)
Pre-test									
Analytic phonics controls, n = 109	5.0 (0.3)	92.5 (15.1)	4.9 (0.1)	5.0 (0.1)	0.9 (4.8)	9.0 (15.4)	4.5 (18.3)	17.9 (30.6)	0.3 (1.8)
Analytic phonics + phonological awareness, n = 78	5.0 (0.3)	90.2 (14.0)	4.9 (0.4)	5.0 (0.1)	2.1 (12.5)	3.9 (8.8)	2.7 (9.9)	21.9 (33.1)	0.6 (4.6)
Synthetic phonics, n = 117	5.0 (0.5)	95.2 (16.8)	4.9 (0.1)	5.0 (0.0)	0.7 (6.2)	6.7 (14.3)	4.1 (14.5)	20.0 (29.1)	0.0 (0.0)
First post-test									
Analytic phonics controls, n = 104	5.4 (0.3)	–	5.4 (0.6)	5.2 (0.4)	37.8 (24.0)	58.1 (24.7)	17.2 (27.4)	26.4 (36.6)	8.8 (22.4)
Analytic phonics + phonological awareness, n = 75	5.4 (0.3)	–	5.4 (0.7)	5.3 (0.5)	23.9 (25.6)	59.9 (24.8)	34.7 (44.6)	36.4 (36.4)	15.8 (29.3)
Synthetic phonics, n = 113	5.5 (0.3)	–	6.04 (0.8)	6.0 (0.7)	53.4 (30.1)	90.1 (14.5)	64.8 (37.9)	46.5 (29.1)	53.3 (41.2)

TABLE 40.4

Mean Percentage Correct on Analogy Reading Task and Irregular Word Reading at End of
Training Programme (First Post-test), Study 2

Research Group	Pre-Test Scores	Clue Word- Reading Scores	Post-Test Scores	Irregular Words
Analytic phonics controls, $n = 104$	2.9	6.3	2.6	21.4
	(12.0)	(18.3)	(9.3)	(19.5)
Analytic phonics + phonological awareness, $n = 75$	4.9	11.4	5.5	15.3
	(15.8)	(27.3)	(16.2)	(23.1)
Synthetic phonics, $n = 113$	16.9	30.5	22.7	30.2
	(25.7)	(32.9)	(23.7)	(25.4)

$F(2, 289) = 57.8$, $p < .001$; Newman–Keuls tests showed that nonword reading was better in the synthetic phonics group than in the other two groups, and the other two groups did not differ from each other. There was also a group difference in the ability to spell dictated words (Schonell & Schonell, 1952), $F(2, 289) = 57.7$, $p < .001$; Newman–Keuls tests showed that the synthetic phonics group had higher spelling ages than did the other two groups, who did not differ from each other. Knowledge of letter sounds was also differentially affected by the training schemes, $F(2, 289) = 74.2$, $p < .001$; Newman–Keuls tests showed that the synthetic phonics group was ahead of the other two groups, although at the pre-test they had been behind the analytic phonics group. There was also a group difference in phoneme segmentation skill as measured by the Yopp–Singer Test (Yopp, 1988), $F(2, 289) = 57.1$, $p < .001$; Newman–Keuls tests showed that, although the analytic phonics + phonological awareness group was significantly better at this task than the analytic-phonics-only group, both of these groups were outperformed by the synthetic phonics group. The groups differed in their ability to produce rhymes for auditorily presented words, $F(2, 289) = 6.8$, $p < .001$. Newman–Keuls tests showed that the synthetic phonics group outperformed the analytic-phonics-only group, but not the analytic phonics + phonological awareness group; the two analytic phonics groups did not differ. Finally, in terms of irregular word reading, the groups were found to differ, $F(2, 289) = 10.3$, $p < .000$. See Table 40.4 for means and standard deviations. Newman–Keuls tests showed that the synthetic phonics children read these items better than the other two groups, who did not differ.

An examination was also made at the first post-test of ability to read words by analogy (see Table 40.4 for means and standard deviations). The children were asked to read a list of 40 words. They then read 5 clue words that would assist them in reading the 40 words by analogy on second showing. For example, prior exposure to 'ring' should facilitate the pronunciation of 'sing'. These clue words were then removed, and the 40 words shown again. The items were taken from Muter, Snowling, and Taylor (1994). The gain in reading skill after exposure to the clue words was assessed. It was found on the analogy task that there was an interaction among groups and pre- and post-test reading performance, $F(2, 289) = 19.1$, $p < .001$. Newman–Keuls tests showed that the synthetic phonics children were the only group to show an increase in reading skill between pre- and post-test, and they also showed superior reading to the other groups in both test sessions. There was a significant difference between groups in clue word reading, $F(2, 289) = 23.5$, $p < .001$, Newman–Keuls tests showing that the synthetic phonics group read the clue words significantly better than the other two groups. Analysis of covariance was therefore used to control for differences in cue reading ability; there was still a significant group difference in gains in word reading at post-test, $F(2, 288) = 7.6$, $p < .001$, in favour of the synthetic phonics group. A similar analysis with reading age as the covariate also showed a significant difference among the groups in gain scores $F(2, 288) = 8.8$, $p < .001$. Thus the ability to read by analogy could not be accounted for in terms of the superior word-recognition ability of the synthetic phonics taught group; it indicates a qualitative difference in their approach to reading.

After the first post-test, the two analytic phonics groups carried out the synthetic phonics programme, completing it by the end of their first year at school. Post-tests are still being carried out on a yearly basis; we report here the performance of the children on reading and spelling tests at the end of their third year at school, 2 years after the intervention ended (see Table 40.5 for means and standard deviations). At this stage, 237 children were still available for testing. In all previous analyses we had found no differences between boys and girls in reading and spelling ability. However, we now found an interaction between reading, spelling, chronological age, and sex, $F(2, 470) = 3.6$, $p < .03$. Newman–Keuls post hoc tests showed that the boys read better than the girls, but that the two groups spelt equally well. Although the boys showed a 5-month advantage in reading over the girls, this did not indicate poor performance by the girls. The girls were reading a significant 15 months ahead of their chronological age, whereas the boys were reading a significant 20 months ahead of chronological age. In terms of spelling, the boys and girls were both a significant 10 months ahead of chronological age. 7.3% of the boys had reading ages 6 or more months below chronological age, whereas 14.9% of girls fell into this category. There were also gains in reading comprehension on the Primary Reading Test scores (France, 1981) for the 232 children who were available. See Table 40.5 for means and standard deviations. Both the boys and the girls were a significant 3 months ahead of their chronological ages, $F(1, 230) = 12.1$, $p < .001$, in reading.

STUDY 3

In contrast to the previous two studies, from Study 3 we have data on 228 5-year-old children in schools in Scotland that were implementing their local education authority's analytic phonics scheme as part of the reading programme (Watson, 1998). We tested the children at the point at which their analytic phonics programme was completed, at the end of the third year at school (see Table 40.5 for means and standard deviations). An interaction was found between reading, spelling, chronological age, and sex, $F(2, 452) = 3.5$, $p < .03$. Newman–Keuls tests showed that the boys were significantly behind the girls in reading and spelling. Both the girls and the boys read significantly above their chronological ages, being 6 months and 3 months ahead, respectively. However, the boys were spelling a significant 3 months below their age level, whereas the girls were at an age-appropriate level on spelling. It was found that 31% of the boys had reading ages 6 or more months below their chronological ages, whereas 26% of girls fell into this category. There were also scores for reading comprehension (France, 1981) on 217 of the children; there was an interaction between sex and comprehension ability, $F(1, 215) = 4.1$, $p < .05$. Newman–Keuls tests showed that the girls read better than the boys.

DISCUSSION

We have found that children can be taught to read English at the grapheme-to-phoneme conversion level right from the start of reading tuition, and that they do particularly well with the

TABLE 40.5

Comparison of Performances of Boys and Girls, Synthetic Phonics (Study 2), and Analytic Phonics (Study 3), at the End of the Third Year at School; Chronological Age, Word-Reading Age, Reading-Comprehension Age, and Spelling Age (Standard Deviations in Parentheses).

| | Synthetic Phonics | | | | | Analytic Phonics | | | |
Participants	Chronological Age	Reading Age (Word Recognition)	Reading Age (Comprehension)	Spelling Age	Participants	Chronological Age	Reading Age (Word Recognition)	Reading Age (Comprehension)	Spelling Age
Girls, n = 114	7.7	9.0	8.0	8.5	Girls, n = 115	7.6	8.1	7.7	7.6
	(0.3)	(1.8)	(1.2)	(1.0)		(0.3)	(1.5)	(1.1)	(0.9)
Boys, n = 123	7.7	9.4	8.0	8.5	Boys, n = 113	7.6	7.8	7.4	7.3
	(0.3)	(2.1)	(1.0)	(1.2)		(0.3)	(1.3)	(1.4)	(1.0)

synthetic phonics approach. In Study 1, even when speed of letter learning and exposure to new print vocabulary was controlled for, the synthetic phonics taught children read and spelt better than the other children. The lack of complete regularity in English orthography was not an impediment to using this approach. In Study 2, the children who were taught through synthetic phonics read irregular words better than the other groups did, and they were the only group that was able to read words by analogy. Again, they read and spelt better than the analytic phonics taught groups, despite exposure to the same new print vocabulary. Furthermore, by the end of the third year at school, the boys read better than the girls (although spelling was equivalent), and a smaller proportion of the boys was falling behind in reading.

The question arises as to why boys taught by a synthetic phonics approach developed an advantage in reading that was detected only at the end of the third year at school, 2 years after the end of the intervention. It is not generally the case that boys read better than girls; in an international comparison, boys read less well than girls in 19 out of 26 countries (Elley, 1992). Indeed, we showed in Study 3 that boys in Scotland taught by an analytic phonics approach read less well than girls by the end of the third year at school. It seems likely that a fundamental developmental change occurs in boys that leads to synthetic phonics becoming particularly effective for them. We propose that synthesising letter sounds for pronunciation is the critical factor, as the boys had no advantage over girls in spelling, a skill that involves phonemic analysis rather than phonemic synthesis. Sounding and blending letters is a sequential skill that would be dealt with primarily by the left hemisphere of the brain. From the time the boys are 6 years old onwards, their brains, although maturing more slowly than those of girls, become more specialised for language skills in the left hemisphere and for visuospatial skills in the right hemisphere (Buffery, 1976). As this specialisation takes place they may start to develop a particular aptitude for the sequential left-to-right letter-to-sound translation and for the synthesis of these sounds for pronunciation, which underpins synthetic phonics. Although this approach was not so effective for girls, they still attained an excellent level of reading skill.

The synthetic phonics approach may have other advantages for boys. Naglieri and Rojahn (2001) have recently shown that boys are less good than girls at attending to or planning how to tackle a cognitive task, and it has been proposed that boys may need to be taught to be more strategic and to focus their attention. Synthetic phonics may encourage them to focus their attention on the information given by letter sounds, whereas they may do this less effectively if taught by an analytic phonics approach. Similarly, children at risk of dyslexia seem to be particularly prone to developing a form of word reading that is not well underpinned by phonological information (Ehri, 1992), so focussing on the sequence of letter sounds in words should be of benefit to them as well.

Thus we conclude that synthetic phonics can be used to teach English-speaking children to learn to read at the start of schooling, and its advantages are not just due to the accelerated letter-sound learning typical of this approach. Synthetic phonics develops phonemic awareness, and gives rise to children's word reading, reading comprehension, and spelling skills being significantly above their chronological ages. Furthermore, it is a method of teaching reading that is particularly beneficial for boys.

ACKNOWLEDGEMENTS

We thank Clackmannanshire Council and the Scottish Executive for their support of Study 2. The opinions expressed here do not necessarily reflect their views. We are very grateful to Bonnie MacMillan and Martin Heil for helpful comments on this chapter.

REFERENCES

Ball, E., & Blachman, B. (1991). Does phoneme awareness training in kindergarten make a difference in early word recognition and developmental spelling? *Reading Research Quarterly, 26*, 46–66.

Bradley, L., & Bryant, P. E. (1983). Categorizing sounds and learning to read—a causal connection. *Nature (London), 301*, 419–421.

Buffery, A. W. H. (1976). Sex differences in the neuropsychological development of verbal and spatial skills. In R. M. Knights & D. J Bakker (Eds.), *The Neuropsychology of Learning Disorders*. Baltimore, MD: University Park Press.

Byrne, B., & Fielding-Barnsley, R. (1989). Phonemic awareness and letter knowledge in the child's acquisition of the alphabetic principle. *Journal of Educational Psychology, 81*, 313–321.

Byrne, B., & Fielding-Barnsley, R. (1991). Evaluation of a program to teach phonemic awareness to young children. *Journal of Educational Psychology, 83*, 451–455.

Clay, M. M. (1979). *The early detection of reading difficulties*. London: Heinemann.

Cunningham, A. E. (1990). Explicit versus implicit instruction in phoneme awareness. *Journal of Experimental Child Psychology, 50*, 429–444.

Dunn, L. M., & Dunn, L. M. (1982). *British Picture Vocabulary Scales*. Windsor, UK: NFER-Nelson.

Ehri, L. C. (1992). Reconceptualising the development of sight word reading and its relationship to recoding. In P. B. Gough, L. C. Ehri, & R. Treiman, (Eds.), *Reading acquisition* (pp. 107–143). Hillsdale, NJ:Lawrence Erlbaum Associates.

Ehri, L. C., Nunes, S. R., Willows, D. M., Schuster, B.V., Yaghoub-Zadeh, Z., & Shanhan, T. (2001). Phonemic awareness instruction helps children learn to read: Evidence from the National Reading Panel's meta-analysis. *Reading Research Quarterly, 36*, 250–287.

Elley, W. B. (1992). *How in the world do students read?* Oxford, UK: Elsevier Science.

Elliott, C. D., Murray, D. J., & Pearson, L. S. (1977). *The British Ability Scales*. Windsor, UK: NFER-Nelson.

Fox, B., & Routh, D. K. (1984). Phonemic analysis and synthesis as word attack skills: Revisited. *Journal of Educational Psychology, 76*, 1059–1064.

France, N. (1981). *Primary reading test*. Windsor, UK: NFER-Nelson.

Fraser, H. (1997). *Early intervention: A literature review*. Edinburgh: Moray House Institute of Education.

Goswami, U. (1994a). The role of analogies in reading development. *Support for Learning, 9*, 22–26.

Goswami, U. (1994b). Phonological skills, analogies and reading development. *Reading, 28*, 32–37.

Goswami, U. (1995). Phonological development and reading by analogy: What is analogy and what is not? *Journal of Research in Reading, 18*, 139–145.

Goswami, U. (1999). Causal connections in beginning reading: The importance of rhyme. *Journal of Research in Reading, 22*, 217–240.

Goswami, U. C., & Bryant, P. E. (1990). *Phonological skills and learning to read*. Hove, UK: Lawrence Erlbaum Associates.

Haddock, M. (1976). Effects of an auditory and an auditory-visual method of blending instruction on the ability of prereaders to decode synthetic words. *Journal of Educational Psychology, 68*, 825–831.

Hatcher, P. J., Hulme, C., & Ellis, A. W. (1994). Ameliorating early reading failure by integrating the teaching of reading and phonological skills: The phonological linkage hypothesis. *Child Development, 65*, 41–57.

Johnston, R. S., & Watson, J. (2004). Accelerating the development of reading, spelling and phonemic awareness skills in initial readers. *Reading and Writing, 17*, 327–357.

Lie, A. (1991). Effects of a training programme for stimulating skills in word analysis in first grade. *Reading Research Quarterly, 26*, 234–249.

Lundberg, I., Frost, J., & Petersen, O.-P. (1988). Effects of an intensive programme for stimulating phonological awareness in preschool children. *Reading Research Quarterly, 23*, 263–284.

Lundberg, I., Olofsson, A., & Wall, S. (1980). Reading and spelling skills in the first school years predicted from phonemic awareness skills in kindergarten. *Scandinavian Journal of Psychology, 21*, 159–173.

Maclean, M., Bryant, P., & Bradley, L. (1987). Rhymes, nursery rhymes and reading in early childhood. *Merrill-Palmer Quarterly Journal of Developmental Psychology, 33,* 255–281.

Morais, J., Bertelson, P., Cary, L., & Alegria, J. (1986). Literacy training and speech segmentation. *Cognition, 24*, 45–64.

Morais, J., Cary, L., Alegria, J., and Bertelson, P. (1979). Does awareness of speech as a sequence of phones arise spontaneously? *Cognition, 7*, 323–331.

Muter, V., Snowling, M., & Taylor, S. (1994). Orthographic analogies and phonological awareness: Their role and significance in early reading development. *Journal of Child Psychology and Child Psychiatry, 35*, 293–310.

Naglieri, J. A., & Rojahn, J. (2001). Gender differences in planning, attention, simultaneous, and successive (PASS) cognitive processes and achievement. *Journal of Educational Psychology, 93*, 430–437.

Schonell, F. J., & Schonell, F. E. (1952). *Diagnostic and attainment testing* (2nd ed.). Edinburgh: Oliver & Boyd.

Share, D. L. (1995). Phonological recoding and self-teaching: *Sine qua non* of reading acquisition. *Cognition, 55*, 151–218.

Share, D. L., Jorm, A. F. Maclean, R., & Matthews, R. (1984). Sources of individual differences in reading acquisition. *Journal of Educational Psychology, 76*, 466–477.

Stanovich, K. E., Cunningham, A. E., & Cramer, B. B. (1984). Assessing phonological awareness in kindergarten children: Issues of task comparability. *Journal of Experimental Child Psychology, 38*, 175–190.

Stuart, M., & Coltheart, M. (1988). Does reading develop in a sequence of stages? *Cognition, 30*, 139–181.

Treiman, R., & Baron, J. (1983). Phonemic-analysis training helps children benefit from spelling-sound rules. *Memory and Cognition*, 383–389.

Vellutino, F. R., & Scanlon, D. M. (1987). Phonological coding, phonological awareness, and reading ability: Evidence from a longitudinal and experimental study. *Merrill-Palmer Quarterly, 33*, 321–363.

Watson, J. (1998). An investigation of the effects of phonics teaching on children's progress in reading and spelling. Unpublished doctoral thesis, University of St. Andrews, Scotland.

Watson, J. E., & Johnston, R. S. (1998). Accelerating reading attainment: The effectiveness of synthetic phonics. *Interchange, 57*, 1–12.

Williams, J. P. (1980). Teaching decoding with an emphasis on phoneme analysis and phoneme blending. *Journal of Educational Psychology, 72*, 1–15.

Yopp, H. K. (1988). The validity and reliability of phonemic awareness tests. *Reading Research Quarterly, 23*, 159–177.

41

Genetic?? and Environmental Influences on the Development of Reading and Related Cognitive Skills

Richard K. Olson
University of Colorado, Boulder

On a global scale and within diverse nations such as the United States, there are large educational and cultural differences related to literacy development. However, significant individual differences in literacy are still present within relatively homogeneous environments for reading development. This chapter explores the balance of genetic and environmental influences on individual differences in reading and on reading disability (extreme poor reading) in generally supportive educational environments. Evidence from identical and fraternal twins' behavior showing strong genetic influences on reading disability is supported with molecular genetic evidence from their DNA. Linkage analyses indicate regions on several different chromosomes where genes related to reading disability are likely to be found. Implications are discussed for current educational policy, possible future diagnosis of risk, and gene therapy for reading disability.

INTRODUCTION

Everyone would agree that there are environmental influences on reading development, consistent with the "environmental" part of my title, but the "genetic" part of the title may raise a few questions and eyebrows. Indeed, there are large cultural differences in levels of literacy both between and within countries that have no relation to genetic differences (D.R. Olson, 2002). However, even within relatively homogenous cultural environments that are strongly supportive of reading development, some children fall far behind their peers. These children may or may not be labeled as "dyslexic," but their most salient characteristic is a reading level that is well below the norm, typically below the local 10th percentile in most research studies. Our research on English reading development in the United States has focused on the average genetic and environmental contributions to membership in this low-reading group without obvious cultural (impoverished schools, English as a second language) or overt biological (i.e., brain damage) constraints on their reading development.

For some critics of genetic research on reading disabilities, our disclaiming of genetic influence on cultural differences in literacy is not enough. These critics insist that individual differences in a complex and culturally dependent human behavior such as reading simply cannot be influenced by genetic factors. For example, a reviewer for one of our papers that was recently submitted to a well-respected European journal had the following comment: "I can understand heritability studies on pigs' weight or cows' milk production or on human height, but what does this strange doubly-normalized sum [combined z scores for two measures of printed word recognition] represent that one can directly relate to biological processes?"

The editor agreed with this reviewer and rejected the paper. It was subsequently published with high editorial praise in another well-respected journal (Castles, Datta, Gayan, & Olson, 1999). The point is that, although some students of human behavior acknowledge the possibility of genetic influence on complex cognitive skills, others do not. Part of their disbelief in genetic influence regarding reading may be that this is a skill that is explicitly taught to young children, and it has become widespread in modern societies only in the past 100 or 200 years. It is hard to see how deficits or broader individual differences in this culturally dependent skill could be related to basic biological processes. Thus a major goal of our research has been to understand the genetic and environmental causes of more basic cognitive deficits that may be causally related to reading disability.

This chapter is a brief and personal narrative account of how our collaborative research group has approached this problem and what we have learned about genetic and environmental influences on reading and related skills over the past 20 years. Since 1990, the group's research efforts have been administered within the Colorado Learning Disabilities Research Center (CLDRC), directed by John DeFries. The separate projects (and their primary investigators) are *Twin Studies* (John DeFries, Sally Wadsworth, Erik Willcutt); *Reading and Language Processes* (Richard Olson and Janice Keenan), *Validity of Subtypes of ADHD* (Bruce Pennington and Erik Willcutt), *Genomic Analyses* (Shelley Smith), and *Early Reading, Language, and Attention Development* (Richard Olson and Brian Byrne). With the exception of the last project that includes preschool twins from the United States and Australia, we all studied the same group of school-age twins and their siblings from across the state of Colorado.

Before beginning the narrative, I would like to emphasize that, in designing our studies and selecting measures, we have stood on the shoulders of giants in the field of reading and language development. To maintain the story line and keep the story reasonably short, I do not mention many of these contributions here. They are gratefully acknowledged in our cited publications.

ORIGINS OF THE RESEARCH: THE COLORADO FAMILY READING STUDY AND A RELATIVE WITH DYSLEXIA

The first behavioral genetic study of reading disability at the University of Colorado was initiated by John DeFries in 1973 at the Institute for Behavioral Genetics. The Colorado Family Reading Study tested 133 children with reading disability, their parents, and siblings on measures of reading and cognitive processes. In addition, 125 typical control children without reading disability, their parents, and siblings were tested on the same measures. The most basic finding from this study, completed in 1976, was the strongest evidence to date for familial transmission of reading and related cognitive disabilities (DeFries, Singer, Foch, & Lewitter, 1978). There was also some evidence, from the apparent pattern of inheritance across family generations, for genetic transmission of reading disability. However, family studies are not ideal for separating the relative importance of genetic and environmental influences on individual differences, because family members share both their genes and their environment.

The demonstrated familial transmission of reading disability raised the possibility of genetic influence, but a more precise method was needed to definitively separate the average relative influence of genes, shared family environment, and nonshared environment on reading disability.

While the results of the Colorado Family Reading Study were being published in the late 1970s, a group at the Institute for Behavioral Genetics was formed to propose a large study of reading disability to the National Institutes of Health. This study would use identical and fraternal twins as subjects to obtain more precise and valid estimates of the genetic and environmental etiology of reading disorders and individual differences. The new research group, headed by John DeFries and Jerry McClearn, asked me to join them at a very opportune time. They had heard that I was using an eye-movement monitor to study cognitive development, and some researchers had suggested that eye-movement problems during reading might be a cause of dyslexia. I was happy to accept their invitation to use this technology on such an interesting and important problem.

Immediately before the invitation to help with this study of reading disability, the importance and the complexity of the problem were impressed on me when I learned to my surprise that an adult relative by marriage had "dyslexia." His compensation for his reading disability was both difficult and impressive. His reading difficulties continued throughout his school years and after, but he graduated from the local state university and went on to become a successful businessman. I never would have suspected that he had serious difficulty reading if he had not told me, sadly, and with great embarrassment.

What an interesting disability this was to a cognitive psychologist, that an intelligent and successful person would have such great difficulty in reading. He said he was telling me about his problem because he thought that, as a psychologist, I might have some insight into his dyslexia, and he had three questions he thought I might be able to answer. The paraphrased questions were (1) what is the cause of my problem in reading, (2) what can I do to get over it, and (3) will my children get it from me (by genes or conveying a bad attitude about reading)? I responded with sympathy but had little to offer for answers. I said "I don't know, I'll look into it." Shortly thereafter, a call came from the group at the Institute for Behavioral Genetics requesting my participation in their twin study of dyslexia, and the rest is history, documented in the narrative and publications subsequently cited.

AN INITIAL STUDY TO VALIDATE MEASURES FOR SUBSEQUENT STUDIES WITH TWINS

Our first project to develop and validate measures of reading and related cognitive and perceptual skills began in 1979. For 3 years, we studied a group of children from 8 to 18 years of age who, based on their poor reading performance, were referred by teachers. (An interesting footnote to this teacher-referred sample is that it was about 80% males versus about 55%–60% males in subsequent nonreferred samples of twins with reading disability). These children were compared with a typical control group matched on gender and age that had no evidence of reading problems. The first clear result from this study was that, contrary to a report by Pavlidis (1981), there were no significant differences between disabled and typical readers' eye movements in nonreading visual tracking or target search tasks, and their abnormal eye movements when reading text were *caused by* their reading difficulties, and not a *cause of* their reading difficulties (Hyona & Olson, 1995; Olson, Kliegl, & Davidson, 1983a, 1983b).

Other researchers have provided evidence that children with dyslexia may have problems in processing low-spatial-frequency visual stimuli that are moving or rapidly flickering (see Stein, 2001, for review). These researchers have suggested that this basic sensory processing deficit may contribute to reading disabilities by disrupting the visual processing of print. We have also explored several basic visual and auditory processes in our reading-disabled and typical twins described in the next section. We found limited support for a relation between individual differences in visual–temporal processing skills and word-reading ability ($r = .3$), though nearly all of this correlation could be accounted for by individual differences in the children's IQ (Olson & Datta, 2002). We have not given up trying to find unique relations between reading and basic visual and auditory processes: A current collaboration with Joel Talcott and Caroline Witton has provided evidence for some modest correlations ($\sim .3$) between word reading and individual differences in dynamic visual motion sensitivity and auditory processing of tone frequency and amplitude modulation (Hulslander et al., 2002). However, these correlations fell below .1 and were no longer significant when controlled for participants' full-scale Weschler IQ.

Other laboratories have attempted to confirm the unique rapid auditory–temporal processing deficit reported by Tallal (1980) for children with weak phonological decoding skills. Recent attempts to replicate the findings of Tallal have instead found a generalized deficit in auditory–temporal processing tasks that is not specific to rapid processing demands and may be related to attention deficits for children with reading disability in psychophysical tasks that are boring (Share, Jorm, Maclean, & Matthews, 2002). Further research is needed to understand the possible contribution of attention deficits present in some poor readers to their deficits in basic visual or auditory processing tasks.

In contrast to the conflicting results from the preceding studies of basic visual and auditory processing in dyslexic and typical readers, we have consistently found that most children with dyslexia have clear deficits in phonological language processes that are independent of any differences in IQ. Results from our initial measure-validation study demonstrated that children with dyslexia had unique deficits in their ability to play a "Pig Latin" language game (Olson, Kliegl, Davidson, & Foltz, 1985; Olson, Wise, Connors, Rack, & Fulker, 1989). This game required children to move the initial consonant or consonant cluster to the end of a word, add the /ay/ sound, and pronounce the result (i.e., "pig" would become "igpay"). Nearly all of the children with dyslexia were below the typical average in this task, and most were also worse than younger typical children who were matched to the dyslexic children's level of reading.

Our initial measure-validation study also found that dyslexic children's phonological decoding or "sounding out" of pronounceable nonwords (e.g., tegwop, framble, calch) was nearly always lower than the typical average, and, similar to results for our "Pig Latin" game, the majority of dyslexics were also lower in phonological decoding skills than younger typical reading children at the same absolute level of word-reading skills (Olson et al., 1985; Rack, Snowling, & Olson, 1992). The fact that dyslexic children's phonological language and phonological decoding skills in reading were worse than expected from their level of reading strongly suggested their causal role in reading disability. However, proving this causal role and understanding its genetic and environmental origins is an ongoing effort that is documented in the subsequent sections.

Before turning to our studies of twins, I would like to mention one more finding from the initial measure-validation study that is particularly relevant to reading English words. Phonological decoding of nonwords and new words encountered in print is certainly an important component skill for learning and reading English words, but for many words, it is not sufficient. English has numerous words that are spelled differently but sound the same (e.g., bare bear), and a large number of single syllable words are "exception" words that violate the most common rules of English orthography (e.g., yacht, said). This may pose special problems for children learning to read and spell English compared with learning other more orthographically regular written languages. The challenging orthography of many printed English words requires that the child remember the specific orthographic patterns for exception words and homophones. This skill has traditionally been assessed by having children read lists of exception words (cf., Coltheart, Curtis, Atkins, & Haller, 1993), but we decided to take a different approach. We had children quickly choose a target word over a phonologically identical foil that was not a word (e.g., rain, rane). We called this skill "orthographic coding." (There are several more recently developed versions of orthographic coding tasks that are reviewed in Olson, Forsberg, Wise, & Rack, 1994).

Our participants with reading disability were nearly always below the average typical reader in their orthographic coding accuracy. However, in contrast to results from the phonological tasks previously described, their orthographic coding accuracy was consistent with that of younger typical readers at the same absolute level of word-reading skill. For this reason, we suggested that orthographic coding deficits may not play a primary causal role in reading disability. We also suggested that orthographic coding deficits may primarily result from lack of print exposure rather than from any fundamental or constitutional deficit in this skill. I show in the remaining narrative how our early view of orthographic coding skills has changed with further evidence from studies of identical and fraternal twins, as well as from molecular genetic studies.

USING IDENTICAL AND FRATERNAL TWINS TO ESTIMATE GENETIC AND ENVIRONMENTAL INFLUENCE

Logic of the Twin Method

With the completion of our initial measurement-validation study, we were ready to employ the measures with identical and fraternal twins. Identical twins are "monozygotic" (MZ) because they derive from the same egg and sperm, so they share all their genes. Same-sex fraternal twins are "dizygotic" (DZ) because they derive from two different eggs and sperm from their two parents, and they share half of their segregating genes (i.e., genes that make us different as individuals) on average. Both types of twins in our study shared their family environments. Thus if the MZ twins turned out to be more similar on average than DZ twins in reading across the typical range or in reading disability, this would provide evidence for genetic influence.

The most familiar and common method for comparing the similarities of MZ and DZ twins is to compare their correlations. This approach is appropriate for assessing genetic and environmental influence on typically distributed individual differences in the population. IQ would be a good example of such a normally distributed variable, and I later mention some results from assessing the heritability of individual differences in reading, which are also normally distributed across the population (Rogers, 1982).

The normal distribution of reading ability in the population is a surprise to many who think of "dyslexia" as a distinct and categorical disorder, and it raises a problem for the diagnosis of "dyslexia": What is the severity criterion that we should use, and should there be other criteria such as a discrepancy with IQ that should be required? I return to these questions in the next section, but first I want to briefly describe a method developed by John DeFries and David Fulker for analyzing the average genetic and environmental influence on extreme-group membership in normally distributed traits.

For the moment, assume that our group with reading disability consists of twins in the low tail of the population reading distribution, say the lower 10%. How should we assess the average genetic and environmental influence on reading deficits in this group? DeFries and Fulker (1985) reasoned that if at least one member of MZ and DZ twin pairs were "probands" selected to be in the low tail of the population distribution, say in the lower 10% (at least −1.5 standard deviations below the population mean), there would be specific expectations for where the other twin (the "cotwin") of the MZ and DZ probands would be in the distribution, depending on the relative magnitude of genetic and environmental influences. For example, if low-group membership were entirely due to genetic factors, the cotwins of MZ probands should also be probands, exactly as deviant as their cotwin, because they share all their genes. On the other hand, cotwins of DZ probands should fall, on average, halfway toward the population mean, because they share half their segregating genes on average.

Now suppose that low-group membership was entirely due to environmental factors that the twins shared, such as books in the home or quality of their school. In this case, MZ probands and their cotwins would all share their low-group membership, but so would DZ probands and their cotwins, because their different genetic similarity does not matter if their deficits were entirely due to shared environment.

A third extreme example of cotwin regression to the mean illustrates the power of this method to assess a second kind of environmental influence, that is, environmental influences that are not shared by members of a twin pair, such as a unique illness, accident, different schooling, or just having a bad day when they took the test (measurement error). If nonshared environmental influences were the only cause of low-group membership, then the cotwins of both MZ and DZ probands should regress all the way to the population mean, on average, because there is no genetic or shared environment influence to make them similar.

The preceding extreme examples are for illustration only. In fact, there is likely to be a mix of genetic, shared environment, and nonshared-environment influences on low-group membership, so average MZ and DZ cotwin positions in the normal distribution are likely to fall between these extremes. Exactly where they fall allows us to estimate the percentage of influence on group membership from genes (group heritability, symbolized as h_g^2), shared environment (symbolized as c_g^2), and nonshared environment (symbolized as e_g^2). Because these are the only three general sources of individual differences, their combined percentages must add to 100%. DeFries and Fulker (1985) presented a regression equation that provided a quantitative estimate and standard error for the h_g^2 parameter, allowing a test of its statistical significance.

It should be emphasized that estimates of genetic and environmental influences are averages for the deviant group and do not pertain to any individual within the group. In fact, it is likely that different individuals within the deviant group have very different genetic and environmental etiologies, both quantitatively (the relative balance of genetic and environmental influence on their disorder) and qualitatively (the specific genetic and environmental mechanisms).

Our Twin Sample

The twin sample in the CLDRC now consists of 2,690 individuals, nearly all between 8 and 18 years of age, and with a mean of 12 years. The twins are ascertained by school personnel in 27 Colorado school districts through records containing the same last names and birthdays. The twins' parents are then mailed a letter requesting their children's participation in the study. Of the 40%–50% who return the letter, the vast majority agree to let us examine their twins' school records further and bring their children to our laboratories in Boulder and Denver for testing on weekends or summer holidays.

Since 1982, we have looked for any evidence of a reading problem in the twins' school records. Since 1996, we also have looked for evidence of attention deficits, hyperactivity, or both (ADHD). Children exhibiting reading or attention problems are invited to the laboratories in Boulder and Denver, Colorado, for testing. We also test a comparison group of typical range twins with no evidence of reading or attention problems in their school records, though some turn out to have such problems when tested in the laboratory.

Twin pairs are excluded from the sample if either member has an uncorrected sensory deficit, neurological signs such as seizures, or limited school attendance. We also exclude children who have learned to read English as a second language, as this is a clear environmental risk factor for poor reading. Nearly all of the subjects' schools were close to or above national norms in average reading skill, suggesting that most twins had generally adequate educational support for learning to read. Until very recently, we did not draw twins from the Denver school district. This district has serious problems with poor schools, poverty, and English as a second language learning, yielding average performance at about the 30th percentile on nationally normed reading tests. Our goal was to explore the etiology of deficits in reading for which there were no clear environmental influences. Thus the conclusions we draw about average genetic influence in this sample should be viewed within the context of our restricted environmental range for reading development. If that environmental range had been broader (e.g., by including the Denver schools), it is likely that our estimates of genetic influence on individual differences would have been lower, and the influence from shared family and school environment would have been higher.

Finally, for most analyses, the twins had to have a minimum verbal or performance IQ score of 85. However, we had no requirement for a discrepancy between reading and IQ when analyzing average genetic influence on the group's reading and related deficits. A discrepancy between IQ and reading performance has traditionally been a requirement in the United States for the delivery of special education services in "specific reading disability" and in some studies of "dyslexia." However, recent evidence suggests that poor readers' IQ is unrelated to their primary phonological processing deficits or their response to intervention, so there is a strong movement in the United States to eliminate the IQ discrepancy criterion for the diagnosis and delivery of remedial services for learning disabilities (Lyon et al., 2001).

Our Initial Behavior Genetic Results

Evidence for genetic influence on reading disability emerged early in the twin study (DeFries, Fulker, & LaBuda, 1987). The DeFries and Fulker (1985) method was sufficiently powerful in our small early twin sample to detect significant genetic influence on the group deficit in a composite word-reading, spelling, and reading-comprehension measure from the Peabody Individual Achievement Test (PIAT) (Dunn & Markwardt, 1970). Two years later, Olson et al. (1989) published results for group deficits in their word-recognition, phonological decoding, phoneme awareness ("Pig Latin"), and orthographic coding skills. When the deviant groups were selected independently on each measure for deficits below −1.5 standard deviations from the typical group mean, all of the measures except for orthographic coding showed statistically significant genetic influence on the average group deficit.

Unfortunately, Olson et al. (1989) were not clear about the implications of the lack of significance for genetic influence on orthographic coding in their small sample. They suggested that phonological decoding might be the uniquely heritable component skill in word reading, whereas orthographic coding deficits might be more due to environmental influences. In fact, the significant heritability for phonological decoding and the nonsignificant heritability for orthographic coding deficits were not significantly different from each other in this small sample of twins. Subsequent analyses described in the next subsection showed little difference in the absolute heritabilities for phonological and orthographic coding, though their relations with phoneme awareness are different and they have significant independent genetic variance.

More Recent Behavior Genetic Results

In the early 1990s, the twin sample grew large enough to more accurately assess heritabilities for group deficits in component reading, spelling, and language skills. Olson, Forsberg, and Wise (1994) found that, with additional twin pairs, deficits in orthographic coding showed significant genetic influence. The sample in this analysis was also large enough to explore bivariate genetic

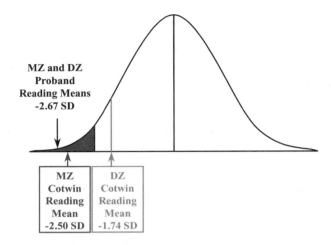

FIG. 41.1.   Cotwin regression for word-reading deficits (from Gayan & Olson, 2001).

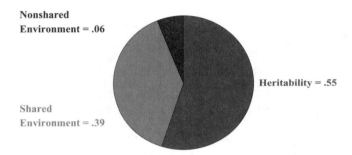

FIG. 41.2.   Genetic and environmental etiology of group word-reading deficit (Gayan & Olson, 2001).

analyses by selecting the proband on one measure, say word recognition, and assessing cotwin regression to the population mean on a second measure, say phonological decoding. We found significant bivariate genetic influence between all pairings of word recognition, phonological decoding, orthographic coding, and phoneme awareness, indicating that group deficits in all these skills were at least partly influenced by the same genes. The pattern of bivariate genetic relations varied somewhat in their strength, but the sample was still too small to detect statistical significance for any *differences* in bivariate heritability.

Our most recent twin analyses, which use the sample collected up to fall 2000, do show significant differences in bivariate heritability for different pairs of variables, and the univariate heritability estimates for each variable are the most reliable to date (Gayan & Olson, 2001). Before considering the bivariate results, I would like to revisit the basis for the univariate estimates of genetic, shared-environment, and nonshared-environment influence. Figure 41.1 shows the proband and cotwin means for printed word recognition within the typical distribution when probands were selected to be below –1.5 standard deviation units from the typical mean. It can be seen that the MZ cotwin mean regresses a bit toward the population mean, and this is the basis for our estimate of nonshared-environment influence shown in Fig. 41.2. (MZ twins share their genes and their environment, so within-pair differences must be due to nonshared environment.) It can also be seen that the DZ cotwins regress a great deal more toward the

TABLE 41.1
Heritability (h_g^2), Shared Environment (c_g^2), and Nonshared Environment (e_g^2) Estimates
for Group Deficits in Each Task

Task	h_g^2	SE	c_g^2	SE	e_g^2	SE
Word recognition	.55	.08	.39	.09	.06	.03
Phonological decoding	.64	.09	.25	.10	.12	.03
Orthographic coding	.67	.12	.17	.12	.16	.04
Phoneme deletion	.72	.14	.15	.14	.13	.06

Note. SE is the standard error for each estimate. (Adapted from Gayan and Olson, 2001)

population mean than do the MZ cotwins, but not the halfway-to-the-mean regression that I earlier stated would be the case if genetic influence accounted entirely for the group deficit. The actual result reflects the joint influence of a bit of nonshared environment (6%), a lot more shared environment (39%), and more still for genetic influence (55%).

Table 41.1 presents the univariate results for word recognition, phonological decoding, orthographic coding, and a new measure of phoneme awareness called phoneme deletion (e.g., say "prot" without the /r/ sound. . . . *pot*). It is clear that the group deficits in all of these skills are substantially influenced by genes, perhaps a bit less so for printed word recognition, for which shared environment influence seems to be stronger than for the other variables. However, these generally small differences between variables in genetic and environmental influence are not statistically significant in the current sample (Gayan & Olson, 2001).

Are the same genes operative on the group deficits across these variables? Gayan and Olson (2001) conducted bivariate genetic analyses to follow up on the previous bivariate analyses by Olson, Forsberg, and Wise (1994). In the new analyses with a larger sample, it was apparent again that, for all of the variable pairings, there was significant bivariate heritability, indicating that at least part of the phenotypic correlations between the variables was due to the same genes. On the other hand, there was also evidence for significant differences in the size of the genetic correlations for different variable pairs. Specifically, the genetic correlation between deficits in phonological decoding and phoneme awareness (.67) was significantly higher than the genetic correlation between orthographic coding and phoneme awareness (.28).

Gayan and Olson (2003) have recently addressed similar bivariate heritability questions for these variables in latent-trait genetic models, but concerning individual differences across the typical range instead of group deficits. Basically, we did these analyses by comparing correlations or covariances for MZ and DZ twins, without selecting a deviant proband group. We obtained the same basic result for individual differences across the typical range as that we found for group deficits. High levels of genetic influence were found for each of the variables, and the genetic correlation between phoneme awareness and phonological decoding (.79) was significantly higher than that between phoneme awareness and orthographic coding (.55). In addition, we found that, although phonological decoding and orthographic coding had a substantial and significant genetic correlation (.82), they also had significant independent genetic variance.

It is tempting to cite the independent genetic variance for phonological decoding and orthographic coding as support for the biological basis of two partly independent routes to the lexicon for reading printed words, as in interactive dual-route models (cf., Coltheart et al., 1993).

However, note also that the genetic correlation between group deficits in word recognition and oral nonword reading was .99 in Gayan and Olson (2001) and the comparable correlation was .97 for individual differences in Gayan and Olson (in press). These high genetic correlations seem to cast some doubt on the separate importance of orthographic coding skills in the genetic basis for individual differences in word reading, at least for those orthographic coding skills that are independent of phonological decoding. On the other hand, the ability to read nonwords may reflect skills in the hypothesized phonological route to reading as well as the orthographic route, thus yielding the very high phenotypic and genetic correlations between word reading and phonological decoding.

SUBTYPES AND THE DIFFERENTIAL GENETIC ETIOLOGY OF READING DISABILITY

Up to this point, I have discussed average genetic and environmental influences on group deficits in reading and related skills without consideration of individual characteristics that might interact with those estimates. An obvious possibility is gender. Wadsworth, Knopic, and DeFries (2000) compared male and female groups on their heritability for deficits in a composite word reading, comprehension, and spelling measure. The heritability for males (.58) was not significantly different from the heritability for females (.59). Another obvious subtype dimension is age, given the broad age range of our twin sample, from 8 to 18 years. DeFries, Alarcon, and Olson (1997) found a significant interaction between age and the heritability of group deficits in word reading versus spelling. The heritability of spelling deficits tended to increase with age whereas the heritability of word-reading deficits tended to decline with age.

We have also explored differences in the genetic etiology of reading disability depending on subjects' profiles of component word-reading skills and nonreading cognitive skills. Castles et al. (1999) found that disabled readers who had relatively low phonological decoding compared with their reading of exception words ("phonological dyslexics") had a significantly higher heritability for their general word-reading deficits when compared with disabled readers with relatively high phonological decoding compared with their exception word reading ("surface dyslexics"). We explained this result by suggesting that the reading of exception or strange words may depend more on environmental differences in print exposure, and that more severe phonological decoding deficits were specifically linked to genetic influences in word-reading deficits.

Nonreading cognitive skills have also been explored for their influence on the genetic etiology of reading deficits. Olson, Datta, Gayan, and DeFries (1999) found that several tasks involving speed of processing showed lower genetic influence for subjects who were slower on these tasks. The tasks ranged from the matching of abstract visual forms to the rapid naming of letters, numbers, colors, and pictures. Olson et al. also found that children with word-reading disability who had lower IQ scores tended to have less genetic influence on their reading deficits compared with children with higher IQ scores. This result was subsequently confirmed by Wadsworth, Olson, Pennington, and DeFries (2000) for a composite measure of word reading, comprehension, and spelling. We suggested that, because the children with lower IQ tended to have mothers with fewer years of education and fewer books in the home, these negative environmental influences may have been more responsible their reading deficits. In contrast, children who read poorly in spite of higher IQ and likely environmental support may have had more constitutional (genetic) constraints on their reading growth. We emphasized, however, that these results do not justify withholding remedial services to poor readers with lower IQ (see also, Lyon et al., 2001; Fletcher et al., 2002).

MOLECULAR GENETICS AND LINKAGE
FOR READING DISABILITY

In the brave new world of molecular genetics and the human genome project, there are new tools for locating genes that influence behavioral disorders. Because behavioral disorders are etiologically complex, there are likely to be several different genes, each accounting for only a portion of the average genetic influence on the group deficit in reading, and they may vary in their relative influence across different individuals and their families.

The method of linkage analysis attempts to locate the general region on a chromosome that may have a gene or genes that influence a disorder. Linkage of a region to the disorder can be assessed by a comparison of the DNA of sibling pairs who share or do not share the disorder. Their DNA is compared for the expression of different "markers" or sequences of base pairs along different positions on the chromosome. If both siblings in a pair inherit the same marker and this is associated with a significantly greater likelihood for their sharing a reading disorder than if the marker is not shared, there is evidence for linkage of a gene or genes in the region to the disorder.

A region on the short arm of chromosome 6 has shown the most significant and replicated evidence for linkage to reading disability (Cardon et al., 1994; Fisher et al., 2002; Gayan et al., 1999; Grigorenko et al., 1997). However, there have been other reported linkages for reading disability on other chromosomes, including chromosomes 1, 2, 15, and 18. Although chromosome 6 seems to show the most reliable linkage at this point, Fisher et al. also found very strong linkage for a region on chromosome 18 by using a whole genome scan in two independent samples. (Both samples also showed evidence for linkage to chromosome 6.) Thus there is accumulating evidence for more than one region of the genome that is linked to reading disability, and we are likely to find that different individuals have different specific genetic etiologies for their reading disabilities.

Finding a region or regions of the genome linked to reading disability is not the same as finding the gene or genes. In fact, a marker that is linked could be millions of base pairs removed from the responsible gene or genes. (The human genome consists of about 3 billion base pairs.) Moreover, the marker cannot be used for diagnosis of genetic risk, as it provides information only about whether the two siblings in a pair happened to inherit the same large chunk of DNA from their parents. The next step is to find a marker that is close enough to the responsible gene that it is directly "associated" with risk for the disorder. (For reliable association, the marker has to be close enough that it does not recombine separately from the gene during meiosis.) This association is typically discovered by "fine mapping" with a large number of markers in the region of linkage. Most recently, Kaplan et al. (2002) found significant evidence for association at the JA04 location within the 6p21.3-22 linkage area. However, this finding needs further replication before we can be confident about this association result.

The preceding association study and some earlier studies of linkage on chromosome 6 used several different reading-related phenotypes, including phonological decoding, phoneme awareness, and orthographic coding. Although there is evidence for linkage from all of these phenotypes, the strongest evidence has come from orthographic coding. This result, along with the high heritability estimate for orthographic coding from recent twin analyses (Gayan & Olson, 2001, 2003), indicates that the early doubts of Olson et al. (1989) about the heritability of orthographic coding deficits were quite wide off the mark. It remains to be seen in much larger sibling pair samples if the linkage and association results for orthographic coding will be significantly stronger than for the other reading phenotypes. The current small samples reported to date do not have sufficient power to detect significant differences between the phenotypes. Such large sibling pair studies with greater power are currently being developed at the Colorado Center for the Study of Learning Disabilities.

A very different way to find genes related to reading disability is to start with a known gene that has different alleles, that is, slightly different patterns of DNA, that may cause differences in gene expression. (An allele difference in only one out of thousands of base pairs is sufficient to cause major changes in expression for some genes.) Likely target genes are those in a demonstrated area of linkage on a chromosome that are known to be expressed in the brain (as the majority of identified genes are). This approach was recently used by Smith et al. (2001), but unfortunately the target gene and its different alleles had no association with reading disability. No doubt there will be more promising target genes discovered for future "top-down" association analyses to complement the "bottom-up" exploration through linkage analyses and fine mapping to locate genes contributing to reading disability.

SUMMARY AND CONCLUSIONS

My relative with "dyslexia" finds our genetic results from the last 20 years "interesting," though less so because I cannot specify the origins of his personal problem with reading: We have estimates only for average group influences from genes and environment, and no specific genes have been found. When we do find genes whose abnormal variation account for some percentage of the group reading deficit, there is much further work to be done to understand how those genes influence brain development and activity in ways that make reading and other related skills difficult to learn. Then we may learn how to modify the genes, their effects, or both, to support typical reading development. I am sure this will be a long and difficult road. Regardless of the difficulty in understanding and modifying genetic pathways to reading disability, having seen the struggles of children with reading and other learning disabilities, I am convinced this understanding will be worth the effort. The prospects for near-term success in finding relevant genes are increasing with rapid improvements and reduced costs in gene mapping technology.

Once we discover variations in genes associated with risk for reading disability, very thorny questions arise about how this information would be used. Would it be used by some parents to selectively abort an embryo with a modestly higher genetic risk for reading disability, as some do for an embryo with a more serious difference that inevitably leads to Downs syndrome? Would the information be used to introduce some sort of gene therapy to channel brain development in a more normal pattern? The first possibility may be more imminent and of greater ethical ambiguity than the second, but both raise the concerns of some people with reading disability and their advocates who believe some special skills that are valuable to the individual and society may be a direct consequence of their different brain development. I do recognize and admire the remarkable personal strengths of individuals who have successfully compensated for their reading disabilities through extraordinarily hard work and careful planning. Maybe this perseverance in overcoming or compensating for their reading disability leads to greater success in other areas. However, most adults with reading disabilities that I have met would have been happy to have effective gene therapy to avoid their learning difficulties. (I do not ask if they would have preferred abortion, as most lead reasonably happy lives.)

In the near term, a much less controversial application of genetic knowledge is at hand. We can now use family history and, I believe in the near future, associated genetic markers, along with behavioral data, to assess risk for reading disabilities before children enter school. If the risk is high, extraordinary environmental intervention during the preschool years may be prescribed to reduce the risk of reading failure in the early grades and to recognize the likely continued need for a supportive reading environment in the later school years.

It is very important to recognize that a significant genetic etiology for reading disability at the individual level does not imply that environmental intervention would not be helpful for that individual, but it may imply that the intervention needs to be extraordinary. Environmental support that is adequate for most typically developing children may be inadequate for many in the low tail of the reading distribution. Much research has been done on the benefits from preschool training in phonological and alphabetic skills for children at risk for reading disability, with positive results for early reading development, and diminishing benefits in the later grades (cf. Byrne, Fielding-Barnsley, & Ashley, 2000). Thus it seems that continued extraordinary environmental support is needed in the later grades for many children with reading disability. Computer programs have shown promise in providing this support to struggling readers through continued reinforcement of phonological skills, and most importantly for children beyond the third-grade reading level, support for their practice in accurate and fluent reading of text (Olson, Wise, Ring, & Johnson, 1997; Wise, Ring, & Olson, 1999, 2000).

At present, for many cases of severe reading disability, there are no special behavioral treatments that result in a normal trajectory for reading growth from a normal amount of reading practice (Olson, 2002). Children who overcome their reading disability usually do so through much more reading practice and perseverance than required by typically developing children. While we continue to search for behavioral and genetic or other biological interventions to ultimately normalize disabled readers' growth from reading practice, we need to recognize, encourage, and honor the extraordinary effort they must make to ultimately reach an adequate level of reading accuracy and fluency. Genes?? Yes, they do matter, but for now we must do our best to optimize the reading environment for children with reading disability.

ACKNOWLEDGMENTS

This work was supported in part by program project and center grants from the National Institute of Child Health and Development (HD-11681 and HD-27802), R01 HD38526, and RO1 HD-22223. The contributions of staff members of the many Colorado school districts that participated in our research, and of the twins and their families, are gratefully acknowledged.

REFERENCES

Byrne, B., Fielding-Barnsley, R., & Ashley, L. (2000). Effects of preschool phoneme identity training after six years: Outcome level distinguished from rate of response. *Journal of Educational Psychology, 92,* 659–667.

Cardon, L. R., Smith, S., Fulker, D., Kimberling, W., Pennington, B., & DeFries, J. (1994). Quantitative trait locus for reading disability on chromosome 6. *Science, 266,* 276–279.

Castles, A., Datta, H., Gayan, J., & Olson, R. K. (1999). Varieties of developmental reading disorder: Genetic and environmental influences. *Journal of Experimental Child Psychology, 72,* 73–94.

Coltheart, M., Curtis, B., Atkins, P., & Haller, M. (1993). Models of reading aloud: Dual route and parallel-distributed-processing approaches. *Psychological Review, 100,* 589–608.

DeFries, J. C., Alarcon, M., & Olson, R. K. (1997). Genetics and dyslexia: Developmental differences in the etiologies of reading and spelling deficits. In C. Hulme & M. Snowling (Eds.), *Dyslexia: Biological bases, identification, & intervention* (pp. 20–37). London: Whurr.

DeFries, J. C., & Fulker, D. W. (1985). Multiple regression analysis of twin data. *Behavior Genetics, 15,* 467–473.

DeFries, J. C., Fulker, D. W., & LaBuda, M. C. (1987). Evidence of a genetic aetiology in reading disability of twins. *Nature, (London), 329,* 537–539.

DeFries, J. C., Singer, S. M., Foch, T. T., & Lewitter, F. I. (1978). Familial nature of reading disability. *British Journal of Psychiatry, 132,* 361–367.

Dunn, L. M., & Markwardt, F. C. (1970). *Examiner's manual: Peabody Individual Achievement Test.* Circle Pines, MN: American Guidance Service.

Fisher, S. E., Francks, C., Marlow, A. J., MacPhie, L., Williams, D. F., Cardon, Lon R., Ishikawa-Brush, Y., Talcott, J. B., Richardson, A. J., Gayan, J., Olson, R. K., Pennington, B. F., Smith, S. D., DeFries, J. C., Stein, J. F., & Monaco, A. P. (2002). Genome-wide scans in independent samples reveal strong convergent evidence for a chromosome 18 quantitative-trait locus influencing developmental dyslexia. *Nature Genetics, 30,* 86–91.

Fletcher, J. M., Lyon, R., Barnes, M., Stuebing, K. K., Francis, D. J., Olson, R. K., Shaywitz, S. E., & Shaywitz, B. A. (2002). Classification of learning disabilities: An evidence based evaluation. In R. Bradley, L. Danielson, & D. P. Hallahan (Eds.), *Identification of learning disabilities—Research to practice* (pp. 185–250). Mahwah, NJ: Lawrence Erlbaum Associates.

Gayan, J., & Olson, R.K. (2001). Genetic and environmental influences on orthographic and phonological skills in children with reading disabilities. *Developmental Neuropsychology, 20,* 487–511.

Gayan, J., & Olson, R. K. (2003). Genetic and environmental influences on individual differences in printed word recognition. *Journal of Experimental Child Psychology, 84,* 97–123.

Gayan, J., Smith, S. D., Cherny, S. S., Cardon, L. R., Fulker, D. W., Kimberling, W. J., Olson, R. K., Pennington, B., & DeFries, J. C. (1999). Large quantitative trait locus for specific language and reading deficits in chromosome 6p. *American Journal of Human Genetics, 64,* 157–164.

Grigorenko, E. L., Wood, F. B., Meyer, M. S., Hart, L. A., Speed, W. C., Shuster, B. S., & Pauls, D. L. (1997). Susceptibility loci for distinct components of developmental dyslexia on chromosomes 6 and 15. *American Journal of Human Genetics, 60,* 27–39.

Hulslander, J., Willcutt, E., Talcott, J., Witton, C., Pennington, B., & Olson, R.K. (2002, June 29). *Reading ability, ADHD, and performance on visual and auditory psychophysical tasks.* Poster presented at the meeting of the Society for the Scientific Study of Reading, Chicago.

Hyona, J., & Olson, R. K. (1995). Eye fixation patterns among dyslexic and normal readers: Effects of word length and word frequency. *Journal of Experimental Psychology: Learning, Memory, and Cognition, 21*(6), 1–11.

Kaplan, D. E., Gayan, J., Ahn, J., Won, T. W., Pauls, D., Olson, R., DeFries, J. C., Wood, F., Pennington, B., Page, G., Smith, S.D., & Gruen, J. R. (2002). Evidence for linkage and association with reading disability on 6P21.3-22. *American Journal of Human Genetics, 70,* 1287–1298.

Lyon, G. R., Fletcher, J. M., Shaywitz, S. E., Shaywitz, B. A., Torgesen, J. K., Wood, F. B., Schulte, A., & Olson, R. K. (2001). Rethinking learning disabilities. In C. E. Finn, A. J. Rotherham, & C. R. Hokanson Jr. (Eds.), *Rethinking special education for a new century* (pp. 259–287). Washington, DC: Progressive Policy Institute and the Thomas B. Fordham Foundation.

Olson, D. R. (2002). Literacy in the past millennium. In E. Hjelmquist & C. von Euler (Eds.), *Dyslexia and literacy: A tribute to Ingvar Lundberg* (pp. 23–38). London: Whurr.

Olson, R. K. (2002). Phoneme awareness and reading, from the old to the new millenium. In E. Hjelmquist & C. von Euler (Eds.), *Dyslexia and literacy: A tribute to Ingvar Lundberg* (pp. 100–116). London: Whurr.

Olson, R. K., & Datta, H. (2002). Visual-temporal processing in reading-disabled and normal twins. *Reading and Writing, 15,* 127–149.

Olson, R. K., Datta, H., Gayan, J., & DeFries, J.C. (1999). A behavioral-genetic analysis of reading disabilities and component processes. In R.M. Klein & P.A. McMullen (Eds.), *Converging methods for understanding reading and dyslexia* (pp. 133–153). Cambridge, MA: MIT Press.

Olson, R. K., Forsberg, H., & Wise, B. (1994). Genes, environment, and the development of orthographic skills. In V. W. Berninger (Ed.), *The varieties of orthographic knowledge I: Theoretical and developmental issues* (pp. 27–71). Dordrecht, The Netherlands: Kluwer Academic.

Olson, R. K., Forsberg, H., Wise, B., & Rack, J. (1994). Measurement of word recognition, orthographic, and phonological skills. In G.R. Lyon (Ed.), *Frames of reference for the assessment of learning disabilities: New views on measurement issues* (pp. 243–277). Baltimore, MD: Brookes.

Olson, R. K., Kliegl, R., & Davidson, B. J. (1983a). Dyslexic and normal readers' eye movements. *Journal of Experimental Psychology: Human Perception and Performance, 9,* 816–825.

Olson, R. K., Kliegl, R., & Davidson, B. J. (1983b). Eye movements in reading disability. In K. Rayner (Ed.), *Eye movements in reading: Perceptual and language processes* (pp. 467–480). New York: Academic Press.

Olson, R. K., Kliegl, R., Davidson, B. J., & Foltz, G. (1985). Individual and developmental differences in reading disability. In G. E. MacKinnon and T. G. Waller (Eds.), *Reading research: Advances in theory and practice, Vol. 4* (pp. 1–64). New York: Academic Press.

Olson, R. K., Wise, B., Conners, F., Rack, J., & Fulker, D. (1989). Specific deficits in component reading and language skills: Genetic and environmental influences. *Journal of Learning Disabilities, 22,* 339–348.

Olson, R. K., Wise, B. W., Ring, J., & Johnson, M. (1997). Computer-based remedial training in phoneme awareness and phonological decoding: Effects on the post-training development on word recognition. *Scientific Studies of Reading, 1,* 235–253.

Pavlidis, G. Th. (1981). Do eye movements hold the key to dyslexia? *Neuropsychologia, 19,* 57–64.

Rack, J. P., Snowling, M. J., & Olson, R. K. (1992). The nonword reading deficit in developmental dyslexia: A review. *Reading Research Quarterly, 27*(1), 28–53.

Rogers, B. (1982). The identification and prevalence of specific reading retardation. *British Journal of Educational Psychology, 53,* 369–373.

Share, D. L., Jorm, A. F., Maclean, R., & Matthews, R. (2002). Temporal processing and reading disability. *Reading and Writing: An Interdisciplinary Journal, 15,* 151–178.

Smith, S. D., Kelley, P. M., Askew, J. W., Hoover, D. M., Deffenbacher, K. E., Gayan, J., Brower, A., & Olson, R. K. (2001). Reading disability and chromosome 6p21.3: Evaluation of MOG as a candidate gene. *Journal of Learning Disabilities, 34,* 512–519.

Stein, J. (2001). The sensory basis of reading problems. *Developmental Neuropsychology, 20,* 509–534.

Tallal, P. (1980). Auditory temporal perception, phonics, and reading disabilities in children. *Brain and Language, 9,* 182–198.

Wadsworth, S. J., Knopic, V. S., & DeFries, J. C. (2000). Reading disability in boys and girls: No evidence for a differential genetic etiology. *Reading and Writing: An Interdisciplinary Journal, 13,* 133–145.

Wadsworth, S. J., Olson, R. K., Pennington, B. F., & DeFries, J. C. (2000). Differential genetic etiology of reading disability as a function of IQ. *Journal of Learning Disabilities, 33,* 192–199.

Wise, B. W., Ring, J., & Olson, R. K. (1999). Training phonological awareness with and without attention to articulation. *Journal of Experimental Child Psychology, 72,* 271–304.

Wise, B. W., Ring, J., & Olson, R. K. (2000). Individual differences in gains from computer-assisted remedial reading with more emphasis on phonological analysis or accurate reading in context. *Journal of Experimental Child Psychology, 77,* 197–235.

42

Maternal Mediation in a Young Child's Writing Activity: A Sociocultural Perspective

Dorit Aram
Tel Aviv University

Ofra Korat
Bar Ilan University

Iris Levin
Tel Aviv University

In this chapter, we review two studies we conducted that focused on mother–child joint writing activity as a function of their sociocultural background and its relation to the child's literacy level in two age groups: kindergartners and second graders. In the first study with second graders, we compared two socioeconomic-status (SES) groups, high SES (HSES) and low SES (LSES), and in the second, with kindergartners, we delved deeper into the LSES by studying SES differences within the LSES group. The most important findings of the two studies described here are the links found between the quality of maternal mediation of writing and children's literacy. In the first study of second graders, LSES differed from HSES on maternal mediation and on children's literacy level. However, the correlations between these variables within each group—HSES and LSES—appeared only in the HSES group. In the second study, in which only LSES kindergartners were studied, these correlations were especially strong. Within this group, even after all sociocultural measures (SES, maternal exposure to children's and adults' books, and literacy-related materials at home), were controlled for, the link between the quality of maternal mediation of writing and the child's reading and writing skills is still substantial.

INTRODUCTION

In this chapter, development is conceived of as embedded in the sociocultural context. It claims that culture shapes the mind, that the original form of higher mental activity is external and social and is then appropriated by the individual in the course of activity in collaboration with more experienced others. This line of thinking is associated with the sociocultural theories of Vygotsky (1978), neo-Vygotskians like Rogoff (1990) and Wertsch (1984), cultural psychologists like Bruner (1996), and the contextual ecological theory of Bronfenbrenner (1979).

Reading and writing are essential cultural tools in modern, technologically oriented cultures. Parental mediation, through which children are introduced to this code, constitutes a central factor in literacy development (Kagicibasi, 1996; Rogoff, 1990). Differences in the quantity and quality of parental literacy mediation reportedly are related to differences in young children's competencies in this area (Adams, 1991; Reese & Cox, 1999; Rogoff, 1990). Research on parental mediation in literacy-promoting contexts has focused mainly on the area of joint story-book reading (Allison & Watson, 1994; Burgess, 1997; DeBaryshe, 1993; DeBaryshe & Binder, 1994; Hale & Windecker, 1993; Mackler, Baker, & Sonnenschein, 1999; Reese & Cox, 1999; Sénéchal, 1997). Parent–child joint storybook reading (nature and amount) was assumed to set the stage for future differences in children's literacy and academic achievements (Teale, 1981).

Bus, van IJzendoorn, and Pellegrini (1995) and Scarborough and Dobrich (1994) reviewed more than three decades of empirical research pertaining to the relationship between storybook reading and the development of literacy skills. These authors concluded that reading to children accounted for 8% of the overall variance in language, emergent literacy, and literacy skills. From this finding, it is apparent that a large amount of the variance remains to be explained, and other factors, such as joint parent–child activities, could be critical. Children share with their parents a variety of literacy-related activities that may enhance their literacy skills (Teale, 1986; Tudge & Putnam, 1997), of which storybook reading is one. Scarborough and Dobrich (1994) suggest that further research may find that other early literacy experiences have a powerful relationship with literacy development.

This chapter reviews two studies that examined another early literacy-promoting activity: parent–child mutual writing. The first study involved second graders and their mothers from two socioeconomic-status (SES) groups engaged in a parent–child writing activity (see details in Korat & Levin, 2002). The second study involved kindergartners and their mothers from only a low-SES (LSES) group, in a collaborative writing activity (see details in Aram & Levin, 2002, 2004). Our purpose in these studies was to analyze the nature of maternal mediation during the joint writing activity as a function of sociocultural background and its relationship to the child's literacy level in the two age groups: kindergartners and second graders.

Preschoolers' experience with writing is important for cultivating literacy. Durkin (1966), who observed precocious readers, found that for many of them writing came before reading. She suggested that reading seemed almost a by-product of writing. When children write, they ask questions about the relationship between speech and print that can help them construct their knowledge about the written system. Observations in homes reveal that children engage in pretend writing, invent spelling, and question their parents about what their parents write (Baker, Fernandez-Fein, Scher, & Williams, 1998; Bissex, 1980; Harste, Woodward, & Burke, 1984; Tudge & Putnam, 1997).

Parental mediation of writing often occurs as an integral part of ongoing day-to-day activity rather than as a ritual, like storybook reading (Weinberger, 1996). Writing interactions among preschoolers are often initiated by children who wish to write and who spontaneously ask their parents how to write or by parents modeling or explaining the spelling of words. Yet the nature of parent–child writing transactions has hardly been studied.

Two case studies on emergent literacy development referred to children's writing interactions with family members, teachers, or age mates. In her seminal study, Bissex (1980) documented longitudinally her son Paul's development of writing at home between the ages of 5 and 11 years. Despite her deep interest in and consistent study of her son's writing, Bissex considered Paul to be his own teacher and she provided only sparse information about the support that she, and presumably her husband, provided for their son's early writing. Gundlach, McLane, Stott, and McNamee (1985), unlike Bissex, assumed that parents and older siblings play an active role in young children's writing development. They describe three case studies of young children beginning to write, emphasizing the social nature of their experience. The first case study is of a 4-year-old boy trying to write at home. The parents supported his writing activity and explained the nature of the written system. The second case study is of a 5-year-old girl writing with her mother and her 7-year-old sister. The role that the older sister plays in her younger sister's writing activities (as a model, a coach, a competitor, and a coconspirator) is emphasized.

The third study shifts the focus from writing at home to writing in a preschool setting, describing writing interactions of three preschoolers among themselves and with their teacher.

Two experimental studies analyzed parent–child joint writing. Burns and Casbergue (1992) examined collaborative writing among 3- to 5-year-olds and their parents. Parental mediation in which high levels of control were demonstrated was related to more conventional products and to parent–child exchanges that focused on spelling. Parental mediation in with lower levels of control was related to less conventional products and to a focus on the letters of the alphabet. DeBaryshe, Buell, and Binder (1996) observed 5- and 6-year-old children attempting to write a letter alone and with their mother's assistance. Children produced more sophisticated products with maternal mediation than in solo writing. Almost all mothers guided their children to use conventional spelling in the dyadic condition, irrespective of the child's solo level.

Compared with the ample research that exists on the role played by parent–child literate activities in emergent literacy, and particularly joint storybook reading, research observing parents assisting schoolchildren in literacy activities are rare. This type of observation is very important because parents of school beginners are highly involved with their children's reading and writing in functional or playful daily activities (Bissex, 1980; Clay, 1975; Heath, 1983; Taylor & Dorsey-Gaines, 1988) as well as in academic activities, such as homework support (Anderson, 1986; Cooper, 1989; Hoover-Dempsy, Bussler, & Burow, 1995; Levin et al., 1997). Yet we do not have a clear picture of the nature of parent–child joint reading or writing with young schoolchildren.

The two studies presented in detail in this chapter examine the sociocultural context of literacy development among young children, focusing on the unique role of mother–child collaborative writing. The sociocultural aspects that we refer to are SES, literacy environment at home, and maternal literacy. There is a stable, well-documented connection between SES and children's literacy. Children who come from a lower SES show a lower level of achievement on such literacy measures as phonological awareness, letter naming, word writing, word recognition, receptive vocabulary, and grammar (e.g., Bowey, 1995; Duncan, 1991; Feitelson & Goldstein, 1986; Lonigan, Burgess, Anthony, & Baker, 1998; Nicholson, 1999; Ogbu, 1990; Reese, 1995; Smith & Dixon, 1995; Walker, Greenwood, Hart, & Carta, 1994; Whitehurst, 1997). Children who have access to literacy-evocative materials and experiences (papers, pencils, books, blackboards, crayons, booklets, journals, dictionaries, cards, visits to the library, etc.) tend to become more proficient readers than children lacking such tools and activities (Hart & Risley, 1992; Neuman & Celano, 2001; Nicholson, 1999; Sonnenschein, Shmidt, & Mackler, 1999; Stuart, Dixon, Masterson, & Quinlan, 1998; Whitehurst, 1999). Mothers from different SES groups differ in their level of language, frequency of reading and writing in their everyday life, and the amount of pleasure they get from reading and writing. Some parents expose their children to positive models of reading; others do not (Heath, 1983; McCormick & Mason, 1986; Teale, 1986).

In our kindergarten sample, we focused on maternal guidance of the graphophonemic code and the child's autonomy in printing the letters and in writing unfamiliar words. In the second-grade sample, we examined child's autonomy in the writing activity while composing and printing a simple text, that is, a shopping list for a birthday party.

THE STUDIES

Study 1: Mothers' Mediation of Text Writing With Their Second-Grade Children: A Comparison Between Two SES Groups

In this study, we examined low-SES (LSES) and high-SES (HSES), second-grade children's independent writing, followed by mother–child collaborative writing of the same text: a shopping list for the child's imaginary birthday party. Our purpose was to analyze the nature of parent–child mutual writing activity as a function of the child's family background and its relation to the child's independent writing level. Our focus was on the child's autonomy in the writing activity while composing and printing the text.

Young children, regardless of their social strata, are frequently exposed to the writing of shopping lists and are aware of their usage. Lists are usually written as a mnemonic device and require planning, organizing, and qualifying items according to the list's function. Young children have been reported to be involved in writing lists on their own or in collaboration with others even before they are of school age (Clay, 1975). Lists can be considered a particular genre. They include nouns, noun phrases, and, sometimes, descriptors rather than complete sentences. They are displayed as single items running from top to bottom rather than as complete lines or paragraphs.

A total of 40 second graders and their mothers took part in this study. They were recruited from two schools located in two urban neighborhoods in the greater area of Tel Aviv, Israel. One neighborhood was populated mainly by LSES families and the other by HSES families. Participants were solicited by letters sent to parents through the school system. From the 75% of the parents who returned permission forms, 10 boys and 10 girls and their mothers from each SES were randomly chosen and invited to participate. The two schools used a program of reading and writing instruction called "No Secrets" (in Hebrew *Bli Sodot*), which is employed by approximately 39% of elementary schools in Israel (Ministry of Education, 2001). "No Secrets" is an eclectic program with an emphasis on phonics, whole-word, and meaning instruction.

Most LSES mothers were Israeli born, with Asian or North African origins. Most HSES mothers were Israeli born, with European origins. In both groups most of the families were intact. The mothers and fathers in the two SES groups differed significantly in the number of school years: mothers, LSES $M = 11.4$ versus HSES $M = 16.7$, $t(38) = 5.63$, $p < .001$; fathers, LSES $M = 10.6$ versus HSES $M = 16.7$, $t(38) = 6.46$, $p < .001$. The LSES and HSES parental occupational levels, measured on a 4-point scale (Roe, 1956) adapted to the Israeli population (Meir, 1978), differed significantly: mothers, LSES $M = 2.3$ versus HSES $M = 3.7$, $t(38) = 7.37$, $p < .001$; fathers, LSES $M = 2.1$ versus HSES $M = 3.4$, $t(38) = 5.83$, $p < .001$. A significant difference between the two SES groups was also found in the number of rooms per apartment, LSES $M = 3.1$ versus HSES $M = 4.5$, $t(38) = 7.15$, $p < .001$, but not in the number of children per family, LSES $M = 2.6$ versus HSES $M = 2.7$; $t(38) = 0.31$, ns.

Data were collected in three sessions. In the first session, the child was invited to a quiet room in the school, given two blank sheets of paper, a pencil, and a set of thin markers, and asked to write a shopping list for a birthday party. The interviewer read out the following instructions: "Imagine that in a week's time you are going to have a birthday party. Please, write a shopping list for this party." The written instructions were left on the table in front of the child. No help was provided. In the second session, 3–4 days after the first session, the researcher visited the child's home for observations of mother–child interactions during the same writing activity. The mother–child collaborative writing occurred in the participants' chosen place at home (in the living room, in the child's room, or in the kitchen) and lasted, on average, for about 25 min ($M = 25$ min; range: 15–40 min). The interviewer gave the child the same writing materials and written instructions as in the independent writing activity. The mother was asked to sit next to the child and to provide help as she deemed fit. A VHS camcorder on a tripod, placed at the far end of the room, videotaped the session. The interviewer left the room while the mother and the child completed the task. In the third session, the researcher revisited the homes for gathering demographic and family literacy information from the mother.

Interviews with the mothers were used to assess the literacy environment at home and maternal exposure to books. The literacy environment at home was measured on a 10-point scale that assessed the existence of literacy tools and activities (e.g., computer, tape recorders, video tapes, arithmetic games, daily newspaper, subscription to adults' and children's magazines, reading and writing activities, library visits). Maternal exposure to books was assessed by the Title Recognition Test (TRT; Stanovich & West, 1989). The checklist task is a proxy indicator of a person's exposure to print. This checklist method presents the participant with a list of book titles, some of which are real book titles and others are foils (fictitious names). Participants scan the list and check the book titles they recognize. The advantages of this measure are its immunity from social desirability, its low cognitive load, and the lack of a necessity for retrospective time judgments. The storybook exposure measure is sensitive to individuals' actual exposure to books. We presented the mothers with two checklists: an Adult's TRT (ATRT) and a Children's TRT (CTRT). The adults' lists predict an adult's vocabulary, verbal fluency, and reading comprehension (Cunningham & Stanovich, 1991; Stanovich & Cunningham, 1993). The children's list, when administered to parents, predicts their childs' language better than traditional self-report measures of storybook reading do (Sénéchal, LeFevre, Hudson, & Lawson, 1996; Sénéchal, LeFevre, Thomas, & Daley, 1998).

Mothers were presented with two lists: one of children's book titles and one of adults' book titles. Each list was composed of 30 titles: 20 recommended popular books and 10 foils that were verified as nonexistent titles in library databases. They were asked to read the lists and indicate the titles that they recognized. To obtain a total score on exposure to print, a correct recognition contributed 1 point and an incorrect one, deleted 2 points so that recognition of all books in the list would result in a zero score.

Results

Literacy Environment at Home and Maternal Books Exposure by SES. Comparisons between the two SES groups regarding literacy-related tools and activities and maternal exposure to adults' and children's books are presented in Table 42.1.

The upper part of Table 42.1 shows that LSES homes were significantly less affluent than HSES homes in literacy tools and activities. Furthermore, LSES mothers recognized significantly fewer children's and adults' books than did HSES mothers.

The child's independent writing of text in school—a shopping list—was scored on four aspects: (a) number of print signs (e.g., letters, numbers, punctuation marks); (b) number of genre elements (the number of products in the list); (c) percentage of spelling errors (calculated as number of spelling errors out of number of letters written in the text); and (d) number of linguistic elements of the written register (i.e., number of descriptors of the products such as tasty bubblegums, 10 bottles of Coca Cola, beautiful candles). The second part of Table 42.1 shows that LSES children produced significantly less advanced texts as measured by all four aspects of writing. These differences were especially large in the percentages of spelling errors.

Videotapes of the mother–child dyadic interactions during the same writing activity in the home were transcribed verbatim, and transcripts, videotapes, and the written texts were all examined together to code the interactions. The interaction was segmented into topic units, that is, the idea or the theme of the discourse (Diamond, 1996; Schiffrin, 1987). Whenever a new topic was raised, it was defined as the beginning of a new unit.

Within each unit, the child's level of autonomy was scored on a 5-point scale in which a score of 5 indicated that the child produced the text unit autonomously (e.g., the child wrote the name of a product in the list, the mother looked at the child's writing and said "very nice." Then the child started writing the next product); a score of 4 indicated that the child produced the text unit autonomously with some help from the mother (e.g., after writing a word the child asked the mother if the word was spelled correctly, and the mother responded to the child); a score of 3 indicated that both parties played an equal part in the text unit production (e.g., the mother asked a question of clarification and the child gave the right answer, which

TABLE 42.1

Means and Standard Deviations of Literacy Tools at Home, Maternal Exposure to Print, Child's
Independent Text Level, Child's Autonomy, and Maternal Reinforcement and Criticism by SES

	Low SES M (SD)	High SES M (SD)	df	t	p<
Literacy tools at home and maternal exposure to print					
Literacy tools and activities at home (possible range of scores = 1–10)	6.5 (1.80)	8.7 (1.07)	38	4.82	.00
Maternal adults' books exposure (possible range of scores = −20–20)	2.60 (3.25)	12.80 (4.23)	38	8.54	.00
Maternal children's books exposure (possible range of of scores = −20–20)	1.35 (3.34)	6.20 (3.70)	38	4.35	.00
Child's independent text level					
No. of written signs	37.00 (21.04)	90.45 (71.70)	38	3.20	.00
No. of genre elements	4.35 (3.08)	8.35 (3.52)	38	3.82	.00
Percentage of spelling errors	17.90 (12.51)	2.46 (2.70)	38	5.39	.00
No. of linguistic elements	4.49 (3.36)	9.15 (5.19)	38	3.43	.00
Child's autonomy in the interaction					
Child's autonomy in the writing interaction (possible range of scores = 1–5)	2.93 (0.77)	3.94 (1.04)	37	3.39	.00
Maternal reinforcement and criticism in the interaction					
Maternal reinforcements	2.25 (2.75)	2.40 (4.06)	38	0.15	.97
Maternal criticism	0.55 (.87)	0.00 (0.00)	38	2.77	.01

progressed the text writing); a score of 2 indicated that the mother produced the text unit
with some help from the child (e.g., the mother asked the child a question but she gave the
answer herself after a very short try of the child, or the mother dictated to the child what
to write); a score of 1 indicated that the mother produced the text unit autonomously (e.g.,
the mother wrote by herself the products in the list.) According to the third part in Table
42.1, LSES children were significantly less autonomous in text writing than were their HSES
counterparts.

The affective aspects that were measured in the writing interaction included maternal reinforcement and criticism. Maternal reinforcements and criticisms were counted throughout
the interaction. Maternal reinforcements included general remarks like "good," "very nice,"
"you are a good boy," as well as specific comments like "you wrote bubblegum beautifully."
Maternal criticism included disapprovals related to the child's performance, like "you wrote it
wrong" or "how many spelling mistakes do you have?" and discipline remarks like "sit still,"
"stop it", or "listen to me." The fourth part in Table 42.1 shows that mothers from the two SES
groups did not differ in the frequency of reinforcing comments. However, only LSES mothers
expressed critical remarks.

Correlational Analyses.   Table 42.2 presents correlations between sociocultural measures, children's text level, children's autonomy, and maternal affective responses across SES groups. The intercorrelations among the sociocultural measures (literacy tools and activities at home and maternal exposure to adults' and children's books) are positive, moderate, and significant.

The intercorrelations among children's text measures range from low moderate to high, and significant. No correlations were found between measures of the mother–child interaction during the writing activity (i.e., child's autonomy and maternal affective responses). Moderate and significant correlations were found between child's autonomy and sociocultural measures and between child's autonomy and child's text level. Negative, low moderate, and significant correlations were found between sociocultural measures and maternal criticism but they were not correlated with maternal reinforcement.

Correlations within SES groups are not presented in the table. Most of them were insignificant. Still, correlations of child's text measures in both SES groups were positive, moderate to high, and significant. Thus correlations were found between number of written signs and number of genre elements (LSES: $r = .60$, $p < .01$; HSES: $r = .90$, $p < .001$); between number of written signs and number of linguistic elements (LSES: $r = .62$, $p < .001$, HSES: $r = .93$, $p < .001$) ; and between number of genre elements and linguistic elements (LSES: $r = .99$, $p < .001$; HSES: $r = .98$, $p < .001$).

In the LSES group, child autonomy in the interaction was positively and significantly correlated with maternal reinforcements ($r = .47$, $p < .04$), and maternal reinforcements were also positively and significantly correlated with maternal criticism ($r = .54$, $p < .01$). In the HSES group, child's autonomy in the interaction with the mother was negatively and significantly correlated with child's independent spelling errors ($r = -.50$, $p < .01$); in the LSES group, maternal exposure to adults' and to children's books were positively and significantly correlated ($r = .56$, $p < .02$).

In sum, our findings demonstrate a clear difference between the two social groups in terms of home literacy environment, maternal exposure to books, children's independent text writing, children's autonomy in the collaborative writing activity with their mothers, and the amount of criticism that the mothers use throughout this activity. Our findings also indicate positive and significant correlations between most aspects across SES, but fewer correlations within SES groups.

To more fully illustrate the relationship between the sociocultural measures, child's independent text level and maternal mediation, we present here two protocols of mother–child interactions, one from each SES group. These protocols were selected for presentation because they were typical for their SES in terms of the interaction.

Ben and Omer.[1]   Ben and Omer are second-grade boys. Ben lives in a LSES and Omer in a HSES neighborhood, both in the greater area of Tel Aviv. In his independent text, Ben listed four products: "presents, a cake, sweets, food," which was about the average number of items in the LSES group ($M = 4.35$, $SD = 3.08$). The independent text of Ben's list appears in upper left-hand panel of Fig. 42.1.

The list's display was not conventional in that it was written horizontally. It was composed of 16 written signs, which is substantially below the average number of signs in the LSES group ($M = 37$, $SD = 21.04$). Seven spelling errors emerged (43%, out of the total number of letters), which is higher than the average percentage in the LSES group ($M = 17.90\%$, $SD = 12.51$). No descriptors appeared in the list.

---

[1] All names are fictitious.

TABLE 42.2

Correlations Among Literacy Tools at Home, Maternal Exposure to Print, Child's Independent Text Level, Child's Autonomy, and Maternal Reinforcement and Criticism Across SES Levels

	Literacy Tools and Activities at Home	Maternal Exposure to Adults' Books	Maternal Exposure to Children's Books	Child's Writing (No. of Signs)	Child's Writing (No. of Genre Elements)	Child's Writing (Spelling Errors)	Child's Writing (Linguistic Elements)	Child's Autonomy in the Interaction	Maternal Reinforcement	Maternal Criticism
Literacy tools and activities at home										
Maternal exposure to adults' books	.56**									
Maternal exposure to children's books	.40*	.49**								
Child's writing no. of signs	.36*	.27	.32*							
Child's writing no. of genre elements	.35*	.34*	.43**	.82***						
Child's writing spelling errors	−.33*	−.60**	−.34*	−.38**	−.28					
Child's writing linguistic elements	.36*	.31*	.37*	.87**	.98**	−.27				
Child's autonomy in the interaction	.42*	.54**	.34*	.26	.40*	−.45**	−.45**	.37*		
Maternal reinforcement	.12	−.03	−.07	.08	.17	−.03	−.03	.18	.18	
Maternal criticism	−.32*	−.39*	−.19	−.20	−.15	.36**	−.15	.36**	−.06	.30

Note. * *p* < .05, ** *p* < .01, *** *p* < .001.

FIG. 42.1.   Examples of independent and mutual texts.

Omer's list (in upper right-hand panel of Fig. 42.1) had a title, "Shopping List," and was also written horizontally. It was in a speech format rather than as names of single items, as required in a list. Omer mentioned four products: "To buy cheesecake and chocolate cake, sweets too and surprises for children." The list included fewer products than the average number in his HSES group ($M = 8.35$, $SD = 3.52$) and only 57 signs, substantially fewer than the average in his HSES group ($M = 90.45$, $SD = 71.70$). The list included four spelling errors (8.7 %), higher than the average percentage in his HSES group ($M = 2.46$, $SD = 2.70$), and three descriptors "cheesecake," "chocolate cake," and "surprises for children," which is below average in his HSES group ($M = 9.15$, $SD = 5.19$).

Ben is the eldest child in a family of two children. His mother completed 10 years of schooling and she is a housewife. His father completed 10 years of schooling and works as a printer. In Ben's home, there are few educational games, several videocassettes, 25 adults' books (about a fifth of the LSES average for number of adults' books, $M = 124.34$, $SD = 128.11$), 20 children's books (less than half the LSES average, $M = 51.47$, $SD = 51.47$), and no computer. Ben's family buys a daily newspaper and subscribes to one periodical for adults and no periodicals for children. The mother reported that her son is being read to about twice a week, mostly by her, and that they do not visit the local library. The mother's score on exposure to adults' books was 3 (about the same as the LSES average, $M = 2.60$, $SD = 3.25$) and exposure to children's books was 4 (higher than the LSES average, $M = 1.35$, $SD = 3.34$).

Omer has three brothers, two older and one younger than he. His mother completed 20 years of schooling and works as a social worker. His father completed 16 years of schooling and works as a computer engineer. In Omer's home there are many educational games, many videocassettes, a computer, about 300 adults' books (about same as the HSES average, $M = 308.75$, $SD = 196.28$) and about 50 children's books (less than the HSES average, $M = 86.25$, $SD = 49.49$).

Omer's family buys and reads the newspaper once a week and subscribes to two periodicals for adults and one for children. The child and his mother have visited the local library for the past 2 years. According to the mother's report, the child is being read to twice a week, usually by the father and sometimes by her. The mother's score on exposure to adults' books was 18 (above the HSES average, $M = 12.80$, $SD = 4.23$) and to children's books was 8 (above the HSES average, $M = 6.20$, $SD = 3.70$).

The mutual text of Ben and his mother included eight products (less than LSES average, $M = 10.65$, $SD = 4.62$) written vertically and was composed of 38 signs (less than LSES average, $M = 85.95$, $SD = 36.70$) with no spelling errors (that is, fewer errors than the LSES average, $M = 3.28$, $SD = 4.79$). No descriptors accompanied the products (much lower than the LSES average, $M = 11.35$, $SD = 5.53$).

Here is an excerpt from the protocol of this dyad's interaction[2]:

(After the first product was written in the list)

M: What else do we need to buy for the party?

C: *Mamtakim* [sweets].

M: Write *mamtakim*. Write it below the cake. *Mam-ta-kim.*

C: (Starts to write. One letter in the beginning of the word—*mɛm*—is missing.)

M: Add one more *mɛm* [the missing letter], do the *mɛm* here . . . *mɛm* . . . *mam-ta-kim.*

C: (Adds *mɛm*.)

M: (Dictates to him before he continues to write): *Yud* [a letter name] and write a final *mɛm* [*mɛm* at the final position of words has a different shape than a regular *mɛm* and is called 'final *mɛm*']

C: (Writes.)

M: What else do we need? What do you think?

C: *Balonim* [Balloons].

M: Write *balonim, ba-lo-nim.*

C: (Writes the two first letters.)

M: (Dictates the end of the word): *Yud* [letter name] and *final mɛm* [letter name].

C: (Writes.)

M: (Erases the first letter, which was not well formed.) Fix here the *bɛt* [letter name]. *Bɛt.* (Erases the letter *lamed* as well.) *Lamɛd*, write *lamɛd. Ba-lo-* . . . .

---

[2] Note that Hebrew words are spelled in International Phonetic Alphabetic symbols.

C: (Writes the letter *bεt*.)
M: Now you need to write the letter *vav*.
C: (Writes.)
M: What else do you think? Try to think (does not wait for the child's answer). Write *matanot* [presents].
C: Yes. OK.
M: OK write, *mεm*, *tεt*, . . . (dictates letter names).

From this example we can see that the child suggests most of the items, with prompting from the mother, but that sometimes she proposes an item. She suggests writing the list vertically and he accepts her suggestion. She erases letters that she considers not well shaped and asks the child to rewrite them, which he does. She monitors and suggests corrections of spelling. The letters of some words are dictated by the mother to the child even without the child's requesting such help. Because correct spelling is important to her and because she knows that the child makes spelling errors, she prefers sometimes to dictate the letters to him rather than to allow him to work independently on his own spelling. Ben's mother does not express any critical remarks during the entire interaction. She provides five reinforcements, more than the average in their LSES group ($M = 2.25$, $SD = 4.06$). The child himself initiated almost nothing during their mutual writing activity but waited for his mother to push it forward. We got the impression that this child did not explore the writing process, neither in terms of composing the text nor in coping with spelling.

The mutual text of Omer and his mother included 17 products (more than the HSES average, $M = 13.85$, $SD = 7.95$) written vertically, with two or three products in a row. It was composed of 284 written signs (more than the HSES average, $M = 133.80$, $SD = 104.60$) and had four spelling errors (2%) (about the HSES average, $M = 1.99$, $SD = 2.41$). The text included 11 descriptors (less than the HSES average, $M = 15.60.65$, $SD = 10.04$).

Here is an excerpt from the protocol of this dyad's interaction:
(After the six first products in the list were written)

M: Do you have something else?
C: Prizes to the children (writes "prizes for the children").
M: (Looks at the text and laughs. It looks like she enjoys her son's ideas.)
C: (Makes a gesture that designates that he remembers something else. He writes, "different types of prizes.")
M: (Looks at the text and smiles). Of course.
C: (Writes, then stops. Looks as if he is contemplative. Goes on writing: "And different types of drinks.")
M: This is something! (says it proudly). In the next birthday party that we'll have, you are going to write the shopping list.
C: (He writes quietly, and suddenly he exclaims) Waw! I forgot something.
M: What?
C: (He writes *ptl*   [red berry juice], Coka-cola and Kinley [Brand names for drinks].)
M: You are really something! What else? What did you have in your last birthday that you liked?
C: (Smiles) Oy!, How could I forget it? (He writes "a magician.")
M: But this. . . you don't buy. It does not seem . . . it is a different thing.
C: Aa Ha (accepts her remark and erases the word.) What else?

From this transcription we can see that Omer was the composer of the text and the scribe. Even if the mother asks, from time to time, "what else?" he actually does not need her encouragement in order to move the text forward. The mother ignores the fact that her son is not writing the list in the conventional vertical direction. However, when the child includes in the shopping list an inappropriate item—a magician—she explains the error and her son accepts her comment. It is clear that the mother enjoys her son's ideas and expresses reinforcing comments. She did not use any critical remarks in the entire interaction and used nine reinforcements, substantially more than the average in their HSES group ($M = 2.40$, $SD = 4.06$). The child seems to feel responsible to move the text production forward and he seems enthusiastic and highly motivated about doing so. He enjoys his mother's support but he neither waits for her to provide guidance nor does he wait for her reaction to his emerging ideas.

Study 2: LSES Mothers' Mediation of Their Kindergartners' Writing of Single Unfamiliar Words

In this study, we examined the cultural context of emergent literacy among LSES kindergartners, focusing on the unique role of mother–child collaborative writing. The study's aims were to reveal the relationship between the cultural context (maternal writing mediation and sociocultural measures) and emergent literacy and to examine the unique relationship between the nature of mother–child joint writing and emergent literacy, controlling for the effects of the other sociocultural measures (SES, literacy-related tools at home, and maternal literacy level).

The sample included 41 children (19 boys and 22 girls) and their mothers, recruited from an Israeli "development town" whose residents are mainly of LSES (National Center for Statistics, 1997). Children were recruited from seven kindergartens in seven neighborhoods in the town. The neighborhoods were ranked on a 7-point scale from the lowest (1) to the highest (7) on their socioeconomic level by the head of the municipal welfare department and by the municipal educational superintendent, both of whom agreed on the assigned rankings. To control for the possible mediating effects of the children's age on children's literacy and on mother–child interaction, we restricted the age range, sampling children born between January and June. The children's average age was 5 years and 8 months ($M = 69.59$ months, $SD = 2.14$). From the 46 parents who received letters describing our study, 41 returned the permission forms and were invited to participate. The parents were Israeli born, with Asian or North African origins; most of the families were intact. The average number of children per family was 3.32 ($SD = 1.42$), which is higher than the national average of 2.20 (National Center for Statistics, 1999). All parents were schooled in Israel. The level of parental education was lower than the national average of their Israeli cohort. The mother's and the father's numbers of school yearswere 11.80 ($SD = 2.00$) and 11.05 ($SD = 2.54$), respectively. Profession and occupation were assessed on a scale adjusted to our sample, considering that, on a national scale (Meir, 1978), the variance of our sample was low and restricted to the low end of the scale. Thus a 5-point scale was developed to assess level of profession and occupation for our sample of parents. The 50 professions found in our study were ranked from highest to lowest by 13 middle-SES adult judges. Interjudge reliability was high (Cronbach $\alpha = .98$). According to their average rank, the professions were divided into five equal groups, based on their scores on the 5-point scale, For example, unemployed, housewife, housemaid, and industrial laborer were scored 1; carpenter, locksmith, and crane driver were scored 3; schoolteacher, practical engineer, and bookkeeper were scored 5.

The children's emergent literacy was assessed in the kindergarten in four sessions. In each of the four sessions, the children were first asked to write 4 pairs of words (for a total of 16 pairs of words); each pair was presented orally and illustrated by two drawings. Then the children were asked to recognize each pair by matching the two oral words to two printed words and to justify the recognition. The 16 pairs of words fell into four groups, each of which encompassed different aspects of children's emergent literacy. In the first group, the longer sounding word in each pair denoted a bigger referent, for instance, *pil–nɛmala* [elephant–ant]. In the second group, the two words in each pair differed in their phonological length but did not differ clearly in the size of their referents, for instance, *ɛt–iparon* [pen–pencil]. We assumed that, in the second group, children would be less biased by the referential dimension than those in the first group, and hence would be more sensitive to phonological length. In the third group, the two words rhymed, for instance *tsinor–kinor* [violin–pipe], such that they differed only in their initial letter. In the fourth group, the two words differed in gender, such that male and female nouns were spelled the same, but the latter were suffixed with *hey*, for instance, *xatul–xatula* [cat (male)–cat (female)].

Each word that the children wrote was scored on a 9-point scale, adapted from Levin, Share, and Shatil (1996). The scale's range consisted of pseudoletters, random letters insensitive to phonological length, random letters sensitive to phonological length, and from basic through partial to advanced consonantal spelling, without and with vowels. The writing score was equal to the sum of the scores attributed to the 32 words comprising the 16 pairs of words (4 pairs [8 words] per each of four sessions).

The number of pairs matched correctly determined the score on word recognition. Their justifications for their recognition of each pair were scored on a 4-point scale to yield an explanation score, as follows: (1 point) prealphabetic explanation: when the child's explanation does not refer to the system of writing (e.g., "because I know," "I guessed"); (2 points) rudimentary incorrect alphabetic explanation: when the child's explanation refers to characteristics relevant to writing, by noting letter names or phonological length, but the child applies them erroneously; (3 points) partial alphabetic, mixed correct and incorrect explanation: when the child's explanation refers to characteristics relevant to writing, but the child applies them both correctly and incorrectly (e.g., provides a correct name to a letter, but derives the conclusion that it should be a word that actually is not spelled with that letter); and (4 points) correct alphabetic explanation: when the child's explanation correctly refers to the written system (e.g., the child maps the longer sounding word onto the longer written word and explains it by reference to phonology, or provides a correct letter name and derives the conclusion that it should be a word spelled with that letter). The explanation score was determined by an average of the scores for the 16 pairs of words. The correlation between word recognition and explanation was highly significant, $r = .84$, $p < 0.001$. The mean Z score served as the reading score.

Maternal writing mediation was assessed at home. The mothers and the children were videotaped in their homes while writing four pairs of unfamiliar words. The mother–child collaborative writing occurred in the participants' chosen place at home (in the living room, in the child's room, or in the kitchen) and lasted, on average, for about 16 min. The dyad was presented with four pairs of words that were presented orally and were illustrated by drawings on four cards (one pair per card). Each pair represented one of the four types of words that the children had been asked earlier to write independently in the kindergarten. The word pairs written with the mothers were not among the pairs written independently by the children. The eight words encompassed altogether 30 letters. The mother was asked to help her child write these words and to provide help as she deemed fit.

The videotapes were analyzed to reveal the mothers' graphophonemic mediation style, child's autonomy in printing the letters, and affective measures (mothers' reinforcements and criticism throughout the interaction).

Maternal Graphophonemic Mediation Scale: This 6-point scale reflects how the mother mediates the writing of letters to her child who attempts to represent a word presented orally in writing. The score reflects the level of mediation of the graphophonemic encoding process, which includes segmenting the word into sounds, connecting a segmented sound with a letter, retrieving the letter's shape, and printing it. The earlier the step in the graphophonemic process that the mother mediates with her child, the higher the mediation score. The score reflects the mother's original mediation level, even when the child needs further assistance at a later step in the process.

A 6-point scale emerged from analyzing mother–child joint writing protocols: (1) mother writes down all the letters of the word for the child; (2) mother writes down all the letters of the word as a model for copying; (3) mother dictates a letter; (4) mother retrieves a phonological unit (syllable, subsyllable, or phoneme) and immediately dictates the required letter name; (5) mother retrieves a phonological unit (syllable, subsyllable, or phoneme) and encourages or helps the child to link this unit with a letter name; and (6) mother encourages or helps the child to retrieve a phonological unit (syllable, subsyllable, or phoneme) and to link it with a letter name. The mediation of each letter was scored, and the average score yielded the mother's graphophonemic mediation score.

Child's Autonomy in Printing the Letters Scale: This scale captured the child's autonomy in retrieving letter shapes and in printing the letters. A 4-point scale was used to score the printing of each letter: (1) mother wrote the letter on her own; (2) mother wrote and child copied the letter; (3) mother scaffolded the child in writing the letter (e.g., the mother commented that the letter appears in the child's name or in the name of a close friend; the mother gave the child spatial directions regarding the letter's shape); and (4) child wrote the letter independently, usually encouraged by mother. The production of each letter was scored according to this scale, and the average score across all the letters yielded the child's autonomy in printing score. Maternal reinforcements and criticisms were counted in the same manner as described previously for the first study and were scored for each pair of words.

The sociocultural factors were measured at home. SES was assessed on the basis of parents' education, profession and occupation, and a ranking of the family's residential area. The mean Z score across all constituents was highly reliable (Cronbach $\alpha = .92$) and served as the SES score.

Home literacy level was based on the Home Observation for Measurement of Environment (HOME) inventory for children ages 3–6 years (Bradley & Caldwell, 1979). We created an instrument for noting the presence of literacy-related materials in the home, the Games and Literacy-Related Materials (GLM). Accompanied by the child and the mother, the interviewer asked if she could look at each of the items on the following list: 10 books, cards for learning numbers, three puzzles, five children's audiocassettes, crayons and pencils, blocks, notebooks, readiness workbooks, and computer. After leaving the home, the interviewer completed a form indicating the presence or absence of each item.

Maternal exposure to adults' books and to children's books was assessed by a Hebrew adaptation of the exposure to adult and to children's TRTs the ATRT and the CTRT (Stanovich & West, 1989), as described previously for Study 1.

Results

Sociocultural Measures, Maternal Mediation, and Emergent Literacy.   The upper part of Table 42.3 presents the correlations between each sociocultural measure and the children's writing and reading scores. All the correlations were of moderate strength and in the positive direction, and all of them but one (mother's exposure to adults' books and the child's writing) were significant. In our LSES sample, children who came from poorer homes in terms of SES, presence of games and literacy-related materials, and maternal exposure to adults' and children's books, scored lower on reading and writing.

The lower part of Table 42.3 presents the correlations between each maternal mediation measure and the children's writing and reading scores. High, positive, and significant correlations

TABLE 42.3

Correlations Between Scores on Sociocultural Measures and Maternal
Writing Mediation and the Child's Emergent Literacy Measures ($N = 41$)

	Child's Literacy	
	Reading	Writing
Sociocultural measures		
SES	.42**	.48***
Games and literate materials	.45**	.46**
ATRT	.33*	.28
CTRT	.54***	.43**
Maternal writing mediation		
Graphophonemic mediation	.77***	.74***
Child's autonomy	.69***	.73***
Maternal reinforcement	.48**	.37*
Maternal criticisms	−.13	−.15

Note. $p < 0.05$; **$p < 0.01$; ***$p < 0.001$

were found between both maternal graphophonemic mediation and the child's autonomy in printing the letters and the child's literacy achievement scores (reading and writing). As to the affective measures of the interactions, maternal reinforcement was significantly and positively correlated with the child's reading and writing scores. Maternal criticism was negatively correlated with the child's reading and writing, but the correlations were very low and did not reach significance. In our LSES sample, children whose mothers used higher mediation strategies scored higher on reading and writing.

Maternal Mediation Measures and Emergent Literacy, With the Sociocultural Measures Controlled.   The significant correlations between both sociocultural measures on the one hand and maternal mediation measures on the other hand, with emergent literacy measures (reading and writing), raise questions regarding the unique contributions of maternal mediation measures to emergent literacy. To examine this unique relationship, a partial correlation between the maternal mediation measures and the child's reading and writing scores was calculated, with all sociocultural measures controlled for (SES, GLM, maternal exposure to adults' books and maternal exposure to children's books).

Table 42.4 reveals significant and moderately high partial correlations between the child's reading and writing scores and both maternal graphophonemic mediation as well as child's autonomy in printing the letters in the interaction, when all the sociocultural measures are controlled for. Maternal reinforcement was significantly and moderately correlated with reading but not with writing, when all the sociocultural measures are controlled for. Maternal criticism was not correlated to the child's reading and writing scores.

The findings demonstrate a strong linkage between sociocultural factors and emergent reading and writing within a LSES group, and a particularly strong relationship between maternal mediation of writing and the child's reading and writing achievement. When children's sociocultural measures are controlled for, maternal mediation measures still explain a substantial amount of variance in their children's emergent literacy.

To illustrate this linkage between sociocultural measures and emergent literacy within a LSES group, and to emphasize the unique contribution of maternal mediation to emergent

TABLE 42.4
Partial Correlations Between Maternal Writing
Mediation and the Child's Emergent Literacy
Measures, With Sociocultural Factors (SES, GLM,
Maternal Exposure to Adults' Books and Maternal
Exposure to Children's Books) Controlled

| | Child's Literacy | |
	Reading	Writing
Maternal writing mediation		
Graphophonemic mediation	.65***	.64***
Child's autonomy	.53***	.60***
Maternal reinforcement	.33*	.19
Maternal criticisms	−.05	−.04

Note. $N = 41$; $*p < 0.05$; $**p < 0.01$; $***p < 0.001$.

literacy above all the other sociocultural measures, we present the protocols of two children. Both children came from families that resembled each other in their sociocultural measures; however, one mother exhibited higher levels of mediation than the other, within her child's zone of proximal development (ZPD), and her child's literacy measures were higher. The other mother mediated below the child's level and the child's emergent literacy measures were lower.

Sharon and Adam

Sharon and Adam lived in the same neighborhood, which scored a 2 on the 7-point SES scale previously described, where 1 = lowest and 7 = highest SES level. They attended the same kindergarten. Both sets of parents shared the same education level. The two mothers had completed vocational high school and the fathers had completed 11 years of schooling (around the sample's average years of schooling; see previous section). Sharon's mother worked as a seamstress and Adam's mother worked as an industrial laborer, both professions ranking 1 on our 5-point professional ranking scale, where 1 = lowest to 5 = highest (maternal mean for the sample was $M = 2.48$, $SD = 1.60$). The fathers of the two children were carvers professionally, ranking 3 on our scale (the paternal sample average was $M = 2.90$, $SD = 1.24$). However, Sharon's father worked as an industrial labor (ranked 1) and Adam's father worked as a maintenance man in a factory (ranked 3). Both families had in their home about half of the cultural tools that were scored in our study. The two mothers recognized two adult's book titles, so their score for exposure to adult's books was 2 (lower than the sample average, $M = 3.85$, $SD = 3.78$). As to children's books, Sharon's mother's score was 9 and Adam's mother's score was 6 (the sample's average score was $M = 6.15$, $SD = 3.52$).

The two mothers differed in the dominant strategy that they used in mediating writing, as well as in the level of autonomy given to the child in printing letters. They also differed in their reinforcement and criticism toward their children's performance.

Sharon's mother frequently encouraged her daughter to segment the word into CV/C units and to provide the letter name (10 out of 30 letters). However, she also tended to segment the word and name the required letter right away, usually when the girl failed to come up immediately with the required letter (16 out of 30 letters). Sharon's mother's score on the graphophonemic mediation (3.83) was higher than the sample's average ($M = 3.11$, $SD = 1.20$). Sharon's mother often expected her daughter to retrieve the letter shapes, and, indeed, many times Sharon succeeded in retrieving the letter shape and in writing it independently (18 out of 30 letters). When Sharon did not succeed, her mother usually wrote the letter on one side and let Sharon copy it (12 out of 30 letters). Her score on autonomy (2.27) was higher than the sample's average ($M = 1.61$, $SD = 0.83$). Sharon's mother used reinforcements frequently (23) and she sometimes criticized her daughter (12). Her reinforcements mean score for each pair of words (5.75) was higher than the sample's average ($M = 4.59$, $SD = 3.54$). Her criticisms mean score for each pair of words (3) also was higher than the sample's average ($M = 1.53$, $SD = 1.68$). Sharon's mother mediated writing within the girl's ZPD, as illustrated by the following example of writing the letters (*yud, dalɛt*) of *yad* [hand]:

M: Good, now you have to write *yad*. Which letters do we have in *yad*? *yad*—what do you hear?

Sharon: *Alɛph* [letter name].

M: /ya/ *yud* [letter name], not *alɛph, yud, yad*.

Sharon: (writes the letter *yud*).

M: *yad*, what do you hear after the Yud?

Sharon: *Dalɛt* [letter name]?

M: Very good.

Sharon: So will I do it alone, the way that I know to write *dalɛt*?

M: O.K, do it your way.

Sharon: (Writes a different letter.)

M: (Looks at the letter) *dalɛt*, Sharon, like in the word *kad* [jar].

Sharon: Ah, *dalɛt*, the first or the second letter in *kad*?

M: The second.

Sharon: (Writes *dalɛt*.)

Adam's mother wrote each pair of words on a sheet of paper and put it in front of him, asking him to copy the words. She used only this strategy during her writing mediation, disregarding Adam's understanding of the alphabetic system. She did not segment the words that Adam was copying, but while he was copying, she looked at his writing and sometimes mentioned the name of the letters that he was copying. Adam's mother's score on the graphophonemic mediation score (2) was lower than the samples' average ($M = 3.11$, $SD = 1.20$). Her score on autonomy (1.36) was about the same as the sample's average ($M = 1.61$, $SD = 0.83$). Adam's mother used frequent criticism (35) and few reinforcements (6). Her criticisms mean score for each pair of words (9.25), was much higher than the sample's average ($M = 1.53$, $SD = 1.68$). Her reinforcements mean score for each pair of words (1.50), was far lower than the sample's average ($M = 4.59$, $SD = 3.54$). She ignored his experience with printing letters and his emerging alphabetic awareness, as illustrated by the following example of writing the letters (*zayin, kuf, nun*) of *zakɛn* [old man].

M: I will write to you and you will copy.

Adam: I don't want. I know (to do it) on my own.

Mother: (Writes the word on a paper and puts it in front of Adam). Write *zakɛn* [old man] like this. Do you see Adam, *zakɛn* [old man]? You have to be more cooperative. Copy it like this.

Adam: I want to do it alone.

Mother: Copy it!

Adam: (Copies the word.)
Mother: (Looks at him while he is writing and uttering the letters' names) *zakɛn, zayin,*
              kuf, nun [letter names].

Sharon and Adam achieved different emergent literacy scores. Out of 16 word pairs, Sharon recognized 13 pairs. When explaining her recognition, she usually gave a phonological explanation, noticing that one word sounded longer than the other or mapping letters onto sounds (11 out of 16). Yet she also used rudimentary incorrect alphabetic explanations (4) and one egocentric explanation (1). Her reading score (82.03) was higher than the sample average ($M = 61.97$, $SD = 22.01$). In her writing (see Fig. 42.2), Sharon used random letters in 75% of the words, but in 60% of these cases the longer sounding word was written with more letters. She used basic consonantal writing in six words: middle consonantal writing in five words, and complete consonantal writing in one word. Sharon did not use vowels in any of the 32 words. Her writing score (41.34) was higher than the sample average ($M = 34.82$, $SD = 20.66$).

Adam correctly recognized 7 pairs of words (out of 16), thereby performing within the chance level. Most of his explanations on word recognition were egocentric (12 out of 16) or rudimentary incorrect alphabetic (3). Still, one explanation was phonological. His reading score (38.28) was lower than the sample average ($M = 61.97$, $SD = 22.01$). Adam wrote most of the words with random letters (95%), and mostly with no indication of sensitivity to the phonological length of the words (60%) (see Fig. 42.2). However, he used basic consonantal writing in one word and middle consonantal writing in another word. His writing score (38.28) was about the same as the sample average ($M = 34.82$, $SD = 20.66$).

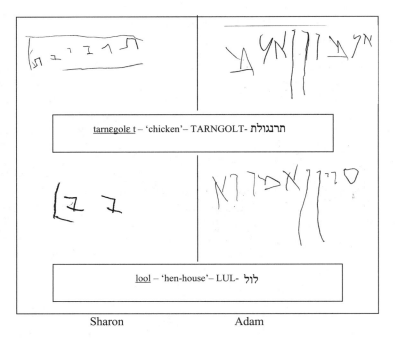

tarnɛgolɛt – 'chicken'– TARNGOLT- תרנגולת

lool – 'hen-house'– LUL- לול

Sharon   Adam

FIG. 42.2. Examples of Sharon's and Adam's independent word writing. Sharon wrote *tarnɛgolɛt* [chicken] with three required consonants—the first two and the last one—and three random letters. She wrote the word *lul* [hen-house] with the same random letter twice (and a sign), explaining that she hears the same sound twice /lu/ /l/. Adam wrote both words with random letters. He used 9 and 10 letters for *tarnɛgolɛt* and *lul*, respectively, disregarding their phonological length.

The qualitative analyses demonstrated the broad range of maternal mediation strategies among these families from a low SES and their links with the children's emergent literacy. This range is illustrated by a case of mediation within the child's ZPD, building on the child's understanding of the written system, and a case of mediation below the ZPD, failing to utilize the child's knowledge.

DISCUSSION

In this chapter, we have reviewed two studies we conducted that focused on mother–child joint writing activity as a function of their sociocultural background and its relation to the child's literacy level in two age groups: kindergartners and second graders. In the first study, with second graders, we compared two SES groups, HSES and LSES, and in the second, with kindergartners, we delved deeper into the LSES by studying SES differences within the LSES group.

LSES mothers recognized fewer adults' book titles as well as fewer children's book titles. Their scores on maternal mediation, reflecting the extent of autonomy of the child, were lower and so was their children's literacy. Although parallel differences between SES groups do not prove a causal relationship between familial factors promoting literacy and the child's literacy level, they suggest the possibility that such a linkage exists. However, this approach may lead to conceiving of LSES cohorts as homogeneous (Holden, 1997; Pflaum, 1986).

To deal with this difficulty, the second study was restricted to LSES families. The focus on LSES families in an Israeli development town enabled us to shed light on differences that may be relevant to literacy development within a LSES group.

SES was assessed within LSES with the same variables typically used to measure discrepant SES groups, only with more finely graded scales. Thus the SES measures within LSES were parental education, profession and occupation, and the family residential area. Despite the narrow range of SES in this group from the general perspective of Israeli society, differences were found between the families on all of the sociocultural measures we used, supporting Renck-Jalongo's (1996) view that LSES cohorts should not be viewed as homogeneous.

Within our LSES group, stable significant correlations were found between the sociocultural measures and the child's emergent literacy. It should be noted that parallel relationships were found between sociocultural measures and children's' emergent literacy both within LSES (our second study) and in comparing LSES with HSES (our first study). In both studies, exposure of parents to print (adults' and children's book titles) and the presence of games and literacy tools at home were related to children's literacy. These findings are congruent with those of previous researchers who compared SES groups (e.g., Bus et al., 1995; Campbell & Ramey, 1994; Hart & Risley, 1992; Reese, 1995; Walker et al., 1994).

The most important finding of the two studies described here are the links found between the quality of maternal mediation of writing and children's literacy. In the first study of second graders, LSES differed from HSES on maternal mediation and on children's literacy. However, the correlations between these variables within each group—HSES and LSES—appeared only in the HSES group. In the second study, in which only one SES group was studied, among the LSES kindergartners, these correlations were especially strong. Within this group, even after all sociocultural measures (SES, maternal exposure to children's and to adults' books, and literacy-related materials at home) were controlled for, the link between quality of maternal mediation of writing and the child's reading and writing is still substantial.

Integrating the results of our two studies yielded three questions. First, why is the quality of mother–child joint writing more strongly related to child's literacy level in kindergarten than in second grade (see Tables 42.2 and 42.3)? Our interpretation is based on the assumption that before formal schooling parents play an especially critical role in promoting their offspring's literacy or, even more broadly, their cognitive competencies. In this vein, Hiebert and Adams (1987) claim that parents are the first teachers of their children in literacy and Meisels (1998) concludes that beyond the many debates about the different ways to promote kindergartners' readiness to school, there is a general consensus that parents are the main mediators of young children's learning. When children enter first grade, school also starts to exert its influence. This is especially true in first grade, in which children intensively concentrate on reading and writing; as a consequence, their literacy is no longer fostered mainly by their parents. Rather, other influences enter the equation, in particular their interactions with their schoolteachers, their classmates, and the curricula they are exposed to (Crone, 1999).

The second question refers to second graders. Why is maternal mediation less related to children's writing level in the LSES group compared with the HSES group? This might be explained by the special contribution that some HSES parents make toward their children's literacy that goes beyond the massive contributions of school. In our interviews with them as well through our observations, it was evident that some HSES mothers exhibited profound knowledge about literacy development and about how to promote literacy in the joint activity with their children. In the long run, these mothers may foster their children's literacy development above and beyond the potent schooling effects. It may be the case that fewer LSES mothers are able to foster their children's development of literacy far beyond school in quite the same way as the HSES mothers.

The final question is pedagogical–educational. What is a good model for parental mediation of writing with kindergarten children and with second graders? From analyses of videotaped interactions collected in the two studies, we conclude that the nature of good models of mediation for children at these two different age levels have both common and different features. A good model in both age groups is characterized by highly autonomous children. Because the interaction is dyadic and hence determined by interplay between the two parties, the child's autonomy reflects the extent to which the mother allows or encourages the child to act autonomously and the extent to which the child is ready to act so or even to demand it.

In many dyads, the extent of autonomy given by the mother and that adopted by the child were balanced. However, in some cases, the child asked to lead the writing activity more than the mother allowed, and in others, the mother urged the child to take a more leading role. In the same vein, some mothers wanted to provide less help than their child asked for whereas some children asked the mother to take a more active role. For example, in one case, a LSES mother tried to convince her second-grade child to write the shopping list by herself, but the girl did not agree to do so. She helped the mother to compose part of the list but insisted on not printing the words in spite of her mother's encouragement throughout the entire interaction. In another case, a HSES mother suggested many shopping list items for the child to write, although the child wanted to do it on his own. This situation drove the child to react negatively to his mother. The same phenomenon occurred in our kindergarten LSES group: One mother encouraged her child to print the letter *zayin* (Z) independently, but her son insisted that she should print it, and eventually she did. In another case, a mother took control and printed letters for her girl to copy, and the child cried that she did not need the model and that she wanted to print the letters independently.

The difference between the good models in the two age groups stems from the distinction in the problem space that children struggle with when they try to write. Writing is a multifaceted activity, which involves meaning-focused and language-focused processes, including linguistic and genre elements. It also includes code-focused processes, such as spelling words, leaving spaces between them, and preserving direction of text and using punctuation marks. Among kindergartners, mother–child dyads focused on the written code, often working on mapping of graphemes onto phonemes. Among second graders, they focused on composing the text and spelling conventionally. It remains an open question whether parents who function as good mediators of writing for their kindergarteners continue to be good mediators when their children enter grade school.

The children in our study were asked to write a list of words. Although second graders typically are able to write words, lists, short answers to written questions, as well as short stories, among the LSES mothers of second graders, there were mothers who composed and printed the list themselves or dictated items to their children, almost letter by letter, even though the children had not requested them to do so. This pattern emerged even though the writing task was deliberately addressed to the child, and the mother was asked only to help. Such a behavior may imply that the mother focuses on obtaining the conventional product, rather than on the child's process of production. Further, it may indicate that the mother underestimates her child's actual achievement level (Marcus & Corsini, 1978). Still, within the kindergarten LSES group, mothers differed in their sensitivity and accommodation to their children's level. Some had difficulty finding the appropriate way for enhancing their children's understanding and knowledge, as required by this specific task, whereas others mediated very skillfully.

The substantial correlations between maternal mediation of writing and children's emergent literacy deserve clarification (see Tables 42.3 and 42.4). Several different interpretations may be suggested. One might assume that the child's literate abilities were crucial in determining maternal level of mediation. This explanation is in line with studies that demonstrate how mothers alter their teaching strategies to adjust to the task demands as well as to their children's level of competencies (Kermani & Brenner, 2000; Kermani & Janes, 1999). DeBaryshe et al. (1996), who observed mother–child joint letter writing, found in a qualitative analysis that mothers were sensitive to their children's emergent literacy level in terms of the letter's length, genre elements, and conventions of punctuation, directionality, and spacing. They concluded that mothers adjust mediation to their children's literacy level.

An alternative explanation conceives the strong relationships between maternal mediation and the child's literacy mainly as a result of parental mediation affecting the child's growing literacy. The nature of parental mediation is considered the strongest predictor of the child's cognitive development. It is a proximal factor that affects children's development beyond all other sociocultural measures and has to be acknowledged as such (Klein, Weider, & Greenspan, 1987; Tzuriel, 1999).

A third explanation for the strong relationships between the nature of maternal mediation of writing and the child's literacy level integrates the former two explanations. Accordingly, mother–child joint writing is a two-way street in which both parties shape the interaction mutually and interactively, in a way that is shaped and reshaped dynamically over time.

However, we claim that the mother, as the expert, has the leading role. Her interaction style is molded by her previous experiences with her children, but not to a lesser extent by cultural beliefs and norms of behavior related to parenting (Lightfoot & Valsiner, 1992). Aram and Levin (2001) demonstrated, in qualitative analyses, that kindergartners who exhibited similar levels of literacy were mediated differently by their mothers. Some mothers were more sensitive to their child's ZPD whereas others were less sensitive. The demonstration suggested that the mothers who showed lower levels of mediation often mediated below their children's ZPD, disregarding their competencies. Mothers who showed higher levels of mediation often mediated beyond their children's actual level of literacy and tried to promote their children's understanding of the written system while affording them higher levels of autonomy.

The leading role of the mother in the interaction is not a local occurrence. We claim that a significant maternal role comprises an ongoing phenomenon affecting the trajectory of the child's literate development. Mothers who mediate literacy on a higher level, from the child's early age on, learn about the child's competencies and use this knowledge to shape their coming interactions. Consistently high-quality mediation is likely to promote children's literacy. This may be a central explanation for the substantial contribution of mediation quality to the prediction of the child's literacy level. This explanation is consistent with the systematic finding that cognitively advanced children tend to have parents who are accurate in attributions of cognitive achievement to their children (Hiebert & Adams, 1987; Miller, Manhal, & Mee, 1991).

The design of the two studies presented in this chapter does not permit determining a causal direction of the relationships between maternal mediation and the child's literacy. Whitehurst and Lonigan (1998) reviewed intervention programs concerning different aspects of emergent literacy. None of these programs dealt with joint writing. Hence there is a need to carry out experimental studies in which parental writing mediation is manipulated and children's literacy performances are compared.

APPENDIX: WRITTEN FORMS OF HEBREW LETTERS TRANSLITERATED INTO LATIN LETTERS

א = alef	ב = bet	ג = gimmel	ד = dalet	ה = heh
ו = vav	ז = zayin	ח = het	ט = tet	י = yud
כ (f) ך = kaf	ל = lamed	מ = (f) ם mem	נ, (f) ן = nun	ס = samech
ע = a'yin	פ, (f) ף = peh	צ (f) ץ = zadik	ק = kuf	ר = reish
ש = sh or shin	ת = taf			

Note: *Shin* is noted by Sh when pronounced /sh/ and by S* when pronounced /s/. *Mem, nun, zadik, peh*, and *kaf* have two written forms: regular and final. Final letters are marked by (f).

REFERENCES

Adams, M. J. (1991). *Beginning to read: Thinking and learning about print.* Cambridge, MA: MIT Press.

Allison, D. T., & Watson, J. A. (1994). The significance of adult storybook reading styles on the development of young children's emergent reading. *Reading Research and Instruction, 34,* 57–72.

Anderson, B. (1986). *Homework: What do national assessments results tell us.* Princeton, NJ: National Assessment of Educational Progress, Educational Testing Service. (ERIC Document Reproduction Service No. 276980).

Aram, D., & Levin, I. (2001). Mother-child joint writing in low SES: Sociocultural factors, maternal mediation and emergent literacy. *Cognitive Development, 16,* 831–852.

Aram, D., & Levin, I. (2002). Mother–child joint writing and storybook reading: Relations with literacy among low SES kindergartners. *Merrill Palmer Quarterly, 48,* 202–224.

Aram, D., & Levin, I. (2004). The role of maternal mediation of writing to kindergartners in promoting literacy achievements in second grade: A longitudinal perspective. *Reading and Writing: An Interdisciplinary Journal, 17,* 387–409.

Baker, L., Fernandez-Fein, S., Scher, D., & Williams, H. (1998). Home experiences related to the development of word recognition. In J. L. Metsala & L. C. Ehri (Eds.), *Word recognition in beginning literacy* (pp. 263–288). Hillsdale, NJ: Lawrence Erlbaum Associates.

Bissex, G. L. (1980). *GNYS AT WRK: A child learns to write and read.* Cambridge, MA: Harvard University Press.

Bowey, J. A. (1995). Socioeconomic status differences in preschool phonological sensitivity and first grade reading achievement. *Journal of Educational Psychology, 87,* 476–487.

Bradley, R. H., & Caldwell, B. M. (1979). HOME observation for measurement of the environment: A revision of the preschool scale. *American Journal of Mental Deficiency, 84,* 235–244.

Bronfenbrenner, U. (1979). *The ecology of human development.* Cambridge, MA: Harvard University Press.

Bruner, J. (1996). *The culture of education.* Cambridge, MA: Harvard University Press.

Burgess, S. (1997). The role of shared reading in the development of phonological awareness: A longitudinal study of middle to upper class children. *Early Child Development and Care, 127–128,* 191–199.

Burns, M. S., & Casbergue, R. (1992). Parent child interaction in a letter writing context. *Journal of Reading Behavior, 24,* 289–312.

Bus, A. G., & van IJzendoorn, M. H. (1988). Mother-child interaction, attachment and emergent literacy: A cross sectional study. *Child Development, 59*, 1262–1272.

Bus, A. G., van IJzendoorn, M. H., & Pellegrini, A. D. (1995). Joint book reading makes for success in learning to read: A meta-analysis on intergenerational transmission of literacy. *Review of Educational Research, 65*, 1–21.

Campbell, F. A., & Ramey, C. T. (1994). Effects of early intervention on intellectual and academic achievement: A follow-up study of children from low-income families. *Child Development, 65*, 684–698.

Clay, M. (1975). *What did I write?* London: Heinemann Educational Books.

Cooper, H. (1989). *Homework.* White Plains, NY: Longman.

Crone, D. A. (1999). Age and schooling effects on emergent literacy and early reading skills. *Journal of Educational Psychology, 91*, 604–614.

Cunningham, A. E., & Stanovich, K. E. (1991). Tracking the unique effects of print exposure in children: Associations with vocabulary, general knowledge and spelling. *Journal of Educational Psychology, 83*, 264–274.

Cunningham, A. E., & Stanovich, K. E. (1998). Early reading acquisition and its relation to reading experience and ability 10 years later. *Developmental Psychology, 5*, 111–123.

DeBaryshe, B. D. (1993, March). *Maternal reading-related beliefs and reading socialization practices in low-SES homes.* Paper presented at the biennial meeting of the Society for Research in Child Development, New Orleans, LA.

DeBaryshe, B. D., & Binder, J. C. (1994). Development of an instrument for measuring parental beliefs about reading aloud to young children. *Perceptual and Motor Skills, 78*, 1303–1311.

DeBaryshe, D. B., Buell, M. J., & Binder, J. C. (1996). What a parent brings to the table: Young children writing with and without parental assistance. *Journal of Literacy Research, 28*, 71–90.

DeLoache, J. S., & Demendoza, O. A. P. (1987). Joint picture book interactions of mothers and 1-year-old children. *British Journal of Development Psychology, 5*, 111–123.

DeTemple, J. M., & Snow, C. (1996). Styles of parent–child book reading as related to mothers' views of literacy and children's literacy outcomes. In J. Shimron (Ed.), *Literacy and education: Essays in memory of Dina Feitelson* (pp. 49–68). Cresskill, NJ: Hampton Press.

Diamond, J. (1996). *Status and power in verbal interaction: A study of discourse in a close-knit social network.* Philadelphia, PA: Pragmatics and Beyond New Series.

Duncan, G. J. (1991). The economic environment of childhood. In A. C. Huston (Ed.), *Children in poverty: Child development and public policy* (pp. 23–50). New York: Cambridge University Press.

Durkin, D. (1996). *Children who read early: Two longitudinal studies.* New York: Teachers College Press.

Echols, L. D., West, R. F., Stanovich, K. E., & Zehr, K. S. (1996). Using children's literacy activities to predict growth in verbal cognitive skills: A longitudinal investigation. *Journal of Educational Psychology, 88*, 296–304.

Evans, M. N., Barraball, L., & Eberle, T. (1998). Parental responses to miscues during child-to-parent book reading. *Journal of Applied Developmental Psychology, 19*, 67–84.

Feitelson, D., & Goldstein, Z. (1986). Patterns of book ownership and reading to young children in Israeli school-oriented and nonschool-oriented families. *Reading Teacher, 39*, 924–930.

Goodist, J., Raitan, J. G., & Perlmutter, M. (1988). Interactions between mothers and their preschool children when reading a novel and a familiar book. *International Journal of Behavioral Development, 11*, 489–505.

Gundlach, R. A., McLane, J. B., Stott, F. M., & McNamee, G. D. (1985). The social foundations of children's early writing development. In M. Farr (Ed.), *Advances in writing research: Vol 1: Children's early writing development* (pp. 1–58). Norwood, NJ: Ablex.

Hale, C., & Windecker, E. (1993, March). *Influence of parent-child interaction during reading on preschoolers' cognitive abilities.* Paper presented at the biennial meeting of the Society for Research in Child Development, New Orleans, LA.

Harste, J. C., Woodward, V. A., & Burke, C. L. (1984). *Language, stories and literacy lessons.* Portsmouth, NH: Heinemann.

Hart, B., & Risely, T. R. (1992). American parenting of language-learning children: Persisting differences in family-child interactions observed in natural home environment. *Developmental Psychology, 28*, 1096–1105.

Haviv, T., & Blum- Kulka, S. (1996). Mekadme orianout basiah hamishpahti [Literate discourse in families]. *Hellcat-Lashon, 22*, 168–171.

Heath, S. B. (1983). *Way with words.* Cambridge, UK: Cambridge University Press.

Hiebert, E. H., & Adams, C. S. (1987). Father's and mother's perceptions of their preschool children's emergent literacy. *Journal of Experimental Child Psychology, 44*, 25–37.

Holden, G. W. (1997). *Parents and dynamics of child rearing.* Boulder, CO: Westview.

Hoover-Dempsy, K., Bussler, O., & Burow, R. (1995). Parents' reported involvement in student's homework: Strategies and practices. *Elementary School Journal, 95*, 435–450.

Kagicibasi, C. (1996). *Family and human development across cultures: A view from the other side.* Hillsdale, NJ: Lawrence Erlbaum Associates.

Kermani, H., & Brenner, M. E. (2000). Maternal scaffolding in the child's zone of proximal development across tasks: Cross-cultural perspectives. *Journal of Research in Childhood Education, 15*, 30–52.

Kermani, H., & Janes, H. A. (1999). Adjustment across task in maternal scaffolding in low-income Latino immigrant families. *Hispanic Journal of Behavioral Sciences, 21*, 134–153.

Klein, S. P., Wieder, S., & Greenspan, S. I. (1987). A theoretical overview and empirical study of mediated learning experience: Prediction of preschool performance from mother–infant interaction patterns. *Infant Mental Health Journal, 8*, 110–129.

Korat, O., & Levin, I. (2001). Maternal beliefs and child development: Comparison of text writing between two social groups. *Journal of Applied Developmental Psychology, 22*, 397–420.

Korat, O., & Levin, I. (2002). Spelling acquisition in two social groups: Mother–child interaction, maternal beliefs and child's spelling. *Journal of Literacy Research, 43*, 209–236.

Lambore, S. D., Mount, N. S., Steinberg, L., & Dorbusch, S. M. (1991). Patterns of competence and adjustment among adolescents from authoritative, indulgent and neglectful families. *Child Development, 62*, 1049–1065.

Levin, I., Levi-Shiff, R., Appelbaum-Peled, T., Katz, I., Komar, M., & Meiron, N. (1997). Antecedents and consequences of maternal involvement in children's homework: A longitudinal analysis. *Journal of Applied Developmental Psychology, 18*, 207–227.

Levin, I., Share, D. L., & Shatil, E. (1996). A qualitative-quantitative study of preschool writing: Its development and contribution to school literacy. In M. Levy & S. Ransdell (Eds.), *The science of writing* (pp. 271–293). Hilldsale, NJ: Lawrence Erlbaum Associates.

Lightfoot, C., & Valsiner, J. (1992). Parental belief systems under the guidance of the construction of personal cultures. In I. E. Siegel, A. V. McGillicuddy De-Lisi, & J. J. Goodnow (Eds.), *Parental belief systems: The psychological consequences for children* (pp. 393–414). Hillsdale, NJ: Lawrence Erlbaum Associates.

Lonigan, C. J., Burgess, S. R., Anthony, J. L., & Baker, T. A. (1998). Development of phonological sensitivity in two- to five-year-old children. *Journal of Educational Psychology, 90*, 294–311.

Mackler, K., Baker, L., & Sonnenschein, S. (1999, April). *How parents interact with their first grade children during storybook reading: Relations to subsequent reding development.* Paper presented at the biennial meeting of the Society for Research in Child Development, Albuquerque, NM.

Marcus, T., & Corsini, D. (1978). Parental expectations of preschool children as related to child gender and socioeconomic status. *Child Development, 49*, 243–246.

McCormick, C. E., & Mason, J. M. (1986). Intervention procedures for increasing preschool children's interest in and knowledge about reading. In W. H. Teale & E. Sulzby (Eds.), *Emergent literacy: Writing and reading* (pp. 90–115). Norwood, NJ: Ablex.

Meir, E. I. (1978). A test of the independence of fields and levels in Roe's occupational classification. *Vocational Guidance Quarterly, 27*, 124–129.

Meisels, S. J. (1998, November 1). Assessing readiness. *Ciera Report #3-002.* Ann Arbor: University of Michigan, center for the improvement of early reading achievement.

Miller, S. A., Manhal, M., & Mee, L. L. (1991). Parental beliefs, parental accuracy, and children's cognitive performance: A search for causal relations. *Developmental Psychology, 27*, 267–276.

Ministry of Education, Internal Committee for Examining Reading and Writing in the Educational System. (2001). *Mapping reading methods in first grade in Israel.* Jerusalem, Israel: Author.

National Center for Statistics. (1997). *The Israeli Municipalities 1995: Physical data.* Jerusalem, Israel: Author.

National Center for Statistics. (1999). *The statistical annual.* Jerusalem, Israel: Author.

Neuman, S. B., & Celano, D. (2001). Access to print in low-income and middle-income communities: An ecological study of four neighborhoods. *Reading Research Quarterly, 36*, 8–26.

Nicholson, T. (1999). Literacy, family and society. In G. B. Thompson & T. Nicholson (Eds.), *Learning to read: Beyond phonics and whole language* (pp. 1–22). New York: Teachers College Press.

Ninio, A. (1980). The naive theory of the infant and other maternal attitudes in two subgroups in Israel. *Child Development, 50*, 976–980.

Ogbu, J. U. (1990). *Minority status and literacy in comparative perspective. Deadalus, 119*, 141–168 .

Olson, D. R. (1984). See jumping! Some oral language antecedents of literacy. In H. Goelman, A. Oberg, & F. Smith (Eds.), *Awakening to literacy* (pp. 185–192). Portsmouth, NH: Heinemann Educational Books.

Pellegrini, A. D., Perlmutter, J. C., Galda, L., Brody, G. H (1990). Joint reading between black Head Start children and their mothers. *Child Development, 61*, 443–453.

Pflaum, S. W. (1986). *The development of language and literacy.* Columbus, OH: Merrill.

Pratt, M., Kerig, P., & Cowan, P. A. (1988). Mothers and fathers teaching 3-year-old: Authoritative and adult scaffolding of young children's learning. *Developmental Psychology, 24*, 832–839.

Reese, E. (1995). Predicting children's literacy from mother–child conversation. *Cognitive Development, 10*, 381–405.

Reese, E., & Cox, A. (1999). Quality of adult book reading affects children's emergent literacy. *Developmental Psychology, 35*, 20–28.

Renck-Jalongo, M. (1996). Editorial: On behalf of children: Pervasive myths about poverty and young children. *Early Childhood Education Journal, 24,* 1–3.

Roe, A. (1956). *The psychology of occupation.* New York: Wiley.

Rogoff, B. (1990). *Apprenticeship in thinking: Cognitive development in social context.* New York: Oxford University Press.

Scarborough, H. S., & Dobrich, W. (1994). On the efficiency of reading to preschoolers. *Developmental Review, 14,* 245–302.

Schiffrin, D. (1987). *Discourse makers.* Cambridge, UK: Cambridge University Press.

Sénéchal, M. (1997). The differential effect of storybook reading on preschooler's acquisition of expressive and receptive vocabulary. *Journal of Child Language, 24,* 123–138.

Sénéchal, M., LeFevre, J., Hudson, E., & Lawson, P. (1996). Knowledge of storybooks as a predictor of young children's vocabulary. *Journal of Educational Psychology, 88,* 520–536.

Sénéchal, M., LeFevre, J., Thomas, E. M., & Daley, K. E. (1998). Differential effects of home literacy experiences on development of oral and written language. *Reading Research Quarterly, 33,* 96–116.

Smith, S. S., & Dixon, R. G. (1995). Literacy concepts of low- and middle-class four-year-olds entering preschool. *Journal of Educational Research, 88,* 243–253.

Snow, C. E., & Goldfield, B. A. (1983). Turn the page please: Situation specific language acquisition. *Journal of Child Language, 10,* 551–569.

Sonnenschein, S., Shmidt , D., & Mackler , K. (1999, April). *The role of the home in improving children's reading during early elementary school,* Paper presented at the meeting of the Society in Research in Child Development, Albuquerque, NM.

Stanovich, K. E., & Cunningham, A. E. (1993). Where does knowledge come from? Specific associations between print exposure and information acquisition. *Journal of Educational Psychology, 85,* 211–229.

Stanovich, K. E., & West, R. F. (1989). Exposure to print and orthographic processing. *Reading Research Quarterly, 24,* 402–433.

Steinberg, L., Elman, J. D., & Mount, N. S. (1989). Authoritative parenting, psychological maturity and academic success among adolescence. *Child Development, 60,* 1424–1436.

Stuart, M., Dixon, M., Masterson, J., & Quinlan, S. (1998). Learning to read at home and at school. *British Journal of Educational Psychology, 68,* 3–14.

Taylor, D., & Dorsey-Gaines, C. (1988). *Growing up literate: Learning from inner-city families.* Portsmouth, NH: Heinemann.

Teale, W. H. (1981). Parents reading to their children: What we know and need to know. *Language Arts, 58,* 902–911.

Teale, W. H. (1986). Home background and young children's literacy development. In W. H. Teale & E. Sulzby (Eds.), *Emergent literacy: Writing and reading* (pp. 173–206). Norwood, NJ: Ablex.

Teale, W. H., & Sulzby, E. (1986). *Emergent literacy: Writing and reading.* Norwood, NJ: Ablex.

Teale, W. H., & Sulzby, E. (1999). Literacy acquisition in early childhood: The roles of access and mediation in storybook reading. In D. A. Wagner (Ed.), *The future of literacy in a changing world* (pp. 131–150). Cresskill, NJ: Hampton.

Tudge, J., & Putnam, S. (1997). The everyday experiences of North American preschoolers in two cultural communities: A cross-disciplinary and cross-level analysis. In J. Tudge, M. J. Shanahan, & J. Valsiner (Eds.), *Comparisons in human development: Understanding time and context* (pp. 252–279). New York: Cambridge University Press.

Tzuriel, D. (1999). Parent–child mediated learning interactions as determinants of cognitive modifiability: Recent research and future directions. *Genetic, Social and General Psychology Monographs, 125,* 109–156.

Vygotsky, L. S. (1978). *Mind and society: The development of higher psychological processes.* Cambridge, MA: Harvard University Press.

Walker, D., Greenwood, C., Hart, B., & Carta, J. (1994). Prediction of school outcomes bases on early language production and socioeconomic factors. *Child Development, 65,* 606–621.

Weinberger, J. (1996). *Literacy goes to school: The parents' role in young children's literacy learning.* London: Paul Chapman.

Wertsch, J. V. (1984). The zone of proximal development: Some conceptual issues. In B. Rogoff & J. V. Wertsch (Eds.), *Children's learning in the "zone of proximal development"* (pp. 19–30). San Francisco, CA: Jossey-Bass.

Whitehead, M. R. (1997). *Language and literacy in early years.* London: Paul Chapman.

Whitehurst, G. J. (1997). Language processes in context: Language learning in children reared in poverty. In L. B. Adamson & M. S. Romski (Eds.), *Research on communication and language disorders: Contribution to theories of language development* (pp. 233–266). Baltimore, MD: Brookes.

Whitehurst, G. J. (1999, April). *The role of literacy environment in the home on language and literacy outcomes of children from low-income families.* Paper presented at the biennial meeting of the Society for Research in Child Development, Albuquerque, NM.

Whitehurst, G. J., & Lonigan, C. J. (1998). Child development and emergent literacy. *Child Development, 69,* 848–872.

43

Foundations for Studying Basic Processes in Reading

Richard L. Venezky*
University of Delaware

Since the revival of cognitive psychology in the 1950s, significant contributions have been made to the knowledge base on the reading processes and on the processes involved in learning to read. From the work of Eleanor Gibson and her colleagues on the role of grapheme–phoneme correspondences in word recognition to the most recent work on phonemic awareness and decoding, much has been learned about different components of reading and learning to read. Nevertheless, many of the problems that drove the earliest studies of reading in Leipzig, Paris, and New York before the 1900s remain unresolved, including the features utilized in competent word or character recognition, the role of subvocalization in reading connected text, and the function of letter–sound or character–sound patterns in reading acquisition. Studies from a number of different orthography–language communities suggest that some components of reading and learning to read, such as the extraction and use of frequency information and automatization of basic processes, are universal, whereas others, such as the relationship of decoding ability to comprehension, are more language specific. One challenge remaining for researchers is to build more powerful models that can predict which orthography–language features contribute to which reading processes. A second challenge is to build such models from the more general concepts, strategies, and mechanisms of cognitive psychology, language development, and linguistics. For example, overgeneralization in letter–sound learning needs to be related to the processing models posited for overextension or overgeneralization in general language processing such as the learning of morphology; phonemic awareness ideas need to be related to the more general findings on the development of recoding of visual stimuli for storage in working memory, the growth of general processing speed, and the use of attentional mechanisms; and models for learning variant letter–sound patterns need to be built on mechanisms posited for other types of rule learning. The more we can base our models on general processing strategies rather than on mechanisms unique to our specific domain, the more compelling will be our claims. Our unified dream should be of a Nobel Prize for reading research, giving international recognition to breakthroughs that demonstrate how simple, general processing strategies can account for learning to read in many different orthographies and languages.

---

*Richard Venezky passed away on June 11, 2004.

FOUNDATIONS FOR STUDYING BASIC
PROCESSES IN READING

Research on basic reading processes appears on the surface to be healthy and thriving. The most up-to-date research tools and methodologies—fMRI, HLM, eye-movement tracking, connectionist modeling, IRT scaling—are being applied regularly; results are being presented at more and more conferences around the world; and new journals are publishing an ever-expanding collection of peer-reviewed offerings. The dominance of studies done in North America on English-speaking participants continues, but studies from other parts of the world and on other languages are also rising dramatically. A wide range of problems is being investigated, stretching from the role of phonemic awareness in early reading acquisition to the nature of orthographic encoding in different languages and scripts to the identification of genetic markers for dyslexia to effective remediation techniques for reading failure. For all this there is much to celebrate.

But there are also forewarnings here and there of potential malfunctions, like an occasional sneeze or cough, a blemish on an otherwise smooth skin, a tightness in the throat. There is, as in too many of the sciences, a Balkanization occurring, with different camps growing farther and farther apart. Those who study comprehension, for example, appear to talk less and less to those who study basic reading skills, and those who study trends in reading performance—subpopulation differences, summer loss, and the like—draw little from the work of those who study reading processes. Of greater concern, however, is the continual drift of the educational psychology of reading from the mainstream of modern experimental psychology and linguistics. Studies on perceptual development applied to faces and familiar scenes in nature are parallel to those done on the learning of words and decoding patterns, yet the reading literature rarely draws on them. Similarly, important work on the development of working memory and on recoding of visual input for retention in working memory could enrich much of the work done on phonemic awareness but rarely are these psychological studies referenced.

At issue is not blind referencing of related work, performed as a ritual to prove one's membership in a professional tribe, but the alignment of reading constructs with those for related learning tasks. From years of research on perceptual learning, for example, we expect that the learning of letters and printed words will be characterized by certain attentional, stimulus imprinting, feature discrimination, and feature combining or unitization characteristics found in the learning of other visual stimuli. To the degree that such alignment is demonstrated, the scientific community will find the results more convincing than when unique constructs are offered. Alternatively, to the degree that reading researchers posit constructs, stages, periods, and processes that are not related to what is found for similar learning tasks, the results will be less convincing and less valuable for constructing general theories of learning.

An additional source of concern is the lack of understanding evidenced in too many reading research reports of related studies from earlier periods. It appears that few reading researchers have examined the history of the fields they study, and the few who do know their history back to only 1966 when the ERIC bibliography system was started in the United States. For the same reasons that developmental psychologists read Claparède, Piaget, Vygotsky, and Bruner, so should researchers of basic reading processes examine Cattell, Javal, Huey, Thorndike, and many others. This concern for the past does not derive from antiquarian interests nor from fear of reliving the past—there is often a value in reinventing or rediscovering. Some do believe, with reasonable cause, that "There is nothing wrong with reinventing the wheel if your interest is in invention and not in wheels." Nevertheless, our interest in the past should be in understanding the theoretical frameworks and the psychological reasoning that accompanied basic process studies, as well as the results of these studies.

The remarkable interest exhibited in the 1960s in the reissue of Edmund Huey's 1908 text, *The Psychology and Pedagogy of Reading* (Huey, 1908/1968), has, unfortunately, dissipated, and few reading researchers who entered the field after around 1980 have any familiarity with this text. In its day it was called "the most readable English work on the reading habit" (cited by Carroll, in Huey, 1908/1968, p. x). Paul Kolers, who wrote the Introduction to the reissue, said of it, "What is amazing to someone reading the book sixty years later is not only the breadth and scope of [Huey's] vision but also the amount of information in it that is still on the 'front lines' of research" (p. xiv).

My task here, however, extends beyond demonstrating that there is more to read from the early 20th and late 19th century than Huey's text. I also examine several current issues in research on basic reading processes and point out how concepts from experimental and cognitive psychology and from linguistics can enrich our investigations of these problems. My strategy is to present first a somewhat eclectic view of the history of research on basic processes, emphasizing the continuing tension between basic and applied research. This leads to a brief discussion on current views of how applied and basic research can be reconciled, and this in turn leads to a discussion of two different frameworks for research on perceptual learning. In the remainder of the chapter I then examine against this background three concerns of basic process research: the Word Superiority Effect, phonemic awareness, and the determination of orthographic regularity.

FROM THE FLOOD TO THE EXODUS

The Antediluvian Period

Research on basic reading processes[1] can be grouped chronologically into four major periods: Antediluvian, Darwinian, Measurement, and Cognitive Revival. The Antediluvian Period extends from the late 1790s until about 1879, when Wundt established at the University of Leipzig the world's first experimental psychology laboratory. What can be called research during this period was atheoretical, driven by practical concerns such as legibility. Theory building was not an issue, and no one, at least as judged from the published record, asked how the mind processed visual information or what caused the eyes to react in different ways when confronted with print. For example, Anison in the French National Printing Office used expert judges and reading distance to compare the legibility of a modern typeface (Didot) with that of an older one (Garamond) (Anison, cited in Wiggins, 1967). Charles Babbage (1792–1871), an English mathematician and the inventor of the first working mechanical computing device, also used expert judges to assess the impact of different colors of paper on readability of print.

Emile Javal's early studies on legibility and on eye movements in reading also began during this period (Javal, 1879). Javal (see Fig. 43.1) was the first to report on the discontinuous or saccadic nature of eye movements in reading. Through observation and introspection, Javal concluded that clear vision occurred only during fixations, that the eyes fixated on about every 10th letter, and that the fixation point was somewhere between the middle and the top of the printed line. The first of these findings, which was a topic of considerable debate for decades, was shown to be true; the other two, however, have not been supported by subsequent work. Although some of Javal's work on reading fits chronologically in the Darwinian Period, Javal's approach was more applied than theoretical, driven by problems related to eye fatigue, myopia, and, as was his own case later in life, blindness.

---

[1] This section is based loosely on Venezky, 1984.

LOUIS EMILE JAVAL, M.D.

FIG. 43.1.   Emile Javal.

Darwinian Period

Wilhelm Wundt, whom Boring (1950, p. 316) calls the founder of experimental psychology, accepted the chair in philosophy at the University of Leipzig in 1875 and within a few years established what most historians of science agree was the first experimental psychology laboratory in the world. According to Cattell (1888), the laboratory's program centered on four areas: (a) analysis and measurement of sensations, (b) duration of mental events, (c) the time sense, and (d) attention, memory, and the association of ideas. Lurking behind this program was Darwin's theory of evolution and in particular natural selection. If variability of features in different species was what allowed change or adaptation over time, then psychologists could contribute to this fundamental understanding by focusing on the measurement of differences in mental processes. Basic reading processes such as naming of individual words were convenient and accessible for this goal.

The primary figure in reading research then was not Wundt, however, but James McKeen Cattell, an American Ph.D. student who was Wundt's first research assistant (see Fig. 43.2). Cattell was interested in individual differences, which he studied through reaction-time

JAMES McKEEN CATTELL, PH.D.

FIG. 43.2. James McKeen Cattell.

experiments (*mental chronometry*), using the subtractive method developed by the Dutch physiologist F. C. Donders (1818–1889).[2] Cattell's work on letter and word recognition, legibility of print, and span of attention are the bedrock of basic process research in reading. In one study, Cattell (1886) mounted letters on a rotating drum that passed by a narrow viewing slit. When only a single letter could be seen, naming time was about half a second. But as the slit was widened so that more and more letters could be viewed simultaneously, the naming time dropped. Individuals who were tested on this paradigm differed in the number of letters that they could process at one time. For some, naming times dropped through the fifth letter but were not decreased further for six; for others decreases occurred only through the fourth letter and for a few, only through the third.

With this study on the "limits of consciousness," Cattell demonstrated that seeing and naming could overlap, thus bringing into question the basis of Donders' subtractive method. The eye–voice span that occurred was also reported by Quantz in 1897 but not studied until almost 23 years later (Buswell, 1920). Cattell's most influential experiment was published a year before this, however. Using brief exposures of letters and words, Cattell demonstrated that, with limited viewing time, skilled readers could read aloud more words that made sentences

---

[2] On Donders and the errors in his method, see Boring (1950, pp. 147–149). Donders subtractive procedure was revived in the 1960s by Sternberg (1969).

than they could read words that had no connection, and more letters that made words than letters that had no connection (Cattell, 1885; see also Dearborn, 1914). The improvement for letters in words over letters in nonsense strings was rediscovered by Reicher in 1969 and became what today is called the Word Superiority Effect (WSE; Reicher, 1969; Wheeler, 1970).

By the end of the 1880s basic reading processes had moved to center stage in experimental psychology, and over the next 20 years many of the major problems investigated today were studied, including the cues for word recognition, the role of peripheral vision in reading, the eye–voice span, the causes of subvocalization, and memory for connected text. During this period Quantz (1897, 1898) published the first systematic study of reading processes and even posited a stage-by-stage reading model. In discussing the eye–voice span, he concluded that "In reading aloud . . . if it is to be intelligent and intelligible, words must be perceived some distance in advance of those which the voice is uttering. The rapid reader has the greatest interval between eye and voice" (Quantz, 1898, p. 436). Dearborn (1906) also published during this period a major treatise on basic processes in reading, covering, among other topics, the number and duration of fixation pauses in reading, perception during eye movements, span of attention, and location of fixations. Dearborn (1906) was the first to use pseudowords in a reading study and spoke of how illegal or odd letter strings "disappoint the association expectancy" (p. 65). His observations about orthographic structure and pronounceability were not taken up again until the work of E. J. Gibson and her colleagues in the 1960s (e.g., Gibson, Pick, Osser, & Hammond, 1962).

Of special interest to many psychologists in both Europe and North America during that period was the nature of printed word recognition. Erdmann and Dodge (1898) found that words could be recognized at a distance at which individual letters could not be recognized and interpreted this result as evidence for a whole-word-recognition strategy. From similar evidence, Cattell drew the same conclusion. In Europe, Goldscheider, and Müller (1893), Messmer (1904), and Zeitler (1900), all using tachistoscopically presented words, found evidence for "dominant" or "determining" letters as mediators of word identity. Huey (1908, p. 102) (see Fig. 43.3), speaking for the entire century, concluded from his review of the evidence available then that "it is very difficult to draw conclusions concerning visual perception in reading."

Other studies during this period—too numerous to be summarized here—examined the field of vision (e.g., Ruediger, 1907), the perceptual span in reading (e.g., Erdmann & Dodge, 1898), span of attention (e.g., Griffing, 1896), the cues for word recognition (e.g., Goldscheider & Müller, 1893), and word blindness (e.g., Morgan, 1896), among many others. All of these and much more were summarized by Huey in 1908 in his textbook. What is significant, however, is the theoretical orientation of most of the work done during this period. Few of the researchers pursued practical or applied applications of their work, and the few who did, such as Huey and Dearborn, did so mostly through speculation rather than through research programs.

The Age of Measurement

After the publication of his book, Huey abandoned reading research, turning his attention to mentally challenged children. By 1911, when the Age of Measurement began, the first volume of the *Journal of Educational Psychology* had been issued, and the attention of this new field had turned from research on basic processing to applied areas and in particular to teaching and testing. According to Boring (1950, p. 574), "By 1910 mental testing had clearly come to stay." In the next 40 years little work, relatively speaking, would be done on basic processes. Behaviorism, arising from functionalism and spurred on by John B. Watson's campaign against introspection, soon became the dominant school in psychology, thus further dampening interest in mental operations. The intensity and excitement of the Darwinian Period was gone, even though pockets of basic research continued here and there.

EDMUND BURKE HUEY, PH.D.

FIG. 43.3.   Edmund B. Huey.

Pinter (1913b) compared silent with oral speed in elementary school pupils and found the former to be significantly faster. Mead (1915) and Oberholtzer (1915) also studied reading speed, and Pinter (1913a) revisited subvocalization during silent reading. Further work was also done on the eye–voice span by Gray (1917), Buswell (1920), and Judd and Buswell (1922). Much of this work was descriptive, however, establishing norms rather than testing theories. Vernon, in her 1931 text *The Experimental Study of Reading,* lamented that "There has been little experimental work since the publication of Huey's *Psychology and Pedagogy of Reading* upon adult perception in reading, and the majority of the work upon children's perception in reading, although possibly of much pedagogical value, has been too disconnected and uncontrolled to provide results of much reliability or psychological interest" (p. xiv).

The Cognitive Revival

The Age of Measurement extended to the revival of cognitive psychology in the 1950s and was a small-scale Dark Ages for research on basic processes in reading. There is much more to this story than I have space for here and many more contributions through this period than hinted at here, particularly in eye-movement studies.[3] With the return of interest in cognitive processes, a variety of new directions appeared for basic reading research. E. J. Gibson and her colleagues examined the features of letters that were critical for recognition and then turned their attention to the role of letter–sound correspondences in word recognition (see Gibson & Levin, 1975, for a summary of this work). Beginning with the information theories of Shannon (1948, 1951), Miller and others studied the role of letter-string redundancy on word recognition and recall (e.g., Miller, Bruner, & Postman, 1954). In the Soviet Union around this same time, Zhurova and Elkonin were exploring children's abilities to manipulate single speech sounds or what is today called phonemic awareness (Elkonin, 1963; Zhurova, 1963/1964). Work also began at a number sites, including the Haskins Laboratories, on the role of speech processes in reading, and new studies of subvocalization were initiated (e. g., Hardyck & Petrinovich, 1969). This Cognitive Revival flowered in multiple directions including verbal learning, mathematical modeling, and information processing. As in the Darwinian Period, in the Cognitive Revival the primary focus was basic understanding. Application may have been somewhat closer to the researchers' vision than in the Darwinian period but it was not the driving force, and few of the researchers ventured beyond their laboratories.

One lesson from this brief historical sketch is that psychologists have pondered the cues for word recognition, the role of orthographic redundancy, the causes of subvocalization, and an array of other basic reading issues since at least the middle 1880s, and their findings and their methods remain important today. Methods for experimentation and especially for data analysis have improved dramatically since Cattell's earliest studies, yet most of the problems studied before 1900 remain problems today. But there is another lesson or paradox that we encounter in examining this history in detail, and this is that in the past the best work on basic processes in reading was done by psychologists who were driven not by a desire to improve the teaching of reading but by general psychological issues—perceptual development, information processing, individual variability, speed of mental events, and so on. Where researchers directed their attentions to applied issues such as vocabulary knowledge, teaching methods, and reading speed, little basic knowledge was gained. The challenge for the coming decades is to have both a solid program of basic research and a solid applied program that leads to major improvements in diagnosis and instruction.

BASIC SCIENCE, APPLIED SCIENCE

For many years a simple, unidirectional linear model was assumed for connecting research to practice. At one end was pure, basic research, pursued without specific goals in mind, and at the other end, practice. In between, according to whose model was presented, might be oriented basic research, applied research, experimental development, or other stages of similar composition. All movement within these models was from pure research to application, with little or no reverse flow. An alternative model featured the categories *pure research*, *strategic research*, and *tactical research*. Within these models, a tension between pure or basic research and applied research was assumed. According to an influential U.S. report on scientific research, issued after World War II, "Applied research invariably drives out pure" (Bush, 1945; cited in Stokes, 1997, p. 3). One might interpret The Age of Measurement described in the previous section as an example of where applied research drove out pure or basic research.

Recently, however, the consensus on pure and applied research has shifted. First, the notion of a linear, one-way relationship has been rejected in favor of a two-way flow in which

---

[3] For a fuller account, see Venezky, 1984.

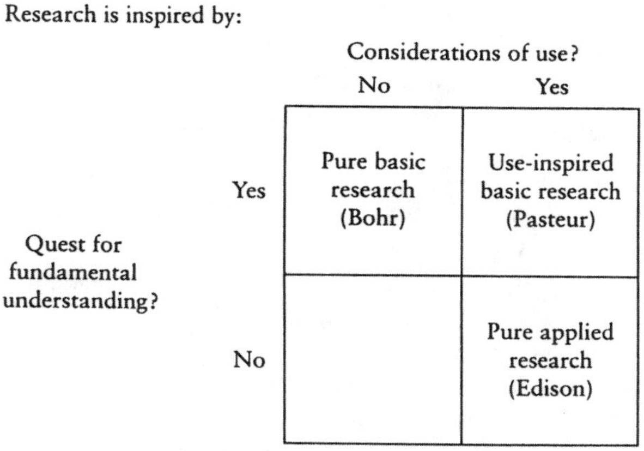

Research is inspired by:

FIG. 43.4.   Quadrant model of scientific research (from Stokes, 1997, p. 73).

application now feeds back to research. Second, in many fields it has been noted that the same people are often involved in both basic and applied work; thus the communities that were once assumed to be distinct actually overlap. The most influential recent work on research programs, however, Donald E. Stokes's *Pasteur's Quadrant: Basic Science and Technological Innovation* (Stokes, 1997), posits a two-dimensional relationship for the various types of research, building on two yes–no questions: Is there a quest for fundamental understanding? and Are there considerations of use? (see Fig. 43.4). Three of the quadrants are named after researchers whose work characterizes the dimensions involved (Bohr, Pasteur, Edison). The lower left-hand quadrant, which involves a quest for neither fundamental understanding nor for use might be called the Peterson quadrant after the birdwatchers' guide, which represents a high level of scientific curiosity but not basic science or application in the sense of problem solving.

Just as Pasteur made significant contributions to basic microbiology in his search for solutions to problems in fermentation and public health, present-day researchers can seek basic understandings in a search for how to improve the reading skills of at-risk students. For public policy, Stokes advocates a focus on use-inspired basic research, knowing that sponsors and researchers may differ in how they classify particular studies. Nevertheless, once an either–or classification system is rejected, use-inspired basic research that contributes both to the solution of real problems and to fundamental knowledge becomes possible, just as it was for Pasteur, for John Maynard Keynes, for the physicists on the Manhattan Project, and for many others.

Although it may be obvious to readers of this chapter why the lower right-hand quadrant in Fig. 43.4 (Pure applied research) should not be the direction of publicly funded educational research programs, others may not accept this premise. Unlike medicine or the physical sciences, for which trial and error has been productive in the past (for example, with Edison's work on the incandescent light bulb), education rarely sees long-term benefits from applications whose underlying properties are not well understood. This is especially true for many preschool and early primary enrichment, prereading, and reading programs from which early improvements often disappeared after a few years. Without an understanding of the factors that lead to independent student learning in any curricular area, little is learned from these failures. Even Edison, in time, was forced to hire technicians trained in electrical theory, admitting that a fundamental understanding of electricity was critical for the continuation of his work.

PERCEPTUAL LEARNING

With a framework of use-inspired basic research to guide our general search for a psychologi-cally sound research program, we turn now to a logical analysis of the object of our concerns. My concern from here on is with a few basic reading processes, particularly those related to the perception of words, both through visual recognition and through conversion to sound (i.e., decoding). This is not meant to be a promotion for a dual-route theory of lexical access, only a statement that, at different times in the normal acquisition of reading, both visual recognition and translation from spelling to sound play roles. Exactly what these roles are I will leave to another time, other than to claim that most reading by fluent adults, whether silent or oral, is driven by visual word recognition whereas for most learners at the earliest stages translation from letters to sounds is essential.

The core task in learning to read is a perceptual learning task. The print environment is composed of symbols encoded at multiple levels. At the lowest level for alphabetic writing systems such as English, Dutch, and Spanish are straight lines, curves, and intersections that distinguish the letters of the Roman alphabet, plus added features for punctuation marks. At a higher level are letters and letter clusters that have special significance for word recognition and letter–sound translation: single letters; digraphs and trigraphs that form functional units within the orthography such as <sch, ch>, and <ee>; common prefixes and suffixes such as <con-, -ed>, and <–ion>; and frequently occurring word beginning and endings such as <prin-, -ado>, and so forth. At even a higher level are words and beyond words are, perhaps, commonly occurring short phrases such as "the man," although the evidence for phrases as basic recognition units is weak.

From a number of studies done over the past 50 years we know that repeated exposure to print leads to the learning of letter and word frequencies as well as positional frequencies of letters and letter combinations within words (e.g., Attneave, 1953; Mason, 1975; Massaro, Taylor, Venezky, Jastrzembski, & Lucas, 1980). Although the deployment of this knowledge in normal reading is not well understood, its existence is firmly established, as is the existence of a general perceptual capacity for continuously encoding frequency of occurrence information from the environment (Hasher & Zacks, 1984). When a child is between the ages of 5 and 20 years there appears to be little change in this ability, and what the child acquires shows little fading across the adult years. (Frequency has a long history in psychology. As early as 1890 William James noted that "Perception is of definite and probable things," and both Brunswick and Thorndike incorporated frequency of occurrence of environmental patterns into general laws of learning.)

One of the challenges for basic process research on reading is to explore the information that experienced readers extract from repeated exposure to printed words. Besides single-letter positional frequency, which has been explored by Mason (1975), empirical studies have also produced some evidence for knowledge of bigram and trigram frequency (e.g., Massaro et al., 1980; McClelland & Johnston, 1977), and tables of such have been published for research use (e.g., Mayzner & Tresselt, 1965). What has not been explored is the nature of the sublexical units that are learned. Are these letter strings of varying lengths (single letters, bigrams, trigrams, etc.), are they word beginnings and word endings of particular structures (e.g., CV, VC, CCV), or are they, as E.J. Gibson speculated in the 1960s, letter strings that had invariant or nearly invariant correspondences to sound (Gibson et al., 1962)?

The pursuit of frequency as a variable in basic reading should be motivated by established foundations in human development and perceptual learning. I invoke two such frameworks here, although others could be substituted. My only purpose is to try to align reading research with more general studies of learning and development so that it can benefit from the perspectives that have been established from similar research. The first derives from the work on human development by Eleanor Gibson and Ann Pick, who characterize human behavior by four hallmarks: agency, prospectivity, perceiving order, and flexibility (Gibson & Pick, 2000).

Agency implies control over one's own behavior. In reading, for example, the movement of the eyes along the line and down the page is controlled by the reader, not by some innate mechanism or external signal. According to the reader's purpose for reading and the familiarity of the text, scanning will be slower or faster, fixations longer or shorter, and regressions many or few. Words will be recognized by strategic processes: visual form, translation to sound, segmentation into meaningful components, all supported or not supported by contextual cues.

Prospectivity implies a goal orientation. We do things for reasons; we have goals. We do not just meander about aimlessly, receiving whatever sensory inputs occur. Instead, we have goals—immediate and longer term—and adjust our behavior to reach them. When confronted with a printed word, we carry through our processing of it all the way to retrieval of meaning, even if the immediate task does not require this: Hence the Stroop effect (Stroop, 1935). Most of the basic processes in reading that we study become automated in fluent readers; however, before they reach that stage these processes need to be planned more explicitly. Prospectivity drives us to consider means to reach ends.

Perceiving order, as just explained, is a built-in human activity. We continually search for regularities, patterns, repetitions of stimuli and events, and utilize this information to control our behavior. The newborn learns quickly to distinguish familiar from unfamiliar faces. By 9 months of age a baby has already formed phoneme classes so that more attention is given to those sound differences that help make meaningful distinctions in the surrounding language than those that are within the same phoneme. By third or fourth grade the young reader can already discriminate regular and irregular orthographic patterns (Golinkoff & Rosinski, 1976).

Flexibility is the ability to adjust to new circumstances and to correct behavior that does not lead to desired ends. Better readers will detect when they are not sure of the meaning of a word or passage and take appropriate remedial action, perhaps rereading the passage or word, pronouncing it aloud. Poorer readers exhibit less flexibility, often applying the same strategic approaches to texts or reading situations that normally require alternative strategies.

This is in brief form a general framework that provides a perspective and a vocabulary for considering learning and development. It derives from an ecological perspective that focuses on human organisms in active engagement with their environments, extracting information according to the resources and opportunities available. A second, more cognitively based framework on perceptual learning, which could be viewed as an elaboration on the third point, perceiving order, attends to mechanisms for perceptual adaptation: attention weighting, stimulus imprinting, differentiation, and unitization (Goldstone, 1998).

Attention weighting is a process through which attention is shifted to the features and dimensions that are important for a task (e.g., naming a letter) and away from those that are irrelevant. In some sense, the irrelevant aspects become less distinguishable. We become, for example, well attuned to features that distinguish lowercase <e> from lowercase <c> but at the same time learn to pay little attention to those features that distinguish a sans serif <m> from a serif <m>. Just as we learn to attend to differences across phoneme classes but to ignore those within classes, we also apply these same strategies to stimuli received by means of other senses.

Stimulus imprinting involves the development of specialized abilities (i.e., detectors) for stimuli that occur frequently in the environment. The more we see a particular word, the higher the probability that we will develop a special facility for recognizing it. This ability might develop through the generation of templates for whole stimuli (e.g., printed words) or for features of these stimuli. This same process applies to pseudowords as demonstrated by Salasoo, Shiffrin, & Feustel (1985).

Differentiation is a process through which distinct familiar objects (i.e., stimuli) become more and more differentiated. According to Gibson and Pick (2000, p. 176), "Perceptual development is a process of differentiation." Before training, most people cannot discriminate a Cabernet Sauvignon from a Merlot or a Chardonnay aged in American oak barrels from one aged in French oak barrels but with training most people can learn to make these discriminations. In first learning to recognize printed words, many children pay little attention to letters in the middle of a word, thus treating pairs such as <then> and <than> as identical. With experience they learn to discriminate these. Similarly, <b> and <d> are treated as the same letter, although not because the child cannot see a difference. Instead, everything in the child's environment up to the first encounters with numbers and letters is invariant to rotation. A cup is still called a cup when it is rotated 180 degrees and now the handle is on the left rather than on the right. There are, however, physical limits to discrimination. Psychophysicists spent decades deriving just-noticeable differences (JNDs) for all types of physical judgments and modern sensory receptor studies have found enormous variability in the numbers of different sensory receptors in humans, such as those for taste.

Unitization is, at first glance, the opposite of differentiation. It refers to the building of larger and larger units that are perceived at once (in some sense). The classic study by Bryan and Harter (1899) on the speed of recognition of telegraphy codes represents a demonstration of unitization. Figure 43.5 shows the learning curve over about 27 weeks for a single telegraphy receiver who was studied.

The slowest speed occurred early in the operator training when the units of recognition were individual letters. With experience, words were perceived as units and speed improved dramatically. With more and more training, the operator could "copy behind" 6 to 12 words, that is, could wait for whole phrases or sentences before writing what was heard. We assume that, in initially learning to read, word length as measured in number of letters, is a good

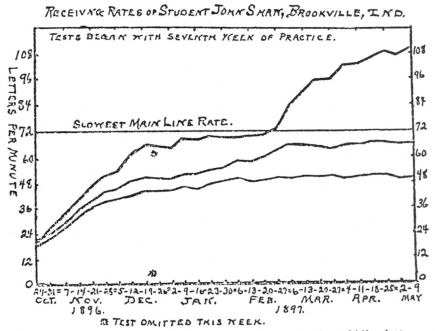

Connected discourse curve at the top; word curve in the middle; letter curve at the bottom.

FIG. 43.5. Telegraphic codes receiving rates for a single receiver during learning (from Bryan & Harter, 1899, p. 350).

predictor of recognition time. However, with experience unitization occurs for familiar words and length no longer is a factor in predicting recognition time.

REVISITING SOME BASIC READING PROCESSES

Several different frameworks for basic reading research having been presented, the time has come to explain how they can be applied to research on basic reading processes. To this end, three problems have been selected: the Word Superiority Effect, phonemic awareness, and the classification of real words and pseudowords as regular or irregular according to the their orthographic patterns. No magic is promised with any of these; instead most of the rhetoric will be in framing questions within broad psychological or linguistic issues.

The Word Superiority Effect

Cattell (1885) was the first to demonstrate that in a brief exposure time (10 ms) adults could recognize more letters in words than in unrelated letter strings. What Cattell actually did was have adults name unconnected letters from a briefly exposed string and then at the same exposure time name short unconnected words. (Cattell also tested short connected words.) Because there were more letters named in the unconnected words than there were in the unconnected letter strings, Cattell concluded that words could not be perceived letter by letter, as was assumed at the time, but as wholes. However, Cattell's methods confounded recognition with memory retention and articulation. Words that are identified in equal time might require different times for retrieval and execution of their articulatory patterns. In addition, everything that was recognized from a briefly exposed display may not have been retained in memory long enough to be retrieved and articulated.

George Sperling's (1960) partial report paradigm provided a technique for demonstrating that much more is available in *iconic* memory at the end of a brief display than can normally be reported orally by a viewer. But the issue of whether letters in words were perceived one after the other independently required a different approach, which was not reported until the late 1960s, when Gerard Reicher at the University of Michigan applied a forced-choice paradigm to the problem and Daniel Wheeler, also at the University of Michigan, replicated these studies with some refinements in the methodology (Reicher, 1969; Wheeler, 1970). Since that time the effect has been called the Word Superiority Effect (WSE) and the paradigm used to explore it, the Reicher–Wheeler paradigm.

Before explaining what Reicher did, however, I want to return to the basic–applied research issue that was already introduced. How do we justify an interest in the WSE if we are concerned with use-inspired basic research? Poor readers in the upper elementary grades typically read slower than students on grade level and also have more limited recognition vocabularies. We do not know, however, how much they differ from fluent readers in basic processing. If basic processing were weak, remediation potentially could focus on it or on compensatory mechanisms. If basic processing were not an issue, however, other reading components would need to be emphasized. A critical component of fluent processing is rapid recognition of letters and words. The Reicher–Wheeler Paradigm, among others, is a tool for probing basic processing skills. As will be explained shortly, it is richer than simple reaction time or other speed measures in that more information can be obtained through various manipulations on the basic paradigm. From the Gibson and Pick (2000) perspective, the Word Superiority Effect is a measure of how well the reader perceives order in the world of print, and from the Goldstone (1998) perspective, it is a measure of perceptual adaptation, tapping, in particular, stimulus imprinting.

Reicher (1969) presented single–letter, single-word, and random letter-string displays at brief exposures to adults, followed by a mask to eliminate any afterimage.[4] The mask was followed by two choices for a letter at a cued position where, for words, both choices would make words. For example, the display might be WORK and the response choices D and K, with dashes indicating that the choices applied to the last letter in the displayed word. A random letter-string display (e.g., OWRD) would also be followed by a two-choice display with a cued position.

Reicher (1969) found that accuracy rates were significantly higher for letters in real words than in random letter strings or alone. The effect was not overwhelming—about a 12% advantage for words—but has held up consistently (e.g,, Gilmore & Egeth, 1976; Thompson & Massaro, 1973; Wheeler, 1970). Subsequent studies showed that the effect could be eliminated by having a constant target set (Bjork & Estes, 1973; Thompson & Massaro, 1973) or by blocking on the stimulus type (words, letters, random letter strings). These manipulations demonstrate that the reader can act strategically, adjusting basic processing to optimize task performance. How well poor readers can make such adjustments, however, remains to be determined. But what interests us here primarily is the types of information that the reader must extract from the orthography for such an effect to occur. Even though some level of guessing is still possible on the word trials, information from other letters in the real words must be utilized to facilitate recognition of the correct response alternative. If the effect came from the reader's ability to utilize partial information from the cued position alone, then accuracy rates for words and random letter strings would be the same. These studies do not tell us, however, whether whole-word templates are utilized or subunit ones, such as WOR or OR.

A clue to what information might be utilized comes from a study by Baron and Thurston (1973) that showed a Word Superiority Effect for legal pesudowords over illegal pseudowords. This information eliminates whole-word templates as an explanation because, presumably, the Baron and Thurston (1973) study participants had never seen the pseudowords before. Therefore some aspects of the regularity of the orthography, what we call *scribal regularity* (Venezky & Massaro, 1987) must be invoked. What scribal regularity is exactly, I'll hold for later in this chapter. For the present it is enough to know that such a concept exists and may account for the Pseudoword Superiority Effect, which itself may be a useful probe for the basic processing abilities of poor readers.

The Baron and Thurston (1973) finding about pseudowords has been supported by recent brain-imaging studies that examined localization of brain activity for passive viewing of different types of letter strings: words (ant, farm, mother, etc.), pseudowords (reld, aldober, etc.), consonants (vsffht, stb, etc.), and false fonts composed of fragments of letters. Although all four types were characterized by activity responses (increased blood flow) in areas of the right hemisphere outside the primary visual cortex, only words and pseudowords produced prominent responses along the inner surface of the left cerebral hemisphere (Posner & Raichle, 1997, pp. 78–81). A two-level processing model is assumed by the authors for passive viewing of words and wordlike strings: an initial level of visual feature analysis, involving multiple areas on both sides of the brain, and a second level of analysis of visual word forms, involving coordinated responses from areas developed through experience with English orthography.

The WSE offers to reading researchers an opportunity to develop deep diagnostic tools while at the same time contributing to a knowledge based on information processing. To do this, studies need to probe a wider array of stimuli than words, letters, and pseudowords to determine which effects are due to the acquisition of reading skills and which are due to general information processing. Tracing the developmental course of the WSE in parallel with the acquisition course of nonverbal stimuli might lead to a better understanding of whether

---

[4] Reicher also presented double-letter and double-word displays but these are not discussed here.

reading failure is a linguistic phenomenon, arising from a failure to process phonological and alphabetic materials, or a more general cognitive fault.

Phonemic Awareness

If the past decade was the decade of whole language in reading instruction, the present decade might be called the Decade of Phonemic Awareness. No other concept from reading research has received as much press as this for decades. But after 50 years of probing, phonemic awareness is still, from a psychological perspective, a black box. We are interested in it because many studies have found a strong correlation between the lack of this ability and later reading failure (National Institute of Child Health, 2000). However, an equal number of careful studies also show that phonemic awareness results from learning to read in school far more than it does from any maturational process or out-of-school experiences (e.g., Morrison, Griffith, & Frazier, 1996; Olson, Wise, & Forsberg, 1996). There are also a number of different ways that phonemic awareness is measured, and each places slightly different demands on the child.

Phonemic awareness has also been investigated in adults, with results similar to those found for children. Morais, Cary, Alegria, and Bertelson (1979) found that Portuguese illiterate and ex-illiterate readers differed dramatically in their abilities to delete or add phoneme segments to the beginnings of words, with those who had learned to read as adults far better at the segmentation tasks. Similarly, Read, Zhang, Nie, and Ding (1986) demonstrated that Chinese adults who learned Pinyin, a romanization for Chinese, could do a phoneme segmentation task far better than those who learned only logographic forms.

From the Gibson and Pick (2000) perspective, phonemic awareness is a demonstration of *flexibility*, that is, an adjustment to new circumstances created by the world of alphabet print. From the Goldstone (1998) perspective it involves differentiation. That is, a spoken word needs to be differentiated into syllables, and then syllables further differentiated into separate phonemes. The tasks for measuring phonemic awareness all require retention of an acoustic string in memory, segmentation of that string at a phoneme level, and (usually) retrieval of a substring, either as a new word or as a sound. These tasks all place large burdens on short-term or working memory and on attention. Over the early school years dramatic changes occur in the child's articulatory rate, acoustical processing, and working memory abilities, changes that might help researchers to understand the acquisition of phonemic awareness (or lack thereof). Reading researchers need to examine the general psychological literature on these phenomena for clues to a deeper understanding of phonemic awareness and for developing more effective diagnostic procedures.

Haith (1971), for example, observed a qualitative change in short-term visual information processing after children were 5 years of age. Whereas adults can recode visual stimuli for retention in working memory and rehearse them, 5-year-olds appear not to do this spontaneously. Although Haith found no evidence for acoustical recoding, more recent work suggests that most recoding for working memory is acoustical (Gathercole & Baddeley, 1993). Almost 30 years ago Conrad (1972) demonstrated that most 3–5-year-olds were not affected by the acoustic similarity of words held in working memory but older children also were. More recent evidence indicates that one of the outcomes of schooling is active, cumulative rehearsal strategies for memory (Morrison et al., 1996).

Gathercole and Baddeley (1993) found that children from the age of about 4 years on possess phonological storage and can do subvocal rehearsal; however, the recoding of visual material into a phonological form for retention in working memory emerges sometime between the ages of 6 and 8 years, on average. Because this form of coding is acoustical in nature, it depends heavily on articulatory facility. The increase in short-term memory for spoken materials that is observed in children over the ages of 4–12 years corresponds roughly to the increase of articulation rate over this same period. Fry and Hale (1996, p. 240), in investigating age-related changes in processing speed, working memory, and fluid intelligence, found that "age-related changes in processing speed mediate most of the developmental increases in working memory capacity." That is, individual differences in processing speed lead to differences in articulation rate, which then show up as differences in working memory, particularly as measured by digit and letter span.

Between the ages 5 and 7 years, the child makes rapid improvements in a wide range of abilities, driven at least in part by the need to cope with the new or changing demands of school, home, and friendship environments (Sameroff & Haith, 1996). Some of these changes, although not appearing similar to the tasks employed for measuring phonemic awareness, may nevertheless be related to its acquisition. For example, White (1965; cited in Haith, 1971) found that the speech of 5-year-olds, unlike that of 7-year-olds, was unaffected by a delay in hearing their own voice. This finding may reflect a special case of the 5-year-old's general inability to attend to all of the components of a stimulus simultaneously (Piaget, 1961). This suggest that tasks parallel to those used for phonemic awareness can be developed, but without a requirement of speech processing, as a control for the attentional demands of the awareness tasks.

The most important lesson to draw from this review is that what reading researchers have labeled "phonemic awareness" and have treated as a property unique to reading may, in fact, reflect more general basic processing limitations. More careful probing is needed of the relationship between phonemic awareness and general processing speed, articulatory rate, and ability to attend to complex features of stimuli. Such a research program might contribute not only to the knowledge base for basic processes in reading but also to the general developmental knowledge base.

Orthographic Regularity

The last area of interest for this chapter, orthography, also fits within the Gibson and Pick (2000) framework under *perceiving order* but the general concepts involved derive in part from cognitive psychology and in part from linguistics. I will save for another time the arguments over deep versus shallow orthographies (terms that I find to be somewhat limiting), rules versus analogies, and whether graphemes are parallel to phonemes, and concentrate instead on the nature of information needed for defining orthographic regularity, using English as an example. One point to be made here is the wide range of knowledge of English orthography needed for such tasks as generating legal pseudowords for experimental studies. Another point to be made is that some orthographies are generally much more complex than the labels "regular" and "irregular" (or "deep" and "shallow") reflect. English is perhaps the prime example. Not only does it contain variant letter–sound correspondences and outright irregularities but it also attempts to preserve morpheme identity so far as the translation to phonology will allow. Although this latter characteristic may add to the difficulties of the initial learner, it is an aid to the advanced or more fluent reader. Thus there are trade-offs for certain orthographic characteristics.

Orthographic regularity has been a concern of psychological studies on word recognition and reading since the late 1950s, although the majority of work of interest here dates from the 1970s. Some of the work has been developmental, looking at either the acquisition of grapheme–phoneme patterns (Venezky, 1976) or of differences across readers of different abilities or languages in processing regular and irregular spellings (e.g., Massaro & Taylor, 1980; Wimmer, Landerl, & Frith, 1999). Dyslexia researchers have found different types of reading disability depending on how irregular orthographic patterns are handled (Patterson & Morton, 1985; Plaut & Shallice, 1993). Work in a variety of languages has also been done (e.g., Monteiro, 1995, reported in Rego, 1999; Ziegler, Jacobs, & Stone, 1996). Probabilities for English grapheme–phoneme correspondences have been reported by Berndt, Reggia, and Mitchum (1987) and a variety of models proposed for processing of orthographic patterns (e.g., Brown, 1987; Glushko, 1979; Parkin, 1984; Waters & Seidenberg, 1985).

In most of this work, *orthographic regularity* has been defined by regularity of grapheme–phoneme patterns even though evidence exists for influence from graphic patterns (e.g., Mason, 1975; Parkin, 1984; Venezky & Massaro, 1987). In particular, there exists a *scribal regularity* to English as much as there does a grapheme–phoneme regularity. For example, *tchif*, although pronounceable, is scribally irregular in that the pseudogeminates <ck>, <dg>, and <tch> do not occur in initial position in English words. Similarly, *cwack* could be pronounced as *quack*, but would still be scribally irregular because <cw> is not found at the beginnings of words or syllables in English; in spelling, only <qu> represents the sequence /kw/. To frame the issue here, the problem of generating regular and irregular pseudowords for English is considered, along with the problem of defining regularly and irregularly spelled real words.

The first type of information needed for these tasks is graphemic and requires a basic decision on processing units. This concern for basic units is parallel to what is faced in measuring the capacity of working memory. English orthography employs 26 letters plus a handful of diacritics to render its lexicon in print. However, the traversal from spelling to sound originates not with the 26 letters but with a larger collection of *functional units*. This distinction between letters (or graphemes) and functional units is critical for most orthographies and has implications that have not been explored for instruction. The functional units for English include, besides the 26 letters, digraphs such as <ch, sh, th, ea> and <oo>, as well as a few trigraphs such as <tch, eau> and <sch>. Functional units are letters or letter sequences whose correspondences cannot be predicted from their separate components. Because letters are the smallest units considered here, they are functional units by definition. Digraphs such as <ch> are functional units because their correspondences cannot be predicted from their separate letters. In contrast, consonant clusters (e.g., <cl>) and geminate consonants (e.g., <pp>) are not because the same rules that predict the correspondences of the separate letters apply also to the letters in these combinations. For vowels, however, the geminate sequences that occur (<ee, oo>, and occasionally <aa, ii> and <uu>) are usually separate functional units because their correspondences cannot be predicted from their constituents.

Functional units, as defined here, are based on translation to sound. Therefore, what is a functional unit in one word might be a sequence of two (or more) separate units in another. Notice, for example, the differences between <th> in "whether" and "hothouse" and <ea> in "clean" and "idea." The exact number of functional units to define for English orthography is somewhat arbitrary, depending on the number of rarer (and mostly foreign) spellings one wants to account for in an English spelling-to-sound system.

Once functional units have been identified, they are divided into two classes: relational units and markers. Relational units are the workhorses of the orthography, the purveyors of sound. Markers are mute cousins of relational units, functioning like museum signage to indicate sound translations, preserve graphotactical patterns, identify morphemic forms, and do other functions. For example, the <u> in "guest" marks <g> as hard (i.e., /g/), just as the <e> in "traceable" marks <c> as soft (cf. blame: blamable). In "glove" and "plague," final <e> preserves graphotactical patterns in that neither <v> nor <u> is tolerated in final position. (A few counterexamples have slipped through the scribal guard, however, including "you" and "Slav.")

The letter <e> is the most common and easily recognizable marker in English orthography. Among other functions, it does a cameo performance in what is called the final-e pattern, marking the free (i.e., long) pronunciation of single-letter, stressed vowels (rate, mete, site, note, flute). It also preserves graphotactical patterns as just explained, separates homophones (bell–belle), and decorates ordinary words with quaintness and historicity, as in Ye Olde Curio Shoppe.

Relational units, although mapped into phonological-level components, may also serve marking functions. The <i> in "city," for example, is mapped into /i/ but at the same time marks the correspondence <c> → /s/. In "trafficking" a slightly different marking relationship occurs, in that the final <c> in "traffic" is replaced with <ck> so that the following <i> in <ing> does not mark <c> as /s/. This substitution is not done in single-syllable words so that in words like *arcing* a highly irregular correspondence for <c> occurs. This irregularity is a result of a marking omission as opposed to the irregularity of <c> in "facade." (But note that the cedilla is used in French and in some English texts to mark "hard" <c>.)

As any appeal to sanity would predict, English orthography is order preserving in translating from spelling to sound. Thus *tap* is pronounced /t p/ and not /p t/ or /pt/. But notice what happens with Midwestern pronunciations of <wh> words like *when*. The initial consonant sounds are reversed in order from their spellings: /hw n/. Similarly, <gn>, as in "cognac" and "poignant" is pronounced in reverse order: /nj/ as it is in French. A far more frequent reversal occurs in final <le> words like "bottle" and "article" when the pronunciations are not blended into a syllabic l. Similarly, final <re> also signals a sound reversal: *acre, metre, centre,* and so forth. These, fortunately, are the only exceptions to the order-preserving rule.

An issue of more importance concerns silent letters that do not function as markers. Consider "receipt," "hymn," and "knowledge." The <p> in *receipt* is not only silent, but was never pronounced in English. It appeared first in the 15th century in a fit of classical atavism that reshaped hundreds of English spellings to approximate more closely their Latin origins (Scragg, 1974). In contrast, the <n> in *hymn* not only retains evidence of a sound once present but also preserves morphemic shape in relation to "hymnal," for which the <n> is pronounced. The <k> in "knowledge" is somewhere between these two cases in that a related form, "acknowledge," exists, although the presence of the *c* makes the alternation less direct than in the "hymn–hymnal" case. To account for these different types of silent spelling units, three classes are posited: fossilized (e.g., <p> in "receipt"; <h> in "heir"); morphophonemic (e.g., <n> in "hymn," "damn," etc.; <b> in "bomb"); and marking (e.g., <e> in "hope").

The patterns or regularities just summarized represent one part of what we call *scribal regularity*. The other part, which is not summarized in detail here, consists of a variety of peculiarities of English spelling: restrictions on gemination and word length, use of <qu> rather than <kw> or <cw> for /kw/, nonuse of digraph vowels before geminate consonants, and so on. These are the patterns that are critical for creating legal pseudowords for English. A much more detailed presentation of them is given in Venezky (1999).

Spelling-to-Sound Patterns

The second major area of concern for labeling words and pseudowords as regular or irregular is how spelling relates to sound. All spelling–sound relationships are based on arbitrary associations of symbols with sounds and most can trace their origins from West Semitic through Greek and Latin. Some of these relationships, however, are modified by English phonotactics, that is, by the allowable sound patterns of English. The pronunciation of <n> in "think," for example, is conditioned by the following velar stop that requires a velar nasal wherever a palatal nasal is indicated by the spelling. This is a component of the English phonological system and is automatic for native speakers. That is, English does not allow /n/ to occur in the same syllable before /g/ or /k/. In "creature," "luxury," "azure," and "cordial," a similar process operates to yield the sounds /c, s, z, j/. This process, palatalization, converts particular consonants, when followed by a high front vowel or glide and then an unstressed vowel into one of the palatals

/c, s, z, j/. It continues to operate today, particularly across word boundaries, in forms like /gac/ [got you] and /rez/ [raise you—as in poker].

A related issue is raised by the pronunciation of the initial <th> in words like "the," "then," "those," and "though." In these and other function words (with the exception of "through," in which <th> is followed by <r>) the initial interdental spirant is voiced (cf. "thin," "think," "thumb"). A rule that accounts for this pattern would be based on the classification of the English lexicon into function words and content words. The former class contains the syntactic glue of the lexicon—the articles, prepositions, and other marking terms—whereas the latter class carries the main burden of semantics—the nouns, verbs, adjectives, and adverbs. Is this a psychologically valid division? For a native speaker, probably yes, given that the function words in English form a small, closed set and are, with rare exceptions, frequently occurring and easily identified (see also Campbell & Besner, 1981).

Form class and stress placement are two of a small group of features that are relevant to the description of spelling–sound patterns. Another feature is morpheme identity. In "dogs," "cats," and "houses," the final <s> has three different pronunciations. These are all predictable from the sound preceding <s> if the <s> stands for noun plural (or third-person singular, present indicative for verbs, or possessive). If, on the other hand, <s> is not a separate morpheme, this rule does not apply (cf. "gas," "has," "chassis"). What might give English orthography an appearance of greater regularity is etymology, in that some patterns apply differently according to word origins. Unfortunately, many (if not most) English words no longer carry any reliable indication of their origins, and in many cases the same origin may have had, over time, two or more pronunciations for the same spelling.

So far the word "rule" has been assiduously avoided. Part of the reason for this timidness is that many spelling–sound patterns are arbitrary and therefore unpredictable. For example, the functional unit <ea> has two high-frequency pronunciations, represented by "bread" and "team." Which will occur in a given environment is generally unpredictable, although a few subpatterns show high regularity (e.g., <ea> before <th> is almost always pronounced as in "bread": "feather," "weather," etc.). Other patterns tend toward a regularity, but with more than a handful of exceptions. A stressed, single-vowel spelling before a simple consonant unit plus final <e> is generally mapped into a free (i.e., long) pronunciation, for example. But exceptions abound: "glove," "give," "machine," "police," etc.

Further complicating the notion of rule is the question of level or range for a pattern. Consider as an example the pronunciation of <d> in words like "Indian" and "obsidian." Because <d> is almost always pronounced /d/, these particular pronunciations seem to follow a general rule. However, when considered in relation to the general palatalization procedure just outlined, these two words have irregular pronunciations, in that /d/ before /i/ plus a following unstressed vowel should palatalize to /j/. A similar problem appears with <g> patterns. The letters <c> and <g> share a number of features, including mappings into so-called hard and soft pronunciations (cozy, ceiling; guard, gym). For <c> these mappings can be predicted by the type of sound that follows <c>; if this sound is a high or mid front vowel, <c> takes its soft pronunciation; otherwise, it is hard (ceiling, cyst, coelacanth; climb, coal, cage). Notice that although the rule "c before e, i, or y is soft . . ." is a good approximation to the real rule, it cannot account for the correct pronunciation of <c> in *coelacanth*.

Against the high regularity of the <c> pattern, <g> appears negligent at best. Notice "gear," "give," "get," "tiger," and "anger" alongside the more "regular" "gem," "ginger," and "ranger." Many borrowings from Scandinavian languages (e.g., "gear," "gift") do not follow the standard <g> pattern, and many other exceptions are respellings of forms that were originally regular (tiger < tigre, target < targat, anger < angr, auger < augur, etc.). The question for rule making is whether to consider the <c> and <g> patterns separately or as part of a larger pattern. The former path could lead to treating <g> as if it had one regular pronunciation, /g/, thus making "gym," and so forth, irregular; the latter to a single hard–soft rule whereby "gym" and related forms would be regular and "get," "girl," and so forth, irregular. Studies of both children and adults indicate that a hard–soft selection rule operates for <c> but not for <g> (Venezky, 1976).

With all of the caveats and complications just given, it is still possible to develop a set of patterns for English orthography. The first division of this set is into three classes: invariant, variant but predictable, and variant and unpredictable. The majority of the consonants fall into the invariant class: <b, ck, dg, f, h, j, k, kh, l, m, p, q, r, sh, tch, v> and <z>. Among the variant, predictable patterns are <c, d, n, t, w, x, y>, and the short–long vowel pattern for monosyllables (e.g., rat:rate, met:mete, sit:site, rob:robe, run:rune). Depending on the specificity allowed, a variety of other patterns fits into this class. For example, a stressed vowel before the suffix <ity> is generally short, even though followed by only a single consonant: "sanity," "divinity," "verbosity," "serenity." More could be said about these classes but the object here is not exhaustion.

Lack of Symmetry in the Spelling–Sound System

If orthographic patterns were symmetrical, pronouncing words from their spellings and spelling words from their pronunciations would be relatively similar tasks, complicated only by homographs (i.e., words like "read" that admit two or more pronunciations with distinct meanings for each) and homophones (i.e., words like "to," "too," and "two" that sound the same but have different meanings and spellings). Such symmetry would allow a collapsing of the teaching of reading and spelling, as well as simplifying the description of orthographic patterns. But alas, English orthography is painfully asymmetrical. Observe in Fig. 43.6 the various spellings for the sound /k/ and in turn the various pronunciations each of these spellings admits.

Excluding anomalous forms like <kh> (khaki), and <cch> (saccharine), six spellings commonly occur for /k/: <q, k, ch, c, cc, ck>. At first glance this is the stuff out of which spelling reform tracts are made, but when positional constraints are considered, far more order can be seen. In addition, it should be noted that <c> represents /k/ in almost 75% of the words in which this sound occurs alone (that is, not in clusters), and nearly 100% of its occurrences are in clusters. <K> represents about 12% of the /k/ spellings and <ck> about 7%. The decoding situation, although less complicated, is by no means simple. The various spellings of /k/ have

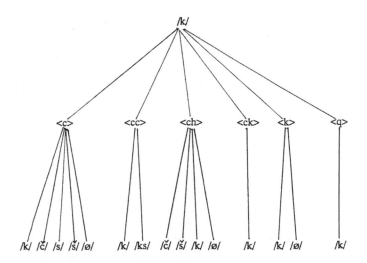

FIG. 43.6.   Spellings for /k/ and the various pronunciations of these spellings.

a variety of pronunciations other than /k/, as shown in Fig. 43.6. This exercise could be extended to almost all of the vowel spellings and sounds, thus providing further demonstrations of asymmetry. Such excess is unwarranted, however, as asymmetry is so obvious.

With all of these conditions and variations, one is tempted to give up on making sense of English orthography. However, this type of linguistic analysis is a prelude and not a substitute for psychological testing. Parkin (1984), among others, has found that the psychological concept of regularity for grapheme–phoneme correspondences does not depend on strict, invariant mappings; instead, it is highly flexible, treating major and minor patterns similarly under certain experimental conditions. In addition, studies of rule and pattern learning from other domains such as language development have a number of parallels with orthographic acquisition. For example, overgeneralization or overextension has been found in the learning of a number of language features, including morphology and semantics (see Harley, 1995, pp. 360–364, for a brief review). This same phenomenon has been found in the child's learning of grapheme–phoneme patterns (Venezky, 1976). The same pragmatic factors affecting language acquisition proposed by Taylor and Taylor (1990) could be applied to the learning of orthography: Simple and short before complex and long, concrete before abstract, frequent and familiar before less frequent and unfamiliar, and so forth. Once again, with a shift in emphasis and an occasional change in vocabulary, the study of orthographic regularity could fit into the mainstream of language and cognitive development

RECAPITULATION

If research on basic reading processes is to gain the respect of psychologists and linguists, then it needs to be aligned more carefully with the mainstream concepts, paradigms, and vocabulary of these areas. At issue is not just respect, however, but the very health of our field. Insularity is rarely a virtue in academic pursuits. Peer review, discussion, and debate are essential ingredients of the scientific process. By examining the history of basic process research and by centering it within the conceptual frameworks of psychological and linguistic research, basic process studies on reading could once again be in the mainstream of psychological studies. The more we can base our models on general processing strategies rather than on mechanisms unique to our specific domain, the more compelling will be our claims. Our unified dream should be of a Nobel Prize for reading research, giving international recognition to breakthroughs that demonstrate how simple, general processing strategies can account for learning to read in many different orthographies and languages.

REFERENCES

Attneave, F. (1953). Psychological probability as a function of experienced frequency. *Journal of Experimental Psychology, 46*, 81–86.

Baron, J., & Thurston, I. (1973). An analysis of the word superiority effect. *Cognitive Psychology, 4*, 207–228.

Berndt, R., Reggia, J., & Mitchum, C. (1987). Empirically derived probabilities for grapheme-to-phoneme correspondences in English. *Behavior Research Methods, Instruments, & Computers, 19*, 1–9.

Bjork, E. L., & Estes, W. K. (1973). Letter identification in relation to linguistic context and masking conditions. *Memory & Cognition, 1*, 217–223.

Boring, E. G. (1950). *A history of experimental psychology* (2nd ed.). Englewood Cliffs, NJ: Prentice-Hall.

Brown, B. D. A. (1987). Resolving inconsistency: A computational model of word naming. *Journal of Memory & Language, 26*, 1–23.

Bryan, W. L., & Harter, N. (1899). Studies on the telegraphic language. The acquisition of a hierarchy of habits. *The Psychological Review, 6*, 345–375.

Buswell, G. T. (1920). An experimental study of the eye-voice span in reading. *Supplementary Educational Monographs, 17.* Chicago: University of Chicago Press.

Campbell, R., & Besner, D. (1981). This and thap—Constraints on the pronunciation of new written words. *Quarterly Journal of Experimental Psychology, 33A,* 375–396.

Cattell, J. M. (1885). Über die Zeit der Erkennung und Benennung von Schriftzeichen, Bildern und Farben. *Philosophische Studien, 2,* 635–650.

Cattell, J. M. (1886). The time it takes to see and name objects. *Mind, 11,* 63–65.

Cattell, J. M. (1888). The psychological laboratory at Leipsig. *Mind, 13,* 37–51.

Conrad, R. (1972). Speech and reading. In J. F. Kavanagh & I. G. Mattingley (Eds.), *Language by ear and by eye* (pp. 205–240). Cambridge, MA: MIT Press.

Dearborn, W. F. (1906). The psychology of reading. *Archives of Philosophy, Psychology, and Scientific Methods, No. 4.*

Dearborn, W. F. (1914). Professor Cattell's studies of perception and reading. *Archives of Psychology, 4,* 34–45.

Elkonin, D. B. (1963). The psychology of mastering the elements of reading. In B. Simon (Ed.), *Educational psychology in the U.S.S.R.* London: Routledge and Kegan Paul.

Erdmann, B., & Dodge, R. (1898). *Psychologische Untersuchungen über das Lesen auf Experimenteller Grundlage.* Halle, Germany: Neimeyer.

Fry, A. F., & Hale, S. (1996). Processing speed, working memory, and fluid intelligence: Evidence for a developmental cascade. *Psychological Science, 7,* 237–241.

Gathercole, S. E., & Baddeley, A. D. (1993). *Working memory and language.* Hove, UK: Lawrence Erlbaum Associates.

Gibson, E. J., & Levin, H. (1975). *The psychology of reading.* Cambridge, MA: MIT Press.

Gibson, E. J., & Pick, A. D. (2000). *An ecological approach to perceptual learning and development.* Oxford/New York: Oxford University Press.

Gibson, E. J., Pick, A., Osser, H., & Hammond, M. (1962). The role of grapheme–phoneme correspondence in the perception of words. *American Journal of Psychology, 75,* 554–570.

Gilmore, G. C., & Egeth, H. E. (1976). When are nonwords easy to see? *Memory & Cognition, 4,* 519–524.

Glushko, R. (1979). The organization and activation of orthographic knowledge in reading aloud. *Journal of Experimental Psychology: Human Perception and Performance, 5,* 674–691.

Goldscheider, A., & Müller, R. F. (1893). Zur Physiologie und Pathologie des Lesens. *Zeitschrift für klinische Medicin, 33,* 131–167.

Goldstone, R. L. (1998). Perceptual learning. *Annual Review of Psychology, 49,* 585–612.

Golinkoff, R. M., & Rosinski, R. R. (1976). Decoding, semantic processing and reading comprehension skill. *Child Development, 47,* 252–258.

Gray, C. T. (1917). Types of reading ability as exhibited through tests and laboratory experiments. *Supplementary Educational Monographs, 5.* Chicago: University of Chicago Press.

Griffing, H. (1896). On the development of visual perception and attention. *American Journal of Psychology, 7,* 227–236.

Haith, M. M. (1971). Developmental changes in visual information processing and short-term visual memory. *Human Development, 14,* 249–261.

Hardyck, C., & Petrinovich, L. F. (1969). Treatment of subvocal speech during reading. *Journal of Reading, 12,* 361–368, 419–422.

Harley, T. A. (1995). *The psychology of language: From data to theory.* Hove, UK: Psychology Press.

Hasher, L., & Zacks, R. T. (1984). Automatic processing of fundamental information. *American Psychologist, 39,* 1372–1388.

Huey, E. B. (1908/1968). *The psychology and pedagogy of reading.* Cambridge, MA: MIT Press. (Originally published 1908 by Macmillan.)

Javal, E. (1879). Essai sur la psyiologie de la lecture. *Annales d'Oculistique, 82,* 242–253.

Judd, C. H., & Buswell, G. T. (1922). Silent reading: A study of the various types. *Supplementary Educational Monographs, 23.* Chicago: University of Chicago Press.

Mason, M. (1975). Reading ability and letter search time: Effects of orthographic structure defined by single-letter positional frequency. *Journal of Experimental Psychology: General, 194,* 146–166.

Massaro, D. W., & Taylor, G. A. (1980). Reading ability and utilization of orthographic structure in reading. *Journal of Educational Psychology, 72,* 730–742.

Massaro, D. W., Taylor, G. A., Venezky, R. L., Jastrzembski, J. E., & Lucas, P. A. (1980). *Letter and word perception: Orthographic structure and word processing in reading.* Amsterdam: North-Holland.

Mayzner, M., & Tresselt, M. (1965). Tables of single-letter and digram frequency counts for various word-length and letter-position combinations. *Psychonomic Monograph Supplements, 1,* 13–32.

McClelland, J. L., & Johnston, J. C. (1977). The role of familiar units in the perception of words and nonwords. *Perception & Psychophysics, 22,* 249–261.

Mead, C. D. (1915). Silent versus oral reading with one hundred sixth-grade children. *Journal of Educational Psychology, 6*, 345–348.

Messmer, O. (1904). Zur Psychologie des Lesens bei Kindern und Erwachsenen. *Archiv für die gesamte Psychologie, 2*, 190–298.

Miller, G. A., Bruner, J. S., & Postman, L. (1954). Familiarity of letter sequences and tachistoscopic identification. *Journal of General Psychology, 50*, 129–139.

Morais, J., Cary, L., Alegria, J., & Bertelson, P. (1979). Does awareness of speech as a sequence of phones arise spontaneously? *Cognition, 7*, 323–331.

Morgan, W. P. (1896). A case of congenital word-blindness. *British Medical Journal, 2*, 1612–1614.

Morrison, F. J., Griffith, E. M., & Frazier, J. A. (1996). Schooling and the 5 to 7 shift: A natural experiment. In A. J. Sameroff & M. M. Haith (Eds.), *The five to seven shift: The age of reason and responsibility* (pp. 161–186). Chicago: University of Chicago Press.

National Institute of Child Health and Human Development. (2000). *Report of the National Reading Panel. Teaching Children to Read: An Evidence-Based Assessment of the Scientific Research Literature on Reading and Its Implications for Reading Instruction* (NIH Publication 00-4769). Washington, DC: U.S. Government Printing Office.

Oberholtzer, E. E. (1915). Testing the efficiency of reading in the grades. *Elementary School Journal, 15*, 313–322.

Olson, R., Wise, B., & Forsberg, H. (1996). The 5 to 7 shift in reading and phoneme awareness for children with dyslexia. In A. J. Sameroff & M. M. Haith (Eds.), *The five to seven shift: The age of reason and responsibility* (pp. 187–204). Chicago: University of Chicago Press.

Parkin, A. J. (1984). Redefining the regularity effect. *Memory & Cognition, 12*, 287–292.

Patterson, K. E., & Morton, J. (1985). From orthography to phonology: An attempt at an old interpretation. In K. E. Patterson, J. C. Marshall, & M. Coltheart (Eds.), *Surface dyslexia: Neuropsychological and cognitive studies of phonological reading* (pp. 15–34). London: Lawrence Erlbaum Associates.

Piaget, J. (1961). *Les mechanismes perceptifs.* Paris: Presses Universitaires de France.

Pinter, R. (1913a). Inner speech during silent reading. *Psychology Review, 20*, 129–153.

Pinter, R. (1913b). Oral and silent reading of fourth-grade pupils. *Journal of Educational Psychology, 4*, 333–337.

Plaut, D. C., & Shallice, T. (1993). Deep dyslexia: A case study of connectionist neuropsychology. *Cognitive Neuropsychology, 10*, 377–500.

Posner, M. I., & Raichle, M. E. (1997). *Images of mind.* New York: Scientific American Library.

Quantz, J. O. (1897). Problems in the psychology of reading. *Psychological Monographs, 2*(1, Whole No. 5).

Quantz, J. O. (1898). Summary—Problems in the psychology of reading. *Psychological Review, 5*, 534–536.

Read, C., Zhang, Y.-F., Nie, H.-Y., & Ding, B.-Q. (1986). The ability to manipulate speech sounds depends on knowing alphabetic writing. *Cognition, 24*, 31–44.

Rego, L. L. B. (1999). Phonological awareness, syntactic awareness and learning to read and spell in Brazilian Portuguese. In M. Harris & G. Hatano (Eds.), *Learning to read and write: A cross-linguistic perspective.* Cambridge, UK: Cambridge University Press.

Reicher, G. M. (1969). Perceptual recognition as a function of the meaningfulness of the stimulus material. *Journal of Experimental Psychology, 81*, 275–280.

Ruediger, W. C. (1907). The field of distinct vision: With reference to individual differences and their correlations. *Archives of Psychology, 1*(5), 1–68.

Salasoo, A., Shiffrin, R. M., & Feustel, T. C. (1985). Building permanent memory codes: Codification and repetition effects in word identification. *Journal of Experimental Psychology: General, 114*, 50–77.

Sameroff, A. J., & Haith, M. M. (Eds.). (1996). *The five to seven shift: The age of reason and responsibility.* Chicago: University of Chicago Press.

Scragg, D. G. (1974). *A history of English spelling.* Manchester, UK: Manchester University Press.

Shannon, C. E. (1948). A mathematical theory of communication. *Bell System Technical Journal, 27*, 379–423, 622–656.

Shannon, C. E. (1951). Prediction and entropy of printed English. *Bell System Technical Journal, 30*, 50–64.

Sperling, G. (1960). The information available in brief visual presentation. *Psychological Monographs, 74*, 1–29.

Sternberg, S. (1969). The discovery of processing stages: Extensions of Donders' method. In W. G. Koster (Ed.), *Attention and Performance II. Acta Psychologica, 30*, 276–315.

Stokes, D. E. (1997). *Pasteur's quadrant: Basic science and technological innovation.* Washington, DC: Brookings Institution Press.

Stroop, V. R. (1935). Studies of interference in serial verbal reactions. *Journal of Experimental Psychology, 18*, 643–662.

Taylor, I., & Taylor, M. M. (1990). *Psycholinguistics: Learning and using language.* Englewood Cliffs, NJ: Prentice-Hall International.

Thompson, M. C., & Massaro, D. W. (1973). The role of visual information and redundancy in reading. *Journal of Experimental Psychology, 98*, 49–54.

Venezky, R. L. (1976). Theoretical and experimental bases for teaching reading. In T. A. Sebeok (Ed.), *Current trends in linguistics. Vol. 12: Linguistics and adjacent arts and sciences*. The Hague: Mouton.

Venezky, R. L. (1984). The history of reading research. In P. D. Pearson (Ed.), *Handbook of reading research* (Vol. 1, pp. 3–38). New York: Longman.

Venezky, R. L. (1999). *The American way of spelling*. New York: Guilford Press.

Venezky, R., & Massaro, D. (1987). Orthographic structure and spelling-sound regularity in reading English words. In A. Allport, D. Mackay, W. Prinz, & E. Scheerer (Eds.), *Language perception and production: Relationships between listening, speaking, reading and writing* (pp. 159–179). London: Academic Press.

Vernon, M. D. (1931). *The experimental study of reading*. Cambridge, UK: University of Cambridge Press.

Waters, G. S., & Seidenberg, M. S. (1985). Spelling-sound effects in reading: Time-course and decision criteria. *Memory & Cognition, 13*, 557–572.

Wheeler, D. D. (1970). Processes in word recognition. *Cognitive Psychology, 1*, 59–85.

Wiggins, R. H. (1967). Effects of three typographic variables on speed of reading. *Journal of Typographic Research, 1*, 5–18.

Wimmer, H., Landerl, K., & Frith, U. (1999). Learning to read German: Normal and impaired acquisition. In M. Harris & G. Hatano (Eds.), *Learning to read and write: A cross-linguistic perspective* (pp. 34–50). Cambridge, UK: Cambridge University Press.

Zeitler, J. (1900). Tachistoskopische Untersuchungen über das Lesen. *Philosophische Studien, 16*, 380–463.

Zhurova, L. E. (1963/1964). The development of analysis of words into their sounds by preschool children. *Soviet Psychology and Psychiatry, 2*, 17–27.

Ziegler, J. C., Jacobs, A. M., & Stone, G. O. (1996). Statistical analysis of the bidirectional inconsistency of spelling and sound in French. *Behavior Research Methods, Instruments, & Computers, 28*, 504–515.

Author Index

Note: italic page numbers denote full reference

Subject Index